COSTA RICA HANDBOOK

SECOND EDITION

CHRISTOPHER P. BAKER

MOON
PUBLICATIONS INC.

COSTA RICA HANDBOOK
SECOND EDITION

Published by
Moon Publications, Inc.
P.O. Box 3040
Chico, California 95927-3040, USA

Printed by
Colorcraft Ltd., Hong Kong

© Text and photographs copyright Christopher P. Baker, 1996.
All rights reserved.
© Illustrations and maps copyright Moon Publications, Inc., 1996.
All rights reserved.

Some photographs and illustrations are used by permission
and are the property of the original copyright owners.

ISBN: 1-56691-035-8
ISSN: 1082-4847

Editor: Karen Gaynor Bleske
Assistant Editor: Michael Raymond Greer
Copy Editors: Deana Corbitt Shields, Asha Johnson
Production & Design: Carey Wilson
Cartographers: Bob Race, Brian Bardwell
Index: Deana Corbitt Shields

Front cover photo: Danalid butterfly *(Lycorea cleobaea),* by Thomas C. Boyden

Distributed in the U.S.A. by Publishers Group West
Printed in Hong Kong

Please send all comments,
corrections, additions,
amendments, and critiques to:

**COSTA RICA HANDBOOK
MOON PUBLICATIONS, INC.
P.O. BOX 3040
CHICO, CA 95927-3040, USA
e-mail: travel@moon.com**

Printing History
1st edition — May 1994
Reprinted — February 1995
2nd edition — March 1996

This book is dedicated with love to my parents.

This book is dedicated with love to my patrons.

CONTENTS

MAPS

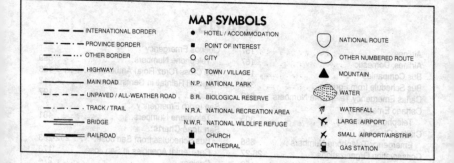

MAP SYMBOLS

- – – – – INTERNATIONAL BORDER
- – · – · – PROVINCE BORDER
- – · · – · · – OTHER BORDER
- ———— HIGHWAY
- ———— MAIN ROAD
- – – – – – UNPAVED / ALL-WEATHER ROAD
- – · – · – · TRACK / TRAIL
- ═════ BRIDGE
- ▬▬▬ RAILROAD

- ● HOTEL / ACCOMMODATION
- ■ POINT OF INTEREST
- O CITY
- N.P. TOWN / VILLAGE
- N.P. NATIONAL PARK
- B.R. BIOLOGICAL RESERVE
- N.R.A. NATIONAL RECREATION AREA
- N.W.R. NATIONAL WILDLIFE REFUGE
- ⛪ CHURCH
- ⛪ CATHEDRAL

- NATIONAL ROUTE
- OTHER NUMBERED ROUTE
- ▲ MOUNTAIN
- WATER
- ⋔ WATERFALL
- ✈ LARGE AIRPORT
- ✕ SMALL AIRPORT/AIRSTRIP
- ⛽ GAS STATION

SPECIAL TOPICS

CHARTS

ABBREVIATIONS

a/c—air conditioning/air-
  conditioned
Apdo.—Apartado (post office
  box)
C—centigrade/Celsius
d—double
F—Fahrenheit

FIT—Fully Independent Travel
4WD—four-wheel drive
ICT—Instituto Costarricense de
  Turismo (Costa Rican
  Tourism Institute)
km—kilometer(s)
km/h—kilometers per hour

m—meter(s)
s—single
Sr.—Señor
tel.—telephone
t—triple

IS THIS BOOK OUT OF DATE?

Inevitably, a book of this size and scope is a long time in the making. While every effort has been made to keep abreast of the rapid pace of change and development in Costa Rica, some information may already be out of date by the time you read this book. A few inaccuracies are also inevitable. You—the reader—are a valuable resource in ensuring that future editions contain the most up-to-date and accurate information. Please let us know about any price changes, new accommodations or restaurants, map errors, travel tips, etc.

To assist future travelers, feel free to photocopy maps in this book: while sightseeing, mark the exact locations of new hotels and other travel facilities, and cross off those that may have closed down. Mail your revised map, along with any information you wish to provide (including a business card, brochure, and rate card for hotels, if possible) to:

Costa Rica Handbook
c/o Moon Publications
P.O. Box 3040
Chico, CA 95927 U.S.A.
E-mail: travel@moon.com

REGARDING PRICE CONVERSIONS

The value of the *colón* has been declining against the U.S. dollar; at press time it had fallen to 190. Prices in this book were converted at 165 *colones* to the dollar, the exchange rate as of July 1995.

ACKNOWLEDGMENTS

I could not have sustained this book without the support—sometimes minor, often colossal—of a coterie of friends and others to whom thanks are due.

Firstly, no number of words can sufficiently express the thanks due to Eldon Cooke, who flung open the doors of the finest hotel in San José—Hotel Grano de Oro—on numerous occasions. His fathomless hospitality added immense pleasure to my capital experience.

Thanks, too, go to Prego Rent-a-Car, and especially to Xinia Novoa Espinoza, for facilitating transportation to research this edition. Also to the public relations staff of LACSA, the national airline, whose willingness to provide air transportation for the first edition contributed in no small way to the flowering of that two-year labor. Due thanks, too, to Peggy Mahoney of Continental Airlines and Maggie Maldonado and Jorge Corella of Aero Costa Rica.

The following also offered miscellaneous assistance, and credit is due to one and all: Milvia Cornacchia Grossi, of Hotel Milvia; Denis Roy, of Villa Caletas; Rodrigo Bedout, of Hotel Fiesta; Don Perry, of Rainforest Aerial Tram; Cecilia Cook, of Hotel Camino Real; Louis Wilson, of Hotel Las Tortugas; Yadyra Simón, of Villas Río Mar; Jim Damalis, of Hotel Si Como No; Amy Bonanata, of Costa Rica Experts; Martha and John, of Casa Sunset; the owners of Hotel Capitán Suizo and Hotel del Rey; and Kurt Kutay, of Wildland Adventures.

To my dear friend Ginny Craven, of Progressive Public Relations, thank you for your support, encouragement, and fun-filled times aboard the *Temptress;* and to *Temptress* owner Tomás Posuelo for acting as congenial host. Natalie Ewing of Costa Rica Expeditions and Marcos Crespos of Costa Rica Temptations provided efficient assistance in tour arrangements.

To friends Shirley Miller and Randy Case, publishers of the *Costa Rica Outlook* newsletter, thank you for anecdotes used herein, and for introducing me to an endless procession of useful contacts. And to friends Rod Garrett and Roger Oyama a special note of appreciation: without their kind assistance the first edition would have been immeasurably delayed.

Others who deserve credit include: Fernando Esquivel, of Ríos Tropicales; Sara Jiménez, of Hotel Punta Leona; Maria del Carmen Viquez, of Hacienda Los Inocentes; Marta Cañas de Burgos, of Hotel Las Espuelas; Marjan de Vargas, of Las Pacífica; Helene Beloín, of Tango Mar; Arturo Otero Ackermann, of Chatelle Country Resort; Jose Luis Cabada; James Seip, of Villa Casa Blanca; Thomas Douglas, of Hotel Santo Tomás; William Parker, of L'Ambiance; Marcello Marongiu, of Jardín del Eden; Michele de Rojas, of Casa Turire; Manuel Montero, of Magil Lodge; Carlo Traversone, of Hotel El Tucán; Maria Batalla, of Hotel Chalet Tirol; Carlos Lobo, of La Providencia; Ricardo Carranza, of Hacienda Lodge Guachipelín; Gabrielle Carazo, of Villablanca; Jim Hamilton, of Tilajari Resort; Margarita Sanabria, of Hotel Maribu Caribe; Erich Barrantes, of Orquídeas Inn; Brian and Milena, of Finca Brian y Milena; Jean Paul Cazedessus, of Tilawa Viento Surf; John and Tony Aspinall, of Costa Rica Sun Tours; David and Cecilia Reid, of Calypso Cruises; John Williams; Joanne Carter; Rocio Lopez, of Café Britt; Joris Brinkerhoff, of the Butterfly Farm; Peter Brennan; George Aron, of Casa 429; Marlene Alvarez, of JGR Associates; Tania D'Ambrosia and Carlos Alberto Silva, of the ICT; Roland Huber, of Rent-a-Rover; and to Bill Baker, for generously allowing me to extract from *The Essential Road Guide to Costa Rica*.

To all others who lent their support but who through my senility or thoughtlessness have not been acknowledged, a sincere apology and a heartfelt thank you are due.

A Special Note on Photography

This book has been lent color and vitality thanks to the gracious support and splendid photography of Jean Mercier and John Anderson. Those with a commercial interest in their photography should contact:

Jean Mercier, Apdo. 1798, Alajuela 4050, Costa Rica, tel. (506) 441-2897 or (506) 441-2282.

John Anderson, 650 N.E. 64th St. #2, Miami, FL 33138, tel. (305) 758-9933, fax (305) 594-1741.

WHY COSTA RICA?

If San Salvador were hosed down, all the shacks cleared and the people rehoused in tidy bungalows, the buildings painted, the stray dogs collared and fed, the children given shoes, the trash picked up in the parks, the soldiers pensioned off—there is no army in Costa Rica—and all the political prisoners released, those cities would, I think, begin to look a little like San José. In El Salvador I had chewed the end of my pipestem to pieces in frustration. In San José I was able to have a new pipestem fitted . . . [Costa Rica] was that sort of place.

—PAUL THEROUX, THE OLD PATAGONIAN EXPRESS

In his highly entertaining and incisive book *The Old Patagonian Express*, describing his journey south by rail from Massachusetts to Tierra del Fuego, Paul Theroux portrays a litany of places one might want to avoid. But Costa Rica is different. One of his characters sums it up. Freshly arrived in San José, the capital city, Theroux finds himself talking to a Chinese man in a bar. The Asian—a Costa Rican citizen—had left his homeland in 1954 and traveled widely throughout the Americas. He disliked every country he had seen except one. "What about the United States?" Theroux asked. "I went all around it," replied the Chinese man, "Maybe it is a good country, but I don't think so. I could not live there. I was still traveling, and I thought to myself, 'What is the best country?' It was Costa Rica—I liked it very much here. So I stayed."

At first sight, Costa Rica appears almost too good to be true. The temptations and appeals of this tiny nation are so many that an estimated 30,000 North American citizens (more than one percent of Costa Rica's population) have moved here in recent years and now call Costa Rica home, attracted by financial incentives and a quality of life among the highest in the Western Hemisphere. *Pensionados* and other Americans-in-residence seem to have known for quite some time what travelers have only recently begun wising up to: Costa Rica is one of the world's best-kept travel secrets, as well as a great place to live.

For years travelers had neglected this exciting yet peaceful nation primarily because of a muddled grasp of Central American geopolitics. While its neighbors have been racked by turmoil, Costa Rica has been blessed with a remarkable normalcy: few extremes of wealth and poverty, no standing army (the army disbanded itself after the 1948 coup d'état by which it gained power), and a proud history as Central America's most stable democracy (the 1994 elections were so trouble-free that crowd control at polling stations was handled in part by schoolchildren). Of the 53 presidents since independence from Spain in 1821, only three have been military men and only six could be considered dictators.

Ticos, as the friendly, warmhearted Costa Ricans are known, pride themselves on having more teachers than policemen, a higher male life expectancy than does the United States, an egalitarianism and strong commitment to peace and prosperity, and an education and social-welfare system that should be the envy of many developed nations. Even the smallest town is electrified, water most everywhere is potable, the roads are generally excellent, and the telecommunications system is the best in Latin America. In 1990, the United Nations declared Costa Rica the country with the best human-development index among underdeveloped nations; in 1992 it was taken off the list of underdeveloped nations altogether. No wonder *National Geographic* called it the "land of the happy medium."

This idyllic vision, however, ignores the country's problems. The truth, of course, is more complex. Costa Rica has mired of late in an economic crisis. The nation's per-capita debt, while improving, ranks among the world's worst. Inflation reached 25% in 1992. One-third of Costa Rica's 520,000 families live in poverty. And in recent years, diseases such as measles and malaria have reappeared. Traffic fatality statistics are frightening. And deforestation outside the national parks is occurring at a rate faster than in the Amazon. Still, one element has set Costa Rica apart from its neighbors: geography is the only true extreme in Central America's most peaceful nation . . .

Despite its diminutive size (about the same size as Nova Scotia or West Virginia), Costa Rica proffers more beauty and adventure per acre

than any other country on earth. It is in fact a kind of microcontinent unto itself. The diversity of terrain is remarkable, most of it as supremely beautiful as Mother Nature ever intended. Costa Rica is sculpted to show off the full potential of the tropics. Anyone who wants to journey, as it were, from the Amazon to a Swiss alpine forest has simply to start in a valley and start walking uphill. Within a one-hour journey from San José, the capital city, the tableau changes with dramatic effect through dense rainforest, airy deciduous forest, and montane cloud forest that swath the slopes of towering volcanoes, to dry open savannah, lush sugarcane fields, banana plantations, and rich cattle ranches set in deep valleys, and to rain-soaked jungle, lagoons, estuaries, and swamps teeming with wildlife in the northern lowlands. The lush rainforest spills down the steep mountains to greet the Pacific and Atlantic oceans, where dozens of inviting beaches remain unspoilt by footprints, and in places offshore coral reefs open up a world more beautiful than a casket of gems (note, however, that few beaches live up to the scintillating beauty of beaches in the West Indies, Thailand, or Cozumel). "Send almost anyone there," the *Weissmann Travel Reports* advises travel agents, but "if they're not turned on by jungles, coffee fields, beaches and volcanoes, they may wonder why they're there."

Though the history buff may be disappointed by the lack of pre-Columbian or colonial sites and structures, Costa Rica's varied ecosystems, particularly its tropical rainforests, are a naturalist's dream. Unlike many destinations, where man has driven the animals into the deepest backwater seclusion, Costa Rica's wildlife seems to love to put on a song and dance. Animals and birds are prolific and in many cases relatively easily seen: sleek jaguars on the prowl, tattered moth-ridden sloths moving languidly among the high branches, scarlet macaws that fall from their perches and go squalling away, coatimundis, toucans, brightly colored tree frogs, and other exotic species in abundance. That sudden flutter of blue is a giant morpho butterfly, that mournful two-note whistle, the quetzal, the Holy Grail of tropical birds. The pristine forests and jungles are full of arboreal sounds that are, according to one writer, "music to a weary ecotraveler's ears." You can almost feel the vegetation growing around you. There is a sense of life at flood tide.

The nation's 12 distinct ecological zones are home to an astonishing array of flora and fauna—approximately five percent of all known species on earth in a country that occupies less than three ten-thousandths of its land area—including more butterflies than the whole of Africa, and more than twice the number of bird species than the whole of the United States . . . in colors so brilliant their North American cousins seem drab by comparison. Stay here long enough and you'll begin to think that with luck you might, like Noah, see all the creatures on earth.

Scuba divers, fishermen, golfers, spa addicts, kayakers and white-water rafters, hikers, surfers, honeymoon romantics, and every other breed of escape artist, too, can find their nirvana in Costa Rica. The adventure travel industry has matured into one of the world's finest under the tutelage of experienced North American operators. About the only adventure activities not possible in Costa Rica are those that involve snow skis or camels.

For better or worse, Costa Rica, too, seems set to burst into blossom as a contender on the international beach-resort scene. The nation's Pacific Northwest coast offers miles of talcum-fine, sugar-white beaches. The nation boasts a number of supremely attractive resorts, civilized hotels, and rustic lodges and cabinas where, lazing in a hammock dramatically overlooking the beach, you might seriously contemplate giving it all up back home and settling down to while away the rest of your days enjoying the never-winter climate.

Fortunately, as yet there are no Acapulcos or Cancúns scarring the coast with their endless discos and concrete beachfronts and vast high-rise condominiums: Costa Rica's progressive conservationist tradition and dedication to development with a genteel face have helped keep rapacious developers at bay . . . until now! The nation's law setting aside its beaches as surfside parks for the people is being eroded. And although Luis Manuel Chacón, the country's first minister of tourism, vowed to allow no buildings "taller than a palm tree" to blight the beaches, megaresort complexes are rising along the jungled shoreline like mushrooms on a damp log, often without heed for existing environmental laws.

The country is finally having to face a paradoxical problem: that of being loved to death. As the word spreads, the more people come. The more, too, the big developers are drawn in. I hope it will be many years before Costa Rica is spoiled, but I say: *GO NOW!*

BOB RACE

Chirique gold image

CATHY CARLSON

INTRODUCTION

THE LAND

A traveler moving south overland through Central America gradually has his choice of routes whittled away until he finally reaches the end of the road in the swamps and forests of Darien, in Panamá, where the tenuous land bridge separating the two great American continents is almost pinched out and the Pacific and Caribbean oceans almost meet. Costa Rica lies at the northern point of this apex: a pivotal region separating two oceans and two continents vastly different in character.

The region is a crucible. There are few places in the world where the forces of nature so actively interplay. Distinct climatic patterns clash and merge; the great landmasses and their off-shore cousins, the Cocos and Caribbean plates, jostle and shove one another, triggering earthquakes and spawning sometimes cataclysmic volcanic eruptions; and the flora and fauna of the North and South American realms, as well as

those of the Caribbean and the Pacific, come together and play Russian roulette with the forces of evolution. The result is an incredible diversity of terrain, biota, and weather concentrated in a country barely bigger than the state of New Hampshire.

At 50,895 square kilometers, Costa Rica is the second smallest Central American nation after El Salvador. At its narrowest point, in the south, only 119 kilometers separate the Caribbean from the Pacific. Even in the north one can savor a leisurely breakfast on the Caribbean and take an ambling five-hour drive to the Pacific for dinner. At its broadest point, Costa Rica is a mere 280 km wide. On the ruler-straight eastern seaboard, barely 160 km separate the Nicaraguan and Panamanian borders. And while the Pacific coast is longer, it is still only 480 km from the northernmost tip to the Panamanian border as the crow flies.

CENTRAL AMERICA

© MOON PUBLICATIONS, INC.

Lying between 8° and 11° north of the equator, Costa Rica sits wholly within the tropics, a fact quickly confirmed in the middle of a rainy afternoon in the middle of the rainy season in the middle of the soddeningly wet Caribbean lowlands or Talamanca mountains. Elevation and extremes of relief, however, temper the stereotypical tropical climate. In fact, the nation boasts more than a dozen distinct climatic zones. Even ice and snow aren't unknown in cooler months atop the highest mountains.

TOPOGRAPHY

A Backbone of Mountains

Costa Rica sits astride a jagged backbone of volcanoes and mountain chains, part of the great Andean-Sierra Madre chain, which runs the length of the western littoral of the Ameri-

cas. From the Pacific coast of Costa Rica great cones and domes dominate the landscape, and in the north one is almost always in sight of volcanoes.

The mountains begin as a low, narrow band of hills that rise from the nation's northwestern-most corner, growing steeper and broader and ever more rugged until they gird Costa Rica coast to coast at the Panamanian border, where they separate the Caribbean and Pacific zones from one another as surely as if these were the towering Himalayas.

Volcanic activity has fractured this mountainous backbone into distinct cordilleras. In the northwest, the **Cordillera de Guanacaste** rises in a leap-frogging series of volcanoes, including Rincón de la Vieja and Miravalles, whose steaming vents have been harnessed to provide geothermal energy. To the southeast is the **Cordillera de Tilarán,** dominated by Arenal, one of the world's most active volcanoes. Rising higher yet to the east is the **Cordillera Central,** with four great volcanoes—Poás, Barva, Irazú and Turrialba. Together, these three cordilleras form the central highlands, within whose cusp lies the Meseta Central, an elevated plateau ranging in height from 900 to 1,787 meters. To the south of the valley rises the **Cordillera Talamanca,** an uplifted mountain region that tops out at the summit of Cerro Chirripó (at 3,797 meters, Costa Rica's highest peak).

Meseta Central

All roads radiate out from the Meseta Central, the heart and heartbeat of the nation. This rich agricultural valley is cradled by the western flanks of the Cordillera Talamanca to the south, and to the north and east by the fickle volcanoes of the Cordillera Central. San José, the capital city, lies at its center. At an elevation of 1,150 meters, San José and neighboring Alajuela, Cartago, and Heredia enjoy year-round temperatures above 70° F, reliable rainfall, and rich volcanic soils—major reasons why almost two-thirds of the nation's population of 3,087,000 lives in the valley.

The Meseta Central—which measures about 40 km north to south, 80 km east to west—is divided into two separate valleys by the low-lying crests of the **Cerros de la Carpintera,**

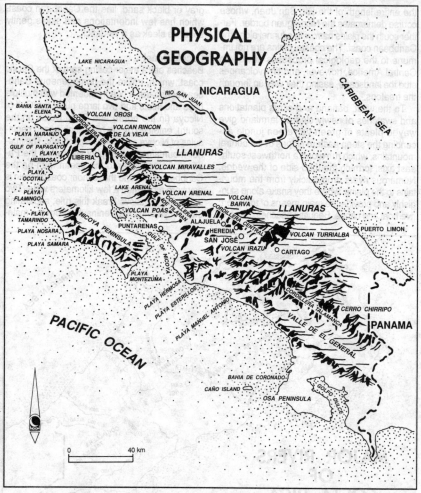

PHYSICAL GEOGRAPHY

NICARAGUA

LAKE NICARAGUA

RIO SAN JUAN

CARIBBEAN SEA

BAHIA SANTA ELENA

VOLCAN OROSI

VOLCAN RINCON DE LA VIEJA

PLAYA NARANJO

GULF OF PAPAGAYO

PLAYA HERMOSA

CORDILLERA DE GUANACASTE

LLANURAS

LIBERIA

VOLCAN MIRAVALLES

PLAYA OCOTAL

LAKE ARENAL

PLAYA FLAMINGO

VOLCAN ARENAL

VOLCAN BARVA

LLANURAS

PLAYA TAMARINDO

VOLCAN POAS

CORDILLERA DE TILARAN

CORDILLERA CENTRAL

NICOYA PENINSULA

PUNTARENAS

ALAJUELA

HEREDIA

SAN JOSÉ

VOLCAN TURRIALBA

PUERTO LIMON

PLAYA NOSARA

VOLCAN IRAZU

CARTAGO

PLAYA SAMARA

GULF OF NICOYA

PLAYA MONTEZUMA

PACIFIC OCEAN

PLAYA HERMOSA

PLAYA ESTERILLOS

PLAYA MANUEL ANTONIO

CORDILLERA TALAMANCA

CERRO CHIRRIPO

VALLE DE EL GENERAL

PANAMA

BAHIA DE CORONADO

CAÑO ISLAND

GOLFO DULCE

OSA PENINSULA

© MOON PUBLICATIONS, INC.

0   40 km

which rise a few miles east of San José. Beyond lies the somewhat smaller Cartago Valley, at a slightly higher elevation. The Carpinteras mark the Continental Divide. To the east the turbulent Reventazón—a favorite of whitewater enthusiasts—slices through the truncated eastern extreme of the Cordillera Central and tumbles helter-skelter to the Caribbean lowlands. The Río Virilla exits more leisurely, draining the San José Valley to the west.

Northern Lowlands and Caribbean Coast
The broad, pancake-flat, wedge-shaped northern lowlands are cut off from the more densely populated highlands by a languorous drape of virtually impenetrable hardwood forest that only the most accomplished outdoor types can penetrate without local guides. The low-lying plains or *llanuras*, which only in a few places exceed 480 meters above sea level and which comprise one-fifth of the nation's land area, extend along

the entire length of the Río San Juan, whose course demarcates the Nicaraguan border. Farther south the plains narrow to a funnel along the Caribbean coast. The coastal plains are not immune to the geological processes at work in Central America, however, and tiny volcanoes stud the landscape, easing their way up through the treetops.

To the west, banana and citrus plantations and swatches of newly cleared farmland give way to pleats of green velveteen jungle ascending the steep eastern slopes of the central mountains, which run along a northwest-southeast axis, forming the third side of the wedge. Numerous rivers drop quickly from the mountains to the plains, where they snake along sluggishly and provide the main means of transport: riverboat and canoe. Beautiful beaches, many of gray or black sand, line the Caribbean coast, which has few indentations and sidles gently south as sleek as a yardstick.

Pacific Coast

Beaches are a major calling card of the Pacific coast, which, unlike the homogeneous Caribbean seaboard, is deeply indented with multiple bays and inlets and two large gulfs: the Gulf of Nicoya (in the north) and Golfo Dulce (in the south), enfolded by the hilly, hook-nosed peninsulas of Nicoya and Osa, respectively. The interior mountains tilt precipitously toward the Pacific, coming closer to the ocean than on the Caribbean side, and the slender coastal plain is nowhere more than a few kilometers wide. Two broad fertile valleys break this rule, separating the Nicoya and Osa Peninsulas from the main-

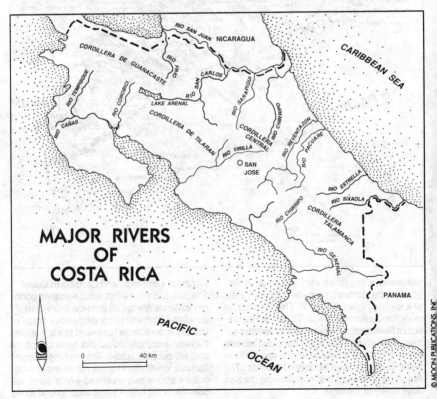

MAJOR RIVERS OF COSTA RICA

0   40 km

© MOON PUBLICATIONS, INC.

PLATE TECTONICS: A WORLD IN UPHEAVAL

Until the 1960s, when the theory of plate tectonics revolutionized the earth sciences, geologists trying to explain the distribution of earthquakes and volcanoes were at a loss. When earthquakes and volcanoes were plotted on a map, geologists realized that the planet is a puzzle—literally. The pieces of the terrestrial jigsaw are some 25 "tectonic plates," interconnected pieces of the earth's crust (the lithosphere), 40-95 miles thick. Seven major plates carry the continents and ocean basins on their backs.

These plates are in continual motion, ponderously inching along on their endless journeys around the surface of the earth at a pace no faster than human fingernails grow, powered by forces originating deep within the earth's bowels. They ride on a viscous layer called the aesthenosphere, whose molten component wells up to the earth's surface on great convection currents fueled by heat from deep within the earth's core.

As the plates move, they pull apart or collide, unleashing titanic geological forces. When two plates slide past each other or converge, as off the Pacific coast of Central America, the geological forces generally drive one plate beneath the other, causing earthquakes. The friction created by one plate grinding beneath another melts part of both crusts, forming magma—molten rock—which wells up under pressure, erupting to form a chain of volcanoes.

many tributaries have carved a deep, steep-sided trough, long isolated from the rest of the nation. The construction of the Pan-American Highway through the valley in the 1950s brought thousands of migrant farmers and their families in its wake.

GEOLOGY

Costa Rica lies at the boundary where the Pacific's Cocos Plate, a piece of the earth's crust some 510 km wide, meets the crustal plate underlying the Caribbean. The two are converging as the Cocos Plate moves east at a rate of about 10 cm a year. It is a classic subduction zone in which the Caribbean Plate is forced under the Cocos, one of the most dynamic junctures on earth. Central America has been an isthmus, a peninsula, and even an archipelago in the not-so-distant geological past. It has therefore been both a corridor and a barrier to landward movements, and it has been an area in which migrants have flourished, new life forms have emerged, and new ways of life have evolved. Yet a semblance of the Central America we know today became recognizable only in recent geological history. In fact, Costa Rica has one of the youngest surface areas in the Americas—only three million years old—for the volatile region has only recently been thrust from beneath the sea.

Earthquakes

In its travels eastward, the Cocos Plate gradually broke into seven fragments, which today move forward at somewhat different depths and different angles. This fracturing and competitive movement causes the frequent earthquakes Costa Ricans contend with (during one two-month period in 1989, seismologists recorded more than 16,000 tremors in Costa Rica; most were imperceptible to people, but 16 registered above 4.0 on the Richter scale). The forces that thrust the Cocos and Caribbean plates together continue to build inexorably.

From insignificant tremors to catastrophic blockbusters, most earthquakes are caused by the same phenomenon: the slippage of masses of rock along earth fractures called faults. Rocks possess elastic properties, and in time this elas-

land. North of the Gulf of Nicoya, the coastal strip widens to form a broad lowland belt of savannah—the Tempisque Basin—drained, appropriately, by the Río Tempisque, and narrowing northward until hemmed in near the Nicaraguan border by the juncture of the Cordillera de Guanacaste and rolling, often steep coastal hills that follow the arc of the Nicoya Peninsula.

Of growing importance to the national economy is the narrow, 64-km-long intermontane basin known as the Valle de El General, which runs parallel to and nestles comfortably between the Cordillera Talamanca and the coastal mountains—**Fila Costeña**—of the Pacific southwest. The rivers General and Coto Brus and their

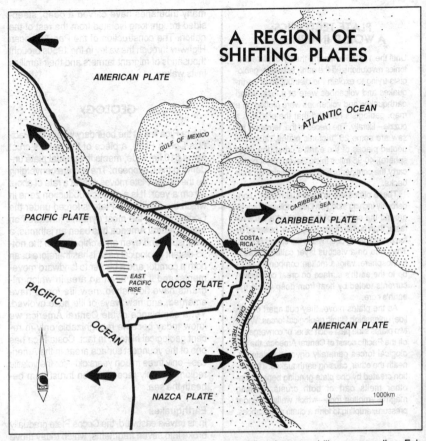

A REGION OF SHIFTING PLATES

AMERICAN PLATE

ATLANTIC OCEAN

GULF OF MEXICO

CARIBBEAN SEA

PACIFIC PLATE

MIDDLE AMERICA TRENCH

CARIBBEAN PLATE

COSTA RICA

EAST PACIFIC RISE

COCOS PLATE

PACIFIC OCEAN

PERU-CHILE TRENCH

EAST PACIFIC TRENCH

AMERICAN PLATE

NAZCA PLATE

0   1000km

ticity allows rocks to accumulate strain energy as tectonic plates or their component pieces jostle past each other. For years friction contains the strain and holds the rocks in place. But eventually, as with a rubber band stretched beyond its breaking point, strain overcomes frictional lock and the fault ruptures at its weakest point. Suddenly, the pent-up energy is released in the form of seismic waves—the earthquake—that radiate outward in all directions from the epicenter, the point of rupture. This rupturing lasts from a fraction of a second to many minutes for a major earthquake. Pressure waves traveling at five miles per second race from the quake's epicenter through the bedrock, compressing and

expanding the ground like an accordion. Following in their wake come waves that thrust the earth up and down, whipping along at three miles per second.

For Costa Ricans the bad news is that the most devastating earthquakes are generally associated with subduction zones, where one tectonic plate plunges beneath another. Ocean trench quakes off the coast of Costa Rica have been recorded at 8.9 on the Richter scale and are among history's most awesome, heaving the sea floor sometimes by scores of feet. These ruptures often propagate upward, touching off other lower-magnitude tremors in a system of overlapping cracks in rock called imbricate faults,

Four survivors of the Cartago earthquake (circa 1910) survey the damage.

THE 22 APRIL 1991 EARTHQUAKE

April 22, 1991—appropriately, Earth Day—is a day most Costa Ricans will never forget. At 3:57 p.m., the country was hit by a massive earthquake that registered 7.4 on the Richter scale and which originated near the Caribbean town of Pandora, 112 km southeast of San José. Although the quake was stronger than the San Francisco earthquake of 17 October 1989, and the strongest earthquake to rattle Costa Rica since 1910, damage was minor in most parts of the country. Structural damage to San José was superficial. And the resort regions of the Pacific coast and montane national parks in the north were not affected. By the time the rocking and rolling were over, however, the quake had left at least 27 people dead, more than 400 injured, 13,000 homeless, and more than 3,260 buildings destroyed in Limón Province.

The port city of Puerto Limón (which rose 1.5 meters), fared badly. The Las Olas and the International hotels were reduced to rubble. Tanks at the nation's only oil refinery burst into flames. And the port sustained almost $20 million in damages, temporarily closing down the nation's leading export industry (bananas) and contributing significantly to the final $170 million bill—a devastating blow for such a small nation.

Roads, too, throughout the Atlantic lowlands were badly damaged, including the road between San José and Puerto Limón, which was closed because of landslides and collapsed bridges. Some 40 km of road were destroyed. The earthquake caused massive landslides in the Talamanca mountains, stripping the hills of all vegetation and causing serious flooding when unusually heavy rains hit in the summer of 1991. The floods did their own damage, washing out a replacement bridge over the Río Estrella, for example.

Despite aid from around the world, hundreds of kilometers of roads still remained in need of repair more than a year later. By year's end, many of the streets and water pipes had still not been repaired. Citizens in the southern Caribbean towns of Sixaola and Bribrí faced the most difficult situations, as the wells that supply these townships became contaminated after the destruction of sewers and aqueducts, resulting in local outbreaks of cholera.

Though economically the country quickly got over the shakes, the physical legacy is lasting. The temblor provides a magnificent example-in-action of the processes that continue to thrust the Central America landmass from the sea. The earthquake caused the Atlantic coastline to rise permanently, in parts as much as 1.5 meters. In consequence, many of the beaches are deeper, and coral reefs have been thrust above the ocean surface and reduced to bleached calcareous skeletons. The bedrock underlying the natural waterways that connect Puerto Limón with Tortuguero on the northern Caribbean coast was also uplifted. Although formerly level with the Atlantic, many of the canals inland from the ocean have also been left high and dry.

HOW EARTHQUAKES ARE TRIGGERED

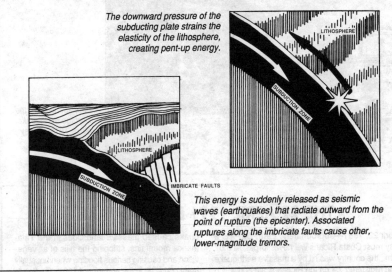

The downward pressure of the subducting plate strains the elasticity of the lithosphere, creating pent-up energy.

This energy is suddenly released as seismic waves (earthquakes) that radiate outward from the point of rupture (the epicenter). Associated ruptures along the imbricate faults cause other, lower-magnitude tremors.

as happened when the powerful 7.4 quake struck Costa Rica on 22 April 1991.

Volcanoes

Costa Rica lies at the heart of one of the most active volcanic regions on earth. The beauty of the Costa Rican landscape has been enhanced by volcanic cones—part of the Pacific Rim of Fire—that march the length of Central America. Costa Rica has seven of the isthmus's 42 active volcanoes, plus 60 dormant or extinct volcanoes. Some have the look classically associated with volcanoes—a graceful symmetrical cone rising to a single crater. Others are sprawling, much-weathered mountains whose once-noble summits collapsed into huge depressions, called calderas. Still others have smooth shield-shaped outlines with rounded tops pockmarked by tiny craters, such as on Cocos Island.

Visitors seeking to peer into the bowels of a rumbling volcano can easily do so. The reward is a scene of awful grandeur, like the fires of Milton's hell. Atop Poás's crater rim, for example, you can gape down into the great well-like vent where pools of molten lava bubble menacingly—

with diabolical, gut-wrenching fumes of chlorine and sulfur, and explosive cracks, like the sound of distant artillery, for good effect.

Several national parks have been created around active volcanoes, with accommodations, viewing facilities, and lectures and guided walks to assist visitors in understanding the processes at work. A descriptive map charting the volcanoes is published by the **Vulcanological and Seismological Observatory** of Costa Rica at the National University in Heredia, which monitors volcanic activity throughout the nation (Librería Lehmann and Librería Trejos, in San José, may sell the map). An excellent descriptive guide, good for travelers, is *Costa Rica; Land of Volcanoes,* by Guillermo Alvarado, which offers a layman's scientific-based how, where, why.

In 1963, Irazú (elev. 3,412 meters) broke a 20-year silence to begin disgorging great clouds of smoke and ash. The eruptions triggered a bizarre storm that showered San José in 13 cm of muddy ash that snuffed out the 1964 coffee crop but enriched the Meseta Central for years to come. The binge lasted for two years, then abruptly ceased. Poás (elev. 2,692 meters) has

been particularly virulent during the past 30 years. In the 1950s, the restless four-mile-wide giant awoke with a roar after a 60-year snooze, and it has been huffing and puffing ever since. Eruptions then kicked up a new cone about 100 meters high. Two of Poás's craters now slumber under blankets of vegetation (one even cradles a lake), but the third crater belches and bubbles persistently. In 1989 and again in May 1994, when new fumaroles appeared, a spate of intense eruptions and gas emissions forced Poás Volcano National Park to close (local residents were even evacuated). During summer 1994, several dramatic if minor eruptions occurred and vulcanologists anticipated that eruptions would continue for a year or two. They monitor the volcano constantly for impending eruptions.

Arenal (elev. 1,624 meters) gives a more spectacular light-and-sound show. After a four-century-long Rip van Winkle-like dormancy, this 4,000-year-young juvenile began spouting in 1968, when it laid a four-square-mile area to waste. Arenal's activity, sometimes minor and sometimes not, continues unabated. Though more placid, Miravalles, Turrialba, and Rincón de la Vieja, among Costa Rica's coterie of coquettish volcanoes, also occasionally fling fiery fountains of lava and breccia into the air.

The type of magma that fuels most Central American volcanoes is thick, viscous, and so filled with gases that the erupting magma often blasts violently into the air. If it erupts in great

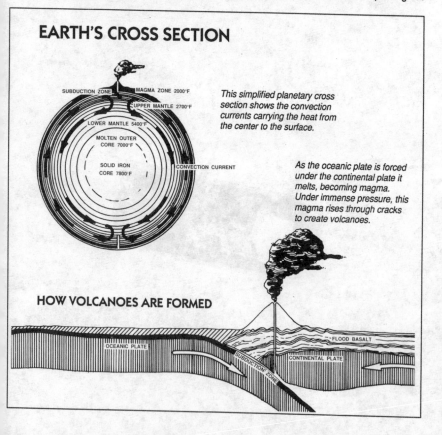

EARTH'S CROSS SECTION

SUBDUCTION ZONE MAGMA ZONE 2000°F
UPPER MANTLE 2700°F
LOWER MANTLE 5400°F
MOLTEN OUTER CORE 7000°F
SOLID IRON CORE 7800°F
CONVECTION CURRENT

This simplified planetary cross section shows the convection currents carrying the heat from the center to the surface.

As the oceanic plate is forced under the continental plate it melts, becoming magma. Under immense pressure, this magma rises through cracks to create volcanoes.

HOW VOLCANOES ARE FORMED

OCEANIC PLATE SUBDUCTION ZONE FLOOD BASALT CONTINENTAL PLATE

quantity, it may leave a void within the volcano's interior, into which the top of the mountain crumbles to form a caldera (from the Portuguese word for caldron). Irazú is a classic example.

Irazú's top fell in eons ago. Since then, however, small eruptions have built up three new volcanic cones—"like a set of nesting cups," says one writer—within the ancient caldera.

CLIMATE

When talk turns to Costa Rica's climate, hyperbole flows as thick and as fast as the waterfalls that cascade in ribbons of quicksilver down through the forest-clad mountains. English 19th-century novelist Anthony Trollope was among the first to wax lyrical: "No climate can, I imagine, be more favorable to fertility and to man's comfort at the same time than that of the interior of Costa Rica." Merlin the wizard couldn't have conjured the elements into a more blissful climate.

The country lies wholly within the tropics yet boasts at least one dozen climatic zones and is markedly diverse in local microclimates, which make generalizations on temperature and rainfall misleading.

Most regions have a rainy season (May-Nov.) and a dry season (Dec.-April). And the rainfall almost everywhere follows a predictable schedule. In general, highland ridges are wet, and windward sides always are the wettest.

When planning your trip, don't be misled by the terms "summer" and "winter," which Ticans use to designate their dry and wet seasons. Since the Tican "summer"—which in broad terms lasts December through April—equates to winter months elsewhere in the Northern Hemisphere, and vice versa, it can be confusing. Don't be put off by the term "rainy season." Costa Rica promotes it as the "green season"—a splendid time to travel, generally.

Temperatures

Temperatures, dictated more by elevation and location than by season, range from tropical on the coastal plains to temperate in the interior highlands. Mean temperatures hover near 22° C (72° F) on the central plateau, average 27° C (82° F) at sea level on the Caribbean coast and 32° C (89° F) on the Pacific lowlands, and fall steadily with elevation (about one degree for every 100-meter gain). They rarely exceed a mean of 10° C (48° F) atop Chirripó, where frost is frequent and enveloping clouds drift dark and ominous among the mountain passes. You'll definitely need a warm sweater or jacket for the mountains, where the difference between daytime highs and nighttime lows is greatest. Balmy San José and the Meseta Central have an average year-round temperature of 23° C (74° F).

This being the tropics, the length of daylight varies only slightly throughout the year. Sunrise is around 5 a.m. and sunset about 6 p.m., and the sun's path is never far from overhead, so seasonal variations in temperatures rarely exceed five degrees in any given location.

Everywhere, March to May are the hottest months, with September and October not far behind. Cool winds bearing down from northern latitudes lower temperatures during December, January, and February, particularly on the northern Pacific coast, where certain days during summer (dry season) months can be surprisingly cool. The most extreme daily fluctuations occur during the dry season, when clear skies at night allow maximum heat loss through radiation. In the wet season, nights are generally warmer, as the heat built up during the day is trapped by clouds.

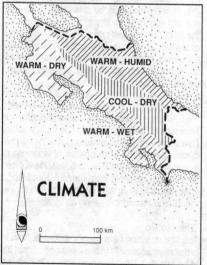

WARM - DRY

WARM - HUMID

COOL - DRY

WARM - WET

CLIMATE

0   100 km

© MOON PUBLICATIONS, INC.

REGIONAL RAINFALL IN CENTIMETERS

LOCATION	JAN.	FEB.	MARCH	APRIL	MAY	JUNE	JULY	AUG.	SEPT.	OCT.	NOV.	DEC.
San José	1.01	1.52	1.01	4.3	20.8	31.7	20.3	26.7	37.3	33.5	16.2	3.56
Barra del Colorado	56.1	26.9	21.8	26.9	41.4	36.6	62.2	47.5	37	42.7	69.1	83.6
Tortuguero	60.4	13.7	25.1	17.5	24.1	52.6	97.3	28.7	29	32.8	14	32.2
Puerto Limón	33	19.3	22.4	32.2	31.5	19.6	34.5	26.9	14	17	41.7	46.7
Puerto Viejo	32.5	16.8	21.6	28.2	43.2	41.1	45.2	42.2	30.2	37.3	46	50
Puntarenas	0.08	1.3	0.5	3	12.4	23.6	19.8	18.8	27.9	28	10.7	2.3
Golfito	15.7	14.7	17	31	49.2	45	50.8	55.1	45	68.1	64.5	33
Liberia	0.1	0.15	0	2.1	17.8	29.2	19	16.8	30.7	35.8	11.2	1.2
Filadelfia	0	0.8	0.1	5.1	19.6	41.7	19	21.8	32.8	39.1	9.1	1.1

Rainfall

Rain is a fact of life in Costa Rica. The winds and weather of two great oceans meet above Costa Rica's jungles and mountains. Oceans—especially in tropical latitudes—spell moisture, and mountains spell condensation. Annual precipitation averages 250 cm (100 inches) nationwide. Depending on the region, the majority of this may fall in relatively few days, sometimes fewer than 15 days a year. The Tempisque Basin in Guanacaste, for example, receives as little as 48 cm (18 inches) in drier years, mostly in a few torrential downpours. The mountains, by contrast, often exceed 385 cm (150 inches) per year, sometimes as much as 7.6 meters (25 feet) on the more exposed easterly facing slopes! And don't expect to stay dry in the montane rainforests even on the sunniest days, for the humid forests produce their own internal rain as water vapor condenses on the cool leaves and falls.

Generally, rains occur in the early afternoons in the highlands, midafternoons in the Pacific lowlands, and late afternoons (and commonly during the night) in the Atlantic lowlands. Sometimes it falls in sudden torrents called *aguaceros,* sometimes it falls hard and steady, and sometimes it sheets down without letup for several days and nights. Sounds like England, doesn't it!

Dry season—"summer"—on the Meseta Central and throughout the western regions is December through April. In Guanacaste, the dry season usually lingers slightly longer; the north-west coast (the driest part of the country) often has few rainy days even during wet season. On the Atlantic coast, the so-called dry season occurs January-April.

Even in the rainy season, days often start out warm and sunny, although *temporales* (morning rainfall) are not uncommon. As in many tropical destinations worldwide, only newly arrived gringos go out without an umbrella after noon during the wet season. In the highlands, rainy season usually means an hour or two of rain midafternoon. Still, be prepared: 23 hours of a given day may be dry and pleasant; during the 24th, the rain can come down with the force of a waterfall. The sudden onset of a relatively dry period, called *veranillo* (little summer), sometimes occurs during July-Aug. or August-Sept., particularly along the Pacific coast.

Be aware, though, that seasonal patterns can vary, especially in years, such as 1990 and 1995, when an occasional weather phenomenon known as El Niño may set in. The freak weather (read: torrential and unseasonal rains) it produces is caused by an abnormal warming of ocean waters off the Pacific coast, most often when warm currents from the Western Pacific shift, resulting in volatile changes in fish movements and moisture-bearing air masses.

When to Go

The first question I am usually asked is, "When is the rainy season?" in the assumption that it's to be avoided. Well, the *best* time weatherwise

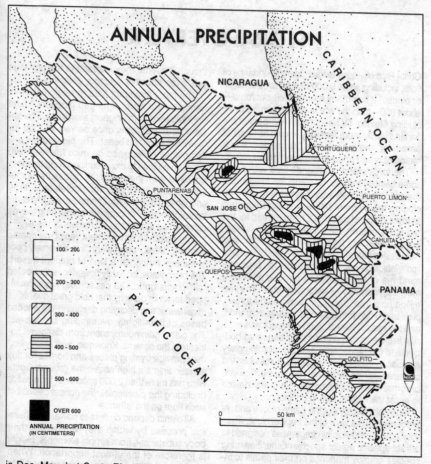

is Dec.-May, but Costa Rica is a year-round destination. Most of my research for this book was undertaken in the wet—or "green"—season. During Christmas week and Easter the whole of Costa Rica seems to descend on the

beach. Otherwise, any time is a good time (but take note of regional variations in weather).

The *Tico Times* (a weekly English-language newspaper) publishes a weather report for the following week.

FLORA: OVERVIEW

Costa Rica offers an extraordinary abundance of flora, including some 9,000-plus species of "higher plants." It has many more species of ferns—about 800—than the whole of North America, including Mexico. Of heliconias, members of the banana family more familiarly known as "birds of paradise," there are some 30 species. It is a nation of green upon green upon green.

The forests and grasslands flare with color, some flamboyantly so, for plants like to advertise the delights and rewards they have to offer, including the ultimate bribe—nectar. Begonias, anthuriums, and blood of Christ, named for the red splotches on the underside of its leaves, are common. My favorite plant is the "hot lips" (labios ardientes), sometimes called "hooker's lips" (labios de puta), whose bright red bracts remind me of Mick Jagger's famous pout or—more appropriately—Madonna's smile. The vermilion poró tree (the bright flame-of-the-forest), pink-and-white meadow oak, purple jacaranda, and the almost fluorescent yellow corteza amarilla are trees that all add their seasonal bouquets to the landscape. And the morning glory spreads its thick lavender carpets across lowland pastures, joined by carnal red passionflowers, unromantically foul-smelling—a crafty device to enlist the help of flies in pollination.

Many plants play out the game of love and reproduction in the heat of the tropical night, when they emit their irresistible fragrances designed to attract specific insect species. Other flowering species employ markings on their petals to indicate the exact placing of the rewards insects seek. Many orchid species, for example, are marked with lines and spots like an airfield, to show the insect where to land and in which direction to taxi (see "Orchids," below). Others display colors invisible to the human eye, yet clearly perceptible by insects whose eyesight spans the ultraviolet spectrum. And a remarkable holly species (Ocotea tenera) occasionally changes sex, being male one year and female the next to increase its chance of pollination. What makes them change sex isn't known, though it seems they respond to the previous year's reproductive success, or lack of it.

The most abundant flora in rainforest environments are ferns, light-gap pioneers found from sea level to the highest elevations. The ancient terrestrial ferns once served as food for many a prehistoric beast. The big tree ferns—sometimes called rabo de mico (monkey-tail) ferns, an allusion to the uncurling young fronds—are relics from the age of the dinosaurs, sometimes four meters tall, with fiddleheads large enough to grace a cello. Others are epiphytic, arboreal "nesters," or climbers whose long leaves can grapple upward for 20 meters or more.

The epiphytic environment (epiphyte comes from the Greek, "upon plants") is extremely poor in mineral nutrients, a kind of nutrient desert. The bromeliads, brilliantly flowering, spiky-leafed "air" plants up to 120 cm across, have developed tanks or cisterns that hold great quantities of rainwater and decaying detritus in the whorled bases of their tightly overlapping stiff leaves. The plants gain nourishment from dissolved nutrients in the cisterns. Known as "tank epiphytes," they provide trysting places and homes for tiny aquatic animals high above the ground. Costa Rica has more than 2,000 species of bromeliads (including the pineapple), the richest deposit of such flora on the isthmus.

All plants depend on light to power the chemical process by which they synthesize their body substances from simple elements. Height is therefore of the utmost importance. When an old tree falls, the strong, unaccustomed light triggers seeds that have lain dormant, and banana palms and ginger plants, heliconias and cecropias—all plants that live in the sunshine on riverbanks or in forest clearings—burst into life and put out big broad leaves to soak up the sun, to flower and to fruit. Another prominent plant is the poor man's umbrella (sombrilla de pobre), whose name you'll remember if you get caught in a downpour while in the rainforest; its giant leaves make excellent impromptu umbrellas.

ECOSYSTEMS

In 1947, the biologist L.H. Holdridge introduced a system of classifying vegetation types or "zones" according to a matrix based on analyzing combinations of temperature, rainfall, and seasonality. Each zone has a distinctive natural vegetation and ecosystem. Costa Rica has 12 such zones, ranging from tidal mangrove swamps to subalpine *paramó*, with its stunted dwarf plants above the timberline atop the high mountains.

Costa Rican Natural History, edited by Daniel Janzen, provides a description of the vegetation types associated with each life zone. You can also obtain a life zone map from the **Tropical Science Center** (Calle 1, Avenidas 4/6), a private nonprofit organization that operates the Monteverde Cloud Forest Reserve.

Costa Rica's tropical situation, in combination with both a remarkable diversity of local relief and climates plus generous infusions since Miocene times of plants and animals from the adjoining continents, has resulted in the evolution of a stupendously rich biota. Some habitats, such as the mangrove swamps, are relatively noncomplex. Others, particularly the ecosystem of the tropical rainforests of the Caribbean lowlands and the Osa Peninsula (the only rainforest still extant on the Pacific side of Central America), are among the most complex on the planet.

There is no barrier in Costa Rica to the entry of South American species of flora, and the lowland rainforests have strong affinities with the *selva* (jungle) of South America and form a distinctive assemblage of species in which the large number of palms, tree ferns, lianas, and epiphytes emphasize the constant heat and humidity of the region. The impressive tropical rainforest of eastern Costa Rica and the Osa Peninsula gives way on the central Pacific to a dry evergreen forest at lower elevations and dry deciduous forest farther north. These, too, are of essentially South American composition. Above about 1,000 meters, the species are fewer and the affinities with North America are stronger. In the Cordillera Talamanca, conifers of South American provenance are joined by North American oaks. Above the treeline (approximately 3,000 meters), hikers familiar with the midelevation flora of the high Andes of Peru and Ecuador will find many affinities in the shrubby open landscape of Costa Rica's cordillera.

In 1898 the German botanist A.F.W. Schimper coined the phrase "tropical rainforest." Since then botanists have distinguished among 30 or so different types of rainforest, whose species content is determined by temperature and rainfall. Tropical evergreen rainforest exists in areas of high rainfall (at least 200 cm) and regular high temperatures averaging no less than 25° C (77° F). In Costa Rica, the lush tropical evergreen rainforest of the Caribbean lowlands gives way on the Pacific side to a seasonally dry evergreen forest in the well-watered south, and tropical deciduous forest—dry forest—in the northwest.

TROPICAL DRY FORESTS

Unlike Costa Rica's rainforests, the rare tropical dry forest is relatively sparsely vegetated, with far fewer tree species and only two strata. Canopy trees have short, stout trunks with large, flat-topped crowns, rarely more than 15 meters above the ground. Beneath is an understory layer of trees with small, open-top crowns, and a layer of shrubs with vicious spines and thorns. Missing are the great profusion of epiphytes and the year-round lush evergreens of the rainforest.

For half the year (Nov.-March), no rain relieves the parching heat. Then, the deciduous dry forests undergo a dramatic seasonal transformation, the purple jacaranda, pink-and-white meadow oak, yellow *corteza amarilla,* scarlet *poró,* and the bright orange flame-of-the-forest exploding in Monet colors in the midst of drought.

Before the arrival of the Spanish in the early 16th century, dry forests blanketed the Pacific coastal lowlands from Panamá to Mexico.

EMERGENT TREE LAYER
HARPY EAGLE
MORPHO BUTTERFLY
SWALLOWTAIL HUMMINGBIRD

CANOPY LAYER
SCARLET MACAW
THREE-TOED SLOTH
CHESTNUT-MANDIBLED TOUCAN

MIDDLE LAYER
OCELOT
WOOLLY OPOSSUM

SHRUB LAYER
SPOT-BACKED ANTBIRD
HELICONIUS BUTTERFLY
LEAF-CUTTING ANT

GROUND LAYER
TAPIR
JAGUAR
CORAL SNAKE

BOB RACE

Today, they cling precariously to some two percent of their former range—a mere 520 square kilometers of Costa Rica in scattered patches centered on the lower Río Tempisque of Guanacaste. Far rarer than rainforests, they are significantly more endangered, especially by fires, which eviscerate whole forest patches, opening holes in which ecological opportunists—weeds and grasses such as African jaragua—rush in. Eventually savannah comes to replace the forest.

Fires set by the Spanish and by generations of farmers and ranchers thereafter spread savannahs across the province, whose flat alluvial plains and rich volcanic soils are perfect for crops and cattle ranchland. Within the last decade or so, the introduction of electricity and irrigation to southern Guanacaste has exacerbated the problem by attracting increasing numbers of farmers to areas where dry-forest patches still exist. The fate of even the preserved dry-forest parcels hinges on the success of two ambitious conservation projects (see special topic "Dry Forest Restoration" in the Guanacaste and the Northwest chapter).

TROPICAL RAINFOREST

Once upon a time, about 140 million years ago, near the beginning of the Cretaceous period in the age of dinosaurs, before the freezing embraces of the Ice Ages, thick evergreen forests blanketed much of the world's warm, humid surface. Today's tropical rainforests—the densest and richest proliferation of plants ever known—are the survivors of these primeval jungles of ages past.

These forests, the largest of which is Brazil's Amazonian jungle, are found in a narrow belt that girdles the earth at the equator. In the tropics, constant sunlight, endless rains and high temperatures year-round spell life. The steamy atmosphere and fast nutrient turnover have promoted favorable growth conditions and intense competition that have allowed the forest flora to evolve into an extraordinary multitude of different species, exploiting to the full every conceivable niche. Nowhere else on earth is biological productivity and diversity so evident:

layers of life in the tropical rainforest

CANOPY ANIMALS

VASCULAR PLANTS

SOIL AND DETRITUS

NONVASCULAR PLANTS

layers of life at the top

BOB KALE

tropical rainforests contain more than half of all living things known to man. Costa Rica alone has as many plant species as the whole of Europe, and the number of insect species in a hectare of rainforest is so great that no successful count has been made. Entomologists have collected from just one species of tree more than 950 different species of beetles!

Only superficially does the rainforest resemble the fictional jungles of Tarzan. Yes, the foliage can indeed be so dense that you cannot move without a machete. But since only about 10% of the total sunlight manages to penetrate through the forest canopy, the undergrowth is generally correspondingly sparse, and the forest floor surprisingly open and relatively easy to move about in. Within the shadowed jungle the dark subaqueous greens are lit here and there by beams of sunlight pouring down from above.

The stagnant air, however, is loaded with moisture. Even the briefest trail walk leaves clothing saturated with sweat, and molds and fungus seem to appear virtually overnight. There is supposedly even a fungus that flourishes in-

side binoculars and cameras and eats away the protective coating of lenses. To a visitor, the tropical rainforest seems always the same: uniform heat and stifling 90% humidity which scarcely varies. But this is true only near the ground. High in the tops of the trees, where the sun comes and goes, breezes blow, and moisture has a chance to be carried away, the swings in temperature between day and night are as much as 15 degrees, whereas the humidity may drop from 95%, its fairly constant nighttime level, to as low as 60% as the sun rises and warms the forest. Thus, within 30 vertical meters, two distinctly different climates prevail.

The Attraction

Costa Rica's tropical rainforests have an allure that abates discomfort. They are places of peace and renewal, like a vast vaulted cathedral, mysterious, strangely silent, and of majestic proportions. As one writer says: "a fourteenth century stonemason would have felt at home [in the rainforest], with its buttressed, moss-columned, towering trees and dark recesses."

The rich rainforest green backdrops the jewel colors of its many inhabitants. Sit still awhile and the unseen beasts and birds will get used to your presence and emerge from the shadows. Enormous morpho butterflies float by, flashing like bright neon signs. Is that vine really moving? More likely it's a brilliantly costumed tree python, so green it is almost iridescent, draped in sensuous coils on a branch.

Plunging deep into the forest, you are soon struck by how much variety there is. While in temperate forests distinct species of flora congregate neatly into distinctive plant "neighborhoods" with few other species interspersed, in the rainforest you may pass one example of a particular tree species, then not see another for half a mile. In between, however, are hundreds of other species. In the rainforest, too, you'll notice that life is piled upon life—literally. The firm and unyielding forest floor is a "dark factory of decomposition," where bacteria, mold, and insects work unceasingly, degrading the constant rain of leaf litter and dislodged fruits into nutrient molecules.

Flora

Strange-shaped umbrellas, curtains, and globes of fungi proliferate, too. They are a key to providing the nourishment vital to the jungle's life cycle. While a fallen leaf from a North American oak may take a year to decompose, a leaf in the tropical rainforest will fully decay within a month. If these precious nutrients and minerals thus released are not to be washed away by the daily drenching of rain, they must be reclaimed quickly and returned to the canopy to restart the cycle of life. The trees suck up the minerals and nutrients through a thick mat of rootlets that grow close to the surface of the soil. To counteract their inherent instability, many species grow side buttresses: wafer-thin flanges that radiate in a ring around the base of the tree like the tail fins of rockets.

The dark nave of the rainforest cathedral is rich with ferns, saplings, and herbaceous plants, seeping in moisture. For every tree in the jungle, there is a clinging vine fighting for a glimpse of the sun. Instead of using up valuable time and energy in building their own supports, these clutching vines and lianas rely on the straight, limbless trunks typical of rainforest tree species to provide a support in their quest for sunlight. They ride piggyback to the canopy, where they continue to snake through the treetops, sometimes reaching lengths of 300 meters (their weight can often cause their hosts to come crashing down). One species spirals around its host like a corkscrew; another cements itself to a tree with three-pronged tendrils.

The bully of the forest, however, is the strangler fig, which isn't content to merely coexist. While most lianas and vines take root in the ground and grow upward, the strangler figs do the opposite. After sprouting in the forest canopy from seeds dropped by birds and bats, the strangler fig sends roots to the ground, where they dig into the soil and provide a boost of sustenance. Slowly but surely—it may take a full century—the roots grow and envelop the host tree, choking it till it dies and rots away, leaving a hollow, trellised, freestanding cylinder.

The vigorous competition for light and space has promoted the evolution of long, slender, branchless trunks, many well over 35 meters tall, and flat-topped crowns with foliage so dense that rainwater from driving tropical downpours often may not reach the ground for 10 minutes. Above this dense carpet of greenery rise a few scattered giants towering to heights of 70 meters or more. This great vaulted canopy—the clerestory of the rainforest cathedral—is the jungle's powerhouse, where more than 90% of photosynthesis takes place.

The scaffolding of massive boughs is colonized at all levels by a riot of bromeliads, ferns, and other epiphytes (plants that take root on plants but that are not parasitic). Tiny spores sprout on the bark, gain a foothold, and spread like luxuriant carpets. As they die and decay, they form a compost on the branch capable of supporting larger plants that feed on the leaf mold and draw moisture by dangling their roots into the humid air. Soon every available surface is a great hanging gallery of giant elkhorns and ferns, often reaching such weights that whole tree limbs are torn away and crash down to join the decaying litter on the forest floor.

Wildlife

The Babylonian gardens of the jungle ceiling—naturalist William Beebe called it an "undiscovered continent"—host a staggeringly complex,

unseen world of wildlife that runs into millions of species. In the canopy, forest trees flower and fruit in the steaming tropical sunshine. Scarlet macaws and lesser parrots plunge and sway in the high branches, announcing their playacting with an outburst of shrieks. Arboreal rodents leap and run along the branches, searching for nectar and insects, while insectivorous birds watch from their vantage points for any movement that will betray a stick insect or leaf-green tree frog to scoop up for lunch. Legions of monkeys, sloths, and fruit- and leaf-eating mammals also live in the green world of the canopy, browsing and hunting, thieving and scavenging, breeding and dying.

Larger hunters live up there too. In addition to the great eagles plunging through the canopy to grab monkeys, there are also tree-dwelling cats. These superbly athletic climbers are quite capable of catching monkeys and squirrels as they leap from branch to branch and race up trunks. There are also snakes here. Not the great monsters so common in romantic fiction, which dangle, says David Attenborough, "optimistically from a branch, waiting to pick up a human passer-by," but much smaller creatures, some twig-thin, such as the chunk-headed snake with catlike eyes, which feasts on frogs and lizards and nestling birds.

Come twilight, the forest soaks in a brief moment of silence. Slowly, the lisping of insects begins. There is a faint rustle as nocturnal rodents come out to forage in the ground litter. And the squabbling of fruit bats replaces that of the birds. All around, myriad beetles and moths take wing in the moist velvet blanket of the tropical night.

ECHO (Environmentally Conscious Holiday Options, Apdo. 7-3290, San José 1000, tel. 255-2693, fax 255-0061) makes it possible for you to get a monkey's eye view of life in the canopy with its "Canopy Tours" in Iguana Park ($35) and Santa Elena Cloud Forest Preserve ($70). With an expert guide, you travel from tree to tree and platform to platform using pulleys on horizontal traverse cables before rappeling back to the jungle floor! If that sounds too frightening, the **Rainforest Aerial Tram** (Apdo. 592, San José 2100, tel./fax 225-8869; in the U.S., 65 Walnut St. #301, Wellesley Hills, MA 02181, tel. 617-239-3626, fax 617-239-3610) provides a 90-minute, Disneyworld-like ride through the canopy aboard motorized trams in a private

rainforest reserve on the fringe of Braulio Carrillo National Park.

MANGROVES

Costa Rica's shorelines are home to five species of mangroves. These pioneer land builders thrive at the interface of land and sea, forming a stabilizing tangle that fights tidal erosion and reclaims land from the water. The irrepressible, reddish-barked, shrubby mangroves rise from the dark water on interlocking stilt roots. Small brackish streams and labyrinthine creeks wind among them like snakes, sometimes interconnecting, sometimes petering out in narrow culs-de-sac, sometimes opening suddenly into broad lagoons. A few clear channels may run through the rich and redolent world of the mangroves, but the trees grow so thickly over much of it that you cannot force even a small boat between them.

Mangroves are what botanists call halophytes, plants that thrive in salty conditions. Although they do not require salt (they in fact grow better in fresh water), they thrive where no other tree can. Costa Rica's young rivers have short and violent courses that keep silt and volcanic ash churned up and suspended, so that a great deal of it is carried out of the mountains onto the coastal alluvial plains. The nutrient-rich mud

BOB RACE

red mangrove

generates algae and other small organisms that form the base of the marine food chain. Food is delivered to the estuaries every day from both the sea and the land so those few plants—and creatures—that can survive here flourish in immense numbers. And their sustained health is vital to the health of other marine ecosystems.

The nutrients the mangrove seeks lie not deep in the acid mud but on its surface, where they have been deposited by the tides. There is no oxygen to be had in the mud either: estuarine mud is so fine-grained that air cannot diffuse through it, and the gases produced by the decomposition of the organic debris within it stay trapped until your footsteps release them, producing a strong whiff of rotten eggs (the mud also clings so tenaciously it can suck the boots from your feet). Hence, there is no point in the mangroves sending down deep roots. Instead, the mangroves send out peculiar aerial roots, like a spider's legs, to form a horizontal platform that sits like a raft, maintaining a hold on the glutinous mud and giving the mangroves the appearance of walking on water. The mangroves draw oxygen from the air through small patches of spongy tissue on their bark.

Mangrove swamps are esteemed as nurseries of marinelife and as havens for water birds—cormorants, frigate birds, pelicans, herons, and egrets—which feed and nest here by the thousands, producing guano that makes the mangroves grow faster. The big birds roost on the top canopy, while smaller ones settle for the underbrush. Frigate birds are particularly fond of mangrove bushes and congregate in vast numbers along the swampy shorelines of the Gulf of Nicoya (see "Birds," below). The bushes in which they build their nests rise some two to three meters above the mudflats—just right to serve as launching pads.

Mangrove swamps, especially those fed by freshwater streams, are marine nurseries of astonishing fertility. A look down into the water reveals luxuriant life: oysters and sponges attached to the roots, small stingrays flapping slowly over the bottom, and tiny fish in schools of tens of thousands. Baby black-tipped sharks and other juvenile fish, too, spend much of their early lives among mangrove roots, out of the heavy surf, shielded by the root maze that keeps out large predators.

High tide brings larger diners—big mangrove snappers and young barracudas hang motionless in the water. Raccoons, snakes, and, as everywhere, insects and other arboreal creatures also inhabit the mangroves. There is even an arboreal mangrove tree crab (Aratus pisonii), which eats mangrove leaves and is restricted to the very crowns of the trees by the predatory activities of another arboreal crab, Goniopsis pulcra.

Mangroves are aggressive colonizers, thanks to one of nature's most remarkable seedlings. The heavy, fleshy mangrove seeds, shaped like plumb bobs, germinate while still on the tree. The flowers bloom for a few weeks in the spring and then fall off, making way for a fruit. A seedling shoot soon sprouts from each fruit and grows to a length of 15-30 cm before dropping from the tree. Falling like darts, at low tide they will land in the mud and put down roots immediately. Otherwise, the seedlings—great travelers—become floating scouts and outriders ahead of the advancing roots.

The seaborne seedling can remain alive for as long as a year, during which time it may drift for hundreds of miles. Eventually, it touches the muddy floor and anchors itself, growing as much as 60 cm in its first year. By its third year a young tree starts to sprout its own forest of arching prop roots; in about 10 years it has fostered a thriving colony of mangroves, which edge ever out to sea, forming a great swampy forest. As silt builds up among the roots, land is gradually reclaimed from the sea. Mangroves build up the soil until they strand themselves high and dry. In the end they die on the land they have created.

ORCHIDS

It's appropriate that the orchid is the national flower of Costa Rica: the country has more than 1,400 identified species, the richest orchid flora in Central America. Countless others await discovery. At any time of year you're sure to find dozens of species in bloom, from sea level to the highest, subfreezing reaches of Chirripó. There is no best time for viewing orchids, although the beginning of both the dry season (especially in the wettest rainforest regions) and wet season are said to be particularly favorable times.

Not only are orchids the largest family of flowering plants, they're also the most diverse: poke around with magnifying glass in hand and you'll come across species with flowers less than one millimeter across. Others, like the native *Phragmipedium caudatum,* have pendulant petals that can reach more than half a meter. Some flower for only one day. Others will last several weeks. Orchid lovers should head for the cloud forests, for the greatest diversity exists in humid—not wet—midelevation environments where they are abundant as tropical epiphytes (constituting 88% of orchid species). One biologist found 47 different orchid species growing on a single tree.

While not all orchids lead epiphytic lives—the Spanish called them *parasitos*—those that do are the most exotic of epiphytes, classics of their kind, so heartachingly beautiful that collectors can't resist their siren call and threaten their existence.

Orchids have evolved a remarkable array of ingenious pollination techniques. Some species self-pollinate. Others attract insects by sexual impersonation. One species, for example, produces a flower that closely resembles the form of a female wasp complete with eyes, antennae, and wings. It even gives off the odor of a female wasp in mating condition. Male wasps, deceived, attempt to copulate with it. In their vigor, they deposit pollen within the orchid flower and immediately afterward receive a fresh batch to carry to the next false female.

Guile seems to be the forte of orchids. Another species drugs its visitors. Bees clamber into its throat and sip a nectar so intoxicating that after the merest taste they become so inebriated they lose their footing and slip into a small bucket of liquid.

Escape is offered up a spout . . . the proverbial light at the end of the tunnel. As the drunken insect totters up, it has to wriggle beneath an overhanging rod, which showers its back with pollen. Pollination techniques have become so species-specific that hybridization of different orchid species is avoided by each having developed its own morphological configuration to attach its pollen, and receive it in return, to a specific part of the insect's body.

Lankester Gardens, part of the University of Costa Rica, features more than 800 orchid species, including the collection of Charles Lankester, who once ran Lankester as a private garden. It's about seven km east of Cartago on the road to Paraíso. **Orchid Alley,** at La Garita in the central highlands, offers a stunning array of orchids for sale, suitably packed for export. Nearby, at Palmares, is **Jardín de Las Guarias,** the largest private orchid collection in the country, all raised by farmer Javier Solorzano Murillo. Orchidologist Eugenio Esquivel has a nursery open to visitors in Puriscal. See the Central Highlands chapter for more information.

An annual orchid show is held each March in San José. **Costa Rica Connections** (958 Higuera St., San Luis Obispo, CA 93401, tel. 800-345-7422, fax 805-543-3626) offers a week-long "Costa Rica National Orchid Show and Tour," with visits to the show and to private orchid collections, Poás Volcano National Park (known for its abundance of epiphytes), Lankester Gardens, and other places of interest to orchid lovers.

If you're serious in your study, check out the *Field Guide to the Orchids of Costa Rica and Panama,* by Robert L. Dressler (Ithaca, NY: Comstock Publishing, 1993).

CONSERVATION

In the time it takes you to read this page, some 32 hectares of the world's tropical rainforests will be destroyed. The statistics defy comprehension. One hundred years ago, rainforests covered two billion hectares, 14% of the earth's land surface. Now only half remains, and the rate of destruction is increasing: an area larger than the state of Florida is lost every year. If the destruction continues apace, the world's rainforests will vanish within 40 years.

By anyone's standards, Costa Rica leads the way in moving Central America away from the soil-leaching deforestation that plagues the isthmus. The country has one of the world's best conservation records: about one-quarter of the country is under some form of official protection. In 1992, Costa Rica received the Cantico a Todas Las Criaturas—"Song to all Creatures"—award given by the Franciscan Center for Environmental Studies, based in Rome; was one of three winners of the first environmental award presented by the American Society of Travel Agents; and was named the most environmentally conscious country in the world by the San Francisco-based News Travel Network. In April 1992, the National Biodiversity Institute was also awarded the Peter Scott Award by the International Union for the Conservation of Nature.

Despite Costa Rica's achievements in conservation, almost the entire country has been deforested outside the national parks and reserves, where deforestation continues at an alarming rate.

DEFORESTATION

The Evidence
Along the Río San Juan, in the heart of the *llanuras* of the Atlantic lowlands, along the border with Nicaragua, is some of the wildest, wettest, most densely canopied rainforest in Costa Rica. It is a crown jewel of Central American jungle, as shining and sweet-smelling and innocent as it must have been in the first light of Creation.

The humid *llanura* is the biggest piece of primeval rainforest left on the Caribbean rim, a tiny enclave of the original carpet that once covered most of lowland Central America. Caimans, manatees, peccaries, and sloths move amid the small sloughs, and deep in the cobalt shadows jaguars and tapirs move unseen. Very wet and isolated, these mist-enshrouded waves of green have been relatively untouched by man until recently. The brief outbreak of peace in Nicaragua created a land rush, and settlers are leapfrogging over the agricultural flatlands and landing in the heart of the forest (see "Megaparks," below). Today, the lowland rainforests resound with the carnivorous buzz of chain saws; in the "dry" season, in isolated patches, they are on fire.

It is a story that's been repeated again and again during the past 400 years. Logging, ranching, and the development of large-scale commercial agriculture have transformed much of Costa Rica's wildest terrain. This is particularly true in the highlands, where the temperate and moist environment is ideal for the production of coffee and tea, and the Pacific lowlands, where beef and cotton have become major export products. Cattle ranching has been particularly wasteful. Large tracts of virgin forest were felled in the 1960s to make way for cattle, stimulated by millions of dollars of loans provided by U.S. banks and businesses promoting the beef industry to feed the North American market. Author Beatrice Blake claims that "Costa Rica loses 2.5 tons of topsoil to erosion for every kilo of meat exported" and that although a "farmer can make 86 times as much money per acre with coffee, and 284 times as much with bananas," cattle ranching takes up more than 20 times the amount of land devoted to bananas and coffee.

The Defense
The nation is making a courageous and costly attempt to protect sufficiently large areas of natural habitat and to preserve most of its singularly rich biota. But it is a policy marked by the paradox of good intent and seemingly poor applica-

DEFORESTATION

	1950	1973	1983	1993
Forested area (sq. km)	26,865	17,500	13,350	8,500
Percent of territory	52.5	34.8	26.1	17.2
Area cut/year (sq. km)	360	450	600	800
Pasture (sq. km)	6,308	15,581	26,674	30,500
Percent of territory	12.4	30.5	52.5	58

tion. Many reserves and refuges are accused of being poorly managed, and the Forestry Directorate, the government office in charge of managing the country's forest resources, has reportedly never functioned efficiently in more than 20 years of existence. While the administration of Oscar Arias Sánchez (1986-90) consolidated conservation efforts by creating a Ministry of Natural Resources, and President Rafael Angel Calderón (1990-94) called for a "New Ecological Order," the country continues to suffer the kind of environmental degradation and deforestation that plague most tropical countries. Environmentalists, with some justification, claimed that the Calderón administration abandoned the ecological principles of preceding administrations, and the 1994 elections were fought with that issue at the forefront; Calderón lost to José María Figueres, who campaigned on a platform of fostering "sustainable development."

It's a daunting battle. Every year Costa Rica's population grows by 2.5%, exacerbating the land-pressure problem and forcing squatters onto virgin land where they continue to deplete the forests that once covered 80% of Costa Rica. Fires set by ranchers today lap at the borders of Santa Rosa National Park. And oil-palm plantations squeeze Manuel Antonio against the Pacific. In the lowlands, fires from slash-and-burn agriculture burn uncontrolled for weeks; in the highlands, cloud forests are logged for timber, roof shingles, and charcoal, while farmers and plantation owners continue to clear mountain slopes to plant coffee, tea, bananas, nuts, and cinchona (for quinine).

In the 1970s, the Costa Rican government banned export of more than 60 diminishing tree species, and national law proscribes cutting timber without proper permits. It happens anyway, much of it illegally, with logs reportedly trucked into San José and the coastal ports at night. In many places the line of cultivation is already at an elevation of 2,000 meters, as lumbermen and squatters move uphill. And wherever new roads are built, the first vehicles in are usually logging trucks, which rumble along the highways loaded high with thick tree trunks. In Costa Rica the remaining tropical forest is disappearing by at least 520 square kilometers a year, and less than 1.5 million hectares of primal forest remain (about 20% of its original habitat). Despite the seemingly sincere efforts of the Costa Rican government, the nation's forests are falling faster than anywhere else in the Western Hemisphere and, as a percentage of national land area, reportedly nine times faster than the rainforests of Brazil. By the year 2000, claims biologist Daniel Janzen, all the forest outside protected areas could disappear completely.

Sadly, the Rafael Calderón administration proved more a friend of agricultural expansionists than environmentalists. In July 1992, for example, the legislature eliminated a key clause in the Forestry Law designed to protect the remaining forests. The signs are encouraging that Costa Rica's current government will break away from the short-term policies of the immediate past and the unregulated development that have called into question the country's conservation record.

The Cost

While many patches of forest will no doubt be saved, many animal and plant species can only survive in large areas of wilderness. Most of the millions of rainforest species are so highly specialized that they are quickly driven to extinction by the disturbance of their forest homes. Isolation of patches of forest is followed by an exponential decline in species; the reduction of original habitat to one-tenth of its original area means an eventual loss of half its species. The decline of a single species has a chain effect on many dependent species, particularly plants, since tropical plants are far more dependent on individual animal and bird species for seed dispersal than are plants in temperate climates. Eventually

these biological islands become depauperate communities.

At the current rate of world deforestation, plant and animal species may well be disappearing at the rate of 50,000 a year; by the end of the 20th century, an estimated one million species will have vanished without ever having been identified. Among them will be many species whose chemical compounds might hold the secrets to cures for a host of debilitating and deadly diseases. The bark of the cinchona tree, for example, has long been the prime source of quinine, an important antimalarial drug. Curare, the vine extract used by South American Indians to poison their arrows and darts, is used as a muscle relaxant in modern surgery. And scientists recently discovered a peptide secreted by an Amazonian frog called *Phyllomedusa bicolor* that may lead to medicines for strokes, seizure, depression, and Alzheimer's disease. In fact, some 40% of all drugs manufactured in the United States are to some degree dependent on natural sources; more than 2,000 tropical rainforest plants have been identified as having some potential to combat cancer.

Nonrenewable Resources

Once the rainforests have been felled, they are gone forever. Despite the rainforests' abundant fecundity, the soils on which they grow are generally very poor, thin, and acidic.

When humans cut the forest down, the organic-poor soils are exposed to the elements and are rapidly washed away by the intense rains, and the ground is baked by the blazing sun to leave an infertile wasteland. At lower elevations, humans find their natural water sources diminishing and floods increasing after removal of the protective cover, for intact the montane rainforest acts as a giant sponge. Thus, indigenous groups such as the Bribrí and Cábecar Indians who inhabit remote regions close to the Panamanian border are finding their tenuous traditional livelihoods threatened.

REFORESTATION AND PROTECTION

Part of the government's answer to deforestation has been to promote reforestation, mostly through a series of tax breaks, which have led to a series of tree farms predominantly planted in nonnative species such as teak. The government, for example, has extended legal residency status to anyone participating in reforestation programs, with a required minimum nontaxable investment of US$50,000. These efforts, however, do little to replace the precious native hardwoods or to restore the complex natural ecosystems, which would take generations to reestablish. Such efforts are being taken up by a handful of dedicated individuals and organizations determined to preserve and even replenish core habitats, such as attempts spearheaded by Daniel Janzen and the Friends of Lomas Barbudal to reestablish the tropical dry forests of Guanacaste.

The most famous of the private reserves is perhaps Rara Avis, 1,200 hectares of prime rainforest 96 km northeast of San José. The reserve, founded by American biologist Amos Bien, was conceived to prove that rainforest can produce more income from such schemes as ecotourism, harvesting ornamental plants, and raising iguanas, pacas, and *tepezcuintles* (the forest-dwelling rodents that make popular bar snacks!) for food than if cleared for cattle.

International Efforts

Private and foreign agencies are becoming increasingly active in the battle to preserve Costa Rica's natural heritage. The country is now home to a plethora of conservation groups and projects, ranging from private nature reserves and children's reforestation projects to a $22.5 million forest-management project for the Central Volcanic Mountain Range funded by the U.S. Agency for International Development. Many of these organizations are attempting to bridge the gap between conservation funding and the nation's massive foreign-debt problems by developing "debt for nature" swaps. Swapping land for debt, for example, the U.S.-based Nature Conservancy has helped swell conservation coffers while curbing the outflow of foreign currency from Costa Rica. Using Conservancy money, the National Parks Foundation bought a share of the nation's debt from a U.S. bank, paying in dollars after the debt was discounted to only 17 cents on the dollar. Costa Rica then paid off the National Parks Foundation with bonds in the

local currency, with the agreement that the money would be used on conservation projects. Like the majority of international agencies involved in conservation, the Nature Conservancy relies heavily on donations and public support.

Private Efforts

Privately owned forests comprise the majority of unprotected primary forest remaining in Costa Rica outside the national parks. "While national programs have attempted to force compliance with Costa Rica's forestry law, little effort has been directed toward encouraging private landowners to willingly conserve and rationally manage their forests," says **COMBOS** (Conservación y Manejo de Bosques Tropicales, or Conservation and Management of Tropical Forests; Apdo. 1456, San Pedro 2050, tel. 253-0889, fax 253-4750), a nonprofit association that promotes the conservation and management of tropical forests through private action. Many of the reserves described in this book are privately owned.

Several organizations sponsor private voluntary action on the part of landowners. For example, COMBOS, working with CEDARENA and the Nature Conservancy, has inscribed "conservation easements," legal agreements whereby property owners guarantee to restrict the type and amount of development that may take place on the property. Any subsequent owners are bound by the agreement. COMBOS maintains a rotating fund to pay private owners for establishing easements to guarantee protection of their forests. In other cases it buys forested properties and establishes easements before resale to private buyers. Money from the sale is returned to the rotating fund.

Working against these valiant philanthropists is a legal system that grants significant inalienable rights to squatters: if they "improve" the land, they are entitled to just compensation; if they are not ejected in good time, the land becomes theirs. The law has given rise to professional squatters acting on behalf of businesspeople; once the former gains legal title it is signed over to the sponsor and then the squatter moves to another plot. Says Tom Huth, in *Conde Nast Traveler:* "If the gringo wants his land back, he has to pay the squatters for having destroyed his forests." The temptation is for foreigners who buy land to *build* right away or hire a caretaker *(cuidador)* to hold squatters at bay (even the *cuidador,* if allowed to live on the property, can legally claim it as his own after six months' tenure). One can see the result up and down the Pacific coast.

New Approaches

The Costa Rican government's own conservation efforts have been undermined by the International Monetary Fund's structural-adjustment program, which requires government departments to cut their budgets and staffs. Particularly worrisome is the fact that much of the land incorporated into the national park system has not yet been paid for and, hence, could revert back to private use.

Partly in response to this pressure, but also in an attempt to improve the efficiency of its conservation programs, Costa Rica is reorganizing management of its protected areas (see "National Parks," below); one of the main components of the reorganization is that each conservation unit will be able to procure international funding and manage its own budget apart from the federal government's coffers. Costa Rica's National Biodiversity Institute recently signed an avant-garde contract with the world's largest pharmaceutical company, the New Jersey-based Merck Co., which calls for the Institute to provide Merck with samples of plant and insect species in exchange for royalties from any marketable products. The objective is to finance the conservation of biodiversity and to ensure that Costa Rica receives a small percentage of the massive profits derived from pharmaceutical extracts. (The U.S. company Lilly, for example, earns some $100 million a year from periwinkle extract used in treating leukemia; Madagascar, where the plant was first collected, receives none of the profits.)

Another concept of land protection evolving in Costa Rica places the needs of local communities in the equation by attempting to integrate their livelihoods into the philosophy and day-to-day operation of the national park system. The intent is to give local inhabitants a vested interest by teaching them that they can earn a living by preserving natural resources rather than by destroying them. Governmental agencies have recently placed an emphasis on such efforts along the Nicaraguan border, where the Si-a-

CONSERVATION ORGANIZATIONS

The following organizations are active in conservation efforts in Costa Rica and urgently need volunteers and/ or contributions to help implement their programs. Twenty-four key environmental groups make up the **Costa Rican Federation for Environmental Conservation** (Federación Costarricense para la Conservación del Ambiente—FECON, tel. 224-0399, fax 234-6175), which publishes a directory listing campaign groups and regional conservation organizations.

Arbofila
Apdo. 512, Tibas 1100. This grassroots organization helps Costa Rican farmers reforest environmentally degraded areas with native tree species.

Asociación Preservacionista de Flora y Fauna Silvestre
Apdo. 1192, San José 1007. Organizes volunteers to patrol wilderness areas to report illegal activities, such as logging and hunting.

ASCONA
Apdo. 8-3790, San José 1000. This organization specializes in investigation of and legal action against environmental infringements. Volunteers with appropriate technical backgrounds are needed, in addition to tax-deductible donations (donations should be made through the World Wildlife Fund, 1250 24th St. NW, Washington, D.C. 20037).

Audubon Society of Costa Rica
P.O. Box 025216-700, Miami, FL 33102. Supports efforts to rear endangered species in captivity for release to the wild, plus lobbies the Legislative Assembly on environmental issues.

Bosque Mundial de La Páz (World Forest Foundation)
Apdo. 2592, San José 1000. Buys rainforest lands, both virgin and partly cut, and preserves them as centers for research and recreational visits. "Godparents" (donors giving more than $400, enough to buy one acre) receive special visitation privileges.

CEDARENA
Apdo. 134, San Pedro 2450. Researches and maintains a database on environmental laws. Volunteers with appropriate backgrounds are needed.

Children's Rainforest
P.O. Box 936, Lewiston, MN 04240. Educates children in Costa Rica and throughout the world on rainforest ecosystems. The Children's Eternal Rainforest is part of the Monteverde Conservation Area.

Conservation International
1015 18th St. NW, Suite 1000, Washington, D.C. 20036.

Department of Responsible Tourism
Apdo. 1524, San Pedro 2050, tel./fax 506-224-8910. Part of the Institute for Central American Studies. Has established a national "Sustainable Tourism

Paz cross-border preserve poses a new challenge, and in so-called buffer zones surrounding existing parks and reserves. And the Monteverde Conservation League is one of several private organizations formed to promote environmentally responsible use of primal land by assisting farmers to increase productivity and promote reforestation.

In recent years, a campaign has also been launched to protect the vitally important wetlands and waterways (see "Mangroves," above).

NATIONAL PARKS

Although contradictions abound, Costa Rica is blessed with a conscientious leadership that appreciates the value of the nation's natural heritage. Past-President Rafael Calderón pledged to make the same kind of efforts on behalf of the environment that his predecessor, Nobel winner Oscar Arias Sánchez, made on behalf of peace. "By destroying species and nature," said Calderón, "man is destroying himself." Alas, environmentalists claim, Calderón did not prove a man of his word. The current president, José María Figueres, campaigned on an environmental ticket, and his early actions suggest that his administration is more earnestly determined to protect Costa Rica's natural heritage.

While much of Costa Rica has been stripped of its forests, the country has managed to protect a larger proportion of its land than any other country in the world. In 1970 there came a growing acknowledgment that something unique and lovely was vanishing, and a systematic ef-

Ranking" and promotes grassroots advocacy for sustainable development.

Fundación Neotrópica

Apdo. 236, San José 1002. Helps promote sustainable development and conservation among local communities. Also sells a wide range of T-shirts, books, maps, postcards, and souvenirs at the Fundación headquarters (Calle 20, Avenida 3), Poás volcano, and elsewhere.

Fundación de Parques Nacional

Apdo. 236, San José 1002. Jointly administered with the Fundación Neotrópica, this private nonprofit organization promotes environmental education, rural development, and sound management of national parks and reserves, and arranges "debt-for-nature" swaps. The foundation matches donations with endowment funds in Costa Rican government bonds.

Instituto Eco de Costa Rica

Apdo. 8080, San José 1000. Works to prevent Costa Rica from "becoming an environmental theme park." Sponsors a think tank of government officials, private developers, and environmental activists to develop responsible tourism planning.

Monteverde Conservation League

Apdo. 10165, San José 1000. Promotes reforestation projects and works to assist farmers to increase productivity. Centered on the Monteverde Cloud Forest Preserve. The league administers the Children's Eternal Rainforest Preserve.

Nature Conservancy

Latin American Division, 1815 N. Lynn St., Arlington, VA 22209. Identifies species in need of protection and acquires land to protect them; the largest private sanctuary system in the world.

Rara Avis

Apdo. 8105, San José 1000. A "conservation-for-profit" organization with a "hotel" and biological station in the rainforest bordering Braulio Carrillo National Park. Researches rainforest use to produce more income than competing uses, such as cattle ranching.

Talamanca Association
of Ecotourism and Conservation

Puerto Viejo de Talamanca, Limón. Welcomes donations and volunteer labor in the fight to halt the destruction of the southern Caribbean coastal zone by the banana industry and uncontrolled hotel development.

fort was begun to save what was left of the wilderness. In that year, the progressive Costa Ricans formed a national park system that has won worldwide admiration. Costa Rican law declared inviolate 10.27% of a land once compared to Eden; an additional 17% is legally set aside as forest reserves, "buffer zones," wildlife refuges, and Indian reserves. Throughout the country representative sections of all the major habitats and ecosystems are protected for tomorrow's generations. The National Parks Service is in charge of managing 20 national parks, eight biological reserves, and a national monument. The Forestry Department and National Wildlife Directorate are responsible for 26 protected zones, nine forest reserves, and seven fauna sanctuaries. In May 1995 the Ministry of Natural Resources announced that it planned to extend the boundaries of existing national parks and reserves to encompass 19% of the country (compared to 11.4% of national territory at the time).

Besides providing Costa Ricans and foreign travelers with the privilege of admiring and studying the wonders of nature, the national parks and reserves protect the soil and watersheds and harbor an estimated 75% of all Costa Rica's species of flora and fauna, including species that have all but disappeared in neighboring countries. They contain active volcanoes and hot springs, high-reaching mountains and mysterious caves, historic battlefields, inviting beaches, and pre-Columbian settlements, and provide last, vital reservoirs of rainforests whose chemical secrets may one day reveal the cures for AIDS and other diseases.

The Yellowstones and Yosemites of Costa Rica—the lure for 90% of all visitors to the park system—are Manuel Antonio, with its beautiful beaches; Braulio Carrillo, with its rainforest beside a highway; Irazú, where on a clear day you can see both the Caribbean and the Pacific; and Poás, where you can peer into a steaming crater and see the earth's crust being rearranged.

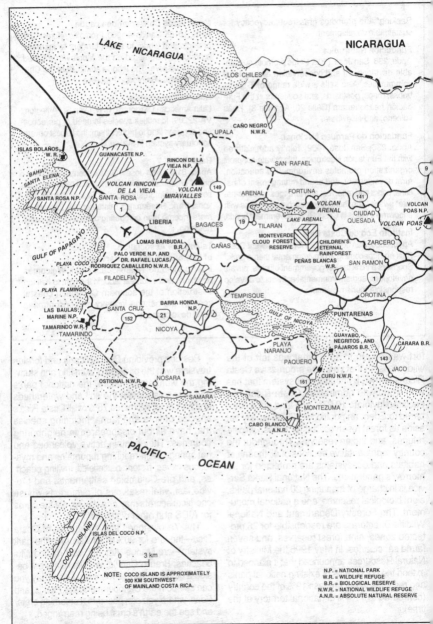

LAKE NICARAGUA

NICARAGUA

LOS CHILES

CAÑO NEGRO N.W.R.

UPALA

SAN RAFAEL

ISLAS BOLAÑOS W.R.

GUANACASTE N.P.

RINCON DE LA VIEJA N.P.

BAHIA SANTA ELENA

VOLCAN RINCON DE LA VIEJA

VOLCAN MIRAVALLES

ARENAL

FORTUNA

149

SANTA ROSA N.P.

SANTA ROSA

LIBERIA

BAGACES

TILARAN

19

Lake Arenal

VOLCAN ARENAL

CIUDAD QUESADA

141

VOLCAN POAS N.P.

VOLCAN POAS

9

GULF OF PAPAGAYO

1

LOMAS BARBUDAL B.R.

CAÑAS

MONTEVERDE CLOUD FOREST RESERVE

CHILDREN'S ETERNAL RAINFOREST

ZARCERO

PALO VERDE N.P. AND DR. RAFAEL LUCAS RODRIGUEZ CABALLERO N.W.R.

PLAYA COCO

FILADELFIA

PEÑAS BLANCAS W.R.

SAN RAMON

1

PLAYA FLAMINGO

TEMPISQUE

OROTINA

LAS BAULAS MARINE N.P.

SANTA CRUZ

BARRA HONDA N.P.

GULF OF NICOYA

PUNTARENAS

TAMARINDO W.R.

TAMARINDO

152

21

NICOYA

GUAYABO, NEGRITOS, AND PAJAROS B.R.

CARARA B.R.

143

OSTIONAL N.W.R.

NOSARA

PLAYA NARANJO

PAQUERO

CURU N.W.R.

JACO

SAMARA

161

MONTEZUMA

CABO BLANCO A.N.R.

PACIFIC OCEAN

ISLAS DEL COCO N.P.

COCO ISLAND

0   3 km

NOTE: COCO ISLAND IS APPROXIMATELY 500 KM SOUTHWEST OF MAINLAND COSTA RICA.

N.P. = NATIONAL PARK
W.R. = WILDLIFE REFUGE
B.R. = BIOLOGICAL RESERVE
N.W.R. = NATIONAL WILDLIFE REFUGE
A.N.R. = ABSOLUTE NATURAL RESERVE

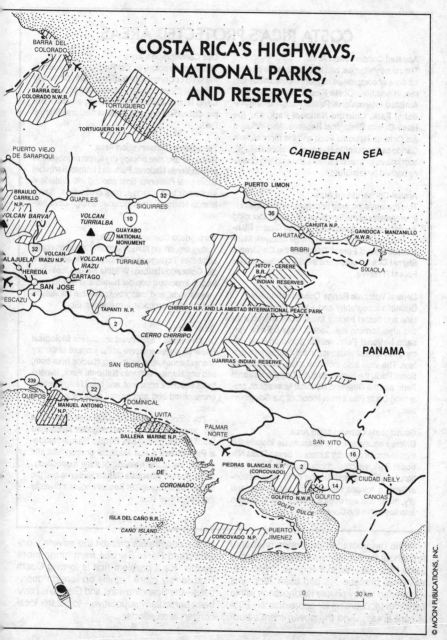

COSTA RICA'S HIGHWAYS, NATIONAL PARKS, AND RESERVES

BARRA DEL COLORADO

BARRA DEL COLORADO N.W.R.

TORTUGUERO

TORTUGUERO N.P.

PUERTO VIEJO DE SARAPIQUI

CARIBBEAN SEA

BRAULIO CARRILLO N.P.

VOLCAN BARVA

GUAPILES

SIQUIRRES

32

PUERTO LIMON

36

VOLCAN TURRIALBA

10

GUAYABO NATIONAL MONUMENT

CAHUITA N.P.

CAHUITA

BRIBRI

GANDOCA - MANZANILLO N.W.R.

VOLCAN IRAZU N.P.

ALAJUELA

HEREDIA

VOLCAN IRAZU

TURRIALBA

32

SIXAOLA

SAN JOSE

4

CARTAGO

HITOY - CERERE B.R.

INDIAN RESERVES

ESCAZU

TAPANTI N.P.

CHIRRIPO N.P. AND LA AMISTAD INTERNATIONAL PEACE PARK

2

CERRO CHIRRIPO

PANAMA

SAN ISIDRO

UJARRAS INDIAN RESERVE

239

QUEPOS

22

DOMINICAL

MANUEL ANTONIO N.P.

SAN VITO

UVITA

16

BALLENA MARINE N.P.

PALMAR NORTE

SAN VITO

BAHIA DE CORONADO

PIEDRAS BLANCAS N.P. (CORCOVADO)

2

CIUDAD NEILY

14

GOLFITO N.W.R.

GOLFITO

CANOAS

ISLA DEL CAÑO B.R.

CAÑO ISLAND

GOLFO DULCE

CORCOVADO N.P.

PUERTO JIMENEZ

0   30 km

© MOON PUBLICATIONS, INC.

COSTA RICA'S PROTECTED AREAS

Amistad Conservation Area

The country's largest and least accessible protected area encompasses rugged, mountainous terrain in southern Costa Rica. It incorporates **La Amistad International Peace Park, Tapantí National Park, Chirripó National Park,** and the **Hitoy-Cerere Biological Reserve.** Also included are **Cahuita National Park** and the more remote **Gandoca-Manzanillo National Wildlife Refuge,** both known for their coral reefs and stunning beaches backed by rainforest.

Arenal Conservation Area

This conservation area encompasses wildlife-rich environments of the Cordillera de Tilarán, including **Arenal volcano, Lake Arenal, Juan Castro Blanco National Park,** and three private reserves: **Monteverde Cloud Forest Reserve,** the **Children's Eternal Cloud Forest,** and the **Santa Elena Cloud Forest Reserve.**

Central Volcanic Range Conservation Area

Dramatic topography and a wide range of montane and humid tropical forest types characterize this area flanking the Central Valley. **Poás Volcano National Park,** with its active drive-up volcano, is the most visited site in the national park system. The area also includes **Irazú Volcano National Park,** the rugged **Braulio Carrillo National Park,** and the **Guayabo National Monument,** preserving Costa Rica's most important pre-Columbian site.

Guanacaste Conservation Area

Diverse ecosystems in Guanacaste include the wildlife-rich tropical dry forests of **Santa Rosa National Park,** which also includes an important national monument, and **Rincón de la Vieja National Park,** a volcano with geysers, hot springs, and dry, moist, and wet tropical forests. **Orosí** volcano also lies within the Conservation Area.

Osa Conservation Area

This humid region, in the Pacific Southwest, is made up of **Corcovado National Park,** protecting a vast rainforest boasting large wildlife populations; **Caño Island Biological Reserve,** an important pre-Columbian site; and **Ballena National Marine Park.**

Tempisque Conservation Area

Wetlands and rare tropical dry forest predominate in **Palo Verde National Park** and **Lomas Barbudal Biological Reserve.** Both abound with waterfowl and other bird species, plus crocodiles. **Barra Honda National Park** includes a large cave network.

Tortuguero Conservation Area

Tortuguero, on the humid northern Caribbean coast, combines **Tortuguero National Park** and **Barra del Colorado National Wildlife Refuge,** both protecting important tropical humid and wet forests, swamplands, and mangroves that are habitats to green turtles, crocodiles, manatees, etc.

Other Areas

On the Central Pacific coast are **Carara Biological Reserve,** a vital preserve at the juncture of the dry and wet zones, and protecting species from both; and tiny **Manuel Antonio National Park,** famous for its beaches, coral reef, and humid forest, where endangered bird and animal species are easily seen.

The Nicoya Peninsula has four important, albeit tiny, protected regions. The contiguous **Tamarindo Wildlife Refuge** and **Las Baulas Marine National Park** protect a vital estuarine environment and nesting site of the leatherback turtle respectively. **Cabo Blanco Absolute Nature Reserve** and the private **Curú Biological Reserve** boast a diversity that belies their size.

While deforestation continues unabated throughout the country, wildlife preservation in Costa Rica—at least in theory—is only a matter of due process . . . and cash. Money is still needed to buy private landholdings within the parks (accounting for approximately 20% of park areas). And the government's budgetary constraints prohibit the severely understaffed Parks Service from hiring more people. It's a problem that is forcing Costa Rica to rely more heavily on foreign donations—the Scandinavians and Germans have been particularly supportive—to bolster local conservation efforts.

PARK VOLUNTEERS

The **Association of National Park Volunteers** recruits foreign volunteers with appropriate skills to work alongside rangers on a temporary basis. If you can handle basic living for a while and would enjoy giving your skills and energies for a noble cause, give it a try. Work might include digging at an archaeological site, life-guard duty at a park beach, or protecting nesting marine turtles. Volunteers receive free transportation and lodging. However, you may need to provide your own food, living conditions are rustic, and the work is often hard, long, and lonely. You must be at least 18 years old and provide two references from relevant organizations or individuals in Costa Rica. Contact Stanley Arguedas, Asociación de Voluntarias de Parques Nacionales, Apdo. 10104, San José 1000.

Facing the Challenge

The parks are in the midst of an important series of changes in which the focus is on increasing the degree of protection—turning poorly managed forest reserves and wildlife refuges into national parks, for example, and integrating adjacent national parks, reserves, and national forests into regional conservation units (RCUs) to create corridors in which wildlife might be able to move with greater freedom over much larger areas (see "Megaparks," below). Since farming, logging, and other activities are allowed within buffer zones on the edge of the parks, the intent is to more carefully manage this land. "We used to manage the parks from their borders inwards, but now we're working from the borders outwards, to avoid isolation," says National Parks Director Alvaro Ugalde. Responsibility for their management is being shifted from central offices in San José to regional offices and, in some cases, to nongovernmental organizations.

To accomplish this, in 1989 the country began reorganizing its parks system. Following the model of the recently created Guanacaste Regional Conservation Unit, big and small parks are being amalgamated to form eight more RCUs based on the premise that larger parks—being more complete ecosystems—are more easily preserved than smaller ones. Each unit is characterized by its unique ecology: Amistad, Arenal, Cordillera Volcánica Central, Isla del Coco, Osa, Pacífico Central, Tempisque, and Tortuguero. The government is also merging the Parks Service, the Fish and Wildlife Service, and the Forest Reserves and Protected Zones into a new body: the Directorate of Conservation Units, responsible to the Ministry of Natural Resources, Energy, and Mines.

Costa Rican tourism is booming so quickly that some parks are beginning to show wear and tear from too much visitation (park visitation increased 500%—from 50,000 to over 250,000 annually—in the years 1988-1992). In 1986, just 20% of foreign tourists visited a park; in 1992 more than half did so. In 1994, a visitor management policy was introduced to control the adverse effects on all the parks. Limits have been set to the number of visitors allowed in each part at any one time. Hence, if you arrive at Manuel Antonio to find that the reserve is full, you will need to wait until a similar number of people leave before being granted access.

Until 1994, the Costa Rican Legislative Assembly had refused to revise its fee system upward despite the fact that the park system has been so short of funds that it could not afford uniforms or vehicles for many park rangers. Revenues generated by park visits ($7 million in 1992) were not available for park use; they were usurped by the Instituto Costarricense de Turismo (in the hullabaloo over the increase in fees in 1994—see below—the ICT magnanimously agreed to provide $400,000 toward operating costs for the parks through April 1995). The **Ecotourism Society,** an organization of travel professionals and conservationists, began a campaign to raise park fees so that the country could afford to maintain the parks (Costa Rica Expeditions and Horizontes Nature Tours also jointly donated $25,000 to open the Tourism For Conservation Park Ranger Fund, to be administered by Fundación Neotrópica). Unfortunately, in September 1994 the bureaucrats overreacted by raising entrance fees more than 1,000% (see "Fees," below). The number of visitors to national parks immediately plummeted.

Information

The **Servicio de Parques Nacionales** (SPN—National Parks Service) has a special telephone

line for tourist information: tel. 192 (from abroad, the same information is offered by fax: 223-6963). Eventually a worldwide toll-free "800" number will be introduced, possibly by the time you read this.

Alternately, you can visit the **public information office** (tel. 233-5673 or 233-5284) in the Parque Bolívar Zoo at Calle 7, Avenida 11 in San José (see San José chapter). The office has maps and a limited stock of brochures. It helps if you speak Spanish. There's also a public information office at the SPN headquarters in the **Ministerio de Natural Resources and Mines** (MIRENEM, Apdo. 10094, San José 1000, tel. 257-0922; open Mon.-Fri. 8 a.m.-4 p.m., located at Calle 25, Avenidas 8/10).

The SPN maintains radio contact with each park through the radio communications office (tel. 233-4160), and can arrange accommodations and meals at many ranger stations on your behalf.

If you need specialized information on scientific aspects of the parks, contact the Conservation Data Center, **Instituto Nacional de Biodiversidad** (tel. 236-4269), in Santo Domingo de Heredia.

Detailed topographical maps of the parks and reserves are available at Librería Lehmann (Calle 3, Avenida Central) and the **Instituto Geográfico Nacional** (Avenida 20, Calle 5/7), both in San José.

Dr. Humberto Jiménez (tel. 231-1236) offers a one-hour slide show on the national parks at cinemas in San José, and to private groups on request.

Fees and Facilities

No permits are required for most national parks; you'll need permits for a few of the biological reserves. These can be obtained in advance from the public information office, or write the Servicio de Parques Nacionales at MIRENEM (see above).

In September 1994, MIRENEM raised the park entrance fees more than 1,000% for tourists, from about US$1.25 to $15 (subsequently offered to tour operators at one-third the price through spring 1995). The increase led to many would-be visitors getting sticker-shock and turning around at the gates. The National Chamber of Tourism reported a 59% drop in visits! Tour operators complained that the whopping rise was killing off some of their business. They correctly argued, too, that a single fee for all parks is ludicrous. It can be justified for some, but not others. A review body was established and revisions made in spring 1995.

Tickets for walk-in visitors remain at $15 and are valid for 24 hours only. However, you can buy advance tickets at a discount (valid for 90 days) at MIRENEM headquarters. Parks are divided into three groups for advance-ticket pricing. Advance tickets to Caño Island, Carara, Chirripó, Irazú, Poás, Manuel Antonio, and Santa Rosa National Parks cost $10. Advance tickets to Arenal, Braulio Carrillo, Cabo Blanco, Corcovado, Guayabo, Palo Verde, Rincón de la Vieja, Tapantí, and Tortuguero cost $7. And advance tickets to Barra Honda, Hitoy-Cerere, and La Amistad cost $5. If you plan to visit several parks, your best bet is to buy a "Green Passport" ($29), good for four admissions to any national parks.

MIRENEM planned to introduce a 24-hour telephone information system—TELEGES-TION—to answer travelers' questions on individual parks. It also planned to invest $8.5 million in 1995 on infrastructure, including free maps and information to be disbursed at park ranger stations.

Most national parks and reserves have camping sites (60 cents for camping), although a few of the more remote wildlife refuges lack even the most rudimentary accommodations. You may be able to stay in park ranger housing or at biological research stations if space permits. Call 233-4070 or fax 223-6369 for information on accommodations at specific parks and reserves. Don't expect hotel service! You'll usually need to

provide your own towels and bedding; there are no restaurants or snack bars, so bring enough food and drink for your anticipated stay.

The national wildlife refuges are administered by the **National Wildlife Directorate** (Calle 25 and Avenidas 8/10, San José, tel. 233-8112 or 221-9533).

MEGAPARKS

Wildlife doesn't distinguish political borders. Birds migrate. Plants grow on each side. "It's not enough to draw lines on a map and call it a park," says Alvaro Ugalde, the National Parks director. "These days, park management is tied into economic issues, war and peace, agriculture, forestry, and helping people find a way to live." With peace breaking out all over Central America, park management increasingly requires international cooperation through the creation of a transnational park network. In this rare interlude of calm and fresh governments, there is an opportunity for neighboring countries to forget ancient border disagreements and see the rivers and rainforests along their borders not as dividing lines but as rich tropical ecosystems that they share.

Paseo Pantera

The idea is fruiting as the Paseo Pantera, a five-year, $4 million project dedicated to preserving biodiversity through the creation of a chain of conservation areas from Belize to Panamá. This cooperative effort of Wildlife Conservation International and the Caribbean Conservation Corporation takes its name from the Path of the Panther, a historical forested corridor that once spanned from Tierra del Fuego to Alaska. The ultimate dream is a Central American "biogeographic corridor," a contiguous chain of protected areas from Mexico to Colombia. Then the isthmus could once again be a bridge between continents for migrating species—"a much more daring and valuable dream," says one writer, "than a canal between seas."

La Amistad

The first and most advanced of the transfrontier parks is the La Amistad Biosphere Reserve, created on 2 February 1982 when the Costa Rican government signed a pact with Panamá to join two adjacent protected areas—one in each country—to create one of the richest ecological biospheres in Central America. La Amistad's remote, unexplored rainforests protect 60% of Costa Rica's fauna species, including large populations of big cats and more than 400 species of birds. In August that year, UNESCO cemented the union by recognizing the binational zone as a biosphere reserve. La Amistad (the Friendship Park) covers 622,000 hectares and includes six Indian reserves and nine natural protected areas.

Si-a-Paz

The idea for a transboundary park along the northern border with Nicaragua germinated in 1974, but little progress was made until 1985, when Nicaraguan President Daniel Ortega seized on the idea as a way to demilitarize the area, which was then being used by anti-Sandinista rebels. Ortega proposed the region be declared an international park for peace and gave it the name Si-a-Paz: "Yes to Peace." Efforts by the Arias administration to kick the rebels out of Costa Rica's northern zone led to demilitarization of the area, but lack of funding and political difficulties prevented the two countries from making much progress on the Si-a-Paz project. Since 1990, presidential elections in Costa Rica and Nicaragua have led to improved relations between the countries, and the end of the Nicaraguan war has allowed the government to dedicate more money to conservation. Si-a-Paz has been rejuvenated (former Costa Rican President Rafael Angel Calderón and Nicaraguan President Violeta Chamorro both cited it as a conservation priority).

Si-a-Paz represents a last chance to save Central America's largest and wettest tract of rainforest. In the north, natural resources once made inaccessible by guerrilla warfare are now being plundered by loggers. In the south, the rainforests have already been severely deforested, and only scattered patches of wilderness remain intact, plus a strip of forest along the Atlantic coast. In the wake of peace in Nicaragua, thousands of people displaced by the war are drifting back to the area, chasing dreams of a better life through the vast dank chambers of the rainforest of the Río San Juan, one of Costa

Rica's last seductive frontiers and the boundary between the two countries. Conservationists must immediately find a way to stabilize this wave, to help this hungry horde develop farming skills.

The idea is to enable people to make a living in one place, to involve them in conservation efforts and provide them with ecologically sustainable livelihoods so that they won't have to keep eating away at the forest's receding edge. The park design requires a full evaluation of existing human and natural resources, social and cultural considerations, demographics, and development potential. Si-a-Paz planners want to

wrap buffer zones of low-impact agriculture and agroforestry around core habitats, with whole communities integrated into the park design.

The goal is to establish a wildlife refuge along the southern shore of Lake Nicaragua, whose Solentiname Islands would be reforested and designated a cultural preserve. Other areas along the Río San Juan would be included in the park, making it a paradigm of ecosystem protection. The Costa Ricans plan to expand Tortuguero National Park to include the eastern part of Barra del Colorado Wildlife Refuge, which would connect the park with Nicaragua's Indio Maíz Biological Reserve.

There are also plans to create a corridor between the Caño Negro Wildlife Refuge and Nicaragua's Los Guatusos Wildlife Refuge and to create a new protected area west of where the Sarapiquí River pours into the San Juan, in Tambor. Also, the two-km-wide protected border zone will be expanded to a width of 10 km on the southern side of the San Juan.

The Nicaraguan part of the project is centered on Indio Maíz, which protects nearly half a million hectares of rainforest—one of the largest areas of undisturbed wilderness in Central America—in the southeast corner of the country. The Si-a-Paz region is such an El Dorado of biodiversity that conservation groups from around the world already have projects pending, from butterfly farms to sophisticated horticulture systems of intercropping. The governments of the Netherlands, Sweden, Switzerland, and Norway have already committed funds, and the IUCN World Conservation Union is helping coordinate the project.

FAUNA: OVERVIEW

Anyone who has traveled in the tropics in search of wildlife can tell you that disappointment comes easy, and often at considerable expense. But Costa Rica is one place that lives up to its word. You don't need to venture far to experience the nation's full panoply of magnificent wildlife. Costa Rica is nature's live theater where the actors aren't shy.

My friend Lynn Ferrin wrote: "the birds are like jewels, the animals like creatures in a Rousseau painting." Noisy flocks of oropendolas, with long tails "the color of daffodils," sweep from tree to tree. The scarlet macaws are like rainbows, the toucans and hummingbirds like the green flash of sunset. The tiny poison-dart frogs, red and evil, are bright enough to scare away even the most dim-witted predator. And the electric-blue morphos, the neon narcissi of the butterfly world, make even the most jaded of viewers gape wide-mouthed in awe.

Then there are all the creatures that mimic other things and are harder to spot: insects that look like rotting leaves, moths that look like wasps, the giant *Caligo memnon* (cream owl) butterfly whose huge open wings resemble the wide-eyed face of an owl, and the mottled, bark-colored *machaca* (lantern fly), which is partly to blame for Costa Rica's soaring birthrate. According to local folklore, if a girl is stung by a *machaca* she must go to bed with her boyfriend within 24 hours or she will die.

Much of the wildlife is glimpsed only as shadows. Some, like the dreaded fer-de-lance, for example, uncurling in the rotten leaves, you'll not want to meet. Well-known animals that you are *not* likely to see are the cats—pumas, jaguars, and ocelots—and tapirs and white-lipped peccaries. With patience, however, you can usually spot monkeys galore, as well as iguanas, quetzals, and three-toed sloths—"long-armed tree-dwelling Muppets"—that, as one guidebook puts it, get most of their aerobic exercise by scratching their bellies.

The **National Institute of Biodiversity,** a private, nonprofit organization formed in 1989, has been charged with the formidable task of collecting, identifying, and labeling every plant and animal species in Costa Rica. The task is expected to take at least 10 years to complete. "After 100 years of work by the National Museum we still only know 10-20% of what we have in the country," says Rodrigo Gómez, director of the NIBR. Over the course of the last 110 years, the National Museum collected some 70,000 specimens. In their first 18 months, the NIBR's hundreds of "parataxonomists" (ordinary citizens trained to gather and preserve specimens) gathered almost two million!

Identifying the species is a prodigious task, which every day turns up something new. Insects, for example, make up about half of the estimated 500,000 to one million plant and animal species in Costa Rica. The country is home seasonally to more than 850 bird species—10% of all known bird species (the U.S. and Canada combined have less than half that number). One source reports there are 5,000 different species of grasshoppers (with an estimated 2,000 yet to be discovered), 160 known amphibians, 220 reptiles, and 10% of all known butterflies (Corcovado National Park alone has at least 220

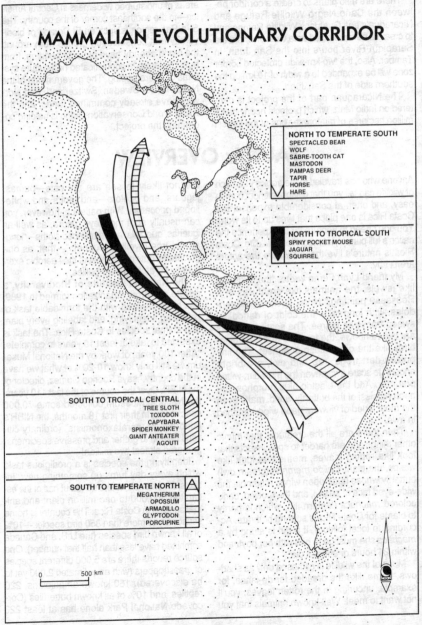

MAMMALIAN EVOLUTIONARY CORRIDOR

NORTH TO TEMPERATE SOUTH
SPECTACLED BEAR
WOLF
SABRE-TOOTH CAT
MASTODON
PAMPAS DEER
TAPIR
HORSE
HARE

NORTH TO TROPICAL SOUTH
SPINY POCKET MOUSE
JAGUAR
SQUIRREL

SOUTH TO TROPICAL CENTRAL
TREE SLOTH
TOXODON
CAPYBARA
SPIDER MONKEY
GIANT ANTEATER
AGOUTI

SOUTH TO TEMPERATE NORTH
MEGATHERIUM
OPOSSUM
ARMADILLO
GLYPTODON
PORCUPINE

500 km

different species). It's like being caught up in a kind of botanical rush hour!

IT ALL BEGAN

About three million years ago, the Central American isthmus began to rise from the sea to form the first tentative link between the two Americas. Going from island to island, birds, insects, reptiles, and the first mammals began to move back and forth between the continents. During this period, rodents of North America reached the southern continent, and so did the monkeys, which found the tropical climate to their liking.

In due course, South America connected with North America. Down this corridor came the placental mammals to dispute the possession of South America with the marsupial residents. Creatures poured across the bridge in both directions. The equids used it to enter South America, the opossums to invade North America. A ground sloth the size of an elephant headed north, too, reaching all the way to what is now Texas before it died out. Only a few South American mammals, notably armadillos, ground sloths, and porcupines, managed to establish themselves successfully in the north. The greatest migration was in the other direction.

A procession of North American mammals swarmed south, with disastrous effects on native populations. The mammals soon came to dominate the environment, diversifying into forms more appropriate to the tropics. In the course of this rivalry, many marsupial species disappeared, leaving only the tough, opportunistic opossums.

The isthmus has thus served as a "filter bridge" for the intermingling of species and the evolution of modern distinctive Costa Rican biota, a fairly recent amalgam as the isthmus has been in existence for only some three million years. Costa Rica's unique location and tropical setting, along with a great variety of local relief and microclimates, have meant that refuge areas for ancient species endangered by changes in environmental conditions have been widely available, and species that have died out elsewhere can still be found here. This, together with generous infusions of plants and animals from both continents, has resulted in a proliferation of species

that in many important respects is vastly richer than the biota of either North or South America. Costa Rica's biota shares much with both.

NUTRIENT RECYCLING AND SPECIES RICHNESS

One of the most important differences between tropical and temperate environments is what biologists call "species richness." A natural forest patch of a few hundred acres in Michigan, for example, might contain 25-30 species of trees; an equivalent tract of Costa Rican rainforest might contain more than 400. Ohio has only about 10 species of bats; Costa Rica has more than 100, although it is less than half Ohio's size. That's species richness.

nutrient recycling in a rainforest

BOB RACE

Why such complexity, such stupefying abundance of *species* in the neotropics—the tropics of the New World? It all has to do with the rapid pace of nutrient recycling and the way the natural world competes most effectively for nourishment.

In the temperate world, with the warm days and sunlight of spring, plants burst forth with protein-rich buds, shoots, and young leaves, which appear simultaneously in a protein "pulse." Animals bring forth their young during this period of protein abundance: birds return from the south to lay eggs and raise their broods, insect eggs hatch, frogs and toads crawl out of hibernation to reproduce. Come autumn, the same plants produce a second protein glut as tender berries, seeds, and nuts, which critters pack in to sustain themselves through the hardships of impending winter. The synchronized budding and fruiting of foliage is so great that all the hungry mouths gobbling protein hardly threaten a plant species's survival.

In the tropics, by contrast, the seasonal cycle is far less pronounced: sunlight, rain, and warm temperatures are constant, and plants germinate, grow, flower, and seed year-round. Hence, there is no distinct protein surplus. Leaf fall, too, occurs continuously and slowly in the tropical rainforest, unlike the autumnal drops of temperate deciduous forests, and the same tropical conditions of heat and moisture that fuel year-round growth also sponsor fast decomposition of dead leaves. The humus that enriches the soils of more temperate latitudes doesn't have a chance to accumulate in the tropics. Thus, soils are thin and, after millions of years of daily rainfall and constant heat, leached of their nutrient content.

Result? The ecosystem of a tropical rainforest is upside down when compared to forests in the temperate zone, where nutrients are stored in the soil. In the tropics they're stored overhead: in the densely leafed canopy. Leaves and young shoots represent a major investment of scarce nutrients, which plants cannot afford to have gobbled up by hungry multitudes of animals, insects, and birds. Hence, says one biologist, "It might be said that the plants 'want' to be different from one another in order to avoid being devoured." Intense competition has pressured tropical plants to diversify greatly, to disperse, and to develop defense mechanisms, such as thorns or sickening toxins. Other species stagger their production of shoots and new leaves throughout the year so that they never expose too much new growth to predation at any one time.

Because plant protein is scarce at any given time, and because plants have evolved stratagems to guard it, animals have been forced to compete fiercely. They've diversified like the plants, and competition has resulted in notable examples of specialization, with individual species staking claims to a narrow ecological niche in which other creatures can't compete. One bird species eats only insects driven up from the ground by army ants, while its droppings provide food for a certain species of butterfly.

Through these intricate associations, specific plants and predators become totally dependent on one another. A perfect example is the ant acacia, a tree common along the Pacific coast. The plant is weak and defenseless, a poor competitor in the upward race for sunlight, and easily overshadowed by faster-growing neighbors. Its tiny nectaries (glands that exude sugar) and leaf-tip swellings filled with proteins and vitamins are tempting morsels for hungry insects and birds. None, however, dares steal a nibble, for a species of tiny yet aggressive ants acts as the acacia's praetorian guard. In exchange for the honeylike food that they love, the ants defend their plant fiercely. Any predator foolish enough to touch the acacia is attacked; if a vine threatens to envelop the tree, the ants cut the vine down. If the branches of a neighboring plant threaten to steal the acacia's sunlight, the ants will prune the interloper; if a neighbor's seeds fall to the ground beneath the acacia, the insects will cart them off before they can germinate. If the ants were to become extinct, the plant would never survive. If the plant disappeared, the ants would starve. Each is inextricably in the debt of the other. Nature's a wonderful thing.

AMPHIBIANS AND REPTILES

Costa Rica is home to approximately 160 species of amphibians and more than 200 species of reptiles, half of them snakes. The most common reptile you'll see is the dragonlike, tree-dwelling green iguana, which seems to have little fear of man and can grow to a meter in length. You'll spot it often in moist deciduous habitats, crawling through the forest leaf litter or basking on branches that hang over water, its preferred route of escape when threatened. There's no mistaking this reptilian nightmare for any other lizard. Its head—the size of a man's fist—is crested with a frightening wig of leathery spines, its heavy body encased in a scaly hide, deeply wrinkled around the sockets of its muscular legs. Despite its menacing *One Million Years B.C.* appearance, it is quite harmless, a nonbelligerent vegetarian. Local gourmands, for reasons you may not wish to know, call the iguana the "tree chicken." Its cousin, the ctenosaur *(iguana negra)* is considered more edible, and you may see them on sale in *mercados* of major cities.

Another miniature dinosaur is *Basilicus basilicus,* or Jesus Christ lizard, a Pacific lowland dweller common in Santa Rosa, Palo Verde, and Corcovado national parks. These, too, have large crests atop their heads, backs, and tails, and use water as their means of escape, running across it on hind legs. (Hence their name.)

Terrestrial turtles are also common in Costa Rica, particularly in the Caribbean lowlands, where you can see them going about their business in the midmorning hours and after heavy rains. One species—the red turtle, found in northern Pacific lowlands—is particularly easy to spot: its high-domed carapace is gaudily patterned in oranges, reds, yellows, and blacks. Several species of aquatic turtles also frequent the swamps and creeks. Look for them squatting on partially submerged logs.

The amphibians are primarily represented by the dozens of species of frogs and toads, most of which you're probably more likely to hear than to see. That catlike meow? That's Boulenger's hyla, one of Costa Rica's more than 20 kinds of toxic frogs (see "Poison-Arrow Frogs," below). That sharp tink, tink that is usually the most prominent sound on damp nights in Costa Rica's midelevation rainforests? That's the tiny tink frog, of course. That insectlike buzz is probably two bright-red poison-arrow frogs wrestling belly-to-belly for the sake of a few square meters of turf. And the deafening choruses of long loud whoops that resound through the night in Nicoya and the adjacent lowlands of Guanacaste? That's an orgiastic band of ugly, orange and purple-black Mexican burrowing toads doing their thing. Should you locate them—the sound carries for miles—don't be surprised to find the horny toads floating like balloons with legs outstretched, emitting their lusty whoops. Love's a strange thing!

CROCODILES AND CAIMANS

Many travelers visit Costa Rica in the hope of seeing crocodiles and caimans, modest-size relatives. One of the smallest of western crocodilians—no more than two meters long—and possibly the most abundant in existence today, the speckled caiman is still relatively common in parts of wet lowland Costa Rica on both the Atlantic and Pacific coasts. Palo Verde and Tortuguero are both good places to spot them in small creeks, playas, and brackish mangrove swamps, or basking on the banks of streams and ponds.

The scales of the caiman take on the blue-green color of the water it slithers through. Such camouflage and even the ability to

red-eyed tree frog

breathe underwater, through raised nostrils, have not protected the caiman. Their nests are heavily disturbed by dogs, foxes, tegu lizards, and humans. And increasingly they are being sought for their skins, which are turned into trivia. Ironically, this is easing the pressure on the crocodiles, which are fast disappearing as humanity takes their hides and habitats.

The crocodile exists in precariously low numbers along both coasts, and the only healthy population is in Corcovado National Park in the Pacific southwest. Only three species of crocodiles—the saltwater croc of Southeast Asia, Africa's Nile crocodile, and the American alligator—are considered man-killers, but it's still a wise idea to check with locals or park rangers before swimming in coastal estuaries and lagoons.

For all their beastly behavior, crocodiles are devoted parents. And despite being relics from the age of the dinosaurs, croc brains are far more complex than those of other reptiles. Perhaps because crocodiles have ugly toothy leers and a stigma of primeval wickedness, there isn't the same love of crocs that has brought international support for the turtles, and their future is much less secure. As biologist David Janzen says: "We may never again see the huge four-meter animals that used to terrify the *campesinos* and eat their dogs."

POISON-ARROW FROGS

Of all Central America's exotic species none are more colorful—literally and figuratively—than the "poison-arrow" frogs, of the type from which Indians extract deadly poisons with which to tip their arrows. Frogs are tasty little fellows to carnivorous amphibians, reptiles, and birds. Hence, in many species, the mucous glands common in all amphibians have evolved to produce a bitter-tasting poison.

In Central and South America at least 20 kinds of frogs have developed this defense still further: their alkaloid poisons are so toxic that they can paralyze a large bird or small monkey immediately. Several species—the dendrobatids, or poison-arrow frogs, which are confined to Costa Rica—produce among the most potent toxins known: atelopidtoxin, bufogenin, bufotenidine, and bufotoxin. Pity the poor snake

that gobbles up *Dendrobatis granuliferus*, a tiny, bright green, red, and black frog that inhabits the lowland forests of the Golfo Dulce region (it is commonly seen on forest floors of Corcovado National Park). Another species, *Bufo marinus*, can even squirt its poison in a fine spray. And some species' eggs and tadpoles even produce toxins, making them unpalatable, like bad caviar!

Of course, it's no value to an individual frog if its attacker dies *after* devouring the victim. Hence, many have developed conspicuous, striking colors—bright yellow, scarlet, purple, and blue, the colors of poison recognized throughout the animal world—and sometimes "flash colors" (concealed when at rest but flashed at appropriate times to startle predators) that announce, "Beware!" These confident critters don't act like other frogs either. They're active by day not night, moving boldly around the forest floor, "confident and secure," says one writer, "in their brilliant livery."

Perhaps the most famous poison frog species is the rare **golden toad**, found only in the Monteverde Cloud Forest Reserve. In fact, the montane rainforest reserve owes its existence in part to the discovery of *Bufo periglenes*. This brilliant, neon orange arboreal toad—discovered in 1964 and so stunning that one biologist harbored "a suspicion that someone had dipped the examples in enamel paint"—is not easily seen, despite being one of the most brightly colored animals in the world. The golden toad is so seldom seen that some naturalists speculate that it may now exist only on the cover of tourist brochures.

April through May, golden toads go looking for love in the rainpools of scarlet bromeliads that festoon the high branches. They're easily distinguished: the males are the orange ones; females are yellow and black with patches of scarlet. Here, high in the trees, tadpoles of arboreal frogs wriggle about.

Adaptive Breeding

Few Costa Rican frog species breed in permanent bodies of water, where fish predation is intense. Above 1,500 meters, where there are no native fish species, stream breeding is more common, although the introduction in recent years of trout into upland streams already threatens whole frog populations.

The frogs instead have evolved away from dependence on bodies of permanent water. Many species, particularly the 39 species of hylids, spend their entire lives in the tree canopies where they breed in holes and bromeliads. The hylids have enlarged suction-cup pads on their toes. They often catch their prey in midair leaps: the suction discs guarantee sure-footed landings. Others deposit their eggs on vegetation over streams; the tadpoles fall when hatched. Others construct frothy foam nests, which they float on pools, dutifully guarded by the watchful male.

Some rainforest species, such as the diminutive and warty eleutherodactylus—its name is longer than its body—live on the ground, where they lay their eggs in moist cups of leaves. The tadpole develops fully within the egg sac before emerging as a perfect, if tiny, replica of its parents: it and 12 of its siblings could easily fit on a man's fingernail. Some tadpole species—the *Hyla zeteki*, for example—are cannibalistic: they eat other frogs' tadpoles. The carnivorous smoky frog (*Leptodactylus pentadactylus*), an aggressive giant (adults can grow up to 20 cm long), can eat snakes up to 50 cm long. It, too, can emit a poisonous toxin, to which some snakes are immune. If the smoky frog's loud hissing, inflated body, and poisonous secretions don't manage to scare off its predator, it has another ingenious defense: when captured it emits a loud scream.

SNAKES

Although rarely seen by the casual tourist in Costa Rica, snakes make up more than half of all reptile species in the nation (135 species, 17 poisonous). It is a fortunate traveler indeed who gets to see in the wild the fantastically elongated, I-beam-shaped **chunk-headed snake**, with its catlike elliptical eyes; the slender, beak-nosed bright green vinelike **vine snake;** or the relatively benign boa constrictor. Many neotropical snake species inhabit a wide range of Costa Rican environments, and wherever you are in the country snakes are sure to be about. Not that you should worry. Fewer than 500 snakebites are reported each year, and less than three percent of these are fatal. Most bites occur among farmworkers.

Still, caution is always the watchword. Never reach into holes or under rocks, debris, or forest-floor leaf litter without first checking with a stick to see what might be quietly slumbering there. And remember that many snakes are well-camouflaged arboreal creatures that snooze on branches, so never reach for a branch without looking. You should even be cautious when peering inside bromeliads: the dark-colored chunk-headed snake likes to doze inside the moisture-collecting plants during the dry season.

Among the more common snake species you are likely to see are the wide-ranging **boas,** which, with luck, you might spot crawling across a cultivated field or waiting patiently in the bough of a tree in wet or dry tropical forest, savannah, or dry thorn scrub. Wild boas vary in temperament and some are aggressive. Though not poisonous, they are quite capable of inflicting serious damage with their large teeth and will not hesitate to bite. Heaven forbid a full-grown adult (three meters or more) should sink its teeth in sufficiently to get its constricting coils around you!

Venomous Snakes

A species of tropical **rattlesnake** is also found in Guanacaste and a few relic areas of the Meseta Central. It produces a venom considerably more toxic than its North American cousin—blindness and suffocation are typical effects on humans—and it rarely uses its well-developed rattle to warn off the unwary.

Among the more colorful snakes are the four species of **coral snakes,** with small heads, blunt tails, and bright bands of red, black, and yellow or white. These *highly* venomous snakes (often fatal to humans) exhibit a spectacular defensive display when approached: they flatten their bodies and snap back and forth while alternately hiding then swinging their heads side to side and coiling and waving their tails.

Along the Pacific beaches, you may sometimes encounter venomous pelagic **sea snakes,** yellow-bellied and black-backed serpents closely related to terrestrial cobras and coral snakes. This gregarious snake has developed an oarlike tail to paddle its way through the ocean. It tends to drift passively with its buddies among driftlines of flotsam, where it feeds on small fish.

The most talked-about snake in Central America is the **fer-de-lance,** much feared for its aggressiveness and lethal venom. One of several Central American pit vipers—another is the bushmaster—the fer-de-lance can grow to a length of three meters and is abundant throughout the country, particularly in overgrown fields and rivercourses in drier lowland regions. Costa Ricans call this lethal creature *terciopelo,* Spanish for "velvet." As juveniles, fer-de-lance are arboreal critters that feed on lizards and frogs, which they attract with a yellow-tipped tail. As adults, they come down to earth, where they move about at night and, by daylight, rest in loose coils of burnished brown on the forest floor.

Give the fer-de-lance a wide berth! Unlike other vipers, the fer-de-lance will bite with little provocation. The snake's powerful venom dissolves nerve tissue and destroys blood cells and artery walls; those fortunate enough to survive may suffer paralysis or tissue damage so massive as to require amputation of the bitten limb.

The **Serpentario** in San José is a good place to learn to identify snakes and their habits and habitats (see "Other Attractions" under "Sightseeing" in the San José chapter). There is also a snake laboratory at the Clodomiro Picando Institute in Coronado, where you can watch snakes being milked for venom (see "San Isidro de Coronado" under "Northeast from San José" in the Central Highlands chapter).

TURTLES

Six of the world's eight species of marine turtles nest on Costa Rica's beaches, and you can see turtles laying eggs somewhere in Costa Rica virtually anytime of year. In "season," turtles can vastly outnumber tourists.

Tortuguero National Park, in northeastern Costa Rica, is one of fewer than 30 places in the world that the **green turtle** considers clean enough and safe enough to lay its eggs. Although green turtles were once abundant throughout the Caribbean, today there are only three important sites in the region where they nest: one on Aves Island, 62 km west of Montserrat, a second at Gandoca-Manzanillo (and occasionally on beaches

north toward Cahuita), and another at Tortuguero, the only major nesting site in the western Caribbean. June-Nov., peaking Aug.-Sept., more than 5,000 greens swim from their feeding grounds as far away as the Gulf of Mexico and Venezuela to lay their eggs at the eons-old nesting site on the oceanside 21-kilometer stretch of beach on Tortuguero's barrier island.

On the Pacific coast, the most spectacular nestings are at Playa Nancite, in Santa Rosa National Park, and Ostional Wildlife Refuge, where tens of thousands of **olive ridley turtles** come ashore July-Dec. in synchronized mass nestings known as *arribadas*. Giant **leatherback turtles,** which can weigh as much as a ton and reach a length of three meters (the largest reptile in the world), nest at Playa Grande, near Tamarindo, Oct.-April. Hawksbills, ridleys, leatherbacks, Pacific greens and occasionally loggerheads (primarily Caribbean nesters) appear in lesser numbers at other beaches along the Pacific coast.

Turtle Turmoils
One hundred years ago, green turtles were as numerous as the bison on the North American plains. They were highly prized for their meat by Central American and Carib Indians, who netted and harpooned them. And British and Spanish fleets, buccaneers, and merchantmen counted on turtle meat to feed their crews while cruising in New World waters. An average adult green turtle weighs 115 kg. They're easy to catch and easy to keep alive for weeks on their backs in a space no bigger than the turtle itself. ("Turtle turners" patrolled nesting beaches, where they wrestled female turtles on to their backs to be picked up next day.)

TURTLE NESTING

SPECIES	SEASON	LOCATION
Hawksbill	March-Aug.	Caribbean
Green	June-Nov.	Caribbean
Leatherback	Feb.-July	Caribbean
	Oct.-April	Pacific
Ridley	year-round (July-Dec. peak)	Pacific

green sea turtle

The end of colonialism offered no respite. Large-scale green turtle export from Tortuguero, for example, began in 1912 when turtle soup became a delicacy in Europe. And the recurrent massing of olive ridley turtles at a few accessible beaches fostered intensive human exploitation. Despite legislation outlawing the taking of turtle eggs or disturbance of nesting turtles, nest sites continue to be raided by humans (encouraged by an ancient Mayan legend that says the eggs are aphrodisiacs).

When not nesting in Costa Rica, Pacific ridleys congregate in Mexican and Ecuadorian waters, where commercial exploitation continues in earnest (in 1968, Mexican fishermen harvested more than one million turtles for the leather trade). Turtle oil is used in the manufacture of cosmetics and perfumes, the shells used in jewelry and ornaments, and the offal dried and processed as fertilizer. Hawksbills, which rarely exceed 55 kg, are hunted illegally for the tourist trade: one occasionally still sees stuffed turtle specimens for sale.

Mother Nature, too, poses her own challenges. Coatis, dogs, raccoons, and peccaries dig up nest sites to get at the tasty eggs. Gulls, vultures, and hungry frigate birds, with their piercing eyes and sharp beaks, pace the beach hungrily awaiting the hatchlings; crabs lie in wait for the tardy; and hungry jacks, barracudas, and sharks come close to shore for the feast. Ridley hatchlings have even been found in the stomachs of leatherback turtles. Of the hundreds of eggs laid by a female in one season, only a handful will survive to reach maturity. (As many as 70% of the hatchlings are eaten before they reach the water.)

Most of the important nesting sites in Costa Rica are now protected, and access to some is restricted. Still, there is a shortage of undisturbed beaches where turtles can safely nest. Most turtle populations continue to decline because of illegal harvesting and environmental pressures, despite the best efforts of conservationists inspired by Dr. Archie Carr, of the University of Florida, who has written and lectured indefatigably on behalf of turtle protection (see "Tortuguero National Park" under "Tortuguero and Vicinity" in the Caribbean Coast chapter).

Turtle Ecology

Turtles have hit on a formula for outwitting their predators, though, or at least for surviving despite them. Each female turtle normally comes ashore two to six times each season and lays an average of 100 eggs on each occasion. Some marvelous internal clock arranges for most eggs to hatch at night when hatchlings can make their frantic rush for the sea concealed by darkness. Often, baby turtles will emerge from the eggs during the day and wait beneath the surface of the beach until nightfall. The young hatch together and dig their way up out through up to a meter of sand as a kind of "simple-minded, cooperative brotherhood," says Archie Carr, "working mindlessly together to lower the penalties of being succulent on a hostile shore." They are programmed to travel fast across the beach to escape the hungry mouths. Even after reaching the sea they continue to swim frantically for several days—flippers paddling furiously—like clockwork toys.

No one knows where baby turtles go. They swim off and generally are not seen again until they appear years later as adults. Turtles are very slow growing; most immature turtles of all species increase in carapace length by less than three cm a year. In fact, little is known about the lives of adult marine turtles. In captivity, a turtle can grow to the size of the smallest fertile nester in about 10 years; in the wild, they grow much slower.

Turtles are great travelers capable of amazing feats of navigation. Greens, for example, navigate across up to 1,500 miles of open sea to return, like salmon, to the same nest site. Guided presumably by stars and currents, thousands of greens arrive at Tortuguero every year from their faraway feeding grounds. (Most Tortuguero greens apparently arrive from the Miskito Bank feeding area of Nicaragua.)

TURTLE WATCHING

Caribbean

Tortuguero: Loggerheads and hawksbills come ashore year-round, but especially in August. The major attraction is green turtles, which nest here June-November. They concentrate in the section of beach between Parismina and the mouth of the Río Tortuguero. Numbers vary year to year, with as few as 3,000 and as many as 8,000 in a season.

Barra de Matina Beach: Leatherbacks, greens, and hawksbills all come ashore at this leatherback sanctuary north of Puerto Limón. April and May are the best months to spot leatherbacks. By July, they are gone, replaced by greens, which can be seen in large numbers through September. Hawksbills also come ashore year-round, mostly March-August.

Gandoca-Manzanillo Wildlife Refuge: Four species of turtles lay their eggs, Jan.-April, on this beautiful beach south of Punta Uva.

Pacific

Curú Wildlife Refuge: Three species of turtles come ashore at this private refuge, on the eastern coast of the Nicoya Peninsula.

Las Baulas Marine National Park: Costa Rica's most stunning beach—Playa Grande—is the pre-eminent nesting site for leatherback turtles. It has evolved into perhaps the nation's best-managed site and is easily reached, with plenty of hotels nearby. Leatherbacks come ashore Oct.-April; up to 100 on any one night. Olive ridley and green turtles can be seen here in small numbers May-August.

Ostional National Wildlife Refuge: This 248-hectare refuge, north of Playa Nosara, is the major nesting site of olive ridleys. Leatherbacks and a small number of Pacific greens (called *negras* locally) also nest here. Solitary nesters can be seen on most nights. Ostional is also one of two sites in Costa Rica where synchronized mass nestings *(arribadas)* of the *lora*, or olive ridley, occur. Ridleys come ashore in massive numbers at two- to four-week intervals (generally between the third quarter and full moon) April-Dec., with a peak in July-September. During each *arribada* (which may last four to eight days), up to 120,000 turtles may nest at Ostional.

Playa Nancite: Located in Santa Rosa National Park, Nancite is the second major site for *arribadas*. Some 200,000 ridleys choose Nancite. Leatherbacks and Pacific greens also nest at Nancite. Peak arrival for ridleys (called *carpentaria* locally) is midsummer, with a peak in October.

Turtles come ashore at many other beaches along the Pacific coast. See regional chapters for details.

Tours

The following operators offer tours to the major turtle nesting sites:

Costa Rica Temptations (1600 N.W. LeJeune Rd., Suite 301, Miami FL 33126, tel. 305-871-2657 or 800-336-8423) has a "Turtles Under the Moonlight" tour during the *arribadas* (from $35). **Tikal Tour Operators** (Apdo. 6398, San José 1000, tel. 223-2811, fax 223-1916) has a three-day turtle-watching tour visiting Playa Grande. **Papagayo Excursions** (Apdo. 35, Santa Cruz de Guanacaste, tel. 680-0859, fax 225-3648) has a one-day "Turtle Nesting Safari" to Playa Grande. **Guanacaste Tours** (Apdo. 55, Liberia 5000, tel. 666-0306, fax 666-0307) has nighttime turtle-watching tours to Playa Grande (Nov.-Feb., $40) and Playa Ostional (July-Nov., $50).

From the U.S., **Extraordinary Expeditions** (P.O. Box 1739, Hailey, ID 83333, tel. 800-234-1569) offers eight departures on a 10-day "Sea Turtles of Playa Nancite" tour in which participants camp out and assist local researchers (from $1015). **Journeys** (4011 Jackson Road, Ann Arbor, MI 48103, tel. 800-255-8735) also offers a 10-day "Tortuguero Jungle Odyssey" timed to coincide with the green-turtle nestings ($1395).

One of the few things known about the intervals between females' trips to the nesting beaches is that a lot of strenuous romance goes on out in the surf. There is no pair-bonding between individual turtles, and each female may be courted by as many as 10 males.

"Sea turtles in love are appallingly industrious," according to Archie Carr. "The male turtle holds himself in the mating position on top of the smooth, curved, wet shell of the wave-tossed female by employing a three-point grappling rig [consisting] of his long, thick, curved, horn-tipped tail and a heavy, hooked claw on each front flipper . . . The female generally stays coy and resistant for what seems an unnecessarily long while. Other males gather, and all strive together

VOLUNTEER PROGRAMS TO SAVE THE TURTLES

If you're interested in helping save turtles, consider volunteering services to the following organizations.

The **Caribbean Conservation Corps** (P.O. Box 2866, Gainesville, FL 32602, tel. 904-373-6441 or 800-678-7853; in Costa Rica tel. 224-9215) enlists volunteers to patrol Tortuguero during nesting season to protect the nests from poaching and help boost the survival rates of newborn turtles. Enclose $1 and a stamped, self-addressed business-size envelope with your request for information to help defray costs for this nonprofit organization.

The **Earth Island Institute** (300 Broadway, San Francisco, CA 94133, tel. 415-788-3666 or 800-859-SAVE) has a "Sea Turtle Restoration Project" in which paying guests count and tag turtles, take radio-transmitter readings, and perform other duties at Playa Nancite and Ostional ($1075-1175, eight days).

Youth Challenge International (11 Soho St., Toronto, ON M5T 1Z6, Canada, tel. 416-971-9846) accepts volunteers for its "Turtle Project" at Playa Ostional.

Volunteers with the **Foundation for Field Research** (P.O. Box 2010, Alpine, CA 92001, tel. 619-445-9264) help biologists in a leatherback turtle study program as well as patrol the beach at Michoacán, Mexico. Five- to 15-day programs are offered at selected times of the year.

over the female in a vast frothy melee." In the frenzy of mating, intelligence seems sadly lacking. Females have been mounted by a male who in turn is mounted by another male while several more jealous males jostle and bite one another to dislodge the successful Casanova.

Most females make their clumsy climb up the beach and lay their eggs under the cover and cool of darkness (loggerheads and ridleys often nest in the daytime, as they seem less timid). They normally time their arrival to coincide with high tide, when they can swim in over the coral reef and when they do not have to drag themselves puffing and panting across a wide expanse of beach. Their great weight, unsupported by water, makes breathing difficult. As a turtle drags her ponderous bulk up the beach, her progress is slow and punctuated by numerous halts to breathe. Some turtles even die of heart attacks brought on by the exertions of digging and laying.

Once she settles on a comfortable spot above the high tide mark, the female scoops out a large body pit with her front flippers. Then her amazingly dexterous hind flippers go to work hollowing out a small egg chamber below her tail and into which white, spongy, golf-ball-size spheres fall every few seconds. After shoveling the sand back into place and flinging sand wildly about to hide her precious treasure, she makes her way back to sea. **Note:** When near nesting sites, respect the turtles' need for peace and quiet. Nesting turtles are very timid and extremely sensitive to flashlights, sudden movements, and noise, which will send a female turtle in hasty retreat to the sea without laying her eggs. Sometimes in desperation she will drop her eggs on the sand without digging a proper nest.

The eggs normally take six to eight weeks to hatch, incubated by the warm sand. The sex of the hatchling is determined by the temperature of the sand: males are predominantly produced in cooler sand; a difference of two to three degrees Celsius will produce females. Thus, hatchlings from any one nest site are usually siblings of the same gender.

MAMMALS

Given the rich diversity of Costa Rica's ecosystems, it may come as a surprise that only 200 mammal species, half of which are bats, live here. And Costa Rica, like most neotropical countries, has "a depauperate marine mammal flora," in the words of one biologist. Several species of dolphins and seven species of whales are common in Costa Rican waters, but there are no seals. And the only endemic species of any significance is the endangered manatee.

Before man hunted them to extinction, there were many more mammal species. Even today all large- and many small-mammal populations are subject to extreme hunting pressure or habitat destruction, and it is only recently that large-mammal populations in the national parks are beginning to recover. Like most large mammals, jaguars and tapirs are shy and stay well clear of people. Sighting one would be cause for great celebration! Still, most visitors can expect to see one or more species of monkeys, one of Costa Rica's four ecologically unique tropical mammals; the others are sloths, anteaters, and noninsectivorous bats. And luck, patience, and the aid of a professional guide can lead to thrilling encounters with other species.

Early morning and late afternoon are the best times for wildlife viewing, particularly around waterholes (the dry regions of Guanacaste offer prime locations). I recommend joining a natural-history tour or guided day tours through one of the many tour companies specializing in wildlife programs (see special topic "Natural-History Cruise Tours" in the On the Road chapter).

The *Costa Rica Mammal Flip Chart,* by Anthony Schmitz, provides a handy, simple guide to 44 mammals ($6 plus $2 shipping; Rebecca Thompson, P.O. Box 1221, Centralia, WA 98531, tel. 206-748-8731). No technical verbiage here; it's an informative little pocket-scale wonder replete with drawings of each mammal, plus range map, drawings of tracks, and other data for laypeople.

MONKEYS

No visit to Costa Rica would be complete without seeing any of its four species of monkeys: the cebus (or capuchin), howler, spider, and squirrel. Along with approximately 50 other species, they belong to a group called New World monkeys, which evolved from a single simian group that appeared about 40 million years ago in Africa and Asia. Some of these early primates migrated to North America and then down the land bridge to Central and South America.

Though the North American monkeys gradually died out, their southern cousins flourished and evolved along lines that differ markedly from those of their ancestors in the Old World. While African and Asian monkeys have narrow noses with nostrils that point down (much like human noses), New World monkeys evolved broad, widely spaced nostrils. New World females, too, evolved a singular ability to bear twins. And, perhaps most important, some New World species—notably the cebus, howler, and spider monkeys—developed long prehensile tails for added purchase and balance in the high treetops.

capuchin monkey

They inhabit a wide range of habitats, from the rainforest canopy to the scrubby undergrowth of the dry forests, though each species occupies its own niche and the species seldom meet. Together, they are the liveliest and most vocal jungle tenants. Beyond the reach of most predators, they have little inhibition about announcing their presence with their rough-housing and howls, chatterings, and screeches. The sudden explosive roar of the howler monkey—a sound guaranteed to make your hair

stand on end!—is said to be the loudest sound in the animal kingdom.

Capuchins

The distinctive-looking capuchin is the smartest and most inquisitive of Central American simians. It derives its name from its black body and monklike white cowl. If they look familiar to you, you've probably seen them dancing at the end of a tether at street fairs in Europe or South America—they're the little guys favored by organ-grinders worldwide. Capuchins range widely throughout the wet lowland forests of the Caribbean coast and the deciduous dry forests of the Pacific northwest below 1,500 meters. Two excellent places to see them are Santa Rosa and Manuel Antonio National Parks, where family troops are constantly on the prowl, foraging widely through the treetops and over the forest floor.

These opportunistic feeders are fun to watch as they search under logs and leaves or tear off bark as they seek out insects and small lizards soon after dawn and again in late afternoon. Capuchins also steal birds' eggs and nestlings. Some crafty coastal residents, not content with grubs and insect larvae, have developed a taste for oysters and other mollusks, which they break open on rocks. The frugal capuchin sometimes hoards his food for "rainy days." While their taste is eclectic, they *are* fussy eaters: they'll meticulously pick out grubs from fruit, which they test for ripeness by smelling and squeezing. And capuchins are not averse to crop-raiding, especially corn, as the farmers of Guanacaste will attest.

Squirrel Monkeys

The smallest Costa Rican primate, the squirrel monkey or titi, which grows to 25-35 cm, plus a tail up to 45 cm, is restricted to the rainforests of the southern Pacific lowlands. Always on the go, day and night, they scurry about in the jungle understory and forest floor on all fours, where they are safe from raptor predators. Squirrels are more gregarious than most other monkeys; bands of 40 individuals or more are not uncommon. Like the larger capuchins, the golden-orange titi (with its face of white and black) is the arboreal goat of the forest. It will eat almost anything: fruits, insects, small lizards. In times of abundance (May-Oct.), the two species have been known to forage together. When food is scarce they become rivals; the heftier capuchin invariably is the victor. The titi is an endangered species well on its way to extinction.

Spider Monkeys

The large, loose-limbed spider monkey—the supreme acrobat of the forest—was once the most widespread of the Central American monkeys. Unfortunately, they are very sensitive to human intrusion and are among the first primate species to decline with disturbance. The last few decades have brought significant destruction of squirrel monkey habitats, and land clearance and hunting—their flesh is said to be very tasty—have greatly reduced spider monkey populations throughout much of their former range. If you inadvertently come across them you'll soon know it: they often rattle the branches and bark and screech loudly to demonstrate their fearlessness.

spider monkey

These copper-colored acrobats can attain a length of a meter and a half. They have evolved extreme specialization for a highly mobile arboreal lifestyle. Long slender limbs allow spider monkeys to make spectacular leaps. But the spider's greatest secret is its extraordinary prehensile tail, which is longer than the combined length of its head and body. The underside is ridged like a human fingertip for added grip at the end of treetop leaps (it is even sensitive enough for probing and picking). You might even see individuals hanging like ripe fruit by their tails.

Gregarious by night (they often bed down in heaps), by day they are among the most solitary of primates. The males stay aloof from the females. While the latter tend to their young, which

they carry on their backs, the males are busy marking their territory with secretions from their chest glands.

Howlers

The howler is the most abundant as well as the largest of Central American monkeys (it can weigh up to five kg). It inhabits both lowland and montane forests throughout Costa Rica. Fortunately, it is less sensitive to habitat destruction than the spider monkey and can be found clinging precariously to existence in many relic patches of forest.

While howlers are not particularly aggressive, they sure sound it! The stentorian males greet each new day with reveille calls that seem more like the explosive roars of lions than those of small arboreal leaf-eaters. The hair-raising vocalizations can carry for almost a mile in even the densest of jungle. The males sing in chorus again at dusk (or whenever trespassers get too close) as a spacing mechanism to keep rivals at a safe distance. Their Pavarotti-like vocal abilities are due to unusually large larynxes and throats that inflate into resonating balloons. Females generally content themselves with loud wails and groans—usually to signal distress or call a straying infant. This noisy yet sedentary canopy browser feeds on leaves (64% of its diet) and fruit. Although capable of eating anything that grows, howlers are extremely selective feeders.

JAGUARS

Worshiped as a god in pre-Columbian civilizations, the jaguar is the symbol of the Central American jungle. *Panthera onca* was once especially abundant in the dense forests, coastal mangroves, and lowland savannahs of Central America. Today, sadly, this magnificent and

howler monkey

jaguar

noble beast is an endangered species, rare except in parts of the larger reserves: Santa Rosa, Tortuguero, and Corcovado National Parks, the Río Macho Forest Reserve, and lower levels of the Cordillera Talamanca.

While a few of the famous black "panther" variety exist, most Central American jaguars are a rich yellow, spotted with large black rosettes. Jaguars are the largest and most powerful of the American members of the cat family—a mature jaguar measures over two meters, stands 60 cm at the shoulders, and weighs up to 90 kg. The animal's head and shoulders are massive, the legs relatively short and thick. An adept climber and swimmer, the beast is a versatile hunter, at home in trees, on ground, and even in water. Not surprisingly, it feeds on a wide range of arboreal, terrestrial, and aquatic animals and is powerful enough to kill a full-grown cow.

Don't be surprised if you come across a jaguar's footprints alongside a mangrove islet or streambed in the gallery forest. Don't get your hopes up, however. You're not likely to see one lying lazily by the riverbank (a favorite pastime), one paw dangling in the water, as it waits to flip out a passing fish or turtle.

Although one source states that they seem not to avoid the scent of man and may follow a man walking a trail, most agree that jaguars are extremely shy creatures, not particularly dangerous, and attack humans very rarely. Although jaguars are legally protected and spotted cat trophies cannot be imported into the U.S., hunting may still occur. However, the main threat to the remaining jaguar population

is deforestation. When roads penetrate the primeval forest, the jaguar is among the first large mammals to disappear.

These splendid beasts are easily seen at the "Cat Zoo of Guanacaste," outside Cañas (see "Las Pumas Mini Zoo" under "Cañas to Liberia" in the Guanacaste and the Northwest chapter), where injured and orphaned jaguars, cougars, ocelots, margay, jaguarundi, and tiger cats are nursed back to health and/or prepared for a second life in the wild.

SLOTHS

Ask anyone to compile a list of the world's strangest creatures and the sloth would be right up there with the duck-billed platypus. And while the creature moves with the grace and deliberation of a tai chi master, few would argue about the beast's ugly looks. The sloth, which grows to about the size of a medium-size dog, has a small head and flat face with snub nose, beady eyes, and rudimentary ears (its hearing is reputedly so poor that one can fire a gun within centimeters and its only response will be a slow turn of the head). Its long, bony arms are well-developed, however, with three curving claws, which hook over and grasp the branches from which it spends almost its entire life suspended upside down.

The arboreal beast pays no attention to personal hygiene. Its shaggy fur harbors algae and mold that make the sloth greenly inconspicuous—wonderful camouflage from prowling

three-toed sloth

jaguars and keen-eyed eagles, its chief predators. Hordes of mites, beetles, and caterpillars graze on its moldy hair. And the sloth even has communities of parasitic moths that live in the depths of its fur.

Lulled by its relative treetop security, the sloth, says naturalist David Attenborough, "has sunken into an existence just short of complete torpor." The creature spends up to 18 hours daily sleeping curled up with its feet drawn close together and its head tucked between the forelimbs. Actually, Costa Rica has two species of sloths: the three-toed sloth (Bradypus variegatus) and the nocturnal two-toed sloth (Choloepus hoffmani). You're more likely to see Bradypus, which is active by day.

At top speed a sloth can barely cover a mile in four hours. On the ground, it is even more awkward and crawls with great difficulty or simply falls on the ground. In fact, there's a very good reason sloths move at a rate barely distinguishable from rigor mortis.

A sloth's digestion works as slowly as its other bodily functions. Its metabolic rate is half that of other animals of similar size, and food remains in its stomach for up to a week. Hence, it has evolved a large ruminant-like stomach and intestinal tract to process large quantities of relatively indigestible food. To compensate, it has sacrificed heavy muscle mass—and, hence, mobility—to maximize body size in proportion to weight. Thus, the sloth has evolved as a compromise between a creature large enough to store and process large quantities of food and one light enough to move about in trees without breaking the branches.

When nature calls (about once a week), the animal descends to ground level, where it digs a small hole with its hind limbs. It then shits into the depression, urinates, covers the broth with leaves, and returns much relieved to its arboreal life. During this 30-minute period, the female "sloth moths" have been busy laying their eggs on the sloth dung. When hatched, the larvae feed and pulpate on the feces. The newly emerged adults then fly off to seek a new sloth.

Sloths, which may live up to 20 years or longer, reach sexual maturity at three years, a relatively old age for mammals of their size. Females give birth once a year (the gestation period is about six months) and spend half their

adult lives pregnant. Although female sloths are never separated by choice from their offspring, they are peculiarly unsentimental about their young: if a baby tumbles, its plaintive distress calls go unheeded. And when the juvenile reaches six months old, the mother simply turns tail on her youngster, which inherits her "home range" of trees.

An easy way to find sloths is to look up into the green foliage of cecropia trees, which form one of the sloth's favorite food staples. More adventurous individuals might even be basking in the sunlight, feigning death halfway up a tree. The sloth's heavy fur coat provides excellent insulation against heat loss. Still, its body temperature drops almost to the temperature of its surroundings at night and, much like cold-blooded reptiles, the sloth needs to take in the sun's rays to bring its temperature to normal mammalian levels. The sight of a sloth languishing in open cecropia crowns is a heavenly vision to harpy eagles, which swoop in to snatch the torpid creature much like plucking ripe fruit.

TAPIRS

Another symbol of the New World tropics is the strange-looking tapir, a solitary, ground-living, plant-eating, forest-dwelling, ungainly mixture of elephant, rhinoceros, pig, and horse. The tapir uses its short, highly mobile proboscis—an evolutionary forerunner to the trunk of the elephant—for plucking leaves and shoveling them into its mouth. This endangered species is the largest indigenous terrestrial land mammal in Central America. Like its natural predator the jaguar, the tapir has suffered severely at the hands of man. The animal was common in Costa Rica and ranged far and wide in the lowland swamps and forests. It was even present in the bamboo thickets up to 3,000 meters elevation in the Talamanca mountains. Hunters have brought it to the edge of extinction.

Today, tapirs are found only in national parks and reserves where hunting is restricted, with the greatest density in Corcovado National Park, which has a population of fewer than 300. They have learned to be wary of man, and few travelers have the privilege of sighting them in the wild. Tapirs live in dense forests and swamps and rely on concealment for defense. They are generally found wallowing up to their knees in swampy waters. In fact, tapirs are rarely seen far from water, to which they rush precipitously at the first sign of danger. The tapir's speed—in the forest it can run as fast as a man in the open—is no protection from hunters. The animals make conspicuous trails in the forest, and because tapirs maintain territories which they mark with dung or scent, they are easily tracked by dogs.

BATS

It won't take you long to discover that the most numerous mammals by far are the bats, found throughout Costa Rica. You may easily come across them slumbering by day halfway up a tree or roosting in a shed. In true Dracula fashion, most bats are lunarphobic: they avoid the bright light. On nights one week before and after the full moon, they suspend foraging completely and stay in their roosts while the moon is at its peak.

Many bat species look more grotesque than any painted demon in a medieval manuscript. Most of these—like the giant **Jamaican fruit bat,** with a wingspan of more than 50 cm—are frugivores (fruit eaters) or insectivores, and quite harmless.

The **vampire bats** are a different matter: they inflict an estimated $100 million of damage on domestic farm animals throughout Central and South America by transmitting rabies and other diseases. The vampire bat's modus operandi is almost as frightening as the stuff of Bram Stoker's *Dracula.* It lands on or close to a sleeping mammal, such as a cow or, yes, even an unsuspecting human. Using its two razor-sharp incisors, it then punctures the unsuspecting beast and, with the aid of an anticoagulant saliva, merrily squats beside the wound and laps up the blood while it flows.

The most interesting of bats, however, and one easily seen in Tortuguero, is the **fishing bulldog bat,** with its huge wingspan (up to 60 cm across) and great gaff-shaped claws with which it hooks fish. It fishes by sonar. Skimming the water surface it is able to detect slight ripples ahead. The bat then drops its hooked feet at just the right moment and—hey presto!—supper.

OTHER MAMMALS

The most commonly seen mammal is the **agouti,** a large rodent related to the guinea pig and which looks like a giant tailless squirrel. Its nocturnal cousin, the **paca,** is a favorite of hunters. Both are easily captured because of the strong anal musks they use to scent their territories and because of their habit of running in circles but never leaving their home turf (pacas, at least, are intelligent enough to leap into water and stay submerged for a considerable time). If you disturb one in the forest, you may hear its high-pitched alarm bark before you see it.

Anteaters, too, are common in lowland and middle-elevation habitats throughout Costa Rica. These are the squirrel-size, tree-dwelling kind called tamanduas. The giant terrestrial anteater, with its huge, bushy tail, is now restricted to the less sparsely forested areas of the Osa Peninsula. At night you may, with a great deal of luck, also see the strictly arboreal silky anteater, which can hang from its strong prehensile tail. Anteaters are purists and subsist solely on a diet of ants and termites, plus a few unavoidable bits of dirt. There is no doubt about what the best tool is for the job—a long, sticky tongue. The anteater's toothless jaw is one long tube. When it feeds, its thong of a tongue flicks in and out of its tiny mouth, running deep into the galleries of excavated ant and termite nests. Each time it withdraws, it brings with it a load of ants, which are scraped off inside the tunnel of its mouth and swallowed, to be ground down by small quantities of sand and gravel in its stomach.

tamandua anteater

Another endearing and commonly seen mammal is the long-nosed **coati,** the most diurnal member of the raccoon family, found throughout the country. Coatis wear many coats, from yellow to deepest brown, though all are distinguished by their faintly ringed tail, white-tipped black snout, and pandalike eye-rings. The animal is at home both on the ground and in the treetops, where it can sometimes be spotted moving from tree to tree. (The name coatimundi refers specifically to lone coatis; the animals are usually gregarious critters.)

Another charming member of the raccoon family is the small and totally nocturnal **kinkajou,** with its large limpid eyes and velvet-soft coat of golden brown. It's a superb climber and spends most of its life feeding on fruit, honey, and insects in the treetops. By day it is very drowsy; if picked up, its first instinct is to cuddle against your chest, bury its head to avoid the light, and drop back off to sleep.

The sleek, long-haired chocolate-brown **tayra**—a meter-long giant of the weasel family—is often seen in highland habitats throughout Costa Rica. Weighing up to five kg, the tayra habitually preys on rodents but can make quick work of small deer, such as the **red brocket deer** and **white-tailed deer,** commonly seen in habitats throughout the country. Keep an eye off the ground, too, particularly in Santa Rosa National Park, where tayras can sometimes be seen stalking squirrels in the crowns of deciduous trees with a motion so fluid they seem to move like snakes.

You may, too, with luck come upon **peccaries,** but preferably at a distance! These wild pigs are notoriously fickle and potentially aggressive creatures whose presence in the rainforest may be betrayed by their pungent, musky odor and by the churned-up ground from their grubbing. Gregarious beasts, they forage in herds and make a fearsome noise if frightened or disturbed. Like most animals, they prefer to flee from human presence. Occasionally, however, an aggressive male may show his bravado by threatening to have a go at you, usually in a bluff charge. Rangers advise that you should climb a tree if threatened. The collared peccary *(saino)* is marked by an ochre-colored band of hair running from its shoulders down to its nose; the rest of its body is dark brown. The white-lipped peccary *(cariblanco)* is all black, or brown, with a white mustache or "beard."

Anyone venturing to Tortuguero National Park will no doubt be hopeful of seeing a West Indian **manatee.** This herbivorous marine mammal has

long been hunted for its flesh, which is supposedly tender and delicious, and for its very tough hide, once used for machine belts and high-pressure hoses. The heavily wrinkled beast looks like a tuskless walrus, with small round eyes, fleshy lips that hang over the sides of its mouth, and no hind limbs, just a large, flat, spatulate tail. Now endangered throughout their former range, these creatures once inhabited brackish rivers and lagoons along the whole coast of Central America's Caribbean shoreline. Today, only a few remain in the most southerly waters of the U.S. and

isolated pockets of Central America. Tortuguero, where the animals are legally protected, has one of the few significant populations. They are not easy to spot, for they lie submerged with only nostrils showing. Watch for rising bubbles in the water: manatees suffer from flatulence, a result of eating up to 45 kg of water hyacinths and other aquatic flora daily. Good fortune may even provide an encounter with groups of manatees engaged in courtship ritual. Interestingly, the manatee is one of very few species in which males engage in homosexual activity.

manatee

ERIN DWYER

BIRDS

In William Henry Hudson's *Green Mansions,* his great romantic novel of the American tropics, the young hero Abel is lured into the jungle by the mysterious call of an unseen bird. So stirred is he by the siren song that he follows the haunting sound deeper and deeper into the forest until he eventually discovers the source: a lovely, half-wild girl called Rima, who has learned to mimic the sounds of the birds. The birdlife of Costa Rica is so rich and so varied—and often so elusive—that at times it seems as if Rima herself is calling.

With approximately 850 recorded bird species, the country boasts one-tenth of the world's total. More than 630 are resident species; the remainder are occasionals who fly in for the winter. Birds that have all but disappeared in other areas still find tenuous safety in protected lands in Costa Rica, though many species face extinction from deforestation. The nation offers hope for such rare jewels of the bird world as the quetzal and the scarlet macaw, both endangered species yet commonly seen in protected reserves.

It may surprise you to learn that in a land with so many exotic species the national bird is the relatively drab *yiquirro,* or clay-colored robin, a brown-and-buff bird with brick-red eyes. You may hear the male singing during the March through May breeding season when, according to *campesino* folklore, he is "calling the rains." Otherwise both sexes are mum.

BIRDWATCHING

Fortunately, Costa Rica's birds are not shy. Seeing them is relatively easy. Depending on season, location, and luck, you can expect to see many dozens of species on any one day. Many tour companies offer guided bird-study tours (see "Special-Interest Travel and Recreation" in the On the Road chapter), and the country is well set up with mountain and jungle lodges that specialize in birdwatching programs. Annual "bird counts" also need volunteers (contact Rafael Campos, tel. 444-6572, or Hector Gonzalez, tel. 710-6897).

The deep heart of the jungle is not the best place to look for birds: you cannot see well amid the complex, disorganized patterns cast by shadow and light. For best results, find a large clearing on the fringe of the forest, or a watercourse where birds are sure to be found in abundance.

keel-billed toucans

JEAN McKULK

MOTMOT: HOW IT GOT ITS TAIL

The long-billed bird that makes his home in a hole in the ground is the motmot. Of nine species of motmot in tropical America, six live in Costa Rica. You'll find them from humid coastal southwest plains to the cool highland zone and dry Guanacaste region and, yes, even San José. You can't mistake this colorful charmer: he (and she) has a pendulous twin-feathered tail with the barbs missing three-quarters-way down, leaving two disc-shaped tips like pendant oval earrings.

According to Bribrí legend, the god Sibo asked all the creatures to help him make the world. They all chipped in gladly except the motmot, who hid in a hole. Unfortunately, the bird left his tail hanging out. When the other birds saw this they picked the feathers from the motmot's tail but left the feathers at the tip.

When the world was complete, Sibo gave all the tired animals a rest. Soon the motmot appeared and began boasting about how hard he had labored. But the lazy bird's tail gave the game away, so Sibo, who guessed what had happened, admonished the motmot and banished him to living in a hole in the ground.

BOB RACE

toucans—"flying bananas"—are a particular delight to watch as they pick fruit off one at a time with their long beaks, throw them in the air and catch them at the back of their throats. Costa Rica's six toucan species are among the most flamboyant of all Central American birds. That loud frog-like croak is the Swainson's toucan; that noisy jumble of cries and piercing creaks could well be a congregation of gregarious chestnut-mandibled toucans.

In fact, many birds are easily heard but not seen. The **three-wattled bellbird,** which inhabits the cloud forests, is rarely spotted in the mist-shrouded treetops, though the male's eerie call, described by one writer as a ventriloqual 'bonk!' (it is more like a hammer clanging on an anvil), haunts the forest as long as the sun is up. And the lunatic laughter that goes on compulsively at dusk in lowland jungles is the **laughing falcon.** Fortunately other species, such as the **tanagers,** brighten the jungle, and you are likely to spot their bright plumage as you hike along trails. The tanagers' short stubby wings enable them to swerve and dodge at high speed through the undergrowth as they chase after insects. By contrast, the great **curassow,** growing as tall as one meter, is almost too big for flight and tends to run through the undergrowth if disturbed. You're most likely to see this endangered bird in Corcovado or Santa Rosa National Park.

The sheer size of Costa Rica's bird population has prompted some intriguing food-gathering methods. The **jacamar** snaps up insects on the wing with an audible click of its beak. One species of epicurean **kite** has a bill like an escargot fork, which it uses to pick snails from their shells. The **attila,** like its namesake a ruthless killer, devours its frog victims whole after bashing them against a tree.

The four major "avifaunal zones" roughly correspond to the major geographic subdivisions of the country: the northern Pacific lowlands, the southern Pacific lowlands, the Caribbean lowlands, and the interior highlands. Guanacaste's dry habitats (northern Pacific lowlands) share relatively few species with other parts of the country. This is a superlative place, however, for waterfowl: the estuaries, swamps, and lagoons that make up the Tempisque Basin support the richest freshwater avifauna in all Central America, and Palo Verde National Park, at the mouth of the Tempisque, is a birdwatcher's mecca.

The southern Pacific lowland region is home to many South American neotropical species, such as jacamars, antbirds, and, of course, parrots. Here, within the dense forests, the air is cool and dank and underwater green and alive with the sounds of birds. The bright-billed

Other birds you might expect to see include the boobies, the rare harpy eagle (the largest of all eagles, renowned for twisting and diving through the treetops in pursuit of monkeys), pelicans, parakeets, oropendolas, woodpeckers, and a host of birds you may not recognize but whose names you will never forget: scarlet-thighed dacnis, violaceous trogons, tody motmots, laneolated monlets, lineated foliage-gleaners, and black-capped pygmy tyrants.

HUMMINGBIRDS

Of all the exotically named bird species in Costa Rica, the hummingbirds beat all contenders. Their names are poetry: the green-crowned brilliant, purple-throated mountaingem, Buffon's plummeteer, and the bold and strikingly beautiful fiery-throated hummingbird. More than 300 species of New World hummingbirds constitute the family Trochilidae (Costa Rica has 51), and all are stunningly pretty. The fiery-throated hummingbird, for example, is a glossy green, shimmering iridescent at close range, with dark blue tail, violet-blue chest, glittering coppery orange throat, and a brilliant blue crown set off by velvety black on the sides and back of the head. Some males take their exotic plumage one step further and are bedecked with long streamer tails and iridescent mustaches, beards, and visors.

These tiny high-speed machines are named because of the hum made by the beat of their wings. At up to 100 beats per second, the hummingbirds' wings move so rapidly that the naked eye cannot detect them. They are often seen hovering at flowers, from which they extract nectar and often insects with their long, hollow, and extensile tongues forked at the tip. Alone among birds, they can generate power on both the forward and backward wing strokes, a distinction that allows them to even fly backward!

Understandably, the energy required to function at such an intense pitch is prodigious. The hummingbird has the highest metabolic rate per unit of body weight in the avian world (its pulse rate can exceed 1,200 beats a minute) and requires proportionately large amounts of food. One biologist discovered that the white-eared hummingbird consumes up to 850% of its own weight in food and water each day. At night, they go into "hibernation," lowering their body temperatures and metabolism to conserve energy.

Typically loners, hummingbirds bond with the opposite sex only for the few seconds it takes to mate. Many, such as the fiery-throated hummingbird, are fiercely territorial. With luck you might witness a spectacular aerial battle between males defending their territories. In breeding season, the males "possess" territories rich in flowers attractive to females: the latter gains an ample food source in exchange for offering the male sole paternity rights. Nests are often no larger than a thimble, loosely woven with cobwebs and flecks of bark and lined with silky plant down. Inside, the female will lay two eggs no larger than coffee beans.

MACAWS

What magnificent creatures these birds are. No protective coloration. No creeping about trying to blend in with the countryside. Macaws—the largest of the neotropical parrots—are dazzlingly colored in jackets of bright yellow and blue, green, or scarlet. Their harsh, raucous voices are filled with authority. "Even moving from branch to branch in the treetops," says one writer, "they seem arrogant and proud as emperors."

Although macaw is the common name for any of 15 species of these large, long-tailed birds found throughout Central and South America, only two species inhabit Costa Rica: the scarlet macaw *(lapa roja)* and the great green or Buffon's macaw *(lapa verde)*. Though the scarlet ranges from Mexico to central South America and was once abundant on both coasts of Costa Rica, today it is found only in a few parks on the Pacific shore, and rarely on the Caribbean side, which is the home of the Buffon's macaw. Both bird populations are losing their homes to deforestation and poaching. The scarlet macaw population has declined so dramatically that it is now in danger of disappearing completely: only three wild populations in Central America have a long-term chance of survival—at Carara Biological Reserve and Corcovado National Park in Costa Rica, and Coiba Island in Panamá—although

macaws can also be seen with regularity at Palo Verde National Park, Santa Rosa National Park, and other forested parts of the Gulf of Nicoya and Osa Peninsula. Even these are below the minimum critical size. An estimated 200 scarlets live at Carara and 1,600 at Corcovado, where as many as 40 may be seen at one time.

As they fly overhead, calling loudly, their long, trailing tail feathers and short wings make it impossible to confuse them with other birds. They are gregarious and rarely seen alone. They are almost always paired male and female—they're monogamous for life—often sitting side by side, grooming and preening each other, and conversing in rasping loving tones, or flying two by two. However, it is impossible to tell male from female. The scarlet's bright red-orange plumage with touches of blue and yellow does not vary between the sexes or with aging.

Macaws usually nest in softwood trees, such as jallinazos, where termites have hollowed out holes. April through July, you might see small groups of macaws clambering about the upper trunks of dead trees at Corcovado, squabbling over holes and crevices. In Carara, nesting season begins in September.

Many bird books mistakenly describe macaws as feeding on fruits—they get their names because they supposedly feed on the fruits of the macaw palms. In fact, they rarely eat fruits, but prefer seeds and nuts, which they extract with a hooked nutcracker of such strength that it can split that most intractable of nuts, the Brazil nut.

Macaw Protection

Several conservation groups are working to stabilize and reestablish the scarlet macaw population. Deep in the forest of the Carara Biological Reserve, Sergio Volio (a former national park superintendent and owner of Geotur) oversees a project to build artificial nests high up in jallinazo trees beyond the reach of poachers. Although macaws are the biggest attraction at Carara, they are threatened with extinction by poachers who take the chicks to sell on the black market in the U.S., despite a ban that prohibits importing the birds. Most die, however, before they reach the United States. Volio estimates up to 95% of natural nests at the reserve are poached. Volio's is the first project that will protect the birds' breeding grounds in their natural habitat. He is forming a

foundation to accept donations to help build the birdhouses, which cost about $100. Contact: **Geotur,** P.O. Box 469 Y Griega, San José 1011, tel. 234-1867, fax 253-6338.

Tsuli/Tsuli, an independent, self-supporting chapter of the Audubon Society, has an Adopte un Ave (Adopt-a-Bird) program. Tsuli/Tsuli means "Many Parrots" in the language of the Cabecar Indians. The group has an environmental education program to teach local Costa Ricans to understand and appreciate their flora and fauna, with a special emphasis on protecting birds, especially parrots, which are symbols of tropical wilderness. Contact: Tsuli/Tsuli, Audubon de Costa Rica, Apdo. 4910, San José 1000, tel. 249-1179 or 240-8775, fax 249-1179; or P.O. Box 025216-700, Miami, FL 33102.

Tsuli/Tsuli supports Richard and Marge Frisius, two experienced aviculturists who have a macaw-breeding program on the grounds of their home in Río Segundo de Alajuela. The Frisiuses have successfully raised many baby macaws using special techniques and cages. By teaching the domestically raised macaws how to find native food and then releasing them into carefully selected wilds of Costa Rica, their goal is to reestablish flocks of these magnificent birds in parts of the nation where there is still appropriate habitat for viable populations to establish themselves. The Frisiuses need at least 15 breeding pairs of macaws to establish a large gene pool. They also need to construct a large cage in which the birds can fly and forage freely (approximate cost $75,000). The Frisiuses have formed their own nonprofit organization, **Amigos de las Aves,** to raise money (send donations to: Apdo. 32, Río Segundo 4001).

Dr. Dagmar Werner—famous as the "Iguana Mama"—heads the **Macaw Program,** a captive breeding program run in collaboration with the World Wildife Fund and Costa Rica's National University's School of Medicine. (See "Iguana Park" under "San José to Puntarenas" in the Central Pacific chapter).

QUETZALS

The quetzal, or resplendent trogon, is a rare jewel of the bird world. Many birdwatchers travel to Costa Rica simply to catch sight of this

magnificent bird. What this pigeon-size bird lacks in physical stature it makes up for in audacious plumage: vivid, shimmering green that ignites in the sunshine, flashing emerald to golden and back to iridescent green. In common with other bird species, the male outshines the female. He sports a fuzzy pink punk hairdo, a scintillating crimson belly, and two brilliant green tail plumes up to 60 cm long, edged in snowy white and sinuous as feather boas.

Its beauty was so fabled and the bird so elusive and shy that early European naturalists believed the quetzal was a fabrication of Central American natives. In 1861, an English naturalist, Osbert Salvin, wrote that he was "determined, rain or no rain, to be off to the mountain forests in search of quetzals, to see and shoot which has been a daydream for me ever since I set foot in Central America." Salvin, the first European to record observing a quetzal, pronounced it "unequaled for splendour among the birds of the New World," and promptly shot it. During the course of the next three decades, thousands of quetzal plumes crossed the Atlantic to fill the specimen cabinets of European collectors and adorn the fashionable milliners' shops of Paris, Amsterdam, and London. Salvin redeemed himself by writing the awesome 40-volume tome *Biologia Centrali Americana,* which provided virtually a complete catalog of neotropical species.

Quetzal Culture

The quetzal has long been revered in Guatemala, where the bird graces the national shield, flag, postage stamps, and currency (which happens to be called the *quetzal*). It is pleasing to know that the former center of the Mayan empire still honors the magnificent bird. Early Mayans and Aztecs worshiped a god called Quetzalcoatl, the Plumed Serpent, and depicted him with a headdress of quetzal feathers. The bird's name is derived from *quetzalli,* an Aztec word meaning "precious" or "beautiful."

Mayans considered the male's iridescent green tail feathers worth more than gold, and killing the sacred bird was a capital crime. Quetzal plumes and jade, which were traded throughout Mesoamerica, were the Mayans' most precious objects. It was the color that was significant: "Green—the color of water, the lifegiving fluid. Green, the color of the maize crop, had special significance to the people of Mesoamerica," says Adrian Digby in his monograph *Mayan Jades,* "and both jade and the feathers of the quetzal were green."

During the colonial period, the indigenous people of Central America came to see the quetzal as a symbol of independence and freedom. Popular folklore relates how the quetzal got its dazzling blood-red breast: in 1524, when the Spanish conquistador Pedro de Alvarado defeated the Mayan chieftain Tecun Uman, a gilt-and-green quetzal alighted on the Indian's chest at the moment he fell mortally wounded; when the bird took off again, his breast was stained with the brilliant crimson blood of the Mayan.

Archaeologists believe that the wearing of quetzal plumes was proscribed, under pain of death, for use except by Mayan priests and nobility: it became a symbol of authority vested in a theocratic elite, much as only Roman nobility were allowed to wear purple silks.

Quetzal Watching

Although Costa Ricans don't worship the quetzal with the same fervor as pre-Columbian Guatemalans, the bird is most easily seen in Costa Rica, where it is protected in four national parks—Braulio Carrillo, Poás, Chirripó, La Amistad—and the Monteverde and Los Angeles Cloud Forest Reserves. Everywhere throughout its 1,000-mile range (from southern Mexico to western Panamá) it is endangered by loss of its cloud-forest habitat. This is particularly true of the lower forests around 1,500 to 2,000 meters, to which families of quetzals descend during breeding season (March-June), and where they seek dead and decaying trees in which to hollow out their nests. This is the best time to see narcissistic males showing off their tail plumes in undulating flight, or launching spiraling skyward flights, which presage a plummeting dive with their tail feathers rippling behind, all part of the courtship ritual.

At other times, the wary birds aren't easily spotted. Their plumage offers excellent camouflage under the rainy forest canopy. They also sit motionless for long periods, with their vibrant red chests turned away from any suspected danger. If a quetzal knows you're close by and feels threatened, you may hear a harsh "weec-

weec" warning call and see the male's flicking tail feathers betray his presence. The quetzal's territory spans a radius of approximately 300 meters, which the male proclaims each dawn through midmorning and again at dusk with a telltale melodious whistle—a hollow, high-pitched call of two notes, one ascending steeply, the other descending—repeated every eight to 10 minutes.

Nest holes (often hollowed out by woodpeckers) are usually about 10 meters from the ground. Within, the female generally lays two light-blue eggs, which take about 18 days to hatch. Both sexes share parental duties. By day, the male incubates the eggs while his two-foot-long tail feathers hang out of the nest. At night, the female takes over.

Although the quetzal eats insects, small frogs, and lizards, it enjoys a penchant for the fruit of the broad-leafed *aguacatillo* (a kind of miniature avocado in the laurel family), which depends on the bird to distribute seeds. The movement of quetzals follows the seasonal fruiting of different laurel species. Time your birdwatching visit, if possible, to coincide with the quetzals' rather meticulous feeding hours, which you can almost set your watch by. They're fascinating to watch feeding: an upward swoop for fruit is the bird's aerial signature.

FRIGATE BIRDS

Black frigate birds, with their long scimitar wings and forked tails, hang like sinister kites in the wind all along the Costa Rican coast. They hold a single position in the sky, as if suspended from invisible strings, and from this airborne perch harry gulls and terns until the latter release their catch (birders have a name for such thievery: kleptoparasitism).

Despite the sinister look imparted by its long hooked beak, the frigate bird is quite beautiful. The adult male is all black with a lustrous faint purplish-green sheen on its back (especially during the courtship season). The female, the much larger of the two, is easily distinguished by the white feathers that extend up her abdomen and the breast, and the ring of bluish mascara she wears around her eyes.

Second only to a frigate bird's concern for food is its interest in the opposite sex. The females do the conspicuous searching out and selecting of mates. The hens take to the air above the rookery to look over the males, who cluster in groups atop the scrubby mangrove bushes. Whenever a female circles low over the bushes, the males react with a blatant display of wooing: they tilt their heads far back to show off their fully inflated scarlet gular pouches (appropriately shaped like hearts!), vibrate their wings rapidly back and forth, and entice the females with loud clicking and drumming sounds.

To walk through a colony of frigate birds courting is a spellbinding experience; the lusty atmosphere is palpable. You may even see pairs entwined, the male with his wings around his mate.

Once the pair is established, a honeymoon of nest-building begins. In the structured world of the frigate birds it is the male's job to find twigs for the nest. The piratical frigates will not hesitate to steal twigs from their neighbors' nests, so the females stay home to guard them.

The female lays a single egg, and each parent takes turns at one-week shifts during the eight-week incubation. They guard the chick closely, for cannibalistic neighbors and predatory hawks and owls make quick feasts of the unwary young. For five months, the dejected-looking youngsters sit immobile beneath the hot sun; even when finally airborne, they remain dependent on their parents for more than a year while they learn the complex trade of air piracy.

Superb stunt flyers, frigate birds often bully other birds on the wing, pulling at the tails of their victims until the latter release or regurgitate a freshly caught meal. Frigate birds also catch much of their food themselves. You may see them skimming the water, snapping up squid, flying fish, and other morsels off the water's surface. (They must keep themselves dry, as they have only a small preen gland, insufficient to oil their feathers; if they get too wet they become waterlogged and drown.)

Frigate birds are easily seen close-up en masse along the mangrove-lined shorelines of Guanacaste and the Gulf of Nicoya, sunning themselves, often in a near vertical position with wings turned "palm up."

INSECTS

The long history of the rainforest has enabled countless butterflies, moths, ants, termites, wasps, bees, and other tropical insects to evolve in astounding profusion. Ant species alone number in the many thousands. Corcovado National Park boasts at least 220 species of breeding butterflies, plus others that simply pass through. And there are so many species of beetles and grasshoppers that no one knows the true numbers. Many, many thousands of insect species still await identification.

The most brilliantly painted insects are the butterflies and moths, some quite tiny and obscure, others true giants of the insect kingdom, dazzlingly crowned in gold and jewel-like colors. In Guanacaste, hundreds of species of bees, moth larvae, and tiger beetles make an appearance in the early dry season. When the first rains come, lightbulbs are often deluged with adult moths, beetles, and other insects newly emerged from their pupae. That's the time, too, that many species of butterfly migrate from the deciduous lowland forests to highland sites.

leaf-cutting ant

Many insect species are too small to see. The hummingbird flower mite, for example, barely half a millimeter long, is so small it can hitch rides from flower to flower inside the nostrils of hummingbirds. Other insects you may detect by their sound. Male wood crickets, for example, produce a very loud noise by rubbing together the overlapping edges of their wing cases.

Many exotic-looking species you can immediately recognize. Guanacaste stick insects are easily spotted at night on low shrubs. The three-inch rhinoceros beetle has an unmistakable long, upward-curving horn on its head. And the number of spiders ornamented with showy colors is remarkable. Some even double them-

selves up at the base of leaf-stalks, so as to resemble flowerbuds, and thus deceive the insects on which they prey.

Of course, a host of unfriendly bugs also exist in great numbers: chiggers, wasps and bees (including aggressive African bees), ticks, mosquitoes, and the famous "no-see-ums." All five insects can inflict irritating bites on humans (see "Health Care" in the On the Road chapter).

ANTS

Leaf-cutting Ants

There's something endearing about the leaf-cutting ant (Atta cephalotes), a mushroom-farming insect found in lowland forests throughout Costa Rica, carrying upright in its jaws a circular green shard scissored from the leaves of a plant. At some stage in your travels you're bound to come across an endless troop of "media" workers hauling their cargo along jungle pathways as immaculately cleaned of debris as any swept doorstep.

The nests are built below ground, sometimes extending over an area of 200 square meters, with galleries to a depth of six meters. Large nests provide a home for up to five million insects. All ant societies are composed entirely of females; males exist only to fertilize the queen and then die. And only the queen, who may boast a thousand times the body weight of a minor worker, is fertile. Hence, all other ants in the colony are her daughters. They set off from their nests, day and night, in long columns to demolish trees, removing every shoot, leaf, and stem section by tiny section and transporting them back to their underground chambers.

They don't eat this material. Instead, they chew it up to form a compost on which they cul-

tivate a nutritional breadlike fungus whose tiny white fruiting bodies provide them with food. So evolved has this symbiosis become that the fungus has lost its reproductive ability (it no longer produces sexual spores) and relies exclusively on the ants for propagation.

The species has evolved different physical castes, each specializing in its own social tasks. Most of the workers are tiny minors ("minimas"), which tend the nest. The cutting and carrying are performed by intermediate-size workers ("medias"), guarded by ferocious-looking "majors" about two centimeters long.

Army Ants

The most terrifying ants of all are the army ants, which march through the forest with the sole intent of turning small creatures into skeletons in a few minutes. They produce a faint hissing sound and distinct ant-army odor. They're like a wolf pack, but with tens of thousands of miniature beasts of prey that merge and unite to form one great living creature.

Hollywood images of mammals and even humans fleeing madly before them are mostly imagination run wild. In truth, while the ants advance across the forest floor driving small creatures in front of them, humans and other large creatures can simply step aside and watch the column pass by—this can take several hours. Even when the ants raid human habitations, people can simply clear out with their foodstock while the ants clean out the cockroaches and other vermin as thoroughly as any exterminator might.

The army ants' jaws are so powerful that Indians once used them to suture wounds: the tenacious insect was held over a wound and its body squeezed so that its jaws instinctively shut, clamping the flesh together. The body was then pinched off.

Larvae carried by workers produce pheromones, which stimulate the army to keep on the move. When the larvae begin to pupate and no longer exude their chemical messages, the ants bivouac in a vast ball in a hollow. They actually cling to one another and make a nest of their bodies, complete with passageways and chambers where the eggs are deposited. Once the queen lays her eggs and these hatch as larvae, a new generation of workers and sol-diers synchronistically emerges from the stored pupae. The larvae begin to secrete their characteristic pheromone, and the army is again stimulated to march off and terrorize the bush.

BUTTERFLIES

With nearly 1,000 identified species (approximately 10% of the world total), Costa Rica is a lepidopterist's paradise. You can barely stand still for one minute without checking off a dozen dazzling species: metallic gold riondinidae; delicate black-winged heliconius splashed with bright red and yellow; orange-striped paracaidas; and the deep neon-blue flash of morphos fluttering and diving in a ballet of subaqueous color. The marvelously intricate wing patterns are statements of identity, so that individuals may recognize those with whom mating may be fertile.

Not all this elaboration has a solely sexual connotation. Some butterflies are ornately colored to keep predators at bay. The bright white stripes against black on the zebra butterfly (like other members of the Heliconid family), for example, tell birds that the butterfly tastes acrid. There are even perfectly tasty butterfly species that mimic the Heliconid's colors, tricking predators to disdain them. Others use their colors as camouflage so that at rest they blend in with the green or brown leaves or look like the scaly bark of a tree. Among the most intriguing, however, are the owl-eye butterflies, with their 13-cm wingspans and startling eye spots. The dull, blue-gray *Caligo memnon*, the cream owl butterfly, is the most spectacular of the owl-eyes: the undersides of its wings are mottled to look like feathers and boast two large yellow-and-black "eyes" on the hind wing, which it displays when disturbed.

The best time to see butterflies is in the morning, when most species are active. A few are active at dawn and dusk, and one species is even active by night. In general, butterfly populations are most dense in June and July, corresponding with the onset of the rainy season on the Pacific side. Butterfly migrations are also common. Like birds, higher-elevation species migrate up and down the mountains with changes in local weather. The most amazing migration—unsurpassed by any other insect in

MORPHO BUTTERFLIES

Undoubtedly the narcissus of the Costa Rican butterfly kingdom is the famous blue morpho, one of the most beautiful butterflies in the world. There are about 50 species of morphos, all in Central and South America, where they are called *celeste común*. The males of most species are bright neon blue, with iridescent wings that flash like mirrors in the sun. Sadly, this magnificent oversized butterfly—it grows 13-20 centimeters—is not as common as it once was, thanks to habitat destruction.

"It used to be a backyard species; now it is found only in reserves," says Maria Sabido, cofounder of the Butterfly Farm, in La Guácima de Alajuela. Still, you can't miss them when they're around and active, particularly in November when they are extremely common along riverbeds and other moist habitats.

The morpho is a modest, nondescript brown when sitting quietly with wings closed. But when a predator gets too close, it flies off, startling its foe with a flash of its beautiful electric-blue wings. (Not that they are always successful. Biologist David Janzen reports that piles of morpho wings are often found under the perches of jacamars and large flycatchers, which are partial to the morpho.)

The subspecies differ in color: in the Atlantic lowlands, the morpho is almost completely iridescent blue; by contrast, one population in the Meseta Central is almost completely brown, with only a faint hint of electric blue. One species, commonly seen gliding about in the forest canopy, is red on the underside and gray above.

Showmen have always used mirrors to produce glitter and illusion. The morpho is no exception. Look through a morpho butterfly's wing toward a strong light and you will see only brown. This is because the scales are brown. The fiery blue is produced by structure, not by pigment, and therefore will never fade. Tiny scales on the upper side of the wing are laid in rows that overlap much like roof shingles. These scales are ridged with minute layers that, together with the air spaces between them, bend (refract) and reflect light beams, destroying all the colors except blue. The Atlantic species have additional glassy scales on top of the others to reflect even more light and give the wings a paler, more opalescent quality.

the neotropics—is that of the kitelike uranidae (this black and iridescent green species is actually a moth that mimics the swallowtail butterfly), in which millions of individuals pass through Costa Rica heading south from Honduras to Colombia.

The best places to see butterflies in all stages are the **Butterfly Farm** (tel. 438-0115), at La Guácima; **Spirogyra** (tel. 222-2937), near the El Pueblo Shopping Center in San José; **Butterfly Paradise** (tel. 221-2015), at San Joaquín de Flores, three km northwest of Heredia; **Wings For Education/Joyeros del Bosque Húmedos** (tel. 223-0343), in Santo Domingo de Heredia; the **Butterfly Garden** at Monteverde; **Butterfly Valley** (tel. 454-4050), in Sarchí; and **Mariposario**

Los Heliconios (tel. 226-2570), 48 km northeast of San José on the road to Puerto Limón.

Selva Verde Lodge offers butterfly-study workshops (one to nine days) at La Selva Biological Station and Los Inocentes in Guanacaste. For information, contact **Costa Rican Lodges** (3540 N.W. 13th St., Gainesville, FL 32609, tel. 904-373-7118 or 800-451-3711, fax 904-371-3710). **Wings for the Earth** is a nonprofit organization dedicated to supporting community-based tropical butterfly and insect-rearing projects worldwide. The group works closely with local conservation organizations in Colombia, Ecuador, and Jamaica. Contact Wings for the Earth (6341 Longcroft Dr., Oakland, CA 94611, tel. 510-531-8959, fax 510-531-6659).

HISTORY

PRE-COLUMBIAN ERA

When Spanish explorers arrived in what is now Costa Rica at the dawn of the 16th century, they found the region populated by several poorly organized, autonomous tribes living relatively prosperously, if wanton at war, in a land of lush abundance. In all, there were probably no more than 200,000 indigenous people on 18 September 1502, when Columbus put ashore near current-day Puerto Limón. Although human habitation can be traced back at least 10,000 years, the region had remained a sparsely populated backwater separating the two areas of high civilization: Mesoamerica and the Andes. High mountains and swampy lowlands had impeded the migration of the advanced cultures. Though these cultures were advanced in ceramics, metalwork, and weaving, there are few signs of large complex communities, little monumental stone architecture lying half-buried in the luxurious undergrowth, no planned ceremonial centers of comparable significance to those elsewhere in the isthmus.

The region was a potpourri of distinct cultures arranged into chiefdoms. In the east along the Caribbean seaboard and along the southern Pacific shores, the peoples shared distinctly South American cultural traits. These groups—the Caribs on the Caribbean and the Borucas and Chibchas and Diquis in the southwest—were seminomadic hunters and fishermen who raised yucca, squash, *pejibaye* (bright orange palm fruits), and tubers supplemented by crustaceans, shrimp, lobster, and game; chewed coca; and lived in communal village huts surrounded by fortified palisades. The matriarchal Chibchas and Diquis had a highly developed slave system and were accomplished goldsmiths, for their habitat was abundant in gold ore. Amulets, awls, tweezers for plucking out facial hair, beads and baubles, pendants and religious icons decorated in fantastical animist imagery were among the many items of gold expertly worked through the "lost wax" technique. These people were famed for their simple clothwork, traded throughout the country. They were also responsible for the fascinating, perfectly spherical granite balls *(bolas)* of unknown purpose found in large numbers at burial sites in the Río Terraba valley, Caño Island, and the Golfito region. Tens of thousands have been unearthed. Some are the

pre-Columbian pottery, Jade Museum, San José

PRE-COLUMBIAN JADE

Ancient Costa Ricans had a love affair with jade. The semiprecious stone first appeared in Costa Rica around 400 B.C., when the Olmecs of Mexico introduced it to the Nicoya Peninsula. It became more prized than gold.

Though early carvings were crude, quality pieces began to appear around A.D. 300, when the indigenous peoples developed the "string-saw" carving technique by drilling a hole in the jade, inserting a string, and sawing back and forth. Pendants, necklaces, and earrings appeared, exquisitely tailored with relief showing human faces and scenes of life. Painstakingly worked monkeys, crocodiles, anteaters, jaguars, reptiles, and owls (symbol of the underworld) appeared as jade figurines. Most common of all was the eagle, worshiped by indigenous peoples throughout the isthmus.

Costa Rican jade comes in green, black, gray, and—rarest of all—blue. Although the quarry for the famous blue jade has never been found, Fidel Tristan, curator of the Jade Museum, believes a local source exists. The nearest known source of green is at Manzanal, in Guatemala.

pre-Columbian
jade figurines

size of a grapefruit. Others weigh 16 tons. One and all are as perfectly round as the moon. Like other indigenous groups, the people had no written language and their names are of Spanish origin, bestowed by colonists, often reflecting the names of tribal chiefs.

The most interesting archaeological finds throughout the nation relate to pottery and metalworking. The art of gold working was practiced throughout Costa Rica for perhaps one thousand years before the Spanish conquest, and in the central highlands was in fact more advanced than in the rest of the isthmus. The tribes here were the Corobicís, who lived in small bands in the highland valleys, and the Nahuatl, who had recently arrived from Mexico at the time that Columbus stepped ashore. The largest and most significant of Costa Ri-

ca's archaeological sites found to date is here, at Guayabo, on the slopes of Turrialba, 56 km east of San José, where an ancient city is being excavated. Dating from perhaps as early as 1000 B.C. to A.D. 1400, Guayabo is thought to have housed as many as 10,000 inhabitants. Rudimentary though it is by the standards of ancient cities elsewhere in the isthmus, it is nonetheless impressive, with wide cobblestone walkways and stone-lined pools and water cisterns fed by aqueducts.

Perhaps more important (little architectural study has been completed) was the Nicoya Peninsula of what is today northwest Costa Rica. In late prehistoric times, trade in pottery from the Nicoya Peninsula brought this area into the Mesoamerican cultural sphere, and a culture developed among the Chorotegas—the most nu-

merous of the region's indigenous groups—that in many ways resembled the more advanced cultures farther north. In fact, the Chorotegas had been heavily influenced by the Olmec culture, and may themselves have even originated in southern Mexico before settling in Nicoya early in the 14th century (their name means "Fleeing People"). The most advanced of the region's cultures, they developed towns with central plazas, brought with them an accomplished agricultural system based on beans, corns, squash, and gourds, had a calendar, wrote books on deerskin parchment, and produced highly developed ceramics and stylized jade figures (much of it now in the Jade Museum in San José) depicting animals, humanlike effigies, and men and women with oversized genitals, often making the most of their sexual functions. Like the Olmecs, they filed their teeth; like the Mayans and Aztecs, too, the militaristic Chorotegas had slaves and a rigid class hierarchy dominated by high priests and nobles. Human sacrifice was part of the cultural mainstay. Surprisingly little, however, is known of their spiritual belief system, though the potency and ubiquity of phallic imagery hints at a fertility-rite religion.

ruins of church at Ujarrás

Alas, the pre-Columbian cultures were quickly choked by the stern hand of gold-thirsty colonial rule, condemned, too, that Jehovah might triumph over local idols.

Costa Rica is just beginning to open up its native-American culture to tourism. Plans are afoot to establish a "Petroglyph Trail," for example, plus a "sound-and-light" show at the Guayabo Monument with archaeo-astronomers to explain the pre-Columbians' sophisticated knowledge of the heavens, nighttime dramatizations of pre-Columbian mythologies atop Irazú volcano, and explorations of the Pacific Southwest to study the mysterious rock spheres found in the rainforests.

COLONIAL ERA

The First Arrivals

When Columbus, 51 years of age, anchored his storm-damaged vessels, the *Captiana, Gallega, Viscaína,* and *Santiago de Palos,* in the Bay of Cariari, off the Caribbean coast on his fourth voyage to the New World in 1502, he was welcomed and treated with great hospitality by indigenous peoples who had never seen white men before. The coastal Indians sent out two girls, "the one about eight, the other about 14 years of age," Columbus's son Ferdinand recorded. "The girls . . . always looked cheerful and modest. So the Admiral gave them good usage . . ." In his *Lettera Rarissima* to the Spanish king, Columbus offered a different tale of events: "As soon as I got there they sent right out two girls, all dressed up; the elder was hardly 11, the other seven, both behaving with such lack of modesty as to be no better than whores. As soon as they arrived, I gave orders that they be presented with some of our trading truck and sent them directly ashore."

The Indian dignitaries appeared wearing much gold, which they gave Columbus. "I saw more signs of gold in the first two days than I saw in Española during four years," his journal records. He called the region La Huerta ("The Garden"). Alas, the great navigator struggled home to Spain in worm-eaten ships (he was stranded for one whole year in Jamaica) and never returned. The prospect of vast loot, however, drew adventurers whose numbers were reinforced after Vasco Nuñez de Balboa's discovery of the Pacific in 1513. To these explorers the name Costa Rica would have seemed a cruel hoax. Floods, swamps, and tropical diseases stalked them in the sweltering lowlands. Fierce, elusive Indians harassed them maddeningly. And, with few exceptions,

there was no pot of gold at the end of the rainbow.

In 1506, Ferdinand of Spain sent a governor, Diego de Nicuesa, to colonize the Atlantic coast of the isthmus he called Veragua. He got off to a bad start by running aground off the coast of Panamá and was forced to march north, enduring a welcome that was less hospitable than that of Columbus. Antagonized Indian bands used guerrilla tactics to slay the strangers and willingly burnt their own crops to deny them food. Nicuesa set the tone for future expeditions by foreshortening his own cultural lessons with the musket ball. Things seemed more promising when an expedition under Gil González Davila set off from Panamá in 1522 to settle the region. It was Davila's expedition, which reaped quantities of gold, that nicknamed the land Costa Rica, the "Rich Coast." Alas, the Indians never revealed the whereabouts of the fabled mines of "Veragua" (most likely it was placer gold found in the still-gold-rich rivers of the Osa Peninsula).

Davila's Catholic priests also supposedly managed to convert many Indians to Christianity with cross and cutlass. But once again, sickness and starvation were the price: the expedition reportedly lost more than 1,000 men. Later colonizing expeditions on the Caribbean similarly failed miserably; the coastal settlements dissolved amidst internal acrimony, the taunts of Indians, and the debilitating impact of pirate raids. When two years later Francisco Fernández de Córdova founded the first Spanish settlement on the Pacific at Bruselas, near present-day Puntarenas, its inhabitants had all died within less than three years.

For the next four decades Costa Rica was virtually left alone. The conquest of Peru by Pizarro in 1532 and the first of the great silver strikes in Mexico in the 1540s turned eyes away from southern Central America. Guatemala became the administrative center for the Spanish main in 1543, when the captaincy-general of Guatemala, answerable to the viceroy of New Spain (Mexico), was created with jurisdiction from the Isthmus of Tehuantepec to the empty lands of Costa Rica.

By the 1560s several Spanish cities had consolidated their position farther north and, prompted by an edict of 1559 issued by Philip II of Spain, the representatives in Guatemala thought it time to settle Costa Rica and Christianize the natives. By then it was too late for the latter. Barbaric treatment and European epidemics—opthalmia, smallpox, and tuberculosis—had already reaped the Indians like a scythe and had so antagonized the survivors that they took to the forests and eventually found refuge amid the remote valleys of the Cordillera Talamanca. Only in the Nicoya Peninsula did there remain any significant Indian population, the Chorotegas, who soon found themselves chattel on Spanish land under the *encomienda* system whereby Spanish settlers were granted the right to forced Indian labor.

Settlement

In 1562, Juan Vásquez de Coronado—the true conquistador of Costa Rica—arrived as governor. He treated the surviving Indians more humanely and moved the few existing Spanish settlers into the Cartago Valley, where the temperate climate and rich volcanic soils offered the promise of crop cultivation. Cartago was established as the national capital in 1563. The economic and social development of the Spanish provinces was traditionally the work of the soldiers, who were granted *encomiendas*, landholdings that allowed for rights to the use of indigenous serfs. Coronado, however, to the regret of his subordinates, never made use of this system; in response, the Indians, led by chief Quitao, willingly subjugated themselves to Spanish rule. Coronado's successor allowed the Spanish to enslave the Indians. Soon, there were virtually no Indians left alive in the region.

After the initial impetus given by its discovery, Costa Rica lapsed into being a lowly Cinderella of the Spanish empire. The gold was soon gone, shipped to Spain. Land was readily available, but there was no Indian labor to work it. Thus, the early economy lacked the conditions that favored development of the large colonial-style hacienda and feudal system of other Spanish enclaves. Without native slave labor or the resources to import slaves, the colonists were forced to work the land themselves (even the governor, it is commonly claimed, had to work his own plot of land to survive). Without gold or export crops, trade with other colonies was infrequent at best. The Spanish found themselves

impoverished in a subsistence economy. Money became so scarce that the settlers eventually reverted to the Indian method of using cacao beans as currency.

A full century after its founding, Cartago could boast little more than a few score adobe houses and a single church, which all perished when Volcán Irazú erupted in 1723.

Gradually, however, prompted by an ecclesiastical edict that ordered the populace to resettle near churches, towns took shape around churches. Heredia (Cubujuquie) was founded in 1717, San José (Villaneuva de la Boca del Monte) in 1737, and Alajuela (Villa Hermosa) in 1782. Later, exports of wheat and tobacco placed the colonial economy on a sounder economic basis and encouraged the intensive settlement that characterizes the Meseta Central today.

Intermixing with the native population was not a common practice. In other colonies, Spaniard married native and a distinct class system arose, but mixed-bloods and ladinos (mestizos) represent a much smaller element in Costa Rica than they do elsewhere in the isthmus. All this had a leveling effect on colonial society. As the population grew, so did the number of poor families who had never benefited from the labor of *encomienda* Indians or suffered the despotic arrogance of *criollo* (Creole) landowners. Costa Rica, in the traditional view, became a "rural democracy," with no oppressed mestizo class resentful of the maltreatment and scorn of the Creoles. Removed from the mainstream of Spanish culture, the Costa Ricans became very individualistic and egalitarian.

Not all areas of the country, however, fit the model of rural democracy. Nicoya and Guanacaste on the Pacific side offered an easy overland route from Nicaragua to Panamá and were administered quite separately in colonial times from the rest of Costa Rica. They fell within the Nicaraguan sphere of influence, and large cattle ranches or haciendas arose. Revisions to the *encomienda* laws in 1542, however, limited the amount of time that Indians were obliged to provide their labor; Indians were also rounded up and forcibly concentrated into settlements distant from the haciendas. The large estate owners thus began to import African slaves, who became an important part of the labor force on the cattle ranches that were es-

tablished in the Pacific northwest. The cattle-ranching economy and the more traditional class-based society that arose persist today.

Some three centuries of English associations and of neglect by the Spanish authorities have also created a very different cultural milieu all along the Caribbean coast of Central America. On the Caribbean of Costa Rica, cacao plantations—the most profitable activity of the colonial period—became well established. Eventually large-scale cacao production gave way to small-scale sharecropping, and then to tobacco as the cacao industry went into decline. Spain closed the Costa Rican ports in 1665 in response to English piracy, thereby cutting off seaborne sources of legal trade. Such artificial difficulties to economic development compounded those created by nature. Smuggling flourished, however, for the largely unincorporated Caribbean coast provided a safe haven to buccaneers and smugglers, whose strongholds became 18th-century shipping points for logwood and mahogany. The illicit trade helped weaken central authority. The illusion of Central American colonial unity was also weakened in the waning stages of the Spanish empire as interest in, and the ability to maintain, the rigid administrative structure declined.

THE EMERGENCE OF A NATION

Independence

Independence of Central America from Spain on 15 September 1821 came on the coattails of Mexico's declaration earlier in the same year. Independence had little immediate effect, however, for Costa Rica had required only minimal government during the colonial era and had long gone its own way. In fact, the country was so out of touch that the news that independence had been granted reached Costa Rica a full month after the event. A hastily convened provincial council voted for accession to Mexico; in 1823, the other Central American nations proclaimed the United Provinces of Central America, with their capital in Guatemala City.

After the declaration, effective power lay in the hands of the separate towns of the isthmus, and it took several years for a stable pattern of political alignment to emerge. The four leading cities

of Costa Rica felt as independent as had the city-states of ancient Greece, and the conservative and aristocratic leaders of Cartago and Heredia soon found themselves at odds with the more progressive republican leaders of San José and Alajuela. The local quarrels quickly developed into civic unrest and, in 1823, to civil war. After a brief battle in the Ochomogo Hills, the republican forces of San José were victorious. They rejected Mexico, and Costa Rica joined the federation with full autonomy for its own affairs. Guanacaste voted to secede from Nicaragua and join Costa Rica the following year.

From this moment on, liberalism in Costa Rica had the upper hand. Elsewhere in Central America, conservative groups tied to the Church and the erstwhile colonial bureaucracy spent generations at war with anticlerical and laissez-faire liberals, and a cycle of civil wars came to dominate the region. By contrast, in Costa Rica colonial institutions had been relatively weak and early modernization of the economy propelled the nation out of poverty and laid the foundations of democracy far earlier than elsewhere in the isthmus. While other countries turned to repression to deal with social tensions, Costa Rica turned toward reform. Military plots and coups weren't unknown—they played a large part in determining who came to rule throughout the next century—but the generals usually were puppets used as tools to install favored individuals (usually surprisingly progressive civilian allies) representing the interests of particular cliques.

Early Liberalism
Juan Mora Fernández, elected the nation's first chief of state in 1824, set the tone by ushering in a nine-year period of progressive stability. He established a sound judicial system, founded the nation's first newspaper, and expanded public education. He also encouraged coffee cultivation and gave free land grants to would-be coffee growers. The nation, however, was still riven by rivalry, and in September 1835 the War of the League broke out when San José was attacked by the three other towns. They were unsuccessful and the national flag was planted firmly in San José (see "History" in the introduction to the San José chapter for more details).

Braulio Carrillo, who had taken power as a benevolent dictator, established an orderly public administration and new legal codes to replace colonial Spanish law. In 1838, he withdrew Costa Rica from the Central American federation and proclaimed complete independence. In a final show of federalist strength, the Honduran general Francisco Morazan toppled Carrillo in 1842. It was too late. The seeds of independence had taken firm root. Morazan's extranational ambitions and the military draft and direct taxes he imposed soon inspired his overthrow. He was executed within the year.

Coffee Is King
By now, the reins of power had been taken up by a nouveau elite: the coffee barons, whose growing prosperity led to rivalries between the wealthiest family factions, who vied with each other for political dominance. In 1849, the *cafetaleros* announced their ascendancy by conspiring to overthrow the nation's first president, José María Castro, an enlightened man who initiated his administration by founding a high school for girls and sponsoring freedom of the press. They chose as Castro's successor Juan Rafael Mora, one of the most powerful personalities among the new coffee aristocracy. Mora is remembered for the remarkable economic growth that marked his first term, and for "saving" the nation from the imperial ambitions of the American adventurer William Walker during his second term (which Mora gained by manipulating the elections). In a display of ingratitude, his countryfolk ousted him from power in 1859; the masses blamed him for the cholera epidemic that claimed the lives of one in every 10 Costa Ricans in the wake of the Walker saga, while the elites were horrified when Mora moved to establish a national bank, which would have undermined their control of credit to the coffee producers. After failing in his own coup against his successor, he was executed—a prelude to a second cycle of militarism, for the war of 1856 had introduced Costa Rica to the buying and selling of generals and the establishment of a corps of officers possessing an inflated aura of legitimacy.

The Guardia Legacy
The 1860s were marred by power struggles among the ever-powerful coffee elite supported by their respective military cronies. General Tomás Guardia, however, was his own man.

THE WILLIAM WALKER SAGA

William Walker was 1.65 meters and 55 kg (five feet five inches and 120 pounds) of cocky intellect and ego. Born in Nashville in 1824, he graduated from the University of Pennsylvania with an M.D. at the age of 19 before going on to study in Paris and Germany. Despite his illustrious start, Walker was preordained to failure. He tried his hand unsuccessfully as a doctor, lawyer, and writer, and even joined the '49ers in the California Gold Rush. Somewhere along the line he became filled with grandiose schemes of adventure and an arrogant belief in America's "manifest destiny" to control other nations. During the next decade the Tennessean freebooter went on to become the scourge of the Central American isthmus.

He dreamed of extending the glory of slavery and forming a confederacy of southern American states to include the Spanish-speaking nations. To wet his feet, he invaded Baja California in 1853 with a few hundred cronies bankrolled by a proslavery group called the Knights of the Golden Circle.

Forced back north of the border by the Mexican army, Walker found himself behind bars for breaking the Neutrality Act. Acquitted and famous, he attracted a following of kindred spirits to his next wild cause.

During the feverish California Gold Rush, eager fortune hunters sailed down the East Coast to Nicaragua, traveled up the Río San Juan and across Lake Nicaragua aboard an exaggerated canoe called a bungo, and thence were carried by mule the last 12 miles to the Pacific, where with luck a San Francisco-bound ship would be waiting. In those days, before the Panamá Canal, wealthy North Americans were eyeing southern Nicaragua as the perfect spot to build a canal to link the Pacific and Caribbean. The conservative government of Nicaragua decided that both the traffic and the proposed canal were worth a hefty fee. U.S. business interests thought otherwise.

Backed by North American capitalists and with the tacit sanction of President James Buchanan,

---

In April 1870, he overthrew the government and ruled for 12 years as an iron-willed military strongman backed up by a powerful centralized government of his own making.

True to Costa Rican tradition, Guardia proved himself a progressive thinker and a benefactor of the people. His towering reign set in motion forces that shaped the modern liberal-democratic state. Hardly characteristic of 19th-century despots, he abolished capital punishment, managed to curb the power of the coffee barons, and tamed the use of the army for political means. He used coffee earnings and taxation to finance roads and public buildings. And in a landmark revision to the Constitution in 1869, he made "primary education for both sexes obligatory, free, and at the cost of the Nation."

Guardia had a dream: to make the transport of coffee more efficient and more profitable by forging a railroad linking the Central Valley with the

Atlantic coast, and thus with America and Europe. The terrain through which he proposed to build his railroad was so forbidding that it gave rise to a saying: "He who once makes the trip to the Caribbean coast is a hero; he who makes it a second time is a fool." Fulfillment of Guardia's dream was the triumph of one man—Minor Keith of Brooklyn, New York—over a world of risks and logistical nightmares (see special topic "Coffee, Bananas, and Minor Keith").

Guardia's enlightened administration was a watershed for the nation. The aristocrats gradually came to understand that liberal, orderly, and stable regimes profited their business interests while the instability inherent in reliance on militarism was damaging to it. And the extension of education to every citizen (and the espousal in the free press of European notions of liberalism) raised the consciousness of the masses and made it increasingly difficult for the patri-

Walker landed in Nicaragua in June 1855 with a group of mercenaries—the "fifty-six immortals"—and the ostensible goal of molding a new government that would be more accommodating to U.S. business ventures. Perhaps some of Walker's men thought they were fighting simply to annex Nicaragua to the United States; others may have believed they were part of the great struggle to establish slavery in Central America. But Walker, it seems, had other ambitions: he dreamed of making the five Central American countries a federated state with himself as emperor. After subduing the Nicaraguans, he had himself "elected" president of Nicaragua and legalized slavery. He spent his source of support, however, when his filibusters seized the transit steamers of Cornelius Vanderbilt's Trans-isthmian Transit Company.

Next, Walker looked south to Costa Rica. In March 1856 he invaded Guanacaste. Warned of Walker's plans, President Mora, backed by the Legislative Assembly, called up an army of 9,000 to join "the loyal sons of Guatemala, El Salvador, and Honduras," who had combined their meager and bickering forces to expel the invaders. President Mora and his brother-in-law José María Cañas took personal charge of Costa Rica's band of *campesinos* and makeshift soldiers (Cornelius Vanderbilt—the pre-financially strapped Donald Trump of

his day—reportedly bankrolled the effort). Armed with machetes and rusty rifles, they marched for Guanacaste where, in a 14-minute battle, the Costa Ricans routed Walker and his cronies, who retreated pell-mell the way they'd come. Costa Rica still celebrates its peasant army's victory over Walker's forces in the Pacific lowlands. The site of the battle—La Casona, in Santa Rosa National Park—is now a museum.

Eventually, the Costa Rican army cornered Walker's forces in a wooden fort at Rivas, in Nicaragua. A drummer boy named Juan Santamaría bravely volunteered to torch the fort, successfully flushing Walker out into the open. His bravery cost the young drummer boy his life; he is now honored as a national hero and a symbol of resistance to foreign interference.

With his forces defeated, Walker's ambitions were temporarily scuttled. He was eventually rescued by the U.S. Navy and taken to New York, only to return in 1857 with even more filibusters. The Nicaraguan army defeated him again, and Walker was imprisoned. Released three years later and unrepentant, he seized a Honduran customs house. In yet another bid to escape, he surrendered to an English frigate captain who turned him over to the Honduran army, which promptly shot him, thereby bringing to an end the pathetic saga.

monial elite to exclude the population from the political process.

Democracy

The shift to democracy was witnessed in the election called by President Bernardo Soto in 1889—commonly referred to as the first "honest" election, with popular participation; women and blacks, however, were still excluded from voting. To Soto's surprise, his opponent José Joaquín Rodríguez won. The masses rose and marched in the streets to support their chosen leader after the Soto government decided not to recognize the new president. The Costa Ricans had spoken, and Soto stepped down.

During the course of the next two generations, militarism gave way to peaceful transitions to power. Presidents, however, attempted to amend the Constitution to continue their rule and even dismissed uncooperative legislatures. Both Rodríguez and his hand-picked succes-

sor, Rafael Iglesias, for example, turned dictatorial while sponsoring material progress. Iglesias's successor, Ascension Esquivel, who took office in 1902, even exiled three contenders for the 1906 elections and imposed his own choice for president: González Víquez. And Congress declared the winner of the 1914 plebiscite ineligible and named its own choice, noncontender Alfredo González Flores, as president.

Throughout all this the country had been at peace, the army in its barracks. In 1917, democracy faced its first major challenge. At that time, the state collected the majority of its revenue from the less wealthy. Flores's bill to establish direct, progressive taxation based on income and his espousal of state involvement in the economy had earned the wrath of the elites. They decreed his removal. Minister of War Federico Tinoco Granados seized power. Tinoco ruled as an iron-fisted dictator and soon squandered the support of U.S. business interests. More im-

Bernardo Soto, progressive president of Costa Rica 1885-1890

portant, Costa Ricans had come to accept liberty as their due; they were no longer prepared to acquiesce in oligarchic restrictions. Women and high-school students led a demonstration which called for his ouster, and Tinoco fled to Europe.

There followed a series of unmemorable administrations culminating in the return of two previous leaders, Ricardo Jiménez and González Víquez, who alternated power for 12 years through the 1920s and '30s. The apparent tranquility was shattered by the Depression and the social unrest it engendered. Old-fashioned paternalistic liberalism had failed to resolve social ills such as malnutrition, unemployment, low pay, and poor working conditions. The Depression distilled all these issues, especially after a dramatic communist-led strike against the United Fruit Company brought tangible gains. Calls grew shrill for reforms.

REFORMISM AND CIVIL WAR

Calderón

The decade of the 1940s and its climax, the civil war, mark a turning point in Costa Rican history: from paternalistic government by tradi-

tional rural elites to modernistic, urban-focused statecraft controlled by bureaucrats, professionals, and small entrepreneurs. The dawn of the new era was spawned by Rafael Angel Calderón Guardia, a profoundly religious physician and a president (1940-44) with a social conscience. In a period when neighboring Central American nations were under the yoke of tyrannical dictators, Calderón promulgated a series of farsighted reforms. His legacy included a stab at land "reform" (the landless could gain title to unused land by cultivating it), establishment of a guaranteed minimum wage, paid vacations, unemployment compensation, progressive taxation, plus a series of constitutional amendments codifying workers' rights. Calderón also founded the University of Costa Rica.

Calderón's social agenda was hailed by the urban poor and leftists and despised by the upper classes, his original base of support. His early declaration of war on Germany, seizure of German property, and imprisonment of Germans further upset his conservative patrons, many of whom were of German descent. World War II stalled economic growth at a time when Calderón's social programs called for vastly increased public spending. The result was rampant inflation, which eroded his support among the middle and working classes. Abandoned, Calderón crawled into bed with two unlikely partners: the Catholic Church and the communists (Popular Vanguard Party). Together they formed the United Social Christian Party.

The Prelude to Civil War

In 1944, Calderón was replaced by his puppet, Teodoro Picado, in an election widely regarded as fraudulent. Picado's uninspired administration failed to address rising discontent throughout the nation. Intellectuals, distrustful of Calderón's "unholy" alliance, joined with businessmen, *campesinos,* and labor activists and formed the Social Democratic Party, dominated by the emergent professional middle classes eager for economic diversification and modernization. In its own strange amalgam, the SDP allied itself with the traditional oligarchic elite. The country was thus polarized. Tensions mounted.

Street violence finally erupted in the run-up to the 1948 election, with Calderón on the ballot for a second presidential term. When he lost to his

COFFEE, BANANAS, AND MINOR KEITH

Costa Rica became the first Central American country to grow coffee when seeds were introduced from Jamaica in 1808. Coffee flourished and transformed the nation; it was eminently suited to the climate (the dry season made harvest and transportation easy) and volcanic soils of the central highlands. There were no rival products to compete for investments, land, or labor. And the coffee bean—*grano d'oro*—was exempt from taxes. Soon, peasant settlements spread up the slopes of the volcanoes and down the slopes toward the coast.

By 1829, coffee had become the nation's most important product: production leapt from approximately 20,000 kilograms in 1829 to four million kilograms in 1841 and 45 million kilograms by the mid-1880s. Export to England was flourishing, and foreign money was pouring in. The coffee elite owed its wealth to control of processing and trade rather than to direct control of land; small farmers dominated production. Thus, no sector of society failed to advance. The coffee bean pulled the country out of its miserable economic quagmire and placed it squarely on a pedestal as the most prosperous nation in Central America.

In 1871, when Guardia decided to build his railroad to the Atlantic, coffee for export was still being sent via mule and oxcart 100 kilometers from the Meseta Central to the Pacific port of Puntarenas, then shipped via a circuitous, three-month voyage around the southern tip of South America and up the Atlantic to Europe.

Enter Minor Keith, a former stockboy in a Broadway clothing store, lumber surveyor in the American West, and raiser of pigs in Texas. Minor had come to Costa Rica in 1871 at the age of 23 at the behest of his brother. Henry Keith had been commissioned by his uncle, Henry Meiggs (the famous builder of railroads in the Andes), to oversee the construction of the Atlantic Railroad linking the coastal port of Limón with the coffee-producing Meseta Central. By 1873, when the railway should have been completed, only a third had been built and money for the project had run dry. (The railroad was to have been financed by a loan of 3.4 million pounds issued by English banks; the unscrupulous British bankers, however, took advantage of the artless Costa Ricans by retaining the majority of the money as commissions.) Henry Keith promptly packed his bags and went home.

The younger brother, who had been running the commissary for railroad workers in Puerto Limón, picked up the standard and for the next 15 years applied unflagging dedication to achieve the enterprise his brother had botched. In London, he renegotiated the loans and raised new money. He hired workers from Jamaica and China, and drove them, and himself, like beasts of burden. The Jamaicans, says one writer, were "a generation freed from slavery only in 1834 . . . proud new British subjects who profoundly identified with what seemed to them the imperial task at hand—so much so that they conferred honorary British citizenship on the white man Minor Keith."

A direct route to the Caribbean had never been surveyed, and as a result some stretches of railway had to be abandoned when progress turned

(continues on next page)

Railroads opened the Caribbean lowlands to banana production; this locomotive was imported from Europe.

COFFEE, BANANAS, AND MINOR KEITH
(continued)

out to be impossible. The workers had to bore tunnels through mountains, bridge numerous tributaries of the Reventazón river, hack through jungles, and drain the Caribbean marshlands. During the rainy season, mud slides would wash away bridges. And malaria, dysentery, and yellow fever plagued the workers (the railroad eventually claimed more than 4,000 lives). In December 1890, a bridge high over the turbulent waters of the Birris River finally brought the tracks from Alajuela and Puerto Limón together. It was a prodigious achievement.

For Keith, the endeavor paid off handsomely. He had wrangled from the Costa Rican government a concession of 800,000 acres of land (nearly seven percent of the national territory) along the railway track and coastal plain, plus a 90-year lease on the completed railroad. And the profits from his endeavors were to be tax-free for 20 years. To help finance the railroad project, Keith planted his lands with bananas. *Musa sapientum* (the "muse of wisdom"), a fruit of Asian origin that had been brought to the New World by the Spaniards, was a popular novelty in North America. Costa Rica thus became the first Central American country to grow bananas. Like coffee, the fruit flourished. Exports increased from 100,000 stems in 1883 to more than a million in 1890, when the railroad was completed. By 1899 Keith, who went on to marry the daughter of the Costa Rican president, had become the "Banana King" and Costa Rica the world's leading banana producer.

Along the way, the savvy entrepreneur had wisely entered into a partnership with the Boston Fruit Company, the leading importer of tropical fruits for the U.S. market. Thus was born the United Fruit Company—La Yunai, as Central Americans called it—which during the first half of the 20th century was to become the driving force and overlord of the economies of countries the length and breadth of Latin America.

The Atlantic Railroad helped transform Costa Rica's traditional subsistence economy into one dominated by commercial agriculture. The railroad and Keith's large-scale banana plantations, which required roads and ports, had involved massive injections of capital. Costa Rica's coffee barons were unwilling to invest in bananas—an enterprise that threatened their interests—and it would otherwise have been impossible for Costa Rica to have financed this infrastructure itself. Hence, foreign money came flooding in. On the one hand, the host country gained, because areas that had previously been outside the national economy were brought into it, and facilities were created that eventually would revert to the national government. But as in most Central American countries, Costa Rica had abrogated certain national rights to United States interests and those of the United Fruit Company.

opponent Otilio Ulate by a small margin, the government claimed fraud. Next day, the building holding many of the ballot papers went up in flames, and the *calderonista*-dominated legislature annulled the election results. Ten days later, on 10 March 1948, the "War of National Liberation" plunged Costa Rica into civil war.

"Don Pepe"—Savior of the Nation
The popular myth suggests that José María ("Don Pepe") Figueres Ferrer—42-year-old coffee farmer, engineer, economist, and philosopher—raised a "ragtag army of university students and intellectuals" and stepped forward to topple the government that had refused to step aside for its democratically elected successor. In actuality, Don Pepe's revolution had been long in the planning; the 1948 election merely provided a good excuse.

Don Pepe had been exiled to Mexico in 1942—the first political outcast since the Tinoco era—after being seized halfway through a radio broadcast denouncing Calderón. Figueres formed an alliance with other exiles, returned to Costa Rica in 1944, began calling for an armed uprising, and arranged for foreign arms to be airlifted in to groups being trained by Guatemalan military advisors.

Supported by the governments of Guatemala and Cuba, Don Pepe's insurrectionists captured the cities of Cartago and Puerto Limón and were poised to pounce on San José when Calderón, who had little heart for the conflict, capitulated. (The government's pathetically trained soldiers—aided and armed by the Somoza regime in Nicaragua—included communist banana workers from the lowlands; they wore blankets over their shoulders against the cold of the highlands,

"Don Pepe" Figueres, leader of the 1948 revolution, at a victory parade

earning Calderón supporters the nickname mariachis.) The 40-day civil war claimed over 2,000 lives, most of them civilians.

THE MODERN ERA

Foundation of the Modern State

Don Pepe became head of the Founding Junta of the Second Republic of Costa Rica. As leader of the revolutionary junta, he consolidated Calderón's progressive social reform program and added his own landmark reforms: he banned the press and Communist Party, introduced suffrage for women and full citizenship for blacks, revised the Constitution to outlaw a standing army (including his own), established a presidential term limit, and created an independent Electoral Tribunal to oversee future elections. Figueres also shocked the elites by nationalizing the banks and insurance companies, a move that paved the way for state intervention in the economy.

On a darker note, Don Pepe reneged on the peace terms that guaranteed the safety of the *calderonistas:* Calderón and many of his followers were exiled to Mexico, special tribunals confiscated their property, and, in a sordid episode, many prominent left-wing officials and activists were abducted and murdered. (Supported by Nicaragua, Calderón twice attempted to invade Costa Rica and topple his nemesis, but was each time repelled. Incredibly, he was al-

lowed to return, and even ran for president unsuccessfully in 1962!)

Then, by a prior agreement that established the interim junta for 18 months, Figueres returned the reins of power to Otilio Ulate, the actual winner of the '48 election and a man not even of Don Pepe's own party. Costa Ricans later rewarded Figueres with two terms as president, in 1953-57 and 1970-74. Figueres dominated politics for the next two decades. A socialist, he used his popularity to build his own electoral base and founded the Partido de Liberacion Nacional (PLN), which became the principal advocate of state-sponsored development and reform. He died on 8 June 1990, a national hero.

The Contemporary Scene

Social and economic progress since 1948 has helped return the country to stability, and though post-civil war politics have reflected the play of old loyalties and antagonisms, elections have been free and fair. With only two exceptions, the country has ritualistically alternated its presidents between the PLN and the opposition Social Christians. Successive PLN governments have built on the reforms of the *calderonista* era, and the 1950s and '60s saw a substantial expansion of the welfare state and public school system, funded by economic growth. The intervening conservative governments have encouraged private enterprise and economic self-reliance through tax breaks, protectionism, subsidized credits, and other macro-

COSTA RICA AND THE NICARAGUAN REVOLUTION

Costa Rica's relations with neighboring Nicaragua have always been testy. During the 1970s, the Nicaraguan revolution brought these simmering tensions to a boil, threatening to destabilize Costa Rica and plunge the whole of Central America into war. Costa Rica was led to the brink by a pathetically myopic U.S. foreign policy. That it was ultimately saved owes much to the integrity of Costa Rican president Oscar Arias Sánchez (1986-90), who earned the 1987 Nobel Peace Prize for bringing peace to the region.

Much of the post-1948 friction between the two nations stemmed from the personal rivalry between Costa Rica's "Don Pepe" Figueres and "Tacho" Somoza, Nicaragua's strongman dictator, who despised Figueres's espousal of social democracy and efforts to rid Central America of tyranny. In 1948, Figueres ousted the *calderonista* government and came to power with the backing of Nicaragua's anti-Somoza opposition. For the next two decades Figueres and the Somoza family conspired against each other.

During Figueres's second term as president (1970-74), relations with Nicaragua briefly improved; enough, in fact, for the Somoza family—now headed by Tacho's son, Anastasio (Tachito)—to acquire three vast properties on the Costa Rican side of the border. (The estates, equipped with airstrips suitable for large aircraft, became training grounds for Cuban exiles planning a military invasion of Cuba; in the 1980s, the lands became training grounds for the contras.)

The Carter administration brought new attitudes toward human rights. U.S. support for right-wing dictatorships temporarily waned, and countries with relatively democratic systems, such as Costa Rica, benefited from increased aid. Buoyed by the new moral stance, the Nicaraguan church and the Sandinista National Liberation Front (FSLN) stepped up

their attacks on the tyrannical Somoza regime. Costa Rica was to play a pivotal role in the revolution and postrevolutionary war that followed.

Most Ticos were sympathetic to the Sandinista cause and supported their government's tacit backing of the anti-Somoza revolutionaries who established guerrilla camps in Costa Rica close to the Nicaraguan border. Many Costa Ricans even took up arms alongside the revolutionaries.

As relations worsened, Somoza launched retaliatory airstrikes on Costa Rican border towns; Civil Guards came under attack, and the dictator threatened a full-scale invasion, prompting Costa Rica to break off diplomatic relations and seize the Somoza estates. As the Sandinistas became more radical, however, fears were raised that the revolution would have a destabilizing effect throughout the isthmus. President Rodrigo Carazo attempted to rid the northern border of guerrilla camps. Meanwhile, he allowed the FSLN to set up a government-in-exile in San José in the apparent hope that he could pressure the Sandinistas into taking a more moderate stance.

The picture was reversed overnight. On 19 July 1979 the Sandinistas entered Managua and toppled the Somoza regime. Thousands of Nicaraguan National Guardsmen and right-wing sympathizers were forced to flee. Many settled in northern Costa Rica, where they were warmly welcomed by wealthy ranchers sympathetic to the right-wing cause. By the summer of 1981, the anti-Sandinistas had been welded into the Nicaraguan Democratic Front (FDN) headquartered in Costa Rica; contras roamed throughout the northern provinces, and the CIA was beginning to take charge of events. Costa Rica's foreign policy underwent a dramatic reversal: the former champion of the Sandinista cause found itself embroiled in the Reagan administration's vendetta to oust the Sandinista regime.

economic policies. The combined results were a generally vigorous economic growth (see "Economy," below) and the creation of a welfare state which had grown by 1981 to serve 90% of the population, absorbing 40% of the national budget in the process and granting the government the dubious distinction of being the nation's biggest employer.

By 1980, the bubble had burst. Costa Rica was mired in an economic crisis: epidemic inflation, crippling currency devaluation, soaring oil bills and social welfare costs, plummeting coffee, banana, and sugar prices, and the disruptions to trade caused by the Nicaraguan war (Costa Rica became a base first for Sandinista and then for contra activities, as its war-torn northern

Costa Rica was in a bind. In February 1982, Luis Alberto Monge Alvarez was elected president. He originally tried to keep his country neutral. In the face of the Sandinistas' radical shift to the left, however, Monge found himself hostage to U.S. and domestic right-wing pressure to support the contras. As his economic crisis deepened, he was forced to bow to U.S. demands in exchange for foreign aid. By 1984, when contra raids had begun to prompt Nicaraguan counterstrikes across the border, the CIA, Oliver North, and his cronies in the National Security Council were firmly in command, the Costa Rican Civil Guard was being trained in Honduras by U.S. military advisors, and roads and airstrips were being built throughout the northern provinces.

In the fall of 1984, when Nicaragua agreed to sign the Contadora Peace Plan brokered by Venezuela, Monge withdrew his support and flew to Washington to endorse Reagan's pro-contra plan. Monge's administration, with right-wingers in the ascendancy, was now giving tacit support to newly formed paramilitary groups that began carrying out acts of domestic terrorism that were intended to implicate the Sandinistas as a key excuse for Monge and the U.S. to militarize Costa Rica's security forces.

As the prospect of regional war increased, the Costa Rican people "stepped back from the brink" and rallied behind peace advocate Oscar Arias Sánchez in the 1986 presidential elections. Arias had been outraged by U.S. attempts to undermine Costa Rica's neutrality and drag the tiny nation into the conflict. Once inaugurated, he immediately threw his energies into restoring peace to Central America.

In February 1987, Arias presented the leaders of the Central American nations a formal peace plan, which called for suspension of all military aid to insurrectionists, cease-fires to all conflicts, general amnesties for political prisoners and for guerrillas who laid down their arms, negotiations between governments and their oppositions, and free and fair elections. Reagan called it "fatally flawed." Despite Washington's best efforts to sabotage Arias's plan, all five Central American presidents—including Nicaragua's Daniel Ortega—signed it in August 1987, rejecting Reagan's inane military "solution" in favor of a solution in which all concerned committed themselves to fundamental reforms in their political systems.

In a speech before the U.S. Congress the following month, Arias told Washington forthrightly that the Costa Rican people "are convinced that the risks we run in the struggle for peace will always be less than the irreparable cost of war."

The costs of the turmoil were great. In addition to tens of thousands killed, a decade of war in the region (and Monge's support for U.S. policy) had eroded international confidence in Costa Rica. Regional trade had declined 60%. There had been a capital flight from the country; by 1984, the national debt had almost quadrupled. As many as 250,000 Nicaraguan exiles and refugees were living in Costa Rica by 1987, and the country's political stability had been seriously—though temporarily—undermined.

"Although we are poor, we have so far been able to reach satisfactory goals," Arias told the U.S. Congress. "This is largely because we have no arms expenditures and because the imbedded practice of democracy drives us to meet the needs of the people. Almost 40 years ago we abolished our army. Today we threaten no one, neither our own people nor our neighbors. Such threats are absent not because we lack tanks, but because there are few of us who are hungry, illiterate, or unemployed."

neighbor swung from rightist to leftist regimes). When large international loans then came due, Costa Rica found itself burdened overnight with the world's greatest per-capita debt.

In February 1986, Costa Ricans elected as their president a relatively young sociologist and economist-lawyer called Oscar Arias Sánchez. Arias's electoral promise had been to work for peace. Immediately, he put his energies into resolving Central America's regional conflicts. He attempted to expel the contras from Costa Rica and enforce the nation's official proclamation of neutrality made in 1983 (much to the chagrin of the U.S. government; see special topic "Costa Rica and the Nicaraguan Revolution"). Arias's tireless efforts were rewarded in 1987, when his Central American peace plan was signed by the five Central American presidents in Guatemala City—an achievement that earned the Costa Rican president the 1987 Nobel Peace Prize, and for which the whole nation is justly proud.

In February 1990, Rafael Angel Calderón Fournier, a conservative lawyer and candidate for the Social Christian Unity Party (PUSC), won a narrow victory with 51% of the vote. He was inaugurated 50 years to the day after his father, the great reformer, was named president. Restoring Costa Rica's economy to sound health in the face of a debilitating national debt was Calderón's paramount goal. Under the aegis of pressure from the World Bank and International Monetary Fund, Calderón initiated a series of austerity measures aimed at redressing the country's huge deficit and national debt (see "Economy," below). Indications were that the attempts were succeeding, although not without social cost.

In March 1994, in an intriguing historical quirk, Calderón, son of the president ousted by Don Pepe Figueres in 1948, lost his re-election bid to Don Pepe's youthful son, José María Figueres, a graduate of both West Point and Harvard.

GOVERNMENT

ORGANIZATION

Government Branches

Costa Rica is a democratic republic, as defined by the 1949 Constitution, which guarantees all citizens and foreigners equality before the law, the right to own property, the right of petition and assembly, freedom of speech, and the right to habeas corpus. As in the United States, the government is divided into independent executive, legislative, and judicial branches, with "separation of powers" consecrated under Article 9 of the Constitution (none of the powers, for example, can delegate to another the exercise of its functions). In 1969 an amendment ruled that neither the incumbent president nor any former president may be reelected (they must also be secular citizens; i.e. not a priest).

The **executive branch** is composed of the president, two vice presidents, and a cabinet of 17 members called the Council of Government (Consejo de Gobierno). Legislative power is vested in the **Legislative Assembly,** a unicameral body composed of 57 members elected by proportional representation. *Diputados* are elected for a four-year term and can be reelected only after four more. The Assembly holds the power to amend the president's budget and to appoint the comptroller general, who checks public expenditures and prevents the executive branch from overspending. Like its U.S. equivalent, the Assembly can override presidential decisions by two-thirds majority vote and reserves unto itself the sole right to declare war. The power of the legislature to go against the president's wishes is a cause of constant friction (Costa Rica is governed through compromise: a tempest may rage at the surface, but a compromise resolution is

generally being worked out behind the scenes), and presidents have not been cowardly in using such tools as the executive decree to usurp power to themselves. The Oduber administration (1974-78), for example, issued 4,709 executive decrees; the legislature enacted just 721 laws in the same period.

The Legislative Assembly also appoints **Supreme Court** judges—"as many Magistrates as are necessary for adequate service"—for minimum terms of eight years. They are automatically reappointed unless voted out by the Legislative Assembly. Twenty-four judges now serve on the Supreme Court. These judges, in turn, select judges for the civil and penal courts. Together, the courts have done much to enforce constitutional checks on presidential power. The courts also appoint the three "permanent" magistrates of the **Special Electoral Tribunal,** an independent body that oversees each election and is given far-reaching powers. The Tribunal appointees serve staggered six-year terms and are appointed one every two years to minimize partisanship (two additional temporary magistrates are appointed a year before each election). Don't expect to buy a drink in the immediate run-up to an election: liquor and beer sales are banned for the preceding three days.

Provincial Organization

The nation's seven provinces—Alajuela, Cartago, Guanacaste, Heredia, Limón, Puntarenas, and San José—are each ruled by a governor appointed by the president. The provinces are subdivided into 81 *cantones* (counties), which in turn are divided into a total of 421 *distritos* (districts) ruled by municipal councils. The provinces play only one important role: as electoral dis-

COSTA RICA'S PROVINCES AND CAPITALS

tricts for the Legislative Assembly. The number of deputies for each province is determined by that province's population, with one member for each 30,000 people; seats are allotted according to the proportion of the vote for each party. In the past three decades, the municipalities have steadily lost their prerogatives to central authority and now are relegated to fulfilling such functions as garbage collection, public lighting, and upkeep of streets, with a marked lack of success in some cases!

POLITICAL PARTIES

Costa Rica has no shortage of political parties. However, only two really count. The largest is the **National Liberation Party** (Partido de Liberacion Nacional, or PLN), founded by the statesman and hero of the Civil War, "Don Pepe" Figueres, and now headed by his son, José María Figueres. In March 1994, Figueres was elected president with a victory of only 30,000 votes. The PLN, which roughly equates with European social democracy and American-style welfare-state liberalism, has traditionally enjoyed a majority in the legislature, even when an opposition president has been in power. Its support is traditionally drawn from among the middle-class professionals and entrepreneurs and small farmers and rural *peones*.

PLN's archrival is the **Social Christian Unity Party** (Partido de Unidad Social Cristiana, or PUSC), which represents more conservative in-

terests and is a loose coalition of four different parties known as La Oposición and led by past-president (1990-94) Rafael Angel Calderón Fournier, a conservative lawyer. (Calderón enjoyed a close friendship with George Bush during the latter's tenure. His 1990 election campaign, which ended the civil niceties traditionally observed in Costa Rican electioneering, was aided by Bush's own campaign mastermind Roger Ailes and carried election promises that much resembled Bush's own "impossible dreams," including cutting taxes.)

Between them, the two parties have alternated power since 1949 (in every presidential election but two, the "ins" have been ousted). Still, enough Costa Ricans switch their political colors every four years to make the outcome of an election hard to predict.

In addition, a number of less influential parties represent all facets of the political spectrum. Together they managed to collect only some two percent of votes and three seats in the Legislative Assembly in the 1990 presidential ballot. Since Costa Ricans tend to vote for the man rather than the party, most minor parties form around a candidate and represent personal ambitions rather than strong political convictions. (Former president Figueres once accused Ticos of being as domesticated as sheep; they are not easily aroused to passionate defense of a position or cause.) The peasantry is the least represented constituency.

ELECTIONS

Costa Rica's national elections, held every four years, always on the first Sunday of February, reaffirm the pride Ticos feel for their democratic system. In the rest of Central America, says travel writer Paul Theroux, "an election can be a harrowing piece of criminality; in Costa Rica [it is] something of a fiesta. 'You should have been here for the election,' a woman told me in San José, as if I had missed a party." The streets are crisscrossed with flags, and everyone drives around honking their horns, throwing confetti, and holding up their purple-stained thumbs to show that they voted.

Costa Rican citizens enjoy universal suffrage—everyone, male and female, over 18 has the vote—and citizens are automatically registered to vote on their 18th birthdays, when they are issued voter identity cards. Since 1959 voting has been compulsory—it is a constitutional mandate—for all citizens under 70 years of age. After being ushered into voting booths by school-children decked out in party colors, voters indicate their political preferences with a thumbprint beneath a photograph of the candidates of their choice. Splitting votes across party lines is common, as separate ballots are issued for the presidency, legislature, and municipal councils; disillusioned voters register their dissent with the dominant parties by turning in blank ballots. If the president-elect fails to receive 40% of the vote, a special runoff election is held for the two top contenders.

The daily press is full of political messages for months preceding an election. Most papers take an overt partisan stance and journalists "print news stories that may be extremely biased, and allow supporters of opposing points of view to reply the next day," say the Biesanzes in their book, *The Costa Ricans.* As in the U.S., campaigns tend to stress personalities rather than issues, with one blessed difference: attacking your opponent's personal life is considered taboo. "Costa Ricans may copy a lot of things Americans do," said Figueres, "but they would never use sex scandals against their worst enemies." The Supreme Electoral Tribunal rules on campaign issues and can prohibit the use of political smears, such as branding an opponent as communist. Given the tone of the two most recent elections, when North American consultants introduced Machiavellianism into the arena, the Tribunal is in danger of losing hold of the reins.

Control of the police force also reverts to the Supreme Electoral Tribunal during election campaigns to help ensure the integrity of all constitutional guarantees. All parties are granted equal air time on radio and television, and all campaign costs are largely drawn from the public purse: any party with five percent or more of the vote in the prior election can apply for a proportionate share of the official campaign fund, equal to 0.5 percent of the national budget. If a party fails to get five percent of the vote, it is legally required to refund the money, though this rarely happens.

BUREAUCRACY

Little Costa Rica is big on government. Building on the reforms of the *calderonista* era, successive administrations have created an impressive array of health, education, and social-welfare programs plus steadily expanding state enterprises and regulatory bodies, all of which spell a massive expansion of the government bureaucracy. In 1949, the state employed only six percent of the working population; today the government pays the salaries of approximately 25%, or one in four employed people. For the nation, this represents a huge financial burden. Public employees are the best paid, most secure, and most highly unionized and vocal workers, and the supposedly neutral bureaucracy has become the largest and most insatiable pressure group in the country. Public employees' repetitive demands for higher pay, shorter hours, and greater fringe benefits (backed up by the constant threat of strikes) are so voracious that they eat up a vast proportion of the government benefits intended for the poor. "The state," says one Tican, "is a cow with a thousand teats and everyone wants a teat to suck."

Unfortunately, Costa Rica's government employees have nurtured bureaucratic formality to

the level of art. Corruption is part of the way things work, though to a lesser degree than in other Latin American countries. And travelers may find a lot of their time being tied up in interminable lines. The problem has given rise to *despachantes*, people who make a living from their patience and knowledge of the bureaucratic ropes: for a small fee they will wait in line and gather the necessary documents on your behalf. Travel agencies can usually arrange a trustworthy *despachante*.

Armed Forces

Simply put, there is no army, navy, or air force. Costa Rica disbanded its military forces in 1949, when it declared itself neutral. You'll question this if you pass through one of the "military" checkpoints along roadways in the northern lowlands. Those guys in army fatigues touting M-16 rifles are members of the Civil Guard (a quasi "National Guard"—trained in paramilitary techniques), a branch of the police force. Costa Rica's police force has traditionally been underpaid and, as such, its ranks have suffered from being little-educated and prone to bribery and corruption. Many senior officers, too, have been political appointees rather than career men and women. The government recently tried to purge the force of its cancer.

ECONOMY

Costa Rica's economy this century has, in many ways, been a model for developing nations. Highly efficient coffee and banana industries, aided by high and stable world prices, have drawn in vast export earnings. Manufacturing has grown rapidly under the protection of external tariffs and the expanding purchasing power of the domestic market (per-capita income doubled between 1960 and 1979). And the nation long avoided amassing a crippling foreign debt.

The 1980s, however, provided a rough ride for Costa Rica. Costa Rica's economy took a serious fall in 1978. World coffee prices plummeted, slashing the country's income. The following year, oil prices rose sharply (Costa Rica spends the equivalent of its *total* coffee income for foreign oil every year) while foreign capital took to its heels with the outbreak of the Nicaraguan Revolution, which slowed commerce throughout the isthmus. Costa Rica is dependent on foreign investment. The welfare state established in the 1960s and 1970s was financed largely through foreign loans, and the industrialization policies of the 1970s based on import substitution were largely funded by foreign sources of investment capital.

In 1980, a large part of the foreign loans came due. Starved for money, the government of President Rodrigo Carazo (1978-82) began to soak up domestic bank credit, devalued the *colón,* the nation's currency, and printed more money to meet its debts. Carazo's government was overwhelmed by the resulting crisis. Inflation soared to 100% by 1982. Industrial production went into decline. Official unemployment rose to 8.2%, with an additional 22.6% officially "underemployed" (unofficial figures were certainly higher). Real wages fell to pre-1970 levels, bringing impoverishment to much of the nation (35% of the nation's families were officially below the poverty line in 1991). By August 1981, when the nation's foreign debt reached US$4 billion, Costa Rica was forced to cease payment on its international loans.

The U.S. and International Monetary Fund (IMF) stepped in with a massive aid program that injected $3 billion into the economy between 1981 and 1984, equivalent to more than one-third of the Costa Rican government's budget and 10% of the nation's gross national product (GNP) for the period (Costa Rica was second only to Israel as the highest per-capita recipient of U.S. aid). Much of the U.S. government aid was tied to Costa Rica's support for the contra cause (see special topic "Costa Rica and the Nicaraguan Revolution"); IMF and World Bank assistance was tied to austerity measures designed to slash government spending, stimulate economic diversification, and sponsor competitive export industries.

Costa Rica *must* diversify to recharge an economy reeling under the impact of plummeting earnings from coffee—in 1991 coffee earnings plummeted to $180 million, down from $300 million the year before—and a debilitating international debt which today, at US$4.6 billion or $1440 for each of its 3.2 million citizens, is one of the world's highest per capita. The good news is that tourism is booming, pulling in previously unknown revenues on a scale that, in 1994, topped those of any other industry ($577.4 million, compared to $531 million from bananas and $203.5 million from coffee).

In spite of a steady growth in GNP during the past decade, real wages remain basically stagnant (inflation was 27% in 1992, 11% in 1993, and 17% in 1994), a growing proportion of resources goes to service the national debt, and the government has found it impossible to meet any of the IMF goals. The trade deficit grew from approximately $800 million in 1993 to more than $850 million in 1994. The *colón* continues to decline in value. And consumption taxes add to the general inflation (at press time, the Legislative Assembly was considering raising the sales tax from 10% to 15%).

The government of Rafael Calderón (1990-94), under strong pressure from the IMF and World Bank, pledged to balance the budget and rectify Costa Rica's structural weaknesses. Albeit halfheartedly, state-owned enterprises were privatized, elements of the social

welfare institutions were being dismantled, some subsidies and tax exemptions—such as those for *pensionados* (foreign residents)—were rescinded, and new taxes were levied on income and savings. In the short run the social costs will be high. On the bright side: The current blossoming in tourism and nontraditional export items is pulling in hundreds of millions of dollars and will increasingly help alleviate the current crisis. Indeed, per capita GNP increased from $1793 to $2400, 1989-93. The country's external debt peaked in 1989 at $4.7 billion and has since been reduced. And dollar reserves have increased to $1.025 billion (1993).

Another bright note was the signing of a bilateral trade agreement with Mexico. Beginning 1 January 1995, 70% of customs duties between the two countries were eliminated (the remaining 30% will be phased out over 10 years). It's anticipated that this will vastly increase Mexican investment in Costa Rica's tourism industry. It also gives Costa Rica access to a Mexican market of 90 million people (in 1993, Costa Rican exports to Mexico soared by 269% to $63 million) and represents a step toward Costa Rica's eventually joining the North American Free Trade Agreement (NAFTA). That would be a culmination of the move, since the late '70s, progressively away from a protectionist attitude and toward a more diversified trading economy (together, coffee, bananas, sugar, and beef represented almost 80% of exports in 1980 (less than 40% today).

MANUFACTURING

Manufacturing still plays a relatively small part in the Costa Rican economy (in 1990 earnings from industrial manufacturing were US$398 million—21.6% of GNP), and there is little to suggest that industrialization is going to transform the essentially agricultural economy in the near future. The market for manufactured goods is largely restricted to a small population with a relatively low purchasing power. Local industrial raw materials are restricted to agricultural products, wood, and a small output of mineral ores. Manufacturing is still largely concerned with food processing, although pharmaceutical and textile exports have risen dramatically in recent years. Major industrial projects also include aluminum processing, a petrochemical plant at Moín, a tuna-processing plant at Golfito, and an oil refinery at Puerto Limón.

Hydroelectricity, though well developed and concentrated in the Arenal area, is the only domestic power source of significance. Costa Rica uses 971,000 kilowatts daily. A newly completed geothermal plant on Miravalles volcano, in Guanacaste, is anticipated to produce about 10% of the nation's electricity need.

AGRICULTURE

Noted Nicaraguan poet Rubén Darío once described Costa Rica as a nation of clerks,

traditional Sarchí oxcart in use near Cartago

LAND REFORM

Despite Costa Rica's reputation as a country of yeoman farmers, land ownership has always been highly concentrated, and there are parts, such as Guanacaste, where rural income distribution resembles the inimical patterns of Guatemala and El Salvador.

In colonial days, Costa Rica's agricultural land was relatively equally distributed among peasant smallholders. The situation began to change with the introduction of coffee in the early 19th century, when many farmers were squeezed off their land. Today, 71% of the economically active rural population is landless. The bottom 50% of all landholders own only three percent of all land. And the top one percent of farm owners own more than one-quarter of the agricultural land.

The Costa Rican government, too, has traditionally been the domain of large landholders and coffee barons. Understandably, they had little reason to reform the agrarian structure so as to eliminate unfair concentration of land and alleviate the lot of the army of landless *campesinos*. Lip service had been paid to the need for rural change, but little had been achieved. Then, in 1959, Fidel Castro gave the elites a big scare. Concerned about the impact of the Cuban revolution in the rest of the continent, the U.S. began to encourage Latin American governments to carry out agrarian reforms aimed at dismantling unjust ownership patterns as a means of easing rural discontent into controllable channels. Costa Rica passed its agrarian reform law on 14 October 1961. Most other Latin American countries followed suit.

Alas, as Professor J.K. Galbraith has pointed out: "A land reform is a revolutionary step; it passes power, property and status from one group in the community to another. If the government of the country is dominated or strongly influenced by the landholding group—the one that is losing its prerogatives—no one should expect effective land reform as an act of grace."

By 1963, the threat of leftist revolution throughout the region had receded, and along with it the will for reform. The original intent had been to expropriate inefficiently farmed land and grant it to landless peasants. Instead, emphasis was placed on colonization schemes aimed at settling the landless on virgin land—a case of dealing with the consequences of inequality in land distribution, not its cause. For the Instituto de Tierras y Colonización, the reform agency, the costs of opening up new land were debilitatingly huge. Land had to be bought and cleared, houses, roads, water and utility systems built.

In the first decade of so-called reform only 1.7% (2,574) of the nation's 145,000 landless peasant families had received titles—to two percent of the nation's farmland. By 1983 the figures had respectively doubled. Colonization schemes, however, have failed to keep up with the growth of the landless. And while the number of smallholdings (farms of less than 25 acres) continues to rise, the percentage of farmland they encompass continues to fall.

lawyers, and oxen. Indeed, while it might *appear* that bureaucrats and legal eagles have the upper hand, agriculture dominates the Costa Rican economy. The fact is obvious everywhere you go, particularly in the central highlands, where a remarkable feature of the land is the almost complete cultivation, no matter how steep the slope. Nationwide, some 12% of the land area is planted in crops, 45% is given to pasture, and only 27% is forested. Despite the ubiquitousness of small family farms, large-scale commercial agriculture is more important in terms of dollar value, even in coffee, where a relatively small number of large farms associated with the coffee *beneficios*

(processing plants) have established their dominance.

Coffee—*grano d'oro* (golden bean)—is the most important crop in the highlands in terms of area (bananas, however, zipped ahead of coffee as the biggest income earner in 1991, after the collapse of world coffee prices, to be outpaced in turn by tourism, now the nation's biggest income earner). The mist-shrouded slopes of the Meseta Central and southern highlands are adorned with green undulating carpets of coffee. The large hacienda is foreign to the traditions of the Meseta Central, and the fabric of the rural landscape, with its thousands of small-size farmsteads, is reminiscent of certain parts of peasant Europe.

Red-tiled and corrugated-roofed houses straggle along the web of farm roads and, by their pattern and numbers, indicate that pressure on the land has mounted. Some relief has been found by intensifying cultivation of coffee and, west of Alajuela and at lower levels, sugarcane; elsewhere in the higher, more temperate areas, carnations, chrysanthemums, and other flowers grow under acres of plastic sheeting, and dairying is becoming more important in a mixed-farming economy that has been a feature of the Meseta since the end of the 19th century. The situation is a far cry from the very limited economy of the Altiplano at similar elevations in Guatemala.

The vast banana plantations that swathe the Caribbean plains produce some 50 million boxes of bananas per year, making Costa Rica the second-biggest exporter of bananas in the world, behind Ecuador. Sugarcane is grown by small farmers all over the country but becomes a major crop on plantations as you drop into the lowlands. Particularly rapid growth in sugar production occurred in the 1960s after the U.S. reassigned Cuba's sugar import quota; production has since gone into decline—in 1981 Costa Rica had to import sugar to meet domestic demand. And cacao, once vital to the 18th-century economy, is on the rise again as a major export crop; the trees, fruit hanging pendulously from their trunks, are everywhere, especially in large plantations around Limón and Upala and to a much lesser degree around Alajuela and increasingly around Golfito and the *llanuras*.

Recent attempts to stimulate nontraditional exports are paying dividends in agriculture. Cassava, papaya, the camote (sweet potato), melons, strawberries, chayote (vegetable pear), eggplant, *curraré* (plantain bananas), pimiento, macadamia nuts, ornamental plants, and cut flowers are all fast becoming important export items.

For tourists with an interest there are several farms where you can learn about agriculture firsthand. The Central American School of Animal Husbandry, for example, is fostering agriecotourism on a working ranch near Atenas (see "West from Alajuela" in the Central Highlands chapter).

Cattle

By far the largest share of agricultural land (70%) is given to cattle pasture. Despite its evolving complexion, Guanacaste remains essentially what it has been since midcolonial times—cattle country—and three-quarters of Costa Rica's 2.2 million head of cattle are found here. They are mostly humpbacked zebu, originally from India and now adapted over several generations; there are also herds of Charolais and Hereford. Low-interest loans in the 1960s and 1970s encouraged a rush into cattle farming for the export market, prompting rapid expansion into new areas such as the Valle de El General and more recently the Atlantic lowlands.

Although Costa Rica is today Latin America's leading beef exporter (it accounts for some five percent of U.S. meat imports), beef has never provided more than nine percent of Costa Rica's export earnings (meat exports earned $44 million in 1992). Sadly, much of the land placed under cattle in recent decades has been on steep hill slopes that have been stripped bare of timber. The scoured slopes bear mute testimony to the greed and folly of man. Destructive floods now common in the *terra caliente* of the Pacific lowlands can be traced to "cattle mania." And the loss of the ready smile of the small farmers who have been driven from their land—cattle ranches need little labor—is a poignant reminder of a cancer that has slowly but inevitably eaten away at the land. All this so that North Americans can enjoy their hamburgers and TV dinners.

Bananas

Costa Rica's banana industry, recently ousted by tourism as the country's number one earner of foreign currency, continues to expand to meet the demand of a growing international market. In 1992, 32,000 hectares were under bananas, a 50% increase since 1985. By the time you read this, bananas will cover at least 45,000 hectares. Most growth is concentrated in the north Atlantic lowlands.

Bananas have been a part of the Caribbean landscape since 1870, when American entrepreneur Minor Keith shipped his first fruit stems—360 bunches—to New Orleans (see special topic "Coffee, Bananas & Minor Keith"). In 1899, his Tropical Trading & Transport Co. merged with the Boston Fruit Co. to form the United Fruit Co., which soon became the overlord of the political economies of the "banana republics." By

the 1920s, much of the chaotic jungle south of Puerto Limón had been transformed into a vast sea of bananas.

Then, as now in some areas, working conditions were appalling, and strikes were so frequent that when Panamá disease and then *sigatoka* (leaf-spot) disease swept the region in the 1930s and 1940s, United Fruit took the opportunity to abandon its Atlantic holdings and move to the Pacific coast, where it planted around Golfito, Coto Colorado, and Palmar (operated by United Fruit's subsidiary Compañía Bananera). Violent clashes with the banana workers' unions continued to be the company's nemesis. In 1985, after a 72-day strike, United Fruit closed its operations in southwestern Costa Rica. Many of the plantations have been replaced by stands of African palms (used in cooking oil, margarine, and soap); others are leased to independent growers and farmers' cooperatives who sell to United Fruit.

The Standard Fruit Co. began production in the Atlantic lowlands in 1956. Alongside ASBANA (Asociación de Bananeros), a government-sponsored private association, Standard Fruit helped revive the Atlantic coast banana industry. Much of the new acreage, however, has come at the expense of thousands of acres of virgin jungle (see special topic "Bananas: Friend or Foe?" in the Caribbean Coast chapter). Banana export earnings rose from $482.9 million in 1992 to $531 million in 1993.

Coffee

Costa Rica's Meseta Central possesses ideal conditions for coffee production, and beans grown here are ranked among the best in the world. The coffee plant loves a seasonal, almost monsoonal climate with a distinct dry season; it grows best, too, in well-drained, fertile soils at elevations between 800 and 1,500 meters with a narrow annual temperature range—natural conditions provided by the Meseta Central. The best coffee—mild coffee commanding the highest prices—is grown near the plant's uppermost altitudinal limits, where the bean takes longer to mature.

The first coffee beans were brought from Jamaica in 1779. Within 50 years coffee had become firmly established; by the 1830s it was the country's prime export earner, a position it oc-

cupied until 1991, when coffee plunged overnight to third place in the wake of a precipitous 50% fall in world coffee prices after Brazil scuttled the International Coffee Agreement quota system in 1989. (Ticos can find satisfaction in the fact that their coffee has an unusually high "liqueur," or coffee essence, content of 86%; Brazilian coffee has a meager 29% content.)

Coffee exports earned $203.5 million in 1993, down from $250 million in 1991 and $150 million lower than 1990. This despite the fact that Costa Rica today has the greatest coffee productivity per acre in the world. In May 1992, Costa Rican coffee growers rioted in towns throughout the highlands; they even briefly suspended exports to protest the low prices. The decline has caused widespread distress for small farmers and the 45,000 poorly paid laborers who rely on work in the harvest season. In 1994, however, international coffee prices skyrocketed after large crop losses in Brazil, signaling a respite—however brief—for Costa Rica's coffee growers.

Population pressure on the land has induced the adoption of the most modern and intensive methods of cultivation, including high-yielding plants. The plants are grown in nurseries for their first year before being planted in long rows that ramble invitingly down the steep hillsides, their paths coiling and uncoiling like garden snakes. After four years they fruit. In April, with the first rains, the small white blossoms burst forth and the air is laced with perfume not unlike jasmine. By November, the glossy green bushes are plump with shiny red berries—the coffee beans—and the seasonal labor is called into action.

The hand-picked berries are trucked to *beneficios* (processing plants), where they are machine-scrubbed and washed to remove the fruity outer layer and dissolve the gummy substance surrounding the bean (the pulp is returned to the slopes as fertilizer). The moist beans are then blow-dried or laid out to dry in the sun in the traditional manner. The leather skin of the bean is then removed by machine, and the beans are sorted according to size and shape before being vacuum-sealed to retain the fragrance and slight touch of acidity characteristic of the great vintages of Costa Rica.

A visit to a coffee *finca* (farm) is an interesting day-trip from San José. **Café Britt** (tel. 237-

5044 or 238-4240, fax 238-1848) offers an hour-long "Coffeetour" of its *finca* and *beneficio*, including an English-language multimedia presentation on the "Story of Coffee." At San Pedro de Barva, 10 km north of Heredia, is a coffee research station and the **Museo de Café** (tel. 237-1975; hours Mon.-Fri. 7 a.m.-3 p.m.). **Aventuras Turísticas de Orosí** (tel. 533-3030, fax 533-3212) offers an "Orosí Coffee Adventure" featuring a tour of a coffee farm and *beneficio* (three hours; $20).

TOURISM

Costa Rica is one of the world's fastest-growing destinations for adventure and nature travel, and travelers of every other persuasion are pouring in, too. The resort industry is blossoming as it realizes the seductive potentials of Costa Rica. Even the cruise lines are taking notice. Above all the country has been adopted as the darling of the ecotourist: the just reward for two decades of foresight and diligence in preserving its natural heritage in national parks and wildlife reserves.

Costa Rica gains more and more fans every year. Tourism even scored a 16% increase in 1991, a remarkable figure for the year of the Gulf War, which devastated the travel industry throughout the rest of the world. In 1992, 610,093 tourists came, an increase of 28% over the previous year. And official statistics claim that tourist arrivals increased 10% in 1994 compared to 1993, when 689,872 tourists visited Costa Rica. However, tourism arrivals suddenly shriveled in the second half of 1994. Experts blame the 1,000% rise in national park fees imposed in September 1994 (see "National Parks" under "Conservation" earlier in this chapter). To put arrivals back on the fast track, the Figueres government planned to spend $7.5 million in 1995 on marketing and promotion, up from $1.4 million in 1994.

The nation's status as a "destination of the '90s" is a boon to the struggling economy. In fact, the government is relying on tourism dollars to help pull the country out of debt. In 1993, tourism generated an estimated $577.4 million (or $114 per capita), boosting it past the banana industry to become the nation's prime income earner. Tourism revenues grew by an unprecedented 34% in 1993, generating an estimated 70,000 jobs in the process (about 12.5% of the labor force works in tourism-related activities); 1994—when tourism generated $685.5 million—posted a 19% increase in revenues. By 1998 (assuming the decline in late 1994 is reversed), the country anticipates receiving 1.2 million visitors who, it predicts, will drop a cool $1.278 billion. It's not simply a matter of tourist numbers: the average stay is up from 6.9 days in 1988 to 10.8 days in 1993, while per diem expenditures per tourist are up, too.

Costa Rica is even looking to sponsor further growth in tandem with its Central American neighbors, including easing immigration restrictions among the Central American nations, creating a Mayan Route for tourists, and even developing a regional tourism card. Five Central American airlines—Aviateca of Guatemala, COPA of Panamá, LASCA of Costa Rica, NICA of Nicaragua, and TACA of El Salvador—have a cooperative "Visit Central America" marketing effort and coupon program that allows travelers to visit the entire region (see "Getting There" in the On the Road chapter).

Costa Rica continues to respond to the growing flood in eager anticipation of the welcome injection of dollars. In May 1990, the country installed its first tourism minister, Luis Manuel Chacón, on the president's cabinet. To accommodate the growing number of visitors, he made expansion of hotel rooms a priority. At the rates of tourism expansion, the country needed to open 500 new rooms each month. While some hotel corridors echo in the rainy-season months, it is still difficult to get beds Nov.-April, when a severe case of room shortage afflicts many of the more popular spots. Overall, the country predicts it will need 30,700 hotel rooms by 1998.

At this rate, Costa Rica is singing the old song, "Yes, We Need No Bananas!" The new addendum, however, is: "Well, maybe the bananas aren't so bad in lieu of a reduction in national park fees!"

The Beach Resort Boom

In its haste to boost the influx of tourist dollars, the government of Rafael Calderón began promoting large-scale resort development on the

shores of the Pacific northwest. More than 50% of visitors in 1991 mentioned that they were visiting Costa Rica to pursue some interest in nature. The government decided to also position Costa Rica as a comprehensive destination for the whole family, and particularly as a beach resort contender to Mexico and the Caribbean.

Sprawling resort complexes began sprouting from the jungled shoreline. Jacó Beach has been pinpointed for redevelopment, and Puerto Limón is expected to prosper as cruise tourism booms. Chief among the projects, however, is the Gulf of Papagayo project encompassing several beaches in Guanacaste (see special topic "Gulf of Papagayo Project" in the Nicoya Peninsula chapter). The megaresort, being constructed by a host of European and Mexican developers (initially led by the Spanish developers Sol Meliá), will be the largest "leisure city" in Central America. Mexico's Grupo Situr alone is planning to build 6,900 rooms in an initial project phase that includes more than 2,000 hotel rooms, 50 luxury villas, 400 family villas, and 700 apartments, complete with shopping center, golf course, and other supporting amenities. In all, more than 20,000 rooms may be developed.

The development covers 4,942 acres close to several national parks and wildlife reserves, and has come under heavy attack from conservation groups (see "The Down Side," below).

Savvy tourism experts speak disparagingly of the so-called "Cancún model" because it also encourages precisely the low-budget mass tourism that Costa Rica has long professed wanting to avoid. "We're really concerned about the direction tourism is taking in Costa Rica," says Kurt Kutay, a director of the Ecotourism Society and president of Seattle-based Wildland Adventures. "There's a place for Mexico-style developments, but it has to be done in a sensitive way, otherwise there's a threat Costa Rica could lose it all . . . Unfortunately, the [Calderón] government espoused ecotourism and then did the opposite."

The Down Side

There has been much debate about how to regulate the impact of tourism on Costa Rica. Concern about whether Costa Rica is growing too fast and shifting from its ecotourism focus toward mass-market tourism led, in 1993, to a

threatened boycott of the country's annual travel trade show, Expotur, by environmentally responsible tour operators and threatens to be a contentious issue for years to come. But everyone agreed on one point: the nation was lacking any sort of coherent tourism development plan to control growth. Consequently, developers large and small were pushing up hotels along Costa Rica's 1,227 kilometers (767 miles) of coastline in total disregard of environmental laws.

In 1977, the country adopted the Maritime Terrestrial Zone Law, which declares the country's entire coastline to be public property, prohibits construction within 50 meters of the point halfway between high and low tides, and restricts construction within 200 meters of the same spot. It happens anyway, without punishment. The sheer volume of violations, said a report in the *Tico Times* (29 May 1992), "bespeaks a massive lack of political will . . . Violations of the coastal law—most noticeably building within the 'inviolable' 50-meter tide line—are out of control." Concerned environmentalists are calling for a prosecutor's office exclusively to enforce the Maritime Terrestrial Zone Law.

Tax credits and other incentives for foreign investors are also pushing the price of land beyond reach of the local population. Up to 40% of Costa Rica's habitable coastline is now owned by North Americans and Europeans, according to Sergio Guillen, an information officer for the Ministry of Planning. "We are selling our land to the highest bidder . . . and the government doesn't seem to care," he says.

What a Mess!

How bad is it? In June 1992, Costa Rica's Ministry of Natural Resources filed charges against Maurice Strong (the *organizer* of the Earth Summit held in Rio de Janeiro in June 1992) and Julio Garcia, his partner in Desarrollos Ecologicos S.A., for building their 12-unit Villas del Caribe on land in the KekoLdi Indian Reserve and Gandoca-Manzanillo Wildlife Refuge without official permits. The Spanish developer Barceló was taken to court for flagrant breaches of environmental codes during construction of a 400-room resort at Playa Tambor, opened in 1992, although the Calderón administration sided with Barceló. And few people were shocked when, in March 1995, twelve ICT officials and even the

tourism minister in the Calderón administration were indicted on a variety of charges relating to violations at Papagayo (see below).

"The current atmosphere is to build first and deal with the legalities later," claims Michael Kaye, president of Costa Rica Expeditions. Ecoconscious tour operators express worry about the degree to which "big" money is beginning to corrupt the democratic process in Costa Rica: they say major corporations who look only at their balance sheets are paying off Costa Rican government officials to get permission to build. "As long as nature unspoiled had the best bottom line, it had at least a fighting chance," noted an article on Costa Rica in *Condé Nast Traveler,* July 1993. "But in the end the big money would come, and what the big money wanted, the big money got, and what the big money wanted was *big.*"

The big money has finally arrived . . . in the Gulf of Papagayo. Alas, history seems to be repeating itself. In October 1993 the Municipality of Liberia ordered Grupo Situr to stop construction of two resorts that are part of the government's Gulf of Papagayo Tourism Project. The Mexican developer lacked the necessary permits and was accused of violating environmental codes. Heeding the requests of local residents, the municipal government formed a special commission to assess complaints that Grupo Situr's subsidiary, Eco-Desarollo Papagayo, was causing environmental damage, including filling in a protected mangrove estuary. In spring 1994, the newly elected Figueres administration also ordered a review; the independent investigation found that the most serious problem was sedimentation in the bay. The company defied a restraining order, according to Michael Kaye. "Construction has not stopped at Papagayo," he says. "The issue will go through the courts for two years, Eco-Desarollo will receive a slap on the wrist, and the damage will have been done."

"Plans in the works suddenly appear on the ground. The question is, have rigorous environmental reviews been done?" asks one ecotour operator. The government's independent ombudsman office thought not. In January 1994, it charged the Calderón administration of issuing a presidential executive decree granting permission for tourism infrastructure to be built inside areas previously defined as "inalienable"

(protected); granting land concessions to foreign developers on preferential terms outside legal provisions; allowing resort development at Papagayo without permits; and ignoring destruction of natural resources at Papagayo.

In September 1994, tourism minister Carlos Roësch, together with developers and members of the local government, met with the ombudsman. They agreed that development should continue under a new master plan and guidelines that don't violate preservation laws. They also decided that local communities should participate in the monitoring process and should be guaranteed a large share of jobs and other benefits generated by the project. However, in March 1995, in the midst of an announcement that the government would move ahead with the project, 12 senior former ICT officials, including former tourism minister Luis Manuel Chacón (who while in office called the ombudsman officials "liars" and refused to accept their findings), were indicted on charges of embezzlement, violating public trust, and dereliction of duty relating to Papagayo!

Ecotour operators have warned that without a conscientious development plan, the government could kill the goose that lays the golden egg. By the time a blueprint is developed it will be too late, says Kaye. Hotels, he says, are going up "so fast and arbitrarily" that there needs to be a moratorium on construction of large-scale resorts until a national plan is in place. "The [Calderón administration's] policy [was] to use eco-development as a smoke screen to get as much foreign exchange as fast as possible without regard for the long-term consequences," he says.

"The [Calderón] policy [was] to talk appropriate-scale tourism and to foster mass tourism. People are *already* beginning to see too many other people," says Kaye, who points to the example of Manuel Antonio National Park, where the problem has reached a crisis. The diminutive (682-hectare) park, midway down the Pacific coast, averages more than 1,000 visitors daily— three times more than it can withstand, according to park director José Antonio Salazar. The shallow lagoon that visitors wade to reach the park is polluted. Trails are showing wear and tear. And hotels have squeezed Manuel Antonio against the Pacific, cutting off migratory corridors

for the park's 350 squirrel monkeys. "Development without concern for sewage or crowding has ruined Manuel Antonio," claims Kaye, whose company has removed Manuel Antonio from its itineraries (as have several other ecotour operators). Says one North American tour operator: "The day mass tourism gets the upperhand, we'll switch our groups to Panamá, Nicaragua, and Venezuela."

"They've got a tiger by the tail here. If they don't start dealing with it in an effective way, it's going to be a catastrophe," concludes Kaye.

The Up Side

The previous tourism minister, Luis Manuel Chacón, pointed out that surging tourism dollars could pull the country out of debt. "Larger projects represent significant investment that the country requires," he said. Costa Rica stands to gain much more than cash from the current boom. Firstly, optimists suggest that the profit potential of tourism encourages private landowners to regard natural areas as long-term assets rather than a source of quick cash, and that resort developers realize that the added expense of building *around* rather than through a forest pays ample dividends in the end. And the employment opportunities are huge. Chacón gained ground in training a broader segment of the Costa Rican population to work in tourism: his five-year goal was to train an additional 15,000 Costa Ricans for the tourism industry (27,600 were so employed in 1991). Chacón claims the Gulf of Papagayo development alone could provide 30,000 jobs by the year 2000.

Alas, when Chacón visited Berlin in March 1993, a German environmental group gave him the "Environmental Devil" award for the Costa Rican government's support of the Tambor and Papagayo projects. Chacón countered that opponents of large-scale resorts are afraid of losing their share of the market. The "greens" who denounce the government's policy, he said, are really leftists: "When you scratch them, the red begins to flow!"

The government is also pouring money into improving road access to popular destinations such as Cahuita, Flamingo, Monteverde, Quepos, Sámara, Tamarindo, and Tambor—which are all sometimes difficult to reach in wet season. Unfortunately, where roads come so do the log-

gers. While many local residents welcome the potential development, others fear that if the roads that lead to more remote natural shrines are paved, more and more tourists will flock, thereby quickening the possible destruction of the very thing they come to worship (see, for example, "Ostional National Wildlife Refuge" in the Nicoya Peninsula chapter).

Most important, collaboration in monitoring tourism growth, as well as Costa Rica's environment in general, is growing. Before leaving office, tourism minister Chacón announced that the government was developing a blueprint for sustainable tourism, as well as a management plan and carrying capacity studies to determine the impact of visitors on protected areas. The *new* tourism minister, Carlos Roesch (a 20-year veteran of the hotel industry), has stated his commitment to launch an ambitious plan for "sustainable tourism development" that includes licensing of tourism companies and visitor quotas for national parks. Roesch has unveiled a multifaceted plan to protect both the country's natural assets and the culture and character of the Ticos. Now that tourism is the country's major income earner, protecting those assets has taken on even greater importance.

One of the keys to Roesch's plan is local community involvement. The ICT is opening five regional offices to make the national tourism board more accessible to small enterpreneurs, and it's working to identify ways to guarantee Costa Ricans greater access to hotels, resorts, and attractions.

Ecotourism

Travel, like fashion, follows trends. In the 1990s the ecological movement has become something of a solar-powered steamroller, changing the way we travel. A 1986 study by the Costa Rican Tourism Institute found that 87% of tourists surveyed cited natural beauty as one of their main motivations for visiting Costa Rica, and 36% specifically cited ecotourism.

More recently, ecotourism—defined as responsible travel that contributes to conservation of natural environments and sustains the well-being of local people by promoting rural economic development—has become to the 1990s what the European Grand Tour was to the 1930s and adventure travel was to the

VOLUNTEER DEVELOPMENT ORGANIZATIONS

Amigos de las Americas (5618 Star Lane, Houston, TX 77057, tel. 800-231-7796) provides health care for villages.

Flying Doctors of America (1951 Airport Rd., Atlanta, GA 30341, tel. 404-451-3068, fax 404-457-6302) arranges short-term medical mercy missions in Central America. Spanish required.

Food First (1885 Mission St., San Francisco, CA 94103, tel. 415-864-8555) publishes *Alternatives to the Peace Corps: Gaining Third World Experience.*

F.O.R. Task Force on Latin America & the Caribbean (515 Broadway, Santa Cruz, CA 95060, tel. 408-423-1626) offers voluntary service in Latin America.

Global Service Corps (1472 Filbert St. #1405, San Francisco, CA 94109, tel. 415-922-5538) offers short-term service programs in Costa Rica.

International Voluntary Service (1424 16th St. NW #204, Washington, D.C. 20036, tel. 202-387-5533) offers voluntary service in Latin America; two to five years' commitment.

Institute for International Cooperation and Development (P.O. Box 103, Williamstown, MA 01267, tel. 413-458-9828, fax 413-458-3323) accepts volunteers for programs in Latin America.

Partners of the Americas (1424 "K" St. NW, Washington, D.C. 20005) provides voluntary service throughout Latin America.

Peacework (305 Washington St. NW, Blacksburg, VA 24060, tel. 703-552-2473) offers work programs in Central America.

1980s. Many adventure enthusiasts of the last decade have discarded their wetsuits, mountain boots, and whitewater rafts; they still want to explore exotic regions, to peer beneath the veneer of the normal mass tourist experience, but in a more relaxed and socially acceptable manner. Bringing only their curiosity, the new wave of ecotourists are leaving their footprints—and their cash.

Costa Rica practically invented the term. In October 1991 the country was chosen as one of three winners of the first environmental award presented by the American Society of Travel Agents (ASTA) and *Smithsonian* magazine. The award was designed to recognize a "company, individual or country for achievements in conservation and environmentalism." Costa Rica shared the prize along with the late Brazilian activist "Chico" Mendez and the country of Rwanda. In 1992 Costa Rica won the Golden Compass Award for its exemplary support of ecotourism. "Since 1979, the country has been defining what conservation in Latin America is and should be," says Steve Cornelius, the Central American program officer for the World Wildlife Fund.

Just because a tour is labeled "ecotour" doesn't mean that it is. The term has become catchy. "Everybody talks about ecotourism to the point where the word is being prostituted," says Sergio Volio, a former Costa Rican national park ranger and now owner of the ecotourism company Geotur. The term can have little meaning if a tour provider doesn't adhere to sound environmental principles.

Fortunately, many tour operators in this fledgling but fast-developing industry are honorable role models. One company has helped build trails that minimize erosion of fragile watersheds. Another makes tour members sign a contract that states they won't touch anything, not even a rock. Other companies hire local guides exclusively. And a key aspect of Seattle-based Wildland Adventures' program to the Caribbean coast is a stay at the Chimuri Lodge, near Puerto Viejo; the lodge is owned and operated by a Bribrí Indian, Mauricio Salazar, who leads groups on rainforest walks.

Filtering tourist dollars into the hands of locals is another problem and, fortunately, one that more and more companies are addressing. In January 1990, the World Wildlife Fund released a two-volume report that found that people interested in nature travel and in visiting fragile environments generally spend more money than other kinds of tourists. Yet Guillermo Canessa, a veteran conservationist and nature guide, found that less than three percent of the profits earned by the tour companies and hotels in Tortuguero actually benefit people of the local community. And conservationists claimed that neither the foreigners flocking to the nation's protected areas nor the tour companies that

WHAT YOU CAN DO YOURSELF

If ecotourism is not in your stars, but camping and hiking are, here are some ways to keep your impact on the environment to a minimum (also see "Personal Conduct").

• Pack it in, pack it out. Try to leave a convenient pack pocket available for carrying out litter you find along the trail.

• Give yourself enough time at the end of the day to find a camping site that will retain the least evidence of your presence.

• Bone up on the types of wildlife you're likely to meet. The more you know, the better you can observe without disrupting them.

• To lessen your visibility, use gear and wear clothing that blend in with the landscape.

• Read books on enjoying the outdoors in environmentally sensitive ways. *Soft Paths,* by Bruce Hampton and David Cole (Stackpole Books), and *Backwoods Ethics,* by Laura and Guy Waterman (Stone Wall Press), are two good choices.

In support of regulated ecotourism and the Code of Environmental Ethics for Nature Travel established by Tsuli/Tsuli (the Costa Rican chapter of the National Audubon Society), the Institute for Central American Studies has formed a Department of Responsible Tourism. The DRT monitors the compliance of tour operators according to the code of ethics, as well as the impact that tourism has on local communities and development in Costa Rica. Based on these investigations, Tsuli/Tsuli and the DRT can recommend "responsible" tour operators and can research complaints about those who are not complying. The DRT, in collaboration with the **Institute for Central American Studies** (Apdo. 1524, San Pedro 2050, tel./fax 224-8910; in the U.S., c/o Mesoamerican Communications, P.O. Box 423808, San Francisco, CA 94142) has launched the "Partnership for Sustainable Tourism" that has resulted in a "Sustainable Tourism Ranking" ($3, including postage and handling) for tour operators, hoteliers, etc.

In the U.S., contact **Ecotourism Society** (801 Devon Place, Alexandria, VA 22314, tel. 703-549-8979, fax 703-549-2920), a watchdog body comprising travel operators and conservationists. In Costa Rica, contact the **Asociación Tsuli/Tsuli** (Audubon de Costa Rica, Apdo. 4910, San José 1000, tel. 240-8775 or 249-1179); the **Department for Responsible Tourism** (Apdo. 300, San José 1002, tel. 233-7112 or 233-7710); or the **Eco-Institute of Costa Rica** (Apdo. 8080, San José 1000, tel. 233-2200, fax 221-2801), which publishes the *Sustainable Tourism Newsletter*.

bring them there had been contributing their share to maintaining the parks (the entrance fee charged for bringing tourists to parks was only $1.50 until 1994, when the Legislative Assembly raised it to $15 per person). The past few years, however, have seen solid efforts to place management of on-site tourism in the hands of local cooperatives whereby the local community gains the benefits (Playa Grande, in Nicoya, and Tortuguero, on the Caribbean, are good examples).

PEOPLE

POPULATION

The July 1989 census recorded a population of 2.92 million, more than half of whom live in the Meseta Central. Approximately 275,000 live in the capital city of San José. Fifty-one percent of the nation's population is classed as urban. The country's annual population growth rate is 2.3% and gradually falling. As recently as the 1960s the rate was a staggering 3.8% per annum, a figure no other country in the world could then match. The impressive decline in recent decades has likewise been matched by few other countries. At press time, the population was estimated at 3.3 million.

All the municipalities of the Meseta Central have gained agricultural migrants for whom there is simply no more room. Hence, emigration from the Meseta Central in recent decades has taken people in all directions, assisted by government incentives. The most attractive areas of settlement in the past 35 years have been on the Nicoya lowlands on the drier part of the Pacific coast, on the northern lowlands, and on the alluvial soils of the Valle de El General in the south. The Pan-American Highway has attracted settlers, and the border between Panamá and Costa Rica is now quite densely settled, with colonists from Italy as well as the Meseta Central grafted onto the local population.

CLASS AND RACE

Most Costa Ricans insist that their country is a "classless democracy." True, the social tensions of class versus class that characterize many neighboring nations are absent. Ticos lack the volatility, ultranationalism, and deep-seated political divisions of their Latin American brethren. There is considerable social mobility, and no race problem on the scale of the United States's. And virtually everyone shares a so-called middle-class mentality, a firm belief in the Costa Rican equivalent of "the American Dream"—a conviction that through individual effort and sacrifice and a faith in schooling every Costa Rican can climb the social ladder and better him- or herself.

Still, despite the high value Ticos place on equality and democracy, their society contains all kinds of inequities. Wealth, for example, is unevenly distributed (the richest one percent of families receive 10% of the national income; the poorest 50% receive only 20%; and at least one-fifth of the population remain *marginados* who are so poor they remain outside the mainstream of progress). And a small number of families—the descendants of the original *hidalgos* (nobles)—have monopolized power for almost four centuries (just three families have produced 36 of Costa Rica's 49 presidents, and fully three-quarters of congressmen 1821-1970 were the offspring of this "dynasty of conquistadores").

Urbanites, like city dwellers worldwide, condescendingly chuckle at rural "hicks." The skewed tenure of an albeit much-diluted feudalism persists in regions long dominated by plantations and haciendas. Tolerance of racial minorities is tenuous, with "whiteness" still considered the ideal (in more remote areas, blacks may experience the all-too-familiar cold shoulder). And the upwardly mobile "elite," who consider menial labor demeaning, prefer to indulge in conspicuous spending and, often, in snobbish behavior (several restaurateurs and hoteliers have told me that the Tico nouveau riche will, as a matter of course, complain about service, food, etc., and that they often treat waiters and service staff with such contempt that the latter may even refuse to serve them).

Though comparatively wealthy compared to most Latin American countries, by developed-world standards most Costa Ricans are poor (the average income is slightly less than US$3000 per annum). Many rural families still live in simple huts of adobe or wood; the average income in the northern lowlands, for example, is barely one-seventh that in San José. And although few and far between, shacks made

from gasoline tins, old automobile tires, and corrugated tin give a miserable cover to poor urban laborers in small *tugurios*—illegally erected slums—on the outskirts and the riverbanks of San José.

However, that all paints far too gloomy a picture. In a region where thousands thrive and millions starve, the vast majority of Costa Ricans are comparatively well-to-do. The country has few desperately poor, and there are relatively few beggars existing on the bare charity of the world. The majority of Costa Ricans keep their proud little bungalows spick and span and bordered by flowers, and even the poorest Costa Ricans are generally well groomed and neatly, even formally, dressed in fedoras and shawls.

Overt class distinctions are kept within bounds by a delicate balance between "elitism" and egalitarianism unique in the isthmus: aristocratic airs are frowned on and blatant pride in blue blood is ridiculed; even the president is inclined to mingle in public in casual clothing and is commonly addressed in general conversation by his first name or nickname. Alas, my experience suggests that such virtues cling by a tenuous and weakening thread.

Costa Rican Ethnicity

Costa Rica is unquestionably the most homogeneous of Central American nations in race as well as social class. Travelers familiar with other Central American nations will immediately notice the contrast: the vast majority of Costa Ricans look predominantly European. The 1989 census classified 98% of the population as "white" or "mestizo" and less than two percent as "black" or "Indian." Native and European mixed blood far less than in other New World countries. There are mestizos—in fact, approximately 95% of Ticans inherit varying mixtures of the mestizo blend of European colonists with Indian and black women—but the lighter complexion of Old World immigrants is evident throughout the nation. Exceptions are Guanacaste, where almost half the population is visibly mestizo, a legacy of the more pervasive unions between Spanish colonists and Chorotega Indians through several generations. And the population of the Atlantic coast province of Puerto Limón is one-third black, with a distinct culture that reflects its West Indian origins.

Blacks

Costa Rica's approximately 40,000 black people are the nation's largest minority. For many years they were the target of racist immigration and residence laws that restricted them to the Caribbean coast (only as late as 1949, when the new Constitution abrogated apartheid on the Atlantic Railroad, were blacks allowed to travel beyond Siquirres and enter the highlands). Hence, they remained isolated from national culture. Although Afro-Caribbean turtle hunters settled on the Caribbean coast as early as 1825, most blacks today trace their ancestry back to the 10,000 or so Jamaicans hired by Minor Keith to build the Atlantic Railroad, and to later waves of immigrants who came to work the banana plantations in the late 19th century.

Costa Rica's early black population was "dramatically upwardly mobile" and by the 1920s a majority of the West Indian immigrants owned plots of land or had risen to higher-paying positions within the banana industry. Unfortunately, they possessed neither citizenship nor the legal right to own land. In the 1930s, when "white" highlanders began pouring into the lowlands, blacks were quickly dispossessed of land and the best-paying jobs. Late that decade, when the banana blight forced the banana companies to abandon their Caribbean plantations and move to the Pacific, "white" Ticos successfully lobbied for laws forbidding the employment of *gente de color* in other provinces, one of several circumstances that kept blacks dependent on the largesse of the United Fruit Company, whose labor policies were often abhorrent. Pauperized, many blacks migrated to Panamá and the U.S. seeking wartime employment. A good proportion of those who remained converted their subsistence plots into commercial cacao farms and reaped large profits during the 1950s and '60s from the rise of world cacao prices.

West Indian immigrants played a substantial role in the early years of labor organization, and their early strikes were often violently suppressed (Tican folklore falsely believes in black passivity). Many black workers, too, joined hands with Figueres in the 1948 civil war. Their reward? Citizenship and full guarantees under the 1949 Constitution, which ended apartheid.

Costa Rica's black population has consistently attained higher educational standards

than the national average and many blacks are now found in leading professions throughout the nation. They have also managed to retain much of their traditional culture, including religious practices rooted in African belief about transcendence through spiritual possession *(obeah)*, their rich cuisine (codfish and akee, "rundown"), the rhythmic lilt of their slightly antiquated English, and the deeply syncopated funk of their music. However, as noted above, in some areas outside the Caribbean and capital city, age-old discriminatory concepts prevail.

Indians

Costa Rica's indigenous peoples have suffered abysmally. Centuries ago the original Indian tribes were splintered by Spanish conquistadores and compelled to retreat into the vast tracts of the interior mountains (the Chorotegas of Guanacaste, however, were more gradually assimilated into the national culture). Today, approximately 9,000 Indian peoples of the Bribrí, Boruca, and Cabecar tribes manage to eke out a living from the jungles of remote valleys in the Cordillera Talamanca of southern Costa Rica, where their ancestors had sought refuge from Spanish muskets and dogs. Eight different Indian groups live on 22 Indian reserves.

Although various agencies continue to work to promote education, health, and community development, the Indians' standard of living is appallingly low, alcoholism is endemic, and they remain subject to constant exploitation. In 1939, the government granted every Indian family an allotment of 148 hectares for traditional farming, and in December 1977 a law was passed prohibiting non-Indians from buying, leasing, or renting land within the reserves.

Despite the legislation, a majority of Indians have gradually been tricked into selling their allotments or otherwise forced off their lands. Poor soils and rough rides have not kept colonists in search of land and gold from invading the reserves. Banana companies have gradually encroached into the Indians' remote kingdoms, buying up land and pushing *campesinos* onto Indian property. Mining companies are infiltrating the reserves along newly built roads, which become conduits for contamination, like dirty threads in a wound. In 1991, for example, an American mining company was accused of illegally exploring within the Talamanca Indian Reserve. And hotel developers are violating the protective laws by pushing up properties within coastal reserves.

Indigenous peoples complain that the National Commission for Indigenous Affairs (CONAI) has proved particularly ineffective in enforcing protections. "When the moment arrives for CONAI to stand up for the Indian people, they don't dare. They duck down behind their desks and wait for their paychecks to arrive," says Boruca Indian leader José Carlos Morales.

The various Indian clans cling tenuously to what remains of their cultures. The Borucas, who inhabit scattered villages in tight-knit patches of the Pacific southwest, have been most adept at conserving their own language and civilization, including matriarchy, communal land ownership, and traditional weaving. For most other groups, only a few elders still speak the languages, and interest in traditional crafts is fading. Virtually all groups have adopted elements of Catholicism along with their traditional animistic religions, Spanish is today the predominant tongue, and economically the Indians have for the most part come to resemble impoverished *campesinos*.

Other Ethnic Groups

Immigrants from many nations have been made welcome over the years (between 1870 and 1920, almost 25% of Costa Rica's population growth was due to immigration). Jews are prominent in the liberal professions. A Quaker community of several hundred people centers on Monteverde, where they produce gouda, cheddar, and *monterico* cheeses. Germans have for many generations been particularly successful as coffee farmers. Italians have gathered, among other places, in the town of San Vito, on the central Pacific coast. Tens of thousands of Central American refugees from El Salvador, Guatemala, and Nicaragua still find safety in Costa Rica, where they provide cheap labor for the coffee fields. The Chinese man quoted in Paul Theroux's *Old Patagonian Express* (see the preface, "Why Costa Rica?") is one of several thousand Chinese who call Costa Rica home. Many are descended from approximately 600 Asians who were imported as contract laborers to work on the Atlantic Railroad (an

1862 law prohibiting immigration by Asians had been lifted on the understanding that the Chinese would return home once the work was complete). The Chinese railroad workers were worked miserably and paid only one-fifth of the going wage. In recent years many *chinos* have immigrated freely and are now conspicuously successful in the hotel, restaurant, and bar trade (Theroux's Chinese man owned one of each), and in Limón as middlemen controlling the trade in bananas and cacao.

THE TICAN IDENTITY

Every nationality has its own sense of identity. Costa Ricans' unique traits derive from a profoundly conscious self-image, which orients much of their behavior as both individuals and as a nation. The Ticos—the name is said to stem from the colonial saying "we are all *hermaniticos*" (little brothers)—feel distinct from their neighbors by their "whiteness" and relative lack of indigenous culture. Ticos identify themselves first and foremost as Costa Ricans and only Central Americans, or even Latin Americans, as an afterthought.

Traditionally, they've been extremely critical of *themselves,* as individuals and as a society. Costa Ricans, regardless of wealth or status, used to act with utmost humility and judge as uncouth boasting of any kind, and for the most part this still holds true. The rise of a young, yuppie, self-conscious nouveau riche is changing all this. Fortunately, it remains true to say that the behavior and comments of most Ticos are dictated by *quedar bien,* a desire to leave a good impression. Like the English, they're terribly frightened of embarrassing themselves, of appearing rude or vulgar (tactless and crude people are considered "badly educated") or unhelpful. As such, they can be exceedingly courteous, almost archaically so (they are prone, for example, to offer flowing compliments and formal greetings). It is a rare visitor to the country who returns home unimpressed by the Costa Ricans' celebrated cordial warmth and hospitality.

Ticos are also peacable. Violence of any kind is extremely rare. The religious fervor common in Mexico and the Central American isthmus is unknown. It has been said that the law-abiding

Ticos respect and have faith in their laws, their police force, and state institutions (except, it seems, on the roads); the worrying statistics on theft and crime suggest that this is a spurious notion. In fact, a distaste for anything that impinges on their liberty or that of their nation is just about the only thing that will make their hackles rise. Attempts to modernize the police force, for example, bring floods of editorial columns and popular outrage protesting "militarism."

Democracy is their most treasured institution, and the ideal of personal liberty is strongly cherished. Costa Ricans are intensely proud of their accomplishments in this arena and show it at 6 p.m. on each 14 September, on the eve of Independence Day, when the whole nation comes to a halt and everyone gustily sings the national anthem.

A progressive people, Ticos revere education. "We have more teachers than soldiers" is a common boast and framed school diplomas hang in even the most humble homes. Everyone, too, is eager for the benefits of social progress. Sociologists, however, suggest that Costa Ricans are also very conservative people, suspicious of experimentation that is not consistent with a loosely held sense of "*tican* tradition." Changes, too, supposedly should be made *poco a poco,* little by little. Ticos share the fatalistic streak common to Latin America, one that accepts things as they are and promotes resignation to the imagined will of God. Many North American and European hoteliers have bemoaned the general passivity that often translates into a lack of initiative.

Many old virtues and values have faltered under the onslaught of foreign influence, modernity, and social change. Drunkenness, drug abuse, and a general idleness previously unknown in Costa Rica have intruded. And theft and burglary are seriously on the rise (see "Safety" in the On the Road chapter). But most Costa Ricans remain strongly oriented around traditional values based on respect for oneself and for others. The cornerstone of society is still the family and the village community. Social life still centers on the home and family bonds are so strong that foreigners often find making intimate friendships a challenge. Nepotism—using family ties and connections for gain—is the way things get done in business and government.

Generally, you can count on a Tico's loyalty, but not on his punctuality. Private companies, including most travel businesses, are efficient and to a greater or lesser degree operate *hora americana:* punctually. But don't expect it. Many Ticos, particularly in government institutions, still tick along on turtle-paced *hora tica. "¿Quien sabe?"* ("Who knows?") is an oft-repeated phrase. So too *"¡Tal vez!"* ("Perhaps!") and, of course, *"¡Mañana!"* ("Tomorrow!"). In fact, *mañana* is the busiest day of the week!

SEX, MACHISMO, AND THE STATUS OF WOMEN

In October 1990 I had dinner in San José with a young North American friend who was studying for a year at the University of Costa Rica. She is tall, beautiful, with hair as blonde as flax (to Tico men, the erotic equivalent of a red rag to a bull) and skin as white as fresh-fallen snow. She was tired, she told me. Tired of the attention-arresting "Sssssst!" of the Tico male. Tired of the silent, insistent stares—of *dando cuerva,* "making eyes." Tired of leeringly being called *guapa, mi amor,* and *¡machita!* To her, Costa Rica was a land of unbridled and ugly machismo.

Everything in life of course is relative. Yes, Tico men make a national pastime of flirting. But by the standards of other Latin American countries—I am constantly assured—Costa Rican men are relatively restrained in their advances, and the nation progressive and moderately successful in advancing the equal rights of women.

That said, legacies of the Spanish Catholic sense of "proper" gender roles are twined like tangled threads through the national fabric. Male and female roles are clearly defined. Machismo, sustained by a belief in the natural superiority of men, is integral to the Costa Rican male's way of life. It "justifies" why he expects to be given due deference by women, why he expects his wife or *novia* (girlfriend) to wait on him hand and foot, why he refrains from household chores, and why he is generally free to do as he pleases, particularly to sleep around. The sexual wanderings of married men are still tolerated by a remarkably high percentage of women, and the faithful husband and male celibate is suspect in the eyes of

his friends. The Latin male expresses his masculinity in amorous conquests. In Costa Rica flirting has been taken to the level of art. "Making love is the number one pastime in Costa Rica, followed by drinking and eating," suggests writer Kent Britt. "*Fútbol* (soccer), the so-called national sport, isn't even in the running."

But it always takes two to tango. San José's stylish young Ticas, with their unbelievably tight jeans and high heels, give as good as they get. Hip urban Ticas have forsaken old-fashioned romanticism for a latter-day liberalism that accepts short-term relationships and sexual pleasure. Even in the most isolated rural towns, dating in the Western fashion has displaced the *retreta*—the circling of the central plaza by men and women on weekend evenings—and chaperonage, once common, is now virtually unknown.

The rules of the mating game, however, are not the same as in Europe or North America. A gradual wooing is expected. Males are expected to adhere to traditional romantic roles; Sir Walter Raleigh would do well here with his cloak. And females can be both outrageously flirtatious and stand-offish as part of the ritual.

Costa Ricans are liberal in their sexual relations, even if some of the mental projections don't quite match up. Women are *supposed* to be loyal and chaste. Sexual freedom is the prerogative of males; sexually liberated women are still looked down on as "loose." You don't need to be Einstein to work out the mathematical inconsistencies and mental delusions this implies. In fact, almost 10% of all Costa Rican adults live together in "free unions," one-quarter of all children are *hijos naturales* (born out of wedlock; one in five of such births list the father as "unknown"), and one in five households is headed by a single mother. Many rural households are so-called Queen-bee (all-female) families headed by an elderly matriarch who looks after her grandchildren while the daughters work. Divorce, once a stigma, is now common and easily obtained under the Family Code of 1974, although desertion remains as it has for centuries "the poor man's divorce."

Compañeras, women in consensual relationships, enjoy the same legal rights as wives. In theory, the law, too, forbids sex discrimination in hiring and salaries, and women are entitled to

maternity leave and related benefits. And urban women have attained considerable success in the political and professional arena: women outnumber men in many occupations and notably in university faculties, the nation's vice-president 1986-90 was a woman (Dr. Victoria Garron), and the current president of the Legislative Assembly is Dr. Rosemary Karpinsky. The 1990 Law to Promote Women's Social Equality should provide one more stepping-stone to real equality.

In reality, discrimination is ingrained. Low-level occupations especially reflect wide discrepancies in wage levels for men and women. The greater percentage of lower-class women remain chained to the kitchen sink and the rearing of children. And gender relationships, particularly in rural villages, remain dominated to a greater or lesser degree by machismo and *marianismo*, its female equivalent. Women are supposed to be bastions of moral and spiritual integrity (to call a wife and mother *abnegado*—self-sacrificing—is the ultimate compliment), to be accepting of men's infidelities, and to "accept bitter pride in their suffering."

RELIGION

Costa Ricans are said to be "lukewarm" when it comes to religion. Although more than 90% of the population is Roman Catholic, at least in name, almost no one gets riled up about his or her faith. Sure, Holy Week (the week before Easter) is a national holiday, but it's simply an excuse for a secular binge. The passing of the parish priest inspires no reverential gestures. And most Costa Ricans respond to the bell only on special occasions, generally when the bell peals for birth, marriage, and maybe for Easter morning, when the mass of men mill by the door, unpiously half in and half out.

The country has always been remarkably secular, the link between Christianity and the state—between God and Caesar—always weak. The Costa Ricans' dislike for dictators has made them intolerant of priests. The feudal peasants of other Central American nations, miserably toiling on large estates *(latifundias)* or their own tiny plots, may have been poor and ignorant, but the Church offered them one great consolation. Theirs would be the kingdom of heaven. And in more recent times, when Catholic organizations attempted to address pressing social problems, they strengthened the Church's bond with the people. In Costa Rica, by contrast, the Church, from the earliest colonial times, had little success at controlling the morals and minds of the masses. While poor peasants can be convinced they'll become bourgeois in heaven, a rising class wants its comforts on earth. Costa Rica's modernity and "middle-class" achievements have made the Church superfluous.

Basílica de Nuestra Señora de Los Angeles, Cartago

Still, every village no matter how small has a church and its own saint's day, albeit celebrated with secular fervor. Every taxi, bus, government office, and home has its token religious icons. The Catholic marriage ceremony is the only church marriage granted state recognition. And Catholicism is the official state religion. The 1949 Constitution even provided for state contributions to the maintenance of the Church, and the salaries of bishops are paid by the state.

Catholicism, nonetheless, has only a tenuous hold; mass in some rural communities may be a once-a-year affair, and resignation to God's will is tinged with fatalism. In a crisis Ticos will turn to a favorite saint, one who they believe has special powers or "pull" with God, to demand a miracle. And folkloric belief in witchcraft is still common (Escazú is renowned as a center for *brujos*, witches who specialize in casting out spells and resolving love problems).

Protestantism has proved even less spellbinding. The Catholic clergy has fiercely protected its turf against Protestant missionaries (even Billy Graham's tour in 1958 was blackballed by the local media), and the Protestant evangelism so prevalent in other parts of Central America has yet to make a dent in Costa Rica. A great many sects, however, have found San José the ideal base for proselytizing forays elsewhere in the isthmus. The nation's black population constitutes about half of Costa Rica's 40,000 or so Protestants, though the archbishop of Canterbury would be horrified at the extent to which "his" religion has been married with African-inspired, voodoo-like *obeah* and *pocomoia* worship.

EDUCATION

The briefest sojourn in San José makes clear that Costa Ricans are a highly literate people: the country boasts of 93% literacy in those 10 and over, the most literate populace in Central America. Many of the country's early father figures, including the first president, José María Castro, were former teachers and shared a great concern for education. In 1869, the country became one of the first in the world to make education both obligatory and free, funded by the state's share of the great coffee wealth (as early as 1828, an unenforced law had made school attendance mandatory). Then, only one in 10 Costa Ricans could read and write. By 1920, 50% of the population was literate. By 1973, when the Ministry of Education published a landmark study, the figure was 89%.

The study also revealed some worrying factors. More than half of all Costa Ricans aged 15 or over—600,000—had dropped out of school by the sixth grade, for example. Almost 1,000 schools had only one teacher, often a partially trained *aspirante* (candidate teacher) lacking certification. And the literacy figures included many "functional illiterates" counted by their simple ability to sign their own name. The myth of "more teachers than soldiers" and the boast of the highest literacy rate in Central America had blinded Costa Ricans to their system's many defects.

The last 20 years have seen a significant boost to educational standards. Since the 1970s the country has invested more than 28% of the national budget on primary and secondary education. President Figueres, elected in March 1994, advocates a computer in each of the nation's 4,000 schools, plus mandatory English classes to coincide with the tremendous boom in tourism (the Program for Foreign Language Education for Development—involving the training of 500 teachers and 100,000 children—began three months later). A nuclearization program has worked to amalgamate one-teacher schools. And schooling through the ninth year (age 14) is now compulsory. Nonetheless, there remains a severe shortage of teachers with a sound knowledge of the full panoply of academic subjects, remote rural schools are often difficult to reach in the best of weather, and the Ministry of Education is riven with political appointees who change hats with each administration. As elsewhere in the world, well-to-do families usually send their children to private schools.

Village libraries are about the only means for adults in rural areas to continue education beyond sixth grade. The country, with approximately 100 libraries, has a desperate need for books and for funds to support the hundreds of additional libraries that the country needs. Books (Spanish preferred) can be donated to the **National Library** (c/o Vera Violeta Salazar Mora,

Director, Dirección Bibliotecas Públicas, Apdo. 10-008, San José, tel. 236-1828).

A new program recently instigated by the **Ministerio de Educación** accepts volunteers to teach English (Departamento de Inglés, San José 1000). **World Teach** (Harvard Institute for International Development, 1 Eliot St., Cambridge, MA 02138, tel. 617-495-5527, fax 495-1239) also places volunteers to teach English in schools that have requested assistance. The local school or community provides housing and a living allowance; you pay a participation fee of $3500 that covers airfare, health insurance, training, and field support.

Universities

Although the country lacked a university until 1940, Costa Rica now boasts four state-funded schools of higher learning, and opportunities abound for adults to earn the primary or secondary diplomas they failed to gain as children.

The **University of Costa Rica** (UCR), the largest and oldest university, enrolls some 35,000 students, mostly on scholarships. The main campus is in the northeastern San José community of San Pedro (UCR also has regional centers in Alajuela, Turrialba, Puntarenas, and Cartago). The **National University** in Heredia (there are regional centers in Liberia and Perez Zeledon) offers a variety of liberal arts, sciences, and professional studies to 13,000 students. Cartago's **Technical Institute of Costa Rica** (ITCR) specializes in science and technology and seeks to train people for agriculture, industry, and mining. And the **State Correspondence University,** founded in 1978, is modeled after the United Kingdom's Open University and has 32 regional centers offering 15 degree courses in health, education, business administration, and the liberal arts.

In addition, the many private institutions include the **Autonomous University of Central America** and the **University for Peace,** sponsored by the United Nations and offering a master's degree in Communications for Peace.

HEALTH

Perhaps the most impressive impact of Costa Rica's modern welfare state has been the truly dramatic improvements in national health. Infant mortality has plummeted from 25.6% in 1920 to only 1.5% in 1990. The annual death rate dropped from 41 per thousand in 1894 to 18 in 1944 and just 3.9 per thousand in 1989. And the average Costa Rican today can expect to live to a ripe 73.2 years—longer than the average U.S.-born citizen. All this thanks to the Social Security system, which provides universal insurance benefits covering medical services, disability, maternity, old-age pensions, and death. These factors, together with considerations on levels of education and standard of living, have elevated Costa Rica to 42nd on the United Nations' "Human Development Index," ahead of 118 other countries (both 1992 and 1993). Despite this, nearly 121,000 Costa Rican families live in poverty, which creates its own health problems.

Costa Rica assigns about 10% of its GNP to health care. The result? A physician for every 700 people and a hospital bed for every 275. In fact, in some areas the health-care system isn't far behind that of the U.S. in terms of the latest medical technology, at least in San José, where transplant surgery is now performed. Many North Americans fly here for surgery, including dental work. And the Beverly Hills crowd helps keep Costa Rica's cosmetic surgeons busy.

One key to the nation's success was the creation of the Program for Rural Health in 1970 to ensure that basic health care would reach the furthest backwaters. The program, aimed at the 50% of the population living in small communities, established rural health posts attended by paramedics. The clinics are visited regularly by doctors and nurses, and strengthened by education programs stressing good nutrition, hygiene, and safe food preparation. Even a few years ago malnutrition reaped young Ticos like a scythe; in the last two decades infant mortality from malnutrition has fallen by more than 80%. In April 1992, the Social Security service initiated a plan aimed at lowering infant mortality to one percent. It's a constant battle, however. Health standards slipped slightly in 1990-91 because of budget cutbacks: the tuberculosis rate doubled in 1991, for example, and that year the nation witnessed its first measles epidemic in many years. But then again, so did the United States. A major problem is the high incidence of

smoking among Ticos. Heated debates in the Legislative Assembly in 1994 augered that it may soon be illegal to light up a cigarette in public offices, hospitals, schools and other places. The proposed law will also ban cigarette advertising.

ON THE ROAD
SIGHTSEEING HIGHLIGHTS

San José

National Theater: Historic landmark with magnificent murals and interior decoration. Classical music, opera, and other performances at night.

Fidel Tristan Jade Museum: Immense collection of jade utensils and jewelry and other artifacts recording Costa Rica's pre-Columbian history.

National Arts and Cultural Center: Housed in the former Liquor Factory, the Center embodies art, architectural and photo exhibitions, and performing arts theaters.

Pre-Columbian Gold Museum: Superb collection of pre-Columbian gold figurines, ornaments, etc.

Contemporary Art Museum: Proof that Costa Rica is *not* a cultural backwater; encompasses paintings, engravings, ceramics, and sculptures spanning the century.

National Museum: Displays recording Costa Rica's history and cultures from pre-Columbian days to the contemporary setting. Housed in an old fort.

Pueblo Antigua: A marvelous re-creation of traditional Costa Rican settings; a living museum on a Williamsburg theme.

Spirogyra: Splendid collection of live butterflies performing daily functions on a lepidopterary theme.

Central Highlands

Poás Volcano: Drive-up volcano with active fumaroles, viewing platforms, good geological displays, nature trails, and stunning views on clear days.

Butterfly Farm, La Guácima: Entertaining and enlightening breeding farm with walk-through display areas and guided tours.

Café Britt, Heredia: Working coffee *finca* with guided tours, folkloric show, and coffee tasting.

Guayabo National Monument: The nation's only pre-Columbian archaeological site of significance; an intriguing entrée into Costa Rica's Indian heritage. Good birding.

Irazú Volcano: The world's highest drive-up volcano. Stunning scenery en route.

Joyeros del Bosque Húmedos, Santo Domingo de Heredia: World's largest butterfly collection, magnificently displayed.

Northern Lowlands and Caribbean Coast

Caño Negro Wildlife Refuge: Remote lagoon surrounded by wetlands protecting vast quantities of birds and other wildlife. Fantastic fishing.

Arenal Volcano: An active volcano that throws out lava and breccia almost daily. Backed by beautiful Lake Arenal. Best enjoyed from Arenal Observatory Lodge or while soaking in thermal hot springs at Tabacón.

Tortuguero National Park: Coastal jungle with vast numbers of birds and animals easily seen on guided boat trips. Turtles come ashore to lay eggs. Superb fishing.

Cahuita National Park: Pretty beaches, coral reefs (sadly depleted), and nature trails leading into coastal rainforest. Popular budget travelers' hangout.

Los Canales: The reward is in the journey up (or down) these narrow canals linking Tortuguero National Park with Moín. Plentiful wildlife viewing en route.

Rainforest Aerial Tram: Dr. Donald Perry's innovative aerial tram provides a unique entrée to the wildlife-rich world of the rainforest upper canopy.

Green Train: Slow-paced train journey follows the lowland route of the old Jungle Train through the banana plantations, complete with tour of processing plant.

Tabacón Hot Springs, Fortuna: A kind of lush, open-air Roman baths, with waterfalls, chutes, and steaming pools fed by waters from Arenal volcano, which looms nearby.

Central and Southwest Pacific

Manuel Antonio National Park: Small rainforest preserve with diverse wildlife, good nature trails, and beautiful beaches. Popular and heavily visited.

Carara Biological Reserve: Easily reached reserve at the meeting point of moist and dry tropical ecosystems. Monkeys, crocodiles, and macaws virtually guaranteed.

Corcovado National Park: Remote pristine rainforest reserve harboring jaguars, macaws, and other rare species. Excellent hiking for the hardy.

Wilson Botanical Gardens: Combines magnificent landscaped tropical gardens and protected rainforest with plentiful wildlife.

Chirripó National Park: Remote and rugged region surrounding Costa Rica's highest peak. Superb, yet strenuous, hiking to the summit.

Guanacaste

Monteverde Cloud Forest: Rare cloud forest environment, with plentiful wildlife and birds, including the quetzal. Lectures. Guided hikes. Superbly maintained reserve.

La Casona—Santa Rosa National Park: Costa Rica's most important historic site, this rustic farmstead, now a museum, has been the setting of three major battles. Nature trails and plentiful wildlife.

Lake Arenal: Scenery reminiscent of England, with quilted patchwork farmland and forest running down to the lake. A favored windsurfing spot, with smoldering Arenal volcano as a backdrop.

Rincón de la Vieja National Park: Remote, scenic volcano with fumaroles, boiling mud pots, and thermal springs reached by nature trails. Excellent hiking.

Nicoya Peninsula

Playa Grande: An important leatherback turtle nesting site. One of the prettiest beaches—great for surfing, too—in Costa Rica.

Cabo Blanco Absolute Nature Reserve: Remote rainforest preserve protecting rare flora and fauna.

Guaitil: Small village maintaining the Chorotega Indian pottery tradition. Beautiful earthenware for sale.

Playa Conchal: Supremely beautiful white-sand beach on the threshold of development; Playa Flamingo, immediately north, gives it a run for its money.

Ostional National Wildlife Refuge: One of two major nesting sites featuring *arribadas* (mass nestings) of the Pacific ridley turtle.

ORGANIZED TOURS

ICT surveys suggest that about 30% of North American tourists to Costa Rica arrived on package tours, and that a majority of the remaining 70% book some form of tour through a company in Costa Rica once they arrive.

A growing number of U.S. tour companies specialize in Costa Rica, and dozens of others offer group tours and/or prepackaged programs for independent travelers based on a wide range of special-interest themes. Joining a group tour offers many advantages over traveling independently, such as the camaraderie of a shared experience and the joys of discovery and learning passed along by a knowledgeable guide. Tours are also a good bet for those with limited time: you'll proceed to the most interesting places without the unforeseen delays and distractions that can be the bane of independent travel. Everything is taken care of from your arrival to your departure, including transportation and accommodations. And the petty bureaucratic hassles and language problems you may otherwise not wish to face are eliminated, too.

Fortunately, the majority of group tours to Costa Rica are operated by companies with a genuine concern for the quality of your experience and the impact on the local environment. That means relatively small groups of no more than 20 people, escorted by a trained guide, often a professional naturalist or other specialist who loves to share his or her knowledge. Use these two criteria when selecting an appropriate tour; the quality of your guide and makeup of your group can be imperative to the rewards of group travel.

Ask, too, about the "difficulty" level of particular tours. Many nature tours involve a certain amount of activity and even discomfort. Certain companies offer "soft adventure" tours that include a lesser degree of discomfort or difficulty than other tours that follow a similar itinerary. Don't be put off by a "hard" adventure unless you're an absolute coach potato or thoroughly detest the slightest physical discomfort, as the rewards of active adventures are truly immense: how otherwise might you see a quetzal in its natural environment, for example?

GUIDES

If, for the sake of comparison, you explore Costa Rica's national parks and wildlife refuges both with and without a professional guide, it will become crystal clear that to fully appreciate your time in the forests and savannahs you need an outstanding guide—an experienced and well-read local who is part animal biologist, part ecologist, and part entertainer.

There's another, equally important, reason to hire a guide. It's one of the best ways to help benefit the people living near the parks and reserves.

Costa Rica has many guides. The standards are generally very high. A handful have been truly outstanding. However, I've been with a few who should be given early retirement or sent back to class. Bad guides tend to anthropomorphize; they're really chauffeurs who clutch a wildlife handbook and merely point at animals and identify them. A good guide provides a lucid, lively, and learned discussion that leaves you wide-eyed in wonder.

Many of the best are former park wardens or farmer's children. The good guides freelance. A recent proliferation of "guides" has diluted the standards. Ask for a "naturalist guide"—a more appropriate term for qualified, professional guides. Ask for recommendations from local tour operators: Costa Rica Expeditions has some splendid guides and even publishes an extensive profile on each, including his or her specialty interest and/or unique approach to guiding; recommended. My favorite, **Rodolfo Zamora** (Apdo. 347, Santa Ana 6150, tel. 282-8538), in 1994 was named "Best Guide in Costa Rica."

World Teach (in Costa Rica, tel. 223-7464) and the **Center for Tropical Conservation** (in the U.S., tel. 215-735-3510) sponsor guide training for youngsters from local communities. Donations are accepted.

NORTH AMERICAN TOUR COMPANIES

Abercrombie & Kent, 1520 Kensington Rd., Oak Brook IL 60521, tel. (800) 323-7308. Offers a deluxe 12-day "Nature of Costa Rica" tour.

Adventure Center, 1311 63rd St., Emeryville, CA 94608, tel. (800) 227-8747 or (510) 654-1879, fax (510) 654-4200. Has monthly departures of a 10-day "Costa Rica Explorer" tour plus other nature and adventure related tours.

Adventure Costa Rica, 16 N. 9th Ave. #2, Bozeman, MT 59715, tel. (406) 586-9942 or (800) 231-7422, fax (406) 586-0995.

Adventure-Dive Travel, P.O. Box 6098, San Mateo, CA 94403, tel. (415) 364-3931 or (800) 938-9767. Specializes in dive packages.

Adventures, 3507 Tully Rd. #5, Modesto, CA 95356, tel. (800) 423-9731, fax (209) 524-1220. Wide range of Costa Rica tours and specialty programs. (Also known as About Costa Rica.)

Aggressor Fleet Ltd., Drawer K, Morgan City, LA 70381, tel. (504) 385-2628 or (800) DIV-BOAT, fax (504) 384-0817. Operates the 120-foot live-aboard dive vessel, the *Okeanos Aggressor,* on 10-day charters to Cocos Island. Also represents the *Temptress* cruise ship.

Ambiance Tours, 27001 U.S. 19 N, Suite 2075, Clearwater, FL 34621, tel. (813) 725-5969 or (800) 466-6244. Independent packages, including fishing, beach resorts, and jungle lodges.

American Express Vacations, 300 Pinnacle Way, Norcross, GA 30071, tel. (800) 241-1700. Independent tour arrangements.

American Way Tours, 152 Madison Ave., New York, NY 10016, tel. (212) 683-3810 or (800) 547-8893. Scheduled group tours specializing in natural history.

Avanti, 851 SW 6th, Suite 1010, Portland, OR 97204, tel. (503) 295-1100, fax (503) 295-2723. Specialists in Central America. San José and beach hotel packages and "eco" extensions.

Bayside Tours, 3925 Alton Rd., Miami Beach, FL 33140, tel. (305) 673-3522 or (800) 821-9726. Custom-designed FIT (fully independent travel) services, independent city and beach packages.

Bentley Tours, 1649 Colorado Blvd., Los Angeles, CA 90041, tel. (213) 258-8451 or (800) 821-9726.

Custom-designed FITs and independent tour packages, including resorts, mountain lodges, and national parks.

Best of Belize and Beyond, 31F Commercial Blvd., Novato, CA 94949, tel. (415) 884-2325 or (800) 735-9520, fax (415) 884-2339 or (800) 405-BEST. Central American experts. Customized FITs, independent city and beach packages. Tours, cruises, and specialist packages.

Big-Five Expeditions, 819 S. Federal Hwy., Stuart, FL 34994, tel. (407) 287-7995 or (800) 345-2445, fax (407) 287-5990. Nature and photography tours.

Biological Journeys, 1696 Ocean Dr., McKinleyville, CA 95521, tel. (707) 839-0178 or (800) 548-7555. Offers a 14-day natural-history tour visiting the major national parks in the company of a naturalist guide.

Calypso Island Tours, 3901 Grand Ave. #304, Oakland, CA 94610, tel. (510) 653-3570 or (800) 852-6242. Occasional Costa Rica specials, such as a 10-day "Christmas in Costa Rica" adventure.

Coral Way Tours, 9745 Sunset Dr., Suite 104, Miami, FL 33173, tel. (305) 279-3252 or (800) 882-4665. FIT fishing packages.

Costa Rica Adventures and Wildlife, 4014 N. 46th Ave., Hollywood, FL 33021, tel./fax (305) 720-9281. Offers rainforest exploration, wildlife and nature safaris, sailboat adventure cruises, whitewater rafting, and biking and hiking trips.

Costa Rica Connections, 975 Osos St., San Luis Obispo, CA 93401, tel. (805) 543-8823 or (800) 345-7422, fax (805) 543-3626. Specializes in naturalist and educational trips to the major national parks. Complete range of independent packages and scheduled group departures for birding, fishing, ecotourism, kayaking/rafting, and dive trips, plus the Costa Rica National Orchid Show.

Costa Rica Experts, 3166 N. Lincoln Ave. #424, Chicago, IL 60657, tel. (312) 935-1009 or (800) 827-9046, fax (312) 935-9252. Specialists in the full panoply of offerings, from hotels, car rentals, and tours to special interest activities for individuals and groups.

Costa Rican Fantasy Travel, 6595 N.W. 36th St., Suite 213-A, Miami, FL 33166, tel. (305) 871-6663 or (800) 832-9449. Independent packages,

including honeymoon, fishing, eco-adventures, and hotel/car rental programs.

Costa Rica Temptations, 1600 N.W. LeJeune Rd., Suite 301, Miami, FL 33126, tel. (305) 871-2657 or (800) 336-8423. Operates weeklong natural-history cruises featuring guided shore visits to major national parks on the Pacific coast aboard the *Temptress*. Also full range of half-day, full-day excursions, beach resort packages, and mountain lodge stays.

Costa Rica Tours And Travel, P.O. Box 2645, Las Cruces, NM 88004, tel. (800) 383-7859, fax (505) 521-4324. Set and customized packages, including nature and special-interest options.

Costa Rica Travel Exchange, 1700 Napoleon Ave., New Orleans, LA 70115, tel. (800) 256-0124. Complete tour services: hotels, car-rentals, tours, special-interest travel, airfares, etc.

Ecotour Expeditions, P.O. Box 1066, Cambridge, MA 02238, tel. (800) 688-1822 or (617) 876-5817, fax (617) 876-3638. Offers a selection of three- to 10-day tours for the naturalist.

Elegant Vacations, 1760 The Exchange, Suite 150, Atlanta, GA 30339, tel. (404) 850-6891 or (800) 451-4398, fax (404) 859-0250. Independent tours and hotel packages.

Extraordinary Expeditions, P.O. Box 1739, Hailey, ID 83333, tel. (800) 234-1569. Offers 10-day turtle-watching tours.

Fantasia Tours, 732 W. Fullerton, Chicago, IL 60614, tel. (312) 929-0577 or (800) 525-1666, fax (312) 878-8534. Wide range of scheduled tour packages plus customized FIT (fully independent travel) service.

Forum International, 91 Gregory Ln., Suite 21, Pleasant Hill, CA 94523, tel. (510) 671-2900. Scheduled natural-history tours, plus packages at mountain lodges and the Rainbow Adventures Lodge near Corcovado.

Fourth Dimension Tours, 1150 N.W. 72nd Ave., Suite 250, Miami, FL 33126, tel. (305) 477-1525. Five-day San José package, including air, with optional one-day extensions.

Friendly Holidays, 575 Anton Blvd. #790, Costa Mesa, CA 92626, tel. (800) 221-9748 or (714) 556-8400. All-inclusive escorted tours, special interest packages, etc.

Geostar Travel, 1240 Century Ct., Suite C, Santa Rosa, CA 95403, tel. (707) 579-2420 or (800) 624-6633, fax (707) 579-2704. Offers seven- and 10-day itineraries focusing on natural history, botany, horticulture, and birds.

Halintours, P.O. Box 49705, Austin, TX 78765, tel. (512) 472-1895, fax (512) 472-1896. Specializes in Costa Rican ecotours, including packages to Marenco Biological Station.

Holbrook Travel, 3540 N.W. 13th St., Gainesville, FL 32609, tel. (904) 377-7111 or (800) 451-7111. Customized FITs and scheduled natural-history group tours.

Imagine Travel Alternatives, P.O. Box 27023, Seattle, WA 98125, tel. (206) 624-7112 or (800) 777-3975. Independent modular packages, plus soft-adventure and scheduled natural-history group tours. Also "Tropical Photo Workshop."

International Expeditions, One Environs Park, Helena, AL 35080, tel. (205) 428-1700 or (800) 633-4734. Independent programs and natural-history group tours.

International Showcase Tours, 833 Hempstead Turnpike, Franklin Square, NY 11010, tel. (516) 437-4923 or (800) 437-4923. A range of independent tours from birdwatching, whitewater rafting, and diving to resorts and golfing.

Intra Tours, 2411 Fountainview, Suite 225, Houston, TX 77057, tel. (713) 952-0662 or (800) 334-8069. Independent air-land packages from Texas, Miami, and Los Angeles.

Ladatco Tours, Ladatco Bldg., 2220 Coral Way, Miami, FL 33145, tel. (305) 854-8422 or (800) 327-6162. Independent packages and customized FITs.

Lost World Adventures, 1189 Autumn Ridge Dr., Marietta, GA 30066, tel. (404) 971-8586 or (800) 999-0558, fax (404) 977-3095.

Marco Polo Vacations, 16776 Bernardo Center Dr. #106A, San Diego, CA 92128, tel. (619) 451-8406 or (800) 421-5276, fax (619) 451-8472.

Mariah Wilderness Expeditions, P.O. Box 248, Point Richmond, CA 94807, tel. (510) 233-2303 or (800) 462-7424. Specializes in whitewater river trips combining rafting, cycling, and sea kayaking, plus scheduled group departures for soft-adventure and nature tours. Also customized FITs.

(continues on next page)

NORTH AMERICAN TOUR COMPANIES
(continued)

Morris Overseas Tours, 418 4th Ave., Melbourne Beach, FL 32951, tel. (407) 725-4809 or (800) 777-6853. Wide range of special adventure packages, including surfing, fishing, rafting, trekking, and golf.

Mountain Travel/Sobek, 6420 Fairmount Ave., El Cerrito, CA 94530, tel. (510) 527-8100 or (800) 227-2384. Monthly group departures for soft-adventure and whitewater-rafting itineraries.

Ocean Connection, 211 E. Parkwood Ave. #108, Friendswood, TX 77546, tel. (713) 996-7800 or (800) 331-2458. Independent packages, fly-drives, and customized FITs.

Ocean Voyages, 1709 Bridgeway, Sausalito, CA 94965, tel. (415) 332-4681. Live-aboard dive trips and luxury yacht charters.

Osprey Tours, P.O. Box 030211, Fort Lauderdale, FL 33302, tel. (305) 767-4823. Customized FITs and custom-group tours for natural-history enthusiasts and ornithologists.

Overseas Adventure Travel, 349 Broadway, Cambridge, MA 02139, tel. (617) 876-0533 or (800) 221-0814. Natural-history and soft-adventure itineraries.

Pan Angling Travel Service, 180 N. Michigan Ave., Chicago, IL 60601, tel. (312) 263-0328 or (800) 533-4353. Independent fishing packages and customized FITs.

Pioneer Tours, P.O. Box 22063, Carmel, CA 93922, tel. (408) 626-1815 or (800) 288-2107, fax (408) 626-9013. Customized independent tours, rafting trips, and fishing packages.

Preferred Adventures, One West Water St., Suite 300, St. Paul, MN 55107, tel. (612) 222-8131 or (800) 840-8687, fax (612) 222-4221. Customized FITs and special-interest group tours, including birdwatching, horticulture, and fishing.

See & Sea Travel Service, 50 Francisco St., Suite 205, San Francisco, CA 94133, tel. (415) 434-3400 or (800) 348-9778. Live-aboard dive trips on the *Undersea Hunter* and *Okeanos Aggressor* to Cocos Island.

Serendipity Adventures, P.O. Box 2325, Ann Arbor, MI 48106, tel. (313) 995-0111, fax (313) 426-5026. Whitewater rafting, jungle riverboat, and ballooning trips.

South American Fiesta, P.O. Box 7947, Hampton, VA 23666, tel. (516) 924-6200 or (800) 334-3782. Independent packages and customized FITs.

Southern Horizons Travel, 6100 Simpson Ave., N. Hollywood, CA 91606, tel. (818) 980-7011 or (800) 333-9361, fax (818) 980-6987. More than 150 package options, including special-interest travel, convertible for independent travel.

Special Expeditions, 720 5th Ave., New York, NY 10019, tel. (212) 765-7740 or (800) 762-0003. Educational and adventure voyages aboard the 80-passenger *Polaris.*

Surf Costa Rica, P.O. Box 90009, Gainesville, FL 32607, tel. (904) 371-8124 or (800) 771-7873. Surfing and windsurfing programs for groups and independent travelers.

Tara Tours, 6595 N.W. 36th St., Suite 306-A, Miami, FL 33166, tel. (305) 871-1246 or (800) 327-0080. Independent city and beach resort packages.

Tauck Tours, 11 Wilton Rd., Westport, CT 06880, tel. (203) 226-6911 or (800) 468-2825). Upscale group tours.

Tico Tours, P.O. Box 90009, Gainesville, FL 32607, tel. (904) 371-8124 or (800) 771-7873. Customized FITs and independent packages.

Tourtech International, 17780 Fitch, Suite 110, Irvine, CA 92714, tel. (714) 476-1912 or (800) 882-2636. Independent air-inclusive and land-only beach and city packages, plus special-interest group tours.

Tropical Travel, 720 Worthshire, Houston, TX 77008, tel. (713) 869-3614 or (800) 451-8017. Wide range of land-only independent packages and customized FITs, including sportfishing and diving. Also nature tours.

Underwater Adventure Tours, 732 W. Fullerton Ave., Chicago, IL 60614, tel. (312) 929-0717 or (800) 621-1274, fax (312) 929-2821. Custom independent and group dive and deep-sea fishing packages; non-dive packages.

Wilderness Travel, 801 Allston Way, Berkeley, CA 94710, tel. (510) 548-0420 or (800) 247-6700, fax (312) 929-2821. Scheduled group departures for two soft-adventure itineraries, one featuring the national parks, one featuring river rafting.

Wildland Adventures, 3516 N.E. 155th St., Seattle, WA 98155, tel. (206) 365-0686 or (800) 345-4453, fax (206) 363-6615. Scheduled group departures

on nature, culture, and camping itineraries; customized FITs. Offers family trips. The company specializes in Costa Rica (more than 60 scheduled tour departures each year) and publishes a comprehensive Costa Rica Travel Planner.

Woodstar Tours, 908 S. Massachusetts Ave., DeLand, FL 32724, tel. (904) 736-0327. Nature tours for birdwatchers.

Many of the programs offered by competing companies are very similar; most feature some focus on natural history, with visits to one or more leading national parks. Often this is because a large number of the North American-based tour companies use the services of only a handful of Costa Rican-based companies or book you into the latter's own tours.

Discounts
Costa Rican Outlook (P.O. Box 5573, Chula Vista, CA 91912-5573, tel./fax 619-421-6002 or tel. 800-365-2342) offers an ID card to subscribers (see "Information," under "Other Practicalities" later in this chapter) good for discounts of up to 15% on tours, cruises, meals, and other services offered by a wide range of Costa Rican companies. *Subscribe now!*

Conexiones Universales (tel. 232-0870, fax 231-5221) claims to be the "most powerful discount travel and investment club south of the border." It offers "super discounts" on tours, hotels, and cruises.

NORTH AMERICAN TOUR COMPANIES

See the chart "North American Tour Companies" for a list of tour companies that offer group tour packages and arrange air tickets and customized programs (FITs, or fully independent travel) for individual travelers. See "Special-Interest Travel and Recreation" below for additional tour companies offering special-interest activities.

Many companies are excellent. Particularly recommended are: **Costa Rica Experts** (3166 N. Lincoln Ave. #424, Chicago, IL 60657, tel. 312-935-1009 or 800-827-9046, fax 312-935-

9252); and **Wildland Adventures** (3516 N.E. 155th St., Seattle, WA 98155, tel. 206-365-0686 or 800-345-4453). Their superb brochures say it all!

BRITISH TOUR OPERATORS

The following companies offer group tours to Costa Rica from the U.K.: **Exodus Expeditions** (9 Weir Rd., London SW12 0LT, tel. 081-675-5550), **Journey Latin America** (14-16 Devonshire Rd., London W4, tel. 081-747-8315, fax 081-742-1312), **South American Experience** (11-15 Betterton St., London WC2H 9BP, tel. 071-379-0344, fax 071-379-0801), **Reef and Rainforest Tours** (3 Moorashes, Totnes, Devon TQ9 5TH, tel. 1803-866965), and **Steamond Latin American Travel** (278 Battersea Park Rd., London SW11 3BS, tel. 071-978-5500, fax 071-978-5603). **Voyages Jules Verne** (21 Dorset Square, London NW1 6QG, tel. 171-723-5066) operates nine-day packages (£745-895), with weekly direct flights from Gatwick airport to Costa Rica. **Trips** (24 Clifton Wood Crescent, Bristol BS8 4TU, tel./fax 0272-292199) specializes in customized tours to Costa Rica, Belize, and Mexico.

COSTA RICAN COMPANIES

The Costa Rican tour industry has grown rapidly in the past decade or so. In 1973 there were just 10 licensed tour and travel agencies in Costa Rica; in July 1994, there were 219! They're a close-knit, supportive, and thoroughly professional community. Many North American-based tour companies use the services of Costa Rican based operators, or book their own

COSTA RICAN TOUR COMPANIES

Aerobiajes, Apdo. 12742, San José 1000, tel. 233-6108, fax 233-6293. Specializes in one-day excursions.

Aventuras Naturales, Apdo. 812, San José 2050, tel. 225-3939. Located at Calles 33/35 and Avenida Central. Offers river-rafting and nature trips.

CATA Tours, Apdo. 10173, San José 1000, tel. 296-2133, fax 296-1995; in San José, tel. 221-5455, fax 221-0200. Specializes in tours of Guanacaste Province.

Central American Tours, Apdo. 531, San José 1000, tel. 255-4111. A range of one-day excursions and multiday tours from San José, as well as whitewater rafting, mountain hiking, beach resort packages, and a Tortuguero jungle adventure.

Costa Rica Expeditions, Apdo. 6941, San José 1000, tel. 257-0766, fax 257-1665, e-mail crexped@sol.racsa.co.cr; or P.O. Box 025216 (Dept. 235), Miami, FL 33102. Its street location is a charming colonial building at Calle Central and Avenida 3. Specialists in natural-history tours, river-rafting, kayak, and fishing trips. Offers a complete range of active and nature-oriented tours from one to 14 days, including volcanoes, Calypso Island cruise, Sarchí, etc. The American-owned company also has its own deluxe lodges at Monteverde and Tortuguero National Park, plus a rustic tent-camp at Corcovado, and offers in-depth "jungle" and "forest odysseys" into the national parks. Costa Rica Expeditions was consistently excellent in making tour arrangements on my behalf. Highly recommended.

Costa Rican Trails, Apdo. 2907, San José 1000, tel. 222-4547 or 221-3011. Tours include a comprehensive 14-day package featuring Sarchí, Poás volcano, Tortuga Island, and Manuel Antonio. Shorter programs focus on individual nature reserves.

Costaricaraft, Apdo. 812, San Pedro 2050, tel. 225-3939. Whitewater rafting specialists offering year-round one- to four-day trips on the Reventazón, Pacuare, Sarapiquí, and Corobicí rivers.

Costa Rica Sun Tours, Apdo. 1195, Escazú 1250, tel. 255-3418, fax 255-4410. Located at Avenida 7, Calles 3/5. A range of fishing trips (including Lake Arenal), beach resort packages, one-day guided excursions, and nature tours. Also operates two private nature reserves: Tiskita Biological Reserve and Arenal Volcano Observatory. Sun Tours offers two- to four-day programs to Tiskita and Arenal featuring accommodation at its own private lodges, or in combination with visits to Monteverde, Manuel Antonio, and a Calypso cruise in the Gulf of Guanacaste.

Costa Rica Temptations, Apdo. 5452, San José 1000, tel. 220-4437, fax 220-2103. Offers a full range of half-day and full-day excursions, beach resort packages, mountain and jungle lodge stays, and special-interest tours, including visits to local farms and coffee *fincas.* Can arrange every type of special-interest travel, hotels, car rental, etc. I received consistently excellent service from Costa Rica Temptations, often at extremely short notice. Recommended. It publishes a travel agents' manual full of "insider tips."

Costa Sol International, Apdo. 7-1880, San José 1000, tel. 239-1025, fax 239-2405. Owns and operates luxury hotels, a 30-meter cruise ship, a fleet of sportfishing boats, a fishing and nature lodge, air-taxi service, tour buses, a marina, whitewater rafting, and a full service tour and travel agency. Offers a wide range of inclusive tour packages using its own facilities. Highly respected.

Cruceros del Sur, Apdo. 1198, San José 1200, tel. 220-1927, fax 220-2103. Operates one-day, four-day, and weeklong natural-history cruises featuring guided shore visits to major national parks on the Pacific coast aboard the 11-meter *Georgiana* and the 68-passenger *Temptress.* Also operates scuba programs aboard the *Okeanos Aggressor.* The company owns both vessels. Highly recommended.

ECHO: Environmentally Conscious Holiday Options, Apdo. 7-3290, San José 1000, tel. 255-2693, fax 255-0061. Offers a range of intriguing ecotours, including a one-day "Edible Forest Products" tour, "Ascent Into the Forest Canopy," and a visit to the ARBOFILIA reforestation and research project.

Eclipse Tours, Apdo. 11057, San José 1000, tel./fax 223-7510. Wide range of one-day and multiday tours.

EcoTreks Adventure Company, tel. 228-4029, fax 289-8191. Specializes in mountain biking, rafting, and scuba trips.

Frontera Tours, Apdo. 1177, Tibas 1000, tel./fax 670-0403. Specializes in tours of Guanacaste Province.

Geo Expediciones, Apdo. 681, San José 2300, tel. 272-2024, fax 272-2220. Specializes in trips to Gandoca-Manzanillo Wildlife Refuge. Operates the Almond-Coral Lodge Tent Camp.

Geotur, Apdo. 469 Y Griega, San José 1011, tel. 234-1867, fax 253-6338. Specializes in one-day visits to Braulio Carrillo National Park and Carara Biological Reserve. Also offers three-day horseback trips through the Guanacaste dry forest, a full-day "Resplendant Quetzal" tour, plus a wide range of one-day and longer excursions and tours to national parks.

Guanacaste Tours, Apdo. 55, Liberia 5000, tel. 666-0306, fax 666-0307. Offers nighttime turtle-watching tours.

Horizontes, Apdo. 1780, San José 1002, tel. 222-2022, fax 255-4513. One of Costa Rica's most respected operators, with a wide range of one- and multiday birdwatching, nature, and walking programs to national parks and nature reserves. Also rafting, sea-kayaking, sailing, cruising, mountain biking, and horseback riding throughout the country in association with other Costa Rican tour operators. Many family vacations.

Interviajes, Apdo. 296, Heredia 3000, tel. 233-4457. A range of nature and special-interest tours. Slightly less expensive than some of the other operators.

Jungle Trails/Los Caminos de la Selva, Apdo. 2413, San José 1002, tel. 255-3486, fax 255-2782. Offers a wide range of one-day and longer nature and hiking tours featuring leading national parks and reserves. Specializes in programs to Barva, Poás, and Rincón de la Vieja volcanoes, with stays at mountain lodges. Also features a unique ecotour called "Let's Plant a Tropical Endangered Tree," in which participants plant their own trees at Carara; plus a "Trek on Your Own" hiking program; birdwatching and turtle-watching programs; and a tour for artists.

Panorama Tours, Apdo. 7323, San José 1000, tel. 233-0233. Offers "New Age" tours (holistic medicine, etc.).

Papagayo Excursions, Apdo. 6398, Santa Cruz de Guanacaste, tel. 680-0859, fax 225-3648. Offers a "Turtle Nesting Safari."

Ríos Tropicales, Apdo. 472, San José 1200, tel. 233-6455, fax 255-4354. Located at Avenida 2, Calle 32. Perhaps the premier river-rafting company in Costa Rica, with one-day trips on the Corobicí, Reventazón, Sarapiquí, and Pacuare rivers. Also longer trips combining rafting with nature programs. Also offers kayaking and sea-kayaking, rock-climbing, caving, trekking, and mountain-biking tours.

SANSA, Calle 24, Paseo Colón/Avenida 1, tel. 222-6561. The nation's domestic airline offers a range of inexpensive tours and three- to four-day beach vacations, including air transportation, transfers, accommodations, and meals. Popular destinations are Nosara, Sámara, Tamarindo, and Manuel Antonio.

Sol Tropical, Apdo. 153-1017, San José 2000, tel. 232-9041, fax 232-9062. Wide range of one-day excursions.

Tikal Tour Operators, Apdo. 6398, San José 1000, tel. 223-2811, fax 223-1916. Daily departures on a wide range of natural-history trips of one day or longer, plus special-interest tours, including diving, surfing, and natural history. Also offers a range of eight-day ecotours under the company name Ecoadventures featuring horseback riding, cycling, canoeing, snorkeling, hiking, and rafting. Tikal is recommended for arranging exit visas for those who overstay their legal limit.

Universal Tropical Nature Tours, Apdo. 4276, San José 1000, tel. 257-0181, fax 255-4274. Special-interest tours, including natural history, birding, etc.

Vesa Nature Tours, Apdo. 476, San Antonio de Belén, Heredia 4005, tel. 239-1049, fax 239-4206. Wide range of one-day excursions.

The above is only a partial listing of local tour operators. There are many lesser known.

clients into the latter's tour packages. The leading operators offer a complete range of tour options, including one-day and overnight excursions to all the major points of attraction. English-speaking guides, private transportation, meals, and accommodations are standard inclusions. This gives you the added flexibility of making your own tour arrangements once you've arrived in Costa Rica and gained a better sense of your options and desires.

Accommodations at the more popular tourist sights, national parks, and reserves are limited, and tours and excursions that feature visits to those sites may therefore already be fully booked when you arrive in Costa Rica, particularly during dry season (Dec.-April), when accommodations can be hard to come by even in San José. I recommend making reservations

well in advance for any visits that include overnight stays at leading parks and wildlife reserves. Many hotels in San José have tour information desks, where you can make inquiries and reservations. Most tours and excursions pick up group tour members at the major hotels, and drop them either at their hotels or outside the Gran Hotel in Plaza de la Cultura. On most day-trips, lunch is included; on longer trips, meals, accommodations, and any equipment are included as part of the package.

See the chart "Costa Rican Tour Companies" for recommended Costa Rican tour operators. The **Asociación Costarricense de Operadores de Turismo** (Costa Rican Association of Tour Operators, Apdo. 1628, San Pedro de Montes de Oca 2050, tel./fax 250-5878) can provide a complete list and additional details.

SPECIAL-INTEREST TRAVEL AND RECREATION

BALLOONING

Serendipity Adventures (P.O. Box 2325, Ann Arbor, MI 48106, tel. 313-995-0111 or 800-635-2325, fax 313-426-5026) offers seven- and 10-day adventures that combine ballooning with rafting and other active adventures. Customized balloon trips are also offered. **Aventuras Naturales** (Apdo. 812, San Pedro 2050, San José, tel. 225-3939, fax 253-6934) plans to introduce **hot-air ballooning**. Pilot **Roberto Kopper** (tel. 222-6722 or 450-0311) also offers balloon float trips.

BICYCLING

The occasional sweat and effort make Costa Rica's spectacular landscapes and abiding serenity all the more endearing from the seat of a saddle. Sure, you'll work for your reward. But you'll never get so close to so much beauty in a car.

Costa Ricans are particularly fond of cycling, and bicycle racing is a major sport, culminating each December in the 12-day-long Vuelta a Costa Rica, which crisscrosses the mountain chain from sea level to over 3,000 meters. Away from the main highways roads are little traveled. However, there are no bike lanes. Potholes are a persistent problem. And traffic can be hazardous on the steep and windy mountain roads. A helmet is a wise investment.

If you're planning your own trip, a good reference source is *Latin America on a Bicycle* by J.P. Panet (Champlain, NY: Passport Press, 1987), which has a chapter on Costa Rica. Airlines generally allow bicycles to be checked free (properly packaged) with one piece of luggage. Otherwise a small charge may apply. Leave your touring bike at home: bring a mountain bike or rent one once you arrive. **Bike N' Hike: One Stop Bike Shop** (tel./fax 289-8191), in

Centro Comercial in Escazú, rents mountain bikes ($29 daily) and offers guided bike tours. **Mountain Biking Costa Rica** (tel. 255-0914) rents 18-speed mountain bikes ($5 per hour), as does **EcoTreks** (tel. 228-4029, fax 289-8191), **Ríos Tropicales** (Apdo. 472, San José 1200, tel. 233-6455, fax 255-4354; its office is on Calle 32, Avenida 2), **Safaris Corobicí** (tel. 669-0544), **C.R. Mountain Biking** (Apdo. 3979, San José 1000, tel. 222-4380, fax 255-4354), and **Tikal Tour Operators** (Apdo. 6398, San José 1000, tel. 223-2811, fax 223-1916).

Several local tour companies offer group tours. Most are suitable for all levels of competence, but check in advance about the kind of terrain and mileages involved. Don't be put off by the fact that the majority of tours involve cycling on the volcanoes: you usually ride down, not up!

It helps to ride a bicycle regularly before such a tour. Even so, the pace is as leisurely or demanding as you wish to make it. You'll feel no pressure to conform to anyone else's pace. Armed with a route map and instructions for safe riding, you can cycle alone if you wish. A support van ("sag wagon") follows in the group's wake to drop off and pick up those wishing to cycle only a part of each day's journey, or those getting a little out of breath. And qualified bilingual guides cycle with you to cure any mechanical, physical, or psychological breakdowns. One-day bicycling tours generally cost $65-75, including lunch and bike rental.

Costa Rican Tour Companies
Aventuras Naturales (Apdo. 812, San José 2050, tel. 225-3939, fax 253-6934) offers one-day mountain biking tours of Irazú, Turrialba, and Guayabo, plus two- and three-day tours of both the Caribbean coast and Arenal volcano. **Costa Rica Adventures and Wildlife** (4014 N. 46th Ave., Hollywood, FL 33021, tel./fax 305-720-9281; in Costa Rica, tel. 255-2463, fax 255-3573) offers a four-day mountain biking trip

through Barra Honda and Palo Verde National Parks in Guanacaste ($399).

Costaricabike (Apdo. 812, San Pedro 2050, tel. 225-3939, fax 253-6934) has a series of one-day mountain bike tours to Turrialba, Irazú, and Guayabo National Monument, and two- and three-day tours to the Caribbean and Arenal volcano ($260 two days, $340 three days).

Costa Rica Tropical Cycling (Apdo. 1195, Escazú 1250, tel. 255-2011, fax 255-3529) has guided mountain-bike tours. **Mountain Biking Costa Rica** (tel. 255-0914) offers a three-day mountain bicycling tour along the Caribbean coast ($275). Also try **C.R. Mountain Biking** (Apdo. 3979, San José 1000, tel. 222-4380, fax 255-4354).

EcoTreks Adventure Company (tel. 228-4029, fax 289-8191), in Escazú, lists a wide range of two- to six-day mountain biking trips nationwide.

Geoventuras (tel. 221-2053, fax 282-3333) has a full-day tour from Cartago into the Orosí Valley and Tapantí refuge. **Horizontes** (Apdo. 1780, San José 1002, tel. 222-2022, fax 255-4513) also has a one-day "Tapantí Cycling Adventure." **Ríos Tropicales** (Apdo. 472, San José 1200, tel. 233-6455, fax 255-4354), at Calle 32 and Avenida 2, has one-day mountain biking tours on both Poás and Irazú volcanoes, plus a three-day Caribbean tour, and eight- to 10-day coast-to-coast cycling tours.

Tikal Tour Operators (Apdo. 6398, San José 1000, tel. 223-2811, fax 223-1916) offers a three-day mountain bike program from Tilarán to Monteverde and around Lake Arenal; a full day of mountain biking in Santa Rosa National Park is part of an eight-day "Ecoadventure Tour." **Tropical Adventure Tours** (Apdo. 1362, San José 1000, tel. 222-8974, fax 255-0306) offers one-day bicycling tours in Santa Rosa National Park and Rincón de la Vieja volcano.

U.S. Tour Companies

Backroads (1526 5th St., Berkeley, CA 94710, tel. 800-245-3874 or 510-527-1555, fax 510-527-1444) has a nine-day mountain-biking tour featuring Monteverde, Arenal, the Nicoya Peninsula, and Manuel Antonio. **Mariah Wilderness Expeditions** (P.O. Box 248, Point Richmond, CA 94807, tel. 510-233-2303 or 800-462-7424)

features cycling on Orosí volcano as part of an eight-day "Tropical Adventure" ($912). **Journeys** (4011 Jackson Rd., Ann Arbor, MI 48103, tel. 800-255-8735) also offers an eight-day "Mountain Bike Odyssey" between Cartago and Cahuita (Dec.-April). **Lost World Adventures** (1189 Autumn Ridge Dr., Marietta, GA 30066, tel. 404-971-8586 or 800-999-0558, fax 404-977-3095) offers a three-day mountain biking package ($429), plus a five-day biking and rafting program ($785). **Specialty Tours** (1925 Wallenberg Dr., Ft. Collins, CO 80526, tel. 800-685-4565) includes Palo Verde, Arenal, and Sámara on its nine-day bicycling tours. It also has an eight-day self-guided tour. And **ExperiencePlus!** (1925 Wallenberg Dr., Fort Collins, CO 80526, tel. 800-685-4565) has nine-day guided tours of Guanacaste and Nicoya ($1495), plus a nine-day "self-guided solo tour" ($995). Lastly, **Canadian BackRoutes** (597 Markham St., Toronto, ON M6G 2L7, tel. 416-588-6139, fax 416-588-9839) has an eight-day tour taking in Lake Arenal, Poás volcano, the Orosí Valley, and an unspecified "jungle" destination; departures are offered Nov.-April ($1699).

BIRDWATCHING

Costa Rica is to birders what Grand Central Station is to pickpockets. Few places in the world can boast so many different bird species in such a small area. Wherever you travel, you're sure to be surrounded by the calls and whistles of scores of exotic species.

Birding, like any outdoor activity, requires some knowledge of where you are going, what you're looking for, and the best season. No self-respecting ornithologist would be caught in the field without his copy of *A Guide to the Birds of Costa Rica* by F. Gary Stiles and Alexander Skutch (Ithaca, NY: Cornell University Press, 1989). Still, even with this in hand, your best bet for seeing and learning about different bird species is to hire a qualified guide or to join a birdwatching tour.

Costa Rican Tour Companies

San José Travel (Apdo. 889, San José 1007, tel. 221-0593, fax 221-5148) and **Geotur** (Apdo.

469 Y Griega, San José 1011, tel. 234-1867, fax 253-6338) both offer one-day quetzal tours. **Horizontes** (Apdo. 1780, San José 1002, tel. 222-2022, fax 255-4513) offers one-day and multiday guided birdwatching trips to selected national parks and reserves. It also offers birdwatching program in May—the mating and breeding season for many species. **Jungle Trails** (Apdo. 2413, San José 1000, tel. 255-3486, fax 255-2782) has one-day birdwatching tours to Poás and Braulio Carrillo National Parks. Serious birders might consider the company's 15-day birdwatching tour.

U.S. Tour Companies
Costa Rica Connections (975 Osos St., San Luis Obispo, CA 93401, tel. 805-543-8823 or 800-345-7422) lists three escorted birdwatching tours (March and Nov.), including a 12-day "Tropical Birding" tour. **Geostar Travel** (6050 Commerce Blvd., Suite 110, Rohnert Park, CA 94928, tel. 707-584-9552 or 800-633-6633) has a seven-day and a 10-day "Birdwatcher's Paradise" tour (from $1090 seven-day, $1460 10-day). **Holbrook Travel** (tel. 800-451-7111) offers a midwinter "Costa Rica Birding Adventure" including Palo Verde, Monteverde, Arenal, and Selva Verde ($1515). **Cheeseman's Ecology Safaris** (20800 Kittredge Rd., Saratoga, CA 95070, tel. 408-867-1371 or 800-527-5330) features birding on a 14-day nature trip that takes in Tortuguero, Tiskita, Arenal, Monteverde, Carara, La Selva, and Selva Verde. **Osprey Tours** (P.O. Box 030211, Fort Lauderdale, FL 33302, tel. 305-767-4823) customizes birding tours for groups. Birdwatching tours are also a specialty of **Questers** (257 Park Ave. S, New York, NY 10010, tel. 212-673-3120).

CRUISES/YACHTING

Tortuga Island and Gulf of Nicoya
A popular day outing for Costa Ricans and tourists alike is a day cruise from Puntarenas across the Gulf of Nicoya to Tortuga Island. The cruise—from one to two and a half hours each way, depending on the vessel—is superlatively scenic. En route you'll pass the island of Negritos, the prison island of San Lucas, Gitana, and

the Guayabo National Park Sanctuary. The cruise provides an opportunity to spot manta rays or pilot whales in the warm waters. Even giant whale sharks have been seen basking off Tortuga Island.

Buses pick passengers up at San José hotels. You'll normally have about two hours on Tortuga Island, with a buffet lunch served on the beach. Costs average $65 from Puntarenas, $75 from San José. The following companies offer Tortuga Island cruises.

Bay Island Cruises (Apdo. 49, San José 1017, tel. 296-5551, fax 296-5095) offers cruises year-round aboard the *Bay Princess,* an ultramodern 16-meter cruise yacht with room for 70 passengers. The ship has a sundeck and music, and cocktails and snacks are served during the cruise.

Calypso Cruises (Apdo. 6941, San José 1000, tel. 233-3617, fax 233-0401) initiated Tortuga Island cruises aboard its 15-meter cruise yacht *Calypso.* In 1994, the venerable vessel was relocated and began operating eco-cruises to Punta Coral, on the southern tip of Nicoya. Replacing it was a huge catamaran, the *Manta Raya,* described as an "ocean-going spaceship" built of high-density, closed-cell waterproof PVC, and a bow of Kevlar (of bullet-proof vest fame), and fitted with $30,000 of NASA-type electronic equipment. It carries up to 100 passengers and features a fishing platform and underwater viewing platform, plus—gosh!—two Jacuzzis, and the amazing ability to "drive" right up onto the beach. After dropping off passengers, it makes a ferry run from Paquera to Puntarenas, placing San José within a three-hour journey of Nicoya. Daily departures are offered during dry season (15 Dec.-15 April), Wednesday, Friday, and Sunday in wet season ($84).

Costa Sol International (Apdo. 7-1880, San José 1000, tel. 239-1029, fax 239-2405; in the U.S./Canada contact Costa Sol International, 1717 N. Bayshore Dr., Suite 3333, Miami, FL 33132, tel. 305-539-1630, fax 305-539-1123) offers a cruise to Costa Sol Beach (on the southern coast of the Nicoya Peninsula) aboard the elegant 30-meter *Costa Sol.* The vessel carries up to 120 passengers and features a sundeck. Snorkels, boogie boards, volleyball, and beach games are included.

Cruises depart every Wednesday, Friday, Saturday, and Sunday.

Sea Ventures (tel. 239-4719 or 255-3022, fax 239-4666; in the U.S. tel. 800-428-3541) operates daily cruises aboard its sleek 29-meter namesake vessel. A three-day "Sailing/Nature Adventure" combines two days sailing in the Gulf of Nicoya and one day at Cabo Blanco National Reserve, with overnights on board (the trip departs and returns to Playa Herradura, north of Jacó; $445).

Pacific Islands Adventures (tel. 255-0791 or 661-0697), **Fantasy Yacht Tours** (tel. 222-4752, 255-0791), and **Blue Seas** (tel. 233-7274, fax 233-5555) also offer cruise tours to Tortuga Island.

Other

If you want to feel the snap of the wind in the sails, Calypso Cruises (see above) has full-day sailing trips aboard a selection of cutters plus a 19-meter yawl. More exciting yet is Calypso's stunning *Star Chaser* catamaran—the fastest commercial cat in the world—which operates day-trips from north of Jacó Beach (see "Playa Malo and Punta Leona" under "Puntarenas to Jacó" in the Central Pacific chapter).

Cruceros del Sur (Apdo. 1198, San José 1200, tel. 220-1927, fax 220-2103) operates one-day cruises from Puntarenas to Manuel Antonio National Park and Curú Wildlife Refuge on alternate days aboard the 11-meter *Geor-*

giana. The company also operates weeklong natural-history cruises to national parks along the Pacific coast aboard the *Temptress.*

Pollux de Golfito (Apdo. 7-1970, San José 1000, tel. 231-4055, fax 231-3030) has a range of daylong and multiday cruises aboard the sleek 16-meter-long *S/Y Pollux.* **Swiss Travel Service** (Apdo. 7-1970, San José 1000, tel. 231-4055, fax 231-3030) also offers one-day trips from Puntarenas to Herradura Bay aboard the *S/Y Pollux.*

Yacht Charters

Way To Go Costa Rica (P.O. Box 81288, Raleigh, NC 27622, tel. 800-835-1223, fax 919-787-1952) has four fully outfitted sailing vessels for rent for five or seven days. Calypso Cruises, Pollux de Golfito, and Sea Ventures (see above) also offer yacht charters. Calypso Cruises also has one- to seven-day coastal charters and a 10-day Cocos Island charter. **Veleros del Sur** (Apdo. 13, Puntarenas 5400, tel. 661-1320, fax 661-1119) charters 14- to19-meter yachts, with skippers and crew if needed.

DEEP-SEA FISHING

When your fishing-loving friend tells you all about the big one—the *really* big one—that got away in Costa Rica, don't believe it. Yes, the fish come big in Costa Rica. But *hooking* trophy contenders

MV Temptress

NATURAL-HISTORY CRUISE TOURS

The *Temptress*

In 1990, Cruceros del Sur introduced the *Temptress,* a 53-meter semi-luxury eco-cruise ship offering natural-history cruises to national parks along the Pacific coast. The ship operates three-, six- and seven-day itineraries out of Puntarenas. Since many of the "ports of call" are difficult to get to by land—or even air—the cruise offers perhaps the most condensed and certainly the most comfortable means of reaching a broad combination of more remote, prime wilderness sites. *Highly recommended!*

There are three itineraries. A four-day "Curú Voyage," which departs Saturday, explores Curú National Wildlife Refuge, with stops at Corcovado National Park, Drake Bay, and Manuel Antonio; a four-day "Caño Voyage" (departs Tuesday) replaces Curú with Caño Island and Carara Biological Reserve. Rates: $695 summer, $795 winter. A seven-day itinerary combines both routes ($1290-1495). I've experienced three trips. All were fantastic.

The vessel departs Puntarenas weekly and travels by evening so that each morning when you awake *Temptress* is already anchored at a different location. You spend a large part of each day exploring ashore, with landings through the surf aboard Zodiacs, the inflatable rubber dinghies popularized by Jacques Cousteau. Two options for land excursions are available: a natural-history excursion guided by a professional biologist and a recreational-cultural excursion (this sometimes means a more relaxed natural-history tour, or perhaps beach hiking). A slide presentation and briefing are given each evening to outline the next day's activities. Tours are led by knowledgeable naturalist guides; their enthusiasm is contagious! And the amenities make all the difference after a day of hiking.

Temptress comfortably accommodates up to 68 passengers in relatively spacious cabins (the vessel was refurbished for the 1995 season with double beds replacing twins in some cabins). Her crew of 16 is all Costa Rican, ultrafriendly, and mostly bilingual. All cabins are outside, with large windows, single beds, and private showers/baths. The ship is fully outfitted with two five-meter sportfishing boats and state-of-the-art diving equipment. Certified divemasters lead certified scuba divers on dives; there's a Resort Course program for non-certified divers. The top deck has a large carpeted sun-deck and a roomy bar where the crew and passengers mingle at night to dance to *salsa* and reggae. The vessel

even has a film-developing lab on-board. And the cuisine is excellent.

This is casual button-down cruising without the formality of most other cruise ships: pack your tux and you'd be with the boys in the band (if there were one). The company offers a "Family Adventure Package" that includes special activities for children. Also new in 1994 was a "Reef Ecology Workshop" for divers and snorkelers. One-way air transfers from San José are available.

The vessel was replaced in December 1995 by the 56-meter *Temptress Explorer,* which carries 99 passengers on similar itineraries as its predecessor, which moved to Belize.

Contact Cruceros del Sur at Apdo. 1198, San José 1200, tel. 220-1927, fax 220-2103; or in the U.S. at 1600 N.W. LeJeune Rd., Suite 301, Miami, FL 33126, tel. (800) 336-8423 or (305) 871-2663, fax (305) 871-2657.

Other Cruises

Clipper Adventure Cruises (7711 Bonhomme Ave., St. Louis, MO 63105, tel. 800-325-0010 or 314-727-2929) features Costa Rica cruises aboard the *World Discoverer* ("hardy expeditions") and 78-meter-long *Yorktown Clipper* ("softer expeditions"). Each ship carries 138 passengers and a team of naturalists, with daily routines similar to the *Temptress*'s. A 14-day "Costa Rica's National Parks, The Darien Jungle and the Panamá Canal" cruise visits San José, Carara Biological Reserve, Manuel Antonio National Park, and Marenco Biological Station, plus the Darien, Panamá Canal, Portobelo, and San Blas islands in Panamá (from $3450 per person).

Special Expeditions (tel. 800-762-0003 or 212-765-7740) has launched three itineraries combining Costa Rica and Panamá aboard the 80-passenger *Polaris,* including a one-week "Journey on the Wild Side" (from $2260) featuring Curú, Marenco, and Poás, as well as a Panamá Canal transit and calls in Panamá (departures in December, January, and March); and an 11-day cruise featuring Corcovado and Manuel Antonio (from $4,380). A 13-day cruise—"From the Panamá Canal to the Maya Coast"—takes in Tortuguero, plus Belize (from $5390). Pre- and post-tours of Costa Rica are available.

Tauck Tours (tel. 800-468-2825 or 203-226-6911) offers a nine-day package of Costa Rica and Panamá aboard the 80-passenger *Aurora II,* with a focus on nature (from $2420).

comes easy; the fish seem to be lining up to get a bite on the hook. The country is the undisputed sailfish capital of the world on the Pacific, the tarpon capital on the Caribbean (see "Inland and Coastal Fishing," below). Fishing varies from season to season, but hardly a month goes by without some IGFA record being broken. (In 1991, anglers caught 1,691 sails and marlin during the 13th Annual International Sailfish Tournament!)

Alas, the sportfishing industry is facing some sharp competition from illegal commercial harvesting: a 1994 report by the Ministry of Agriculture and Livestock estimates "conservatively" that 28,000 marlin and sailfish are being killed annually by longline fleet; *Marlin* magazine says more than 88,000 Costa Rican marlin and sailfish were exported to the United States *in the first eight months* of 1994. Fishing experts talk of a possible catastrophe, such as befell sportfishing in Puerto Rico and Baja California. Regulation is a problem for cash-strapped Costa Rica: it cannot police its 1,227-kilometer (767 mile) coastline. Fishing expert Jerry Ruhlow reports a significant drop in the number of sails raised during the 1993 and 1994 Annual International Sailfish Tournament, as well as a drop in the number of competitors, who are complaining that they must compete with commercial purse seiners who are ruining sportfishing. The Figueres administration, elected in 1994, promises to give the issue high priority. The good news, says Ruhlow, is that "1995 is shaping up to be one of the best fishing years in recent memory . . . Conditions have been virtually ideal."

Boat charters run $250-400 a half day, and $350-650 for a full day for up to four people, with lunch and beverage included. Most fishing resorts are similar in their approach to servicing anglers, providing world-class boats and equipment; most operators now operate only catch-and-release.

Ruhlow has an excellent column on fishing in the weekly *Tico Times* and *Costa Rica Today,* and also publishes *Costa Rica Outdoors,* a slick full-color bimonthly magazine dedicated to fishing and outdoor sports (see "Information," in this chapter).

Carlos Barrantes, the "father of Costa Rican fishing" (and also founder of the Tarpon Rancho and Casa Mar fishing lodges), runs a **tackle shop,** Gilca Casa de Pesca, in San José at Calle 1, Avenidas 16/19 (tel. 222-1470, fax 223-8223).

The Pacific

No place in the world has posted more "super grand slams"—all three species of marlin and one or more sailfish on the same day—than the Pacific coastal waters of Costa Rica, where it's not unusual to raise 25 or more sailfish in a single day. In May 1991, fishermen posted the highest catch record in tournament history when 120 anglers caught and released 1,691 sailfish and marlin in the four days of the 13th Annual International Sailfish Tournament. And in early 1991, an angler out of Gunamar caught the first Pacific blue marlin taken on a fly (at 92 kilograms, it's also the largest fish ever caught on a fly).

The hard-fighting blue marlin swims in these waters year-round, although this "bull of the ocean" is most abundant in June and July, when large schools of tuna also come close to shore. June-October is best for dorado (another year-round fish). Then, too, yellowfin tuna weighing up to 90 kilograms offer rod-bending action. Wahoo are also prominent, though less dependable. Generally, summer months are the best in the north; the winter months the best in the south.

To meet the ever-increasing demand for fishing on the west coast, local operators have been upgrading their fleets with bigger and better boats. And the development of a marina at Flamingo Beach has served as a major catalyst for the arrival of ever-increasing numbers of world-class fishing yachts from other countries.

Flamingo and Tamarindo are the two most prominent fishing centers in the northern Pacific. A 20-minute run puts you in 180 meters of water. However, northern Guanacaste is largely unfishable Dec.-March beacuse of heavy northern winds (boat operators at Flamingo and Tamarindo move boats south to Quepos during the windy season, when Quepos posts its best scores). Boats out of Puntarenas and resorts near the tip of the Nicoya Peninsula can fish areas protected from the winds year-round.

Quepos is a year-round sportfishing center. The coastal configuration protects these waters from the winds that batter Guanacaste. Many operators offer multiday trips from Quepos to the waters off Drake Bay and Caño Island, with overnights at one of the local wilderness camps or nature lodges. Golfito is the base for another popular fishing paradise, the Golfo Dulce, with calm seas and light winds the rule. Many rivers empty into this 56-kilometer-long by 16-kilometer-wide body of water, providing nutrients and an abundant food source for a wealth of baitfish.

Costa Rican Tour Operators
Additional operators advertise in the publications listed above (in particular see *Costa Rica Outdoors*). See regional chapters for more specific listings on operators and lodges.

Costa Rican Dreams (Apdo. 79, Belén 4005, Heredia, tel. 239-3387, fax 239-3383) offers half-day and full-day specials out of Quepos using two eight-meter center-console open-cockpit sportfishing boats and a 12-meter sportfishing yacht. Dreams also offers multiday charters to Drake Bay and Caño Island.

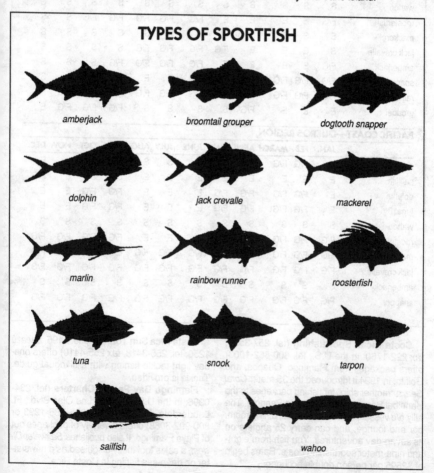

TYPES OF SPORTFISH

amberjack

broomtail grouper

dogtooth snapper

dolphin

jack crevalle

mackerel

marlin

rainbow runner

roosterfish

tuna

snook

tarpon

sailfish

wahoo

FISHING SEASONS

S = Slow   F/G = Fair/Good   E = Excellent

PACIFIC COAST—NICOYA

	JAN.	FEB.	MARCH	APRIL	MAY	JUNE	JULY	AUG.	SEPT.	OCT.	NOV.	DEC.
marlin	S	S	F/G	E	E	F/G	E	E	S	S	F/G	S
sailfish	S	S	F/G	F/G	E	E	E	E	F/G	F/G	S	S
dolphin	S	S	F/G	F/G	E	E	E	E	F/G	F/G	S	S
tuna	E	E	F/G	F/G	F/G	F/G	F/G	F/G	S	S	S	E
wahoo	S	S	S	S	S	S	S	S	S	S	S	S
roosterfish	F/G	E	E	E	E	F/G	F/G	F/G	F/G	F/G	S	S
mackerel	S	S	S	S	S	S	S	S	S	S	S	S
jack crevalle	S	E	E	E	F/G	F/G	F/G	F/G	S	S	S	S
amberjack	F/G	E	E	E	E	F/G	F/G	F/G	F/G	S	S	S
snapper	F/G	F/G	F/G	F/G	E	E	E	E	F/G	F/G	S	S
rainbow runner	F/G	F/G	F/G	F/G	F/G	F/G	F/G	F/G	F/G	F/G	F/G	F/G
grouper	E	E	E	F/G	S	S	S	S	F/G	F/G	F/G	E

PACIFIC COAST—QUEPOS REGION

	JAN.	FEB.	MARCH	APRIL	MAY	JUNE	JULY	AUG.	SEPT.	OCT.	NOV.	DEC.
marlin	E	F/G	F/G	F/G	S	S	S	S	S	S	S	E
sailfish	E	E	E	E	E	E	E	E	S	S	S	F/G
dolphin	E	F/G	F/G	F/G	F/G	E	E	E	F/G	F/G	E	E
tuna	E	F/G	F/G	F/G	F/G	E	E	E	F/G	F/G	E	E
wahoo	S	S	S	S	S	S	S	S	S	S	S	S
roosterfish	F/G	F/G	F/G	F/G	E	E	E	E	F/G	F/G	F/G	F/G
mackerel	F/G	F/G	F/G	F/G	F/G	F/G	F/G	F/G	E	E	E	F/G
jack crevalle	F/G	F/G	F/G	F/G	F/G	F/G	F/G	F/G	F/G	F/G	F/G	F/G
amberjack	S	S	S	S	S	S	S	S	S	S	S	S
snapper	F/G	F/G	F/G	F/G	F/G	F/G	F/G	F/G	F/G	F/G	F/G	F/G

Costa Rican Sportfishing (tel. 257-3553, fax 222-1760; in the U.S., tel. 800-862-1003) offers packages from Flamingo, Quepos, and Golfito. In 1994 it introduced the 35-meter *Coral Sea*, a "mother ship" for fishing packages to the Hannibal Bank and Isla Coiba, in Panamá. The fully a/c vessel has 11 staterooms, dining room, bar and lounge, and can carry 25 anglers on its seven-day adventures. You fish from eight- and nine-meter sportfishing boats. Rates begin at $2695 per person double occupancy.

Costa Rica Sun Tours (Apdo. 1195, Escazú 1250, tel. 255-3418, fax 255-4410) offers one-day light-tackle fishing with a bilingual guide. Tackle is provided.

Flamingo Bay Pacific Charters (tel. 234-0906; in the U.S., 1112 E. Las Olas Blvd., Ft. Lauderdale, FL 33301, tel. 305-765-1993 or 800-992-3068) offers a variety of packages out of Playa Flamingo. It also publishes *Saltwater Digest,* a sales tool thinly disguised as a newsletter on deep-sea fishing in Costa Rica.

PACIFIC COAST—GOLFITO, DRAKE BAY, CAÑO ISLAND

	JAN.	FEB.	MARCH	APRIL	MAY	JUNE	JULY	AUG.	SEPT.	OCT.	NOV.	DEC.
marlin	F/G	E	E	F/G	S	S	S	S	S	S	S	S
sailfish	E	F/G	F/G	E	F/G	S	S	S	S	S	E	E
dolphin	F/G	F/G	F/G	F/G	F/G	F/G	F/G	F/G	F/G	F/G	F/G	F/G
tuna	E	E	E	F/G	F/G	F/G	F/G	S	S	S	F/G	F/G
wahoo	S	F/G	S	S	S	E	E	E	F/G	F/G	F/G	F/G
roosterfish	E	F/G	F/G	F/G	S	S	S	S	S	S	E	E
mackerel	F/G	F/G	F/G	F/G	F/G	F/G	F/G	F/G	F/G	F/G	F/G	F/G
jack crevalle	F/G	F/G	F/G	F/G	F/G	F/G	F/G	F/G	F/G	F/G	F/G	F/G
amberjack	F/G	F/G	F/G	F/G	F/G	E	E	E	S	S	F/G	F/G
snapper	E	E	E	E	E	E	E	E	E	E	E	E

CARIBBEAN

	JAN.	FEB.	MARCH	APRIL	MAY	JUNE	JULY	AUG.	SEPT.	OCT.	NOV.	DEC.
tarpon	F/G	E	E	E	E	E	F/G	F/G	S	S	F/G	F/G
snook	E	F/G	S	S	S	F/G	F/G	F/G	E	E	E	E

JP Tours (Apdo. 66, Tibas 1100, tel. 235-3490, fax 236-9252; in the U.S., SJO 950, P.O. Box 025216, Miami, FL 33102-5216, tel. 800-308-3394) offers sportfishing packages from Flamingo, Drake Bay, Quepos, and Golfito using a wide range of seven- to 11-meter boats.

Pacific Coast Charters (tel./fax 654-4210; in the U.S., 4905 S.E. Dixie Hwy., Stuart, FL 34997, tel. 407-287-4626, fax 220-4851) operates out of Flamingo Bay with the *Tijereta,* a custom-built 12-meter boat skippered by Capt. James "Bubba" Carter.

Papagayo Excursions (Apdo. 35, Santa Cruz de Guanacaste, tel. 680-0859, fax 680-0859) operates out of Tamarindo Beach using fully equipped seven- to nine-meter sportfishing boats; half-day and full-day programs.

Phoenix Charters (tel./fax 575-0735; in the U.S., tel. 800-733-4742 or fax 504-872-3230) offers live-aboard sportfishing adventures out of Golfito aboard the 19-meter *Cheoy Lee.*

Pisces Boat Tours (Apdo. 239, San Isidro 8000, P.Z., tel. 221-2053, fax 221-2053) runs full-day offshore packages out of Playa Dominical.

Sportfishing Costa Rica (Apdo. 115, La Uruca 1150, tel. 233-9135, fax 223-6728) claims the largest fleet of sportfishing boats based at Flamingo Beach, Quepos, and Drake Bay. It also offers Caribbean ocean fishing.

Starseeker (tel. 228-6946, fax 228-6950) is a 13-meter sailboat that promises "no motor noise, no diesel exhaust, less rolling in waves, and 270 degree fighting area." Live-aboard accommodations are provided for a fishing party of four.

Tamarindo Sportfishing (tel./fax 654-4090; in the U.S., tel. 800-308-3394) offers charters aboard a 12-meter Topaz and seven-meter Boston Whaler.

War Eagle Sportfishing (tel./fax 575-0838; in the U.S., tel. 714-632-5285, fax 714-632-1027) offers multiday charters from Golfito and also serves Flamingo, Quepos, Caño Island, and Drake Bay aboard the 16-meter Hattera *War Eagle.*

Fishing expert Wayne Nordstrom recommends Steve Lino and his two boats, the nine-meter *Lucky Strike* and seven-meter *Show Time* (Apdo. 73, Golfito, tel. 288-5083, fax 775-0373).

PACIFIC FISHING LODGES

The following specialize in sportfishing and are a handful selected from resorts offering fishing.

Bahía Pez Vela (Apdo. 7758, San José 1000, tel. 221-1586, fax 221-3594) nestles in its own tiny, secluded cove. Six basic but adequate a/c cabinas on a small rise catch the breeze. Each has two double beds, lots of light, and a private bathroom with hot water, plus a veranda looking out over the ocean. Sportfishing runs are made in fully equipped nine-meter Boston Whalers and 11-meter Blue Marlins. Package rates (per boat) include transfers, accommodation, meals, liquor, tackle, and fishing. Rate: $1575 (four nights, three days fishing).

Golfito Sailfish Rancho (tel. 235-7766; in the U.S., P.O. Box 290190, San Antonio, TX 78280, tel. 800-531-7232, fax 512-377-0454) nestles against a jungle backdrop in the Golfo Dulce. It has 10 rooms, each with beamed ceilings and soaring roofs. The landscaped grounds contain sea-view terraces and paved trails leading back into the jungle. The lodge offers a guarantee for anglers spending more than three days at the lodge: if you don't get at least one sailfish, you come back and stay free. Several IGFA world records have been set from the lodge. The lodge operates catch-and-release sportfishing trips. Rates: $1395 d for three days; $2395 d seven days, all-inclusive of alcohol, laundry, meals, etc.

Guanamar Beach and Sportfishing Resort (Apdo. 7-1880, San José 1000, tel. 220-0722, fax 220-2095; in the U.S., Costa Sol International, 1717 N. Bayshore Dr., Suite 3333, Miami, FL 33132, tel. 800-245-8420 or 305-539-1630, fax 305-539-1123) is a deluxe resort at Playa Carrillo, just south of Sámara, on the Nicoya Peninsula. About 40 cabinas—some thatched—cascade down the hillside. The resort has a romantic rough wood-and-thatch restaurant, and even a small casino. Boats regularly report "Super Grand Slams"—all three species of marlin and one or more sailfish taken on the same day. Rates: $110-120 s/d, $165 suite, $10 each additional person.

Villas Pacífica (Apdo. 10, Santa Cruz, tel. 680-0932, fax 680-0981; in the U.S., 6387-B Camp Bowie Blvd., Suite 333, Fort Worth, TX 76116, tel. 817-738-1646, fax 817-738-9240) is one of the finest deluxe resorts in the country. The complex enjoys a lofty and luxurious setting overlooking the ocean. The resort has five deluxe two-bedroom villas (two people per room minimum), each with a/c, twin bathrooms, full American kitchen, dining room, large living room, and veranda. Each sleeps six guests. The hotel specializes in anglers' packages (inquire for special rates) and offers a wide range of charter boats from $550 to $950 half day, $750 to $1250 full day. Rates: $105 s/d, $125 t, $150 quad.

INLAND AND COASTAL FISHING

Part of the beauty of fishing Costa Rica, says one fisherman, is that "you can fish the Caribbean at dawn, try the Pacific in the afternoon, and still have time to watch a sunset from a mountain stream." Forget the sunset! There're fish in them thar' mountains. A freshwater fishing license is mandatory; the limit is a maximum of five specimens (of any one species) per angler per day. The closed season is Sept.-Dec., inclusive.

Lakes and Mountain Streams
More than a dozen inland rivers provide lots of action on rainbow trout, *machaca* (Central America's answer to American shad), drum, *guapote, mojarra* (Costa Rica's bluegill with teeth!), *bobo* (a moss-eating mullet that adapted to fresh water thousands of years ago), and other freshwater and tidal species in season. Not too many rivers are easily reached, however. Your best bet is the **Río Savegre** and other streams around San Gerardo de Dota, Copey and Cañon (see "South of San José" at the end of the Central Highlands chapter).

Caño Negro Lagoon and the waters of the Río San Juan are virtually untouched but represent fabulous horizons for powerful snook and tarpon. Lake Arenal is famed for its feisty rainbow bass *(guapote)* running 3.5 kilograms or more. Lake Arenal boasts the world record for guapote (5.2 kilograms), set in 1986, although everyone expects the record to be broken here soon.

CARIBBEAN FISHING LODGES

Casa Mar (Apdo. 825, San José, tel. 441-2820, fax 433-9287; or, in the U.S., P.O. Box 787, Islamorada, FL 33036, tel. 800-327-2880 or 305-664-4615), at Barra del Colorado, offers 12 comfortable duplex cabins set in attractive landscaped grounds in fishing season, Sept.-Oct. and Jan.-May.

Isla de Pesca (Apdo. 8-4390, San José 1000, tel. 223-4560, fax 221-5148; in the U.S., Costa Sol International, 1717 N. Bayshore Dr., Suite 3333, Miami, FL 33132, tel. 800-245-8420 or 305-539-1632, fax 305-539-1123), on a private tropical island close to the mouth of the Río Colorado, offers 20 thatched A-frame cabins with porches, ceiling fans, and hot water. Open year-round; offers three-, five-, and seven-day packages for $999-1375.

Parismino Tarpon Rancho was recently taken over by Sportsfishing Costa Rica (Apdo. 115, La Uruca, San José 1150, tel. 233-3892 or 257-3553, fax 223-6728 or 222-1760; in the U.S., tel. 800-862-1003). It sits on six hectares of landscaped grounds fronting the lagoon and features a two-story building housing a bar, gift shop, and restaurant where hearty meals are served at big homely tables. Five additional structures house 30 private rooms built in hardwoods, with two full-size double beds, ceiling fans, and hot-water showers. A full fleet of sportfishing boats caters to anglers year-round. Offshore fishing is offered from the hulking steel-hulled *King Kong*, a "mothership" that ferries the resort's fishing boats beyond the dangerous breakers at the mouth of the Río Parismina. Rates: $225 per person, two nights; $420 three nights, including fishing.

Río Colorado Lodge (12301 N. Oregon Ave., Tampa, FL 33612, tel. 800-243-9777 or 813-931-4849, fax 813-933-3280; in Costa Rica, Apdo. 5094, San José 1000, tel. 232-8610 or 232-4063, fax 321-5987), right at the mouth of the Río Colorado, is the most upscale sportfishing lodge on the Caribbean. Its 18 comfortable individual rooms are open to the breeze and have private baths, hot showers, electric fans, and daily laundry service. The lodge is equipped with a complete tackle shop, plus a large fleet of 5.5-meter boats with two fighting chairs. It offers five-, six-, and seven-night packages, including air transfers from San José ($1275-1945). Extra fishing days are $375. Rate for nonfishing guests is $75 per day.

Silver King Lodge (tel. 288-0849, fax 288-1403; in the U.S., Aerocasillas, Dept. 1597, P.O. Box 025216, Miami, FL 33102, tel. 800-847-3474 or 813-942-7959, fax 813-943-8783) offers 10 spacious duplexes, widely spaced and linked by covered catwalks. All cabins have queen-size beds with orthopedic mattresses, plus private baths with their own water heaters and large showers. Other features include a Jacuzzi, well-equipped tackle shop, plus a spacious bar and restaurant in hardwoods with a wide-screen TV and VCR. Free beer, rum, and soft drinks are included. Fishing is from 10 six-meter Carolina skiffs and offshore boat (and five-meter aluminium canoes for rainforest fishing). Package prices—from $1195 (single) for three days fishing to $2245 (double) for five days—include roundtrip air from the U.S., alcoholic drinks, meals, transfers, and laundry service.

Tortuga Lodge (Apdo. 6941, San José 1000, tel. 257-0766, fax 257-1665), owned and operated by Costa Rica Expeditions, is an upscale jungle lodge in the heart of Tortuguero National Park, on the Río Tortuga. Highly recommended. The lodge has 18 spacious and comfortable riverfront cabinas on 20 hectares of attractive landscaped grounds replete with ornamental plants. Standard and "deluxe" rooms (each with ceiling fans plus fully equipped bathrooms) are in thatched lodges made of attractive hardwoods and fronted by wide verandas with leather rocking chairs. English-speaking staff and superb guides are under the assured management of Eduardo Brown Silva, who holds the world cubera snapper record. Good-quality meals are served family-style. Rates: $50-66 s, $59-79 d, $70-92 t.

Lodges can obtain your freshwater fishing permit. Or, you can obtain one from the Department of Agriculture in San José (Ministerio de Agricultura, Calle 1 and Avenida 1, tel. 223-0829). Reportedly, permits can also be obtained from the Banco Nacional de Costa Rica (Avenida 1, Calles 2/4; 9 a.m.-3 p.m. weekdays). Cost is approximately $12.

Caribbean

Costa Rica's northeastern shores, lowland lagoons, and rivers offer the world's hottest tarpon

and snook action for the light-tackle enthusiast. At prime fishing spots, tarpon average 35 kilograms (sometimes reaching up to 70 kilograms). These silver rockets are caught in the jungle rivers and backwater lagoons, and ocean tarpon fishing just past the breakers is always dependable. Wherever you find them, you'll have your hands full; no other fish jumps, leaps, twists, and turns like the tarpon. Often, the fish will leap four meters and jump five or six times before you get it to the boat to be lipgaffed, hoisted for a photo, and released. When you tire of wrestling these snappy fighters, you can take on snook—another worthy opponent.

Fall, when the rain tapers down and winds swing onshore, flattening the rivermouths, is the best time to get a shot at the trophy snook that return to the beaches around the rivermouths to spawn. Anglers stand knee-deep in the surf and cast at five- to nine-kilogram snook. "Talk about excitement, there's nothing like it!" says Chet Young, owner of Angler's Connection. Snook will hit lures trolled or cast along the riverbanks, but the biggest fish are usually taken from the surf. The all-tackle IGFA record came from Costa Rica, which regularly delivers 14-kilogram fish.

Tarpon are caught year-round. Snook season runs from late August into January, with a peak Aug.-November. November-Jan. the area enjoys a run of *calba*, the local name for small snook that average two kilograms and are exceptional sport on light tackle, with 20 or more *calba* per angler in a typical day's catch. Jacks are also common year-round in Caribbean waters. They are voracious predators, and because they are extremely strong and have great endurance, they can be a challenge for any fisherman using light tackle.

Alas, the past few years have seen an alarming drop-off in numbers of snook caught because of "rampant" gillnetting. New regulations due to go into effect in 1995 should ease the situation.

The Río Colorado Lodge began experimenting with Caribbean offshore fishing in 1992. It may catch on. For now, most offshore fishing is relegated to the Pacific coast.

In addition to the many fishing lodges, another option is the *Rain Goddess* (c/o Blue

U.S. SPORTFISHING OPERATORS

Angle Adventures, P.O. Box 872, Old Lyme, CT 06371, tel. (203) 434-9624 or (800) 628-1447

Angler's Connection, 3220 W. Sepulveda Blvd. #B, Torrance, CA 90505, tel. (213) 325-9628 or (800) 624-8429

Coral Way Tours, 9745 Sunset Dr. #104, Miami, FL 33173, tel. (305) 279-3252 or (800) 882-4665.

Costa Rican Adventures, 2221 Palo Verde Avenue, Suite 1D, Long Beach, CA 90815, tel. (800) 451-6997 (in CA) or (800) 458-3688, fax (213) 596-5666

Dockside Tours, 339 Hickory Ave., Harahan, LA 70123, tel. 504-734-5868 or (800) 235-DOCK, fax (504) 737-2998; four-day packages, including two days fishing

Fishing International, P.O. Box 2132, Santa Rosa, CA 95405, tel. (707) 542-4242 or (800) 950-4242; FIT fishing packages

Fishing Travel, 2525 Nevada Avenue N, Golden Valley, MN 55427

Rod and Reel Adventures, 3507 Tully Rd. #5, Modesto, CA 95356-1020, tel. (209) 524-7775 or (800) 356-6982, fax (209) 524-1220). Wide range of options in Costa Rica.

Wing International, Apdo. 850, Escazú 1250, tel. 231-4299, fax 231-3816; in the U.S., tel. 800-308-3394), a luxurious 20-meter a/c houseboat dedicated to fishing the San Juan and Colorado rivers on three- to seven-day excursions.

GOLFING

Pack your bags and head south! Costa Rica is about to put itself on the golfing map!

Before 1995, Costa Rica had just two courses worth the time, both associated with luxury resorts—the **Hotel Cariari and Country Club** outside San José, and the **Hotel Tango Mar** overlooking the Gulf of Nicoya on the Pacific coast. **Morris Overseas Tours** (418 4th Ave., Melbourne Beach, FL 32951, tel. 407-725-4809

or 800-777-6853) is the exclusive U.S. representative for golfing adventures at the two resorts.

The Cariari course is Costa Rica's championship golf course. Tom Watson, Greg Norman, Raymond Floyd, and Chi Chi Rodriguez have played the annual Friendship Golf Tourney and American Professional Golf Tourney held here. The Tango Mar resort course is the Pebble Beach of Costa Rica. It's a nine-hole layout on 1,765 meters, but a good challenge for the average golfer. The longest hole is 270 meters, the shortest only 110, but some of the holes have 15-meter trees blocking the middle of the fairway—when teeing off, do you go over or under?

Three other nine-hole courses are at the **Costa Rica Country Club** in Escazú; the **Los Reyes Country Club** in La Guácima, near Alajuela; and the **El Castillo Country Club** above Heredia.

At press time, two 18-hole courses were close to completion in **Bahía Culebra** and another at the **Meliá Playa Conchal Hotel,** in Guanacaste. Work was half-complete, too, on an 18-hole championship course at Playa Grande, part of the Rancho Las Colinas Golf and Country Club, also in Guanacaste (the front nine were due to be ready for play by mid-1995; the back nine by mid-1996; tel. 293-4644). Another course was slated to open soon as part of the Pueblo Real resort complex north of Quepos. The biggest development of all, however, is a 27-hole resort—**La Roca Beach Resort and Country Club**—to be constructed two miles north of Puerto Caldera.

Costa Sol International (Apdo. 7-1880, Ciudad Cariari, San José 1000, tel. 239-1025, fax 239-2405), one of the country's most respected tour operations, offers a four-day "Golf Escape" and a weeklong "Golf n' Surf" package.

HIKING

Surprisingly few organized tours cater to the hiking enthusiast. Those that exist are mostly one-day hikes of the upland slopes of volcanoes. Half-day or full-day hiking tours with a professional guide can generally be arranged

through jungle and mountain lodges or by travel agencies and tour operators in San José.

Be sure to prepare fully for your foray: a map, sunscreen, sun hat, insect repellent, protection against chiggers (see "Health Care"), and plenty of water. Raingear and a warm sweater or jacket are essential for hiking at higher elevations. In the rainy season, hiking can resemble mud-wrestling. The **Army & Navy Surplus Store** in Moravia, northeast of San José, can outfit you with lightweight thermal sleeping bags, hiking boots, water canteens, rain ponchos, and other hiking and camping equipment.

Most reserves and national parks maintain marked trails. However, hiking in the more remote parks may require stamina, a high degree of self-sufficiency, knee-high rubber boots, and, says one writer, "a guide so comfortable with a machete he can pick your teeth with it."

The hardy and adventurous might try a strenuous hike to the peak of Chirripó, Costa Rica's tallest mountain (see special topic "Climbing Chirripó" for full details).

A word of warning for those setting out alone to hike through the mountain-forests of the Caribbean: the *duendes* dwell here—little men covered with long gray hair who will cut off your thumbs if they get a chance because they have none of their own!

Jungle Trails (Apdo. 2413, San José 1000, tel. 255-3486, fax 255-2782) specializes in hiking tours, including a one-day "Walk in the Cloud Forest" on Barva Volcano (within Braulio Carrillo National Park), and two-day hikes on Barva and Poás volcanoes. **Wildland Adventures** (3516 N.E. 155th St., Seattle, WA 98155, tel. 206-365-0686 or 800-345-4453) has an 11-day "Hiking Safari" that includes Palo Verde, Arenal, Cahuita, and the remote Cocles Indian Reserve and Manzanillo Wildlife Reserve (camping). You'll hike, too, on the company's 10-day "Tropical Trails Odyssey" and eight-day "Pacific Highlands and Jungles" trips. *Recommended!*

Backroads (1526 5th St., Berkeley, CA 94710, tel. 800-245-3874 or 510-527-1555, fax 510-527-1444) offers a seven-day walking trip that includes Lake Arenal, Fortuna Falls, Monteverde Cloud Forest, Cabo Blanco Nature Reserve, and Curú. Departures are Dec.-April (about. $1550). **Country Walkers** (P.O.

Box 180, Waterbury, VT 05676-0180, tel. 802-244-1387, fax 802-244-5661) likewise features an eight-day walk in Costa Rica, with departures January, March, April, October, and November.

No one was offering llama treks, but you *can* hike with "earless goats" as your trusty companions and guides. Contact **Para Las Orejas** (tel./fax 279-9752).

Adventure Expeditions (21346 St. Andrews Blvd. #411, Boca Raton, Fl 33433, tel. 800-497-3422 or tel./fax 407-487-4465) features hiking in its five- to 20-day "Sports Safaris."

HORSEBACK RIDING

Horseback riding is very popular in Costa Rica, especially in Guanacaste Province, the nation's "old west" cattle-ranching area where horses are still the traditional means of transportation. The native horse of Costa Rica is the *crillo*, a small, big-chested creature of good temperament, resistant to ticks and the pesky *torsalo* fly. Taller, heavier horses from the north don't work well in the tropics, although Lipizzans, Peruvians, and Andalusians are common.

In Santa Ana (about nine km west of San José), **Club Paso Fino** (tel. 249-1466) provides instruction in riding, and the **Club Hípico la Caraña** (tel. 228-6106) offers intensive riding clinics. The latter, known simply as La Caraña, boasts two covered exhibition and practice arenas, an open-air jumping ring, and more than 100 stables. It even has an Olympic-size swimming pool for a refreshing dip after riding. The club also offers guided horseback tours into the Santa Ana mountains, or simply canter around the club's 15 acres.

Travel agencies and tour operators in San José can arrange half- or full-day rides at ranches and mountain lodges throughout the country. Prices average $70 for a full-day tour, including lunch. **Rico Tours** (Apdo. 883, San José 1002, tel. 233-9658, fax 233-9357; in the U.S., 13809 Research Blvd. #606, Austin, TX 78750, tel. 512-331-0918, fax 512-331-8765) offers a number of interesting horseback tours, including a 10-day "Horse Trekking Adventure."

Ranches and Lodges
The following ranches and lodges specialize in horseback rides. The horses are usually the same ones used by the ranch *sabaneros*, so they're not the downtrodden mounts typical of so many horses for rent.

In Guanacaste: Finca San Antonio (c/o Las Espuelas, Apdo. 1056, San José 1007, tel. 666-0144, fax 233-1787); **Hacienda Los Inocentes,** near La Cruz; **Dundee Ranch Hotel** and **Hacienda Doña Marta,** near Orotina; **Hacienda Guachipelín,** on the flanks of Rincón de la Vieja volcano; and **Finca Los Angeles** (c/o Central American Tours, Apdo. 531, San José 1000, tel. 255-4111, fax 255-4216), near Orotina.

Elsewhere: Hacienda San Miguel (tel. 229-1094), at Rancho Redondo, offers horseback rides through cloud forest. **Hacienda Santa María** (Apdo. 463, San José 1000, tel. 253-6514, fax 234-0958) is a working ranch midway between San José and the central Pacific. Horseback rides through Braulio Carrillo National Park are offered from **La Posada** (tel. 237-2116, fax 237-1976), and at **Hacienda Retes** (c/o Magic Trails, tel. 253-8146).

There are dozens of other options (see regional chapters). Wherever you are, ask around. Someone local is sure to rent horses.

Costa Rican Tour Operators
Horizontes (Apdo. 1780, San José 1002, tel. 222-2022, fax 255-4513) lists a one-day ride on Orotina Ranch, with lunch at a beach on the Pacific ocean. **Jungle Trails** (Apdo. 2413, San José 1000, tel. 255-3486, fax 255-2782) has two horseback riding tours: a three-day program in Rincón de la Vieja National Park, and a one-day trip in the central Pacific.

Horseback riding at San Antonio Ranch is featured in a series of three- to eight-day tours offered by **L.A. Tours** (Apdo. 492, Centro Colón 1007, tel. 224-5828). **Papagayo Excursions** (Apdo. 35, Santa Cruz de Guanacaste, tel. 680-0859, fax 680-0859) has half-day guided horseback "nature safaris." **Tikal Tour Operators** (Apdo. 6398, San José 1000, tel. 223-2811, fax 223-1916) features horseback riding (with options for beginners and more experienced riders) at its Ecoadventure Lodge at Coter Lake. **Tipical Tours** (tel. 233-

Hacienda Guachipelín offers horseback rides up Rincón de la Vieja.

8486) has horseback tours in the Talamanca mountains. **Magic Trails** (tel. 253-8146) offers rides on the flanks of Irazú volcano; **Rainbow Tours** (tel. 233-8228) has tours at Rancho Nuevo, near Carara Biological Reserve; and **Robles Tours** (tel. 237-2116) offers riding adventures on its farm near Sacramento, bordering Braulio Carrillo National Park.

On the Atlantic coast, **Tropical Adventure Tours** (Apdo. 1362, San José 1000, tel. 222-8974, fax 255-0306) has a series of half-day guided horseback tours, including to the Keko-Ldi Indian Reserve and Gandoca-Manzanillo Wildlife Refuge.

U.S. Tour Operators
Mariah Wilderness Expeditions (P.O. Box 248, Point Richmond, CA 94807, tel. 510-233-2303 or 800-462-7424) includes horseback riding on Barva volcano as part of an eight-day adventure tour of Costa Rica, plus a full day on horseback at Gandoca-Manzanillo Wildlife Refuge during an eight-day "Jungles Off-the-Beaten-Track" tour of the Caribbean.

Playing the Marlboro Man
City slickers longing to be the Marlboro Man can pay perfectly good money to work hard and get coated with dust and manure at **Los Vaqueros** (Apdo. 627, San José 2100, tel. 233-3435, fax 221-5884), near Punta Morales, in Guanacaste. The farm offers one-day cattle drives led by workaday cowboys, and greenhorns are welcome to tag along for the ride. The chorus of mooing and slapping of Levis against leather saddles combines with a rest on the beach as you drive cattle to where the grass is greener to get them ready for the American supermarkets.

MOTORCYCLE TOURING

Motorbike enthusiasts haven't been left out of the two-wheel touring business. A Peruvian off-road racer named Larrabure established Costa Rica's first motorcycle touring service: **Moto Aventura** (Apdo. 4188, San José 1000, tel. 255-4174, fax 221-9233). The company uses Husqvarna four-stroke 610s for a variety of enduro rides from one day ($50) to two weeks, all-inclusive. Its office is 150 meters west of the Sala Garbo Theater (Avenida 2, Calles 30/32).

In 1995, **Costa Rican Trails** (tel. 233-0557 or 221-5800, fax 257-4655) introduced a 10-day "Trails' Fly-N-Ride" tour using gleaming new BMW F650 Fonduro motorcycles and guided by Wilhelm von Breymann, whose father happens to have the San José BMW concession. Poás, Arenal, Caño Negro, the Nicoya peninsula, and central Pacific coast are included. Cost of $1500 includes all breakfasts, support van, hotels, etc. A 16-day tour of Costa Rica and Panamá is also offered.

Getting in on the act, too, is **Eko-Alternativo Tours** (Apdo. 1287, San José 1002, tel. 221-6476, fax 223-7601), which offers an eight-day motorcycle tour of the central highlands, Arenal, and Nicoya ($675).

NATURAL HISTORY

Costa Rica is replete with tour operators offering natural-history programs to suit every interest,

NATURAL-HISTORY TOURS (U.S. COMPANIES)

Abercrombie & Kent, 1520 Kensington Rd., Oak Brook, IL 60521, tel. (800) 323-7308. Features a 12-day "Nature of Costa Rica" tour focusing on the country's diverse ecosystems.

Academic Study Associates, P.O. Box 38, Armonk, NY 10504, tel. (800) 752-2250. Offers both a "Family Rain Forest Exploration" and "Student Rain Forest Workshop."

Big Five Tours & Expeditions, 110 Route 110, S. Huntington, NY 11746, tel. (516) 424-2036 or (800) 445-7002. Nature tours include a nine-night "Costa Rica Explorer" that includes Monteverde Cloud Forest Preserve, Arenal volcano, Caño Negro National Wildlife Refuge, Tortuguero National Park, plus whitewater rafting (from $1303).

Cheeseman's Ecology Safaris, 20800 Kittredge Rd., Saratoga, CA 95070, tel. (408) 867-1371 or (800) 527-5330. Annual 14-day nature tour that covers a diversity of ecosystems ($2925).

Geostar Travel, 1240 Century Ct., Suite C, Santa Rosa, CA 95403, tel. (707) 579-2420 or (800) 624-6633, fax (707) 579-2704. Offers three nature tours with departures year-round: "Costa Rica Naturally" (seven days, from $1295), "Costa Rica Explorer" (10 days, from $1225), and "Costa Rica Odyssey" (10 days, from $1225).

Holbrook Travel, 3540 N.W. 13th St., Gainesville,

FL 32609, tel. (904) 377-7111 or (800) 451-7111. Has customized natural-history and educational itineraries for individuals, including a nine-day "Tropical Forest" trip ($1468) and a seven-night "Costa Rica Wildlife Adventure" ($1282).

International Expeditions, One Environs Park, Helena, AL 35080, tel. (205) 428-1700 or (800) 633-4734. Offers a 10-day nature tour that includes Tortuguero, Monteverde, Santa Rosa, and Palo Verde National Parks ($2198).

Latour, 15-22 215th St., Bayside, NY 11360, tel. (718) 229-6500 or (800) 825-0825. Features a nine-day "Eco-Explorer" (from $1925) to Carara, Monteverde, Caño Negro, Arenal, and the Quetzal Forest Preserve; and an eight-day "National Parks" tour (from $1575) including Los Angeles Cloud Forest, Manuel Antonio, and Carara.

Mariah Wilderness Expeditions, P.O. Box 248, Point Richmond, CA 94807, tel. (510) 233-2303 or (800) 4-MARIAH. Offers a nine-day "Volcanoes and Rainforests" program centered on Arenal volcano and Corcovado National Park ($1020), plus an eight-day "Cloud Forests and Caribbean" tour ($828), as well as a series of Costa Rica tours for the active traveler.

Mountain Travel/Sobek, 6420 Fairmount Ave., El Cerrito, CA 94530, tel. (510) 527-8100 or (800)

and the nation boasts scores of bilingual naturalist guides (Costa Rica has more American field biologists than anywhere else in the world). Professional guides generally know where the wildlife is at any given moment; they have an uncanny ability to identify the most well-camouflaged birds and beasts (in Manuel Antonio, I once stood for 20 minutes trying to spot a sloth that folks I'd met on the trail told me was sunning itself nearby; when a professional guide passed by, he identified it within moments). And you'll gain great pleasure from the knowledge they impart. Most nature tours are from one to four days; one-day tours cost $40-85, including lunch.

Nature tours are not for lounge lizards. They're often get-your-feet-wet kind of tours. You may be expected to endure hard treks through rainforest. The line between athleticism

and ecology in Costa Rica is tenuous at best. Just remember one caveat: you won't see much wildlife if you're moving quickly or noisily. Think slow, think small, think quiet.

Costa Rica Expeditions (Apdo. 6941, San José 1000, tel. 257-0766, fax 257-1665, e-mail, crexped@sol.racsa.co.cr) has a complete range of natural-history tour packages to destinations throughout Costa Rica. In addition to guided tours offered daily to eight prime forest habitats, the company offers specialist natural history and birding trips from its acclaimed Monteverde Lodge (Monteverde Cloud Forest) and Tortuga Lodge (Tortuguero National Park). CRE also offers "Women in Conservation," featuring field workshops to nature reserves such as Ostional, Monteverde, and Gandoca-Manzanillo Wildlife Refuge; trips are led by prominent fe-

227-2384, fax (510) 525-7710. Lists five departures on a nine-day "Natural History of Costa Rica" tour featuring visits to Tortuguero, Caño Island, Corcovado, Monteverde, and Poás (from $2095).

Natural Habitat Adventures, 2945 Center Green Ct. S., Boulder, CO 80301, tel. (303) 449-3711 or (800) 543-8917, fax (303) 449-3712. Offers a rainforest adventure to Tortuguero, Tiskita, and Monteverde.

Nature Expeditions International, P.O. Box 11496, Eugene, OR 97440, tel. (503) 484-6529 or (800) 869-0639. Lists a 15-day "Costa Rica Wildlife" tour featuring Monteverde, Poás, Santa Rosa, Tortuguero, and Corcovado (departures in Jan., March, July, and Dec., $2390).

Overseas Adventure Travel, 349 Broadway, Cambridge, MA 02139, tel. (617) 876-0533 or (800) 221-0814, fax (617) 876-0455. Offers a 15-day "Costa Rica Tropical Adventure" combining visits to Poás, Monteverde, Marenco, Corcovado, and Caño Island, and rafting on the Reventazón and Pacuare (from $2590). Departures Feb., March, April, June, Nov., and Dec. An eight-day tour is also listed ($1290).

Tropical Travel, 720 Worthshire, Houston, TX 77008, tel. (713) 869-3614 or (800) 451-8017, fax (713) 869-2540. Offers four natural-history programs, among them an eight-day "Naturalist's

Costa Rica" ($550-750); and a rugged seven-day "Caribbean Jungles Off the Beaten Path" ($889).

Wilderness Travel, 801 Allston Way, Berkeley, CA 94710, tel. (510) 548-0420 or (800) 247-6700. Has two natural-history programs: a 14-day "Costa Rica Wildlife" trip focusing on Tortuguero, Selva Verde, Monteverde, and Corcovado (from $2490); and a nine-day "River and Rainforests" tour, combining rafting on the Pacuare and Reventazón with visits to Monteverde, Carara, and Poás (from $1590).

Wildland Adventures, 3516 N.E. 155th, Seattle, WA 98155, tel. (206) 365-0686 or (800) 345-4453. Offers a "Wildlands Family Odyssey" (10 days, $1680) with visits to national parks throughout the country, plus three trips emphasizing wildlife and tropical ecology: an 11-day "Tropical Trails Odyssey" featuring visits to Monteverde, Carara, Manuel Antonio, Marenco, and Corcovado ($1595); a nine-day "Tortuguero Jungle Odyssey" timed to coincide with the green turtle nestings ($1395); and a 12-day "Wildlands Camping Safari" combining visits to national parks as far afield as Santa Rosa and Cahuita ($1545).

Many museums, universities, and zoos also offer natural history tours to Costa Rica. The **Cincinnati Zoo** (3400 Vine St., Cincinnati, OH 45220, tel. 513-281-4701), for example, features a springtime, 11-day tour to a diversity of national parks (about $2750).

male conservationists. The company was honored with a *Condé Nast Traveler* 1995 Ecotourism Award.

Costa Rica Experts (3166 N. Lincoln Ave. #424, Chicago, IL 60657, tel. 312-935-1009 or 800-827-9046, fax 312-935-9252) offers two- and three-day packages to various nature lodges, plus a 10-day "Costa Rica Explorer" (soft adventure) and 10-day "Odyssey" (hardy adventure) for nature lovers.

Horizontes (Apdo. 1780, San José 1002, tel. 222-2022, fax 255-4513) has a wide range of tour options at nature lodges nationwide, plus horseback riding and rafting; its stunning brochure—which includes a handy "Key to Adventure" chart showing which programs highlight birdwatching, and other special activities—should convince you to put your money down! **Jungle Trails** (Apdo. 2413, San José 1000,

tel. 255-3486, fax 255-2782) offers both a two-day "Rainforests of the Caribbean" tour and a six-day rainforest study-tour in Corcovado National Park. **Eko-Alternativo Tours** (Apdo. 1287, San José 1002, tel. 221-6476, fax 223-7601) calls itself a "National Park Specialist," and has a series of tours to national parks and reserves.

Adventure Expeditions (21346 St. Andrews Blvd. #411, Boca Raton, Fl 33433, tel. 800-497-3422 or 407-487-4465) offers a series of "Nature Getaways" (five to seven days) that can be customized to your specific adventure travel interests.

Other companies specializing in nature tours include: **Costa Rica Sun Tours** (Apdo. 1195, Escazú 1250, tel. 255-3418, fax 255-4410), **Geotur** (Apdo. 469 Y Griega, San José 1011, tel. 234-1867, fax 253-6338), **Costa Rica Temp-**

tations (Apdo. 1199, San José 1200, tel. 220-
4437 or 220-3169, fax 220-2792), **Costa Rican
Trails** (Apdo. 2907, San José 1000, tel. 222-
4547 or 221-3011), **Tikal Tour Operators**
(Apdo. 6398, San José 1000, tel. 223-2811, fax
223-1916), **Exotur** (Apdo. 1394, Y Griega, San
José 1011, tel. 227-5169, fax 227-2180), and
Tropical Adventure Tours (Apdo. 1362, San
José 1000, tel. 222-8974, fax 255-0306).

Fantasía Ecológica (Apdo. 1500, San José
1002, tel. 220-2515, fax 222-3216) offers three-
to 14-day ecological study tours in association
with the International University of the Americas,
with lectures provided by university faculty, who
also act as guides.

An exciting recent addition is the **Route of
Biodiversity**, a 24-night comprehensive off-the-
beaten-path tour to a variety of ecosystems,
many quite remote, with travel by 4WD. In the
U.S., contact **Costa Rica Experts** (3166 N. Lincoln Ave. #424, Chicago, IL 60657, tel. 800-827-
9046 or 312-935-1009, fax 312-935-9252). In
Costa Rica, contact **Costa Rica Temptations**
(see above), which divides the Route (which incorporates the entire country) into regional sections; you can choose certain sections according
to interest and schedule. The ratio of participants to guides is never more than six per guide.
Lecturers accompany the tour. Cost is approximately $187 per day, all-inclusive.

I highly recommend a four- to six-day natural-
history cruise tour aboard the *Temptress Explorer* (see "Natural-History Cruise Tours," this
section).

For Orchid Lovers
Costa Rica Connections (975 Osos St., San
Luis Obispo, CA 93401, tel. 805-543-8823 or
800-345-7422) has an annual Costa Rica National Orchid Show tour ($1795 from Miami), in-
cluding excursions to several national parks.
Geostar Travel (6050 Commerce Blvd., Suite
110, Rohnert Park, CA 94928, tel. 707-584-9552
or 800-633-6633) also offers both seven- and
10-day botanical trips to Costa Rica, with a special focus on orchids. The **Brooklyn Botanic
Garden** (1000 Washington Ave., Brooklyn, NY
11225) offers a 14-day Costa Rica trip for orchid
lovers and botanists each January. Also see "Orchids," in the section on "Flora" in the Introduction.

SCUBA DIVING

Less than a decade ago, Costa Rica was virtually unknown as a destination for diving. Suddenly it is being applauded for the vast variety
and abundance of its marinelife. Operators are
opening up miles of undisturbed coastline and
inshore islands. New facilities along the Pacific
coast now offer first-class dive boats and fully
stocked dive shops. And divers have the excitement of truly virgin diving in areas never before explored. Visibility, unfortunately, ranges
only 6-24 meters, but water temperatures are a
steady 24-29° C (75-85° F) or higher. That said,
people looking for underwater adventure *may* be
happier in Belize, the Bay Islands of Honduras,
or in the Caribbean.

Would-be divers will find plenty of one-day
resort courses and PADI certification courses. A
wise investment is to join **Divers Alert Network**
(P.O. Box 3823, Duke University Medical Center, Durham, NC 27710, tel. 919-684-8111),
which provides emergency medical evacuation,
treatment, and referral services.

Pacific
Most recent dive-site development has been
along the Pacific coast of Guanacaste Province.
You'll see little live coral and few reefs. In their
place divers find an astounding variety and number of fish, soft corals, and invertebrates—a result of the abundant plankton and other marine
organisms that thrive in the warm tropical waters.
Most diving is around rock formations: the typical site is alongside a rocky island or partially
submerged rocky pinnacles a mile or more offshore. Visibility can often be obscured (particularly in rainy season, May-Nov., where rivers
enter the ocean; where rivers are absent, visibility is enhanced during this period), but on
calm days you may be rewarded with densities
of marinelife that cannot be found anywhere in
the Caribbean.

Favored dive destinations in the Pacific northwest include Murcielagos Island and the Catalina
Islands. Both locations teem with grouper, snapper, jacks, sharks, and giant mantas, as well as indigenous tropical species. Dozens of morays peer
out from beneath rocky ledges. And schools of

tang, Cortez angelfish, bright yellow butterflies, and eagle rays are common. Great bull sharks congregate at a place called "Big Scare," at the farthest point of Murcielagos (the place is aptly named and is recommended for advanced open-water divers: it can scare the hell out of neophytes!). The two island chains are challenging because of their strong currents and surges.

Quality dive operations to the Murcielagos and Catalinas are offered by **Dive Safaris de Costa Rica** (P.O. Box 121, Playa del Coco, Guanacaste 5019, tel./fax 670-0012), based at El Ocotal (see "The Northern Beaches" in the Nicoya Peninsula chapter). PADI instructors provide certification, resort dive courses, and a wide range of specialty dives. Daily dive trips leave at 9 a.m. and 1:30 p.m. Divers go off from an 8.5-meter dive platform boat, 10-meter yacht, and 10-meter dive pontoon. You can rent cameras and strobes. The company also provides the diving services offered at La Costa in Playa Hermosa, Costa Smeralda in Playa Panamá, Malinche Real in Playa Arenilla (just north of Playa Panamá, and Vista Ocotal and Villa Casa Blanca in Playa Ocotal. **Condovac La Costa** resort in Playa Hermosa (see "The Northern Beaches" in the Nicoya Peninsula chapter) has local dive spots that are home to huge schools of tropical fish, unusual hogfish, parrot fish, giant jewfish, turtles, and an array of starfish, crustaceans, clown shrimp, and shellfish.

At the Punta Gorda dive site, six km west of El Ocotal, thousands of eagle rays have been known to swim by in columns that take more than 10 minutes to pass from start to finish. And divers can drop into select spots where whale sharks bask on the bottom at a depth of 12 meters. Divers also report seeing black marlin cruising gracefully around pinnacle rocks; at Las Corridas, only one km from El Ocotal, you're sure to come face to face with one of the 180-kilogram jewfish that dwell here.

Mario Vargas Expeditions (tel./fax 670-0351) and **Rich Coast Diving** (tel. 670-0176, fax 670-0165) also offer dive trips and PADI instruction at Playa del Coco.

Tropic World Diving Station (tel. 661-1915, fax 661-2069) operates diving programs, including PADI certification courses, out of Playa

---

U.S. SCUBA TOUR OPERATORS

Go Diving!, 7630 West 78th St., Minneapolis, MN 55435, tel. (612) 942-9687 or (800) 328-5285, fax (612) 942-8591

Ocean Connection, 211 E. Parkwood Ave. #108, Friendswood, TX 77546, tel. (713) 996-7800, fax (713) 996-1556

See & Sea Travel Service, 50 Francisco St., Suite 205, San Francisco, CA 94133, tel. (415) 434-3400 or (800) 348-9778

Tropical Adventures Travel, 111 2nd N., Seattle, WA 98109, tel. (206) 441-3483 or (800) 247-3483, fax (206) 441-5431

Underwater Adventure Tours, 732 W. Fullerton Ave., Chicago, IL 60614, tel. (312) 929-0717 or (800) 621-1274, fax (312) 929-2821

Tambor Beach Resort, near Cabo Blanco at the southern tip of Nicoya. South of Puntarenas, Bahía Herradura has an area known as El Jardín, famed for its formations of soft coral and sea fans. Charters operate from Puntarenas and Quepos, and **Mutra Tours** (Centro Comercial El Cruce, Escazú, tel. 232-6324, fax 231-2145) offers a one-day diving excursion ($125) from San José.

Farther south, Caño Island, just off the Osa Peninsula, has a reef that hosts a large variety of tropical fish, as well as groupers, snappers, wahoo, roosterfish, jacks, and tuna. About two km out from Caño is a near-vertical wall and parades of pelagic fish, including manta rays. The island is serviced by dive boats out of **Águila de Osa Inn** and **Marenco Biological Station** (see "The Osa Peninsula" in the Pacific Southwest chapter). Charters can also be arranged out of Quepos, and the deluxe cruise ship *Temptress Explorer* (see special topic "Natural History Cruise Tours," this section) offers scuba diving for certified divers at Caño during its one-week natural-history itineraries.

Escenarios Tropicales (Apdo. 2047, San José 1000, tel. 224-2555, fax 234-1554) specializes in dive tours, from one-day Tortuga Island to 10-day Cocos Island, using the *Undersea Hunter* (see below). **EcoTreks Adventure Company** (tel. 228-4029, fax 289-8191), with of-

fices in Escazú and Flamingo Beach, similarly offers a wide range of diving trips to a wide number of destinations, as does the yacht *S/Y Pollux* (tel. 231-4055, fax 231-3030).

Cocos Island

Divers from around the world descend on Costa Rica to make the journey to Cocos Island (550 km off the nation's southern Pacific coast), the subject of a Jacques Cousteau special. Its reputation for big animal encounters—whale sharks, hammerheads (sometimes 500 at a time), and mantas—have made it renowned.

Dive trips are available to Cocos Island aboard the *Okeanos Aggressor* and *Undersea Hunter,* which operate 10-day itineraries out of Puntarenas. The *Okeanos*—one of the world's classiest live-aboard dive vessels—is a 34-meter, nine-cabin ship with complete facilities for 18 divers, including an E-2-film processing lab. It is operated through **Cruceros del Sur** (Apdo. 1198, San José 1200, tel. 220-1927, fax 220-2103; in the U.S. contact Aggressor Fleet Ltd., P.O. Drawer K, Morgan City, LA 70381, tel. 504-385-2628, fax 504-384-0817). The *Hunter* is a 27-meter steel-hull ship with two compressors and 50 tanks, plus seven cabins and capacity for 12 divers; for information, contact **See & Sea Travel** (50 San Francisco St., Suite 205, San Francisco, CA 94133, tel. 415-434-3400 or 800-DIV-XPRT/348-9778) or **Escenarios Tropicales** (Apdo. 2047 San José 1000, tel./fax 224-2555).

The **Oceanic Society** (Fort Mason Center, Bldg. E, San Francisco, CA 94123, tel. 415-441-1106 or 800-326-7491, fax 415-474-3395) offers a "Biodiversity Study" trip as part of its marine science research project. No research experience is necessary; basic scuba certification is required.

S/Y Pollux (see above) offers eight- and 10-day Cocos Island diving adventures.

Tropical Adventures (111 2nd Ave. N, Seattle, WA 98109, tel. 800-247-3483 or 206-441-3483, fax 206-441-5431) also offers a Cocos Island package from the U.S.

Caribbean

The Caribbean coast has yet to develop a serious infrastructure catering to sport divers, despite good coral reefs. At Isla Uvita, just off-shore from Limón, are tropical fish, sea fans, and a coral reef, plus the wreck of the *Fenix,* a cargo ship that sank about a mile off the island years ago. There is a compressor in Puerto Limón, and you can rent boats for the run out to the island.

Farther south, at Cahuita, is Costa Rica's most beautiful coral reef, extending 500 meters out from Cahuita Point. The fan-shaped reef covers 593 hectares and has 35 species of coral, including the giant elkhorn. Two old shipwrecks—replete with cannons—lie on the Cahuita reef, seven meters down, playgrounds for more than 500 species of fish. The reef has suffered significant damage in recent years from sedimentation running down from the banana plantations, and there is concern that rapidly expanding hotel development will do further damage (see special topic "Coral Reef Destruction" in the Caribbean Coast chapter). The Gandoca-Manzanillo Wildlife Refuge protects a southern extension of the reef.

Best time for diving is during dry season (Feb.-April), when visibility is at its best. Check with park rangers for conditions, as the area is known for dangerous riptides.

Cahuita Tours & Rental (tel. 758-1515) can provide scuba-diving gear. If undersea caverns are your thing, check out Puerto Viejo, 20 km south of Cahuita. **Viajes Aventura Tropical** (Tropical Adventure Tours; Apdo. 1362, San José 1000, tel. 222-8974, fax 255-0306) has full-day and half-day diving packages to Cahuita, Puerto Viejo, and Punta Uva. **Mutra Tours** (Centro Comercial El Cruce, Escazú, tel. 232-6324, fax 231-2145) also has diving trips to Punta Uva, where you'll also find **Buceo Aquatour** (tel. 257-4466, ext. 8127), claiming to be the area's "only full service aqua-sport tour operator." The latter has a Zodiak launch boat ($45 one-tank; $350 four-day PADI certification).

SEA KAYAKING

This sport is quickly catching on in Costa Rica, and no wonder. The sea kayak's ability to move silently means you can travel unobtrusively, sneaking close up to wildlife without freaking it out. Dolphins and even turtles have been known

to surface alongside to check kayakers out. The long, slender one- and two-man craft provided are remarkably stable and ideally suited for investigating narrow coastal inlets and flat-water rivers larger vessels cannot reach. They allow you access to places you can't hope to reach by land.

The modern kayaks used for group-tour programs are seaworthy boats of fiberglass and plastic, with built-in watertight compartments to provide added buoyancy. And the basics of kayaking are easy to learn. Experienced guides give beginners introductory instruction on handling the craft, including a "dunk" test (deliberate rolling). The kayaks have rudders operated by foot pedals, which make steering in wind and waves remarkably easy. You'll paddle from one secluded beach to another or explore the shorelines of national parks. At night, you'll normally camp on an idyllic beach. An accompanying support boat generally carries the camping gear and personal belongings. The Gulf of Nicoya is particularly kind to sea kayakers, with sheltered waters and easily accessible parks to explore.

Tour Operators and Rentals

For rentals, try **Gulf Island Kayaking** (tel. 661-2392; in Canada, R.R. #1, Galiano Island, B.C., V0N 1P0, tel. 604-539-2442) or **Isla Gitana/Gypsy Island** (Apdo. 340, Puntarenas; or P.O. Box 250-C2, Selma, CA 93662).

Baja Expeditions (2625 Garnet Ave., San Diego, CA 92109, tel. 619-581-3311 or 800-843-6967) offers 10-day trips on the jungle-lined Río Cañas through Palo Verde National Forest and along the Pacific coast. Departures year-round. Six-day trips ($795) of Guanacaste and Nicoya, outfitted by Baja Expeditions, are also available Oct.-May through **American Wilderness Experience** (P.O. Box 1486, Boulder, CO 80306, tel. 303-444-2622 or 800-444-0099, fax 303-444-3999).

Mariah Wilderness Expeditions (P.O. Box 248, Point Richmond, CA 94807, tel. 510-233-2303 or 800-462-7424) features sea kayaking at Manuel Antonio as part of an eight-day "Tropical Adventure" trip that also includes cycling, rafting, and hiking.

Ríos Tropicales (Apdo. 472, San José 1200, tel. 233-6455, fax 255-4354), at Calle 32 and

Avenida 2, offers one-, two-, and three-day tours along the mangrove-lined tidal zone of Damas (five km north of Quepos), Manuel Antonio National Park, and remote Mogote Island. Prior kayaking or paddling experience is a must for the Manuel Antonio trips, as rough ocean conditions are often encountered. A 10-day kayaking trip in the Gulf of Nicoya is also offered, Dec.-May.

SURFING

Dedicated surfers are constantly in search of the perfect wave. For many, the search has ended in Costa Rica (the "Hawaii of Latin American surf"), where uncrowded beaches and a tantalizing array of waves have convinced devotees that this is as close to Nirvana as they'll ever get. Long stretches of beaches provide thousands of beach breaks. Numerous rivers offer quality sandbar rivermouth breaks, particularly on the Pacific coast. And coral reefs on the Caribbean coast, says Costa Rican surf expert Peter Brennan, "take the speed limit to the max." The reef breaks often hold more size and get more hollow (they're also shallower and more consistent) than the beach breaks.

Every level of surfer will find plenty of choice spots. If the surf blows out or goes flat before you are ready to pack it in for the day, you can simply jump over to the other coast, or—on the Pacific—head north or south. If one break isn't working, another is sure to be cooking. The water is warm. The beaches are uncrowded. And the waves are world class. You'll rarely see monster-size Hawaiian waves (except on the Caribbean coast south of Puerto Limón). Waves are generally smaller, although they occasionally grow to three-plus meters. They're nicely shaped, long, and tubular, and in places never-ending—often nearly a kilometer!

Approximately 10,000 foreign surfers annually make a pilgrimage to Costa Rica in search of waves, and many hotels and car rental companies offer discounts to surfers. Note, though, that the word is out, and many of the more popular surf spots are beginning to look crowded. The **Costa Rican Surf Association** (P.O. Box 393, Puntarenas 5400, tel. 661-0344) also sponsors four to six events a year. SANSA airline's

policy on carrying surfboards is subject to change; at last check it would not accept them.

Note: Beware riptides! Costa Rica's beaches are beautiful and the surf top-notch, but every year many tourists and surfers lose their lives to treacherous riptides. Lifeguards can be found at Jacó Beach and Manuel Antonio National Park. Elsewhere, you're on your own. (See "Riptides," under "Safety," below.) A free 24-hour **Costa Rican Surf Report** (tel. 233-7386) provides information on latest conditions. *Surf Guide* magazine provides information on virtually every beach in Costa Rica, and is published every six months by Consultoria Ecar Ltda. (Apdo. 694, 1100 Tibas, San José, tel./fax 253-3966). Also see *Costa Rica Outdoors* (Apdo. 199-6150, Santa Ana, tel./fax 282-6743; in the U.S., Dept. SJO 2316, P.O. Box 025216, Miami, FL 33102-5216), which has an update column on the surf scene.

Rentals

Surf shops are opening up throughout the country, and rentals can be arranged at coastal towns such as Jacó, Quepos, and Tamarindo. In San José, try **Mango Surf Shop** (tel. 225-1067) and **Keola Surf** (tel. 225-6041), both near the Banco Popular in San Pedro; and **Tsunami** in Los Yoses. **Shaka-Bra Dake** is a surf information center that also rents boards; it has offices in San Pedro (tel./fax 234-7508) and Escazú (tel. 289-8589). Also in Escazú is **EcoTreks** (tel. 228-4029, fax 289-8191), which rents and sells surf equipment and beachwear. It also has an outlet in the Flamingo Marina Hotel (see "Playa Flamingo" under "The Northern Beaches" in the Nicoya Peninsula chapter).

The **Beach Surf Shop** in Jacó (tel. 643-3036) is also reputedly good. Don't rely on being able to rent boards away from the most popular surf centers, however. If you have a board, bring it. Airline carriers require that you pack your board in a board bag. Generally, you will be allowed to count your board bag as one piece of luggage for international flights. Many surfers sell their boards in Costa Rica before returning home.

Tour Operators

Surf Costa Rica (P.O. Box 9009, Gainesville, FL 32607, tel. 904-371-8124 or 800-771-7873) offers surf tour packages for groups and individuals. Its "Surf Surfaris" (from $453 one week to $631 two weeks) include roundtrip airfare, free board travel, the 24-hour Costa Rican Surf Report, hotel lodging at the surf break of your choice, and fully surf-rigged 4WD rental vehicle. The company (founded and operated by Donald Larsson, organizer of the Da Bull's Annual Surfing Classic) also offers a 14-day "surf camp" (at the Tamarindo Resort Club) where you can learn to surf or learn to improve your technique ($1390 from Miami; $1625 from Los Angeles).

Tricolor Rent-a-Car (tel. 222-3333 or 800-949-0234, fax 221-4444) has a series of 11- and 16-day "4x4 Surfing Tours" promising "Good Waves, Good Climate, Virgins, and Wild Beaches." Sign me up! **Toucan Surf Tours** (2822 Newport Blvd., Suite 101, Newport Beach, CA 92663, tel. 714-673-2785, fax 714-675-1331) also offers surf tours to Costa Rica.

Caribbean

If you think there are no waves in the Caribbean, come to Costa Rica. Surfers in the know generally agree that the Caribbean coast is for experienced big-wave riders; the timid and inexperienced should stay on the Pacific coast. Although the Caribbean has only some 130 kilometers of surfable coast and fewer breaks than the Pacific, it's more accessible and offers great surfing during winter and spring. On the Caribbean, waves are short yet heartstoppingly powerful rides with sometimes Hawaiian-style radical waves. Occasionally massive swells sweep over the coral reefs, creating demanding tubes. You'll also experience exciting offshore cloud breaks, reef breaks, point breaks, and more than 80 kilometers of beach breaks.

The best time to surf this coast is late May through early September (hurricane season) and December through March (when Atlantic storms push through the Caribbean, creating three-meter swells).

Just north of Playa Bonita is Potrete, with a hollow right break at the south end of a small bay. It's very shallow. A 20-minute boat ride from Puerto Limón is Isla Uvita, with a strong and dangerous left. Farther south there are innumerable short breaks at Cahuita. Closing in on the Panamanian border, things really heat up!

Puerto Viejo has the biggest rideable waves in Costa Rica (up to seven meters at times, mostly in December), although these have diminished in size because of coastal uplift caused by the April 1991 earthquake. The mecca for surfers is Salsa Brava (so named for the "juice" the huge, tubular waves contain). The waves are now said to be a lot "tubier" since the 'quake and offer a right slide that "pitches out in a nasty manner that surfers love."

One expert recommends avoiding the Tortuguero region, where sharks are abundant.

Guanacaste

You're spoilt for choice here, although access to some surf beaches is difficult in rainy season. Accommodations, too, are often limited. The Pacific northwest offers more than 50 prime surf spots. The best time is during the rainy season (May-Oct.), when the surf can build to three meters; there are large offshore winds thoughout the dry season (Nov.-April), but the waves are smaller. Tamarindo is the surfing capital of Guanacaste (and Costa Rica), with lots of good surf spots within a short driving distance; it also offers good hotels and is an excellent jumping-off place for a surf safari south to more isolated beaches.

Hot spots such as Playa Naranjo (one of the best beach breaks in the country, with very strong offshore winds Dec.-March) in Santa Rosa National Park require 4WD or boat for access. You can rent a boat from Playa del Coco and other beach resorts for visits to Naranjo and Potrero Grande (also in Santa Rosa National Park), which has a right break, very fast and hollow. Here you'll find Ollie's Point, named after Oliver North, who masterminded a secret airstrip nearby to ferry weapons to the Nicaraguan rebels in the 1980s. "What Ollie probably never knew," says Peter Brennan, "is that just off the coast there's a hot right point."

Just north of Tamarindo is Playa Grande, with a five-km-long beach break acclaimed as one of the best in the world. Tamarindo itself has three main points, including Pico Pequeño, a rocky right point in front of the Hotel Tamarindo; El Estero, an excellent rivermouth; and Henry's Point, another rocky point in front of the **Third World Bar.**

There's fine surfing the whole way south from Tamarindo, including at Avellanas, with a "very hollow" beach break called "Guanacasteco," and breathtakingly beautiful Playa Negra, a narrow beach with very fast waves breaking over a coral- and urchin-encrusted shelf—definitely for experts only when the waves are big. Continuing south you'll find Nosara, Sámara, Camaronal, Coyote, Manzanillo, and Mal País, all with good surf.

Central Pacific

March through June are good. The best time, however, is during the heart of the rainy season (July-Dec.) when the Caribbean dies down and conditions along the central Pacific create a full spectrum of kilometer-long lefts, reef breaks, and powerful beach breaks.

The fun begins at Boca de Barranca, at the mouth of the Barranca River, a few kilometers south of Puntarenas (it's the closest surfing spot to San José). Boca reportedly has one of the world's longest—albeit slowest—lefts, which can run Malibu-style for more than a kilometer! Unfortunately, it has lost some of its luster because of its polluted water, but a new sewage-treatment plant for Puntarenas should restore Boca's image. Two miles south is Caldera, with a very good left called "Jetty Break." Playa Tivives and Valor also offer good beach breaks.

Central Pacific surfing centers on Jacó, though the waves really appeal to beginners and intermediates. Farther south lie Playa Hermosa (known as "Boom Boom Beach" to the locals), which has miles of expert beach breaks and an international contest every August, plus Escondida, Esterillos Este and Oeste, and Boca Damas.

Southern Pacific

Manuel Antonio has beach breaks, lefts, and rights. What it lacks in consistency it more than makes up for in natural beauty. Farther south lies Playa Dominical, which has "militant" sandbars and long point waves in an equally beautiful and classically tropical setting.

The Osa Peninsula has many virtually virgin surfing beaches. The cognoscenti head to Pavones, on the southern shore of the Golfo Dulce, to conquer, or at least encounter, what

one writer calls the "temple of zoom." On a decent day, the very fast, nearly one kilometer left break (one of the longest in the world) is "so long it will make your legs wobbly," according to Peter Brennan. Getting there in rainy season can be problematic. That doesn't stop the diehards, who pour in in droves. Then the waves are at their grandest, and the long left point can offer a three-minute ride.

WHITEWATER RAFTING/ CANOEING/KAYAKING

Whitewater rafting is the ultimate combination of beauty and thrill—an ideal way to savor Costa Rica's natural splendor, diverse ecosystems, and exotic wildlife, which have made river running here only slightly less popular than in the United States. A rafting trip is simply pure joy: a sort of bucking-bronco ride with soft pillows instead of a saddle.

Tour operators offer a wide range of whitewater programs, with ground transportation from San José and professional, bilingual guides. Generally, no experience is necessary. Families are catered to. Guests' desire for comfort is met with quality meals, and roomy tents and thick pads for sleeping on overnight trips. And unlike most other places, Costa Rica regulates its tourist industry, so all who conduct tours, including whitewater outfitters, are held to strict standards.

Because the land is so steep, streams pass through hugely varied landscapes within relatively short distances. A few Costa Rican rivers even have their sources in glacial lakes. At high elevations, Costa Rican rivers closely resemble those of California. Farther downstream, the water is warmer and rainforest lines the riverbanks. You'll tumble through a tropical fantasia of feathery bamboos, ferns, and palms as good as Walt Disney can offer: a rollercoaster ride amid glistening jungle entwined with vines and perhaps a green python or two. The sense of isolation is complete. Everything is as silent as a graveyard, except for the chattering monkeys and birds. With luck, you may even see small caiman in pools and shallows at lower elevations. Fear not if you fall in: piranhas are one South American fish species that hasn't reached Costa Rica. Just mind the crocodiles!

Everyone planning on running rivers themselves (as opposed to with an organized tour) should obtain a copy of *The Rivers of Costa Rica: A Canoeing, Kayaking, and Rafting Guide* by Michael W. Mayfield and Rafael E. Gallo (Menasha Ridge Press, 3169 Canaba Heights Rd., Birmingham, AL 35243; 1988). I won't attempt to replicate this splendid guide, which provides detailed maps plus a technical blow by blow account of virtually the entire river system.

What to Bring
Rafters are required to wear helmets and life jackets, which are provided by the tour operators. Generally, all you need bring is a swimsuit, a T-shirt, and tennis shoes or sneakers. Sunscreen is a good idea, as you are not only in the open all day but also exposed to reflections off the water. You'll also need an extra set of clothing, and perhaps a sweater or jacket, as you can easily get chilled if a breeze kicks up when you're wet. And you will get wet! Most operators provide a special waterproof bag for cameras, though you may wish to buy a waterproof bag for your camera before leaving the United States.

rafting on the Río Corobicí

WHITEWATER RAFTING

COSTA RICAN TOUR OPERATORS

One- to four-day trips are offered through the following Costa Rican-based whitewater specialists. Trips up to 10 days combine river rafting with a variety of other activities: hiking, bicycling, birdwatching, and/or kayaking, etc. Bookings can be made from North America or at most hotels and travel agents in San José. Prices start at $65 per person for one-day trips. Longer trips and class IV-V runs on the Guayabo and Upper Reventazón vary in price according to number of people.

Aventuras Naturales, Apdo. 812, San José 2050, tel. 225-3939, fax 253-6934

Costa Rica Expeditions, Apdo. 6941, San José 1000, tel. 257-0766, fax 257-1665

Costaricaraft, Apdo. 812, San Pedro 2050, tel. 225-3939, fax 253-6934

Costa Sol Rafting, Apdo. 8-4390, San José 1000, fax 233-6881; in North America, tel. (800) 245-8420

Pioneer Raft, Apdo. 29, Sabanilla, San José 2070, tel. 253-9132, fax 253-4687

Ríos Tropicales, Apdo. 472, San José 1200, tel. 233-6455, fax 255-4354

Safaris Corobicí, Apdo. 99, Cañas, Guanacaste, tel./fax 669-0544

U.S. TOUR OPERATORS

Mariah Wilderness Expeditions, P.O. Box 248, Point Richmond, CA 94807, tel. (510) 233-2303, (800) 4-MARIAH. A nine-day "Tropical Jungle Rafting" trip includes trips on the Corobicí, Reventazón, and Pacuare; $949. Departures are offered year-round. The company also features an eight-day cycling, rafting, and rainforest adventure program ($912).

Mountain Travel/Sobek, 6420 Fairmount Ave., El Cerrito, CA 94530, tel. (800) 227-2384, fax (510) 525-7710. The company offers a 10-day "Costa Rican Explorer," which features one-day rafting on the Reventazón as part of a soft-adventure package: $1325 (land only). A nine-day "Rivers of Costa Rica" tour combines rafting on the Chirripó and Pacuare rivers (wet season) and Pacuare and Reventazón (dry season); $1235 (land only).

Pioneer Raft, P.O. Box 22063, Carmel, CA 93922, tel. (408) 626-1815, (800) 288-2107, fax (408) 626-9013. Pioneer offers one-day tours on the Reventazón, Pacuare, Sarapiquí, and Corobicí rivers, and multiday tours on the Reventazón, Pacuare, and Chirripó.

In San José, you can buy or rent rafting and kayaking equipment from **Centro de Aventuras** (Paseo Colón, Calles 22/24).

When and Where

Generally, May-June and Sept.-Oct. are the best times for high water. Trips on the Reventazón, Pacuare, and Corobicí are offered year-round, although in dry season the latter two rivers can be barely runnable. Most other rivers are seasonal and become too low to paddle during dry season. Rivers are rated from class I to VI in degree of difficulty, with V considered for true experts only. The only class V river in the country is the Guayabo section of the Reventazón. Rafting experience is required for this trip; all other trips are generally offered to be-

ginners and intermediates. New rivers are constantly being opened up and additional options may be available by the time you read this. The following are the most popular runs.

Río Reventazón: Whitewater rafting enthusiasts will get more than their money's worth of excitement on the Reventazón (class II-V)—the name means "Bursting" in Spanish. The river tumbles out of Lake Cachí and cascades to the Caribbean lowlands in an exciting series of rapids, plus stretches of tranquil waters that provide the perfect combination of soothing calm and adventure. Beginners can savor class II and III rapids on the "Mid-Section," the most popular run for one-day trips. The Guayabo section offers extremely difficult class V runs: one rapid, El Horrendo, drops an awesome seven

THE FIGHT TO SAVE THE PACUARE

In 1985, the Costa Rican government recognized the Pacuare Gorge's scenic quality by making it a *zona protectora*, the first designated wild-and-scenic river in the country. But the national electricity agency, ICE, already had plans to dam the Pacuare in the gorge, which is one of the country's best potential sites for hydroelectric power generation. As ICE has pursued feasibility studies on its dam site—bulldozing riverbanks and blasting tunnels—the Pacuare has become the focus of a classic development-versus-preservation face-off.

The conflict flared up publicly during a commemoration ceremony for Earth Day 1990 in San José, when river activists interrupted speeches by Nobel Peace Prize laureate and then-President Oscar Arias Sánchez. Other activists began a camp-in the gorge in defiance of ICE's attempts to close it. The project—known as the Siquirres Hydroelectric Project—will inundate a 14-kilometer stretch of river and 1,250 hectares of surrounding wilderness. The ICE was to decide in 1994 whether or not to build the dam, after the feasibility study was completed, but at press time a decision was still pending. The project will cost an estimated $1 billion, presumably with a loan from the World Bank. The ICE dam has not been funded yet and will take at least 10 years to construct. In the meantime, significant erosion and deforestation goes on as exploratory mining takes place.

It is a hard decision for the country. The only alternative to such dams is for the nation to build diesel-powered electricity plants, which it can ill afford to do for both environmental and economic reasons.

If you're interested in helping save the Pacuare, contact the **Costa Rican Association for the Protection of the Rivers,** a nonprofit group of concerned citizens trying to promote "positive, environmentally compatible and sustainable alternatives" to ICE's project (CRAPR, Apdo. 4600, San José 1000, tel. 223-1925, fax 222-9936).

---

meters in one hundred meters. Constant rainfall allows operators to offer trips year-round; June and July are considered the best months.

Río Chirripó: The majestic Chirripó (class III-IV) runs down the slopes of the southwest Pacific and is recommended for two- to four-day trips. The river, which tumbles from its source on Mt. Chirripó, has been compared to California's Tuolomne and Idaho's Middle Fork of the Salmon, with massive volumes of water and giant waves. It produces more than 100 class III and IV rapids in its first 65 kilometers. The river runs into the Río General. Trips are offered Aug.-December.

Río General: This high-volume river is famous for its large, challenging rapids and big waves (including a six-meter wave at Chachala) ideal for surfing. Its "outlandish scenery" includes narrow, dramatic gorges and waterfalls, and giant iguanas by the score. Complex rapids follow in quick succession. Worth the trip in itself is The Whirlpool, which, say Mayfield and Gallo, "obligingly pulls entire boats underwater for several seconds before dissipating. Boats often spend two or three hours here spinning down the eddy line, giggling the afternoon away."

Río Sarapiquí: The Sarapiquí (class III) runs along the eastern flank of the Cordillera Central and drops to the Caribbean lowlands. It is noted for its crystal-clear water, variable terrain, and exciting rapids. Trips are offered May-December.

Río Corobicí: The Corobicí (class II) provides more of a float trip and makes an ideal half-day trip for families, with superb wildlife viewing and calms the whole way. The river is lined its whole length by a thin strip of tropical jungle, and howler monkeys, iguanas, coatis, boat-billed herons, egrets, and a host of other birds are common. The river flows westward through Guanacaste into the Gulf of Nicoya. It is runnable year-round.

Río Pacuare: For an in-depth immersion in nature, the Pacuare (class III-IV) is the best choice, a stunner even among all the other beauties as it slices through virgin rainforest, plunging through mountain gorges to spill onto the Caribbean plains near Siquirres. Toucans, monkeys, and other animals galore make this journey unforgettable. Overhead loom cliffs from which waterfalls drop right into the river, drenching rafters as they pass. Black tongues of lava stick out into the river, creating

large, technically demanding rapids such as Doble Piso, Pinball, and Huacas, and making great lunch beaches. And steep drops produce big waves. Best of all is the stunning Dos Montañas Gorge (the proposed site of a controversial dam project; see special topic "The Fight to Save the Pacuare"). Though run year-round, the best months are June and October.

Río Naranjo: A recent addition to the rafting scene, this river in the mountains above Manuel Antonio, on the central Pacific coast, is a corker in high water. However, it's inconsistent, with dramatic changes in water level. During low water you'll need to look elsewhere for thrills. In high water, however, such rapids as Satan's Gut offer swirling class V action. The upper section runs through rainforest; lower down, it slows as it passes through ranchland before winding through Manuel Antonio National Park—what a bonus!—and exiting into the Pacific.

Canoeing and Kayaking

Aventuras Naturales (Apdo. 10736, San José 1000, tel. 225-3939, fax 253-6934) has guided kayaking trips on the Río Savegre, which flows through the moist tropical forest of the central Pacific ($70). Class III, moderate. No experience necessary. Kayak Jungle Tours (Rancho Leona, La Virgen de Sarapiquí, tel. 761-1019) offers five-day kayaking trips on the Sarapiquí river and through Caño Negro National Wildlife refuge, in the northern lowlands. The trips are available year-round and include lodging at Rancho Leona, a thatch-roofed lodge in the village of La Virgen. No experience is necessary.

Ríos Tropicales (Apdo. 472, San José 1200, tel. 233-6455, fax 255-4354), on Calle 32 and Avenida 2, offers kayaking trips for experienced kayakers on the Sarapiquí, Sucio, Grande de Orosí, Peñas Blancas, Chirripó (all class IV), and the Pacuare (class V). Costa Rica Expeditions (Apdo. 6941, San José 1000, tel. 257-0766, fax 257-1665; e-mail, crexped@sol.racsa.co.cr) rents kayaks and canoes, plus offers guided programs on the Chirripó, Reventazón, and Pacuare. Neither provides paddles, sprayskirts, helmets, or lifejackets.

Omniglobe Vacations (tel. 800-468-5151) features an eight-day kayaking package on the Reventazón and Pacuare rivers.

If you prefer a non-challenging paddle in a canoe, American Wilderness Experience (P.O. Box 1486, Boulder, CO 80306, tel. 303-444-2622 or 800-444-0099, fax 303-444-3999) offers two 10-day canoeing trips Nov.-April: one in the Northern Lowlands, with stays at lodges; the other in the remote Talamancas of the southeast, using lodges and "safari-style" base camp.

WINDSURFING

Despite the strong winds that sweep along the coast of the Pacific northwest in summer, ocean windsurfing in Costa Rica has yet to take off. Bahía Salinas, five km west of La Cruz in the extreme northwest, is recommended for the funnel effect.

Inland it's a different story. For windsurfing aficionados, Lake Arenal is paradise, with 23-35 km/h easterly winds funneling through a mountain corridor virtually year-round. Strong winds rarely cease during the dry season (Dec.-April). The lake has acquired an international reputation as one of the best all-year freshwater windsurfing spots in the world. Despite the publicity blitz, it is *not* a rival to Oregon's Columbia Gorge, I'm assured: the waves are too choppy.

Windsurfing at nearby Coter Lake is also superb. For taking off at high speed during the high-wind season (Nov.-April), experienced windsurfers can use four- to five-square-meter sails with short boards; even during the low-wind season, long boards with six- to six-and-a-half-square-meter sails can give a good ride.

Rentals and Tours

North American windsurfers recommend hiring equipment locally. If you plan on testing ocean waters, equipment is in short supply. If you rent at Arenal, try negotiating to use the same equipment at the coast.

Most of the hotels at Lake Arenal and Tilarán rent equipment. The following are recommended: Hotel Puerto San Luis, Aventuras Tilarán (tel. 695-5008), Rock River Lodge, and Tilawa Viento Surf. On the coast, Aqua Sports at Playa Hermosa rents Windsurfers. See regional chapters for telephone numbers and additional information.

Windsurf Costa Rica (P.O. Box 9009, Gainesville, FL 32607, tel. 904-371-8124 or 800-771-7873) offers windsurfing packages, including a "Paradise on a Shoestring" package ($275, with roundtrip air from Miami). Destination Costa Rica (Apdo. 590, San José 1150, tel. 223-0676, fax 222-9747) offers three-day windsurfing packages from San José, with two nights at the Rock River Lodge. Tikal Tour Operators (Apdo. 6398, San José 1000, tel. 223-2811, fax 223-1916) offers windsurfing from its Ecoadventure Lodge at Lake Coter. Also contact Windsurfing Vacations (tel. 800-635-1155, fax 215-348-2341) and Windsurfing World Travel (tel. 800-936-3333).

MISCELLANEOUS

Bungee Jumping
Tropical Bungee (tel. 233-6455) and Saragundí Specialty Tours (tel. 255-0011) both offer bungee jumping on weekends year-round.

Motoring
Pro Motor (Apdo. 150, San José 1002, tel. 233-3166, fax 233-3341) offers tour packages to the Costa Rica Grand Prix (Formula 3), held at La Guácima Race Track.

Mysticism
Costa Rica Rainbow Connection (Apdo. 7323, San José 1000, tel./fax 240-7325) offers an "11-day journey through the wonders and wisdom of magical Costa Rica," focusing on healing arts, meditation, etc.

Culture
Costa Rica Adventures and Wildlife (tel. 800-497-3422; in Costa Rica, tel. 255-2463, fax 255-3573) offers a four-day "Chorotega Culture" tour in Guanacaste combining folkloric traditions with studies of pre-Columbian culture ($339). Myths & Mountains (251 Cheswold Lane, Haverford, PA 19041, tel. 610-896-7780, fax 610-896-9897) specializes in tours designed to introduce you to the culture, religion, history, and art. A 12-day "Culture, Crafts and National Parks," for example, includes visits to a Bribrí Indian village and the pottery-making center of Guaitil. Another tour focuses on medi-

pre-Columbian gold lobster

BOB RACE

cinal plants and traditional healing practices.

Seeking greater cross-cultural understanding? VNA Humanitarian Tours (Gail Nystrom, Apdo. 458, Santa Ana Centro, tel. 282-7368) provides visitors opportunities to explore the often troubling downside of Costa Rica, with day-trips to a women's prison, an orphanage, a girls' shelter, a boys' detention center, and a children's hospital. Longer, multiday trips include visits to indigenous people's reserves and even a street kids' project in Puerto Limón, with time included for relaxation on the beach or in the forests. Company owner Gail Nystrom also runs an annual Eco-Camp for children aimed at enriching the youngsters' perspectives and appreciation of Costa Rica's indigenous peoples.

Cooking
Vantage Adventures (P.O. Box 5774, Greensboro, SC 29661, tel. 800-826-8268, fax 803-233-3864) offers an eight-day package with five days of "tropical gourmet" cooking classes hosted by Maria Batalla, a member of the prestigious Chaine des Rotisseurs (from $1409).

Spelunking
Costa Rica Adventures and Wildlife (tel. 800-497-3422; in Costa Rica, tel. 255-2463, fax 255-3573) offers a four-day "Caverns of Barra

Honda" trip, with equipment and support provided ($437).

Horse Racing

Costa Rica's two race tracks, **Hipódromo del Sol** on the southern outskirts of San Rafael de Alajuela, 20 km west of San José, and **Hipódromo Nacional San Isidro** in Cartago, were both shut at press time because of financial problems, with hopes to reopen. When del Sol is open it offers thoroughbred action every Saturday. Post time is 1 p.m. (150 *colones;* 90 cents).

pre-Columbian gold musician

ARTS AND CULTURE

Interest—and excellence—in the arts has been slow to develop. Costa Rica, with its relatively small and heterogeneous pre-Columbian population, had no unique culture with powerful and unusual artforms that could spark a creative synthesis where the modern and the traditional might merge. Costa Rica's postcolonial development, too, was benign, and the social tensions (often catalysts to artistic expression) felt elsewhere in the isthmus were lacking. And more recently, creativity has been stifled by the Ticos' desire to *quedar bien* (leave a good impression), praise the conventional lavishly, and criticize rarely.

Hence, Costa Rica has been relatively impoverished in native arts and crafts. In Costa Rican literature there has never been anyone of the stature of Latin American writers such as Gabriel García Márquez, Octavio Paz, Jorge Amado, Pablo Neruda, Isabel Allende, or Jorge Luís Borges. And much of the modern art that exists has been patronized by the tourist dollar, so that art and craft shops now overflow with whimsical Woolworth's art: cheap canvas scenes of rural landscapes, rough-hewn macaws gaudily painted, and the inevitable cheap bracelets and earrings sold in market squares the world over.

In recent years, however, artists across the spectrum have found a new confidence and are dismissing rigid social norms to experiment with new paintings and sculptures and movements that metaphorically express the shape of their thoughts. The country's artistic milieu doesn't have the same vibrancy as Argentina's, say, but beneath the patina exciting things are happening for a country long dismissed as a cultural backwater. The performing arts are flourishing. A young breed of woodcarvers and carpenters is transcending the relegation of native-style crafts to mere airport art. Artists are tearing free from a straitjacket of conformity. And the National Symphony Orchestra sets a high standard for other musical troupes to follow. Ticos now speak proudly of their latter-day "cultural revolution," which strikes a vital chord in the national tempo.

The new sophistication in culture is amply demonstrated by the introduction of an **International Art Festival** in March 1992. Featuring dance troupes, theater, experimental music, puppets, jazz, folklore, classical music, etc., from around the world, the annual marathon event has already won a place among the arts festivals of the continent (in 1994, the artistic banquet included displays of talent by 53 foreign groups alongside 62 from Costa Rica). When March comes around, you can almost feel the country's pulse begin to quicken. Then, theaters, parks, and plazas are flooded with color and motion. The festival has brought inspiration and new ideas while raising the quality of local groups by allowing them to measure themselves against international talent.

ART

Santa Ana and neighboring Escazú, immediately southwest of San José, have long been magnets for artists. Escazú in particular is home to many contemporary artists: Christina Fournier; the brothers Jorge, Manuel, Javier, and Carlos Mena; and Dinorah Bolandi, who was awarded the nation's top cultural prize. Here, in the late 1920s, Teodorico Quiros and a group of contemporaries provided the nation with its own identifiable art style—the Costa Rican "Landscape" movement—which expressed in stylized version the flavor and personality of the drowsy little mountain towns with their cobblestone streets and adobe houses backed by volcanoes. The artists, who called themselves the Group of New Sensibility, began to portray Costa Rica in fresh, vibrant colors.

Quiros had been influenced by the French impressionists. His painting *El Porton Rojo* ("The Red Gate") hangs in the Costa Rican Art Museum. In 1994, aged 77, he was awarded the *Premio Magón* award for lifetime achievement in the "creation and promotion of Costa Rican artistic culture." The group also included Luisa Gonzales de Saenz, whose paintings evoke the style of

Craftsmen, such as this yoke-maker, still thrive in Sarchí.

Magritte; the expressionist Manuel de la Cruz, the "Costa Rican Picasso"; as well as Enrique Echandi, who expressed a Teutonic sensibility after studies in Germany.

One of the finest examples of sculpture from this period, the chiseled stone image of a child suckling his mother's breast, can be seen outside the Maternidad Carit maternity clinic in southern San José. Its creator, Francisco Zuñigo (Costa Rica's most acclaimed sculptor), upped and left for Mexico in a fit of artistic pique in 1936 when the sculpture, titled *Maternity*, was lampooned by local critics (one said it looked more like a cow than a woman).

By the late 1950s many local artists looked down on the work of the prior generation as the art of *casitas* (little houses) and were indulging in more abstract styles. The current batch of young artists have broadened their expressive visions and are now gaining increasing international recognition for their "eclectic speculations into modernist and contemporary art."

Many of Costa Rica's new breed of artists have won international acclaim. Isidro Con Wong, from Puntarenas, is known for a style of "magic realism," with works in permanent collections in several U.S. and French museums. Once a poor farmer of Mongolian descent, he started painting with his fingers and *achiote,* a red paste made from a seed. "Children, drunk bohemians, or the mentally regressed—in other words the innocent chosen by God—are those

who understand my works," he says. Imagine the Nicoya landscape seen on LSD! His paintings sell for about $35,000 each.

In Puerto Limón, Leonel González paints images of the Caribbean port with figures reduced to thick black silhouettes against backgrounds of splendid colors, "overtaken if not fully embraced by the design," says art critic Pau Llosa. The most irreverent of contemporary artists is perhaps Roberto Lizano, who collides Delacroix with Picasso and likes to train his eye on the pomposity of ecclesiastics.

Alajeulan artist Gwen Barry is acclaimed for her "Moveable Murals"—painted screens populated by characters from Shakespeare and the Renaissance. Rafa Fernández is noted throughout the Americas; his work, heavily influenced by his many years in Spain, has been defined as "magic realism, where the beauty and grandness of women is explored with a sense of intimacy and suggestion." His ladies often appear in quasi-Victorian guise wearing floral hats. And Rolando Castellón, who won acclaim in the U.S. and was director of the Casa España de Bellas Artes and also a director of the New York Museum of Modern Art before returning to Costa Rica in 1993, translates elements of indigenous life into 3-D art. His studio gallery in Zapote, Moyo Coyatzin, is named for the indigenous deity of creativity. Castellón was recently named curator of Costa Rica's Museum of Contemporary Art and Design. And you can't travel far in Costa Rica these

days without seeing examples of the works of another Escazú artist, Katya de Luisa, whose stunning photo collages are complex allegories. Katya has recently initiated "Encounters With Art," a collaborative effort in which artists from different media contribute to a single work.

The government-subsidized House of Arts helps sponsor art by offering free lessons in painting and sculpture. The Ministry of Culture sponsors art lessons and exhibits on Sundays in city parks. University art galleries, the Museo de Arte Costarricense, and the many smaller galleries scattered throughout San José exhibit works of all kinds. The **Centro Creativo,** opened in 1991 in Santa Ana west of Escazú, offers courses and studio space for local and visiting artists (tel. 282-6556 or 282-8769).

The Ministry of Culture was considering founding a Museum of Latin American Art with a collection of 1,000 works, plus cultural, study, and conference centers.

CRAFTS

Here's an example of what the tourism revolution can launch! As recently as 1993, I wrote: "Costa Rica doesn't overflow with native crafts. Apart from a few notable exceptions—the gaily colored wooden *carretas* (oxcarts) which have become Costa Rica's tourist symbol, for example—you must dig deep to uncover crafts of substance. There are few villages dedicated to a single craft or crafts, as in Mexico or Guatemala. Much that is sold for home decoration or to tourists reflects a mediocre kitsch culture that is imitative rather than creative (frankly, much is cheap junk). And, other than the *carretas,* there is nothing distinctly and recognizably *costarricense.*"

The tourist dollar, however, has spawned a sudden renaissance in crafts, and many new forms (many of them experimental) have emerged in the past few years. The revival is most remarkable in the traditional realm. At Guaitil, in Nicoya, not only is the Chorotega Indian tradition of pottery retained, it is booming, so much so that neighboring villages are installing the potters' wheels, too. Santa Ana is also famous for its ceramics: large greenware bowls, urns, vases, coffee mugs, and small *típico* adobe houses fired in brick kilns and clay pits on the patios of some 30 independent family workshops, such as **Cerámica Santa Ana** (see "Santa Ana" under "Escazú and Vicinity" in the Central Highlands chapter). In Escazú, master craftsman Barry Biesanz (see "Sights" under "Escazú" in the Central Highlands chapter) skillfully handles razor-sharp knives and chisels to craft subtle, delicate images, bowls as hemispherical as if turned with a lathe, and decorative boxes with tight dovetailed corners from carefully chosen blocks of tropical woods: lignum vitae (ironwood), *narareno* (purple heart), rosewood, satinwood, and tigerwood.

Many of the best crafts in Costa Rica come from Sarchí. Visitors are welcome to enter the *fabricas de carretas* and watch the families and master artists at work producing exquisitely contoured bowls, serving dishes, and—most notably—miniature versions of the *carretas* for which the village is now famous worldwide. Although an occasional full-size oxcart is still made, today most of the *carretas* made in Sarchí are folding miniature trolleys—like little hot-dog stands—that serve as liquor bars or indoor tables, and half-size carts used as garden ornaments or simply to accent a corner of a home. The carts are painted in dazzling white or burning orange and decorated with geometric mandala designs and floral patterns that have found their way, too, onto wall plaques, kitchen trays, and other craft items. Sarchí and the Moravia suburb of San José are also noted for their leather satchels and purses.

There's not much in the way of traditional clothing. However, the women of Drake Bay are famous for *molas,* colorful and decorative hand-sewn appliqué used for blouses, dresses, and wall hangings. Of indigenous art there is also little, though the Boruca Indians carve balsa-wood masks—light, living representations of supernatural beings—and decorated gourds, such as used as a resonator in the *quijongo,* a bowed-string instrument.

I predict the next few years will see a wholesale revival in cultural pride.

LITERATURE

Though the government, private donors, and the leading newspaper *La Nación* sponsor literature

SARCHÍ OXCARTS

Sarchí is famous as the home of gaily decorated wooden *carretas* (oxcarts), the internationally recognized symbol of Costa Rica. The carts, which once dominated the rural landscape of the central highlands, date back only to the end of the 19th century. Sadly, they are rarely seen in use today, though you might spot a cart bringing coffee beans into Escazú.

At the height of the coffee boom and before the construction of the Atlantic Railroad, oxcarts were used to transport coffee beans to Puntarenas, on the Pacific coast, making the journey in 10-15 days. In the rainy season, the oxcart trail became a quagmire. Costa Ricans thus forged their own spokeless wheel—a hybrid between the Aztec disc and the Spanish spoked wheel—to cut through the mud without becoming bogged down. In their heyday, some 10,000 cumbersome, squeaking *carretas* had

A Sarchí artisan paints an intricate design on a wooden wheel.

a dynamic impact on the local economy, spawning highway guards, smithies, inns, teamsters, and crews to maintain the roads.

Today's pretty and masterly crafted *carretas* bear little resemblance to the original rough-hewn, rectangular, cane-framed vehicles covered by rawhide tarps. Even then, though, the compact wheels—about four or five feet in diameter—were natural canvases awaiting an artist. Enter the wife of Fructuoso Barrantes, a cart maker in San Ramón, in Alajuela Province, with her paintbrush and novel idea. She enlivened her husband's cartwheels with a geometric starburst design in bright colors set off by black and white. Soon every farmer in the district had given his aged *carreta* a lively new image.

Oxcart art evolved along established lines. By 1915, flowers had bloomed beside the pointed stars. Faces and even miniature landscapes soon appeared. And annual contests—still held today—were arranged to reward the most creative artists. *Carretas* became every farmer's pride and joy. They had ceased to be purely functional. Each cart, too, was designed to make its own "song," a chime as unique as a fingerprint, produced by a metal ring striking the hubnut of the wheel as the cart bumped along. Supposedly, the intention was to allow the farm owner to hear his laborers. Once the oxcart had become a source of individual pride, greater care was taken in their construction and the best-quality woods were selected to make the best sounds.

Today the *carretas,* forced from the fields by the advent of tractors and trucks, are almost purely decorative, but the craft and the art form live on in Sarchí, where artisans still apply their masters' touch at *fabricas de carretas* (workshops), which are open to view (see "Sarchí" under "Grecia to Los Angeles Cloud Forest" in the Central Highlands chapter). A finely made reproduction oxcart can cost up to $5000.

The **Ox-cart Museum** (tel. 259-7042; open 8 a.m.-4 p.m.), in Salitral de Desamparados, has displays of *campesino* life, including a collection of hand-painted oxcarts, in a typical old adobe house. Also, the Pueblo Antigua, outside San José, has a living museum featuring the carts.

through annual prizes, only a handful of writers make a living from writing, and Costa Rican literature is often belittled as the most prosaic and anemic in Latin America. Lacking great goals and struggles, Costa Rica was never a breeding ground for the passions and dialectics that spawned the literary geniuses of Argentina, Brazil, Mexico, Cuba, and Chile, whose works, full of satire and bawdy humor, are "clenched fists which cry out against social injustice."

Costa Rica's early literary figures were mostly essayists and poets: Roberto Brenes Mesen and Joaquín García Monge are the most noteworthy. Even the writing of the 1930s and '40s, whose universal theme was a plea for social progress, lacked the pace and verisimilitude and rich literary delights of other Latin American authors. Carlos Luis Fallas's *Mamita Yunai,* which depicts the plight of banana workers, is the best and best-known example of this genre. Other examples include Fallas's *Gentes y Gentecillas,* Joaquín Gutierrez's *Puerto Limón* and *Federica,* and Carmen Lyra's *Bananos y Hombres.*

Much of modern literature still draws largely from the local setting, and though the theme of class struggle has given way to a lighter, more novelistic approach it still largely lacks the mystical, surrealistic, Rabelaisian excesses, the endless layers of experience and meaning, and the wisdom, subtlety, and palpitating romanticism of the best of Brazilian, Argentinean, and Colombian literature. An outstanding exception is Julieta Pinto's *El Eco de los Pasos,* a striking novel about the 1948 civil war.

An excellent compendium of contemporary literature *on* Costa Rica is *Costa Rica: A Traveler's Literary Companion,* edited by Barbara Ras (see "Booklist"), which brings together 26 stories by Costa Rican writers spanning the 20th century. The essays have been selected to provide a sense for Costa Rica's national psyche and are arranged "according to the geographical allusions they contain." Says former President Oscar Arias: "This anthology offers an accurate synthesis of the literary perceptions that accompanied Costa Rica's transition from a rural, rather isolationist, society . . . to a highly urbanized society increasingly open to the cultural and commercial currents of the present decade of globalization." Highly recommended as a pre-

lude and accompaniment to your journey, for as Arias notes, you gain a more profound impression of Costa Rica when traveling in the company of these writers.

MUSIC AND DANCE

Ticos love to dance. By night San José gets into its stride with discos hotter than the tropical night. On weekends rural folks flock to small-town dance halls, and the Ticos' celebrated reserve gives way to outrageously flirtatious dancing befitting a land of passionate men and women. Says *National Geographic:* "To watch the viselike clutching of Ticos and Ticas dancing, whether at a San José discotheque or a crossroads *cantina,* is to marvel that the birthrate in this predominantly Roman Catholic nation is among Central America's lowest." Outside the dance hall, the young prefer to listen to Anglo-American rock, like their counterparts the world over. When it comes to dancing, however, they prefer the hypnotic Latin and rhythmic Caribbean beat and bewildering cadences of *cumbia, lambada, marcado, merengue, salsa, soca,* and the Costa Rican swing, danced with sure-footed erotic grace.

Many dances and much of the music of Costa Rica reflect African, even pre-Columbian, as well as Spanish roots. The country is one of the southernmost of the "marimba culture" countries, although the African-derived marimba (xylophone) music of Costa Rica is more elusive and restrained than the vigorous native music of Panamá and Guatemala, its heartland. The guitar, too, is a popular instrument, especially as an accompaniment to folk dances such as the Punto Guanacaste, a heel-and-toe stomping dance for couples, officially decreed the national dance. (The dance actually only dates back to the turn of the century, when it was composed in jail by Leandro Cabalceta Brau.)

Costa Rica has a strong *peña* tradition, introduced by Chilean and Argentinian exiles. Literally, "circle of friends," *peñas* are bohemian, international gatherings—usually in favored cafes—where moving songs are shared, and the wine and tears flow.

On the Caribbean coast music is profoundly Afro-Caribbean in spirit and rhythm, with plenti-

ful drums and banjos, a local rhythm called *sinkit,* and the *cuadrille,* a maypole dance in which each dancer holds one of many ribbons tied to the top of a pole: as they dance they braid their brightly colored ribbons. The Caribbean, though, is really the domain of calypso and reggae. Bob Marley is king!

At least three dance academies can teach you the basics of dancing *a la costarricense:* **Danza Viva** (tel. 253-3110) offers courses in *salsa* and *merengue,* the two dances most popular at discos, as well as the *lambada,* the more formal *bolero* and *marcado,* the Caribbean *mambo,* and ballet, jazz, and modern dance. An offshoot of Danza Viva is **Merecumbe** (tel. 224-3531), which specializes in popular dancing. And the **Academia de Bailes Latinos** offers more intensive courses in ballroom and formal dancing.

Folkloric Dancing

Guanacaste is the heartland of Costa Rican folkloric music and dancing. Here, even such pre-Columbian instruments as the *chirimia* (oboe) and *quijongo* (a single-string bow with gourd resonator) popularized by the Chorotega Indians are still used as backing for traditional Chorotega dances such as the Danza del Sol and Danza de la Luna. The more familiar Cambute and Botijuela Tamborito—blurring flurries of kaleidoscopic, frilly satin skirts accompanied by tossing of scarves, a fanning of hats, and loud lusty yelps from the men—are usually performed on behalf of tourists rather than at native *turnos* (fiestas). The dances usually deal with the issues of enchanted lovers (usually legendary coffee pickers) and are mostly based on the Spanish *paseo,* with pretty maidens in white bodices and dazzlingly bright skirts being circled by men in white suits and cowboy hats.

A number of folkloric dance troupes tour the country, while others perform year-round at such venues as the Melico Sálazar Theater, the Aduana Theater, and the National Dance Workshop headquarters in San José. Of particular note is Fantasía Folklorica, a colorful highlight of the country's folklore and history from pre-Columbian to modern times (see "Nightlife," in the San José chapter).

Vestiges of the half-dead Indian folk dancing linger by a hair's breadth elsewhere in the nation. The Borucas still perform their Danza de los Diablitos, and the Talamancas their Danza de los Huelos. But the drums and flutes, including the curious *dru mugata,* an ocarina (a small potato-shaped instrument with a mouthpiece and finger holes which yields soft, sonorous notes) made of beeswax, are being replaced by guitars and accordions. Even the solemn Indian music is basically Spanish in origin and hints at the typically slow and languid Spanish *canción* (song) which gives full rein to the romantic, sentimental aspect of the Latin character.

Classical Music

Costa Rica stepped onto the world stage in classical music with the formation, in 1970, of the **National Symphony Orchestra** under the leadership of an American, Gerald Brown. The orchestra, which performs in the Teatro Nacional, often features world-renowned guest soloists and conductors. Its season is April through November, with concerts on Thursday and Friday evenings, plus Saturday matinees. Costa Rica also claims the only state-subsidized youth orchestra in the Western world. The **Sura Chamber Choir,** founded in 1989 with musicians and vocalists from the country's two state universities, is the first professional choir in Central America, with a repertoire from sacred through Renaissance to contemporary styles. The **Goethe Institute, Alliance Française,** the **Museo de Arte Costarricense,** and the **Costa Rican-North American Cultural Center** (call 253-5527 for information on the Center's U.S. University Music Series) all offer occasional classical music evenings.

Costa Rica holds an **International Festival of Music** during the last two weeks of August. In 1992, performances included the Costa Rican Chamber Orchestra, a Brazilian chamber orchestra, a string, woodwind, and harpsichord sextet, and Costa Rican music for two guitars. There's also an annual six-week-long **Monteverde Music Festival** (tel. 645-5125), each Jan.-Feb., combining classical with jazz and swing. It's held at the Hotel Fonda Vela, in Monteverde (see "Entertainment" under "Monteverde and Vicinity" in the Guanacaste and the Northwest chapter). Book early!

THEATER

A nation of avid theater lovers, Costa Rica supports a thriving acting community. In fact, Costa Rica supposedly has more theater companies per capita than any other country in the world. The country's early dramatic productions gained impetus and inspiration from Argentinian and Chilean playwrights and actors who settled here at the turn of the century, when drama was established as part of the school curriculum.

The streets of San José are festooned with tiny theaters—everything from comedy to drama, avant-garde, theater-in-the-round, mime, and even puppet theater. Crowds flock every night Tuesday through Sunday. Performances are predominantly in Spanish, although some perform in English. The English-speaking **Little Theater Group** is Costa Rica's oldest theatrical troupe; it performs principally in the Centro Cultural's Eugene O'Neill Theater. The prices are so cheap—you could go once a week for a year for the same cost as a single Broadway production—that you can enjoy yourself even if your Spanish is poor. Theaters rarely hold more than 100 to 200 people and often sell out early. Shows normally begin at 7:30 or 8 p.m. The *Tico Times* and *Costa Rica Today* offer complete listings of current productions and whether a play is in Spanish or English. Also see the "Viva" section in *La Nación*.

HOLIDAYS

Costa Rica is a Catholic country and its holidays *(feriados)* are mostly church-related. Most busi-

---

OFFICIAL HOLIDAYS

1 January	New Year's Day
19 March	St. Joseph's Day (patron saint of San José)
Easter	Holy Week (Wednesday noon through Easter Sunday)
11 April	Juan Santamaría Day
1 May	Labor Day
June (variable)	Corpus Christi
29 June	St. Peter and St. Paul Day
25 July	Guanacaste Day
2 August	Virgin of Los Angeles Day
15 August	Mother's Day
15 September	Independence Day
12 October	Día de la Raza (Columbus Day)
8 December	Immaculate Conception
25 December	Christmas Day

---

nesses, including banks, close on official holidays. The country closes down entirely during the biggest holiday time, **Easter Holy Week** (Wednesday through Sunday). Buses stop running on Holy Thursday and Good Friday. Banks and offices are closed. And hotels and rental cars are booked solid months in advance as everyone seems to head for the beach. Avoid the popular beaches during Easter week. Most Ticos now take the whole **Christmas** holiday week through New Year as an unofficial holiday.

Easter is a tremendous opportunity to see colorful religious processions. Individual towns also celebrate their patron saint's day: highlights usually include a procession, plus bullfights (benign), rodeos, dancing, and secular parades. Fireworks and firecrackers *(bombetas)* are a popular part of local fiestas *(turnos)* and church celebrations. Often they'll start at dawn. Ticos can't resist sirens and horn-honking during celebrations. The *Tico Times* provides weekly listings of festivals and events nationwide.

FESTIVALS

January

Alajuelita: Fiesta Patronales; oxcart parade and pilgrimage

Santa Cruz: Fiestas de Santa Cruz; folk dancing, marimba music, bullfights

February

San Isidro de El General: Fiestas Cívicas; agricultural fair, bullfights, orchid exhibition

Rey Curre (Talamancas): Fiesta de los Diablos; Indian festival, masked dancing

March

Escazú: National Oxcart Day (2nd Sunday); oxcart festival and competitions

Tierra Blanca: Farmers' Day (15 March)

Paraíso (Ujarrás): pilgrimage (midmonth)

San José: Bonanza Cattle Show; bullfights, rodeos, horse races

April

Alajuela: Día de Juan Santamaría; marching bands

San José: Earth Day; Indian handicrafts

Cartago, Escazú, Heredia, San José, San Joaquín de Flores: Semana Santa (Holy Week); processions of effigies

Cartago, Santo Domingo: Procession of the Holy Burial (Good Friday)

May

Puerto Limón: May Day (1 May); cricket matches, quadrille dances

University of Costa Rica: University Week (1st week); beauty contests, bands, sports events

Escazú, San Isidro: Día del Boyero (15 May); oxcart parades

July

Alajuela: Mango Festival; parades, music, craft fairs

Playa del Coco, Puntarenas: Carnival (Saturday nearest 16 July); parades, concerts, dancing, beauty contest, fireworks

Liberia, Santa Cruz: Guanacaste Day (25 July); folk dancing, marimba music, bullfights, rodeos

August

Cartago: Virgin of Los Angeles (2 August); religious procession

San Ramón: Día de San Ramón (31 August); religious procession

San José: Semana Afro-Costarricense; cultural displays honoring International Black People's Day

September

Nationwide: Independence Day (15 September); lantern (farole) parades, marching bands

October

Puerto Limón: Carnival (10-12 October); floats, dancing

Upalá: Fiesta de Maíz; Corn Queen contest, corn festival

November

Nationwide: All Souls' Day (2 November); church parades

Meseta Central: Coffee Picking Tournament; coffee picking, songs

San José: International Theater Festival; plays, street theater, puppet shows

December

Boruca: Fiesta de los Negritos (8 December); costumed dancing

Nationwide: Día de la Pólovra (8 December); fireworks

Nicoya: Fiesta de la Yeguita (12 December); processions, bullfights, fireworks, concerts

Nationwide: Los Posadas (15 December); caroling

San José: Year-end Fiestas (25 December); bullfights, tope (horse procession)

San José: New Year's Eve (31 December); dance in Parque Central

ACCOMMODATIONS

At press time Costa Rica officially had about 800 "lodging establishments" representing 22,791 rooms, the majority in properties with no more than 50 rooms (only 7.3% had more). Of these, 10,794 rooms met the Costa Rican Tourism Institute standards to be licensed as "tourist-quality." Only eight hotels had more than 200 rooms.

Accommodations run the gamut from cheap *pensiones,* beachside cabinas, and self-catering *apartotels* to rustic jungle lodges, swank mountain lodges, homestays, and glitzy resort hotels with casinos. "Motels" are cheap hotels, usually on the outskirts of San José, used for sexual trysts. Cabinas range from truly horrendous, spartan, and ill-equipped hovels to upscale, fully equipped units that would do any hotelier proud. The moniker hides a lot; check around before making a reservation if at all possible. And don't be afraid of looking at several rooms in a hotel (particularly in budget hotels) before making your decision: this is quite normal and accepted in Costa Rica. Rooms in any one hotel can vary dramatically.

Reservations
Hardly a week goes by without two or three new hotels springing onto the scene; until recently it was hardly fast enough to keep pace with tourism growth. The sudden blossoming of several name-brand hotels to the inventory is beginning to ease booking headaches (at press time, the government had permits on the books for at least 27 new hotels; the Gulf of Papagayo Project alone will *double* the country's hotel inventory). Indeed, tourism officials are beginning to worry that the rapid growth of hotels will bring a new crisis—that of *too many* rooms!—as the tourism boom shows signs of slowing down. The sudden, unexpected drop in visitors in late 1994 has left many hotels struggling to fill their rooms.

Still, during dry season planning is recommended for the more popular parks, reserves, and other select destinations. Christmas, Easter week, and weekends in dry season (Dec.-April) are particularly busy. And nature lodges tend to be heavily booked May-Nov. too. (Hotel occupancy, for example, ran a very high 85% in February 1994, but dropped to 45% in June.) Make your reservations well in advance for the busier months.

Virtually every hotel (except budget hotels) has a fax, so you can easily book directly from the United States. Take your fax copy with you and reconfirm reservations a few days before arrival.

A **Hotel Information & Reservation Office** (tel. 231-5848) is open 24 hours to advise on hotels and assist with reservations. Outside Costa Rica, **My Favorite Sunset,** which specializes in Costa Rica, offers a **travel agents' reservation service** (tel. 800-361-3931 or 416-225-2200, fax 416-225-2580) on-line through Sabre, Apollo, System One, Amadeus, and Gemini reservation networks (hotel designator code **CU**). The company has brochures and a Hotel Preview Video and CD-ROM.

Honor your reservations! Or at least call as far in advance as possible if you have to cancel. Someone else may have been turned away.

Rates and Facilities
Many hotels offer discounts of 20% or more off-season. Upscale properties also have "shoulder-season" rates. If no single rooms are available, you'll usually be charged the single rate for a double room. And couples requesting a *casa matrimonial* (i.e., wishing to sleep in one bed) will often receive a discount off the normal double rate. Ask to review several rooms if possible, particularly in cheaper hotels, since standards can vary widely room to room. Rates are subject to fluctuation. A 13% tax is added to your room bill.

Note that prices in general continue to escalate with demand and may have increased by the time you read this book. However, the sudden downturn in tourism arrivals in late 1994 and the sense that there is now a glut of hotels had stalled increases in room rates, and the law of supply and demand had come into effect with a vengeance by April 1995, when many hotels were posting "specials" with rates up to

50% below those quoted in the first edition of this book! Others had upgraded their properties and increased their rates. The situation is fluid. Every attempt has been made to ensure that prices given were accurate at time of going to press.

Rates are normally quoted for single or double. Rates for additional guests are shown below as *additional;* e.g. "$10 s ($5 additional)."

Subscribers to the *Costa Rican Outlook* newsletter (see "Newspapers and Magazines" under "Communications" in this chapter) receive 10-15% discounts at a wide range of upscale hotels.

In cheaper hotels and even the better hotels in some areas, be prepared for cold-water showers. You'll soon get used to it and come to look forward to a refreshingly icy shower. Hot water, often little more than tepid, may be available only at certain times of the day. Shower units are often powered by electric heating elements, which you switch on for the duration of your shower (don't expect steaming-hot water, however). Beware! It's easy to give yourself a shock from any metal object nearby, including the water pipes. Upscale hotels usually have "U.S. standard" showers, plus flushing toilets capable of handling toilet paper. Cheaper hotels do not: trying to flush your waste paper down the toilet will cause a blockage. Waste receptacles are provided for paper. Unhygienic, yes! But use the basket unless you fancy sloshing about in your own waste.

Though not as bad as in many countries, theft is a problem. Before accepting a room, ensure that the door is secure and that your room can't be entered by someone climbing through the window. *Always* lock your door. Never leave valuables in your room if you can avoid it and *always* lock your possessions in your baggage (many hotel workers are abysmally low-paid and the temptation to steal may be irresistible; I've had favorite shirts and other items "disappear" because I trustingly left them lying around). Take a padlock to use in cheaper hotels.

Those concerned to stay in "environmentally conscious" accommodations have been presented an easy means of identifying appropriate properties. In 1994, the government initiated an **Eco-Seal** program: a standardization system for recognizing hotels that meet certain environmental standards.

HOTELS

Budget ($10 and below)
Many of the bottom-end hotels, though often sparsely furnished with no more than a bed and a dresser, are usually clean and adequate. They can be great places to meet other budget travelers. Many budget hotels—often called *pensiones* or *hospedajes*—have only communal bathrooms. Still, you can often find a room with

Cariari Hotel and Country Club

JOHN ANDERSON

private bathroom for $5, and even as low as $2. Be warned: Some are ghastly hovels.

Inexpensive ($10-25)
Generally, inexpensive hotels will have private bathrooms, but don't bet on it. Standards vary markedly, with prices in direct relationship to a destination's popularity.

Moderate ($25-50)
Sometimes there may be little to distinguish these from less expensive hotels. But there are also some wonderful bargains in this category: spacious, with plentiful facilities, and, with luck, a charismatic atmosphere. These hotels normally accept credit-card payment.

Upscale ($50-80)
There's a wide and growing choice of upper-end hotels. Many properties can hold their own on the international hotel scene. Often what you're paying for, however, is the extra space and furniture. Shop around. Many expensive hotels can't justify their price: where this is the case, I've said so.

Deluxe ($80 and above)
The good news is that most of Costa Rica's fistful of deluxe hotels, most of them new on the scene, live up to expectations. They run the gamut from beach resorts, mountain lodges, and haciendas-turned-hotels to San José's plusher options. Perhaps two dozen proffer remarkable ambience; a fistful are truly superb (I've profiled these especially noteworthy cases in separate boxes).

APARTOTELS

The equivalent of drive-in motels in the U.S., apartotels offer rooms with kitchens or kitchenettes (pots and pans and cutlery are provided) and sometimes small suites furnished with sofas and tables and chairs. One- or two- bedroom units are available, and weekly and monthly rates are offered. Apartotels are particularly economical for families. In San José, they are concentrated in Los Yoses, 10 minutes' walk east of downtown. Most are characterless; it's all a matter of taste.

BEACH RESORTS

The majority of beachside hotels are not what you may be accustomed to when you think of a "resort" vacation, though recent years have seen a litter of stellar resorts open their doors. Beach resorts here are used more for three- or four-day vacations-within-a-vacation, a little sun and sand after touring jungles and mountains. But things are changing. International resort developers are pushing up deluxe resorts in Guanacaste, all-inclusive of golf courses and water sports.

CAMPING

Costa Rica is not greatly endowed with established campsites. Still, that doesn't stop the locals, for whom camping on the beach during national holidays is a tradition. Several of the national parks have basic camping facilities. And there are a growing number of commercial camping areas at popular beach sites. At more remote beaches camping is the only option, even though there are often no facilities.

The nation's maritime zone law, which maintains 50 meters of beachfront in the public domain, means that you should be able to camp on any beach without permission. However, ask locals if you're unsure; you may need to pass through private land to reach the beach. You may also need to pack everything in and out. Remember: *Leave only footprints.* Also, don't camp near riverbanks. And make sure you camp *above* the high-tide line.

Theft is a problem at many sites. If possible, camp with a group of people so one person can guard the gear. You'll need a warm sleeping bag and a waterproof tent for camping in the mountains, where you are more likely to need permission from local landowners or park rangers before pitching your tent. Generally, a Gore-Tex bivouac bag or even a tarp will suffice in the lowlands. You'll also need a mosquito net and plenty of bug repellent for many locations. If you really want the "local" flavor, buy a hammock (widely available) and sleep between two coconut trees. A hammock also suspends you safely beyond the reach of most creepy crawlies. Avoid grassy pastures: they harbor chiggers and ticks.

In San José you can buy camping equipment from **ARO** (Avenida 8, Calles 11/13), **Armerio Polini** (Calle 2, Avenidas Central/2), **Centro de Aventuras** (Paseo Colón, Calles 22/24), **El Palacio del Deporte** (Calle 2, Avenidas 2/4), or **Alquileres y Toldos Fiesta** (one block north of Banco Anglo, in San Pedro, tel. 224-9155).

Staying in National Parks
Most national parks and reserves have camp sites ($2 fee for camping), although a few of the more remote wildlife refuges lack even the most rudimentary accommodations. Others, such as Ballena Marine National Park, are now discouraging camping in the park in an attempt to have you support locals who offer camping and support services. You may be able to stay in park ranger housing or at biological research stations if space permits. Call toll-free 192, or 233-4070, or fax 223-6369 for information on accommodations at specific parks and reserves. Don't expect hotel service! You'll usually need to provide your own towels and bedding. There are no restaurants or snack bars, so bring enough food and drink for your anticipated stay. A food contribution for the low-paid rangers is appreciated.

NATURE LODGES

Costa Rica is richly endowed with off-the-beaten-track mountain and jungle lodges and cabinas at private reserves, biological stations, and prime nature-rich locations throughout the nation. Some are working scientific centers. Most have naturalist guides and arrange special activities, such as nature hikes, horseback riding, etc. They're a perfect opportunity to immerse yourself in Costa Rica's diverse ecosystems. Some offer basic facilities only. Others are relatively luxurious. Most are moderately expensive—despite which they're heavily booked. Reservations are highly recommended in dry season (Dec.-April) well in advance.

HOMESTAYS AND BED AND BREAKFASTS

More and more bed and breakfasts are opening, with live-in hosts to cosset you. And more and more Costa Rican families are welcoming foreign travelers into their homes as paying guests. Staying with a local family provides a wonderful cross-cultural exchange and a great insight into the Tico way of life. It's also an opportunity to improve your Spanish. Many local hosts advertise in the *Tico Times* and *Costa Rica Today*. Also, contact the ICT office below the Plaza de la Cultura. Judy Tattersall Ryan's book, *Simple Pleasures: A Guide to the Bed and Breakfasts and Special Hotels of Costa Rica,* has descriptions of select hostelries (Apdo. 2055, San José 1002, fax 222-4336).

Bell's Home Hospitality, run by Vernon and Marcela Bell, lists more than 70 host homes in the residential suburbs of San José, plus a few in outlying towns (Apdo. 185, San José 1000, tel. 225-4752, fax 224-5884; in the U.S., P.O. Box 025216, Miami, FL 33102). Rates are $30 s, $45 d (dinners $5). The company arranges accommodations for singles, couples, and families of up to five people, and will match you with an English-speaking family if you wish. The Bells

---

YOUTH HOSTELS

Hostel Toruma, San José, tel. 224-4085, fax 224-4085; 95 beds, $5

Hostel El Plástico, Sarapiquí, tel. 253-0844, fax 253-0844; 29 beds, $35

Hostel Cabinas San Isidro, Puntarenas, tel. 221-1225, fax 221-6822; 260 beds, $9

Hostel La Casona de Lago, Tilarán; 20 beds, $15

Hostel Rincón de la Vieja, Rincón, tel. 666-0473, fax 257-2070; 40 beds, $48

Hostel Islas del Río, Sarapiquí, tel. 710-6898; 20 beds, $35

Hostel Tilarán, Tilarán, tel. 695-5008; 16 beds, $7

Hostel Burío, Fortuna, tel./fax 479-9076; 20 beds, $10

Hostel Guanacaste Travel Lodge, Guanacaste, tel. 666-2287, fax 666-0085

Hostel Maraparaíso, Jacó, tel. 221-6544, fax 221-6601; 70 beds, $9

will also arrange airport transfers and offer a free information service. *Recommended* for a home-away-from-home!

Costa Rican Homestays Bed & Breakfast (Apdo. 8186, San José 1000, tel. 240-6829) also offers lodging in private homes. And **Costa Rica Home & Host** (2445 Park Ave., Minneapolis, MN 55404, tel. 612-871-0596, fax 612-871-8853) offers homestay packages with English-speaking families who also act as chauffeur-guides.

TurCasa (tel. 221-6161) represents hosts who take guests. They have uniform pricing and offer a variety of services, including airport transfers for stays of five nights or more. Soledad and Virginia Zamora (tel. 224-7937 or 225-7344) specialize in finding accommodation for **long-term renters** (expect to pay $250 monthly, including meals and laundry).

The **Costa Rican Bed and Breakfast Group** (call Pat Bliss, tel. 228-9200, or Debbi McMurray, tel. 223-4168) can provide information on where to stay.

YOUTH HOSTELS

The **Costa Rican Youth Hostel Association,** RECAJ (Red Costarricense de Albergues Juveniles), operates 12 "youth hostels" throughout Costa Rica (RECAJ, Apdo. 1355, San José 1002, tel./fax 224-4085). The Hostel Toruma in San José (Avenida Central, Calles 29/31) serves as association headquarters. Most of the hostels are actually standard hotels that honor YHA rates (one is a campsite). Some offer horseback riding, windsurfing, hiking, and guided tours. Toruma, Casona, and Rincón de la Vieja also allow camping. Reservations are recommended. (See chart.)

You can reserve youth hostel accommodation up to six months in advance through the **International Booking Network** ($2 booking fee), with booking centers worldwide (contact any participating hostel or travel center). **Hostelling International** (733 15th St., N.W. #840, Washington, DC 20005, tel. 202-783-6161 or 800-444-6111, fax 202-783-6171), the U.S. affiliate of the International Youth Hostel Federation (IYHF), offers reservation services on the Internet through Global Network Navigator: http://gnn.com/gnn/bus/ayh/.

HEALTH SPAS

Costa Rica offers four dedicated health spas. The **Nosara Retreat** (see "Nosara" under Tamarindo to Playa Nosara" in the Nicoya Peninsula chapter) is an upscale holistic resort run by renowned yoga practitioners Amba and Don Stapleton, both teachers at the Kripalu Center for Yoga and Health in Massachusetts. Sunrise Yoga on the beach, anyone? The most complete spa is **Tara Resort Hotel & Spa** in the hills above Escazú (see "Escazú" in the Central Highlands chapter). Its "Scarlett's Fountain of Youth Spa" offers a complete range of rejuvenation programs, from aromatherapy and mud cocoons to lymphatic drainage and "Sun Lover's Facials."

Also in the central highlands are the **Healthy Day Inn** (see "Grecia to Los Angeles Cloud Forest Reserve" in the Central Highlands chapter), and **Hearty Hands Health Home** (Apdo. 185, Ipis, San José, tel. 253-1162, fax 234-9469), in San José's Barrio Escalante. The latter offers everything from mud baths and massages to herbal treatments to dietary programs, naturalist routines, and reflexology. Take your pick from residential courses from one week to one year, including programs for seniors and handicapped people. Bedrooms with private baths are said to be "comfortable."

Centro Creativo (tel. 282-6556, fax 282-6959), near Santa Ana, offers residential holistic-living courses and treatments in massage, chiropractic, etc., as well as art, writing, and textiles.

Also to consider: **Costa Rica Rainbow Connection** (Apdo. 7323, San José 1000, tel./fax 240-7325) offers courses in Kripalu Yoga and the healing arts; **Centro de Balance Integral** (tel. 224-5806) and **Acu Yoga** (tel. 253-1614) both offer short- and long-term yoga and massage courses; **Hare Krishna Farm** (tel. 551-6752 or 227-4505) holds meditation and yoga classes; and **Integree Clínica de Bienestar Corporal** (tel. 233-3839) and **Instituto Bienestar** (tel. 226-4975) have massage and spa facilities and beauty treatments.

A large number of hotels and nature lodges feature Jacuzzis, and a few have beauty salons and massage parlors. A growing number of places specialize in holistic health and self-improvement.

FOOD AND DRINK

COSTA RICAN CUISINE

First a generality before I eat my words! *Disappointing!* Gourmands, for example, who like a good tongue-lashing won't find the spices associated with Mexican food. Costa Rican cuisine is simple and chefs shun spices. Says *Weissmann Travel Reports:* "It's almost easier to find an American fast food outlet than a restaurant serving good, native cuisine." *Comida típica,* or native dishes, rely heavily on rice and beans, the basis of many Costa Rican meals. "Home-style" cooking predominates. But meals are generally wholesome and reasonably priced. *Gallo pinto,* the national dish of fried rice and black beans, is as ubiquitous as is the hamburger in North America, particularly as a breakfast staple. I never tire of *gallo pinto* for breakfast *(desayuno).* Many meals are derivatives, including *arroz con pollo* (rice and chicken) or *arroz con tuna* (a favorite of mine when eating at the terrace cafe of the Gran Hotel). At lunch, *gallo pinto* becomes the *casado* (married): rice and beans supplemented with cabbage-and-tomato salad, fried plantains, and meat. Vegetables do not form a large part of the diet.

Food staples include *carne* (beef, sometimes called *bistek), pollo* (chicken), and *pescado* (fish). Beef and steaks are relatively inexpensive, but don't expect your steak to match its North American counterpart; at its worst you may be served a leathery slab cooked in grease. They're also lean (cattle is grass-fed). Despite 1,227 kilometers (767 miles) of coastline, seafood—especially shrimp *(camarones)* or lobster *(langosto)*—is expensive, because Costa Rica exports most of its seafood. Travelers on tight budgets should stick with the set meal—*casado*—on lunchtime menus ($2-3). *Sodas,* open-air lunch counters, also serve inexpensive snacks and meals ($1-3).

Eating in Costa Rica doesn't present the health problems that plague the unwary traveler elsewhere in Central America, but you need to be aware that pesticide use in Costa Rica is unregulated. I've *never* become sick in Costa Rica. *Always* wash vegetables in water known to be safe. And ensure that any fruits you eat are peeled yourself; you never know where someone else's hands have been. Otherwise, stick to staples such as bananas and oranges. Remember, too, that the kitchen of a snazzy restaurant with candelabra and silverware may not live up to its facade. Eat where the locals eat. Usually that means tasty and trustworthy food.

Dining in Costa Rica is a leisurely experience, befitting the relaxed pace of a genteel vacation. Restaurants normally open 11 a.m.-2 p.m and 6 p.m.-11 p.m. or midnight. Some restaurants stay open 24 hours. If desperation sets in, you have plentiful fast-food options—McDonald's, Pizza Hut, Kentucky Fried Chicken, and the like.

Now for the good news: In San José, many fine restaurants serve the gamut of international cuisines at reasonable prices. And though culinary excellence in general declines with distance from the capital city, a growing number of hoteliers and gourmet chefs are opening restaurants worthy of note in even the most secluded backwaters. Take the Caribbean coast, for example, where the local cuisine reflects its Jamaican heritage with mouthwatering specialties such as ackee and codfish (ackee is a small, pink-skinned fruit tasting like scrambled eggs), johnnycakes, curried goat, curried shrimp, and pepperpot soup, with its subtle, lingering flame. Here, simple restaurants such as Defi's, in Cahuita, and The Garden, in Puerto Viejo, are worthy of a review in *Bon Appetit.*

Many bars in Costa Rica have a delightful habit of serving *bocas*—savory tidbits ranging from *ceviche* to *tortillas con queso* (tortillas with cheese)—with each drink. Some bars provide them free, so long as you're drinking. Others apply a small charge. Turtle *(tortuga)* eggs are a popular dish in many bars. The eggs *may* have been legally taken with the first *arribadas* (mass turtle nestings) of the season. Turtles, however, are an endangered—and protected—species, and the eggs may have been taken illegally. Don't support the decimation of turtle populations.

COSTA RICAN SPECIALTIES

arreglados—sandwiches or tiny puff pastries stuffed with beef, cheese, or chicken. Greasy!

arroz con pollo—a basic dish of chicken and rice

casado—*arroz* (rice), *frijoles* (black beans), *carne* (beef), *repollo* (cabbage), and *plantano* (plantain). Avocado *(aguacates)* or egg may also be included.

ceviche—marinated seafood, often chilled, made of *corvina* (sea bass), *langostinos* (shrimps), or *conchas* (shellfish). Normally served with lemon, chopped onion, garlic, and sweet red peppers.

chorreados—corn pancakes, often served with sour cream *(natilla)*

elote—corn on the cob, either boiled *(elote cocinado)* or roasted *(elote asado)*

empañadas—turnovers stuffed with beans, cheese, meat, or potatoes

enchiladas—pastries stuffed with cheese and potatoes and occasionally meat

gallo—tortilla sandwiches stuffed with beans, cheese, or meat

gallo pinto—the national dish (literally "spotted rooster"), made of lightly spiced rice and black beans. Traditional breakfast *(desayuno)* or lunch dish. Sometimes includes *huevos fritos* (fried eggs).

olla de carne—soup made of squash, corn, *yuca* (a local tuber), *chayote* (a local pear-shaped vegetable), *ayote* (a pumpkinlike vegetable), and potatoes

palmitos—succulent hearts of palm, common in salads

patacones—thin slices of deep-fried plantain. A popular Caribbean dish. Served like French fries.

pescado ahumado—smoked marlin

picadillo—a side dish of fried vegetables and meat

sopa negra—a creamy soup, often with a hard-boiled egg and vegetables soaking in the bean broth

sopa de mondongo—soup made from tripe (the stomach of a cow)

tamales—boiled cornmeal pastries stuffed with corn, chicken, or pork, and wrapped in a banana or corn leaf. A popular Christmas dish.

tortillas—Mexican-style corn pancakes or omelettes

DESSERTS *(POSTRES)* AND SWEETS

cono capuchino—an ice-cream cone topped with chocolate

dulce de leche—a syrup of boiled milk and sugar. Also thicker, fudgelike *cajeta*—delicious!

flan—cold caramel custard

mazamorra—corn starch pudding

melcocha—candy made from raw sugar

milanes—chocolate candies

pan de maíz—corn sweet bread

queque seco—pound cake

torta chilena—multilayered cake filled with *dulce de leche*

If you wish to cook for yourself, the best places to buy fresh food are the Saturday morning street markets *(ferias de agricultor)*.

FRUITS

Costa Rica grows many exotic fruits. The bunches of bright vermilion fruits on the stem found at roadside stalls nationwide are *pejibayes,* teeny relatives of the coconut. You scoop out the boiled avocadolike flesh; its taste is commonly described as falling between that of a chestnut and that of a pumpkin. Not for me. The *pejibaye* palm (not to be confused with the *pejibaye* above) produces the *palmito* (heart of palm), used in salads. *Guayabas* (guavas) come into season Sept.-Nov.; their pink fruit is used for jams and jellies. A smaller version—*cas*—finds its way into *refrescos* (see "Drink," below) and ice cream. The *marañón,* the fruit of the cashew, is also commonly used in *refrescos. Mamones* are little green spheres containing grapelike pulp. And those yellowish red, egg-size fruits are *granadillas* (passion fruit).

Most of the tropical fruits you'll find in the stateside Safeway were grown in Costa Rica. The sweetest and most succulent *sandías* (wa-

termelons) come from the hot coastal regions. Be careful not to confuse them with the lookalike *chiverre,* whose "fruit" resembles spaghetti! *Piña* (pineapple) is common. So too are *mélon* (cantaloupe) and mangos, whose larger versions are given the feminine gender, *mangas,* because of their size! Papayas come in two forms: the round, yellow-orange *amarilla* and the elongated, red-orange *cacho. Moras* (blackberries) are most commonly used for refrescos.

DRINK

Costa Rica has no national drink, perhaps with the exception of *horchata,* a cinnamon-flavored cornmeal drink, and *guaro,* the *campesino*'s near-tasteless yet potent drink of choice (see "Alcoholic Drinks," below); friends joke about my predilection for this cheap liquor. And **coffee,** of course, Costa Rica's *grano d'oro* (grain of gold). Most of the best coffee is exported, so don't expect consistently good coffee everywhere you go. What you're served may have been made from preground coffee that has been in a percolator for an hour or two. That said, I've been served some excellent coffee in restaurants. Coffee is traditionally served very strong and mixed with hot milk; it can sometimes be half coffee, half milk. When you order coffee with milk *(café con leche),* you'll generally get fifty-fifty. If you want it black, you want *café sin leche.* Herb teas are widely available. **Milk** is pasteurized.

The more popular North American soda pops, such as Pepsi and Coca-Cola, as well as sparkling water, called *agua mineral* or *soda,* are popular and widely available. The Costa Rican refreshers are *refrescos,* energizing fruit drinks served with water *(con agua)* or milk *(con leche).* They're a great way to taste the local fruits, such as *tamarindo* (the slightly tart fruit of the tamarind tree), mango, and papaya. They come in cartons, or made to order, in which case ask for *sin azucar* (no sugar). Some are made from oddities such as *pinolillo* (roasted corn flour). *Refrescos* are usually highly sugared.

Sugar finds its way into all kinds of drinks, even water: *agua dulce,* another popular *campesino*'s drink, is boiled water with brown sugar—energy for field workers. Roadside stalls also sell *pipas,* green coconuts with the tops chopped off. You drink the refreshing cool milk from a straw.

Alcoholic Drinks

Imported drinks are expensive; stick with the local drinks. Lovers of **beer** *(cerveza)* are served locally brewed pilsners and lagers that reflect the early German presence in Costa Rica. Imperial and Bavaria are the two most popular brews. If you're watching your diet, try Tropical, a low-calorie "lite" beer. Heineken is also brewed under license. Cheaper bars charge about 60 cents for a local beer; fancy hotels charge about $2. Most bars charge $1.

Even the poorest *campesino* can afford the native red-eye, *guaro,* a harsh, clear spirit distilled from fermented sugarcane; a large shot costs about 40 cents. My favorite drink? Guaro mixed with Café Rica, a potent coffee liqueur akin to Mexican Kahlúa.

The national liquor monopoly also produces vodka and gin (both recommended), rum (so-so), and whiskey (not recommended). A favorite local mix is Cuba libre (rum and coke). Imported whiskeys—Johnnie Walker is very popular—are less expensive than other imported liquors, which are super-expensive (often $8 or more a shot).

Avoid the local wines. The most memorable thing about them is the hangover. Imported wines are expensive with the exception of Chilean and Argentinian wines, of which there are some superb options.

Costa Rica, you'll often hear, is a nation of drinkers. Most nations are. Costa Ricans, by the way, deplore drunks; it goes against the grain of *quedar bien* (the cultural characteristic that calls for making a good impression). Still, drinking is not restricted to lunch and the evening hours. Don't be surprised to find the Tico at the table next to yours washing his breakfast down with whiskey.

GETTING THERE

BY AIR

Costa Rica's tourism boom is fueling an increase in air traffic to the capital, San José. Nearly 20 international airlines provide regular service to Costa Rica (see chart); 123 flights a week come from the U.S., either directly or with stopovers in Mexico, Nicaragua, Guatemala, Honduras, and/or El Salvador. Virtually all flights land at San José's Juan Santamaría International Airport (six km, 20 minutes by taxi from the city center. As of early 1995, the airport was undergoing extensive expansion, including a new terminal to mostly handle charter flights. A second international airport was inaugurated in February 1992 at Liberia, in Guanacaste, but as of April 1995 the airport was not completed and no scheduled service offered.

See section on "Transportation" in chapter on San José for information on airport arrival and departure.

Fares
Airline fares are in constant flux in these days of deregulation. The cheapest scheduled fares are APEX (advance-purchase excursion) fares, which you must buy at least 21 days before departure and which limit your visit to 30 days (from U.S.). From Europe, you must stay a minimum of 14 days and return within 180 days. Penalties usually apply for any changes after you buy your ticket. Generally, the further in advance you buy your ticket, the cheaper it will be. Buy your return segment before arriving in Costa Rica, as tickets bought in the country are heavily taxed.

If you fly to a U.S. gateway on a carrier with no service to Costa Rica, try to have your ticket issued on the stock of the airline on which you'll fly to Costa Rica; the latter will have an office in San José, which makes having your ticket reissued much easier if needed.

Keep your eyes open for introductory fares. Central American carriers are also usually slightly cheaper than their American counterparts but

stop over at more cities en route. The cheapest flights generally are via Miami. Midweek and low-season travel is often cheaper. And you may be able to obtain lower fares by changing planes and/or carriers in Mexico City. If you're flexible, consider traveling **stand-by,** where you do not make a reservation, but turn up at the airport and hope for an empty seat, preferably at a last-minute discount fare (if there's a seat). The **Last Minute Travel Club** (tel. 617-267-9800) specializes in last-minute airfares.

If you really want to know how to save money, invest in a copy of *The Worldwide Guide to Cheap Airfares* by Michael McColl ($14.95 plus postage; Insider Publications, 2124 Kittredge St., San Francisco, CA 94704, tel. 510-276-1532 or 800-78-BOOKS, fax 510-276-1531), which gives a complete profile on how to travel the world without breaking the bank.

Charters and Consolidators
Charter flights from the U.S. to Costa Rica are slim pickings. However, you may save money by buying your ticket from a **consolidator** (similar to a "bucket shop" in England), which sells discounted tickets on scheduled carriers. Consolidators usually have access to a limited number of tickets, so book early. The Sunday travel sections of major city newspapers are the best source. Some consolidators are unethical, though these are the rarity. The following offer cut-rate fares to Costa Rica: **Cut Rate Travel** (1220 Montgomery Drive, Deerfield, IL 60015, tel. 800-388-0575 or 708-405-0575, fax 708-405-0587); **Buenaventura Travel** (595 Market St., San Francisco, CA 94105, tel. 800-286-8872 or 415-777-9777, fax 415-777-9871); **Access International** (101 W. 31st St., Suite 1104, New York, NY 10001, tel. 212-465-0707 or 800-825-3633); and **UniTravel** (P.O. Box 12485, St. Louis, MO 63123, tel. 314-569-2501 or 800-325-2222). Many tour operators offer air and hotel packages that provide excellent bargains. Try **Costa Rica Sun Tours** (tel. 415-759-6604) and **Costa Rica Experts** (tel. 800-827-9046).

AIRLINES

AIRLINES SERVING COSTA RICA FROM THE U.S.

AIRLINE	FROM	TELEPHONE
Aero Costa Rica	Atlanta, Orlando, Miami	(800) 237-6274
Aeronica	Miami	(800) 323-0856
American	Dallas, Miami	(800) 433-7300
Aviateca	Houston, Miami	(800) 327-9832
Continental	Houston	(800) 525-0280
LACSA	Los Angeles, Miami, New Orleans, Orlando, New York, San Francisco	(800) 225-2272
Mexicana	Denver, Los Angeles	(800) 531-7921 (in Canada: 800-531-7923)
SAHSA	Houston, Miami, New Orleans	(800) 327-1225 (in Canada: 416-675-2007)
TACA	Houston, New Orleans, Miami, San Francisco, Washington, D.C.	(800) 535-8780
United Airlines	Miami	(800) 241-6522

AIRLINES SERVING COSTA RICA

AIRLINE	LOCATION IN SAN JOSÉ	TEL.	FAX	AIRPORT TEL.
Aero Costa Rica	200 meters north of La Hispanidad	253-4753	253-8098	442-0545
American	Calles 26/28, Paseo Colón	257-1266	222-5213	441-1168
Aviateca	Juan Santamaría Airport	255-4949	223-4238	441-7641
Continental	Calle 19, Avenida 2	233-0266	233-4146	442-1904
COPA	Calle 1, Avenida 5	223-7033	221-6798	441-4742
Iberia	Calle 40, Paseo Colón	221-3311	223-1055	442-1932
KLM	Calle 1, Avenidas Central/1	221-0922	220-3092	442-1922
LACSA	Calle Central/1, Avenida 5	221-4579	441-3994	
Ladeco		641-1444		
LTU	Calles 1/3, Avenida 9	257-2990	233-3508	
Mexicana	Calle 1, Avenidas 2/4	222-1711	222-7847	441-9377
NICA		222-1744		
SAHSA	Calles 1/3, Avenida 5	221-5561	221-5459	441-1064
SAM	Calles 1/3, Avenida 5	233-3066	255-0940	
TACA	Calle 1, Avenidas 1/3	222-1790	223-4238	441-5090
United Airlines	Sabana Sur	220-4844	220-4855	
Varig	Calles 1/3, Avenida 5	221-3087	221-3087	
Viasa	Calle 1, Avenida 5	231-0033	441-6244	

Especially for
Students and Teachers, Etc.

Council Travel, an affiliate of the Council on International Education Exchange (205 E. 42nd St., New York, NY 10017, tel. 212-661-1414), with a worldwide network of travel agencies in the U.S., Europe, and Japan (see "Council Travel Offices" chart), caters to students, teachers, and youths. Another CIEE affiliate, **Council Charter** (tel. 212-661-0311 or 800-800-8222) sells discounted air tickets on scheduled flights. Council Travel issues the International Student Identification Card, good for special fares (see "Notes for Students," under "Other Practicalities" later in this chapter).

STA Travel also caters to students. More than 120 offices worldwide (see "STA Offices" chart) offer low-price airfares (as well as the ISIC and a **STA Travel Card** good for travel discounts). Also try **International Student Exchange Flights** (5010 E. Shee Blvd. A-104, Scottsdale, AZ 85254, tel. 602-951-1177).

Courier Flights

Here, you deliver or accompany a package on behalf of a company for a much-discounted ticket. Delivery of the package usually takes priority over your personal travel plans upon arrival. **Discount Travel** (P.O. Box 331, Sandy, UT 84091, tel. 800-344-9375) issues *A Simple*

COUNCIL TRAVEL OFFICES

Arizona
Tempe . . . . tel. (602) 966-3544

California
Berkeley . . . . tel. (510) 848-8604
Davis . . . . tel. (916) 752-2285
La Jolla . . . . tel. (619) 452-0630
Long Beach . . . . tel. (310) 598-3338
Los Angeles . . . . tel. (310) 208-3551
Palo Alto . . . . tel. (415) 325-3888
San Diego . . . . tel. (619) 270-6401
San Francisco . . . . tel. (415) 421-3473
Sherman Oaks . . . . tel. (818) 905-5777

Colorado
Boulder . . . . tel. (303) 447-8101

Connecticut
New Haven . . . . tel. (203) 562-5335

District of Columbia
Washington . . . . tel. (202) 337-6464

Florida
Miami . . . . tel. (305) 670-9261

Georgia
Atlanta . . . . tel. (404) 377-9997

Illinois
Chicago . . . . tel. (312) 951-0585
Evanston . . . . tel. (708) 475-5070

Indiana
Bloomington . . . . tel. (812) 330-1600

Louisiana
New Orleans . . . . tel. (504) 866-1767

Massachusetts
Amherst . . . . tel. (413) 256-1261
Boston . . . . tel. (617) 266-1926
Cambridge . . . . tel. (617) 497-1497

Michigan
Ann Arbor . . . . tel. (313) 998-0200

Minnesota
Minneapolis . . . . tel. (612) 379-2323

North Carolina
Durham . . . . tel. (919) 286-4664

New York
New York . . . . tel. (212) 661-1450

Ohio
Columbus . . . . tel. (614) 294-8696

Oregon
Portland . . . . tel. (503) 228-1900

Pennsylvania
Philadelphia . . . . tel. (215) 382-0343
Pittsburgh . . . . tel. (412) 683-1881

Rhode Island
Providence . . . . tel. (401) 331-5810

Texas
Austin . . . . tel. (512) 472-4931
Dallas . . . . tel. (214) 363-9941

Utah
Salt Lake City . . . . tel. (801) 582-5840

Washington
Seattle . . . . tel. (206) 632-2448

Wisconsin
Milwaukee . . . . tel. (414) 332-4740

STA TRAVEL OFFICES

California
ASUC Travel Center
MLK Jr. Building, 2nd Floor
University of California
Berkeley, CA 94720
tel. (510) 642-3000

7202 Melrose Ave.
Los Angeles, CA 90046
tel. (213) 934-8722

920 Westwood Blvd.
Los Angeles, CA 90024
tel. (310) 824-1574

51 Grant Ave.
San Francisco, CA 94108
tel. (415) 391-8407

Massachusetts
297 Newbury St.
Boston, MA 02115
tel. (617) 266-6014

65 Mt. Auburn St.
Cambridge, MA 02138
tel. (617) 576-4623

New York
Travel Center
103 Ferris Booth Hall
Columbia University
New York, NY 10027
tel. (212) 854-2224

10 Downing St.
New York, NY 10014
tel. (212) 627-3111

Guide to Courier Travel ($17.95, including shipping). The *Air Courier Directory* also lists courier companies ($5; Pacific Data Sales Publishing, 2554 Lincoln Blvd., Suite 275, Marina del Rey, CA 90291). Also see *The Worldwide Guide to Cheap Airfares,* listed above.

The following companies offer courier flights: **Courier Travel Service** (530 Central Ave., Cedarhurst, NY 11516, tel. 516-374-2299 or 800-922-2359); **Now Voyager** (74 Varick St., Ste. 307, New York, NY 10013, tel. 212-431-1616); **Trans-Air System** (tel. 305-592-1771) in Miami, and **Travel Unlimited,** which publishes a monthly schedule (P.O. Box 1058, Allston, MA 02134). You might also try **LACSA Courier** in Los Angeles (tel. 310-607-0100), Miami (tel. 305-591-8080), New Orleans (tel. 504-467-2973), or New York (tel. 718-526-5300); or in Costa Rica (tel. 221-0111). Other courier companies advertise in the Sunday travel sections of the *Los Angeles Times, New York Times,* and other large newspapers.

Practicalities

Ensure that you make your reservation as early as possible (several months in advance would be ideal), especially for the dry season, as flights are often chronically oversold. Take account, too, of *hora tica*—Latin time. Always reconfirm your reservation within 72 hours of your departure (reservations are frequently canceled if not reconfirmed, especially during Dec.-Jan. holidays), and arrive at the airport with *at least* two hours to spare. Avoid reservations that leave little time for connections, as baggage transfers and customs and immigration procedures can be infuriatingly slow.

I recommend using a travel agent for reservations (travel agents do *not* charge a fee, but derive their income from commissions already costed into the airlines' fares). The agent's computer will display all the options, including seat availability and current fares, and they have the responsibility to chase down refunds in the events of overbooking, cancellations, etc.

Especially recommended for budget travelers is **CIEE/Council Travel Services** (205 E. 42nd St., New York, NY 10017, tel. 212-661-1414); see the "Council Travel Offices" chart.

From the U.S.

American Airlines (tel. 800-433-7300), **Continental** (tel. 800-525-0280 or 800-231-0856), and **United Airlines** (tel. 800-722-5243 or 800-241-6522) all offer daily service to Costa Rica (see chart). American, for example, offers as many as four flights daily in high season.

At press time, Costa Rica's national airline, **LACSA** (1600 N.W. LeJeune Rd., Suite 200, Miami, FL 33126, tel. 800-225-2272 or 305-876-6583), offered three daily flights from Miami; once daily from Orlando, New York, Los Angeles, and San Francisco; and five times weekly from New Orleans. Additional service is constantly being added. Some flights are non-stop; others make the "milk run" through Central America. Service is excellent, with free beverages. LACSA's route network serves 21 cities in 15 countries throughout the Americas and the Caribbean. Service is aboard four Airbus Industries wide-body A310s (240 passengers) and five narrow-body A320s (168 passengers).

LACSA offers an "EcoPass," which offers up to 50% savings on LACSA's Central America routes for travelers originating in the U.S.; it's valid year-round, with no blackout periods or minimum stays (maximum stay is 30 days), and must be purchased with the originating ticket. Also, students can get a 40% discount on LACSA flights with an **International Student Identification Card** ($14; send for the Student Travel Catalog, c/o Council on International Educational Exchange, 205 E. 42nd St., New York,

NY 10017, tel. 212-661-1414). With card in hand, you must buy your discounted ticket through a student travel agency. See "Notes for Students," under "Other Practicalities" later in this chapter.

Aero Costa Rica (700 S. Poinciana Blvd., Suite 705, Miami Springs, FL 33166, tel. 800-237-6274 or 305-888-2622; in Chicago, Aero Costa Rica, 100 S. Greenleaf, Gurnee, IL 60031, tel. 708-249-2111, fax 708-249-2772; in San José, tel. 234-6013) offers daily nonstop service to San José via Managua from Miami (plus

---

LACSA TICKET OFFICES

U.S.

Los Angeles, 2500 Wilshire Blvd., Suite 510, Los Angeles, CA 90057, tel. (800) 225-2272 or (213) 646-1210 (airport), fax (213) 384-1245

Miami, 1600 N.W. LeJeune Rd., Suite 200, Miami, FL 33126, tel. (800) 225-2272 or (305) 876-6581 (airport), fax (305) 871-4585

New Orleans, 2002 20th St., Suite B-104, Kenner, LA 70062, tel. (800) 225-2272 or (504) 466-1799 (airport), fax (504) 466-8268

New York, 630 5th Ave., Suite 242, New York, NY 10111, tel. (800) 225-2272 or (718) 917-6658 (airport), fax (212) 245-3901

San Francisco, 870 Market St., Suite 654, San Francisco, CA 94103, tel. (800) 225-2272 or (415) 692-2212

LATIN AMERICA

Bogota, Carrera 10, Numero 27-51, Suite 213, Bogota, Colombia, tel. 28-67471

Buenos Aires, Viamonte 920, Capital 1053, Buenos Aires, Argentina, tel. 393-5546

Cancún, Quintana Roo Edifico Suites, Atlantis Local #4, Av. Bonampak, Mexico, tel. 7-3101, 7-5101, or 6-0041 (airport)

Caracas, Centro Ciudad Comercial Tamanaco, Nivel C-2, Caracas, Venezuela, tel. 57-21611, 255-1041 (airport)

Guatemala, Edificio La Galeria, No. 7, Ave. 14-44 Locales 3 y 4, Guatemala Zona 9, tel. 34-6905, 31-8747 (airport)

Lima, Pasaje Telle 145, Lima, Peru, tel. 46-8273

Managua, Frente Porton Antiguo Hospital, El Retiro, Camino Real, Nicaragua, tel. 66-8268, 31-253 (airport)

Mexico City, Esquina con Leibnitz, Colonia Anzures, CP 11590, Mexico, tel. 5-250025, 5-713489 (airport)

Panamá City, Avenida Justo Arosemena, #31-44, Ciudad de Panamá, Panamá, tel. 25-0194, 38-4118 (airport)

Quito, Avenida 12 de Octubre #394, Quito, Ecuador, tel. (593) 2-504-961

Rio de Janeiro, Av. N.S. Copacabana, 500 GR 504/516, Rio de Janeiro, Brazil, tel. (021) 255-6466

San Juan, Miramar Palza Centre, Ave. 954 Ponce de Leon, Suite 207-A, Santurce, Puerto Rico 00909, tel. (800) 225-2272 or (809) 791-6400

San Pedro, Edifico Romar, 8 Ave. S.O. 1-2 Calle, San Pedro Sula, Honduras, tel. 52-6688, 56-2391 (airport)

San Salvador, 43-A Ave. Norte #216, San Salvador, El Salvador, tel. (503) 24-6222 or (503) 39-9470

EUROPE

Madrid, Princesa 1, Torre de Madrid, Pta. 31 #4, Spain, tel. 54-24-378

Paris, Costa Rican Embassy, 74 Ave. Paul Doumer, 75016 Paris, France, tel. 4504-5093

Frankfurt, Eisenbahnstrasse 204, P.O. Box 210, 6072 Dreieich 2, Germany, tel. (06103) 64010

additional flights on Thursday and Sunday); from Orlando on Tuesday, Friday and Saturday; and Atlanta on Monday, Wednesday, and Friday, using Boeing 727-200s. Superb service; free drinks include champagne.

LACSA and four other Central American carriers—Aviateca (Guatemala, tel. 800-327-9832), TACA (El Salvador, tel. 800-535-8780), COPA (Panamá, tel. 800-359-2672), and NICA (Nicaragua; 800-831-6422)—have formed a joint marketing company, **America Central Corp.** (P.O. Box 590628, Miami, FL 33159, tel. 305-526-8236), and will eventually integrate their services. Together, they offer a **"Visit Central America Air Pass"** valid with a roundtrip ticket from the United States. The fare allows purchase of three to 10 coupons (two to arrive and depart Central America) to cities throughout Central America over a 45-day period. Presstime prices started at $399 low season, $549 high season from Miami, Houston, Orlando, or New Orleans, with one stopover allowed. A fourth and fifth coupon cost $50 each (high season); a sixth and seventh cost $80 each. "High season" is July 1 to August 31 and November 1 to December 31. *A great bargain!* You can combine services of participating carriers. Here are numbers for information and reservations in Europe: England, tel. (0293) 553-3330; France, tel. (1) 4451-0165; Germany, tel. (49) 6103-81061; Holland, tel. (23) 291-723; Italy, tel. (6) 559-4342. In Australia, tel. (03) 654-3233.

LACSA, TACA, and Aviateca have a similar deal called **Mayan Airpass** for travel between Guatemala, Flores, San Salvador, Belize, Cancún, Mérida, San Pedro Sula, La Ceiba, Tegucigalpa, and Roatan. You must buy your ticket before arrival, buy a minimum of four coupons ($75 apiece), and arrive on any of the three airlines from any gateway city in the U.S. or Mexico.

USAir and 14 Latin American carriers, including LACSA, have a **LatinPass** (1600 N.W. LeJeune Rd., Miami, FL 33116, tel. 800-44-LATIN or 305-870-7500, fax 305-870-7676) program whereby members of the individual carriers' frequent flyer programs can accrue miles on other LatinPass member airlines. (To enroll, mail your last statement from *any* U.S. airline's frequent flyer program and LatinPass will match the last three one-way flights between U.S. and Latin America.)

Aero Costa Rica and COPA, the airline of Panamá, have a joint "circle fare," Miami-San José-Panamá-Miami ($399).

SAHSA (tel. 800-327-1225), the airline of Honduras, has a "Maya World Fare" from U.S. gateways that allows visits to five Central American destinations, including Costa Rica; it is valid for 21 days and you must make a minimum of three stopovers.

From Europe

American Airlines, British Airways, Continental, United Airlines, and Virgin Atlantic fly from London to Miami, from where you can connect with an airline serving Costa Rica. **Aeroflot** flies to Miami from Shannon (tel. 62-299), Stockholm (Sveavagan 20, tel. 217-007), and Luxembourg (35 rue Glesener, L-1631, tel. 493-291), with onward flight aboard Aero Costa Rica.

KLM flies to Costa Rica direct from Amsterdam on Sunday and Wednesday (some flights stop in Curaçao and Aruba); **Iberia** flies daily from Spain via Puerto Rico or the Dominican Republic; and **LTU** and **Condor** fly charters direct from Dusseldorf and Munich. In Germany, discount fares are available through **Council Travel** in Dusseldorf (tel. 2113-29088) and Munich (tel. 0898-95022); and, in Frankfurt, **STA Travel** (tel. 6943-0191, fax 6943-9858). Charter service from Milan may be offered by the time you read this.

In England, **Voyages Jules Verne** (21 Dorset Square, London NW1 6QG, tel. 171-723-5066) offers a weekly charter from Gatwick, Dec.-May. "Bucket shops" advertise in London's *What's On* and *Time Out* and leading Sunday newspapers. **Trailfinders** (42 Earl's Court Rd., London W8 6EJ, tel. 071-938-3366) is a reputable budget travel agency; it also publishes *Trailfinder* magazine, which lists fares. **Journey Latin America** (16 Devonshire Rd., Chiswick, London W4 2HD, tel. 081-747-3108) specializes in cheap fares throughout Latin America. **STA Travel** (74 Old Brompton Rd., London SW7, tel. 071-937-9971, fax 071-938-5321) specializes in student fares. STA also has offices at 25 Queens Rd., Bristol; 38 Sydney St., Cambridge; 75 Deansgate, Manchester; and 19 High St., Oxford. Alternately, try **Council Travel** (28A Poland St., London W1V 3DB, tel. 071-437-7767).

In Switzerland try **Sindbad Travel** (3 Schoffelgasse, Zurich 8025, Switzerland). In France try **Uniclam** (63 rue Monsieur Le Prince, Paris 75006); **Council Travel** (31 rue St. Augustin, Paris 75002, tel. 1-4266-2087); or **Voyages Découvertes** (21 rue Cambon, Paris, tel. 1-4261-0001).

Also see "Visit Central America Air Pass" in section on "From the U.S.," above.

From Canada

LACSA was "ready to expand northward to Montreal and Toronto." **Air Transat** (tel. 233-8228) offers direct flights every Saturday from Montreal (US$549 roundtrip). The following companies offer inexpensive charter flights and one-, two-, and three-week air/hotel packages: **Fiesta Wayfarer Holidays** (tel. 416-498-5566), in Toronto; **Fiesta West** (tel. 604-688-1102), in Vancouver; and **Go Travel** (tel. 514-735-4526), in Montreal. **Canadian Universities Travel Service** (Travel Cuts; 187 College St., Toronto, ON M5T 1P7, tel. 416-979-2406) sells discount airfares to students and has 25 offices throughout Canada.

From Australia and New Zealand

You'll find no direct service to Costa Rica or destinations close by, nor any bargain fares. The easiest and cheapest route is to fly to California or Miami and from there to Costa Rica. Specialists in discount fares include **STA Travel**, whose offices include: 220 Faraday St., Carlton, Melbourne, Victoria 3053, tel. (03) 347-4711 or (03) 347-6911, fax (03) 347-0608; and 1A Lee St., Railway Square, Sydney 2000, tel. (02) 212-1255. In New Zealand, contact STA at 10 High St., Auckland, tel. (09) 309-9723, fax (09) 309-9829; 10 O'Connell St., Auckland, tel. (09) 309-9191; or 207 Cuba St., Wellington, tel. (04) 385-0561.

Also see "Visit Central America Air Pass" in section "From the U.S.," above.

BY BUS

With political stability breaking out throughout Central America, the overland route is now an attractive alternative for patient travelers who can take the rough with the smooth and for whom time is no object. Whether by bus or self-drive, allow at least three weeks (the journey is well over 3,500 kilometers from the U.S. and the going is slow). Obtain all necessary visas and documentation in advance. Accommodation is plentiful all along the route.

Central America is well-served with local bus systems. However, buses are often crowded to the hilt, and you may end up standing for parts of your journey. Rest stops are infrequent. You can travel from San Diego or Texas to Costa Rica by bus for as little as $100 (with hotels and food, however, the cost can add up to more than flying direct). Where possible, book as far in advance as possible—the buses often sell out well in advance.

Watch your baggage; consider keeping it with you on the bus. Passports are often collected by the driver to present en masse to immigration. You will need to provide passport and visas when buying your ticket.

Two detailed resources on bus schedules are *Mexico and Central American Handbook,* edited by Ben Box (Prentice Hall, New York), and *Central America on a Shoestring* (Lonely Planet, Berkeley, CA). Vivien Lougheed's *Central America by Chickenbus* (Respository Press, Quesnel, B.C., Canada) may provide useful reading.

Buses serve Mexico City from the U.S. border points at Mexicali, Ciudad Juárez, and Laredo. **Cristóbal Colón** line serves Mexico City to Tapachula on the Guatemala border, where local buses connect to Guatemala City. **Ticabus** (also known as TICA, tel. 221-8954 in San José) provides direct service to San José from Guatemala City via Nicaragua (departs Managua on Tuesday, Thursday, and Saturday at 7 a.m.; $25; 11 hours); **Sirca** (tel. 222-5541) offers service from Managua on Monday, Wednesday, and Friday at 6:30 a.m. ($5). TICA also offers service to San José from Tegucigalpa in Honduras daily at 7:30 a.m. From Panamá, **Tracopa** (tel. 221-4214 in San José) buses depart David daily at 7:30 a.m. and noon; **TICA** operates buses from Panamá City daily at 11 a.m. Note that Panamá time is one hour ahead of Costa Rica!

BY CAR

It's a long haul, but you can follow the Pan-American Highway all the way from the U.S. to San José and into Panamá (don't let the fancy name

RULES OF THE ROAD

- U.S. license plates are collector's items—take them off and display them inside your vehicle.

- Good tires are a must, as is a sackful of spare parts.

- Make sure your car is in tip-top condition before leaving.

- Gas stations are few and far between—keep your tank topped up. Have a lock on your gas cap.

- Unleaded gas is hard to come by. Disconnect your catalytic converter.

- Be patient and obliging at customs/immigration posts.

- Never leave anything of value in your car.

- Always secure your parked vehicle with one or more anti-theft devices. Apply locking nuts to the wheels.

- Also see "By Car" under "Getting Around."

fool you, however; parts are horrendously potholed). The road ends abruptly in southern Panamá; no road link exists into South America. Don't anticipate fast driving! It's 3,700 kilometers minimum, depending on your starting point. Experienced travelers recommend skirting El Salvador and the Guatemalan highlands in favor of the coast road through Guatemala and Honduras. Allow three weeks at a leisurely pace. High ground clearance is useful. Apparently, cars are sometimes fumigated at borders.

Drive the Pan-American Highway is a guidebook that offers practical advice and tips ($12.50 plus $2.50 postage; Apdo. 208, Heredia 3000; in the U.S., Interlink 209, P.O. Box 526-770, Miami, FL 33152).

Documentation

You'll need passport, visas, driver's license, and vehicle registration. It's also advisable to obtain tourist cards (good for 90 days) from the consulate of each country before departing. A U.S. driver's license is good throughout Central America, although an International Driving Permit—is-

sued through the American Automobile Association—can be handy, too. You'll need to arrange a transit visa for Mexico in advance, plus car entry permits for each country (cars freely pass across international borders without paying customs duty; duty becomes payable, however, if your car is stolen). The AAA can provide advice on carnets, permits, etc., as well as a good area map. Also check with each country's consulate for latest information.

Insurance

A separate vehicle liability insurance policy is required for each country. Most U.S. firms will not underwrite insurance south of the border. **American International Underwriters** (700 Pine St., New York, NY, tel. 212-770-7000) can arrange insurance; inquire several months in advance of your trip. **Sanborn's** (P.O. Box 310, McAllen, TX 78502, tel. 210-686-0711, fax 210-686-0732) is a reputable company specializing in insurance coverage for travel in Mexico and Central America. They publish a very handy booklet, *Overland Travel,* which is full of practical information. The company has the Sanborn's Mexico Club. Reportedly you can buy insurance for Mexico at the border. Note, however, that insurance sold by AAA (American Automobile Association) covers Mexico only, not Central America.

Upon arrival in Costa Rica, foreign drivers *must* buy insurance stamps for a minimum of three months (approximately $15). There's also a $10 road tax payable upon arrival in Costa Rica. Vehicle permits are issued at the border for stays up to 30 days. You can extend this up to six months at the Instituto Costarricense de Turismo (travel agencies in San José can help with paperwork). Don't plan on selling your car in Costa Rica—you'll be hit with *huge* import duties.

BORDER CROSSINGS

See section on "Immigration and Entry" for information on visas, etc. Since requirements are always in flux, check in advance with the Nicaraguan or Panamanian embassies. Likewise, borders are open only at specific times and these, too, are subject to change.

Peñas Blancas

Virtually everyone arriving from Nicaragua does so at Peñas Blancas, in northwest Costa Rica. This is a border post, not a town. It's open 8 a.m.-noon and 1-5 p.m daily (the Nicaraguan post closes at 4 p.m.). Taxis are available for the five-km journey between the border posts. If asked for proof of onward ticket, simply buy a cheap bus ticket (valid 12 months) back to Nicaragua. They're available at the ticket booth next to the tourist information office at the Costa Rican border post. Opposite, in the same building, are a bar and restaurant plus Oficina de Imigración (tel. 679-9025). You can change money here (you'll get better rates for U.S. dollars than if exchanging *colones* for *córdobas,* or vice versa).

You may or may not be required to pay an exit fee ($1-2) leaving either country.

The tourist information office sells bus tickets to San José (departs 10:30 a.m. and 3 p.m.) via La Cruz (19 km), the nearest town with accommodations (see "La Cruz and Vicinity" in the Guanacaste and the Northwest chapter). The last San José-bound bus is at 3 p.m. Local buses also run to Liberia ($1.25; last bus at 5 p.m.).

Buses from San José to Peñas Blancas operate from the Coca-Cola Terminal (Calle 14, Avenidas 3/5; CARSOL, tel. 224-1968) daily at 5 and 7:45 a.m., and 1:30 and 4:15 p.m. ($5; six hours); and from Liberia at 5:30, 8:30, and 11 a.m, and 2 and 6 p.m. ($1.25). **TICA** (tel. 221-8954) operates buses from San José (Avenida 4, Calles 9/11) to Managua daily on Monday, Wednesday, Friday, and Saturday at 7 a.m.; $25; 11 hours); to Tegucigalpa, in Honduras, daily at 7:30 a.m. from Calle 9, Avenida 4; and to Guatemala City from Avenida 4, Calles 9/11, daily at 7:30 a.m. **Sirca** (tel. 222-5541) offers service to Managua on Wednesday, Friday, and Sunday at 5 a.m. ($5) from Calle 7, Avenidas 6/8. (See "By Bus," above, for information on bus service from Nicaragua and beyond.)

Buses run between the border and Rivas, the nearest Nicaraguan town (37 km) with accommodations. Buses fill fast—get there early. Allow lots of time for border delays. The TICA and Sirca buses between Managua and San José are often delayed for hours, as the bus usually waits for all passengers to be processed. (See "Peñas Blancas," under "La Cruz and Vicinity" in the Guanacaste and the Northwest chapter, for information on crossing into Nicaragua.)

Los Chiles

In 1994, Costa Rica and Nicaragua signed an agreement to establish a border post at Los Chiles (14 km south of San Carlos, on the southeast tip of Lake Nicaragua). Though things have settled down in this region since 1990, border officials are still touchy about the fact that contras operated out of this region, and they have traditionally been *very* picky about who they let through. Until recently, foreigners have automatically been turned away and had to enter Nicaragua via Peñas Blancas. Word is that the immigration post is open again. You might be able to breeze through by the time you read this.

Paso Canoas

Paso Canoas, the crossing point into Panamá, is on the Pan-American Hwy. about 20 km east of Ciudad Neily. The border posts have been open 24 hours, but are subject to change (recent hours, for example, were 6-11 a.m. and 1-11 p.m.). Budget accommodation is plentiful in Paso Canoas (see under "Ciudad Neily and Vicinity" in the Pacific Southwest chapter). No visas are issued at the border, so ensure that you arrive with correct documentation (U.K. and certain European nationals are excepted: check with the Panamanian consulate in San José). There's a fee of $10 upon entering Panamá (good for 30 days with visa, five days without). Tourist cards *may* be available at Paso Canoas, but don't trust to it. Moneychangers abound. A bus terminal on the Panamanian side of the border offers service to David, the nearest town (90 minutes), every hour or two until 7 p.m. Buses leave from David for Panamá City (last bus 5 p.m.; seven hours).

Entering Costa Rica from Panamá, you may need to show proof of onward ticket. You can buy a Tracopa bus ticket in David to Paso Canoas and back. David also has a Costa Rican consulate.

TICA (tel. 221-8954 in San José) operates a/c buses from Panamá City direct to San José from the Hotel Ideal (Calle 17 Este) at 11 a.m. Panamá time ($25). **Transchiri** (Calle 17 Este and Balboa) has departures daily from Panamá

City to David at noon and midnight ($11, or express $15; five hours); you can connect with **Tracopa** (tel. 221-4214 in San José) buses departing David at 7:30 a.m. and noon. Book at least two days ahead. Tracopa (tel. 221-4214) buses depart San José for Paso Canoas from Avenida 18, Calles 2/4, daily at 5 and 7:30 a.m. and 1, 4:30, and 6 p.m. (eight hours). TICA buses depart San José from Avenida 4, Calles 9/11 at 10 p.m. Buses also run frequently from Ciudad Neily to the border (about 25 cents).

Sixaola/Guabito

Sixaola, a one-street hamlet on the Caribbean coast, lies at the end of the gravel road from Bribrí. The crossing is open 7-11 a.m. and 1-5 p.m., Mon.-Thurs. (and sometimes on Friday and Saturday if officials show up), although a recent report suggests occasional lapses for excessively long "lunch." Reports are that officials may demand a malaria test or ask to see your malaria tablets. Sixaola dissolves into Guabito on the Panamanian side of the border. Minibuses operate a regular schedule from here to Changuinola (16 km); a narrow-gauge train also runs daily to Almirante (30 km), the end of both rail and road. For access to the rest of Panamá, you can either fly to David from Changuinola or take a boat from Almirante to Bocas del Toro and then Chiriquí Grande, where a road traverses the mountain to David.

Buses depart San José for Sixaola from Avenida 11, Calles Central/1 (Transportes Mepe, tel. 257-8129) daily at 6 a.m. and 1:30 and 3:30 p.m.

BY SEA

Costa Rica is appearing with increasing frequency on the itineraries of luxury cruise ships. However, stops are often no more than one day, so don't expect more than a cursory glimpse of the country. The country was given a boost as a port-of-call when the superliner *QEII* made her first visit to Puerto Limón in January 1986 (another of Cunard's cruise ships, *Vistafjord,* also visits Costa Rica on a regular basis; the company even maintains an office in San José, tel. 223-5111). By 1994, more than 60,000 passengers stepped ashore for at least a short visit, typically on a trans-canal itinerary. That year, the newly elected Figueres administration announced that it would build a port facility for international cruise lines near Puntarenas (now served by a cargo terminal at Puerto Caldera).

Cruises from Fort Lauderdale or Tampa, Florida, usually stop off at various Caribbean islands and/or Cozumel before calling in at Moín, which serves the town of Puerto Limón. Cruises from San Diego or Los Angeles normally stop off in

---

CRUISE LINES SERVING COSTA RICA

Clipper Cruise Line, 7711 Bonhomme Ave., St. Louis, MO 63105, tel. (314) 727-2929

Costa Cruises, World Trade Center, Miami, FL 33130, tel. (305) 358-7330

Crystal Cruises, 2121 Ave. of the Stars, Los Angeles, CA 90067, tel. (800) 446-6645

Cunard Lines, 555 5th Ave., New York, NY 10017, tel. (212) 880-7500

Holland America, 300 Elliott Ave. W, Seattle, WA 98119, tel. (800) 426-0327

Ocean Cruise Line, 1510 S.E. 17th St., Fort Lauderdale, FL 33316, tel. (305) 764-3500

Princess Cruises, 10100 Santa Monica Blvd., Los Angeles, CA 90067, tel. (213) 553-7000

Royal Caribbean Cruise Line, 1050 Caribbean Way, Miami, FL 33132, tel. (305) 539-6000

Royal Viking Line, 95 Merrick Way, Coral Gables, FL 33134, tel. (800) 422-8000

Seabourn Cruise Line, 55 Francisco St., San Francisco, CA 94133, tel. (415) 391-7444.

Sitmar Princess Cruises, 10100 Santa Monica Blvd., Los Angeles, CA 90067, tel. (800) 421-0522

Sun Line Cruises, One Rockefeller Plaza, Suite 315, New York, NY 10020, tel. (800) 872-6400

Puerto Caldera after visits to various Mexican ports. Many itineraries include the Panamá Canal and the San Blas Islands. No scheduled passenger service links Costa Rica and other Central American nations. (**Temptress Cruises** offers cruise programs from Costa Rica to Panamá: see special topic "Natural-History Cruise Tours.")

Tour options while in port (normally one or two days) usually include a San José tour, sightseeing and shopping in Sarchí, a rafting expedition, a nature walk in Carara Biological Reserve, a banana plantation tour, maybe even golfing or horseback riding.

Finally, interest in dedicated cruises to Costa Rica is increasing steadily and expedition cruise ships that specialize in natural history are now cutting a wake to Costa Rica. See special topic "Natural-History Cruise Tours."

Adventurous travelers might be able to book a passage on a "tramp" steamer plying ports up and down the Americas. Some have limited passenger accommodations. This can be tremendous fun, and passengers are normally fed and looked after very well. Itineraries, however, can change without notice, and your interests will always be secondary to commercial freight considerations. **Marcon Lines** takes 10 passengers aboard the *Nedlloyd Hong Kong* on journeys from Lázaro Cárdenas (Mexico) and Puerto Caldera. The cruises, up to 150 days long, travel as far as Japan. Contact **Freighter World Cruises** (180 South Lake Ave. #335, Pasadena, CA 91101, tel. 818-449-3106, fax 818-449-9573), which also books passage on the MV *Maya Tikal,* which began three-week roundtrip cruises between Long Beach and Central America in 1994, with room for five passengers in one double and three single cabins.

Ford's Freighter Travel Guide (a semi-annual directory; 19448 Londelius St., Northridge, CA 91342, tel. 818-701-7414) and *Ford's International Cruise Guide* (published quarterly) provide comprehensive listings on freighters that take passengers.

Departing Costa Rica

See section on "Transportation" in chapter on San José for information on departure by air.

GETTING AROUND

BY AIR

Surprise! Traveling by air in Costa Rica is supremely economical, a quick and comfortable alternative to often long and bumpy road travel—and a great way to nip back to San José between forays by road to other places. The government-subsidized domestic airline **SANSA** has inexpensive flights to points throughout Costa Rica (SANSA, Calle 24 and Paseo Colón/Avenida 1; reservations, tel. 233-5330, 233-0397, or 233-3258, fax 255-2176). Flights are short—only 20-40 minutes. However, planes are small (22-35 passengers) and sell out quickly. SANSA reservation staff reportedly often fill all the seats with people making over-the-counter bookings before honoring requests for reservations from travel agents.

Note: Book well in advance. Reservations have to be paid in full and are nonrefundable. Check in at SANSA's San José office at least an hour before departure—it provides a free minibus transfer to Juan Santamaría Airport. SANSA baggage allowance is 11 kilograms. Delays and flight cancellations are common. And check the current schedules. *Schedules change frequently* as well as between seasons.

Travelair (Apdo. 381, San José 2100, tel. 232-7883 or 220-3054, fax 220-0413) flies from Tobías Bolaños Airport, near Pavas, three km west of San José. Its rates are higher than SANSA's, but unlike SANSA, you can confirm reservations without prepayment and the airline is somewhat more reliable. Travelair initially accepted surfboards and fishing poles, but this may have changed.

Air-Taxi: You can rent small charter flights from Tobías Bolaños Airport. **Aero Costa Sol** (Costa Sol International, 2490 Coral Way, Ste. 301, Miami, FL 33145, tel. 800-245-8420 or 305-858-4567, fax 305-858-7478; in Costa Rica, Apdo. 782, Alajuela 4050, tel. 441-1444, fax 441-2671) offers charter, ambulance, and executive flights to 23 destinations throughout Costa Rica using twin-engine five-passenger Aztecs, seven-passenger Navajos, and Lear Jets. Also try **Aeronaves de Costa Rica** (tel. 231-2541), **SAETA** (tel. 232-1474), **Taxi Aereo** (tel. 232-1579, fax 232-1469), **Trans Costa Rica** (tel. 232-0808), or **VEASA** (tel. 232-1010). **Air Taxi** (tel. 441-1444, fax 441-2671) flies out of Juan Santamaría. Rates range from $150 per hour upward. You may have to pay for a roundtrip if no one else is returning from your destination.

Helicopter: Yes, you can now get a bird's-eye view of Costa Rica by whirlybird, courtesy of **Helicopters of Costa Rica** (Apdo. 144, San José 2300, tel. 231-6564 or 232-1251, 24 hours, fax 232-5265), based at Tobías Bolaños Airport. Prices range from $25 for a 10-minute tour of the Meseta Central to $300 for a two-hour tour of Nicoya. Direct flights are offered to a variety of destinations on Bell Jet Rangers. Charter services are offered. **Helisa** (tel. 222-9219 or 255-4138, or **Diamante Tropical Tours** at 232-7532) likewise offers helicopter sightseeing trips; its choppers seat six "in comfort." A one-hour tour of Arenal costs $60; a 10-minute paronamic of the Meseta Central is $36.

DOMESTIC AIRLINES

AIRLINE	LOCATION	TELEPHONE
Aeronaves	Tobías Bolaños Airport	232-1413
SACSA	Juan Santamaría Airport	441-1444
SANSA	Calle 24, Paseo Colón	233-5330
SAETA	Tobías Bolaños Airport	232-1474
Travelair	Tobías Bolaños Airport	232-7883
Taxi Aereo	Juan Santamaría Airport	441-1626
VEASA	Tobías Bolaños Airport	232-1010

SANSA is the only airline that provides a free bus shuttle to/from the airport. Check in at the Paseo Colón office one hour before departure.

SANSA SCHEDULE

FROM/TO	DAYS	DEPARTURE TIME
San José-Quepos	Mon.-Sat.	8:15 a.m. and 3:45 p.m.
	Sun.	11 a.m.
Quepos-San José.	Mon.-Sat.	8:50 a.m. and 4:20 p.m.
	Sun.	11:35 a.m.
San José-Quepos	Mon., Wed., Fri., Sat.	9:30 a.m.
Quepos-Palmar Sur		10:05 a.m.
Palmar Sur-San José		10:35 a.m.
San José-Coto 47	Tues., Thurs., Sat.	8 a.m.
Coto 47-Puerto Jiménez		9 a.m.
Puerto Jiménez-Palmar Sur		9:30 a.m.
Palmar Sur-San José		10:05 a.m.
San José-Coto 47	Mon., Wed., Fri.	8:45 a.m.
Coto 47-Puerto Jiménez		9:45 a.m.
Puerto Jiménez-Palmar Sur		10:15 a.m.
Palmar Sur-San José		10:50 a.m.
San José-Golfito	Daily except Sun.	6 a.m.
	Wed., Thurs., Fri.	1:45 p.m.
Golfito-San José.	Daily except Sun.	7 a.m.
	Wed., Thurs., Fri.	2:45 p.m.
San José-Barra del Colorado	Tues., Thurs., Sat.	5:30 a.m.
Barra del Colorado-San José		6:15 a.m.
San José-Tamarindo.	Mon., Wed., Fri.	6 a.m.
Tamarindo-Nosara		6:55 a.m.
Nosara-Sámara		7:25 a.m.
Sámara-San José		7:50 a.m.
San José-Tambor.	Daily except Sun.	11:15 a.m.
Tambor-Tamarindo		11:50 a.m.
Tamarindo-Sámara		12:35 p.m.
Sámara-Tambor.		1:05 p.m.
Tambor-San José		1:45 p.m.
San José-Tambor	Sun.	8 a.m.
Tambor-Tamarindo		8:40 a.m.
Tamarindo-Sámara		9:20 a.m.
Sámara-Tambor.		9:50 a.m.
Tambor-San José		10:20 a.m.

Schedules often change; check current timetables. Extra flights are often announced in dry season.

FARES (ONE-WAY)

San José-Quepos	$24	San José-Palmar Sur	$41
San José-Tamarindo	$47	San José-Coto 47	$47
San José-Nosara	$41	San José-Golfito	$47
San José-Tambor	$36	San José-Barra del Colorado	$36

TRAVELAIR SCHEDULE (HIGH SEASON)

FROM/TO	DAYS	DEPARTURE TIME
San José-Barra del Colorado	Daily	6 a.m.
Barra del Colorado-Tortuguero		6:45 a.m.
Tortuguero-San José		7:05 a.m.
San José-Carrillo (Sámara)	Daily	8:45 a.m.
Carillo-Nosara		9:35 a.m.
Nosara-San José		10 a.m.
San José-Golfito	Daily	11 a.m.
Golfito-Puerto Jiménez		12:05 p.m.
Puerto Jiménez-San José		12:25 p.m.
San José-Liberia	Mon., Thurs., Fri., Sat.	7:30 a.m.
Liberia-San José		8:40 a.m.
San José-Quepos	Daily	7 a.m., noon, and 3:30 p.m.
Quepos-San José		7:40 a.m., and 12:40 p.m and 4:10 p.m.
San José-Quepos	Daily	11 a.m.
Quepos-Palmar Sur		11:40 a.m.
Palmar Sur-San José		12:15 p.m.
San José-Tambor	Daily	8:30 a.m. and 3 p.m.
Tambor-San José		3:40 p.m.
San José-Tamarindo	Daily	7:30 a.m. and 2 p.m.
Tamarindo-San José		8:40 a.m. and 3 p.m.

Schedules often change; check current timetables.
Note: A reduced schedule is in effect during green season.

FARES (ONE-WAY/ROUNDTRIP)

San José-Barra del Colorado	$74/$117	San José-Puerto Jiménez	$81/$136
San José-Carrillo	$75/$122	San José-Quepos	$45/$72
San José-Golfito	$76/$129	San José-Tambor	$62/$98
San José-Liberia	$82/$136	San José-Tamarindo	$82/$136
San José-Nosara	$82/$122	San José-Tortuguero	$72/$110
San José-Palmar Sur	$73/$119		

Sea Plane: For the ultimate thrill, you can fly with **Alas Anfibias** (Apdo. 247, San José 1017, tel. 232-9108, fax 232-9567), which offers the "only authorized seaplane charter in Costa Rica" to virtually anywhere in the country with water (hotel swimming pools excepted).

BY RAIL

Railway lines, originally built to serve the banana industry, run from San José to Puntarenas on the Pacific, and Puerto Limón on the Caribbean. No scheduled passenger trains run along them. The train to Puntarenas stopped service in October 1991 after a locomotive was stolen and the hijacker ran it off the rails! Actually, that was just the final blow—the railroad had been running at a loss for years. And the infamous and highly popular Jungle Train to Puerto Limón—one of the world's wildest train rides—was discontinued in November 1990 after a massive landslide covered the track. Landslides during the April 1991 earthquake sealed its fate.

SILVER TRAIN SCHEDULE

DEPARTS	ARRIVES
San José .... 5:45 a.m. .... Heredia ..... 6:15 a.m.	
Heredia ..... 6:30 a.m. .... San José .... 6:45 a.m.	
San José ... 12:15 p.m. .... Heredia .... 12:30 p.m.	
Heredia ..... 1:00 p.m. .... San José .... 1:15 p.m.	
San José .... 5:30 p.m. .... Heredia ..... 5:45 p.m.	
Heredia ..... 6:00 p.m. .... San José .... 6:15 p.m.	
Heredia ..... 6:15 a.m. .... San Pedro ... 7:00 a.m.	
San Pedro .... 12 noon .... Heredia ... 12:30 p.m.	
Heredia ..... 1:00 p.m. .... San Pedro ... 1:30 p.m.	
San Pedro ... 5:15 p.m. .... Heredia ..... 5:45 p.m.	

For information, call Intertren (tel. 226-0011)

You can still take part of the journey, however. **Swiss Travel Service** (tel. 231-4055), which operated the Jungle Train, now runs a day tour to Braulio Carrillo National Park, from where its private Banana Train runs to Siquirres. Lunch, a swimming stop, and a banana-plantation tour are included ($69). In the same vein,

Before it was disbanded after the April 1991 earthquake, the five-car, narrow-gauge Jungle Train ran between San José and Puerto Limón.

M. SILVER ASSOCIATION

TAM Travel Co. (tel. 222-2642) launched its Green Train, featuring two fully restored 1930s-style carriages with a/c. It follows the same route as the old Jungle Train, with a stop at Río Frío for a tour of the Dole banana plant ($70). It departs San José Tuesday and Saturday at 8 a.m.

Reportedly, local service on the Pacific Railroad is still offered between Salinas, Orotina, and Ciruelas, and on the Atlantic Railroad between Siquirres and Puerto Limón. A passenger train also still clunks between Limón and Estrella, a 55-km journey through banana country and a throwback to a more leisurely era. And the Pachuco Tico Tren Company may have reinstated service between Turrialba and Lake Bonilla by the time you read this. There's also local service from San José's Pacific Station to the western suburb of Pavas (Mon.-Fri. at 6 a.m. and 12:15 and 5:15 p.m.; Sunday 10 and 11:15 a.m.)

In April 1992, a service was initiated three times daily between Heredia, San José, and San Pedro (see "Silver Train Schedule" chart). The Silver Train, pulling sparkling silver carriages, departs the Atlántico Station at Avenida 3 and Calles 17/19, on the north side of Parque Nacional.

In 1994, an international consortium began negotiations with the government for a possible new railway to be constructed between Puntarenas and Puerto Limón.

BY BUS

The Meseta Central is well provided with good roads and local transportation. Both diminish the farther you travel from San José, the hub for services to the rest of the nation. However, most Costa Ricans use the nation's comprehensive bus system as their daily transport, and buses generally serve even the most remote towns. Generally, if there's a road there's a bus. More popular destinations are served

BUS COMPANIES

COMPANY	DESTINATION	TELEPHONE
Autobuses del Pacífico	Puntarenas	261-2158
Autotrans Mata	Orosí Valley	551-6810
Autotransportes Ciudad Quesada	Ciudad Quesada, Zarcero	255-4318
Autotransportes MEPE	Cahuita, Bribrí, Sixaola	221-0524
Autotransportes Tilarán	Tilarán, Monteverde	222-3854
Buses Metropoli	Irazú	272-0651
Carsol	Santa Rosa NP, Peñas Blancas	224-1968
CNT	Nicaragua (Peñas Blancas), Upala, Santa Cruz	255-1932
Coopelimón	Puerto Limón	223-7811
Coopetragua	Guápiles, Rara Avis	223-1276
Empresa Alfaro	Guanacaste, Nicoya, Nosara, Tamarindo, Sámara, Santa Cruz	223-8229 or 222-2750
Empresa Esquival	Playa Panamá, Hermosa	666-1249
Empresarios Unidos	Puntarenas	222-0064
Garaje Barquero	Fortuna	232-5660
Jacó	Carara, Jacó, Herradura	223-1109 or 441-5890
Mi Bus	Puntarenas	222-1867
Microbuses Rapidos	Heredia	233-8392
Pulmitán	Cañas, Bagaces, Liberia, Coco	222-1650
SACSA	Cartago	233-5350
Sirca	Nicaragua	222-5541
TICA	Panamá, Guatemala, Honduras, Nicaragua	221-8954
Tracopa	Golfito, Palmar Norte, Paso Canoas, San Isidro, Panamá	221-4214 or 223-7685
Tralapa	Nicoya, Santa Cruz, Tamarindo, Flamingo, Junquillal	221-7202
Transportes Blanco	Puerto Jiménez	771-2550
Transportes la Cañera	Cañas	222-3006
Transportes Morales	Jacó, Quepos	223-5567 or 223-1109
Transportes Rojas	Nosara, Sámara	685-5352
Transportes Quepos	Quepos, Manuel Antonio	223-5567
Transportes Musoc	San Isidro	222-2422 or 223-0686
Transtusa	Turrialba	556-0073
Tuan	Sarchí	441-3781
Tuasa	Alajuela, Poás	222-4650 or 222-5325

PURA NATURA SHUTTLE SERVICE

Saragundí Specialty Tours operates 15-seat Ford microbuses that service a network of about 100 hotels nationwide. You can buy an **ECOPass** good for the duration of your vacation ($115, seven tickets/ two weeks; $150, 10 tickets/three weeks). Buses depart San José at 7 a.m. Times below are for departures.

ROUTE 1/NORTHERN LOWLANDS

9 a.m.	Horquetas
9:30 a.m.	Puerto Viejo
10 a.m.	Chilamate
11:30 a.m.	Pital
Noon	Muelle
2 p.m.	Fortuna
4 p.m.	San Ramón

ROUTE 2/NORTHERN LOWLANDS

9:30 a.m.	San Ramón
1:30 p.m.	Fortuna
2:30 p.m.	Muelle
3:30 p.m.	Pital
5 p.m.	Chilamate
5:15 p.m.	Puerto Viejo
5:45 p.m.	Horquetas

ROUTE 3/CENTRAL PACIFIC

8:30 a.m.	Atenas
9:30 a.m.	Carara
10:30 a.m.	Jacó
1:30 a.m.	Manuel Antonio
4 p.m.	Jacó
5 p.m.	Carara
5:45 p.m.	Atenas

ROUTE 4/GUANACASTE

9:30 a.m.	Puntarenas
11:30 a.m.	Liberia
2 p.m.	Tamarindo
3 p.m.	Liberia
5 p.m.	Puntarenas

ROUTE 5/CARIBBEAN

8:10 a.m.	Braulio Carrillo (Aerial Tram)
8:45 a.m.	Bosque Lluvioso
9:05 a.m.	Guápiles
10:05 a.m.	Puerto Limón
11:25 a.m.	Río Estrella
1 p.m.	Cahuita
1:40 p.m.	Río Estrella
2:35 p.m.	Puerto Limón
4 p.m.	Guápiles
4:20 p.m.	Bosque Lluvioso
4:55 p.m.	Braulio Carrillo (Aerial Tram)

ROUTE 6

8 a.m.	Fortuna
8:50 a.m.	Lake Arenal (Los Héroes)
9:40 a.m.	Lake Coter
10:05 a.m.	Lake Arenal (Tilawa)
10:30 a.m.	Cañas
3 p.m.	Liberia
3:25 p.m.	Cañas
3:50 p.m.	Lake Arenal (Tilawa)
4:15 p.m.	Lake Coter
5:05 p.m.	Lake Arenal (Los Héroes)

You can make reservations until 6 p.m. one day in advance at participating hotels or Pura Natura (Edificio Cristal at Avenida 1, Calles 1/3, tel. 233-9709, fax 223-9200; in the U.S., GL Tours, tel. 800-334-5832 or 414-275-6873, fax 414-275-3996; in Canada, tel. 800-667-1221 or 604-681-1221, fax 604-681-2754).

by both fast buses *(directo)* and slower buses *(normal* or *corriente),* which stop en route. You can travel to most parts of the country for less than $6. Some popular national parks are not included on bus schedules; take a bus as close as you can, then take a taxi. Manfred Melchinger, of Mainz in Germany, wrote to say "We can recommend travel by bus, even for older people, like we are."

Standards of service vary widely, from modern, ultracomfortable Volvos to smoking, run-down old-timers. Most buses serving major towns from San José are up to par with Greyhound. Farther afield, many local buses are old U.S. high-school buses with arse-numbing seats.

Information about the bus system is fragmentary. Most bus stops are unmarked, and there are virtually no published schedules or

route information. The ICT information office beneath the Plaza de la Cultura (Calle 5, Avenida Central) provides an up-to-date bus schedule. Both *Costa Rica Today* and the *Tico Times* publish bus schedules.

San José has no central terminal. Many buses leave from the Coca-Cola "terminal" (centered on Calle 16 and Avenida 1, but spread around many streets), named after the defunct Coca-Cola bottling factory. Beware pickpockets here, and avoid it at night if possible. Other buses leave from the bus company office or a streetside bus stop—*parada.* Many street departure points are unmarked: ask the locals. The Ministry of Public Works and Transport is planning to build a bus terminal in San José's Barrio Tournón district to serve the northern and eastern parts of the country. Buses from San José are particularly crowded on Friday and Saturday. So, too, are those returning *to* San José on Sunday and Monday. (See the San José chapter for bus schedules.)

You should buy tickets in advance from larger bus companies; others you'll have to pay for when getting aboard. Fare cards are posted near the driver's seat. *Don't display wads of money!* Get there at least an hour before departure for long-distance buses. Locals pack aboard until there isn't even standing room left and the rush for seats can be furious. Some buses have storage below; local buses do not. Luggage space inside is usually limited to overhead racks. Stops on *normal* buses are frequent—everyone seems to have a couple of boxes and perhaps a chicken or two to load aboard. Travel light. Consider leaving some luggage at your hotel in San José.

If possible, sit toward the front. Conditions on local buses can get very cramped and very hot; the back tends to be hottest. Aisle seats usually provide more leg room. Don't drink too much coffee or other liquids if you anticipate a long journey; toilet stops are few and far between. Often, the bus won't have a buzzer. To get off, whistle loudly or shout *"¡Parada!"* In the Meseta Central, bus stops are marked by yellow lines on the roadside, rectangular signs, or shelters. Elsewhere, you can usually flag down rural buses anywhere along their routes. Long-distance buses don't always stop when waved down. Locals will direct you to the correct bus stop if you ask.

Men and women relinquish their seats gladly to pregnant women, the handicapped, elderly people, and mothers with small children. Set a good example: do the same.

Bill Baker's *The Essential Road Guide for Costa Rica* provides comprehensive information on traveling by bus, including San José bus routes.

Tourist Buses

The tourist boom is spawning new bus shuttle services (most operated by specific tour companies) between points on the tourist circuit. Monteverde and Jacó Beach, for example, are served by the Silver Bullet (Exotur) from San José, and Manuel Antonio is served by the American VIP Coach Service, although reports are in that both had ceased. And Saragundí Specialty Tours operates the **Pura Natura** shuttle services on six popular routes (see chart "Pura Natura Shuttle Service"), including a three-week pass.

BY CAR

Nearly half of all foreign tourists to Costa Rica rent a car. Exploring the country by car allows total freedom of movement. You can cover a lot of turf without the time delays of buses, and you can stop off for sightseeing anywhere you want. The exception is San José, where a car can be a distinct liability. Says *National Geographic:* "Japanese compacts play daylong dodg'em with bullyboy buses . . . Rush hour is a bullfight on the streets, with every car a blaring beast and every pedestrian a torero."

Costa Rica has some 29,000 kilometers (18,000 miles) of highway (14% paved). A two-lane "freeway" links many of the major towns in the Meseta Central, where roads are well marked (four-lane roads into San José are toll roads). Most popular beaches can be reached by car. Beyond the Meseta, however, roads generally deteriorate with distance. Even much-traveled roads, such as those to Monteverde Reserve and Manuel Antonio National Park, are still not paved and can shake both a car and its occupants until their doors and teeth rattle. In the rainy season, such roads become deeply potholed or even totally flooded. Condi-

HIGHWAY SIGNS

Adelante—Ahead
Alto—Stop
Alto Adelante—Stop Ahead
Area de Descanso—Rest Area
Calle Sin Salida—Dead-end Street
Carril para Transito Lento—Lane for Slow Traffic
Ceda El Paso—Yield
Control por Guia—Tow-away Zone
Curva Adelante—Curve Ahead
Derrumbes—Landslides
Desvio—Deviation
Hundimiento—Dip
Mantenga su Derecha—Stay to the Right
Mirador—Scenic View
No Adelantar—No Passing
No Estacionar—No Parking
No Hay Paso—Do Not Enter
No Virar En U—No U-turn
Peaje Adelante—Toll Ahead
Peligro—Danger
Puesto de Control—Control Post
   (Guardia Rural)
Ruta Pesada—Truck Route
Siga con Precaución—Proceed with Caution
Trabajos en La Via—Roadworks
Transito Entrado—Traffic Entering the Highway
Transito Lento por La Derecha—Slow Traffic Keep Right
Transito Público—Public Transportation

tions improve December onward, although roads may not be regraded for months. Parts of the Nicoya Peninsula are often impenetrable by road during much of the rainy season.

In 1994, the newly elected Figueres administration promised to invest one billion *colones* ($6.5 million) for road improvements nationwide, with a large percentage dedicated to the Nicoya Peninsula.

If you've only a short time, a figure-eight-shaped drive looping east and west of San José allows you to see much of the nation's splendid scenery, along with "enough hairpins and foggy mountain passes to give drivers a sense of adventure."

Traffic Regulations
You must be at least 21 years old and hold a passport to drive in Costa Rica. Foreign driver's licenses are valid for three months upon arrival.

For longer, you'll need a Costa Rican driver's license. Apply at Calle 5 and Avenida 18 in San José. The speed limit on highways is 80 km/h (50 mph), and 60 km/h on secondary roads. Speed limits are vigorously enforced (see "Traffic Police," below). A law enacted in 1992 raised speeding fines from $10 to a whopping $150 and higher! Seat belt use is mandatory, and motorcyclists must wear helmets. Insurance—a state monopoly—is also mandatory. Car rental companies sell insurance with rentals (see "Insurance," under "By Car" under "Getting There," above).

Note, too, that it's illegal to: 1) enter an intersection unless you can exit; 2) make a right turn on a red light unless indicated by a white arrow; and 3) overtake on the right; pass only on the left. Cars coming uphill have right of way.

If you see a speed sign ahead, it's a good idea to slow down immediately. I once got a speeding ticket for exceeding 50 km/h as I *approached* a 50 km/h zone; the cop was standing by the sign, pointing his radar gun at traffic still in the 70 km/h zone! He wanted me to pay a fine on the spot for his crafty subterfuge—an illegal act that you should *never* fall for.

Driving Safety
Costa Ricans *boast* about having the world's highest auto fatality rate (18 deaths per 100,000 kilometers, compared to 2.7 per 100,000 km in the U.S.). A total of 41,908 accidents were reported in 1991; the 1,946 registered taxis had an

SPEED LIMITS

Toll roads/Primary Highways . . . . . 70-90 km/h
Primary/Secondary roads . . . . 40-60 km/h
School zones . . . . 25 km/h
   Speed limits vary as posted. Heed them.
   Penalties are heavy.

TRAFFIC SIGNS

NO VEHICULOS AUTOMOTORES
no motorized vehicles

ANCHO MAXIMO (18 m)
maximum width (number)

NO ESTACIONAR
no parking

VELOCIDAD MAXIMA (60 KPH)
maximum speed (number)

PARADA DE TAXIS
taxi stand

NO ADELANTAR
no passing

PEATONES POR LA IZQUIERDA
pedestrians to the left

SILENCIO
quiet

ALTURA MAXIMA (3 m)
maximum height (number)

NO VIRAR EN U
no U-turn

SE PERMITE VIRAR EN U
U-turn permitted

MANTENGA SU DERECHA
stay to right

CEDA EL PASO
yield

ESTACIONAMIENTO UNA HORA 6 AM - 6 PM
parking permitted (hours)

ALTO
stop

accident rate of 174%—or nearly two accidents for every taxi!

A sizeable share of Costa Ricans are appalling drivers capable of truly unbelievable recklessness. They drive at warp speed, flaunt traffic laws, hold traffic lights in total disdain, and love to crawl up your tailpipe at 100 km/h. Worse, everybody overtakes at the slightest chance—they seem to suffer feelings of inadequacy knowing there's a car in front of them. Costa Ricans positively thrill to overtaking on blind corners and narrow overhangs, so beep your horn before sharp bends. And keep your speed down, especially on rural roads, with their potholes from hell. Roads usually lack sidewalks, so pedestrians—and even livestock—walk the road. Be particularly wary at night. And treat mountain roads with extra caution: they're often blocked by thick fog, floods, and landslides. The road from San José to Puntarenas, the new road linking San José and Guápiles, and the long and winding road between Cartago and San Isidro de General are particularly bad: steep, fog-ridden, narrow, and as serpentine as coiled snakes. Still, that doesn't faze local drivers, who even in the worst conditions drive with an almost feline disdain for mortality.

Watch out for piles of leaves or boulders at the roadside—they indicate a stalled car ahead. Check old wooden bridges before crossing: you may need to go around if tire tracks lead into the watercourse. Narrow bridges *(puente angosto)*, which usually accommodate only one vehicle at a time, are first-come, first-served. And slow down whenever you see the sign *topes* or *túmulos*, meaning "road bumps." The first time you barrel over them heedlessly will serve notice to respect the warning next time.

Potholes are a particular problem. "Hit a big one," says Bill Baker in *The Essential Road Guide for Costa Rica,* "and it's not unusual to damage a tire or even destroy a wheel . . . Nor is it unusual to have a driver suddenly swerve to avoid one just as you're passing him." Beware buses, too. They'll often stop without warning. *Drive slowly. And give everyone else on the road lots of room!*

Another good tip is to drive with your lights on at *all times,* as they do by law in Scandinavia (where vehicular accidents have been signifi-cantly reduced as a consequence). Oncoming drivers will flash their lights at you in response, even in gloomy conditions, but so what: they've acknowledged your presence!

Accidents and Breakdowns

The law states that you must carry fluorescent triangles in case of breakdown. Locals, however, generally pile leaves, rocks, or small branches at the roadside to warn approaching drivers of a car in trouble. If your own car is involved, **Coopetaxi Garage** (tel. 235-9966) in San José is recommended for towing and repair. If your car is rented, call the rental agency: it will arrange a tow.

After an accident, *never* move the vehicles until the police arrive. Get the names, license plate numbers, and *cedulas* (legal identification numbers) of any witnesses. Make a sketch of the accident. And call the **traffic police**—*tráfico* (in the Meseta Central, tel. 227-7150 or 227-8030; in rural areas call 127).

Do *not* offer statements to anyone other than the police. In case of injury, call the **Red Cross ambulance** (tel. 221-5818). Outside towns, call 118 for **emergency rescue** and 117 for an **emergency patrol** car. Try not to leave the accident scene, or at least keep an eye on your car: the other party may tamper with the evidence. And don't let honking traffic—there'll be plenty!—pressure you into moving the cars.

Show the *tráfico* your license and vehicle registration. Make sure you get them back: he is not allowed to keep any documents unless you've been drinking (if you suspect the other driver has been drinking, ask the *tráfico* to administer a Breathalyzer test, or *alcolemia*). Nor can the *tráfico* assess a fine. The police will issue you a green ticket or "summons." You must present this to the nearest municipal office *(alcaldia)* or **traffic court** *(tribunal de tránsito)* within eight days to make your *declaración* about the accident. Wait a few days so that the police report is on record. Don't skip this! The driver who doesn't show is often found at blame by default. Then, take your driver's license, insurance policy, and a police report to the **INS,** the state insurance monopoly in San José (Avenida 7, Calles 9/11, tel. 223-5800), to process your claim. Car rental companies will take care of this if your car is rented.

Car Rentals

The leading U.S. car rental companies have offices in Costa Rica. You also have a wide choice of reputable local rental companies, usually with slightly cheaper rates. I can recommend Prego Rent-a-Car (tel. 221-8680, fax 221-8675) based on my own experiences.

Most agencies are in San José, usually west of downtown. Some have offices at Juan Santamaría Airport and/or representatives at major hotels in more popular resort towns. Minimum age for drivers ranges from 21 to 25. You'll need a valid driver's license plus a credit card. Without a credit card you'll have to pay a hefty deposit, normally around $700.

The government fixes a ceiling on rental rates. Most agencies charge the maximum during the high season (Nov.-April) and offer discounts during the low season (May-Oct.). You'll normally get better rates (up to 10% discount) by making your reservations in the U.S. at least one week before departure, though I've heard several reports of extra charges appearing, and other complications. **Note:** During my most recent research trip, I received a worrisome report: upon returning his car, one reader was advised by counter staff that there were payment issues to resolve, although the car had been fully prepaid and no "problems" were mentioned when he picked up the car. After a one-hour delay at the counter, the reader and his wife found that their possessions had been stolen from their vehicle parked outside. Police records show similar reports on file. The reader had booked with Elegante Rent-a-Car.

Reserve as far in advance as possible, especially in dry season and for Christmas and holidays. Make sure you clarify any one-way drop-off fees, late return penalties, etc. Take a copy of your reservation with you. And be prepared to defend against mysterious new charges that may be tagged on in Costa Rica. You must rent for a minimum of three days to qualify for unlimited mileage. Stick shift is the norm. Some agencies will rent camping and surfing equipment, too.

Rates: Small cars such as the Subaru Justy, Nissan 1300, or Toyota Corolla begin at about $30 daily/$180 weekly plus 21 cents per kilometer, or $45 daily/$270 weekly with unlimited mileage. **Midsize** cars such as the Toyota Corolla, Nissan Sentra, and Daihatsu Applause begin at $35 daily/$215 weekly plus 29 cents per kilometer, or $60 daily/$350 weekly with unlimited mileage. (See also "Insurance," below.) It behooves you to get unlimited mileage if you plan on driving more than 500 km per week. And regardless where you plan to go, my advice is to rent a 4WD vehicle.

Consider a pre-arranged package such as **Costa Rica Experts'** "Flexipak," which includes roundtrip airfare from Miami, seven nights' accommodation, and choice of vehicle with unlimited mileage (from $715 double, per person; 3166 N. Lincoln Ave. #424, Chicago, IL 60657, tel. 312-935-1009 or 800-827-9046, fax 312-935-9252). **Adventure Tours** (10612 Beaver Dam Rd., Hunt Valley, MD 21030-2205, tel. 800-892-9894) also offers a fly/drive program with two itineraries from $625 pp, double occupancy, including airport transfers, upscale accommodations, and car rental.

Four-Wheel Drive

Most agencies offer a range of small-size to full-size four-wheel-drive vehicles. 4WDs are essential for Nicoya and other off-the-beaten-path destinations. In fact, I recommend them, *period!* Some agencies will insist you rent a 4WD for specific regions, especially in rainy season. Fortunately, you may get an off-season discount then. The smaller models (Suzuki Sidekick, Samurai, etc.) begin at about $35 daily/$250 weekly with unlimited mileage and insurance. Rates rise to about $450 per week for larger models (e.g., Toyota Land Cruiser). The smaller 4WDs are ideal for most conditions, but may be too lightweight for more rugged conditions.

Even hardy 4WDs can be reduced to a tormented standstill by Costa Rica's dirt roads and unpaved highways. The prospect of getting inextricably stuck in fender-deep mud midway to a remote jungle lodge is very real, especially in wet season.

If you intend exploring off the beaten track, and/or want to travel away from paved roads in wet season with complete assurance, a lightweight vehicle won't do! I strongly recommend a heavy-duty 4WD. My personal preference is to rent a Range Rover—a vehicle as prized in Costa Rica as it is in the capitals and countryside of Europe. They were assembled in Costa Rica in

CAR-RENTAL AGENCIES IN SAN JOSÉ

ADA Rent-a-Car, Plaza Gonzalez Víquez, tel. 233-7733

Adobe Rent-a-Car, Calle 7, Avenidas 8/10, tel. 221-5425

American Rent-a-Car, Centro Colón, tel. 221-5353, fax 221-8667.

Amigo Rent-a-Car, Calle 3, Avenida 13, tel. 255-4141, fax 223-0660

Avis, Calle 42, Avenida Las Americas, tel. 222-6066; U.S. (800) 331-1212

Budget, Calle 30, Paseo Colón, tel. 223-3284; fax 255-4966; U.S. (800) 472-3325

Coral Rent-a-Car, tel. 240-1085, fax 240-1293

CrUSA Rent-a-Car, tel. 442-6642, fax 442-6642.

Dollar, Calle Central, Avenidas 7/9, tel. 233-3339; U.S. (800) 421-6868

Ecological Rent-a-Car, Barrio Aranjuez, tel./fax 233-6558

Economy Rent-a-Car, Sabana Norte (next to Datsun), tel. 232-9130, fax 231-5410

Elegante Rent-a-Car, Calle 10, Avenidas 13/15, tel. 221-006, fax 233-8605; U.S. (800) 582-7432

El Indio Rent-a-Car, Calles 40/42, Avenida Central, tel. 223-4955

Exotico Rent-a-Car, tel. 253-0762, fax 253-0776.

Gemini Rent-a-Car, Escazú, tel./fax 228-9629

Global Rent-a-Car, Calles 7/9, Avenida 7, tel. 223-4056, fax 222-4823

Happy Rent-a-Car, Calle 3, Avenidas 5/7, tel. 233-3435, fax 221-5884

Hertz, Calle 38, Paseo Colón, tel. 223-5959; U.S. (800) 654-3131

Holiday Rent-a-Car, tel. 255-1333, fax 223-4525

Jeeps R Us, tel. 289-9920

Mapache Rent-a-Car, tel. 255-1640, fax 256-1869

Meir Rent-a-Car, Calle 11, Avenida 14/18, tel. 257-4666, fax 222-7447

Nacho Rent-a-Car, tel. 221-8261, fax 223-3225

National, Calle 36, Avenida 7, tel. 233-4044, fax 233-2186; U.S. (800) 227-7368

Paz Rent-a-Car, Calle 42, Avenida 2/4, tel. 255-1491, fax 255-4257

Pilot Rent-a-Car, Calle 30, Avenida 1, tel. 222-8715, fax 222-9080

Prego Rent-a-Car, Paseo Colón, Calle 32, tel. 221-8680, fax 221-8675

Rent-a-Rover, Apdo. 77, Paraíso de Cartago, tel./fax 533-3037

Santos Rent-a-Car, Calle 40, Avenidas 3/5, tel. 257-0035

Tico Rent-a-Car, Calles 24/26, Paseo Colón, tel. 222-8920, fax 222-1765. Also offices at the Hotel San José Palacio and next to Burger King in the Plaza de la Cultura.

Toyota Rent-a-Car, Paseo Colón, Calles 30/32, tel. 223-2250

Tricolor Rent-a-Car, tel. 222-3333 or (800) 949-0234, fax 221-4444

U-Haul Rent-a-Car, Paseo Colón, 100 meters west of Toyota, tel. 222-1110, fax 222-1242

Vetrasa, La Uruca, tel. 257-2211, fax 255-0621

Wabe Rent-a-Car, Calle 24, Paseo Colón, tel. 221-7004, fax 221-6964

Walker Rent-a-Car, Paseo Colón, 100 meters south of Mercedes-Benz, tel. 257-0193, fax 257-0194

The following have offices at Juan Santamaría Airport: **ADA** (tel. 441-1260), **Budget** (tel. 441-4444), **Santos** (tel. 441-3044), **Hertz** (tel. 441-0097), **Tico** (tel. 443-2078), and **Wabe** (tel. 442-0884).

the late 1970s and are still going strong. The Range Rover's massive power, formidable traction, and suspension system are unmatched by any other off-road vehicle. The vehicle is so superbly engineered and supremely versatile that *4 Wheel & Off-Road* magazine called it "the best of any 4 wheel drive we've ever driven." I explored the most remote corners of Costa Rica in wet season, making headway across terrain that would have crippled lesser vehicles. Range Rovers got me up, over, around, and across terrain that would have challenged a pack mule. Although heavy, the Range Rover generally handles on-road with ease and agility. I loved the vehicle's commanding height. And it has enough room in back for a refrigerator's worth of food . . . and the refrigerator, too!

Rent-a-Rover—a family-run company owned by a Swiss, Roland Huber—offers Range Rovers for about the same price as ordinary 4WDs. Cost is about $490 a week, including unlimited mileage and insurance (collision deductible is approximately $450). Special rates are available for two or more weeks. Cars are dropped off and picked up free of charge in the San José area, and elsewhere for a small fee.

However, that said, the rental vehicles are more than a decade old and although rebuilt and completely reupholstered, reliability seems to be an issue. The company supposedly provides a specialized technician on call 24 hours. This proved true in my case when my vehicle broke down. I've received two complaints from readers about mechanical and other problems (hoods—bonnets—shaking loose and worn clutches seem typical), delays for repairs, etc.

Contact Rent-a-Rover, Apdo. 77, Paraíso de Cartago, tel./fax 533-3037.

Most other companies offers a range of 4WD rentals, including hefty Toyota Land Cruisers, etc. Companies that specialize in these are **Jeeps R Us** (tel. 289-9920) and **Tricolor Rent-a-Car** (tel. 222-3333 or 800-949-0234, fax 221-4444), which also offers a series of "4x4 Tours." I've heard of complaints regarding U-Haul Rent-a-Car, which is *not* affiliated with the U.S. company of that name.

An increasing number of car rental and tour companies are offering 4WD tours. **Southern Horizons Travel** (6100 Simpson Ave., N. Hollywood, CA 91606, tel. 818-980-7011, fax 818-980-6987) offers an eight-day 4WD package. **Costa Rica Experts** (3166 N. Lincoln Ave. #424, Chicago, IL 60657, tel. 800-827-9046 or 312-935-1009, fax 312-935-9252) has a 24-day 4WD tour following the "Route of Biodiversity" to remote national parks.

Motor Homes
ATA Motor Home Rentals (tel. 288-2011; in the U.S., c/o Dockside Tours, tel. 800-235-3625) offers rentals with tax and insurance included. Prices based on two people: three days $405 ($30 per day each additional person), seven days $875 ($25 per day each additional person), $120 per day for over seven days ($20 per day each additional person).

Siesta Campers (tel. 487-7066) offers fully equipped VW campers, as does **VW Campers,** with vehicles from $320 weekly (tel. 232-7532, 231-5905).

Motorcycles
Prego Rent-a-Motorcycle rents Honda XL125 trail bikes from $20 daily and Honda 200 Fourtrax from $30 (tel. 265-1400, fax 257-1158). **Moto Rental S.A.** (tel. 257-0193) has Honda XR200 motorcycles ($42 per day, $250 weekly) and Suzuki TS185 ($36 per day, $210 weekly); four-day minimum. **Rent-a-Moto** (tel. 442-1534) offers Kawasaki Ninjas and Suzuki 185s.

Insurance
The sample rates above do *not* include insurance. However, many rates quoted by rental agencies now include insurance. Check carefully. Only Adobe, Budget, and National accept American Express auto-rental insurance (check in advance). Because auto insurance is mandatory in Costa Rica, you will need to accept the obligatory C.D.W. (collision damage waiver) charged by car rental companies. It does not cover your car's contents or personal possessions. Rates range $10-15 per day, depending on car and agency. Each company determines its own deductible—ranging $500-1000—even though the INS sets this at 20% of damages.

Inspect your vehicle for damage and marks before departing, otherwise you may be charged for the slightest "damage" when you return. Note even the smallest nick and dent on the diagram you'll be presented to sign. And

don't forget the inside, as well as the radio antennae. Heaters and defrosters often don't work (you'll need to bring a rag for your frequently steamed-up windows). **Note:** *Don't* use your a/c to clear up condensation as it cools the windows and actually fosters condensation. Don't assume the rental agency has taken care of oil, water, brakes, fluids, or tire pressures: check them yourself before setting off. Most agencies claim to provide a 24-hour road service. (Is the moon made of cheese?)

The English-language *Tico Times* and *Costa Rica Today* advertise private car rentals and guide services in the classified sections. Recommended are Flor de María Castro (tel. 235-1072); Javier Cambronero Alfaro (tel. 236-5044); and Evelio Fonseca Mata (tel. 661-0958; Spanish only). All have minivans for one- to multi-day tours countryside.

See also "Insurance" under "By Car" in the "Getting There" section, above, for more information on insurance.

Gasoline

Unleaded gasoline was introduced in July 1994 in an attempt to reduce pollution. In Costa Rica it is called Super. Most rental cars take regular, although all cars imported to Costa Rica beginning 1 January 1995, had to use unleaded gas. Service stations *(bombas)* are far apart; in rural areas they're usually open dawn to dusk only. It's a wise idea to always fill up whenever you pass a service station. At press time, gasoline cost 45 cents a liter ($1.75 a gallon), down from 50 cents a litre a few years ago. Expect to pay double at off-the-beaten-track spots where gas may be poured from a can. If you don't see a gas station there's sure to be someone nearby willing to sell from private stock.

Maps and Directions

Costa Rican roads have few signposts (the Figueres administration has promised to rectify this). Those that exist are generally easy to understand. However, many crucial signs are located where you'd never think of looking or are otherwise obscured. Others often point in the wrong direction or lead you off on the longest route simply because they were placed by folks who want to direct tourists past their sundry business establishments.

Ask directions whenever in doubt. And check with locals about conditions down the road. Costa Ricans tend to be optimistic about whether roads are passable in excessive rain and fog, so double-check with foreigners if possible. Roadside ads for Delta cigarettes also include brief directions to major destinations.

You'll need the best map you can get hold of. The **ICT** tourist information office (below the Plaza de la Cultura) has a basic road map, as do car rental agencies. Neither are much use for beyond the Meseta Central. **World Wide Books And Maps** (736A Granville St., Vancouver, B.C., Canada V6Z 1G3, tel. 604-687-3320, fax 604-687-5925) sells the best map: the *International Travel Map of Costa Rica* (scale 1:500,000), showing minor roads and service stations (see "Maps," in the "Other Practicalities" section of this chapter). I recommend also buying a copy of the *Red Guide to Costa Rica* and/or the *Costa Rica Nature Atlas-Guidebook,* which has detailed 1:200,000 road maps; they're not always accurate, but they're the best around. (See the San José chapter for bookstores with map sections.)

Consider buying a copy of Bill Baker's *Essential Road Guide to Costa Rica* (see Booklist). An alternative is audiocassettes for the independent traveler produced by **Audio Turismo de Costa Rica** (Apdo. 1214, San José, tel. 233-8751; in the U.S., Interlink #217, P.O. Box 526770, Miami, FL 33152). It offers three tapes: one describes a self-drive tour from San José to Atenas, Orotina, Jacó, Parrita, Quepos, Manuel Antonio, and Dominical; another covers San José to Monteverde via Grecia and Sarchí; a third leads via Grecia and Sarchí to the beaches of Guanacaste. They give specific driving directions, plus driving tips, side trips, information on national parks, etc. en route. Each tape comes with a map of the route. Available in hotel gift stores ($15 each).

Traffic Police

Traffic police patrol the highways to control speeding drivers. They pull people over at random to check documentation. In the past they've been fond of rental cars (the TUR on rental car license plates gives the game away) in the hope of extorting bribes. The government has initiated an anti-corruption campaign that includes a crackdown on this despicable act, and there

TRAFFIC POLICE TELEPHONES

Central Radio 227-8030, 227-1750
Alajuela 441-7411
Cartago 551-7475
Heredia 238-1966
Liberia 666-1116
Puerto Limón 758-3943
Puntarenas .661-1825
San Carlos .460-1838
San Isidro 717-1313
San José . . . . .227-2188, ext. 506
San Ramón 445-5288
Siquirres 768-8476
Southern Zone 789-9050

are even plans to do away with the plates, which are red flags to car thieves.

If you're stopped, the police will request to see your license, passport, and rental contract. *Tráficos* use radar guns. Speeding fines (see "Traffic Regulations," above) are paid at a bank; the ticket provides instructions. Don't think you can get away with not paying a fine. Delinquent fines are reported to the immigration authorities and people have been refused exit from the country (reportedly, police also have the right to take your license away until you pay the fine). Often, the car rental agency will handle the tickets, although you remain responsible for paying the fine. The best bet is: *don't speed!*

It's important to know your rights and respond accordingly. *Never* pay a fine to police on the road! The police cannot legally request payment on site. If he (I've never seen a female traffic cop) demands payment, note the policeman's name and number from his M.O.P.T. badge (he is legally required to show his carnet upon request). Report the incident to the Aesoría Legal de Tránsito of M.O.P.T., 150 meters east of the Pacific train station in San José (Calle 2, Avenida 20, tel. 227-2188, ext. 546).

Traffic police cars and pickups are dark blue with white tops and doors. Oncoming vehicles will often flash their lights to indicate traffic police—or an accident or disabled vehicle—ahead.

HITCHHIKING

Hitchhiking is reasonably safe and straightforward, though it may be slow going; if buses don't go where you're going, cars are not likely to either. Ticos are used to picking up pedestrians in areas where bus service is infrequent, and locals often hitchhike in more remote regions. They'll also unabashedly ask you for a ride; don't be afraid to be "brazen." Simply sticking out your thumb won't do it! Try to wave down the car. Politely ask if there's room, as you've "been waiting for ages for a bus," etc. Politeness and gratitude, too, demand you offer to pay for your ride—"*¿Cuanto le debo?*"—after you're safely delivered.

Generally, Ticos are immensely civil and trustworthy and will go out of their way to help out of goodwill. Still, caution is always a watchword when hitchhiking, especially for women. I do not recommend that women hitchhike alone. Try to "get the measure" of the driver *before* getting in a car. If you feel uncomfortable, don't get in. My instincts have always served me well when hitchhiking. Trust yours!

TAXIS

Costa Rica has an excellent nationwide taxi system. Taxis are inexpensive by U.S. standards, so much so that they are a viable means of touring for short trips, especially if you're traveling with two or three others. Generally, taxis will go wherever a road leads. Most taxis are radio dispatched. A white triangle on the front door contains the taxi's license plate number.

You can hire a taxi by the hour or half day; the cost normally compares favorably to hiring a car for the day. Many national parks are served infrequently by bus, or not at all; hence you may be inclined to take a taxi, for example, to Poás volcano (110 km roundtrip), which should cost about $40 with perhaps two hours at the volcano. Jeep-taxis are common in more remote areas, particularly the Nicoya Peninsula.

Agree on the fare *before* setting off, as taxi drivers are notorious for overcharging. Don't be afraid to bargain. How you dress might make a difference: the more downbeat you dress the

less likely it is that you'll receive an inflated price. Outside San José, few taxis are metered and taxi drivers are allowed to negotiate their fare for any journey over 15 kilometers.

Taxi drivers are required by law to use their meters *(marías)*. In San José, however, drivers rarely use them (many will do so in the morning; the later it gets, the less they like to do so). Insist on it being used. If there isn't one, agree on the rate before getting in the taxi. Check rates in advance with your hotel concierge. Official rates, introduced in November 1994, were: 100 *colones* (60 cents) for the first kilometer, 45 *colones* (about 25 cents) each kilometer thereafter. Nighttime fares cost 20% more. Journeys longer than 12 km, or on unpaved roads outside San José, are charged at a previously agreed amount. (See the "Transportation" section in San José for more information.) Fares quoted by taxi drivers who don't use their meters tend to be inflated 20-30%. Consider getting out if after a few blocks the meter doesn't start advancing; taxi drivers are now being fined, so your ruse may work.

Outside San José, you'll usually find taxis around the main square of small towns. Here, you'll be dependent on taxis after, say, 10 p.m., about the time most rural buses stop running. Few taxis outside San José have *marías*. You'll get a better deal if you speak Spanish and know local customs. You do not tip taxi drivers.

It may be you prefer to travel in style. Then give **All American Limousines** (tel./fax 273-

3818) a call. Bilingual drivers provide airport transfers, city tours, etc., with 24-hour service.

FERRIES

On the Pacific, three ferries link the Nicoya Peninsula with mainland Guanacaste. A car/passenger **ferry** (tel. 661-0397) links Puntarenas to Playa Naranjo. Another ferry for both passengers and vehicles also operates from Puntarenas to Paquera on the southeastern corner of the Nicoya Peninsula, from where buses will take you to Tambor and Montezuma. Further north, the **Tempisque Ferry** (tel. 662-0147) crosses the Gulf of Nicoya from the mouth of the Tempisque River. A passenger ferry also departs Golfito daily for Puerto Jiménez, near Corcovado National Park on the Osa Peninsula; and there are small-boat services run to Montezuma and other points in Nicoya and between destinations along the Pacific coast. (See regional sections for schedules and details.)

BY BICYCLE

See "Bicycling" under "Special-Interest Travel and Recreation." **Bike N' Hike** (tel./fax 289-8191), in Centro Comercial, in Escazú, rents high-performance Canadian mountain bikes ($29 daily).

IMMIGRATION AND ENTRY

DOCUMENTS AND REQUIREMENTS

Tourist Cards and Passports

Citizens of Canada, the U.S., and Panamá may enter Costa Rica with just a tourist card, valid for 30 days, and one other piece of identification, such as a passport, a driver's license, or a birth certificate. No passport or visa is required. Citizens of all other countries require a valid passport to enter Costa Rica. If you plan on staying longer than 30 days, a valid passport enables Canadian and American citizens to stay for up to 90 days, in which case no tourist card is required (your passport will also make life easier when changing money and/or renting cars). Business travelers should travel with a passport regardless of length of stay.

Tourist cards ($3) may be obtained in advance through any Costa Rican embassy or consulate, or, on your day of departure, upon production of a valid airline ticket at the airport ticket counter on your way to Costa Rica (airlines issue them free); you will also need to present a birth certificate and a driver's license or other

photo identification. The card can be renewed monthly for up to three months from the immigration office in San José (Calle 21, Avenidas 6/8), but since this can be a time-consuming hassle (see below), it's one more reason to take your passport. British citizens need a 10-year passport (a visitor's passport is insufficient); no visa is required.

The law requires that you carry your passport or tourist card with you at all times during your stay. An influx of undocumented refugees from Nicaragua and El Salvador beginning in the 1980s has led to an increase in the activity of plainclothes immigration inspectors, who may stop you on the street to request to see your documentation. In 1992 the police were instructed *not* to stop tourists unless they had broken, or were suspected of breaking, the law. Still, carry your papers with you to help avoid the possibility of being hauled off to the immigration office for a verification check (fortunately, officials will usually accept photocopies of your passport; be sure to include your photo, passport number, and entry stamp). It's a good idea in any case to make photocopies of all documentation and to keep them with you, separate from the originals.

Legal entry requirements often change, so contact your travel agent or the Costa Rican Tourism Institute or consulate before you leave home.

SPECIAL NOTE FOR TRAVELERS WITH CHILDREN

Regardless of nationality, children under 18 who stay for more than 30 days in Costa Rica become subject to the nation's child-welfare laws and will not be allowed to leave unless both parents request permission to take the child out of the country. For this, contact the **National Child Protection Agency** (Patronato Nacional de Infancia; Calle 19 and Avenida 6).

If your child is traveling with only one parent or with someone other than his or her parent, then you must obtain notarized permission from the Costa Rican consulate in the child's country of residence. Two passport-size photos (Costa Rican size) plus the child's passport must accompany the application form.

Visas

Citizens of the following countries may enter Costa Rica for up to 90 days *without* a visa (a passport *is* required): Argentina, Austria, Canada, Colombia, Denmark, Finland, Germany, Israel, Italy, Japan, Luxembourg, Netherlands, Norway, Panamá, Romania, South Korea, Spain, United Kingdom, United States, Yugoslavia.

Citizens of the following countries may enter Costa Rica for up to 30 days *without* a visa (a passport *is* required): Australia, Belgium, Brazil, Ecuador, Guatemala, Honduras, Iceland, Ireland (Eire), Liechtenstein, Mexico, Monaco,

EMBASSIES AND CONSULATES IN COSTA RICA

The following nations have embassies/consulates in San José. Note, however, that phone numbers and addresses change frequently. For up-to-date phone numbers, check the phone book under "Embajadas y Consulados." If you plan on visiting, call to confirm the address and opening hours.

Argentina, Avenida 6, Calles 21/25, tel. 221-6869; Mon.-Fri. 8 a.m.-3 p.m.

Australia, Centro Colón Bldg., Paseo Colón, Calles 38/40, tel. 221-5566 or 221-5816; Mon.-Fri. 8:30 a.m.-1 p.m.

Austria, Avenida 4, Calles 36/38, tel. 255-3007

Belgium, Avenida 3, Calles 35/37, tel. 225-6633 or 225-0484; Mon.-Fri. 8 a.m.-2 p.m.

Belize, Pavas, tel. 231-7766

Bolivia, Avenida 2, Calles 19/21, tel. 232-9455

Brazil, Avenida Central, Calles 20/22, tel. 257-5484 or 233-1544; Mon.-Fri. 8 a.m.-5 p.m.

Canada, Calle 3, Avenida Central (Kronos Bldg.), tel. 255-3522; Mon.-Fri. 9 a.m.-noon and 12:45-4:30 p.m.

Chile, Barrio Dent, tel. 225-0413

China, Republic of (Taiwan), San Pedro, tel. 225-2510

Colombia, Calle 29, Avenida 1, tel. 253-0819 or 221-0725

Cyprus, Barrio Francisco Peralta, tel. 234-9512

Denmark, Centro Colón Bldg., Paseo Colón, Calles 38/40, tel. 257-2695

Dominican Republic, Lomas de Ayarco, tel. 272-2398

Ecuador, Sabana Sur, tel. 232-1903

El Salvador, Los Yoses, tel. 224-9034 or 225-3861

Finland, Centro Colón Bldg., Paseo Colón, Calles 38/40, tel. 257-0210

France, road to Curridabat (from Indoor Club, 200 meters south, 25 meters west), tel. 225-0733 or 253-7027; Mon.-Fri. 8:30 a.m.-noon

Germany, Rohrmoser, tel. 232-5533; Mon.-Fri. 9 a.m.-noon

Great Britain (see "United Kingdom")

Greece, Los Yoses, tel. 225-9413

Guatemala, Barrio California, tel. 283-2555

Haiti, Desamparados, tel. 259-4920

Honduras, Los Yoses, tel. 234-0949 or 234-9502

Hungary, Los Yoses, tel. 224-3045 or 253-4445

Israel, Central Park Bldg., Calle 2 and Avenidas 2/4, tel. 221-6011 or 221-6444; Mon.-Fri. 10 a.m.-3 p.m.

Italy, Avenida 10, Calles 33/35, tel. 234-2326 or 224-6574; Mon.-Fri. 8:30 a.m.-noon

New Zealand, Sweden, Switzerland, Vatican, Venezuela.

Citizens of the following countries may enter Costa Rica for up to 30 days *with* a passport and a visa ($20), obtainable through any Costa Rican consulate: Andorra, Barbados, Belize, Bermuda, Bolivia, Chile, Cyprus, Dominican Republic, Grenada, Grenadines, Greece, Guadalupe, Guyana, Haiti, Jamaica, Malta, Martinique, Morocco, Paraguay, Peru, San Marino, St. Lucia, St. Vincent, Saudi Arabia, Surinam, Taiwan, Trinidad and Tobago, Uruguay.

Citizens of all other countries may be allowed entry into Costa Rica on a restricted visa subject to approval by a Costa Rican consulate (passports are required). This includes nationals of

communist countries, former Soviet republics, and other countries with extremist governments. (I've heard reports of tourists with entry stamps from communist countries being refused entry into Costa Rica, but the political changes of recent years seem to have eased this situation. I've never had a problem.)

Visa Extensions

Extending your stay beyond the authorized time is like entering the Minotaur's maze. Anticipate bureaucratic headaches and a heavy toll on your time and patience. Permission to extend your 30- or 90-day stay *(prórroga de turismo)* must be requested from the immigration office (Migración) in the Irazemi Bldg. on Calle 21 and

Jamaica, Urbana Los Anones, tel. 228-0802

Japan, Rohrmoser Blvd. (400 meters west, 100 meters north from Nunciatura Apostolica), tel. 232-1255 or 296-1706; Mon.-Fri. 8:30 a.m.-5 p.m.

Korea, Rohrmoser, tel. 220-3160; Mon.-Fri. 8 a.m.-5 p.m.

Lebanon, Los Yoses, tel. 222-7762

Malta, Paseo Colón, Calles 38/40, tel. 223-2597

Mexico, Avenida 7, Calle 13/15, tel. 283-2333 or 222-5528; Mon.-Fri. 9 a.m.-noon.

Monaco, Paseo Colón, Calle 38, tel. 223-5017

Netherlands, Sabana Sur, tel. 296-1490; Mon.-Fri. 9 a.m.-noon

Nicaragua, Avenida Central, Calles 25/27, tel. 223-2373

Norway, Centro Colón Bldg., Paseo Colón, Calles 38/40, tel. 257-1414; Mon.-Fri. 10 a.m.-4 p.m.

Panamá, San Pedro (600 meters south from Higueron), tel. 225-3401; Mon.-Fri. 8 a.m.-1 p.m.

Paraguay, San Ramón-Tres Ríos, tel. 234-3794

Peru, Los Yoses, 200 meters south and 50 meters west of Auto Mercado, tel. 225-9145

Poland, Calle 33, Avenida 9, tel. 225-1481

Puerto Rico, Avenida 2, Calles 11/13, tel. 257-1769

Romania, Paseo Colón, Calles 38/40, tel. 231-0724

Russia, one block south from entrance to Lomas de Ayarco Sur, Curridabat, tel. 272-1021; Mon.-Fri. 8:30 a.m.-noon

South Africa, Calle 2, Avenidas 16/18, tel. 222-1470

Spain, Paseo Colón, Calle 32, tel. 222-1933 or 221-7005; Mon.-Fri. 8 a.m.-1 p.m.

Sweden, La Uruca, tel. 232-8549, 332-3128

Switzerland, Centro Colón Bldg., Paseo Colón, Calles 38/40, tel. 233-0052 or 221-4829; Mon.-Fri. 9 a.m.-noon

United Kingdom, Centro Colón Bldg., Paseo Colón, Calles 38/40, tel. 221-5566 or 221-5816; Mon.-Fri. 8:30 a.m.-1 p.m.

United States, in front of Centro Comercial, road to Pavas, tel. 220-3939; Mon.-Fri. 8 a.m.-4:30 p.m. (The bus for Pavas leaves from Avenida 1, Calles 16/18. Mailing address: Apdo. 10053, San José. It is reportedly quicker to write c/o U.S. Embassy in Costa Rica, APO Miami, FL 34020.)

Uruguay, Los Yoses, tel. 253-2755 or 234-9909

Venezuela, Los Yoses, one block south and one half block west from fifth entrance, tel. 225-8810; Mon.-Fri. 8:30 a.m.-2:30 p.m.

Yugoslavia, Calles 21/25, Avenida 8, tel. 221-7362

Avenidas 6/8 (open 8:30 a.m.-3:30 p.m. weekdays), which may also require you to obtain an affidavit from the Justice Tribunal (Calle 17, Avenidas 6/8) stating that you have no dependents in Costa Rica. If they're busy, you could wait all day. Check first with a reputable local travel agent or tour operator: they can usually obtain what you need for a small fee. Since you'll need to allow three days minimum—plus an additional four days or more if you are asked to submit to a blood test for AIDS (see below)— it may be just as easy to travel to Nicaragua or Panamá for 72 hours and then reenter with a new visa or tourist card.

The following are required with your application for an extension via the immigration office: three passport-size photos, a ticket out of the country, and adequate funds in cash or traveler's checks. The processing fee is approximately $1.50 (revenue stamps to attach to your application are available outside the immigration office at a booth on Calle 21), plus $12 for the visa if you leave by air, $30 if you leave by land.

You no longer need to show documentary proof that you owe no taxes, haven't sired or given birth to a child, and don't owe child support. Check to ensure these requirements have not been reintroduced. If the immigration authorities request that you submit to an AIDS test, the Ministerio de Salud (Ministry of Health, Calle 16 and Avenidas 6/8) can oblige. Exit visas take 48 hours or more to process.

Don't overstay your 30- or 90-day entry terms without obtaining an extension, as you will quite

possibly end up in the Minotaur's maze (Migración) anyway. Although the fine is small ($5 for each month or part of a month extra), you will not be allowed to leave without first obtaining an exit visa ($14), which means a trip back to the immigration office, plus a visit to the Tribunales de Justicia for a document stating you aren't abandoning any offspring or dependents in Costa Rica. The exit visa is valid for an additional 30 days' stay. Travel agencies in San José can arrange exit visas for a small fee.

Other Documentation

All tourists may be required to demonstrate adequate finances for their proposed stay upon arrival (at least $400). This is normally requested only of those travelers intent on staying 30 days or more. In addition, you may be asked to show a return or onward ticket. Technically, you must have an exit ticket out of the country, but immigration officials rarely request to see it. Airlines, however, frequently will not let you board without proof of a return or onward ticket.

If you're traveling overland you need an onward bus ticket (you can buy one at the border immigration office or even from the driver on TICA international buses), and you will need to show at least $400 in cash or traveler's checks. Check with other overland travelers you meet to see how they fared.

Note: Ease of entry may well depend on your looks. Costa Rican immigration officials—like Costa Ricans in general—are sensitive to appearance, so be aware that you can help your own cause by looking neat and tidy.

Immunizations

Costa Rican authorities do not require travelers to show proof of immunizations or an international vaccination card (see "Health Care," below). However, if you plan on staying beyond 30 days, you may be required to show proof of being free from AIDS or its precursor, HIV. Again, check with your travel agent or Costa Rican consulate for the latest updates. Travelers arriving from Nicaragua report being tested for malarial infection at the border.

To Nicaragua

Canadians and U.S. citizens, as well as citizens of Belgium, Denmark, Finland, the Netherlands, Norway, Spain, Sweden, Switzerland, and the United Kingdom, do not require visas; others—including Australians and New Zealanders—do. This may have changed by the time you read this.

To Panamá

U.S. citizens, as well as citizens of the Dominican Republic, El Salvador, Germany, Honduras, Spain, Switzerland, and the United Kingdom, do not require visas; all others do. Do not rely on obtaining visas/entry permits at border crossings; obtain them in advance. Regulations for entry into Nicaragua and Panamá are subject to frequent change, so check in advance.

CUSTOMS

Travelers arriving in Costa Rica are allowed 500 cigarettes or 500 grams of tobacco, plus three liters of wine or spirits. You can also bring in two cameras, binoculars, electrical and video equipment, plus camping, scuba, and other sporting equipment duty-free. You may be asked to prove that your personal computer is for personal use. A nominal limit of six rolls of film per person is rarely enforced. I don't recommend bringing in pets. If you wish to bring your dog, write the Jefe de Departamento de Zoonosis (Ministerio de Salud, San José 1000) for an importation form.

Exiting Costa Rica

Travelers exiting Costa Rica are charged $15 (or its equivalent in *colones*) departure tax on international flights out of San José. No departure tax applies for overland or sea. You may change no more than $50 worth of *colones* into U.S. currency at the airport. Costa Rica prohibits the export of pre-Columbian artifacts.

Returning to the U.S.

U.S. citizens can bring in $400 of purchases duty-free. You may also bring in one quart of spirits plus 200 cigarettes (one carton). Live animals, plants, and products made from endangered species will be confiscated by U.S. Customs (you'll also be fined for bringing in items made from endangered species). Tissue-cultured orchids and other plants in sealed vials are okay.

COSTA RICAN EMBASSIES AND CONSULATES

IN THE U.S.

Chicago, 8 South Michigan Ave., Suite 1312, Chicago, IL 60603, tel. (312) 263-2772

Los Angeles, 3540 Wilshire Blvd., Suite 404, Los Angeles, CA 90010, tel. (213) 380-7915, fax (213) 380-5639

Kenner, 2002 20th St., Suite B-103, Kenner, LA 70062, tel. (504) 467-1462

Miami, 1600 N.W. LeJeune Rd., Suite 300, Miami, FL 33126, tel. (305) 871-7458

New Orleans, 2002 20th St., Suite B-103, New Orleans, LA 70130, tel. (504) 467-1462, fax (504) 466-8268

New York, 80 Wall St., Suite 1117, New York, NY 10005, tel. (212) 425-4620, fax (212) 785-6818

San Francisco, 870 Market St., San Francisco, CA 94102, tel. (415) 392-8488

Washington, D.C., 1825 Connecticut Ave. NW, Suite 3211, Washington, D.C. 20009, tel. (202) 234-2945, fax (202) 265-4795

IN CANADA

Montreal, 1155 Dorchester Blvd. West, Suite 2902, Montreal, Quebec H3B 2L3, tel. (514) 866-8159

Ottawa, 15 Argule St., Ottawa, ON K2P 1B7, tel. (613) 234-5762, fax 230-2656

Toronto, 164 Avenue Rd., Toronto, ON M5R 2H9, tel. (416) 961-6773, fax 961-6771

IN ENGLAND

Costa Rica Embassy, Flat 1, 14 Lancaster Gate, London W2, tel. 071-723-1772

The Caribbean Basin Initiative scheme raised the customs exemption for member countries, including Costa Rica, to $600. Granting you the added allowance is at the discretion of the Customs agent. Costa Rica is also listed under the U.S. Customs Service's Generalized System of Preferences (GSP) program, which provides for duty-free importation of arts, handicrafts, and other select items from Third World countries.

The U.S. Department of State (2210 C St. NW, Washington, D.C. 20520, tel. 202-647-4000) publishes *Your Trip Abroad;* and the U.S. Customs Service (Department of the Treasury, 1301 Constitution Ave. NW, Washington, D.C. 20229, tel. 202-566-5286) publishes *GSP and the Traveler,* both of which outline what may and may not be brought into the United States.

Returning to Canada

Canadian citizens are allowed a $300 annual "exemption," or $100 per quarter for goods purchased abroad, plus 1.1 liters of spirits and 200 cigarettes.

Drugs

It goes without saying that trying to smuggle drugs through customs is not only illegal, it's stupid. Travelers returning from Central and South America are particularly suspect. Trained dogs are employed to sniff out contraband at U.S. airports as well as at Juan Santamaría Airport in San José. Be warned, too, that recent years have seen a concerted effort to stamp out drug trafficking and use within the country.

HEALTH CARE

Sanitary standards in Costa Rica are very high, and although occasional outbreaks of tropical diseases occur, the chances of succumbing to a serious disease are rare. As long as you take appropriate precautions and use common sense, you're not likely to incur serious illness. If you do, you have the benefit of knowing that the nation has a superb health-care system. There are English-speaking doctors in most cities, and you will rarely find yourself far from medical help. *Medical Systems of Costa Rica*, by Frank Chalfont (Dept. 257-SJO, P.O. Box 025216, Miami, FL 33102-5216) "gives English-speaking foreigners a feel" for Costa Rica's "interactive combination of socialist-private medical systems."

Dental and medical check-ups may be advisable before departing home, particularly if you intend to travel for a considerable time, partake in strenuous activities, or have an existing medical problem. Take along any medications, including prescriptions for eyewear; keep prescription drugs in their original bottles to avoid suspicion at customs. If you suffer from a debilitating health problem, wear a medical alert bracelet. Pharmacies can prescribe drugs (be wary of expiry dates, as shelf life of drugs may be shortened under tropical conditions).

A basic health kit is a good idea. Pack the following (as a minimum) in a small plastic container: alcohol swabs and medicinal alcohol, antiseptic cream, Band-Aids, aspirin or pain killers, diarrhea medication, sunburn remedy, antifungal foot powder, calamine and/or antihistamine, water-purification tablets, surgical tape, bandages and gauze, and scissors.

Information on health concerns can be answered by **Intermedic** (777 3rd Ave., New York, NY 10017, tel. 212-486-8974) and the **Department of State Citizens Emergency Center** (tel. 202-647-5225). The **International Association for Medical Assistance to Travellers** (IAMAT, 417 Center St., Lewiston, NY 14092, tel. 716-754-4883; in Canada, 40 Regal Rd., Guelph, ON N1K 1B5, tel. (519) 836-0102; in Europe, 57 Voirets, 1212 Grand-Lancy, Geneva, Switzerland) publishes helpful information, including a list of approved physicians and clinics. A useful pocket-size book is *Staying Healthy in Asia, Africa, and Latin America* (Moon Publications, P.O. Box 3040, Chico, CA 95927, tel. 800-345-5473), which is packed with first-aid and basic medical information.

Medical Insurance

Medical insurance is highly recommended. Check to see if your health insurance or other policies cover you for medical expenses and/or baggage loss while abroad. Your American Express credit card service may provide coverage too. Traveler's insurance isn't cheap, but it can be a sound investment. Travel agencies can sell you traveler's health and baggage insurance, as well as insurance against cancellation of a prepaid tour. The best coverage I've found is through **American Express** (P.O. Box 919010, San Diego, CA 92190, tel. 800-234-0375), and **Wallach and Company** (P.O. Box 480, Middleburg, VA 22117, tel. 703-687-3166 or 800-237-6615). The following companies also offer travel insurance: **Travelers** (1 Tower Square, Hartford, CT 06183, tel. 203-277-0111 or 800-243-3174), **Access America International** (P.O. Box 90315, Richmond, VA 23286, tel. 800-284-8300), **International Underwriters** (243 Church St. W, Vienna, VA 22180, tel. 703-281-9500), **TravelGuard International** (1145 Clark St., Stevens Point, WI 54481, tel. 715-345-0505 or 800-782-5151), and **Carefree**

RED CROSS (CRUZ ROJA) AMBULANCE

Alajuela	441-2939
Cartago	551-0421
Heredia	237-1115
Liberia	666-0994
Puerto Limón	758-0125
Puntarenas	661-0184
San José	221-5818

Travel Insurance (P.O. Box 310, 120 Meola Blvd., Mineola, NY 11501, tel. 516-294-0220 or 800-323-3149).

The **Association of British Insurers** (51 Gresham St., London BC2V 7HQ, tel. 071-600-3333) and **Europ Assistance** (252 High St., Croyden, Surrey CR0 1NF, tel. 081-680-1234) can provide advice for obtaining travel insurance in Britain.

Costa Rica's Social Security system (Instituto Nacional de Seguros) introduced a **Traveller's Insurance** program in 1992 specifically for foreigners. As well as loss or theft of possessions, it covers emergency medical treatment (hospitalization and surgery, plus emergency dental treatment are covered; services for pre-existing conditions are not), plus repatriation of a body. You can choose coverage between 500,000-10 million *colones* for the number of weeks you desire (from one to 12 weeks). You can buy coverage at travel agencies, language schools, the Organización Internacional Cultural de Intercambios (tel. 257-0680), or the Instituto Nacional de Seguros (tel. 223-5800).

MEDICAL EMERGENCIES

In emergencies, call 911. Alternately, call 122 for the Red Cross or Emergency Rescue Unit (or tel. 221-5818) in San José (see the "Red Cross Ambulance" chart); outside the capital, call 118 (the equivalent of 911 in the U.S.). For the police, outside San José call 127. No coin is required.

The following private hospitals in San José have emergency medical facilities available for foreigners at reasonable rates: **Clínica Bíblica** (Avenida 14, Calles Central/1, tel. 223-6422), **Clínica Catolica** (Guadalupe, tel. 225-9095), **Clínica Americana** (Avenida 14, Calles Central/1, tel. 222-1010), and **Clínica Santa Rita** (Avenida 8, Calles 15/17, tel. 221-6433). Normally you will have to pay by cash or credit card and seek reimbursement from your insurance company once you return to the United States.

The following hospitals in San José can provide free emergency health care on the Social Security system: **Calderón Guardia** (Calle 17, Avenida 9, tel. 222-4133), **Children's Hospital** (Calle 20, Paseo Colón, tel. 222-0122), **Hospital Mexico** (Autopista General Cañas, tel.

232-6122), and **San Juan de Dios** (Calle 14, Avenida Central, tel. 222-0166).

Air Ambulance (Apdo. 256, San José 1017, tel. 225-4502, fax 235-8264, 24-hour beeper 225-2500) offers 24-hour coronary and mobile critical care for surgical and medical emergencies, using either a twin Learjet or a helicopter.

Medical Evacuation
Traveler's Emergency Network (P.O. Box 238, Hyattsville, MD 20797, tel. 800-275-4836) provides worldwide ground and air evacuation and medical assistance, as does **International SOS Assistance** (P.O. Box 11568, Philadelphia, PA 19116, tel. 215-244-1500 or 800-523-8930). The following companies also provide emergency evacuation and other services: **Carefree Travel Insurance, Travel Guard,** and **Wallach and Company** (see "Medical Insurance," above).

VACCINATIONS

No vaccinations are required to enter Costa Rica. Epidemic diseases have mostly been eradicated throughout the country. However, a few isolated cases of cholera broke out in 1992 and again in 1994, and the incidences of measles and tuberculosis have risen in recent years. Consult your physician for recommended vaccinations. Travelers planning to rough it should consider vaccinations against tetanus, polio, cholera, and infectious hepatitis.

Infectious hepatitis is endemic throughout Central America, although only infrequently reported in Costa Rica. Main symptoms are stomach pains, loss of appetite, yellowing skin and eyes, and extreme tiredness. Hepatitis A is contracted through unhygienic foods or contaminated water (salads and unpeeled fruits are major culprits). A gamma globulin vaccination is recommended. The much rarer Hepatitis B is usually contracted through unclean needles, blood transfusions, or unsafe sex.

If you're traveling overland, it may be wise to carry an **International Certificate of Vaccinations,** available from the Superintendent of Documents, U.S. Government Printing Office, Washington, D.C. 20402, tel. 202-783-3238 ($2). The **Ministerio de Salud** (Ministry of Health, Calle 16 and Avenida 4) can provide

yellow fever vaccinations. Also recommended: Dr. Rodrigo Jiménez Monge (Calle 5, Avenida 4, tel. 221-6658) in San José.

HEALTH PROBLEMS

Infection

Even the slightest scratch can fester quickly in the tropics. Treat promptly and regularly with antiseptic and keep the wound clean.

Intestinal Problems

Water is safe to drink virtually everywhere, although more remote rural areas, as well as Escazú, Santa Ana, Puntarenas, and Puerto Limón, are suspect. Water systems in the Caribbean lowlands were disrupted by the April 1991 earthquake and in the more off-the-beaten-track places might not yet have been restored. A few areas, such as the waters around Puntarenas in particular, are too polluted for swimming. If you want to play it safe, drink bottled mineral water *(agua mineral* or *soda)*. Remember, ice cubes are water too. And don't brush your teeth using suspect water. Always wash your hands, too, before eating.

Food hygiene standards in Costa Rica are generally very high. Milk is pasteurized, so you're not likely to encounter many problems normally associated with dairy products. However, the change in diet—which may alter the bacteria that are normal and necessary in the bowel—may cause **diarrhea** or **constipation.** (In case of the latter, eat lots of fruit.) Fortunately, the stomach usually builds up a resistance to unaccustomed foods. Most cases of diarrhea are caused by microbial bowel infections resulting from contaminated food. Common-sense precautions include not eating uncooked fish or shellfish (which collect cholera bugs), uncooked vegetables, unwashed salads, or unpeeled fruit (peel the fruit *yourself)*. And be fastidious with personal hygiene.

Diarrhea is usually temporary and many doctors recommend letting it run its course. Personally, I like to plug myself up straightaway with Lomotil or a similar "solidifier." Treat diarrhea with rest and lots of liquid to replace the water and salts lost. Avoid alcohol and milk products while suffering from diarrhea. If conditions don't improve after three days, seek medical help.

Clínica Americana in San José (tel. 222-1010) can analyze stool samples (there are clinical laboratories in most towns).

Diarrhea accompanied by severe abdominal pain, blood in your stool, and fever is a sign of **dysentery.** Seek immediate medical diagnosis. Tetracycline or ampicillin is normally used to cure bacillary dysentery. More complex professional treatment is required for amoebic dysentery. The symptoms of both are similar. **Giardiasis,** acquired from infected water, is another intestinal complaint. It causes diarrhea, bloating, persistent indigestion, and weight loss. Again, seek medical advice. **Intestinal worms** can be contracted by walking barefoot on infested beaches, grass, or earth.

Sunburn and Skin Problems

Don't underestimate the tropical sun! It's intense and can fry you in minutes, particularly at higher elevations. It can even burn you through light clothing or while you're lying in the shade. The midday sun is especially potent. Even if you consider yourself nicely tanned already, *use a suncream or sunblock*—at least SPF 8 or higher. Zinc oxide provides almost 100% protection. Bring sun lotions with you; they're expensive in Costa Rica. If you're intent on a tan, have patience. Build up gradually, and use an aloe gel after sunbathing; it helps repair any skin damage. The tops of feet and backs of knees are particularly susceptible to burning. Consider a wide-brimmed hat, too. Calamine lotion and aloe gel will soothe light burns; for more serious lobster-pink burns use steroid creams.

Sun glare—especially prevalent if you're on water—can cause conjunctivitis. Sunglasses will protect against this. **Prickly heat** is an itchy rash, normally caused by clothing that is too tight and/or in need of washing. This, and **athlete's foot,** are best treated by airing out the body and washing your clothes. And the tropical humidity and heat can sap your body fluids like blotting paper. Drink regularly to avoid dehydration. Leg cramps, exhaustion, and headaches are possible signs of dehydration.

Snakebite

Snakes are common in Costa Rica. Always watch where you're treading or putting your hands. Be particularly wary in long grass. And avoid streams

at night. The majority of bites occur from people stepping on snakes; most of the rest occur to people who play macho with them.

Death from snakebite is extremely rare; fear of the consequences is one of your biggest enemies, so try to relax. Do not move unless absolutely necessary. Commercial snakebite kits are normally good only for the specific species for which they were designed, so it will help if you can definitively identify the critter. But don't endanger yourself further trying to catch it.

If the bite is to a limb, immobilize the limb and apply a tight bangage between the bite and body. Release it for 90 seconds every 15 minutes. Ensure you can slide a finger under the bandage; too tight and you risk further damage. Do *not* cut the bite area in an attempt to suck out the poison unless you are an expert. Many snake poisons are anticoagulants; cutting your blood vessels may cause you to bleed like a hemophiliac. Recent recommendations to use electric shock as snakebite treatment have gained popular favor recently in Costa Rica; do *not* follow this medically discredited advice.

Symptoms include swelling, bruising around the bite (which will show two puncture marks), soreness of the lymph glands, nausea, vomiting, and fever. Worst-case scenarios normally involve numbness and tingling of the face, muscular spasms, convulsions, and hemorrhaging. Seek medical attention without delay. Rural health posts and most national park rangers have antivenin kits on-site.

Insects and Arachnids

Sweet blood or sour blood, at some stage during your visit to Costa Rica the creepy crawlies will get you. Fortunately, only a few people will have fierce reactions. Check your bedding before crawling into bed. Always shake out your shoes and clothing before putting them on. Keep beds away from walls. And, for true paranoids, look underneath the toilet seat before sitting down.

Repellent sprays and lotions are a must. Apply regularly in jungle areas, marshy areas and coastal lowlands (particularly the Caribbean). Take lotion to apply to the body, and aerosol spray for clothing. Avon Skin-So-Soft oil is such an effective bug repellent that U.S. Marines use it by the truckload ("Gee, private, you sure smell nice, and your skin's so soft!").

Bites can easily become infected in the tropics, so avoid scratching! Treat with antiseptics or antibiotics. A baking-soda bath can help relieve itching if you're badly bitten, as can antihistamine tablets, hydrocortisone, and calamine lotion. Long-sleeved clothing and full-length pants will help keep the beasties at bay.

Chiggers *(coloradillas)* inhabit grasslands, particularly in Guanacaste. Their bites itch like hell. Mosquito repellent won't deter them. Dust your shoes, socks, and ankles with sulphur powder. Sucking sulphur tablets *(azufre sublimado)* apparently gives your sweat a smell that chiggers find obnoxious. **C&C Laboratories** (P.O. Box 7779, Dallas, TX 75209, tel. 214-748-7953) sells Chigarid, for relief of chigger bites. Nail polish apparently works, too (on the bites, not the nails) by suffocating the beasts. It's best to use clear, as you might imagine).

Ticks *(garrapatas)* hang out near livestock. They bury their heads into your skin. Don't try to pull them out; you'll most likely snap their bodies off, leaving their heads in your flesh, where they'll fester. Extract ticks by holding a lighted match near them. They should pop out quickly. Applying gasoline or even alcohol also should do the trick (though *not* in conjunction with the lighted-match treatment).

Tiny, irritating **no-see-ums** (truly evil blood-sucking sandflies about the size of a pinpoint, and known locally as *purrujas*) inhabit marshy coastal areas: pour sulphur powder on your shoes, socks, and ankles, and avoid walking the beach barefooted around dusk. They're not fazed by bug repellent with DEET, but Avon's Skin-So-Soft works a treat. Sandflies on the Atlantic coast can pass on leishmaniasis, a debilitating disease: seek urgent treatment for non-healing sores.

Insect larvae, such as that of the botfly, can cause growing boils once laid beneath your skin (you'll see a clear hole in the middle of the boil or pimple). Completely cover with Vaseline and a secure Band-Aid or tape and let it dry overnight. All being well you should be able to squeeze the culprit out next day. If stung by a **scorpion**—not normally as bad as it sounds—take plenty of liquids and rest. If you're unfortunate enough to contract **scabies** (a microscopic mite) or **lice,** which is possible if you're staying in unhygienic conditions or sleeping with unhygienic

bedfellows, use a body shampoo containing gamma benzene hexachloride. You should also wash all your clothing and bedding in very hot water, and toss out your underwear. The severe itching caused by scabies infestation appears after three or four weeks (it appears as little dots, often in lines, ending in blisters, especially around the genitals, elbows, wrists, lower abdomen, and nipples).

Avoid **bees'** nests. African bees have infiltrated Costa Rica in recent years. They're very aggressive and will attack with little provocation. Running in a zigzag is said to help in fleeing. If there's water about, take a dunk and stay submerged for a while.

Many bugs are local. The bite of a rare kind of insect found along the southern Caribbean coast and locally called *papalamoya* produces a deep and horrible infection that can even threaten a limb. It may be best to have such infections treated locally (and certainly promptly); doctors back home (or even in San José) might take forever to diagnose and treat the condition.

AIDS and Sexually Transmitted Diseases

AIDS is on the rise throughout Central America. Since 1983, more than 500 cases of AIDS have been reported. The Costa Rican government conducts an exemplary anti-AIDS campaign. The Ministry of Health distributes 800,000 condoms a month in nationalized clinics, billboards promoting condom use are everywhere, and even a prime-time TV ad shows an animated condom "person" educating a couple dancing in a disco about the necessity of safe sex.

Avoidance of casual sexual contact is the best prevention. This being the real world, if you succumb to the mating instinct, use condoms. Though readily available, Costa Rican condoms tear easily; to be safe, bring your own. Prostitution is legal in Costa Rica, and though prostitutes supposedly have regular health checks, many prostitutes aren't registered and may constitute a particular risk. Blood transfusions and unclean needles, such as those shared in drug use, are other potential sources of AIDS infection. Remember that gonorrhea, syphilis, and other sexually transmitted diseases are no less prevalent than elsewhere in the world. Practice safe sex!

Malaria

An increase in the incidence of malaria has been reported recently in the Caribbean lowlands, particularly the area south of Cahuita (more than 6,000 cases were reported in 1992, the highest number in 20 years; the majority of cases were due to poor health practices on banana plantations). Malaria is not a serious problem elsewhere in the country. Consult your physician for the best type of antimalarial medication. Begin taking your tablets a few days (or weeks, depending on the prescription) before arriving in an infected zone, and continue taking the tablets for several weeks after leaving the malarial zone. Malaria symptoms include high fever, shivering, headache, and sometimes diarrhea.

Chloroquine (called Alaren in Costa Rica) and Fansidar are both used for short-term protection. Chloroquine reportedly is still good for Costa Rica, although Panamanian mosquitoes have built up a resistance to the drug. Fansidar may be a safer bet for travel south of Puerto Limón. **Note:** Fansidar can cause severe skin reactions and is dangerous for people with a history of sulfonamide intolerance. If you take Fansidar and suffer from such skin and mucuous-membrane ailments as itching, rash, mouth or genital sores, or a sore throat, seek medical help immediately.

The best mosquito repellents contain DEET (diethylmetatoluamide). Use rub-on repellent directly to the skin; use sprays for clothing. DEET is quite toxic; avoid using on small children. And avoid getting this on plastic—it melts it. Use mosquito netting at night in the lowlands (you can obtain good hammocks and "no-see-um" nets in the U.S. from **Campmor,** P.O. Box 997, Paramus, NJ 07653, tel. 800-526-4784). A fan over your bed and mosquito coils *(espirales)* also help keep mosquitoes at bay. Coils are available from *pulperías* and supermarkets (don't forget the metal stand—*soporte*—for them). Avoid breathing in the fumes.

The Ministerio de Salud (Calle 16, Avenida 4) can supply free malaria tablets from the information desk to the left of the ministry.

Long-sleeved shirts and long pants will help reduce the number of bites you collect.

Other Problems

A serious outbreak of **dengue fever** occurred in mid-1994 and spread to many areas of the

nation by year's end before abating somewhat. Transmitted by mosquitoes, the illness can be fatal (death usually results from internal hemorrhaging). Its symptoms are similar to malaria, with additional severe pain in the joints and bones (it is sometimes called "breaking bones disease"), but, unlike malaria, is not recurring. You can spray your clothing with the insecticide *permethrin*. **Rabies,** though rare, can be contracted through the bite of an infected dog or other animal. It is always fatal unless treated. You're extremely unlikely to be the victim of a vampire bat, a common rabies vector that preys on cattle. If you're sleeping in the open (or with an unscreened window open) in areas with vampire bat populations, don't leave your flesh exposed! Their bite is said to be painless. They're particularly fond of toes.

You're not likely to suffer from **altitude-related problems** unless you intend climbing Chirripó (3,819 meters), in which case you should ascend slowly and take plenty of liquids. If you experience nausea, severe headaches, fatigue, a rapid pulse, and/or irregular breathing, you've probably got altitude sickness. Rest! Don't go higher until the symptoms clear. If they don't clear after a day, waste no time: turn around and descend.

If you need a rejuvenating (nonsexual) **massage,** contact Charlotte Gramms (tel. 296-0020) for an appointment. Other masseurs and masseuses advertise in the classified sections of the *Tico Times* and *Costa Rica Today*.

SAFETY

With common sense, you are no more likely to run into problems in Costa Rica than you are in your own backyard. The vast majority of Costa Ricans are supremely honest and friendly people. However, there is a growing problem of petty theft and muggings. That said, there are more murders and muggings in San Francisco in a year than in the whole of Costa Rica, with 10 times the population. In fact, until December 1994 it was the only country in Latin America that hadn't been listed in the U.S. State Department's Travel Advisory. (My friend Shirley Miller, co-publisher of *Costa Rican Outlook* newsletter, reports there were "65 murders in Costa Rica in 1994, 500 incidents of street thieves taking jewelry, cash and other valuables in San José, and other crimes such as auto theft, street assaults and house robberies for a total of 35,587 crimes." She then called the San Diego police and "found that in our relatively quiet city—I didn't dare contact Los Angeles—there had been 20,594 crimes in the first three months of 1994!" Of that number, 19 murders and 3,218 violent crimes were committed.)

Traffic is perhaps the greatest danger. Be especially wary when crossing the street in San José. Tico drivers do not like to give way to pedestrians and they give no mercy to those still in the road when the light turns to green. Stand well away from the curb, especially on corners, where buses often mount the curb. (Also see "Driving Safety," under "By Car" in the "Getting Around" section, above.) And sidewalks are full of gaping potholes and tilted curbstones. Watch your step!

Outside the city you need to be savvy to some basic precautions. Hikers straying off trails can easily lose their way amid the rainforests. And don't approach too close to an active volcano, such as Arenal, which may suddenly hiccup lava and breccia far and wide. Remember that atop the mountains, sunny weather can turn cold and rainy in seconds, so dress accordingly. And be extra cautious when crossing rivers; a rainstorm upstream can turn the river downstream into a raging torrent without any warning. Ideally, go with a guide.

If things go wrong, contact the U.S. embassy or consulate (Apdo. 10035, San José, tel. 220-3939), in front of the Centro Comercial, on the road to Pavas, in the western suburbs of San José. (Other nationalities should refer to the "Embassies and Consulates in Costa Rica" chart.) Consulate officials can't get you out of jail, but they can help you locate a lawyer, alleviate unhealthy conditions, or arrange for funds to be wired if you run short of money. They can even authorize a reimbursable loan—the Department of State hates to admit it—while you arrange for cash to be forwarded, or even lend

you money to get home. Don't expect the U.S. embassy to bend over backward; it's notoriously unhelpful. The *Handbook of Consular Services* (Public Affairs Staff, Bureau of Consular Affairs, U.S. Department of State, Washington, D.C. 20520) provides details of such assistance. Friends and family can also call the Department of State's **Overseas Citizen Service** (tel. 202-647-5225) to check on you if things go awry.

Travelers venturing overland through Central America should contact the **Central American Resource Council** (1407 Cleveland Ave. N, St. Paul, MN 55108, tel. 612-644-8030). It publishes *Centroamérica: The Month in Review*, a digest of information not readily available or widely reported on current conditions in Central America. Suscriptions cost $25 a year.

Americans Traveling Abroad: What You Should Know Before You Go, by Gladson Nwanna (World Travel Institute Press, P.O. Box 32671-1A, Baltimore, MD 21208; $39.99 plus $3 shipping) is an invaluable resource on safety, healthy, money tips, etc. It includes a chapter on Central America.

THEFT

Costa Rica's many charms can lull visitors into a false sense of security. Like anywhere else, the country has its share of social ills, with rising street crime among them. The recent economic crisis and influx of impoverished refugees has spawned a growing band of petty thieves and purse slashers that blossomed into a sudden

EMERGENCY NUMBERS

All emergencies		911
Police		117
Police—Rural Areas	Rural Guard (Guardia Rural)	127
Fire Department	(San José Metropolitan Area only)	122
Fire Department (Bomberos)		118
Traffic Accident	Traffic Police (Policia de Tránsito)	222-7150
Red Cross Ambulance (Cruz Roja)	accidents	221-5818
Hospital México	emergencies	232-6122
Hospital San Juan de Dios	emergencies	222-0166
Hospital Dr. Calderón Guardia	emergencies	222-4133
Hospital National de Niños	poison control	223-1028
Clínica Bíblica	private hospital	223-6422
Air Ambulance	surgical and medical emergencies	225-4502
	(24-hour beeper)	225-2500
U.S. Embassy	8 a.m.-4:30 p.m.	220-3939
U.S. Embassy	evenings and weekends	220-3127
Canadian Embassy		255-3522
British Embassy		221-5566
German Embassy		232-5533
American Express	loss or theft	233-0044
MasterCard		253-2155
Visa International		223-2211

IF TROUBLE STRIKES

Report theft and assault and similar crimes to the **Judicial Police (OIJ)** in the middle courthouse on Avenida 6, Calles 17/19 (tel. 221-5337 or 255-0122). If you are sold counterfeit dollars or *colones* contact the Crime Prevention Unit (UPD, tel. 233-5083).

Report complications with restaurants, tour companies, hotels, etc., to the main office of the **Costa Rican Tourism Institute (ICT)** at Avenida 4, Calles 5/7 (tel. 223-1733).

Report theft or demands for money by traffic police to the **Ministry of Public Works and Transport** at Calle 9, Avenidas 20/22 (tel. 227-2188). Report similar problems with Radio Patrulla police to the OIJ; then try to identify the policeman at the Radio Patrulla headquarters (tel. 226-2242) in front of Centro Comercial del Sur.

The U.S. State Department maintains a **Citizens' Emergency Center** (tel. 202-647-5225, fax 202-647-3000; computer bulletin board, tel. 202-647-9225). Defense attorney Richard Atkins specializes in **international legal defense** (111 S. 15th St., Packard Bldg., Philadelphia, PA 19102, tel. 215-977-9982). Of course, there's always the possibility that you'll need a lawyer *in* Costa Rica. Chris Howard's *Golden Door to Retirement and Living in Costa Rica* provides particularly valuable information on finding and dealing with lawyers, and is good preparation.

spree in winter 1994/5 (in December 1994, Costa Rica was listed for the first time ever on a U.S. Consular Information advisory). And since the arrest of Noriega in 1990, Costa Rica is replacing Panamá as a distribution point for cocaine, thereby fostering a concomitant increase in larger-scale crime. Still, most crime is opportunistic, and thieves seek easy targets. Don't become paranoid. A few common-sense precautions, though, are in order.

The Instituto Costarricense de Turismo publishes a leaflet—*Passport For Your Security*—listing common-sense precautions and a list of emergency phone numbers. In January 1995 the National Chamber of Tourism (CANATUR) and Ministry of Public Security announced a pilot program to reduce crime aimed at tourists by beefing up policing and security in central San José, Puerto Limón, and other key areas popular with tourists. A 24-hour tourist information line—(800) 012-3456—was touted to begin in April 1995, but was not yet in service.

Make photocopies of all important documents: your passport (showing photograph and visas, if applicable), airline ticket, credit cards, insur-

ance policy, driver's license. Carry the photocopies with you, and leave the originals in the hotel safe where possible. If this isn't possible, carry the originals with you in a secure inside pocket. Don't put all your eggs in one basket! Prepare an "emergency kit," to include photocopies of your documents and an adequate sum of money to tide you over if your wallet gets stolen. If you're robbed, immediately file a police report. You'll need this to make an insurance claim.

For credit card security, insist that imprints are made in your presence. Make sure any imprints incorrectly completed are torn up. Don't take someone else's word that it will be done. Destroy the carbons yourself.

In San José, be especially wary in and around the Coca-Cola bus terminal (centered on Calle 14, Avenida 1), particularly the streets to the north (Calles 8-16 and Avenidas 3-5). Avoid the area at night. After dusk, don't walk in Parque Central and be particularly wary in the red light district (between Calles 4-8 and Avenidas 4-10). Don't use buses at night, and be alert on buses by day. Crowded places are the happy hunting grounds of quick and expert crafty crooks. If you sense yourself being squeezed or jostled, don't hold back—elbow your way out of there *immediately*. Better safe than sorry!

Large-scale scams are common. I know several foreigners who lost huge sums by investing in bogus macadamia farms and other schemes. I've heard cautionary reports that "Newcomers' Seminars" advertised in *Costa Rica Today* and elsewhere have shills in the audience to inspire attendees to part with their dollars.

If you pick up hitchhikers, locals, etc., *always* take the car keys with you if you get out of the vehicle. One of my friends had his rental car and possessions stolen by a local guide he had hired—after a full week together!

Some policemen are less than honest, and there have been many reports of tourists being

SPECIAL TRICKS TO BEWARE

There's no need for paranoia in Costa Rica. Enjoy it with the same caution you'd apply in any foreign country. However, tourists occasionally find themselves victims of contrived crime. Here are a few special tricks to beware.

Guys! Beware the bevy of amorous ladies who may approach you and start running their hands over your body and crotch. Alas, they're not impressed by your looks. They walk away giggling while you struggle to compose yourself. Only later do you realize that they walked off with your wallet. Hasn't happened to me yet, but you never know your luck!

Be wary of "plainclothes policemen." Ask to see their identification. Never relinquish your documentation or give money. And be especially wary if he asks a third party to verify his own credentials; they could be in league.

Never allow yourself to be drawn into arguments. And don't be distracted by people spilling things on you. These are ruses meant to distract you while an accomplice steals your valuables. An acquaintance of mine, a well-known travel writer to boot, fell for a beauty. She was hit on the head and shoulders by birdshit! Two young men, seeing her plight, came rushing to her aid with handkerchiefs. They coo-cooed all over her until the stains were removed. Of course, they niftily lifted her wallet amid the pandemonium. The two rogues had contrived the whole pantomime—it was they who had spattered her.

Remain alert to the dark side of self-proclaimed good samaritans. Another acquaintance had her luggage neatly stolen by two men who offered to help her as she struggled to cross a street in Puntarenas with two suitcases. Convinced of their samaritan nature, she went off to look for a taxi while they "looked after" her luggage. When she returned, they and her suitcases were gone.

Beware of drinks or candies offered by strangers. They may be laced with drugs. When you awake hours later you'll be poorer in possessions and in spirit. Never accept a drink from an open bottle while in a bar.

Remember, these are the rarities. Most Ticos have the integrity of saints.

---

shaken down for money. Never pay a policeman money. If a policeman asks for money, get his name and badge number and file a complaint to the **Judicial Police** (OIJ, tel. 255-0122) in the middle courthouse, Avenida 6, Calles 17/19; or, if it's a traffic policeman, to the **Ministry of Public Works and Transport** (tel. 227-2188) at Calle 9, Avenidas 20/22. If you are stopped by policemen wanting to see your passport or to search you, insist on its being done in front of a neutral witness—*"solamente con testigos."*

Common-Sense Precautions

Don't wear jewelry, chains, or expensive watches. They mark you as a wealthy tourist. Leave them with your ego at home. Wear an inexpensive digital watch.

Never carry more cash than you need for the day. The rest should be kept in the hotel safe. If you don't trust the hotel or if it doesn't have a safe, try as best you can to hide your valuables and secure your room. The majority of your money should be in the form of traveler's checks, which can be refunded if lost or stolen.

Never leave your purse, camera, or luggage unattended in public places. And always keep a wary eye on your luggage on public transportation, especially backpacks: sneak thieves love their zippered compartments.

Never carry your wallet in your back pocket. Instead, wear a secure moneybelt. Alternatively, you can carry your bills in your front pocket. Pack them beneath a handkerchief. Carry any other money in an inside pocket, a "secret" pocket sewn into your pants or jacket, or hidden in a body pouch or an elasticated wallet below the knee. Spread your money around your person.

Don't carry more luggage than you can adequately manage. Limit your baggage to one suitcase or duffel (see "What to Bring," under "Other Practicalities," below). And have a lock for each luggage item. Purses should have a short strap (ideally, one with metal woven in) that fits tightly against the body and snaps closed or has a zipper. Always keep purses fully zipped and luggage locked.

Don't leave anything of value within reach of an open window.

Don't leave anything of value in your car.

Don't leave tents or cars unguarded.

Be particularly wary after cashing money at a bank.

Have fun and don't worry!

RIPTIDES

On average, four people drown every week in Costa Rica. Rip currents are responsible for three-quarters of those ocean drownings. And most victims are caught in water barely deeper than waist-high. Most victims died because they *unnecessarily* panicked and struggled against the tide until they became exhausted. Yet surfers and strong swimmers rely on rip currents to carry them beyond the breakers. If you understand how rip currents function, you too can use their forces to get to safety.

Rip currents form where a large volume of wave-borne water attempting to return to sea is blocked by the mass of water coming ashore; the excess water rushes back to sea via a narrow fast-flowing "river" channel that relieves the build-up. Sometimes they run parallel to shore before turning out to sea. They can carry a swimmer out to sea for several hundred yards before they lose their strength.

Remember: Rip currents will always deliver you to calm waters, the "head" (a mushroom-shaped plume of muddy water), a short distance from shore.

Put your ego aside. Call for help *immediately* if you sense something wrong. *Don't* try to swim against the current. It is far, far stronger than you, and you'll only exhaust yourself while being carried out. Float. Alternatively, gently swim or wade parallel to the shoreline (many victims are pulled out by rip currents while wading close to shore); with luck you may reach the edge of the rip current and break free. Conserve your energy. And above all, don't panic! Rip currents do *not* pull you under. Once the current subsides, you can return to shore by swimming obliquely (at a 45-degree angle) to the beach.

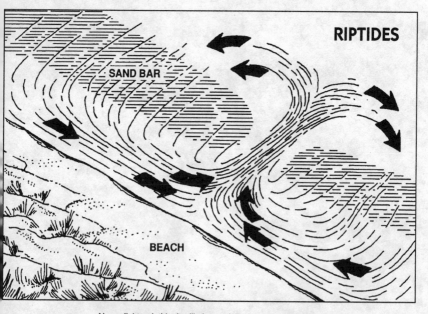

Never fight a riptide; it will always deliver you to calm water.

Rip currents sometimes have a discolored brown surface; others may display a mirror-like, deceptively smooth surface. An area of low incoming waves or a break in a surf line is another good indicator. Some rip currents migrate up and down a beach. They can also change location with the tides and weather. What seemed safe yesterday may not be today. Avoid wading or swimming on surf-swept beaches, where rip currents often occur during lulls in wave action. Also avoid rivermouths and jetties, which form their own rip currents.

The **Costa Rican Lifesaving Association** (tel. 777-0345) can provide more information. Remember: There are very few lifeguards on duty at Costa Rican beaches. Educate yourself, and always check the sea's behavior or ask about local conditions before venturing in.

Beaches to Beware
The following popular beaches are particularly renowned for their riptides:

• Cahuita National Park (beach near entrance)
• Espadilla (Manuel Antonio)
• Jacó Beach
• Playa Barranca (Puntarenas)
• Playa Bonita (Puerto Limón)
• Playa de Doña Ana (Puntarenas)
• Playa Savegre (Manuel Antonio)

MONEY

Currency

Costa Rica's currency is the *colón* (plural *colones*), which is written ¢ and sometimes colloquially called a *peso*. Notes are issued in the following denominations: 20 (brown), 50 (light green), 100 (gray), 500 (purple), 1,000 (red), and 5,000 (blue) *colones;* coins come in one, two, five, 10, 25, and 50 *colones*. New 50 and 100 *colones* coins were to be introduced in October 1995, replacing bills, while the "silver" one, five, and 10 coins will be replaced with smaller "gold" issues. The *colón* is divided into 100 *centimos,* though these coins are being taken out of circulation. You may hear money referred to colloquially as *pista* or *plata. Menudo* is loose change; *caña* is one *colón;* a 1,000-*colón* bill is called a *rojo.*

The five *colones* bank note is considered obsolete as a form of currency and is popularly sold as a souvenir ($1). It's a very beautiful note with a portrait of late-19th-century president Don Rafael Yglesia Castro on the face side and, on its reverse, a colorful reproduction of the pretty mural on the ceiling of the foyer of the National Theater in San José. Your dollar supposedly goes toward upkeep of the theater.

Watch out! A large quantity of counterfeit 5,000-*colones* bills are in circulation. Look for the watermark above the 5,000 to the right of the official signature, absent on fakes. There are even fake traveler's checks on the market. Be particularly wary if changing money on the street.

Most hotels will accept payment in U.S. dollars, as do car rental companies and taxis (for larger fares). For most other items, use *colones.* Other international currencies are generally not accepted as direct payment.

Exchange Rates

The Costa Rican government regularly devalues the *colón.* As a result, its value has fallen steadily against the U.S. dollar over the past few years. Spring 1992 ushered in a dramatic reversal after the government eliminated exchange controls, forcing the Central Bank to lower interest rates in an attempt to slow the *colón's* rise. The exchange rate stabilized for a while at approximately 135 *colones* to the dollar. However, by 1994 the slide resumed. By press time the official exchange rate was approximately 190 *colones* to the dollar (prices in dollars have been converted at 165 *colones* to the dollar, the rate as of July 1995), and predictions were that the dollar would reach 200 *colones* by early 1996. A yearly devaluation of 20% is expected (hence, a dollar will be worth about one *colón* more every week). All prices in this book are quoted in U.S. dollars unless otherwise indicated.

CHANGING MONEY

Legally, money may be changed only at a bank or hotel cash desk. You can change money at Juan Santamaría Airport upon arrival; the bank is inside the departure terminal but service can be abominably slow and complicated (hours: Mon.-Fri. 8 a.m.-4 p.m., weekends and holidays 7 a.m.-1 p.m.). Travelers arriving from countries other than the U.S. may find it easier to buy U.S. dollars before arriving in Costa Rica. Small towns may not have banks or moneychangers: change money beforehand. And travel with sufficient small bills.

You are allowed to convert only $50 of *colones* to dollars when departing, so spend all your local currency before leaving.

Banks

Banks are normally open 9 a.m.-3 p.m. Their foreign-exchange departments are often open longer. In San José, **Banco Metropolitan** (Avenida 2, Calle Central) specializes in foreign currency transactions. The **Banco Nacional**

(Avenida 3, Calles 2/4) is open weekdays 7 a.m.-6.30 p.m., Saturday 9 a.m-noon. The Banco Nacional will change German *marks*. And the **Banco Anglo Costarricense** (Calle 3, Avenida 2, tel. 222-3322) is open weekdays 9 a.m.-7 p.m. and Saturday 10 a.m.-2 p.m. The Banco Anglo and Banco Lyon (Calle 2, Avenida Central) will change sterling. Banks are allowed to charge what they wish for foreign-exchange transactions. Shop around if changing a large amount.

Don't expect fast service. Costa Rican banks can be infernally slow bureaucracies. At most banks, you'll have to stand in two lines: one to process the transaction, the other to receive your cash. It can sometimes take more than an hour. Ask to make sure you're in the correct line. Banks tend to give large bills: have them broken down. Automated teller machines are beginning to appear. The automated teller machine at the Banco Anglo will supposedly accept Visa and MasterCard for cash withdrawals. Banks (including at Juan Santamaría Airport) close during Easter, Christmas, New Year, and other holidays, so plan carefully.

Hotels
Large hotels and travel agencies offer similar exchange rates to banks. Normally, you must be a hotel guest to change money in hotels, although I've managed to change money as a nonguest. Often, hotels will only change small amounts, but the benefit is you'll avoid the long lines that are the plague of banks.

Street Changers
Illegal but common. You'll find plenty of moneychangers outside the terminal at Juan Santamaría Airport. They also congregate around the Mercado Central and Avenida Central (between Calles 2 and 6). You'll get between two and five percent—and perhaps even 10% if you're a great bargainer—more than the official exchange rate. Traveler's checks get less than cash.

Travelers illicitly changing money—as well as the vendors—can face heavy fines. **Note:** The moneychanger may be an undercover policeman. Occasionally police sweeps try to clean out the moneychangers.

The Judicial Police say they receive between 10 and 15 complaints a day from people who have been ripped off while changing money on the street. Most victims are tourists. Some rip-off artists work as pairs. Tricks include going to a car to "change dollars"; instead of returning, they flee. Always count your money before handing over your U.S. dollars (street changers won't change other currencies). Note that many counterfeit 5,000-*colones* bills were in circulation in 1992 and 1993 and that moneychangers have been implicated.

Chris Howard, author of *The Golden Door to Retirement Living in Costa Rica,* recommends **Villalobos Brothers Money Traders** (tel. 233-0090, fax 223-8838), on the second floor of the Schyfter Bldg, 75 meters south of the post office, next to the Banco Lyon.

Traveler's Checks
Traveler's checks can be readily cashed, though some banks may refuse or will change only a specific kind. You'll usually need your passport, and you may also need to show your proof-of-purchase slip. You'll receive one or two *colones* less per dollar than if changing cash. Take small-denomination checks, and stick to the well-known international brands, such as American Express, Citibank, Barclays, and Thomas Cook. Banks will deduct a small commission. **Thomas Cook Currency Services** (630 5th Ave., New York, NY 10111, tel. 212-757-6915) specializes in traveler's checks. The **American Express** (see below) office will also issue U.S.-dollar traveler's checks.

Credit Cards
Most larger hotels, car rental companies, and travel suppliers, as well as larger restaurants and stores, will accept credit card payment by Visa and MasterCard (American Express is not widely accepted). Conversion is normally at the official exchange rate, although a small service charge may be added. You can also use your credit cards to buy *colones* at banks (minimum $50); try the **Banco de San José,** Calle Central and Avenidas 3/5, tel. 221-9911. The automated teller machine at the Banco Anglo will supposedly accept Visa and MasterCard for cash withdrawals. There's a Rapidbank **autoteller** (hours: 3-6 p.m.) on the south side of the main post office at Calle 2, Avenida 1. **American Express's** Express Cash sys-

tem (tel. 800-227-4669 for information) also links your AmEx card to your U.S. checking account. You can withdraw up to $1000 in a 21-day period; a $2 fee is charged for each transaction and the money is usually issued in traveler's checks. The local American Express representative is **TAM Travel Agency** (Calle 1, Avenida Central, Edificio Alde, 4th floor, tel. 223-5111 or 233-0044, fax 222-8092; open 8 a.m.-5:30 p.m. weekdays). It will also provide cash against Visa or MasterCard, as will the following **Credomatic** offices in San José: Credomatic San Pedro (Avenida Central, Calles 31/33, tel. 224-2155), Credomatic Omni Building (Avenida 1, Calles 3/5, tel. 233-2156), Credomatic Center (Avenida Central, Calles 3/5, tel. 257-0155), and Credmatic Rohrmoser (tel. 220-2563). There are also Credomatic offices in Alajuela (Avenida 3, Calles Central/2, tel. 441-2080), Cartago (one block west of El Carmen church, tel. 552-3155), Heredia (in front of McDonald's, tel. 260-2000), and Moravia (tel. 235-3184).

Both **Visa** (tel. 257-1357 or 222-4611) and **MasterCard** (tel. 253-2155) maintain offices in San José. The local **Thomas Cook** representative is Intertur, 50 meters east La Toruma Youth Hostel, in Los Yoses.

Money Transfers

Major banks in San José will arrange cash transfers from the U.S. for a small commission fee. Ask your home bank for the name and details of a "correspondent" bank in San José. If you need money transferred while traveling, simply telex your home bank to arrange a wire transfer to the correspondent bank. You can also wire or receive up to $10,000 via **American Express MoneyGram** (to send, the full amount must be paid in advance; only $1000 can be charged to a credit card). Call (800) 543-4080 for information. **Western Union** has representatives in the San José suburbs of Tibas (tel. 257-1150), Los Yoses, and San Francisco dos Ríos (tel. 227-1103), as well as Escazú, Liberia, San Isidro de El General, and Puntarenas.

In an emergency, you may be able to cull money from your parent's Visa Gold or Business Card via the 24-hour **Visa Assistance Center** (call collect 919-370-3203; in the U.S., tel. 800-759-6262).

COSTS

Costa Rica may be more expensive than you thought, and certainly is more so than the rest of Central and much of South America. However, it should be possible to get by on $15 a day by being frugal. Budget hotels will cost $2-10 per night. A breakfast or lunch of *gallo pinto* will cost $1-4, and a dinner with beer at an inexpensive restaurant should cost no more than $5. I normally travel in a little more style and average $30-50 a day, usually with a hefty bar bill included!

Travelers used to at least a modicum of comfort will probably pay $35-100 a day, depending on the standard of accommodation, mode of transportation, and where they choose to eat. Day tours featuring sightseeing and first-class hotels average $75-100, all-inclusive. Moderate hotels will cost $20-60 per night. Popular mountain and jungle lodges and upscale beach resorts and hotels can cost up to $100 or more. Outside San José, you'll find prices lower. Remember, too, you can fly anywhere in the country for less than $80, or travel by bus for less than $10. Renting a car will send your costs skyrocketing—a minimum of $30 a day, plus insurance and gas.

Limit your Costa Rican purchases to souvenirs, as foreign-made goods are subject to a whopping 100% import duty. I recommend bringing everything you think you'll need.

Discounts

A subscription to *Costa Rican Outlook* ($19 in U.S., $22 outside U.S.; P.O. Box 5573, Chula Vista, CA 91912-5573, tel./fax 619-421-6002, or tel. 800-365-2342 with Visa/MasterCard orders) includes an ID card good for discounts of 5-15% at select hotels, restaurants, car rental companies, etc.

Access Costa Rica Network (tel. 231-3637, fax 231-5221) produces a **Passport Discount Card** ($20) offering discounts of 10-30% on a wide range of tourist facilities.

The main ICT information office in San José, beneath the Plaza de la Cultura, has lots of hotel and other leaflets and coupons offering discounts upon presentation. Likewise see ad coupons in the *Tico Times* and *Costa Rica Today*.

Tipping

Taxi drivers do not receive tips. Tipping in restaurants is *not* the norm; restaurants automatically add both a 13% sales tax and a 10% service charge to your bill. Don't add an additional tip except as a reward for exceptional service. Bellboys in classy hotels should receive 25 cents to 50 cents per bag. And don't forget your chambermaid—the often-forgotten workhorses who have worked hard on your behalf—when you leave. Tour guides normally are tipped $1-2 per person per day. Again, do not tip if you had only mundane service. Be fair.

COMMUNICATIONS

BROADCASTING

Costa Rica has twelve TV broadcasting stations. Four TV channels provide 24-hour satellite coverage from the United States. Much Spanish-language programming is of trite soap-opera and ass-kicking mayhem variety—either the worst of Los Angeles with Spanish translations, or cheap Costa Rican imitations. Upscale hotels also beam in C-Span, CNN, ESPN, etc. There are 119 radio stations (102 are commercial and 17 belong to public service institutions). Classical music fans are served by **Radio Universidad** (870 AM and 96.7 FM), and by **Radio FM 96**. For New Age and jazz, tune to **Radio Estereo Azul**, on 99 FM). BBC World Service and Voice of America provide English-language news, as does **Radio 2** on FM 99.5. The latter offers 24-hour, all-English-language programming, with trivia contests, weather, music, and a special Friday morning segment devoted to tourist information.

NEWSPAPERS AND MAGAZINES

Costa Rica has three major dailies. *La Nación* offers a distinctly right-wing bias (the publisher also published the contra newspaper, *Nicaragua Hoy*). *La República* and *La Prensa Libre* offer slightly less biased news accounts. For a leftist perspective, read *Libertad*. I recommend the Spanish-language weekly *Esta Semana* for its solid and clear-minded news coverage. Evening newspapers include *La Prensa Libre*.

No Spanish? The family-run English-language *Tico Times* will edify you. It is consistently more analytical than its Costa Rican peers and diligently covers environmental issues. It's published each Friday and is a particularly good source of information on cultural events. You'll find it at newsstands nationwide (25 cents). A six-month subscription costs U.S. residents $26.50; one year costs $45 (*Tico Times,* Dept. 717, P.O. Box 025216, Miami, FL 33102).

Costa Rica Today is an English-language weekly newspaper geared specifically to foreign travelers and published in full color. Longtime Costa Rica resident Jerry Ruhlow, formerly a reporter with the *Los Angeles Times,* is editor. Excellent! It is available free at hotels. U.S. subscriptions cost $32.95 for six months (P.O. Box 0025216, Miami, FL 33102).

The government has its own official organ: *La Gazette*. International newspapers and magazines are available at newsstands, bookstores, and upscale hotels.

For advance information, I highly recommend the *Costa Rican Outlook* (P.O. Box 5573, Chula Vista, CA 91912, tel./fax 619-421-6002, or tel. 800-365-2342), a wonderful bimonthly newsletter replete with useful information. Annual subscriptions ($19) include a money-back guarantee plus a discount card valid for restaurants and other businesses in Costa Rica.

In German: *Costa Rica aktuell* (subscription 139DM or $79; Apdo. 3264, San José 1000, tel. 257-0232, fax 257-0237) is a superb monthly newspaper combining practical information for travelers with news and profiles on every aspect of the country. The same company publishes a color magazine, *Focus Zentral-Amerika,* (subscription 139DM or $45) listing country profiles and essential telephone numbers for German travelers in Central America.

Also see "Information" under "Other Practicalities" below.

MAIL

The nation's mail service is only moderately efficient and has faced some severe criticism in recent years for internal fraud. A recent investigation of CORTEL (the Costa Rica postal service) revealed a frightening degree of mail theft. Even when mailing out of Costa Rica, don't enclose anything of value.

Airmail *(correo aereo)* to/from North America averages five days to one week, though two or even three weeks is not unknown. To/from Europe, anticipate a minimum of one week to 10 days; sea mail *(marítimo)* takes anywhere from six weeks to three months. Postcards to North America cost 30 *colones* (approximately 20 cents); letters cost 40 *colones* (about 25 cents). Add 10 *colones* (six cents) to Europe. Registered mail costs 30 *colones* extra. Hotels usually can provide stamps and will often take care of mailing for you. Or go to the central post office (Calle 2, Avenida 1/3). The post office is open Mon.-Fri. 7 a.m.-6 p.m. and Sat. 7 a.m.-noon. Current postal rates are posted to the left of the main entrance on Calle 2.

Mailing packages overseas is expensive. *Don't* seal your package. You must first take it to the central post office for customs inspection. The office is to the left of the main entrance.

It is much faster and surer to fax than to mail.

Receiving Mail

Street addresses are rarely used in Costa Rica. Most people rent a post office box *(apartado—* abbreviated Apdo.). You may wish to do the same if you plan on staying a few months or more. Mailboxes are in short supply, so you may find an individual or company willing to share—it's common. Costa Rican postal codes sometimes appear before the name of the town, or even after the *apartado* number (e.g., Apdo. 890-1000, San José, instead of Apdo. 890, San José 1000). Embassies generally will not hold mail for you.

You can receive international mail c/o **Lista de Correos** at the central post office in San José (Lista de Correos, Correos Central, San José 1000) or any other large town. Each item costs 10 cents. You must pick up your mail in person at window 17 in the hall at the southern end of the building on Calle 2. Bring your passport; you won't get your mail without it.

Incoming letters are filed alphabetically. If the clerk can't find your name under the initial of your surname try other initials, such as those of your first or middle name. Tell anyone you expect to write to you to *print* your surname legibly and to include the words "Central America." Also tell them not to send money or anything else of monetary value.

Tell friends and family not to mail parcels larger than a magazine-size envelope. Receiving them is a hassle. You'll need to make two or more visits to the Aduana (Customs) in Zapote, on the outskirts of San José; one visit to declare the contents, the second to pay duty. The fee is hefty: at least equal to the value of the goods, however minor they may be.

Private Mail Services

The incidence of mail theft has spawned private mail services. American Express cardholders can have mail sent to them c/o the **American Express** office (Calle 1, Avenidas Central/1, tel. 223-5111). In the U.S., call (800) 528-2121. **Trans-Air Express Interlink** (tel. 232-2544) lets you mail or receive up to four pounds of mail a month for $15; the **Association of Residents** (tel. 233-8068) offers a courier service to Miami; and **Aerocasillas** (Apdo. 4567, San José 1000, tel. 255-4567, fax 257-1187) also offers courier service ($25 per month for accounts). Two other companies recommended are **AAA Express Mail** (tel. 233-4993, fax 221-5056) and **Star Box** (Apdo. 405, San José 1000, tel. 221-9029, fax 233-0448).

DHL Worldwide Express (Paseo Colón, Calle 30/32, tel. 223-1423) offers express document and parcel service.

The **Business Center** (tel. 257-1138, fax 257-1345) has a message service; you can send or receive mail, faxes, or phone messages. It offers complete business services, including secretaries.

TELEX AND FAX

Most moderate and upscale hotels will send a fax or telex for you for a small fee. You'll find a public telex in San José at **Radiográfica**

Costarricense, one block west of the National Theater (Calle 1, Avenida 5; hours 7 a.m.-10 p.m.; tel. 287-0513 or 287-0462); its telex number is Costa Rica 1050. Not cheap: approximately 50 cents a word! You can also send and receive faxes via Radiográfica (fax 223-1609 or 323-7932), which also has e-mail service; or the **ICE Office** (Avenida 2, Calles 1/3, tel. 255-0444; hours 7 a.m.-11 p.m.). The fax or telex must indicate your name and Costa Rica address or telephone number or you'll not be advised of its arrival; it's best to call anyway to check if you've received a fax or telex. Fax transmissions cost $7 per page to Europe, $5 to the United States.

Cheaper by far is CORTEL, the Costa Rican postal and telegraph system. A window in the most southerly office in the main post office (see above) is marked CORTEL Fax, where you can obtain a fax form. After filling this out, take it to the main lobby and follow the arrow marked Servicio de Fax upstairs to the telex office. The fax office is in an anteroom. A clerk will send your fax.

TELEPHONES

Costa Rica has an efficient direct-dial telephone system. The country boasts more telephones per capita than any other Latin American nation. Public phones are all over the country, even in the most implausible places.

International Calls

When calling Costa Rica from North America, dial 001 (the international dial code), then 506 (the country code), followed by the number. AT&T has a "Language Line" that will connect you with an interpreter (800-843-8420 in North America; 408-648-7174 in Costa Rica); interpreter time is billed at $3.50 per minute.

For outbound calls to the U.S. or Canada, dial 001, then the area code and number. You can dial direct to most countries from public phone booths, or via an English-speaking international operator (dial 116). You'll need to call 116 to make collect calls (reverse charges) or charge to a telephone credit card. The operator will call you back once he/she has connected you. Hotel operators can also connect you, although charges for calling from hotels are high.

Better yet, you can also make direct calls to the U.S. (and bill to your credit card or phone card) via the **AT&T** operator (dial 114), **MCI** (dial 162), **Sprint** (dial 163), **Telecom Canada** (dial 161), and **British Telecom** (dial 167). **USADirect** phones automatically link you with an AT&T operator. You'll find USADirect phones at Juan Santamaría Airport, in the lobbies of the **Aurora Holiday Inn** and other top-class ho-

---

NEW TELEPHONE NUMBERS

Seven-digit telephone numbers replaced the old six-digit numbers on 30 March 1994. In 85% of cases, existing numbers were simply prefixed by an additional digit. The rest received either an additional digit or two digits to replace an existing one. For example, numbers 49-1000 through 49-2999 were preceded by 2 (thus 49-1234 became 249-1234); but for numbers 49-3000 through 49-3999, the second digit was replaced by 63 (thus 49-1234 became 463-1234).

ICE, the Costa Rican Electricity Institute, made the transition in just one evening during Holy Week, when the telephone system was little used.

Some of the numbers used in this book are based on a conversion table provided by ICE before publication of the first edition. Every effort has been made since to assure accuracy of these conversions. Nonetheless, we recommend that readers double-check telephone directories and other reference sources for accuracy. We would appreciate learning about any discrepancies.

Note: Just before press time, ICE disconnected all telephone lines operated by Millicom—a division of the U.S. company Millicom International, which pioneered cellular communications in Costa Rica—in response to a Costa Rican Supreme Court ruling that confirmed a constitutional clause stating that only the state may operate phone lines. One hotelier called to say that his telephone was therefore no longer valid. The ruling may affect other numbers listed in this book.

tels, and at **Radiográfica Costarricense** (see above, tel. 287-0513). For **international information,** dial 124. Many private and hotel phones do not have international access. International calls to North America cost $2-3 per minute, depending on where you're calling. Calls to the U.K. cost $5 per minute; to Australia $8 per minute. Cheaper rates apply between 8 p.m. and 7 a.m. and on weekends.

Local Calls

Local calls are very cheap. You can call anywhere in the nation for three minutes for 50 cents from public phone booths. Calls from your hotel room may be considerably more expensive than normal long-distance rates. There are no area or city codes; simply dial the seven-digit number. There is one telephone directory for the whole country, plus a separate directory for San José. In some villages you will reach the local operator, who will connect you with your party. For **local information,** dial 113.

Public Phone Booths

Street signs with telephone symbols point the way to public phone booths. Pay phones in San José are usually on noisy intersections (the phone booth next to the ICT office beneath the Plaza de la Cultura is quiet). There's often a lengthy line. If no one else is standing in line, the phone is probably *malo* (broken)!

Public phones accept only the new two-, five-, 10-, and 20-*colones* coins (some accept only two-*colones* coins). You may need a stack of coins. Wait for the dial tone before inserting your coin. The dial tone is similar to that of U.S. phones. The coin will drop when your call is connected. Two *colones* give you two minutes. Have your second and subsequent coins ready to insert immediately when the beep indicating "time up" sounds, or you'll be cut off. Some phones allow you to "stack" coins in an automatic feeder.

It's a good idea to give your phone booth telephone number to the person you're calling so he or she can call you back (it is usually indicated on a yellow sign above the phone). Phone booths do not have telephone books; your hotel front desk should have one.

Where public phones are absent, local hotels, corner stores, or *pulperías* will usually allow use of their phones for a charge. They'll dial for you and meter your call; you'll be charged by the minute.

Cellular Phones

The Costa Rican division of Millicom Corp. (tel. 257-2527) offers cellular phone rentals for $7.50 per day. A fax attachment can also be rented (you provide the fax machine). Rentals can be charged to an American Express account.

OTHER PRACTICALITIES

INFORMATION

Tourist Information Offices

The chaotic era of 1991-94, when the Calderón administration closed the two North American offices of the Costa Rican Tourism Institute (Instituto Costarricense de Turismo—ICT), is improving. The toll-free tourist information line—(800) 343-6332—is now manned by real people. Three lines (based in the San José headquarters of the tourist board's publicity agency) were being answered by bilingual staff, 7 a.m.-6 p.m. (local time), Mon.-Friday. Two additional lines were planned. You can request brochures, but anticipate that it will take weeks or months before they arrive.

And the Figueres administration was looking at opening two or three tourist offices in the U.S., including the main office: 1101 Brickel Ave., Suite 801, Miami, FL 33131, tel. 305-358-2150 or 800-327-7033.

There are no ICT offices in Canada or the United Kingdom. The Costa Rican embassies can provide limited tourist information (see the "Embassies and Consulates in Costa Rica" chart).

In Costa Rica, the ICT head office is at Apdo. 777, San José 1000, tel. 223-1733. The **main ICT information office** is below the Plaza de la Cultura, at Calle 5 and Avenida Central (Apdo. 777, San José 1000, tel. 222-1090, fax 223-5452; open Mon.-Fri. 8 a.m.-4:30 p.m.). It issues a very basic ICT road map (free) and a San José city map, plus a copy of *Enjoying Costa Rica* (a monthly leaflet that lists tourist attractions as well as the events for each month).

You'll also find an ICT information booth (next to the taxi stands outside Customs) at Juan Santamaría Airport (tel. 442-1820 or 441-8542; open 8 a.m. until 9 p.m. every day except major holidays). The ICT was planning to open regional offices, starting with Liberia, San Carlos, Golfito, Puntarenas, and Limón.

Also in San José is **INFOtur** (tel. 223-4481, fax 223-4476), whose main office is on the corner of Avenida 2 and Calle 5, facing the National Theater.

Telephone Information Services

A 24-hour, multilingual **Tourist Tele-Info Line** (tel. 257-4667) provides information on a wide range of tourist facilities that include restaurants, accommodations, adventures, etc. Only paying business subscribers are listed. The *Tico Times* newspaper also operates a 24-hour bilingual **Tourist Information Line** (tel. 240-6373).

National Parks

You can receive free information on national parks nationwide by calling 192. At press time, a toll-free "800" number was to be introduced some time in the future for worldwide calls. The headquarters of the Servicio de Parques Nacionales has a public information office (Calle 25, Avenidas 8/10, tel. 257-0922), open Mon.-Fri. 8 a.m.-4 p.m. There's also an SPN public information office at the rear of the Simón Bolívar Zoo in San José, at Calle 7, Avenida 11 (tel. 233-5673 or 233-5284), though so far I've not encountered an English-speaking staff-member here. Also see "National Parks" in the "Conservation" section of the Introduction.

Other Sources

One of the best resources is the *Costa Rican Outlook,* a superb bimonthly newsletter (P.O. Box 5573, Chula Vista, CA 91912-5573, tel./fax 619-421-6002, or tel. 800-365-2342 with Visa/MasterCard orders). It's full of useful tidbits and excellent feature articles. *Highly recommended!* The annual subscription ($19 in U.S., $22 outside U.S.) includes an ID card good for discounts of 5-15% at select hotels, restaurants, car rental companies, etc.

Another option is *Adventures in Costa Rica* (subscription $48; Starflame Productions, P.O. Box 508, Jackson, CA 95642), with lots of first-person reportage and a strong focus for would-be retirees to Costa Rica. *Costa Rica Outdoors* (Dept. SJO 2316, P.O. Box 025216, Miami, FL 33102; in Costa Rica, Apdo. 199, Santa Ana

6150, tel. 282-6743) is a color magazine dedicated to fishing and outdoor sports, and published twice-monthly (annual subscription, $39.50). Also new, *Costa Rica Adventure & Business* (12416 Hymeadow Dr., Austin, TX 78750, tel. 512-250-9023) was launched as a quarterly full-color magazine in December 1994 ($19.95 a year), and includes features articles and news reports. I also recommend subscribing to **Latin America Travel Tribune** (Apdo. 661, Alajuela; $25 per year in U.S.), which has a strong focus on Costa Rica, with plenty of news features, tourism profiles, and tongue-in-cheek humor.

Horizontes, a Costa Rican tour company, publishes *Horizontes News,* more for tourism industry folks than travelers. Nonetheless, those with a serious interest in environmentalism may find it useful (Apdo. 1780, San José 1002, tel. 222-2022, fax 255-4513).

Adams Enterprises (P.O. Box 18295, Irvine, CA 92713-8295, tel. 714-857-8079, fax 714-786-8079) distributes a "Costa Rica Information Packet" containing dozens of brochures on hotels, tour packages, Spanish language schools, real estate, etc., as well as a video and a magazine on Costa Rican real estate ($8 postpaid).

The **South American Explorer's Club** (1510 York St., Denver, CO 80206, tel. 303-320-0388) publishes the quarterly *South American Explorer* magazine, containing a list of guidebooks, maps, trip reports, and resources for sale, as well as feature articles and advice for travelers and explorers. Annual membership costs $25.

The **Central American Information Center** (P.O. Box 50211, San Diego, CA 92105, tel. 619-583-2925) publishes *Travel Programs in Central America;* the **Resource Center** (P.O. Box 4506, Albuquerque, NM 87196, tel. 505-842-8288) publishes "Country Guides" for Central American countries; and **Third World Resources** (464 19th St., Oakland, CA 94612) publishes a quarterly review listing contact organizations.

Also try the **Asociación Costarricense de Agencias** (Costa Rica Travel Agents Association; Apdo. 8076, San José 1000) for information on specific tour companies and tour options. The **Latin American Travel Association** (6175 N.W. 153rd St., Suite 332, Miami Lakes, FL

33014, tel. 305-557-5221) is a professional body representing the interests of tour companies and travel suppliers.

The **South America Travel Association** (c/o Creative Resources, 12830 N.W. 9th St., Miami, FL 33182) is geared to travel industry personnel though it accepts memberships from anyone (rates vary); it publishes *The News of Latin America* ($20).

Many excellent travel videos provide an insight into Costa Rica's delights (see "Booklist"). **LACSA,** the national airline, provides superb destinational profiles and literature on Costa Rica.

Lastly, of course, are a wide range of excellent and lesser guidebooks, including several of special-interest focus (see "Booklist"). Make sure you obtain the latest edition. Many recent editions still list the useless old telephone numbers, for example. The *Pocket Traveler's Guide to Costa Rica* (American Research Service Corp., P.O. Box 025216, Dept SJ-316, Miami, FL 33102-5216, tel. 221-6408, fax 223-3811) is a thin, 28-page pamphlet listing essential information and telephone numbers.

In Costa Rica, my friend, *Tico Times* reporter Peter Brennan, hosts "Costa Rica Update" at 7 p.m. every Thursday on Channel 19 (it's rebroadcast on Saturday, 1 p.m.). And **Radio 2** has a Friday-morning tourist information segment, broadcast in English on FM 99.5.

Online Information
Phil Greenspun's *Travels With Samantha* and other tales provide a fabulous information service on the **Internet's World Wide Web Travel Review** (http://ww-swiss.ai.mit.edu/cr/), based largely on his own anecdotal travels. I'm pleased to report that much of the first edition text from the *Costa Rica Handbook* is online. Thanks, Phil! The **Macintosh online service, eWorld,** features "TravelTalk," produced by Ana Wagner-Hoffman.

General Information
Consumer Reports (101 Truman Ave., Yonkers, NY 10703; $8.95) publishes the *Travel Buying Guide* (Ed Perkins, ed.), which provides information on "How to Get Big Discounts on Airfares, Hotels, Car Rentals, and More."

Also of use is the monthly *Consumer Reports Travel Letter* ($37 annual subscription). I also recommend the **Alternative Travel Directory** (Transitions Abroad, P.O. Box 1300, Amherst, MA 01004, tel. 800-293-9373, fax 413-256-0373; $16.95) for practical information on travel, learning and working abroad.

MAPS

The Costa Rican Tourism Institute (ICT) and most moderate hotels provide single-sheet street maps of San José. Car rental agencies provide a basic 1:1,000,000 ICT road map of the country, though this is not much use for driving beyond the Meseta Central.

The best road map is a detailed topographical 1:500,000 sheet published by **International Travel Map Publications** (P.O. Box 2290, Vancouver, B.C. V6B 2WF, Canada). The map shows gas stations and features a 1:250,000 "Environs of San José" inset. It is available in the U.K. through **Bradt Publications** (41 Nortoft Rd., Chalfont St. Peter, Bucks SL9 0LA, England), and at **Stanford's** (12-14 Long Acre, London WC2E 9LP, tel. 071-836-1321, fax 071-836-0189). Most travel bookstores in the U.S. stock it or can order it. **Jitan** also publishes a reasonable quality 1:800,000 "General Map of Costa Rica" ($2) and a 1:670,000 road map ($4), available by mail order from Jimenez and Tanzi, Apdo. 2553, San José 1000, tel. 233-8033, fax 233-8294 (add $1 for postage and handling; do *not* send cash by mail).

The *Red Guide to Costa Rica: National Map Guide* (San José: Guias de Costa Rica, 1991) provides detailed regional maps, as does Wilberth S. Herrera's *Costa Rica Nature Atlas* (San José: Editorial Incafo), which I've found the most detailed—scale 1:200,000—and trustworthy of maps (it also has the advantage of providing detailed and lucid accounts of virtually every natural site of attraction in the country, beautifully illustrated with color photography). Delineations of national parks and reserves aren't always accurate

Major bookstores in San José carry the above maps and books. **The Bookshop, Chispas Books, Lehmann's,** and **Librería Trejos** (see "Publications" under "Shopping" in the San José chapter for addresses) have an excellent stock of maps; prices at Librería Trejos tend to be cheaper. Quality topographic maps can be bought from the Ministry of Public Works on Calles 9/11 and Avenida 20 (Mon.-Fri. 8:30-11:30 a.m.). If you can't obtain an ITMP map, the Institute publishes a less detailed topographical map at the same scale. More detailed maps include a 1:200,000 nine-sheet map, and 1:50,000 topographical maps, which hikers will find particularly useful.

WHEN TO GO

Costa Rica has distinct wet and dry seasons. The best weather is during dry season (December through April), with December, January, and February perhaps the ideal months. This is the busiest time, however, and many hotels and coastal resorts tend to be fully booked. Easter is the very busiest period, closely followed by Christmas and New Year, when accommodations tend to be booked solid months in advance. Advance reservations—several months ahead—are strongly recommended for dry season.

Consider traveling off-season. The rainy season—now promoted by the ICT as the "green season"—normally begins in late April or early May. While many dirt roads (particularly in Nicoya) can be washed out, and many regions temporarily inaccessible by road, don't let this put you off. Advantages to green-season travel are endless. Prices are often lower, and it is usually much easier to find vacant hotels rooms, especially in more popular destinations. The more popular parts of the country remain accessible by road at this time of year. And the country is magnificently green. Rain normally means short-lived afternoon and evening showers or rainstorms (the Golfito and Caribbean lowlands, both of which can be lashed by the whip of tropical storms in the wet season, don't have a distinct dry season anyway). The highlands can be especially delightful at this time of year. In Costa Rica temperatures in any locale remain the same year-round; temperatures generally vary with elevation, not season. (See "Climate" in the Introduction)

WHAT TO BRING

Pack light! A good rule of thumb is to lay out everything you wish to take—then cut it by half. Most often I've regretted packing too much, not too little. Remember, you'll need some spare room too for any souvenirs and books you plan on bringing home. *Leave your jewelry at home;* it invites theft.

Most important, *don't forget your passport, airline tickets, traveler's checks, and other documentation.* You'd be amazed how many folks get to the airport before discovering this "minor" oversight.

Rule One

Space on buses and planes is severely limited. Limit yourself to one bag (preferably a sturdy duffel bag or internal-frame backpack with plenty of pockets), plus a small day-pack or camera bag. Avoid suitcases, as well as backpacks with external appendages: they catch and easily bend or break. Believe me! One of the best investments you can make is a well-made duffel bag that doubles as a backpack and can be carried by hand and/or on the back. Reputable outdoor-equipment companies such as North Face and REI make superb bags. A small day-pack allows you to pack everything for a one- or two-day journey. Then, you can leave the rest of your gear in the storage room of a San José hotel and return frequently as you travel around the country using the capital as a base.

Rule Two

Limit the number of changes of clothing. Pack items that work in various combinations—preferably darker items that don't show the inevitable dirt and stains you'll quickly collect on your travels. Note, though, that dark clothes tend to be hotter than khaki or light clothing. Bright clothing tends to scare off wildlife; pack khakis and sub-

---

ESSENTIALS TO BRING

GENERAL

address book and notebook
beach towel
cord (at least three meters; useful for clothesline and/or repairs)
electrical adapter
first-aid kit (see "Health")
flashlight (ideally pocket-size), plus spare batteries
hat with sun visor
insect repellent and sulphur powder
nylon zippered bag
padlock
pocketknife
sunglasses
travel alarm
universal sink plug
water bottle
Ziploc plastic bags (variable sizes; for laundry, wet clothing, and lotions)

TOILETRIES

contraceptives (locally made condoms tear easily)
facecloth
hand mirror (budget hotels often lack mirrors)
hand towel
shampoo, conditioner, soap, toothbrush and toothpaste, shaving gear, dental floss, Q-tips, etc.
sun creams and sunblock
tampons and feminine-hygiene products (expensive in Costa Rica)
toilet paper (rarely supplied in hotels or restaurants)

---

dued greens if you plan on nature viewing. Some people recommend packing just one set of clothes to wash, and one to wear. Two sets of clothing seems ascetic. Two T-shirts plus two dressier shirts, a sweatshirt and sweatpants, a polo shirt, a pair of Levi's, "safari" pants, two pairs of shorts, and a "safari" or photographer's jacket with heaps of pockets suffice me. Women may wish to substitute blouses and mid-length skirts. Don't forget your bathing suit.

Rule Three

Pack plenty of socks and underpants. Socks get wet quickly and frequently in Costa Rica. You may need a daily change. Wash them fre-

quently to help keep athlete's foot and other fungal growths at bay.

Hot or Cold?

Remember, Costa Rica can be both hot and cold. If you plan on visiting a volcano or cloud forest, pack a warm sweater and/or a warm windproof jacket; you'll want one for San José and the highlands at night, anyway. In the mountains, cold winds are common, and it gets very chilly and wet when the clouds set in. The lowlands, of course, are humid and warm to hot. Expect to sweat—a lot! You'll want light, loose-fitting shirts and pants. And if you plan on hiking in the forests, loose-fitting cotton canvas shirt and pants will help protect against thorns and biting bugs.

Note: Here's a handy tip for handling changes in environment. Whenever you move from, say, the relatively cool central highlands to hot, dry Guanacaste, or from Guanacaste to the humid Pacific Southwest, *take a shower!* Don't delay. This leaves the human body at the local temperature. You'll be amazed at how much more quickly you'll adjust.

Wet or Dry?

In the wet season, plan on rain—plenty of it! An inexpensive umbrella is best (you can buy one in San José). Raincoats are heavy and tend to make you sweat. For the rainforests at any time of year, you'll find a hooded poncho an invalu-able asset. Make sure it has slits down the side for your arms, and that it is large enough to carry your small day-pack underneath. Breathable Gore-Tex rainproof jackets also work fine.

I like to travel with denim jeans. But they take forever to dry when wet. I also always pack a pair of light cotton-polyester-blend safari-style pants, which are cooler, dry quickly, and have plenty of pockets. Ideally, everything should be drip-dry, wash-and-wear.

Jackets, Ties, and Cocktail Dresses

Most travelers will not need dressy clothes. However, Costa Ricans love to dress in jacket and tie for dinner or the theater, as well as for business functions, where hip designer suits and shoes by Giorgio Armani and Fratelli Rosetti are displayed by wealthier Ticos. You may wish to take jacket and tie or cocktail dress for dinners in more expensive hotels and restaurants, and for the theater. Otherwise, Costa Ricans dress informally, but always very neatly. Shorts for men are gradually becoming acceptable wear in San José. Save shorter style runner's shorts for the beach.

Footwear

Normally a comfortable, well-fitting pair of sneakers will do double-duty for most occasions. In the wet season and any time in the rainforests, your shoes will get wet. Rubber boots *(botas de hule)* are a godsend on tropical trails. In fact, they're

local laundry, Cahuita

standard wear for many rural dwellers. You can buy them in Costa Rica for $10. (Ticos have small feet; if you take size 9 or above, plan on bringing your own.) If you go hiking, you'll also want a plastic water bottle and sturdy walking shoes. If hiking in the wet season or rainforest, protect your spare clothing in a plastic bag inside your backpack.

PHOTOGRAPHY

Equipment
You are allowed to bring two cameras plus six rolls of film into Costa Rica (don't worry about the official film limit; I've never heard of its being enforced). Film is susceptible to damage by X-ray machines. You should always request that film (including your camera loaded with film) be hand-checked by airport security rather than having it go through the X-ray machine. Reports are that the machines at Costa Rica's international airport are "vicious."

Decide how much film you think you'll need to bring—then double it! I recommend one roll per day as a minimum, much more if you're even half serious about your photography. Film is very expensive in Costa Rica. If you do need to buy in San José, check the expiry date; the film may be outdated. And the film may have been sitting in the sun for months on end—not good! One exception is the **IFSA** store (Avenida 2, Calles 3/5), which usually has fresh film stock, as well as batteries, etc. Also try **Ilford Dima** (Calle 5 and Avenida Central, tel. 222-3939). Kodachrome 64 and Fujichrome 50 give the best color rendition in Costa Rica's bright, high-contrast conditions. You may need ASA 200 or 400 for the dark conditions typical within the gloomy rainforest sanctum. **The Glamour House** (Calle 1, Avenidas 7/9, tel./fax 221-3470) is a professional photography studio that can supply batteries and film, plus passport photos.

Keep your film out of the sun. If possible, refrigerate it. Color emulsions are particularly sensitive to tropical heat, and film rolls can also soften with the humidity so that they easily stretch and refuse to wind in your camera. Pack both your virgin and exposed film in a Ziploc plastic bag with silica gel inside to protect against moisture.

Bring extra batteries for light meters and flashes. Protect your lenses with a UV or skylight filter, and consider buying "warming," neutral-density, and/or polarizing filters, which can dramatically improve results. Your local camera shop can help you understand their applications.

Avoid processing your film in Costa Rica. Wait until you get home (try to keep your film cool). Or buy film with prepaid processing. It comes with a self-mailer and you can simply pop it in a mailbox; the prints or slides will then be mailed to your home.

Keep your lenses clean and dry when not in use (believe it or not, there's even a tropical mildew that attacks coated lenses). Silica gel packs are essential to help protect your camera gear from moisture; use them if you carry your camera equipment inside a plastic bag. Cameras are valuable goods. Never turn your back on your camera gear. Watch it at all times.

If you need urgent repairs, **Taller de Equipos Fotográficos** (Avenida Central, Calles 3/5, tel. 223-1146) in San José is recommended.

Shooting Tips
Don't underestimate the intensity of light. Midday is the worst time for photography. Early morning and late afternoon provide the best light; the wildlife is more active then, too. Use rubber hoods on all your lenses to screen out ambient light. And a good idea is to "stop down" one or two f-stops to underexpose slightly for better color rendition when photographing in bright sunlight. In the forest, you'll need as much light as possible. Remarkably little light seeps down to the forest floor; use a tripod, slow shutter speed, wide-open aperture, and higher-speed film. Use a flash in daytime to "fill in" shaded subjects (such as the forest) or dark objects surrounded by bright sunlight.

Ticos enjoy being photographed and will generally cooperate willingly. Never assume an automatic right to take a personal photograph, however. Ask permission to take a photograph as appropriate. And respect an individual's right to refuse.

Two recommended books are *The Wildlife & Nature Photographer's Field Guide* by Michael Freeman (Cincinnati: Writer's Digest Books, 1984) and *The Traveler's Photography Hand-*

book by Julian Calder and John Garrett (New York: Fielding/Morrow, 1985).

Photography Tours

The following companies offer photography workshops in Costa Rica: **Close-Up Expeditions** (1031 Ardmore Ave., Oakland, CA 94610, tel. 510-465-8955, fax 510-465-1237) offers tours for amateur photographers; its Costa Rica programs are escorted by natural-history photographer Thomas Johnson. **Photo Adventure** (P.O. Box 5095, Anaheim, CA 92814, tel. 714-527-2918, fax 714-826-8752) offers eight-day photographers' workshops. **Photo Safaris** (Apdo. 7812, San José 1000, tel. 267-7070, fax 267-7050) offers seven-day photo workshops. **Rico Tours** (Apdo. 833, San José 1002, tel. 233-9658, fax 233-9357; in the U.S., 13809 Research Blvd. #606, Austin, TX 78750, tel. 512-331-0918, fax 512-331-8765) offers an eight-day Costa Rican "Photo Safari."

WEIGHTS AND MEASURES

Costa Rica operates on the metric system. Liquids are sold in liters, fruits and vegetables by the kilo. Some of the old Spanish measurements still survive in vernacular usage. Street directions, for example, are often given as 100 *varas* (the Spanish "yard," equal to 33 inches) to indicate a city block. See the chart at the back of the book for metric conversions.

TIME

Costa Rica time is equivalent to U.S. central standard time (i.e., six hours behind Greenwich mean time, one hour behind New York, two hours ahead of the U.S. west coast). There is little seasonal variation in dawn (approximately 6 a.m.) and dusk (6 p.m.). Hence, Costa Rica has no daylight-saving time.

BUSINESS HOURS

Businesses are usually open Mon.-Fri. 8 a.m.-5 p.m. A few also open Saturday morning. Government offices close between 3:30 and 4:30 p.m. Lunch breaks are usually two hours; businesses and government offices may close 11:30 a.m.-1:30 p.m. Banks are open 9 a.m.-3 p.m. (see the section on "Money" for exceptions). Most shops open Mon.-Sat. 8 a.m.-6 p.m., often with a lunch break. Some restaurants close Sundays and Mondays. Most businesses also close on holidays (see "Holidays" under "Arts and Culture.")

ELECTRICITY

Costa Rica operates on 110-volts AC (60-cycle) nationwide. Some remote lodges are not connected to the national grid and generate their own power. Check in advance to see if they run on direct current (DC) or a nonstandard voltage. Two types of U.S. plugs are used: flat, parallel two-pins and three rectangular pins. A two-prong adapter is a good idea (most hardware stores in Costa Rica—*ferreterías*—can supply them). **Magellan's** (P.O. Box 5485, Santa Barbara, CA 93150, tel. 800-962-4932) can supply appropriate plugs, as well as dozens of other handy travel items featured in a 36-page catalog.

Never allow your personal computer or disks to pass through an airport X-ray machine. The magnets can wipe out all your data and programs. Insist on having it hand-checked. You will need to turn your computer on to show that it's what you say it is and not a bomb.

SPECIAL NOTES

NOTES FOR MEN

The lure of women is the likeliest source of problems for men. Things haven't changed since Genesis!

Ticas are renowned for their beauty and a reputation for pampering their men; the *Tico Times*'s classifieds are full of advertisements from Europeans and North Americans seeking a pretty Tica with whom to settle down in blissful union for a week or a lifetime. Agencies that provide bilingual companions for dining, etc., advertise in the classifieds of the *Tico Times* and *Costa Rica Today*. A book called *Happy Aging With Costa Rican Women,* by James I. Kennedy (Box Canyon Books, Canoga Park,

CA), provides a feel for the trials and tribulations you, the amorous gringo, can expect if you lose your head and your heart to a Tica.

But be careful of scams pulled by prostitutes, or other salacious Ticas, who may have a pecuniary gain in mind above any stated fees. Watch out for prostitutes who work in tandem. One may start to grope you while her partner lifts your wallet. Some sources warn that prostitutes have been known to lure you into a dark spot where you may be jumped by a male accomplice(s). Be aware, too, that some prostitutes may roll you while you're sleeping—there are several reports of johns being unwittingly drugged and robbed. Oh! That beauty giving you the wink near the Clínica Bíblica is probably a transvestite.

PROSTITUTION

Prostitution is not only legal in Costa Rica, it's looked upon with a general acceptance (many Latin American fathers still initiate sons into sex, for example, by introducing them to prostitutes), and many innocent tourists find it is a staple of bar life in San José. In "Gringo Gulch," the exotic becomes the erotic (see "Nightlife," in the San José chapter).

Ostensibly, the government tries to maintain a tight control on health standards. It provides regular health checks for prostitutes, who are issued *carnets de salud* to attest to their cleanliness. Many prostitutes, however, are not registered. Be aware that AIDS is gathering pace in Costa Rica. Other venereal diseases are prevalent, as elsewhere in the world. Prostitutes pose a particular risk (see "AIDS and Sexually Transmitted Diseases," in the section on "Safety," this chapter). And police warn tourists to beware of scams worked by prostitutes (see special topic "Special Tricks to Beware" and "Notes for Men").

The women are independent, for their legal status protects prostitutes from the development of pimping. And unlike places in Asia, where many prostitutes are underage, the women plying their bodies in Costa Rica are past the age of consent (a scandal made headlines, however, in 1993, when a brothel serving homosexual pedophiles was exposed in Puntarenas). The **Instituto Eco de Costa Rica** (Apdo. 8080, San José 1000, tel. 221-2801, fax 222-3300) sponsors job training for youngsters and works to mitigate the negative impacts of tourism in promoting prostitution.

NOTES FOR WOMEN

Most women stress the enjoyment of traveling in Costa Rica. The majority of Tico men treat foreign women with great respect. True, Costa Rica is a *machismo* society and the wolf-whistles can grate, but sexual assault of women is almost unheard of. *Women Travel: Adventures, Advice, and Experience,* by Niktania Jansz and Miranda Davies (Real Guides), is full of practical advice for women travelers.

If you do welcome the amorous attentions of men, Costa Rica is heaven. The art of gentle seduction is to Ticos a kind of national pastime: a sport and a trial of manhood. They will hiss in appreciation from a distance like serpents, and call out epithets such as *guapa* (pretty one), *machita* (for blondes), or *mi amor.* Be aware that many

Ticos think gringas are an "easy" *conquista.*

Take effusions of love with a grain of salt; while swearing eternal devotion, your Don Juan may conveniently forget to mention he's married. And when your Romeo suggests a nightcap at some romantic locale, make sure he doesn't mean one of San José's motels.

On the Caribbean coast are many "beach boys"—"rent-a-Rastas"—who earn their living giving pleasure to women looking for love beneath the palms.

If you're not interested in love in the tropics, unwanted attention can be a hassle. Pretend not to notice. Avoid eye contact. An insistent stare—*dando cuervo* or "making eyes"—is part of their game. You can help prevent these overtures by dressing modestly. Shorts, boob tubes, or strapless sundresses in San José invite attention. And avoid deserted beaches, especially at night. (See also "Sex, Machismo, and the Status of Women," in the "People" section of the Introduction.)

Casa de la Nueva Mujer (House of the New Woman, tel. 225-3784) provides a forum for women to meet and discuss issues ranging from arts and self-defense to women's issues. Accommodation is provided if needed ($9 per night). Located on Calle Sabanilla, about 250 meters north and 100 meters east of La Cosecha market. **Mujer No Estás Sola** (Woman, You're Not Alone) and its parent organization, **CE-FEMINA** (Apdo. 5355, San José 1000, tel. 224-4620) are feminist organizations that can provide assistance to women travelers. CEFEMINA publishes the quarterly *Mujer.*

NOTES FOR GAYS AND LESBIANS

San José has been described as a "very actively gay city" and is well-known for its active, if relatively underground, gay scene. Despite the *machismo* of Latin American societies, Costa Rica seems to be tolerant of homosexuality and has laws to protect gays from discrimination. Although Costa Rica is nominally a Roman Catholic nation, you may be surprised to learn that homosexual intercourse is legal (the consensual age is 17; for heterosexuals it's 15). However, the Costa Rican government is zealous in protecting minors and since the age of

majority is 18, gay travelers are advised against fraternizing with anyone under 18.

Despite legal protections, discrimination clearly exists and the general feeling is that Costa Rican gays (particularly lesbians) remain, for the most part, in the closet. Gay tourists should feel no discrimination "if you don't indulge in foolish [overt] behavior." These words of advice are from *Pura Vida!: A Travel Guide to Gay & Lesbian Costa Rica* by Joseph Itiel (1993), a practical guidebook that also provides a no-holds-barred look at the author's experiences in Costa Rica ($19.95; Orchid House, 2215-R Market St., San Francisco, CA 94114, tel. 415-749-1821, fax 415-928-1165).

To understand the sociology of Latino homosexuality, readers of Spanish may wish to browse *Hombres que aman hombres,* by Jacobo Schifter Sikora and Johnny Madrigal Pana (San José: Ediciones Illep-Sida, 1992).

Transvestis (transvestites) are part of the gay and prostitution scene, much more so in Latin American countries than, say, North America. Itiel describes a world of "brutal fights, drugs, unsafe sex, and robberies." A majority of *transvestis,* he says, are involved with drugs. Beware!

Confidencial (Publicaciones Unicornos, Apdo. 601, Curridabat, San José 2030) is a Costa Rican gay magazine.

Meeting Places

San José has several gay bars and discos (see "Nightlife" in the San José chapter). Wednesday is supposedly a "cruising day" at **Ojo de Agua,** a water-park outside San José that is also popular with families (see "San Antonio de Belén" under "West of Escazú" in the Central Highlands chapter). **Troyanos** is a gym "with a gay reputation." Itiel recommends the following steam baths: **Leblon** (Calle 9, Avenidas 1/3), **Decameron** (Avenida 10, Calles 7/9), and **Jano** (Calle 1, Avenidas 4/6). Gay men and women also advertise in the classified section of the daily newspaper, *La Nación.* **Soda La Perla** (Avenida Central, Calle 1) is supposedly a gay hangout after hours. Itiel strongly advises against "cruising" the parks where "you can get yourself into real trouble."

Away from San José, Manuel Antonio is the gay meeting place of choice (see Central Pacific chapter). Here, a tiny, nude beach north of Playa

Espedilla, the main beach, is a gathering spot, especially during holidays.

Accommodations

San José: The city has at least two dedicated gay hotels. **Colours Costa Rica** (Apdo. 341, San José 1200, tel./fax 232-3504; in the U.S., tel. 800-964-5622 or 305-532-9341, fax 305-534-0362), in the quiet residential Rohrmoser district, is a small colonial-style property operated by a U.S. travel agency. Most rooms have shared bath (more private baths are planned). The hotel hosts occasional social events. Women are encouraged. Rates: $75-130, including breakfast. At **Apartamentos Escocia,** near the Pizza Hut in San José's Barrio La California ($495 per month), is owned by a trans-op, Gianna. Each apartment has a large living room with TV, and bedroom plus kitchenette. Itiel describes it as "rundown and dirty" but with a nice view. He lists the **Hotel L'Ambiance** and **Hotel Santo Tomás** as "gay-friendly." **Casa Yemayá** (tel. 223-3652, fax 225-3636), in Barrio Guadalupe, though not overtly gay, is a hostel for women and a center for the feminist movement.

Elsewhere: In Manuel Antonio, Itiel lists the **Casa Blanca, Vela Bar Hotel,** and **Hotel Mariposa** (although the gay owners recently sold the property, many of the gay staff have been retained); and in Puntarenas, **Hotel Cayuga.** See relevant chapters.

Nightlife

Dejavú (Calle 2, Avenidas 14/16) is a gay disco—spacious, elegant, with two dance floors—for both men and women (entrance $3.50). Better known to foreign gays is **La Torre** (also called "Tonite Disco," Calle 7, Avenidas Central/1; cover charge varies from free to $4; open Wed.-Sun.), popular with men, women, and straight couples. Its disco has flashing lights, smoke, and great music. **La Avispa** (Calle 1, Avenidas 8/10, tel. 223-5343) was once exclusively lesbian but now caters to both men and women (entrance $2-4). It has a disco playing mostly techno and Latin music, plus pool room, bar, and snack bar. Drag queens flock on show night. Two predominantly lesbian bars are **Unicornio** (Avenida 8, Calles 1/3) and, in Barrio San Pedro, **Bar De La Tertulia** (tel. 225-0250). A mixed gay and straight crowd hangs out at **Risas** (Calle 1, Avenidas

Central/1) and at **El Churro Español El Puchito** (Calle 11, Avenida 8).

In Puntarenas, Itiel lists **Bar Viena, Bar de Belleza,** and **Bar Miraflores,** and in Puerto Limón, **Bar & Disco Palmelier** and **Bar & Restaurante Tuta.**

Tours

Toto Tours (1326 W. Albion Ave. #3W, Chicago, IL 60626, tel. 312-274-8686) offers a gay tour to Costa Rica for both men and women. **Mariah Wilderness Expeditions** (P.O. Box 248, Point Richmond, CA 94807, tel. 800-4-MARIAH) is a women-owned company specializing in Costa Rica. It offers women-only and lesbian active adventures that include whitewater rafting, sea kayaking, and nature cruises. In Costa Rica, **Exotur** (tel. 227-5169, fax 227-2180) and **Costa Rica Sun Tours** (tel. 255-3418, fax 255-4410) are listed as "gay-friendly."

The **Gay & Lesbian Travel Services Network** (2300 Market St. #142, San Francisco, CA 94114, tel. 415-552-5140, fax 415-552-5104; Internet gaytvlinfo@aol.com) and **Odysseus: The International Gay Travel Planner** (P.O. Box 1548, Port Washington, NY 11050, tel. 516-944-5330 or 800-257-5344, fax 516-944-7540) lists hotels and tours, etc. worldwide.

Organizations

The **International Gay Travel Association** (P.O. Box 4974, Key West, FL 33041, tel. 800-448-8550) and the **International Gay & Lesbian Association** (208 W. 13th St., New York, NY 10011, tel. 212-620-7310; in Europe, 81 Rue Marche au Charbon, 1000 Brussels, Belgium, tel. 32-2-502-2471) can provide information on gay organizations in Costa Rica, where the gay movement has been late in blossoming. Only in 1986, when Costa Rican authorities attempted to tackle the AIDS problem by "harassing" gay bars, did the gay movement coalesce.

Gay organizations include **Colectivo Gay Universitario** (tel. 222-3047) and **Las Entendidas** (Apdo. 1057, San José 2050; fax 233-9708), a local lesbian/feminist group that meets the last Wednesday of each month at La Avispa (see "Nightlife" in the San José chapter below). The **International Gay & Lesbian Association** has a local chapter (tel. 234-2411). There are several support groups for HIV-positive gays,

including **Asociación de Lucha Contra el SIDA** (Apdo. 1412, San José 1000, tel. 222-3047). Supposedly, there's even one for English-speaking foreign residents.

NOTES FOR STUDENTS AND YOUTHS

Student Cards
An **International Student Identity Card** (ISIC; for information call 800-GET-AN-ID) could be the most valuable item in your wallet. The card entitles students 12 years and older to discounts on transportation, entrances to museums, etc. When purchased in the U.S. ($15), ISIC even includes $3000 in emergency medical coverage, limited hospital coverage, and access to a 24-hour, toll-free emergency hotline. Students can obtain ISICs at any student union. Alternately, in the U.S., contact the **Council on International Educational Exchange** (CIEE, 205 E. 42nd St., New York, NY 10017, tel. 212-661-1414, fax 212-972-3231), which arranges ISICs ($14) and also arranges study vacations in Costa

Rica. (CIEE publishes a 72-page *Student Travel Catalog* and operates **Council Travel,** a travel agency for U.S. students, with offices at most major campus cities throughout the U.S.; see "Getting There," in this chapter). In Canada, cards (C$13) can be obtained from **Travel Cuts** (187 College St., Toronto, ON, tel. 416-979-2406). In the United Kingdom, students can obtain an ISIC from any student union office.

In Costa Rica, **OTEC,** a student travel agency in San José (Edificio Ferencz, Avenida 3 and Calle 3, tel. 222-0866), can arrange an ISIC for a small fee; you'll need two passport photos and proof of student status.

The **Youth International Educational Exchange Card** provides similar benefits for students and nonstudents under 26. In the U.S., contact CIEE (see above); in Europe, contact **Federation of International Youth Travel** (81 Islands Brugge, DK-2300, Copenhagen S, Denmark).

Work Study
Students wishing to study in Costa Rica have a wide choice of options. The **University of Costa**

DRUGS

Marijuana and cocaine are available in Costa Rica, which is a transshipment point between South America and the United States. Drug trafficking and laundering of drug money has increased markedly since the ouster of Noriega from Panamá. A sting operation carried out by the U.S. Drug Enforcement Agency (DEA) and the Costa Rica Judicial Police in March 1994 uncovered a money laundering racket that handled more than $180 million a year (several other major drug syndicates were busted that year). And indications are that the Buenos Aires region of southern Puntarenas province is overrun with traffickers who have been able to entice impoverished farmers to turn to growing marijuana and cocaine. The dramatic rise in car theft in Costa Rica is believed to be linked to drug trafficking, with stolen cars being used to ship goods.

The Costa Rican government is strictly opposed to drugs and initiated an on-going anti-narcotics operation in 1986. Penalties for possession or deal-

ing are stiff. If offered drugs on the street, be aware that you may be dealing with a plainclothes policeman. If caught, you will receive no special favors because you're foreign. A trial could take many months, in which case you'll be jailed on the premise that you're guilty until proven innocent.

Article 14 of the Drug Law stipulates: "A jail sentence of eight to 20 years shall be imposed upon anyone who participates in any way in international drug dealing." That includes anyone caught distributing, producing, supplying, transforming, refining, extracting, preparing, cultivating, transporting, or storing. The jail sentence also applies to anyone buying or otherwise involved in financial dealings involving drugs.

Looking unkempt and dirty signals a high possibility that you may be using drugs in the eyes of officialdom. If you roll your own cigarettes, consider leaving your papers at home; they are considered highly suspect. Stick to commercial brands. Or use it as an opportunity to give up smoking!

Rica offers special *cursos libres* (free courses) during winter break (Dec.-March). It also grants "special student" status to foreigners. Contact the Oficina de Asuntos Internacionales, Ciudad Universitaria Rodrigo Facio, San José, tel. 224-3660). The **University for Peace** and **Organization for Tropical Studies** also sponsor study courses. (Language students should see the appendix, "Language," for language schools.) Work abroad programs are also offered through **CIEE's Work Abroad Department** (205 E. 42nd St., New York, NY 10017, tel. 212-661-1414, ext. 1130), which publishes a series of reference guides, including *Work, Study, Travel Abroad* ($12.95 plus $1.50 book-rate postage, $3 first-class) and *The High School Student's Guide to Study, Travel, and Adventure Abroad* ($13.95 plus $1.50 postage; Publications Dept., 205 E. 42nd St., New York, NY 10017; or e-mail message to books@ciee.org), an invaluable resource for young travelers.

Transitions Abroad (18 Hulst Rd., Box 344, Amherst, MA 01004, tel. 413-256-0373) provides information for students wishing to study abroad, including advertisements from universities offering study programs in Costa Rica. The *Directory of Study Abroad Programs* ($17.95 including shipping) lists university bodies that offer international study courses. Contact **Renaissance Publications,** 7819 Barkwood Dr., Worthington, OH 43085, tel. 614-885-9568, fax 614-436-2793.

In Costa Rica, **Ecole Travel** (Apdo. 11516, San José 1000, tel. 223-2240), in Chispas Books at Calle 7 and Avenidas 1/Central, offers **international student exchange** programs, including 28-day packages ($1600 with accommodation) that have a strong focus on ecology and include a visit to Panamá's San Blas islands. It also offers language study for students.

NOTES FOR SENIORS

The **American Association of Retired Persons** (AARP, 601 E St., Washington, D.C. 20049, tel. 202-434-2277) has a "Purchase Privilege Program" offering discounts on airfares, hotels, car rentals, etc. Check also to see if any of the airlines serving Costa Rica are offering seniors discounts. The AARP also offers group tours for seniors through **AARP Travel Experience from American Express** (400 Pinnacle Way, Suite 450, Norcross, GA 30071, tel. 800-927-0111); annual membership, open to anyone over 50, is $8.

I recommend the "Retirement Tour" offered biannually by *Costa Rican Outlook* (P.O. Box 5573, Chula Vista, CA 91912-5573, tel. 800-365-2342 or tel./fax 619-421-6002). You'll meet with retirees, get a thorough look at Costa Rica, and generally have a great time with tour escorts Shirley Miller and Randy Case, two lively, warm-hearted folks who know Costa Rica as well as I or anyone else. Two other companies specialize in tours especially for retirees considering living in Costa Rica: **Lifestyle Explorations** (World Trade Center, 101 Federal Ave. Suite 1900, Boston, MA 02210, tel. 508-371-4814, fax 508-369-9192), and **Retirement Expedition Tours** (P.O. Box 6487, Modesto, CA 95355, tel. 209-577-4081).

ElderHostel (80 Boylston St., Suite 400, Boston, MA 02116, tel. 617-426-7788) offers relatively inexpensive educational tours to Costa Rica for seniors. Toronto-based **ElderTreks** (tel. 416-588-5000) offers a 10-day "Nature & Adventure Tour" in Costa Rica for travelers 50 years of age and older. In 1995, tours were offered in June, November and December.

Useful information sources include *The Mature Traveler* (P.O. Box 50820, Reno, NV 89513), a monthly newsletter ($24.50 subscription); and *The International Health Guide for Senior Citizen Travelers,* by Robert Lange, M.D. (New York: Pilot Books).

TRAVELING WITH CHILDREN

Generally, travel with children poses no special problems, and virtually everything you'll ever need for younger children is readily available. Costa Ricans adore children and will dote on your youngsters. There are few sanitary or health problems to worry about. However, ensure that your child has vaccinations against measles and rubella (German measles), as well as any other inoculations your doctor advises. Bring cotton swabs, Band-Aids, and a small first-aid kit with any necessary medicines for your child. The **Hospital de Niños** (Children's

CODE OF ETHICS

The **North American Center for Responsible Tourism** (P.O. Box 827, San Anselmo, CA 94979, tel. 415-258-6594 or 800-654-7975, fax 415-454-2493) suggests travelers abide by the following Code of Ethics for Tourists:

• Travel with a spirit of humility and a genuine desire to meet and talk with local people.

• Be aware of the feelings of others. Act respectfully and avoid offensive behavior, particularly when taking photographs.

• Cultivate the habit of actively listening and observing rather than merely hearing and seeing. Avoid the temptation to "know all the answers."

• Realize that others may have concepts of time and attitudes which are different—not inferior—to those you inherited from your own culture.

• Instead of looking only for the exotic, discover the richness of another culture and way of life.

• Learn local customs and respect them.

• Remember that you are only one of many visitors. Do not expect special privileges.

• When bargaining with merchants, remember that the poorest one may give up a profit rather than his or her personal dignity. Don't take advantage of the desperately poor. Pay a fair price.

• Keep your promises to people you meet. If you cannot, do not make the promise.

• Spend time each day reflecting on your experiences in order to deepen your understanding. Is your enrichment beneficial for all involved?

• Be aware of why you are traveling in the first place. If you truly want a "home away from home," why travel?

Costa Rica has developed its own set of guidelines for tourists. Contact the **Department of Responsible Tourism** (Apdo. 1524, San Pedro 2050, tel./fax 506-224-8910) for its leaflet: *Code of Ethics for Sustainable Tourism.*

Hospital) is at Paseo Colón and Calle 14 (tel. 222-0122). Proceeds from the **Parque Nacional de Diverciones** (tel. 231-2072)—a children's amusement park in La Uruca, west of San José—go to the hospital.

Children under two travel free on airlines; children between two and 12 are offered special discounts (check with individual airlines). Children over three are usually charged half the adult rate at moderate and expensive hotels. Cheaper hotels may charge an extra-bed rate. Baby foods and milk (radiated for longevity) are readily available in San José. Disposable diapers, however, are expensive (consider bringing cloth diapers; they're ecologically more acceptable). Bring baby wipes. If you plan on driving around, bring your own children's car seat—they're not offered for rental cars. Costa Rican TV features children's programs.

An increasing number of hotels and tour companies now feature children's facilities (amusements, entertainment, babysitting, etc.), and

special attractions are coming on line. The various butterfly farms, for example, are fabulous for youngsters. So, too, the **Children's Museum,** an interactive forum in the former penitentiary at the north end of Calle 4 in San José (see "Museums" under "Sightseeing" in the San José chapter). It has workshops on weekend mornings (call to register: tel. 223-7003 or 233-2734, ask for the Education Dept.) as well as exhibits.

The *Temptress* (see special topic "Natural-History Cruise Tours,") for example, offers a "Family Adventure Program" on its four- and six-day natural-history cruises. And **Costa Rica Learning Adventures** of New Orleans offers a "Family Cloud Forest Adventure" to Monteverde. **Wildland Adventures** (3516 N.E. 155th St., Seattle, WA 98155, tel. 206-365-0686 or 800-345-4453, fax 206-363-6615) offers a 10-day "Costa Rica Family Odyssey."

If you plan on staying for more than 30 days, you will need special permits for your children to leave the country (see the section on "Entry Re-

quirements," under "Immigration and Entry"). This applies to all children under 18 years old. **LAPA Vacations** (13260 S.W. 131st St. #123, Miami, FL 33186, tel. 305-255-8140, fax 305-255-8143) offers one-week family ranch vacations at various haciendas; children under 12, free.

Travel With Your Children (45 W. 18th St., New York, NY 10011, tel. 212-206-0688) publishes the *Family Fun Times* newsletter 10 times a year ($35 subscription). It also operates an information service. *Great Vacations with Your Kids* (New York: E.P. Dutton), by Dorothy Jordan and Marjorie Cohen, is a handy reference guide to planning a trip with children. *Let's Discover Costa Rica* is a 64-page children's book that sponsors intercultural understanding using puzzles, cut-outs, paint-by-number pictures, etc. ($7.50 including shipping; Bandanna Republic, Apdo. 1-6100 Mora, Ciudad Colón, tel./fax 249-1179).

PERSONAL CONDUCT

Generally, Costa Ricans are immensely respectful and courteous, with a deep sense of integrity. Politeness is greatly appreciated, and you can ease your way considerably by being both courteous and patient. Always greet your host with *"Buenas días"* or *"Buenas tardes."* And never neglect to say *"gracias"* (thank you). Honor local dress codes as appropriate. Don't flaunt flesh! Nude bathing is neither allowed nor accepted. Short shorts should generally be relegated to beachwear; longer shorts are now gaining acceptance on urban streets.

Costa Ricans have an understandable natural prejudice against anyone who ignores personal hygiene.

Respect the natural environment. Take only photographs; leave only footprints.

axe-shaped jade pendant

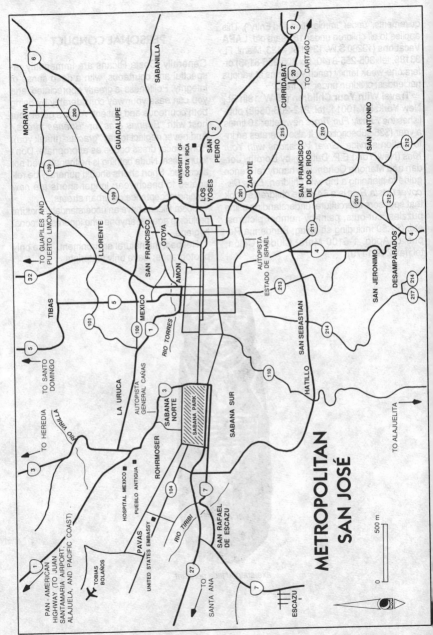

METROPOLITAN SAN JOSÉ

0   500 m

CATHY CARLSON

SAN JOSÉ
INTRODUCTION

San José, the nation's capital, squats on the floor of the Meseta Central, a fertile upland basin 1,150 meters (3,773 feet) above sea level in the heart of Costa Rica. The basin is a tectonic depression some 20 km wide and 70 km long, with volcanoes rising like a meniscus on every side, their slopes quilted with dark green coffee and pastures as bright as fresh limes. It's an enviously magnificent setting!

Nature is never far away. Earthquakes regularly give San José a shaking. The last major temblor, in April 1991, did significant damage to the Teatro Nacional. Cracks in hotel walls are evident everywhere.

San José's central position makes it an ideal base for forays into the countryside. Virtually every part of the country is accessible within a four-hour drive; applying the "hub and spoke" system of travel, you can use San José as a node to return to between excursions to the national parks and beaches.

San José, or "Chepe," as the locals call it,

dominates national life. Two-thirds of the nation's urban population lives in greater or metropolitan San José, whose population of 1.3 million represents 30% of the nation's total (central San José had an official population of 278,373 in 1991). The city's gravitational pull continues to attract those from outlying regions in search of a better life. Nearby towns such as Heredia have become virtual dormitory towns from which many people commute daily into San José.

THE FEEL OF THE CITY

San José is a retiring city. Urbane, not flashy; relatively prosperous, but not ostentatious. It's a compact city, congested and bustling, yet still manageably "small town" in scale and feel. The Plaza de la Cultura is its teeming vortex.

One of the first things you note is the relative lack of a colonial or even a pre-20th-century

legacy. Sure, its chaos of architectural styles is part Spanish, part Moorish, and many streets in the older neighborhoods are still lined with one- or two-story houses of wood, even adobe— many with ornamental grillwork—abutting the sidewalk and opening onto inner patios in the colonial style. But what few older structures remain are of modest interest (see "Sightseeing," below). If it's "colonial quaint" that you're seeking, skip San José!

Equally lacking is any vestige of an Indian heritage, such as gives Guatemala its characteristic feel. Only west of the Plaza de la Cultura is there a bustling market area that presents a stereotypically Central American aspect, with gaily colored fruit and produce stalls spilling from the sidewalks onto the streets. Almost every street corner has its vendor carts bursting with mangos, bananas, coconuts, pineapples, and papayas. And the neighborhood corner store *(pulpería)* remains the locus of social life, much as two generations ago.

Far more, however, San José mirrors North America: its commercial center dominated by hotels, offices, and countless shops stocked with the latest fashions; its narrow streets clogged with cars, trucks, and buses; its appallingly ugly modern high-rise architecture; and its neon signs advertising Kentucky Fried Chicken, McDonald's, and Pizza Hut contending with billboards touting condoms, Mercedes-Benzes, and the Moulin Rouge-style lures of Josephines, Hollywood International, and Olympus nightclubs. Together, they have sapped the inner city of a distinctive identity. *¡Que lastima!*

The Josefinos' (as San José residents like to be called) passion for the motor vehicle has added to the detrimental effects. Downtown San José's traffic scene is the stuff of Steven Spielberg movies. Despite staggering import duties that can run the cost of a Japanese compact to $30,000, the cramped city streets grow more choked every year with honking cars, buzzing mopeds, and trucks and gaily painted buses spewing diesel. Fortunately, in late 1994, a force of 60 traffic inspectors began patrolling as part of a campaign to improve traffic flow and enforce traffic laws in the center.

And what of the people? Despite their casual, unprepossessing ways, Josefinos are a relatively progressive and cosmopolitan cityfolk.

"Shopping," says one commentator, "is a social pastime," and on weekends suburbanites flock into San José to stroll down Avenida Central. Businessmen sport expensive suits to rival those of San Francisco. Women make a contemporary statement with tight miniskirts and high heels. And the city is large enough, and its occupants cosmopolitan enough in outlook, to support a vital cultural milieu and vivacious nightlife.

Fortunately—though the city is not without its share of homeless and beggars—there are very few of the ghoulish *tugurios* (slums) that scar the hillsides of so many other Latin American cities. The modest working-class *barrios* (neighborhoods), such as the newer regions of Hatillo, San Sebastian, and Zapote to the southwest, are almost everywhere clean and well ordered. And the tranquil residential districts such as Sabana Sur, San Pedro, and Rohrmoser, and more so the burgeoning middle-class suburbs of La Granja and Peralta with their gracious houses, green lawns, and high metal fences, have come to resemble those of Miami or outer Los Angeles.

Now the good news! San José has been undergoing a facelift in recent years under a Ministry of Culture concerned to improve the city's image. The first tuck-and-lift was to Parque Morazán which, like a butterfly, metamorphosed from blight to beauty. Next came Parque La Merced (also known as Parque Braulio Carrillo), on Avenida 2 (Calle 14), then Parque Central, an erstwhile ugly duckling that has emerged as a true Cinderella. Such edifices as the Catedral Metropolitan were receiving rejuvenating cosmetic surgery too, not least bright new color schemes. Hurrah!

CLIMATE

For first-time visitors the mild climate is surprising in a place so tropical. The weather is refreshingly clear and invigorating, which partly explains why the greater part of Costa Rica's population—and a majority of expatriates— choose to live here. Affectionately referred to by locals as "perpetual tropical spring," San José's climate earned the *National Geographic*'s stamp of approval as one of the best three in the world.

There's never a need for air-conditioning. San José's daily temperatures are in the 70s virtually year-round, with very little monthly variation (the average annual temperature is 20° C/68° F). A heat wave is when the mercury reaches the 80s; if it falls below 65° F, it's considered cold. Rest assured, there's never a frost. It has never snowed in San José. Nights are usually in the 60s year-round: bring a sweater. The record high for San José is only 92° F; the low is 49° F.

However, there *is* a distinct wet season—May to October—when rain can be expected at some time almost every day. Bring your umbrella during these months. Rain generally falls in midafternoon and evening, and long rainy days are a rarity. November through April are dry months when rain virtually never falls.

HISTORY

Colonial Times

Until little more than 200 years ago, San José was no more than a few muddy lanes around which clustered a bevy of ramshackle hovels. The village first gained stature in 1737 when a thatched hermitage was built to draw together the residents then scattered throughout the valley. Inauspiciously, the first wholesale influx was composed of Spaniard and Creole smugglers, who, say Biesanz et al., "having rebelled against the royal monopoly of commerce by resorting to contraband, were punished by being 'exiled' from Cartago," the colonial capital city founded in 1564 by Juan Vásquez de Coronado. The new settlement was christened Villa Nueva de la Boca del Monte del Valle de Abra, a real tongue twister later changed to San José, the name of the local patron saint.

Thanks to its occupants' freewheeling mercantilist ways, San José flourished and quickly grew to equal Cartago in size: by the 1820s, Cartago and San José each had slightly more than 5,000 inhabitants, Heredia half that number, and Alajuela a little more than 1,800. San José quickly developed a lucrative monopoly on the tobacco trade and made the most, too, of the booming coffee trade. Tobacco profits funded civic buildings; by the close of the 18th century, San José already had a cathedral fronting a beautiful park, a currency mint, a town council building, and military quarters.

Independence

When the surprise news of independence from Spain came by mail to the Meseta Central in October 1821, the councils of the four cities met to determine their fate, and a constitution—the Pacto de Concordia—was signed, its inspiration derived from the 1812 Spanish Constitution. Alas, says historian Carlos Monge Alfaro, early Costa Rica was not a unified province, but a "group of villages separated by narrow re-

Avenida Central at the intersections of Calles 5 and 7 in San José, circa 1870

DISTRICTS—*BARRIOS*—OF SAN JOSÉ

The names of San José's most important neighborhoods, or *barrios*, will come in handy if you plan on extensive sightseeing. Here are the most important.

Barrio Amón

This historic neighborhood (see "Sightseeing," this chapter) is replete with venerable buildings. It is in the midst of revival after going to seed. Many intriguing facades now sport hotel signs. Makes for an interesting walking tour. Between Avenidas 3-11 and Calles Central and 17.

Barrio México

To the north of Avenida 7, west of Calle 16, this residential area provides a slice of local color. Few tourist facilities, but an important church and a growing number of upscale bars and restaurants are finally garnering tourists' attention.

Escazú

Eight km southwest of San José, and distinctly different in ambience and tempo, this historic suburb (dating back to 1561) retains strong hints of the past. A wide selection of fine bed-and-breakfast hostelries, restaurants, and contemporary shopping centers add to the appeal. See Central Highlands chapter.

Los Yoses

East of downtown, Avenida Central leads to this bustling residential and commercial center that is off the tourist path, yet contains some fine historic bed-and-breakfast hotels, restaurants, and upscale shopping malls. Due east of Los Yoses is Barrio Monterrey.

Moravia

Strictly a separate entity from San José (see Central Highlands chapter), this quiet residential suburb, six km from downtown, is now on the tourist map as a center for art and handicrafts.

San Bosco

Although rarely referred to as San Bosco, its main thoroughfare—Paseo Colón—is the vitally important western extension of Avenida Central. A large number of car rental and airline companies have headquarters here. The area contains several select restaurants and historic hotels.

San Pedro

Beyond Los Yoses, about three km east of downtown, this residential enclave replete with bohemian nightclubs and restaurants owes its vitality to the presence of the University of Costa Rica. It offers some fine bed-and-breakfast hotels.

Rohrmoser

This upscale neighborhood, due west of Sabana Park, is the setting for fine mansions (many of them housing embassies), a growing number of quality restaurants, and the U.S. embassy.

---

gionalisms." Each of the four cities felt and acted as freely as had the city-states of ancient Greece. The conservative and aristocratic leaders of Cartago and Heredia, with their traditional colonial links, favored annexation into a Central American federation led by Mexico; the more progressive republican forces of San José and Alajuela, swayed by the heady revolutionary ideas ascendant in Europe, argued for independence. A bloody struggle for regional control soon ensued.

On 5 April 1823, the two sides clashed in the Ochomogo Hills. The victorious republican forces, commanded by an erstwhile merchant seaman named Gregorio José Ramírez, then stormed and captured Cartago. In a gesture that set a precedent to be followed in later years, the civilian hero Ramírez relinquished power and retired to his farm, then returned to foil an army coup.

San José thus became the nation's capital city. Its growing prominence, however, soon engendered resentment and discontent. In March 1835, in a conciliatory gesture, San José's city fathers offered to rotate the national capital among the four cities every four years. Unfortunately, the other cities—Alajuela included—had a bee in their collective bonnet. In September 1837 they formed a league, chose a president, and on 26 September attacked San José in an effort to topple the Braulio Carrillo government. The Josefinos won what came to be known as La Guerra de la Liga ("The War of the League"), and the city has remained the nation's capital ever since.

By the mid-1800s the coffee boom was bringing prosperity, culture, and refinement to the once-humble backwater. San José developed a substantial middle class eager to spend its newfound wealth for the social good. The mud roads were bricked over and the streets illuminated by kerosene lamps. Tramways began to appear. The city was the third in the world to install public electric lighting. Public telephones appeared well ahead of most cities in Europe and North America. By the turn of the century, tree-lined parks and plazas and sumptuous buildings catering to a burgeoning bourgeoisie—libraries, museums, the Teatro Nacional, and grand neoclassical mansions and middle-class homes—graced the city. Architects, influenced by the Paris and Crystal Palace Expositions and aided by coffee income, were erecting great monuments and schools built of imported prefab metals. Homes and public buildings, too, adopted the in-vogue, French-inspired look of New Orleans and Martinique. The city was . . . *respectable!*

Of course, the city had its slumlike suburbs formed of *puertas ventanas,* tiny workers' houses in which several families often lived side by side. Industrial zones rose on the periphery of the urban center. And isolated sections were populated by blacks who had defied segregationist laws and settled in the Meseta Central.

Modern Times

Still, as recently as the 1940s San José had only 70,000 residents, a mere tenth of the country's population. After WW II ended, however, the capital city began to mushroom, growing haphazardly, encroaching on neighboring villages such as Guadalupe and Tibas. Sadly, many of the city's finest buildings felt the blow of the demolition crane in postwar years. In their stead have come monstrous examples of modern architecture. Uncontrolled rapid growth in recent years has spread the city's tentacles farther afield until the suburban districts have begun to blur into the larger complex and neighboring towns such as Heredia and Alajuela are threatened with being engulfed. At night the surrounding hills twinkle with the lights of suburban villages that are slowly being drawn into the city's fold.

SIGHTSEEING

As a drawing card in itself, the capital city has been disparaged ever since Anthony Trollope, passing through in 1858, observed that "there is little more interest to be found in entering San José than in driving through . . . a sleepy little borough town in Wiltshire." Things have improved since then (and continue to do so month by month), but I've often heard tourists say that San José can be "done" in two days. It's true, although you can certainly occupy a third day. Bona fide tourist attractions can be counted on one hand: the Jade Museum, the National Museum, the National Theater, the Gold Museum, the Museum of Art, and the recently opened National Cultural Center (including the Museum of Contemporary Art and Design, and the theaters of the National Dance Company and the National Theater Company), and a smattering of other additions.

The capital city has its small yet pretty tree-shaded plazas and its block-square Mercado Central ("Central Market"), a dark, century-old maze of stalls where vendors hawk everything from T-shirts and chickens to medicinal herbs and Christ figurines done in plaster (nearby is the seamier Mercado Borbón, and in outlying *barrios* are *ferias,* open-air produce markets). At sunset on a Sunday evening, San José's small parks fill with strolling families and youths. But it's hardly a romantic or endearing city, though it's getting more so day by day as city fathers foster the on-going facelift. Baroque or Renaissance-style buildings are few. And excepting the Teatro Nacional, San José's late-19th-century belle-epoque National Theater whose interior drips with opulence, the city is wholly lacking the grand colonial structures of, say, Mexico City, Santiago, or even Buenos Aires.

You will find some architectural gems, however, as you stroll the narrow streets, and I'm happy to report that these jewels are being saved from the wrecking ball and given new polish. **Barrio Amón** and **Barrio Otoya,** in particular, extending north and west of the old Na-

SUGGESTED ITINERARIES

One-Day Itinerary

Begin with breakfast at the **Café Parisienne,** in front of the Gran Hotel on Avenida 2. First stop should be the nation's cultural pride and joy: the **Teatro Nacional,** to the left, in front of the Gran Hotel. Stop at the ticket booth on the way out and buy your *boletas* for a performance that night (symphony season only). Turn right and cross the plaza to Calle 5 and descend the steps to the **ICT** tourist information office (below the plaza) for a San José map. Next door to the ICT office is the **Pre-Columbian Gold Museum,** with 22,000 troy ounces of gold adornments and artifacts to peruse. Emerging back into sunlight, turn right onto Avenida Central and walk five blocks to the **National Museum,** housing national treasures tracing the history of the country. A little shopping for arts and crafts is in order at the stalls at the foot of the plaza.

Turn left (north) from the main entrance of the museum and follow Calle 15 past the Moorish-style Legislative Assembly building to **Parque Nacional.** On its northeast corner is the old Atlantic Railway Station, now the **National Railroad Museum,** after which you should stroll back down Avenida 3 to the **National Arts and Cultural Center,** with art galleries, exhibits, and performing arts theaters.

For lunch, exit the center on the west side and cross Parque España to Calle 9. Turn left and head to the popular **Balcón de Europa** (turn right on Calle 9), serving some of the best Italian food in town.

Suitably revived, retrace your steps along Calle 9 to **Parque España** and the **Fidel Tristan Jade Museum,** on the 11th floor of the INS Building, facing the park on Avenida 7. Note the **Edificio Metálico** on the left, and the **Casa Amarilla** on the right.

Assuming you still have time and energy, two options to close out the day include a walking tour through the historic **Barrio Amón** behind and to the east of the INS Building (turn left as you exit); or a visit to the **Simón Bolívar Zoo** (turn right out of the INS Building, right on Calle 7, and right on Avenida 11).

If the day seems packed, remember that all the above-mentioned places are within a few blocks of each other, and the museums are relatively small, allowing you to fully savor each in an hour or less.

In the evening, don your fineries for a performance at either the National Theater or **Teatro Melico Salazar** (Avenida 2, Calles Central/2). An absolute must before departing San José is a late-night visit to **La Esmeralda** restaurant (Avenida 2, Calles 5/7) for live mariachi music.

Two-Day Itinerary

Assuming you followed the itinerary above, day two should start with a peek inside the **Catedral Metropolitan,** on the west side of Parque Central (Avenida 2, Calle Central). Then, follow Avenida 2 west to Calle 6, turn right, and walk one block to the **Mercado Central** (Central Market), with its chaotic jumble of stalls and vocal hawkers. Emerging onto Avenida 1, tread east to the **Serpentario** (Calles 9/11), displaying a robust collection of live snakes and poison-arrow frogs. This may only fuel your interest in bugs. If so, stroll (or take a taxi) north along Calle 3 to Avenida 13, where you should follow the road uphill to the right a few hundred meters to **Spirogyra,** a live-butterfly farm opposite the Centro Comercial shopping center (better known as **El Pueblo**).

Before heading to Spirogyra, have an inexpensive lunch at the **Hotel Amstel** or **Café Parisienne.** Later, you may wish to walk west along Paseo Colón to **Sabana Park** and the **Costa Rican Art Museum** (this is a lengthy walk; you may prefer a taxi). Finally, enjoy a snooze back at your hotel before a dinner . . . perhaps of traditional Costa Rican fare at the **Cocina de Leña** in El Pueblo. Energy left to spare? Great! El Pueblo is full of discos to choose from. Alternately, you can try your chance with Lady Luck at any of San José's many casinos.

tional Liquor Factory (now the National Cultural Center), are together an aristocratic residential neighborhood founded at the end of the last century by a French immigrant, Amón Fasileau Duplantier, who arrived in 1884 to work for a coffee enterprise owned by the Tournón family, which lent its name to an adjacent region. Until recently, it had suffered decline and stood on the verge of becoming a slum. An atmosphere of revitalization was inspired by the restoration of Parque Morazán in 1992, prompting investors to refurbish the neighborhood's grand historic homes (the Barrio Amón Conservation and Development Association was formed in 1992). A

burst of newfound civic pride is leading to closure of disreputable bars and a renaissance of the area as the region of choice for intellectuals and nouveau riche. Of particular note are the **Bishop's Castle** (Avenida 11, Calle 3), an ornate Moorish, turreted former home of Archbishop Don Carlos Humberto Rodriguez Quirós, and the **Casa Amarilla,** immediately north of the beautifully renovated Parque España.

The most appealing aspect of San José is the view across the roofs of the city to the mountains that cradle the Meseta Central. Still, after two or three days you'll know it is time to move on. (See the special topic "Suggested San José Itineraries.")

See "Orientation" under "Transportation," below for help in finding your way around.

A handy pocket-size guide is *Vern Bell's Walking Tour of Downtown San José, With Some Glimpses of History, Anecdotes, and a Chuckle or Two,* available at hotel gift stores in San José, or directly from Mr. Bell (tel. 225-4752, fax 224-5884), who leads you by the hand, providing erudition and tongue-in-cheek humor along the way.

MUSEUMS

While San José has nothing to compare with the Smithsonian or Louvre, it does have a number of excellent museums that provide a good perspective on the history and culture of Costa Rica.

Fidel Tristan Jade Museum

On the 11th floor of the National Insurance Institute (Instituto Nacional de Seguro) or INS Building (Calle 9, Avenida 7), San José's world-famous Jade Museum houses the largest collection of jade in the Americas. The displays (mostly carved adzes and pendants) include a full panoply of pre-Columbian artifacts and reconstructions and are well-organized, with some mounted pieces backlit to show off the beautiful translucent colors of the jade to best effect. The museum also displays a comprehensive collection of pre-Columbian ceramics and gold miniatures organized by culture and region, as well as special exhibits of jewelry by important national and foreign artists.

Humankind's eternal preoccupation with sex is evidenced by the many enormous clay phalluses and figurines of men and women masturbating and copulating. The museum's 11th-floor vantage point offers splendid panoramic views over the city through the large windows: bring your camera. (Open Mon.-Fri. 9 a.m.-3 p.m.; admission is free, tel. 223-5800, ext. 2581.)

National Museum

A large collection of pre-Columbian art (pottery, stone, and gold) and an eclectic mix of colonial-era art, furniture, costumes, and documents highlight the Museo Nacional, in the old Bellavista Fortress, on the east side of Plaza de la Democracia at Calle 17 and Avenida Central/2. Separate exhibition halls deal with history, archaeology, geology, religion, and colonial life. Only a few exhibits offer translations in English. The National Institute of Biodiversity also has a small but interesting display of insects downstairs. The towers and walls of the fortress, an old army barracks, are pitted with bullet holes from the 1948 civil war. The museum surrounds a beautiful landscaped courtyard featuring colonial-era cannons. There's a small gift shop. (Hours: Tues.-Sun. 9 a.m.-5 p.m.; admission 45 cents, students free, tel. 257-1433.)

Pre-Columbian Gold Museum

Given the paucity of pre-Columbian sites in Costa Rica, the Museo del Oro Precolombiano—run by the state-owned Central Bank—comes as a pleasant surprise. The more than 2,000 glittering pre-Columbian gold artifacts (frogs, people, etc.) weigh in at over 22,000 troy ounces. A collection of old coins is also displayed in an adjoining room in the Museo Numismática, while a small exhibit hall features works from the bank's art collection.

The museum is adjacent to the ICT tourist information office in the basement beneath the Plaza de la Cultura (Calle 5 and Avenida Central/2). The entrance is at the base of the steps beside the large silver, funnel-shaped air vents at the east side of the plaza. Free guided tours presented by bilingual guides are offered Tuesday and Thursday at 2 p.m., and on weekends at 11 a.m. and 2 p.m. Bring your passport or other identification for the security check upon entry. (Hours: Fri.-Sun. and holidays, 10 a.m.-5

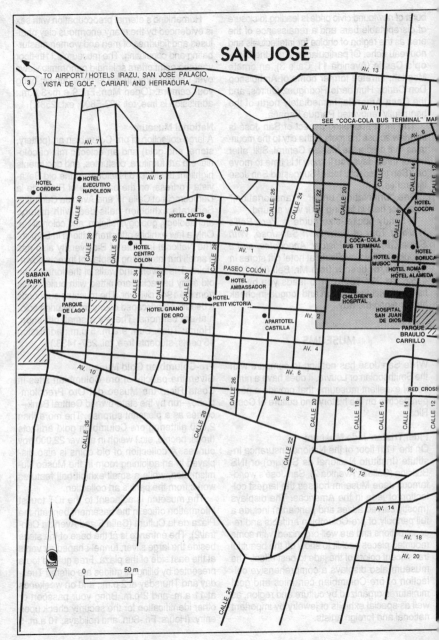

SAN JOSÉ

TO AIRPORT / HOTELS IRAZU, SAN JOSE PALACIO,
VISTA DE GOLF, CARIARI, AND HERRADURA

3

SEE "COCA-COLA BUS TERMINAL" MAP

AV. 13

AV. 11

AV. 9

AV. 7

AV. 5

AV. 3

AV. 1

HOTEL
COROBICI

HOTEL
EJECUTIVO
NAPOLEON

HOTEL CACTS

HOTEL
CENTRO
COLON

PASEO COLÓN

HOTEL
AMBASSADOR

HOTEL
GRANO
DE ORO

HOTEL
PETIT VICTORIA

APARTOTEL
CASTILLA

SABANA
PARK

PARQUE
DE LAGO

CHILDREN'S
HOSPITAL

HOSPITAL
SAN JUAN
DE DIOS

PARQUE
BRAULIO
CARRILLO

COCA-COLA
BUS TERMINAL

HOTEL
COCORI

HOTEL
MUSOC

HOTEL
BORUCA

HOTEL ROMA
HOTEL ALAMEDA

RED CROSS

AV. 2

AV. 4

AV. 6

AV. 8

AV. 10

AV. 12

AV. 14

AV. 18

AV. 20

CALLE 40

CALLE 38

CALLE 36

CALLE 34

CALLE 32

CALLE 30

CALLE 28

CALLE 26

CALLE 24

CALLE 22

CALLE 20

CALLE 18

CALLE 16

CALLE 14

CALLE 12

N

0   50 m

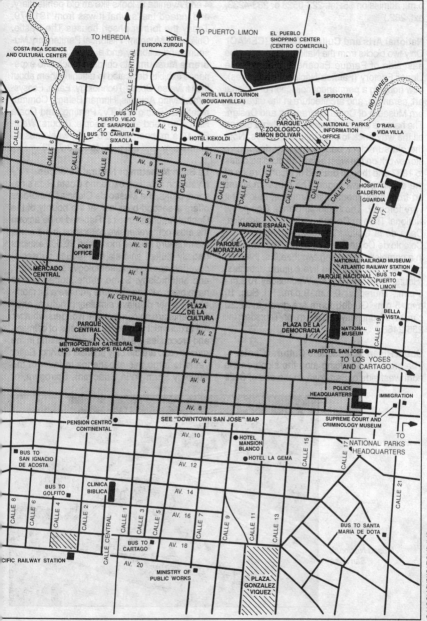

TO HEREDIA

TO PUERTO LIMON

EL PUEBLO SHOPPING CENTER (CENTRO COMERCIAL)

HOTEL EUROPA ZURQUI

COSTA RICA SCIENCE AND CULTURAL CENTER

CALLE CENTRAL

HOTEL VILLA TOURNON (BOUGAINVILLEA)

SPIROGYRA

RIO TORRES

BUS TO PUERTO VIEJO DE SARAPIQUI

BUS TO CAHUITA-SIXAOLA

HOTEL KEKOLDI

PARQUE ZOOLOGICO SIMON BOLIVAR

NATIONAL PARKS INFORMATION OFFICE

D'RAYA VIDA VILLA

CALLE 8
CALLE 6
CALLE 4
CALLE 2

AV. 13

CALLE 1
CALLE 3
AV. 11
CALLE 5
CALLE 7
CALLE 9
CALLE 11
CALLE 13
CALLE 15

AV. 9

AV. 7

HOSPITAL CALDERON GUARDIA

AV. 5

CALLE 17

PARQUE ESPAÑA

POST OFFICE
AV. 3

PARQUE MORAZAN

NATIONAL RAILROAD MUSEUM/ ATLANTIC RAILWAY STATION

MERCADO CENTRAL
AV. 1

PARQUE NACIONAL

BUS TO PUERTO LIMON

AV. CENTRAL

PLAZA DE LA CULTURA

BELLA VISTA

CALLE 19

PARQUE CENTRAL
AV. 2

PLAZA DE LA DEMOCRACIA

NATIONAL MUSEUM

METROPOLITAN CATHEDRAL AND ARCHBISHOP'S PALACE

AV. 4

APARTOTEL SAN JOSE

TO LOS YOSES AND CARTAGO

AV. 6

AV. 8

POLICE HEADQUARTERS

IMMIGRATION

PENSION CENTRO CONTINENTAL

SEE "DOWNTOWN SAN JOSE" MAP

SUPREME COURT AND CRIMINOLOGY MUSEUM

TO

AV. 10

HOTEL MANSION BLANCO

CALLE 15
CALLE 17

NATIONAL PARKS HEADQUARTERS

BUS TO SAN IGNACIO DE ACOSTA

HOTEL LA GEMA

AV. 12

BUS TO GOLFITO

CLINICA BIBLICA

AV. 14

CALLE 8
CALLE 6
CALLE 4
CALLE 2
CALLE CENTRAL
CALLE 1
CALLE 3
CALLE 5
CALLE 7
CALLE 9
CALLE 11
CALLE 13

AV. 16

CALLE 21

BUS TO SANTA MARIA DE DOTA

BUS TO CARTAGO
AV. 18

PACIFIC RAILWAY STATION

AV. 20

MINISTRY OF PUBLIC WORKS

PLAZA GONZALEZ VIQUEZ

© MOON PUBLICATIONS, INC.

p.m.; admission $5; tel. 223-0528 or 233-4233, ext. 282.)

National Arts and Cultural Center (CENAC)

Only two blocks from the National Library, on the east side of Parque España is the erstwhile Liquor Factory (Fábrica Nacional de Licores), now housing a permanent collection of national art, ceramics, and architecture in the ultramodern Museum of Contemporary Art and Design. The name is a little misleading as exhibits extend all the way back to pre-Columbian days. Note the old sun clock and exemplary decorative stonework on the west side. The building dates to 1887 and though drained of alcohol, relics of the distilling days linger. The museum spans art from throughout Latin America, much of it very forceful. The National Dance Company, National Theater Company, Cultura Hispanica, Casa de la Cultura Iberoamericana, and the Colegio de Costa Rica are all housed here, too, in a complex comprising two theaters, three art galleries, a library, and live cultural activities. (Hours: Tuesday 1-5 p.m., Wednesday 10 a.m.-5 p.m., Thursday 10 a.m.-9 p.m., Fri.-Sun. 10 a.m.-5 p.m. Guided tours are given at 12:30 p.m. on Wednesday and 6 p.m. on Thursday; tel. 255-2468.)

Costa Rican Science and Cultural Center

The prominent building atop the slope on the northwest side of San José, at the end of Calle 4 and Avenida 9, looks like an old penitentiary, and indeed that's what it was from 1910-79. Today the former prison houses The Castle, Children's Museum, Historical Penitentiary Museum, and a library and auditorium. The **Children's Museum** lets children touch and experience exhibits dedicated to teaching them about the Universe, Space Technology, Earth, Ecosystems, Living Animals, Human Beings, Communications, Radio and TV, Printing, and Costa Rica: The Land and the People. (Hours: Wed.-Fri. 10 a.m.-noon and 2-5 p.m.; weekends 10 a.m.-1 p.m. and 2-5 p.m.; tel. 223-7003).

La Salle Museum of Natural Sciences

If you don't plan on exploring Costa Rica's national parks, the Museo de Ciencias Naturales offers a second-best look at the bounty of the Central American tropics. Reputed to be among the most comprehensive collections in the world, the museum houses more than 22,500 exhibits (mostly stuffed animals and mounted insects) covering zoology, paleontology, archaeology, and entomology. Some of the stuffed beasts have been ravaged by time and are a bit motheaten; other displays simulating natural environments are so comical one wonders whether the taxidermist was drunk. A coterie of caimans and crocodiles that live on a small island in the *museo* patio are the only animals moving. Better yet is to forgo this experience in favor of the Butterfly Farm (in la Guácima), Spirogyra, or

Museo Nacional, San José

Wings for Education (in Santo Domingo de Heredia).

The museum is administered by the Ministry of Agriculture and is in the old Colegio La Salle on the southwest corner of Sabana Metropolitan Park. Walk, take a taxi ($2), or the Sabana-Estadio bus, which departs from the Catedral Metropolitana on Avenida 2; ask the driver to drop you at Colegio La Salle. (Hours: Mon.-Fri. 7 a.m.-3 p.m.; Saturday 7.30 a.m.-noon; admission 30 cents; tel. 232-1306.) If it looks closed, simply ring the buzzer and hope that the curator appears to open the door and switch on the lights.

Criminology Museum
Reflecting a national concern with public awareness and responsibility, the ostensible rationale of the Museo Criminologico is to prevent crime through education. This the museum attempts to achieve by featuring pictures and displays of Costa Rica's more famous crimes, along with weapons involved in the diabolical deeds, a jar containing an embalmed severed hand, and an illegally aborted fetus. The stuff that good nightmares are made of. The museum is in the Judicial Police headquarters in the Supreme Court Building at Calle 17/19 and Avenida 6. (Hours: Monday, Wednesday, and Friday 1 p.m.-5 p.m.; tel. 223-0666, ext. 2378.)

Postal, Telegraphic, and Philatelic Museum
On the second floor of the main post office in downtown San José, the Museo Postal, Telegráfico y Filatélico (Calle 2, Avenidas 1/3) features postage stamps and philatelic history displays. (Hours: Mon.-Fri. 8 a.m.-4 p.m.; admission free; tel. 223-9766, ext. 269.)

National Printing Office Museum
A motley yet interesting collection of printing presses, typesetting machines, typefaces, and other print-related objects represents the history of printing in Costa Rica during the last 150 years. Founded in 1985, the museum is in the La Uruca district, just behind the Capris S.A. Corporation Complex. Tours are guided. (Hours: Tues.-Fri. 8 a.m.-3 p.m.; admission is free.)

Entomology Museum
There's no explaining why this museum is housed in the basement of the School of Music (Facultad de Artes Musicales) of the University of Costa Rica in San Pedro. (You can take a bus from the National Theater on Avenida 2 and Calle 5 to the church in San Pedro, from where the faculty and museum are signposted; a taxi from downtown San José will cost approximately $2.) The Museo de Entomología features an immense variety of Costa Rican and Central American insects, including a spectacular display of butterflies. Knowledgeable guides are available, but call ahead to check availability and opening times, which reputedly vary. Don't be discouraged if the door is locked. Ring the bell for admission. (Hours: Mon.-Fri. 1-5 p.m.; admission is free; tel. 225-5555, ext. 318.)

National Railroad Museum
The ornate, pagodalike Atlantic Railway Station, built in front of Parque Nacional (Avenida 3, Calle 21) in 1907, is now a museum tracing the history of railroads in Costa Rica. It displays a small collection of memorabilia plus old photographs and even vintage rolling stock and an old steam locomotive, *Locomotora 59* (or *Locomotora Negra*), imported from Philadelphia in 1939 for the Northern Railway Company. One room traces the history of railway development. Note the beautiful if aged tile floor and ornately carved ceiling. The museum seems to keep irregular hours (perhaps because it is severely underfunded), but is officially open Mon.-Fri. 9 a.m.-4 p.m. Entrance: 60 cents.

ART GALLERIES

National Gallery of Contemporary Art
Costa Rica has a thriving community of artists, some producing stunning work. The Galería Nacional de Arte Contemporaneo shows revolving displays by leading contemporary Costa Rican artists. It's in the basement on the east side of the National Library at Avenida 3, Calle 15. (Hours: Mon.-Sat. 10 a.m.-1 p.m. and 1:45-5 p.m.; admission is free; tel. 233-4919.)

Costa Rican Art Museum
Founded in 1977, the museum houses a permanent collection of some of the most important works in the history of the fine arts in Costa Rica. Besides a diverse, robust, and outstanding permanent collection of woodcuts, wooden

DOWNTOWN SAN JOSÉ

CALLE 10
CALLE 8
CALLE 6
CALLE 4
CALLE 2
CALLE CENTRAL
CALLE 1

AV. 9

JOSEPHINE'S

BUS TO HEREDIA

GARDEN COURT HOTEL

HOTEL MARLYN

HOTEL AMERICA

AV. 7

AV. 5

PENSION OTOYA

LACSA AIRLINES

HOTEL COMPOSTELA

HOTEL CENTRAL

HOTEL CAPITAL

MERCADO BORBON

AV. 3

HOTEL BIENVENIDO

POST OFFICE

BANCO NACIONAL

AV. 1

MERCADO CENTRAL

BANCO CENTRAL

AV. CENTRAL

HOTEL LA GRAN VIA

HOTEL DIPLOMAT

HOTEL GRAN HOTEL CENTROAMERICANO

BANCO DE COSTA RICA

MELICO SALAZAR THEATER

GRAN HOTEL

BUS STOP TO HEREDIA (MINIBUS)

NUEVO HOTEL TALAMANCA

AV. 2

LA MERCED CHURCH

HOTEL DORAL

AV. 4

PARQUE CENTRAL

BUS TO IRAZU

METROPOLITAN CATHEDRAL AND ARCHBISHOP'S PALACE

0   25 km

AV. 6

HOTEL FORTUNA

HOTEL PRINCIPE

HOTEL BOSTON

AV. 8

RITZ

CALLE 6
CALLE 4
CALLE 2
CALLE CENTRAL
CALLE 1
CALLE 3

CALLE 10
CALLE 8

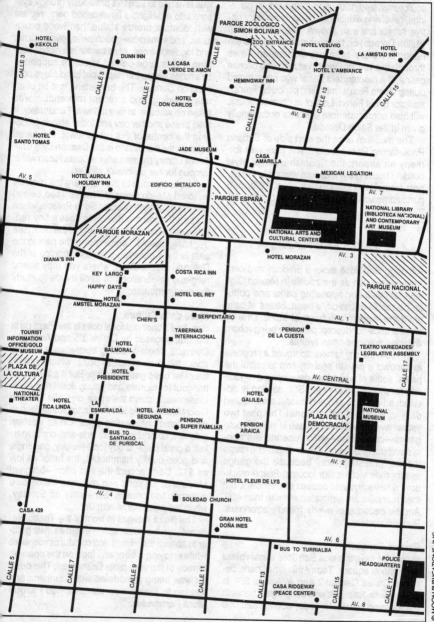

HOTEL KEKOLDI

DUNN INN

LA CASA VERDE DE AMON

PARQUE ZOOLOGICO SIMON BOLIVAR

ZOO ENTRANCE

HOTEL VESUVIO

HOTEL LA AMISTAD INN

HEMINGWAY INN

HOTEL L'AMBIANCE

HOTEL DON CARLOS

AV. 9

HOTEL SANTO TOMAS

JADE MUSEUM

CASA AMARILLA

MEXICAN LEGATION

HOTEL AUROLA HOLIDAY INN

AV. 5

EDIFICIO METALICO

PARQUE ESPAÑA

AV. 7

NATIONAL LIBRARY (BIBLIOTECA NACIONAL) AND CONTEMPORARY ART MUSEUM

PARQUE MORAZAN

NATIONAL ARTS AND CULTURAL CENTER

HOTEL MORAZAN

AV. 3

DIANA'S INN

KEY LARGO

HAPPY DAYS

HOTEL AMSTEL MORAZAN

COSTA RICA INN

HOTEL DEL REY

PARQUE NACIONAL

CHERI'S

SERPENTARIO

AV. 1

TABERNAS INTERNACIONAL

PENSION DE LA CUESTA

TOURIST INFORMATION OFFICE/GOLD MUSEUM

HOTEL BALMORAL

TEATRO VARIEDADES/ LEGISLATIVE ASSEMBLY

PLAZA DE LA CULTURA

HOTEL PRESIDENTE

AV. CENTRAL

NATIONAL THEATER

HOTEL TICA LINDA

LA ESMERALDA

HOTEL AVENIDA SEGUNDA

HOTEL GALILEA

PLAZA DE LA DEMOCRACIA

NATIONAL MUSEUM

BUS TO SANTIAGO DE PURISCAL

PENSION SUPER FAMILIAR

PENSION ARAICA

AV. 2

HOTEL FLEUR DE LYS

CASA 429

AV. 4

SOLEDAD CHURCH

GRAN HOTEL DOÑA INES

AV. 6

BUS TO TURRIALBA

CASA RIDGEWAY (PEACE CENTER)

POLICE HEADQUARTERS

AV. 8

CALLE 3

CALLE 5

CALLE 7

CALLE 9

CALLE 11

CALLE 13

CALLE 15

CALLE 17

CALLE 5

CALLE 7

CALLE 9

CALLE 11

CALLE 13

CALLE 15

CALLE 17

© MOON PUBLICATIONS, INC.

sculptures, and 19th- and 20th-century paintings, revolving exhibitions of contemporary native artists are also shown. The Golden Hall (Salón Dorado) on the second floor depicts the nation's history from pre-Columbian times through the 1940s. Done in stucco and bronze patina, the resplendent mural was constructed during Costa Rica's "muralist" period by French sculptor Louis Feron. Lovers of chamber music will also appreciate free concerts occasionally given in the Salón Dorado.

The museum is on the east side of Sabana Park, facing Paseo Colón. The park was formerly an airport; the Spanish-colonial style building housing the museum was once the airport terminal! (Hours: Tues.-Sun. 10 a.m.-5 p.m.; admission is 50 cents, free on Sunday; tel. 222-7155.)

PARKS AND PLAZAS

Although San José lacks a predominant central square such as the zócalo in Mexico City, several small and appealing parks and popular plazas lie at the city's heart, oases of calm amid the incessant hubbub of traffic. One by one the once-nondescript parks are being reborn with new spic-and-span liveries.

In 1994, the city fathers approved a proposal to contract a private security firm to patrol the parks, some of which had developed a reputation for muggings at night. Still, caution is advised: an average of five criminals are arrested daily in Parque Central alone! The past two years have brought an increase in violent youth gangs—chapulines—which operate like Fagin's urchins in Dickens' Oliver Twist. The name means "grasshoppers," because the gangs swarm their victims like locusts. Police crackdowns have arrested dozens of offenders, but their numbers are estimated at more than 400. And be cautious of overly friendly strangers. Remain alert!

Parque Central

In colonial days this was San José's main plaza and market square. Today this small park, between Calles Central/2 and Avenidas 2/4, is popular with Josefinos who congregate beneath the looming palms. In 1993, about $325,000 was lavished to turn this previously grungy eyesore into a delightful landscaped gem, replete with fountain, bronze statue, hardwood sculptures, and venerable guachipelín, guanacaste, and higueron trees. At its center is a raised platform with a large domed structure supported by arches where the municipal band plays concerts on Sunday. The bandstand is a bit of an ugly duckling, and a recent referendum was taken on whether to tear it down. Fortunately, it lived to see another day and today stands proudly in the center of this urban jewel. Hunkered beneath the bandstand is the Carmen Lyra Children's Library (named after a Costa Rican writer famous for her children's stories).

Across the road to the north are the recently restored Melico Salazar Theater (see below) and the garish yet popular Soda Palace, which is open 24 hours a day. San José's tiny redlight district lies just to the south of the park (see "Nightlife," below). Looming over the park to the east is the Corinthian-columned portico of the Catedral Metropolitan, where you may attend religious celebrations or stroll inside to study the ornamentation.

Plaza de la Cultura

San José's unofficial focal point is the Plaza de la Cultura, encased by Calles 3/5 and Avenidas Central/2. There's nothing aesthetically exciting about this drab concrete plaza, which gathers litter like bees gather pollen. But it's a popular hangout for tourists and young Josefinos alike. Underneath, down the steps on Calle 5, is the Gold Museum and ICT (Instituto Costarricense de Turismo) information office. On its western side is a colorful open-air arts-and-crafts market: a great place to buy local jewelry, paintings, and good-quality hammocks, the latter as low as $12. Don't accept the first price—bargain! Musicians, jugglers, and marimba bands also entertain the crowds, especially on Sunday, when the plaza hums with life.

The plaza extends in front of the Teatro Nacional—on the south side—where tourists gather to absorb the vibrant and colorful atmosphere while enjoying a beer and food on the open-air terrace of the venerable Gran Hotel. This quarter was being remodeled with fountains and seating to form a new plaza named **Parque Mora Fernandez.**

Parque Morazán

This pretty, petite park lies directly south of the ultramodern Aurola Holiday Inn (Calle 5, Avenida 5). The park's four quadrants—beautifully relandscaped in 1992—surround the domed Temple of Music, which was supposedly inspired by Le Trianon in Paris. A small Japanese garden lies in the northeast quadrant, which also contains a children's playground. The infamous Key Largo night spot sits on the southeastern corner. On the northeast side of the park is the ochre-colored Edificio Metálico (see below).

Parque España

The diminutive Spanish Park, due east of Parque Morazán, is a beautiful and pleasant place to rest your feet after visiting the Jade Museum, in the INS (Instituto Nacional de Seguros) Building on the north side of the park. The park was recently renovated. Its tall and densely packed trees have been adopted by birds, and their chorus is particularly pleasing just before sunrise and sunset. Note the quaint colonial-style tiled "pavilion" on the northeast corner, donated, in 1947, by the National Liquor Factory. A colorful outdoor art market is held here on Sunday. On the north side of the park you will see an old, ornately stuccoed, ochre-colored colonial building, **Casa Amarilla,** which once housed the Court of Justice and today is the Chancellery, or State Department.

Parque Nacional

The largest and most peaceful of the city's central parks graces a gentle hill that rises to the south of the National Library, between Calles 15/19 and Avenidas 1/3. At the park's center, under towering, shady trees, is the massive National Monument, one of several statues commemorating the War of 1856. The statue depicts the spirits of the Central American nations defeating the American adventurer William Walker. Like several other San José edifices, the monument originated in France: it was made in the Rodin studios. On Parque Nacional's southwestern corner is a statue of Juan Santamaría, the national hero.

Plaza de la Democracia

Immediately southwest of the Legislative Assembly you come upon the thoroughly unin-spiring Plaza de la Democracia, stairstepping to the south of Bellavista Fortress. It was built in 1989, reportedly to receive visiting presidents attending the Hemispheric Summit. Dominating the dreary plaza is the crenellated historic Bellavista fortress, which today houses the Museo Nacional. The main entrance is on the east side of the fortress. However, you may also enter by ascending the steps on the west from the plaza, where you'll find a concrete monument (with bronze statue and waterfall) to Don Pepe Figueres, completed in 1994. Note the etchings of some of the former president's favorite sayings. To the south are the buildings of the "Judicial Circuit," including the Supreme Court and Immigration buildings. You'll find an artisans' market one block west and one block south, on the east side of Soledad Church, and stalls, too, at the base of the plaza.

Parque Sabana

The only park of any real scale in San José, this favorite weekend getaway for Josefinos used to be the national airport (the old terminal now houses the Costa Rican Art Museum). Today, it's a focus for sports and recreation and one of the few places within San José where you may jog without being hassled by traffic. Sabana Park contains both the Estadio Nacional (on the northwest corner) and the National Gymnasium (southeast corner), which features an Olympic-size swimming pool. There are also basketball, tennis, and volleyball courts,

---

SCENIC DRIVES FROM SAN JOSÉ

San José—Santa Ana—Ciudad Colón—Tabarcia—San Ignacio de Acosta—Aserrí—San José. Lightweight 4WD recommended, though not essential. Powerful mountain vistas. Time your journey to arrive in San Ignacio at sunset. Four hours.

San José—Aserrí—Tabarcia—San Pablo de León Cortez—San Marcos—Santa María—Cartago—San José. Beautiful mountain scenery on a little-touristed route. Lightweight 4WD recommended, though not essential. Six hours.

a baseball diamond and a soccer field, and tree-lined paths for jogging and walking. Even fishing folks are catered to. A small lake on the south side is stocked with fish, and fishing is permitted. And a small hill has been piled up from Sabana ("Flatlands") for kite flyers. The park entrance is at the end of Paseo Colón. The Sabana-Cementerio bus, which leaves from Calle 7 and Avenida Central, will take you there. Otherwise, it's a pleasing, brisk, 30-minute walk.

Parque Braulio Carrillo

Most Josefinos call this small park (not to be confused with Braulio Carrillo National Park) on Avenida 2 and Calle 14 La Merced Park, because it faces La Merced church. A new, improved park emerged in 1993 after a yearlong facelift. Among the new features unveiled were a gothic-arch-shaped fountain to match the arched windows of La Merced church and a monument honoring the astronomer Copernicus.

Parque del Este

On the outskirts of the city, in the hills three km east of San Pedro, this rural retreat provides a close-at-hand escape from the city. Trails lead through landscaped grounds to a panoply of facilities: children's playhouses, basketball courts, volleyball nets, two pools, and clearings with barbecue pits and benches. Trails lead uphill into wild woodlands, where you may settle beneath tall pines and listen to the needles and branches sighing in the wind. Josefinos flock at weekends. You reach it via the suburb of Sabanilla (turn north—left—at the large roundabout in San Pedro, then right at the road immediately before Friday's restaurant. Beyond Sabanilla the road ends; turn left and head uphill to the park). Open 8 a.m.-4 p.m. daily except Monday. Entrance: 60 cents.

OTHER ATTRACTIONS

Edificio Metálico

One of San José's more intriguing edifices, this ochre-colored prefabricated building is made entirely of metal. Designed by the French architect Victor Baltard (some attribute it to Charles Thirio), who also designed Les Halles in Paris, the structure was shipped piece by piece from Belgium in 1892 and welded together in situ. The facade is dressed with a bust of Minerva, the "goddess of wisdom." The building, on the northwest corner of Parque España between Avenidas 5 and 7, is now a school.

Legislative Assembly/Blue Castle

The pretty white Moorish structure on Calle 15, opposite the National Museum, was originally the Presidential Palace, built in 1912 by presidential candidate Maximo Fernández in anticipation of victory in the 1914 elections. He lost. Nonetheless, he lent his home—known as the Blue Castle (Castillo Azul—to President-elect Alfredo González Flores as his official residence. The Tinoco brothers (Federico and Joaquín) ousted Flores in a coup in 1917 and took possession of the home. Eventually it was returned to Fernández, who sold it to the U.S. State Department as the site of the U.S. Diplomatic Mission. It was a private residence between 1954-89, when the Costa Rican government bought it. Today it houses the National Legislative Assembly and features a tiny library and history exhibit open to the public via a side door.

General Cemetery

When you've seen everything else, and before heading out of town, check out the final resting place of Josefinos, with its many pleasing mausoleums of Italian design. The cemetery, on the south side of Avenida 10 between Calles 20 and 36, is particularly worth seeing 1 and 2 November, when vast numbers of people go to leave flowers at the tombs of their relatives.

Mercado Central

San José's most colorful and authentically Central American offering is the Central Market, at Calle 6 and Avenida 1. While it lacks the native quality of, say, Guatemalan markets, it's heady on atmosphere nonetheless. Everything but the kitchen sink seems on offer: baskets, flowers, hammocks, spices, meats, vegetables, souvenirs. There are fish booths selling octopus, dorado, and shrimp; butchers' booths with oxtails and pigs' heads on display; flower stalls, saddle shops, and booths selling medicinal herbs guaranteed to cure everything from sterility to common colds. Outside, street hawkers call out their wares sold from brightly colored barrows. The

market is a good place to order *olla de carne,* a steaming beef-and-vegetable stew, at a bustling *soda.* Pickpockets thrive in crowded places. Watch your valuables!

Catedral Metropolitan

Dominating the east side of Parque Central is the city's main cathedral: whitewashed, with a blue domed roof more reminiscent of a Greek Orthodox church than a Catholic cathedral. The original cathedral was toppled by an earthquake in 1821; the current edifice dates from 1871. In and out it's a statement in modesty. The interior is relatively unremarkable, bar its lofty barrel-arched ceiling, and there is little of the ostentatious baroque influence found in cathedrals elsewhere on the continent. Tucked neatly in its shadow to the south is the marvelously mellowed Archbishop's Palace dating from the 18th century.

Teatro Nacional (National Theater)

Truly a national treasure and unquestionably the nation's most impressive architectural showpiece, the National Theater (on the south side of Plaza de la Cultura, on Avenida 2 between Calles 3 and 5) is a study in harmony and regal splendor, a testimony to the Costa Ricans' high degree of culture, and justifiably a great source of national pride. Costa Rica's Central American brethren jokingly remark that "Ticos do not make revolutions for fear of breaking the panes on the National Theater."

The theater was conceived in 1890 when a European opera company featuring the prima donna Adelina Patti toured Central America but was unable to perform in Costa Rica because there was no suitable theater. Jilted, the ruling *cafelateros* (coffee barons) voted a tax on coffee exports to fund construction of a theater, and craftsmen from all over Europe were imported. Built under the direction of presidents Dr. José Rodríguez and his son-in-law and successor Rafael Iglesia, it was inaugurated on 19 October 1897 to a performance of *Faust* by the Paris Opera and its great Ballet Corps.

Outside, the classical Renaissance facade is topped by statues symbolizing Dance, Music, and Fame. Inside, the foyer, done in pink marble, rivals the best of ancient Pompeii, with allegorical figures of Comedy and Tragedy, stunning

JEAN MERCIER

the Teatro Nacional

murals depicting themes in Costa Rican life and commerce (if the giant mural showing coffee harvesting looks familiar, it's probably because you've seen it on the old five-*colón* note), and triptych ceiling supported by six-meter-tall marble columns topped with bronze capitals.

Art and good taste are lavishly displayed on the marble staircase, with its gold-laminated ornaments sparkling beneath bronze chandeliers. A grandiose rotunda—painted in Milan in 1897 by Arturo Fontana—highlights the three-story auditorium, designed in a perfect horseshoe and seating 1,040 in divine splendor. The ceiling fresco depicts naked celestial deities surrounding a giant crystal chandelier.

The theater is an art gallery unto itself. Magnificent frescoes abound. Much of the mahogany furniture is gold-leafed, and the floor is fashioned in local hardwoods. Uniquely, the auditorium floor was designed to be raised to stage level by a manual winch so that the theater could be used as a ballroom. Downstairs, to the left of

the entrance foyer, is a coffee shop no less resplendently gilded than the theater itself. The delightfully peaceful cafe serves, too, as an art gallery for modern works. This is *the* place to linger over coffee and wonderful desserts.

A visit to a performance is an absolute must on any visit to Costa Rica. The theater was fully reopened in early 1995 after a four-year restoration to repair severe damage sustained in the April 1991 earthquake. You can buy tickets for performances at a ticket booth next to the entrance (expect to pay $3-15). Be sure to dress for the part: Josefinos treat a night at the National Theater as a distinguished social occasion.

Admission: $1. Guided tours are offered.

Pueblo Antiguo

This 12-acre Disney-style attraction, in La Uruca, one km east of Hospital México on the western outskirts of San José, opened in December 1994 and is the Williamsburg of Costa Rica. The theme park recreates the locales and dramatizes the events of Costa Rican history. Buildings in traditional architectural style include a replica of the National Liquor Factory, Congressional Building, church, market, fire station, and the Costa Rican Bank. The place comes alive with oxcarts, horsedrawn carriages, live music, folkloric dances, and actors dramatizing the past. The park has three sections: the capital city, coast (including a replica of the Tortuguero Canals), country (with original adobe structures moved to the site, including a sugar mill, coffee mill, and milking barn). The venture is operated by the Association for the National Children's Hospital and profits fund improvements to the hospital. You can visit craft shops and a restaurant that serves typical Costa Rican cuisine. Entrance: $10, or $20 including historic show (Apdo. 730, San José 1150, tel. 296-2212, fax 231-6529).

Serpentario

If you don't intend to venture into the wilds, this is the place to get a close-up look at some of Costa Rica's most colorful reptiles. The small but interesting collection is quite impressive, despite its peculiar location above the El Gran Chaparral restaurant on the second floor of the Radamida building (Calles 9/11 and Avenida 1). The displays include poison-arrow frogs,

iguanas, and Costa Rica's most feared poisonous species safely on view behind glass cages. After seeing the nasty forearm-thick fer-de-lance, you'll probably not want to venture into the jungle! Signs are offered in English for some exhibits, others only in Spanish. (Hours: Mon.-Sat. 9 a.m.-6 p.m.; admission $1.20; tel. 255-4210.)

Simón Bolívar Zoo

What a pity a country renowned for conscientiousness regarding its natural heritage should have been shamed for so long by what was until recently an appalling zoo. The zoo's all-too-obvious problems reflect a severe shortage of funds that has resulted in understaffing and an inability to provide the animals with adequate nutrition and veterinary care. Now the good news . . .

A $3 million fund-raising and five-stage reconstruction project began in mid-1992, aided by private donations from individuals and major corporations led by McDonald's. A **Friends of the Zoo** and **Adopt an Animal** program (FUNDAZOO, Apdo. 11594, San José 1000, tel. 223-1790, fax 223-1817) were initiated in 1993 sponsored by *Costa Rica Today* with the aim of collecting money to improve conditions. The zoo (founded in 1916 and retaining many of its original, inadequate cages and facilities) is becoming more of an educational experience, too. A Nature Center, for example, opened in 1994, containing a video room, library, and work area for schoolchildren. The amphibians and reptiles recently received a new home—the Joyeros del Bosque Húmedos—designed by the Baltimore Aquarium. The alligators and tapir will receive a new lagoon, and other beasts will get their own new enclosures. The non-native species were scheduled to move to Zoo Ave, near Garita (see "West from Alajuela," in the Central Highlands chapter), by 1997. The current zoo is gradually being turned into a national exhibition and visitor center with re-creations of Costa Rica's various ecosystems.

The relatively small number of Costa Rican species on display includes spider and capuchin monkeys, most of the indigenous cats, plus a small variety of birds, including toucans and tame macaws. The zoo's finest exhibits, surprisingly, are a male lion and a handsome Bengal tiger. Sadly, they and the other cats are

housed in depressingly austere and small metal cages. Two times I visited the 14-acre zoo, the cages were foul with urine. The lion had to be re-housed after he had learned to piss on people passing his cage. Who can blame him! Maybe they'll have more pleasing new homes by the time you visit.

The zoo has a small *soda*. The national parks system information office is also located inside the zoo, at the rear. A small selection of books and pamphlets (mostly in Spanish) is for sale here, and there is a moderately sized reference library.

The zoo's entrance is hidden away at Calle 7 and Avenida 11 (turn right at Avenida 11 and follow the curving road for 100 meters). Avoid the zoo on weekends if possible, when the locals flock in droves. (Hours: Tues.-Fri. 8 a.m.-4 p.m., weekends and holidays 9 a.m.-5 p.m.; admission is $1.)

Spirogyra Butterfly Garden

Butterfly lovers no longer have to venture beyond San José to see butterflies in their natural setting. Opened in 1992, this small butterfly garden and farm is 100 meters east and 150 meters south of the El Pueblo shopping center (it's signed from El Pueblo). Bilingual tours are offered every half-hour by biologist Javier Baltodano, or you can opt for a 30-minute self-guided tour. More than 30 species flutter about in the 350-square-meter garden, which is sheltered by a net. In the center is a small waterfall surrounded by orchids, heliconias, and trees. A separate section houses cages where eggs and caterpillars develop, protected from nature's predators. The small natural forest is being protected as a private botanical garden. A restaurant is planned. (Hours: Wed.-Mon. 8 a.m.-4 p.m.; admission $4; tel. 222-2937, fax 296-3964.) Another gem on the theme of lepidoptera is Wings For Education, in Santo Domingo de Heredia, only four km away (see "Heredia and Vicinity" in Central Highlands chapter).

Teatro Melico Salazar

Dating to the 1920s, this unprepossessing theater opposite Parque Central on Avenida 2 has a quaint appeal. It's no contender to La Scala, but its fluted Corinthian columns, high balconies, and gilding provide a study in understated period detail. Symphony season normally runs April through October, but after the April 1991 earthquake, which forced the closure of the Teatro Nacional, the Teatro Melico Salazar for a few years did double-duty year-round with plays, dances, and classical concerts.

University of Costa Rica

The university campus, in the suburb of San Pedro, is a fine place to get a take on Costa Rica's youthful bohemianism. U.C. Berkeley it's not, but the plentiful *sodas* and bars and bookstores nearby hint at Berkeley's famed Telegraph Avenue. Concerts, exhibitions, etc. are given at the gallery of the Facultad de Bellas Artes (College of Fine Arts). The last week of March, during **Semana Universitaria,** students shirk studies for a rambunctious fiesta.

The reverse of the five colones note shows the mural on the Teatro Nacional's foyer ceiling.

ACCOMMODATIONS

San José's hotels are not, overall, the bargains one usually associates with other Central and South American destinations. But what changes are happening! The once motley and dowdy hotels of a few years ago have been upstaged by a blossoming of deluxe, boutique, and bed-and-breakfast hotels. And skyrocketing demand for hotel rooms in recent years has fostered the arrival of large name-brand hotels. Budget hotels, however, are for the most part still uninspired, though a few gems shine. In San José, steeper prices don't always equal better quality, especially among hotels in the so-called upscale and moderate price brackets. My recommendation is to opt for one of the small and atmospheric boutique hotels, which offer superb value for the money and for which you'd be wise to make advance reservations.

San José is a noisy city; it is wise to ask for a room away from the street. Also consider staying outside San José, where you'll find dozens of superb options close enough for forays into the capital and further afield (see "Escazú and Vicinity" and "Heredia and Vicinity" in the Central Highlands chapter; also see "Arrival" under "Transportation," this chapter, for airport hotels).

Christmas and Easter are particularly busy periods. If you'll be in San José during these times, plan on making reservations several months in advance. Reservations are also strongly advised for dry-season months (Dec.-April). Don't rely on mail to make reservations; it could take several months to confirm. Instead, call direct, send a fax, or have your travel agent make reservations for you. It may be necessary to send a deposit, without which your space may be released to someone else. Check on this when you make your reservation.

The ICT (Instituto Costarricense de Turismo) office beneath the Plaza de la Cultura provides a computer printout listing recommended hotels (tel. 222-1090). If you arrive without reservations, the ICT office can help. The Costa Rican Hotels Association issues an annual *Costa Rican Hotel Guide,* available from the ICT. Your local travel agent may have a copy. If seeking something exclusive and quiet, check the classified ads in the back of the *Tico Times* or *Costa Rica Today* for private houses and rooms.

Most hotels supply towels and soap, but unless you're staying in the deluxe hotels, you'll need to bring your own shampoos and conditioners. Bringing a sink plug is also a good idea if you plan on using budget accommodations.

If you anticipate carousing until midnight or later, make sure in advance that the hotel provides late access. Many of the better hotels discourage unregistered guests. Gay and lesbian hotels are listed separately in "Notes for Gays and Lesbians" under "Special Notes" in the On the Road chapter.

Hotels are arranged below by price category: **Budget** $10 or less; **Inexpensive** $10-25; **Moderate** $25-50; **Upscale** $50-80; **Deluxe** $80+. Prices were as accurate as possible at time of writing. Please bear in mind that prices may have increased by the time you read this book. A 14.3% tax is added to all hotel bills. Some hotels charge extra (as much as six percent) for paying by credit card. Check!

BUDGET

San José has a heavy sprinkling of budget hotels offering clean rooms in areas that are quite safe, many on the fringe of downtown. A number of super-cheap hotels can also be found in the less savory area near the Coca-Cola bus station (Calle 16, Avenidas 1/3). Caution is needed here at night. The bevy of cheap hotels between Calles 6/10 and Avenidas 3/5 is surrounded by drunks and dozens of bars with cheap hookers for the desperate, desperately poor, or too drunk to care. Many of the hotels themselves are little more than brothels. Away from this area, for a few dollars extra you can have greater peace of mind.

Don't take cleanliness and comfort for granted. Compare! Since walls in budget hotels are often merely wooden partitions, noise can be a major problem, especially in those budget hotels

that also rent by the hour to prostitutes and have more comings and goings.

Reservations are accepted with a prearranged arrival time (no deposit). However, you must arrive on time, or your room may be given away. Hot (more likely, heated) water is never guaranteed. These hotels usually will not change dollars.

There are several super-cheap hotels along Avenida 2, between Calles 7 and 15. **Hotel Tica Linda** (Avenida 2, Calles 5/7, tel. 233-0528 or 255-0425, fax 255-0444) is probably the cheapest place in San José. This basic hostel next to La Esmeralda has shared bedrooms—alas tiny, noisy, and dingy—a small garden and, amazingly, a Jacuzzi. It's popular with the bare-bones crowd. Rates: dorm $3.50, private double $7. The music is free!

On the next block, **Hotel Avenida Segunda** (Avenida 2a, Calles 7/9, tel. 222-0260) has been acclaimed the best budget hotel in San José by one guidebook, despite reportedly doing double-duty as a "love shack." It's almost always full. The 10 rooms are well lit, with shared baths. Those facing the road are noisy. Rates: $5 s, $8 d. Next door is the equally popular **Pensión Super Familiar** (tel. 223-1102 or 257-0486), a favorite of penny-pinchers and Central Americans. The 14 rooms are clean but spartan. Shared bath. Rates: $3-6. On the same block are the **Hotel Lilimani** (tel. 222-0607) and **Pensión Salamanca** (next door to Tropical Tiny's Bar and Restaurant), with tiny rooms with cold showers for $4.

One block east is **Pensión Araica** (Calles 11/13, tel. 222-5233). Rate: $2.50. Between Calles 13 and 15 is the family-operated **Hotel Nicaragua** (tel. 223-0292), with clean and quiet, though somewhat dingy, rooms. Popular with Central American travelers. Cold-water showers. Rates: $3.

Pension Otoya (Calle Central, Avenidas 5/7, tel. 221-3925) comes recommended for its location and as "good value for money." 14 rooms. Clean, large but dingy. TV in lobby. Popular with foreigners. The owner says it's a "family hotel"—no unregistered guests! Rates: $7 s, $12 d, shared bath; $10 s, $14 d, private bath. Also winning laurels is **Pensión Villa Blanca** (Avenida 7, Calles 2/4, tel. 223-9088), with 12 spotless rooms, some with equally clean private bath with cold water. Reportedly, owner Don Sergio turns away "undesirables" but gets rave reviews for being friendly and helpful. Rates: $6.

Hotel Boston (Avenida 8, Calles Central/2, tel. 221-0563). Popular as a gathering spot for budget travelers. Noisy; inside rooms less so. Staff are lauded for helpfulness. Private baths have hot water. Black and white TV. Rates: $10 s, $16 d. **Casa Leo** (Avenida 6 bis, Calles 13/15, tel. 222-9725) has also been recommended as a favorite of the backpacking crowd. The owners are said to be friendly, plus there are hot water and kitchen privileges. Rates: $9 per person, dorm; $11 private room.

Last, but not least of the recommended options, almost hidden behind an iron door at Calle 8, Avenidas Central/1, is **Gran Hotel Imperial** (tel. 222-7899), another favorite of the backpacking crowd. Step down the stairwell and you'll find basic yet clean rooms for $3 a night (its restaurant offers filling meals for a pittance). No room in the inn? Step north a few meters to **Hotel Moderno** (tel. 221-2572), where basic rooms with cold water cost $4 per person.

Others to Consider

Hotel América (Avenida 7, Calles 2/4, tel. 221-4116). Eleven rooms. Clean, good value. Reportedly accepts hourly guests. Rates: $6 s, $8 d.

Hotel Asia (Calle 11, Avenida Central/1, tel. 223-3893). Clean, well lit, communal showers, thin particle-board walls; downstairs is a spawning ground for prostitutes and their johns. One room with private bath. Rates: $6 s, $8 d.

Hotel Astoria (Avenida 7, Calles 7/9, tel. 221-2174, fax 221-8497). Popular, clean and airy, private bathrooms with hot showers, small garden; noisy. Good location in Barrio Amón. Some rooms in the back have communal baths. Rates: from $8 s, shared bath, to $20 d, private bath.

Hotel Aurora (Avenida 4, Calle 8). Good value, hot showers, clean. Rates: from $10 s/d.

Hotel Bienvenido (Calle 10, Avenida 1/3, Apdo. 389, San José 2200, tel. 221-1872 or 233-2161). An erstwhile movie house-turned-hotel with 44 rooms. Clean, pleasant, private bath, hot water; excellent value. On the fringe of the red-light district. Rates: $16 s, $20 d. Advertised rates have often been considerably less.

Hotel Boruca (Calle 14, Avenidas 1/3, tel. 223-0016). Clean, shared bath, restaurant, popular with Peace Corps. Near Coca-Cola bus station; noisy. Rates: $5.

Pensión Centro Continental (Calle Central, Avenidas 8/10, tel. 233-1731). Clean, communal showers, kitchenette. Rates: $8 s, $14 d, $4 additional.

Hotel Compostela (Calle 6, Avenidas 3/5, tel. 221-0694). Family-run. Very quiet. Rooms with shared bath dingy. Doors close at 11 p.m.; no guests. Rates: $6 dorms with shared bath, $12 s/d rooms with private bath.

Hotel Generaleño (Avenida 2, Calles 8/10, tel. 233-7877), has large, dingy, basic rooms (45 in all) with cold showers. Rates: $7.50 s with communal shower, from $11 d with private shower.

Hotel Gran Hotel Centroamericano (Avenida 2, Calles 6/8; Apdo. 3072, San José 1000, tel. 221-3362). Forty-five small, cell-like rooms, telephone, private bath, hot water. TV in lobby. Self-service restaurant, laundry. Noisy, musty. Rates: $15 s, but $4 each extra person.

Hotel Marlyn (Calle 4, Avenidas 7/9, tel. 233-3212). Small, dark, but clean rooms, hot showers. Rates: $6 s with communal bath, $10 with private bath.

Hotel Morazán (Avenida 3, Calles 11/13, tel. 221-9083). Clean, large rooms, spartan. Rates: from $5 s in low season; $8/15 s/d in high season.

Hotel Principe (Avenida 6, Calle Central/2, tel. 222-7983). Thirty-four spacious rooms, private bath, hot water, noisy on street side. Very popular. Rates: $11 s, $16 d.

Hotel Rialto (Calle 2, Avenida 5). Clean. Occasional hot water. Rates $5 shared bath, $7 private.

Hotel Roma (Calle 14, Avenidas Central/1, tel. 223-2179). Clean but barebones. No hot water. Rate: $4.

Hotel San José (Calle 14, Avenida 5). Clean, showers.

Pensión Familiar (Avenida 6, Calles 6/8). Clean, good value.

Pensión Americans (Calle 2, Avenidas Central/2, tel. 221-4171). Large rooms. Dingy. Cold showers. Rates: $7 per person.

Hostels

Headquarters of the Costa Rican Youth Hostel Association is the **Toruma** hostel (RECAJ, Apdo. 1355, San José 1002, tel./fax 224-4085), a beautiful old colonial-style structure sitting above Avenida Central, Calles 29/31, about a half-kilometer east of the National Museum. No age restrictions. Segregated dormitories accommodate 95 beds in eight rooms. Family rooms are available. Advance booking required, weeks ahead in peak season. Laundry and restaurant. It's popular with the backpacking crowd, and a great place to meet other travelers. Hours: 6 a.m.-11 p.m. You can stay out later with a pass. Rates: from $5 per person for members, $12 nonmembers; breakfast included.

Another good bet is the much smaller **Casa Ridgeway** hostel attached to the Friends Peace Center (Calle 15, Avenidas 6/8, tel. 233-6168). Dormitories and private rooms provide clean accommodation in a relaxed and friendly environment. Basic kitchen facilities and communal showers. No alcohol or smoking. And drugs? Are you stoned? Rates: dorm $7 per person; $15 d, private room.

INEXPENSIVE

There's a shortage of inexpensive hotels offering reasonable quality: safety, cleanliness, and hot water. Quality varies remarkably. Many hotels in this bracket are little better than the absolute bottom-price hotels; a few rival those twice the price.

The recently renovated **Hotel Fortuna** (Avenida 6, Calles 2/4, Apdo. 7, San José 1570, tel. 223-5344, fax 223-2743) offers a good bargain, clean and quiet, with 32 large rooms plus a reasonable Chinese restaurant and bar. Rates: $17 s; $21 d.

A better bargain might be the **Ritz** (Calle Central, Avenidas 8/10, Apdo. 6783, San José 1000, tel. 222-4103, fax 222-8849), with 25 rooms with private baths. No TVs or phones. One report says it's run-down; a more recent one says "very clean." There's a large second-floor lounge with a book exchange. Rates from $20 s, $25 d with private bath (less with shared bath).

The **Pensión de la Cuesta** (Avenida 1, Calles 11/13, tel. 255-2896, fax 223-6808) is clean, cozy, charmingly eccentric, and ideal for those who like offbeat hotels. Nicola Bertoldi, the Italian manager, presides over this 1930s house full

of antiques and potted plants. Owned by local artists Dierdre Hyde and Otto Apuy, whose original artworks adorn the walls. There are seven rooms plus a furnished apartment for up to six people. Shared, well-kept baths and self-service laundry. Coupons good for a 20% discount are available at the ICT office beneath the Plaza de la Cultura. Rates: from $20 s, $32 d, including breakfast.

In Barrio Amón is the **Joluva Guesthouse** (tel. 223-7961; in the U.S., tel. 800-296-2418 or 619-298-7965, fax 619-294-24180, on Calle 3 bis, Avenidas 9/11. Rooms have private baths and cable TV, and include continental breakfast.

A reasonable option is the **Hotel Capital** (Calle 4, Avenidas 3/5, Apdo. 6091, San José 1000, tel. 221-8583, fax 221-8497), offering 15 completely remodeled rooms with tiled bathrooms. Eight rooms have king-size beds; some have no windows. No TVs or phones. Antique photographs adorn the walls. Rates: from $20. A nearby alternative is the **Hotel Central** (Avenida 3, Calle 6, tel. 222-3509), with 45 spacious rooms. Rates: from $8 s with shared bath; $17 d with private bath.

Several inexpensive hotels lie near the disreputable Coca-Cola bus terminal. The two best are the **Hotel Cocorí** (Avenida 3, Calle 16, tel. 233-0081) and **Hotel Musoc** (Calle 16, Avenidas 1/3, Apdo. 1049, San José 1000, tel. 222-9437, fax 231-4814 or 239-1657). The former has 26 rooms with private baths and hot water. The recently renovated Musoc has 45 rooms. Rates for both: $11 s, $17 d with communal bath, $13 s, $18 d private bath.

The **Hotel Johnson** (Calle 8, Avenidas Central/2, Apdo. 6638, San José 1000, tel. 223-7633, fax 222-3683) has long been a favorite of budget travelers, Peace Corps volunteers, and Central American businessmen. Rooms—57 in all—are moderately clean, but timeworn and spartan. Restaurant and bar. Rates: $14 s, $17 d.

East of downtown is the **Costa Rica Inn** (Calle 9, Avenidas 1/3, Apdo. 10282, San José 1000, tel. 222-5203, fax 223-8385; in the U.S., tel. 800-637-0899), a favorite of gringos and erstwhile home of ex-president Tinoco (the decor has been described as "like a '50s horror movie—not gothic, just cheesy." The 35 rooms are small and dingy yet clean, comfortable, and

quiet. Each has private bath, hot water, and telephone. Rates: from $25 d. The **Hotel Galilea** (Avenida Central, Calle 13, tel. 233-6925, fax 223-1689), off Plaza de la Democracia, has 23 basic rooms with hot showers. Discounts for students. The Dutch owner speaks English, German, French, Dutch, and Malay! Rates: $18 s, $22 d. Farther east still is the popular **Bella Vista** (Avenida Central, Calles 19/21, tel. 223-0095), described as being as close as you get to a "surfers' hangout" in San José. The 30 carpeted rooms are spic-and-span if stuffy; walls are reportedly thin. Private bathrooms, plus a restaurant. Rates: from $16 s, $24 d.

To the west is the **Hotel Petit** (Paseo Colón and Calle 24, Apdo. 357, San José 1007, tel. 233-0766, fax 233-1938), which, appropriately, has only 11 rooms, all with hot showers and cable TV. Kitchen facilities and laundry service are available. An immensely popular hotel which I find very basic, unappealing, and vastly overpriced. Rates: $24 s/d with shared bath, $28 s, $32 d private bath.

Hidden away across Paseo Colón from Hotel Petit is **Posada Tropical;** not reviewed, but it has been described as sleeping "34 persons in lockable louvered cabinets" for $13 apiece! A better bet is the **Hotel El Crucero** (Calle 4, Avenidas 7/9, tel. 233-3124). It has 12 rooms, with private bath and hot water. Rates: $15 s, $23 d.

The intimate **Hotel Aranjuez** (Apdo. 457, San José 2070, tel. 223-3559, fax 223-3528), at Calle 19, Avenidas 11/13, has been recommended. It has 23 admirably and eclectically decorated rooms with private or shared bath with hot water. It's formed of four contiguous houses, each with its own personality; the original home is in Caribbean style. Relax on wicker and rattan furniture in the inner courtyards or shady patios, enjoying the limes and heliconias adorning the grounds. Rates: from $25 s, $35 d, including breakfast. One block east, in Los Yoses, on Avenida 2 and Calles 19/21, is the English-owned **Hotel Troy** (tel. 222-6756). You can't miss its blue-and-ochre exterior. Inside, there's lots of bamboo and tropical colors in counterpoint to the general gloom. Rates: $15 s/d.

MODERATE

For atmosphere, try the **Hotel Don Carlos** (Calle 9, Avenidas 7/9; Apdo. 1593, San José 1000, tel. 221-6707, fax 255-0828. U.S. mailing address: Dept. 1686, P.O. Box 025216, Miami, FL 33102-5216), founded by pre-Columbian art expert Don Carlos Balser in an aged colonial-style mansion. The hotel is replete with Sarchí oxcarts and archaeological treasures (many of the artifacts in Costa Rica's Jade Museum across the street were originally part of his collection). Magnificent wrought-iron work abounds, there are bronze sculptures on the sun-deck, and one wall is covered with 272 hand-painted tiles showing San José at the turn of the century.

The Boutique Annemarie, which has a splendid collection of artwork and souvenirs, is in the foyer. The hotel has live marimba music three nights a week, plus a small gym and restaurant lit by an atrium skylight. Some of the 15 rooms and suites are long in the tooth, however, with drab decor and furniture. And the noise of buses and trucks negotiating the hill on which the hotel stands is constant. Newer and more appealing rooms at the back, reached by a rambling courtyard, partly escape this intrusion and are more pleasing. Cable TV. Room rates: from $48 s, $58 d, including continental breakfast, English-language newspaper, and welcome cocktail.

The **Hotel Mansion Blanco** (Calle 9, Avenida 10, Apdo. 8-5570, San José 1000, tel./fax 222-0423) is handily located on a busy street corner five blocks from the National Theater. A beautiful hardwood staircase leads to a reception lounge festooned in plants and cascades of curtains. There're a TV and phone in the lounge, none in the rooms. The reception area displays handicraft souvenirs. Delightful touches include walls decorated with oil paintings of Costa Rican scenes. The 11 adequately sized bedrooms are pleasingly decorated in muted pastels. Comfortable beds. Tiny sinks, however, ridiculously inadequate shelf space, and teeny mirrors in the bathrooms. Room 9 is much larger, with two double beds and TV, but the bathroom has the same deficiencies. The highly conscientious staff all speak fluent English. The hotel has its own car park. Rates from $40.

Another intriguing option is **Casa 429** (direct postal address: Calle 5, Avenidas 4/6, tel. 222-1708, fax 233-5785), boasting a perfect location just two blocks from Plaza de la Cultura. Czech-born George Aron, the owner, spent a year and considerable effort to conjure a tiny gem from a dilapidated 1940s-era house. Six pleasingly intimate rooms differ in size but are all of a theme, with ornate white rattan furniture and matching, deep maroon-and-sea-green curtains, lampshades, and cushions on the sofas and chairs. Belgian "Oriental" throw rugs adorn the beautiful colonial-tiled and lacquered hardwood floors. Large ceiling fans keep things pleasingly cool. In the small entrance lounge, tabletops are adorned with beautiful ceramics of grotesque surrealistic fish. And the owner's aesthetic taste is reflected in the handsome original paintings—every one in colors as bright as Matisse's—that adorn the walls. Some rooms have shared baths, albeit spacious and beautifully tiled. The single suite opens onto its own patio—an excellent spot for sunbathing. Another has French doors onto a narrow veranda. Avoid the downstairs room with no outside windows (one reader says it's "damp and smells sour"). The dining area features a deep eight-foot-square, colonial-tiled, floodlit Jacuzzi with a waterfall-fountain and potted plants in abundance, plus a lemon tree. Rooms have VCRs. Drawbacks? Noise from the traffic outside. And George tends to hang out wearing only a towel and his pet snake, which can appear intimidating. Rates: from $50 s/d.

Hotel Vesuvio (Apdo. 477, San José 1000, tel. 221-7586, fax 221-8325) is a newly opened property in Barrio Otoya, immediately east of the zoo on Avenida 11, Calles 13/15. The modern structure hints at Spanish colonial. The 20 rooms have spic-and-span, if soulless, all-pink decor, with remote control TV, safety deposit box, telephone, and private bath. It has an intimate restaurant and a pleasing tiled patio out front for literally watching the world go by. Rates: $40 s, $50 d, $60 t, $75 deluxe.

Nearby is another newly opened property, **Hotel Kekoldi** (Apdo. 12150, San José, tel. 223-3244, fax 257-5476) on Avenida 9 and Calle 3 bis, in Barrio Amón. Wow! The jade-green wooden house was built in 1914 and today, after a thorough restoration, offers 14 large

though simply furnished rooms (each named from the Bribrí Indian language) with king-size beds, polished hardwood floors, and private baths. That, though, tells you nothing of the ambience . . . fantastically decorated from head to toe in a rainbow of tropical Caribbean hues, including *trompe l'oeil* paintings by renowned English artist Helen Eltis. Even the curtains have not been left out. The place reminds me of something you might see in a painting by David Hockney. The dining room abounds in hardwoods. Rates: $29-36 s, $38-47 d, $55-66 t.

The modest **Hotel Amstel Morazán** is an adequate yet very popular downtown option (Calle 7, Avenida 1, Apdo. 4192, San José 1000, tel. 222-4622, fax 233-3329). Its bar/restaurant is a popular lunch spot for the city business crowd. One plus: Breakfasts and lunches are among the best bargains in San José. The 52 rooms have a/c and TV. Rates from $39 s, $46 d.

Another pleasing alternative is the **Garden Court Hotel** (Avenida 7, Calles 6/8, Apdo. 1849, San José 1000, tel. 255-4766, fax 232-3159), with 70 clean and comfortable rooms; TV, a/c, and phones are standard. It has a swimming pool and a self-service restaurant. One major drawback: It's on the edge of a terrible area full of cheap bars-cum-brothels. Rates: $33 s, $45 d, $51 t, including American breakfast.

Alternatively, try the soulless **Hotel Royal Garden** (Calle Central, Avenidas Central/2, Apdo. 3493, San José 1000, tel. 257-0022, fax 257-1517), with dowdy utility furniture. The 54 recently decorated rooms come with a/c and TV. The hotel's saving graces are its convenient location one block from Parque Central and a Chinese restaurant serving dim sum breakfasts. Gamblers may appreciate the 24-hour casino. Rates from $35 s, $40 d.

Also in the center, the **Hotel La Gran Vía** (Avenida Central, Calles 1/3, Apdo. 1433, San José 1000, tel. 222-7737, fax 222-7205) has 32 rooms with twin double beds and TV, some with a/c. Those with balconies overlooking the street can be noisy; inside rooms are quieter. There are a restaurant and coffee shop. Rates: $35 s, $45 d.

Others have raved about the **Hemingway Inn** (Calle 9, Avenida 9; Apdo. 1711, San José 1002, tel./fax 222-5741), in a twin-story colonial-era building. I found it disappointing. The

nine rooms are small and fairly basic, though with bright floral decor. Some rooms have hardwood walls. The Hemingway Suite has a canopied bed and pleasing maroon decor plus a spacious bathroom. Continental breakfast is served on a small patio. Rates: $35 s, $55 d, $65 t, $80 Hemingway Suite.

The family-operated **Hotel Alameda** (Avenida Central and Calle 12, Apdo. 680, San José 1000, tel. 223-6333, fax 222-9673), a stone's throw from the Coca-Cola bus terminal (a questionable district), has 52 rooms with TV. There's a second-floor restaurant and bar. Some rooms are terribly small and dowdy, with lots of noise off the street. Rates: $33 s, $39 d.

Other centrally located options are the **Hotel Doral** (Avenida 4, Calle 8, Apdo. 55-30, San José 1000, tel. 233-0665, fax 233-4827), with 42 clean, bright rooms from $30; the pleasing **Hotel Plaza** (Avenida Central, Calles 2/4, Apdo. 2019, San José 1000, tel. 222-5533, fax 222-2641), with 40 rooms from $20 s; the '70s-era **Hotel Diplomat** (Calle 6, Avenida Central/2, Apdo. 6606, San José 1000, tel. 221-8133), with 29 rooms from $21 s, $30 d, plus restaurant and most services; and the **Hotel Park** (Avenida 4, Calles 2/4, tel. 221-6944), a clean hotel with 16 rooms and bar. **La Gema** (Avenida 12, Calles 9/11, tel./fax 222-1074) is a pleasant new offering in a quiet downtown street, with rooms at the back facing a lush courtyard. Bar and restaurant. Rates from $30.

The **Nuevo Hotel Talamanca** (Avenida 2, Calles 8/10; Apdo. 11661, San José 1000, tel. 233-5033, fax 233-5420) reopened in 1994 after a complete facelift that lends a previously unknown modern elegance. The 46 a/c rooms and four junior suites (with Jacuzzi and mini bar) are tastefully appointed, and have TVs and telephones. Four junior suites have been described as "a vision in chrome and black, emphasizing sharp lines and minimalist furnishings." Other rooms are done in slate cool greens. It has already established itself as a popular business hotel. Rates: $43 s, $56 d, $70 t, $86 suite, including tax and breakfast.

The relaxed **Hotel Cacts** (Avenida 3, Calles 28/30; Apdo. 379, San José 1005, tel. 221-2928, fax 221-8616) has 12 spacious rooms with satellite TV. It offers a tour agency and provides airport pick-up. Some rooms have shared bath.

Rates: $31-60, including breakfast. In the same neighborhood is the newly opened **Belmundo Hotel** (Calle 20, Avenida 9, tel. 222-9624), a restored mansion. The rooms have cable TV and private baths. Dinners are served. Rates: $25 s, $35 d, including breakfast.

The 24-room **Britannia Hotel** (Apdo. 3742, San José 1000, tel. 223-6667, fax 223-6411) is a newly restored Victorian mansion in Barrio Amón, at Calle 3 and Avenida 11. The boutique hotel features "tropical courtyards," coffee shop, and room service. Not reviewed. Full? Not to worry: one street away on Avenida 11 is **Hotel Hilda** (Apdo. 8079, San José 1000, tel. 221-0037, fax 255-4028). This refurbished home has clean, airy rooms with private bath and hot water. Rates: from $30.

Farther Afield

Very few of San José's hotels offer such a fanfare of trumpets and drums as the pretty exterior of the **Hotel Petit Victoria** (Calle 28, Avenida 2, tel. 233-1812, fax 233-1938), resembling a New England home painted in daffodil yellow with white trim. The intriguing entrance hall—approached through a Chinese-style circular doorway with intricate woodwork—has fancy colonial tiles illuminated by a venerable chandelier. The basically appointed bedrooms, however, are very disappointing. The melancholy blue color scheme is reminiscent of a youth hostel. Bathrooms are spacious and airy. There's a very basic kitchenette and an untidy garden-cum-parking area for guests' use. Vastly overpriced! Rates: $50 s, $60 d, including breakfast and tax.

You don't have to be a tennis and fitness fan to check into the **Hotel Tennis Club** (Apdo. 4964, San José 1000, tel. 232-1266, fax 232-3867) in Sabana Sur, on the south side of Sabana Park. The 27 spacious rooms, each with king-size beds, cable TVs, and pleasing bathrooms, are complemented by 11 tennis courts, a gym, a pool, a spa, and a sauna. Hotel guests get free use of sports facilities. Some rooms have kitchenettes. Secure parking; childcare includes a children's playground. A bargain! Rates: $50 s, $60 d; $71-81 junior suite; $74-84 senior suite.

Also for sports fans is the **Vista de Golf** (Apdo. 379, San Antonio de Belén 4005, tel.

293-4330, fax 293-4371), 250 meters east of the Cariari on the Airport Highway. This quiet, modern hotel offers a Jacuzzi, a heated swimming pool, and access to the Cariari Hotel and Country Club, with golf course and tennis courts. Most of the 35 rooms have king-size beds; some have singles. Also has self-catering "studios" with fully equipped kitchens. Rates: $70/75 standard/large double, breakfast included; $80 junior suite, $100 master studio. Low-season discounts.

Lastly, **Health Homes** (tel. 253-1162, fax 234-9469), on Avenida 1, Calles 33/35, has rooms with private bath with hot water, laundry service, and professional massage on site. Rates: $100 three nights, including breakfasts.

UPSCALE

Most hotels in this category are overpriced and offer little that you can't find in less expensive hotels. A clear exception is the delightful and very *moderne* **Hotel Villa Tournon,** formerly the Bougainvillea (Apdo. 6606, San José 1000, tel. 233-6622, fax 222-5211). It's full to the brim with magnificent and eclectic artworks and sculptures and is with good reason a popular favorite of North American tourists. It's situated opposite the copper-windowed COFISA Building, in Barrio Tournón, north of the town center, within a short distance of El Pueblo, one of San José's most interesting nightlife areas (10 minutes' walk from downtown). The 84 mammoth rooms are graciously appointed. An acclaimed restaurant offers fireside dining. A Jacuzzi and swimming pool in a splendidly decorated garden round out the offerings. Ask for rooms off the street. Rates: $58 s, $65 d standard; $69 s, $75 d, $85 t superior.

Its new neighbor is the **Hotel Europa Zurquí** (tel. 257-3257, fax 221-3976), across Calle 3. This spic-and-span object is a modern five-star hotel with 100 superior rooms, six executive suites, and one presidential suite, all with 24-hour room service, direct-dial telephones, cable TV, mini-bars and safes. It also offers a pool and spa with Jacuzzi, plus small gym, an art gallery and shops, and the inevitable casino. Very nice decor, but soulless character. Rates: from about $50.

Downtown

The granddaddy of San José's upscale hotels is the venerable **Gran Hotel** (Avenidas Central/2, Calle 3; Apdo. 527, San José 1000, tel. 221-4000, fax 221-3501; in the U.S., tel. 800-949-0592), opened in 1930. Its 105 rooms were recently renovated but *two* readers complain of fleas! Rooms facing the plaza can be noisy. Rooms vary from spacious to small and have a/c and cable TV. Junior suites are very elegant. There is a small casino on the ground floor, plus the basement Bufo Dorado Restaurant. The Gran enjoys a superb position in front of the Teatro Nacional, where the hotel's Café Parisienne is a favorite hangout for tourists. Rates: $60 s, $75 d. A $32 special rate (per person, double occupancy, including breakfast) was also available.

Another steps-to-everything option for those seeking a moderately priced room downtown is the **Hotel Balmoral** (Avenida Central, Calles 7/9, Apdo. 3344, San José 1000, tel. 222-5022, fax 221-7826; toll-free in the U.S. 800-327-7737), one block east of Plaza de la Cultura. The Balmoral offers 121 recently renovated rooms, all with a/c, appealing modern decor, and color TV. However, rooms are small, bathrooms are very small, and walls are so thin you can hear your next-door neighbor brushing his/her teeth. There are a sauna and mini-gym, plus a restaurant and casino on the ground floor. Swiss Travel Service, Hertz, and several other

car rental agencies have offices in the lobby. Popular with business travelers. Rates: $75 s, $89 d.

Opposite the Balmoral on Avenida Central is the **Hotel Presidente** (Apdo. 2922, San José 1000, tel. 222-3022, fax 221-1205; in the U.S. 800-972-0515), with 150 rooms with a/c and cable TV, including 100 in a new wing. The older rooms are spacious but dowdy (by one report, they were recently remodeled; if so, my room had caught up with the 1960s). Otherwise pleasant. The hotel has a discotheque, casino, and bar, plus a restaurant serving Italian cuisine. Free airport pick-up. You can do better for the price. Rates: $65 s, $75 d, $85.

Nearby is a splendid option: the **Hotel Del Rey** (Apdo. 6241, San José 1000, tel. 221-7272, fax 221-0096), a newly renovated neoclassical building, long on history (many of the bullet-holes on the face of the Bellavista Fortress were fired from this building in the 1948 revolution), splendidly located on Avenida 1, Calle 9, one block south of Parque Morazán. The beautiful five-story, 104-room structure is a National Heritage Treasure that boasts a lively casino, bar, a 24-hour restaurant, a well-stocked gift shop, travel agency and one small meeting room. Seventeen rooms are deluxe (five with balconies); all rooms are large and come with king-size bed and cable TV. Rooms range from singles to suites for six people. Some facing the street may be too noisy for you. If so, take one

Gran Hotel, San José

GRAN HOTEL COSTA RICA

facing the inner atrium. Note the superb hand-crafted wooden doors and the watercolors by local artists. There's a restaurant, too: a joy to eat in, albeit dim-lit, with its trickling waterfall. Your coffee for breakfast comes not by the cup, but in a large thermos with a separate thermos full of piping hot milk; six cups in one! The hotel, which opened in 1994, is superbly run by an English diamond-in-the-rough, Timothy Johnson, and has become a favorite of gringos, especially fishermen. So, too, the Blue Marlin Bar, where you can sup, eat *bocas*, be wooed by local beauties, and listen to mariachis who wander in off the street. An added bonus is the unique free guided city tour aboard the hotel's own modern tour-bus . . . a great way to get your bearings. Justifiably popular with tourists. A bargain! Rates: $55-75 s, $68-75 d, $125 suites with living room and balconies.

The recently refurbished **Hotel Europa** is also conveniently located (Calle Central and Avenidas 3/5, Apdo. 72, San José 1000, tel. 222-1222, fax 221-3926; toll-free in U.S. 800-223-6764). Rooms, 72 in all, are spacious. Some have a/c. Beds are very comfortable. Avoid lower-floor rooms facing onto the street, as noise from traffic is horrendous (quieter inner-facing rooms are more expensive). The tiny pool is for dipping only. The hotel restaurant and efficient service make amends. Rates from $58 s, $72 d.

The **Hotel Ambassador** (Apdo. 10186, San José 1000, tel. 221-8155, fax 255-3396) on Paseo Colón offers a good location away from the hubbub of downtown yet is within a 20-minute walk of both the city center and Sabana Park. The 74 rooms are clean and spacious, if uninspired. TV and a/c. Amenities include a restaurant, a coffee shop, and a bar with dance floor. Rates: from $65 s, $75 d for standard rooms with a choice of king-size bed or twins. Rates include continental breakfast.

One of the best options in this category is the Swiss-owned and-operated **Hotel Fleur de Lys,** at Calle 13, Avenidas 2/4 (Apdo. 10736, San José 1000, tel. 224-0505, fax 253-6934). This marvelously restored mansion offers guests a choice from the 20 individually styled rooms, each named for a species of flower. All have private bath with hot water, plus phone and cable TV. A restaurant serves Italian cuisine, and

there's a tour agency in the lobby. Its enviable location, one block from the National Museum, is a plus. And the decor is quite exquisite. Rates: $65 s, $70 d, $80-105 suites, including breakfast.

Farther Afield

The **Hotel Torremolinos** (Avenida 5, Calle 40; Apdo. 114, San José 2000, tel. 222-5266, fax 255-3167) is pleasingly situated off Paseo Colón in a quiet neighborhood near Sabana Park. Its 70 rooms—recently renovated in contemporary style—are modest but attractive and comfortable. All have large TVs. It offers a pool and sauna, plus a courtesy bus to downtown. The beautiful restaurant has hints of Italian and Japanese decor. Rates: $55 s, $65 d. Farther out is **Hotel Americano del Este** (tel. 224-2455 or 225-3022, fax 224-2166), 200 meters north of Agencia Subaru in Los Yoses. It's a lovely property with 29 large and comfortable bedrooms with cable TV and direct-dial phone. There are a swimming pool, bar, and cafe. Rates: $65 s, $75 d, including buffet breakfast.

It may once have looked like a Motel 6, but the **Hotel Ejecutivo Napoleon** (Avenida 5 and Calle 40, Apdo. 8-6240, San José 1000, tel. 223-3252, fax 222-9487) today sports a marvelous new livery. The entrance foyer sets the tone with its rich mahogany and deep green color scheme, reception desk adorned with a wraparound rug, and fake stream and bridge leading to a well-stocked kitchenette. It is well placed in a quiet residential neighborhood near Sabana Park. The 27 exceedingly spacious rooms—each with two double beds, cable TV, and direct-dial phone—are arrayed around an outdoor swimming pool and small horseshoe-shaped open bar. No restaurant. The hotel was formerly an apartotel. Rates: $85 s, $95 d with a/c, $75 s, $85 d without. Includes buffet breakfast.

Also worth considering is the small and homey **Gran Hotel Doña Inés** (Calle 11, Avenidas 2/6, tel. 222-7443, fax 223-5426), a good bet, with luxury bathrooms with full-size tubs and TV and phones in the bedrooms, which are furnished in hardwoods. Rates: from $60. Also try the **Hotel Boulevard Ejecutivo** (Apdo. 3258, San José 1000, tel./fax 232-9839), in Rohrmoser. Not inspected. The hotel's brochure suggests exquisite decor. Rates: $55 s, $68 d, from $85 suites.

In 1994, Choice Hotels (see "Quality Hotel," below) began construction of a 100-room **Plaza Esmeralda,** a "limited-service economy" hotel northeast of downtown.

DELUXE

Large Scale

Two deluxe properties adjacent to each other at Ciudad Cariari, about 10 km northwest of San José (about five minutes from Juan Santamaría Airport) are the **Cariari Hotel and Country Club** and **Hotel Herradura.** It's a 20-minute taxi journey to downtown. Both hotels offer spacious rooms with modern decor and complete deluxe resort facilities, including access to the Cariari Country Club (next door) featuring a championship golf course and 10 tennis courts. I prefer the elegant and appealing layout of the Cariari (Apdo. 737, Centro Colón, San José 1007, tel. 233-0022, fax 239-2803; in the U.S. 800-344-1212), which centers on an outdoor swimming pool with swim-up bar. There's a casino and small disco. Rates: from $105.

Formerly part of the Sheraton chain, the **Hotel Herradura** (Apdo. 7-1880, San José 1000, tel. 239-0033, fax 239-2292; in the U.S. 800-245-8420, fax 305-539-1123) offers impressive entertainment facilities, including the elegant Krystal Casino and the 51,000-square-foot conference center (Julio Iglesias has performed there). There are a Jacuzzi and a spa, plus an outdoor swimming pool. Magnificent hardwoods abound. Rooms were refurbished in late 1994. The Herradura is replete with restaurant options: Sakura for Japanese, Bon Vivant for international cuisine, and Tiffany's 24-hour coffee shop for Costa Rican food. New in 1995 were the Sancho Panza restaurant, appropriately serving Spanish dishes, and the Tropicana health-food restaurant. A "San José by Night" *folklorica* show is presented on weekends in the Bon Vivant. An 89-room addition brings the total to 234 rooms. Satellite TV is standard. Rates: from $108 s, $118 d. Children under 17 stay free with parents.

Closer to town—10 minutes by taxi—is the **Hotel San José Palacio** (Apdo. 458, San José 1150, tel. 220-2034, fax 231-1990), a large-scale property with 254 rooms flush with hardwoods and pleasing decor. It offers a large swim-

ming pool, tennis and racquetball courts, health spa and gym, sauna and Jacuzzi, plus a casino popular with the San José elite. A lively casino and elegant and reasonably priced restaurant are countered by a drab bar. The hotel is one mile north of Sabana Park on Autopista General Cañas; an awkward location. Rates: from $110 s, $118 d.

The **Hotel Irazú** (tel. 232-4811, fax 232-3159; in the U.S., Costa Rica Fantasy Travel, tel. 800-832-9449) is the largest urban hotel in the country, with 350 rooms, some nonsmoking. All rooms were remodeled in early 1993, though the rooms remain so-so. Most rooms have a balcony overlooking the pool or gardens, plus direct-dial telephone, cable TV, and a/c. The hotel features all the amenities of a deluxe property: tennis courts, sauna, swimming pool, restaurant, Costa Rica's largest casino, plus a small shopping mall. It is popular for tour groups. Its location—next door to the San José 2000 Shopping Center, in La Uruca—has little to recommend it. There's an hourly shuttle bus to downtown. Rates: $65-80 s, $75-90 d, $85-110 t.

Looking a little like a set from *Star Trek* is the **Hotel Corobicí** (Apdo. 2443, San José 1000, tel. 232-8122, fax 231-5834; in the U.S., tel. 800-CARIARI, fax 305-876-9837), on the northeastern corner of Sabana Park. You may hate its inward-sloping exterior, but its soaring atrium design, with tier upon tier of balconies festooned with ferns, is impressive. The 179 spacious rooms in this former Playboy Club were recently remodeled and have a/c and cable TV. There's a 24-hour cafeteria, plus an authentic Japanese restaurant with a native cook. The Corobicí's spa is one of the best in the country. It's within walking distance of downtown (30 minutes), and there's a courtesy shuttle. It offers the Epocas Night Club and casino for those who don't want to wander far at night. Rates: from $99 s, $110 d.

Dominating the downtown skyline is the **Hotel Aurola Holiday Inn** (Apdo. 7802, San José 1000, tel. 233-7233, fax 255-1036), with its bronze-tinted windows. The modern high-rise overlooking Parque Morazán, in the heart of San José (Avenida 5 and Calle 5), offers sumptuous accommodations and is the most sophisticated of downtown hotels by far. Literally topping off the hotel's attractions is the Mirador restaurant on the 17th floor, adjacent to the casi-

FOUR GEMS: SAN JOSÉ'S NEW BREED OF BOUTIQUE HOTELS

Travelers to Costa Rica have long bemoaned the lack of charming boutique hotels in the nation's capital city. Finally, a new breed of intimate and gracious hotel has emerged to blow the dust off San José's dowdy hotel scene. Of a dozen or so gems to choose from, the following are my pick.

Hotel Grano de Oro

Opened in February 1992, this gracious turn-of-the-century mansion turned thoroughly modern hotel immediately acquired a staunch American clientele. The guest book is a compendium of compliments. "What charm! What comfort!" one guest effused. "The best hotel we've stayed in—ever!" said several more. "We would love to keep it a secret, but we promise we won't," said another. And no wonder . . . the Grano de Oro exudes charm and superlative service. Unquestionably my hotel of preference whenever I stay in San José.

The hotel, in a quiet, tree-lined residential neighborhood (Calle 30 and Avenida 2) and a pleasing 20-minute walk from the bustling city center, is operated by Eldon and Lori Cooke, who act as congenial hosts. Together, they have overseen the creation of a real home away from home.

Comfort is the keynote. In the 36 faultlessly decorated guest rooms, firm mattresses and plump down pillows guarantee contented slumber beneath sturdy beamed ceilings. Each is done up in flattering combinations of soft gray, peach, and coral, with Latin American watercolors and tapestries adorning the walls. Locally hand-crafted furniture and gleaming hardwood floors add to the sense of elegant refinement. And bedside lamps you can actually read by, satellite TV, and direct-dial telephones reflect North American savoir-faire. A downstairs suite plays on period details, including mahogany wall panels, Jacuzzi bathtub, and French doors that open onto a private garden.

Extravagant bathrooms are adorned with hand-painted colonial tiles, brass fittings, fluffy towels, torrents of piping-hot water, and cavernous showers and deep bathtubs where one can relax with bubbles up to the nose.

One look at the mammoth-scale, rooftop "Vista de Oro" suite and you'll immediately wish to splurge ($140) on what vies with the suite at Finca Rosa Blanca for *best hotel room in the country* . . . with its plate-glass window running the full width of one wall, proffering views of three volcanoes . . . its Jacuzzi, elevated, nose-up to the window with one of two TVs at hand . . . its king-size bed, its sofas lushly decorated in Turkish fabrics . . . its sensual papaya, maroon, and deep blue color scheme . . . its sense of overwhelming romantic indulgence.

All rooms are nonsmoking. Hurray! And no request is too much for the mustard-keen, English-speaking, ever-smiling staff.

Soothing classical, South American, and Peruvian flute music, the sound of trickling water from a patio fountain, and soft chorale chants from the chapel next door waft through the hallways, lounge, and courtyard restaurant lush with palms, orchids, ephiphytes, and yucca—a perfect place to eat. The "Gringo" breakfast—granola with bananas, and thick slices of freshly baked whole-wheat toast—is one of the best breakfasts in Costa Rica. And the gourmet dinner menu is also a temptation in its own right. If you're not staying here, you at least owe it to yourself to eat here (see "Restaurants," this chapter).

no. The hotel contains a gym, a sauna, and an indoor pool. "A giant hermetically sealed container with windows that don't open," says my friend Gregg Calkin. The 201 rooms have a/c and cable TV. Rates: from $128 s, $140 d.

An addition to the scene is the **Amstel Amón** (Apdo. 4192, San José 1000, tel. 257-0191, fax 257-0284; in the U.S., 800-575-1253), on Avenida 11, Calle 3 Bis, in the historic Barrio Amón area downtown. The modern four-story, "neo-Victorian" hotel has 90 rooms, including 24 junior and six deluxe suites. Rooms have a/c, telephone, cable TV, safety deposit boxes, and hair dryer. An unusually elegant marble lobby decorated with artwork hints at the upscale decor throughout. It features an office center with computers, plus conference center, spa, casino, and underground parking. The Danubio Restaurante is *muy elegante*. Overpriced? Rates: from $98 to $235 for a luxury suite with living room and Jacuzzi.

The 129-room **Quality Hotel Centro Colón,** operated by Choice Hotels (10750 Columbia Pike, Silver Spring, MD 20901, tel. 301-236-5032 or 800-228-5151; in Costa Rica, Apdo. 433, San

Hotel Grano de Oro, Apdo. 1157, San José 1007, Costa Rica, tel. 255-3322, fax 221-2782; or, in the U.S., SJO 36, P.O. Box 02516, Miami, FL 33102-5216. Room rates are $70 standard, $82 superior, $92 deluxe, $120 suite, $140 Vista de Oro suite. What a bargain!

Hotel Milvia

Another shining example of the genre, this delightful time-capsule-cum-outer-city-hotel in San Pedro, three km east of downtown San José, offers a discreet yet sophisticated European charm. The exquisitely detailed Caribbean-style wooden home has been restored to its original turn-of-the-century splendor by offspring of the original family. Within, relaxed intimacy is the watchword, aided by classical music adding notes of soothing calm.

There are four rooms upstairs in the original home, five more downstairs in a contemporary add-on built like hand-and-glove in the original style around a tiny triangular garden courtyard. Hardwood floors glisten downstairs (rooms upstairs are carpeted). Oriental throw-rugs abound. Walls are festooned with family portraits and original paintings. A chess table, backgammon, and a fish tank keep you amused.

The individually styled rooms are spacious, luxurious, and each furnished with elegant antiques and tasteful fabrics dominated by blacks, verdigris, and rose . . . speaking of which, you'll find a fresh rose in your bathroom, along with cookies on your table, and a chocolate on your pillow with nightly turn-down service. Grand bathrooms gleam (the white tiles with floral decoratives were hand-painted by Milvia). There are fluffy towels, and even baskets replete with toiletries—a rarity among Costa Rican hotels. No tubs, however. But the showers are voluminous. Fans, remote-control cable TVs, phones, and minibars are standard.

Downstairs are a dining room, small lounge, and a little boutique selling hand-painted porcelain vases, plates, and figurines, as well as traditional ceramics, T-shirts, etc. Upstairs, a terrace perfect for alfresco breakfasts provides views over the hotel's mango trees and garden full of bright yellow lirios, with Irazú volcano in the near distance, brooding under cloud, or basking in golden sunlight at dusk.

And no words can praise highly enough the attentive and caring concern of live-in owners Milvia and Mauricio and their staff. Milvia, a former tour guide, is Italian and the hotel is popular with Italians.

Following Avenida 2 east from San José, turn left 100 meters beyond Centro Comercial M&N in San Pedro (you'll see the hotel signed here), then the first right. The hotel is 50 meters on the left.

Apdo. 1660, San Pedro 2050, tel. 225-4543, fax 225-7801. Rates: $60 s, $65 d, $70 t, including continental breakfast. Another marvelous bargain!

ALSO HIGHLY RECOMMENDED

Hotel L'Ambiance

In the historic Barrio Otoya district, one block south of the Simón Bolívar Zoo and a block north of the Jade Museum, the Hotel L'Ambiance (Calle 13 and Avenida 9) offers the best of both worlds: the tranquility of a residential setting as well as the uproar of San José close at hand, proving that a fine house, like a jewel, is made complete by its setting.

American owner William Parker has restored the former colonial mansion with the same taste, impressive effort, and attention for period detail that he lavished on his previous success, Shiretown Inn, in Martha's Vineyard.

Six individually styled bedrooms and one suite—with names such as Esperanza and Amor—come with stylish colonial furnishings: massive antique

(continues on next page)

José 1007, tel. 257-2580, fax 257-2582), opened in mid-1994 in one of the towers of the Centro Colón complex on Paseo Colón. The 130 a/c rooms (76 standard, six studios, 34 suites, six junior suites, and a Presidential Suite) are "extra-large" and come with cable TV, safety box, hair dryer, and telephone. There are also a restaurant, casino, and nightclub/bar done up in dazzling eye-popping pink and neon! All very contemporary; very nice! Rates: $74 studio, $90 s/d standard, $116 junior suite, $126 suite.

The colonial-style **Costa Rica Marriott Hotel** was under construction with plans to open in 1996. It should be quite showy, boasting a ballroom for 1,000 people, plus golf practice range, swimming pool, three restaurants, tennis courts, and gym.

Small Scale

My favorite hotel in San José—**Hotel Grano de Oro**—is described in a separate box, along with a handful of other gems.

FOUR GEMS: SAN JOSÉ'S
NEW BREED OF BOUTIQUE HOTELS
(continued)

wardrobes and gilt-framed mirrors. Genuine Currier and Ives prints decorate the bathrooms. Cable TV and ceiling fans are standard. (Poor marks, however, for the minimal attention paid to some bathrooms' decor.)

The hub is the open-air Spanish-style colonial courtyard awash with tropical plants. Vibrant tropical colors abound, not least from tasteful modern art pieces that grace the dining-room walls.

Superb cuisine, too! Meals—stylish and light on the palate—have been given the attention they merit, with assured and tempting continental dishes presented with flair.

In my first edition, I wrote that Hotel L'Ambiance scores high for its impeccable service: friendly but stopping short of familiarity, relaxed but always professional. Alas, service is now a concern. Recent feedback (enhanced by personal observation) suggests that a certain haughtiness may have set in.

Hôtel Le Bergerac

Last but not least is this pretty colonial home in Los Yoses, on Calle 35, 50 meters south of Avenida Central, with views south toward the Cordillera Talamanca. Le Bergerac is a full-service hotel that serves breakfast, *not*, the owners hasten to add, a bed-and-breakfast hotel. What does that mean?

Well, how about a sequestered conference room complete with video, bar, telephone and fax service, computer hook-ups, and rooms with private gardens for solace and quiet contemplation.

Business travelers and guests of the diplomatic missions hereabouts gravitate to this piece of the Parisian Left Bank designed by the architect Bartoldi and named for the famous long-nosed French novelist Cyrano de Bergerac. The French influence originates in Québec with its two French Canadian owners, James Elhaleh and Diane-Alexis Fournier. Service is discreet, the atmosphere a curious blend of aloofness and warmth enhanced by the deep maroon-rust and gray color scheme.

The hotel has 18 rooms in three buildings (five in the original home, reached via a sweeping spiral staircase), all with cable TV, direct-dial telephone, and safety boxes, plus hardwood floors and classical furniture constructed by local craftsmen. Plants and prints by Monet abound, displayed amid oodles of light. Rooms vary in size. James brings to **Aux Fines Herbes** (the airy dining terrace) an accomplished background along with gourmet French cuisine. Breakfast is served here, as well as *bocas* and drinks in the evening. Le Bergerac, Apdo. 1107, San José 1002, tel. 234-7850, fax 225-9103. Rates: (standard room) $58 s, $68 d, $78 t; (deluxe) $68 s, $78 d, $88 t.

Another newcomer is the **Parque de Lago** (Avenida 2, Calles 40/42; Apdo. 624, San José 1007, tel. 257-8787 or 222-1577, fax 223-1617; in the U.S., Dept. 1634, P.O. Box 025216, Miami, FL 33102), which opened in March 1993 with 39 exquisitely decorated rooms, plus suites with kitchenettes. Woods, ceramics, plants, and Costa Rican artworks combine to create a nostalgic ambience. Sound-insulated windows and a/c, while doffing a cap to North American standards, detract from the traditional ambience. How much better to be able to throw open the windows! Rooms have cable TV, direct-dial phones with fax, and coffeemakers. The hotel is within a few minutes' stroll of Sabana Park and the Museum of Costa Rican Art and is perfect for both the business and tourist traveler. Rates: $75 s, $85 d; suites from $90 s, $105 d. Children under two stay free.

Note: The distinction between "Deluxe" and "Upscale" (and even "Moderate") is particularly tentative regarding small-scale hotels; compare each category.

BED AND BREAKFASTS

Several hotels include breakfast in their rates but are not true to the purist's concept of a bed and breakfast: small, atmospheric hotels with a homey ambience and congenial, often live-in, hosts. Pricing should be your guide to quality. The **Bed and Breakfast Association** can provide recommendations (tel. 223-4168 or 228-9200).

The Canadian-run **Hotel Santo Tomás** (Avenida 7, Calles 3/5, tel. 255-0448, fax 222-

3950) is an exceptionally fine bed and breakfast with 20 rooms in an elegant turn-of-the-century plantation home—built from a termite-proof mahogany and recently restored to haughty grandeur. The 14-foot vaulted ceiling and original hardwood floors are impressive. Though the street outside is noisy, you'll hardly notice: rooms are off the street. Bedrooms vary considerably: some are mammoth. All beds are queen-size and orthopedic, with crisp linen sheets. Mahogany antique reproduction King Louis XV-style furniture, Persian rugs, watercolors by a local artist, and personal touches abound. All rooms feature a large-scale touring map on the wall. Rooms have cable TV and direct-dial phones, plus there are three separate TVs in the public lounges. Laundry service. All staff are bilingual. No guests at night. A bargain! More rooms, a garden, and a pool were planned on adjoining land. Rates from $50-75 d, including continental breakfast served in an airy patio conducive to mingling.

Nearby, splendidly situated on a corner of Parque Morazán (Calle 5, Avenida 3) is **Diana's Inn** (tel. 223-6542, fax 233-0495), with a/c rooms with private bath, phone, and color TV. The three-story pink building, now in a tatterdemalian state, was once home to an ex-president of Costa Rica. Rates: from $25 s, $35 d. A/c rooms cost more.

The **Hotel La Amistad Inn** (Avenida 11, Calle 15, tel. 221-1597, fax 221-1409) is a restored old mansion with 18 rooms, each with two queen-size beds with orthopedic mattress, ceiling fan, cable TV, and black marble baths. The hotel has a small garden. Good, quiet location, just east of the zoo on the edge of the historic Barrio Otoya district. Under multilingual German ownership (the influence is there in the breakfasts). Rates: from $25 s, $30 d, $60 suites.

*Hotel Grano de Oro,
a hidden treasure
of San José*

In a more colorful vein, and just around the corner, is the strangely named **Cinco Hormigas Rojas** ("Five Red Ants," on Calle 15 and Avenidas 7/9, tel. 257-8581), a small, eight-room bed and breakfast run by local artist Mayra Guell. The place vibrates with Mayra's paintings and drawings. Not content to display her works, she applied her talent to turning the enamel toilet seat and other mundane objects into a calliope of color. Rooms appropriately have their own color schemes. Hardwood floors gleam. There are thick patterned curtains and rattan furnishings. And tiny animal replicas abound, peeping out from nooks and crannies. A Costa Rican breakfast is served in a dining area described as "a jungle in miniature." Rates: $25 s, $30 d.

Another intriguing and tasteful conversion is the **Don Paco Inn** (Calle 33 and Avenidas 9/11, Apdo. 29-2970, Sabanilla, San José, tel. 234-9088, fax 234-9588; in the U.S., tel. 800-288-2107), a cozy bed and breakfast blending *moderne* decor into the setting of a colonial-style mansion. The hotel lies in a quiet upper-class residential area and once served as a United Nations office building. The 10 comfortable bedrooms are decorated in light and cheery colors, with plump comforters, fluffy pillows, and cable TV. The hotel has a small souvenir shop. Full breakfast included. Rates: from $50 s, $60 d.

Hotel Rosa del Paseo (Apdo. 287, San José 1007, tel. 257-3213, fax 223-2776) has 20 nicely decorated rooms in a completely remodeled century-old residence on Paseo Colón. Architectural details combine tilework-and-hardwood floors, original artwork, and art-nouveau flourishes with "Victorian Caribbean." Rates: $60 s, $70 d, $80 t, $130 suite, including breakfast.

In Los Yoses is the **Tres Arcos** (Apdo. 161, San José 1000, tel./fax 225-0271), a pleasing B&B run by longtime residents Eric and Lee Warrington in an area of old houses on Avenida 10, 200 meters south and 50 meters west of the Auto Mercado. Individually styled rooms all have large windows overlooking the southern mountains beyond a large walled garden with trees festooned with orchids, bromeliads, and fruits. The living room has a stone fireplace plus cable TV. Breakfast is served on the outside "birdwatching terrace." Rates: $45 d with shared bath, $55 with private bath; minisuites for four cost $90.

Nearby, at Calle 37 and Avenida 8, is the **Hotel Don Fadrique** (Apdo. 4225, San José 1000, tel. 225-8186, fax 224-9746), claiming 20 "luxuriously furnished rooms" and "lush tropical gardens." Not reviewed. The rooms are decorated in tropical pastels, with works by local artists on the walls. Each has telephone, cable TV, safety deposit box, and fan. Apparently you can enjoy breakfast beneath the shade of a mango tree. Rates: from $65 standard, $78 deluxe.

The **Casa de Finca** (Apdo. 1071, San Pedro 2050, tel./fax 225-6169) is farther out, surrounded by coffee plantations and tropical gardens on the outskirts of San Pedro. This beautifully restored and elegant 1926 mansion features splendid tile floors, hardwoods, and king-size beds in bright pastel-colored bedrooms. Rates: $63 s, $73 d, $83 t.

Barrio Amón, just north of Parque Morazán, has several B&Bs to consider, including the popular **Dunn Inn** (Calle 5, Avenida 9, tel. 222-3232, fax 221-4596) operated by Patrick Dunn, a Texan who used to run the old Nashville South bar. Rooms—13 in the original Spanish-colonial home; 17 in a newer addition—have cable TV and telephone. It features a Jacuzzi plus lounge (with stunning stained-glass window) and a patio restaurant lush with greenery, including a philodrendron that climbs to the second floor. Rates: from $45 (seventh night free). Nearby is the **Hotel Rey** (Avenida 7, Calles 7/9; Apdo. 7145, San José 1000, tel. 233-3819, fax 233-1769), a refurbished mansion with original tile floors, high ceilings, and cable TV in the 13 bedrooms. Rates: $35 s, $50 d, with breakfast and airport pick-up.

La Casa Verde de Amón (Calle 7, Avenida 9, tel./fax 223-0969; in the U.S., P.O. Box 025216, Dept. 1701, Miami, FL 33102-5216) is another elegantly restored Victorian mansion, once the home of Don Carlos Saborio, an influential figure in turn-of-the-century Costa Rica. The building, constructed in red pine, was traded for coffee and imported from New Orleans! It was recently restored by American Carl Stanley. The Victorian lounge is lit by a soaring *tragaluz* (skylight) and features Chinese rugs, silk wallpaper, and a resplendent centenary grand piano. Lots of antique detailing. Breakfast is served on a tiny garden patio, with coffee supplied from beans growing out front. There are three suites and five deluxe rooms, all huge with a distinctly aged feel, though a little dowdy. Hangar-size suites are replete with living room and king-size bed, and bathrooms feature Victorian claw-foot tubs. Rates: $70 d, $90 suite.

Also in Barrio Amón (at Calle 9 and Avenida 7) is **Hotel Rey Amón,** a centenarian structure, formerly the Pensión Rey, that converted to a hotel in 1992. Not reviewed. Nearby is **Taylor's Inn** (tel. 257-4333, fax 221-1475) on Avenida 13 and Calles 13/15. Note the pretty ceramic tiles on this 1908 property, which opened as a hotel in December 1993. Ten non-smoking rooms each have private bath and cable TV. A "Tropical" breakfast is included.

The **D'Raya Vida Villa** (Calle 15, Avenidas 11/13, tel. 223-4168, fax 23-4157) is a lovely restored mansion—described as "antebellum" of pre-U.S. Civil War—tucked in a cul-de-sac in Barrio Otoya. Three rooms are somewhat offbeat but delightful. There's a small patio with fountain, and a mirrored reading room with fireplace and chandeliers. Rates: $85 d, with breakfast and airport pick-up. Nearby, on Avenida 9, Calles 13/15, is the new **Hotel Edelweiss** (tel. 221-9702, fax 222-1241), with clean, comfortable rooms with telephones and private bath with hot water. Bamboo and rattan abounds in the **Ara Macao Inn** (Apdo. 839, San José 2050, tel. 323-2742), a restored early-century house 50 meters south of Pizza Hut, in Barrio La California, five minutes' walk from the National Museum. Sunny rooms. A singular attraction: poison-arrow frogs in specimen tanks! Rates: $50 d.

The **Majestic Inn** (tel. 232-9028, fax 296-3967) has seven spacious, deluxe rooms in residential Rohrmoser, west of Sabana Park. It has a bar and restaurant, plus library and TV room.

In Barrio México, at Avenida 7 and Calles 18/20, is **Hotel Surú** (tel. 222-4151, fax 221-

7917), with seven rooms with private bath. There's a TV room, plus bar and terrace with cafe. Rates: $30 s, $40 d, $50 t. Nearby, opposite the Irazú Hotel, is the **Kalexma Inn** (tel./fax 232-0115), with a choice of shared ($20 s, $30 d) or private bath ($30 s, $40 d).

The **Hotel Amaranto Inn** (Apdo. 230, San Pedro 2010, tel. 225-0542, fax 224-5747), in Zapote, has 12 rooms, some with shared bathroom. Nearby, in Barrio La Granja, near the university, is **Maripaz Bed & Breakfast** (tel./fax 253-8456; in Canada, tel. 613-747-7174), with rooms with either private or shared bath (from $20 per person). **Versalles Inn** (tel./fax 235-3735) is in Tibas. Not reviewed. Rates: from $23 s, $36 d. Two other unreviewed options are **Being Home** (tel. 283-0101, fax 225-3516), in Los Yoses, with a/c rooms with private bath, cable TV, telephone from $22; and **Doña Merce Bed and Breakfast** (Apdo. 3660, San José 1000, tel. 223-1582, fax 233-1909), on Avenida 14, Calles 13/15.

HOMESTAYS

Another option is to stay with a Costa Rican family—an ideal way to experience the legendary Tico hospitality and warmth, and a pleasing opportunity to bone up on your Spanish. You may choose English-speaking hosts if you wish. Dinners ($5) are not included.

Two companies that specialize in this are **Bell's Home Hospitality,** run by Vernon and Marcela Bell (Apdo. 185, San José 1000, tel. 225-4752, fax 224-5884), and Steve Beaudreau's **Costa Rican Homestays** (tel. 240-6829). The Bells offer a selection from 70 homes in the San José area, most in the suburbs ($30 s, $45 d or twin share, with breakfast; $5 extra for private bath; monthly rates are available). Beaudreau offers two classes of accommodation in and around San José: "A" class in upper-middle-class homes, with private baths ($28 d per day up to 15 days, less after that); and "B" class in more humble homes, with shared baths.

Families also advertise rooms for rent in the classifieds of the *Tico Times* and *Costa Rica Today.*

Also see "Accommodations" in the On the Road chapter.

APARTOTELS

A hybrid of hotels and apartment buildings, apartotels resemble motels on the European and Australian model. These self-catering units come fully furnished, with kitchenette and TV. Most offer daily maid service and are available for rent by the day, week, or month. Decor ranges from pleasing to dingy and austere. Most are on the fringe of the city, with many concentrated in Los Yoses. (The Apartotel Napoleon no longer exists: it is now the Hotel Ejecutivo Napoleon.)

The **Apartotel Castilla** (Calle 24, Avenidas 2/4, Apdo. 944, San José 1007, tel. 222-2113, fax 221-2080) offers 15 spacious one- and two-bedroom units with pleasingly simple decor and color TVs. Free parking. Rates: $35 s, $40 d. Farther west, the **Apartotel Ramgo** (two blocks west and one block south of Hotel Tennis Club, Sabana Sur, Apdo. 1441, San José 1000, tel. 232-3823, fax 232-3111) has 16 rooms, each with two double beds and cable TV. Rates from $40.

On the other side of Sabana Park, the clean and modern **Apartotel Cristina** (300 meters north of ICE, Sabana Norte, Apdo. 1094, San Pedro 2050, tel. 231-1618, fax 220-2096) has 25 furnished apartments, each with cable TV. Swimming pool, garage parking, laundry, and free continental breakfast. Also in Sabana Norte is **Apartotel La Sabana** (Apdo. 11400, San José 1000, tel. 220-2422, fax 231-7386), with a/c double rooms and apartments with cable TV and telephone, plus pool and sauna. Rates from $39, including breakfast. Nearby, too, is **Apartotel El Sesteo** (tel. 296-1805, fax 296-1865), 200 meters south of McDonald's. Twenty one- and two-bedroom units rent from $35. It offers a pool and Jacuzzi.

Apartments Intertex (tel. 232-9620), in La Uruca near the Hotel Irazú, has small furnished apartments, plus a TV room and small pool. Rates: $200 monthly s, $250 d.

Apartotels Residencia de Golf (Apdo. 379, San Antonio de Belén 4005, tel. 239-4330, fax 239-4371), 250 meters east of the Cariari on the Airport Highway, is a quiet, modern complex offering Jacuzzi, heated swimming pool, and membership in the adjacent Cariari Country Club (golf course and tennis courts). One- to

four-bedroom apartments. Fans. Most rooms have king-size beds; some have singles. Beautiful landscaped views.

About three km north of Sabana is **La Perla,** east of Hospital México on Autopista General Cañas (Apdo. 2148, San José 1000, tel. 232-6153, fax 220-0103). The 14 one- and two-bedroom apartments come with living and dining rooms, kitchen, cable TV, phone, and fax. Rates: from $34. Nearby, too, is the Italian-owned and operated **Hotel Siena** (tel./fax 231-1791), which, needless to say, has a strong Italian following.

Across town to the east is **Apartotel Los Yoses** (25 meters east of the Pollos Kentucky, Apdo. 1597, San José 1000, tel. 225-0033, fax 225-5595), with 23 rooms, swimming pool, free parking, and daily housekeeping. Rates: from $25 s, $30 d. Adjoining it is **Apartotel Don Carlos** (Calle 29, Avenidas 6/8, Apdo. 1593, San José 1000, tel. 221-6707, fax 255-0828; in the U.S., Dept. 1686, P.O. Box 025216, Miami, FL 33102). Its owner is Don Carlos Balser, who also owns the Hotel Don Carlos. Satellite TV, parking. Rates: $25 s, $30 d, $220 weekly, $750 monthly. Nearby is **Apartotel El Conquistador** (Apdo. 303, San Pedro 2050, tel. 224-2455 or 225-3022, fax 224-2166), whose 29 rooms have ugly furnishings (sickly green bedspreads and wallpaper). Open-air swimming pool, TVs in rooms. Rates: $29.

Apartotel Llama del Bosque (100 meters south and 50 meters west of Plaza del Sol shopping center, Curridabat, tel. 224-0681) is one of the better options. Rooms surround a lush patio and pool. Rooms have cable TV. Rates: from $40.

Also to consider: **Apartotel Miami** (250 meters east of Casa Italia, Avenida 8 and Calles 33/35, Los Yoses, tel. 225-7209), with 27 rooms. **Apartamentos Scotland** (Avenida 1, Calle 27, tel. 223-0833) has luxury one-bedroom apartments for weekly and monthly rental. Less expensive furnished studios are also available. Rates: $175 weekly, $380 monthly.

In San Pedro, **D'Galah** (Apdo. 208, San José 2350, tel. 234-1743) faces the gardens of the University of Costa Rica and absorbs noise from the street. Some rooms are suites with fully equipped kitchenette and loft. Sauna bath, swimming pool, and coffee shop. Rates: from $26. Al-

ternately, try **Apartotel The Palm Trees** (200 meters west, 100 meters north, then 100 meters east of San Pedro church, tel. 253-0182). Units have color TV and phone; Jacuzzi and pool on site. Rates: $39 daily, $850 monthly.

Downtown San José has a choice of aparto-tels. The modern **Apartotel San José** (Apdo. 4192, San José 1000, tel. 222-0455, fax 221-2443; in the U.S., 800-575-1253), across from the National Museum, offers 12 small one- and two-bedroom suites with living room and fully equipped kitchenette, cable TV, phone, and parking. Rates: from $40 d. Its neighbor is the **Apartamentos Lamm** (Avenida 1, Calle 15, Apdo. 2729, San José 1000, tel. 221-4920, fax 221-4720), with 21 one- to three-bedroom apartments. Rates: $32 s, $35 d, $39 t.

APARTMENTS AND HOME RENTAL

The *Tico Times, Costa Rica Today, Costa Rican Outlook,* and *Adventures in Costa Rica* all publish ads listing private apartments for rent (see "Information" under "Other Practicalities" in the On the Road chapter). Usually these are on the outskirts of town and in adjacent towns. Examples include: **"Barrio Dent;** Nice apartment complex, furnished and equipped, 24 hrs security, $1,000, tel. 224-1223"; **"Barrio Escalante;** Furnished apartment for rent, garage, $600, tel. 234-6501 or 758-2364"; **"Rohrmoser;** New apts., 2 bdr., 2 baths, $550/mo. & $600/mo. Condominium 3 bdr., 2 baths, $700/mo. House 3 bdr, 3 baths, completely furnished, $1,000/mo."; **"Sabana;** 3 bdr., 2 baths, maid quarters, stove & fridge, garage, $650/mo., tel. 237-3826, fax 260-7320."

Two properties in the residential neighborhood of San Pedro de Coronado, 10 minutes east of downtown, include a "furnished cottage for four people" for $1000 a month (tel. 225-6895, call noon-1 p.m.); and fully furnished, "luxuriously decorated" apartments, with living room, dining area, etc. for $250 a week (tel. 225-6565).

If you're tempted by the idea of luxury living, consider **The Penthouse** (tel. 233-2958), a three bedroom, three bathroom luxury penthouse suite with full bar and huge living area, plus maid, etc.

NEAR THE AIRPORT

Several airport hotels have recently opened or are under construction for those who want the convenience of the airport nearby. The **Hampton Inn** (Hoteles Marta Apdo. 962, San José 1000, tel. 442-0043, fax 442-9532; or Resertel, tel. 800-272-6654, fax 232-3159) opened in January 1995, a "two-minute" drive east of the airport terminal. The 100-room (75% nonsmoking) property features a swimming pool. Rooms are soundproofed and feature king or two double beds, cable TV with in-room movies, telephones, and lighting you can actually read by. It offers a dedicated handicap-accessible room. The hotel guarantees "100 percent satisfaction" or your money back! Rates begin at $59 s, $65 d, $7 extra (low season) including continental breakfast (children under 18 free)

A 245-room colonial-style **Marriott** (tel. 800-831-1000, fax 800-325-9714) hotel was to open in 1996 on a 30-acre site commanding panoramic views over the valley, four km east of the airport (13 km from downtown San José). Planned are 200 square meters of retail space, a health club, business center, outdoor pool, three tennis courts, a golf practice range, three restaurants, and the obligatory casino.

A more intimate option is the **Posada Aeropuerto** (tel./ fax 441-7569; in the U.S., tel. 800-330-HOME), about two km south of the airport. Not inspected. Rate: $38 d, including breakfast.

The Mexican company Grupo Situr was due to begin construction of a 280-room **Hilton Hotel** with direct walkway to the terminal.

Otherwise, the closest hotels to the airport are the Cariari and Herradura (both deluxe), adjacent to each other about five km south of the airport on the road into town; or various hotels in and around Alajuela and Heredia, two somnolent towns north of the airport. **La Aurora de Heredia** is a private home with a bed and breakfast service, about two km east of the Cariari Hotel. Kitchen privileges, cable TV; $250 a month (tel. 293-1655).

TRAILER PARKS

The only RV trailer park "in" San José is the American-owned facility at San Antonio de Belén, eight km west of the capital. Hot showers and laundry, plus hookup facilities. The site is served by bus service into downtown San José. Rates: $4 per day, $60 monthly. See "San Antonio de Belén," under "Escazú and Vicinity" in the Central Highlands chapter.

MOTELS

In Costa Rica, as throughout Latin America, "motels" are explicitly for lovers. Rooms—complete with adult movies, Jacuzzis, and ceiling mirrors that would outshine Las Vegas's five-star hotels—are rented out by the hour. Originally aimed at providing privacy for young couples, today's motels more commonly serve as meeting places for adult trysts. Hence, they're usually hidden behind high walls with private garages for each room to protect guests from inquisitive eyes and chance encounters with the neighbor or spouse. Ooops! Reportedly, many married couples frequent the motels in search of like-minded others seeking an added sense of adventure. They concentrate in the southeast suburb of San Francisco de Dos Ríos.

FOOD

A surprisingly cosmopolitan range of cuisines awaits in San José. With few exceptions, however, you'll pay relatively high prices for a truly good meal. Shrimp and lobster, in particular, will seriously damage your wallet. Expect to pay $10 and up for even modest shrimp cocktails, and at least $15 for lobster. If you're willing to pay these prices, you may as well opt for the best restaurants in town. Chinese restaurants are an exception and offer inexpensive shrimp dishes. Wines and other imported drinks are very expensive, up to triple what you might pay at home.

Don't neglect the many fine **hotel restaurants**. The Hotel Amstel is a favorite for inexpensive lunches; Grano de Oro is a homey treat for those seeking a good meal (eat here once and you may decide to stay); L'Ambiance would be another choice on a more upscale budget. The Bon Vivant in the Hotel Herradura is also particularly notable; in the Cariari Hotel are the Los Vitrales, serving a wide range of continental cuisines, and the Tropical Terrace and Marisquería, serving seafoods. The restaurant of the Hotel Villa Tournon (formerly the Hotel Bougainvillea) is noteworthy as much for its original art—including Chagall—as for its superb cuisine, not least its corvina (sea bass).

Hours are generally 11:30 a.m.-2:30 p.m. and 6-10:30 p.m. *Sodas* generally stay open throughout the day. Call ahead to check.

Smoking is treated as a national right in Costa Rica. Few restaurants boast a nonsmoking section, and few Costa Ricans would give a second thought to lighting up while you're still eating, even if you're at the same table. You might politely ask smokers around you to refrain. Good luck! Failing that, you could grab your throat and fall to the floor in a histrionic choking fit.

Upscale restaurants automatically add a 14.8% service charge to your bill. Refreshingly, **tipping** is not expected. However, a small tip is generally appreciated as a reward for good service and is sure to be remembered if you return.

The **American Research Service Corp.** (Apdo. 1008, Desamparados 2400, tel. 233-5127; in the U.S., P.O. Box 025216, Dept. 316, Miami, FL 33102) publishes a booklet offering discounts of 5-20% at 51 restaurants in San José. Also see "Cost" under "Money" in the On the Road chapter for additional sources of "reduced-rate" meals.

The *Tico Times* and *Costa Rica Today* carry advertisements and restaurant reviews. The following recommendations provide a small sampling of good possibilities.

RESTAURANTS

Costa Rican
You can't go wrong at the **Restaurante Grano de Oro** (tel. 255-3322), in the splendid hotel of that name on Calle 30, Avenidas 2/4. Chef Francis Canal (formerly of Chalet Tirol and Fleur de Lys) has successfully merged Costa Rican into French, conjured the tropical into a European context. Creative interpretations using Costa Rican ingredients include a fabulous spicy enchilada pie ($5), tenderloin in green peppercorn sauce ($11), and sweet curry chicken sprinkled with coconut ($8; Canal needs to add more curry). The menu is quite vast; the prices exceedingly fair. So, too, the specialty cocktails and an array of desserts that are renowned far and wide. You can dine within in a perfectly romantic setting, or alfresco on an intimate patio festooned with epiphytes.

La Cocina de Leña (tel. 255-1360), in the El Pueblo shopping center, in Barrio Tournón, stands out for more traditional Costa Rican fare. Here, you'll dine by candlelight, surrounded by the warm ambience of a cozy rural farmhouse. Dishes include such traditional Tico fare as Creole chicken, *olla de carne* soup, and square *tamales* made with white corn meal, mashed potatoes, and beef, pork, or chicken, wrapped tightly in a plantain leaf. The menu is written on the back of a brown paper bag! Entrees average $10. Its sister restaurant, **El Fogón de Leña** (tel. 233-9964), next door offers slightly more

exotic Costa Rican fare in a setting that resembles a farmhouse (complete with clay-tile floors and even "laundry" from the ceiling). Expect to pay around $20 for a complete dinner.

The open-air **Restaurant Lukas,** also in El Pueblo (tel. 233-8145), serves familiar local cuisine with a dashing touch and stays open until dawn to capture the danced-out patrons of the discos. Light jazz and a guitarist strumming Latin melodies accompany such dishes as mixed tacos and *picadillos* (small chopped-vegetable platter), fried pork, mixed meats, and grilled corvina in garlic butter. Most dishes are prepared al dente over a large grill. Lukas offers a **Pasaporte** ($33) good for a complete dinner (including wine, dessert, and coffee), plus free admission with drinks and snacks to both Chavetas nightclub and Cocoloco discotheque, next door.

Restaurante Regio, on the west side of the Estadio Nacional in Sabana Park (tel. 232-2887), serves rack-roasted meats, chicken, and fish. There's a *chorizo* (carvery). Roasted chicken is the name of the game at **Restaurante Campesino** (Calle 7, Avenidas 2/4, tel. 255-1438 or 222-1170). You can watch your bird being cooked Tico style over wood coals. The restaurant serves its chicken with mashed potatoes (optional). Down-home ambience and good food for less than $4. Chinese dishes are also served.

Las Tunas (tel. 232-6730) is Costa Rica's answer to Tex-Mex for those seeking barbecued beef, seafood, and Tico-Mex fare (tacos, for example, offer shredded beef rolled in a tortilla and deep fried). For what it's worth, Las Tunas has drive-in service. A bar-disco next door stays open until 4 a.m. on weekends. Las Tunas is housed in a large log cabin overlooking Sabana Park, 500 meters west of the ICE Building, in Sabana Norte.

Nearby is **Bembec** (tel. 221-8631), in a columned colonial house at Calle 40 between Paseo Colón and Avenida 4. Popular as both cafe and bar, Bembec serves excellent sea bass in garlic ($5), Mexican dishes ($2 up), and such simple fare as *montaditos,* a filling tortilla sandwich of miscellaneous fillings, including beans and cheese, and meats and salad.

Barbecue Los Anonos (tel. 228-0180), on the road to Escazú, is *the* place for barbecued meats. A healthy (weightwise, that is) steak will

cost less than $10. Closed on Mondays. The **Poás Taberna y Restaurant** (Avenida 7, Calles 3/5, tel. 221-7802) specializes in the "native platter" ($5), including excellent soups and regional dishes from Central America. Exotic tropical foliage and live birds surround diners. The setting truly is a piece of the urban jungle. Don't surprised if Indiana Jones steps in for a drink at the long wooden bar. A waterfall was even planned inside! Amid the palms is a wooden dance floor, and a romantic ill-lit bar upstairs is a great place for sneaking kisses.

If penny-pinching, try **La Vasconia** (Avenida 1, Calle 5), good for an extensive menu of local fare for $2 or less; or **El Cuartel de la Boca del Monte** (tel. 221-0327; Avenida 1, Calles 21/23), popular as a lively bar by night but an excellent source of good food, reasonably priced, by day; or **Restaurante Che Pato** (tel. 234-2866), a cozy, down-home eatery opposite La Toruma Youth Hostel in Los Yoses. The latter has several intimate rooms decorated with posters, prints, and photos from the local theatrical scene. It serves wholesome health foods and mammoth-size *refrescos*. No smoking. Yeah!

I've also heard good things of **Restaurante Bratsi,** in the Nuevo Talamanca Hotel (Avenida 2, Calles 8/10, tel. 233-5033), with cuisine prepared by acclaimed chef Juan de la Cruz Espinoza.

For the most down-home experience of all, check out the **Mercado Central** (see *"Sodas,"* below), but watch for pickpockets.

Spanish

Old wooden wine casks and Moorish screens are part of the appealing decor at **Casino Español,** which recently moved to a new location (Calle 9, Avenidas Central/1, tel. 222-9440). The leather-bound menu contains more than 150 options: everything from octopus in ink sauce ($5) and tongue in prune sauce ($5.50) to more traditional classics such as chateaubriand flambé ($12 for two), lobster thermidor ($21), and Spanish dishes such as *zarzuela de mariscos* and paella a la Valenciana.

Chef Emilio Machado works wonders at the small but beautifully appointed **Marbella Restaurant** (Centro Comercial de la Calle Real in San Pedro, tel. 224-9452). The large selection of seafood dishes includes paella Marbella

(shellfish and sea bass), paella Valenciana (chicken and seafood). The paella Madrilena (rabbit, chicken, and pork) is particularly good.

Restaurant Reggio (tel. 232-2887), opposite the Estadio Nacional in Sabana West, is an elegant place with large horseshoe booths. It's run by Spaniard José Luis Garcia, who boasts among his 70 dishes a famous paella. The special lunch will cost you $4.

Also recommended: **La Masia de Triquell** (Avenida 2, Calle 40, tel. 296-3524; closed Sunday), recommended for its Catalonian-inspired paella and steak-in-garlic ($10 average); and the atmospheric **Goya** (Avenida 1, Calles 5/7, tel. 221-3887), which provides generous *bocas* as well as excellent Spanish cuisine, including a splendid paella plus rabbit in wine, at moderate prices.

Not quite Spanish, but almost, is **Cocina de Borodlino** (Calle 21, Avenidas 6/8), serving excellent, cheap Argentinian *empanadas* to the local crowd.

Mexican

Antojitos (west of Sabana Park, in Rohrmoser, on the road to Pavas, tel. 231-5564) has excellent fare, plus mariachi on Friday and Saturday. Inexpensive yet classy. Antojitos has three other restaurants: in Los Yoses (tel. 225-9525), in Centro Comercial del Sur (tel. 227-4160), and on the road to Tibas (tel. 235-3961).

Restaurante El Tapatio, in the San José 2000 Shopping Center, 100 meters north of Hotel Irazú, offers a $14.50 special: margarita, beer or wine, plus house filet or Mexican entree, coffee, and dessert.

Bar México, on Calle 16 and Avenida 13, is an upscale favorite of the cognoscenti. Live mariarchi music forms a backdrop for excellent Mexican cuisine. Generous *bocas* are offered with drinks at the bar.

Also to consider: **La Hacienda de Pancho** (200 meters east of La Rotonda del Zapote, tel. 224-8261); and **Sus Antonos** (tel. 222-9086), on Paseo Colón and Calles 24/26.

French

Top marks go to the **Restaurante Grano de Oro** (see "Costa Rican," above) for its French-influenced international menu conjured by the former chef for the Hotel Chalet Tirol.

Cognoscenti craving classical French head to **Le Chandelier** (tel. 225-3980), which has moved from Paseo Colón, where it was once a landmark, to San Pedro, in a restored Mediterranean-style mansion complete with beamed ceiling and fireplace, just behind the high-rise ICE Building. It has 10 separate dining areas, including the sculpture garden. The world-class gourmet restaurant is under the watchful eye of chef Claude Dubuis, who conjures up exceptional and imaginative French cuisine featuring imported French mushrooms, stunning sauces, and even Dubuis's own version of typical Costa Rican fare: roasted heart of palm, cream of *pejivalle* soup, *gratin* of corvina with avocado. The restaurant is adorned with murals and the chef-owner's own works of art. Appetizers average $4; entrees range from $8 to $15. Closed Sunday.

La Bastille (Paseo Colón, Calle 22, tel. 222-0243) is the oldest French restaurant in San José. Chef Hans Pulfer produces superb French cuisine. Closed Sunday. Elegant and expensive. **El Jardín de Paris** (Avenida 10, Calle 21, tel. 22-6806) is located in the Casa Matute Gómez, a venerable downtown mansion turned into a complex of bars and eateries. Chef Vincente Fromont whips up classic French dishes that will set you back more than $20 per head for dinner.

Three other highly recommended options for those feeling flush are the cozy **L'Ile de France** (Calle 7, Avenidas Central/2, tel. 222-4241), run by Chef Jean Claude Fromont (vichyssoise, tournedos, and regional dishes are typical); the **Restaurant El Mirador,** on the top floor of the Hotel Aurola Holiday Inn (tel. 233-7233); and **Bromelias** (Calle 23, Avenida 3, tel. 221-3848), with a wide menu, elegant decor, and live music in the Executive Bar of an old customs building. A jacket is in order. Main entrees start at around $10 at all three.

In San Pedro, the tiny and moderately priced **Le Bistro** (200 meters north and 100 meters east of San Pedro church, tel. 253-8062) serves French cuisine Dijon style. Closed Monday.

Italian

The **Balcón de Europa** is one of the oldest (since 1909) and more revered culinary shrines in the country. It recently moved from next to

the Hotel Presidente to Calle 9 and Avenidas Central/1 (tel. 221-4841). Chef Franco Piatti presents moderately priced cuisine from central Italy in an appropriately warm, welcoming Italianate setting of wood-paneled walls festooned with historical photos and framed proverbs. Potted plants abound. You can eat well for less than $10 on steaks, for example, or such superb pasta dishes as the *pasta a la boscaiola*, with tuna, tomatoes, and mushrooms. A bread plate and tangy cheeses are served as *bocas*. At night, a line of tourists often develops—a reflection not so much of food quality, but of recommendations in guidebooks.

Another popular option is the acclaimed **La Piazzetta** (Paseo Colón, Calle 40, tel. 222-7896). Such decadent dishes as risotto with salmon and caviar and filet mignon in white truffle sauce are served in atmospheric surroundings illustrated by authentic Italian paintings. Live music. Closed Sunday, Monday, Tuesday. Three inexpensive options on Paseo Colón are **Ana** (Calles 24/26, tel. 222-6153), with pleasing ambience and the usual Italian fare of lasagne, spaghetti, and veal; **Piccolo Roma** (Calle 24), with home-style cooking; and **Giardina,** a new Italian restaurant on the south side of Sabana Park.

A relatively new kid on the block is **Il Ponte Vecchio** (200 meters west and 25 meters north of San Pedro church, tel. 225-9399). Moderately priced, tasty Italian cuisine cooked with imported Italian ingredients: sun-dried tomatoes, porcini mushrooms, and basil. Of course, there's plenty of Costa Rican inspiration, too. Pastas are homemade by chef Antonio D'Alaimo, who as a child learned to weave culinary magic in the tiny village of Spinoso and, later, in Florence and New York. A Roman arch doorway and a mural of Venice's famous Ponte Vecchio add to the ambience. Closed Wednesday. In the same area is **Ristorante Caruso** (Centro Comercial de la Calle Real in San Pedro, tel. 224-4801), with gnocchi, homemade pastas, and vegetarian dishes.

One of my more moderately priced favorites is **Peperoni** (Rohrmoser/Sabana East, on the road to Pavas, tel. 232-5119), serving superb pastas, pizzas, and roasted meats. Hidden away in the freezer and known only to the cognoscenti is the house liqueur, *eneldo verde,* a tasty,

bright green knock-you-down concoction distilled from sweet green peppers! Try it. It's better than it sounds.

At the other end of San José is, in San Pedro, **Il Pomodoro** (100 meters north of the church, tel. 224-0966), serving authentic Italian food. It's a popular hang-out for university types who seem to favor the pizzas. A meal should cost $4-8.

Emilia Romagna (tel. 233-2843), 25 meters west of Pollo Kentucky on Paseo Colón, is a romantic restaurant that doubles as San José's hippest jazz club. *Tres chic,* as the Jaguars and Mercedes outside attest. Closed Sunday.

Others to consider include **Via Veneto,** in Curridabat (tel. 234-2898). Elegant and moderately priced. Pastries are delicious. **Miro's Bistro** is also recommended for its mix of Italian and Hungarian dishes. This cozy and inexpensive restaurant is next to the railroad tracks, 300 meters west of Pulpería La Luz in Barrio Escalante.

Swiss

Appropriately, the "Switzerland of the Americas" has several Swiss restaurants. **Chalet Suizo** (Avenida 1, Calles 5/7, tel. 222-3118) is the big boy in town, with yummy Swiss and French fondues as well as international specialties such as *rippli mit sauerkraut* (smoked pork chop with sauerkraut) from Germany, coq au vin from France, and *zarzuela de mariscos* from Spain. It's the hot, gooey pot of bubbling cheeses that makes dining at Chalet Suizo so much fun. The beautifully detailed building has a flagstone floor, handsome oak-lined walls, and a massive walk-in brick fireplace decorated with Swiss cowbells and antique armaments. Waiters dress in native Swiss costume. You can't miss it: the delightful exterior looks like a Swiss chalet. Set lunches cost $5. Dinner entrees avarage $10.

Another option is **Zermatt** (Calle 23 and Avenida 11, tel. 222-0604), with its locally famous *fondue bourguignonne* and Chicken Supreme Zermatt. Closed Saturday. Expensive.

Chinese

Before we begin, you should know that "chopsticks" in Spanish is *palillos*. The chopstick-impaired will do fine with silverware.

My favorite Chinese restaurant is the very popular **Tin Jo** (Calle 11, Avenidas 6/8, tel. 221-7605). The decor is quaintly colonial Costa Rican, but the food is distinctly Oriental: exquisitely tasty Mandarin and Sichuan specialties at moderate prices. The booths have waiters' bells. I'm delighted to report that since my first edition, Tin Jo has added **Thai** food!

Next door is the more homey **Don Wang**, serving generous, reasonably priced portions. It offers Taiwanese dishes and small *bocas*. Seafoods are a particular bargain ($4 to $6). Food quality isn't quite up to par with Tin Jo. Pleasing classical music and attentive Chinese owner.

Flor del Loto (opposite Colegio Los Angeles, behind the ICE Building in Sabana Norte, tel. 232-4652) is the place if you like your Chinese food hot and spicy. Mouth-searing Hunan and Sichuan specialties include *mo-shu-yock* (Shi Chuen-style pork) and *ma po tofu* (vegetables, bamboo shoots, and tofu stir-fried in a sizzling hot-pepper oil). Moderate.

Ave Fénix (200 meters west of the San Pedro church, tel. 225-3362) is a very popular Chinese restaurant acclaimed for its original sauces: soy sauce spiced with crushed garlic, minced onion, and sesame oil; and sweet-and-sour sauce with lemon juice and the juice of maraschino cherries. Mmmm! The Taiwanese chef conjures more than 100 entrees that include some exotic offerings as well as staples. In the same area is **Nueva China** (Avenida Central, opposite Banco Popular, tel. 224-4478), an elegant favorite of aficionados of Chinese cuisine, prepared by a chef from Hong Kong. Among its specialties is dim sum, served on weekends. My garlic-honeyed chicken was a winner! Quintessential Oriental decor.

Another acclaimed option is **King's Garden** (tel. 255-3838), on the second floor of the Centro Comercial Yaohan, opposite the Hotel Corobicí. The head chef is from Hong Kong; the menu features many favorites from the city, as well as Cantonese and Sichuan dishes. A set dinner for two costs about $14.

Penny-pinchers might try the **Restaurant Kian Kok** (Calle 1, Avenida Central/2), on the same block as Soda La Perla. Uninspired decor, but hefty portions of Chinese cuisine with a Costa Rican twist—ask for it spicy if that's how

you like it. The **Lai Yuin** restaurant in the Hotel Royal Garden (Calle Central, Avenida Central, tel. 257-0023) serves dim sum on weekends. Many other inexpensive Chinese restaurants are scattered around town. Another good option is **Restaurante Palacio Real** (tel. 235-4487), in Tibas. Farther afield is **Beijing City** in Escazú (tel. 228-6939; closed Monday).

Japanese

Two expensive options—sorry, folks, Japanese cuisine here responds to the law of supply and demand—are the **Sakura** sushi bar and restaurant in the Hotel Herradura (tel. 239-0033, ext. 33; closed Monday), with superb Teppani-style Japanese cooking; and **Fuji,** in the Hotel Corobicí (tel. 232-8122; closed Sunday), with tatami-covered private dining rooms for six.

Korean

Arirang (Paseo Colón, Calles 38/40, tel. 223-2838) caters to those who love grilled eel, *kimch'i, chu'sok,* and other Korean specialties. Inexpensive to moderately priced (most dishes less than $10).

Thai

Tin Jo (see "Chinese," above) introduced Thai food to San José recently. I tried the *pad thai,* which proved "different" from Thai food I'd had before but was, after I got used to it, quite excellent. **El Exotico Oriente** (tel. 232-4444), in Sabana West, followed suit with all the classics from Thailand and Indonesia: *rystaffel, pad thai,* etc. Li-ket, the chef, is Thai, and his dishes have all the sweet zing you expect of Thai cuisine. Top it off with delicious homemade coffee ice-cream.

Steaks

Recommended for charbroiled surf-and-turf for less than $10 is **La Hacienda** (Calle 7, Avenidas Central/2, tel. 223-5493), a renovated barn with rough-hewn beams, walls decorated with sombreros, horseshoes, and paintings, and a fountain fashioned from an antique *paila* (sugar cauldron).

El Chicote (400 meters west of ICE in Sabana Norte, tel. 232-0936) is another lovely restaurant serving chateaubriand, shrimp-stuffed tenderloin, and filet mignon basted with honey

and served with breaded bananas and mashed potatoes. Steaks are cooked over a large open fire. Palms and ferns abound. Nearby is **Los Ranchos** (tel. 232-7757), formerly known as "West Ranch." Prime ribs, meats, and seafood dishes begin at around $6. Meats are served Argentinian-style—*chimichurri*.

"TR's," or **Tony's Ribs** (Avenida 6, Calles 11/13, tel. 223-2957), offers genuine Texas barbecue, marinated beef and pork ribs, and finger-food appetizers. Also downtown is **Kamakiri Steak House** (Avenida 1, Calles 3/5, tel. 223-7171). **Lancer's Steak House** (tel. 222-5938), in the El Pueblo shopping center, Barrio Tournón, has Texas-style cuts from $6, plus seafoods. Similar is **Rias Bajas** (tel. 221-7123), also in El Pueblo. Of course, you can't do any better than **La Esmeralda** (Avenida 2, Calles 5/7, tel. 221-0530) for a unique atmosphere to eat by. And its food ain't bad either (see "Nightlife," below).

Seafood

San José's most celebrated seafood restaurant is the posh **Lobster's Inn** (Paseo Colón and Calle 24, tel. 223-8594), with fresh fish dishes from $8, namesake lobsters more than twice that. Chicken and beef dishes, too. Great things have been written, too, about **Restaraunte Bratsi**, in the Nuevo Hotel Talamanca (Avenida 2, Calles 8/10, tel. 233-5033), where lobster and shrimp can be had for $12.

The **Jacaranda**, in the Hotel Corobicí (tel. 232-8122), and **La Fuente de Mariscos** (tel. 231-0631), in the San José 2000 Shopping Center adjacent to the Hotel Irazú, also specialize in seafoods at moderate prices.

Oceanos (tel. 293-0622), between the Herradura and Cariari hotels, receives rave reviews. I've not eaten here, so can't pass judgment. But its international menu, strong on seafood, is apparently superbly executed.

Vegetarian

San José is well blessed with monuments to healthy dining. Perhaps the best known is **Soda Vishnu**, with three locations (Avenida 1, Calles 1/3; Calle 14, Avenida Central/2; and Calle 1, Avenida 4). Meals are generous in size and low in price. Get there early for a seat. Glaring neon lights, sure, but who can argue with a tasty, filling meal for $2. A sibling, **Restaurante Vishnu**

(Avenida 1, Calles 1/3, tel. 222-2549), is a chip off the old block: great health-food breakfasts.

Somewhat more upscale and very popular, **Mordisco,** in a palm-filled courtyard at Paseo Colón, Calles 22/24 (tel. 255-2448), conjures such delicious and elegant dishes as cashew chicken and corvina in heart of palm sauce. Try its desserts, including fresh-fruit mousses. Servings are on the small side, but very tasty. Dishes can run up to $10. Closed Sunday.

Two blocks east of the Jade Museum is **Don Sol** (Avenida 7, Calle 15), inexpensive, with a pleasing ambience and totally macrobiotic dishes, including a filling *plato fuerte* (lunch of the day). The delicious fruit salad is particularly recommended. A more upscale, bohemian macrobiotic restaurant is **La Mazorca** (100 meters north and 200 meters east of San Pedro Church, San Pedro, tel. 224-8069), a favorite of the university crowd. You can feast on superb health food and fresh-baked breads and desserts for $5. Closed Sunday.

Also try **La Macrobótica** (Avenida 1, Calles 11/15), **Soda Yure** (Avenida 2, Calle 3), **La Nutrisoda** (Calle 3, Avenida 2, tel. 255-3959), with homemade natural ice cream a sure draw, and **Shakti** (Calle 13, Avenida 8).

Pizza

Many Italian restaurants serve pizza. "Dedicated" pizza palaces include **Valerio's,** in Los Yoses, which also has a highly recommended lasagne and good desserts. **Pizza Hut** has a franchise, with outlets at Calle 4, Avenidas Central/2, and Paseo Colón, Calle 28. Also try **San Remo** (Calle 2, Avenidas 3/5); **Pizzería da Pino,** formerly Piccola Roma, (Avenida 2, Calle 24, tel. 223-4985), serving a range of tasty Italian dishes in a down-home Italian setting; and **Pizza Metro** (Avenida 2, Calles 5/7). **Pizza Pizza** is housed in a beautiful, ochre-colored Georgian-style building at the end of Paseo Colón, opposite the Hotel Corobicí. Downtown you'll find **Pizza Pucci** (tel. 255-0998) at Calle 6 and Avenidas 4/6; and **Mr. Pizza** (tel. 223-1221) at Avenida 1, Calles 7/9. The latter is San José's most venerable pizza parlor. A bargain!

Other

At cozy **Ambrosia** (75 meters east of Banco Popular in San Pedro, tel. 253-8012), chef Janie

Murray conjures up soufflés, quiches, and other moderately priced vegetarian and nonvegetarian dishes. Also in San Pedro is **La Galería** (125 meters west of the ICE Building, tel. 234-0850), famed for its sauces complementing continental cuisine with a heavy Teutonic slant. Soothing classical music. Very popular—reservations essential. Closed Sunday. Your bill should come in at under $10.

If South American is your bag, check out **Machu Picchu** (Calle 32, Avenidas 1/3, tel. 222-7384), with delicious authentic Peruvian dishes and pisco sours and *spicy* sauces! Particularly noteworthy seafood includes the *picante de mariscos* (a seafood casserole with onions, garlic, olives, and cheese), enjoyed in a suitably nautical ambience. Moderately priced (some potato entrees are less than $4; garlic octopus is $5).

Beirut (Avenida 1, Calle 32, tel. 257-1808), a stone's throw away, brings a taste of the Levant to San José with noteworthy Middle Eastern specialties such as shish kebob and falafel created by Chef Tony Mouakar. Other irresistible dishes include *michi malfuf* (stuffed cabbage) and *kafta naie* (marinated ground beef). Open Tues.-Sat.; there's a belly-dancing show nightly at 8 p.m. On a similar theme are **Las Pirámides** (tel. 257-8818), on Paseo Colón, serving Lebanese and Middle Eastern dishes; and **Lubnan** (tel. 257-6071), a Lebanese restaurant on Paseo Colón and Calles 22/24.

SODAS—INEXPENSIVE DINING

Sodas—cheap snack bars serving typical Costa Rican fare—are a dime a dozen downtown. You can usually fill up for $2. They're good for mixing with the "working classes."

HEARTY LUNCHES UNDER $2

Many eateries serve a hearty, all-inclusive *almuerzo ejecutivo*, or businessman's lunch special, on which you can fill your stomach for 200-250 *colones* ($1.20-1.50). Look for a hand-lettered sign in the window announcing an *almuerzo, plato del día,* or *casado*. Lunch specials normally contain vegetables, plus a meat, fish, or chicken dish, and most often a natural fruit drink. You have dozens of inexpensive restaurants and sodas to choose from.

Most big corporations and government buildings also have cafeterias for their staffs. Many are open to the public and offer a *plato del día* for as little as $1.

Among the more popular places are:

ABC, Avenida Central, Calles 9/11. A three-course Chinese meal with fried rice and a meat dish with mixed vegetables costs 200 *colones*.

Central Market, Calle 6, Avenida Central. You'll find many *sodas* and cheap restaurants in this labyrinth, all serving specials for 200 *colones* or less.

Chaplin, Calle 33, Avenida Central. This popular outdoor cafe has a steak-and-vegetables *casado* dish for 230 *colones*.

Fogata, Avenida Central, Calle 13. A superb chicken special, with wood-roasted chicken, fries, corn tortillas, and drink costs 250 *colones*.

Frenchy's, Calle 33, Avenidas 2/4. Frenchy's even has a hamburger special, including fries and a papaya-banana drink, for 160 *colones*.

Mino's Express, Avenida 7, Calles 9/11. The spaghetti *plato del día* with *frijoles molidos* (mashed black beans) costs 160 *colones*, and pork-chop *casados* are 230 *colones*.

Pollo Campesino, Calle 7, Avenidas 2/4. For 225 *colones* you get wood-roasted chicken, mashed potatoes, and *frijoles molidos*.

Soda Tico, Avenida 3, Calles 3/5. Mixed-plate specials for 180 *colones* feature fresh-squeezed orange juice.

Soda Winny, Calle 11, Avenidas Central/1. A tiny *soda* offering meals with good soups and stews for 180 *colones*.

Toruma, Avenida Central, Calles 33/55. The youth-hostel restaurant offers a complete lunch with salad, main course, and dessert for 225 *colones*.

Vishnu, Avenida 1, Calles 3/5. San José's most popular vegetarian restaurant has a five-vegetable special for 220 *colones*.

(previous page) view across the Gulf of Papagayo from Ocotal (John Anderson);
(this page, top) Surfing is popular on both coasts; (above, left) The big one that didn't get away;
(above, right) Costa Rica's beauty comes in many forms (all photos by John Anderson)

My favorite is **Soda La Perla** (tel. 222-7492), on an always-lively junction facing Parque Central (Avenida Central, Calle 1). It's particularly popular with the after-theater crowd from the Teatro Melico Salazar, next door. Basic but good-value, filling Costa Rican fare: everything from a refreshing *refresco* to *gallo pinto, arroz con pollo,* and *torta española,* an inch-thick omelette with everything but the kitchen sink. Soups are outstanding. Free *bocas* are served with drinks. Friendly waitresses. Virtually everything is below $5.

Two blocks north is the **Soda Palace,** highly popular with both locals—some a little eccentric—and budget travelers. The garish lighting is enough to scare me off. Often noisy. Mariachis sometimes appear impromptu. Slightly more expensive than La Perla. Both are open 24 hours.

Also nearby, at Avenida Central and Calles Central/2, is another local favorite: **Manolo's.** Try the *churros,* greasy Mexican donuts, at the streetside stall. Upstairs you can fill up on sandwiches and other fare for less than $5; the third-story is more elegant and double the price. On the northeast corner of the Plaza de Cultura is **Soda B&B,** a popular haunt for both locals and tourists; it serves American and *típico* fare.

Other popular *sodas* include **Soda Central** (Avenida 1, Calles 3/5), where *gallo pinto* still costs about $1; **Soda Tapia,** at the end of Avenida 2, opposite Sabana; the small **Soda La Casita** (Avenida 1, Calles Central/1), with its homey feel; and **Soda Ciudades de Italia** (Calle 6, Avenida 1), the latter a good place to see some of the local machismo color. Two bargain places close to the Toruma Youth Hostel include **Soda Magaly** (Avenida Central, Calle 23) and **Soda Pulpería** (Avenida 3, Calle 23), with meals for about $2.

You have another 1,001 to choose from, many in the Mercado Central (Avenidas Central/1 and Calles 6/8), which is filled to overflowing with inexpensive eateries. The market is a bustling beehive, and *sodas* are often packed. Late afternoon is a good time to sit down. Remember not to display jewelry, wads of money, etc. as pickpockets are common here.

CAFES AND PASTRY SHOPS

The place to see and be seen as a tourist is the **Café Parisienne,** the open-air terrace cafe fronting the Gran Hotel. Besides snacks and coffee, it serves full lunches (Costa Rican cuisine) at a reasonable price. The hustle and bustle of the Plaza de la Cultura provides never-ending entertainment while you sip on a cappuccino or beer. My favorite daytime hangout!

Outdoing all other contenders for most refined coffee shop in the country is the **Café Ruiseñor** inside the foyer of the National Theater. Marble-topped tables, magnificent tilework, a gilded and mirrored serving counter, classical music, and artwork adorning the walls are topped by tempting desserts.

The coffee renaissance is catching up with Costa Rica. **La Esquina del Café** (tel. 257-9868, on Avenida 9 and Calle 3), is dedicated to serving fine coffees and has free tastings and an excellent selection of pastries. Two other pleasing options are **Café Gourmet** (Avenida 9, Calle 3), and **Trangada Coffee Shop,** directly opposite The Bookshop, on Avenida 1 and Calles 1/3. The latest hit, however, is **La Maga** (one block east of the church on the main road in San Pedro), a trendy cafe that serves coffee to an art-thirsty crowd. Magazines from around the world keep the literary crowd happy. The cafe shows films and rents videos and CDs. An experimental theater and art workshop is planned. And the cafe offers computer buffs access to the Internet over a cup of fine blend. The members-only ($25) cafe is so popular that lines form to get in. Yes, sandwiches and desserts are served.

If you've a sweet tooth, check out **La Miel** (tel. 223-3193, at Avenida 6, Calles 13/15); a delightful pastry shop offering cheap yet delicious desserts and pastries. Likewise, try **Panadería Schmidt** (Avenida 2, Calle 4 and Avenida Central, Calle 11), while **Churrería Manolo's** (Avenida Central, Calles Central/2, tel. 221-2041) is known for its *churros,* or cream-filled doughnuts.

Most ubiquitous of coffee shops is **Spoon.** Over the past decade, a small take-out bakery run by four women has grown into a chain with four locations in the metropolitan area. The original shop one block off Avenida Central in Los Yoses (tel. 224-0328) was joined by another on Avenida Central near the Plaza de la Cultura (221-6702), a third in Rohrmoser (tel. 231-6359), and one in the town of Heredia. In addition to desserts, Spoon serves sandwiches, salads,

lasagnes, soups, *empañadas* (pastries stuffed with chicken and other meats), and *lapices,* a Costa Rican equivalent of submarines.

Bromelias Cafe and Grill, kitty-corner to the old Atlantic Railway Station (Calle 23, Avenida 3, tel. 221-3848), is also much more than a cafe. Creative dishes—corvina with avocado and *beurre blanc,* and steak Diane with a green pepper sauce light on the palate—rival those of the better restaurants. Nearby, opposite the station, at Calle 21 and Avenida 3, is **Café Verde.**

Los Yoses has several good coffee shops, among them **Azafrán, Giacomán,** and **Café Ruiseñor,** which has outdoor tables.

Note: Most Ticos drink their coffee black. If you take your coffee with milk, make sure you tell the waiter to pour only a little—*poquito*—or you'll end up with half milk (albeit hot) and half coffee. Few cafes serve decaffeinated coffee or herbal teas.

If you're craving ice cream, check out **Baloons,** a new chain with several outlets nationwide, including on Avenida 2 (Calles Central/1), and Calle 5 and Avenida 1.

FAST FOOD

There's no shortage of American fast-food joints for those who hanker for a taste of back home. Inevitably, they have become icons for Tico teenagers, who pay homage here. **Mc-Donald's** has outlets at Calle 4, Avenidas Central/1, and on Avenida Central, on the north side of the Plaza de la Cultura. Its Costa Rican

clones are **Archi's** (serving fried chicken as well as burgers), also on the north side of the plaza; **A/S,** open 24 hours on Calle 1 and Avenida 2; and **Woopy's,** on Avenida 2 and Calle 2. **Hardee's** is at Calle 1 and Avenidas Central/1, and **Burger King** has an outlet on the east side of Plaza de la Cultura, opposite the entrance to the Gold Museum, and another next to Soda Palace, on Avenida 2 and Calle Central.

Colonel Sanders **(Pollo Kentucky)** is represented at Avenida 2, Calle 6; at Avenida 3, Calles 1/3; on Paseo Colón and Calles 32/34; and in Los Yoses at Avenida Central and Calle 31. The latter two outlets are landmarks that everyone knows. The Nicaraguan equivalent, **Rosti Pollo,** is represented on Avenida Central, in San Pedro. Tasty and cheap.

Every city should have a **Taco Bell,** too, of course, and San José is no exception. It's at Calle 5 and Avenidas Central/2. The local equivalent is **Don Taco,** at Avenida 1, Calle 2.

Friday's Restaurant (tel. 224-5934), in the suburb of La Paulina, bills itself as the "Great American Bistro." Tex-Mex here, folks, plus your favorite cocktails. It's very popular with the younger crowd.

BREAKFAST

San José is sadly lacking in good breakfast haunts. *The* place for a late breakfast is definitively the open-air Café Parisienne of the Gran Hotel (see above).

NIGHTLIFE

If anyone tells you that San José is a city of hearth and home, not one that prizes nightlife, he's dead wrong. True, many Josefinos would rather cozy up behind closed doors than paint the town red. But whatever your nocturnal craving, San José has something to please. Look for a copy of *Info-Spectacles,* which lists forthcoming music and entertainment events; it's published each Tuesday and can be obtained at bars, nightclubs, and from the ICT office. The *Tico Times, Costa Rica Today,* and the "Viva" section of *La Nación* have comprehensive listings of what's on in San José, from classical symphony and theater to cinema showings, concerts, and discos hotter than the tropical night. Many of the deluxe hotels also host concerts, though the hotel bars are generally soulless.

In fact, San José's entertainment is coming on strong. Casinos are multiplying. A nascent blues and jazz scene is gaining strength. A handful of upscale men's nightclubs now proffer burlesque shows. And suddenly bohemian areas such as San Pedro, the university turf east of downtown, are being likened to New York's Greenwich Village in the '60s for their bohemian bars and clubs.

With the exception of one or two areas (particularly around the Coca-Cola bus station and any of the city parks), walking is generally safe at night. Be aware, however, that muggings are on the increase and you should always use common-sense caution (see "Safety" in the On the Road chapter). If you have any qualms, consider using the **Night Life Tour Service** (tel. 256-3807).

BARS AND NIGHTCLUBS

There's a bar on every block, or at least it seems that way. The liveliest, most touristed bars congregate around Gringo Gulch (Calles 5/9, Avenidas Central/3) and in San Pedro, on San José's eastern margin. It's generally quite acceptable for women to drink at bars and nightclubs, at least until midnight, when many local women slip home for an unwritten curfew. Farther out from the center, bars devolve into the spit-and-sawdust variety, women are few and far between, and gringos are virtually unknown. The classic "local" *pulpería* often doubles as a combination of bar, family room, and front porch.

Many bars stay open until the last bleary-eyed patrons go home . . . which could be about the time the sun comes up!

All but the fancier bars offer locally brewed beers for about $1 (prices are generally higher in the Gringo Gulch area), and Heineken and other imported beers are usually available. *Bocas* (bar snacks) are often served free; sometimes a small charge applies. Don't be afraid to ask. Penny-pinchers should stay away from hard liquors and foreign wines, which carry a hefty price tag, and stick with *guaro,* the local sugar-cane firewater that has been likened to everything from a cross between tequila and vodka to a mix of nail-polish remover and turpentine. I like it, particularly chilled or with Café Rica (coffee liqueur) on the rocks. Funnily, I don't recall having had a hangover from it . . . but then the lack of recollection may be one of its nasty side effects!

La Esmeralda
Perhaps the best-known San José institution is La Esmeralda (Avenida 2, Calles 5/7, tel. 221-0503). This lively 109-year-old restaurant and bar is headquarters of the mariachis' union. On any night you may count 50 flamboyantly dressed mariachis wandering through the high-ceilinged ballroom. They warm up to applause from the diners while awaiting calls to action to serenade on some lover's behalf or to enliven a birthday party or other event: the telephone rings, a mariachi band is requested, and off the band goes. The bands expect tips or will charge a set fee per song. It is perfectly acceptable to decline a song if a band approaches your table. A house specialty is the mixed *boca* plate. Stays open past 4 a.m.

Casa Matute Gómez

This beautiful building, formerly the home-in-exile of Venezuelan dictator Juan Vincente Matute Gómez on the corner of Avenida 10 and Calle 21, was recently restored to former glory and turned into a complex of bars and restaurants connected by wide corridors and stately stairways. Downstairs, three bars merge together: the **Vino Bar** with more than 50 different wines available by the glass; the **Whiskey Bar,** where Dutch owner Peder Kolind intends to serve more than 100 brands; and the **Gran Bar.** Here, too, is the **Café Matute** for coffee lovers, and the Jardín de Paris French restaurant. Upstairs you'll find the romantic and elegant **Salon Caracas** hosting live music, and the **Terraza Bar** boasting great views. A minimum charge of $5 applies (tel. 222-6806, fax 257-9752). While here, take time to learn a little of the colorful history of the building and particularly of the somewhat sordid doings of Matute Gómez.

Gringo Gulch

In the area known as Gringo Gulch, virtually every bar that attracts gringos attracts, too, its share of Ticas, a goodly percentage being prostitutes, who face little stigma and hardly raise an eyebrow in liberal Costa Rica.

Key Largo (Calle 7, Avenidas 1/3, tel. 221-0277), once the most colorful bar in San José and one of the city's best-known nocturnal landmarks, has lost its gleam of late. A cross between an elegant Victorian bordello and a raffish Western saloon, this lively bar, housed in a handsome colonial mansion, is a favorite of voyeuristic tourists and anyone with prurient interests. Female tourists and couples also enjoy Key Largo, if for no more than an eyebrow-raising entree to a more rakish side of Costa Rican life. Three large rooms have ceilings sculpted in Tudor fashion and a dark-wood oval bar. There's live music, dancing in a separate room, and cable TV above the bars. Many of the characters propping up the bar could have stepped straight out of a Hemingway novel. The hassle-free atmosphere is very comfortable and lighthearted. Old ladies move among the crowd selling roses. Open through 5 a.m. Cover charge $3.50. Beers cost around $2.

Happy Days is a narrow bar on two levels, next door to Key Largo. The bar gets lively enough on weekends, but Key Largo has more atmosphere. No cover charge. The garishly lit **Chelle's Bar** (Calle 9 and Avenida Central, tel. 221-1369) is open 24 hours. Despite its reputation as a longstanding local favorite, I find it has no great appeal. **Chelle's Taberna,** around the corner on Avenida Central, is marginally more appealing. One block away is **Lucky's Piano Blanco Bar** (Avenida Central, Calle 7, tel. 222-8385), with ESPN on TV, and live piano music. **Tropical Tiny's** (Avenida 2, Calles 7/9) also shows ESPN and CNN on three large TV screens and is understandably popular with North American tourists and expat residents. It gets packed during major sporting events, particularly during Super Bowl. Its St. Patrick's Day party is also legendary.

Nashville South (Calle 5, Avenidas 1/3, tel. 233-1988) caters to country-and-western fans. Around the corner on Avenida 1 (Calles 5/7) is **Pat Dunn's Bar** (formerly "The New Nashville South"), whose claim to fame is that it possesses the longest bar in Costa Rica. Saloon-style swinging doors and Jimmy Buffett tunes drive in the down-home feel. Two blocks east and south is **Charleston** (Calle 9, Avenidas 2/4), offering pleasant 1920s quasi-Deep South decor replete with a stereo pumping out jazz classics and live jazz on weekends ($2).

One block south of Key Largo is the **Bikini Club.** A narrow bar at the front shows risque movies on TV screens above the bar. The barmaids, appropriately, are bikini-clad. Upstairs has striptease. No cover charge; beers $2.

If this is all too much, check out the **Amstel Hotel Bar** (Calle 7, Avenidas 1/3, tel. 222-4622),

a comfortable place for a quiet drink. Even better is the **Blue Marlin Bar** in the Hotel Del Rey (Calle 9, Avenida 1). Fishermen particularly gather here to tell each other big lies, and the place has been adopted as the unofficial expatriate gathering spot. ESPN and MTV show on TV. Guaranteed to be lively, helped along by the flirtatious local lasses. Across the way is **Roger's Bar,** well-lit, intimate, and another popular drinking joint. One block west, between Calles 5/7, is **Yesterday's** (tel. 233-1988), where you can play darts or backgammon, watch a weekly comedy and magic act, or simply listen to the '60s and '70s oldies over a drink or two.

Where the Locals Go

To mingle with the locals, poke your nose inside **Soda Palace,** on Avenida 2 opposite Parque Central (Calle 2, tel. 221-3441). Supposedly, the 1948 Revolution was planned here over beers and *bocas*. The *soda*-cum-watering hole is popular with colorful local characters and budget travelers as well as the odd bohemian intellectual. I find its garish fluorescent lighting and cold ambience totally unappealing. However, there's no doubting it does have character: it's noisy with debate, arguments, and mariachi music.

For a slightly more upscale experience in a down-home setting, head to hip **El Cuartel de la Boca del Monte** (Avenida 1, Calles 21/23, tel. 221-0327), which is a very popular hangout for young Josefinos and the late-night, post-theater set who crowd elbow to elbow. The brick-walled bar is justly famous for its 152 inventive cocktails, often served to wild ceremony and applause. It's a restaurant by day. Monday and Wednesday the bar packs 'em in with live music. A great place for singles who wish to meet Ms. or Mr. Right.

Close by is **Akelare** (Calle 21, Avenidas 4/6), a sprawling old house with secluded alcoves and backyard garden, and a venue for live bands on weekends.

In April 1995 I discovered the newly opened **Cocktail's,** opened and run by Soley and Mayra Starson, from Sweden. The place, kitty-corner to Super Triangulo, in Pavas, attracts a more intellectual crowd mingling locals, expats, and plenty of foreign tourists. Open Tues.-Sunday. Intellectuals also gather to sup at **La Villa** (tel. 225-9612), 100 meters north of the Banco Anglo

in San Pedro. The atmospheric bar drips with political posters and understandably draws leftists who will massage your brain with a healthy discourse on the contemporary political scene. Another popular spot, nearby in Los Yoses but at the other end of the spectrum, is **Benigan's,** one of San José's trendiest spots for the younger crowd. Its eclectic decor keeps you amused. Noisy and *very* lively. Cover charge on Friday ($2.50) is worth three beers.

In San Pedro there's **El Cocodrilo** (opposite Banco Anglo, tel. 225-3277), a popular hangout for university students. A stuffed crocodile presides menacingly over the bar. If you tire of the video screen don't be shy to step onto the dance floor. **Balearas,** also in San Pedro (100 meters west of the Mas x Menos), has backgammon tourneys on Monday, plus live jazz, and *peñas* with Latin folk music. **Los Andes** (opposite the entrance to the University of Costa Rica, in San Pedro) offers South American folk music. **Tequila Willy's** is a hip Mexican bar and restaurant with a hip clientele and occasional live bands. Nearby is **Contravía** (tel. 253-6989), 100 meters south of Nueva China restaurant, another favorite of university students, who add to the bohemian atmosphere. Contravía has live bands on Friday and Saturday and specializes in Nueva Trova (modern Latin folk music). Reservations recommended.

Last but not least in Los Yoses, between downtown and San Pedro, is **Río** (tel. 225-8371), a lively American-diner-style place bristling with TVs showing music videos. No dancing, but a hip young crowd gathers, especially for occasional all-day musical events when the street outside is closed and the party spills out onto the road. Often open until the last guest goes home!

In the northern suburbs, **Bar México** (kitty-corner to the Barrio México church, Calle 16 and Avenida 13, tel. 221-8461) serves excellent *bocas* and Mexican cuisine washed down with superb margaritas and mariachi music. The surrounding area is run-down, but the bar and restaurant—upgraded under the ownership of Joachim Hofer—is full of life and extremely popular with the well-heeled cognoscenti. Thursday is Singles' Night. Music videos light up a giant screen. Nearby is **Liverpool** (500 meters north of La Granja, Barrio México), which plays oldies: mostly Motown and blues. Also playing

1950s and '60s oldies, and closer to town, is **Rock Cafe** on Paseo Colón. Heavy-metal freaks should head to **Bar Rock,** in San Pedro.

"Gentlemen's Nightclubs"

San José has acquired an upscale, no-holds-barred nightlife in the past few years, exemplified by three "gentlemen's clubs" where women amply display their attributes in "dental floss" string bikinis—*tangas*—that would fit in a matchbox and are really no more than two dots and a dash! The three clubs are popular with foreign businessmen, monied Ticos, and even couples. After a visit here you'll have no doubts that Ticos—male and female alike—enjoy celebrating the body as much as the mind.

EL PUEBLO

What San José may lack in the picturesque is made up for at El Pueblo shopping center (Centro Comercial) in Barrio Tournón, a recently constructed and endearing entertainment and shopping complex pleasingly designed to resemble a Spanish colonial town. Wrought-iron lamps, whitewashed walls, red-tiled roofs, and lofty beamed ceilings are the order of the day. El Pueblo's warren of alleys harbors fashionable upscale restaurants, boutiques, and lively discos, which bring a trendy new flavor to its humbler surroundings. It even has a skating rink. There are maps. However, the only ones with accompanying directories are located beside Cocoloco (on the steps leading up to Calle 16) and next to the Tango Bar Che Molinari. For information, call 257-0277.

Getting There: The Calle Blancos bus departs from Calles 1/3 and Avenida 5. Get off a half a kilometer after crossing the river. El Pueblo—now a landmark—is close enough to walk from downtown in 15 minutes. Use a taxi by night. Taxis to and from El Pueblo often overcharge: settle on a fee before getting into your cab ($1 to downtown hotels, $2 to Sabana would be appropriate at night; slightly more after midnight). There's free parking and 24-hour security.

Visa a Cocoloco (tel. 233-8145, 233-2309, 222-8782, fax 233-6410) is a "passport" ($33) good for free admission to Chavetas (including beverages and snacks), Lukas (including dinner with wine), and Cocoloco (including beverages).

Bars

Babaloo Bar (tel. 222-5746) hums well into the night, from 9:30 p.m. until dawn. Bossa nova on Tuesday, live music on Wednesday, Latin jazz fusion on Thursday, and Brazilian on Friday and Saturday. Closed Sunday. **Bar Tango Che Molinari** (tel. 226-6904) is a tiny, smoke-filled hole-in-the-wall that is something of a San José institution. Oscar Molinari plays hot-blooded Argentinian tangos to match the blood-red curtains. Opens at 8:30 p.m. Closed Sunday.

Chavetas (tel. 233-2309) is also popular for its live music. The Chavetas Group performs Tues.-Sat.; the violinist María Lourdes Lobo performs on Wednesday. There's also a comedy routine Friday and Saturday at 11 p.m. **El Escondite de Morgan,** otherwise known as Jerry Morgan's Piano Bar, has—you guessed it—live piano music. **Los Balcones** (tel. 223-3704) is a barbecue restaurant that features live music. The Bolivian folk group Khrisol, the Peruvian group Musica Andea, and the Cuban group Nueva Trova often play in the small bar. No cover. **Salon Musical Lety's** (tel. 273-4236) also has live Latin music.

Restaurants

Pick of the restaurants includes **Rías Bajas** (tel. 233-3214; closed Sunday), one of the city's finest seafood restaurants, and **La Cocina de Leña** (tel. 255-1360), whose exceptionally good traditional Costa Rican dishes are enhanced by the warm and welcoming surrounds (see review under "Restaurants" in the "Food" section). **Lukas** (open 24 hours) also serves typical Costa Rican cuisine. There are many more to choose from.

Discos

Cocoloco (tel. 222-8782) is well established as one of the hottest spots in town, with two dance floors and live bands on weekdays. A two-hour comedy show is offered nightly at 6 p.m. Closed Monday and Sunday. Virtually next door is **Infinito** (tel. 223-2195), another in spot guaranteed to get your hips and feet moving with a choice of three dance floors playing *salsa*, rock, and Latin sounds. **La Plaza Disco Club** (tel. 233-5516), in front of El Pueblo, has live music every Thursday. Two others to consider are **Choza Recuerdo** (tel. 223-2195) and **Kakatua** (tel. 233-3288), which features live reggae and calypso.

Josephine's (Avenida 9, Calles 2/4, tel. 257-2269) is Costa Rica's original answer to the Moulin Rouge; this lavishly decorated Gentleman's Supper Club promises the "splendor of Paris with a Latin flavor." It's a sister club to the famous original in Panamá City. Exotic high-heeled dancers gaudily feathered in ostrich plumes and scant else perform presentations called *San José Nights* and *Panamá Nights*. The floor shows have reportedly grown more risque of late. They even advertise "Erotic Dancing in our Hot Tub." There're private VIP rooms and private parking. Hours: 9 p.m.-2 a.m. nightly except Sunday.

Night Club Olympus, in the same vein as Josephine's and attempting to outdo it (Calle Central, Avenida 5, tel. 223-4058), promises "the most gorgeous dancers in the country" and three VIP rooms overlooking the main stage. Voluptuous Vegas hedonism really has come to Costa Rica!

Last but not least of the trio is **Hollywood International** (400 meters west of McDonald's La Sabana, tel. 232-8932, fax 296-1483), which, not to be outdone, boasts the "best show in Latin America." The show here is about as risque as things can get west of Bangkok. If you go, pack wads of money . . . and scrutinize your bill thoroughly. I had $40 tacked onto my tab for spurious miscellany! Open Mon.-Sat. 9 p.m. to 4 a.m.

Reportedly another club in this genre, though less swanky, is **Casa de Muñecas** ("Doll's House"), one of San José's original exotic dance clubs.

Red-Light District

The so-called red-light district lies south of Parque Central, between Calles Central-8 and Avenidas 6-10. It hardly deserves the moniker. A dozen bars and clubs are interspersed with hotels, shops, homes, and street stalls. It's a modestly run-down area, with a large number of homeless on the streets. Be cautious at night! Girlfriends and wives often accompany their men to the bars and men's striptease clubs.

Metro Metropolitan (Calle Central, Avenidas 6/8) is one of only two cinemas I know in San José that show sex on screen. There may be more. Two blocks west of the Metro is **Femme Internacional** bar and cocktail lounge, with a naked lady on the sign in case you miss the point (Avenida 8, Calles 2/4). Next door, on the corner, is **Salon Típico 77,** with a bar in front and dancing in the rear. Flashing neon signs advertise strip shows at **Tabernas Juniors** (Calle 2, Avenida 8/10), the most substantial of the strip joints. Half a block south is the **Night Club Molino Rouge.**

Nightclub Los Globos (Avenida 10, Calles 6/8), in an aged colonial building; **Tabernas Colt** (Avenida 6, Calles 6/8); **Tabernas Daiquiri** (Avenida 8, Calle Central/2); and **Tabernas El Azteca** (corner of Calle 2 and Avenida 8) all offer striptease, as does the **Arcadas** nightclub (Calle 2, Avenidas 8/10), which also has male strippers for the female crowd on Wednesday (see below). Other lively bars include **Taberna Rex** (Avenida 6, Calles Central/2) and **Bar Atlas** (Avenida 4, Calles 2/4).

Strictly for Women

Male strip shows for women—called *maripepinos,* a naughty play on words combining the Spanish word for cucumber with the name of the cabaret dancer Maripepa—are enjoying popularity, despite having provoked a hypocritical public debate as to the morality of male strip shows when they first appeared in 1992. *Maripepinos* perform on Saturday at **Kilates Discoteque** in Tibas, and Wednesday at **Arcadas** nightclub, which has female strippers on other nights of the week. Unlike some of the female strip joints, male strippers are not for sale at the end of the show, nor do they remove their G-strings. However, for a bill slipped into a bikini, eager women may hop on stage to dance with the macho men of their choice.

DISCOS

Josefinos love to dance. Their first love is *salsa,* but you'll find a gamut of discos playing hip-hop, rap, new wave, reggae, and almost any other dance music that gets you on your feet. Discos stay open later than is usual in North America, often not closing until dawn. Most apply some sort of unwritten dress code. Shorts are never allowed, and jeans at some are definitely not kosher. Call ahead to check. Most discos charge a cover, generally about $2-5. Several of

the most popular discos—including Cocoloco and Infinito (described by one reader as "more an upscale dance club for couples")—are found at El Pueblo shopping center (see special topic "El Pueblo").

Many bars also have music and dancing. See "Bars" (above) and "Music" (below).

Club Panda, a large disco on Paseo Colón, is popular with the surfing set, no doubt because of the screen showing surfing videos. No cover charge except when live bands play. Also on Paseo Colón is **Members** (second floor of Centro Colón, tel. 223-4911), a new kid on the block, playing everything from rock to *salsa,* plus live music by the band Los Bandoleros. **O Key** (Calle 4, Avenidas 6/8) is also new. **New Leonardo's** is in the same building (tel. 223-7310).

A favorite of the younger crowd is **Disco Salsa 54** (Calle 3, Avenidas 1/3, tel. 233-3814), Costa Rica's answer to New York's snooty Studio 54, with one exception; here you can get in! (No! Don't expect any of the infamous "goings-on" of the club in New York.) It's two-discos-in-one. One favors romantic Latin sounds; the other is World Beat and techno. Live bands on Monday. The same owners operate **Zadidas** (200 meters north of the National Theater, tel. 221-4454), playing techno and reggae. Also downtown is **El Tunel de Tiempo** (Avenida Central, Calles 11/13), with a light show as loud as the music.

La Torre (Calle 7, Avenidas Central/1), also known as Tonite, is for the gay crowd, although everyone else is welcome. It's a popular dance spot, too, for women who don't want to be hassled by men trying to pick them up. Musical taste is heavy on funk and rap. High energy and fun!

If Caribbean riffs are your thing, check out the **Showbar** (Calle 7 and Avenidas 1/2), which has reggae on Wednesday. One of San José's most famous discos, **Dynasty** (Centro Comercial del Sur, near the Pacific Railway Station, tel. 226-5000), also plays reggae. This is the place to get down to James Brown, Hammer, and funk. A relatively young crowd, but soul and R&B don't get better than this. **Parthenon** is another disco in Centro Comercial del Sur.

Across the street from the El Pueblo shopping center is **La Plaza** (tel. 233-5516), where you can practice *merengue* and *salsa* on its massive dance floor.

Discos farther out include **Las Tunas,** in Sabana Norte; **Equus** (tel. 323-6966), on the road to Tibas; **Kahlúa** (tel. 253-5181), in Plaza del Sol, in Curridabat; **Kilates** (tel. 240-3215), in Tibas; and **Castro's** (tel. 223-8577), in Barrio México.

CINEMAS

If you missed that Hollywood blockbuster back home, you can catch it in San José. More than a dozen movie houses show American and other foreign movies with English soundtrack and Spanish subtitles. Very few are dubbed into

CINEMAS

CINEMA	ADDRESS	TELEPHONE
Bellavista	Calles 17/19, Avenida Central	221-0909
California	Calle 23, Avenida 1	221-4738
Capri	Calles 9/11, Avenida Central	223-0264
Central	Calle 2, Avenida 2	221-3641
Cinema 2000	Calle 9, Avenidas 8/10	223-6997
Colon	Calle 38, Paseo Colón	221-4517
Hilton	Calle 11, Avenidas 10/12	222-4083
Magaly	Calle 23, Avenida Central	223-0085
Metropolitan	Calles 26/28, Paseo Colón	222-9188
Metro	Calle Central, Avenidas 6/8	221-0963
Omni	Calles 3, Avenida Central/1	221-7903
Real	Calle 11, Avenidas 6/8	223-5972
Reina	Barrio Tournón	222-9861
Rex	Calle Central, Avenida 4	221-0041
Sala Garbo	Calle 28, Avenida 2	222-1034
Universal	Calles 26/28, Paseo Colón	221-5241
Variedades	Calles 9/11, Avenida Central	222-6108

THEATERS

Teatro de la Aduana, Calle 25, Avenidas 3/5, tel. 221-5205. State-sponsored. The award-winning National Theater Company performs here.

Teatro del Ángel, Avenida Central opposite the National Museum, tel. 222-8258. Mostly comedy.

Teatro Bellas Artes. Offers student productions on the campus of the University of Costa Rica.

Teatro Carpa, Avenida Central, Calles 29/33, tel. 234-2866. Family-owned and internationally acclaimed.

Teatro Chaplin, Avenida 12, Calles 11/13, tel. 223-2919. Offers original comedies, dramas, and mime.

Teatro la Comedia, Avenida Central, Calles 11/13, tel. 233-0307. Specializes in comedy.

Teatro Vargas Calvo, Calle 3, Avenida Central, tel. 222-1875. High-quality theater-in-the-round.

Teatro Eugene O'Neill, in the Centro Cultural on Calle los Negritos, tel. 225-9433. Productions by the Little Theater Group and other performances.

Teatro Laurence Olivier, Calle 28, Avenida 2, tel. 223-1960. Films and jazz and other offerings as well as theater.

Teatro la Mascara, Calle 13, Avenidas 2/4, tel. 255-4250. Offbeat comedy and alternative dramas.

Modern Puppet Theater, 200 meters north, 100 meters east of the Santa Teresa Church, tel. 225-6926. The only puppet theater in the nation.

Teatro Melico Salazar, Calle Central, Avenida 2, tel. 221-4952. Everything from dramas to ballet and opera.

Teatro Tiempo, adjacent to the Cartago bus terminal, Calle 13, Avenida Central, tel. 222-0792.

Most movie houses charge about $1.50. They generally have large screens and—good news for nonsmokers—are just about the only places in San José where smoking is not permitted.

THEATER

As might be expected, theatergoing here is still light years from the status-mongering of Broadway. San José, nonetheless, is a theatrical cornucopia, with a score of remarkably varied and professional working theaters putting on original plays as well as classics, and lively, traditional Spanish productions such as *Ay Carmela!* Josefinos' love of theater supports a viable "fringe"—often called "theater-in-the-round"—serving more controversial soup.

By Broadway standards, prices are ludicrously cheap: rarely much more than $2. Theaters are tiny and often sell out early. Reservations are usually possible. Book early! Theater productions normally run Thursday through Sunday and begin at 7:30 or 8 p.m.

Most performances are in Spanish (even if you speak little Spanish you'll have an interesting and worthwhile experience). The **Little Theater Group** (tel. 234-3643) is made up of North American residents and presents English-language musicals and comedies throughout the year in the Centro Cultural's Eugene O'Neill Theater and occasionally at the Teatro Laurence Olivier. It's supposedly the oldest English-language theatrical group in Latin America.

The *Tico Times* offers a complete listing of current productions, including whether they're in Spanish or English; also see the "Viva" section in *La Nación.*

MUSIC, DANCING, AND *FOLKLORICA*

Folklorica

One of the most colorful "cabaret" shows in town is the **Fantasía Folklorica,** which depicts traditions, legends, and history of Costa Rica's seven provinces. The spectacular dance program blends traditional Costa Rican dances with avant-garde choreography and stunning stage

Spanish. (Movies with Spanish soundtracks are advertised as *hablado en Español.*) *La Nación* and the *Tico Times* list current movies. **Sala Garbo** (Calle 28 and Avenida 2) shows avant-garde international movies.

backdrops. Every Tuesday, 8 p.m. at the Melico Salazar Theater (Avenida 2, Calle Central, tel. 222-2653). Tickets at the door: $3-9.

A similar show—**Folklorico**—is put on by the Compañía de Danza Folklorica Zurquí every Thursday at 9 p.m. at the **Bon Vivant Restaurant** in the Hotel Herradura (tel. 239-0033). **Salon Musical de Lety** also has traditional Costa Rican dancing and music (see the "El Pueblo" special topic).

Classical

April through December is the season for the **National Symphony Orchestra,** which performs at the Teatro National on Thursday and Friday (8 p.m.) and Sunday mornings (10:30 a.m.). You can hobnob with cafe society at the symphony or opera for as little as $2, or as much as $20 for the best seats.

The Centro Cultural Costarricense Norteamericano presents the **U.S. University Musicians Series,** with concerts each month (tel. 232-1145). The **National Lyric Opera Company** (Compañía de Lírica Nacional) presents operas, June through mid-August, in the Teatro Melico Salazar (tel. 222-3071).

Also see "Arts and Culture," in the On the Road chapter for further information on classical music.

Live Music

Boleros de Rafa (Centro Cocorí, Los Yoses, tel. 225-6259) has *bolero* singers and dancing, Wednesday through Saturday. **Tony's Ribs** (formerly Los Lechones, behind the La Soledad Church) has live calypso music on Friday and Saturday. For rock, head to **Classic Rock and Roll** (50 meters north of Antojitos restaurant in Tibas), which bills itself as the only rock and roll bar in Costa Rica.

Mariachi bands, though not quite the institution they are in Mexico, do abound. Their undis-

puted headquarters is **La Esmeralda** (see "Bars," above). **Bar México** (Calle 6 and Avenida Central) also features mariachis. **Aida's Sala Musical** (opposite the Barrio California's Pizza Hut) has traditional Costa Rican serenades.

Among the more popular bars with live music are **El Cuartel de la Boca del Monte, Tequila Willy's, Lucky's Piano Blanco Bar, Akelare,** and **Contravía** (see "Bars," above).

Popular local bands to watch out for include Cantoamerica, a fusion band blending *salsa,* calypso, and reggae. Jaque Mate, La Mafia, Los Bandoleros, La Pandilla, and Marfil are also popular *salsa* bands. For jazz lovers, there's Oveja Negra, which blends jazz with a Latin beat. The most well-known and well-loved rock band is Liverpool.

Jazz

The nascent jazz scene is now fairly robust, though it takes out some seeking out. Check out

---

CASINOS

Casino Amstel, Hotel Amstel, Calle 7, Avenidas 1/3, tel. 222-4622, ext. 32

Casino Aurola Holiday Inn, Avenida 5, Calles 5/7, tel. 233-7233, ext. 280

Club Colonial, Avenida 1, Calles 9/11, tel. 233-0112

Club Domino, Hotel Balmoral, Avenida Central, Calles 7/9, tel. 222-1103

Club Triangulo, Calle 7, Avenidas Central/1, tel. 233-7081

Gran Hotel, Avenida Central, Calle 3, tel. 221-9917

Hotel Cariari, Autopista General Cañas, tel. 239-0022

Hotel Centro Colón, Paseo Colón, tel. 257-2582

Hotel Corobicí, La Sabana Norte, tel. 232-8122

Hotel Del Rey, Avenida 1, Calle 9, tel. 221-7272

Hotel Europa Zurqui, Calle 3, Avenida 17

Hotel Irazú, Airport Highway, near Centro Comercial 2000, tel. 322-7910 or 232-4811

Hotel Herradura, 10 km north of San José, tel. 239-0033

Hotel Presidente, Avenida Central, Calles 7/9, tel. 222-3022

Hotel San José Palacio, Airport Hwy., tel. 220-2034

Le Chambourd, Avenida 11, Calle 3, tel. 233-7122

Royal Garden, Avenida Central, Calle Central, tel. 257-0022

the **Shakespeare Gallery,** in the Teatro Laurence Olivier (next door to Sala Garbo, on Calle 28 and Avenida 2). The cognoscenti head to **Emilia Romagna** (25 meters west of Pollos Kentucky on Paseo Colón, tel. 233-2843), an elegant restaurant-cum-jazz club featuring the Orpheus Trip and guest artists (Mon.-Sat. from 8 p.m.; no cover, two-drink minimum). **La Mecca de Jazz** stages live jazz bands Mon.-Sat. (El Pueblo shopping center, tel. 234-0743). **Charleston** (Calle 9, Avenidas 2/4) features live jazz on weekends ($2). Bambu Jazz plays at **El Tablado** (opposite Pollos Kentucky on Avenida Central) on Monday; weekends feature live Latin jazz (Nueva Canción). **Bar Argentina** (at Centro Comercial Calle Real, in San Pedro) also reportedly has jazz music. And **Bromelia's Cafe and Grill** (100 meters north of Cine Magalay at Calle 23 and Avenida Central, tel. 221-3848) offers live jazz nightly 8-11 p.m. Private parking. No cover. **La Habanera** features live jazz and classical music in a suitably jazzed-up classical colonial structure on Avenida 9 and Calles 11/13, behind Casa Amarilla (tel. 233-8383, 8:30 p.m. until the last guest leaves). And **El Caracol** (tel. 253-4407), on Calle 16 between Avenidas 1/3, offers occasional jazz in a laid-back and often crowded atmosphere.

Great times are guaranteed at **Soda Blues** (Calle 11, Avenidas 10/12, tel. 221-8368), which sprang onto the scene in May 1994. Hip blues, jazz, and R&B are sponsored by a zany Brit-Yank duo, Jimmy Forstner and David Scott, horn-tooting owners. Dave and Jim have been in the music business for more than 30 years (Scott opened London's infamous Pink Panther Club at the tender age of 16!). The club is already one of the most happenin' scenes in town.

CASINOS

If two fiery-throated hummingbirds move roughly in the same line, Costa Rica punters will likely place a bet on the winner. Every street corner has two or three touts selling tickets for the National Lottery, the provider—God willing!—of imagined millions. And virtually every major hotel has a small casino. They're not quite the

flirting with Lady Luck, Club Cariari

JOHN ANDERSON

glitzy palaces of Monte Carlo nor the noise-filled gambling houses of Las Vegas, but the familiar sounds of roulette, craps, and blackjack continue well into the night.

Rummy, canasta (a form of roulette, but with a basket containing balls replacing the roulette wheel), craps, and *tute* (a local variant of poker) are the casino games of choice. Slot machines, once prohibited by law, have grown popular, too. Bingo is a favorite pecuniary pursuit in less cosmopolitan terrain.

The casinos were closed down in 1979 and reopened in 1980 after the government formulated more stringent regulations. However, government oversight supposedly remains relatively weak, and house rules and payoffs are stacked far more heavily in the house's favor than in the United States.

The atmospheric casinos of **Club Colonial** and **Royal Garden** will evoke images of a

Humphrey Bogart movie. Some, such as **Club Domino,** serve free drinks and *bocas*. The tiny and unappealing casino in the entrance foyer of the **Gran Hotel** is open 24 hours. That of the **Hotel Del Rey** is modest yet particularly popular. The largest, plushest, and most lively hot spot is the **San José Palacio,** which stays open until dawn and like other upscale casinos has a dress code. The 17th-floor casino at the **Hotel Aurola Holiday Inn** provides a stunning view over the city and is for those feeling flush. **Note:** The casino in Key Largo no longer operates.

SOMETHING COMPLETELY DIFFERENT

Candil Cultural Center (Calle 13, Avenida 7 bis; open Mon.-Fri. 2-9 p.m., Saturday 9 a.m.-9 p.m.) offers a medley of entertainment: everything from poetry readings, art classes, and New Age workshops to live music and hit movie screenings (7 p.m.) preceded by coffee hour.

You can sing your own song at **King's Garden Restaurant** (tel. 255-3838), where *karaoke* is going down big with the local yuppie crowd.

SHOPPING

Shopping in San José, concentrated along Avenida Central and Avenidas 1 and 2, lacks scope and imagination for those with big dollars to spend. A growing number of stores sell superb quality arts and crafts. You can also bargain at the market stalls on Plaza de la Cultura for tourist items or, if you want to live like a local, the Mercado Central, San José's answer to London's Petticoat Lane. In 1993 police began to enforce city codes restricting the Plaza's hawkers to Friday through Sunday. This situation is fluid and you will undoubtedly find stalls set up any time of the week.

Shop hours are usually Mon.-Fri. 8 a.m.-6 p.m. Many places close at noon for a siesta; a few stay open until late evening. Most shops close on Sunday, and many on Saturday too. The local neighborhood store is a *pulpería,* which often doubles as a local bar. They usually sell most household essentials. There's no sales tax.

The United States Mission Association's book *Living in Costa Rica* (available at The Bookshop, Calles 1/3 and Avenida 1, tel. 221-6847) has a comprehensive listing of where to buy specialty items and foods.

Photography

Although expensive ($12 for a 36-exposure roll), most types of film are available. Beware of film that has been sitting in the sun. Buy refrigerated film if possible. **IFSA Industrias Fotograficas** usually has fresh film and batteries in stock (Calle 2, Avenida 5, tel. 223-1444; and Avenida Central, Calle 5, tel. 222-5442). Also try **Kim Color** (Paseo Colón, Calle 38, tel. 223-9257). Photographic equipment and accessories are very expensive.

Also see the section on "Photography," under "Other Practicalities" in the On the Road chapter.

PUBLICATIONS

Books

Two English-language bookstores stand out. The first is **The Bookshop** (Calles 1/3 and Avenida 1, tel. 221-6847), with books on virtually all sub-

jects, including a broad range of travel and nature guidebooks. Books here are pricey but the good news is that they stock the *Costa Rica Handbook.* New upstairs is a giftstore with beautiful local handicrafts. Second, and another source of the *Costa Rica Handbook,* is **Chispas Books** (Calle 7 and Avenida Central/1, tel. 223-2240, fax 224-9278), which has an equally wide variety of new and used books in English, including a well-stocked section of travel, nature, and science books. Chispas has a travel agency—Ecole Travel—in the back, specializing (although not exclusively dealing) in student travel.

Also check both the **Travelers Stores** (Calle Central, Avenida 3, tel. 257-0766) and **Librería Trejos** (Avenida Central, on the north side of the Plaza de la Democracia, tel. 221-7055), which stocks many of the same travel guidebooks as well as a wide array of maps at prices generally 25% below those elsewhere in town.

The largest book selection in Spanish is at **Librería Lehmann** (Calles 1/3 and Avenida Central, tel. 223-2122). Its magazine racks are well stocked with North American magazines, from *National Geographic* to more esoteric journals. Upstairs, it sells a large range of maps and pamphlets on Costa Rica. Also try **Librería Quijote** (in the Arcatas Mall, Calles Central/2 and Avenida 1), with a small selection of new and used English-language books; and **Librería Universal** (Calles Central/1 and Avenida Central, tel. 222-2222), which has a small supply of books in Spanish. **Staufer Books** has two stores, one in La Uruca (tel. 232-0810), the other on Calle 37, 100 meters south of the Centro Cultural Costarricense Norteamericano in Los Yoses (tel. 224-5170).

If all you're after is a cheap paperback or a rare find, try **Casey's Book Exchange** (Calle Central, Avenida 7/9), or **Book Traders** (Avenida 1, Calles 5/7, tel. 255-0508), which sell inexpensive used books as well as new books traded at 25% less than cover price. You can linger here over coffee. Operated on the same basis is **Shakespeare & Co.** (Calle 3, Avenidas 5/7; tel. 233-4995), which also has its own coffee shop.

Newspapers and Magazines

Most major hotel gift stores sell international favorites. Adolescents hawk the day's *Miami Herald, New York Times,* and *USA Today* at the Café Parisienne, in front of the Gran Hotel. Once you've finished reading, they'll buy the paper back from you for half price. The **Candy Shop**, around the corner on the north side of the Plaza de la Cultura, sells a range of English-language newspapers and magazines, as does **Librería Lehmann** (Calle 1/3 and Avenida Central) and **The Bookshop** (Calle 1/3 and Avenida 1). If you can't find your favorite magazine at Lehmann's, try *La Casa de las Revistas* (Calle Central, Avenidas 4/6).

Maps

Check the English-language bookstores listed above for a variety of tourist maps. **Lehmann's** department store, **Librería Universal**, and **Librería Trejos** (usually up to 25% cheaper) also sell large-scale topographical maps. You can also obtain topographical maps from the **National Geographic Institute** (Ministry of Public Works, at Avenida 20, Calles 9/11; Mon.-Fri. 8:30 a.m.-3:30 p.m.). One block north on Avenida 18 is the Ministry of Transport, which has detailed street maps of towns. A bus marked "Barrio La Cruz" departs from Avenida 2 at Parque Central; the Institute is to the left inside the ministry gates, with a sign reading Mapas.

You can mail-order maps from **Jimenez & Tanzi, Ltda.** (Apdo. 2553, San José 1000, tel. 233-8033, fax 323-8294) with prepayment. Maps include: "General Map of Costa Rica" (1:800,000; $2), "Greater Metropolitan San José" (1:200,000; $1.50), a "Center of San José" map for walkers (1:10,000; $2), "Downtown San José," more suited to drivers (1:12,500; $3), and a three-map "Road Map" ($4). Add $1 postage and handling for up to four maps. Postage is free for more than four maps.

Also see the section on "Maps" under "Other Practicalities" in the On the Road chapter.

FOOD

Within the warren of the **Mercado Central** (Calles 6/8, Avenidas Central/1) are stands selling poultry, flowers, meat, fish, medicinal herbs, fresh produce, as well as baskets and souvenirs.

It's a kind of Moroccan *souk* transplanted. An equally colorful alternative across the way is **Mercado Borbón** (Calle 8, Avenidas 3/5). Both are also happy hunting grounds for national costume dresses. Remember that nonpackaged foods will be confiscated by U.S. Customs. However, good preserves that will make it into the U.S. include *palmito* (heart of palm) and *pejibaye* (a rather bland fruit with a chestnutty taste).

The farmers' market *(feria del agricultor)* is held every Saturday morning on the west side of Plaza Víquez (Calles 7/9, Avenidas 16-20). Try to get there before 7 a.m. for the best buys.

Bakeries

The aromas of freshly baked breads and pastries are irresistibly tempting, for San José is replete with good bakeries every few hundred yards. **Pastelería Francesca** (Calle 30 and Paseo Colón), **Giacomin** (Calle 2 and Avenidas 3/5), and **Pastelería Don Simon** (Calle 28 and Paseo Colón) are among the best.

Coffee

Coffee is perhaps the best bargain in Costa Rica. The best deal is to buy whole beans roasted before your eyes; head to the Mercado Central and **El Trebol** (Calle 8, Avenidas Central/1). Ask for whole beans, otherwise you'll end up with superfine grinds. One pound of beans costs about $1! These beans aren't of the finest export quality. Stores throughout the city sell prepackaged premium coffees. When buying these, make sure the package is marked *puro*. Otherwise the coffee will already be laced with sugar—enough to make even the most ardent sugar-lover turn green. **La Esquina del Café** (Avenida 9, Calle 3 bis, tel. 233-4560, fax 221-1048) sells a wide variety of gourmet coffees as well as roasters, *chorreadors* (traditional cotton strainers on a wooden frame), and other paraphernalia. Free tastings to go with pastries! **Café Gourmet** (Avenida 9, Calle 3) also specializes in all things coffee-related, as does the **Trangada Coffee Shop,** directly opposite The Bookshop, on Avenida 1 and Calles 1/3.

Liquor

I always save space in my rucksack for a bottle of Café Rica, the local equivalent of Kahlúa, and *guaro,* the local sugarcane drink that makes

another great souvenir. Don't be tempted to buy your alcohol at a *pulpería*. Prices per bottle here are four or five times more than you'll pay at a supermarket such as Yaohan (opposite the Hotel Corobicí), Auto Mercado (Calle 3, Avenida 3), or Mas x Menos (Paseo Colón).

ARTS AND CRAFTS

Handicrafts

San José is replete with arts and crafts, with choices aplenty to fill even the largest suitcase. Most hotels of substance have gift stores selling arts and crafts.

My favorite place is the Plaza de la Cultura, which any day of the week teems with colorful stalls selling T-shirts, paintings, trinket jewelry, and superb-quality hammocks (excellent bargains at $20-30). Sundays are best. "Unlicensed" vendors have been forced to move to the Plaza de la Democracia, beside the National Museum. Since few tourists flock here, you may find prices lower.

Don't fail to check out the craft market held daily 9 a.m.-5 p.m. at **Parque de las Garantías Sociales** on Calle 5. Everything you'll find at Plaza de la Cultura is here, too, and much more. Many of the items—from jewelry and miniature oxcarts to chairs and carved gourds—are sold by the artists themselves. The sellers are members of the National Association of Independent Artisans.

Specialty handicraft stores include **Atmósfera** (Calle 5, Avenidas 1/3, tel. 222-4322), where a gallery on the second floor displays fantastic Indian masks, carved fantasy beasts, and paintings. Among my favorite items are the brightly painted ceramic buses laden with people (about $7). Wooden and gold-plated brooches and pins are other good buys.

Anne Marie's Boutique in the Hotel Don Carlos (Avenidas 7/9, Calle 9) offers a complete array of souvenirs, handicrafts, and artwork of every description, including Panamanian *molas* and silk-screen scarves by Bandanna Republic. **Suríska Gallery** (Calle 5, Avenida 3, tel. 222-0129) sells top-quality woodcarvings and furniture. The works of renowned North American artists/carpenters Barry Biesanz and Jay Morrison are on sale here; not cheap, but they're superb creations in exotic woods, with incredible execution of detail. Jay Morrison owns **Magia** (Calle 5, Avenidas 1/3, tel. 233-2630), which also stocks his work. The upscale **La Galería** (Avenida 1, Calle 1, tel. 221-3436) has a fine selection of quality handicrafts and also features Barry Biesanz woodworks along with reproduction pre-Columbian 14-karat gold jewelry. And don't fail to check out the upstairs crafts store at **The Bookshop** (Avenida 1, Calles 1/3).

Another sure bet is the **Mercado Nacional de Artesanías** (National Artisans' Market, tel. 223-0122) at Calle 1 and Avenidas 2/4. One block away is **Artesanía CANAPI** (Avenida 2, Calle 1, tel. 221-3342), the artisan's guild, selling reproduction pre-Columbian gold jewelry, hammocks, woodcarvings, and the famous brightly painted miniature oxcarts. A handful of handicrafts stores cluster together on two levels at **La Casona** flea market (Calle Central and Avenida Central), lent atmosphere by its stone floor. The cross-section of crafts include Guatemalan textiles, woodcrafts from Honduras, and the popular Costa Rican nativity figures and Christmas crèches in ceramics and wood. **ANDA** (Avenida Central, Calles 5/7) also has a fine collection of Indian artifacts—gourds, pottery, maracas, and fantastic balsa-wood masks—as well as native Costa Rican weavings and ceramic tea sets.

If you're in Centro Comercial El Pueblo and/or in search of high-quality art, visit **Alba Art Gallery** (tel. 239-4324), where owner Mustehsan Farooqi retails fabulous pieces by Central America's leading painters (works run up to $10,000). Also here is a high-class leather shop, **Del Río**.

Farther out, in the Los Yoses district, is **Galerías Casa Alameda,** a touch of Beverly Hills come to the tropics. Fine art mingles with fashion in this upscale commercial center that includes **Galería Real** art gallery and **Villa del Este** (tel. 224-1261), selling Peruvian and Mexican silver work, pewter, Turkish rugs, and more.

Other places to consider include **Casa del Artesano** (Calle 11, Avenidas 4/6), **Arte Rica,** next to the Teatro Melico Salazar on Avenida 2, **La Buchaca** (Centro Comercial El Pueblo, tel. 233-6773), the **Amir Art Gallery** (Calles 1/3, Avenida Central, tel. 255-3261), **Sapito Dorado** (southwest corner of Parque Morazán, and the **Tienda de la Naturaleza** (Calle 20, Avenidas 3/5), operated by the Neotropica Foundation.

SHOPPING WITH A CONSCIENCE

Think twice before buying something exotic: the item may be banned by U.S. Customs and, if so, you could be fined. Even if legal to import, consider whether your purchase is an ecological sin. In short, shop with a conscience! Don't buy:

- Combs, jewelry, or other items made from tortoise shells.
- Coral, coral items, or shells. Costa Rica's coral reefs are being gradually destroyed. And every shell taken from a beach is one less for the next person to enjoy.
- Jewelry, artwork, or decorated clothes made of feathers. The bird may well have been shot simply for its plumage—and it may well be endangered.
- Furs from jaguars, ocelots, etc. Such furs are illegal. Your vanity isn't worth the life of such magnificent and endangered creatures.
- Think twice, too, about buying tropical hardwood products. Help protect Costa Rica's forests.

For more information, contact the **U.S. Fish and Wildlife Service** (Dept. of the Interior, Washington, D.C. 20240), which puts out a booklet, Buyer Beware; or the **U.S. Customs Service** (1301 Constitution Ave., Washington, D.C. 20229).

The suburb of Moravia (see under "Turrialba and Vicinity" in the Central Highlands chapter), northeast of San José, is a major center for arts and crafts, with a wide array of shops.

Rugs

My friends Shirley Miller and Randy Case, publishers of the *Costa Rican Outlook* newsletter, turned me on to the custom-made rugs of Cecilia Tristán Telles and her sister Ana Gabriela Tristán at their C-Tris Alfombras factory (100 meters east of Plaza del Sol, tel. 273-3554 or 273-3594, fax 273-3624) in the hills of San Ramón Tres Ríos, in Curridabat. The two can make heavy-duty rugs to match any design you give them, with a 3-D effect to boot! They're fabulous—and cost less than $200 per square meter.

Guitars and Violins

On the hunt for a handmade guitar or violin? Guzmán Mora conjures classical compositions from wood ("I used wood from the base and middle of trees because it is the strongest and

best"). His Spanish-style guitars in various styles and sizes sell for about $80. You can try them out in his showroom—**Aristides Guzman Mora, Ltd.**—in Tibas (tel. 223-0682). Alternately, **Martin Prada** continues a family heritage of hand-crafting world-class violins in his San José studio (many members of Costa Rica's acclaimed National Symphony play Prada instruments).

Clothing

If you admire the homely Tico look, check out the **Mercado Central** (Central Market) on Calle 6 and Avenida 1, where you'll find embroidered shirts and blouses and cotton *campesino* hats. **La Choza Folklórica** (Avenida 3, Calle 1) specializes in replicas of national costumes. You can also buy Costa Rican dresses (bright red, blue, and green designs on white cotton) at **Bazaar Central Souvenir** (Calle Central, Avenida 3). A good place to find handmade appliquéd blouses and fabrics—*molas*—from the Drake's Bay region and the San Blas Islands of Panamá is **Antic** (Edificio las Arcadas, Avenida 2 and Calle 1, tel. 233-4630), next door to the Gran Hotel. **La Galería, Suraska**, and **El Caserón** (Calle Central, Avenidas Central/1, tel. 222-7999) also sell *molas*.

Leather

Personally, I find much of Costa Rica's leather goods disappointing, although high-quality leatherwork has emerged of late. There are also some nice soft yellow leather satchels and purses to be had. The northeastern suburb of Moravia is well-known for producing leather goods. In town, try **Galería del Cuero** (Avenida 1, Calle 5, tel. 223-2034), **Marroquinería Del Río** (Calle 9, Avenidas Central/2, tel. 238-2883), and **Artesanías Malety** (Avenida 1, Calles 1/3, tel. 221-1670), all with reasonable quality leather goods, including purses, attaché cases, etc. **Costa Rica Expeditions Travelers Store**

(Avenida 3 and Calle Central) sells the cozy leather rockers from Sarchí, as well as beautifully carved walking sticks, Café Rica liqueurs, posters, and painted ceramic toucans.

You may well be tempted, too, to buy a snazzy pair of handmade leather boots. Shoe-making abounds in San José, and almost everywhere downtown you can come upon rows of boots made from 50 or so different leathers, including dandy two-tones. Stay clear of snakeskin and crocodile skins. A bevy of high-quality shoemakers can be found on Paseo Colón and Avenida 3 between Calles 24 and 26.

Jewelry

Much of what you'll see is actually gold-washed,

not solid gold. Three trustworthy places are: **La Casa del Indio** (Avenida 2, Calles 5/7, tel. 223-0306), which offers reproductions of Indian art, as well as fine jewelry; **La Galeria,** selling 14-carat gold earrings, brooches, etc., much of it in the fabulous pre-Columbian forms; and **18K Esmeraldas y Creaciones,** near Spoon's restaurant in Los Yoses, selling pre-Columbian reproductions in solid gold, plus pins, rings, earrings, etc., created with Colombian emeralds and semiprecious stones.

The best place for cheap trinket jewelry is the Plaza de la Cultura, where you'll find attractive ethnic-style earrings and bracelets. For semiprecious stones check out **Blue Diamond,** on the south side of Parque Morazán.

SERVICES AND INFORMATION

MONEY

San José has no shortage of **banks,** but they're hardly worth the hassle (for speed and ease, I recommend using your hotel cashier and accepting the marginal difference in exchange rates). Hours are usually Mon.-Fri. 9 a.m.-3 p.m., though some stay open longer: the Banco Anglo Costarricense (opposite the National Theater, at Calle 3 and Avenida 2, and other locations) stays open until 7 p.m. weekdays, and 10 a.m. until 2 p.m. on Saturday; the Banco de Costa Rica Office at Calle 7 and Avenida 1 is open until 6:30 p.m. weekdays. Both Banco Metropolitan (Calle Central, Avenida 2) and Banco Lyon (Calle 2, Avenidas Central/1) have been recommended. Banco Metropolitan specializes in foreign currency transactions. You'll need your passport—and a good deal of patience—for all bank transactions.

Electronic tellers are available outside the Banco de Costa Rica (Avenida Central, Calles 4/6) and Banco Nacional (Avenida 3, Calles 2/4). You can also receive cash against your Visa or MasterCard at Banco de San José, Credomatic, or TAM Travel Agency (Calle 1 and Avenidas Central/1); and against your American Express card at the AmEx office (Calle 1, Avenidas Central/1, tel. 233-0044; open Mon.-

Fri. 8 a.m.-5:30 p.m.). **Credomatic** has four locations in San José: in the Omni Bldg., Avenida 1 and Calles 3/5 (tel. 233-2155); in front of Banco San José, Calle Central and Avenidas 3/5 (tel. 257-0155); Edificio Irma at Avenida Central and Calles 31/33 in San Pedro (tel. 224-2155); and half a block west of CEMACO, in Rohrmoser (tel. 220-2563).

Bureaus de change *(casas de cambio)* were closed down several years ago but at least one operates legally and has been recommended: Valorinsa (tel. 257-1010; open Mon.-Fri. 9 a.m.-5 p.m.), on Calle 9, Avenidas Central/2. **Moneychangers,** though illegal, congregate around Calle Central and Avenida Central. They'll call out "dólares" or "cambio" (change) in hushed tones as you pass: moneychanging is strictly illegal, and there are regular police sweeps. Beware of fake notes, and always count your money when it's given to you. You'll perhaps lose five percent on the exchange, but at least it saves lost time standing in long bank lines.

Traveler's checks are widely accepted throughout San José. And most deluxe and moderate hotels will change up to $100 for guests. The government sets the rate, and the rate at hotels is rarely more than two or three *colones* worse than the bank rate.

For further details see "Money" in the On the Road chapter.

MEDICAL SERVICES

Many hospitals and private clinics in San José offer 24-hour emergency care, X-rays, etc. Foreigners receive the same service as Costa Ricans in public hospitals. While the standard of service is generally good, lines are often very long. Private hospitals offer faster treatment.

Use public hospitals for life-threatening emergencies only; private clinics and doctors are recommended for all other emergencies and health needs (a large deposit may be requested on admittance). Doctors—many of them U.S.-trained—are listed by specialty in the Yellow Pages under "Médicos." *Living in Costa Rica,* a guidebook published by the United States Missions Association, provides a comprehensive listing of doctors by specialty; available from the Bookshop (Avenida 1, Calles 1/3, tel. 221-6847).

Hospital San Juan de Dios (Paseo Colón and Calle 16) is the most centrally located medical facility. The Children's Hospital (Hospital Nacional de Niños) is adjacent, to the west. Many private medical services are concentrated west of the Children's Hospital.

Private office visits are usually $20-30. Hospitals and clinics accept credit-card payment. U.S. insurance is not normally accepted, but you can send your bill to your insurance company for reimbursement. Clínica Bíblica reportedly accepts U.S. Medicare.

LAUNDRIES

Self-service laundromats are growing in number, though they're still few and far between and very expensive (count on $4 per wash and dry). The most central is **Sixaola** (Avenida 2, Calles 7/9, tel. 221-2111). Nearby is **Sol y Fiesta Lavaropa** (tel. 257-7151), on Calle 9, Avenidas 8/10 (open Mon.-Sat. 8 a.m.-7 p.m.). **Betamatic** (Calle 47, Avenida 2, near Burger King in Los Yoses) offers both self-service or drop-off and pick-up service ($1.50 per kilogram). Note that it closes at 4:30 p.m. for self-service, though you can drop off laundry until 6 p.m. (closed Sunday). **Lavandería Lava-Mas,** in Los Yoses (tel. 225-1645), is on the same street, between Calles 43 and 45, next to Spoon's. **Lavandería Doña Anna** is next to the Ministerio de Obras Publicas y Transportes (Calle 13, Avenida 20), 100 meters east of Plaza Gonzalez. There are also two *lavanderías* on Paseo Colón: **La Margarita** (Calle 36, tel. 222-5094) and **Sixaola** (tel. 223-2527). Farther out, in Tibas, is **Lavandería Americana** (tel. 236-8724). American-owned **Lavanderías de Costa Rica** (tel. 237-6273) will pick up and deliver ($4.50); cold wash costs $1.75, hot wash $2.25, dry $1.75.

Dry cleaning is a more risky business: you drop off your clothes and keep your fingers crossed. Note that many *lavanderías* only do dry-cleaning. Try **Drycleaning y Lavandería General** (Avenida 16, Calle 18, tel. 221-8641).

Most hotels can arrange to do your laundry for a fee, though the fee is hefty in more expensive hotels. Many budget hotels have a laundry sink and drying area (don't wash your clothes in the large water tank; instead draw water from the tank and wash your clothes in the sink).

LIBRARIES

The **National Library,** Biblioteca Nacional (Avenida 3, Calles 15/17, tel. 221-2436), has more than 100,000 volumes. It is open to foreigners. The main index and information desk is upstairs on the second floor. You'll find the national newspaper collection here, should the muse strike. Another useful source is the **Biblioteca Universidad de Costa Rica** (Ciudad Universitaria Rodrigo Facio, tel. 225-7372). The **Mark Twain Library**—part of the Centro Cultural Costarricense Norteamericano (on Calle Negritos, 200 meters north of Centro La Mufla near the Los Yoses Auto Mercado, tel. 225-9433)—has English-language books and reference materials. You must be a member to check books out. Membership is open to the public. There's also a specialized library in the **Centro Cultural de Mexico** (Calle 21, Avenida Central; hours: Mon.-Fri. 3-5 p.m.).

In addition, **Bibliomania** (200 meters west of San Rafael Church, in Escazú, tel. 228-4537) and **Casey's Book Exchange** (Calle Central, Avenidas 7 and 9) have used-book exchanges.

HOSPITALS, CLINICS, AND DENTISTS

PRIVATE MEDICAL CENTERS

Clínica Americana, Calles Central/1 and Avenida 14, tel. 222-1010
Clínica Bíblica, Calles Central/1 and Avenida 14, tel. 223-6422
Clínica Católica, Barrio Guadalupe, tel. 225-5055 or 225-9095
Clínica Santa Rita (Gynecology), Calles 15/17 and Avenida 8, tel. 221-6433

PUBLIC MEDICAL CENTERS

Hospital Calderón Guardia, Calle 17 and Avenida 9, tel. 222-4133
Hospital México, La Uruca, Highway to Juan Santamaría Airport, tel. 232-6122
Hospital Nacional de Niños, Calles 18/20 and Paseo Colón, tel. 222-0122
Hospital San Juan de Dios, Calle 14 and Paseo Colón, tel. 222-0166

CLINICAL LABORATORIES

Laboratorio Clínica American, Calles Central/1 and Avenida 14, tel. 222-1010
Laboratorio Clínica Bíblica, Calle Central and Avenida 14, tel. 221-8107
Clínica Santa Rita, Calles 15/17 and Avenida 8, tel. 221-3111

PHARMACIES

Farmacia Clínicablica, Calle 1 and Avenida 14, tel. 223-6422
Farmacia Hospital, Calle 16 and Paseo Colón, tel. 222-0985
Farmacia Fischel, Calle 2 and Avenida 3, tel. 222-7322

DENTAL SERVICES

Dr. Jorge Aragon, Calle Central and Avenida 14, tel. 223-6481
Dr. Carlos Lehmann, Edifico Irma, Avenida Central, tel. 225-1818
Dr. Rafael Lachner, Calles Central/1 and Avenida 5, tel. 223-6763
Dr. Dobles Tinoco, Calle 26 and Avenidas 2/4, tel. 222-8555
Dr. Edgar Céspedes, Calles 12/14 and Avenida 10, tel. 223-4686
Dr. Roberto Cob, Calles 27/29 and Avenida 2, tel. 224-6734

MAIL, TELEGRAMS, FAX

The main post office *(correo)* is on Calle 2 between Avenidas 1 and 3. It's a beautiful structure, built in French classical style in 1914. Take the middle entrance to buy stamps; the postal slots are on the left. Are these really the only postal boxes in San José? Probably! Otherwise, you can post your mail at a hotel front desk.

Getting incoming mail is very time consuming. To collect incoming mail, go to window 17 through the entrance nearest Avenida 1. You'll need to bring identification. Mail should be addressed to you using your name as it appears on your passport or other I.D., c/o Lista Correos, Correos Central, San José. There's a small charge per letter. Hours: Mon.-Fri. 7 a.m.-midnight, Saturday 7 a.m.-noon.

To send and/or receive a telegram or fax, go to the ICE's **Radiográfica** office, one block west of the National Theater, at Calle 1 and Avenida 1. Of course, your hotel should be able to send a fax, too. See "Communications" in the On the Road chapter for additional information.

San José has several photocopy centers, including **Copicentro,** on Avenida 1, Calle 1.

SPORTS FACILITIES

Sabana Park, at the western end of Paseo Colón, has facilities for sports and health enthu-

MEDICAL VOCABULARY

AIDS—*SIDA*
arm—*brazo*
ankle—*tobillo*
aspirin—*aspirina*
back—*espalda*
blood—*sangre*
to bleed—*sangrar*
chest—*pecho*
chest trouble—*enfermedad del pecho*
chills—*escalofríos*
a cold—*resfriado, catarro*
constipated—*esterñido*
cough—*tos*
diarrhea—*diarrea*
doctor—*médico*
elbow—*codo*
ear—*oreja*
earache—*dolor de oídos*
eye—*ojo*
finger—*dedo*
foot—*pie*
groin—*ingle*
hand—*mano*
it hurts—*duele*
injection—*inyección*
knee—*rodilla*
laxative—*laxante*

leg—*pierna*
medicine—*medicina*
nauseated—*mareado*
needle—*aguja*
nose—*nariz*
nosebleed—*echar sangre por las narices*
nurse—*enfermera*
operate—*operar*
painkiller—*quitadolores*
pill—*pastilla*
poison—*veneno, tóxico*
prescription—*receta*
recuperate—*recuperar*
to rest—*descansar*
to set in a cast—*enyesar*
to stay in hospital—*internarse*
to stay in bed—*guardar cama, guarda reposo*
to twist—*torcese*
stomach—*estómago*
suppository—*supositorio*
syringe—*jeringa*
throat—*garganta*
tooth—*diente*
treatment—*tratamiento*
venereal—*venéreo*
x-ray—*rayos X* (pronounced "ray-ose e-kis")

---

siasts. Hewn from the former airfield and interspersed among the grass and trees are baseball diamonds, basketball courts, jogging and walking trails, soccer fields, tennis and volleyball courts, plus an Olympic-size swimming pool (open noon-2 p.m.; $3) and showers.

Bicycling: Contact the Federación Costarricense de Ciclismo (tel. 232-7093), which organizes group cycling. You rarely see bicycles in use on San José's streets, with good reason. It's plain suicide! **Mountain Biking Costa Rica** (tel. 255-0914) rents mountain bikes for those heading out of town. Also see "Bicycling" under "Special-Interest Travel and Recreation" in the On the Road chapter.

Bowling: El Boliche Dent (tel. 234-2777) is the local bowling alley in Los Yoses.

Gyms and Health Clubs: The following have facilities for those wanting to slim down or buff up:

Edificio Cristal (Avenida 1, Calles 1/3), Gimnasio Troyanos (Avenida 6, Calle 4, tel. 222-1641), and Gimnasio Usekar (Avenida 10, Calle 14, tel. 222-0333). Club Olimpico operates fitness clubs in Escazú (tel. 228-5051) and Los Yoses (tel. 224-3560). Monthly membership averages $25. Los Cipreses, in the suburb of Curridabat, has a gym as well as three swimming pools, basketball courts, and a half-size soccer field. Most upscale hotels also have Nautilus and spa facilities: Hotel Corobicí is particularly noteworthy. Also see "Gimnasios" in the telephone directory.

Mountaineering: Club de Montañismo de la Universidad de Costa Rica (tel. 235-3147) meets monthly and is open to the public.

Racquetball/Squash: Club Squash Monterreal (tel. 232-6777) in Sabana Norte, Club Olimpico, Top Squash (tel. 220-1108) in Sabana Sur, and San José Indoor Club (tel. 225-

9344) in San Pedro all have racquetball courts. You'll need to become a member.

Running: Sabana Park's trails provide a peaceful, traffic- and pollution-free environment for running. It has showers. Avoid the streets. San José has a chapter of the internationally famous Hashhouse Harriers (tel. 228-0769), which organizes cross-country runs.

Soccer: Watching a soccer game in Costa Rica is quite an experience. On the day of a major game, Josefinos throw their usual decorum out the window and indulge in a general fiesta. The San José team plays at the Estadio Nacional, in Sabana Park; call 221-7677 for a schedule of games. Its archrivals, Saprissa, plays in Tibas; call 235-3591.

Softball: *Bolo lento* or *sofbol* games are played each weekend in Sabana Park; see the "Síntesis Deportiva" section of *La Nación* for schedules.

Tennis: You'll find public courts in Sabana Park. You must be a guest to play on hotel courts, or a member to play at private clubs. Private clubs include the Costa Rica Country Club (tel. 228-9333), Costa Rica Tennis Club (tel. 232-1266), and San José Indoor Club (tel. 225-9344).

For additional information, see the section on "Special-Interest Travel and Recreation" in the On the Road chapter.

TOURIST INFORMATION

The Costa Rican Tourism Institute (Instituto Costarricense de Turismo) has an information booth upstairs to the left immediately after you exit the customs and arrival hall at Juan Santamaría Airport (tel. 442-1820). The main ICT information office is downtown, adjacent to the Gold Museum beneath the Plaza de la Cultura (Calle 5 and Avenida Central, tel. 222-1090). It provides an updated list of hotels, bus schedules, embassies, etc. Other information is tucked away in its file cabinets. The staff are fluent in English, and very gracious and helpful. The ICT office provides free maps of both San José and a touring map of the country. The touring map is too small-scale to be much use as a road guide (see "Maps" in the "Shopping" section, above). Hours: Mon.-Fri. 9 a.m.-5 p.m.; Saturday 9 a.m.-1 p.m.

SAN JOSÉ EMERGENCY NUMBERS

Dial 911 (or 122) for Police, Red Cross, Emergency Rescue Unit, Fire (San José Metropolitan Area only). English-Spanish spoken.

Candil is a bilingual cultural center at Calle 13 and Avenida 7B. A bulletin board lists information on hotels, arts events, community activities, etc. There's also a video show on Costa Rica. Open Mon.-Sat. 8 a.m.-noon and 2-10 p.m.

You'll find an **INFOtur** office (tel. 223-4481, fax 223-4476) on the corner of Avenida 2 and Calle 5, facing the National Theater.

The dozens of travel and tour agencies throughout the city also provide information services.

TRAVEL AGENCIES

You'll find dozens of English-speaking travel agencies in central San José and in the lobbies of moderate and upscale hotels. They can arrange city tours, one- and multiday excursions, beach resort vacations, air transportation, etc. Most tours and excursions are operated by local tour companies, in which case you may wish to make your reservation direct (see "Organized Tours" in the On the Road chapter). I've found **Costa Rica Expeditions** (Avenida 3, Calle Central, tel. 257-0766, fax 257-1665, e-mail, crexped@sol.racsa.co.cr) and **Costa Rica Temptations** (east of the ICE Building, Sabana Norte, tel. 220-4437, fax 220-2103) very knowledgeable, helpful, and efficient. Both are highly recommended and can offer all the same services as travel agencies in addition to their own tours and specialist guides. Costa Rica Expeditions publishes a splendid 66-page catalog listing a zillion tour options. The company was honored with a *Condé Nast Traveler* 1995 Ecotourism Award.

Two recommended travel agencies of note are:

Swiss Travel (Apdo. 7-1970, San José 1000, tel. 231-4055): The head office is in the Corobicí Hotel. This widely respected company offers customized itineraries to fit every budget. It has offices in most of the leading hotels in San José,

including the Amstel, Balmoral, Corobicí, Irazú, and Hotel Herradura.

TAM Travel (Apdo. 1864, San José 1000, tel. 222-2642, fax 221-6465): You'll find it at Calle Central, Avenida Central/1. Like Swiss Travel, it offers a complete range of excursions plus its own version of the famous but defunct Jungle Train (see "Banana Train" under "San José to Puerto Limón" in the Caribbean Coast chapter). It's also the local agent for American Express. TAM recently opened **AdventureLand** (tel. 222-3866, fax 222-3724), a full-service agency for one-stop travel shopping at Avenida 1, Calles 1/3. It maintains a 24-hour bilingual answering service, plus free parking, and has an atmospheric outdoor restaurant.

Ecole Travel (tel. 223-2240, fax 223-4128) specializes in international student exchanges. Their office is in Chispas Books, on Calle 7 and Avenida 1/Central.

jade amulet

TRANSPORTATION

ARRIVAL

All international flights arrive at **Juan Santa-maría Airport,** 17 km northwest of San José (tel. 441-0744). Small charter planes and air-taxis use **Pavas Airport**—also known as To-bías Bolaños—just west of San José (tel. 232-2820). A second international airport was opened at Liberia, in Guanacaste Province, in 1992 but is not yet fully operational.

Immigration proceedings take no more than 10-15 minutes. A **tourist information** booth sits to the left at the top of the stairs as you exit customs (there's another information booth in the departure lounge). The information office staff can provide maps and, if required, help you se-cure accommodations (hotel reservations *before* departing the U.S. are highly recommended, however). The airport has no baggage storage.

You'll find a **post office** (next to the departure tax office) and a **bank** upstairs in the departure ter-minal (hours: Mon.-Fri. 6:30 a.m.-6 p.m., week-ends and holidays 7 a.m.-1 p.m.). Note, though, that the bank can be a grim introduction to Costa Rica's bureaucratic maze of banking (taxis will happily accept dollars; save changing money until you arrive at your hotel). You'll need local cur-rency if you plan on taking the public transport into San José. Most hotels, tour companies, and language schools will pick you up free at the air-port; you'll need to prearrange before arriving.

At press time, a major airport expansion was about to get under way, and a new terminal for charter flights had opened.

Getting into Town

Taxis: Taxi drivers congregate at the top of the stairs as you exit the customs area. The situation isn't as bad as the mayhem at many other des-tinations, but expect to be hustled for taxi rides. Airport taxis that operate between the airport and downtown are orange (local San José taxis are red). The standard daytime fare into down-town San José is $10 (slightly more late at night), although I've been charged everything from $8 to $15. If your cabbie quotes more than $10 by day, don't be afraid to tell him *"demasiado!"* ("too much!") and suggest $10. It normally takes 20-30 minutes to reach downtown.

Buses: A Tuasa company (tel. 222-5325) bus from Alajuela runs about every 15 minutes via the airport into downtown San José via the Cariari Hotel until 11:30 p.m. The Alajuela-San José bus stop is opposite the departure terminal between the two entrance points to the parking lots, and is clearly marked: turn left at the top of the stairs when you exit the customs hall. The fare is 65 *colones* (40 cents). The driver will make change, but you'll need small bills or change. The journey takes about 30 minutes, and ends in the heart of downtown on Avenida 2, between Calles 10 and 12. **Note:** Luggage space is limited. Be sure to ask the bus driver for "San José?", as the buses also go to Alajuela and Heredia from here.

A new bus system operated by a consortium of car rental companies should have been in-troduced by the time you read this. The bus will pick you up at the airport and deliver you direct to the offices of Economy, Pilot, Poás, Tropi-cal, Thrifty, and U-Haul agencies (more com-panies may be added). They'll also return you to the airport at the end of your trip.

Car Rental: A number of car-rental compa-nies have offices at the airport. Some are in mobile units on the far side of the taxi car park at the top of the stairs after you exit customs; additional ones face the departure terminal. If you plan on spending a few days in San José before heading off to explore the country, you'll be better off using taxis and local buses in San José. Rental cars are in very short supply. Make your reservations as soon as you arrive, or much better yet, make reservations *before* departing home. (See the "Car-Rental Agencies in San José" chart).

ORIENTATION

Theoretically, San José's grid system should make finding your way around easy. In actuality,

STREET GRID

Avenida Central and Calle Central divide the city into four quarters as follows (Avenidas run west-east; Calles run north-south):

Northwest: odd number Avenidas, even number Calles
Northeast: odd number Avenidas, odd number Calles
Southwest: even number Avenidas, even number Calles
Southeast: even number Avenidas, odd number Calles

it can be immensely frustrating. Hence, a little orientation lesson is in order.

Streets and Avenues

Streets *(calles)* run parallel north to south. Avenues *(avenidas)* run parallel east to west. Downtown San José is centered on **Calle Central** and **Avenida Central.** To the north of Avenida Central, *avenidas* ascend in odd numbers (Avenida 1, Avenida 3, etc.); to the south they ascend in even numbers (Avenida 2, Avenida 4, etc.). West of Calle Central, *calles* ascend in even numbers (Calle 2, Calle 4, etc.); to the east they ascend in odd numbers (Calle 1, Calle 3, etc.).

Almost all streets are one-way. Often, no sign indicates which direction the traffic is flowing. Pedestrians need to be particularly wary before stepping off the sidewalk (see "Getting Around," below).

Finding Addresses

Addresses are written by the nearest street junction. Thus, the Bar Esmeralda, on Avenida 2 midway between Calles 5 and 7, gives its address as "Avenida 2, Calles 5/7." In telephone directories and advertisements, *calle* may be abbreviated as "c," and *avenida* as "a."

Street names are usually hung on buildings at street corners, about five meters off the ground. Unfortunately, many street corners have no signs at all. And although officially buildings have numbers, they're rarely posted and almost never used. Thus, there's no telling which side of the street the building you're seeking is on.

While the *calle* and *avenida* structure seems easy enough, once you start asking directions you'll discover another problem: Josefinos rarely refer orally to street addresses by *avenida* and

calle. Instead, they usually give a distance in meters *(metros)* from a particular landmark: "100 meters north and 300 meters west of Auto Mercado," for example. Alternately, distances are sometimes expressed in *varas,* an antediluvian Spanish measurement roughly akin to 100 meters *(cien metros).* Fortunately, *"cien metros"* usually refers to one block. *"Cinquenta metros"* (fifty meters) is sometimes used to mean half a block.

The navigational guidance systems of many taxi drivers is linked to particular "landmarks." State a specific street address, and he may give you a confused look! To make matters worse, many reference landmarks still in common use disappeared years ago. Most are not marked on maps. The edifice may have disappeared, but the "landmark" remains. The Coca-Cola bottling plant is a classic example. The Coca-Cola factory was long ago replaced by a "bus terminal," but the area is still called "Coca-Cola." (See the chart, "Common Landmarks.")

Downtown

The focal point of the city is the **central business district,** bisected by Avenida Central and Calle Central and bounded on the north by Avenida 9, on the south by Avenida 4, on the west by Calle 14, and on the east by Calle 11. Avenida Central has been turned into a pedestrian mall between Calles Central and Plaza de la Cultura.

West of Calle 14, Avenida Central widens into a broad, busy, Parisian-style boulevard called **Paseo Colón,** running two and a half kilometers west to Sabana Park. Paseo Colón is known for its elegant restaurants and colonial-style buildings, some of which are being restored; others, sadly, are being torn down to make way for more fast-food restaurants and car dealerships. The large building between Calles 38 and 40 on the north side of Paseo Colón is Centro Colón, a favorite landmark for directions.

Getting out of Town

Paseo Colón, Avenida 1, and Avenida 8 run east to west to Sabana Park and feed right onto the Pan-American Highway, which leads west to Ala-

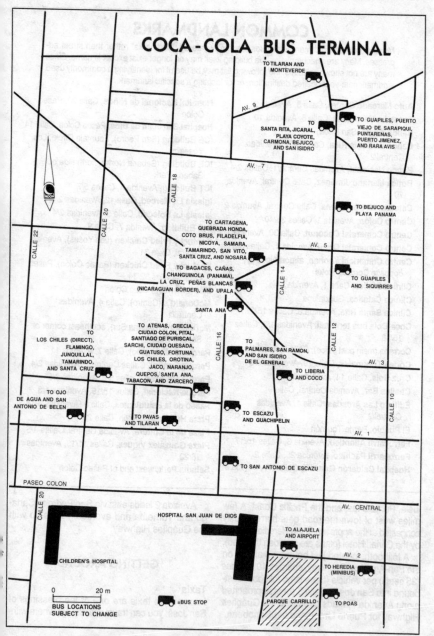

COCA-COLA BUS TERMINAL

TO TILARAN AND MONTEVERDE

AV. 9

TO SANTA RITA, JICARAL, PLAYA COYOTE, CARMONA, BEJUCO, AND SAN ISIDRO

TO GUAPILES, PUERTO VIEJO DE SARAPIQUI, PUNTARENAS, PUERTO JIMENEZ, AND RARA AVIS

AV. 7

TO BEJUCO AND PLAYA PANAMA

CALLE 22

CALLE 20

CALLE 18

TO CARTAGENA, QUEBRADA HONDA, COTO BRUS, FILADELFIA, NICOYA, SAMARA, TAMARINDO, SAN VITO, SANTA CRUZ, AND NOSARA

AV. 5

CALLE 14

TO GUAPILES AND SIQUIRRES

TO BAGACES, CAÑAS, CHANGUINOLA (PANAMA), LA CRUZ, PEÑAS BLANCAS (NICARAGUAN BORDER), AND UPALA

SANTA ANA

CALLE 16

CALLE 12

TO ATENAS, GRECIA, CIUDAD COLON, PITAL, SANTIAGO DE PURISCAL, SARCHI, CIUDAD QUESADA, GUATUSO, FORTUNA, LOS CHILES, OROTINA, JACO, NARANJO, QUEPOS, SANTA ANA, TABACON, AND ZARCERO

TO
LOS CHILES (DIRECT), FLAMINGO, JUNQUILLAL, TAMARINDO, AND SANTA CRUZ

TO PALMARES, SAN RAMON, AND SAN ISIDRO DE EL GENERAL

TO LIBERIA AND COCO

AV. 3

TO OJO DE AGUA AND SAN ANTONIO DE BELEN

CALLE 10

TO ESCAZU AND GUACHIPELIN

TO PAVAS AND TILARAN

AV. 1

TO SAN ANTONIO DE ESCAZU

PASEO COLON

CALLE 20

HOSPITAL SAN JUAN DE DIOS

AV. CENTRAL

TO ALAJUELA AND AIRPORT

CHILDREN'S HOSPITAL

AV. 2

TO HEREDIA (MINIBUS)

0   20 m

BUS LOCATIONS SUBJECT TO CHANGE

🚐 =BUS STOP

PARQUE CARRILLO

TO POAS

COMMON LANDMARKS

Most taxi drivers and many other Josefinos navigate by "landmarks" rather than street addresses. Many are anachronistic—the building itself may no longer exist except in name. Since many are not shown on maps, the following list may be useful for identifying a commonly used landmark near your desired destination, or for locating a specific landmark.

Auto Mercado Centro, Calle 3, Avenida 3

Autos La Castellana, Calle 8, Avenida 10

Banco Anglo, San Pedro

Banco de Costa Rica, Calles 4/6, Avenidas Central/2

Banco Nacional, Avenidas Central/1, Calles 2/4

Botica Mariano Jiménez, Calle Central, Avenida 10

Catedral Metropolitana, Calle Central, Avenida 2

Centro Colón, Avenida 1, Calles 38/40

Centro Comercial Coconut, Calle 30, Avenida 1

Centro Comercial Omni, Avenida 1, Calles 3/5

Centro Comerical Yaohan, airport highway, opposite Corobicí Hotel

Clínica Bíblica, Calle 1, Avenida 14

Clínica Católica, Guadalupe

Clínica Santa Rita, Avenida 8, Calles 15/17

Coca-Cola bus terminal, Avenidas 1/3, Calles 16/18

Correos (main post office), Calle 2, Avenidas 1/3

Cortes/Tribunales, Calle 19, Avenidas 6/8

Cruz Roja, Calle 14, Avenida 6/8

Chelles Bar, Avenida Central, Calle 9

Edificio Las Arcadas, Calle 1, Avenidas Central/2

El Pueblo, Barrio Tournón

Ferrocarril Atlántico, Avenida 3, Calles 15/17

Ferrocarril Pacífico, Avenida 20, Calle 2

Hospital Calderón Guardia, Calle 17, Avenida 9

Hospital Nacional de Niños, Calle 20, Paseo Colón

Hospital San Juan de Dios, Paseo Colón, Calle 14

ICE Building (San Pedro), Fountain Circle, Los Yoses

ICE Building (Sabana Norte), north side of Sabana Park

ICT Building, Avenida 4, Calles 5/7

Iglesia La Merced, Calle 12, Avenidas 2/4

Iglesia La Soledad, Calle 9, Avenidas 2/4

INS Building, Avenida 7, Calle 9

Kentucky Fried Chicken (Los Yoses), Avenida Central, Calle 31

Kentucky Fried Chicken (Paseo Colón), Paseo Colón, Calles 32/34

Más x Menos, Paseo Colón

McDonald's (Centro), Calle 4, Avenidas Central/1

McDonald's (Sabana Sur), southeast corner of Sabana Park

Parque Bolívar (zoo), Calle 7, Avenida 11

Parque Central, Calles Central/2, Avenidas 2/4

Parque Morazán, Calles 5/9, Avenidas 3/5

Parque Nacional, Calles 15/19, Avenidas 1/3

Paseo de la Estudiantes, Calle 9 (Avenidas 8-14)

Pizza Hut, Paseo Colón, Calle 28

Plaza de la Cultura, Avenida Central, Calles 3/5

Plaza González Víquez, Calles 11/13, Avenidas 18/22

Sabana Park, west end of Paseo Colón

---

juela, Puntarenas, and the Pacific Coast. A few miles west of town the road gets horrendously congested at the approach to the Heredia junction, by the Cariari Hotel (plans are to widen the road).

A tollbooth, located just before the airport on the Pan-American Highway, charges 40 *colones* (25 cents) per vehicle (there is no tollbooth eastbound into San José). Calle 3 (best approached along Avenida 7) leads directly to the Guápiles Highway for Puerto Limón and the Caribbean.

Avenida 2 leads east via San Pedro to Cartago and Turrialba and eventually links up with the Guápiles Highway.

GETTING AROUND

Taxis

Inexpensive taxis are one of the blessings of San José: you can travel virtually anywhere with-

TAXI COMPANIES

Coopetaxi, Tibas, tel. 235-9966

Coopetico, Calle 2, Avenidas 9/11, tel. 221-2552

Taxis Alfaro, Calle 19, Avenida 6, tel. 221-8466

Taxis San Jorge, Calle 9, Avenidas 8/10, tel. 221-3434

Taxis Unidos (Airport service), Calles 12/14, Avenida 7, tel. 221-6865 (241-0333 airport)

in the city for less than $3. Fares are fixed by the government, and by law taxi drivers must use their meters—*marias*—for journeys of less than 12 km. Hardly anyone does (this may change with the tighter regulations introduced in mid-1995). Many drivers will tell you it is "broken." The rule is to negotiate an agreeable fare before getting in the cab or setting off, otherwise you could have a rude awakening at your destination. You're well within your rights to demand that the taxi driver use his meter. Ask *"Hay un maria?"* but don't be surprised if he flatly refuses to do so. There's a 20% surcharge after 10 p.m. You do not tip taxi drivers in Costa Rica.

In mid-1995 the government established strict regulations. Taxi drivers must now wear uniforms. They must also have experience and a clean driving record before being issued a license (their vehicles must pass inspection, too). And every taxi driver must now have a business card with his name, license plate, and other details.

Finding a taxi is usually no problem, except downtown during rush hour. Many taxi drivers also take the weekend off. The number of taxis more than doubled from 1990 to 1992 to more than 3,000. One of the best places to find a taxi is Parque Central, where they line up opposite the Teatro Melico Salazar on Avenida 2. Note that taxis in front of the Gran Hotel and National Theater beside the Plaza de la Cultura generally charge slightly more than taxis taken a few blocks away. This is also true of the Aurola Holiday Inn and other deluxe hotels. Penny-pinchers should consider walking one or two

blocks before hailing a taxi. Likewise, when traveling *to* a deluxe hotel, name a location one or two blocks away.

Taxis are painted bright red. If it is any other color, it is a "pirate" taxi operating illegally.

Buses

San José has an excellent network of local bus services. Buses are ridiculously cheap: fares are about 15 *colones* (nine cents) downtown and under 30 *colones* elsewhere within the metropolitan area. The standards, however, may not be quite what you're used to back home. While some routes are served by slick new Mercedes, other buses are decrepit old things belching fumes, with wooden, uncushioned seats. But most are clean and comfortable enough for short journeys. And since almost all Josefinos use them, they play every note on the social scale: a bus journey in San José is a kaleidoscopic vignette of social life.

I've found it virtually as quick as the bus and far more pleasant to walk downtown if a journey is less than three kilometers.

Most buses begin operating at about 5 a.m. and run until at least 10 p.m. The frequency of bus service is determined by demand. Downtown and suburban San José buses leave their principal *paradas* (bus stops) every few minutes. The wait is rarely very long, except during rush hours (7-9 a.m. and 5-7 p.m.), when there are often long passenger lines and buses can get woefully crowded. Also, buses to outer suburbs often fill up straightaway: I recommend boarding at their principal downtown *parada*, designated by a sign, Parada de Autobuses, showing the route name and number. General *paradas* where all buses may stop do not usually display any signs (you may need to ask locals): once they leave the downtown area buses will usually stop at any *parada*, assuming they have space.

The ICT (Instituto Costarricense de Turismo) office (tel. 222-1090) beneath the Plaza de la Cultura publishes a listing of current bus schedules, including the bus company and telephone numbers. It also provides a listing of out-of-town services. The most comprehensive information source for both San José and provincial bus routes is *The Essential Road Guide* by Bill Baker (available from the Bookshop, at Calles 1/3 and

BUS SCHEDULES FROM SAN JOSÉ

Check current schedules, which change often. The ICT information office (Plaza de la Cultura, Calle 5 and Avenida Central) provides a bus schedule. Departures are normally punctual. Bus companies do not take reservations by phone.

DESTINATION; DEPARTURE POINT; TIME; DURATION; COMPANY, TELEPHONE

MESETA CENTRAL AND NORTHERN LOWLANDS

Alajuela and Airport; Avenida 2, Calles 10/12; every 10 minutes, 5 a.m.-midnight; 30 minutes; Tuasa; 222-4650 or 222-5325

Braulio Carrillo; use Guápiles bus (above, under "Caribbean"). Get off at the Botarrama Trail *(sendero)*.

Caño Negro; as per Los Chiles

Cartago; Calle 5, Avenida 18; every 10 minutes, 5 a.m.-7 p.m.; 45 minutes; SACSA; 233-5350

Ciudad Quesada (San Carlos); Calle 16, Avenidas 1/3; hourly, 5 a.m.-7:30 p.m.; 3 hours; Autotransportes Ciudad Quesada; 255-4318

Fortuna; Calle 16, Avenidas 1/3; 6:15, 8:40, and 11:30 a.m.; 4 1/2 hours; Garaje Barquero; 232-5660

Heredia; Calle 1, Avenidas 7/9; every 10 minutes, 5 a.m.-10 p.m.; also Avenida 2, Calles 10/12; every 15 minutes; Microbuses Rapidos; tel. 233-8392

Irazú; Avenida 2, Calles 1/3; 8 a.m. (Sat., Sun., holidays only); 90 minutes; Buses Metropoli; 234-0344 or 252-1138

La Selva; as per Puerto Viejo.

Los Chiles; Calle 16, Avenidas 3/5; 5:30 a.m. and 3:30 p.m.; 5 hours

Poás; Calle 12, Avenidas 2/4; 8:30 a.m. (Sun. and holidays only); 90 minutes; Tuasa; 222-4650 or 222-5325

Puerto Viejo de Sarapiquí; Avenida 11, Calles Central/1; 7, 9 and 10 a.m., 1, 3 and 4 p.m; 4 hours

Rara Avis; Calle 12, Avenidas 7/9; Coopetragua Co.; 223-1276

San Ignacio de Acosta; Calle 8, Avenida 12; hourly, 5:30 a.m.-10:30 p.m.

San Ramón; Calle 16, Avenidas 3/5; hourly, 6 a.m.-10 p.m.

Santa María de Dota; Avenida 16, Calles 19/21; 6 and 9 a.m., 12:30, 3, and 5 p.m.

Sarchí; Calle 16, Avenidas 1/3; daily 12:15 and 5:30 p.m.; 90 minutes; Tuan; 441-3781

Turrialba; Calle 13, Avenidas 6/8; hourly, 5 a.m.-10 p.m.; 90 minutes; Transtusa; 556-0073

Zarcero; Calle 16, Avenidas 1/3; hourly, 5 a.m.-7:30 p.m.; 90 minutes; Autotransportes Ciudad Quesada; 255-4318

CARIBBEAN

Cahuita/Sixaola; Avenida 11, Calles Central/1; 6 a.m., and 1:30 and 3:30 p.m.; 4 hours; Autotransportes MEPE; 221-0524

Guápiles; Calle 12, Avenidas 7/9; every 45 minutes, 5:30 a.m.-7 p.m.; Coopetragua; 223-1276

Puerto Limón; Avenida 3, Calles 19/21; hourly, 5 a.m.-7 p.m.; 2 1/2 hours; Coopelimón; 223-7811

CENTRAL AND SOUTHERN PACIFIC

Carara Biological Reserve; use Jacó bus

Golfito; Avenida 18, Calles 2/4; 7 and 11 a.m., and 3 p.m.; 8 hours; Tracopa; 221-4214

Jacó; Calle 16, Avenidas 1/3; 7:15 a.m. and 3:30 p.m.; 2½ hours; Transportes Morales; 223-5567 or 223-1109

Manuel Antonio; as per Quepos

Palmar Norte; Avenida 18, Calles 2/4; 5, 6:30, 8:30, and 10 a.m., and 2:30 and 6 p.m.; 5 hours; Tracopa; 221-4214

Paso Canoas; Avenida 18, Calles 2/4; 5 and 7:30 a.m., and 1, 4:30, 6 p.m.; 8 hours; Tracopa; 221-4214

Puerto Jiménez; Calle 12, Avenidas 7/9; 6 a.m. and noon; 8 hrs; Transportes Blanco; 771-2550

Puntarenas; Calle 16, Avenidas 10/12; every 40 minutes, 6 a.m.-7 p.m.; 2 hours; Empresarios Unidas; 222-0064

Quepos; Calle 16, Avenidas 1/3; 6 a.m., noon and 6 p.m.; 3½ hours; Transportes Morales; 223-5567 or 223-1109

San Isidro; Calle 12, Avenidas 7/9; hourly, 5:30 a.m.-5:30 p.m.; 3 hours; Transportes Musoc; 222-2422 or 223-0686

GUANACASTE

Cañas; Calle 16, Avenidas 3/5; 8:30 and 10:30 a.m., and 1:30, 2:15, 4:30 p.m.; 3 hours; Transportes la Cañera; 222-3006

Coco; Calle 14, Avenidas 1/3; 10 a.m.; 5 hours; Pulmitán; 222-1650

Flamingo; Calle 20, Avenida 3; 8 and 11 a.m.; 6 hours; Tralapa; 221-7202

Hermosa; Calle 12, Avenidas 5/7; 3:20 p.m.; 5 hours; Empresa Esquivel; 666-1249

Junquillal; Calle 20, Avenida 3; 2 p.m.; 5 hours; Tralapa; 221-7202

La Cruz/Peñas Blancas; Calle 14, Avenidas 3/5; 5 and 7:45 a.m., and 1:30 and 4:15 p.m.; 6 hours; Carsol; 224-1968

Liberia; Calle 14, Avenidas 1/3; 7, 9, and 11:30 a.m., and 1, 3, 4, 6, and 8 p.m.; 4 hours; Pulmitán; 222-1650

Monteverde; Calle 14, Avenidas 9/11; 2:30 p.m. (Mon.-Thurs.) and 6:30 a.m. (Sat.-Sun.); 4 hours; Autotransportes Tilarán; 222-3854

Nicoya; Calle 14, Avenidas 3/5; 6, 8, and 10 a.m., noon, and 1, 2:30, 3, and 5 p.m.; 6 hours; Empresa Alfaro; 222-2750

Nosara; Calle 14, Avenidas 3/5; 6:15 a.m.; Empresa Alfaro; 222-2750

Sámara; Calle 14, Avenidas 3/5; noon; 6 hours; Empresa Alfaro; 222-2750

Santa Cruz; Calle 20, Avenidas 1/3; 7:30, 10:30 a.m., and 2, 4, 6 p.m.; 5 hours; Tralapa; 221-7202

Santa Rosa; use La Cruz/Peñas Blancas bus

Tamarindo; Calle 14, Avenidas 3/5; 3:30 p.m.; 6 hours; Alfaro; 222-2750

Tilarán; Calle 14, Avenidas 9/11; 7:30 a.m. and 12:45, 3:45, 6:30 p.m.; 4 hours; Autotransportes Tilarán; 222-3854

Departures daily unless indicated. For **Juan Santamaría International Airport,** use the Alajuela bus.

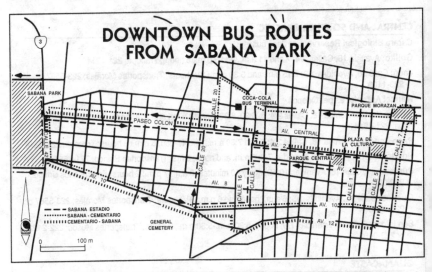

DOWNTOWN BUS ROUTES
FROM SABANA PARK

Avenida 1; or from Apdo. 1185, San José 1011, tel./fax 220-1415), which provides detailed route maps plus a complete listing of metropolitan bus stops and services.

There are many bus routes within San José. A sign in the windshield tells the bus name, route number, and destination. Fares are marked by the doors and are collected when you board. Drivers provide change and tend to be scrupulously honest. Buses—most of them garishly painted, with improbable names such as *Guerrero del Camino* ("Road Warrior"), *Desert Storm, Tico Tex,* and *Titanic*—are equipped with turnstiles.

Private or cooperative bus services operate across the city from east to west, linking the center with Sabana Park and San Pedro, and north and south, from Guadalupe, Moravia, San Juan, and other nearby towns. Many take a circular routing that can provide a good introductory sightseeing experience. From the west, the most convenient bus into town is the Sabana-Cementerio service (route 2), which runs counterclockwise between Sabana Sur and downtown along Avenida 10, then back along Avenida 3 (past the Coca-Cola bus station) and Paseo Colón. The Cementerio-Sabana service (route 7) runs in the opposite direction along Paseo Colón and Avenida 2 and back along

Avenida 12. Both take about 40 minutes to complete the circle.

Many buses serve Los Yoses and the popular eastern suburb of San Pedro from Avenida 2, including the following: Barrio Pinto (route 52), Calle Siles (route 54), Cedros (route 52), Cipreses (route 60A), Curridabat (routes 60 and 61), Granadilla (route 57), Monterrey (route 51), and Santa Marta (route 50).

Most provincial cities and towns are linked to San José by a loosely organized bus system. The main station for buses to the outlying regions is on the site of the old Coca-Cola bottling plant—the bus station is referred to as "Coca-Cola"—at Calle 16 and Avenidas 1 and 3 (see the chart "Bus Schedules from San José" for a listing of provincial bus services).

Note: Be wary of pickpockets on buses, especially in crowded scenarios. Be especially suspect of anyone pushing you or pushing against you.

A **free sightseeing tour** of San José is offered by the Hotel Del Rey (tel. 221-7272, ext. 444) using special tour buses. The one-hour tour includes most major places of historic interest downtown. You are picked up at various points in the city center: Hotel Del Rey, 10:30 a.m.; Holiday Inn, 10:45 a.m.; Gold Museum, 10:50 a.m.; and National Theater, 11 a.m.

Limo Service

If the thought of city touring with in-car TV turns you on, **Limo Servi** (tel. 250-8012, fax 250-2620) can provide 24-hour service. I recommend avoiding the U.S.-made stretch limos, which are cramped, claustrophobic, and nauseating on winding roads.

Car Rental

In a word . . . don't even think about it for travel *within* San José! Parking can be a problem. Traffic jams are frequent. The traffic lights will give you neck-ache. The one-way system can run you ragged. The competitive, free-for-all mentality of Josefino drivers can fray your nerves. And, anyway, most places are quickly and easily reached by taxi, bus, or on foot.

But if you insist on driving, a few tips and precautions are in order. San José's road network is made up of alternating one-way streets. Avenida 2 and Avenida 10 are good west-to-east routes. Avenida 1 and Avenida 8 are good east-to-west routes to Sabana Park. Note that Avenida Central between Calles Central and 5 is closed to traffic, with the exception of delivery and pick-up . . . great for pedestrians, but a nightmare on adjacent streets, where traffic jams are frequent. A peripheral highway *(circunvalación)* encircling San José, scheduled for completion in 1994, was still not complete a year later. When finished it promises to make getting from one side of the city to another considerably quicker.

Bill Baker's book *The Essential Road Guide* provides detailed directions for navigating by car around San José: I recommend it highly.

Parking can be a nightmare. Parking spaces are at a premium, and you may end up having to park so far away you may as well have walked in the first place. Parking meters take five-*colón* coins (30 minutes) as well as tokens *(ficas)*. Forget the tokens! If you really love waiting in line, however, you can obtain these at the Departamento de Parquémetros, in the administrative offices of the Mercado Central (Calle 6, Avenidas Central/1, second floor); or at the Banco de Costa Rica, at the window where municipal taxes are paid. Never park in a no-parking zone, marked Control por Grúa ("Controlled by tow truck"). Regulations are efficiently enforced.

Break-ins and theft are common (rental cars are especially vulnerable; make sure your insurance covers loss). In one 10-day period of July 1994, 52 cars were reported stolen! Never leave anything of value in your car—even in the trunk. Many **public parking lots** offer secure 24-hour parking. You must leave your ignition key with the attendant (it's not necessary to tip except in special circumstances). Elsewhere, young men and boys may offer to watch your car for 40 or 50 *colones*. Usually, it's a worthwhile investment.

Most **car-rental agencies** are strung out along Paseo Colón and parallel streets west of downtown. See "Getting Around" in the On the Road chapter for more driving information and a listing of car-rental agencies.

Walking

Having lived in London—a walker's city if ever there was one—I soon learned to disregard the advice of Prime Minister Gladstone, who said, "The way to see London is from the top of a bus, the top of a bus, gentlemen." I *walked* everywhere and grew to know the city intimately. I apply the same rule to San José, a city on a Lilliputian scale ideal for walking. The city is compact, with virtually everything of interest within a few blocks of the center.

DISTANCES FROM SAN JOSÉ

Alajuela	20 km
Cahuita	202 km
Cañas	188 km
Ciudad Quesada	104 km
Cartago	21 km
Golfito	342 km
Heredia	11 km
Liberia	220 km
Monteverde	168 km
Nicoya	329 km
Puerto Limón	160 km
Puntarenas	110 km
Quepos	277 km
San Isidro	136 km
Tamarindo	321 km

However, a few words of warning:

First, sidewalks everywhere are in horrendous repair. Use the same philosophy as in the rainforests: when walking, look down; look up when standing still. Supposedly, the sidewalks are the responsibility of adjoining property owners. Few, if any, seem to take their responsibility seriously. As a consequence, you'll need to keep an eternal vigil for great potholes, tilted flagstones, and gaping sewer holes.

Second, pedestrians and automobiles mix about as well as oil and water. Says *National Geographic:* "Rush hour is a bullfight on the streets, with every car a blaring beast and every pedestrian a torero." Josefinos treat both pedestrians and traffic lights with total disdain. They love to jump the gun on green lights and sail through heedlessly on red. Don't expect traffic to stop for you if you get caught in the middle of the road when the light changes; drivers will expect you to act like a local—run! To make matters worse, a single stoplight usually hangs above the center of the narrow junctions, where it is far too high for pedestrians to see. Watch the cars, not the lights. Don't take your eyes off the traffic for a moment!

Other than traffic hazards, walking is generally safe everywhere, although pickpockets and muggings are on the increase (see "Safety" in the On the Road chapter). Avoid the parks at night, and use particular caution if exploring the red-light district (bordered by Calles Central and 8, and Avenidas 6 and 10) or the streets around—particularly north of—the Coca-Cola bus terminal.

Vernon Bell, a well-known figure in Costa Rica, publishes the *Walking Tour of Downtown San José,* ($7.50 including postage; Dept. 1432, P.O. Box 025216, Miami, FL 33102, tel. 225-4752, fax 224-5884). It's a whimsical guide to exploring the city, with all the main sites included.

DEPARTING COSTA RICA

The San José **bus** for Alajuela stops at Juan Santamaría Airport and departs from Calles 10/12 and Avenida 2 every 15 minutes or so. Any **taxi** will take you to the airport. To order an airport taxi in advance, call Taxis Unidos (Calles 12/14 and Avenida 7), tel. 221-6865. For Pavas Airport, take bus 14B from the Coca-Cola bus station (Avenida 1, between Calles 16 and 18). The bus stops in Pavas, a short walk from the airport. A taxi will cost about $10 from downtown San José.

The airport bank will give no more than $50 in dollars for *colones.* Change the rest before you arrive at the airport, as the Banco de Costa Rica here is a bureaucratic curse (I once waited 15 minutes in line to have a teller calculate the conversion and then hand me a slip of paper with a number; I then stood in another line for 10 minutes, when a second teller repeated the conversion and cashed my *colones* for dollars—the first line was a total waste). Otherwise, there are two small gift shops, one just outside and one inside the snack bar on the second floor, which also has a full-service restaurant and a separate bar. You can spend your last *colones* here. The duty-free store beyond the immigration post prefers payment in dollars.

Airport departure tax, payable after checking in (the booth is to the left of the LACSA check-in counter), has been increased to $15 (350 *colones*—$2—additional for each month you may have overstayed). You can pay in U.S. dollars.

A four-year airport expansion program finally broke ground in 1994, to include the relocation of the airline check-in counters (renowned for their notoriously cramped quarters), a new terminal, new boarding arms, and a reorganization of passenger arrival and departure routes.

Buses to Nicaragua

TICA (tel. 222-8954) operates service to Managua from Avenida 4, Calle 9/11 on Monday, Wednesday, Friday, and Saturday at 7 a.m. (about $17; 11 hours). **Sirca** (tel. 222-5541) operates a cheaper service from Calle 7, Avenidas 6/8 on Wednesday, Friday, and Sunday at 5 a.m. ($7). Service on Sirca is reportedly unreliable. **Carsol** (tel. 224-1968) operates buses to Peñas Blancas, at the Nicaraguan border, daily at 5 and 7:45 a.m. and 1:30 and 4:15 p.m.

Buses to Panamá

TICA operates daily to Panamá City, departing Avenida 4, Calles 9/11 at 10 p.m. ($40; 20

(top) scarlet macaw; (above) keel-billed toucan (photos by Jean Mercier)

(top) ocelot in Corcovado National Park (Jean Mercier); (bottom) The Rainforest Aerial Tram takes visitors through the rainforest canopy (Rainforest Aerial Tram).

hours). **Tracopa** (tel. 221-4214; opposite the Pacific railway station on Avenida 18, Calles 2/4) has buses to Paso Canoas (at the Panamá border) at 5 and 7:30 a.m., and 1, 4:30 and 6 p.m. ($7; nine hours); and onward to David in Panamá at 7:30 a.m. and noon (nine hours).

A **Via Caribbean** bus leaves daily (10 a.m.) from the Hotel Cocorí (Calle 16 and Avenida 3) via the Caribbean coast and the Sixaola-Guabito border post and travels as far as Changuinola ($6, payable to the driver; six to seven hours).

CENTRAL HIGHLANDS

INTRODUCTION

The central highlands region is stunningly beautiful and replete with sights to see. The large, fertile central valley—sometimes called the Meseta Central ("Central Plateau")—is held in the cusp of verdant mountains that rise on all sides. Almost 70% of the nation's populace lives here, concentrated in the four colonial cities of San José, Alajuela, Cartago, and Heredia, though settlements are found far up the mountain slopes. Though variations of climate exist—the valley floor has been called a place of "perpetual summer" and the upper slopes a place of "perpetual spring"—an invigorating, salubrious climate is universal.

The abundant and marvelous beauty owes much to the juxtaposition of valley and mountain. The ethereal landscapes—the soaring volcanoes and impossibly green coffee terraces—lift the spirits. The serenity beguiles. You can reach virtually any point within a two-hour drive of San José; roads are narrow, unlit, and poorly marked, though almost all are paved and in reasonably

good condition. And though outside San José cities are not well served by hotels, many fine lodges and bed and breakfasts are scattered throughout the highlands, so that you can spend a week or more touring the region without having to retire to San José to rest your head.

THE LAND

The Meseta Central is really two valleys in one, divided by a low mountain ridge—the Fila de Bustamente—which rises immediately southwest of San José. West of the ridge is the larger valley of the Poás and Virilla rivers, with flanks gradually rising from a level floor. East of the ridge the smaller Guarco Valley is undulating, more tightly hemmed in, and falls away to the east, drained by the Río Reventazón.

Volcanoes of the Cordillera Central arc around the central valley to the north, forming a meniscus of smooth-sloped cones. To the south

lies the massive, blunt-nosed bulk of the Cordillera Talamanca. The high peaks are generally obscured by clouds for much of the "winter" months (May through November). When clear, both mountain zones offer spectacularly scenic drives, including the chance to drive to the very crest of two active volcanoes! Poás and Irazú still periodically dump millions of tons of ash on the central valley, which benefits from their eruptions.

When the Spaniards arrived, broad-leafed evergreen forest covered the valley floor. Pine forests blanketed the slopes. The Spaniards first stripped the timber. Today, barely an inch of virgin forest remains. Sugarcane, tobacco, and corn smother the valley floor, according to elevation and microclimate. Dairy farms rise up the slopes to over 2,500 meters. Small coffee *fincas,* too, are everywhere on vale and slope, the dark green, shiny-leafed bushes often shaded by *erythrina* trees, which can be planted simply by breaking off a branch and sticking it in the ground; every manicured row flows into the next like folds of green silk, with blazing orange flame-of-the-forest and bright red African tulip adorning the hedgerows. Pockets of natural vegetation remain, however, farther up the slopes and in protected areas such as Braulio Carrillo National Park and the Tapantí National Park, lush nurseries where quetzals, tapirs, pumas, ocelots, monkeys, toucans, and other treasured species can be seen in the wild.

CLIMATE

Refreshingly clear and invigorating, the weather of the central highlands has been termed idyllic, which partly explains why the greater part of Costa Rica's population has always lived here. As a rule of thumb, mornings are clear and the *meseta* and adjacent valleys bask under brilliant sunshine. In the dry season, things stay this way all day. In the wet—"green"—season, clouds form over the mountains in the early afternoon, announcing the possible arrival of rain. Temperatures average in the mid-20s C (mid-70s F) year-round in the valley and cool steadily as one moves into the mountains, where coniferous trees lend a distinctly alpine feel. The valley—with an average high of 25° C (77° F) and average lows of 16° C (61° F)—has a pronounced dry season December through April, with monthly rainfall averaging less than one inch. Monthly rainfall May through October averages 25-30 centimeters, when moist westerlies begin bearing in from the Pacific. Long rainy days are a rarity.

Things are different on the mountain slopes. Western-facing slopes have a distinct dry season that roughly corresponds to North America's winter months; temperatures increase, however, peaking in February, March, and April, when temperatures are generally three to five degrees (five to 10 degrees F) warmer than in

view toward Meseta Central from Poás volcano

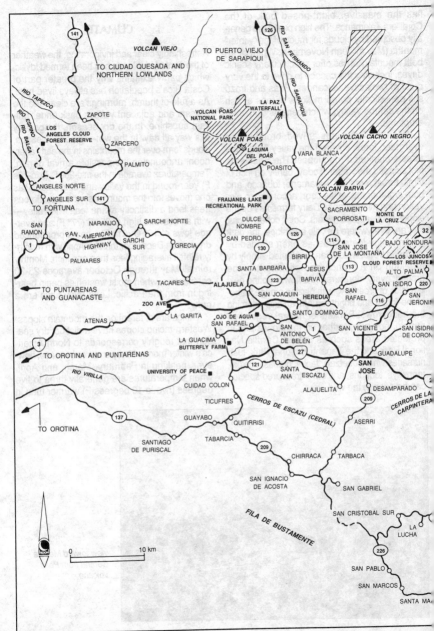

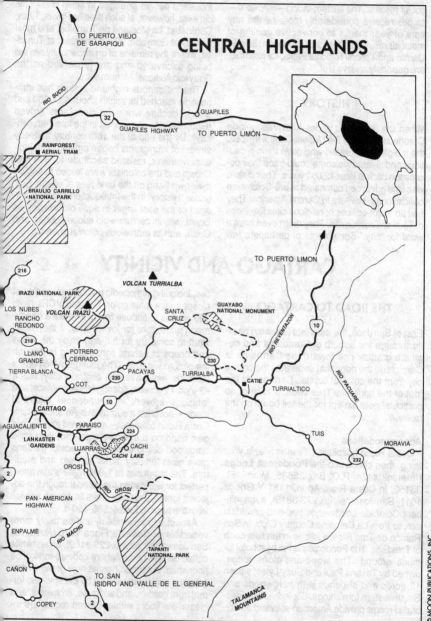

CENTRAL HIGHLANDS

TO PUERTO VIEJO
DE SARAPIQUI

RIO SUCIO

32

GUAPILES

GUAPILES HIGHWAY

TO PUERTO LIMÓN

RAINFOREST
AERIAL TRAM

BRAULIO CARRILLO
NATIONAL PARK

216

IRAZU NATIONAL PARK

LOS NUBES
RANCHO
REDONDO

VOLCAN IRAZÚ

VOLCAN TURRIALBA

SANTA
CRUZ

GUAYABO
NATIONAL MONUMENT

TO PUERTO LIMON

218

LLANO
GRANDE

TIERRA BLANCA

POTRERO
CERRADO

230

PACAYAS

RIO REVENTAZON

RIO PACUARE

COT

230

TURRIALBA

CATIE

10

CARTAGO

224

TURRIALTICO

AGUACALIENTE

PARAISO

LANKASTER
GARDENS

UJARRAS

CACHI

CACHI LAKE

TUIS

OROSI

MORAVIA

2

RIO OROSI

232

PAN - AMERICAN
HIGHWAY

RIO MACHO

TAPANTI
NATIONAL PARK

ENPALME

CAÑON

COPEY

TO SAN
ISIDRO AND VALLE DE EL GENERAL

2

TALAMANCA
MOUNTAINS

© MOON PUBLICATIONS, INC.

cooler months. The eastern-facing—windward—slopes receive considerably more rainfall any time of year thanks to convective cooling of moist air moving in from the Caribbean. Braulio Carrillo and Tapantí National Parks, for example, are generally always wet.

HISTORY

When the Spaniards under Juan Vásquez de Coronado arrived in the Meseta Central in 1562, the indigenous peoples who gave them a cautious and ill-fated welcome could trace their occupation back at least 12,000 years. Their culture was little advanced compared to pre-Columbian civilizations elsewhere in Central America. They had no major edifices or religious sites like those of Tikal or Teotihuacán. They didn't even have a word for "city." Settlements of perhaps a few

thousand people arranged in small chiefdoms did exist, however, at such sites as Pavas, Tibas, Curridabat, La Montaña de Turrialba, and most notably at Guayabo, 20 km northeast of Turrialba, where the remains of an ancient city are still being excavated and are preserved as the Guayabo National Monument.

The indigenous highland culture had supposedly reached its zenith about A.D. 600 and was in decline when the Spaniards arrived (Guayabo was abandoned in the late 14th century). By the end of the 16th century a steady stream of immigrants began arriving. The Indians, however, resisted servitude to God and Crown and the colonists were forced to secure their own living off the land (see "Colonial Era" under "History" in the Introduction chapter). Images of the past linger in such old villages as Barva, with its centuries-old adobe houses, and Orosí, with its marvelous colonial church.

CARTAGO AND VICINITY

THE ROAD TO CARTAGO

East of San José, the *autopista* (freeway) passes through the suburb of Curridabat and begins a gradual rise toward the Cerros de la Carpintera, the ridge that separates the capital city from the colonial capital, Cartago. At the foot of the ridge sits **Tres Ríos**, a town of no particular note except for the toll booth on the freeway.

Accommodations

If Costa Rican hospitality, Texan style, is your thing, then check into the **Ponderosa Lodge** (Interlink #424, P.O. Box 25635, Miami, FL 33152; in Costa Rica, Apdo. 1151 Y Griega 1011, San José, tel./fax 273-3818), a magnificent Colorado Lodge-style bed-and-breakfast across from La Campina Country Club, in San Ramón de Tres Ríos, a village in the hills north of Tres Ríos. The Ponderosa is the best hotel for miles around. The wood-and-stone lodge, owned by Texans Paul and Suzy Lyles, sits on 12 acres and abounds with hardwoods and Southwestern furnishings. Six individually decorated rooms provide American-standard ameni-

ties, including orthopedic mattresses, oodles of closet space, plus color TVs and VCRs (with 200 movies to choose from). There's a honeymoon suite, too, for lovers who, if they don't want to come up for air, can enjoy the views and heaps of natural light flooding in through the picture windows. The lounge, which offers fabulous views over the central valley, has a 42-inch TV screen, soaring stone fireplace, and fabulous artwork in abundance! Gourmet meals—not least a sumptuous American-cum-Costa Rican breakfast—are served from Suzy's own hand on a massive eight-foot-long solid hardwood dining table. The peaceful gardens have quiet "privacy parks" to relax and meditate. The lodge sits at 1,300 meters elevation: perfect for wandering the paths through the adjacent forest. The hotel offers limousine service from the airport. Rates: $65-150 d.

Almost as resplendent, and certainly more venerable, is **Casa de Finca 1926** (Apdo. 29, San José 1000, tel./fax 225-6169), an erstwhile coffee baron's home (where coffee beans once flourished, suburban homes now grow) whose gracious heyday is recalled by the splendid formal front garden, and antiques, archways, and glazed-tile floors within. Eleven rooms are in-

dividually furnished with wicker and, in some, open-air showers and private interior gardens. Rates: $75 d, including breakfast.

Bello Monte (Apdo. 8-5630, San José 1000, tel./fax 273-3879), also in San Ramón de Tres Ríos, reportedly has rooms for $40 upward. Not inspected.

Last but not least among the atmospheric newcomers is **Carpintera Lodge** (tel. 573-7014, fax 573-8125). Not inspected.

CARTAGO

Cartago, about 21 km southeast of San José and reached along the Autopista Florencio del Castillo (50-cent toll), is a peaceful and parochial town founded in 1563 by Juan Vásquez de Coronado, the Spanish governor, as the nation's first city. "I have never seen a more beautiful valley, and I laid out a city between two rivers," he wrote to the king. Cartago—a Spanish word for Carthage, the ancient North African trading center—reigned as the colonial capital until losing its status to San José in the violent internecine squabbles of 1823 (see "History" in the "Introduction" to the San José chapter). In 1841 and again in 1910 earthquakes toppled much of the city. Virtually no old buildings are extant: the remains of the ruined cathedral testify to Mother Nature's destructive powers. Volcán Irazú looms over Cartago and occasionally rubs salt in the wounds by showering ash on the city.

Despite its woes, Cartago has kept its status as the nation's religious center and home of Costa Rica's patron saint: La Negrita, or Virgen de los Angeles. Fittingly, she "lives" in the most impressive church in the nation—one of only two sights of interest in Costa Rica's second-largest city (pop. 30,000). The city is a traditional stopping point and transportation center, however, en route to many points of interest nearby.

Sights
Cartago's central landmark (Avenida 2, Calle 2) is the ruins (Las Ruinas) of the **Church of La Parroquia,** fronted by lawns and trees shading a statue of Manuel Salazar Zunca, the "immortal tenor." Completed in 1575 to honor Saint James the Apostle, the church was destroyed by earthquakes and rebuilt a number of times before its final destruction in the earthquake of 1910. Today, only the walls remain. The interior is now a garden (closed to the public).

The gleaming blue-and-white Byzantine, cupola-topped **Basílica de Nuestra Señora de los Angeles** ("Cathedral of Our Lady of the Angels"), ten blocks east of the main plaza, is one of Costa Rica's most imposing structures. There's a unique beauty to the soaring, all-wooden interior, with its marvelous stained-glass windows, its columns and walls painted in floral motifs, and its miasma of smoke rising from votive candles and curling about the columns like an ethereal veil. Every 2 August, hundreds of Costa Ricans walk from towns far and wide to pay homage to the country's patron saint, La

Las Ruinas, Cartago

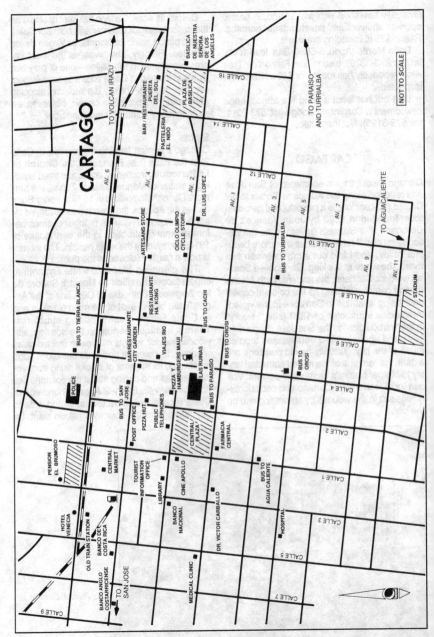

CARTAGO

NOT TO SCALE

TO VOLCAN IRAZU

TO PARAISO
AND TURRIALBA

TO AGUACALIENTE

TO TURRIALBA

TO OROSI

TO
SAN JOSE

TO AGUA
CALIENTE

BASILICA
DE NUESTRA
SEÑORA
DE LOS
ANGELES

BAR / RESTAURANTE
PUERTA
DEL SOL

PLAZA DE
BASILICA

PASTELERIA
EL NIDO

DR. LUIS LOPEZ

ARTESANS STORE

CICLO OLIMPIO
CYCLE STORE

RESTAURANTE
HA KONG

BAR/RESTAURANTE
CITY GARDEN

VIAJES RIO

PIZZA Y
HAMBURGERS MAUI

LAS RUINAS

BUS TO CACHI

BUS TO OROSI

BUS TO OROSI

BUS TO PARAISO

BUS TO SAN JOSE

POST OFFICE

PIZZA HUT

PUBLIC
TELEPHONES

BUS TO TIERRA BLANCA

POLICE

FARMACIA
CENTRAL

CENTRAL /
PLAZA

PENSION
EL BRUMOSO

CENTRAL
MARKET

TOURIST
INFORMATION
OFFICE

LIBRARY

CINE APOLLO

BANCO
NACIONAL

DR. VICTOR CARBALLO

HOTEL
VENECIA

OLD TRAIN STATION

BANCO DE
COSTA RICA

BANCO ANGLO
COSTARRICENSE

MEDICAL CLINIC

HOSPITAL

STADIUM

TO
SAN JOSE

CALLE 16

CALLE 14

CALLE 12

CALLE 10

CALLE 8

CALLE 6

CALLE 4

CALLE 2

CALLE 1

CALLE 3

CALLE 5

CALLE 7

CALLE 9

AV. 6

AV. 4

AV. 2

AV. 1

AV. 3

AV. 5

AV. 7

AV. 9

AV. 11

Negrita. The event attracts pilgrims from throughout Central America. Many crawl all the way from San José on their knees, starting at dawn! Others carry large wooden crosses. On any day you can see the devout crawling down the aisle, muttering their invocations, repeating the sacred names, oblivious to the pain.

The basilica houses an eight-inch-high black statue of La Negrita, embedded in a gold- and jewel-encrusted shrine above the main altar. According to superstition, in 1635 a mulatto peasant girl named Juana Pereira found a small stone statue of the Virgin holding the Christ child. Twice Juana took the statue home and placed it in a box, and twice it mysteriously reappeared at the original spot where it was discovered. The message in the miracle? Obviously God wanted a church built at the site. The cathedral marks the spot (the original cathedral was toppled by an earthquake in 1926). Beneath the basilica, well protected by a civil guard, is the rock where the statue was supposedly found, plus a small room full of ex-votos or *promesas:* gold and silver charms, sports trophies, and other offerings for prayers answered, games won, amorous conquests, etc. Many are in the shape of various human parts, left by devotees seeking a cure for afflictions or in thanks for a miraculous healing. Outside, a spring that flows beneath the basilica is thought to have curative powers. You can buy a receptacle at a shop across the street and take home a vial of holy water if so inclined; you can also buy ex-votos and other religious trinkets here.

Cartago's only museum of note, albeit a motley collection, is the **Elias Leiva Museum of Ethnography** (tel. 551-1110), at Calle 3, Avenida 3/5, where you'll find pre-Columbian and colonial artifacts, furniture, etc.

On the northeastern outskirts of Cartago is **San Rafael de Oreamuno,** site of Costa Rica's venerable if diminutive cigar-making industry.

CARTAGO EMERGENCY TELEPHONE NUMBERS

All emergencies	911
Hospital	551-1600
Police	551-1619
Transport police	551-7575

Chircagres cigars have been made hereabouts since the 17th century from locally grown tobacco. The indigenous population had been growing it since pre-Columbian days, of course. Columbus himself recorded how in September 1502, an Indian maiden had blown smoke in his face when he anchored at Cariay—now Puerto Limón—on his fourth voyage to the New World. The first tobacco factory built by the Spanish Crown was erected in 1781 on the present site of the Central Bank in San José; by the end of the 18th century tobacco production was second only to coffee.

Cigar-lovers may be intrigued to journey to San Rafael to watch cigars being hand-produced in time-honored fashion. It is a treat to watch the workers and to marvel at their manual artistry and dexterity as their highly skilled fingers conjure yet one more perfect cigar with their *chavetas,* rounded, all-purpose knives for smoothing and cutting leaves, tamping loose tobacco, and snipping the tips. The cigar roller, *torcedore,* fingers his or her leaves and according to texture and color chooses two to four filler leaves, which are laid end to end and gently yet firmly rolled into a tube and enveloped by the binder leaves to make a "bunch." The rollers' hands move with precise regularity as they roll cigars on tabletops blackened by oily tobacco leaves and scarred by thousands of tiny knife cuts. You will forever remember the pungent aroma.

Accommodations
Pickings in town are slim. A palmful of cheap and very basic budget hotels—the **Hotel Venecia, Pensión El Brumoso,** and **Familiar Las Arcadas**—lie near the old railway station on Avenida 6. Don't be surprised to find the room next to yours rented by the hour. The particleboard walls guarantee you'll hear every moan and groan. Definitely a refuge of last resort for those stranded. The Venecia offers the luxury of grimy rooms with shared bath with cold water for $7 double; El Brumoso charges $5. Reportedly **Motel Casa Blanca** (tel. 551-2833) in Barrio Asís is a better option. I say, move on!

Food
You have several Chinese restaurants on Avenida 2 to choose from. Best bet is the hangar-size **Restaurante City Garden** (Avenida 4, Calle

2/4). The **Salón Paris**—decorated with scenes of Venice—is recommended for Costa Rican fare. **Puerta del Sol** (Avenida 4, Calle 16) is the best of several eateries near the basilica. **Pastelería El Nido** is a pleasing sit-down bakery at Avenida 4, Calle 12. There are **Pizza Hut** (Calle 2, Avenidas 2/4, tel. 551-9276) and **Pizza y Hamburgers Maui** (tel. 552-0808) around the corner on Avenida 2.

East of town, on the road to Paraíso, is a reasonable *soda* called **Casa Vieja** (tel. 591-1165).

Services
The **tourist information office** (Avenida 2, Calles 1/3, tel. 223-1733) is in the municipal building on the north side of the plaza. The entrance is on Calle 1 (otherwise known as Calle 29 de Octubre). The **post office** is at Calle 1, Avenida 2/4. **Banks** include the Banco de Costa Rica, at Avenida 4, Calles 5/7; the Banco Nacional on Avenida 2, Calle 3; and the Banco Anglo Costarricense at Avenida 4, Calles 7/9. You can get a cash advance against Visa or MasterCard at Credomatic (one block west of El Carmen Church, tel. 552-3155).

Hospital Dr. Max Peralta (tel. 551-0611) is at Avenida 5, Calle 3/5. Many **medical clinics** and doctors' offices are nearby. Two to try are Dr. Luis Lopez (Avenida 2, Calle 10, tel. 551-2930) and Dr. Victor Carballo (Avenida 1, Calles 1/3, tel. 551-9906; hours: 8 a.m.-noon, and 2-6 p.m.). **Pharmacies** include Farmacia Central (Avenida 1, Calles 1/2, tel. 551-0698) and Farmacia Santa Ana (Avenida 2, Calle 11, tel. 552-1521). There are more **dentists** than you would care to count. **Taxis** hang out on the north side of Las Ruinas. Otherwise, call Taxis El Carmen (tel. 551-0247) or Taxis San Bosco (tel. 551-5151).

Getting There
Express buses depart San José from Calle 5, Avenida 18 (SACSA, tel. 233-5350), every 10 minutes 5 a.m.-7 p.m.; every 30 minutes 7 p.m. to midnight; and hourly midnight to 5 a.m. Return buses to San José depart Cartago from Avenida 4, Calles 2/4.

Buses to several destinations around Cartago stop on Avenida 3. Those for Turrialba depart Avenida 3, Calles 8/10 every 30 minutes 6-10:30 a.m. and hourly thereafter until 10:30 p.m. Hourly buses also serve the following destinations, with departure points in parentheses: Aguacaliente (Calle 1, Avenida 3); Cachí (Calle 6, Avenidas 1/2); Lankester Gardens and Paraíso (Avenida 1, Calles 2/4); Orosí (Calle 4, Avenida 1); and Tierra Blanca (Calle 4, Avenida 6/8).

SOUTH OF CARTAGO

Aguacaliente Hot Springs
About three km south of Cartago, beyond Tejar, is the village of Aguacaliente, which has a *balneario* (swimming pool) fed by hot springs and surrounded by an exotic plant collection. Local tours operate from San José and include Cartago, Lankester Gardens, the Orosí valley, a coffee plantation, and Aguacaliente hot springs ($60, tel. 221-3778, fax 257-2367).

Getting There
Buses depart Cartago from Calle 1, Avenida 3.

EAST OF CARTAGO

Lankester Gardens
Orchid lovers will be in heaven here. Covering 10.7 hectares of exuberant forest and gardens, Lankester (seven km east of Cartago, just before Paraíso) is one of the most valuable botanical centers in the Americas, with more than 800 native and exotic orchid species. Visitors will find species in flower throughout the year, with peak blooming in February, March, and April.

The garden attracts a huge number of butterflies and birds and has been declared a refuge for migratory birds. The gardens were conceived by an Englishman, Charles Lankester Wells, who arrived in Costa Rica in 1898 to work in coffee production. Wells also dedicated himself to the conservation of the local flora and the preservation of a representative collection of Central American species. He established the garden in 1917 at a site called Las Cóncavas. After his death, the garden was acquired by the North American Orchid Society and the English Stanley Smith Foundation. It was donated to the University of Costa Rica in 1973. Hours: Gates open hourly 8:30 a.m.-3:30 p.m. After an orientation, you're allowed to roam freely.

Getting There

Buses depart Cartago for Paraíso from the south side of Las Ruinas on Avenida 1 (tel. 574-6127) every 30 minutes, 4:30 a.m.-10.30 p.m. Get off at the Camp Ayala electricity installation and walk approximately 600 meters to the south.

PARAÍSO TO TAPANTÍ NATIONAL PARK

Paraíso, eight km east of Cartago, is of no particular interest, although the park is pleasant (a chapel built here in 1561 was reportedly made of straw). The hamlet was originally called Pueblo de Ujarrás and was renamed in 1832. Just east of Paraíso is the **Auto Vivero del Río,** featuring a private zoo. It charges no fee to see the coatimundis, agoutis, pizotes, and bird collection, but donations are gratefully accepted. Closed Monday.

Two km south of Paraíso on the road to Orosí and Tapantí—turn right at the town square—is the **Mirador Orosí,** an ICT park with lawns and picnic tables overlooking the valley. Steep steps lead up to a riot of shrubbery (usually ablaze in color) which together with the views lure Ticos on weekends, when the park hums with traffic. Entrance is free. Beyond the *mirador,* the road winds down into the Orosí Valley and the village of Ujarrás.

Accommodations

The **Sanchiri** (tel./fax 533-3210) has eight basic yet delightful and secluded hillside cabinas made of rough-hewn logs and bamboo, with telephone and views over the valley. The bathroom, of natural stone, has hot water. Rate: $45 d, including breakfast.

Hacienda del Río (tel./fax 533-3308) sits in the Orosí valley bottom via a steep dirt road about 400 meters beyond Mirador Orosí. This architectural stunner is a Spanish colonial-style mansion initially designed as a country club, later a den of iniquity for a drug baron, and today the home of professional hoteliers, Mark and Sonya Hayward (Sonya being Mark's mum). Ponds and pools, including a fish-filled moat, abound on the lodgelike property. You may prefer to swim in the Olympic-size pool being excavated at press time (the drug baron had had it filled in; I'll let you know in the next edition

whether any cocaine and bodies were found). Each of seven rooms is unique in shape, size, and character. Upstairs, you may laze in soft-cushioned sofas in the lounge, where a log fire may blaze on chill nights. Yes, downstairs are a restaurant and bar. After a meal, hop into a hammock on the wide veranda and listen to the rushing Ríos Agua Caliente and Orosí. Don't mind the pheasants, geese, chickens, and dogs . . . they're part of the family. Rosie the puma, you'll be glad to know, is caged. But the horses run free and may carry you on rides farther afield along trails that lead through the 36-hectare property and into surrounding fruit orchards and forest. Rates: $55-65. A bargain!

Also nearby, but up high, is **Orosí Valley Inn** (tel./fax 574-7893), a bed and breakfast operated by North American Julia Green, opened in May 1994 atop a perch overlooking her 12-hectare farm-cum-private reserve (with nature trail), which slopes down toward the valley and Bridal Veil waterfall. The five rooms with shared bath have picture windows and private patios with fabulous vistas (the corner room proffers a magnificent view down over the waterfall). Rates: $29-49 d, including breakfast.

A 50-room upscale hotel was apparently nearing completion next to the Orosí Valley Inn.

Food

In town, the **Restaurante Continental** dishes up reasonable seafood and homemade strawberry mousse. One km south of Paraíso are the open-air **Restaurant Las Encinas,** surrounded by pines, and **Parque Doña Anacleto** (closed Monday), with magnificent views over the Orosí valley. One hundred meters beyond, a dirt road on the right leads to the **Bar/Restaurant Mirador Sanchiri,** serving *comidas típica* and a miraculous view over the Orosí valley and the wide Río Reventazón glistening in the mountain light. The **Lost in Paradise Cafe,** run by Americans-in-exile Karen and Jim Read at the Mirador Orosí, is the place to stock up on homemade chocolate chip cookies and cakes before exploring further. Don't let pet parrots Petunia and Penelope steal your cookies, though they *will* steal the show.

Complejo Turístico Picacho (tel./fax 574-6322) not only offers Costa Rican cuisine, it has jazz and blues on Wednesday, Friday and Saturday nights.

colonial church at Orosí

CHRISTOPHER P. BAKER

OROSÍ VALLEY

South of Paraíso, you drop steeply into the Orosí valley, replete with sites of interest and yet, remarkably for its proximity to San José, far from the beaten tourist path. The valley is drained by the Río Reventazón and has abundant attractions: coffee *fincas,* hot springs, a large lake for fishing, two stunning colonial churches (Ujarrás and Orosí), an important national park (Tapantí), and—not least—stunning scenery. The valley makes a fine full-day circular tour, described below in counter-clockwise direction.

Tours

Most tour operators in San José offer day tours. **Tours Colón** (tel. 221-3778 or 233-1090) offers a tour that includes visits to Cartago, Lankester Gardens, Mirador de Orosí, Orosí church, a tour of Las Chucaras coffee *finca,* and lunch at Las Chucaras restaurant, with time to bathe in the hot springs. Rate: $60. Reservations essential.

OROSÍ

A must-see on any tour of the central highlands is the intimate village of Orosí, originally settled by Indians forced from the central valley by the Spaniards.

Sights

The charming **Church of San José de Orosí** was built by the Franciscans in 1735 of solid adobe with lime-covered walls adorned with gilt icons and a simple interior with rustic timbered roof, terra-cotta tiled floor, and wooden pews. The altar moved even this atheist to reverence! The recently restored church has withstood earth tremors with barely a mark for nigh three centuries. Note the old bell in the cracked church tower. The church is still in use today.

The church adjoins a small **religious art museum** located in what were once living quarters for the friars. The museum (tel. 533-3051) houses furniture, paintings, icons, and even a monk's cell. Photography is not allowed without prior permission. Hours: 9 a.m.-5 p.m. Closed Monday. Entrance: 30 cents.

About one km south of Orosí is the **Los Patios Balnearios,** with well-kept thermal mineral pools (50° C), changing rooms and showers, and a bar and restaurant. Hours: 8 a.m.-4 p.m. Entrance: $1.50. Another hot springs, **Balnearios Termales,** is two blocks from the plaza in town (open Wed.-Mon. 7 am.-4 p.m.; $1.25).

Literally a stone's throw south of Los Patios is a coffee mill *(beneficio),* where an **"Orosí Coffee Adventure"** is offered Mon.-Sat. through Aventuras Turísticas de Orosí (Apdo. 45, Paraíso 7100, tel. 533-3030, fax 533-3212). The basic plantation and *beneficio* tour costs $15 ($20 with lunch at the Balneario/Motel Río Palomo; see

below); a full-day option combines the coffee tour with a horseback tour of Tapantí National Park ($45). Other tour options are offered.

Accommodations

The owners of the Soda Coto run **Albergue Montaña Orosí** (tel. 533-3028, fax 228-1256), with basic rooms ($15) with shared bath and hot water in an old house. **Montaña Linda** (Apdo. 1180, Cartago, tel. 533-3345), next to Balnearios Termales, has a double room and a small dorm ($5 per person), plus a bamboo rancho with hammocks ($2). It accepts campers ($2) and features a shared kitchen plus Jacuzzi, rents bicycles for $3 a day, and offers massage ($3.50 one hour) and horseback rides ($12 half-day). Meals are provided.

The **Balneario Río Palomo** (Apdo. 220, Cartago 7050, tel. 533-3128, fax 533-3173, or tel./fax 533-3057) has seven modest cabinas with private bath, some with kitchenettes ($20 s, $27 d). It's immediately east of a suspension bridge over the Río Orosí—a small toll is collected on Sunday—two km south of Orosí (turn left at the T-junction just beyond the coffee *beneficio*). The two large swimming pools are open to nonguests (sorry: cold water).

Food

Several places at which to eat include the **Bar/Restaurant El Nido, Soda Coto** (which has a public telephone outside), and **Centro Social Reventazón,** a large and popular *soda* one block east of the soccer field. The hot spot

in town is the **Balneario Termal Orosí,** a large restaurant and bar with small pools filled with thermal water: a good spot for kiddies. A better bet is the **Balneario/Motel Río Palomo,** with an elegant and popular riverside bamboo restaurant. The restaurant serves free coffee tastings. You need a reservation for dinner.

Information

There's a **tourism office** opposite Los Patios (tel. 533-3333).

Getting There

Buses depart Cartago for Orosí from Calle 4, Avenida 1/3 (tel. 551-6810) every 90 minutes, Mon.-Fri. 6 a.m.-10 p.m.; hourly on weekends. Buses stop at Mirador Orosí. Return buses depart Orosí 4:30 a.m.-10:30 p.m.

Getting Around

South of Orosí, if you continue straight at the T-junction next to the coffee *beneficio,* the dirt road leads past the Río Macho hydroelectricity plant and ends at Tapantí (nine km), formerly Refugio de Fauna Silvestre Tapantí. En route you'll pass through endless rows of coffee plants and, just beyond the Río Macho, a fabulously landscaped garden on the right with tropical plants cascading down a hill.

If you take the left fork at the T-junction, the road continues over the Río Orosí and swings north and then east along the southern shore of Lake Cachí via the hamlet of Cachí before crossing a dam on the northeast corner of the lake,

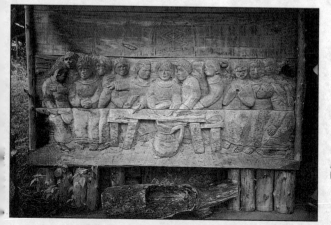

Macedonio Quesada's
Last Supper, *Cachí*

from where you can return to Paraíso via Ujarrás, or continue to Turrialba.

Note: Buses do not complete a circuit of Lake Cachí; you'll have to backtrack to Paraíso to visit Ujarrás and the Cachí dam by public bus.

LAKE CACHÍ

Lake Cachí was created by a dam across the Río Reventazón. About 13,000 years ago a lava flow blocked the Ríos Reventazón and Orosí to form a natural lake. Over the years, the rivers found a way through the natural dam. Thousands of years later, the Costa Rican Institute of Electricity built the Cachí Dam in the same place to supply San José with hydroelectric power.

Sights

Just east of Cachí village, on the banks of the Río Naranjo, is **Casa El Soñador** ("Dreamer's House"), the unusual home of woodcarver Macedonio Quesada and his son Hermes, who carve crude figurines from coffee plant roots. The house—with carved figures leaning over the windows (these, apparently, represent the town gossips)—is made entirely of rough-cut wood, with carvings adorning the outside walls. Upstairs is decorated with historical relics. Check out the *Last Supper* on one of the walls. Macedonio, now elderly and frail, once taught at the University of Costa Rica though he had not even had an elementary education. His work adorns galleries throughout San José. Take time to read the

newspaper clippings on the walls that tell about his life. Hermes continues the tradition and will gladly give you a tour. You can buy carvings.

The road crosses a one-lane suspension bridge paralleling the dam and doubles back on the other side of the lake and winds uphill to Paraíso. Stop at the Ujarrás Lookout Point southeast of Paraíso for a stunning view of the valley and the hamlet of Ujarrás, one of the earliest Spanish settlements in the country (see "Ujarrás," below).

Paradero Lacustere Chavarra

Chavarra is a planned ICT recreational complex beside the lake, one km east of Ujarrás. A basketball court, soccer field, and swimming pools are set amid landscaped grounds. It has camping areas (50 cents per person) plus picnic tables ($1), bathrooms, and a restaurant and bar. Hours: Tues.-Sun. 8 a.m.-5 p.m. Entrance: 80 cents ($1.50 extra for autos).

UJARRÁS

Ujarrás is famous as the site of the ruins of the **Church of Nuestra Señora de la Limpia Concepción,** built out of limestone between 1681 and 1693 to honor the Virgen del Rescate de Ujarrás. The church sits on the same site as a shrine built after an Indian fisherman saw an apparition of the Virgin in a tree trunk. When he attempted to carry the trunk to Ujarrás, it became so heavy that a team of men couldn't move it, a sign that the local priests interpreted as an indication

colonial church at Ujarrás

from God to build a shrine where the trunk lay.

The church, however, reportedly owes its existence to another "miracle." In 1666, the pirates Mansfield and Morgan led a raiding party into the Turrialba valley to sack the highland cities. They were routed after the defenders prayed at Ujarrás (there was more bluff than blunderbuss on the part of the defending forces). The victory was thought to be a miracle worked by the Virgin. The church was abandoned in 1833 after the region was flooded. A pilgrimage is held each mid-March from Paraíso to commemorate how the Virgin saved Ujarrás from the pirate invasion. The ruins—set in a beautiful walled garden and surrounded by coffee and banana plants—are open daily. There's a bathroom. Entrance is free.

Opposite the entrance to the church is Balnearios de Ujarrás, with a small swimming pool.

Food
Try the **Restaurant Típico la Pipiola,** 100 meters before the entrance to the ruins.

Getting There
Buses departs Cartago for Cachí via Ujarrás from one block east and one block south of Las Ruinas. Ask the driver to let you off.

TAPANTÍ NATIONAL PARK

Tapantí, 27 km southeast of Cartago, sits astride the northern slopes of the Cordillera Talamanca, which boasts more rain and cloud cover than any other region in the country. Average rainfall for the Orosí region is 324 cm (128 inches); Tapantí gets much more—almost 800 cm (330 inches) of rain at the intermediate peaks. February through April are the driest months. Not surprisingly, there are many fast-flowing rivers and streams excellent for fishing, permitted in designated areas April through October.

The 6,080-hectare park (formerly Tapantí Wildlife Refuge), on the headwaters of the Río Reventazón, climbs from 1,200 to 2,540 meters above sea level and forms a habitat for resplendent quetzals (often seen on the western slopes near the ranger station), toucans, parrots, great tinamous, squirrel cuckoos, and more than 260 other bird species, plus mammals such as Neotropic river otters, tapirs, jaguars, ocelots,

jaguarundis, howler monkeys, silky anteaters, and multitudinous snakes, frogs, and toads. Birdwatching is fabulous, particularly at dawn.

The park possesses two life zones: lower montane rainforest and premontane rainforest. Terrain is steep and rugged and prone to landslides. Well-marked trails begin near the park entrance ranger station, which has a small nature display. The Oropendola Trail, which begins about 800 meters from the ranger station, leads to picnic shelters and a deep pool by the Río Macho where the hardy can swim in ice-cold waters. There's a vista point—a short trail leads from here to a waterfall viewpoint—about four km along. A trailhead opposite the beginning of the Oropendola Trail leads for miles into the mountains. You can also enter Tapantí at its southwest corner via the Pan-American Highway south of Cartago. Hours: 6 a.m.-4 p.m. Check to see if the park is open on Thursday and Friday. Entrance: $15 walk-in, $7 advance purchase.

Tours
Aventuras Turísticas de Orosí (Apdo. 45-7100, Paraíso, tel. 533-3030, fax 533-3212) offers a three-hour horseback tour to Tapantí ($25). **GeoVenturas** (tel. 221-2053, fax 282-3333) has a mountain-biking tour of Tapantí and the Orosí valley. Most other tour operators in San José can arrange guided tours.

Accommodations
The ranger station has a *hospedaje* with a kitchen and bunk beds ($7.50 per day, students $2). You'll need your own sheets and blankets or sleeping bag. A short distance before the park entrance, about 400 meters up a dirt road, is **Cabinas Kiri** (tel. 533-3040), boasting private baths with heated water and a restaurant specializing in trout culled from its own trout ponds. Rates: $40 per person, including all meals.

Getting There
Buses depart Cartago at 6 a.m. and go via Orosí as far as Purisil, five km from the park entrance. You can hike or take a jeep-taxi from here with Co-Opetaca (tel. 533-3087; $5 each way). Later buses go only as far as Río Macho, nine km from Tapantí. If you befriend the park ranger before setting off to explore, he or she may call for a taxi to pick you up at a prearranged time.

TURRIALBA AND VICINITY

East from Cartago, past Paraíso, vast carpets of sugarcane swathe the rolling landscape. The road falls gradually eastward before a final steep descent into Turrialba. You can choose the low route via **Cervantes,** or a higher route via **Pacayas.**

You won't regret stopping off for a bite to eat at **La Posada de la Luna,** west of the church in Cervantes. The restaurant is chock-a-block full of intriguing bric-a-brac from around the world. Homemade specialties include *tortilla de queso* (cheese tortilla) and *cajeta* (fudge) washed down by hot *agua dulce con leche* (a sugarcane drink with hot milk).

TURRIALBA

A town of no notable contemporary note, Turrialba, 65 km east of San José, was until recently an important stop on the old highway between San José and the Caribbean. The road still snakes down through the valley of the Río Reventazón but is little used since the Guápiles Highway via Braulio Carrillo National Park was opened two decades ago. Turrialba—once an important railroad stop—was further insulated when train service to the Caribbean was ended in 1991. (However, the **Pachuco Tico Tren Company** had plans to operate a small locomotive from Turrialba to Lake Bonilla. Contact the Hotel Wagelia; see "Accommodations," below.)

In the first decades of the century, black engineers on their way from Puerto Limón to San José were compelled to hand over their trains in Turrialba to white engineers, who completed the trip, the black men being prohibited by the country's then-racist policy from entering the highlands. The now-rusted tracks still dominate the town, which squats in a valley bottom—thought to have been a lake bed millennia ago—on the banks of the Río Turrialba at 650 meters above sea level.

Sights

In town, the **Parque la Dominica** (600 meters west of the church) and **Balneario Las Améri-** cas (east of town, on the road to the CATIE agricultural research station)—the former with swings, the latter with two large swimming pools—are okay for kids. Several sites of interest lie nearby, including the Guayabo National Monument archaeological complex and Volcán Turrialba to the north, the tropical agriculture research center at CATIE, the Ríos Reventazón and Pacuare (both great for whitewater trips), and the valley of the Pacuare (great for birding and with two excellent places to stay) to the east.

Accommodations

Budget: Two run-down and dingy hotels lie on the south side of the railway tracks: **Hotel Central** ($3 with shared bath, $3.75 private bath with cold water) and the **Hotel Chamanga** (tel. 556-0623; $4 with shared bath with cold water). Next door is the slightly more upscale **Hotel Interamericano** (tel. 556-0142), with clean rooms and a large restaurant and bar ($6 s, $9 d with shared bath; $9 s, $12 d with private bath with cold water). Kayakers and rafters congregate here. Three other budget options are the **Hotel Primavera**—very basic, but a friendly hostess—with shared bath with hot water ($3 s, $6 d); the **Hotel La Roche** (tel. 556-1624), with shared bath with cold water, and a tidy restaurant with TV downstairs ($6 s, $8.50 d); and—opposite La Roche—the **Pensión Chelita** (tel. 556-0214), which is less clean but has hot water ($6 per person, shared bath).

Moderate: The pleasant though not very atmospheric **Hotel Wagelia** (tel. 556-1566, fax 556-1596) is the only class act in town. It has 20 rooms with a/c, private bath, TV, and telephone. Rooms surround a courtyard full of tropical plants and are tastefully if unremarkably decorated with pleasant fabrics, with lots of light. The hotel offers tours to Volcán Turrialba , Guayabo National Monument, and CATIE. The restaurant is one of Turrialba's best. Rates: $35 s, $51 d standard; $50 s, $64 d superior.

You'll find four atmospheric lodges east of Turrialba, including an excellent nature lodge,

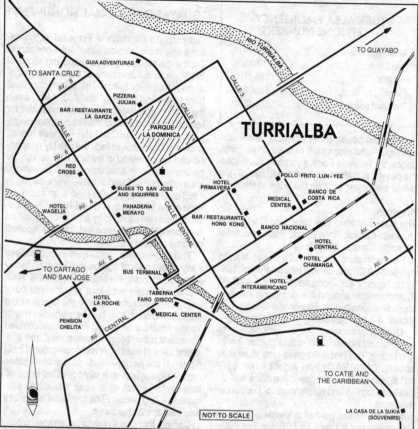

Rancho Naturalista, and **Casa Turire,** near Tuís, sharing honors as the finest hotel in the country (see "Tuís and Moravia," below).

Food and Entertainment
Kingston's (tel. 556-1613), on the right as you exit town heading east, is a large, renowned restaurant with a breezy outdoor dining terrace. A reader has recommended **El Caribeño,** one block south of the railway tracks on the road to CATIE. Lacking in ambience, but great food. Owner Lazel Loyt Lanis—*"El Rey del Buen Sabor"*—has spiced his large menu with a healthy dose of Caribbean dishes. **Bar/Restaurante La Garza**—good for seafood—and the **Hotel Wagelia** are also good. There are several Chinese options, not least **Restaurante Hong Kong** (tel. 556-0286), **Nuevo Hong Kong** (tel. 556-0593), and **Pollo Frito Lun-Yee.** The **Panadería Merayo** sells an excellent selection of breads and cookies. Pizza lovers might check out **Pizzería Julian** (tel. 556-1155).

For the best views, drive out to Turrialtico, where the Mirador Turrialtico and Pochotel both offer stunning views from their alfresco restaurants (see "Turrialtico and Pochotel," below).

TURRIALBA EMERGENCY TELEPHONE NUMBERS

All emergencies	911
Red Cross	556-0191
Hospital	556-1133
Police	556-0030
Transport police	556-1503

The town boasts three cinemas, one—surprisingly—showing adult movies. If ya gotta dance, try **Taberna Faro**. If ya gotta swim, take the plunge at **Balneario Las Américas** ($1), a public swimming pool on the edge of town.

Services
The **banks** in town are Banco de Costa Rica (Avenida Central, Calle 3) and Banco Nacional (Avenida Central, Calle 1).

For **medical** help, you'll find a Centro Médico (tel. 556-0923) and clinical laboratory (tel. 556-1516; hours: 7 a.m.-noon and 2-6 p.m.) on Calle 3, and another around the corner on Avenida Central opposite the Banco de Costa Rica (hours: 3-7 p.m., Saturday 11 a.m.-1 p.m.).

Guia Adventuras (no telephone) rents kayaks and horses and offers guided hikes and rafting. The **Hotel Wagelia** runs tours (see above). **COSASA Travel Agency** (tel. 556-1513) acts as a tourist information office and offers birdwatching and nature tours for five people minimum.

For **souvenirs** go half a kilometer east of Kingston's to La Casa de la Sukia (tel. 556-1231), selling *figuras pre-Columbiana* in stone. Another artisans' store sits opposite the Hotel Wagelia.

Getting There and Around
Buses depart San José from Calle 13, Avenidas 6/8 (tel. 556-0073) hourly 5 a.m.-midnight via Cartago. Buses depart Cartago for Turrialba from Avenida 3, Calle 4. In Turrialba, buses for San José depart hourly from Avenida 4, Calle 2. Buses for nearby towns and villages, including to Guayabo, Santa Cruz, Santa Teresita, and Tuís, leave from Avenidas 2/4, Calle 2.

For a **taxi,** contact Taxis Don Carlos (tel. 556-1593).

GUAYABO NATIONAL MONUMENT

Guayabo, 19 km north of Turrialba, is the nation's only archaeological site of any significance. Don't expect anything of the scale and scope of the Maya and Aztec ruins of Guatemala, Honduras, Mexico, or Belize. The society that lived here between 1000 B.C. and A.D. 1400, when the town was mysteriously abandoned, was far less culturally advanced than its northern neighbors. No record exists of the Spanish having known of Guayabo. In fact, the site lay uncharted until rediscovered in the late 19th century by naturalist/explorer Anastasio Alfaro. Systematic excavations—still under way—were begun in 1968 by Dr. Carlos Aguilar Piedra, an archaeologist at the University of Costa Rica. The excavations are partly funded by a tax of one *colón* on each box of bananas exported. The site received national monument status in 1973.

The 218-hectare monument encompasses a significant area of tropical wet forest on valley slopes surrounding the archaeological site. Well-maintained trails lead to a hilly lookout point from where you can surmise the layout of the pre-Columbian village, built between two rivers. To the south, a wide and impressive cobbled pavement resembling a Roman road and estimated to be at least eight km long—most of it still hidden in the jungle—leads past ancient stone entrance gates and up a slight gradient to the village center, which at its peak housed an estimated 10,000 people. The total area of the city was perhaps 20 hectares.

Conical bamboo living structures were built on large circular stone mounds *(montúculos),* with paved pathways between them leading down to aqueducts—still working after 2,000 years—and a large water tank with an overflow so that the water was constantly replenished. About four hectares have been excavated, of which about two are open for the public via the "Mound Viewing Trail." Note the square tombs, plundered years ago, now covered with mosses and encroached by slithering tree roots. The cobbled pavement *(calzada)* is in perfect alignment with the cone of Volcán Turrialba. It is being relaid in its original form. Maps are sometimes available from the ranger booth. A large map shows the layout. Nearby is a monolithic rock carved with

petroglyphs of an alligator and a jaguar.

You must have a guide to visit the excavation site. I highly recommend Jonathan Sequeria, who guided me on a tour arranged by Costa Rica Expeditions (Apdo. 6941, San José 1000, tel. 257-0766, fax 257-1665). Jonathan once worked on the excavation project. He also has an encyclopedic knowledge of birds. Birding at Guayabo is superb, but it helps to have a guide versed in birdlife. Among the many species we identified were the crowned wood-nymph hummingbird, rufous-crested coquette hummingbird, a family of collared aracari (members of the toucan family), a green honeycreeper, and oropendolas, whose pendulous nests are everywhere hereabouts.

Opposite the ranger booth are a picnic and camping area with shelters, an exhibition and projection hall, a miniature model of the site, plus a hut stuffed to the rafters with pre-Columbian finds. Many of the artifacts unearthed here are on display at the National Museum in San José. **Souvenir Karrol,** 200 meters below La Calzada Lodge, sells pre-Columbian replicas and other souvenirs. Hours: 8 a.m.-3 p.m. daily. Entrance: $15 ($7 with advance ticket from MIRENEM headquarters, Calle 25 and Avenidas 8/10 in San José).

Accommodations

La Calzada Lodge (Apdo. 260, Turrialba 7150, tel. 253-0465), about 500 meters before the park entrance, has seven rooms (three with private bath), each with a table and twin beds. The hotel, which has a hint of the Alps, is named after the Indian road *(calzada)* that runs through the area. The thatched restaurant serves reasonable meals, including organic, home-grown produce. The owner, José Miguel, offers tours to a local *trapiche* (oxen-powered sugar mill), a coffee *finca,* and a cheese factory. There's a children's playground. Expect a wake-up call from the roosters, and beware the vicious goose! Rates: $15 s/d (less with International Youth Hostel card).

The monument's eight campsites (see above; $3 per person) feature access to flush toilets, cold-water showers, and barbecue pits.

Food

You'll find a couple of places at which to eat in the hamlet of Guayabo, plus **Soda La Orquídea** and

Bar Calipso, 1.5 km downhill from the monument.

Getting There

Buses depart Turrialba for Guayabo village from Avenida 4, Calle 2 (from 100 meters south of the main bus terminal), Mon.-Fri. at 11 a.m. and Mon.-Sat. at 5 p.m. Return buses depart 6 a.m. and 1 p.m. You can also take a "Santa Teresita" bus from Turrialba (departs daily at 10:30 a.m. and 1:30 and, possibly, 6:30 p.m.), from where it's a three-mile uphill walk to the monument. You'll need to overnight if you take the 5 p.m. bus. Otherwise, **Taxis Don Carlos** (tel. 556-1593) will take you from Turrialba for about $30 roundtrip. The owner of La Calzada Lodge will meet the bus if you call ahead.

CATIE

The Centro Agronómico Tropical de Investigación y Enseñanza, four km east of Turrialba, is one of the world's leading tropical agricultural research stations. It was established in the 1930s and today covers 880 hectares of magnificent landscaped grounds surrounding a lake full of water birds. CATIE is devoted to experimentation and research on some 335 species of tropical plants and crops, including more than 2,500 coffee varieties. Besides conducting experiments into breeding tropical plants, animals, and crops, CATIE contains the largest library on tropical agriculture in the world.

Several trails provide superb birding, and the laboratories, orchards, herbarium, and husbandry facilities are fascinating. Individual visitors are allowed on a limited basis. Sign up for a group tour with any travel agent or tour operator in San José. Alternatively, call Viviana Sánchez, chief of administration for CATIE (tel. 556-1149, fax 556-1533) to arrange a personal visit. Guided five-hour tours cost $10. Lunch (from cafeteria buffet to a la carte service) costs $5-15.

Reportedly, there's a hotel on-site ($30 s, $40 d).

Getting There

Buses depart for CATIE from the railroad tracks near Taberna Faro in Turrialba. You can also catch the bus to Siquirres from Avenida 4, Calle 2, and ask to be dropped off at CATIE.

RÍO REVENTAZÓN

Beyond CATIE, you come to a bridge over the Río Reventazón ("Exploding River" or "Flatulence"!), from where you can look down upon kayakers running the permanent slalom course. This is the traditional put-in point for rafting trips on the Río Reventazón. The river begins at the Lake Cachí Dam and cascades down the eastern slopes of the Cordillera Central to the Caribbean plains, a drop of more than 1,000 meters. On a good day it serves up class III-IV rapids, with the rainy season understandably providing the most exciting run. Highly recommended.

To the east is the valley of the Río Pacuare, an even more thrilling river that plunges through remote canyons and rates as a classic. Highlights include waterfalls and wildlife galore. Most of the companies below offer two- and three-day trips (June through October are considered the best months). The river is protected as a wild and scenic river, but nonetheless faces the threat of being dammed for its hydrolectric potential (for information, contact the **Friends of the Pacuare,** Apdo. 6941, San José 1000).

Rafting Tours

The following companies have offices on the eastern bank of the Río Reventazón: **Pioneer Raft** (tel. 225-8117 or 253-9132, fax 253-4687;

in the U.S., tel. 800-288-2107); **Costaricaraft** (tel. 225-3939); and **Costa Rica White Water** (tel. 257-0766, fax 257-1665). **Ríos Tropicales** (tel. 233-6455) and **Costa Rica Expeditions** (tel. 257-0766) also specialize in rafting trips on the Reventazón and Pacuare. The latter maintains a rustic and isolated lodge at the head of the Pacuare Canyon, with rooms in Indian-style ranchos, and flush toilets. Those who've stayed here on rafting trips report "superb meals." **Mariah Wilderness Expeditions** (P.O. Box 248, Point Richmond, CA 94807, tel. 510-233-2303 or 800-4-MARIAH) specializes in whitewater packages to Costa Rica from the United States.

Note: For more information on rafting, see the section on whitewater rafting under "Special-Interest Travel and Recreation" in the On the Road chapter.

TURRIALTICO AND POCHOTEL

The road east of the Río Reventazón continues one km to a Y-junction with a police checkpoint. Veer left for Siquirres and the Caribbean. The road switchbacks steeply uphill to tiny Turrialtico, eight km east of Turrialba. There's nothing of note here, but the views over Turrialba and valley toward Volcán Turrialba and the Talamancas are superb. Beyond Tres Equis, east of Pochotel, the road begins its fall to Siquirres and the Caribbean lowlands.

whitewater rafting on the Reventazón

Food and Accommodations

At Turrialtico you'll find the **Mirador/Albergue Montaña Turrialtico** (tel. 556-1111), a very pleasant restaurant-cum-lodge with fabulous views over the Reventazón Valley, and tables made from Sarchí oxcart wheels. The landscaped grounds are beautiful. The 12 rustic and basically furnished rooms are atmospheric (but have "yukky" beds, according to one reader) and have private baths with hot water ($30 per room). Another kilometer brings you to the **Pochotel Hotel/Restaurant** (Apdo. 258, Turrialba 7150, tel. 556-0111, fax 556-6222), on the right. A dirt road climbs steeply to a basic but pleasant restaurant (popular with whitewater rafters) with wide-open vistas and a tall *mirador* from which to admire the volcanoes and Talamanca mountains, with drinks served on a pul-ley-system. The *cansados* are only $4. The six cabins, each of a different size, have private baths with hot water, but a reader reports them "freezing" and "very drafty" ($30-45 d). Both Oscar García of Pochotel and Hector Lezama of Montaña Turrialtico offer transfers from/to Turrialba.

Getting There

Buses for Siquirres depart Turrialba from Avenida 4, Calle 2; ask to be let off at Turrialtico.

TUÍS AND MORAVIA

The road to the right at the Y-junction east of CATIE leads to Tuís, Bajo Pacuare, and the off-the-beaten-track hamlet of Moravia del Chirripó

CASA TURIRE

Stay once at Casa Turire and you may decide next time that if you can't get a room here, you just won't bother visiting Costa Rica. Quiet, relaxing, romantic, and upscale without being pretentious, Casa Turire (Apdo. 303, Turrialba 7150, tel. 731-1111, fax 731-1075) is my number-one choice for a hotel east of San José. *Hideaway Reports* agreed: it named Casa Turire Country House Hotel of the Year, and *Discoveries* magazine named it Best Resort.

The hotel is built on the right bank of the Río Reventazón on the grounds of Hacienda Atirro, about 15 miles southeast of Turrialba, at the foot of the Talamancas (it was from Hacienda Atirro that the first known whitewater run in Costa Rica was made). Follow the road for La Garita and Tuís; turn right at the sign for Hacienda Atirro (there is no sign for the hotel) and continue past fields of lime-green sugarcane until you reach the driveway lined with palms and bougainvillea.

The classical-styled Casa Turire, which opened in December 1991, is the jewel in the crown of a working coffee, sugarcane, and macadamia plantation that commands magnificent views of the mist-haunted Talamanca massif. A trail through primary forest leads down to the river; horseback rides and bike rental are also offered ($15 half day).

You sense the sublime the moment you enter the breathtaking lobby of the modern Spanish-cum-California plantation home, with its colonial-tiled floors, Roman pillars, and sumptuous contemporary leather sofas and chairs.

Outside, a wide, colonial-tiled, wraparound veranda supported by eucalyptus columns opens onto manicured lawns and a small lake out front, a small figure-eight pool and sunning deck surrounded by palms and an arbor of hibiscus, and—out back—a six-hole golf course, which leaps uphill and careens back down rippling fairways.

Upstairs, 12 deluxe rooms with direct-dial telephones enclose the courtyard with a wraparound balcony. Each spacious, lofty-ceilinged room bespeaks romantic indulgence, with divinely comfortable mattresses, sleek tiled bathrooms with thick towels, toiletries, and hair driers, and decor that reflects exceptional taste. Three truly regal suites have wide French doors opening onto spacious private verandas.

The Mediterranean-style dining room proffers good service and artistically arranged food. Culinary treats include fresh homemade bread, spicy *gallo pinto*, and sublime coffee. An intimate English-style "pub" has Edwardian hints. Further pluses? Soothing classical music echoing softly.

One guest from California wrapped herself around a lamppost in the atrium lounge and refused to leave. Could that be you?

Rates: $95 s, $110 d, $125 junior superior suite, $150 junior suite, $200 master suite. Breakfast $6, lunch $13, dinner $15.

before petering out in the foothills of the Cordillera Talamanca. You can hire guides in Moravia for excursions into the Talamancas and **La Amistad International Peace Park.** There's no accommodation, though you may be able to stay with a local family. Near Tuís, however, are two gems in which to lay your head (see special topic "Casa Turire").

Accommodations
Albergue de Montaña (Apdo. 364, San José 1002, tel. 267-7138; in the U.S., Dept. 1425, P.O. Box 025216, Miami, FL 33102), one km beyond Tuís, is a surprisingly elegant if rustic hilltop hacienda-lodge (owned by an American) on a 50-hectare ranch—**Rancho Naturalista**—surrounded by premontane rainforest at 900 meters' elevation at the end of a steep dirt-and-rock road that is "not user-friendly." The mountain retreat is popular with nature and birding groups (more than 340 bird species have been recorded by guests) and has a minimum-three-days-stay policy.

Nine spacious rooms have heaps of light (four have large private baths with hot water). Upstairs rooms open through French doors onto a veranda—telescopes and Sarchí leather rockers provided—with sweeping views down over the Reventazón Valley to Irazú. One room has a canopy bed and a bathroom large enough to wash a Boeing 747. The upstairs also has a lounge with library. Outside are two cabins with shared bath, plus a small alligator in a small pond. Decor is of hardwoods, with beamed ceilings, and—downstairs—a huge hanging lamp made from cattle yokes. Horse riding is included. The ranch has an extensive trail system. You can also see a small *trapiche* (ox-powered sugar mill) on a neighboring *finca*. Rates: $90 per person, including three meals; one-week package costs $450 June-November, $550 December-May, including transfers, local tours, and horseback rides.

Getting There
Buses for Tuís depart from the bus center at Calle 2 and Avenida 2/4 in Turrialba.

TURRIALBA AND IRAZÚ VOLCANOES

The slopes north of Cartago rise gradually up the flanks of Volcán Irazú. The views from on high are stupendous. Every corner reveals another picture-perfect landscape. You'll swear they were painted for a Hollywood set. The slopes are festooned with tidy little farming villages with brightly painted houses of orange, yellow, green, and light blue. I even saw a young boy sweeping the lawn! Dairying is an important industry and you'll pass by several communities known for their cheese. Many of the vegetables that end up on your plate originate here. The fertile fields around Cot look like great salad bowls: carrots, onions, potatoes, and greens are grown intensively. At a Y-junction just below Cot, seven km northeast of Cartago, is a **statue of Jesus**, his arms outstretched as if to embrace the whole valley. The road to the right leads to Pacayas, Santa Cruz, and Guayabo National Monument. That to the left leads to Irazú Volcano National Park (turn right before Tierra Blanca; Irazú is signed). The paved road leads all the way to the mountaintop via Potrero Cerrado.

Prusia Forestry Preserve

This reserve, five km north of Potrero Cerrado, is a reforestation project with a recreation area—Ricardo Jiménez Oreamuno—which features hiking trails and camping and picnic sites set amid pines. Reportedly, there's a "mushroom forest" here, too.

VOLCÁN TURRIALBA

Volcán Turrialba (3,329 meters), the country's most easterly volcano, is a twin volcano to Irazú and part of the Irazú massif. It was very active during the 19th century but today slumbers peacefully. Spaniards baptized the volcano Torre Alba ("White Tower") for the great columns of white smoke it spewed out during eruptions. A rough road suitable for 4WD vehicles winds north from Santa Cruz, about 12 km north of the town of Turrialba, to Bar Canada (three km), where a sign next to the bar marks the beginning

of the trail. It climbs through cloud forest to the summit, which features three craters, a *mirador* (lookout point), and guard house topped by an antennae. You'll find a campsite and additional trails at the summit, including one that leads to the crater floor! You can follow a path all around the summit (there are active sulphur emissions on the western side). You can also hike from the hamlet of Santa Teresa, reached by direct bus from Cartago.

Queseria El Cyprasel, a cheese factory 800 meters east of Santa Cruz, welcomes visitors. The road continues to Guayabo National Monument. It's easy to get lost trying to find Guayabo via this route. An easier option for reaching Guayabo is via the recently paved road that snakes northeast from Turrialba (signs mark the way).

Several local farmers, including La Central dairy farm, will let you camp on their property. Ask! You can also buy fresh homemade tortillas and cheese but are best advised to bring provisions.

Accommodations

Guayabo Lodge (tel. 556-0133 or 234-2878, fax 234-2878), 400 meters west of Santa Cruz on the grounds of Finca Blanco y Negro, is basic but a pleasant and homey atmosphere pervades. It has four double rooms of earthtone cinder block and hardwood construction, with airy and light bathrooms, plus laundry and kitchen. When not exploring the 80-hectare *finca* settle yourself in a hammock on the patio and enjoy the superb views down over the town of Turrialba and across to the Cordillera Talamanca. The *finca* has its own dairy and cheese factory. Rates: $31 s, $40 d. The owner, José Antonio Figueres, also operates a *mirador* restaurant (with a view)—**Casa Bene**—100 meters west of Guayabo Lodge.

Volcán Turrialba Lodge (Apdo. 1632, San José 2050, tel./fax 273-4335) sits in the saddle between Irazú and Turrialba volcanoes, about two miles north of Esperanza and five miles northwest of Santa Cruz. This hidden-

away lodge offers homey comforts and was built from an old milking shed on the family farm of owner Tony Lachner. The twelve rooms each have private bath. Costa Rican meals are cooked over a wood fire and served in a cozy lounge and dining room heated by a wood stove. Guided hikes and horseback rides are offered (Turrialba's crater is about one hour away, and thermal pools are nearby, too), or you can choose a mountain bike or ox-drawn cart for exploration. Guides at the lodge speak only Spanish. You'll need 4WD to get there; transfers by 4WD are provided. The lodge is at 3,300 meters. It can be very cold and rainy up here—bring sweaters and raingear! Rates: $55 per person, including all meals. Transfers from San José are $25.

Nearby, **Esperanza Reserva** (tel. 223-7074, fax 233-5390; in the U.S., tel. 800-213-0051 or 401-295-0690, fax 401-295-8912) squats on the flanks of the Río Atirro, with spring waters diverted into the pools of cabinas. The renovated farmhouse also has rooms with private bath and hot water. Hiking and horseback riding are offered. Rates: from $100 including meals.

Getting There

Buses depart Cartago for Pacayas and Santa Cruz from south of Las Ruinas, and from the bus center at Calle 2, Avenidas 2/4, in Turrialba. From Santa Cruz, you'll need to take a taxi or hike to Bar Canada.

IRAZÚ VOLCANO NATIONAL PARK

Volcán Irazú, about 21 km northeast of Cartago, tops out at 3,432 meters. Its name comes from two Indian words: *ara* (point) and *tzu* (thunder). The volcano has been ephemerally active. The first recorded eruption was in 1723. More recently, on 13 March 1963, the day that John F. Kennedy landed in Costa Rica on an official visit, Irazú broke a 20-year silence and began disgorging great columns of smoke and ash. During the next two years, it showered ash as far away as San José, choked the skies of Cartago, blocked sewers and water pipes, and caused untold short-term damage to crops. At one point, ash-filled vapor blasted up into overhanging clouds and triggered a storm that rained mud up

to five inches thick over a widespread area. After the eruptions, part of the crater collapsed. No further activity was recorded until 8 December 1994, when Irazú unexpectedly hiccuped gas, ash, and breccia.

The windswept 100-meter-deep Diego de la Haya crater contains a sometimes-pea-green, sometimes-rust-red, mineral-tinted lake. Fumaroles are occasionally active. A larger crater is 300 meters deep. Two separate trails lead from the parking lot to the craters. Follow those signed with blue-and-white symbols (*don't* follow other trails made by irresponsible folks whose feet destroy the fragile ecosystems). The crater rims are dangerously unstable. Keep your distance.

A sense of bleak desolation pervades the summit, like the surface of the moon. The weather is often "foggy withal," as Charles Dickens might have said. Even on a sunny day expect a cold, dry, biting wind. Dress warmly. The average temperature is a chilly 7.3° C (45° F). Little vegetation lives at the summit, though stunted dwarf oaks, ferns, lichens, and other species are making a comeback. Best time to visit is March or April, the two driest months.

Don't be put off if the volcano is shrouded in fog. Often the clouds lie below the summit of the mountain—there's no way of telling until you drive up there—and you emerge into brilliant sunshine. On a clear day you can see both the Pacific and Atlantic oceans. The earlier in the morning you arrive the better your chances of getting clear weather.

The ranger booths and facilities are open 8 a.m.-4 p.m., but you can visit at any time. A mobile *soda* serves food and drinks on weekends, and the site has toilets, and picnic benches beside the crater, but no camping or other facilities. Entrance: $15 walk-in, $10 advance purchase.

Tours

Most tour operators in San José offer half-day or day tours to Irazú. **Magic Trails** (Apdo. 5548, San José 1000, tel. 253-8146, fax 253-9937) and **Universal Tropical Nature Tours** (Apdo. 4276, San José 1000, tel. 257-0181, fax 255-4274) both offer tours of Irazú and the Prusia Forestry Reserve, with stays, horseback riding, and/or hikes at Hacienda Retes (see "Accommodations," below).

JEAN MERCIER

*main crater,
Irazú volcano*

Accommodations

Not much to choose from, alas. **Restaurant/ Hotel Irazú** (tel. 253-0827), also known as Hotel Gestoria, near Potrero Cerrado, looks very pleasing from the road. Inside, however, the restaurant smells of urine. The decor is dismal. Smoke stains darken the ceiling. And the hotel rooms will appall all but the most hardy budget traveler. To add insult to injury, the rooms are ridiculously overpriced at $22 double.

Hacienda Retes, a centennial oak-log farmhouse bordering the Prusia Reserve, has accommodations for special-interest groups as well as horseback and hiking tours.

The best bet lies on the lower western flank of the mountain at **Hacienda San Miguel** (tel. 229-5058, fax 229-1094), at Rancho Redondo. This rustic yet modern and cozy lodge boasts a fireplace, Jacuzzi, games room with pool table, and giant screen TV/VCR. Rooms are comfortable enough and even have electric blankets for chilly nights. The hacienda is a working dairy farm on 480 hectares. Horseback rides and guided hikes lead through the pastures to forests and waterfalls. Rates: $60 per person, including breakfast. The drive from San José through Rancho Redondo is spectacular. If you don't drive, a bus departs San José from Avenida 5, Calle Central.

Food

North of Potrero Cerrado is the **Bar/Restaurant Linda Vista** (tel. 225-5808), which, as its name suggests, offers magnificent views. It claims to be the highest restaurant in Central America (2,693 meters/8,835 feet). Take your business card to add to thousands of others pinned on the walls. Don't even *think* about eating at the **Restaurant/Hotel Irazú** (see above)!

Getting There

Buses depart San José for Volcán Irazú from opposite the Gran Hotel on Avenida 2, Calles 1/3 (tel. 272-0651), at 8 a.m. on weekends and holidays (and Wednesday, Nov.-April), returning at 1 p.m. ($5). You can also hop aboard this bus in Cartago, by Las Ruinas. There's no public bus service on weekdays. Then, take a bus to Tierra Blanca or Linda Vista, and from there walk (18 km) or take a taxi. A bus departs Avenida 5, Calle Central in San José for Rancho Redondo daily at 12:20 and 6:20 p.m. Buses to Linda Vista depart Cartago at 5:45 a.m. Monday and Thursday. Buses to Tierra Blanca depart Cartago from one block north of the ruins Mon.-Thurs. at 7 and 9 a.m. and 1 p.m., Sunday 7 a.m. A **taxi** from Cartago will cost upward of $20. I recommend a guided tour from San José ($30 half day; $50 full day, including Orosí and/or CATIE or Lankester Gardens).

By Car: If you drive, the most scenic route east from San José is via the suburb of Guadalupe, then Vista de Mar, and Rancho Redondo, flanking the mountain. Splendid! If you drive via Cartago, the road leading northeast from the basilica continues to Irazú.

NORTHEAST FROM SAN JOSÉ

This little-touristed area encompasses a fistful of charming little towns and villages east of the Guápiles Highway, which climbs inexorably up the southeastern flank of Volcán Barva. A good starting point is the turnoff, about three km north of San Josá, for San Vicente de Moravia. Continuing uphill you'll enjoy fabulous views of the volcano and valley. A gamut of new restaurants, including Restaurant Las Orquídeas and more rustic Restaurante Cerros Verdes (both 10 km, on the left), let you soak in the views over a soda or beer. One km farther is **Hotel Villa Zurquí** (Apdo. 11534, San José, tel. 222-3078 or 268-8856, fax 257-3242), 150 meters east of the Zurquí gas station. This "mountain hotel" has charming chalet-style cabins with stove, refrigerator, and hot water. Horseback riding takes you into the surrounding forest, or along trails through the orchard.

SAN VICENTE DE MORAVIA

Moravia—properly San Vicente de Moravia (it appears as San Vicente on maps)—lies seven km northeast of San José and is known for its handicraft stores centered on the pretty plaza. The village moves at a slower pace than the capital city and is an alternative to touristy Sarchí for craft bargains, especially leather and wicker furniture. **Las Garzas Handicraft Market** (tel. 236-0037), 100 meters south of the Red Cross Station, contains 28 indoor craft stores. The **Caballo Blanco** (tel. 235-6797), on the plaza, is also recommended. Also try **La Rueda** and **La Tinaja** (tel. 325-7787), and the **Palette Souvenirs** arts-and-crafts gallery (tel. 235-3464). Most stores close on Sunday. If you need cash, you can get an advance against your Visa or MasterCard at **Credomatic** (half-a-block south of St. Francis College, tel. 235-3184).

Accommodations and Food
Victoria Inn (Apdo. 6280, San José 1000, tel. 240-2320, fax 323-7932), three blocks east of the town hall, is a bed and breakfast in a large

home with an atrium lounge and wicker furniture and potted plants in profusion. Of the five rooms, two have private bath and kitchen and private garden in their own apartment. Romantic touches include lace bedspreads. Rates: $20 s, $25 d with shared bath, or $25 s, $35 d private bath, including breakfast. **El Verolis** (Apdo. 597, Moravia 2150, San José, tel. 236-0662) is a bed and breakfast with seven comfortable rooms with cable TV. Rates: $40 d with shared bath, $60 with private bath. Also recommended is **Casa Rosa Inn** (Apdo. 155, Moravia 2100, tel./fax 235-9743), a bed-and-breakfast under new Canadian management, one block south of La Guaria Club, to which guests have privileges. The seven rooms, including a larger unit for up to five people, have private bath and cable TV. Two rooms are small singles. Several rooms have private balconies. Secure parking. Rates: $35-55.

For lunch, try the **Soda San Martín** or **Restaurante Rincón Europeo.**

Getting There
A bus departs San José from Avenida 3, Calles 3/5. A microbus reportedly departs from Avenida 7, Calle 6.

SAN ISIDRO DE CORONADO

The road continues six km uphill eastward from Moravia to San Isidro de Coronado, a somnolent country town supposedly popular as a summer resort with Josefinos. The Gothic church is impressive, but not worth the visit in its own right. A fiesta is held here each 15 February. A turnoff two km south of San Isidro de Coronado on the main road back to San José leads eastward via Rancho Redondo, Laguna, and Tierra Blanca to Volcán Irazú. The route is magnificently scenic.

For lunch, try the **Club Mediterráneo** (tel. 229-0661).

The "Snake Farm"
Coronado is most famous as the site of the **Instituto Clodomiro Picando**—the "snake farm"—

of the University of Costa Rica, which is dedicated to snake research. You'll see snakes of every kind, including the fearsome and infamous fer-de-lance, or *terciopelo*. The institute was founded by Clodomiro Picando Twight, a Costa Rican genius born in 1887 and educated in Paris, where he later worked at the Pasteur Institute before returning home to work on immunizations, vaccinations, and serums. Evidence suggests he may have discovered penicillin before Alexander Fleming, the British scientist to whom its discovery is credited. Visitors are welcome (hours: 8 a.m.-noon and 1-4 p.m.). Particularly interesting is to watch snakes being milked for venom (Friday afternoons only). Snake-feeding time is not for mice-lovers. The institute is about one km southwest of Coronado.

Gothic church in San Isidro

Getting There
Buses marked "Dulce Nombre de Coronado" depart San José from Calle 3, Avenidas 5/7.

LOS NUBES, SAN JERÓNIMO, AND ALTO PALMA

Immediately north of San Isidro de Coronado is a crossroads. The road straight ahead deadends. The road to the right leads uphill past cattle pasture and strawberry fields to **Los Nubes,** where you can sample strawberry desserts as well as pizzas and *típico* dishes at Cronopios (tel. 229-0517), a cozy restaurant warmed by an open fire. The road to the left leads to **San Jerónimo,** where begins a cobblestone road: the remains of the old **Carretera Carrillo** that still runs, in much-dilapidated condition, via **Alto Palma** to Bajo Hondura and Braulio Carrillo National Park and was once used by oxcarts carrying coffee to the railway line that ran to Puerto Limón. The route was recently closed because of landslides and for restoration of the old road, and it may be open again when you

read this. The Alto Palma entrance to Braulio Carrillo is 10 km northeast of San Jerónimo.

Getting There
Buses depart San José for San Jerónimo from Avenida 3, Calles 3/5. You can walk or take a taxi to Alto Palma from here. Inquire about local buses.

LOS JUNCOS CLOUD FOREST RESERVE

Los Juncos is a 200-hectare reserve area of virgin cloud forest straddling the Continental Divide on the Caribbean slopes of Irazú volcano, in the mist-shrouded mountains above San Isidro. Its node is a metal-walled farmhouse once the home of former presidents Federico Tinoco and Mario Echandi. Trails through Los Juncos forest connect with the adjacent Braulio Carrillo National Park. Guides lead hikes, followed by a home-cooked lunch served family style at the farmhouse (where overnight stays can be arranged). Rubber boots and raingear are provided for hikes. The trails have been left in a semi-natural state. It's very misty up here, with everything covered in spongy moss and epiphytes. Quetzals are among the many bird species you may see if the magical mists aren't too dense. If you're considering Monteverde but don't like clouds, consider Los Juncos. Reportedly a Biological Station has rustic accommodations for up to 20 in a combination of single and bunk beds. Senderos de Iberoamérica (tel. 255-2859), in San José, has sole rights to use of the trails and offers guided one-day tours from San José ($65).

BRAULIO CARRILLO NATIONAL PARK

Rugged mountains, dormant volcanoes, deep canyons, swollen rivers, and seemingly inter-

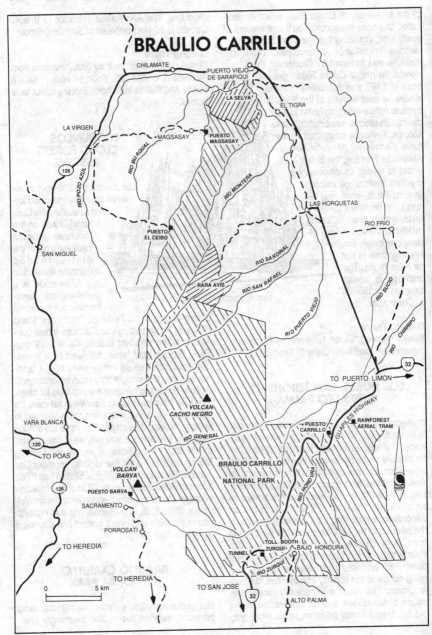

BRAULIO CARRILLO

minable clouds, torrential rains, and persistent drizzles characterize Braulio Carrillo National Park, 20 km northeast of San José. The park was established in 1978 as a compromise with environmentalists concerned that the construction of the Guápiles Highway to the Caribbean would lead to deforestation of the important watershed region. It was named in honor of the president who promoted the cultivation of coffee.

Despite its proximity to San José and the fact that the Guápiles Highway cuts right through it, Braulio Carrillo is both relatively inaccessible and inhospitable. The area—44,099 hectares, 84% of which is primary forest—extends from 2,906 meters above sea level atop Volcán Barva down to 36 meters at La Selva, in Sarapiquí in the Caribbean lowlands. This represents the greatest altitudinal range of any Costa Rican park.

Temperature and rainfall vary greatly and are extremely unpredictable. At higher elevations, temperatures range from 15° to 22° C. At the Carrillo, Magsasay, and El Ceibo biological stations, in the Atlantic lowlands, the average temperature is much warmer, ranging from 22° to 30° C. Annual rainfall is between 400 and 800 centimeters. Rains tend to diminish in March and April. With luck, you might even see the sun!

Encompassing five life zones ranging from tropical wet to cloud forest, Braulio Carrillo provides a home for 6,000 identified species of trees, more than 500 species of birds, and 135 species of mammals, including howler and capuchin monkeys, tapirs, jaguars, pumas, ocelots, deer, pacas, raccoons, and peccaries. Highlights include hundreds of butterfly species and excellent birding opportunities. Quetzals are common at higher elevations. The rare solitary eagle and umbrella bird live here. And toucans, parrots, and hummingbirds are ubiquitous.

The park protects several tree species fast disappearing elsewhere from overharvesting: among them, the palmito, valued for its "heart," and the tepezcuintle, which has been chosen as the park's official mascot. Those elephant-ear-size leaves common in Braulio Carrillo are *sombrilla del pobre* (poor man's umbrella).

Entrances

The main entrance is approximately 19 km northeast of San José, where there is a tollbooth (200

colones—$1.20) on the Guápiles Highway. **Zurquí,** the main ranger station, is described in most literature as being 500 meters south of the Zurquí tunnel. If so, it eluded me. Instead, I found it on the right two km north of the tunnel. Drive slowly; you come upon it suddenly on a bend. The station has maps (not much good) for sale, and a basic information center. The **Puesto Carrillo** ranger station is 22.5 km farther down the road. It has a tollbooth in the center of the road for those entering the park from Limón; it's several km inside the park boundary.

Two other stations—**Puesto El Ceibo** and **Puesto Magsasay**—lie on the remote western fringes of the park and you reach them by rough trails from just south of La Virgen, on the main road to Puerto Viejo de Sarapiquí (see the Northern Lowlands chapter). You can also enter the Volcán Barva sector of the park via the **Puesto Barva** ranger station three km northeast of Sacramento, and via Alto Palma and Bajo Hondura (see above), accessible from San José via San Vicente de Moravia or from the Guápiles Highway at a turnoff about three km south of the main park entrance.

Entrance costs $15 walk-in, $7 advance purchase from MIRENEM headquarters in San José.

Trails and Facilities

Two short trails lead from Puesto Carrillo: **Los Botarramas** is approximately 1.6 km; **La Botella,** with waterfalls and views down the Patria Canyon, is 2.8 km. Says the national park trail map: "For additional exercise as you head down La Botella, turn left at a sign labeled 'sendero.' This path takes you 30 minutes deeper into the forest to the river Sanguijuela." South of Puesto Carrillo is a parking area on the left (when heading north) with a lookout point and a trail to the Río Patria, where you can camp (no facilities). Another parking area beside the bridge over the Río Sucio ("Dirty River") has picnic tables and a short loop trail.

A one-km trail leads from south of the Zurquí Tunnel to a vista point. The entrance is steep, the rest easy. Another trail—the **Sendero Historico**—is shown on the national park map as following the Río Hondura all the way from Bajo Hondura to the Guápiles Highway at a point

near the Río Sucio. Check with a ranger.

A trail from Puesto Barva leads to the summit of Volcán Barva and loops around to Porrosatí (no ranger station). From the summit, you can continue all the way downhill to La Selva in the northern lowlands (see "Volcán Barva" under "Heredia and vicinity," below, for details). Of course, it's a lengthy and arduous hike that will take several days. Recommended only for experienced hikers with suitable equipment. There are no facilities. You can join this trail from Puesto El Ceibo and Puesto Magsasay; reportedly you can drive in a short distance along a 4WD trail from Puesto Magsasay.

Bring sturdy raingear, and preferably hiking boots. The trails will most likely be muddy. Several hikers have been lost for days in the fog and torrential rains. Remember: It can freeze at night. If you intend to do serious hiking, let rangers know in advance, and check in with them when you return.

Note: There were a series of armed robberies in the park in 1992-93. Hike with a park ranger if possible. Thefts from cars parked near trailheads

have also been a problem. Watch for snakes!

Tours

Most tour operators in San José can arrange half-day or full-day tours. **Jungle Trails** (Apdo. 2413, San José 1002, tel. 255-3486, fax 255-2782) has a full-day guided birdwatching tour departing at 5:30 a.m.

Getting There

Buses for Guápiles and Puerto Limón will drop you off (and pick you up) at the Zurquí or Puesto Carrillo ranger stations. Buses depart every 30 minutes 5:30 a.m.-7 p.m. from Calle 12, Avenidas 7/9 (tel. 223-1276). For Alto Palma, take a bus from San José for San Jerónimo from Avenida 3, Calles 3/5. You can walk or take a taxi to Alto Palma from here (there may be local bus service). For Sacramento and the Puesto Barva entrance, take a bus marked "Paso Llano" from the Mercado Central in Heredia, Mon.-Fri. at 6.30 and 11 a.m., and 3 p.m. (4 p.m. on Saturday). See "Volcán Barva" under "Heredia and Vicinity," below.

HEREDIA AND VICINITY

Heredia, a modest-size town (pop. 32,000) and capital city of Heredia Province, lies about 11 km northwest of San José on the lower slopes of Barva volcano amidst a sea of coffee plantations. A pleasant, slow-paced, nostalgic atmosphere pervades the neat and orderly grid-patterned town with its old adobe houses with tile roofs and corridors. It has undergone several name changes from its inception in 1706 as Barrio Lagunilla. Officially, it has been known as Heredia only since 1824. It is colloquially known as La Ciudad de las Flores ("City of Flowers"). The **National University**—famed particularly for its veterinary courses—is here, on the east side of town. It enrolls many foreign students, giving the city a cosmopolitan feel.

Heredia looks set to blossom on the tourism scene. Recent years have introduced several prime attractions. And upscale hotels have opened and will be given a major boost when both the Marriott and Meliá hotel chains open their colonial style properties in the hills of Heredia in 1996.

SIGHTS

Heredia is centered on a pleasing if unremarkable and small cathedral—the **Basílica de la Imaculada Concepción**—containing beautiful stained-glass windows as well as bells delivered from Cuzco, Peru. The church was built in 1797. It is rather squat and thick-walled and has thereby remained standing through several earthquakes. The church faces west onto **Parque Central,** shaded by large mango trees. Concerts are held on Thursday evenings in the peculiarly shaped music temple.

The streets have many other fine examples of colonial architecture, the most important of which is **El Fortín,** a circular fortress tower bordering the north side of the central plaza. A curious piece of military-textbook heresy are the gun slits that widen to the outside. In a classic piece of military ineptitude, the eccentric ex-president Alfredo González Flores (president 1914-17) got it all wrong: the gunports allow bullets in easily, but make it difficult for defenders to shoot out.I

The **Casa de la Cultura,** next to El Fortín on the north side of the park, contains art and historical exhibits. It was once the residence of González Flores, who was exiled in 1917 after a coup d'etat. (He was later welcomed back.) He ran much of his presidency from his home, where he lived until his death in 1962. Flores is the father of social reform in Costa Rica, and the founder of its income tax and the state-run insurance system. The house was declared a National His-

Heredia's stout Basílica de la Imaculada Concepción, built in 1797, has eased through several earthquakes.

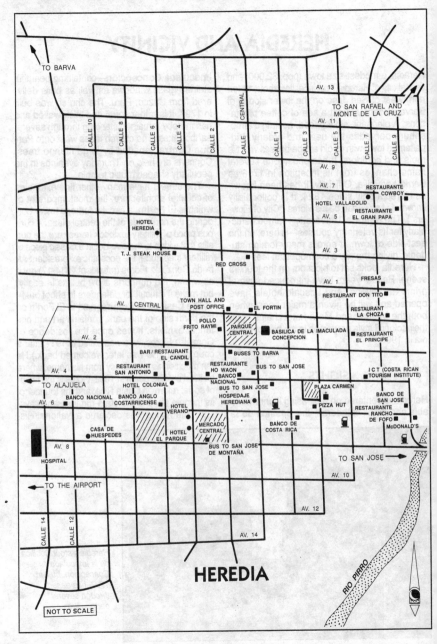

TO BARVA

AV. 13

TO SAN RAFAEL AND
MONTE DE LA CRUZ

AV. 11

CALLE 10 CALLE 8 CALLE 6 CALLE 4 CALLE 2 CALLE CENTRAL CALLE 1 CALLE 3 CALLE 5 CALLE 7 CALLE 9

AV. 9

AV. 7

RESTAURANTE
COWBOY

HOTEL VALLADOLID

AV. 5

RESTAURANTE
EL GRAN PAPA

HOTEL
HEREDIA

AV. 3

T. J. STEAK HOUSE

RED CROSS

FRESAS

AV. 1

RESTAURANT DON TITO

AV. CENTRAL

TOWN HALL AND
POST OFFICE

EL FORTIN

RESTAURANT
LA CHOZA

POLLO
FRITO RAYMI

PARQUE
CENTRAL

BASILICA DE LA IMACULADA
CONCEPCION

AV. 2

RESTAURANTE
EL PRINCIPE

BAR / RESTAURANT
EL CANDIL

BUSES TO BARVA

AV. 4

RESTAURANT
SAN ANTONIO

RESTAURANTE
HO WAON

BUS TO SAN JOSE

BANCO
NACIONAL

I C T (COSTA RICAN
TOURISM INSTITUTE)

TO ALAJUELA

HOTEL COLONIAL

BUS TO SAN JOSE

AV. 6

BANCO NACIONAL

BANCO ANGLO
COSTARRICENSE

HOSPEDAJE
HEREDIANA

PLAZA CARMEN

BANCO DE
SAN JOSE

HOTEL
VERANO

PIZZA HUT

RESTAURANTE
RANCHO
DE FOFO

CASA DE
HUESPEDES

HOTEL
EL PARQUE

MERCADO,
CENTRAL

BANCO DE
COSTA RICA

McDONALD'S

AV. 8

HOSPITAL

BUS TO SAN JOSE
DE MONTAÑA

TO SAN JOSE

AV. 10

TO THE AIRPORT

AV. 12

CALLE 14 CALLE 12

AV. 14

HEREDIA

RIO PIRRO

NOT TO SCALE

toric Monument in 1981, when it was refurbished, although part of the structure had been converted to a restaurant (El Gran Chaparral).

Don't leave Heredia before roaming through the **Mercado Central** ("Central Market"), brimful with locally grown produce. The School of Marine Biology at the National University houses the **Marine Zoological Museum** (tel. 237-6363, ext. 2240), with 1,900 specimens of native marina flora and fauna. Hours: Tues.-Fri. 8 a.m.-4 p.m.

ACCOMMODATIONS

El Fortín

The town is not blessed with hotels, though budget travelers will find a fistful of basic accommodations, and a couple of upscale properties have recently opened. Several superb upscale hotels lie in the hills outside Heredia (see relevant sections below).

Budget

The **Hotel Verano** (Calle 4, Avenida 6, tel. 237-1616), upstairs on the west side of the market, has clean rooms with shared bath and cold water. Disturbed by the noise? Don't worry; your neighbors took their room only for a hour. Rates: $10 d. Some rooms have private baths for $18. The **Hotel El Parque** (tel. 238-2882), on the same block, and the **Hotel Colonial** (tel. 237-5258), on Avenida 4, Calles 4/6, are of a similar standard. The latter has hot water, the former does not. Both charge $8 to $10. Cheaper yet is the family-run **Hospedaje Herediana** (tel. 237-3217) on Calle Central, Avenidas 4/6, with shared baths with hot water ($4). **Casa de Huéspedes** (tel. 238-3829) also has both shared and private baths; $8 and $10. Not inspected, but reportedly clean and a good value.

Another very basic option is the **Hotel Berlin Toronto,** west of San Joaquín en route to the airport.

Inexpensive

Hotel Ramble (tel. 238-3829), on Avenida 8, has 15 beautiful wood-paneled rooms. Bathrooms (some are shared) have hot water. And, best yet, you get ambience at a low price. Rates: $14 d.

A less attractive, but not unappealing, alternative is the **Hotel Heredia** (tel. 237-1324), on the north side of town at Calle 6, Avenida 3/5. It has 10 rooms with private baths and hot water ($12 s, $20 d).

Moderate

A contemporary architectural stunner is the **Hotel America** (Apdo. 1740, Heredia 3000, tel. 260-9292, fax 260-9293), 50 meters south of Parque Central. It features 40 a/c rooms with cable TV, telephone, and private bath and hot water, plus laundry service and souvenir shop. Decor (mauves, blues, and creams) is pleasing. It had no restaurant, but one is planned (meanwhile, the Restaurant Vienna, next door, provides 24-hour room service and has a 24-hour bar). Head to the glassed-in rooftop to admire the city and mountain vistas. A mini-mall of 10 shops was also planned. Rates: $30 s, $40 d, suite $100 (up to six people).

On the outskirts of town, in Santa Lucía, is **Los Jardines** (tel. 260-1904). See "Barva and Vicinity," below.

Upscale

The class act in town is the **Hotel Valladolid** (Apdo. 93, Heredia 3000, tel. 260-2905, fax 260-2912), in a historic building at Avenida 7, Calle 7, with 11 rooms with a/c, cable TV, phone, and kitchenette. The hotel has a sauna, a Jacuzzi, a rooftop solarium with great views, plus a bar and a restaurant. Not reviewed. Rates: $77 s, $86 d, $90 t, $100 suite.

A 245-room colonial-style **Marriott** hotel was to open in 1996 on a 10.5-hectare site commanding panoramic views over the valley, in La Asunción de Belén. Planned were 200 square meters of retail space, a health club,

Heredia's Mercado Central rouses the senses.

business center, outdoor pool, three tennis courts, a golf practice range, three restaurants, and the obligatory casino.

Apartotels

The **Apartotel Vargas** (Apdo. 87, Heredia 1300, tel. 237-8526, fax 223-9878) has eight fully equipped apartments with private baths in a residential setting opposite coffee fields. It's 800 meters north of Colegio Santa Cecilia near Sacramento, north of Heredia. Rates: $60.

Apartotel Valle Verde (Apdo. 1746, San Pedro 2050, tel. 260-2228, fax 237-7365), one mile southeast of Heredia at San Pablo on the road to Santo Domingo, has 13 apartments with kitchen, telephone, cable TV, and safety deposit boxes. It has a Jacuzzi, plus sauna and small gym.

FOOD

Heredia lacks notable eating places. Most interesting is **Fresas** (Calle 7, Avenida 1, tel. 238-4074), which serves all things strawberry as well as meals for less than $5. Nearby are several fast-food joints, including **Pizza Hut** (Calle 3, Avenida 6, tel. 237-7080) and **McDonald's** (three blocks south of the National University), and bars popular with students: try **El Bulevar** and **La Choza**. Fried-chicken addicts might try **Pollo Frito Raymi** (tel. 328-3828), on Calle 2, Avenidas Central/2. And there's a **T.J. Steak House** (tel. 237-9115) at Avenida 3, Calle 4/6.

Restaurante El Gran Papá (tel. 237-4432), on Calle 9, Avenidas 5/7, and **Restaurante El Príncipe** (Calle 5, Avenida Central/2, tel. 238-1894) have also been recommended for *típico* food. For seafood, try **Restaurant San Antonio**, on Avenida 4, Calle 6.

Don't leave before relaxing in the park with an Italian ice cream from **Azzurra,** where you may select from 25 flavors.

INFORMATION AND SERVICES

The **Costa Rican Tourism Institute** (tel. 223-1733) has an office at Avenida 4, Calles 5/7.

Banks

There are Banco Nacionals at Calle 2, Avenidas 2/4, and Calle 12, Avenida 6; a Banco Anglo Costarricense at Calle 6, Avenida 6; and a Banco de Costa Rica at Calle 1, Avenida 6. You can get a cash advance against Visa or MasterCard at Credomatic (in front of McDonald's; tel. 260-2000).

HEREDIA EMERGENCY TELEPHONE NUMBERS

All emergencies	911
Hospital	238-1699
Police	237-0438
Transport police	238-1966

Medical

Hospital San Vicente can be reached at 237-1091. There are plenty of **pharmacies,** including Farmacia Bolaños (Calle 2, Avenida 2/4, tel. 237-0282), Farmacia Imperial (Avenida 5, Calles 1/3, tel. 237-8410), and Farmacia Rayo Azul (tel. 238-3677).

Other

Lavandería La Margarita (Avenida 6, Calles Central/2, tel. 237-0529) offers **laundry** and dry-cleaning service.

Taxis can be found beside Parque Central. Otherwise call Taxis Coopemargarita (tel. 238-3377) or Taxis Coopetico (tel. 237-6163).

GETTING THERE AND AROUND

By Bus

Microbuses Rapido (tel. 238-8392 or 238-0506) offers service to Heredia every 10 minutes 5 a.m.-10 p.m., from Calle 1, Avenidas 7/9 in San José. Buses depart Heredia for San José from both Calle Central and Avenida 4. Microbuses also depart San José from Avenida 2, Calles 10/12 every 15 minutes, and hourly midnight to 6 a.m. from Avenida 2, Calles 4/6.

By Train

A five-car train operated by Intertren (tel. 226-0011) departs from the Atlantic Railway Station in San José (Avenida 3, Calle 21) at 5:45 a.m. and 12:15 and 5:30 p.m., Mon.-Friday. It travels via the University of San José in San Pedro. Return trains depart from the railway station opposite the Mercado Florence in Heredia at 6:30 a.m. and 1:30 and 6 p.m. (30 cents).

From Heredia

Buses to Barva depart from Calle Central, Avenidas 1/3; Ojo de Agua from Avenida 6, Calle 6; and hourly to San José de la Montaña from Avenida 8, Calles 2/4.

SANTO DOMINGO DE HEREDIA

Santa Domingo de Heredia, midway between Heredia and San José, has many colonial houses restored to creamy grandeur. Its prime attraction, however, and a stunner at that, is . . .

Joyeros del Bosque Húmedos/ Wings for Education

Joyeros del Bosque Húmedos (Apdo. 353, Santo Domingo 3100, tel. 223-0343, fax 223-0372), 100 meters east of the cemetery, three miles north of San José on Calle Central, houses the Whitten Collection of more than 50,000 butterflies—truly "Jewels of the Rainforest"—from around the world. The accumulation of Richard Whitten's more than 50 years of collecting, it is claimed to be the largest collection of butterflies in the world. It surely is the most colorful—a veritable kaleidoscope of shimmering greens, neon blues, startling reds, silvers, and golds. A visit here is a must! The truly stunning displays make the Smithsonian's fabulous collection look moth-ridden by comparison. The creativity is sheer choreography. Exhibits glitter against a background of opera and classical music, the climactic highs of the arias and ponderous lows of the cellos seemingly rising and falling to the drama of the displays. One room is dedicated to a collection of every species in the country. Other exhibits include shimmering beetles displayed against black velvet, like opal jewelry, and boxes of bugs majestically turned into caskets of gems. One wall of bugs is informally called the Escher Wall for its resemblance to the artist's work. No normal bugs, these. Some beetles are bigger than your fist; some moths outsize a salad plate! A "rainforest theater" is planned for lectures. For now, it remains an undiscovered secret. An unexpected treat may be an impromptu performance by Whitten (a former professional concert performer) displaying his talents on the glockenspiel, accordina, piano, or organ. Hours: Tues.-Sat. 9 a.m.-1 p.m. for group tours; 2-5 p.m. for general admission (all day Sunday). Entrance: $3.60 (half-price, locals and children).

Accommodations

Hotel Bougainvillea Santo Domingo (Apdo. 69, San José 2120, tel. 240-8822, fax 240-8484) is a sister hotel to the Hotel Villa Tournón in San José. This attractive three-story hotel is set in landscaped grounds surrounded by a sea of coffee plants, with a beautiful view of the mountain ranges. The 44 spacious rooms each have a/c, two double beds, TV, and balcony. Sarchí oxcarts, local handicrafts, and vibrant artwork decorate the public areas. There are a swim-

ming pool and a tennis court. A shuttle service runs into San José. Rates: $65 s, $72 d.

SAN ISIDRO

San Isidro, eight km due east of Heredia, has a landmark white church, very Gothic with lots of pointed spires—English in inspiration, but far less impressive than that of San Rafael (see below). The town is known for its Easter procession.

Cerámica Chavarris

At Cerámica Chavarris (tel. 268-8455), Doña Frances makes "California-style" ovenproof pottery. Nice, but nothing you can't buy in the States. Cross the narrow iron bridge on the northeast corner of the plaza and head uphill to the left. You can't see the house from the road; look for the little white sign on the right. The road eventually loops west to San Rafael.

Accommodations

La Posada de la Montaña (Apdo. 1, San Isidro de Heredia 3017, tel./fax 268-8096; in the U.S., P.O. Box 308, Greenfield, MO 65661, tel./fax 417-637-2066), 400 meters north of Cerámica Chavarris, is a relaxing, 12-bedroom bed and breakfast set amid almost six acres of pretty landscaped gardens and coffee and fruit orchards at 1,500 meters (4,900 feet) elevation, with marvelous views up to Braulio Carrillo National Park. The place, which is family-run by John and Barbara Watkins from Missouri, is spacious and spic-and-span, with lots of light and closet space. Hardwoods abound. Guests have full access to the large living-dining area with TV. Thin partition walls in small economy rooms with shared bath may be a noise problem. Some rooms have queen beds. Three twin-bedroom suites at the bottom of the garden have large kitchens and dining rooms with fireplaces. Guests can use the large barbecue pit in the garden. Reportedly a great breakfast, and a restaurant was planned. Good for handicapped folks. The owners will meet you at the airport or arrange a taxi. Good bargain! Rates: $32 s, $38 d for economy rooms; $42 s, $48 d for deluxe rooms; $69 d to $133 for six for a suite.

The North American owners of Wa Da Da Farm operate **Debbie King's B&B** (Apdo. 465, Heredia 3000, tel. 268-8284), a small bed and breakfast on a coffee *finca* with fabulous views over San José. Two large wood-paneled bedrooms have private baths. Upper rooms have wraparound balconies. Two cottages have kitchens and private baths and sleep four. Dinners on request. The hotel's greatest asset is Debbie, erstwhile Beverly Hills restaurateur, and her equally affable husband. Rates: $20 s, $35, d, $49 cabinas.

Food

Las Orquídeas Restaurante (tel. 268-8686, fax 268-8989), about three km southeast of San Isidro at San Luis on the Guápiles Highway, is a rustic yet elegant and charming eatery with a large international menu. **Al Piel del Monte** is a short walk from Debbie King's B&B—you can enjoy a delicious *casado* here for $3.

Getting There

Buses depart San José from Calle 4, Avenidas 7/9 every half hour.

SAN RAFAEL

Two km northeast of Heredia lies San Rafael. A medieval stonemason would be proud of the town's stunning, recently restored, cream-colored Gothic church, with its buttresses and magnificent stained-glass windows. The church is of surprisingly late vintage; it was completed only in 1962. It is visible from throughout the Meseta Central and bears strong hints of Notre Dame. Turn left (north) in San Rafael for **Monte de la Cruz;** continue east for San Isidro.

North of San Rafael, the land begins to rise up the slopes of Volcán Barva, the temperatures begin to drop, and the first hints of the Swiss Tyrol begin to appear, with pine and cedar forests and emerald-green pastures grazed by frisian and jersey cattle. Remnants of ancient oaks and other primary forests remain, however, and a San Rafael community group has campaigned for more than a decade in an effort to save them. In 1995 their efforts were rewarded with creation of the 100-hectare **Chompipe Biological Reserve** and construction of a scientific research center: **The Center for Earth Concerns.** Tapirs, deer, coyotes, sloths, and kinkajous are among the wildlife species that inhabit the mountainside forests.

Accommodations

The **Meliá Costa Rica** (tel. 232-2025, fax 232-1815; in the U.S., 800-336-3542), a 124-room, four-star property under construction on 15 acres outside town, was due to open in summer 1995. Rooms have a/c plus color TV, telephone, hair drier, safety deposit box, minibar, and full bath. Business facilities include an executive center and conference room. The hotel also features a Jacuzzi, indoor pool, gym, beauty salon, massage, tennis courts, children's playground, and trails for hiking and horseback riding. Yes, of course there's a casino!

Getting There

Buses depart Heredia from the Mercado Central hourly, 8 a.m.-8 p.m.

BOSQUE DEL RÍO AND EL CASTILLO COUNTRY CLUB

Halfway up the hill to Volcán Barva is Parque Residencial del Bosque del Río de la Hoja (two km down a dirt road to the left; look for the sign reading "Bar las Chorreras"), with hiking trails through the forests that protect the water supply for Heredia. Just beyond the turnoff for Bosque del Río is the upscale Club Campestre El Castillo, or El Castillo Country Club (tel. 267-7115), with stunning views over the central valley. Recreational possibilities include basketball, soccer, sauna, swimming pool, go-carts, and the country's

only ice rink. A restaurant serving *típico* cuisine offers magnificent views and the warm glow of logs flaming in a large hearth. You need it at this height, as temperatures are considerably cooler. The club has camping and picnic tables. It's open to foreign tourists. Entrance: $3.50 per person weekends, $2.50 weekdays.

Food

About two km north of San Rafael are **Pollos del Monte,** an open-air roadside *soda* with grilled and roasted chicken, and **Complejo Turístico Bar y Restaurant Añoranzas** (tel. 267-7406), in a wooded park setting with views down the mountain. Two km farther, a road to the left leads uphill to **El Expresso del Bosque,** a rustic restaurant with children's playground and a small, narrow-gauge steam engine, and, beyond, to **Los Peroles,** a tiny restaurant in a meadow, with rustic log tables and seats. The main road from San Rafael continues past **Stein Biergarten** (tel. 267-7021), which specializes in German cuisine. The best meals for miles, however, are served at the **Hotel Chalet Tirol** and **Hotel Le Barbizón** (see below); either is worth the culinary excursion in its own right.

MONTE DE LA CRUZ RESERVE

This private forest reserve eight km north of San Rafael is superb for nature hikes along trails choked with ferns and wild orchids through

Hotel Chalet Tirol

pine forests and a cloud-forest environment with lush epiphytes and bromeliads. One trail along the Río Segundo leads to Braulio Carrillo National Park, another leads to a complex of waterfalls. Trails open out onto stunning views of the valley. It is often cloudy and usually exhilaratingly crisp, if not cold and wet; bring warm waterproof clothing (also bring binoculars—the birding is superb). Popular with weekend hikers from San José. There are barbecue grills. Take the right-hand fork two km north of El Castillo. The fork to the left leads to the Parque Residencial del Monte and Hotel Chalet Tirol (see below).

Accommodations

Hotel Chalet Tirol (Apdo. 7812, San José 1000, tel. 267-7371, fax 267-7050) is an incredibly atmospheric hotel, with one of the finest French restaurants in the country. The immaculate hotel—an authentic replica of a Swiss chalet—whisks you to the Alps. It is set at 1,800 meters (5,900 feet) and surrounded by pine and cypress forest. Rustic yet charming twin-level alpine cabins—hand-painted in Tyrolean fashion—surround a small lawn. A new wing with 20 hotel-style rooms (each with a fireplace), pool, sauna and massage/fitness room, plus two tennis courts, was added in 1991. The modern complex is less appealing, though more expensive.

The hotel, which was once owned by a former Costa Rican president, Alfredo González Flores (1914-17), is worth a visit just to eat in the rough-hewn timbered dining room, with its pretty curtains, window boxes, blazing log fire in an old-world fireplace, brass chandeliers, romantic candlelight, and superbly executed French nouvelle cuisine: *conejo en salsa de ciruelas* (rabbit marinated in prune sauce), *corvina al fondue de aguacate* (sea bass with melted avocado), *camarones a la creme fenouillette au Pernod* (shrimps in fennel Pernod sauce).

The hotel offers a wide selection of tours to local attractions. Day tours, including horseback riding and gourmet lunch, cost $65. The hotel was once featured on a *Lifestyles of the Rich and Famous.* Rates: Chalets $80 s/d, $10 each additional person; suites from $100 d, $20 additional.

About 300 meters along the fork to Monte de la Cruz is **Hotel Le Barbizón** (tel. 267-7449; hotel reservations 267-7451), which was functioning as a restaurant only at press time. The marvelous Spanish colonial-style restaurant, with great views over cloud-shrouded Barva, has been slated to open as a hotel for several years and will surely be one of the country's finest. There are 10 romantic rooms—each with a fireplace and double bath—and a suite with a Jacuzzi. Prices in the $50 range should guarantee a superb bargain. A beautiful reception lounge has a lush tropical pool and fountain. Rough-hewn timbers re-create the feel of an English country inn. Tasteful art decorations, expensive furnishings, and stained glass abound. The bar is lit by cathedral-scale windows, and the elegant dining room is centered on a mammoth open-hearth fireplace. A second dining room has a wall of fiery-red volcanic stone and an open-hearth fireplace with copper chimney. Recommended!

Hotel Monte Alpino, half a kilometer before Parque Residencial del Monte, is a massive modern apartment-style complex with views down the mountain. It, too, was closed, awaiting renovation.

Getting There

Buses to El Castillo and Bosque de la Hoja depart Heredia from the Mercado Central hourly, 8 a.m.-8 p.m. For Monte de la Cruz, take a bus departing 9 a.m., noon, or 4 p.m.

BARVA AND VICINITY

The region north and west of Heredia is coffee country par excellence. Barva, about two km north of Heredia, is about as quaint and colonial as any town in Costa Rica. A major restoration effort was begun in 1992 to spruce up one of the oldest settlements in the country. The town was named for a famous chief of the Huetar Indians who lived in the area when the Spanish arrived in 1568. The crumbling **Basílica de Barva,** which dates back to 1767, sits atop an ancient Indian burial ground and faces onto a square surrounded by red-tiled colonial-era adobe houses. They were built of cane, wood, brick, animal dung, and mud using a pre-Columbian method

called *bahareque*. On one side of the church is a grotto dedicated to the Virgin of Lourdes.

Buildings facing the square open onto pretty inner courtyards with fountains and fruit trees hidden behind thick walls. One of these—the former home of Cleto González Víquez, twice president of Costa Rica—was declared a national landmark in 1985. The village was originally a rest stop for mule trains and was officially named San Bartolomé de Barva in 1613.

The **Museum of Popular Culture** (tel. 260-1619), in Santa Lucía de Barva, presents a picture of rural life at the turn of the century, complete with enormous mortar and pestle and a large clay oven. It is housed in a recently renovated, red-tile-roofed, mustard-colored home that dates back to 1885 and was once owned by former president Alfredo González Flores (1914-17). The landscaped gardens include a fruit orchard—a timeless setting with fabulous views. Down the hills is the restaurant La Fonda. Guided tours are offered on the hour (you can also wander at will). Plans are afoot to add a **Museo del Peón** dedicated to the farm worker. The museum is signed. Open Saturday noon-7 p.m. and Sunday 9 a.m.-6 p.m. Entrance: $2.

The **Galería Huetar** sells local crafts.

Accommodations

At press time, I learned of **Los Jardines** (Apdo. 64, Barva de Heredia 3011, tel. 260-1904), a Canadian-run bed-and-breakfast in a contemporary home with four rooms and two baths. Not reviewed. Rates: $20 s, $32 d. Long-term discounts.

Getting There

Buses depart Heredia for Barva from Calle Central, Avenidas 1/3.

Café Britt

On the northern outskirts of Heredia, on the road to Barva, is the *finca* and *beneficio* of Café Britt (Apdo. 528, Heredia 3000, tel. 260-2748, fax 238-1848; in the U.S., tel. 800-GO-BRITT), where you can learn the story of Costa Rican coffee. The company, which roasts, packs, and exports to specialty stores around the world, has opened its factory and farm to visitors. The "Aventura de Café Tour" ($17) includes an educational tour of the *finca* and roasting plant,

complete with live-theater skit (very commercial, but amusing) telling the history of coffee. You conclude in the tasting room, where you are shown how the experts taste coffee. When you taste the classic light and dark roasts and espressos, you're sure to pull out your wallet! The factory store, where coffee goes for a song, can arrange mail-order delivery to the United States. A full-day "Organic Coffee Farming Tour" is also offered. Tours are offered daily at 10 a.m., Sunday at 10 a.m. and noon May through October; and 9 and 11 a.m. and 3 p.m. November through April ($50). Café Britt will pick up tour guests in San José with the "Britt Bus," colorfully decorated with coffee themes. Call for locations and times.

Getting There: Follow the road north from the McDonald's near the National University in Heredia. Turn left at the end of the road, then right at the first stop sign. Café Britt is signposted from here. Watch for El Castillo, a castlelike house on the left; Café Britt is immediately beyond, on the left.

NORTH OF BARVA

Half a kilometer north of Barva, the road forks: the road to the left leads to Birrí, Vara Blanca, La Paz Waterfall, and the northern lowlands; that to the right leads uphill to San José de la Montaña and Braulio Carrillo National Park (signposted) through countryside surprisingly reminiscent of the Lake District of England. Beyond San José de la Montaña (1,550 meters), with its pretty church, the air becomes decidedly chilly and the road, still paved, decidedly steeper.

Eight km above Barva is the hamlet of **Porrosatí** (also known as Paso Llano), where a turnoff to the left from the Guardia Rural post leads to Sacramento, gateway to Volcán Barva and Braulio Carrillo National Park. The paved road ends at Sacramento. A 4WD vehicle will get you the rest of the way uphill to the park ranger station (three km) along a very steep, deeply rutted, rocky dirt road.

A separate road leads northwest from Barva two km to San Pedro de Barva. This small village is home to the Instituto de Café research laboratory and **Coffee Museum** (tel. 237-1975), 400 meters north of the San Pedro church. The

museum building is an adobe house dating from 1834. Inside are displays of antique coffee-making paraphernalia: pulp extractors, toasters, grinders, etc. Hours: Mon.-Fri. 7 a.m.-4 p.m. Café Britt has stolen the museum's thunder and the latter may be closed by the time you read this.

Getting There
A bus marked "Santa Bárbara por Barrio Jesús" departs Heredia from Avenida 1, Calles 1/3 every 15 minutes, Mon.-Friday.

BIRRÍ AND VICINITY

The left fork at the Y-junction 800 meters north of Barva leads to the village of Birrí. Here, a road to the right from **Restaurante Las Delicias** leads uphill to a series of mountain resort hotels especially popular with Ticos.

Accommodations
Cabinas: You'll find cabinas for rent about 400 meters below Hotel Cypresal (take the right fork at the sign for Urbanizacion El Cypresal), and others (tel. 238-4242) opposite El Portico. Also try **Cabaña de las Ardillas** (tel. 222-8134), directly opposite the Cypresal. Las Ardillas has five log-and-brick cabinas with kitchens surrounded by forest, plus a restaurant and children's play area. Rates: $55 small unit, $90 large.

At press time, I learned about **Mountain Cabins La Catalina** (Apdo. 12742, San José 1000, tel. 233-6108, fax 233-6293; not reviewed), with 13 modern cottages, each with a small living room and two bedrooms, plus volleyball, swimming pool, and gardens. Rates: $42 s, $45 d, $55 t.

Moderate: A stone's throw below Hotel Cypresal is the homey **Posada del Ingles** (tel. 225-1245 or 226-5326), with three small rooms with hardwood floors, pleasant artwork, and vaguely Japanese-style windows providing plentiful light. There's nothing particularly English about the place: it's named after an Englishman, John Hale, who in 1826 established a colony hereabouts and later wrote a travelogue called *Six Months of Residence & Travels in Central America*, a hardbound copy of which is proudly on display in the hotel.) The small dining terrace has windows open to the mountain. The owners are adding two more rooms and an outside dining patio. Rates: $37 s/d, including tax.

Expensive: Five km north of Birrí is the **Hotel Cypresal** (Apdo. 7891, San José 1000, tel. 223-1717 or 237-4466, fax 221-6244), an alpine lodge with views down the mountain. It has 24 rooms, 13 with a fireplace. Take one with a fireplace—you may need it. The log cabins are very pleasant; the brick structures have ugly terraces and are more basic. Rooms have tiled floors, small TVs, and telephones. There are a volleyball court, a small and grungy swimming pool, and a modestly elegant restaurant and bar with a large open fireplace. Lacks atmosphere. Rates: $50 s, $55 d, $60 t.

A much better bet is **Hotel El Portico** (Apdo. 289, Heredia 3000, tel. 237-6022, fax 238-0629), 200 meters uphill from Cypresal. The atmospheric lodge has 13 rooms with rough-stone tiled floors and a beautiful and spacious lounge with leather sofas and a large stone fireplace and vast windows proffering views down the mountainside. There's also a cozy TV lounge, plus an atmospheric Swiss-style restaurant with bar. Beautiful artwork abounds. Pretty landscaped grounds contain a small swimming pool and lake. Rates: $55 s, $65 d, $73 t, including tax.

Cabañas La Milenas (Apdo. 44, Heredia 3009, tel./fax 260-2172) is a health resort set amid pine forests at Guacalillo, near San José de la Montaña, with romantic, rustic log cabins. It offers "stress management," massage, hydrotherapy, mud baths, Tai Chi, and horseback riding. It's reminiscent of a log cabin in the California Sierras!

VOLCÁN BARVA

Barva volcano (2,906 meters/9,534 feet), on the western extreme of Braulio Carrillo National Park, sleeps placidly in majestic surroundings. The mountain's botanical treasures range from mosses to giant oaks, cypress, and cedar. A loop trail leads to the summit from Porrosatí (the trail is marked as "BCNP Sector Barva") and circles back to the ranger station three km northeast of Sacramento (four or five hours hiking, roundtrip). The summit is three km from the

ranger station. The trail leads up through cloud forest—good for spotting resplendent quetzals and black-faced solitaires—to the crater and a lookout point from which, on a clear day, you can see forever. Fog, however, is usually the order of the day.

You can also follow marked trails on a four-day hike from the summit all the way to Puerto Viejo de Sarapiquí, in the northern lowlands. Apparently there are huts en route. Check with the National Parks headquarters (tel. 257-0922). Take an Instituto Geográfica map and a compass, plus high-quality waterproof gear and warm clothing, and—of course—sufficient food and water. Several people have been lost for days in the park. You can camp beside the crater lake, behind the ranger station, or at two picnic areas with barbecue grills on the trail (no facilities).

Tours
Jungle Trails (Apdo. 2413, San José, tel. 255-3486, fax 525-2782) offers a "Walk in the Cloud Forest" hiking tour on Barva volcano, including tours of Heredia, Barva, and a coffee plantation; four hours hiking, with picnic lunch served in a spot favored by quetzals.

Accommodations
Restaurante La Campesina and **Restaurante Sacramento,** north of Porrosatí, have basic cabinas. A round stone building in Porrosatí also offers cheap cabinas for rent. A selection of moderate and expensive accommodations is available north of Barva, on the road via Birrí to Vara Blanca (see "Birrí and Vicinity" above).

Finca Sacramento (tel. 237-2116, fax 237-1976) recently opened its doors nearby. Comfortable and rustic rooms on the family farm, "one-of-the-family" treatment from the gracious hosts, *típico* cuisine, and hiking and horseback rides through the forest combine to guarantee a rewarding experience. Rates: $40 per person.

Food
Chago's Bar, 50 meters uphill from the Guardia Rural post in Porrosatí, is funky but nonetheless popular with locals. The next few kilometers to Sacramento are lined with *sodas* and basic restaurants: **Restaurant El Ranchito** (with an open fireplace), **Bar y Restaurant La Campesina** (with outdoor tables), **Bar y Restaurant Sacramento,** and **Soda El Bosque.**

Getting There
Buses marked "Paso Llano" depart Heredia at 6:30 a.m., noon, and 3 p.m. for Porrosatí and Sacramento via San José de la Montaña from Avenida 8, Calles 2/4 (check times in advance). Hourly buses also go to San José de la Montaña (on Sunday you may need to alight here and take a 7 a.m. bus to Porrosatí). The last bus from Porrosatí departs for Heredia at 5 p.m. weekdays, 4 p.m. Sunday.

Macadamia farm, Central Highlands

JOHN ANDERSON

FINCA ROSA BLANCA

Imagine if Goudy and Frank Lloyd Wright had combined their talents and visions. The result would be an architectural stunner as eclectic and electrifying as Finca Rosa Blanca (Apdo. 41, Santa Bárbara de Heredia 3009, tel. 269-9392, fax 269-9555; in the U.S., tel. 800-327-9854). This is one of Costa Rica's—nay, the world's!—preeminent boutique hotels, opened in 1990. Inspired by Goudy's architectonics and the Santa Fe style, the hotel is conceived as if from a fairy tale. *Que linda!*

Its hillside position, at 1,300 meters above sea level and one km northeast of Santa Bárbara de Heredia, has vistas as romantic and visionary as the house itself, with row upon row of coffee plants cascading down the slopes, and mountains almost mauve in the distance. Tall 200-year-old higuerones trees and effusive tropical plants—bougainvilleas and fuchsia—provide a magnificent frame for the snow-white house with its bridge-of-the-starship-Enterprise turret.

To open the hand-carved wooden front door is like walking into the pages of *Architectural Digest*. Focalpoint is an open-plan, circular atrium lounge with wraparound deep-cushioned sofas and a huge open-hearth fireplace that—imagine!—resembles a mushroom. Light pours in through countless windows to feed the profusion of tropical plants. Flowers and creeping vines are everywhere.

The whole is contrived in rough-worked, whitewashed plaster and finely crafted hardwoods, not least the magnificent dining table and uniquely curled diners and leather casual chairs. The place is like a museum, with imaginative and tasteful statuettes, prints, New Mexican artifacts, and lamp-

Finca Rosa Blanca

SAN JOAQUÍN

San Joaquín de las Flores, four km west of Heredia, is famous for its colorful Easter-week procession and has a colonial-era church still in use. The village is a popular upscale residential area replete with villas hidden behind bougainvillea hedges. It has several nightspots for dining and dancing. The **Galería Vivero** is a very elegant and popular restaurant with din-

ing alfresco. Nearby are **Bicho's Bar, Bar La Frontera,** and **Music Discotheque.**

Butterfly Paradise
Butterfly Paradise (tel. 221-2015 or 224-1095) is a live butterfly "museum" one km to the north of San Joaquín, on the road to Santa Bárbara. Here, you can observe the life cycle of the butterfly in the breeding laboratory. Follow the signs from San Joaquín; distances are greater than indicated. Hours: 9 a.m.-4 p.m. daily.

shades shaped like Japanese fans on the walls and in every delightful nook and cranny.

There are six suites and a master suite, plus a three-bedroom "colonial cottage" (on the grounds). Each bedroom is as different as a thumbprint. Genuine hardwood antiques stand on rough stone floors. Walls are painted with trompe l'oeil landscapes; mine was of an idyllic coffee *finca.* The "Blanco y Negro" Room has a black-and-white checkerboard floor and stylish, contemporary furnishings.

The suite—a fantasy come true—has a bathroom with walls painted to resemble a tropical rainforest, with water that tumbles down a rocky cascade into the fathoms-deep tub shaped liked a natural pool. A hardwood spiral staircase—each step shaped like a petal—twists up to the coup de grace: a rotunda bedroom that caps the turret, with a full-canopied bed and wraparound windows that let in enough light to bring the ships home.

Exceptional cuisine comes with service to match. Four-course dinners ($25) are served with candlelight and soothing classical music, with free-flowing wines poured in generous portions. Careful! Drinks are proffered freely without a hint that they'll appear on your bill at sticker-shock prices.

A nine-passenger van provides transfers to the airport and throughout the Meseta Central.

Ownership has changed since I last visited. But I imagine it's still impossible not to fall head-over-heels in love with this fantasy in stone conjured from the remains of an abandoned farm.

Rates: from $104 s, $122 d to $183-204 (s/d) for the Rosa Blanca Suite. Includes full American breakfast.

SANTA BÁRBARA DE HEREDIA

Santa Bárbara de Heredia, three km north and uphill from San Joaquin, is a lively and compact town with lots of colonial-era adobe houses set amid colorful gardens. The El Banoco de Mariscos is a popular seafood restaurant; the owners catch their own fish and ship it fresh daily under ice. The road east from Santa Bárbara to Jesús and Barva leads past Finca Rosa Blanca, the most architecturally stunning hotel in the country (see special topic "Finca Rosa Blanca"): one km east of Santa Bárbara turn left at the "Chantelle" factory and continue 0.8 km to the hotel.

Getting There

A bus marked "Santa Bárbara por Barrio Jesús" departs Heredia from Avenida 1, Calles 1/3.

ALAJUELA AND VICINITY

A smaller version of San José, with a warmer climate, Alajuela (pop. 35,000) is worth a day's visit. The city rises gently northward up the lower slopes of Volcán Poás. It's approximately 20 km northeast of San José and two km north of Juan Santamaría Airport, and it is easily reached via Calle Ancha from the Pan-American Highway.

Memories of "Erizo," alias Juan Santamaría, the homegrown hero of the Battle of 1856, figure prominently in Alajuela. Erizo means "hedgehog," and refers to Santamaría's bristly hair. Every year, **Juan Santamaría Day** (11 April) is cause for serious celebration, with parades, bands, dancing, and arts-and-crafts fairs lasting a full week. The town also hosts the annual nine-day **Mango Festival** in July.

First named La Lajuela in 1657, the town's name was changed to Villa Hermosa, then San Juan de Nepomuceno, and finally to Alajuela in 1825, though it's also called "La Ciudad de los Mangos." Today, Costa Rica's "second city" is a modestly cosmopolitan town with strong links to the countryside. Saturday is market day, and hundreds of people gather to buy and sell produce fresh from the farm. Soccer is played in the city stadium (home of La Liga soccer team) most Sundays.

SIGHTS

Juan Santamaría
Cultural-Historical Museum
Housed in the former colonial city jail on the northwest corner of the Parque Central (Avenida 3, Calles Central/2, tel. 441-4775), this small but interesting museum tells the story of the War of 1856 against the no-good American adventurer William Walker (see special topic "The William Walker Saga" in the Introduction chapter). The two rooms of permanent exhibits are full of maps, paintings, war-era mementoes, and other historical bric-a-brac relating to the war and to the life of Alajuela's drummer-boy hero. There's also an exhibit room for local handicrafts. The museum has a good library, plus an auditorium where historical films are shown. Call ahead to arrange a screening of an English-language film. Hours: Tues.-Sun. 8 a.m.-4:30 p.m. Entrance free.

Parque Central
Most pleasant of Alajuela's parks is the Plaza del General Tomás Guardia, or Parque Central, the hub of social activity and a popular hangout for retired folk who sit under the mango trees (favored by blue-gray tanagers), watching the pretty girls and giving nicknames to the passersby. Local wags call it El Parque de las Palomas Muertas ("Park of the Dead Doves" . . . doves in this case referring to the old men's penises). Some of the park benches have chess sets built into them. Twice weekly, you can sit and listen to classical—and sometimes pop—music played in the domed bandstand. Any day, look for the resident sloths. Notice, too, the pretty 19th-century structures with fancy iron grilles surrounding the park.

The square is backed by a red-domed colonial-era cathedral, quite ornate within, where the bodies of ex-presidents Tomás Guardia and León Cortés Castro are buried. The cathedral was badly damaged—the faux-painted dome, for example, cracked like an eggshell—by an earthquake in December 1990 and reopened after repairs in 1993. It has some impressive religious statuary, including an image of La Negrita (see "Sights" under "Cartago" in the "Cartago and Vicinity" section) and a glass cabinet brimful of eclectic and macabre offerings.

Juan Santamaría Park
Two blocks south of Parque Central is Parque Juan Santamaría, with its dynamic statue of the national hero rushing forward with flaming torch and rifle. The volunteer soldier knew well he might die: the first volunteer to try torching the building in which Walker's army was holed up was shot and wounded; the second was killed. Juan Santamaría was killed, too, after successfully putting flame to the house. A rumor suggests that the statue is actually that of a French soldier and looks nothing like Santamaría. A

monument to the hero Juan Santamaría in Alajuela, inaugurated September 1891

small company, it is said, sent the wrong statue, but the city fathers put it up anyway.

Other Sights

Alajuela has several other appealing churches, including a simple baroque structure five blocks east of the main plaza.

At Río Segundo de Alajuela, Richard and Margot Frisius breed scarlet macaws for eventual release into the wild. Their home and breeding center, which features three massive aviaries adjoining their house, was not open to tourists when I visited, but may be now. The Frisiuses have formed a nonprofit organization—**Amigos de las Aves**—and welcome donations to expand their aviary (Apdo. 32, Río Segundo de Alajuela 4001). Also see "Macaws" under "Birds" in the Introduction chapter.

ACCOMMODATIONS

Budget

Hotel Rex (Avenida 1, Calles 6/8, tel. 441-6778) is a bottom-tier place to rest your head. Communal bathrooms—none too clean—have cold showers. Rates: $4 d. In a similar vein are **Hotel Chico** (tel. 441-0572), at Calle 10 and Avenidas 1/Central, and **Hostal Villa Real** (tel. 414-4856), one block east; both in the $5 bracket. The latter also has five rooms with shared bath ($12 s, $22 d, $30 t). All are close to the bus terminal. The **Hotel Moderno,** nearby, has also been recommended for budget travelers.

A new addition is the **Mango Verde Hostel** (tel. 441-6330, fax 442-6527), 50 meters west of the Juan Santemaría Museum. Rooms have private and shared baths, plus shared kitchen.

Inexpensive

Pensión Alajuela (Calle 4, Avenida 9, tel. 441-6250) offers 10 clean but simple rooms, plus a snack bar and laundry service. Rates: $17 d, shared bath; $20 d, private bath. **Hospedaje La Posada,** at Avenida 3, Calle 5, is a bed and breakfast, recommended but not reviewed. Also not reviewed is **Los Andes,** another bed-and-breakfast that was slated to open as I prepared this book; it's associated with the Peruvian restaurant at Avenida 1 and Calle 4.

La Rana Holandesa (tel. 381-3662) sits in a garden near Carrizal, in the hills above Alajuela (you reach it via the road that passes the soccer stadium on the northeast edge of town). The Dutch owners—John and Hennie Dekker—offer three clean rooms ($10 per person, including breakfast; dinners are $3 extra). Two have shared bathroom with hot water. The Dekkers provide free airport pick-up and laundry, plus guided tour for $60.

Moderate

Hotel Alajuela (Apdo. 110, Alajuela 4050, tel. 441-1241, fax 441-7912), on the southwest corner of Parque Central, has 50 clean and nicely furnished rooms, with private bath with hot water.

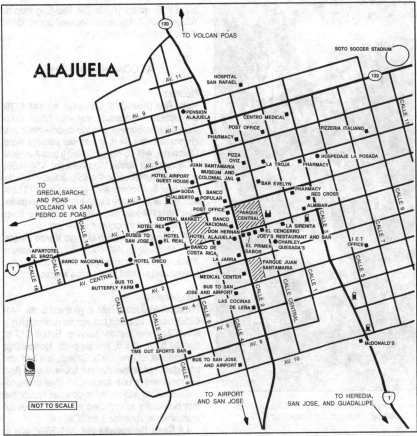

ALAJUELA

TO VOLCAN POAS

SOTO SOCCER STADIUM

HOSPITAL SAN RAFAEL

PENSION ALAJUELA

CENTRO MEDICAL

POST OFFICE

PIZZERIA ITALIANO

PHARMACY

PIZZA OVIZ

LA TROJA

HOSPEDAJE LA POSADA

JUAN SANTAMARIA MUSEUM AND COLONIAL JAIL

PHARMACY

HOTEL AIRPORT GUEST HOUSE

BAR EVELYN

TO GRECIA, SARCHI, AND POAS VOLCANO VIA SAN PEDRO DE POAS

PHARMACY RED CROSS

BANCO POPULAR

SODA ALBERTO

PARQUE CENTRAL

ALMIBAR

CENTRAL MARKET

BANCO NACIONAL

LA SIRENITA

HOTEL REX

DON HERNAN

EL CENCERRO

HOTEL EL REAL

HOTEL ALAJUELA

JOEY'S RESTAURANT AND BAR

BUSES TO SAN JOSE

BANCO DE COSTA RICA

CHARLEY QUESADA'S

I C T OFFICE

APARTOTEL EL ERIZO

BANCO NACIONAL

EL PRIMER SABOR

LA JARRA

HOTEL CHICO

PARQUE JUAN SANTAMARIA

AV. CENTRAL

MEDICAL CENTER

BUS TO BUTTERFLY FARM

BUS TO SAN JOSE AND AIRPORT

LAS COCINAS DE LEÑA

McDONALD'S

TIME OUT SPORTS BAR

BUS TO SAN JOSE AND AIRPORT

TO AIRPORT AND SAN JOSE

TO HEREDIA, SAN JOSE, AND GUADALUPE

NOT TO SCALE

© MOON PUBLICATIONS, INC.

Apartment rooms with kitchen in the old section are dark. It's the only decent downtown hotel. Laundry service. No restaurant. Good bargain. Rates: $26 s, $32 d, $37 t.

Three bed and breakfasts to consider are **La Rana Dorada** (tel. 442-5360), with private bath and cable TV and laundry service (rates: $25); **Charly's Place** (tel./fax 441-0115), a bed and breakfast with 11 rooms with private bath and hot water ($30 d), 200 meters north and 25 meters east of Parque Central; and **Hotel el Colibri** (Apdo. 64, Alajuela 4030, tel./fax 441-4228), a pretty family-operated bed and breakfast in Barrio San José, two km west of Ala-

juela. Its 11 rooms in four bungalows are set in tropical gardens and modestly yet elegantly furnished. Each has TV, fan, private bath, and terrace. Breakfast is served in a garden pavilion. Rates include use of a pool and tennis court and free airport transfer.

Another unknown to me is the **Colón Mini Hotel,** which reportedly has spacious rooms with a/c, two double beds, and private baths with hot water. It's run by the same folks who operate Colón Rent-a-Car (tel. 441-1661). Rates: $15 s, $20 d.

A recommended hostelry in the hills, three km above Alajuela, is the American-run **El Tuetal**

Lodge (tel. 442-1804), offering six spacious cabins, including three with kitchenettes, private baths, and solar-heated water ($35 s, $40 d; $10 less without kitchen). Airy, bamboo-framed "treehouses" cost $9 s, $12 d, and offer sweeping views over coffee plantations. It has 30 **campsites** ($5, plus $2 for a second person and additional people). Campers have access to toilets, showers, and laundry. The restaurant serves organic fare from home-grown produce, and the eight-acre grounds include an orchard.

Upscale

The **Hotel Airport Guest House** (tel. 442-0354), a luxurious colonial-style hostelry, opened in December 1994 downtown on Avenida 3 and Calle 4. It offers 24 a/c, carpeted rooms with cable TV and that rare Costa Rican jewel—real bathtubs! The hotel is set in beautiful grounds with a pool and restaurant. Rates: $55-75 d.

You have several excellent options outside Alajuela, especially the highly recommended Orquídeas Inn (see "San José de Alajuela," below) and Finca Rosa Blanca (see special topic "Finca Rosa Blanca").

Apartments

The **Apartotel El Erizo** (tel./fax 441-2840) has eight fully furnished apartments with full kitchens, plus cable TV and laundry service. It also has four rooms ($54, up to three people). No restaurant. It's on the western outskirts of town. Follow the road signs for Grecia. You'll pass a Hotel 400m sign, which will guide you to El Erizo. Rates: $84, up to four people (seventh night free).

FOOD AND ENTERTAINMENT

Joey's Restaurant and Bar (tel. 441-9222), an open-air cafe on the south side of the central plaza, is popular with gringos and good for *típico* and American dishes and a helluva good time. Alajuela's small but lively colony of Peruvians add a touch of authenticity to the **Rincón Peruano Restaurant** (tel. 442-3977), a favorite hangout of locals at Avenida 1 and Calle 4. For less than $5 you can feast on Peruvian dishes, including the restaurant's famous *papa relleno*. Dancing on Tuesday. The chef, intriguingly, is Russian; she'll make Russian dishes upon request.

Try **El Cencerro** ("The Cowbell"), facing the plaza on Avenida Central, for inexpensive charbroiled steaks; or **Don Hernán** (tel. 441-4680), next to the Hotel Alajuela, for hamburgers and hot dogs. **La Jarra** (tel. 441-8877) at Calle 2 and Avenida 2 is another steak house restaurant, airy and lush with potted plants, and upstairs balconies overlook the northwest corner of Parque Juan Santamarí. **La Sirenita Restaurant** (tel. 441-9681), on the south side of the cathedral, also specializes in seafoods and steaks. Vegetarians should head to **Soda Alberto** (tel. 441-7499), Calle 4, Avenidas 1/3.

Las Cocinas de Leña (Calle 2, Avenida 6, tel. 442-1010) prepares *típico* dishes over coffee-wood fires and has an extensive beef and seafood menu. An abundance of potted plants, but basic decor. **La Esquina de los Mariscos** (tel. 433-8077), on the south side of the main square, has seafood at budget prices. **Soda El Parque,** on the same block, is recommended for inexpensive, filling breakfasts.

Best of the Oriental options include the **Restaurant El Primer Sabor** (Avenida Central, Calles Central/2, tel. 441-7082), a classy restaurant with a wide range of dishes. For pizzas try **Pizza Oviz** (Calle Central, Avenida 3, tel. 441-4328), **Pizzeria Italiano** (Calle 9, Avenida 3, tel. 442-0973), or **Pizza Hut** (Avenida 2, Calle Central, tel. 441-2222).

Almibar coffee and pastry shop (Calles 1/3, Avenida Central) has desserts, gourmet cakes, and breads and rolls. Of course, if like me you're an ice-cream addict, head to **Monpik,** on the southeast corner of the main square.

Entertainment

Nightlife seems restricted to cinemas (there are three along Avenida Central) and bars. **La Troja** is a funky jazz bar and restaurant popular with younger folk. It's housed in a colonial-era building that was once a *troja* (corn warehouse). **Bar Evelyn** (Calle Central, Avenida 1/3, tel. 441-2867) has live guitar music daily except Friday. And **Joey's** (see "Food") is always lively. Ladies' Night on Thursday, and two-for-the-price-of-one on Saturday, when there's live music (country and classic rock 'n' roll predominate). The **Kalahari** dance club and disco, next to Joey's, is a good place to learn a few *salsa* and *merengue* moves. More down-to-earth local color is pro-

vided at **Indianapolis Taberna** (Calle 8, Avenidas 1/3), where the scene reportedly can get fairly rowdy.

SERVICES AND TRANSPORT

Banks
The Banco Nacional has two branches along Avenida Central at Calle 12 and Calle 2; Banco de Costa Rica is at Calle 4 and Avenida Central, and Avenida 10 and Calle 2/4; Banco Popular is on Calle 2 at Avenida 1; and Banco Anglo Costarricense is at Calle Central and Avenidas 1/3. You can get a cash advance against Visa or MasterCard at Credomatic (Avenida 3, Calles Central/2, tel. 441-2080).

Medical
You have plenty of medical **clinics** to choose from. Right downtown is the Clínica Medical Juan Santamaría (tel. 441-6284) and Laboratorio Biopsias (tel. 221-4545), opposite the statue of the national hero. Alternatively, try Dr. Soto Brenes (tel. 442-2608) and Dr. Carlos Vasquez (tel. 442-1467); or the Centro Medical (tel. 441-1971) at Calle 3, Avenidas 5/7. Hospital San Rafael (tel. 441-5011) is at Avenida 9, Calles Central/1.

Pharmacies include Farmacia Chavarría (tel. 441-1231) on Calle 2 and Avenida Central; Farmacia el Hospital (tel. 441-3231) on Calle Central and Avenida 5; and Farmacia Internacional (tel. 442-1343) at Avenida 1 and Calles 1/3.

Tourist Information
The **Costa Rican Tourism Institute** (ICT, tel. 223-1733) has an office on Avenida 4 and Calle 5/7. Ray Nelson and Wade Plymate operate the **Alajuela Welcome Center** (tel./fax 441-1141) on Avenida 2, Calles 2/4. The Center provides travelers' information and acts as a full-service travel agency.

Police
The Guardia Rural (tel. 441-5277) is at Calle 2, Avenida 1. For the transport police—"highway patrol"—call 441-7411.

Laundry
La Margarita (tel. 441-0116) on Avenida Central and Calles 2/4 offers laundry and dry-cleaning service.

Getting There
Buses depart San José from Avenida 2, Calle 10/12 (tel. 222-4650), every 10 minutes, 5 a.m.-midnight; and every 40 minutes from Calle 2, Avenida 2, midnight to 4:20 a.m. Return buses depart from Calle 8, Avenidas Central/1.

SAN JOSÉ DE ALAJUELA

The road west from Alajuela leads to San José de Alajuela, a pretty little town with a historic tumbledown church and the wonderful and very popular thatch-roofed **Restaurant Típico las Tinajitas** (tel./fax 433-8668); the road to the left leads to La Garita. Beyond San José de Alajuela, the road cuts a meandering and leisurely path through the central calley's northern foothills via Tacares, Grecia, Sarchí, and San Ramón en route to Puntarenas, or to Zarcero en route to the northern lowlands. The route is splendidly scenic. Coffee *fincas* gradually give way to field after field of sugarcane and, beyond Naranjo, dairy pastures that could have been transplanted from Europe. The road bears only light to moderate traffic as the majority of travelers heading to Puntarenas and the Pacific coast use the Bernardo Soto Expressway and Pan-American Highway via Atenas.

Driving north from San José to Poás, you'll pass through the pretty little village of **San Pedro,** highlighted by its blue church. One km south of San Pedro the Costa Rica Tourism Institute (ICT) has a lookout point situated where the Ríos Carracha and Poás join; you'll have reasonable views of two waterfalls. A trail—**Sendero Carracha**—follows the river to picnic tables in the forest.

Accommodations and Food
If you tire of Third World toilet paper, towels, and service, stay at the **Orquídeas Inn** (Apdo. 394, Alajuela, tel. 433-9346, fax 433-9740), a gringo-owned gem of a hotel managed to all-American standards. First impression is of a Spanish hacienda, contemporary in style, surrounded by lush landscaped grounds thick with plantains and palms, with a pleasing swimming pool in an enclosed courtyard. Each of the 12 tile-floored rooms is large, with marvelously designed arched windows, arched doors hand-carved with orchid motifs, and matching arched

bed heads. Vases full of orchids and stunning Guatemalan bedspreads and paintings add a note of bright color. Breakfast is truly superb: toast and jam to die for, and spicy *gallo pinto* with *huevos rancheros* and marinated red peppers. A late afternoon coffee tasting energizes tourists en route to Poás. And for dinner, guests are given kitchen access and encouraged to conjure their favorite recipes for other guests.

Afterward, retreat to the hotel's famous Marilyn Monroe Bar, open to the breezes on three sides and festooned with posters, T-shirts, and photos immortalizing the pinup queen. Buffalo wings and popcorn are on the house. Check out the king-size ice-cream piña coladas! The napkins are printed with Marilyn kisses. And there's even Marilyn Monroe wine from California's Napa Valley. A large souvenir store stocks a collection representing the finest of national artisan work. The inn offers limousine service to/from the airport. A friendly toucan, parrots, and a scarlet macaw play tricks on the guests. Rates: $50 s, $60 d, $70 t.

Orquídeas Inn is a great place to stop for lunch or dinner. Alternately, stop off for refreshment at the **Russian Tea Terrace** (tel. 433-9257), in Tambor, seven km beyond Orquídeas Inn on the road to San Pedro. Here, Jhanna Sosenskay serves a healthy dose of Russian culture along with borscht, strudel, etc. and Russian tea served from a genuine *samovar* (turn right at Bar Veranera). Dinners are offered at 5 p.m.

LOS CHORROS

Los Chorros ("The Spouts") is a 38-hectare recreational park with trails leading into a forest preserve where the lucky hiker might spot porcupines, opossums, armadillos, and even margays and jaguarundis. The entrance is in the Quebrada del León Quarry, three km north of the Corazón de Jesús Church in Tacares (from Alajuela, turn right at the church and follow the road that goes uphill to the left). You'll pass **Bar Los Chorros** on the right. The road turns into a rocky path and ends at a fence. A path leads from here down to the quarry where the park is signed. Trails lead to two waterfalls and a *mirador* (lookout point) but are slippery and not well maintained. A rickety rope bridge leads to one of the waterfalls in Indiana Jones fashion. Rainbows sometimes shimmer at the base of the falls. The place is popular on weekends: go midweek. A sign warns you to resist any temptation to skinny-dip. Hours: 7 a.m.-5 p.m. Entrance: 60 cents.

PARQUE LAGUNA FRAIJANES
AND POÁS VOLCANO NATIONAL PARK

Above Alajuela, coffee plantations give way to dairy farms and fields of ornamental plants, ferns, and strawberries separated by forests of cedar that form important watersheds and edge up to the rim of Poás volcano.

PARQUE LAGUNA FRAIJANES

This 18-hectare recreation area of forested parkland (tel. 448-5322) surrounds a 1.5-hectare lagoon good for fishing and swimming. I've heard, however, that the *agua* can get so green it's more fitting for reptilian reproduction than swimming. You'll find basketball courts, a volleyball court, a soccer field, a children's playground, picnic tables and grills, plus trails, and horses for rent ($3 per hour). Alcohol is not allowed. The park is run by the Ministry of Culture, Youth, and Sport. Hours: Tues.-Sun. 9 a.m.-3:30 p.m.

Accommodations
Jaulares Restaurant (see below) has five cabinas ($37 d). A trail leads down to the river.

Restaurants
The road to Poás offers several superb places to eat.

Just north of Sabana Redondo, eight km north of San Pedro, is **Bar/Restaurant Las Fresas** (tel. 661-2397), hidden off the road on the left, replete with shining hardwoods, and justifiably renowned for its Italian specialties. You can't go wrong with the calzone, hamburgers, or pizza (anticipate up to a 30-minute wait for pizza; call ahead to order). It's very popular with wealthier Ticos and gets full at lunchtime. A short distance down the hill is the recently opened **L'Aldea,** a family-run restaurant serving quality Costa Rican dishes for less than $3. Trails lead through a patch of primary forest.

Continuing uphill, you'll come to the atmospheric rancho-style **Jaulares Restaurant** (tel./fax 482-2155), with meals cooked on an open wood-burning stove. It's a popular spot at night, when it has live music. Just below the Jaulares Restaurant, a turnoff to the right leads to Parque Laguna Fraijanes and one of Costa Rica's most famous *típico* restaurants—**Chubascos,** alias **Restaurant Poás** (Apdo. 618, Alajuela 4050, tel. 441-1813, fax 253-4320). It has a large indoor dining area and a covered front porch for dining alfresco. The menu includes an endless list of *gallitos* (tortillas with various toppings), *refrescos* made from strawberries, and even homemade cheesecake. Closed Monday.

One km north of Jaulares is **Restaurant El Recreo,** down-to-earth but serving superb *típico* cuisine cooked in an open kitchen. Sadly, it's been discovered by the tour buses. Arrive early to find a place. The restaurant is set back from the road, but you can't miss it. You'll see a large souvenir shop on the roadside immediately in front of the restaurant.

Getting There
Buses depart Alajuela from Avenida Central, Calle 10 (three blocks west of the Mercado Central) Tues.-Fri. at 9 a.m. and 1, 4:15, and 6:15 p.m. Return buses depart at 6 and 10 a.m., and 2 and 5 p.m. (tel. 449-5141). Buses operate hourly, 9 a.m.-5 p.m. weekends. If you're driving, Calle 2 leads due north from downtown Alajuela to Parque Laguna Fraijanes. About three km beyond Fraijanes, the road merges with the road to Poás volcano from San José de Alajuela (see "West from Alajuela," below) via San Pedro de Poás.

POASITO

Poasito, about 18 km north of San Pedro, is no more than an agglomeration of *sodas* and restaurants, and roadside stalls selling fresh strawberries *(fresas)* and freshly baked cookies.

The road to the right leads east to **Vara Blanca,** four km east of Poasito, in the saddle of Poás and Barva volcanoes. Beyond Vara Blanca, the road veers sharply south and heads back downhill to Alajuela and Heredia. A road to the left at Vara Blanca leads downhill to the La Paz waterfall and Puerto Viejo de Sarapiquí, in the northern lowlands.

Accommodations

Two km east of Poasito is an alpine-style cabina for rent in the middle of a cow pasture (tel. 239-0234). Lauren Fonseca, who owns the Restaurant Vara Blanca, also has two cabinas for rent: one for six people, the other for two, and each with fireplace, kitchen, and hot water ($30 d; $35 cabin for six).

Poás Volcano Lodge (Apdo. 5723, San José 1000, tel./fax 441-9102), 800 meters west of Vara Blanca, east of Poasito, gets two thumbs up. The magnificent rough stone mountain lodge, stunningly situated amid emerald-green pastures at 1,900 meters midpoint between Poás and Barva volcanoes, might have been conceived by Frank Lloyd Wright. Actually, it was built as a farmhouse by an English family that still owns the dairy farm, El Cortijo. Merging Welsh and American influences, the unusual design lends immense atmosphere to the lodge. Centerpoint is a timber-beamed lounge with walls hung with Indian weavings and sunken chairs in front of a massive open fireplace. French doors open onto a patio with fabulous views over the Caribbean lowlands.

The eight bedrooms are rustic yet supremely comfortable, with thick down comforters to ward off the cold and superior bed linens. The large suite (at $80 a superb bargain) has a stunning bathroom with a fathoms-deep stone bathtub shaped like a pool; the bedroom has its own fireplace, plus two bunks and a double bed of rough timbers. Smaller rooms in the house have shared but voluminous baths. Rooms in an adjacent block have the advantage of reliable piping-hot water. The hotel is close to special birdwatching sites. Guests commonly see quetzals. The lodge serves filling breakfasts, and dinners by request. Rates: $55 to $85 d, including breakfast.

You have several options above Poasito, on the last leg to Poás. **Lo Que Tu Quieros** has three cabinas with private baths and hot water ($12 s, $18 d). Camping is also allowed. A short distance beyond is **Lagunillas Lodge** (tel. 448-5506), which has eight simple cabins that proffer splendid views down the mountainside ($16 d with shared bathroom). There are trails for horseback rides, plus a homey Hansel-and-Gretel-type restaurant.

Albergue Ecológico La Providencia (tel. 232-2498, fax 231-2204), only half a kilometer below the park entrance, is a rustic jewel with five lonesome cabañas spread out among 50 hectares of forested hillside pasture on the upper flanks of Poás at 2,500 meters. You can hike or take a horse or a traditional cart to the huts. Views are mesmerizing and include the Gulf of Nicoya, Volcán Arenal, Sarchí, Grecia, the Talamanca mountains, and even Nicaragua! Each cabin has a small kitchenette with butane stove, plus hot water from a HEP generating plant. Or you can eat meals cooked on a traditional stove in a wonderful little restaurant with all-around windows. Horses are available for rides ($25) to sulfur springs and waterfalls with the incredibly gracious and friendly owner, Carlos. The property even has a small dairy for those who want to pull their own pints of warm milk. Reserve now—this place will soon be discovered. Rates: $55 d.

Restaurants

The **Bar/Restaurant Familiar** is notable for its fabulous murals on the outside walls. The **Steak House El Churrasco,** on the corner, is a popular spot for meat dishes ($4 upward). The tiny **Soda Familiar Poasito** next door is more rustic but less expensive.

The **Restaurant Vara Blanca** (tel. 260-2366), at the T-junction for La Paz and Puerto Viejo, is an atmospheric eatery of bamboo and rough-hewn wood, popular with locals.

Above Poasito is **Quetzal Souvenirs,** which lures clients with free coffee; and, 100 meters farther, **Lo Que Tu Quieras** (tel. 448-5213), a rustic restaurant with a large and inexpensive menu of *típico* dishes ($3 for *casados*) served at rough-hewn benches and tables overlooking the whole valley. Marvelous views here. So, too, at the restaurants of **Lagunillas** and **Albergue Ecológica,** farther up the mountain (see "Accommodations").

POÁS VOLCANO NATIONAL PARK

A must see! Few volcanoes allow you to drive all the way to the rim. Poás does . . . well, at least to within 300 meters, from where a short stroll puts you at the very edge of one of the world's largest active craters (1.5 km wide). The viewing terrace gives a bird's-eye view not only 320 meters down into the hellish bowels of the volcano, with its greenish sulfuric pool, but also magnificently down over the northern lowlands.

Poás (2,708 meters) is a restless giant with a 40-year active cycle. It erupted moderately in the early 1950s and was briefly active in 1989, when the access road was closed, and again in May 1994, when the park was temporarily closed. In July and August 1994 it rumbled dramatically.

Over the millennia it has vented its anger through three craters. Two now slumber under a blanket of vegetation; one even cradles a lake. But the main crater bubbles persistently with active fumaroles and a simmering lake. The sulfuric pool frequently changes hues and emits a geyser up to 200 meters into the steam-laden air. The water level of the lake has gone down about 15 meters during the past decade, one of several indications of a possible impending eruption. In the 1950s a small eruption pushed up a new cone on the crater floor; the cone is now 200 feet high and still puffing.

Oft as not it is foggy up here and mist floats like an apparition through the dwarf cloud forest draped with bromeliads and mosses. Clouds usually form midmorning. Plan an early-morning arrival to enhance your chances of a cloud-free visit. Temperatures vary widely. On a sunny day it can be 21° C (70° F). On a cloudy day, it is normally bitterly cold and windy at the crater rim, even freezing. Dress accordingly.

Poás is the most visited park in the country and is particularly popular at weekends with local Ticos who arrive by the busload with their blaring radios. Visit midweek if possible. The park is sometimes closed to visitors because of pungent and irritating sulfur gas emissions—many plants bear the scars of acid attacks.

Trails

The **Botos Trail** just before the viewing platform leads to an extinct crater filled with a cold-water lake—Botos. This and the **Escalonia Trail,** which begins at the picnic area, provide for pleasant hikes. The park protects the headwaters of several important rivers, and the dense forests are home to emerald toucanets, coyotes, resplendent quetzals, sooty robins, hummingbirds, frogs, and the Poás squirrel, which is endemic to the volcano.

Information and Services

Poás National Park is the most developed within the Costa Rican park system. It offers ample

Poás volcano from lookout point

parking, toilets, and a superb exhibit hall and auditorium, where audiovisual presentations are given on Sunday. Upstairs is the **Heliconia Nature Store** run by the Fundación Neotropica. There's wheelchair access to the exhibits and trails. The **Soda El Volcán**, to the left beyond the car park, serves snacks. The park has no accommodations, and camping is not permitted (check with the National Park headquarters—tel. 233-5284—as camping has reportedly been allowed in prior years). Hours: 8 a.m.-3:30 p.m. Entrance: $15 walk-in, $10 advance purchase.

Tours

Most travel agents and tour operators in San José arrange day-trips to Poás (average $30 half day, $50 full day). Many arrive fairly late in the morning, which reduces the chances of seeing anything before the clouds set in. The best bet is to rent a car so that you can arrive early in the morning. A Poás and Sarchí full-day tour offered by **Costa Rica Temptations** (Apdo. 5452, San José 1000, tel. 220-4437, fax 220-2103) is recommended.

Getting There

There's no scheduled public bus service to Poás. However, a full-day excursion bus operated by Tuasa departs at 8:30 a.m. on Sunday from Calle 12, Avenidas 2/4 in San José (tel. 233-7477; $2.50); and from the main square in Alajuela at 9 a.m (tel. 441-0631). Buses fill quickly; get there early. The bus makes a short rest stop at Poasito. You arrive at the volcano about 11 a.m. and depart at 2:30 p.m.

A bus for Poasito reportedly departs Alajuela daily at 5 a.m. and 1:30 p.m. (check times) and goes to San Pedro de Poás, from where you can hire a taxi ($25 roundtrip). If driving, follow Calle 2 north from Alajuela (35 km), or take the road west to Grecia and turn right at the Orquídeas Inn, one km west of San José de Alajuela.

GRECIA TO LOS ANGELES CLOUD FOREST RESERVE

GRECIA AND VICINITY

Grecia's claim to fame is its unique, rust-colored, twin-spired metal church made of steel plates imported from Belgium in 1897. The church is an intriguing amalgam, with steps of pumice, a wooden interior, and a white, arched wooden ceiling with glass chandeliers, a beautiful tiled floor, stained-glass windows, and an all-marble altar that rises fancifully like one of Emperor Ludwig's fairy-tale castles. Birds fly in and out through open doors. The church is fronted by a pretty park with tall palms, an obelisk erected to commemorate the foundation of Grecia in July 1864, fountains, and a domed music temple. The Cultural Center in Grecia houses a regional museum (tel. 444-6767) tracing the development of the area during the last 200 years. Doll collectors or anyone seeking an intriguing souvenir should stop off at **Rincón de Salas**, just off the Pan-American Hwy. six km south of Grecia, where a collective of local women operate a doll-making workshop called Mono Azul.

Northeast of Grecia

The road to San Pedro and Poás via Santa Gertrudis leads to **Balneario Victoria**, a popular swimming spot for Tico families. If the hordes of people don't put you off, the canned music just might. Five km farther brings you to **Complejo Turístico Los Trapiches** (tel. 444-6656), another congested tourist haunt popular with Ticos but with little to recommend it. A restaurant, lawns, a children's pool, picnic sites, and playing fields surround an old sugar mill—much in need of restoration—and a duck pond with fountains. The *trapiche* (traditional sugarcane press) was imported from Scotland in the 1880s and is powered by an equally venerable waterwheel. It wasn't working when I called in. Call ahead to check operating times.

Bungee Jumping

About eight km southwest of Grecia, two km beyond the Grecia turnoff from the Pan-American Highway to Puntarenas, is a sign for bungee jumping. Thrill seekers can jump off the 83-meter Puente Negro bridge over the Río Colorado on

Saturday and Sunday. Two companies—**ASP Eurobungy** (c/o Saragundí Specialty Tours, tel. 255-0011 or 222-4547, fax 255-2155) and **Tropical Bungee** (tel. 233-6455)—offer bungee jumps under the guidance of "jump masters" using an 11-meter bungee cord that stretches 400% (i.e., to 44 meters), with a rebound of 80%. ASP charges $55 per jump; Tropical Bungee (which will also arrange jumps midweek for groups of five or more) charges $40 per jump or $65 for two. **Note:** Anyone with back, neck, or heart problems is advised not to jump. I promptly got a doctor's note! The San José-Puntarenas bus from Calle 12 and Avenida 7 or San José-Naranjo bus from Calle 16 and Avenida 1 will drop you off at "Salon Los Alfaro," from where it is a short walk north to the bridge.

Accommodations

Not much to choose from. In town, nonsmoking travelers could try **La Posada de Grecia** (tel. 444-5354, fax 444-5321) facing the park, above the Tienda Raul Vega store. Three rooms have private bath. Not inspected. Rates: $30, including breakfast. A cheaper alternative is **Pensión Familiar** (tel. 444-5097).

Near town is **Healthy Day Inn** (tel./fax 444-5903), described as a "naturistic health home." The hotel offers therapeutic massage, reflexology, facials, sauna, hydrotherapy, and supervised macrobiotic diets. Amenities include a Jacuzzi, swimming pool, and lighted tennis court. Tastefully decorated rooms have a TV and telephone. The inn offers car rental ($20 daily) and tour guides. Rates: $40 s, $55 d, $65 t, including breakfast and airport transfers.

Somewhere close by, too, is **Finca Mirador** (Apdo. 110, Grecia, tel. 444-6260). Not inspected. Rates: $30 d.

There are reportedly two inexpensive options nearby: **Cabañas Los Cipreses** and the basic **Pensión Quirís.**

Food and Services

The south side of the park in Grecia has several pleasant restaurants, including **Bar Kennedy, Bar/Restaurant Rendezvous,** and the **Bar/Restaurant Oasis.** There's a **hospital** (San Francisco de Asis, tel. 444-5045), and **Red Cross** (tel. 444-5292).

Getting There

Buses depart San José hourly from the Coca-Cola bus terminal. The bus station in Grecia is at Avenida 2, Calles 4/6.

SARCHÍ

Every country has its major artisan center. The internationally famous town of Sarchí (29 km northwest of Alajuela) is Costa Rica's crossroads of crafts. Sarchí is famous for the intricately detailed, hand-painted oxcarts that originated here in the middle of the 19th century. You can still see them being pulled along back roads of the country by plodding bovines led by leather-skinned old men. Hand-crafted souvenirs—from chess sets and salad bowls, leather sandals and rockers, to miniature oxcarts decorated in traditional geometric designs—are sold at shops all along the road of Sarchí Sur, which sits atop a steep hill about one km east of the much larger Sarchí Norte.

Sarchí church

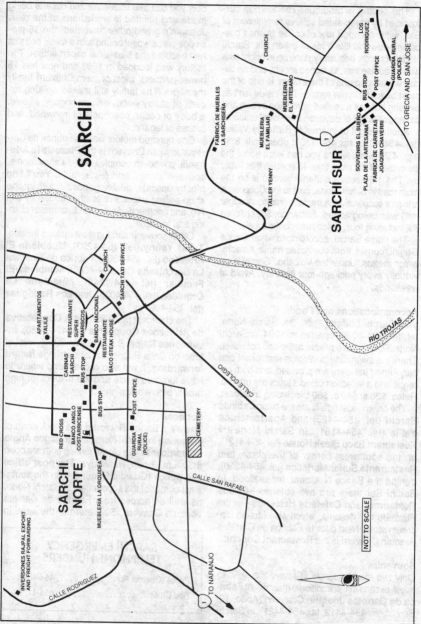

The setting is fabulous. The town is surrounded by steep-sided valleys reminiscent of Bali, with row upon row of coffee bushes cascading downhill like folds of green silk. Sarchí Norte's church, beautifully done up in bright pink with turquoise trim, stuccoed motifs, and an oxcart wheel atop one of the towers, is one of the most beautiful in the nation. The inside isn't as exciting but has a vaulted hardwood ceiling and carvings—a gift of devotion from local artisans.

Another sight of interest is **Butterfly Valley** (tel. 454-4050, fax 454-4300; open daily 8:30 a.m.-4:30 p.m.), where you can learn about the life cycles of the more than 40 species that flutter by. The 1.6-hectare butterfly garden is on the main road in Sarchí Norte, next to the Coopearsa artisan's cooperative. A *trapiche* (traditional sugar mill) was being added. Entrance: $6; children $3, including tour, which runs continuously.

The name Sarchí, according to writer Carlos Gagini, comes from the Aztec name Xalachi, which means "Under the Volcano." Sarchí is on virtually every package-tour itinerary. Avoid at weekends.

Accommodations and Food

Villa Sarchí Lodge (Apdo. 34, Sarchí Norte, tel./fax 454-4006) opened in 1994 in Sarchí Norte. Rooms have private baths and hot water. There's a swimming pool, plus restaurant and bar. Airport transfers are provided, and both car rental and a selection of local tours are offered. Rates: $30 s, $40 d, $60 t, including breakfast.

The only budget hotels are the basic **Cabinas Sarchí** (tel. 454-4425) and **Apartamentos Yalile** (tel. 454-4161). In Sarchí Norte try **Restaurant Baco Steak House** (tel. 454-4121), on the southwest corner of the plaza, and **Restaurante Super Mariscos** (tel. 454-4330), behind the Banco Nacional, for seafood. In Sarchí Sur there are two eateries—**Cocos Restaurant** and **Cafeteria Helechos**—in the Plaza de la Artesanía, which also has an ice-cream store. Next door to Fábrica de Carretas Joaquín Chaverrí is the **Restaurant Concha.**

Souvenirs

Only two men in Sarchí still have the skills to make oxcarts in the traditional manner. At **Fábrica de Carretas Joaquín Chaverrí** (Apdo. 19, Sarchí, tel. 454-4412, fax 454-4421), in Sarchí Sur, you can see souvenirs and oxcarts being made and painted in workshops at the rear. Joaquín's grandfather "invented" the 16-pie-wedge-piece wheel bound with a metal belt that has become the traditional oxcart wheel. The factory was founded in 1903 and now has 15 owner-partners, most of them Chaverrí family members. The family still makes working oxcarts of sturdy wood, with mahogany wheels, a body of cedar, coachpole of ironwood, and braces of lagarto.

One hundred meters west of Fábrica de Carretas Joaquín Chaverrí is the **Plaza de la Artesanía**, a modern complex with 34 showrooms, souvenir stores, and restaurants. You'll find mostly upscale, quality goods, including one shop selling expensive leather goods by Del Rio, and another dedicated to Guatemalan clothing and textiles.

Other souvenir and furniture makers include: **Taller Yenny** (tel. 454-4293), **Mueblería El Artesano** (tel. 454-4304), **Fábrica de Muebles La Sarchiseña** (tel. 454-4062), **Mueblería El Familiar** (tel. 454-4243), **Mueblería La Orquídea** (tel. 454-4035), and **Los Rodriguez** (tel. 454-4097).

The cheapest place in town is **Cooperativa de Artesanos Coopearsa** (tel. 454-4050). **Inversiones Rajpal S.A.** (tel. 454-3250), west of town on Calle Rodriguez, can arrange **freight forwarding**. It will also recommend where to have furniture made and will inspect for high quality before shipping.

Services

There's a **Banco Nacional** one block north of the square in Sarchí Norte, and a **Banco Anglo Costarricense** two blocks farther; both are open 8:30 a.m.-3 p.m., weekdays. The **post office** and **police** (Guardia Rural) are on the southwest corner of the soccer field in Sarchí Norte, as well as across from Fábrica de Carreta Joaquín Chaverrí, 50 meters to the east, in

---

SARCHÍ EMERGENCY TELEPHONE NUMBERS

Police (Guardia Rural) 454-4021	
Red Cross 454-4139	

Sarchí Sur. **Taxis:** try Sarchí Taxi Service (tel. 454-4028).

Getting There

Buses depart Alajuela every 30 minutes, 5 a.m.-10 p.m., from Calle 8, Avenidas Central/1 (Tuan, tel. 441-3781). An express Tuan bus departs San José from Calle 16, Avenidas 1/3, at 12:15 and 5:30 p.m.; return 5:30 and 6:15 a.m. and 1:45 p.m. You can also take a San José bus to Naranjo and change there.

NORTH OF SARCHÍ

From Sarchí a road climbs up the mountain slopes via Luisa and Angeles to the saddle between Poás and Viejo volcanoes before dropping sharply into the **Valle Bajos del Toro**, where at the head of the valley of the Río Toro you'll find the **Magic Kingdom of Nahuatá,** a new ecological resort. Stay tuned!

WEST OF SARCHÍ

From Sarchí the road leads west to **Naranjo** (five km), a substantial and pleasant town with a pretty, twin-towered, cream-colored, red-roofed baroque church worth a browse. Within, thick limestone Corinthian columns support a fine ceiling. Notice the splendid religious paintings to the sides. From Naranjo you can continue southwest via Palmares to San Ramón (see below) or head north 25 km to Zarcero—one of the most scenic drives in the country.

Palmares is renowned for its lively weeklong agricultural and civic fiesta held each mid-January, with bullfights, carnival rides, and general merriment. The stone village church, built in 1894, is attractive in its ornamental setting. Venture within, where the nave is as cool as a well, to inspect the impressive mosaic floor and stained-glass windows.

At Cocaleca, near Zaragoza, one km south of Palmares, is **Jardín de Las Guarias** (tel. 452-0091), a private orchid collection and the largest such in the country. Owner Javier Solórzano Murillo has more than 180 orchid species on display, but it is Costa Rica's national flower, the violet *guaria morada* orchid, that blossoms most pro-

fusely—more than 40,000 of them! Javier planted his first orchid here in 1941. At least a dozen species are always in bloom. Best time, however, is January to April. A small restaurant (closed Monday) serves Costa Rican dishes, which you can enjoy beneath a shady amate tree. A butterfly garden may be completed by the time you read this. Open: 8 a.m.-5 p.m. Entrance: $2.

Accommodations

Posada Las Palomas (Apdo. 185, Alajuela 4003, tel. 661-2401), in the mountain hamlet of Rosario, eight km southeast of Palmares, provides a fabulous bed and breakfast on a working citrus and coffee *finca* owned by two Californians, Johanna and Michale Bresnan. The hotel is hewn of hardwood on a hillside overlooking a river chasm with glorious views across the central valley. Trails lead steeply down to the river. Two guestrooms with private bathrooms are in the main building and three more in two cottages have private bathrooms and kitchens and hints of Tokyo and Kyoto in the decor and furnishings. The place is flooded with light. Fresh-brewed coffee and fresh-squeezed orange juice are delivered to your room in the morning. There's a pool plus Jacuzzi. Room rates: $65-85, including breakfast; dinner $10.

ZARCERO

This pleasant mountain town, 52 km west of Alajuela, is one of the prettiest in the country. Zarcero is like an Emerald City of Oz. Its setting beneath the gaze of green mountains is impressive. Dominating the town, though, is the whitewashed church, made more beautiful by the fabulous topiary that fills the park. The mark of the scissors is on every plant and bush. The work is that of Evangelisto Blanco, who has unleashed his wildest ideas in leafy splendor: a cat riding a motorcycle along the top of a hedge, an elephant with lightbulbs for eyes, corkscrews whose spiral foliage coils up and around the trunks like serpents around Eden's tree, even a bullring complete with matador, charging bull, and spectators. On virtually any day you can see Blanco snapping his pruning shears, evenly rounding off the rabbits and clipping straight the great cascading archway arbor that leads

Zarcero church
and topiary garden

to the steps of the church. Zarcero is also famous for its fresh cheese—called *palmito*—and peach preserves.

Midway between Naranjo and Zarcero you'll pass through **San Juanillo,** where the rustic Soda el Mirador—as its name suggests—proffers staggering views over the central valley, topped with excellent *típico* food that'll fill you up on a dime and that should be washed down with a refreshing ice-cool, fresh-fruit *refresco.* North of San Juanillo you enter true alpine country. The scenery changes abruptly, with black-and-white holstein and frisian dairy cattle munching contentedly on the mountain slopes. Many tight hairpin bends climb the steep uphill stretch of road north of Llano Bonito. Drive carefully. Zarcero is about 10 km north of Llano Bonito.

A road to the left just beyond the hamlet of **Palmita,** about three km south of Zarcero, is signed to San Ramón and **Villablanca.** You won't find Villablanca on any maps, but the hotel is perhaps the only one in the country with official road signs, creating the impression that the hotel is a town: such is the influence of being owned by an ex-president (Rodrigo Carazo)! Actually, it is the center of the Los Angeles Cloud Forest Reserve (see below). The road to Los Angeles is very little traveled and lovely as a fairy tale. Topiary hedges begin to appear. And the brooding scenery reminds me of the English Lake District . . . without the lakes. A dirt road (unsigned) to the right just beyond Alto Villegas leads to Villablanca.

North of Zarcero the drive is replete with looming mountains to left and right, happy heifers snoozing in emerald fields, and—beyond the Continental Divide—sweeping vistas of the northern lowlands far below.

Accommodations
I know of no hotels in town.

Food
Options in Zarcero include the **Restaurant Geranios,** opposite the church; **Pizzeria/Restaurant Casa el Campo,** opposite the Banco Nacional; another pizzeria on the south side of the plaza; the **Soda/Restaurant Jardín,** one block south, next to **Bar Amigos;** and, next to Casa el Campo, a *panadería* selling wonderful breads, scones, and sticky buns.

Services
Zarcero has two **banks:** Banco Nacional, one block north of the church, next to the Red Cross; and Banco de Costa Rica, two blocks north of

---

ZARCERO EMERGENCY TELEPHONE NUMBERS

All emergencies 911
Police (Guardia Rural) 463-3231
Red Cross 463-3131

the church. You'll find **public telephones** on the west side.

Getting There

Buses depart San José hourly 5 a.m.-7:30 p.m. from Calle 16, Avenidas 1/3 (tel. 255-4318). Buses depart Zarcero for San José and north to Ciudad Quesada (San Carlos) from the northwest corner of the topiary park. The red bus stop for San José is opposite the church.

SAN RAMÓN

San Ramón, about 12 km due west of Naranjo, is an agricultural town known for its Saturday *feria del agricultor* (farmer's market). Take a close look at the impressive church. It's built of steel manufactured by the Krups armament factory in Germany. Next to the plaza is the **San Ramón Museum** (open Mon.-Fri. 1-5 p.m.), focusing on local history; it features a re-created turn-of-the-century *campesino* home. A wonderful place to take a break and to refresh yourself is **Balneario Las Musas,** a small swimming complex with a waterslide and a waterfall reached by a trail that continues into primary forest. A restaurant and dance hall is open weekends. Only the locals seem to know about this place, about three km north of town, on the road to Piedades Sur (the last two km are rough dirt road). Entrance: $1.75.

The Pan-American Highway runs past the southern outskirts of San Ramón, from where you can turn west to Puntarenas and Guanacaste Province or return to Alajuela and San José via La Garita.

San Ramón is also a gateway to the northern lowlands via a new road cut through the mountains and providing a tantalizing and dramatic descent to La Tigra and Fortuna. You could spend an eternity trying to find it if you go by the road maps; head *east* out of town to reach the La Tigra road. The road winds magnificently uphill past the turnoff for Los Angeles Cloud Forest Reserve, eventually crests the cordillera, then begins a long sinuous descent to the northern lowlands. A real treasure of a hotel-cum-working *finca*—Valle Escondido Lodge—is on the lee slope (see "An Alternate Route from the Highlands" under "West from Ciudad Quesada" in the Northern Lowlands chapter).

Accommodations

Two budget options listed in the phone book but not reviewed are **Hotel Gran** (tel. 445-6363) and **Hotel El Viajero** (tel. 445-5580). Reportedly, San Ramón also boasts the **Hotel Nuevo Jardín.**

Services

Two **taxi** services are Taxis San Ramón (tel. 445-5966), and Taxis Unidos San Ramón (tel. 445-5110).

Getting There

Buses depart San José hourly from Calle 16, Avenidas 3/5, 6 a.m.-10 p.m. (one hour).

LOS ANGELES CLOUD FOREST RESERVE

If you've planned on visiting Monteverde Cloud Forest Reserve, consider instead the equally fabulous but relatively unknown Los Angeles Cloud Forest Reserve. You'll have the same experience without the crowds. The private 800-hectare reserve was opened in 1991 on part of the Villablanca *finca,* a cattle ranch owned by former president Rodrigo Carazo, north of San Ramón (follow the paved road north to Angeles Norte, from where Villablanca is signed along a dirt road; nine km). It begins at 700 meters' elevation and tops out at 1,800 meters. The hills are covered with thick cloud forest, with the reveille calls of howler monkeys emanating from its dark, shrouded interior. Some 210 bird species were identified in the first 12 months, including bellbirds, quetzals,

---

SAN RAMÓN EMERGENCY TELEPHONE NUMBERS

Hospital Carlos Luis Valverde 445-5825
Police (Guardia Rural) 445-5619
Transport police 445-5288
Red Cross 445-5484

and other trogons. Monkeys—howlers, capuchins, and spiders—abound. Other mammals include ocelots, jaguars, and jaguarundi.

Two short, though still fairly demanding, trails (1.5 and two km) have wooden walkways with nonslip surfaces. A third, hard-hiking trail (six to nine hours) descends past waterfalls and pools to the junction of the Ríos Balsa and Espino. The Alberto Brenes Trail begins immediately behind the Hotel Villablanca. Ivan Brenes and Giovanni Bello (former administrator of the Monteverde Cloud Forest Reserve) are exceptional guides. Forest entrance is $14 per person, a guided walk $7 more. Horseback rides cost $9 per hour.

Accommodations

Hotel Villablanca (tel. 228-4603, fax 233-6896), a reclusive hacienda, sits atop a hill—the very rim of the Continental Divide—on the edge of the reserve. Features include a large restaurant, a lounge with TV, antique furnishings, and a mammoth open kitchen that could feed the Ritz. The main hotel resembles a colonial farmhouse and has a few guest rooms upstairs. Thirty-one cozy chalets for up to six people surround the hacienda and feature rocking chairs and other dainty decor befitting Hansel and Gretel. A small fireplace decorates one corner and saloon swing doors open onto a colonial tiled bathroom. Very quaint. Rates: $77 s, $101 d, *casitas;* $59 s, $83 d, hotel rooms; $17 each additional person.

Sarchí oxcart wheel

WEST FROM ALAJUELA

QUINTA EL COYOL

Quinta el Coyol, about eight km west of the airport on the south side of the Autopista Bernardo Soto, is the locale for **Rodeo Jaiza** (Apdo. 469, San José 1007, tel. 232-8480, fax 231-4723), a "Typical Rodeo and Costa Rican Fiesta" where *sabaneros* (cowboys) demonstrate deep-rooted traditions of Costa Rican culture: bullriding, bronco riding, homestyle "Tico" bullfighting, fancy rope tricks, and demonstrations of the Costa Rican saddle horse. It's great fun to watch the cowboys ride bareback and hang on to angry, jumping, twisting, 700-kilogram bulls with only one hand or none at all (free style). Quieter interludes include the music of a "Cimarrona" band and a folkloric show by dancers in traditional costume. Quinta el Coyol has a swimming pool and restaurant.

Accommodation and Food
Hotel Aeropuerto (tel. 442-0354, fax 441-5922), on the highway four km west of the airport, was constructed in 1994 in colonial style with 24 a/c rooms with fans, telephone, and TV, plus private bath with hot water. Airport transfers are offered. It features **Restaurant Las Planchas.**

ZOO AVE

For anyone who has seen and been disappointed with the Simón Bolívar Zoo in San José, Zoo Ave (tel. 433-9140) will come as a pleasing surprise. The zoo covers 59 hectares of landscaped grounds. The fantastic bird collection includes dozens of toucans, cranes, curassows, and parrots. Lots of macaws fly free. And peacocks strut their stuff on the lawns. You'll also see crocodile, deer, turtles, and spider monkeys in an open-air cage with lots of trees. Noah would be proud: most creatures are in pairs. The goal is to breed national species for reintroduction into the wild. The zoo has more than

70 native bird species and has successfully bred the scarlet macaw, curassow, green macaw, and the guan with the help of a human-infant incubator. The zoo in San José is scheduled for relocation here over a span of four years, with tropical humid, tropical dry, and tropical rainforest environments to be re-created in miniature. Zoo Ave has a small *soda* and bathrooms, but no information tableaux. Hours: 9 a.m.-5 p.m. daily. Entrance: $3.50.

Getting There
Take either the Atenas or the La Garita bus from Alajuela (see below). Both pass by the zoo. If you're driving, the zoo is 3.5 km east of the Atenas exit from the Pan-American Highway to Puntarenas. The zoo is at Dulce Nombre, about three km northeast of La Garita on the road leading to Alajuela via San José de Alajuela.

LA GARITA

La Garita has a distinct climate; *National Geographic* claims it's the third best in the world. The city is surrounded by bananas and citrus. Roads and gardens are fringed with bougainvilleas, *madero negro*, and *poró*, of carnal plum purples and reds. And there are lots of ornamental-plant farms known as *viveros*. You'll see them, covered in black protective tarps, as you fly in to the airport. Group tours can be arranged to the nursery of **Orchid Alley** (tel. 487-7086), which grows more than 100,000 orchids on site. It sells blooms packaged in plastic boxes to last one month ($10 for a dozen blooms). You can also buy live *guaria morada* orchids (the national flower) in sealed vials suitable for import into the United States.

The area is popular among the well-to-do. You'll see lots of upscale villas, at least one of which is for rent: tel. 441-2826 or 433-9464. Bosque Encantado—Costa Rica's answer to Disneyland—has been closed since 1992.

Accommodations

Bed and Breakfast: Villa Raquel (tel. 433-8926) is a bed and breakfast country inn with a tennis court and large swimming pool, with lots of fresh-cut flowers, wicker and antique furniture, spacious living areas, and 12 bedrooms tastefully decorated in lively pastels. A large, modern kitchen is open to guests, and the pleasing grounds are good for relaxing. Rates: $65 d.

About two km south of La Garita, near Turrúcares (take the first left after Fiesta del Maíz restaurant when heading west), is **La Piña Dorada** (tel./fax 487-7781 or tel./fax 487-7220), a spacious and elegant modern Spanish colonial-style, American-operated home-turned-bed-and-breakfast hotel set in a one and one half-hectare garden with fruit trees, with a swimming pool fronting the house. It has a formal library, plus pool table and large projection TV in the lounge. Each room is individually furnished. Most have king-size beds. And original artwork abounds. Spacious suites have private baths. Rates: from $50 d with breakfast and airport pick-up.

Expensive: About 400 meters south of La Piña Dorada is the supremely elegant **Hotel Río Real** (tel. 487-7022, fax 442-1233), a converted *quinta* (villa) featuring a bar and beautiful restaurant with bamboo roof, plus swimming pool and 12 nicely appointed rooms (including two a/c junior suites and a master suite) surrounded by lush tropical plants. Rates: $75.

Chatelle Country Resort (Apdo. 755, San José 1007, tel. 487-7781, fax 487-7095), one km south of Fiesta del Maíz, though pleasant, is not quite the exclusive country club that the brochure proclaims. First the good points. Hexagonal rooms—spaced amid landscaped grounds—are very cozy, atmospheric, and large, with lofty, radial-beamed ceilings, and two supremely comfortable queen-size beds. Showers are huge, and TVs are standard. The views toward Poás and Barva volcanoes are splendid. And the complex is a quiet retreat with a relaxing ambience. Owner Arturo Otero, ex-president of the National Chamber of Commerce, is from Bolivia, has lived in Argentina, Canada, Mexico, and the U.S., and has tried to combine hints of each. The amalgam is a disappointing mismatch, exemplified by some "hippie-style" cabins (they *may* be to *your* taste) and a poorly designed and constructed restaurant with a Bolivian-style roof and tacky tumbledown air. Redeeming factors include superb spicy corvina (sea bass) and a small pool and breezy sunning terrace with views over the mountains. Arturo is adding a health spa, a conference center, and maybe a tennis court. Rates: $60-90 daily, $392 weekly, including continental breakfast and airport transfers.

Food

Centro Turístico Mi Quinta (tel. 487-7065) is a restaurant with a *mirador* lookout, on the right just west of La Garita. It serves the locally acclaimed Chicken Mi Quinta. A great place to fill your stomach is the **Fiesta del Maíz** (tel. 487-7057), a large, cafeteria-style restaurant famous for its very tasty corn meals: *chorreadas* (corn fritters), *tamales* (corn pudding), corn on the grill, very tasty rice with corn and chicken, and other tempting morsels. Free tastings are offered. No plate costs more than $2.75. Now open seven days a week. Fiesta del Maíz is west of La Garita on the main road to Atenas and Orotina.

Delicias del Maíz is another, more rustic corn restaurant, on the road between La Garita and Alajuela. Opposite Fiesta del Maíz is the **BBQ Restaurant Sanabría.** The road south from Fiesta del Maíz leads to **Restaurant Las Campañas** (tel. 487-7021, fax 487-7020), an American-run operation serving high-standard international dishes. **Las Campañas** (tel. 487-7021), near Turrúcares, serves seafood to the accompaniment of live music.

West from the Fiesta del Maíz on the road to Atenas are **La Casita de Campo Steak House** (tel. 487-7408) and the **Green Parrot** (tel. 487-7846), another nationally acclaimed restaurant under a bamboo roof. The Green Parrot—La Lora Verde—specializes in barbecued meats: Caribbean chicken, T-bone, filet mignon, grilled chicken, and Southwest dishes and burgers. Dining is elegant. There's an open-air dining terrace, plus a dance floor (live music on Friday and Saturday).

Getting There

Buses depart San José for La Garita from the Coca-Cola bus terminal and leave Alajuela from Avenida Central, Calle 10. The bus stops outside the Fiesta del Maíz restaurant.

ATENAS

West of La Garita the road rises steeply to balmy Atenas, an agricultural town renowned for its quality fruits and popular with Josefinos on weekends. Although thus far bypassed by tourists, in the past few years several splendid hotels have opened their doors. Watch for the statue of the Virgin Mary on a hill to the right, one km east of town, and an artisan's store on the left, on the outskirts of town. In town there's a beautiful church surrounded by palms. In 1994, *National Geographic* declared that the city had the best climate in the world!

The **Central American School of Animal Husbandry** is pioneering agri-ecotourism and welcomes visitors, who get a first-hand look at dairy operations, reforestry programs, iguana farming, etc., on the 530-hectare property. Besides its own research, the center teaches courses in environmental studies, reforestry, natural history, etc., to farmers interested in hosting tourists. You can saddle up for rides into the mountain forests on horses otherwise used to train *sabaneros* (cowboys) the ropes. The full-day guided tour costs $60, including lunch at an old hacienda *con* marimba music. Reservations must be made a week in advance (tel. 446-5050 or 446-5250).

Accommodations

Wow adequately expresses your first and lasting impressions of **El Cafetal Inn** (Apdo. 105, Atenas, tel. 446-5785, fax 446-5140), a spectacular bed and breakfast with all the elegance and luxury of a no-expense-spared five-star hotel. It's on a small coffee *finca* in Santa Eulalia, about five km north of Atenas. What taste owners Romy and Lee Rodríquez have displayed in their 10-bedroom hostelry. Light streams in through glass doors and huge, rounded bay windows that proffer miraculous vistas. The open-plan lounge even has marble floors and cascading fountains and thick white pillars holding the bedrooms aloft! Outside is just as impressive, with a patio and steps that lead down to a large, tiled swimming pool and a sand-floored, shady ran-

cho. There's no restaurant, though dinners ($13) are prepared by advance order (of course, the breakfasts are hearty). Fancy a tour? Take the chauffeur ($60) along on any of 15 options! Rates: $50 or $65 (with luxury bathroom) d, including breakfast. What a bargain!

Ana's Place (Apdo. 66, Atenas, tel. 446-5019), more properly known as Pensión Villa Los Malinches, is a cozy and quiet home away from home. Italianate steps lead up to the house, with its spacious lounge and beautiful hardwood parquet floors. Some of the 11 rooms are prettier than others; some have shared baths. Macaws and a coatimundi roam free in the pretty back lawn, which has an outside restaurant. Turn left opposite the gas station as you enter Atenas from the east; follow the signs from here. Rates: $35 s, $45 d. Weekly and monthly discounts.

Villa Tranquilidad (Apdo. 28, Alajuela 4013, tel. 446-5460) lives up to its name. This Canadian-run ranch-style bed and breakfast, surrounded by coffee bushes on a private *finca,* has four pleasant rooms with private baths and soft couches, plus a swimming pool set in grounds full of bougainvilleas and orchids. Local monkeys and other wildlife think the inn is a cool place to visit. Rates: $50 d, including breakfast.

El Cafetal Inn (tel. 446-5785, fax 446-5140) is a new bed and breakfast (not reviewed).

American Kevin Hill (SJO 1858, P.O. Box 025216, Miami, FL 33102-5216; in Costa Rica, fax 446-5055) offers two one-bedroom ($675 per month on a six-month basis) and one two-bedroom houses ($775) built "Spanish colonial/Costa Rican rustic" style with antique colonial furniture, plus swimming pool on his 10-acre farm property. Rates are higher on a month-by-month basis.

Food and Services

The rustic **Don Tadeo Restaurant Parrilla,** on the west side of the park in Atenas, has lots of ambience. Also recommended is **Ekalís Pizzeria,** on the park's east side, serving whopping pizzas and milkshakes.

There's a local **Red Cross** (tel. 446-5161).

Buses depart San José hourly from the Coca-Cola bus terminal.

ESCAZÚ

It's remarkable that a place such as Escazú can be found so close to the capital city. The town, only four km west of Sabana Park, is one of the oldest settlements in the country and a favorite with English-speaking expatriates drawn by its climate, its view, and the sleepy *campesino*-town ambience hand-in-hand with the glitziest quarter in all Costa Rica. The place, too, is full of fancy homes and restaurants and ultrachic shopping plazas. The American Legion Post is the largest such post outside the U.S. and is a social center for the many North American residents in the area. (It's with good reason that the U.S. embassy and ambassador's home are here.)

Yet amid the luxury living, time seems to have stood still for a century. Bucolic beauty still blooms, despite the incursions. Swank cars roll past rickety wooden oxcarts weighed down with coffee beans and pulled by stately oxen. Cows wander down the road. And there are still a few cobblestone streets with houses of adobe (sun-dried brick made of mud, cattle blood, egg white, lime, grass, and horse dung), among the oldest in the country. The **Chavez's** house is a fine example.

"Maybe," says author and resident innkeeper Harvey Haber, "it is just what you were hoping to discover in a small Latin country, but really did not dare hope that it would exist." He says the site was originally a crossroads on trails between Indian villages. The Indians found it the perfect place to spend the night on their journeys and gave it its name, Itzkatzu, which means "Resting Place." There have been some changes since those days, but the sense of a place to rest, to experience tranquility, is still there.

According to Haber, the town was first settled by the Spanish in the early 1700s, when cattle ranches were established in the highlands. A small chapel constructed in 1711 became the first public building. Many of the original adobe houses still stand, including those around the village plaza with its red-domed church of San Miguel de Escazú, built in 1799 and painted with a traditional strip of color at the bottom to ward off witches.

Escazú is famous as the *bruja*, or witch capital of the country. The Tiribi River, which flows east of Escazú, is said to be haunted, and old men still refuse to cross the Los Anonos Bridge at night for fear of La Zegua and Mico Malo, the magic monkey. Some 60 or so witches are said to still live in Escazú, including Doña Estrella, who says that "any woman who lives in Escazú long enough eventually becomes a *bruja*." Amorous tourists should beware La Zegua—an incredibly beautiful enchantress. When the (un)lucky suitor gets her to bed, she turns into a horse!

There are actually three Escazús: San Rafael de Escazú, the ultramodern, lower town nearest the freeway, with chic shopping centers (including the landmark, El Cruce) and also a beautiful old church; San Miguel de Escazú, the center of town, midway up the slope, also blending old and new; and San Antonio de Escazú, higher up and the center of bed and breakfast hotels. Each has its own church and patron saint. An annual celebration—Día del Boyero—is held on the soccer field in front of the church of San Antonio each second Sunday in March to honor the oxcart drivers. It features a parade of decorated oxcarts pulled by great oxen, and a blessing by local priests. On Christmas Day, a hydraulic engine is employed to move singular figures, part of a Nativity celebration in front of Iglesia San Antonio, including a headless priest, the devil spinning a ferris wheel, the corpse who opens his coffin, and a carousel.

SIGHTS

Mountain Hikes

The clear mountain air and sense of tranquility owe much to Escazú's lofty position. The town climbs up the lower slopes of soaring mountains, including La Cruz (topped by an imposing 15-meter-tall iron cross), Piedra Blanca, Cerro Rabo de Mico (at 2,455 meters, the tallest), and Cerro de Escazú, fluted with waterfalls. You can hike to the La Cruz cross from the small pueblo

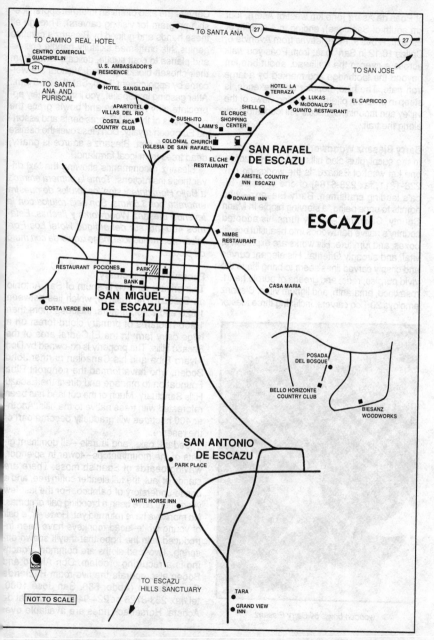

NOT TO SCALE

of Poás de Aserrí (one km west of Aserrí, four km south of San José), ending in Alajuelita or Escazú. A bus to Poás leaves from Avenida 6, Calles 10/12 in San José; from Poás you walk across a river to the trailhead, about one km beyond the footbridge and marked by a large iron gate. The hike, popular on weekends, is steep in parts but offers staggering views of the valley and mountains. Locals sell food and drink along the trail.

Barry Biesanz Woodworks

In the eucalyptus-clad hills of Bello Horizonte, one km west of Escazú, is the workshop (tel. 228-1811, fax 228-6184) of one of Costa Rica's leading craftsmen. Barry Biesanz—who admits to once being "a starving hippie in Marin County, California"—today turns his adopted country's native hardwoods into beautiful bowls, boxes, and furniture. His works are expressive, vital, and strongly Oriental. His elegant curves and crisply carved lines seem to bring life to the vivid purples, reds, and greens of purple heart, rosewood, amaranth, and lignum vitae. Biesanz employs 20 Tico carvers, including three Master

wooden bowls by Barry Biesanz

Carvers (he also offers an informal apprenticeship program for visiting carvers). Through all these hands and guided by Biesanz's creative genius, his craftsmen skillfully handle chisels and planes to craft subtle, delicate forms from their chosen blocks of wood. Visitors are welcome by appointment, Mon.-Sat. 9 a.m.-5 p.m.. After gasping in disbelief, you'll immediately appreciate why his boxes and bowls grace the collections of three U.S. presidents and assorted European royalty. Don't fuss over the demise of the rainforest. Biesanz's source is gnarly, dead trees from local farmland.

Biesanz recommends showing the taxi driver these instructions: *Tome la primera entrada a Bello Horizonte y siga los rótulos de nuestra empresa por 3.5 kms. Son seis rótulos con la leyenda Biesanz Woodworks y flechas. Estamos 400 mts sur del antiguo Hotel Los Portales, casa residencial mano izquierda con muro de piedra.*

Escazú Hills Sanctuary

This private reserve is south of San Antonio de Escazú. The reserve, which lies between 1,820 and 2,400 meters, includes more than 1,900 hectares of primary cloud forest on a large dairy farm in the El Cedral area of the Escazú Hills. The property is co-owned by Don Alvaro Riba and his Canadian partner John Boden, who have formed the nonprofit Riba Foundation to manage and direct the Escazú Hills Sanctuary. Much of the cut land has been reforested with trees native to the hills. Another 400 hectares will gradually become part of the reserve.

Cedars, oaks, and laurels—all dominant giants of the mountaintops—tower in splendor, waving beards of Spanish moss. There are stands of jaul, the tall slender coffin tree, and a dense understory of bamboo. For the last few years there have been a breeding pair of pumas. No monkeys have returned yet. However, a pair of young white-faced monkeys have been introduced with the hope that they'll spawn offspring. Two-toed sloths are common. Poaching is a recurring problem. Don Alvaro and Boden also operate the five-room **Hacienda Cerro Pando** (Apdo. 586, San José 1000, tel./fax 253-8726 or 224-9405), in Cedral de Acosta. Horseback rides are available over

mountain trails into cloud forest, and you can also explore on little all-terrain four-wheelers.

National Boyero's Day

Held every second Sunday of March since 1983, this festival pays homage to the *boyeros,* the men who guide the traditional oxcarts to market. More than 100 *boyeros* from around the country trim their colorful carts and gather for this celebration, which includes an oxcart parade helped along by a supporting cast of women and children in traditional garb, plus a musical accompaniment of *cimarronas,* the traditional instrument mandatory for popular feasts. Bells toll. There's lots of waving and clapping, and plenty of maize, rice, potatoes, and meat for eating. Lencho Salazar, an local folklorist, regales crowds with tales of *brujas*. Grupo Auténtico Tradicional Tiquicia treats onlookers to much-loved local melodies. And young girls perform ancestral dances.

ACCOMMODATIONS

Budget

Hotel Tapezco Inn (tel. 228-1084, fax 289-7026) is a colonial-style property with modern rooms boasting hot water, telephone, TV, and fans. It offers a Jacuzzi and sauna, plus small restaurant.

Deluxe

Hotel Sangildar (Apdo. 1511, Escazú 1250, tel. 800-758-7234 or 289-8843, fax 228-6454), set in lush grounds adjoining the Costa Rica Country Club on the western outskirts of Escazú, is a very handsome contemporary Spanish-style building named for San Gildar, the Father of Triumph, whose effigy was placed in a private chapel in Escazú in 1834 (today it can be seen in the parish church). Note the plaque that tells his tale in the lobby. The hotel—an architectural gem—is as splendid within as without. Hardwoods and stonework abound, and the 30 luxurious rooms (each with cable TV, plus telephone in bedroom and bathroom, and hair dryer) reflect tasteful decor. Amenities include a swimming pool, small shop, bar, and elegant "Terraza del Sol" restaurant, which is earning its own acclaim. Airport transfers are provided. You can rent the hotel minivan. Rates: $80 s, $90 d, $100 suite.

The five-star **Camino Real** (Apdo. 11856, San José 1000, tel. 800-521-5753 or 289-7000, fax 289-8998; in North America, tel. 800-722-6466), one of the slickest hotels to open in Costa Rica in 1994, is two km west of Escazú just off the freeway, 10 minutes from downtown San José (locals know it by its location next to the Multi-Plaza shopping center). First impressions are of Hong Kong hotel standards, with contemporary opulence hinted at by the five-story atrium lobby. Alas, the service is far from Asia. When I arrived, the doorman was too engrossed in social chit-chat to open the door, and I thought I was hallucinating when the bellboy watched me carry my own bags!

The hotel is shaped like the Mercedes-Benz logo without the circle, set in landscaped grounds including a clover-shaped pool with swim-up bar. Each of the 261 a/c rooms is luxuriously carpeted, with 25-inch TV, electronic key locks, direct-dial telephone with voice mail, safety box, hair dryer, and other niceties that include king-size beds high off the ground, plus lounge chair and a writing desk with classical hints. Bathrooms are a Hallelujah chorus of magnesium-bright lighting and marble. Go on, indulge . . . wallow in the deep, deep bathtub. Neutrogena toiletries are standard.

A few flourishes appear on the top floor—the Camino Real Club—where 54 rooms have bathrobes, daily newspaper, concierge and valet services, and a daily cocktail party. Here, too, are five junior suites and the posh presidential suite. The hotel has a fully equipped business center, plus a conference center adjacent. The Azulejo Café is done in tropical colors and serves surprisingly reasonably priced meals. Contemporary fades to classical in the Restaurant Mirage, with a splendidly Baroque feel and a pianist to add mood. Even here you may feast on gourmet French-inspired cuisine for $10 or less. The bar (upholstered in tropical fabrics that might have been conceived by Paul Klee) is popular with wealthy Ticos. A health and fitness center, massage parlor, beauty center, stores, car rental agency, and travel agency complete the picture. A regular shuttle runs between the hotel and downtown San José. To get there from Escazú, take the Santa Ana road to Centro

Comercial Guachipelín, turn right, and right again after 800 meters. Rates: $150 standard, $180 Club, $325-540 suites.

Bed and Breakfasts

Take your pick from a plethora of bed and breakfasts. Many are exemplary of the hotel genre, each one quite different, and most gringo-owned and -run.

Pico Blanco Inn (Apdo. 900, Escazú 1250, tel. 228-1908 or 228-3197, fax 228-5189) is up in the hills, in San Antonio de Escazú, at the end of a cobbled drive. The English owner has stamped a very British imprint: lots of wicker furniture and an English-theme bar. The 20 comfortable colonial-tiled rooms all feature private balconies with great views and private baths with hot water. Swimming pool. There are also two, two-bedroom cottages. Rates: $35 d, $45 two-bedroom apartments. **Posada Pegasus** (Apdo. 370, Escazú 1250, tel. 228-4196) is another intimate and similarly priced American-run mountain hideaway with large rooms, a Jacuzzi, TV and stereo in the lounge, hammocks on the wide veranda, and beautiful views. Somewhat stuffy decor. Closed Dec.-March and July-August.

Posada del Bosque (Apdo. 669, Escazú 1250, tel. 228-1164, fax 228-2006) is another excellent option. The irrepressibly animated Gilbert Aubert and his charming wife run this intimate home away from home—opened as a bed and breakfast in June 1992, and once the home of the U.S. commercial attaché. The beautiful lounge has a large open fireplace, a bamboo-lined roof, a terra-cotta tiled floor, and a wide veranda overlooking the expansive garden, which has a barbecue pit. Seven spacious rooms are well lit and ventilated, with roomy bathrooms (some shared) with colonial-tiled showers. A games room has cable TV and a small workout machine. Those more rigorously inclined have free access to the nearby Bello Horizonte Country Club. Fruit trees in the garden attract lots of birds, including the endangered motmot. Lunch and dinner cost $6. No smoking, but children are welcome. The hotel is well signposted from town. Rates: $48 s, $54 d.

Park Place (Apdo. 1012, Escazú, tel./fax 228-9200), owned by American Pat Bliss, is a modern, quasi-Swiss-chalet-style, 370-square-meter bed and breakfast with four rooms with two shared bathrooms. A huge lofty-ceilinged lounge with tall windows lets in heaps of light. You can warm yourself on cool evenings beside the small open-hearth fireplace, prepare a do-it-yourself breakfast in the full kitchen, and sit anytime and admire the view out over the valley from the interior veranda upstairs. Bedrooms are very homey, with hardwood floors and ceilings and mammoth walk-in showers. Opposite the house, oxcarts filled with coffee beans rattle through a weigh-station. Bus service to San José is right outside the door. Rates: $35 s, $40 d.

Rhett and Scarlett would be aghast to find **Tara** (Apdo. 1459, Escazú 1250, tel. 228-6992, fax 228-9651) a bed and breakfast. But there it is, four-square on the hill above Escazú. Who said the South's plantation lifestyle has gone with the wind? The Greek-revival plantation mansion—complete with Corinthian columns, period-piece furnishings, dark hardwoods, and 12 resplendent bedrooms with antique rosewood tester beds and private verandas—makes it easy to sense the whole opulent antebellum mystique. I even fancied I heard the swish of silk on the handsome mahogany staircase, but it was no more than the sound of the wind. Tara offers a completely equipped workout room, pool and gazebo with Jacuzzi and recently added barbecue terrace, and black-and-white-tiled pavilion patio and croquet lawn with staggering views over the central valley, with the meniscus of Poás and Barva volcanoes in full view. You'll like Tara's orderliness and its lush gardens with tropical plants perfuming the air. Guests eat in a formal dining room, set with silver, crystal, candles, and fresh flowers. And health nuts will love **Scarlett's Fountain of Youth Spa**, newly added for 1995. It's just the tonic, with gym, aerobics rooms, saunas, steam rooms, massage, and a wide range of inclusive programs from the "Jet-lag Special" to "Bonnie's Beauty Bounty." The basic "Novia" program includes aerobics class, sauna, body polish, body cocoon, and manicure ($59). Professional staff offer a range of fitness programs. Cellulite, anti-stress, reflexology, lymphatic drainage, eye-lifting, acupuncture, aromatherapy, and mud treatments are all on hand. A conference center was recently added, too. Room rates: $72-90 single room, $100-125 stan-

dard suite, $124-155 junior suite, $152-190 superior suite, $200 poolside bungalow, including continental breakfast.

Casa María (Apdo. 123, Escazú 1250, tel. 228-2270, fax 228-0015) is a large house that claims to be the first bed and breakfast hotel in the country. It's very popular with the older crowd. The 12 very pretty rooms have hardwood floors and hand-carved beds and sliding doors opening onto the courtyard and an acre of landscaped grounds with swimming pool. The suite has a mammoth bathroom. Rooms upstairs share a bath. One larger upstairs room has a private veranda overlooking the gardens. Features include a "vacation-planning" room, a wide-screen TV in the lounge, a serve-yourself bar, and lots of storage space. The constantly attentive owner is adding a dance floor and outdoor Jacuzzi. So-so decor: The tacky paintings have got to go! Full English breakfast with macadamia pancakes. Rates: from $40 s, $50 d, $100 suite. Airline and business personnel are given "special consideration."

Costa Verde Inn (SJO 1313, P.O. Box 025216, Miami, FL 33102-5216; in Costa Rica, tel. 228-4080, fax 289-8591) is a very beautiful, atmospheric, and peaceful bed and breakfast long on creature comforts. The lofty-ceilinged house is creatively conceived. Hardwoods abound, including a stunning hardwood floor. Walls are festooned with hand-colored historic photos. Decor is simple, romantic, and bright, the furnishings tasteful. The lounge has a plump leather sofa, an open fireplace, and a large-screen TV. Twelve individually styled bedrooms come with king-size bed, built-in hardwood furniture, and huge, beautifully tiled bathrooms. Room 6 has a bathroom in natural stone with an open pit shower at its center. There's not a room I wouldn't want to sleep in. Economy rooms have small singles and shared bath. Outside are a tennis court and a shaded terrace with rough-hewn supports and open fireplace. Added in 1994 were a swimming pool, sundeck, and outdoor gym. A solid bargain. Rates: varies by room, from $45 (single with shared bath) to $70 (suite), including breakfast and tax.

Villa Escazú's (Apdo. 1401, Escazú 1250, tel./fax 228-9566) stunning all-hardwood interiors mix rusticity and tasteful modern decor in a pretty Swiss-style chalet. A "minstrel's gallery" balcony overhangs the lounge, with its fireplace and wide chimney of natural stone. Five rooms include a deluxe room with private bath, and two bedrooms with shared bath on both the main and third floors. The solid and superbly crafted house is enhanced by an all-around outside veranda with chunky wicker chairs for enjoying the view. Landscaped lawns cascade downhill to a fruit orchard. There's an open barbecue at the back, and a stone patio with outdoor seating out front. Villa Escazú is run by friendly Floridians Mary-Anne and Inez, who prepare full American breakfasts in the large kitchen. Rates: $40 s, $57 d, $74 t; $68 d, $80 t, deluxe, including breakfast.

Bonaire Inn (tel. 228-0866, fax 289-8107) has been recommended by a reader, Sandra Leuer Bish. The inn is owned by retired Costa Ricans Fernando and Lil Rosich and offers seven rooms (some with a/c) with private and semi-private bath. Breakfast is served in a sun-filled room with "a magnificent view of the valley." A lounge has cable TV. It is 350 meters south of El Cruce shopping center, in front of La Licorera la Bruja. Rates: from $29 s to $54 d, $5 extra person, including breakfast.

A recent and magnificent addition is the **Puesta del Sol** (P.O. Box 02516, Dept. 305, Miami, FL 33102, tel. 289-9043, fax 289-6581), a colonial hacienda formerly owned by a German ambassador and recently converted into a magnificent inn by Harvey Haber, author of the *Insight Guide to Costa Rica*. Puesta del Sol offers rooms with telephones, king-size beds, and private baths big enough for a house party. The grand old estate boasts a restaurant, plus swimming pool and Jacuzzi amid tropical gardens complete with burbling mountain stream. Recommended. Rates: approximately $60 d.

American-run **Posada El Quijote** (Apdo. 1127, Escazú 1250, tel. 289-8401, fax 289-8729; Dept. 239-SJO, P.O. Box 025216, Miami, FL 33102, tel. 800-570-6750, ext. 8401) is a splendid Spanish colonial home that has been totally renovated and stocked with marvelous works of modern art. Tastefully appointed rooms look out over beautiful gardens, and have queen- or king-size beds, telephones, cable TV, and private baths with "hot, high-pressure" water. You can order light lunches and dinners, and take a nip at the bar. It's one km east of Nimbé Restaurant. Rates:

$55 s, $65 d, $12.50 extra person (add seven percent for credit card transactions).

Las Golondrinas (tel. 228-6448, fax 228-6381) is a secluded "B&B cabaña" amid a half-hectare orchard with panoramic view. Another, unnamed, four-bedroom country house set amid fruit trees is offered for rent for $1000 per month (tel. 228-2395 or 227-1869).

Others to Consider

The **Linda Vista Lodge** (Apdo. 785, Escazú 1250, tel. 228-5854, fax 228-8010) has cozy rooms and a wonderful valley view. Rates: $25 d. The **Grand View Inn** (Apdo. 1012, Escazú, tel. 228-1895, fax 228-9200), 200 meters above Tara, is easily missed. It's a Spanish-style villa with panoramic views and a courtyard with pool. No smoking. Rates: $50 s, $55 d. The **White Horse Inn** (tel. 228-4290, fax 228-9200), run by an amiable Englishman, Mark, lacks the character of other bed and breakfasts. Still, it's thoroughly modern and fitted with all conveniences. Four rooms are well lit, if modest. Two bathrooms are shared. There's a TV in an upstairs lounge. Laundry service. No smoking. Rates: $40 s/d. Three newer hotels (not reviewed) include the **Casa de Las Tías** (tel. 289-5517, fax 289-7353), one block east of Restaurant Ché, which bills itself as a "country bed and breakfast in town" and is amply decorated with Latin American art (rates: $55 s, $70 d); **Posada Ananda** (tel. 228-2802, fax 228-6381); and the **Parvati Mountain Inn** (Apdo. 20, Escazú 1250, tel. 228-4011), with four rooms with shared bath. Yoga and meditation classes are given.

A relatively new and very pleasant addition to the scene is the **Amstel Country Inn Escazú** (Apdo. 4192, San José 1000, tel. 228-1764, fax 228-0620; in the U.S., 800-575-1253), 200 meters south of the El Cruce shopping mall, with 14 cozy, character-filled rooms and two deluxe suites, all with telephone, plus a swimming pool with its own fountain in beautifully landscaped grounds. Some rooms have king-size beds. Rates: $45 s/d standard, $75 suite. Breakfast included. Also new is the **Pine Tree Inn** (tel. 289-7405, fax 228-2180); rooms have TV, telephone, safety box. The inn has a pool and solarium. Last but not least, consider the **Riscos de Guacamaya Country Inn** (Apdo. 351, Escazú 1250, tel. 228-9074, fax 289-5776), with one suite, two

double rooms (two with shared bath), and three singles, each with cable TV and private bath. There's also a pool and restaurant. Rates: $45-60 d, $75 suite, including continental breakfast.

Forest BnB-Hostel-Hotel (tel./fax 228-0900), another American-run hostelry, comes recommended. Surrounded by two acres of lush, landscaped gardens with pool, this nicely furnished property has 14 rooms, including a suite. You can watch cable TV in the lounge, visit the exercise room, and rent mountain bikes. The hotel is part of the IYH hosteling chain and has bunks in a dormitory with full kitchen privileges. Rates: from $15 per person bunk, or $39-65 room, including a hearty breakfast.

Apartments

Apartotel María Alexandra (Apdo. 3756, San José 1000, tel. 228-1507, fax 228-5192) offers 14 completely furnished luxury apartments with a/c and cable TV, plus a lounge and restaurant, pool, sauna, and mini-golf. Rate: $80.

Apartotel Villas del Río (Apdo. 2027, San José 1000, tel. 289-8833, fax 289-8627) was near completion on the south side of the Costa Rica Country Club, with one-, two- and three-bedroom a/c apartments, plus suites and penthouses, each with cable TV and VCR, fully equipped kitchen, and computer message center. Other features include a kiddies' playground, plus pool with swim-up bar, gym and sauna, and rental car and tour agency.

FOOD

My favorite eatery is the **Nimbé Restaurant,** a New England-style house with outdoor dining terrace and very elegant turn-of-the-century decor. Recommended: spicy Pakistani Chicken Quorma ($7), Penne Emperor Style (pasta with shrimp, sea bass, and various seafoods sautéed in olive oil; $10), and meat fondue ($11.50). The vegetables alone are worthy of the visit. The **Atlanta Restaurant** (tel. 228-6992) of the Tara Hotel, favored by former President Rafael Ángel Calderón and First Lady Gloria Bejarano, offers grand elegance, spectacular views, *and* good food. It has an all-you-can-eat "Pasta Night" each Sunday, and a "Family Fun" Sunday brunch (11 a.m.-2 p.m.) with free balloons and a magician.

Four other top-notch choices are the **Restaurant Pociones,** next to the plaza in San Miguel, **Lukas** and **El Capriccio** in San Rafael, and the very exclusive and expensive **Arlene Restaurant** (tel. 228-0370), opposite the Costa Rica Country Club on the road to Santa Ana. The **Restaurante María Alexandra** (tel. 228-4876) also offers reasonably priced European cuisine in a warm, friendly ambience. The tiny restaurant has an enviable reputation. Dutch chef Hans van Gelder came here to prepare the official banquets for President John F. Kennedy's state visit in 1963 more than 30 years ago and has been here ever since. Acclaimed cuisine is enhanced by an elegant setting that includes a lush courtyard and floodlit pool.

The highly acclaimed **Restaurant Beijing City** (tel. 228-6939; closed Monday) is down from Arlene's, on the road to Santa Ana. A little farther along is **El Strivos,** where *típico* Tico barbecued dishes are served alfresco while owner Roberto entertains with guitar and song.

You won't regret a visit to **Rancho Macho** (tel. 228-7588), in the hills above town (you'll see it signposted on the Santa Ana road heading west). It serves some of the best Tico cuisine in the country—sweet fried onion, barbecued chicken *(la plancha de gallo)* and the like cooked over a coffee-wood fire—accompanied by mariachi music, with magnificent views from the candlelit dining room. Very popular with locals. A similar rustic abobe eatery in the hills, this one above San Antonio de Escazú, is **Tíquicia,** where your meal is prepared over charcoal. **Lamm's** is a venerable steak house in San Rafael.

Also recommended is the **Terraza del Sol** restaurant (tel. 289-8843) in the Hotel Sangildar, serving international cuisine with a strong French and Italian flair. Choose to dine in or out to a backdrop of classical music. Great desserts. A good place for Sunday champagne buffet brunch.

At **El Ché Restaurant** you can watch traditional Argentinian delicacies being prepared in front of your eyes on an open barbecue rotisserie. For steak and seafood, try **La Cascada** (tel. 228-0906) or **Los Anonos** (tel. 228-0301). You'll find a **Pizza Hut** in the Los Anonos Shopping Center. **Órale** (tel. 228-6437 or 228-6436) claims the "best margaritas south of Mexico." Best? Maybe not. Good, certainly. And the food

ain't too bad, either. You'll find it in the Centro Comercial Trejos.

Lastly, I recommend **Café el Sol Restaurant** (tel. 228-1645), two blocks east of the church in central Escazú. It serves a wide range of salads, seafoods, sandwiches, pastas, and fish and meat dishes. And don't leave Escazú without checking out **Rincón de la Calle Real,** a bookshop-cum-cafe run by American artist Meredith Paul. The place looks as if it just fell from a painting of a *campesino* home, and is replete with fine works of art. You can sip coffee and read your favorite newspaper or a good book (Meredith stocks leading U.S. journals and bestsellers) at wrought iron tables, and even enjoy live jazz and classical music on full moon nights. The turnoff is on the road to Santa Ana, next to Pizzeria Il Pomodoro.

ENTERTAINMENT

Costa Rica has been behind the eight ball in the pool-hall renaissance sweeping the United States. However, **Mac's American Bar** (tel. 228-2237), opposite the El Cruce Shopping Center, has taken its cue. No floor-spitting, cigar-sucking pool sharks here, thank goodness. The place gets crowded weekdays and weekends with upscale young Ticos; even women are trading in discos on Saturday night for pool. I like the sensual way their lips purse when they chalk up and blow the powder off the tip. No doubt they think the same of the men. Suddenly, pool seems so sexy! The place is run—surprise—by two Brits. When I called in it had four tables, but plans to expand. Tables rent for $2 for 30 minutes, or $3 an hour. Burgers, hot dogs, and fries are served. A great place for a break.

Otherwise, entertainment in Escazú mostly revolves around restaurant musicians. **Russel's** (tel. 228-6740), in the Centro Comercial Trejos, has musicians to entertain while you eat. **Vivaldi** (tel. 228-9332) features an Argentinian guitarist, plus karaoke (and the antipasto bar is recommended). Or hop down the road to Santa Ana on Wednesday to hear an irreverent expat blues band, Blind Pig, at the **Cebolla Verde** (tel. 282-8905). How irreverent? Well, lead guitarist Fat Boy Fowler, "though a thin man," reportedly "takes his name from the way his guitar emu-

lates the moans and groans of large-bodied women, for whom he has a fondness."

SERVICES AND TRANSPORT

El Sabor Tico (tel. 228-7221) souvenir and gift store has a large collection of fine crafts from Costa Rica, Guatemala, and El Salvador. You can rent or buy surf and mountain bike equip-

ment at **EcoTreks Adventure Co.** (tel. 228-4029, tel./fax 289-8191; in the U.S., Dept. 262, P.O. Box 025216, Miami, FL 33102) in Centro Comercial El Cruce. It also sells beachwear but, more important, offers a wide range of biking, scuba, and adventure packages.

Buses depart San José from Avenida 6, Calle 14, every 15 minutes. Minibuses leave from Avenida 6 near the San Juan de Dios Hospital.

WEST OF ESCAZÚ

SANTA ANA

The road west from Escazú leads to Santa Ana (turn right at El Cruce in Escazú), set in a sunny mountain valley. It was named after the daughter of an early landowner and was previously known as the "Valley of Gold," because local Indians mined gold here. The church dates from 1870, and there are still many old adobe homes and old wooden houses clad in bougainvillea. Many of the patrician houses hark to a time when Santa Ana was *the* place to live and vacation. Back then it was known as "sin city," since many of the secluded country villas were used for illicit trysting. Today it is more famous for ceramics and its onions and garlic and locally made honey. Look for braided onions hanging from restaurant lintels and roadside stands. A good place to try roasted onions is the down-to-earth, open-air **El Estribo,** an Argentinian restaurant on the old Santa Ana road. You can watch your fare being prepared over a blazing open grill behind a sturdy wall of logs. The restaurant serves *típico* dishes, including *punta de lomito El Estribo,* steak permeated with a coffee smoke flavor. The locals wash their meals down with rum; the wine is considered cheap plonk.

Tierra Rica is a large *cerámica artística* workshop, on the left, halfway between Escazú and Santa Ana. In town, the artisans of **Cerámica Santa Ana** still use an old-fashioned kick-wheel to fashion the pots. You'll find some 30 independent potteries in the area. The town is also famous as the home of American craftsman Jay Morrison, who turns out fine furniture from hardwoods. Morrison owns two large plots of land at Tárcoles and Turrúcares that he is reforesting in native timber. His showroom, **Tierra Extrana** (tel. 282-6697), is full of chests, desks, mirrors, tables, and chairs rendered with forceful majesty from cristóbal, cenizaro, cocobolo, and lace wood. Tierra Extrana is two miles west of Santa Ana; turn left at Bar la Enramada as you enter Piedades. From here, signs direct you to the showroom.

The **Cerro Pacacua** is an 8,000-hectare forest preserve and bird sanctuary that sits above the town. Mineral springs bubble up from the ground at **Salitral** in the mountains three km south of Santa Ana.

The highly regarded **Club Hipico La Caraña** equestrian school (tel. 282-6934 or 282-7850) is here, too. Besides classes in dressage and jumping, the club offers guided horseback tours in the mountains south of Santa Ana.

Continuing west from Santa Ana will bring you to Ciudad Colón.

Accommodations and Food

Llama de Bosque (tel. 282-6342), behind the village church, is a venerable house of traditional Costa Rican design run by brother and sister Miguel and Katia Obregon, who were raised here and have turned their childhood home into a charming bed and breakfast. The cool and airy rooms are pleasingly if simply decorated and have wood-lined walls, black-and-white tiled bathrooms, and a wide wrap-around veranda. A souvenir shop specializes in locally made crafts. Out back, amid a riot of bougainvillea and heliconias, is the Bosque Café, with hammocks and chairs for relaxing. The restaurant is acclaimed for its *refrescos,* pizzas, and *típico* cuisine. One of Costa Rica's most notable jazz musicians, Manuel Obregon, plays nightly. Rates: $25 s, $50 d, including breakfast.

Apartotel Paradiso Canadiense (Apdo. 68-6151, Santa Ana 2000; tel./fax 282-5870) is, as its name suggests, a Canadian-run unit with one two-bedroom and four one-bedroom apartments. Each is fully furnished and has a TV. Daily rates are $50-60, weekly rates are $225-250.

A few km west of Santa Ana, in the hamlet of La Trinidad, is **Guest House Marañon** (Apdo. 1880, San José 1000, tel./fax 249-1761), surrounded by an orchard. Children welcome. Rates (per person): $28 s, $20 d with private bath ($5 less with shared bath). It offers two-week language courses.

For those seeking a healing retreat there's the **Centro Creativo** (tel. 282-8769, fax 282-6959), which offers yoga, meditation, and art classes, along with basic accommodations. Four basic rooms share baths. Predictably, it serves health food. Rates: $18 s, $28 d, including breakfast.

Tony's Ribs (tel. 282-5650), at the west end of the Santa Ana shopping center, fires up its grill nightly. Ribs, chicken, seafoods, and steaks—and *bocas* with drinks (including exotic cocktails)—are accompanied by music and views of the valley from the open-air terrace. If you're passing through on Sunday, call in for the grand buffet lunch at **Casa Quitirrisi** (tel. 282-5441; $10), a venerable adobe house with outside dining patio. I hear rave reviews about the food. Open for dinner only, Tues.-Sat., with live music on Friday and Saturday.

Also see 'Escazú and Vicinity," above.

Getting There
Buses depart San José from Calle 16, Avenida 1, every 15 minutes. Driving, take the Santa Ana exit off the Carretera Prospero Fernandez freeway, which begins in San José on the south side of Sabana Park; or, from Escazú, take the road west past the U.S. ambassador's residence.

SAN ANTONIO DE BELÉN

About five km north of Santa Ana, San Antonio de Belén is the gateway to the newly opened Acua Mania waterpark and to the Ojo de Agua resort, about three km farther west at San Rafael de Alajuela.

Acua Mania
This 12-hectare, $10 million aquatic amusement complex (tel. 293-2033) made a big splash in January 1995. The open-air water park is centered on a massive 1,300-square-meter pool with volleyball, waterslide, and rope swing. There's even an underwater cave. You'll find at least one dozen water slides, an artificial river, a wave pool, and other attractions to keep kids and kids-at-heart amused. Watch out for the water-guns! The grounds have been landscaped with tropical foliage and include picnic areas, mini-golf, go-cart track, plus play areas for chil-

dren. Acua Mania also has a video arcade and, appropriately, a swimwear shop plus restaurant. Additional theme settings are in the works. The park is 500 meters west of the exit for San Antonio de Belén on Autopista General Cañas. Hours: Tues.-Thurs. and Sunday 10 a.m.-5:30 p.m., Fri.-Sat. 10 a.m.-10 p.m. Admission: $9 adults, $6 children.

Ojo de Agua
Southeast of the Juan Santamaría Airport, and three km west of San Antonio de Belén—watch for the signs—is the Ojo de Agua ("Eye of Water") swimming resort *(balneario)*. The popular resort features a series of swimming pools, a smaller children's pool, and a natural lake fed by a subterranean river that delivers 24,000 liters of water per minute from the ground. Much is siphoned off to supply Puntarenas, on the Pacific coast. The resort has a waterfall surrounded by a lush forest, and picnic areas, sauna, bar and restaurant, plus volleyball, tennis, and soccer facilities. You can hire boats on the lake. Working class Ticos flock, though you may find the pools could do with what my father, speaking of my ears, used to call a "damn good clean out." Entrance: 60 cents (60 cents extra for parking).

Hipódromo del Sol
This thoroughbred racetrack, also in San Rafael, offers horse racing every Saturday at 1 p.m. (90 cents). Alas, it closed down just before press time because of financial difficulties, but had plans to reopen.

Accommodations
Belén Trailer Park (tel. 239-0421, fax 239-1316) is 200 meters beyond the Rancho Guaitil, on the left. Costa Rica's only fully equipped RV and camper site, it has hookups with electricity and water for 30 vehicles, plus a dump station, shady lawns for camping, a washing machine, and showers. The owner was considering converting an old house on the premises into a bed and breakfast with communal kitchen. Rates: $6.50 camping, $8.50 RV per night (seventh day free).

Food
Restaurant Rancho Guaitil (tel. 239-1106), west of San Antonio, is a popular restaurant under a large *palenque* roof. It serves a good

choice of salads, seafood dishes, and meats at reasonable prices. Also try the colonial-style **Restaurant Las Tajiles,** on the left, 100 meters before the church in San Antonio; or the **Marlin Marisquería,** which has very good Italian seafoods. Several restaurants lie along the road on each side of the *balneario.*

Getting There

Buses depart San José for Ojo de Agua from Avenida 1, Calles 20/22, hourly on the half hour, every quarter hour on weekends. Buses also depart Alajuela from Calle 10, Avenida Central. Driving, you can reach San Antonio directly from the Pan-American Hwy.; turn left at the traffic lights by the Herradura Hotel, 10 km northwest of San José. Alternately, take the road that curls around the southern side of Juan Santamaría Airport.

LA GUÁCIMA

The road west from San Antonio de Belén continues to La Guácima. **La Guácima Race Track** has motor races on weekends and hosts the Grand Finale of the International F3 Championship; a Costa Rica Grand Prix (Formula 3) is held in December. **Pro Motor Costa Rica** (Apdo. 150, San José 1002, tel. 233-3166, fax 233-3341) offers tourist packages. Two km south of La Guácima is the **Los Reyes Country Club** (tel. 438-0004), where on weekends (and occasionally midweek) you may settle with champagne and cucumber sandwiches to watch a chucker or two of polo, a game introduced to Costa Rica in 1898 by the British who came to build the Atlantic Railroad. November through August is polo season, when six national teams compete; the club also hosts international competitions. The social scene here is quite the thing. Pip-Pip!

Opposite Los Reyes, and clearly signed all the way from San Antonio de Belén, is the Butterfly Farm, an essential visit on a day-trip from San José.

Butterfly Farm

An absolute must! Established in 1983, the farm (Apdo. 2132, Alajuela 4050, tel./fax 438-0115) has grown to be the second-largest ex-

porter of living pupae in the world. An educational 90-minute tour begins with a video documentary introducing the world of butterflies, followed by a guided tour through the gardens and laboratory, where you witness and learn all about each stage of the butterfly life cycle. Hundreds of butterflies representing 60 native species bred for export flit about in an endless ballet. Educational signs are posted throughout the garden. Serpentine paths lead to a miniature waterfall where many of the butterflies choose to mate. Photographers should bring a macro lens or telephoto lens with macro (close-up) capability.

Among the fascinating snippets of butterfly lore you'll learn is that the butterfly's two antennae allow it to keep flying steady even when half its wings have been chomped by hungry predators, and that the male can detect a single molecule of female pheromone at two kilometers' distance.

In the wild, the survival rate to adult phase is estimated to be only two percent. Raised under controlled conditions within the netted garden, the survival rate on the farm is 90%, ensuring an ongoing supply for the 30,000 pupae exported annually to a London distributor. Eggs are harvested daily by farm employees. The guides will show you the tiny eggs and larvae which, you're informed, are coded to "eat and grow, eat and grow." The guide will thrust out a fat, four-inch caterpillar to show the point. If a newborn human baby ate at the same rate it would grow to the size of a double-decker bus in two months! You'll also see the pupae hanging in stasis and, with luck, witness a butterfly emerging to begin life anew. Occasionally, butterflies are released into the wild. Because of their relatively short lifespan—an average of two to three weeks after becoming butterflies—there's an ongoing demand for replenishment among zoos and butterfly gardens worldwide. Although butterfly activity is greatly reduced in late afternoon, that's the time to enjoy the spectacular show of the *Caligo memnon* (giant owl butterfly), which fly only at dawn and dusk.

Owner Joris Brinkerhoff and his wife María Sabido have a real honey of an attraction—a **bee farm!** A traditional oxcart pulled by Precioso and Cariño ("Precious" and "Affection") will take you down to the bottom of the garden to

LA GUÁCIMA

TO POAS

TO LA GARITA

TO PUNTARENAS

ALAJUELA

SAN JOAQUIN
HEREDIA

SAN ANTONIO
DE BELEN

OJO DE AGUA · AQUAMANIA

HERRADURA
CARIARI HOTEL AND
COUNTRY CLUB

PANASONIC

PAN - AMERICAN HIGHWAY

LA GITANA
STORE

LA GUACIMA

LOS REYES
COUNTRY CLUB

BUSES TO SAN JOSE

THE BUTTERFLY FARM

BUS TO ALAJUELA

SANTA ANA

SABANA
PARK

ESCAZU

TO SAN JOSE

CIUDAD COLON

TO PURISCAL

0   3 km

© MOON PUBLICATIONS, INC.

find out what's buzzing in the bee world. Among the interesting exhibits are a log hive of the type favored by the Mayan Indians and still seen hanging outside homes in Guanacaste, where it's a tradition to start a hive in celebration of the birth of a child, and a glass-sided hive which provides a rather intimate view of day-to-day life in the bee world. Those bees wiggling their bottoms? They're signaling the direction and distance of the sun. The harder they shake the greater the distance. And the direction? The excited bee angles her abdomen (all workers are female) relative to the sun.

A "Tropical Ecology Tour" (Monday, Wednesday, and Friday afternoons) explains the dynamics of the tropical forest, including the differences between temperate and tropical forest, the interrelationships between flora and fauna, the consequences of deforestation, etc.

A large souvenir store sells a million items on a lepidopterian theme. A restaurant features Costa Rica cuisine. Hours: daily 9 a.m.-5 p.m. The last tour starts at 3:30 p.m. Bee tours are offered at 10:30 a.m., noon, and 1:30 and 3:30 p.m. Entrance: $10 adult, $5 children (children under four free).

Accommodations
Country Inn La Guácima (Apdo. 807, Alajuela 4050, tel. 438-0179, fax 221-8245) is a small bed-and-breakfast with two rooms with private bath for $60 d. Not inspected.

Getting There
From San José: The Butterfly Farm offers direct bus service Mon.-Sat. from main hotels

three times daily Dec.-30 April, and twice daily May-30 Nov. Alternately, public buses marked "La Guácima" depart at 11 a.m. and 2 p.m. (except Sunday) from the stop marked "San Antonio/Ojo de Agua" on Avenida 1, Calles 20/22. Take the bus until the last stop (about 60 minutes), from where you walk—follow the signs—about 400 meters. The bus to San José departs at 3:15 p.m.

From Alajuela: Buses marked "La Guácima Abajo" depart from Calle 10 and Avenida 2 in Alajuela at 6:20, 9, and 11 a.m., and 1 p.m.; and return at 9:45 and 11:45 a.m., and 1:45, 3:45, and 5:45 p.m. Ask the driver to stop at La Finca de Mariposas.

By Car: Follow the Pan-American (General Tobías) Hwy. west from Sabana Park to the Herradura Hotel. Turn left at the traffic light for San Antonio de Belén. Just beyond the church in San Antonio, turn right for one block, then left. Continue straight. Signs for the farm are all along the route.

CIUDAD COLÓN

Continuing west from Santa Ana (or south from La Guácima), you reach **Piedades,** with a beautiful church with impressive stained-glass windows, and **Ciudad Colón,** a very scenic, pretty, and incredibly neat little town famous as the home of the University for Peace. Also in Colón is retired Chicagoan Jim Moberg, who lovingly maintains a **menagerie** of more than 140 tropical birds, including toucans and macaws. The "Birdman of Colón" welcomes visitors by advance arrangement (tel. 249-1402).

University for Peace

The university was the dream of Emilio Ramírez Rojas and his uncle Cruz Rojas Bennett, two conservationists, philosophers, and idealists who in the late 1970s donated 350 hectares of primary forest on an untouched part of their cattle estate—Rancho Rodeo—to the nation. They donated an adjoining 100 hectares to the United Nations. From that wellspring came the University for Peace, where students from many lands come to pursue disciplines designed to make the world a better place. Visitors are welcome.

The land is today the **Reserva Forestal el Rodeo,** 2.5 km west of town; supposedly, it's the largest remaining tract of virgin forest in the Meseta Central. Crossing it are several unmarked trails, one of which leads to the university, on the other side of the hill.

Getting There: A bus marked "Ciudad Colón" runs from the Coca-Cola bus terminal in San José. Get off 400 meters before the central plaza in Colón and walk north to the town cemetery *(cementerio),* from where a road to the right leads to El Rodeo. You'll pass Finca Ob-La-Di, Ob-La-Da on your right.

Services and Accommodations

Splendid is the word for **Hotel Posada Canal Grande** (Apdo. 84, Santa Ana, tel. 282-4089, fax 282-5733), opened in December 1994 in the heart of an old coffee *finca* at Piedades, four km west of Santa Ana. The gleamingly new two-story Italianate villa-hotel is operated by a Florentine art collector. The hardwood floor is a stunner, as are the 12 bedrooms with king-size beds, cable TV, and marvelous armoires and desks. A fireplace keeps things warm if a chill sets in at night. Italian taste is everywhere, from the ultra-chic furniture and halogen lamps to the classical vases full of bouquets of flowers, the ceramic bowls full of fruit, and the antique Italian prints gracing the walls. The hotel embraces a large pool. Gazing out from the upper veranda you might imagine yourself looking over the sweeping hillscapes of Tuscany, with sepia-toned farmhouses suffused in golden light. The grounds are mantled in groves of grapefruit, bananas, mango, and other fruits; the rows undulate like a long, swelling sea. A restaurant was under construction. Horse rides are offered; the hotel also has a sauna and tour agency. Airport transfers provided. Rates: $45-60 s, $55-70 d, including breakfast.

The well-known **Finca Ob-La-Di, Ob-La-Da** nature lodge closed its doors to guests in 1990. Owners Andy and Avie Gingold operate the **Go Bandanna Gift Shop** (Apdo. 1, Mora 6100, Ciudad Colón, tel. 249-1179), which sells "medicinal cosmetics, soaps, and herbal first aid from Costa Rica's cornucopia," plus beach bags, tote bags, and other paraphernalia printed with beautiful natural-history prints.

SANTIAGO DE PURISCAL AND LA GARITA

South of Colón the road climbs past the hamlet of Ticufres to **Quitirissi,** where you crest a ridge of **Cerro de Cedral Escazú.** Suddenly the Talamancas spring into view, wildly scenic, forested and unfarmed, sculpted and scalloped in rugged relief. If you turn left (south) two km beyond Quitirrisi, you can enjoy one of the most splendid drives in the country, perfect for an afternoon journey from San José. The rough roads are little traveled. And the landscapes are truly spectacular. Despite some steep, enduring grades, the circuit grants a joyous communion with one of Costa Rica's most splendid regions. Follow the road south to Tabarcia, and turn left for Chirraca and the **Balneario Valle Cantado** (open Fri.-Sun.). East of the *balneario,* the road is unpaved all the way to San Ignacio de Acosta (see "Route of the Saints," below), from where you can return to San José via Aserrí or turn south and follow the "Route of the Saints."

The main road from Ciudad Colón continues west via Guayabo to **Santiago de Puriscal,** a quiet town (called Puriscal by locals) noted for its intense seismic activity and as a center for a major reforestation project—**Arbofilia** (tel. 235-5470)—which involves local *campesinos* and which you can visit for educational tours (contact Jungle Trails, tel. 255-3486). Santiago is centered on a large square with lots of "monkey

puzzle" trees (araucaria pine) and overlooked by a large and pretty if threadbare church surrounded by bougainvillea. Jeep-taxis line the south side of the square. An orchid hobbyist, Eugenio Esquivel, tends a nursery (300 meters north of the post office) with more than 350 orchid species. Visitors are welcome.

Nearby, at Km 30, the **Guayabo Indian Reserve** of the Quitirrisi Indians lies on the slopes of Cerro Turrubares. This remnant indigenous community lives relatively marginalized (reportedly, many of its members can barely speak Spanish, though several members eke livings as weavers; you may see some of their fine baskets on sale at roadside stalls.

From Santiago you can turn north and follow a dirt road to Turrúcares and La Garita, or follow a road southwest as far as Salitrales, from where the road descends steeply to the Pacific coast, crossing the Fila Coyolar and Fila Cangreja mountains and meeting the coast road just north of Parrita. I've not driven beyond Salitrales (the map shows a dirt road from here on, but it may be paved). Alternately, a newly paved and fabulously scenic road (great views northward across the valley) stretches west from Santiago all the way to Orotina, the gateway to the central Pacific. This route promises a traffic-free descent and for that reason is probably far safer (and of equal distance) than either of the two traditional routes from San José by way of Santiago.

Buses depart San José for Santiago from Calle 16, Avenidas 1/3 hourly.

SOUTH OF SAN JOSÉ

South of San José lies one of Costa Rica's most splendid areas, perfect for a full-day drive along the fabulously scenic "Route of the Saints," which leads to Santa María de Dota via San Gabriel, San Cristóbal Sur, San Pablo de León Cortés, and San Marcos de Tarrazú. The roads rise and fall, sometimes gently, sometimes steeply. The tiny villages cling precariously to the steep mountainsides; others nestle in the valley bottoms. The route is virtually unsullied by tourist footprints.

SAN JOSÉ TO SAN IGNACIO DE ACOSTA

Desamparado, a working-class suburb on the outskirts of San José, at the base of the mountains, is worth a stop. Its superb church is one of the most impressive in the country. There's the **Oxcart and Rural Life Museum** (tel. 259-7042) in an aged house, with lots of artifacts profiling the traditional peasant lifestyle (hours: Tues.-Sun. 8 a.m.-noon and 2-6 p.m.); and the **Homage to Joaquín García Monge Museum** (tel. 259-5072), dedicated to the Costa Rican intellectual and writer (hours: Mon.-Fri. 1-4 p.m.).

From Desamparado the road rises toward **Aserrí,** a very pretty hillside town famed for its equally pretty church, for its simplistic hand-crafted dolls, and for La Piedra de Aserrí (a massive boulder with, at its base, a cave once inhabited by a witch). The gradient increases markedly to the crest of the mountains just north of **Tarbaca.** En route you gain a breathtaking view of Volcán Irazú. Three km south of Tarbaca is a Y-junction. The road to the right drops westward to **San Ignacio de Acosta,** a charming little town nestled on a hillside. You can see its whitewashed houses for miles around. The sun sets dramatically on its steep west-facing slopes, and if approaching from Ciudad Colón (see under "Santiago de Puriscal and La Garita" above) you should time your

drive for sundown. The road to the left at the Y-junction is the gateway to the "Route of the Saints" (see below), with San Gabriel at its doorstep, high on the hillside five km southeast of Tarbaca.

Accommodations
An unnamed, fully furnished **mountain chalet** (tel. 259-0840) is available for rent above Desamparados; it includes a pool, phone, and panoramic view; $1000 per month.

Food
El Alcazar (tel. 259-5114), two blocks south of the Bank of Costa Rica in Desamparado, serves good *típico* cuisine. **Restaurant Chicharronera La Tranca** high on the mountain road above Aserrí, has a very windy outdoor patio from where you can admire, mouth agape, the stunning views down over San José and the far-off volcanoes. The restaurant also has a tremendous rustic ambience, with food prepared on an open hearth grill. (Don't mistake this restaurant for the far smaller and less well-situated Chicharronera Ranchita or Mirador Ram Luna, farther down the hill.) **Mirador Ram Luna** is in a similar vein: fireplace, hanging plants, fantastic views, and heaps of warm rusticity to go with the *típico* fare (heavy on Mexican-style steaks). **Las Doñitas Restaurant** (tel. 230-2398), in Tarbaca, also serves traditional Costa Rican cuisine cooked on a woodstove.

Entertainment
In Aserrí you'll find **Chicharroenera Cacique Asserí** (tel. 230-3088), with an "Aserriceñas" night featuring *marimba* music and traditional dancing every Friday and Saturday.

Getting There
Buses from San José depart from Calle 2, Avenidas 6/8, for Aserrí; and hourly 5:30 a.m.-10:30 p.m. from Calle 8, Avenida 12 for San Ignacio. There's bus service for San Ignacio from Aserrí.

"ROUTE OF THE SAINTS"

Until recently relatively off-the-beaten-tourist-path, the area known as the "Route of the Saints" is with good reason enjoying newfound favor as a stunning drive and as a base for mountain vacations. The easiest and most popular approach to tackling these saintly villages is to drive south from Cartago along the Pan-Am Hwy. and to turn right (south) at the Enpalme gas station. At Vara de Roble (two km north of Enpalme), another access road leads west to San Cristóbal via **La Lucha Sin Fin** ("The Endless Struggle"), the *finca* of former president and national hero "Don Pepe" Figueres, who led the 1948 revolution. Another dirt road leads from just south of Cañon on the Pan-American Hwy. to Santa María via Copey.

SANTA MARÍA DE DOTA

This tranquil and pretty village full of gaily painted wooden houses with neat trims is ideal for nature hikes, including one to a nearby lake full of waterbirds. A pleasing square has a small monument honoring those who died in the 1948 revolution. Should you stay overnight here, you'll find the local *cantinas* provide for familiarity with local farmers. For the local Red Cross, call 541-1037; for the local police, call 541-1135.

Accommodations
The inexpensive **Hotel Santa María** (tel. 541-1193) has rooms with private bath; the **Hotel Marieuse** (tel. 541-1176) has rooms with shared bath; the **Hotel Dota** (tel. 541-1193), adjacent to the plaza, has nine rooms and a restaurant-cum-bar but is more interesting for its eclectic collection of armaments and farm implements adorning the walls. Rates: $10 s.

For eats, try **El Arbolito** (tel. 541-1111), on the southwest corner of the plaza, or **Las Tejas,** 200 meters east of the church.

San Marcos de Tarrazú also has several modest hotels.

Getting There
Autotransportes Los Santos (tel. 227-3597) buses to Santa María depart San José from Aveni-da 16, Calles 19/21, at 6 and 9 a.m., and 12:30, 3, and 5 p.m. Return buses San José depart Santa María at 5, 6 and 9 a.m., and 1 and 4 p.m.

COPEY

Copey is a small agricultural village at about 2,121 meters, reached either from Santa María or the Pan-Am Hwy., south of Cañon. The climate is brisk. The region is good for exhilarating walks through hills clad in native oak, and leaving your vehicle by the roadside you may hike in search of resplendent quetzals, which are common hereabouts. You'll see waterfalls and a tiny lake. There's a trout farm, too, run by Don Fernando Elizondo. (If you don't catch your own, enjoy a trout lunch at William Rodríguez's *soda*.)

Accommodations
Don Elizondo's next-door neighbor, Chema, has a single room with stained-glass window and shared bath ($7 with breakfast). He also rents horses and may guide you on horseback or foot to the Río Macho Reserve. The American-run **Cabinas Copey** (tel. 541-1177) reportedly has three spartan and drafty concrete cabinas with kitchenette and private bath (not inspected).

Near Enpalme is **Albergue de Montaña** (c/o Aeroviajes, tel. 233-6108, fax 233-6293), at Km 62 of the Pan-American Highway. It offers cozily furnished cabinas for two, three, or five people, each with private bath with hot water, plus heater, living room, and private terrace. The lounge has a small library, and a restaurant serves Costa Rican meals and the lodge's specialty, "Tapantí Trout."

Getting There
Take the San Isidro bus (Calle 16, Avenidas 1/3) to Cañon, on the Pan-American Highway. Get off at the yellow church, 800 meters beyond Km 58. It's an eight-km walk from here to Copey down a dirt road. The road continues west to Santa María (see above).

CAÑON AND SOUTH

South of Cañon, the Pan-American Hwy. climbs steeply toward Cerro de la Muerte ("Death Moun-

tain"; 3,491 meters) before dropping down into the Valle de El General and the Pacific southwest. The route is fantastically scenic! The vistas are staggering and in parts you'll swear you're in the European Alps. Few tourists seem to venture to this easily accessible yet remarkable region, which only now is being "discovered."

Proceed carefully. The road zigzags uphill, sometimes greatly turning, at other times continuing in a predictable line for a distance only to trap the unwary driver with a sudden, vicious turn. The Pan-Am Hwy. is deeply potholed, so keep your speed down. You'll want to dawdle anyway, for the vistas are superb.

One source says you can enter Tapantí National Park (see "Cartago and Vicinity" earlier in this chapter) via the **Río Macho Forest Reserve,** reached at Trinidad, five km south of Cañon. (Steve Friedman, of Genesis II—see below—says that the *only* entrance to the refuge is from the Orosí valley.) The reserve comprises more than 80,000 hectares of critical forest. Seven of the 12 life zones classified by Holdridge (see "Ecosystems," in the Introduction chapter) have been documented here. Together they provide a vital habitat for the quetzal, the Holy Grail of the tropical cloud forest, and such endemic species as the copper-headed emerald hummingbird, silky fly-catcher, cerise-throated hummingbird, red-billed finch, the *cipresillo* oak, the mountain-needle, and the blueberry.

At the Km 80 marker, 30 km south of Empalme, a turnoff to the right leads downhill to the hamlet of **San Gerardo de Dota** along a snaking and breathtakingly beautiful! mountain road (4WD vehicle highly recommended). The San Gerardo valley is a center for apples and peaches, fed by the waters of the Río Savegre. Quetzals abound (the bird particularly enjoys a type of laurel that grows hereabouts).

The summit, known as **Cerro de la Muerte,** is at Km 85, where you may rest at **Las Torres,** part truck-stop/*soda*/restaurant. From here, a path leads uphill to communications towers from where on a clear day you may enjoy commanding views through the stunted trees (see "Cerro de la Muerte" under "San Isidro and Vicinity" in Pacific Southwest chapter). Back at Km 76 you'll pass a couple of refuge huts built for early pioneers who had to cross the mountains before a road existed

to bring their produce to market in San José. The adobe hut is now a small museum displaying maps and historical information.

Accommodations
Genesis II (Apdo. 10303, San José, tel. 381-0739, fax 221-2053), just north of Cañon, is a rustic nature lodge surrounded by 38 hectares of primary forest on the slopes of the Talamancas. The forest borders the Tapantí National Forest near the village of La Damita, at an elevation of 2,360 meters. One-third lies within the Río Macho Forest Reserve. You reach the lodge—run by an Englishman, Steve Friedman, and his Dutch-born wife Paula—along a rough, three km dirt trail; turn east at Cañon Church (near Km 58 on the Pan-American Hwy.) and right again at La Damita School. You'll need a 4WD vehicle. It's a great spot for sighting resplendent quetzals, hummingbirds, and other birds (more than 200 species have been recorded). You can even see quetzals from the porch March-June. The excellent trail system is well-maintained by volunteers from all over the world—you could be one (boots are provided). The Friedmans run a volunteer program; you can volunteer for trail building and reforestation. The rough-hewn lodge has a wood stove, plus five bedrooms (one with double bed, the rest single) with shared toilets and hot showers. Reader Yvonne Hodges reports the food is "excellent." Rate: $75 per person, $35 students with ID, including all meals and guides (10% discount for weeklong stays). Entrance to the reserve only is $10 (students $5).

Six km south of Cañon, at Km 62 at Macho Gaff, is **Tapantí Lodge** (Albergue de Montaña Tapantí, Apdo. 1818, San José 1002, tel. 233-0155 or 232-0133, fax 233-0778), a comfortable small chalet-style hotel with 10 cabinas on a grassy ridge overlooking the Tapantí National Parks. The rustic but cozy cabins sleep up to five people, with private bathroom with hot water, plus electric heater, living room, and balcony. A lounge has a TV, fireplace, bar, and deep-cushioned red velvet chairs. The hotel offers a small conference room with a library, a bar-cum-restaurant, plus trails for hiking and horseback riding. Also available are a trout-fishing special, quetzal hikes, and tours to Tapantí, several hours' hike away. I'm informed that several people have

gotten lost trying to hike to Tapantí National Park: if you go, take a guide! Rates: $60 s/d, $75 t, $85 quad. Breakfast $5, lunch/dinner $15.

About nine km from the Pan-American Hwy. on the dirt road to San Gerardo de Dota is **Albergue Río Savegre** (Apdo. 482, Cartago, tel. 771-1732 or 284-1444). The basic lodge (also known as Cabinas Chacón) has 14 rustic cabinas on a family farm owned by Don Efraín Chacón. The farm, in a narrow mountain valley at 1,900 meters, grows apples and peaches and is high enough to attract a healthy population of resplendent quetzals, especially during the April and May nesting season. As such, it hosts the Quetzal Education Research Complex in association with the Southern Nazarene University of Oklahoma. The *finca* offers horseback riding, plus trout fishing in the Río Savegre (bring your own tackle), but don't expect prize-size fish. Cabins are basic but clean, with private baths and hot water, but no stoves. Rates: $55 per person, including three meals.

Another Chacón family member, Rolando (tel. 771-2376), has two cabinas—**Cabinas El Quetzal**—nearby. One has four bedrooms. Each has hot water. "We slept so well there with the wood stove going," reports one reader. Rates: $25-33 per person, including meals.

Nearby, too, at Km 70 on the Pan-Am Hwy., is **Finca de Eddie Serrano** (tel. 534-4415), a recently opened, rustic yet cozy eight-room hostel set amid cloud forest where quetzals congregate to nest. Eddie and his wife and three children were pioneers, settling in this area more than 45 years ago. He and his family continue to work their 100-hectare dairy farm, cut decades ago from virgin forest, while collecting wild blackberries for sale in San José and raising trout for local hotels. Up to 20 pairs of quetzals have

been seen feeding in treetops near the *finca!* "We can almost guarantee that visitors will see quetzals," says Serrano. Rates: $25 per person, including breakfast, dinner, and quetzal tour. **El Quetzal** (tel. 771-2376) is supposedly another option. The remote and spartan concrete cabin sleeps up to eight and has a veranda with hammocks, plus bath. Meals included.

Trogon Lodge, also in the San Gerardo de Dota valley, has been referred to me as a family farm with six rustic cabins, each with two bedrooms and private bathroom with hot water. This place of "pure peace and quiet" serves home-cooked meals, family-style. Two horseback tours lead into the forest. Note: It *could* be another name for Albergue Río Savegre.

Tours

Costa Rica Expeditions (Apdo. 6941, San José 1000, tel. 257-0766, fax 257-1665) offers a "Cerro de la Muerte Tropical Forest Adventure" ($65). **San José Travel** (Apdo. 1237, San José 1002, tel. 231-4808, fax 232-7284) offers a "Quetzal Tour," including lunch ($65). **Geostar Travel** (1240 Century Ct., Santa Rosa, CA 95403, tel. 707-579-2420 or 800-624-6633) features two nights at Finca Chacón during a 10-day "Birdwatcher's Paradise" tour (from $1460). **Bio Tours** (tel. 272-4211 or 541-1034) offers "Dota Green Valley" packages.

Getting There

Take the San Isidro bus from San José and ask the driver to drop you off at Cañon (Km 58; it's a four-km hike to Genesis II from the road), or at the *"entrada a San Gerardo"* at the Km 80 marker. If you're staying at Albergue Río Savegre, Don Efraín will pick you up with advance notice ($6).

NORTHERN LOWLANDS
INTRODUCTION

With all the hyperbole about Costa Rica's magnificent beaches and mountains, the northern lowlands must in comparison have felt forlorn and forgotten until recently. During the colonial period the region was a no-man's-land marked only by murky rivers cutting through the vast forested plains that sweep across most of northern Costa Rica. In one regard, today, from your lofty perch atop Poás or Barva volcano, the vision northward toward Nicaragua is no less dismal. Much of the magnificent forests has given way to great cattle *fincas* and sweeping banana plantations forming a huge triangle-shaped, seemingly featureless plain, as green and as flat as a billiard table.

But this first impression is not a fair one. Skirting the foothills of the cordillera, the vistas southward are as grandiose as any in the country. For the naturalist there are some splendid sites: crocodile farms, remote national parks, and plenty of private reserves. For the explorer with time to spare, there are trails to off-the-beaten-track treasures: caves, waterfalls, and rivers for rafting and kayaking. Arenal volcano looms magnificently and well within reach. And the past few years have seen a blossoming of marvelous hostelries. With good reason, the northern lowlands are finally on the tourist map, as the ritzy new look of Fortuna, the most important town, attests.

The places of greatest tourist interest can be reached along well-paved roads. More remote spots are approached along appalling roads that can shake both a car and its occupants until their doors and teeth rattle, but the routes are comparatively straightforward. Most places of interest are within a short drive of one another, and all are readily accessible on a day's journey from San José. On a visit in April 1995, I was delighted to find that many roads that were rock-and-dirt two years prior had been paved.

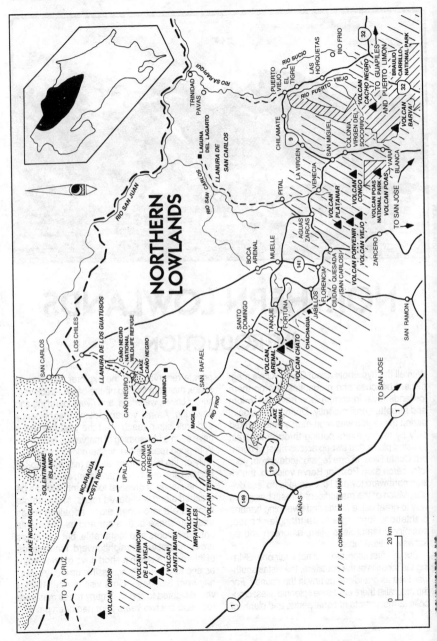

THE LAND AND CLIMATE

Once you pass through the mountains you drop quickly down the steep north-facing slopes and onto the lowlands, which constitute a 40,000-square-kilometer watershed drained by the Ríos Frío, San Carlos, and Sarapiquí and their tributaries, many of which are navigable by shallow-water craft.

The lowlands extend north to the Río San Juan and beyond into southern Nicaragua, where much of the fighting took place during the counterrevolution of the 1980s. This border zone is now an agrarian front in the battle to establish the Si-a-Paz transnational park (see "Megaparks," in the "National Parks" section in the Introduction chapter).

The region is made up of two separate plains (*llanuras*): the **Llanura de los Guatusos** in the west, and the **Llanura de San Carlos** farther east. The Guatusos plain was formed by sediments washed down from the Cordillera de Guanacaste and Cordillera de Tilarán and deposited as part of the Lake Nicaragua basin millions of years ago. The San Carlos plain was formed of fluvial sediments from the basins between the San Carlos and Chirripó rivers.

These rivers meander like restless snakes and commonly flood in the wet season, when much of the landscape is transformed into swampy marshlands epitomized by Caño Negro National Park, southwest of Los Chiles, near the Nicaraguan border. Such terrain provides perfect conditions for rice cultivation, and much of the rice that is the staple of the Costa Rican diet is grown here.

ROAD ROUTES TO THE LOWLANDS

The northern lowlands are separated from San José and the rest of Costa Rica by the great backbone of volcanoes and mountains that girdles the country. Five routes slice through the cordillera and descend to the plains. Combining any two makes for a perfect loop trip. Which you choose may depend on your desired destination in the lowlands.

The most easterly route—good for access to Rara Avis, La Selva, and Puerto Viejo—is via the San José-Limón Highway through Braulio Carrillo National Park. About five km after exiting the park (10 km before Guápiles), a dirt-and-rock road leads northward to Río Frío, Horquetas, and Puerto Viejo de Sarapiquí. This is the least scenic route.

A more appealing route to Puerto Viejo is via Heredia and Vara Blanca, and over the saddle between Poás and Barva volcanoes, then a descent with the hulking mass of Volcán Viejo (2,060 meters) on your right. The route is superbly scenic on a clear day as you descend the switchbacks via the La Paz waterfall: watch for pedestrians on the road as you approach the bridge on the hairpin bend. Of interest to birders is the dirt road—some seven km north of La Paz—that leads east to Colonia Virgen del Socorro: the region is famous for its excellent birding. (Costa Rica Expeditions offers one-day guided birding trips: $65 per person.) At San Miguel you can turn left and follow the foothills to Aguas Zarcas, Ciudad Quesada, and the rest of the lowlands.

Most scenic of all is the route via Alajuela, Sarchí, and Zarcero, skirting the western flank of Volcán Poás, to Ciudad Quesada, the true gateway to the lowlands. North of Zarcero the road begins to drop beyond the Continental Divide, and moist air rises up from the lowlands, forming clouds that drift among the bright emerald-green pastures and forest-clad mountains. The setting, with its whitewashed red-roofed houses, is as pleasingly scenic as any aspect of the Swiss Alps.

A fourth road, new and thereby freshly paved, ascends from San Ramón and descends sinuously and very dramatically to La Tigra. It's fabulously scenic, though there are very few places at which to stop to catch your breath over the views. One such, however, is Valle Escondido Lodge (highly recommended). It gives access to the Children's Eternal Forest Reserve (see "Monteverde and Vicinity," in the Guanacaste and the Northwest chapter).

The fifth route descends into the lowlands via Tilarán and Lake Arenal via Fortuna.

You can also reach Upala (and thence the lowlands to the east) directly from the Pan-American Hwy. via a road that crests the saddle between Volcán Miravalles and Volcán Tenorio, or via a rock-and-dirt road running east from Santa Cecilia, linked to the Pan-American Hwy. by a paved road from La Cruz, in the extreme northwest.

THE RÍO SAN JUAN CANAL

Were it not for volcanoes, the Panamá Canal would probably have been built along the Río San Juan, the broad, easygoing river that murmurs with commerce and forms the international boundary between Costa Rica and Nicaragua. Its gaping mouth (where Barra del Colorado is today) and ample flow quickened the pulse of early European explorers seeking a short route between the Atlantic and Pacific Oceans, for its source is Lake Nicaragua, which at 72 km wide and more than 160 km long is the largest body of fresh water between Lake Michigan and Lake Titicaca. Lake Nicaragua is so immense that it almost links the two oceans, and although its waters drain into the Caribbean, it is separated from the Pacific only by a narrow 17-km-wide strip of land.

By 1551, the Spanish, Dutch, and Portuguese were all surveying this fortuitous piece of real estate for a direct route from sea to sea. For the next four centuries, engineers debated the feasibility of the Río San Juan Canal.

In 1850, at the height of the California gold rush, Gordon's Passenger Line opened the first commercial passenger service on the river. Gordon's shipped eager fortune-seekers from New York to Nicaragua, then ferried them up the Río San Juan and across the lake aboard an oversized canoe called a *bungo*. A mule then carried the argonauts to the Pacific coast, where a San Francisco-bound ship waited.

Transport magnate Cornelius Vanderbilt opened a rival ferry service in 1851 with a grander vision in mind: a canal across the isthmus. Events forestalled his dream, however. The Nicaraguans levied transit fees for use of the river. Vanderbilt called in the U.S. Navy to "protect American interests." The Navy reduced to rubble the unfortunate rivermouth town of San Juan del Norte (then called Greytown), and ushered in a century of strife for Nicaragua, not

least an invasion by the imperialist freebooter William Walker (see special topic "The William Walker Saga" in the Introduction chapter). After naming himself president of Nicaragua, Walker invaded Costa Rica in 1856-57 partly to control the proposed canal. After his ouster, Presidents Juanito Mora of Costa Rica and General Martínes of Nicaragua signed an agreement on 1 May 1858 for the construction of the canal, to be financed with European capital. Unfortunately, the U.S. had a fit of jealous pique and used strong-arm tactics to ensure that the project was stillborn.

U.S. interests in the Río San Juan canal were aroused again in the late 19th century, when the idea gained influential backing in Congress. Teams of engineers and tons of equipment were shipped to Greytown, railroad and machine shops were built, dredges brought in, and around a thousand meters of canal were excavated. But the U.S. got cold feet again in 1902, when Mount Pelée erupted in Martinique, killing 30,000 people (an enterprising promoter of the Panamá route sent each member of Congress a Nicaraguan stamp bearing the picture of a volcano as a reminder that a Río San Juan canal would forever be menaced by geological catastrophe). Thus in November 1903, the U.S. signed an agreement that recognized Panamá's independence from Columbia and was granted in exchange the right to dig a canal (completed in 1914) at a much inferior site.

Even this fait accompli did not deter the dreamers. The fickle Americans tried twice to revive the project: in 1916, when the U.S. paid $3 million to Nicaragua for the right to build a canal and establish a naval base in the Gulf of Fonseca (Nicaragua's neighbors protested and the U.S. backed down); and during the post-WW II "Atoms for Peace" craze, when the U.S. Army Corps of Engineers proposed using nuclear bombs to open up the San Juan waterway!

Just two decades ago these plains were rampant with mixed tropical forest. Today, only a few pockets remain as "charred and lonely sentinels," says one writer, "over kilometers of scraggly pasture." The western lowlands have been transformed into a geometrical patchwork of cattle pastures, fruit *fincas*, and rice paddies. Farther east, much of the land was cleared early in this century to make way for bananas, a crop espe-

cially suited to the region. Deforestation continues apace, and sawmills and huge piles of logs stacked ready for transportation line the routes every few kilometers. Still, there *are* plenty of pockets of rainforest on the lowlands sheltering private reserves and plentiful wildlife. The same holds true on the north-facing slopes of the cordillera whose scarp face encusps the lowlands. Allen M. Young's book, *Sarapiquí Chronicle:*

A Naturalist Guide in Costa Rica, is a splendid book telling of 20 years of natural history study in the region (Washington, D.C.: Smithsonian Institution Press, 1991).

Very few towns are of any size, and in some places accommodations are few and far between, with many miles between lodgings. A handful of upscale resorts and fabulous nature lodges, however, lie at the base of the highlands. Buses serve most destinations.

Climate

The climate bears much in common with the Caribbean coast: warm, very humid, and consistently wet. Temperatures hover at 25-27° C year-round. The climatic periods are not as well defined as those of other parts of the nation, and rarely does a week pass without a prolonged and heavy rain shower (it rains a little less from February to the beginning of May). Annual rainfall can exceed 450 cm in some parts. Precipitation tends to diminish and the dry season grows more pronounced northward and westward.

HISTORY

Early Exploration

Corobicí Indians settled the western lowland region several thousand years ago and were divided into at least 12 distinct tribes (see special topic "Guatuso Indians"). This indigenous population was decimated by internecine warfare with Nicaraguan tribes in the early Spanish colonial period.

As early as the 16th century, Spanish galleons were navigating the Río San Juan all the way from the Caribbean to Lake Nicaragua, a journey of 195 km. Pirates also periodically sailed up the river to loot and burn the lakeside settlements. One of the very few colonial remains in the region is El Castillo de la Concepción, a fort erected by the Spanish in 1675 to keep English pirates from progressing upstream (the ruins are in Nicaragua, three km west of where the Costa Rican border moves south of the river).

This early exploration was limited to the broad river channels, and colonization of most of the region has only occurred within this century. Only between 1815 and 1820 was the first access link with the Río Sarapiquí made, via a mud-and-dirt trail that went from Heredia via Vara Blanca. The river, which descends from Barva volcano, became in the early heyday of coffee the most traveled route for getting to the Caribbean Sea from the central highlands.

The Spanish first descended from the central highlands on a foray into the lowland foothills in 1640. They called the region San Jerónimo de los Votos. But almost 200 years were to pass before the foothills were settled. The first pioneers—the Quesada family from San Ramón—formed a village, then known as La Uniá and today called Ciudad Quesada (colloquially called San Carlos). The Quesadas contributed greatly to the rapid development of the region: Ramón Quesada worked for more than a half century on behalf of the progress of this region; his greatest effort supposedly went into an unsuccessful attempt to form a company to open a railroad from the center of the country.

Development

The area has remained isolated for years. Only about 40 years ago the first organized farming extended below Ciudad Quesada onto the edge of the flatlands, and throughout much of this century the prime influence has been that of Nicaraguans traveling south along the rivers from Lake Nicaragua. Beginning in the 1950s the government, as part of its policy to promote new settlements outside the Meseta Central, helped finance small cattle farmers, and settlement began to edge slowly north. Meanwhile, construction by banana companies of new feeder railways in the eastern lowlands opened up unexplored, virgin land for production.

Only in 1948 was a highway built that reached the Río Cuarto (a little over 48 km due north of San José). The road didn't reach Puerto Viejo de Sarapiquí until 1957. And places such as Upala and Los Chiles continued to use rivers for transportation to Limón until the late 1970s, when the construction of paved highways and bridges granted access to the Inter-American Highway and the rest of the country.

ECONOMY

The northern lowlands have been called the breadbasket of the nation, and most of the working population is employed in agriculture.

CATTLE: FRIEND OR FOE?

"There was so much jungle twenty years ago, individual farmers had no concept of the cumulative damage," Jim Hamilton told me over a beer at the Tilajari Resort Hotel, which he owns. Though an American, Jim is typical of the small-scale farmers who have turned the lowlands from jungle to the nation's breadbasket in all of 20 years. Contrary to a popular perception, the story is not one of cattle barons and rapacious greed.

Jim was an atypical American: a poor gringo who started with nothing. He came to Costa Rica with the Peace Corps in 1969 and carried out the first census in Upala Province. After his work was finished he decided to clear a few acres and farm, "for the unique experience." He cleared his own land, milked his own cows, cooked his eggs on hot rocks, and learned his cattle skills from the locals.

Back then, the region was served only by horseback trails and an airstrip often inoperable for days on end because of weather. It used to take Jim three days by river and horseback to travel between his two plots of land; in 1992 I made the same journey by road in two hours. "Cattle was the only type of product that could be got to market. Cattle can walk," Jim explained. "There was no other way of making money." Hence, the land was cleared by hundreds of impoverished squatters and homesteaders like Jim who each raised a few head and grew corn to feed pigs, which could also be walked to market.

Cattle brought in cash but condemned the rainforests. "Poor farmers can't make a living by holding

their land in jungle," Jim said ruefully. The initial ranchers were forced to sell their lumber to pay for the cost of their land and loans. (Interest rates for cattle farmers 20 years ago were subsidized by the World Bank, as agricultural economists saw the most hopeful future for Central American economies in beef.)

Once the area was developed, the government eventually brought in roads and electricity. Suddenly, other alternatives were possible. Since cattle is the least remunerative agribusiness (the return per hectare from cattle farms is only about one-quarter that from growing produce), very little land has been cleared for cattle within the last decade. Tropical fruits began to oust the hooved locusts. Alas, citrus fruits and bananas, which take up the best agricultural land in the lowlands, have pushed up land values enormously, and land is increasingly passing out of the hands of small-scale farmers and into those of the large fruit companies.

Today, Jim Hamilton is active in conservation. Although most of his own land at Tilajari (240 hectares) was cleared long ago, he is hopeful of buying 160 hectares of virgin forest and turning it into a protected reserve. To finance it, he is developing and selling lots of about one hectare each on cleared land near the Tilajari Resort Hotel. The purchase deed will also include nearly two hectares of the forest, which will be preserved in trust as communal property (see special topic "Two Deluxe Resort Hotels").

Along the cordillera foothills, the lands are dedicated to cattle farming. The plain of San Carlos, centered on Ciudad Quesada, devotes almost 70% of its territory to cattle and produces the best-quality milk in the nation. In the lowlands proper, dairy cattle give way to beef, and other agricultural products predominate the farther one travels from the foothills: plantations of *pejibaye* palm and pineapples, bananas in the east, and citrus fruits farther north. The can-

tons of San Rafael de Guatuso and Puerto Viejo de Sarapiquí devote less than half their land to cattle. In Los Chiles Canton, the fruit *fincas* of TicoFrut predominate and cattle ranching takes up less than one-third of farmland.

A considerable percentage of the farmers in Guatuso, Upala, and Los Chiles cantons are little more than subsistence farmers who make their livings raising corn, beans, tubers, cacao, rice, and a few head of livestock.

CIUDAD QUESADA (SAN CARLOS)

Gateway to the northern lowlands, Ciudad Quesada (known locally as San Carlos and denoted on the front of buses and on bus routes as such) is 23 km north of Zarcero, on the midelevation, north-facing slopes of the Cordillera de Tilarán overlooking the lowlands. It is surrounded by lush farmland—some of the richest and most developed in the country—grazed by prize-spec-

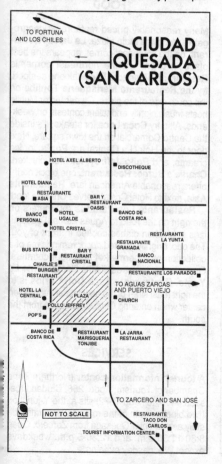

TO FORTUNA
AND LOS CHILES

CIUDAD QUESADA (SAN CARLOS)

HOTEL AXEL ALBERTO

DISCOTHEQUE

HOTEL DIANA

RESTAURANTE ASIA

BAR Y RESTAURANT OASIS

BANCO PERSONAL

HOTEL UGALDE

BANCO DE COSTA RICA

HOTEL CRISTAL

RESTÁURANTE LA YUNTA

BUS STATION

BAR Y RESTAURANT CRISTAL

RESTAURANTE GRANADA

BANCO NACIONAL

CHARLIE'S BURGER RESTAURANT

RESTAURANTE LOS PARADOS

HOTEL LA CENTRAL

PLAZA

TO AGUAS ZARCAS AND PUERTO VIEJO

POLLO JEFFREY

CHURCH

POP'S

BANCO DE COSTA RICA

RESTAURANT MARISQUERIA TONJIBE

LA JARRA RESTAURANT

TO ZARCERO AND SAN JOSÉ

RESTAURANTE TACO DON CARLOS

NOT TO SCALE

TOURIST INFORMATION CENTER

imen dairy cattle. Indeed, the annual **Cattle Fair** *(Feria del Ganado)* in April is one of the largest in the country; colorful, too, with a horse parade and general merriment.

The bustling market town is the hierarchial center of the entire northern region and the only town of any significance in the northern lowlands, which lie at its feet. You may find the main church of Ciudad Quesada of interest; the square to its west is a good place for repose to watch the world go by. Opposite, on the northwest side of the square, is an *artesanía* cooperative selling local arts and crafts, and next to it a colorful fruit and vegetable market. You may find the *talabarterías* (saddle shops) in the center of town interesting; here you can watch elaborately decorated saddles being made and sold. Otherwise, there's nothing here of tourist concern, but it is important as the main gateway to Arenal volcano and Tabacón Hot Springs, Caño Negro National Park, Puerto Viejo de Sarapiquí, and **Juan Castro Blanco National Park,** Costa Rica's youngest national park. Juan Castro Blanco, about five km southeast of Ciudad Quesada, was created to protect the vital watershed on the slopes of Volcán Platanar (2,183 meters). Several endangered species, including the quetzal, curassow, red brocket deer, and black guan exist in the 14,258-hectare park, which is covered in mixed primary forest and clearings in the process of regeneration. Most notable species are lancewoods, oaks and *yayo*. At higher elevations the vegetation is stunted and, given the moister climate, epiphytes abound. The park is not yet developed for tourism.

ACCOMMODATIONS

Budget
You'll find several budget hotels on the block northwest of the plaza. The **Hotel Cristal** (tel. 460-0541) has very basic, dirty rooms with shared bath for $4 s, $7 d; $6 s, $10 d with private bath. Across the road is **Hotel Ugalde** (tel. 460-0260), with rooms with private baths for $3

s, $5 d. In a similar price bracket and one block north is the **Hotel Axel Alberto** (tel. 460-1423), with private bathrooms and fans ($10 s/d). Between the blocks is the **Hotel Diana** (tel. 460-0903). The **El Retiro** (tel. 460-0403) has clean and comfortable rooms with baths overlooking the main plaza; $10 s, $18 d. **Hotel del Valle** (tel. 460-0718), two blocks northwest of the square, is of a similar standard and price.

Other budget hotels include **Los Fernandos; Lily** (tel. 460-0616); **Hotel Los Helechos;** and **Hotel Terminal** (tel. 460-2158), the latter conveniently located in the bus terminal, southwest of the plaza, and thereby noisy.

Moderate

Though basic, the **Hotel La Central** (tel. 469-9179, fax 460-0391), on the west side of the plaza, has clean rooms (some with balconies), with hot-water showers. There's a casino and restaurant; $14 s, $27 d. Nearby is the new **Hotel Don Goyo** (tel. 460-1780), offering clean rooms in bright pastels, each with private bath, hot water, and heaps of light streaming in ($20 s, $25 d). Another acceptable bet is the **Hotel Conquistador** (tel. 469-0546), half a km south of the plaza; room with a bath costs $13 s, $20 d. **Balneario San Carlos** (tel. 460-0747), on the northern outskirts, has a restaurant, weekend entertainment, and basic cabins with baths but no fans ($20 d), and a swimming pool that doubles as a skating rink.

Four km north of Quesada is the **Hotel La Mirada** (tel. 460-2222), astride a ridge beyond which a final steep descent leads onto the level plains. The sweeping vistas from the open-air restaurant are truly stupendous; travelers familiar with Tanzania's Ngorongoro Crater will feel a touch of déjà vu as they look along the forested flanks of the escarpment. Each room each has a carport, a telephone, hot water, and a private bath; $25 d.

Deluxe

El Tucano Resort and Spa provides deluxe accommodations (see special topic "Two Deluxe Resort Hotels").

FOOD

Many reasonably priced restaurants congregate around the main plaza. **La Jarra Restaurant,** on the southeast corner, appears the best place in town. On the northeast corner is **Restaurante Granada.** For steak and seafood, try the **Restaurante Marisquería Tonjibe** on the south side of the plaza. Owner Victor Murillo hosts music nightly and talent contests on weekends. Also try **Coca Loca** for steaks; it's inside the Centro Comercial on the town square. Next door to the Hotel La Central are **Pop's,** for ice creams, and **Pollo Jeffrey,** for fried chicken. **Charlie's Burger Restaurant,** one block north, offers reasonable American fare. **Restaurante Asia,** next to Hotel Cristal, serves Chinese food.

Restaurante Los Parados (50 meters on the right on the road to Aguas Zarcas) specializes in chicken dishes cooked in front of you. The odd, brightly colored decor reminds me of a collection of supermarket checkout counters. Opposite, up the street, is the **Restaurante La Yunta. Restaurante Taco Don Carlos** is to the right (east side) of the new tourist information center when entering Ciudad Quesada from the south.

SERVICES

A **tourist information center** (Northern Zone Chamber of Tourism; Apdo. 256, Ciudad Quesada 4400, tel. 460-1672) sits at the Y-junction (two blocks south of the main square) immediately as you enter Quesada from Zarcero. Open 8:30-11:30 a.m. and 12:30-5 p.m. weekdays except Wednesday evening.

CIUDAD QUESADA EMERGENCY TELEPHONE NUMBERS

All emergencies	911
Hospital San Carlos	460-0533
Red Cross	460-0101
Clínica Dental	
Murillo y Rodriguez	460-0097
Farmacia El Hospital	460-0493
Laboratorio Clínico	
Dr. Ema Zamora Segura	460-1678

There are four **banks** in the center of town. **Budget Rent-a-Car** has an office here, tel. 460-0650.

GETTING THERE

Express buses depart San José every hour 5 a.m.-7:30 p.m. from the Coca-Cola bus station at Calle 16, Avenidas 1/3 (three hours via Zarcero; Autotransportes, tel. 255-4318). Slower buses for Ciudad Quesada and Fortuna also depart Coca-Cola at 6:15, 8:40, and 11:30 a.m. ($1.50; Garaje Barquero, tel. 232-5660). Buses to San José depart Ciudad Quesada hourly 5 a.m.-7 p.m.

The bus terminal is on the block immediately northwest of the plaza. Buses serve most destinations in the northern lowlands: to Arenal and Tilarán (via Fortuna) at 6 a.m. and 3 p.m.; to Fortuna at 5 and 9:30 a.m. and 1, 3, and 10 p.m.; to Los Chiles every two hours, 5 a.m.-5 p.m.; and to Puerto Viejo (tel. 460-0630) daily at 6 and 10 a.m. and 3 p.m. (Also see cities and destinations below for details.)

CIUDAD QUESADA TO LOS CHILES

Dropping down from Ciudad Quesada, the switchback road brings you onto the flat (the road is prone to landslides during rains) as you approach the small town of Florencia. At the stop sign, the road to Fortuna and Arenal veers left; the road for Los Chiles bears right.

The landscape, you'll note, has dramatically changed. Mountain cedars and oaks have given way to palms and wispy bamboos, which reflect the warmer, humid, "more tropical" climate. And holstein and Brown Swiss dairy cattle have been replaced by Brahmas and zebus and their ever-present courtesans, snow-white cattle egrets.

The crossroads hamlet of Muelle is 12 km north, with a Texaco gas station (there's another Texaco station 27 km farther north, 55 km south of Los Chiles) and a store.

Beyond Muelle, the land begins to roll endlessly in a sea of lime-green pastures and waves of citrus—those of the TicoFrut company, whose *fincas* stretch all the way to the Nicaraguan border—with tidy little hamlets in between. The colors are marvelous, the intense greens made more so by soils as red as bright lipstick.

The road fizzles out a few hundred meters beyond Los Chiles, about one km south of the Nicaraguan border.

ACCOMMODATIONS

Budget
The only place offering budget accommodations is the basic **Cabinas La Violeta** ($4.50),

two km north of the Muelles intersection (100 meters beyond the **Bar Los Tres Gatos,** immediately before the bridge over the Río San Rafael). I've heard an unconfirmed report that it rents rooms by the hour.

Moderate
Lodge La Quinta (tel./fax 475-5260 or 460-0731), at Platanar, four km south of the Muelle crossroads, is a very pleasant if modest hotel run by Jeanette and Bill Ugalde. Accommodations include two cabinas, each with hostel-style bunks for 10 people, with shared bath/shower ($12 per person); a spacious triple room ($35) with attractive wood paneling and a roomy shower; and, upstairs, two triples ($35) with private baths and lounges. The Ugaldes will also rent the whole house for families of up to 10 ($110 per day). Meals are cooked and served in an open-air restaurant overlooking a swimming pool. Outdoors you'll find a sauna and basketball and volleyball courts. And—best of all—the bathrooms come festooned with that most prized of rarities in Costa Rica: oversized fluffy towels!

At Boca Arenal, six km north of Muelles, is the **Río San Carlos Lodge** (Apdo. 345, Ciudad Quesada 4400, tel. 469-9179 or 460-0766, fax 460-0391) hidden on the left, 100 meters after the blue hotel sign, on the banks of the Río San Carlos. The old *quinta,* or country home, is built of dark hardwoods. Five handsome, individually decorated rooms (some with a/c) overlooking the river have private baths, hot water, fans, and hammocks that beg to be used. One room has a sunken tub. The lodge has a restaurant

TWO DELUXE RESORT HOTELS

Slim pickings, I'm afraid, for luxe in the lowlands. These two gems make amends . . .

Tilajari Resort Hotel

You don't have to travel far at Tilajari to get your wildlife thrills. Crocodiles sun themselves on the banks of the Río San Carlos in plain view of guests, waiting (no doubt) for a tidbit thrown from the dining room terrace or a careless guest to lean a little too far over the rail. Iguanas roost in the treetops. Hummingbirds feed at the trumpet vines and hibiscus that emblazon the 16 hectares of groomed gardens replete with tropical fruit trees.

The resort hotel-cum-country club is one km west from the Muelles crossroads and is ideally situated for exploring throughout the lowlands.

The Tilajari is as well conceived and equipped as a Palm Springs resort. The 56 a/c, double rooms and four family suites are magnificent, abounding with beautiful hardwoods and featuring private terraces overlooking the river. The wide-open grounds grant unimpeded vistas south across the lush San Carlos Valley toward Volcán Arenal.

Owner Jim Hamilton built the resort with active guests in mind: it offers three tennis courts, a beautifully sculpted swimming pool, a children's pool, two racquetball courts, and horses for rent, too. A sauna, hot tub, and Jacuzzi are available for soothing weary muscles or minds. There's an open-air bar and lounge with satellite TV, and the open-air riverside restaurant is breezy, bright, and lush with tropical air-plants and lipstick-red blossoms. Craving some nightlife? Easy, there's the Jacaré Discotheque!

Tour packages from Tilajari include guided walking tours into the adjacent tropical forests, an agricultural tour, horseback riding through Jim Hamilton's 240-hectare cattle ranch, tours to Volcán Arenal and the Fortuna waterfall, as well as river trips to Caño Negro.

Room rates (low/high season): $50/$60 s, $60/$70 d, $70/$80 t, $75/$85 suite.

Contact Tilajari Resort Hotel, Apdo. 81, Ciudad Quesada, San Carlos, tel. 469-9091, fax 469-9095.

Hotel El Tucano Resort and Spa

I'm not sure what a "prophylactic cure" is (perhaps it's akin to a self-sealing tire), but the Hotel El Tucano Resort and Spa claims this curious healing as one benefit for those dipping their toes—and presumably more—into the thermo-mineral waters (read: hot springs) that hiccup out of clefts in the rocks on which the hotel is built.

El Tucano is eight km east of Ciudad Quesada on the road to Aguas Zarcas. The riverside hotel—built around a courtyard patio and large open-air swimming pool—is styled loosely as a Swiss chalet complex, with pretty, arched, wooden-framed windows, wrought-iron lanterns, and windowboxes full of flaming red flowers. Peaceful and elegant, the hotel has gained popularity as a gathering place for San José's elite, reminiscent of 18th- and 19th-century Europe when water longings swept everyone to the spas.

The hotel has built its reputation on health tourism. Facilities include a Jacuzzi with natural hot springs water, and a hot spring pool in the river, perfect for a morning dip. A scenic walk along the ravine leads past mossy rocks and tumbling cascades to the pool. The river is cool, but the deep pool is fed by piping-hot water trickling down from fissures in the riverbank. Caution: Watch your footing and stay away from the center channel, as the rocks are slippery and the river velocity can change in a second. If you do not want to immerse yourself in the river you can try the natural steam bath built above the river.

The 59 guest rooms reflect European savoir faire. Though small, they're exquisitely and contemporarily furnished in beautiful hardwoods and soothing pink pastels: beds are divinely comfortable. The water in your bathroom comes from the river. Luxury suites accommodate up to five. A four-story addition includes nine suites, a casino, plus 20 additional rooms. Rates: $55 s, $66 d, $77 t, $88-175 suites.

Facilities also include tennis, mini-golf, horseback riding ($5 per hour), and a cavernous restaurant known for its Italian cuisine (I found the food disappointing). Tours are available to Poás, Arenal, Caño Negro, and up the Río Sarapiquí. Paths meander through the woods for cheery hikes.

"Mark Twain and Freud, and Gogol and Nietzsche, lost their skepticism in the steam room" wrote G.Y. Dryansky. And so did I. El Tucano proves that there's true luxe in Costa Rica.

El Tucano: tel. 460-1822, fax 460-1692; in San José, tel. 221-9095, fax 221-9095.

and a swimming pool plus kiddies' pool. Rates: $60 d, including breakfast.

Upscale

Hotel La Garza (tel. 475-5222 or 222-7355, fax 475-5015 or 222-0869), at Platanar, has four beautifully kept cabins with polished wood floors, ceiling fans, Guatemalan fabrics and bamboo furnishings, heaps of potted plants, and verandas with tables and chairs overlooking the Río Platanar. Additional cabins were being added, along with a pool, restaurant, and a three-km hiking/jogging trail. The hotel is part of a 600-hectare working cattle and horse farm where you can hop in the saddle to explore the private lands, or opt for trips to Caño Negro National Wildlife Refuge, etc. Meals are served in a charming old farmhouse. Delightful. Rates: $68 d.

Deluxe

The **Tilajari Resort Hotel** is one km west of the Muelle crossroads (see special topic "Two Deluxe Resort Hotels").

Getting There

Buses to/from Los Chiles and San Rafael can drop you in Muelles. Saragundí Specialty Tours (tel. 255-0011, fax 255-2155) operates a **Pura Natura** shuttle service, departing San José at 7 a.m. ($17 to Muelles via San Ramón and Fortuna; $24 via Horquetas and Puerto Viejo).

LOS CHILES

Unless you're curious to see what a frontier town during the Nicaraguan counterrevolution looks like, there's only one reason to travel the road to Los Chiles: to visit Caño Negro National Wildlife Refuge, about 25 km southwest of town (see below), for the fishing or nature.

Los Chiles is on the Río Frío, about 100 km north of Ciudad Quesada and four km south of the Nicaraguan border. It developed as a minor river port for traffic on the Ríos San Juan and Frío, which remain moderately busy jungle highways. Water-taxis ply to and from Los Chiles loaded with trade goods and families traveling downriver to the Nicaraguan town of San Carlos, which sits at the point where the Río Frío empties into Lake Nicaragua and the Río San Juan flows out.

The **police station** (tel. 471-1103) is on the main road from Muelle, on the right just before you turn left into town. You'll find a **Banco Nacional** in the village center.

Crossing into Nicaragua

Don't hold your breath if you're planning on crossing into Nicaragua from here. This was a sensitive region during the Nicaraguan conflicts of the 1980s: the Río Frío was a contra supply line, and for a while Los Chiles was a boomtown flush with CIA dollars and C-ration wrappers. Many local residents fled the fighting and only in the past few years have begun to drift back.

In June 1994, Costa Rican President José María Figueres and his Nicaraguan counterpart Violeta de Chamorro signed an agreement to establish a new border crossing at Los Chiles (and 14 km inside Nicaragua, at San Pancho). Reports were that this is now operating. A *migración* office has reportedly been opened in the center of town (open Mon.-Fri. 8 a.m.-4 p.m.). When I visited, the office (tel. 471-1061) was at the western end of the village, 100 meters east of the wharf alongside the Río Frío.

Note, though, that this is a sensitive area and the situation fickle. In 1993, a friend was arrested by Nicaraguan police after being refused entry into Costa Rica near Los Chiles and attempting to cross farther upriver!

The only other place foreigners can legally cross into Nicaragua is Peñas Blancas, on the Pan-American Highway (see "Border Crossings"under "Getting There" in the "On the Road" chapter). You can reach Peñas Blancas from Los Chiles by road via Caño Negro, Upala, and Santa Cecilia.

Accommodations

Nothing grandiose here! The **Hotel Río Frío** (tel. 471-1127), between the park and river, has 10 rudimentary rooms with cold-water showers ($2.25; tel. 471-1127). Just around the corner heading back into town is the **Apartamientos Onasis,** on the west side of the soccer field in the village center. The **Hotel Central** is 200 meters farther, on the east side. **Las Carolinas Hotel** (tel. 471-1151), one block west of the police station near the entrance to town, is about the best, but, says local fishing authority Jerry Ruhlow, "It's not the Sheraton." Basic

rooms are clean and have fans plus private bathrooms. Rates: $6 per person. Also try the **Los Chiles Hotel** (not inspected).

The **Restaurant El Parque,** opposite the soccer field, serves basic Costa Rican fare (open 6 a.m.-9 p.m.).

Getting There

Los Chiles is easily reached by car along the all-weather road, built in the 1980s. The small airstrip has no scheduled air service. You can charter from San José (see "Getting Around" in the On the Road chapter).

Seven buses run daily between Ciudad Quesada and Los Chiles. Express buses depart San José from Calle 16 and Avenidas 1/3 at 5:30 a.m. and 3:30 p.m. (return buses same time).

CAÑO NEGRO NATIONAL WILDLIFE REFUGE

One of the undiscovered gems of Costa Rica, Caño Negro National Wildlife Refuge, 25 km southwest of Los Chiles, is a remote tropical everglade teeming with wildlife. The 9,969-hectare reserve protects a lush lowland basin of soft, knee-deep watery sloughs and marshes, *holillo* groves, and tan carpets of sturdy sedge. Life here revolves around Lago Caño Negro, a seasonal lake fed by the fresh waters of the Río Frío, which snake down from the flanks of Vol-

cán Tenorio and collect in this basin, where they slow almost to a standstill.

In the wet season, when the region is flooded and great pools and lagoons form, vast numbers of migratory waterfowl flock in, turtles and crocodiles in abundance bask on the banks, and as you look down into waters as black as Costa Rican coffee you may see the dim forms of big snook, silver-gold tarpon, and garish garfish lurking in the shadows.

In February the dry season sets in (it generally lasts through April), Caño Negro dries out, and the area is reduced to shrunken lagoons. Caiman gnash and slosh out pools in the muck, and wildlife congregate in abundance along the watercourses.

Attractions

Caño Negro is a birdwatcher's paradise. The reserve protects the largest colony of neotropic cormorants in Costa Rica and the only permanent colony of Nicaraguan grackle. Cattle egrets, wood storks, anhingas, roseate spoonbills, and other waterfowl gather in their thousands. The bright pink roseate spoonbill is one of Caño Negro's most spectacular wading birds. It is named for its spatulate bill, some 15-19 centimeters long, which it swings from side to side as it munches insects or small shellfish. Another of my favorites is the anhinga, a bird as adept underwater as in the air. You can see it solo or by the dozen, preening way up in the cypress trees.

crocodile, Caño Negro

JEAN MERCIER

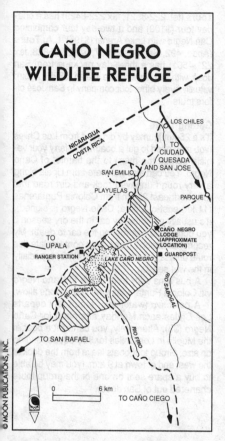

CAÑO NEGRO
WILDLIFE REFUGE

LOS CHILES

NICARAGUA
COSTA RICA

SAN EMILIO

PLAYUELAS

TO
CIUDAD
QUESADA
AND SAN JOSE

PARQUE

CAÑO NEGRO
LODGE
(APPROXIMATE
LOCATION)

GUARDPOST

TO
UPALA

RANGER STATION

LAKE CAÑO NEGRO

RIO MONICA

RIO SABOGAL

RIO FRIO

TO SAN RAFAEL

0   6 km

TO CAÑO CIEGO

© MOON PUBLICATIONS, INC.

The anhinga goes by three aliases: snakebird, for its serpentine neck; American darter, for its jerky movements; and water turkey, for the way its tail spreads in flight.

The reserve is remarkable, too, for its healthy population of endangered mammal species, including jaguars, cougars, tapirs, ocelots, and tayras. There are always sure to be plenty of monkeys playacting. And the crocodile colony of Caño Negro is perhaps the best-protected in Costa Rica.

Everything has its price! The mosquitoes—though tiny—eye your arrival greedily, awaiting that secret signal for their Blitzkreig Stuka attack. Bring plenty of repellent.

The Río Frío, which cuts through the refuge, makes an ideal waterway for guided boat tours into Caño Negro. You can hire a boat and guide in Los Chiles. In dry season, you can explore on foot or on horseback (you can rent a horse in Los Chiles or in the tiny hamlet of Caño Negro, 20 km southwest of Los Chiles; ask around).

Fishing

The Río Colorado may steal the show when it comes to hooking that feisty freshwater gargantuan "silver rocket," the tarpon, but the secret is finally leaking out: Caño Negro and the Río Frío are just as good. A handful of anglers have long known that the region is a sleeper, with waters that almost boil with tarpon, snook, drum, *guapote, machaca,* and *mojarra* jostling for space. Fishing expert Jerry Ruhlow says, "Most tarpon will jump three to five times, often coming 12 feet out of the water and doing a 360-degree twist in the process."

The unexplored fishing frontier is now being opened for commercial fishing trips. Fisherman Richard Krug offers guided "No Frills" fishing trips (tel. 228-4812 or 289-8139, or c/o Dunn Inn Hotel in San José, tel. 222-8134, fax 221-4596) from San José, with accommodation at the Los Chiles Hotel ($300, including tackle, lunch, etc.). Krug has reportedly been planning to build a fishing lodge with a/c cabinas and a swimming pool in Los Chiles; stay tuned. **Americana Fishing Charters** (tel. 222-8134, fax 221-4596), run by Americans Martin Bernard and John Mills, also offers a "No Frills" fishing package with transfers from San José, boat, guide, tackle, and accommodation in Los Chiles ($400 for two days); a "Full Frills" package with nights at Tilajari Resort Hotel costs $550.

Fishing trips on the Río Frío are also offered by most hotels in the lowlands, plus all the tour companies in Fortuna (see below).

Fishing season is July-March and licenses are required.

Accommodations and Food

The **Albergue Caño Negro Lagoon** (tel. 460-0124 or 240-5460, fax 234-1676) opened in 1994, 15 km south of Los Chiles. It is reached by boat or via a very rough six-km-long dirt road from the Muelles-Los Chiles highway (the turnoff is at the hamlet of El Parque). The thatched

lodge and 10 simple yet spacious and comfortable rooms (with private bath) sit on an artificial island on the banks of the Río Frío, and are built entirely of bamboo and rich red hardwoods with blue bedspreads and curtains in counterpoint. The restaurant, open to all sides, has a rustic elegance. Rates: $42 d.

A family-run restaurant—a kind of "drive-in" for boats—perches on stilts over the water at the north end of the lagoon. It serves cold beers and *gallo pinto*.

Camping is allowed; there are no facilities.

You can also stay overnight in the Caño Negro ranger station if space is available (about $7; meals $5). You'll need a sleeping bag and, ideally, a mosquito net. Call the National Parks Service radio dispatcher in San José (tel. 233-4070, fax 223-6369). If your Spanish is good, you may be able to get through to the refuge by calling the public telephone in Caño Negro (tel. 460-1301), or via channel 38 on the SPN radiotelephone (tel. 233-4160).

Tours

Virtually every hotel within a 65-kilometer radius offers guided day-trips down the Río Frío to Caño Negro (prices depend on number of people; average price is $45, including lunch; see "Fortuna," below). **Tropical Adventure Tours** (Apdo. 1362, San José 1000, tel. 222-8974, fax 255-0306) offers a one-day tour to Caño Negro from both San José ($85) and Limón ($99). **Tico**

Tours (tel. 222-8521, fax 222-8429) has a one-day tour ($100) and a two-day tour combining Cañ Negro with Lake Arenal ($195). **L.A. Tours** (Apdo. 492, San José 1007, tel. 224-5828, fax 221-4501) has a three-day package from San José, with two nights at the Tilajari ($325). Again, virtually every other tour company in San José offers tours.

Getting There

It's a 25-km journey by dirt road from Los Chiles (you may need to get a boatman to ferry your vehicle across the river) to the hamlet of Caño Negro. You can also get there from Upala along a very rough unpaved rock-and-dirt road that runs northeast 25 km from Colonia Puntarenas (11 km east of Upala; Caño Negro is signed). It's usually passable by car in the dry season if you don't mind hammering the car to death. My recommendation? Don't even contemplate this route unless you have a sturdy 4WD, especially in the wet season.

A bus runs daily from Upala to Caño Negro via Colonia Puntarenas when conditions allow.

A *colectivo* (water-taxi) reportedly departs Los Chiles each Monday afternoon for Caño Negro ($3). Alternately, you can rent a boat at the Muelle in Los Chiles for $40-90, depending on size. Group tour boats leave from the dock at the west end of town at 9 a.m. (you may be able to buy a spare seat on one of the group tours chartered out of San José).

(top) village square, Potrero, Nicoya (Christopher P. Baker); (bottom left) riding into the sunset, Drake Bay (John Anderson); (bottom right) green turtle, Tortuguero (Christopher P. Baker)

(top left) frigate bird, Isla Chira (Christopher P. Baker); (top right) Tabacón Hot Springs and Arenal volcano (Tabacón Hot Springs); (bottom) iguana, Santa Rosa National Park (Jean Mercier)

WEST FROM CIUDAD QUESADA

West from Ciudad Quesada the road zigzags past lime-green pastures, always with the great bulk of Volcán Arenal—mystical, mist-shrouded—looming ominously and magnificently on your left. From on the lowlands, Costa Rica's volcanic landscapes are almost ethereal; they remind me of Bali. Pastures tumble down the mountainsides like folds of green silk. The plains are thick with chartreuse wands of rice. And the colors are like a painting by Matisse: emerald greens flowing into burning golds, soft pastels, and warm ochres relieved periodically by brilliant tropical colors, houses as blue as the morning sky and flower petals and rich soils as red as ripe, luscious tomatoes.

Passing through Florencia and Jabillos, where the road (full of potholes) swings north, you arrive at Tanque (37 km from Ciudad Quesada), where a turnoff to the right leads via San Rafael to Upala. Continuing straight, you arrive at Fortuna (seven km farther), northern gateway to Volcán Arenal, the Tabacón Hot Springs, and Lake Arenal (described in the Guanacaste and the Northwest chapter). A much swifter route from Florencia to Fortuna is via Jabillos, San Isidro, and Chachagua along a smooth-as-silk newly laid road (see below).

Before we continue, let me digress . . .

AN ALTERNATE ROUTE FROM THE HIGHLANDS

You can reach the western northern lowlands directly from the central Highlands via a new road that transcends the mountains north from San Ramón and drops through the Valle Escondido to La Tigra, San Isidro, and La Fortuna.

The road provides an exhilarating switchback descent to the flatlands and the hamlet of **Bajo Rodriquez.** Two km north is **Eco-Tourist Project Valle Azul,** on the banks of the Río Azul, with cabinas, camping, a restaurant, and swimming. Soon you arrive at **La Tigra,** a gateway to the Bosque Eterno de los Niños (Children's Eternal Rainforest) and Monteverde Cloud For-

est Reserve; you'll see a sign about 800 meters south of La Tigra and an **information office** one km north of town.

You'll cross a high suspension bridge before arriving, about three km north of La Tigra, in **San Isidro.** Jabillos is about four km to the right (east) at the T-junction in town. The paved road northwest from San Isidro leads to Fortuna via Chachagua, where there's a gas station. A dirt road leads west from Chachagua and deadends at the Chachagua Rainforest Lodge (see below). A bus service runs between Chachagua and Fortuna.

Accommodations and Food

A highly recommended stop for a drink, meal, and/or overnight stay is the modern **Valle Escondido Lodge** (Apdo. 452, La Uruca 1150, tel. 231-0906, fax 232-9591), in a valley tucked into the slopes of the cordillera. A steep and very rugged dirt road winds dramatically downhill through a working *finca* whose grandiose mountainside perch is unrivaled. All around are cleaves and valleys clad in dark forest primeval. Arriving at the restaurant, you may dine in or out on *típico* cuisine with a European flair (my sea bass with garlic was splendid; $7). Note the tiny butterfly and insect collection. It will probably be cloudy, but warm nonetheless, and it is tantalizing to join the workers moving among the rows of citrus and ornamental plants. The hotel has 25 elegant, spacious cabinas with handsome, hand-crafted hardwood furniture, and terrace for relaxing and tallying the many bird species. Cool off in the swimming pool or visit the cocktail bar, which features live musicians and draws a local crowd on weekends. Guided horseback riding and hiking are offered on the 60-hectare plantation and 400 hectares of ranchland and primary forest, and mountain bikes can be rented. Trails lead down to the Río La Balsa, a good spot for swimming. Roundtrip transfers from San José are offered ($25). Rates: $55 s, $66 d, $77 t.

Cabañas Los Ríos (not reviewed) offers basic rooms in La Tigra, as does **Hotel Chach-**

agua, with simple, clean rooms in the $10 range. If you've dollars to spare, you won't regret savoring a night or two at Valle Escondido Lodge (above) or at Chachagua Rain Forest Lodge.

CHACHAGUA RAIN FOREST LODGE

Chachagua Rain Forest Lodge (c/o Vesa Nature Tours, Apdo. 476, San Antonio de Belén 4005, tel. 239-1049, fax 239-4206) is an architecturally stunning and tranquil getaway on a 80-hectare cattle ranch nestled at the foot of the Tilarán mountain range, with a gurgling brook cascading down through the property. Seventeen wooden cabins, simple yet magnificently designed, are replete with appointments befitting a four-star hotel. A deck with picnic tables and benches for dining alfresco are surrounded by lush, landscaped greenery with the wild forest close at hand. Each has two double beds. You'll want to return just to take another shower under the skylight in front of mirrored windows with bromeliads and potted plants sharing the waters. The atmospheric natural-log restaurant with pretty pink place settings looks out upon a corral where guests can watch the *sabaneros* testing their skills in the saddle or even riding bulls bareback! There's a swimming pool, designed to resemble a natural pool with rocks and effusive plants, plus horse riding, and nature and birding hikes led by an on-site naturalist guide, Otto Calvo.

You don't have to wander far to spot the wildlife. White-faced monkeys, toucans, bright red poison-arrow frogs, peccaries, and ocelots all inhabit the surrounding terrain, and you can encounter many fabulous species while hiking or riding along the forest trails. Ducks and geese waddle freely through the grounds, and there's a rare green macaw and boxer-hound for good measure. The country hacienda also produces yucca, banana, papaya and pineapple, and has an experimental fish farm (the fish—tilapia, an East African species much favored for its delicate flavor—may find their way onto your dinner plate). The 50-hectare private forest reserve abuts the Children's Eternal Rainforest Reserve. Highly recommended. Rates: $76 s/d, $86 t.

FORTUNA AND VICINITY

Fortuna, the gateway to Arenal volcano, is a pleasant and picturesque little town dominated by the perfectly conical volcano, which lies about six km to the southwest. The town lies at the very foothills of Arenal; from here, the road begins its gradual ascent around the north side of the volcano to Tabacón Hot Springs and Lake Arenal. Fortuna is thriving on the tourist traffic passing through, and the growing choice of decent hotels includes budget options and some great bargains. Fortuna, however, gets crowded on weekends and it would be wise to book ahead. By the time you read this, there'll undoubtedly be more options.

Sights
There's nothing whatsoever in town to see except, perhaps, the village church on the west side of the soccer field.

About five km east of town is the **Catarata Fortuna,** a pretty waterfall that is worth the drive. The falls are reached by taking the paved road to Chachagua (0.7 km south from Cabinas Rolopz) to the turnoff. The falls are signed at regular intervals along a rocky road that combines with a series of hills (slippery as ice when wet) to fox all but the most hale of 4WDs. Eventually you'll have to abandon your vehicle and continue on foot uphill three-fourths of a kilometer, then negotiate a slippery and precipitous trail (20 minutes' walk) that leads down a steep ravine to the base of the cascade. The dirt-and-rock road, meanwhile, continues along the foothills of the Cordillera de Tilarán to La Tigra—a pleasingly scenic drive. Four-wheel drive is definitely recommended. An excellent way to reach the waterfall is on horseback.

Jungla y Senderos Los Lagos (tel. 479-9126), south of town, on the road to the volcano, is a small private nature reserve and quasi-theme park: a large *finca* that includes 400 hectares of primary forest through which five km of trails wind intestinally, providing views of Arenal, Tenorio, and Miravalles volcanoes. You can rent horses ($3 per hour) and paddle boats or water bicycles ($1 for 30 minutes) to

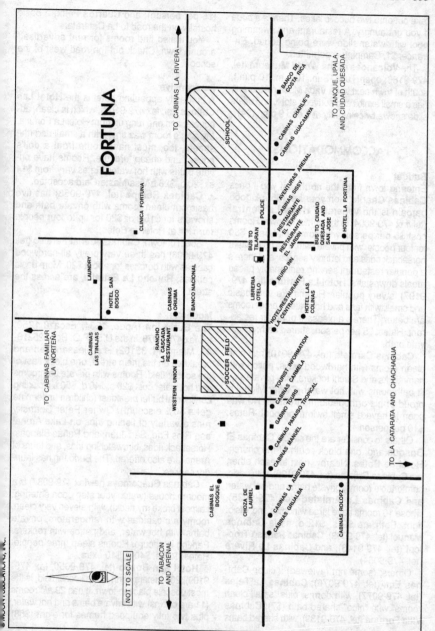

FORTUNA

TO CABINAS LA RIVERA

TO TANQUE, UPALA,
AND CIUDAD QUESADA

SCHOOL

- Banco de Costa Rica
- Cabinas Charlie's
- Cabinas Guacamaya
- Aventuras Arenal
- Cabinas Sissy
- Restaurante El Terruño
- Restaurante El Jardín
- Police
- Bus to Ciudad Quesada and San José
- Hotel La Fortuna

Clinica Fortuna

Bus to Tilaran

Laundry

Hotel San Bosco

Cabinas Oriuma

Banco Nacional

Rancho La Cascada Restaurant

Cabinas Las Tinajas

Western Union

TO CABINAS FAMILIAR
LA NORTEÑA

Libreria Otelo

Burio Inn

Hotel-Restaurante La Central

Hotel Las Colinas

SOCCER FIELD

Tourist Information

Cabinas Carmela

Gabino Tours

Cabinas Paraiso Tropical

Cabinas Manuel

TO LA CATARATA AND CHACHAGUA

Cabinas El Bosque

Choza de Laurel

Cabinas La Amistad

Cabinas Grialba

Cabinas Rolopz

TO TABACON
AND ARENAL

NOT TO SCALE

© MOON PUBLICATIONS, INC.

take out onto two bucolic lakes. There's a *soda* if you get hungry. A restaurant and swimming pool with water slide were being added. Entrance: $1. Camping is permitted.

The **Volcanoes of the World Museum** (tel. 479-9186; open Tues.-Sun. 10 a.m.-10 p.m.), south of town next to La Vaca Muca restaurant, has a small exhibit and souvenir store, and offers slide shows twice nightly at 6 and 9 p.m. ($4).

ACCOMMODATIONS

Budget
Entering town from the northeast you'll pass **Cabinas Charlie's** on your left ($5). A good bargain is the venerable **Hotel La Central** (tel./fax 479-9004) in the center of town. Rooms cost $5 per person with communal bath; $30 for four people, with private bath. The hotel offers horseback rides and laundry service, and there's a popular restaurant serving reasonably priced meals downstairs. **Hotel La Fortuna** (tel. 479-9197) is very popular. Rooms are very basic and small, with fans and hot water. Larger rooms are better. There's a pleasant open-air restaurant. Rates: $5 per person, shared bath; $9 private bath.

Cabinas Carmela (tel. 479-9010) has nine clean rooms with hardwood walls, patios with hammocks and Sarchí rockers, plus private skylit bathrooms with hot water. Owner Miguel is proud of his orthopedic mattresses. He was soon to have a small swimming pool. Rates: $10 per person.

Others to consider are the simple **Cabinas El Bosque** and, one block south of the church, **Hotel de Botes.** Nearby, next to each other, are **Cabinas Grijalba** (tel. 479-9129), with basic, comfortable rooms, private baths and hot water; and **Cabinas La Amistad** (tel. 479-9035), whose 10 rooms have large windows and lots of light. Both are $9 s, $12 d, as is **Cabinas Manuel** (tel. 479-9069), **Cabinas Paraíso Tropical** (tel. 479-9143), and **Cabinas La Rivera** (tel. 479-9084).

Others, (some not reviewed) include **Cabinas Emi** (tel. 479-9076); **Cabinas La Tejas** (tel. 479-9077), with dorms, plus "small clean rooms" with "nice" shared bath ($7); **Cabinas Villa Fortuna** (tel. 479-9139), with shared baths ($6 per person); and **Cuartos Felix,** a basic hostelry on the road to La Catarata.

You'll also find rooms for rent advertised around town. Check out the road west of the school.

Inexpensive
A modestly appealing hotel is the **Hotel Las Colinas** (tel./fax 479-9107), which is clean, adequate, and one rung up from Hotel La Fortuna. My single room was tiny, with a small bed (the sheets, too, must have come from a doll's house) and cheap furniture. Rooms have private baths with hot water. Rates vary from $14 s, $20 d, $28 t; Visa/MasterCard accepted.

Cabinas Rolopz (tel. 479-9058) has five basic but clean rooms with private bath and showers for $15 s or $20 for up to four people (turn left at Hotel de Botes).

South of town, **Cabinas Arenal Paraíso** (tel. 479-9006) has three very pretty all-hardwood cabinas with porches for about $20. More basic cabinas, **Rancho La Estrella,** are across the street.

Moderate
The **Burio Inn** (Apdo. 1234, Escazú 1250, tel./fax 479-9076; in the U.S., P.O. Box 025218-47, Miami, FL 33102) is a pleasant bed and breakfast on the main street, one block east of the soccer field. Rooms with private bathrooms and hot water cost $20 s, $40 d, $50 t, including continental buffet breakfast (children under nine get a 50% discount). Owner Peter Gorinsky runs a variety of fishing trips on Lake Arenal and Ríos Frío, San Juan, and Peñas Blancas. Horseback rides, birdwatching trips, and tours of Arenal are also offered. The Burio Inn has laundry service.

Cabinas Guacamaya (tel./fax 479-9087) is a modern house (watch your step upon entering; I almost broke my neck!), with eleven very clean, roomy a/c cabinas with refrigerators, private baths with hot water, and patios with rockers. Parking is secure. Rooms sleep three people. Rates: $25 s, $40 d, $10 extra.

Hotel San Bosco (tel. 479-9050, fax 479-9109), 200 meters north of the soccer field, is the most upscale place in town. It has 29 a/c rooms (11 are cabins) with private baths and hot water, plus two fully equipped homes for eight ($68)

and 14 people ($104). A two-story annex offers verandas, plus a *mirador* above for viewing the volcano. A pool was being added. Rates: $24 d, cabins; $45 d, rooms; $60 d, suite.

Kitty-corner to San Bosco is **Cabinas Las Tinajas** (tel. 479-9145, leave a message), with four very handsome rooms with attractive tiled floors. Modern and clean, with lots of light and private baths with hot water. Beds boast beautiful hardwood frames and headboards. Rates: $25 s, $30 d, including tax.

Less attractive but pleasant and roomy is **Cabinas Oriuma** (tel./fax 479-9111), with six large rooms for four people, plus two doubles with private bath, hot water, fans, and a common balcony with views of the volcano. Rates: $25 d, $40 quad.

Cabinas Rossi (tel./fax 479-9023), about two km south of Fortuna, offers 16 simple but pretty white-and-blue cabinas with private baths and hot water; one has a full kitchen and sky-lit bathroom. Rooms are light, and vary in size. "Immaculate and comfortable," reports a reader, but walls are "see-through" thin. There's a tiny restaurant plus kiddies' pool and swings. Rates: $20 s, $26 d, $34 t, including breakfast.

The **Hotel Rancho Corcovado** (tel./fax 474-4090) is a cabina-style property with pool and souvenir store on a working farm about 200 meters west of Tanque, five km northeast of Fortuna. The 30 rooms and five suites are described as "clean and cheery," and an open-air restaurant overlooks two pools and a small lake. Fishing is offered, as well as horseback riding. If the screech of howler monkeys sounds too close for comfort, fear not. It's merely Errol Flynn, the hotel's quite tame pet, just one of several beasts and birds in the "animal refuge." Rates: $45 d. A private airstrip was planned.

Six km south of Fortuna is **Montaña de Fuego** (tel. 479-9106), whose fistful of handsome hardwood cabinas sit on a hillock with splendid views of the volcano from a veranda enclosed in glass. The finishing touches were being made when I passed by. Rates: $40 d; $33 for four people in an older cabin. The owners offer horseback trips to hot springs and lava flows.

Upscale
Las Cabanitas (Apdo. 5, San Carlos 4417, tel./fax 479-9091) is an elegant, modern-style

hotel with 30 cozy and comfortable wooden cabinas surrounded by lawns with trim borders, about two km east of Fortuna. Each bungalow has two double beds or one queen-size bed, plus private bathrooms with hot water. The hotel has a swimming pool, tennis court, laundry service, and bar and restaurant with *palenque*-style dining room. You can relax on your porch and watch the volcano erupt. Rates: $75 d. Perhaps it's overpriced.

Camping
There are several options for camping south of town. You can camp at **Fiesta del Mar** restaurant, opposite the cemetery, or, near the cemetery, at **Ojo de Agua** and also at **Finca de Cito,** one kilometer south of Fortuna. About seven km south is **Casa de Campo** ("Camping House," tel. 479-9006), surrounded by cattle pasture. You can rent horses here. A little farther uphill, on the right, is the **Centro Campero las Palmas** (tel. 479-9106), with camping and rooms for five people.

Food
I liked the quaint **Choza de Laurel** (tel. 479-9077, fax 479-9178), a rustic Tican country inn with cloves of garlic hanging from the roof and an excellent *plato especial* (mixed plate) of Costa Rican dishes ($4). Grilled chicken ($2-6) and *casados* ($3) are other good bets. The **Restaurante La Central** is trustworthy (steaks and seafoods from $5). I enjoyed a granola and banana breakfast here.

The soaring thatch-roofed **Rancho La Casada Restaurant** dominates the town square. Its menu boasts *típico* dishes, plus pastas ($3) and burgers ($2).

Other recommended options include **Restaurant La Fortuna** and the popular **Restaurant El Jardín,** opposite each other in the town center, where you can eat for less than $5 (*casados* cost $2.50). Pizza recently has come to town, too, in the form of **Restaurant Pizza Italian.**

One of the best bets going, though, is **El Catalán,** about nine km north of town on the Muelle road. Despite the restaurant's down-at-heels looks, the Spanish cuisine is excellent. Owner Alex Castellón boasts that his paella is the "number one in Costa Rica," and well it may be! He even serves real *sangría*. Alternately, head-

ing south to the volcano, stop off at the rustic yet atmospheric **La Vaca Muca** (just beyond Cabinas Rossi) for good *típico* dishes (average $5). Within shouting distance is **Restaurante Rancho La Pradera,** a handsome, tall thatched *palenque* with Sarchí oxcart as decor. The **Restaurante Marisquería Los Lagos,** about 1.5 km farther, also provides for dining alfresco under a canopy.

Souvenirs
Fortuna has several excellent stores, including a gallery next to Librería Otelo with marvelous Guiatil pottery and high-quality crafts. **Paraíso Tropical** has a good display of locally made jewelry.

BUS SCHEDULE FROM FORTUNA

6:00 a.m.	. . . . Ciudad Quesada via Muelles
6:30 a.m.	. . . . Ciudad Quesada via Los Angeles
7:30 a.m.	. . . . Ciudad Quesada via Chachagua (very slow)
8:00 a.m.	. . . . . . Tilarán (connects to Monteverde at 12:30)
9:00 a.m.	. . . . Ciudad Quesada
9:30 a.m.	. . . . Ciudad Quesada (from Tilarán)
10:00 a.m.	. Ciudad Quesada (from San Rafael de Guatuso)
1:30 p.m.	. . . . . San José (direct via Fortuna from Guatuso)
2:30 p.m.	. . . . San José (direct)
3:15 p.m.	. . . . Ciudad Quesada (from Tilarán)
4:00 p.m.	. . . . Tilarán via Arenal
6:00 p.m.	. . . . San Rafael de Guatuso via Tanque

---

Tours
There's no shortage of tour options, including hiking, horseback riding, fishing and other trips with professional English-speaking guides. A full-day Caño Negro tour—mostly a river trip down the Río Frío—averages $45. Several places in town have signs reading Tourist Information; most also can arrange horse and bike rentals. Among the many providers are **Sunset Tours** (tel. 479-9199, fax 479-9099); **Aventuras Arenal** (tel./fax 479-9133); **Tipical Tours** (tel. 479-9004; fax 479-9045) and, next door, the **Tourist Shop** (tel. 479-9096); the self-proclaimed **tourist information office** (tel. 479-9058), south of the soccer field. **Paraíso Tropical** offers a cloud forest trip, plus trips to Caño Negro and also hot springs on the higher, middle slope of Arenal volcano, including dinner at Tabacón. It also has a horse stable, and Thomas, the American guide, was planning to offer water-skiing on the lake.

The store behind the *veterinario,* on the north side of the gas station, also rents bikes. Horse stables are about two km, on the left, and at **Los Lagos,** about four km south of Fortuna en route to Arenal. **Rapid Rivers of Costa Rica,** next to La Choza Laurel, arranges trips on the Sarapiquí, as well as mountain bike and kayak trips. Alvaro Castro offers a three-day "Nicoya Tour Express" ($60; ask at the Hotel La Central).

You may be approached on the street by so-called guides. The local chamber of commerce warns tourists "not to take tours or information off the street." Instead, it urges you to use tourist offices, hotel services, etc. If you need recommendations, contact **AMITUFOR** (tel. 479-9077, fax 479-9091), the Association of Small Tourist Businesses of Fortuna.

Services
You'll find a **Banco Nacional** on the east side of the soccer field and a **Banco de Costa Rica** as you enter town from Tanque. The Financiera office (tel. 479-9041), next to Rancho La Cascada, has a dollar exchange and **Western Union** service (open Mon.-Fri. 8 a.m.-4 p.m., Saturday 8 a.m.-noon). The **police station** is on the right as you enter town from the east. The **Clínica Fortuna** is two blocks northeast of the gas station. A laundry service operates opposite Hotel San Bosco. Restaurante El Jardín has a **public phone** with international access.

Getting There
Buses depart San José via Ciudad Quesada daily at 6:15, 8:40, and 11:30 a.m. from the Coca-Cola bus station (Calle 16, Avenida 1/3; Garaje Barquero, tel. 232-5660). Buses from Ciudad Quesada depart from the Parada Municipal (tel. 460-0326) at 6 a.m. and 3 p.m.; a separate bus departs at 5 and 9:30 a.m. and 1, 3, and 6 p.m., returning from Fortuna at 6, 7, 9:30, and 10 a.m. and 1, 2:30 and 4 p.m.

The Hotel San Bosco runs a shuttle bus to San José daily at 2 p.m., and to Tamarindo at 8 a.m. The Pura Natura shuttle service operated by Saragundí Specialty Tours (tel. 255-0011, fax 255-2155) departs San José at 7 a.m. (arrives Fortuna at 1:30 p.m.; $12). A second shuttle bus departs Puerto Viejo for La Fortuna at 9:30 a.m. ($9), and another from Liberia via Arenal at 3 p.m. ($18).

You may be able to fly to Fortuna by the time you read this.

TABACÓN HOT SPRINGS

At the base of Arenal volcano, 13 km southwest of Fortuna, is Tabacón Hot Springs, where steaming waters of the Río Tabacón tumble from the lava fields and cascade alongside the road. A dip here is supposedly good for treating skin problems, arthritis, and muscular pains. You can either experience this in style at the Tabacón Resort, or try the more funky (if penny-pinching) route via a booth on the north side of the road—100 meters downhill from the resort—that charges entrance ($2) to a 100-meter section of the river where shallow bathing pools are backed by rainforest. There are toilets and changing rooms but no towels.

Tabacón Resort

This delightful Spanish colonial-style *balneario* (bathing resort) features five natural mineral pools (27-39° C/80-102° F) and natural hot springs set in exotic landscaped gardens. The main stream (hot) and a side stream (cool) have been diverted through the grounds in a series of descending pools of varying temperatures, and steam rises moodily amid lush beautifully landscaped vegetation. Even adults laugh as they whiz down the water slide! You can sit beneath a 20-meter-wide waterfall—like taking a hot shower—and lean back inside the falls, where it feels like a sauna (warns my friend Gregg Calkin: "Ladies often misjudge the force of the falls and if they are wearing suits without straps they can find their tops joining their bottoms very quickly, making a clean breast of things, so to speak.") The complex also has an indoor hot tub, plus a restaurant (meals $5-12) and three bars, including a swim-up bar in the main

pool. Towels, lockers, and showers are available for a small deposit. Massages ($18 per hour) and mud pack treatments complete the picture. "We LOVED Tabacón, and this coming from serious tightwads!" reports a reader. You'll fall in love with Tabacón by night, too, when a dip becomes a romantic indulgence . . . and a jaw-dropping experience if the volcano is erupting. It could well be the most popular place in Costa Rica judging by the tour buses outside. Entrance: $12 ($9 after 6 p.m.). Open 10 a.m.-10 p.m.

Hotel rooms have long been in planning but were no nearer fruition in April 1995 despite existence of a slick brochure boasting about the hotel facilities (Apdo. 181, San José 1007, tel. 222-1072, fax 221-3075).

ARENAL VOLCANO

As picture-perfect as volcanoes come, this one looks as if it were plucked from its own picture postcard. Volcán Arenal (1,633 meters) is a perfect cone. It's also Costa Rica's most active volcano and a must-see on any tourist's itinerary. Arenal was sacred to pre-Columbian Indians (it is easy to imagine sacrifices being tossed into the inferno!), but it slumbered peacefully throughout the colonial era. On 29 July 1968 it was awakened from its long sleep by a fateful earthquake. The massive explosion that resulted wiped out the villages of Tabacón and Pueblo Nuevo, whose entire populations perished. The blast was felt as far away as Boulder, Colorado.

Although it hasn't erupted with any serious force in the past 20 years, it is regarded as one of the world's most active volcanoes. Its lava flows and eruptions have been constant and on virtually any day you can see smoking cinderblocks tumbling down the steep slope from the horseshoe-shaped crater that opens to the northwest, west, and southwest, or, at night, watch a fiery cascade of lava spewing from the 140-meter-deep crater. Some days the volcano blows several times in an hour, spewing house-size rocks, sulfur dioxide and chloride gases, and red-hot lava. The best views are from the Arenal Observatory Lodge (see below), although a designated viewing point en route to the lodge

can be reached by ordinary car and is sign-posted from the main road two km south of Tabacón. One trail leads atop a lava flow from 1992 that is still steaming and will take years to cool completely (follow directions to Arenal Observatory Lodge—see below—and two km after fording the river, park on the grassy clearing on the right; the trail begins here). *Hiking too close to the volcano is not advisable.* A sign at the base reads: Volcano influence area. Do not exceed established security limits. If you notice abnormal activity, run away from the area and report it to the closest authority.

Guides

Hotels in Fortuna can arrange guides. Guides are also available in Tabacón, Tilarán, and Nuevo Arenal. Most guides take tourists up the western slope above Tabacón to a point at about 1,000 meters' elevation. Signs in Spanish warn of the dangers of climbing any higher.

One guide, Gabino Hidalgo, leads hiking trips ($38) to the very rim of the volcano for the truly adventurous, foolhardy, and somewhat suicidal! Hidalgo has led dozens of treks to the summit with tourists in tow. The trek takes about six hours. He follows a trail up the eastern slope which he claims is "ninety percent safe." About 400 meters from the summit, Hidalgo pauses long enough to ascertain whether or not an eruption is imminent. Hikers stay "sheltered" by a large rock before the rush to the summit. The volcano's active vent is on the western side, and the normal easterly wind blows much of the effluvia westward. Explosions and eruptions, however, occur on all sides. **Be warned:** *The volcano is totally unpredictable, and there is a strong possibility of losing your life.* In 1988 a U.S. tourist was killed when hiking to the rim. As another writer has pointed out, you also risk the lives of Red Cross personnel who must look for your body. *Not* recommended.

Tours

Costa Rica Sun Tours (Apdo. 1195, Escazú 1250, tel. 255-3418 or 255-2011, fax 255-4410 or 255-3529) offers a series of two- and three-day tours to Arenal with nights at the company's Observatory Lodge (see below). A two-day tour with a local guide costs $110 upward, depending on number of passengers; two-day tours with a bilingual naturalist guide goes for $165 upward, including a hike and canoeing on Lake Chato, plus an optional horseback ride. Departures Monday to Friday. A three-day tour combines Arenal with a visit to Caño Negro National Wildlife Refuge, in the northern lowlands ($280). Another combines Arenal with a day cruise in the Gulf of Nicoya with a night at the Hotel Fiesta in Puntarenas and a visit to the Observatory Lodge ($280). The company also offers an Arenal Volcano Night Tour Tuesday, Thursday, and Saturday ($69).

Most other tour operators in San José and local hotels can arrange volcano tours.

Accommodations

Arenal Observatory Lodge (Costa Rica Sun Tours; Apdo. 1195, Escazú 1250, tel. 255-3418 or 255-2011, fax 255-4410 or 255-3529; direct tel./fax 695-5033; for reservations, tel. 257-9489, fax 257-4220) is a modern, rustic lodge on a macadamia farm, with immaculate views over the lake and volcano, which looms menacingly only two km to the north. A deep valley safely separates the lodge from the volcano. A stay here should prove one of your most cherished memories of Costa Rica. The lodge—which was built in 1987 as an observatory for the Smithsonian Institution and the University of Costa Rica—is operated by Costa Rica Sun Tours. The dining room and outside terrace have floor-to-ceiling windows facing the volcano's south-west slope, dark with recent lava spills.

The Observatory Lodge is surrounded by a densely forested, 120-hectare private reserve. The rainforests to the southwest join the Mon-teverde Cloud Forest Preserve and abound with wildlife. Trails lead to Cerro Chato, a lagoon-filled extinct crater. The Lava Trail offers "howler monkeys, good birding, dangerous lava." A fear-some fer-de-lance *(terciopelo)* snake is exhibited in a cage near the trailhead, so you know what to watch out for! The lodge also offers horseback rides ($5 per hour), fishing and boat tours ($25 per hour), 8:30 a.m. lava flow guided walk and Night Lava Tour ($10), and canoeing on Lake Chato (free).

Accommodation is bunk-style in modern wooden alpine chalets surrounded by pine trees. Five cabins have private baths and hot water. Home-cooked meals are served family-style in

the dining room. The lodge is closed one week in April and July each year for scientific monitoring. Rates: $49 s, $61 d, $72 t, including meals; $1.50 for day visits. Children's discounts are offered.

Getting There: The lodge is reached by a rough and rocky dirt road from the Arenal-Fortuna road, about four km southwest of Tabacón Hot Springs; a road sign reads, "1 km Parqueo." It's nine km to the lodge. A large orange sign gives information and directions at a Y-fork (if in doubt, follow the pylons). From here, you must cross the 50-meter-wide and fairly deep Río Agua Caliente (beyond the river, take the left at another fork where a sign reads "Macadamia"; a road to the right at the Y-split leads to Tilarán). Four-wheel drive is definitely recommended, though ordinary sedans can usually ford the river. If you don't have 4WD, you can leave your car at Fortuna and take a local jeep-taxi to the lodge. The lodge provides minibus transfers from San José ($150 one-way, split between passengers).

Camping

Camping is allowed at the western base of the volcano, on the road to Arenal Observatory Lodge, reached by turning hard left at the first Y-fork (described above). There are no facilities. Heed the warning signs. Do not camp any closer to the volcano! Note that tour buses park here, too.

SAN RAFAEL DE GUATUSO

From Tanque (seven km east of Fortuna), the road continues northwest to San Rafael de Guatuso, on the Río Frío. Five km north of Tanque the road enters rolling countryside and gradually deteriorates, with more and more potholes. Drive with caution! The road may have been paved by the time you read this.

There is little of interest in San Rafael de Guatuso (often simply called Guatuso), the center of the local canton, which exists almost entirely on cattle ranching and subsistence farming. Still, you can rent boats and guides for trips down the Río Frío to the Ujuminica Crocodile Farm, Caño Negro National Wildlife Refuge, and other points of interest nearby, not least

three Maleku Indian villages where you will be greeted enthusiastically. You'll note distinctive features among the cowboys roaming this snoozy town—a mix of Maleku Indian, Nicaraguan, and Spanish. Things are beginning to happen hereabouts, however, particularly now that the locals have formed the Asociación de Microempresarios Turísticos to put Guatuso on the map.

El Venado Caverns

About 15 km southeast of San Rafael, a dirt road leads south to the mountain hamlet of **Venado**, near which are limestone caverns with stalactites, stalagmites, and underground streams. The chambers weren't discovered until 1945, when the owner of the farm fell into the hole! The main mouth of the caverns is on the farm of Sr. Julio Solís, reached via a mud-and-gravel road that leads south from Venado uphill to Lake Arenal. You'll need to park at the farm, where a guide will lead you on a two-hour exploration of the caverns (about $3 entrance). You'll need sturdy footwear, a flashlight, and ideally a safety helmet. Bats and tiny, colorless frogs and fish inhabit the caves, which also contain seashell fossils, and a "shrine" that glows luminously. Expect to get soaked and covered with ooze. **Cabinas Las Brisas** (tel. 460-1954), in the hamlet of Venado, is very basic. A **bus** departs Ciudad Quesada for Venado daily at 2 p.m.

La Paz Waterfall and El Arbol de la Paz

This narrow though magnificent waterfall plunges 50 meters into the jade-colored Río Celeste, whose waters are "dyed" a jewel-like turquoise by volcanic minerals. Be prepared for an exhilarating though daunting hike but muddy terrain. Guides in Guatuso will take you on horseback through the rolling countryside and then into misty primary forests until you reach the towering El Arbol de la Paz ("Peace Tree"), one of the oldest and largest trees in the nation, dedicated by former President Oscar Arias Sánchez in 1989 as a symbol of peace. Two hours into your journey you reach a tiny hamlet where Doña Marielos Villalobos will refuel you with steaming coffee, tortillas, and fruit under a *ranchito* for the uphill hike through dripping forest to the waterfall.

GUATUSO INDIANS

"We were of 12 communities until the Nicaraguans searching for rubber came to our land and fought with us," Eliécer Velas Alvarez, a member of the El Sol tribe of the Guatuso clans of Corobicí Indians, told reporter Wendy Schmidt.

Only three of the tribal communities—El Sol, La Margarita, and Tongibe—survived the withering encroachments of the last few centuries; the Nicaraguans slaughtered the men and took the women and children back to their homeland, where Bishop Lorenzo de Tristan reported seeing them sold into slavery. In 1783, the Nicaraguan bishop journeyed into the Guatuso region—the first European to do so—to found a mission and convert the Indian clans to Catholicism.

About 400 of the natives survive on the Tongibe reservation *(palenque)* on the plains at the foot of Volcán Tenorio, near San Rafael, on land ceded to them by the government in the 1960s. Today, they are mostly farmers who grow corn and a type of root called *tiquisqui.*

Only one generation ago Guatuso Indians strolled through San Rafael wearing only loincloths made of cured tree bark, called *tana.* These lowlands once rang with the sound of women pounding away at soggy *tana* bark, like metal-beaters hammering gold.

"When I was a little girl, we used *tana* cloth and nothing else," recalls Rebecca Lizondo Lizondo, a pure-blood Tongibe, who learned the art from her mother who, in turn, had learned from her mother. "This is how my grandmother would have made *tana,*" Rebecca explains, as she reaches for a slender strip of moist bark, lays it across a small wooden block, and raises a heavy mallet to beat the bark into thin tissue. Stripped of its outer casing, the bark is first soaked in a stream to render it soft and malleable. "The strips are then hammered to any degree of thinness desired," says Rebecca, striking quickly with a resounding rat-a-tat-tat. When the bark felt like soft corduroy felt, it was ready to be spread out to bleach and dry in the strong sun, then stitched together like leather.

Of course, no one wears *tana* these days. But the Guatuso Indians take great pride in their heritage. Most continue to speak their native dialect, Maleku. Radio Sistema Cultural Maleku airs programs and announcements in Maleku, and Eliécer Velas Alvarez instructs the youngsters in Maleku at the elementary school in Tongibe. Alvarez, reports Wendy Schmidt, "has to buy chalk and books and erasers from his own pocket," and when it rains the schoolroom floods.

The San Rafael area has many ancient tombs (the best place to see them is at Magil Lodge), and jade arrowheads and other age-old artifacts are constantly being dug up. The Guatusos developed jade ornaments and carvings, bowls of terra-cotta, and bows and arrows of *pejibaye,* a tree of the palm family.

Ujuminica Crocodile Farm

Among the newest attractions in the region is this crocodile farm on the banks of the Río Frío, about eight km north of Guatuso. You can see young caimans and crocodiles swimming around in pens. They're not raised for commercial reasons, but will be released into the wild as adults. *Ujuminica* is a Maleku Indian word meaning "crocodile fell in the trap." Until a few years ago, the area was favored as a place to shoot crocodiles; only a few of the antediluvian beasts survived the slaughter. In the wild, a female lays about 20 eggs a year, of which barely one percent survive. The farm attains a hatch and brood survival rate of 95%.

Accommodation at **Ujuminica Lodge** is available in rustic huts, and a Maleku Indian-style *palenque* houses a small restaurant serving homemade meals. Two garfish, also antediluvian leftovers, swim in an upturned boat that serves as a tank. Tours can be arranged at hotels in San Rafael, or in advance by calling La Central Hotel (tel. 460-0766) or ARA Agencia de Viajes (Apdo. 799, San José 1007, tel. 222-2900, fax 222-5173), which offers a choice of two three-day/two-night tours from San José that include visits to Ujuminica and Caño Negro (from $299 s, $229 d, per person). You can rent boats at Ujuminica for the journey downriver to Caño Negro.

Accommodations and Services

Albergue Tío Henry (tel. 460-2058) is a 10-room hotel above the local veterinary store;

each room has a double bed or two singles with shared bath and a balcony ($10). More spacious a/c doubles with private baths cost $18. Henry offers tours to Caño Negro, the Río Celeste, Venado, and Ujuminica.

There are at least three other places to stay: **Hotel Las Brisas** (tel. 460-2087), **Cabinas El Gordo** (tel. 460-2017), and **Cabinas Shirley** (tel. 460-2098).

The **Salon La Pista** is immediately on the right when you enter town from the east. Next door is the **Restaurante el Gordo**. The **Bar/Restaurante Turístico** is in the center of town and has been recommended for its *casado* (set lunch) for $2.

There's a Texaco **gas station** at a Y-intersection 27 km before San Rafael. You'll find a **Banco de Costa Rica** and **Banco Nacional** in San Rafael.

MAGIL RESERVE

Magil is a 414-hectare private farm protecting more than 280 hectares of virgin cloud forest on the flanks of Volcán Tenorio near Río Celeste de Guatuso. The property, 19 km southwest of San Rafael, is owned by Dr. Manuel Emilio Montero, former president of the Costa Rican Tourism Institute (ICT). His objective is to conserve the primary forest and the varied endangered species found on the refuge.

Magil Forest Lodge
Centerpiece is the Magil Forest Lodge, a rustic yet irresistibly appealing ecotourist lodge opened in September 1990 by President Rafael Ángel Calderón. The three-story lodge is made entirely of rough-hewn woods and magnificently adapted to its natural surroundings. It is set against the mountain slope overlooking a rushing stream, with wide views out over the lowlands. On three sides are cattle pasture; behind, mahogany and mountain cedar rise up the slope.

The forests provide a precious habitat for red-and-green and red-and-black poison-arrow frogs, monkeys, oropendolas, toucans, and at least 250 other bird species, including the very rare white eagle, which has found a safe refuge in the Magil forest. The especially lucky guest may spot a black leopard, a jaguar, or even a tapir.

The lodge is superbly managed by ever-friendly Oswaldo Castro and his wife Jessica. There are 12 rooms (four doubles, six quadruples, and two suites). Each four-person room has two singles and a bunk bed. All rooms have baths, toilets, closets, washstands, and writing desks, plus tiny verandas with hammocks and rockers. Rates: from $26 s to $80 for suites, including three meals.

The airy dining room features a massive rough-hewn dining table fit for a Viking feast (supposedly, it's the biggest one-piece table in Costa Rica), plus smaller tables made from *pilon* wood, a tight-grained, mauve-colored species as hard as a petrified log. Jessica prepares delicious, wholesome meals on an open-hearth stove. Surprise! There's even a television and a stereo, powered by a hydroelectric unit—driven by the transmission from a 1940 Chevy—that squats over the stream.

Oswaldo leads horseback rides, hikes, and butterfly walks into the forest. One horseback ride leads to waterfalls and boiling hot springs. A lookout point reveals a view as far away as the Solentiname Islands in Lake Nicaragua. The fit and hale can even climb the impressive massif of Tenorio.

Archaeological sites abound on the property. Only 50 meters downhill from the lodge is an interesting stone formation believed to be a collection of ancient tombs of Indian chiefs. The giant rocks have been cut into surreal shapes and slotted together like some great three-dimensional jigsaw puzzle. The stonemasons' precision was such that it is virtually impossible to slide a knife blade between them.

Dr. Montero has unearthed jade arrowheads and even a beautifully carved jade ornament now housed at the Jade Museum in San José. Local Tongibe Indians told Dr. Montero that they knew of the tombs and were concerned about their remaining intact. A small museum is being created to house the finds. Archaeology students from the National Youth Movement and the Canadian-based Youth Challenge International have begun excavations. The **Magil Archaeological Excavation Project** welcomes donations.

Information

Contact Hotel de Montaña Magil, Apdo. 3404, San José 1000, tel. 221-2825 or 233-5991, fax 233-3713 (in the U.S. c/o PCI Tours, 8505 N.W. 53rd St., Suite A-108, Miami, FL 33166, tel. 305-594-5678, fax 305-594-2149). **Costa Rica Temptations** offers three-day ($350) and four-day ($450) excursions to Magil (Apdo. 5452, San José 1000, tel. 220-4437, fax 220-2103).

Getting There

You reach Magil by a rough 19-km stone-surfaced road that begins immediately after you cross the steel bridge to Upala on the north side of San Rafael (a sign on your left after the bridge reads Hotel de Montaña "Magil"). The road deteriorates into a slippery mud track. The last kilometer is through pasture along a thin muddy trail that had me convinced I had lost my way and was trespassing on a farm (don't attempt this without a 4WD with high ground clearance). Keep going: You'll crest a hill with what looks like a simple farmstead to your right halfway up a slope. That's the lodge. There is no bus service.

UPALA

Upala, 40 km northwest of San Rafael de Guatuso, is a small agricultural town at the center of the local rice and dairy industries (82% of the working population is employed in agriculture). The town received plumbing only in 1976 and electrical power in 1978. It was recently linked by paved road running south to the Pan-American Highway. A bus runs daily to Caño Negro via Colonia Puntarenas; the road is appalling, and if you drive it, 4WD is strongly advised.

Upala is only 10 km south of the Nicaraguan border (the first settlers came from Nicaragua). Dirt roads lead north to Lake Nicaragua, but foreigners are not allowed to enter Nicaragua here or at any other point along the border except Peñas Blancas. If entering Upala by car, you'll be stopped by armed security personnel just before the bridge south of town. Don't be alarmed; it's a routine check for contraband. If you wish to enter Nicaragua, you'll have to continue west along the rough dirt road via Santa Cecilia to La Cruz (81 km).

UPALA EMERGENCY TELEPHONE NUMBERS

Red Cross	470-0080
Hospital de Upala	470-0181
Farmacia Upala	470-0047

Accommodations and Services

The **Cabinas y Restaurant Buena Vista** (tel. 470-0063) is on the right, north of and immediately after crossing the bridge. It has basic rooms for $4 per person, plus a large open-air restaurant overlooking the river. Across the road is the **Hotel Rosita** (tel. 470-0198), which also has basic rooms for the same price. The **Hotel Restaurante Upala** (tel. 470-0169) also has basic rooms with private baths but cold water only. Rates: $5 s, $7 d. It's near the bus station, as is **Cabinas del Norte** (tel. 470-0061). I've not seen inside this hotel, nor inside **Cabinas Buena Vista,** on the left as you enter town from Cañas, or the very basic **Hospedaje Rodriguez.**

There's a **Banco Nacional,** and the **police station** (Guardia Rural, tel. 470-0134) is on the left, 100 meters north of the bridge.

Getting There

Upala is served daily by express **bus** (five to six hours) from San José via Cañas and the Pan-American Hwy.; departs Calle 16 and Avenida 3/5 at 6:30 a.m. and 3 p.m. (call CNT, tel. 255-1932). Return buses depart Upala at 5 and 9 a.m. and 2 and 3:30 p.m. Local buses also link Upala with San José via San Rafael and Ciudad Quesada (departs Ciudad Quesada at 3:30 p.m.; returns from Upala at 9 a.m.); and from Cañas at 5:45, 9, and 11 a.m. and 2 and 5 p.m. (returning from Upala at 6, 9, and 11 a.m. and 1 and 4:30 p.m.). Buses also run daily to Caño Negro Wildlife Refuge when conditions permit.

Nothing of interest lies between San Rafael de Guatuso and Upala. If driving, note: The unpaved road is deeply rutted and provides a very uncomfortable ride for those without 4WD (I passed a bus and trucks stuck neck-deep in mud at one spot). Likewise, you can reach Upala by 4WD via a dirt-and-rock road from La Cruz

and the Pan-American Hwy. via Hacienda Los Inocentes and Santa Cecilia; or from Los Chiles via Caño Negro and Colonia Puntarenas.

Although there's no scheduled air service, there's an **airstrip** east of town just before the bridge over the Río Zapote; you can charter an air taxi from San José (see "Getting Around" in the On the Road chapter).

CIUDAD QUESADA TO PUERTO VIEJO

East from Ciudad Quesada, the road coils downhill through the rolling foothills to **Aguas Zarcas** ("Blue Waters"), a town with less appeal than its name. En route, you'll pass El Tucano Resort and Spa on your left (see special topic "Two Deluxe Resort Hotels").

La Marina Zoológica

This private zoo, opposite the gas station about three km west of Aguas Zarcas, houses jaguars, tapirs, agoutis, monkeys, and other mammal species, as well as birds from around the world. Although opened to the public in 1989, the owners have been taking in orphaned animals for more than 20 years, and today have more than 200 animals and birds, many confiscated by the government from owners who lacked permits to keep them. The zoo is nonprofit; donations are appreciated. Open 8 a.m.-4 p.m. daily. Entrance: $1.50.

Accommodations and Food

If you want to stay overnight in Aguas Zarcas and El Tucano is beyond your budget, try **Cabinas Adriana,** up the hill on the right, just before the church in the center of town. Basic rooms with shared bath cost $4 per person. The **Hotel La Violeta** (tel. 474-4015) is similarly priced for rooms with shared bath, but has private baths, too, for $8. Somewhere nearby is the **Hotel Pájaro Azul** (tel. 225-3479). The brochure suggests a very attractive, moderate lodge set in large grounds with a pool, sheltered outside dining area, and hammocks slung between trees. I couldn't find it!

LAGUNA DEL LAGARTO

This private reserve is about 45 km northeast of Aguas Zarcas, seven km beyond Boca Tapada via Pital along a gravel road. Turn right just north of Chiles, three km north of Aguas Zarcas. You can reach Lagarto by ordinary car, but 4WD is recommended. The reserve protects 500 hectares of virgin rainforest and bayou swamps harboring crocodiles, caimans, turtles, thousands of red-and-green poison-arrow frogs, as well as ocelots, sloths, and all kinds of colorful bird species. The University of Science and Technology of Latin America helps maintain the ecology of the area and uses the reserve for research.

The **Laguna del Lagarto Lodge** (Apdo. 995, San José 1007, tel. 289-5295, fax 289-5295) offers 20 rustic yet comfortable rooms in two separate buildings (18 with private baths, two with shared bath; hot water was being installed) on a hillock overlooking the lagoon, which resembles the bayou of Louisiana. Each has a large terrace with a view overlooking the San Carlos river and forest. A natural lake surrounds the lodge, which has two large decks where you can relax and sip cocktails (canoes are available, as are boat trips on the Río San Juan). There are miles of forest trails for hiking and horseback rides, plus a restaurant serving hearty Costa Rican meals. Reveille call—often the scream of howler monkeys—comes around 6:30 a.m. Don't fatten up too much, as crocodiles can be seen at night in the lagoon waiting for something tasty to pass by. Rates: $53 per person, including three generous buffet-style meals.

Universal Tropical Nature Tours (Apdo. 4276, San José 1000, tel. 257-0181, fax 255-4274) offers a three-day Laguna del Lagarto and San Juan River Boat Adventure ($285).

VENECIA TO LA VIRGEN

About 10 km east of Aguas Zarcas on the road from Ciudad Quesada is **Venecia,** two km beyond which a dirt track (accessible by hiking or 4WD) leads to **Ciudad Cutris,** an archaeologi-

cal site with pre-Columbian tumuli and hints that this was once a settlement with wide, well-ordered streets. The site has yet to be excavated and restored. The one hotel in Venecia is reportedly basic but clean and friendly. The bus from Ciudad Quesada will stop in Venecia (60 cents); or take the three and a half hour bus ride from San José ($2.50).

The road eastward passes the hamlet of Río Cuarto, from where a rugged dirt road to the right leads uphill to an impressive waterfall. About 12 km east of Venecia you reach a T-junction in **San Miguel**. The road to the right leads south to San José via the saddle of Poás and Barva volcanoes. About six km south of San Miguel is **Laguna Hule,** just before the hamlet of Cariblanco, which has a gas station. The lake, set in a dormant volcanic crater and reached via a rough dirt road, is surrounded by lush forest. Fisherfolk should bring their tackle. Four-wheel drive is recommended. One km farther south is **Colonia Virgen del Socorro.** (See special topic "Road Routes to the Lowlands").

Turn left at the T-junction in San Miguel for Puerto Viejo and the Llanura de San Carlos. The descent from San Miguel is sometimes dangerous, with sharp bends and steep drops; take one of the bends too fast and you'll end up amid fields of tropical fruits. Watch for cattle crossing the road.

La Virgen is gateway to the lowland plains. Here, the land flattens out and tropical fruit farms and banana plantations begin to appear. The Llanura de San Carlos extends north and east without a dimple. Rivers crawl sinuously across the landscape, vast sections are waterlogged for much of the year, and the waterways to this day remain a vital means of communication.

Accommodations and Food

If you don't mind bunk beds, I recommend **Rancho Leona** (tel./fax 711-1019 or tel. 710-6312) for its family atmosphere, surprisingly cosmopolitan menu, and eclectic decor that includes stained-glass windows, homemade Tiffany lamps, a kayak and oropendola nests hanging from the roof, and cushioned tree stumps for stools. Rancho Leona serves wholesome health food, including wholemeal bread, brown rice, and Italian dishes. The accommodations offered by Leona Wellingon and Ken

Upcraft, two charming hosts, are particularly comfortable. Both are artists, as the stained-glass work attests. Ken is also a kayaker and offers full-day kayaking trips on the Río Puerto Viejo. When you return, hop into the hot tub for a soothing soak. They plan to build geodesic domes as cabins on their large mountain farm. Rates: $75 with two nights' accommodations. Buses to/from Puerto Viejo will drop you off at the front gate.

La Virgen has a couple of other good restaurants, including **Restaurant Tia Rosarita,** and the **Centro Turisto Los Venados**—about one km north of La Virgen—which has a popular restaurant specializing in *chicharrones,* plus music nightly (it also has a small swimming pool and nature trails leading into a nature reserve).

A few kilometers beyond La Virgen, at Bajos de Chilamate, is **Islas del Río** (tel. 710-6898 or 233-0366, fax 233-9671) where owners Dr. Sonia Ocamp and Dr. Arturo Salazar offer 34 rooms in both a lodge and cement cabinas (from $42 d, with shared bath; $57 s with private bath) on seven hectares of forested property divided into tiny islets along the banks of the Río Sarapiquí. There's an open-air restaurant. Hikes, horseback trips, and all meals are included in the price. IYH members receive discounts.

Five km beyond La Virgen is **La Quinta de Sarapiquí Lodge** (Apdo. 11021, San José 1000, tel./fax 761-1052), a family-run venture on the banks of the Río Sardinal. Ten cozy rooms have private baths with hot water and ceiling fans. An a/c dining room and bar, plus a riverside trail for hikes and mountain bikes or horseback rides complete the picture. Birding is said to be particularly good, and past guests speak well of the food and "congenial atmosphere." Rates: $35 s, $45 d, $60 t.

SELVA VERDE

Selva Verde is a private reserve protecting some 192 hectares of primary rainforest adjacent to Braulio Carrillo National Park and the Organization for Tropical Studies' field station, La Selva. It's seven km west of Puerto Viejo de Sarapiquí, at Chilamate.

Selva Verde, founded in 1985, is owned by U.S.-based Holbrook Travel, which operates a

RAINFOREST LODGES AND RESERVES

PUERTO VIEJO
SELVA VERDE
EL GAVILAN
LA QUINTA
DE SARAPIQUI
RANCHO LEONA
LA SELVA
SARAPIQUI
ECOLODGE
LAS VIRGENS
TO CIUDAD QUESADA
LAS HORQUETAS
SAN MIGUEL
RARA AVIS
TO
PUERTO
LIMON
BRAULIO
CARRILLO
NATIONAL
PARK
32
120
VARA BLANCA
130
126
32
ALAJUELA
HEREDIA
SAN JOSE

0   15 km

© MOON PUBLICATIONS, INC.

nature lodge on the property. The lodge—one of the most impressive in the nation—is popular with academic and tour groups, so book well in advance. There's no advance warning sign, so keep your eyes open on the right if you're driving from San Miguel.

The reserve is renowned for its birdlife, including oropendolas, motmots, parrots, jacamars, and other exotic lowland tropical birds. Poison-arrow frogs are common and easily spotted amid the leaf litter. There's also a butterfly garden. Walking trails lead through the forests: trail maps are provided, and the lodge has a fine staff of naturalist guides. The Río Sarapiquí flows through

the property. Selva Verde Lodge offers trips up the river by canopied boat ($15), or you can rent canoes to explore on your own. Guided hiking ($24 for four hours; $36, six hours), horseback trips, and mountain bikes are also available.

Accommodations and Transportation

The superbly conceived and excellently run 45-room lodge—divided into the River Lodge and the Creek Lodge—is set in 20 acres of landscaped grounds on the banks of the Río Sarapiquí. It has a very comfortable, manicured feel. Thatched walkways lead between the luxury cabins, which are raised on stilts and constructed of beautiful hardwoods. All rooms are large, airy, and screened, with verandas for wildlife viewing.

You have a choice between cabins with private baths at the River Lodge ($60 s, $52 d) and slightly smaller but no less appealing rooms with shared bathrooms at the Creek Lodge ($55 s, $44 d, $39 t). Each room has two large single beds. Five new bungalows (each for four people: $74) were recently opened on separate grounds across the street. Rates include three meals and tax.

Highlights include a large, cozy library and games room, a conference room with scheduled lectures, and a new, larger dining room to replace the older, more crowded one. Meals are served buffet-style at set times. The lodge offers laundry service and provides rubber boots and oversized umbrellas.

Contact Selva Verde Lodge, Chilamate de Sarapiquí, tel. 710-6459. In the U.S., contact Costa Rican Lodges, 3540 N.W. 13th St., Gainesville, FL 32609, tel. 800-451-7111 or 904-373-7118, fax 904-371-3710.

Buses from San José to Puerto Viejo will stop at Selva Verde if you ask. Saragundí Specialty Tours (tel. 255-0011, fax 255-2155) operates a **Pura Natura** shuttle service, departing San José at 7 a.m. (one bus travels clockwise via Muelle, Chilamate, Puerto Viejo, Horquetas; another runs counter-clockwise, continuing to Fortuna).

PUERTO VIEJO AND VICINITY

Unbelievably, this small landlocked town was, in colonial times, Costa Rica's main shipping port. It lies at the confluence of the Ríos Puerto Viejo and Sarapiquí. Before the advent of the Atlantic Railroad linking the central valley with Puerto Limón on the Caribbean, cargo boats ferried goods down the Río Sarapiquí to Barra del Colorado and Puerto Limón. Much of the community today is dependent on the local banana plantations spreading westward from the Guápiles region.

Now that the contras' and Sandinistas' guns lie silent, you can follow the same route as colonial traders (the Río Sarapiquí was once called the contras' Ho Chi Minh Trail); you can still negotiate passage aboard a river launch, which will take you all the way down the San Juan to Barra del Colorado, Tortuguero, and Moín. Several hotels and nearby lodges offer one-day boat trips on the Sarapiquí through tropical wet forest that stretches north to the Río San Juan, linking the northern arm of Braulio Carillo National Park with the rainforests of the Nicaraguan lowlands. Fishing reportedly is good on the Río Sarapiquí, and there are plenty of crocodiles and river turtles, plus sloths, monkeys, and superb birdlife to see. Puerto Viejo is also the gateway to La Selva Biological Station and Rara Avis (see below).

The paved road ends in Puerto Viejo. From here, potholed rock-and-dirt roads push north to Pavas (10 km south of the Río San Juan), and a paved road leads south to Guápiles and the San José-Limón Hwy., where a sea of banana plantations has greedily swamped the land. The railways of the big banana companies opened up this region decades ago. The map tells the story. From Puerto Viejo east to Tortuguero National Park is a gridwork maze of dirt roads and rail tracks linking towns named Finca UCR, Finca Paulina, Finca Agua, Finca Zona Siete, and Fincas 1, 2, 3, etc.

Budget Accommodations
Cabinas and Restaurant Monteverde (tel. 766-6236) is 150 meters west on the right (the office is on the left, opposite the Ministerio de Agricola) and has six very simple but clean, well-maintained rooms with fans and hot water ($7 s, $10 d, $15 t). **Hotel Gonar** (tel. 766-6196) has basic rooms ($6 d, without bath; $9 with). **Restaurant/Cabinas La Paz** (tel. 766-6257) offers a choice of funky older rooms ($6 s, $10) and nicer, newer rooms ($8 s, $12 d), both with private bath.

Hotel El Antiguo (tel. 717-6901 ext. 205) and **Hotel Santa María** are both basic *pensiones* in the $4 per person bracket, as are Las Brisas and Gonzales, the latter above the hardware store *(ferretería)*.

Moderate Accommodations
Immediately west of the soccer field in Puerto Viejo is the modern **Mi Lindo Sarapiquí** (tel. 766-6281), with six clean rooms with private baths and hot water ($45 d, including breakfast) plus a pleasing open-air restaurant. Also in town is **Hotel Bambú** (Apdo. 1518, Guadalupe 2100, tel. 766-6005, fax 766-6132) with nine clean, modern rooms with ceiling fans, TV, and private baths with hot water. Rates: $45 d, including breakfast. It also has two self-sufficient apartments, plus a restaurant. Transfers ($20 per person) from San José can be arranged.

About four km southeast of Puerto Viejo is the **El Gavilán Lodge,** owned by Wolf and Mariamalia Bissinger. The rustic lodge is set in five hectares of landscaped grounds beside the river on 180 hectares of private reserve bordering banana plantations. A pet toucan called Pancho keeps guests company, and plenty of wild birds flock in and out. There are four rooms in the main two-story structure, with hardwood verandas and rockers, plus eight very basic, dark, dingy rooms with smaller bathrooms in two bungalows in the grounds. Simple meals are served in an open-air restaurant beneath a bamboo roof (no alcohol; bring your own). Rooms cost $30 per person, including breakfast. Lunches and dinners cost $8.

The lodge has horses for rent ($15 per person), or Manuel Sánchez, the youthful and irre-

pressibly conscientious manager, will guide you along the forest trails. Boat rides cost $20; or $50 down the Río San Juan to Barra del Colorado. Fishing trips are available. The filthy hot tub looked more fitting for reptilian reproduction than soaking when I was there (another report suggests this is still the case).

There is no telephone on the property. For reservations contact the Bissingers at Apdo. 445, Zapote, San José 2010, tel. 234-9507, fax 253-6556.

El Gavilán is confusing to get to. It took me almost two hours to find the elusive Holy Grail! Turn right at the sign for Río Frío just before entering Puerto Viejo from the west (there's a sign for El Gavilán on the corner, but it is very difficult to spot). About two km down the potholed road you'll see a sign for El Gavilán; turn left here. Immediately, you'll come to a T-intersection. Take the left fork and follow the winding road for one km until you come to a 90-degree bend, with a muddy lane leading straight on at the apex of the bend. The entrance for El Gavilán is 100 meters on the left down this lane. The Bissingers will arrange transfers from San José: $15 one-way/$20 roundtrip.

Accommodations North of Puerto Viejo
The Bissingers also own the **Oro Verde Station** (tel. 233-6613, fax 223-7479), accessible from Puerto Viejo by a two-hour journey down

the Río Sarapiquí ($40) and just 3.5 km from the Río San Juan. This very rustic lodge is surrounded by a 2,500-hectare reserve, some of it cleared but the majority still forested. Indian-style thatched huts offer simple accommodations for up to 40 people. One unit has four small dorm-style rooms with shared bathroom but no electricity: candles and kerosene lamps add to the reclusive and rustic atmosphere. Four two-room family-size cabins with private baths have kitchens, including propane stoves. Oro Verde is managed by Rafael "Chino" Molina, who is replete with knowledge on local lore, medicinal plants, and wildlife. Simple but tasty meals are served on an open-air dining terrace. Rafael and local guides lead fishing trips, trail walks, and explorations by dugout canoes through the rainforests, lagoons, and on the Ríos Sarapiquí and San Juan, just three km downstream. Rates: $195 per person, three-day package including meals, transportation, and lodging.

You'll find cheap cabinas in **La Trinidad**, a hamlet at the junction of the Río Sarapiquí and Río San Juan.

Food
The restaurant at **Mi Lindo Sarapiquí** has an extensive menu. **Pip's Restaurant** is also reportedly good. And the restaurants of **Cabinas Monteverde** and **Hotel Bambú** have both been recommended.

SHARKS IN THE RÍO SAN JUAN?

If you see a shark fin slicing the surface of the Río San Juan, you would be forgiven for thinking you've gone down with heatstroke—there *are* sharks in the freshwater river! The creatures, along with other species normally associated with salt water—tarpon and sawfish, for example—migrate between the Atlantic Ocean and the crystal-clear waters of Lake Nicaragua, navigating 169 kilometers of river and rapids en route. All three fish are classified as euryhaline species: they can cross from salt water to fresh and back again with no ill effects.

For centuries scientists were confounded by the sharks' presence in Lake Nicaragua. The lake is separated from the Pacific by a 19-km-wide chunk of land, and since rapids on the Río San Juan seemingly prevent large fish a clear passage from the Caribbean, surely, the thinking went, the lake must

have once been connected to one or the other ocean. Uplift of the Central American isthmus must have trapped the sharks in the lake.

Studies in the early 1960s, however, showed that there were no marine sediments on the lake bottom. Thus, the lake was never part of the Atlantic or the Pacific. (It was actually formed by a huge block of land falling between two fault lines; the depression then filled with water.)

Then, ichthyologists decided to tag sharks with electronic tracking devices. It wasn't long before sharks tagged in the Caribbean turned up in Lake Nicaragua, and vice versa. Incredibly, the sharks, and presumably the tarpon and sawfish, are indeed able to negotiate the rapids and move back and forth between lake and sea. Don't ask me how! Perhaps sharks are descended from salmon?

Services

There's a **Banco Nacional** opposite the soccer field, and a **Banco Anglo Costarricense** at the east end of town. The **post office** and **police** (Guardia Rural) are opposite the Banco Anglo Costarricense. The road to the right leads to a wharf, where **ferry boats** leave for El Gavilán Lodge and the Río Sarapiquí. You'll find a **taxi stand** on the main street. **Red Cross:** tel. 710-6901, ext. 212.

Tours on the Río Sarapiquí

Evelio Solano, who runs the dockside *soda* (open 5:30 a.m.-6 p.m.), can assist with one-way passage or day-trips on the long narrow boats that ply the river. A regular water-taxi departs the dock at 11 a.m. for Oro Verde and the Río San Juan ($2). Several locals are happy to act as guides and to hire out their boats; William Rojas (tel. 766-6260) has been recommended, and has a boat for up to 10 passengers. Expect to pay $200 or more for a journey all the way down the Río San Juan to Barra del Colorado and Tortuguero National Parks.

In addition to trips offered by the lodges mentioned elsewhere in this section, the following operators offer river trips: **Costa Rica Expeditions** (Apdo. 6941, San José 1000, tel. 257-0766, fax 257-1665) has a one-day whitewater trip (class III), May through mid-December, on the upper Sarapiquí; $65 per person. **Ríos Tropicales** also offers whitewater trips; classes I-II and class III (Apdo. 472, San José 1200, tel. 233-6455, fax 255-4354). **American Wilderness Experience** (P.O. Box 1486, Boulder, CO 80306, tel. 303-444-2622 or 800-444-0099, fax 303-444-3999) offers a 10-day paddling trip through the northern lowlands, including the Ríos Sarapiquí, Tres Amigos, San Juan, Carlos, and Toro ($1676, including accommodation at wilderness lodges). **Swiss Travel Service** (tel. 231-4055) in San José offers a two-hour boat trip on the Río Sarapiquí, ending with lunch and a nature hike at Selva Verde Lodge. Operates Tuesday and Thursday. **Turavia** (Apdo. 458, San José 1150, tel. 296-1223, fax 220-2197) offers a similar boat tour ending at El Gavilán Lodge.

Getting There

Buses (four hours) from San José depart from Avenida 11, Calles Central/1 daily at 7, 9 and 10 a.m., and 1, 3, and 4 p.m., via the Guápiles Hwy. and Horquetas. You can also take a slower bus through Heredia from the same bus stop at 6:30 a.m. and noon (this bus returns to San José via La Selva and continues to Rara Avis). Buses also reportedly leave from Calle 12, Avenidas 7/9 at 6:30 a.m. and 2 p.m., returning at 7:30 a.m. and 12:30 p.m.

Saragundí Specialty Tours (tel. 255-0011, fax 255-2155) operates a **Pura Natura** shuttle service, departing San José at 7 a.m. (arrives Puerto Viejo 9:30 a.m. via Horquetas, $20; another bus arrives 5:15 p.m. via Chilamate, $23).

LA SELVA BIOLOGICAL STATION

South from Puerto Viejo, the newly paved road leads past La Selva ("The Jungle"), a biological research station. It's run by the Organization of Tropical Studies (OTS), an international educational body founded in 1963 by almost 50 universities and museums to foster understanding and rational use of rainforests and other natural resources in the tropics. The station, which includes laboratories, teaching facilities, and experimental plots, is centered on a 1,500-hectare biological reserve—mostly premontane rainforest—linked to the northern extension of Braulio Carrillo National Park. La Selva, four km south of Puerto Viejo, is the most important of OTS's stations worldwide, and leading scientists and graduate students work here year-round.

Both day ($18 entrance) and overnight visitors are welcome with notice: impromptu appearances are not welcome! Only 65 people at a time are allowed in the reserve, including scientists. It is often booked solid months in advance. Hence, reservations are essential, even for day visits (see below).

Almost 50 km of trails snake through the reserve. Many are no more than dirt trails, which deteriorate to muddy quagmires after heavy rain. Annual precipitation is over 400 cm; even the driest months (February and March) each receive almost 20 cm of rain! Rubber boots or waterproof hiking boots are essential. So, too, is adequate raingear (an umbrella is extremely useful for photographers wishing to protect their cameras). Some trails have boardwalks, and most are marked with distance markers at reg-

ular intervals. The gift shop sells maps, as well as *Walking La Selva* (R. Whittall and B. Farnsworth), a handy guide to the trails. Keep a wary eye out for snakes. A good rule of thumb to remember is "Watch your step; look up when you stop." In other words, follow the ground with your eyes at all times while walking.

Birds are particularly profuse. More than 400 species have been identified here. Several birders have seen more than 100 species in a single day—an astonishing number considering the difficulty of spotting birds in the dank forest. An annual Audubon Society "Birdathon" is held, with money for each species seen in the one-day event pledged to a fund aimed at protecting Braulio Carrillo.

Accommodations

La Selva has comfortable yet dormitory-style accommodations with communal bathrooms. It has a few singles and doubles, but researchers and students get priority. In fact, tourists are allowed to stay here only on a space-available basis. Reservations are essential. Rates: $88 per person, including three meals served family-style in the dining room (researchers half-price, students less). Word is that meals are served bang-on time and latecomers get the crumbs. Laundry service is offered. For reservations, contact the OTS, Apdo. 676, San Pedro 2050, tel. 236-6696 or 240-6696, fax 240-6783. Day visits are $15, including lunch (tel. 710-6897).

The Murrillo family offers very rustic lodging in bunk beds at **Sarapiquí Ecolodge** (morning tel. 766-6122, fax 766-6247), a ranch house on an 80-hectare farm across the river from La Selva. Rates: $15 per person, including three meals. Hiking, horseback riding ($5 per hour), and boating ($20 per hour) are available. Shared bathrooms.

Getting There

The OTS operates a shuttle van from San José on Monday, Wednesday, and Friday ($10), space permitting (researchers and students have priority). A van shuttle also operates between La Selva and Puerto Viejo Monday through Saturday. Taxis from Puerto Viejo cost about $4.

Buses from San José will drop you off at the entrance to La Selva (see "Getting There" under "Puerto Viejo," above for schedules). You'll need

to walk from the road to La Selva (two km). There are no bellboys: pack light!

LAS HORQUETAS

Las Horquetas, 17 km south of Puerto Viejo (and a similar distance north from the Guápiles Highway, on the Caribbean lowlands), is the gateway to one of Costa Rica's most famous private reserves: Rara Avis. Horquetas, which lies 500 meters west of the road, is a sleepy little one-street hamlet. The **Hotel Buenos Aires** is very basic (about $5).

En route from Puerto Viejo you'll pass through **El Tigre,** where MUSA, a women's cooperative, sells native medicinal herbs and herb products such as chamomile and rosemary shampoos; you can tour their farm. The almost ruler-straight road between Guápiles and Horquetas and north was recently paved its entire length. The road had a "military" barrier and civil guard checkpoint. If it's still there, don't be fazed by the camouflage jackets and M-16s. Just hit the gas pedal and smash your way through! *I'm kidding!* Stop, show your papers, and all will be fine. It's a legacy of the Nicaraguan civil war days when security was tight around here. Today they search for drugs, contraband, illegal immigrants, etc. No sweat!

RARA AVIS

This unique 1,280-hectare rainforest reserve, founded in 1983 and abutting Braulio Carrillo National Park and La Selva, contains a rustic lodge, a more comfortable lodge, a biological research station, and a host of novel projects designed to show that a rainforest can be *economically* viable if left intact, not cut down. Projects include producing exportable orchids and ornamental air-plants, seedlings of popular timber trees for reforestation projects, macadamias, the rare *Geonoma epetiolata* palm, philodendrons for wicker, *pacas* for meat, and ecotourism.

"The objective," says founder Amos Bien, a former administrator of La Selva (see above), "was to demonstrate that we could take a piece of rainforest . . . and make it economically productive and safe from the chainsaw for the indefinite fu-

three-toed sloth

GERRY ELLIS / SOCIETY EXPEDITIONS

ture. We hope to be a model for many other similar projects, but more importantly to change the way people think about endangered resources." Bien hopes to show the surrounding communities that a cottage industry can be borne by the forest, so that they see the forest not "as something they must cut down in order to earn a living, but rather as the source of that living." You, too, can support the project by buying shares in Rara Avis SA Corporation ($1800 for three shares; it hopes eventually to pay dividends).

The two lodges sit at about 600 meters in elevation, 15 km from Las Horquetas along a mud trail that is probably the worst you'll experience in Costa Rica. Even 4WDs won't make it uphill when the road is halfway bad. You're transported there either on a cart (with cushioned seats) pulled by a tractor, or on horseback. Sometimes, the trail is so muddy that the tractor gets bogged down (there are two rivers to cross; these are often so high that you have to leave the tractor behind and cross by a swinging rope bridge) and even the horses can't make it. Then you have to hike. *The journey is not comfortable!* Some people I've spoken to consider the experience of getting there part of the fun; others have stated that no reward is worth hours of bumping about on the back of an open flatbed followed by an hour tramping knee-deep in mud in the pouring rain (Rara Avis gets up to a phenomenal 5.5 meters of rain a year; it has no dry months).

The area has remained pristine because of its inaccessibility, and the rewards are tremen-

dous. More than 330 bird species—including snowcap hummingbirds, great green macaws, toucans, blue-and-gold tanagers, and umbrella birds—inhabit the reserve. There are jaguars, tapirs, monkeys, anteaters, coatimundis, butterflies galore, and a zillion other wildlife species. Until recently you could thrill to the experience of dangling six stories high in the air, marveling at the superabundance of species in the forest canopy from Dr. Donald Perry's "Automated Web for Canopy Exploration," a radio-controlled aerial tramway designed for treetop exploration. Perry's book, *Life Above the Jungle Floor* (Simon & Schuster, 1986), describes his AWCE project. Alas, the tram no longer operates (Perry has built another aerial tram for tourists near Guápiles; see "San José to Limón" in the Caribbean Coast chapter), but you can view the canopy from two platforms ($35, including two-hour guided hike), including one at the foot of a spectacular double waterfall. A canopy walkway was to be installed.

Trails range from easy to difficult. Rubber boots are highly recommended: hiking the muddy trails is akin to wading through soup (the lodge has boots to lend for those with U.S. shoe sizes of 12 or smaller). Recently, many of the trails have been improved so as to prevent the erosion and root damage prevalent in earlier years.

Accommodations

El Plástico, the more rustic of two lodges, is named for an abandoned jungle prison colony

where the prisoners slept under plastic tarps. The lodge was formerly the penal-colony headquarters. Restored and upgraded, it now features flush toilets and showers plus accommodations for 30 people in bunk beds in seven rooms. Rates (two nights): $90 per person; students $30 a night. Extra nights, $36. Costa Rican citizens and International Youth Hostel members receive a 30% discount.

A little more comfortable is the **Waterfall Lodge,** three km farther into the forest at the end of the corduroy road. It features eight corner rooms, each with a private bathtub and hot water, and a wraparound balcony overlooking the rainforest and lowlands. Only 200 meters away is a spectacular 55-meter double waterfall—the site of the canopy tramway. **Note:** You can swim at the falls, but be aware that flash floods can pour over the break unannounced, as happened in the spring of 1992, when three Canadians were swept to their deaths. Rates: $85 per person d, $75 t, $65 quad.

Room rates include lodging, meals, naturalist guide, and tractor or horse transport from Las Horquetas. A two-night minimum stay is required. You can rent horses ($20). Reservations are essential: Apdo. 8105, San José 1000, tel. 253-0844, fax 221-2314.

Getting There

Buses from San José depart Calle 12 and Avenida 9 daily at 7 a.m. via the Guápiles Highway (do *not* take the bus via Heredia). Buses also run later, but you'll need the 7 a.m. bus to meet the transfer to Rara Avis from Las Horquetas. Get off at **El Cruce para Horquetas,** where a taxi—arranged through Rara Avis's San José office—will take you to Las Horquetas. If driving, you can leave your car in a parking lot at the Rara Avis "office" in Las Horquetas. This is a wooden shack and stockade 200 meters along the most northerly of two dirt roads into Horquetas.

The tractor leaves Las Horquetas daily at 9 a.m. You should be in Las Horquetas by 8:30 a.m. It's a four-hour journey, although delays are not unusual. You can rent horses ($10) for later arrivals, but not after noon; you must walk the last three km. (The tractor leaves Rara Avis for Las Horquetas at 2 p.m. Buses for San José leave Las Horquetas at 7 and 11:30 a.m., and 3 and 5:15 p.m.)

RÍO FRÍO

Virtually the entire route between Puerto Viejo and the Guápiles Hwy. is lined with banana trees that brush up against the road. Rutted dirt roads and rail-tracks criss-cross the land, connecting plantation settlements and banana processing plants with names such as Finca UCR, Finca 1, Finca 3, etc. **Río Frío** is the main settlement and is reached by a dirt road that runs eastward for nine km from the Puerto Viejo-Guápiles road (the turnoff is two km south of Horquetas). There's an airstrip, and because the town sat astride the main route to Puerto Viejo before the new paved road was laid, Río Frío is still visited by buses.

The Guápiles Hwy. is 12 km south of Río Frío.

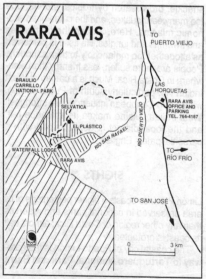

Accommodations

In town, there's the basic **Pensión Ana.** Not reviewed. Also not reviewed, but close at hand, is **Morpho Lodge** (Apdo. 3153, San José 1000, tel. 221-9132, fax 257-2273), a rustic lodge ($15) with dorm bordering Braulio Carrillo National Park. Trails lead into the jungle. Apparently you cook for yourself. More salubrious accommodation may be available by the time you read this.

CATHY CARLSON

THE CARIBBEAN COAST

INTRODUCTION

Part of the Mosquito Coast, which reaches from Puerto Barrios in Guatemala to Colón, Panamá, Costa Rica's Caribbean coast extends some 200 kilometers southward from Nicaragua to Panamá. The coastal zone—wholly within Limón Province—is divided into two distinct regions. To the north of Puerto Limón is Tortuguero ("Land of the Turtles"), a long, straight coastal strip of broad alluvial plain separated from the sea by a series of freshwater lagoons. South of Puerto Limón is the Talamanca coast, a narrow coastal plain broken by occasional headlands and coral reefs and backed by the looming Cordillera Talamanca, whose mountains encroach progressively southward. *Talamanca* is a Miskito Indian word meaning "place of blood," referring to the seasonal slaughter of turtles.

Life along the Caribbean coast of Costa Rica is fundamentally—almost comically—different than in the rest of the country. What few villages and towns lie along the coast are ram-shackle, browbeaten by tropical storms, one too many earthquakes, and the curse of an economic miasma. Here, among the hurricanes and swamps and jungles, life itself is perceived as altogether too melancholy to take seriously. People are more sullen, less friendly than elsewhere in Costa Rica. Much is a cameo of West Indian life, particularly south of Puerto Limón, where Afro-Caribbean influences are strongest, West Indian cuisine makes its influence felt, and the local dialect is richly spiced with a parochial patois English.

SIGHTS

Limón Province boasts a higher percentage of its area preserved in national parks and reserves than any other region of Costa Rica; almost half its coast is protected.

The coastal city of Puerto Limón is the gateway to **Tortuguero National Park** and **Barra**

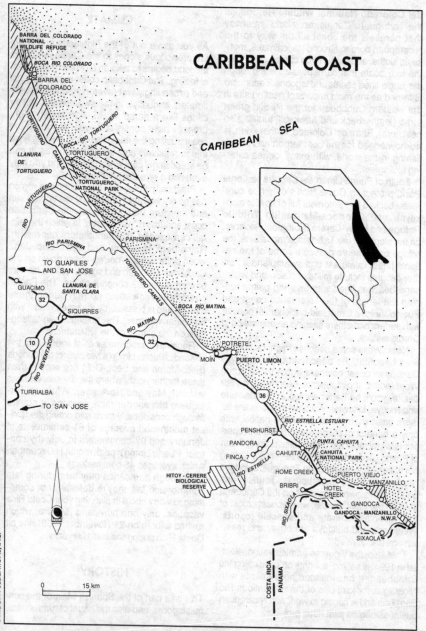

CARIBBEAN COAST

CARIBBEAN SEA

BARRA DEL COLORADO NATIONAL WILDLIFE REFUGE

BOCA RIO COLORADO

BARRA DEL COLORADO

TORTUGUERO CANALS

LLANURA DE TORTUGUERO

BOCA RIO TORTUGUERO

TORTUGUERO

TORTUGUERO NATIONAL PARK

RIO TORTUGUERO

RIO PARISMINA

PARISMINA

TO GUAPILES AND SAN JOSE

GUACIMO

32

LLANURA DE SANTA CLARA

TORTUGUERO CANALS

BOCA RIO MATINA

SIQUIRRES

10

RIO MATINA

32

RIO REVENTAZON

POTRETE:

MOIN

PUERTO LIMON

TURRIALBA

TO SAN JOSE

36

RIO ESTRELLA ESTUARY

PENSHURST

PANDORA

PUNTA CAHUITA

FINCA 7

CAHUITA

CAHUITA NATIONAL PARK

HITOY-CERERE BIOLOGICAL RESERVE

RIO ESTRELLA

HOME CREEK

PUERTO VIEJO

BRIBRI

HOTEL CREEK

MANZANILLO

GANDOCA

GANDOCA-MANZANILLO N.W.R.

RIO SIXAOLA

SIXAOLA

COSTA RICA
PANAMA

0   15 km

© MOON PUBLICATIONS, INC.

del Colorado National Wildlife Refuge via the Tortuguero Canals, an inland waterway that parallels the coast all the way to the Nicaraguan border. Crocodiles, caimans, monkeys, sloths, and exotic birds can be seen from the tour boats that carry passengers through the jungle-lined canals and lagoons. Tortuguero is famed as the most important nesting site in the western Caribbean for the Pacific green turtle (leatherback and hawksbill turtles also nest here); Barra del Colorado, farther north, is acknowledged for the best tarpon and snook fishing in the world, with many lodges catering to anglers.

South of Puerto Limón are Cahuita National Park, protecting Costa Rica's only true coral reefs (backed by rainforests full of howler monkeys), and Gandoca-Manzanillo Wildlife Refuge and Hitoy-Cerere Biological Reserve, on the slopes of the Talamanca mountains; the refuge and reserve preserve some of the nation's finest rainforest and swamplands. Further delights include miles of black- and white-sand beaches lined with swaying palms running the length of the Talamanca coast and Puerto Viejo, a funky, laid-back hamlet popular with surfers and others seeking an immersion in Creole culture.

Note: While some beaches might be considered beautiful, the beaches of Costa Rica's Caribbean coast nowhere equal those of the West Indies. If picturesque beaches are your desire, you'll be better served in Guanacaste and Nicoya. Likewise, accommodations are far more basic than elsewhere in the nation, with only a handful of moderately upscale properties (several more are under construction). South of Puerto Limón, modest cabinas—many lacking hot water—are the norm; in Tortuguero, lodges range from basic to first class. Tourism has been much slower to take off on the Caribbean than on the Pacific coast, which boasts most of the nation's moderate and upscale resorts. Weekends and holidays are busy, and reservations are advised.

That said, the Figueres administration, elected in 1994, is setting its sights on developing the Caribbean. It has initiated agreements with Nicaragua for joint use of the contentious Río San Juan and is hoping to work with Nicaraguan businessmen on joint hotel projects.

CLIMATE

As you move out of the highlands and down the precipitous slopes to the Caribbean plains the land begins to take on a distinctly equatorial feeling. The Caribbean coast is generally hot and exceedingly wet (averaging 300-500 centimeters annually); in the swamps the still air clings like a damp shawl. Fortunately, light breezes blow consistently year-round on the coast, rustling the mangroves and helping keep things relatively cool along the shores. It can be surprisingly cool when cloudy, and you may even find a sweater necessary.

Practically speaking, the Caribbean region has no dry season. Nurtured by the tropical sun and moisture from sea winds, the Caribbean coast endures a "wet season" in which the rainfall can exceed 100 centimeters per month. Rains peak May-Aug. and again Dec.-Jan., when polar winds—nortes—bear down on the Caribbean seaboard and sudden storms blow in, bowing down the coconut palms. The Pacific coast receives almost no rain during these months and is blessed (by the same winds) with fine clear weather. The heaviest rain falls inland on the slopes of the Talamancas.

Regional microclimates exist even within the lowlands. Puerto Limón's two distinct dry periods (Feb.-March and Sept.-Oct.) are shorter than those farther north, where the dry seasons can last into May and November. Whereas Tortuguero has shorter rainy seasons, it suffers through considerably more rain during the rainiest months: an average of 61 centimeters in January and 97 centimeters in July (by contrast, Puerto Limón's peak month is December, which averages 46 centimeters).

Although hurricanes may form during late summer and fall, they're definitely not something to worry about in planning your Costa Rica vacation: only one hurricane (Martha, which rushed ashore on 21 November 1969) has hit Costa Rica during the last 100 years.

HISTORY

This was part of the Spanish Main of the conquistadores, and also the haunt of rumrunners,

gunrunners, mahogany cutters, and pirates, mostly British, attracted by the vast riches flowing through colonial Central America. Between raids, buccaneers found safe harbor along the wild shorelines, where they allied themselves with local Indians. Because of them, the Caribbean coast was never effectively settled or developed by the Spanish.

In 1502, Columbus became the first European to set foot on this coast when he anchored at Isla Uvita on his fourth and last voyage to the New World. Twenty-two years later, Hernán Cortés mapped the coast. The records the early Spaniards left tell of contact with indigenous tribes: subsistence hunters and farmers, and skilled seamen who plied the coastal waters and interior rivers in carved longboats in excess of 12 centimeters (Cortés even mentioned Aztec traders from Mexico visiting northern Costa Rica in search of gold).

Recent evidence suggests that settlement along the coast dates back almost 10,000 years. The indigenous culture was condemned, however, that Jehovah might triumph over local idols; Spanish priests rabidly destroyed much of the documentation and tangible evidence of the indigenous realms of gods and deities. One group, the Votos, apparently had female chiefs. Shamans, too, were an important part of each tribal political system. Their influence is seen today in the National Museum in San José, where pottery from the region bears unusual symbols believed to have been painted by shamans under the influence of hallucinogens.

Cacao was grown here in the late 17th century and was Costa Rica's first export from Costa Rica, an activity financed by well-to-do citizens of Cartago. This made now-derelict Matina such an important town that Fort San Fernando was built here in 1742, the first and last bulwark erected by the Spaniards in the Caribbean zone. Despite this, the region remained virtually uninhabited by Europeans until the Atlantic Railroad was built in the 1880s and a port at Limón was opened for coffee export in 1890 (see special topic "Coffee, Bananas, and Minor Keith" in the Introduction chapter).

In 1882, the government began to offer land grants in the region to encourage migration. The cultivation of bananas was also encouraged, and the plantations prospered until the 1930s, when they were hit by disease: Panamá blight, mold, and sigatoka (see special topic "Bananas: Friend or Foe?").

ECONOMY

Not until the end of the 19th century, with the new railroad and the banana industry, did development begin to take hold. Bananas and cacao for export brought a relative prosperity. With the demise of the banana industry beginning in the 1930s, the region went into decline. During the 1960s, plantations began to grow bananas again using more advanced technologies, and the industry now dominates the region's economy. The government has assisted these efforts with new infrastructure and services, resulting in a rapid population increase during 1960-90.

The port development complex in Puerto Limón, along with its sister port of Moín, is the chief driving force of the urban economy. Beyond the city's hinterland, most people make their livings from farming or as plantation laborers, and there are few and only small industries: sawmills, ceramics, cabinetmaking, bakeries. Fishing is a quite prosperous local industry. A few small farmers cling to a precarious living growing cacao (a blight in 1979 wiped out most of the commercial crop), whose plump, bobbinlike pods are everywhere in the region. Others make a living from lobster fishing. Increasingly, however, locals are being drawn into the tourism industry as guides and hotel workers. And in Cahuita and Puerto Limón, every second person seems to be building rooms for rent or a restaurant, and local entrepreneurship is thriving.

PEOPLE

More than anywhere else in Costa Rica, the peoples of the Caribbean reflect a mingling of races and cultures. There are Creoles, of mixed African and European descent; black Caribs, whose ancestors were African and Caribbean Indian; mestizos, of mixed Spanish and Amerindian blood; people of purebred Spanish descent; more Chinese than one might expect; and, living in the foothills of the Talamancas, approximately 5,000

NO-SEE-UMS

I have been lucky on my visits to the Caribbean and suffered few mosquito attacks. However, come prepared! The insect population is formidable. Chiggers and mosquitoes flourish here, and their hordes have been reinforced by sandflies—no-see-ums—which you don't even know are on you until you rub an idle hand across your thigh and swatches of blood appear (later come the red lumps that can drive you crazy with itching). No-see-ums have shaped the architecture of the coast: since they fly only a few feet above the ground, houses—generally, rickety, jerry-built shacks—are built on stilts (a good precaution, too, against snakes, which are also abundant).

Bribrí and Cabecar indigenous peoples.

The early settlers of the coast were British pirates, smugglers, logcutters, and their slaves who brought their own Caribbean dialects with words that are still used today. During the late 19th century, increasing numbers of English-speaking Afro-Caribbean families—predominantly from Jamaica—came to build and work the Atlantic Railroad and banana plantations. After Panamá's War of Independence in 1903, a further influx of Afro-Caribbeans settled along the coast, grouping themselves into regions that they named after natural landmarks and after themselves. They built their homes by the creeks, which became property boundaries known by the family name (maps today still bear their names: Ben Humphries, Kelly, Duncan, Louis Hudson, and so on). Their dialect is replete with lilting phrases familiar to travelers in the West Indies: "whoppen" is a common greeting; adiós gives way to "all right" or "okay" used as farewells.

The black costeños (coast dwellers), who form approximately one-third of Limón Province's population of 220,000, have little in common with the sponyamon, the "Spaniard man" or highland mestizo who represents the conservative Latin American culture. The Rastafarians—specialists in coolness, composure, and witty repartee—one meets in Cahuita and Puerto Viejo typify the difference.

GETTING AROUND

Except for the Turrialba-Siquirres-Puerto Limón and San José-Guápiles-Siquirres highways, the coastal highway south of Puerto Limón, and the canals of Tortuguero, routes throughout the region are generally in poor condition.

Until the late 1970s, the southern Caribbean coast was virtually isolated from the rest of Costa Rica, as the only route was by slow train or canoe. With the opening of the coastal road the region is now readily accessible, although roads may be washed out during heavy rains (as in 1991 and 1992, when at least 17 bridges were washed away). Local roads are quite deteriorated and often impassable because of flooding.

Behind the shores north of Puerto Limón, sluggish rivers snake through swampland and flooded forests. The winding inland waterways have stymied would-be road builders (a few roads have penetrated to the northern frontier far inland of the coast but they are often impassable except for brief periods in the dry season). Safe anchorage is also denied to marine traffic by strong coastal currents and onshore winds as well as by the lack of protective banks or reefs. Hence, travel is via outpost traders resembling the African Queen (they make the mail and pulpería runs daily), and motorized dugout canoes called cayucos or canoas. The canoes are the main means of getting about the swampy waterways that meander from lagoon to lagoon through the dense, mostly uninhabited jungles between Puerto Limón and the Nicaraguan border.

INFORMATION

The **Pococí Regional Tourist Association** information office (tel. 710-2323) is in Guápiles.

SAN JOSÉ TO PUERTO LIMÓN

The two routes to Puerto Limón are both fantastically scenic. The first is a mountainous switchback road via Turrialba and Siquirres. Although sometimes washed out by rains and landslides, the two-lane road is little trafficked. It follows the powerful Río Reventazón. An hour out of San José, the valley narrows and the road snakes through sheer-sided canyons once negotiated by the Jungle Train. Beyond Turrialba, the road opens onto a hillocked plain before joining the main Puerto Limón highway at Siquirres.

A speedier and far more traveled—and even dangerous—route is via the Braulio-Carrillo (or Guápiles) Highway, built in 1987. The drive (160 km) takes two and a half hours. Leaving San José along Calle 3, the road turns into a divided expressway that climbs Volcán Barva. You'll pay a 200-*colones* ($1.20) toll just before Braulio Carrillo National Park. Beyond the ominously unlit Zurquí Tunnel, you emerge in the mist-enshrouded cloud forest of the park.

Drive carefully! The road coils downhill through thick clouds, landslides are frequent, and even in the worst conditions, Costa Rican drivers display the most insane recklessness. With luck, there'll be no clouds and, if so, you are blessed with perhaps the most staggeringly scenic drive in the country.

The road descends through the forested hills to whale-backed sugarcane fields and cattle ranches, which give way to flatlands of banana plantations and, now and again, farms cultivating macadamia nuts. Here and there, nestled in the bush, are zinc-roofed houses built on stilts with wide verandas and shuttered windows, and adjacent shacks where cacao beans are spread out to dry. In quiet little villages—Las Lomas, La Junta, Cimarrones (the Spanish word for intransigent runaway slaves)—black people begin to appear with greater frequency, letting you know you are now in the Caribbean proper. Once you reach the flatlands, watch your speed. It's easy to go zooming along above the speed limit. Speed cops laze beneath shade trees in wait of heedless tourists.

The turnoff for Moín and the boats to Tortuguero National Park is three km before Puerto Limón, just past the RECOPE storage tanks on your left.

PARK PRACTICALITIES

Río Danta Lodge (Apdo. 10980, San José 1000, tel. 223-2421, fax 555-4039) is actually within the boundaries of Braulio Carrillo National Park (see "Braulio Carrillo National Park" under "Northeast from San José" in Central Highlands chapter). Six duplex structures are surrounded by eight hectares of forest and landscaped grounds overlooking the Río Danta. Rooms have private bathrooms, fans, hot water, plus balconies with rockers for quiet meditation. The lodge also offers a bar and family-style restaurant, plus pool and sundeck. Trails lead along the riverbanks.

Mariposario Los Heliconios (tel. 226-2570), 48 km northeast of San José, immediately east of the Quebrada Grande ranger station, is a nature reserve with live butterfly exhibits. Visitor facilities were being built. Half a kilometer farther is the . . .

RAINFOREST AERIAL TRAM

The Rainforest Aerial Tram (Apdo. 592, San José 2100, tel. 257-5961, fax 225-8869; in the U.S., 65 Walnut St. #301, Wellesley Hills, MA 02181, tel. 617-239-3626, fax 617-239-3610) is a "must-experience" on a 354-hectare private nature reserve on the northeastern boundary of Braulio Carrillo National Park. Constructed at a cost of more than $2 million by Dr. Donald Perry, author of the fascinating book, *Life Above the Jungle Floor,* the tram takes visitors on a guided 90-minute excursion ($47.50) through the rainforest canopy, home to two-thirds of all rainforest species. The site possesses one of the richest canopy communities in the world. It's a 1.3 km ride on any of 20 cable cars that travel

150 meters apart (each holds six people, including a guide armed with walkie-talkie to communicate with other cars and the tram operator, who stops the tram upon request) in the manner of a ski-lift, giving you a truly unique vantage of the "spectacular hanging gardens of the rainforest roof." The 30-meter-tall F-shaped towers were lifted into place by helicopters of the Nicaraguan Air Force, which took off their machine guns and pitched in. The mysteries of the lush canopy unfold with each passing tree.

The tram, the first of its kind in the world (and an astounding achievement), serves Perry in his continued scientific investigations, but most important, it is an educational vehicle, so to speak. Perry hopes that by showing people the wonders of the rainforest, the tram will inspire people to help save the forests (he originated the concept after building the "Automated Web"—funded by a Rolex Award For Enterprise—near Rara Avis to support his research). "We liked the idea of putting people in cages, rather than animals," he says. There are short loop trails for hikes. Bird excursions are also offered (bring a flashlight for nocturnal excursions). The fee ($47.50) includes as many tram rides as you wish. Don't miss this vital experience!

The office in San José is on the corner of Avenida 7 and Calle 7. The tram is on the main Guápiles Highway. The parking lot is on a dangerously fast bend, eight km east of the Río Sucio (four km past the ranger station, 15 km west of Guápiles). There were no advance signs when I called in in March 1995. Keep your speed down or you could leave tire marks as you brake hard into the parking lot! The Guápiles bus (see below) will drop you off at Chichorronera la Reserva or "El Teleférico" ($1.50). You're driven from the parking lot 1.5 km along a gravel road to the visitor center (you must walk a brief trail and rope bridge over a river).

Accommodations and Food

Cabins were being planned; students and researchers get preference. Anticipated rates (per person): $125 s, $100 d, $80 t, including night excursions and unlimited trips on the tram. A restaurant serves breakfast, lunch, and dinner (about $7).

Free coffee, fruit drinks, and cookies are served to day visitors.

MORPHO RESERVE

A couple of kilometers east of the Aerial Tram, you'll pass the turnoff to the left for Horquetas, Río Frío, and Puerto Viejo (see "Puerto Viejo and Vicinity" in the Northern Lowlands chapter). Continuing straight, one km brings you to the Río Corinto, where a turnoff to the right leads 800 meters (4WD only) to the Morpho Reserve. Keep your eyes peeled for the turnoff. The reserve maintains trails through a rainforest (good for birding) and a butterfly garden (hence the name) where you can watch *mariposas* of a thousand hues flitting about the heliconias and other luxuriant plants. Swimming and fishing are other options.

The reserve doubles as a science center: medicinal plant science and guide-training are among the dozens of courses offered. Rattan and other products "harvested" on the reserve are sold to locals to foster crafts and conservation. It's popular with schoolchildren and students, some of whom are researching an inventory of species. A "frog garden" (the first in the nation) and organic farm are planned. A Frog Trail is one of many that lace the reserve.

The very rustic 10-room **Morpho Lodge** (tel. 221-9132) is on the rocky banks of the Rí Corinto, a sometimes turbulent river that forms a natural swimming pool in front of the lodge. Rates: $20 per person. Meals cost $7. Two-day/one-night packages cost $99, including transportation and meals. Also, a **tent-camp** offers top-quality tents (lamp-lit at night) on wooden platforms and shaded from rain. No sleeping bags here . . . instead, beds with fresh cotton sheets and night tables. A "backpackers special" ($15) includes lodging, guided tour, and use of a kitchen.

A one-day all-inclusive tour from San José costs $60. Entrance: $10; guided tours, $10 extra. Morpho Reserve has an office in San José on the third floor of Edificio Murray, at Calle 7, Avenidas 1/3 (tel. 221-9132).

BOSQUE LLUVIOSO

About six km before Guápiles at Km 56, and 400 meters east of the bridge over the Río Costa Rica, a road to the right leads three km via Rancho

Redondo to Bosque Lluvioso (Apdo. 10159, San José 1000, tel. 224-0819, fax 225-1297), a private 170-hectare rainforest reserve, reached via a rope-bridge, with well-manicured trails that provide a chance to see poison-arrow frogs, sloths, oropendola birds and other arboreal critters without any of the discomforts associated with more rugged locales. Guided walks are offered, but you can walk yourself (none of the trails are strenuous), for the trails are fitted with self-guided information posts that correspond to information in a guide booklet ($2). One trail leads past herbs: lemon grass, rosemary, etc. Another—the Hidden Pond Trail—leads to a pool. The ranch also has a fruit plantation and orchid garden, plus a visitors center and a restaurant where you may regain your strength (lunch, $8). Admission: $12 (children, $6). Closed Wednesday, low season.

Accommodations and Food

Bosque Lluvioso owners Alfredo and Maria Gallegos were planning to build cabinas.

Meanwhile, **Casa Río Blanco** (Apdo. 241, Guápiles 7210, tel. 710-1958 or 710-6982, fax 710-6161; in the U.S., tel. 713-292-6796, fax 713-292-7681), on the banks of the turbulent Río Blanco near Patricia, about two km east of the Río Costa Rica (turn right and follow the dirt road 1.5 km), has five pleasant rooms—two in the main lodge, plus three cabins—with private bath with hot water. From your rooms you can look directly out into the rainforest canopy and the river, bubbling away below and reached easily by trails. Owner Thea Gaudette, a former Audubon guide, will make you feel right at home. She'll also happily lead you by the hand on birding and nature hikes (including nocturnal frog walk) to hidden waterfalls and a cave full of bats. Leave your cigarettes behind: the American-owned and -operated hotel is nonsmoking. It's justly popular with birders and has nesting hummingbirds in the grounds, and motmots, aracaria, kingfishers, etc., are common sights. The only noise you'll hear is the rush of the river . . . and birds.

The simple and charming all-hardwood cabins have screened windows to all sides and a small raised porch. Each is a different size, with beds to match. Bathrooms have heaps of light pouring in from above and *real* hot water systems. Solar lamps mark pathways at night. A marvelous curiosity is the collection of pickled insects, snakes, and miscellany, including an albino bat and the head of a boa constrictor, which was caught by a *campesino* while the snake was lazing with a coatimundi in its belly (ask to see the photo). From the patio bar, you can watch the fireflies flit by and bats in pursuit. Guests receive a $5 discount off the Rainforest Aerial Tram. Rates: $40 s, $55 d, $70 t, including American breakfast (lunches and dinners by advance notice) and rainforest tour.

Happy Rana Lodge is farther up the dirt road. Not reviewed.

The **Restaurante Río Blanco** (tel. 710-7857), 200 meters east of the river, on the north side of the Guápiles Hwy., also has cabinas. One km west of the river is **Restaurante Ponderosa** (tel. 710-7144), which specializes in smoked meats.

GUÁPILES

Guápiles, 60 km east of San José, is a center for the expanding Río Frío banana region to the north and has gained importance with the opening of the Guápiles Highway. There is no reason to visit unless you are heading north from the Puerto Limón highway for Rara Avis, Puerto Viejo de Sarapiquí, or other points in the northern lowlands. As you enter town, you'll see huge woven baskets and hanging chairs made of bamboo and *cucherría* for sale. Great buys if you can get them home! Call the Pococí Regional Tourist Association **information office** (tel. 710-2323) for tourist information.

One of several attractions between Guápiles and Guácimo, **Jardín Botánico Las Cusingas** (Las Cusingas Botanical Garden, tel. 710-0114) is a reforestation project that preserves a region of tropical wet forest, undertakes medicinal plant and other botanical research, and raises ornamentals. You can hike the trails and bathe in the refreshing waters of the Río Santa Clara. Horseback rides are available to the village of Buenos Aires. The birding is excellent. Accommodation is provided (see below). Turn right at Soda Buenos Aires, a short distance east of Guápiles. Las Cusingas is about four km up a dirt road (4WD recommended). Entrance: $5.

Accommodations

The **Hotel Suerre** (Apdo. 25, Guápiles 7210, tel. 710-7551, fax 710-6376; in the U.S., tel. 800-758-7234), opposite Colegio Agropecuario de Pococí, just east of Guápiles, is an elegant, modern hacienda-style property with 30 spacious, air-conditioned rooms, beautifully appointed with hardwoods. Each has satellite TV. The hotel features a full-size swimming pool; tennis, basketball, and volleyball courts; restaurant; two bars; and pool-side cafe. Rates: $60 s, $75 d, $100 suite.

In town, the **Hotel Keng Wa** (tel. 710-6235) and **Hotel As de Oro** both have double rooms with private baths, as does the **Hotel Hugo Sanchez** (tel. 710-6197), each charging approximately $10 d. The **Hospedaje Guápiles** (tel. 710-6179) offers clean rooms. Other cheap hotels include the **Hotel Cariari** and **Hotel Alfaro**.

Las Cusingas (see above) has a rustic two-bedroom cabin complete with kitchen, bathroom, firewood stove, and "the best cotton sheets we saw the whole trip," reports one reader, who was also "fed very inexpensively and deliciously." She also recommends eating beneath thatch at **Los Lagos**, on the main road as you enter Guápiles. It has a lake with rickety Japanese bridges and a sorry-looking tethered monkey.

Getting There

Buses from San José depart from Calle 12 and Avenidas 7/9 every 45 minutes between 5:30 a.m. and 7 p.m ($1.50). Buses from Puerto Limón depart hourly from Calle 2 and Avenidas 1/2 ($1.20). Guápiles is also connected by hourly buses to Puerto Limón and from/to Río Frío, Puerto Viejo de Sarapiquí, and other points in the northern lowlands (depart Guápiles 4:30 and 7:30 a.m., and 2 p.m.). A daily train service also operates to Siquirres and Puerto Limón.

GUÁCIMO

Guácimo is a small village and important truck stop about 12 km east of Guápiles and has two sights of interest. Signs in Guácimo point the way north to **Costa Flores,** a tropical flower farm said to be the largest in the world, with more than 600 varieties of plants blossoming gloriously across 120 blazingly colorful hectares. Costa Flores (Apdo. 4769, San José 1000, tel. 716-5047 or 220-1311, fax 220-1316) welcomes visitors. You can buy plants, of course, to brighten your hotel room. A restaurant sits amid beautifully laid-out pathways. **Siempre Verde** is another horticultural farm nearby (ask for details at Las Palmas, below).

EARTH (Escuela de Agricultura de la Región Tropical Húmeda, tel. 255-2000, fax 255-2726) is a university that teaches agricultural techniques to students from thoughout Latin America. More than that, it specializes in researching ecologically sound, or sustainable agriculture. EARTH has its own banana plantation and 400-hectare forest reserve with nature trails. Visitors are welcome. **Costa Rica Expeditions** (Apdo. 6941, San José 1000, tel. 257-0766, fax 257-1665) offers a full-day guided tour ($69 including lunch).

A sign for "Artesania," about four km east of Guácimo, gives heed of a roadside hut selling impressive wicker swing chairs, seats, etc.

Accommodations

Cabinas la Higuito (tel. 716-5025), 500 meters before the turnoff for Guácimo, has basic rooms. Alternately, you can stay overnight at **EARTH** (tel. 255-2000; ask for *relaciones externas*) in any of 32 double rooms with private baths with hot water. Rates: $30 s, $40 s. Meals are in the campus refectory.

One of the nicest places at which to eat and rest your head is the **Hotel and Restaurant Las Palmas** (tel. 716-5289, fax 716-518), 400 meters east of EARTH. It sits shaded by tall trees on the banks of the Río Dos Novillos, a pool of which has been stocked with tasty talapias (African bass). Catch your own and the chef will happily prepare to order. The American-run hotel has 31 rooms with private baths and hot water. There's a laundry. Trails lead into the nearby forest. A heliconia garden is planned. Rates: $10 s, $14 d, economy; $16 s, $22 d, standard; $30 s, $35 d, superior.

BANANA TRAIN

Swiss Travel Service (tel. 231-4055), pioneers of the now defunct Jungle Train, has rescued a Costa Rican tradition with the Banana Train,

which takes you on a leisurely ride through the banana plantations of the Caribbean lowlands near Guápiles. The main highlight is a visit to a banana packing plant at Río Frío. You're transported in two restored and air-conditioned 1930s-era carriages on a narrow-gauge track. Transportation from San José is provided. Departures daily except Sunday. Light breakfast is included, plus lunch and beverages on the train.

The same trip—known as the **Green Train** and billed as a "Premier Train Adventure"—is offered by TAM Travel (tel. 222-2642) on Tuesday and Saturday for a half-day journey; $70, including lunch.

SIQUIRRES

Siquirres, 99 km from San José, two km after crossing the Río Reventazón bridge, is also a major railroad junction, echoing to a calliope of clanging bells—those of locomotives pulling freight cars leased by the banana companies. The railway lines run through the north end of town. The name Siquirres derives from an Indian word meaning "reddish colored." The town has several historical buildings, as well as three monuments, two of which are dedicated to important local patrons, and the other, Mártires del Codo del Diablo, in honor of those who lost their lives in the revolution of 1948. The roads are one-way: you must turn right immediately as you enter town and follow the road in a counter-clockwise direction. There's a lively little **Mercado Central** facing the railway station. The **Siquirres Tourist Association** has an office (tel. 768-8002).

About 28 km east of Siquirres is **Matina** (four km north of the highway; the turnoff is at Bristol), from where you can hire boats to take you to Tortuguero. Reportedly a bus from Matina journeys as far as San Rafael (also called Freeman) and Parasmina.

Accommodations

On the northeast corner of town, facing the railway station, is the **Hotel Garza,** above the **Restaurant Vidal** (ask in the restaurant for hotel rooms; $10 d). On the other side of the market is the **Hotel Las Brisas,** with rooms in need of a good scrubbing. Rates: $5 s, $10 d. Much nicer, but in the same price range, is the **Hotel Central** (tel. 768-8113), 50 meters on the right.

The **Melissa,** directly across the railway tracks from the Mercado Central, has a lively bar—stinking hot!—plus rooms with private baths. The **Hotel Mireya** (tel. 768-8178) is on the same block; **Henry's Bar** is adjacent. Both offer basic rooms for $4-6. Other budget hotels include the **Colerán, Wilson, Idamar,** and **Cocal.** Also to consider are **Cabinas Las Palmas,** two km after the turnoff for Siquirres; and **Hotel 9 Millas,** about 10 km before Puerto Limón.

Food

Siquirres offers plenty of modest restaurants and bars, though nothing outstanding. Immediately when one enters town is the **Hidalgo Bar,** at the crossroads. Go right four blocks and you'll come to **Restaurant Andrea.** Up the street from the Hotel Central is the **Restaurant Típico Goyito.** On the main street leading back to the Puerto Limón highway are **Restaurant Kings, Restaurant Hong Kong, Nano's Bar,** and **Lalo's Bar,** a lively and popular hangout. The **Los Castellanos Restaurant** facing the soccer field offers good-quality Tico food at reasonable prices. The Mercado Central, facing the railway station, has lots of *sodas.*

The **Caribbean Dish Restaurant,** immediately west of Siquirres, is popular with rafters.

Services

The **police** (Guardia Rural) post is a small booth adjacent to the railway tracks facing the *mercado.* A **Banco de Costa Rica** is on the left as you head back toward the San José-Puerto Limón highway.

Transportation

Buses for Siquirres leave San José hourly from Avenida Central and Calles 11/13 ($1.50). Buses depart hourly for Guápiles, Puerto Limón, and San José from two blocks south of the railway station. Trains to Guápiles depart daily at 3:20 p.m. ($1). Check for latest schedules.

PUERTO LIMÓN AND VICINITY

Navigating off these shores, hopelessly lost, half a millennium ago, Columbus had assumed that the region was really Siam. Columbus's son, Ferdinand, 14 at the time, described the area as "lofty, full of rivers, and abounding in very tall trees, as also is the islet [Uva Island] where they grew thick as basil . . . For this reason the Admiral [Columbus] called it La Huerta [The Garden]." Knowing this, Limón, as most Ticos call the town, may come as a sad disappointment to the modern visitor.

Except for Carnival, when Puerto Limón (pop. 65,000) gets into the groove, this teeming tropical port is merely a jumping-off point for most travelers; tourist facilities are limited and there is little of interest to see. The colorful street life is really about the only thing that piques my interest. Puerto Limón has been described as a town of "sleazy charms." Until a few years ago it had more sleaze than charm. True, its decayed buildings with ironwork balconies are still badly in need of a paint job, and the wide streets are still potholed, though the garbage which vultures once fed upon greedily had been cleared when I called by in 1995. The earthquake of 22 April 1991 dealt Puerto Limón a blow below the belt and its effects are still paramount, with broken pavements and toppled houses adding to the city's gone-to-seed appearance. Limonians (predominantly black) justifiably feel neglected by federal officials and display a lingering resentment at being treated as second-class citizens.

Still, the city has come a long way since I first visited in 1992, and city fathers seem to be making a genuine effort—reflected in the razing of decrepit buildings (not least two notorious dens of iniquity) and a sense of newfound prosperity—to pull the city up by its bootstraps. The city is in flux. Some hotels and restaurants will inevitably have closed by the time you read this.

The name "Puerto Limón" goes back to when a big lemon tree grew where the Town Hall is today. The town, which is usually referred to simply as "Limón," was originally built in a swampy area (yellow fever was once rampant) near the site of an ancient Indian village, Cariari;

it was later moved to rocky terrain in front of La Uvita islet, the only island on Costa Rica's Caribbean side and a pleasant place for a hiking excursion while killing time in Puerto Limón. The town is centered on a lively market (Avenida 2, Calles 3/4), focus of Puerto Limón's social action. Note the mixing of blood: Chinese with black with Latin.

The harbor (there are four docks) handles most of the sea trade for Costa Rica and, with Moín, its modern sister port, is the only seaport offering direct docking and ferrying. The city has never fully recovered from the slump in the banana industry in the 1950s. The town moves with the lassitude of a tropical port. Still, people rise early to beat the heat and businesses stay open late. Many bars—some of them colorful hangouts for sailors and prostitutes—stay open 24 hours. The pious head for a church, worth seeing for its beautiful stained glass, three blocks west of the *mercado*.

Limonians hope to get back the steam train—shipped from England to Puerto Limón in 1939—which, restored, now graces the Atlantic Railway station in San José.

Warning: Beware of pickpockets by day and muggings at night. The city is now often referred to as Piedropolis ("Crack City") because of the rising influence of drug traffic. Just as Mark Twain said that tales of his demise "are greatly exaggerated," so, too, Limón's evils have been greatly inflated. Still, I recommend constant vigilance.

SIGHTS AND ACTIVITIES

There's not much to hold you in town. About as interesting as things come around here is the cemetery spanning the road into town (note La Colonia China, the Chinese quarter).

Parque Vargas

The most commonly touted attraction is Parque Vargas (Calle 1, Avenida 2), literally an urban jungle, with palm promenades, looming hardwoods, and a tangle of vines and bromeli-

(top) view over Central Valley from Irazú volcano (Christopher P. Baker);
(above) Río Colorado (John Anderson)

(top) Las Ruinas, Ujarrás (Christopher P. Baker);
(above) church, Sarchí (John Anderson)

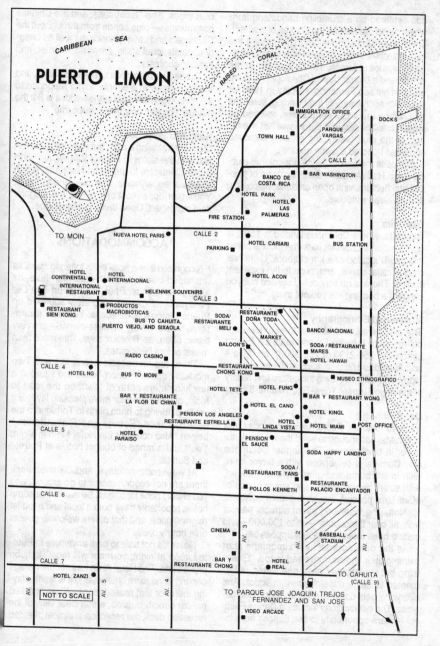

CARIBBEAN SEA

PUERTO LIMÓN

RAISED CORAL

TO MOIN

DOCKS

IMMIGRATION OFFICE

PARQUE VARGAS

TOWN HALL

CALLE 1

BAR WASHINGTON

BANCO DE COSTA RICA

HOTEL PARK

HOTEL LAS PALMERAS

FIRE STATION

NUEVA HOTEL PARIS

CALLE 2

PARKING

HOTEL CARIARI

BUS STATION

HOTEL CONTINENTAL

HOTEL INTERNACIONAL

HOTEL ACON

INTERNATIONAL RESTAURANT

HELENNIK SOUVENIRS

CALLE 3

RESTAURANT SIEN KONG

PRODUCTOS MACROBIOTICAS

SODA/ RESTAURANTE MELI

RESTAURANTE DOÑA TODA

BANCO NACIONAL

BUS TO CAHUITA, PUERTO VIEJO, AND SIXAOLA

MARKET

BALOON'S

SODA / RESTAURANTE MARES

RADIO CASINO

RESTAURANT CHONG KONG

HOTEL HAWAII

CALLE 4

HOTEL NG

BUS TO MOIN

MUSEO ETHNOGRAFICO

HOTEL TETE

HOTEL FUNG

BAR Y RESTAURANTE LA FLOR DE CHINA

BAR Y RESTAURANT WONG

HOTEL EL CANO

HOTEL KINGL

PENSION LOS ANGELES

RESTAURANTE ESTRELLA

HOTEL LINDA VISTA

HOTEL MIAMI

POST OFFICE

CALLE 5

HOTEL PARAISO

PENSION EL SAUCE

SODA HAPPY LANDING

SODA/ RESTAURANTE YANS

CALLE 6

RESTAURANTE PALACIO ENCANTADOR

POLLOS KENNETH

BASEBALL STADIUM

CINEMA

CALLE 7

BAR Y RESTAURANTE CHONG

HOTEL REAL

HOTEL ZANZI

TO CAHUITA (CALLE 9)

AV. 6

AV. 5

AV. 4

AV. 3

AV. 2

AV. 1

NOT TO SCALE

TO PARQUE JOSE JOAQUIN TREJOS FERNANDEZ AND SAN JOSE

VIDEO ARCADE

ads centered on a crumbling bandstand from which paths radiate like the spokes of a wheel. Three-toed sloths move languidly among the high branches. A bust of Balvanera Vargas Molina (governor of Limón, 1883-1905) sits in the center, and a bronze bust of Christopher Columbus and his son Fernando, erected in 1990 for the 500th anniversary of their landing, faces the sea. Since the 1991 earthquake, the sea no longer crashes against the seawall at the far end of the park (sadly, the recently exposed coral had become a dump ground).

Opposite the park is the cream-colored stucco **Town Hall** (Alcádia), a fine example of tropical architecture, with open arcades, balconies, and louvered windows.

Isla Uvita

Isla Uvita, where Columbus landed in 1502, is now a national landmark park (the Indians called it Quiribrí) located one km offshore. Uvita has craggy cliffs, caves, and, reportedly, excellent surfing. There is no scheduled service but you can hire a boat to take you out there.

Museum of Ethnography

The only museum in town is the ethnohistorical museum (Museo Ethnográfico de Puerto Limón, tel. 758-2130 or 758-3903), on Calle 4 and Avenidas 1/2, displaying artifacts, photography, and exhibits tracing the culture and history of the region (open: Tues.-Sat. 10 a.m.-5 p.m.)

Carnival

Each 12 October, Puerto Limón explodes in a bacchanal hot enough to send them running for cover in Los Alamos. The annual Columbus Day Carnival is celebrated with a fervor more akin to the bump-and-grind style of Trinidad, with street bands, floats, and every ounce of Mardi Gras passion, though in a more makeshift fashion. The weeklong event attracts people from all over the country—up to 100,000—and getting hotel rooms is virtually impossible.

As the date approaches, Limonians start painting their bodies from head to toe. "Everything but insecticide," says one writer, is fermented to make napalm-strength liquor. And everyone gets down to reggae, *salsa,* and calypso. The celebrations include a Dance Festival—a rare opportunity to see dances from Indian tribes, Afro-Caribbeans, and the Chinese communities—plus bands from throughout the Caribbean and Latin America, as well as beauty contests, craft stalls, fireworks, theater, and calypso contests.

The seductive tempos lure you to dance, and life is reduced to a simple, joyful response to the most irresistible beat in the world. It is like the plague: you can only flee or succumb!

Hotel Matamas Zoo

"Zoo" is stretching it a bit, but if you're not satisfied with the sloths in Parque Vargas, nip north a few kilometers to the Hotel Matamas, which boasts a jaguar, apes, macaws, and toucans. You'll tear up, almost cry, to see the magnificent cat caged. Open daily. Entrance free.

ACCOMMODATIONS

"I recognized it as a hotel by its tottering stairs, its unshaded bulbs, its moth-eaten furniture, its fusty smell." Thus, Paul Theroux (in *The Old Patagonian Express*) accurately summed up Puerto Limón's hotel scene. With few exceptions, hotels—many Chinese-owned—are very basic; often, as Theroux says, little more than "nests of foul bedclothes."

There are no upscale hotels in town. Two modestly upscale resort hotels are situated a few kilometers north of town, on the road to Moín, and provide a far more pleasing layover if you're planning to head north to Tortuguero the next day (see "Potrete and Playa Bonita," below). Also consider the Hotel Moín in Moín. You'll find a range of budget hotels at Potrete and Bonita.

At weekends, holidays, and Carnival week there are not enough rooms to go around, and you should book far ahead. Be aware that some hotels reportedly have both a local and a tourist (higher) price, and that others welcome guests on a hourly basis.

Note: It's not safe to park anywhere in Puerto Limón at night; your car will most likely be broken into. The Hotel Acón has secure garage parking at no extra charge, and it is worth staying there for that reason alone. When I parked my car directly outside, within clear view of the reception desk, the receptionist almost pleaded

with me not to park there; she insisted it would be broken into! The Hotel International also has secure parking.

Budget

You'll find a wide selection of budget hotels in the center of town, though nothing to write home to Mum about. Compare before taking a room; many hotels cater to prostitutes doing short-time business (rates given below are for overnight), and there's a wide discrepancy in cleanliness.

I've heard good things of the **Hotel El Caño** (tel. 758-0894), on Avenida 3 between Calles 4/5. Rooms are fairly dingy, as is the shared bathroom, but the owner otherwise runs a tight ship. Rates: $9 d, with private bath.

On Avenida 2, there are three hotels to choose from between Calles 4 and 5, one block west of the central market. The **Hotel Fung** (tel. 758-3309) has 22 rooms. Rates: $5 s, $10 d. The **Linda Vista** (tel. 758-3359) has 35 small but well-kept rooms, some with private bath. Rates: $5 s without bath, $8 with; $11 d. Opposite is the **Hotel Kingl.** Also try the fairly basic **Hotel Galaxy** (tel. 758-2828), one block west.

The **Hotel Cariari** (Calle 2, Avenida 3, tel. 758-1395) has 30 decent rooms for $11 s, $7 per person double. On the same block (Calle 2) are the similarly priced **Hotel Familiar** and **Hotel Palace,** which has plant-festooned balconies with chairs (tel. 758-0419; rooms with communal baths $6 per person; or private bath, $10 per person), and the slightly cheaper **Hotel Río** (tel. 758-4511), with basic rooms for $4.

Gone is the white-and-green building on the corner of Calle 2 and Avenida 4 containing the erstwhile Hotel Venus, replaced by a new complex that includes **Nueva Hotel Paris.** It's adequate, clean, with lots of light and an airy balcony. Rates: $9 s, $18 d.

On Avenida 5, the **Hotel Ng** has very basic rooms (the room I inspected had three beds but no other furniture; wall decorations were limited to two fist-size holes). Rates: $7 s; $10 d. The **Hotel Lincoln** (Avenida 5, Calles 2/3, tel. 758-0074) competes in price and equally uninspiring decor; worse, some rooms lack windows. **Hotel Paraíso** (tel. 758-0684) has 26 rooms that are no more than a box with a bed (shared baths). Also epitomizing Paul Theroux's warning are

Hotel Real, a true dive, and the very run-down **Pensión El Sauce.**

For a much better deal, try the **Hotel Zanzi,** a little out of the way on Calle 7, but with nine small but clean rooms with overhead fans and communal bath ($4 per person).

Moderate

The **Hotel Miami** (Apdo. 266, Puerto Limón, tel. 758-0490, fax 758-1978), between Calles 4/5 on Avenida 2, offers well-kept if sparsely furnished rooms with overhead fans and private baths. Rates: $12 s, $18 d; $15 s, $22 d with a/c. The restaurant serves Chinese food. **Hotel Continental** (Avenida 5, Calles 2/3, tel. 798-0532) has 20 rooms with private baths and hot water. It's Chinese-run and spotlessly clean. Rooms are simple but spacious. Rates: $11 s, $15 d, $19 t. The **Hotel Internacional** (tel. 758-0434), across the road, is of a similar standard. Rates: $12 s, $20 d.

The best bet in town is the four-story **Hotel Acón** (Avenida 3, Calle 2/3, Apdo. 528, Puerto Limón, tel. 758-1010, fax 758-2924), popular with businessmen from San José. Rooms have a/c and are clean and spacious, though dowdy. The hotel has a reasonable restaurant. Take a fourth-floor room. Otherwise, don't expect to sleep from Thursday through weekends—there's a disco on the second floor! Reservations may be a good idea. Rates: $21 s, $30 d.

Another popular hotel is the rather jaded **Hotel Park** (Apdo. 35, Puerto Limón, tel. 758-3476, fax 758-4364), with 30 rooms with private bath overlooking the ocean at the corner of Calle 1 and the frontage road. Prices vary according to room standard and view. More expensive ocean-view rooms catch the breeze and, hence, are cooler. Rates: $13-17 s, $20-25 d.

Others to consider include **Hotel Las Palmeras** (tel. 758-0241), with 18 rooms for $11 per person, and the slightly more expensive **Hotel Tete** (Apdo. 401, Puerto Limón, tel. 758-1122), with 14 rooms featuring modern bathrooms and balconies with chairs.

Hotel Jardín Tropical (tel. 798-1244), on the highway into Limón, 600 meters from the turnoff to Moín, has 32 a/c rooms with TV and telephone, plus larger "family rooms" with kitchens. The lush grounds boast two swimming pools.

FOOD

One of the pleasures of the Caribbean coast is the unique local cuisine: *pan bon* (good bread) laced with caramelized sugar and a very sharp yellow cheese, banana brownies, fresh ginger cookies, fresh ice cream flavored with fresh fruits, and ceviche made with green bananas. You can sample many of these tasty goodies at the open-air *sodas* that ring the Mercado Central and offer filling meals for as little as $2. **Restaurant Springfield** (tel. 758-1203), about one km north of town, on the road to Moín, is a favorite of locals. It doubles as a lively nightspot and offers zesty Caribbean dishes at about $4 and up (including a good garlic shrimp, fish in curry sauce, and, alas, turtle meat).

My favorite place to eat is **Soda Mares**—more a restaurant than a *soda*—on the market's south side. Popular with locals and tourists alike, it's about the only place in town with even a hint of the cosmopolitan. *Gallo pinto* here costs about $1.50, and you can have a shrimp dish and beer for $5. Also recommended is the **Restaurant Doña Toda**, around the corner on the east-facing side of the market; and the **Milk Bar La Negra Mendoza**, serving good milkshakes and snacks.

At the junction of Calle 3 and Avenida 5 and worth trying is the **International Restaurant**, which has appealing decor and hearty meals from $3. The **Restaurante Arrecife**, 100 meters beyond Springfield on the road to Moín, is another good bet for seafood.

The ground-floor restaurant in the **Hotel Acón** offers reasonably priced meals (average $5), including basic American breakfasts. The restaurant in the **Hotel Park** is also recommended.

For a pleasing break from *típico* Costa Rican dishes, think Oriental. There's no shortage of clean, inexpensive Chinese restaurants. The **Restaurant Chong Kong**, facing the market on the west side, is one of the best. Around the corner on Avenida 2 is **Restaurant Wong** and, on the next block, **Soda Happy Landing, Palacio Encantador,** and the popular **Soda Restaurante Yans,** all offering meals for $2 upward. Two other reasonably priced restaurants to consider are **Restaurante Chong** (Avenida 3, Calles 6/7) and **Restaurante La Flor de China** (Avenida 4, Calles 4/5). Playing a more expensive note on the scale is the elegant **Restaurant Sien Kong** (Calle 3 and Avenida 6), with meals from $5.

Fast food, as everywhere, has reared its head in Puerto Limón. **Restaurante Estrella,** a tiny and pleasing open-air restaurant behind wrought-iron grilles on the corner of Calle 5 and Avenida 3, offers reasonably good and reasonably priced burgers and perhaps the best atmosphere in town. **Pollos Kenneth** (Calle 6, Avenida 3) is the local contender for Colonel Sanders. Hankering for pizza? Try **Pizza Mia** on Calle 5 and Avenida 3. Lastly, **Café Verde** (Avenida 3, Calles 19/21) serves from a truly international menu that features Italian, German, and Tican cuisines.

Avenida 4 (between Calles 4/7) is given over to a lively **fruit market** on weekends. **Productos Macrobióticas** (Avenida 5, Calles 3/4) sells organic foods.

Baloons, on the north side of the *mercado,* and **Mönpik,** opposite the Hotel Acón, can satisfy your ice cream craving, as can **Pops,** next to Café Rey, in the new complex on the corner of Calle 2 and Avenida 4. For coffee, try the **Café Rey. Soda/restaurante Meli,** opposite the north side of the *mercado,* is clean.

ENTERTAINMENT

Basic and colorful describes the **Bar Washington** (Calle 1 and Avenida 2, opposite Parque Vargas), awash with prostitutes and sailors. **Bar Mamajora** (tel. 798-0874), on Avenida 2 between Calles 1/2, is popular with locals. Most bars—of which there's no shortage—have a decidedly raffish quality, and an aura of impending violence pervades many. Some open by 8 a.m. **Bar Mamón** is a lively place, popular with the locals. It looks safe.

The weekend disco in the **Hotel Acón** is jampacked, fun, and safe. Emphasis is on the Latin beat (admission $1, free to hotel guests). **Discoteque Roxelle** is above Soda Mares. At **Springfield,** on the road to Moín, you can step out to calypso and reggae (the disco is unseen, at the back of the restaurant). Just up the road, at Potrete, the seafront, open-air **Johny Dixon Bar** can get equally lively. In town, the **Mark 15 Disco** is also recommended.

The **Cine Atlantic** offers American movies for $1. For theater, try the **Teatro Hong Kong** on Calle 9 and Avenida 1 (tel. 758-0034).

SERVICES

Banks

You'll find a **Banco Anglo Costarricense** (open Saturday morning, tel. 758-0351) and a **Banco de Costa Rica** (tel. 758-3166) on Calle 1 and Avenida 2, a **Banco Nacional de Costa Rica** (tel. 758-0094) next to the Puerto Limón-San José bus terminal (Calle 2, Avenida 1), and a **Banco de San José** (Calle 2, Avenida 4). **Moneychangers** hang around the Mercado Central. There's only one bank south of Puerto Limón, and none to the north; if you're spending more than a few days on the coast, change as much as you'll need here, as the bank in Bribrí is a long drive and can take hours to change money. The better hotels and some bars and tour operators in Tortuguero, Cahuita, and Puerto Limón will also change dollars and traveler's checks.

Tourist Information

The local ICT (Instituto Costarricense de Turismo) office is on Avenida 4, between Calles 5/7. **Helennik Souvenirs** (tel. 758-2086), on Calle 3 and Avenidas 4/5, acts as an informal information office, too.

Medical

The **Hospital Dr. Tony Facio** (tel. 758-2222), at the north end of the seafront *malecón,* is the only hospital in Puerto Limón; for **emergencies,** call 758-0580. There's also a small clinic—**Clínica Santa Lucía**—in the town center on

---

Calle 2 and Avenidas 4/5 (tel. 758-1286). Dr. Eric Castro Vega has a **clinical laboratory** on Calle 4 and Avenidas 3/4 (tel. 758-3106).

If you need urgent dental treatment, Dr. Cheryl Cunningham Dehanny has a **dental clinic** on Calle 6 and Avenidas 5/6 (hours: Mon.-Fri. 3-7 p.m.; tel. 758-0193). The following dental clinics may also be able to help: Dr. Javier Walters Brown (tel. 758-0810), Dr. Marcos Arley Leon (Calle 2, Avenidas 4/5, tel. 758-2635), and Dr. Juanita Chacón (Avenida 4, Calles 3/4, tel. 758-3994).

There are five **pharmacies** in the center of town: Farmacia Britannica (Calle 2, Avenidas 2/3, tel. 758-3362), Farmacia Buenos Aires (Avenida 2, Calles 2/3, tel. 758-0067), Farmacia Kingston (Avenida 3, Calles 4/5, tel. 758-0329), Farmacia Limonense (Avenida 4, Calle 3/4, tel. 758-0654), and Farmacia Super Cariari (Calle 4, Avenidas 3/4, tel. 758-1064).

Other

The **post office** is one block west of Soda Mares, on the corner of Calle 5 and Avenida 1.

The town has three **gas stations:** one on the corner of Calle 3 and Avenida 6, where the frontage road to Moín begins; an Esso station at Calle 7 and Avenida 2, just before the junction for Cahuita when exiting Puerto Limón; and a RECOPE station just outside town on the highway from Guápiles. Fill up here as there are only two gas stations south of Puerto Limón, both off the beaten track—one at Pandora, in the Valle de Estrella, and the other near the Panamanian border, halfway between Bribrí and Sixaola (gas is also sold, however, by freelancers at inflated prices).

TRANSPORTATION

Getting There

Direct buses (two and a half hours; COPELIMóN, tel. 223-7811) depart San José hourly 5 a.m.-7 p.m. from Avenida 3 and Calles 19/21, opposite the Atlantic Railway station. Buses to San José depart Puerto Limón on the same schedule from Calle 2 and Avenida 2, one block east and half a block south of the municipal market ($2). Buses also serve Guápiles and Siquirres throughout the day. **Saragundí Specialty Tours** (tel. 255-

---

PUERTO LIMÓN EMERGENCY TELEPHONE NUMBERS	
All emergencies	911
Police	758-1148
Organismo de Investigación Judicial	758-1865
Hospital	758-0580
Red Cross	758-0125

0011, fax 255-2155) offers a daily tourist shuttle to Limón (departs San José 7 a.m.). It stops at the hotels Tata, Matama, and Maribu Caribe.

Buses for Cahuita (85 cents), Puerto Viejo ($1.25), and Sixaola ($2) depart from opposite Radio Casino on Avenida 4 daily at 5 and 10 a.m., and 1 and 4 p.m. Buy tickets in advance at the *soda* beside the bus stop, as buses get crowded (advance tickets are reportedly only offered for the 10 a.m. and 4 p.m. departures). Buses also serve Penshurst and the Valle de Estrella regularly throughout the day from Calle 2. Around the corner on Calle 4 to the north is the bus stop for Playa Bonita and Moín.

Train service to San José was suspended after the April 1991 earthquake. However, you can savor a down-to-earth journey by "rustic rail" to Estrella (see "Puerto Limón to Cahuita," below).

There are no scheduled flights to Puerto Limón, but **Travelair** (tel. 232-7883 or 220-3054, fax 220-0413) keeps toying with the idea. You can arrange charters to the airstrip four km south of town (see "By Air" under "Getting Around" in the On the Road chapter).

Getting Around
From San José, you enter town along Avenida 1, paralleling the railway track that runs to the docks on the right. The *avenidas* (east-west) are aligned north of Avenida 1 in sequential order. The *calles* (north to south) are numbered sequentially and run westward from the waterfront. Avenida 2 ("Market Street") is the main street and runs from the railway station (Calle 8) to Parque Vargas (Calle 1). All streets except Avenida 1 are one-way.

Although the streets have numbers, they're unposted. Limonians don't use them anyway; instead, they use local landmarks. Avenida 2 is commonly referred to as Market Street, and virtually all addresses and directions are given in distance from the market or Parque Vargas.

For Moín take Calle 2 or Avenida 6, which merge into the coast road heading north. For Cahuita, turn right from Avenida 1 at the traffic lights at the junction with Calle 9 (just beyond the tiny Parque José Joaquín Trejos Fernandez).

You'll find plenty of taxis on the south side of the market. Expect to pay $20-25 for a taxi to Cahuita.

POTRETE AND PLAYA BONITA

Playa Bonita, four km north of Puerto Limón, boasts an attractive golden sand beach encusped by palms and popular with Limonians, with nary a tourist in sight. Reportedly, swimming is safe only at the northern end. The surf is good, but unreliable; it can be excellent on a good swell, or flat calm for weeks. There are two *sodas*—**Restaurant Joy** and **Bar y Restaurant Kimbamba.** The former is run by a colorful character, Johnny Dixon, a former musician who says he's "as well known throughout Costa Rica as *gallo pinto*." His breezy bar and restaurant is a good place to hang and watch the surf pump ashore while savoring a shrimp cocktail ($9), ceviche ($6), snapper ($9), or rice and beans "Caribbean style" ($6). There's a public telephone here. (En route, you'll pass the ruins of the **Hotel Las Olas,** destroyed by the April 1991 earthquake.)

Adjoining Playa Bonita to the north is Potrete, an unsightly bay interesting only for the flocks of vultures that gather to feed on lobster scraps left by the local fishermen. **For surfers:** The cove supposedly has good right points on its southern end.

Between Playa Bonita and Potrete is **Parque Recreativo Cariari,** an overgrown and untended public park with little to recommend it, although trails reportedly offer sightings of sloths, toucans, iguanas, and parrots.

Budget Accommodations
The tiny, bare-bones **Cabinas Mar Bella** are just before Playa Bonita, 50 meters north of Cabinas Cocori. Rates: $10. Also try the funky **Apartotel Temporal Inn,** two km north of Puerto Limón, immediately past the popular **Bar y Restaurant Arrecife,** on the left; the **Nuevo Hotel Lux,** about 400 meters farther and looking anything but luxe; and **Cabinas Getsemani** (tel. 758-1123), which reportedly has cabins with a/c and bath.

Moderate Accommodations
Cabinas Maeva Caribe (tel. 758-2024), on the left 100 meters before the Maribu Caribe, is very attractive, with six appealing bamboo-lined octagonal cabins set in a lush hillside garden

full of palms. The swimming pool contains an enchanting statue, and the restaurant is open-air. Additional cabins are planned. Rates: $27 d.

Two km farther north, directly across from the Hotel Matama, is **Cabinas Cocori** (tel. 758-2930 or 257-4674), which has metamorphosed from simple cabins to a modern hotel complex with a pleasing ocean-view terrace restaurant—**Bar/Restaurante Tía María**—open to the breezes. It offers 15 simple but pleasing rooms, plus six apartments sleeping up to six. Rates: $24 s, $36 d, fans; $30 s, $45 d with a/c; $55, apartment. It might be overpriced.

Upscale Accommodations
More pleasing by far than a night in Puerto Limón is to splurge at any of the following three upscale resort-style hotels within a 10-minute drive or one hour's walk of Puerto Limón. **Hotel Maribu Caribe** (Apdo. 1306, San Pedro 2050, tel. 253-1838, fax 234-0193; direct line, tel. 758-4543) is on your right 100 meters beyond Cabinas Maeva, with round, thatched, African-style cabins peeking over the top of the hill. The hotel enjoys a scenic setting above the ocean, although views are somewhat obscured by palm trees. The resort is centered on a swimming pool, with steps leading up to a restaurant for alfresco dining. A second, more romantic open-air restaurant overlooks the ocean and catches the breeze. The hotel offers 17 bungalows and 56 rooms, each with a/c, telephone, and private bath with hot water. Rooms are disappointingly basic, with narrow beds and unappealing decor. Roomy showers make amends with piping hot water. The Maribu can arrange sportfishing ($125) and scuba-diving ($50) trips, Tortuguero tours ($70), and boat trips on the Pacuare ($45) and Parismina rivers ($60). Rates: $65 s, $75 d, $107 family suite.

Slightly more appealing is the **Hotel Matama** (Apdo. 686, Puerto Limón 7300, tel. 758-1123, fax 758-4499), two km farther north, with rooms and four-person and six-person villas with loft bedrooms, set in lush, beautifully landscaped gardens on a rise set back from the shore. The wide open-air restaurant overlooks the gardens and swimming pool and features an array of seafood dishes. Rooms are spacious and clean, with comfortable wicker furniture, a/c, and large showers along with their own solarium gardens.

Some units have lofts. Rates: $50 s, $60 d, $75 t, or $90-120 for four to six.

Villas Cacao (Apdo. 3565, San José 1000, tel. 223-1126, fax 222-0930) is a resort development of villas and condominiums. The bulldozers moved in in early 1995. Stay tuned.

Last but not least is **Hotel Jardín Tropical Azul** (tel. 798-1244, fax 798-1259), 200 meters beyond Villa Cacao and half a km before Moín. It's a beautifully landscaped resort set in a hollow backing onto forest, with 32 rooms in eight attractive modern fourplex bungalows abutting the forest. It has a quality open-sided thatched restaurant and a bar atop a bluff overlooking a small pool and sundeck. Rates: $45 s, $55 d, from $65 family.

Getting There
From Puerto Limón, the bus to Playa Bonita, Potrete, and Moín operates hourly from Calle 4 and Avenida 4, opposite Radio Casino. It is often crowded; arrive early to secure a seat. Alternatively, take a taxi from the south side of the *mercado* ($4). If you're feeling adventurous, the one-hour coastal walk provides good exercise. Plenty of vehicles travel along the road, so you should have no problem hitchhiking.

MOÍN

Moín Bay, five km north of Puerto Limón, has a recently built port where Costa Rica's crude oil is received for processing (RECOPE has its main refinery here) and bananas are loaded for shipment to Europe and North America. Just north of Moín is a recently developed experimental fish farm where tilapia and carp are raised (the tilapia is a low-cost market fish; the carp, it is hoped, will help control the growth of water hyacinth that clogs Los Canales). Sea turtles come ashore to nest at Playa Barra de Matina, 23 km farther north.

The only reason to visit Moín is to catch a boat to Tortuguero. The dock is along a dirt road across the railway tracks from Restaurante Papa, at the base of the hill below Hotel Moín. After crossing the track, turn left immediately behind the funky restaurant and follow the sinuous dirt road. Keep left and go through the open gates into a compound behind a mesh fence; follow

the fence. You'll see lots of canopied boats, and touts will descend on you to offer rides to Tortuguero (expect to pay $50 per person roundtrip). Also see "Tortuguero and Vicinity," below.

Accommodations

Moín Caribe (Apdo. 483, Moin, tel. 758-2436, fax 758-1112), atop the hill above the dock to Tortuguero, is the only place around. Its steak house restaurant downstairs is surprisingly elegant. Its 15 L-shaped rooms, though not unappealing, are more modest (some are quite dark despite being large, so check several rooms before choosing; room #204 has heaps of light). A wide breezy veranda has sofas. The intriguingly named **Banana Power** disco downstairs opens on weekends. Private parking and laundry service. Rates: $21 s, $27 d.

Getting There

From San José, you can reach Moín by a spur on the San José-Puerto Limón highway (six km before Puerto Limón, immediately after the RECOPE storage tanks on the left; three km further, turn right); or by the coast road from Puerto Limón via Playa Bonita (Calle 2 and Avenida 6 both merge into the coast road). **By Bus:** See "Potrete and Playa Bonita," above.

PARISMINA

This small, haphazard village on a small strip of land at the mouth of the Río Parismina, 45 km north of Moín on the way to Tortuguero, is very popular with North American anglers. Parismina suffered severely in the April 1991 earthquake. One of its three fishing lodges, Tarpon Rancho, was flattened! All is well once again.

Accommodations

The Tarpon Rancho re-opened in 1994 as the **Parismino Tarpon Rancho** (it had been slated to re-open as the Happy Monkey Jungle Resort), and was recently taken over by Sportsfishing Costa Rica (Apdo. 115, La Uruca, San José 1150, tel. 233-3892 or 257-3553, fax 223-

6728 or 222-1760; in the U.S., tel. 800-862-1003). It sits on six hectares of landscaped grounds fronting the lagoon. The new resort retains some of the old charm, including its blue wooden livery. It features a two-story building housing a bar, gift shop, and restaurant where hearty meals are served at big homely tables. Five additional structures house 30 private rooms built in hardwoods, with two full-size double beds, ceiling fans, and hot-water showers. The swimming pool measures 140 square meters, and nature trails lead into a private jungle reserve behind the lodge. Don't fail to take the popular night-time crocodile safari. A full fleet of sportfishing boats caters to anglers year-round. Offshore fishing is offered from the hulking steel-hulled *King Kong*, a "mothership" that ferries the resort's fishing boats beyond the dangerous breakers at the mouth of the Río Parismina. Rates: $225 per person, two nights; $420 three nights, including fishing.

The **Río Parismina Lodge** (P.O. Box 460009, San Antonio, TX 78280, tel. 800-338-5688; in Costa Rica, tel. 222-6633, fax 221-9127), is also strongly oriented to sportfishing, with an inventory of 6.5-meter V-hulls. It features 12 attractive rooms, plus swimming pool, Jacuzzi, and airy, screened dining room and bar. Rates: from $60 per person; sample package rate, $1499 (five nights, with three days' fishing).

Serving the budget-conscious is the **Parismina Lodge** (tel. 768-8636), which offers basic accommodations in a twin-story waterfront structure; six of the nine rooms share bathrooms.

Also for those traveling on a dime is **Bar y Cabinas Madre de Dios,** an open-air eatery a few kilometers south of Parismina. It's a popular stopover for hungry and thirsty boaters traveling the canals.

Also somewhere in this area (it may be farther north, along the canals) is **Samay Lagoon Lodge** (tel./fax 236-7154). It claims to be the "only lodge in the area located right at the Caribbean waterfront." A three-day package from San José includes roundtrip boat journey from Puerto Viejo de Saripiquí plus all meals ($199). Not inspected.

TORTUGUERO AND VICINITY

All along the Caribbean coast from the Colorado to the Río Matina, a series of lagoons and swamps makes the region impassable. Many rivers meander through this region, carrying silt that the coastal tides conjure into long, straight, brown-sand beaches. These shores, which are pounded by wild surf, are the ideal places for sea turtles to lay their eggs. The 35-km beach of Tortuguero is favored by the hawksbill, Pacific green, and leatherback, the world's largest sea turtle. Tortuguero National Park protects these turtles, as well as a vast diversity of other critters. The park, and adjacent Barra del Colorado Wildlife Refuge, are the only attractions of the Caribbean north of Puerto Limón, the only city of any significance.

Somnolent, idyllically funky Tortuguero is an 80-km, three-hour journey upriver from Moín; by small plane, it's a 30-minute flight that sets you down on a thin strip of land between canal and ocean. The village of 500 inhabitants is little more than a few stilt houses on a spit of sand, with the ocean crashing on one side and the lagoon and the jungle on the other. It's a budget traveler's haven. Waves pile up white foam on the beach. The waters here are not safe for swimming because of rip currents and the large number of sharks, mostly nurse sharks in the two-meter range; the photo of the vicious-looking shark that hangs in the dining room of the Tortuga Lodge will dissuade skeptics from swimming! Barracuda—silvery assassins, terrifyingly dentured—also abound in the warm, shallow waters. That rusting hulk of saw-blades and metal framework was once a lumber mill that between the 1940s and 1972 provided steady work to the villagers, who supplemented their meager income selling turtle meat and shells, as had their forebears. When the mill closed—the same year the village's sole telephone arrived—the population began drifting away. Now tourism is booming, and so is the local population.

Every hotel and tour company in San José pushes Tortuguero, with good reason. About 30,000 tourists a year come here to explore the forests and swamps of Tortuguero National Park and to see any of four species of turtles that nest on the beach. The recent boom had spawned fears that the park was becoming overloaded with tourists. The rise in the park entrance fee to $15 in 1994 has helped alleviate the pressure (fewer people are visiting).

You can walk the entire 35-km length of the beach.

A note of interest: By one report, Fidel Castro and Che Guevara were erstwhile visitors on supply runs here before their return to Cuba as revolutionaries.

ACCOMMODATIONS

Tortuguero has only a limited number of rooms to rent. It's best to reserve well in advance. You can make reservations for any of the budget hotels via Olger Rivera at the community phone (tel. 710-6716) in the *pulpería;* you'll need to provide a return telephone number so that hotel owners can confirm your reservation. If you arrive without reservations, make it a priority to secure accommodations immediately.

If it's within your budget, I highly recommend a tour package that includes accommodations at one of the more upscale lodges (see "Guided Tours" under "Tortuguero National Park," below).

Budget

Budget travelers have several rustic options, most notably the **Cabinas Sabina,** with 35 basic rooms, plus a bar and rudimentary restaurant, and three newer rooms with private baths and fans facing the beach. Sabina, says another guidebook author, is not "the friendliest of souls." Surly, say I! Rates: $5 per person, $7 with bath. Simple rooms near the beach are also reportedly provided by Miss Junie and the **Brisas del Mar,** which has a five-person room ($15) and offers live music in the bar on Wednesday and Saturday nights. The **Cabinas Tortuguero,** adjacent to the beach, has simple but clean hostel-style rooms with communal outside bathroom-cum-toilet. Rates: $5 per person. Another option is

LOS CANALES—"THE WATERWAYS"

During the Tejos administration (1966-70), four canals were dug from solid ground to link the natural channels and lagoons of the coastal swamplands stretching north of Moín to Tortuguero and the Río Colorado. Today, these canals form a connected "highway"—virtually the only means of getting around along the coast—and one can now travel from Siquirres eastward along the Río Pacuare to Moín, then northward to Tortuguero, and from there to the Río Colorado, which in turn connects with the Río San Juan, which will take you westward to Pavas and Puerto Viejo de Sarapiquí. Most people simply travel between Tortuguero and Moín (see "Tortuguero National Park" under "Tortuguero and Vicinity"), and dozens of vessels ply this main channel.

The three-hour journey provides a superb experience. All along the riverbanks are the ramshackle shacks of settlers who come and go with the river level, subsisting on corn and the canal's swarming fish, such as tarpon and gar. Mingling with the tour boats and puttering tuglike launches are slender nine-meter-long canoes—each carved from a single log—powered by outboard motors and sometimes piled high with coconuts.

The easygoing waterway is lined with rainforest vegetation in a thousand shades of green. The deep verdure of the foliage, the many brilliant flowers, the graceful festoons of the vines and mosses intertwining themselves make for an endlessly fascinating journey. Noisy flocks of parrots speed by doing barrel rolls in tight formation. Several species of kingfishers patrol the banks; the largest, the Amazon kingfisher, is almost 30 centimenters long. In places the canopy arches over the canal and howler monkeys sounding like rowdy teenagers may protest your passing. Keep a sharp eye out, too, for mud turtles and caimans absorbing the sun's rays on logs.

Los Canales,
Tortuguero
National Park

Cabinas Meryscar, where clean yet tiny rooms with communal bathrooms rent for $4 per person. Pastor Centeno and his wife reportedly take in guests and provide all meals; ask around.

Southeast of town is **Cabinas Riversal,** with four cabins with bathroom for $20 (available through the grocery next to Soda Caribbean).

The **John H. Phipps Biological Field Station,** formerly the Casa Verde Green Turtle Research Station (contact the Caribbean Conservation Corporation, Apdo. 6975, San José 1000, tel. 238-8069; or P.O. Box 2866, Gainesville, FL 32602, tel. 904-373-6441) has dormitory accommodations for up to 24 people, with communal kitchen and bathroom. **Camping** is allowed here, and at the park headquarters at the southern end of the village. Remember, it rains torrentially at Tortuguero, the ground is

often waterlogged, and fer-de-lance snakes are abundant at night—hardly ideal conditions for camping!

The **Canadian Organization for Tropical Education and Rainforest Conservation** (COTERC, P.O. Box 335, Pickering, ON L1V 2R6, tel. 416-683-2116; or, in Costa Rica, beeper tel. 296-2626) has a research field station at Caño la Palma, about eight km north of Tortuguero. A dorm has bunk beds. You may also camp or sleep in hammocks. Rates: $40 including all meals and guided walk on trails into the rainforest and swamps.

Moderate

You have six moderately priced jungle lodges to choose from. Most basic is the **Hotel Ilan Ilan,** just north of and across the canal from Tortuguero; 20 large and comfortable but somewhat spartan rooms feature private baths, fans, and ice coolers. The small dining room serves *típico* Costa Rican meals. The lodge is owned and operated by Agencia Mitur (Apdo. 91, San José 1150, tel. 255-2262, fax 255-1946), which promotes a three-day/two-night package ($180, including transfers, meals, and guided tours aboard the *Colorado Prince* or *Tortuguero Prince*). Tour departures are offered from San José every Tuesday, Friday, and Sunday. The Mitur office in San José is at Calle 20 and Paseo Colón.

Slightly more upmarket is the **Jungle Lodge,** about one km south of Ilan Ilan. The lodge is owned and operated by Cotur (Apdo. 1818, San José 1002, tel. 233-0133, fax 233-0778), which promotes its three-day/two-night package featuring guided tours aboard the *Miss Caribe* and *Miss América* tour boats. Accommodation is in 16 rustic red-roofed cabinas, all with private bath and fans, linked by covered walkways. Oropendolas nest in the grounds. You can hire canoes *(cayucas)* for $5. Rates: same as Ilan Ilan, above.

Since the above lodges are both owned by tour companies, priority goes to people on the companies' own package tours. You may be able to secure last minute reservations if room is available.

About 800 meters north of the village is the **Mawamba Lodge** (tel. 233-9964 or 758-4915, fax 225-8613). Accommodation is slightly more upscale than at Ilan Ilan in 12 rooms with private baths and fans. The restaurant and bar is airy and spacious. A two-day/one-night package ($140) and a three-day/two-night package ($165) include tours and motorboat transfer from Moín.

More modest, and about five minutes by canoe from the village, is **Tatane Lodge** (Apdo. 7433, San José 1000, or c/o Ecole Travel, tel. 223-2240), with five small but pleasant A-frame huts (16 beds) on the bank of the canal leading to Barra del Colorado. Showers and toilet are in a separate hut. There's a restaurant. Rates: $85 per person, including transport to/from Moín, lodging (one night), plus jungle excursions.

The most recent addition is the **Manatí Lodge** (tel. 221-6148), with eight rooms with private bath and fan, including two-room suites with bunks. You can rent canoes and kayaks. The lodge is near the turtle research station. Not reviewed. Rates: $200 per person, two-night stay, including transfers.

Also new, and not reviewed, is the **Laguna Lodge** (tel./fax 225-3740), between the village and airstrip. Four hardwood units each have four airy rooms with heaps of light, ceiling fans, and private baths plus verandas. If you wish to relax in the grounds, simply hop into a hammock beneath a little *ranchita*. The lodge serves basic *típico* cuisine family-style. Rates: $219 for three days/two nights.

Upscale

The most atmospheric and appealing place in Tortuguero is **Tortuga Lodge,** owned and operated by Costa Rica Expeditions (Apdo. 6941, San José 1000, tel. 257-0766, fax 257-1665). Highly recommended. The lodge, which is the only one in the region to include park visits in its room rates, and which has 18 spacious and comfortable riverfront cabinas, is opposite the Casa Verde Turtle Research Station on 20 hectares of attractive landscaped grounds replete with ornamental plants. Howler monkeys often provide a reveille call, the wharf is a preferred spot for fishing bats that swoop and scoop in the wharf lights, and a nature trail that leads from the gardens offers good sightings of brightly colored frogs and other wildlife. You almost expect Tarzan and Jane to swing down from the trees and greet you as you dock.

Standard and "deluxe" rooms (each with ceiling fans plus fully equipped bathrooms) are in thatched lodges made of attractive hardwoods and fronted by wide verandas with leather rocking chairs. Elegant it is not. However, I was told of a possible impending upgrade, including construction of a more upscale restaurant. English-speaking staff and superb guides are under the assured management of Eduardo Brown Silva. Good-quality meals are served family-style. Rates: $50-66 s, $59-79 d, $70-92 t.

Tortuga Lodge is also acclaimed for its wide range of highly recommended guided nature tours (see "Exploring Tortuguero" under "Tortuguero National Park," below). Tortuga is the only fishing lodge in Tortuguero (there are others at Barra del Colorado and Parismina). Both world-record snook and tarpon were taken a short distance from Tortuga Lodge, and lodge manager Eduardo Silva—one of the finest fishermen on the east coast—holds the world's cubera snapper record.

FOOD AND SERVICES

The **park headquarters office** is 200 meters south of the village. The *pulpería* at the southern end of the village houses the community **telephone** (tel. 710-6716). Not to be missed is dinner at **Miss Junie's**, whose mother, Sibella, used to feed the famed turtle-conservationist Archie Carr (ironically, his favorite dish was green turtle soup). Today, $5 will buy you a platter of fish, chicken, and steak, with rice and beans simmered in coconut milk. **Soda Liliana,** adjacent, offers *típico* Costa Rican meals for $1 to $3. You can buy breads, cakes, cinnamon rolls, omelettes, and lasagne at **Pancaca Restaurant.** And Evelyn, in the **Soda Caribbean** to the south end, proffers *casados* for $4.

Soda Dolar, the **post office,** and the **police station** are in the village center, where there is also an **information booth** explaining the natural history of the area. The biological field station and visitors center, adjacent to the airstrip four km north of the village, can provide additional information on the turtles. For T-shirts and souvenirs, check out the **Jungle Shop** in the village center, or—better still—**Paraíso Tropical,** 50 meters farther north. The latter has a surprisingly excellent selection of shirts, swimwear, posters, jewelry, hammocks, etc. Owner Antoinette Gutierrez donates 10% of her profits to the local school. She may be able to cash traveler's checks.

For night owls tired of turtle watching and stargazing, there's a disco—**Disco El Bochinche**—100 meters north of Cabinas Sabina.

For those journeying to Tortuguero on the canals, a relaxing midway port-of-call—**Rancho Turístico el Tres,** alias Armando's Bar—features tree trunks as tables to complement the rustic bamboo restaurant. Local dishes (about $3) include shrimp and rice, breaded fried fish, chicken, and *gallo pinto.*

TRANSPORTATION

By Boat

JAPDEVA, the port authority, retired its old *Gran Delta* launch a few years ago; the vessel has not been replaced. A colorful variety of private boats, however, waits at the JAPDEVA dock in Moín (tel. 758-1106, 758-3286, or 758-3417) for passengers with or without reservations (see "Moín," above). The *Riverboat Francesca,* piloted by Modesto Watson (Apdo. 218, San Francisco de Dos Ríos, San José, tel. 226-0986) is recommended; for $70 he'll take you to Tortuguero and back, with lunch and snacks and a guided cruise of the park. Carlos Bruno (Apdo. 2482, San José 1000, tel. 758-1210) offers a similar service from Limón.

Cargo-cum-passenger boats also run irregularly via Parismina (3-10 hours, depending on vessel; $4-15). Try to arrange your trip the day before; otherwise get to Moín docks early in the morning and ask around. You may find yourself sitting atop the cargo (bring raingear and something warm; it can get quite cool in cloudy weather).

Alternately, river transport is also available as part of tour packages to Tortuguero offered by several tour companies in San José and jungle lodges in Tortuguero (see "Guided Tours" under "Tortuguero National Park," below).

See Moín, above, for direction to the JAPDEVA dock.

By Air

Travelair offers flights from San José's Pavas Airport via Barra del Colorado, daily at 6 a.m. ($6 one-way). Return flights depart Tortuguero at 7:05 a.m. **Costa Rica Expeditions** (Apdo. 6941, San José 1000, tel. 257-0766, fax 257-1665) operates a private plane to a beach landing strip four km north of Tortuguero village. Tour members get priority, but you may be able to get a spare seat ($60 one-way). You can also arrange charter flights from San José (see "By Air" under "Getting Around" in the On the Road chapter for a listing of air-taxi companies).

TORTUGUERO NATIONAL PARK

Drenched by 500 centimeters of rain a year, Tortuguero's 18,800 hectares—one of the last great stands of tropical rainforest in Central America—shelter a fabulous array of wildlife, including more than 300 bird species, among them the great green macaw; 13 of Costa Rica's 16 endangered mammal species, not least jaguar, tapir, ocelot, cougar, and manatee, plus three species of marine turtles. Commonly seen birds include toucans, aricarias, oropendolas, swallow-tailed hawks, several species of herons, kingfishers, anhingas, parrots, and jacanas. The wide-open canals with their great forested walls make viewing easier than at many other parks.

Tortuguero National Park is basically a mosaic of deltas on an alluvial plain nestled between the Caribbean coast on the east and the low-lying volcanic hills of Coronel, Caño Moreno, and 300-meter-high Las Lomas de Sierpe—the Sierpe Peaks—on the west.

The park—one of the most varied within the park system—has 11 ecological habitats, from high rainforest to herbaceous marsh communities. Fronting the sea is the seemingly endless expanse of beach. Behind that is a narrow lagoon, connected to the sea at one end and fed by a river at the other, which parallels the beach for its full 35-km length. Back of the lagoon is a coastal rainforest threaded by an infinite maze of serpentine channels and streams fed by rivers flowing from the central mountain ranges and by the torrential rains that fall in the area (the rains can last for days at a time, usually

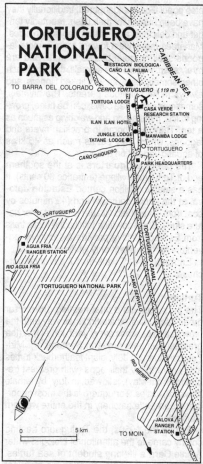

subsiding briefly in March). On the periphery of the forest lies a complex of swamps.

The western half of the park is under great stress from logging and hunting, which have increased in recent years as roads are cut into the core of the rainforest from the west, north, and south. The local community and hotel and tour operators are battling a proposed highway sponsored by banana and logging interests into the region between Tortuguero and Barra del Colorado. Particularly threatened is the large mammal population. Tortuguero's fragile man-

atee population is endangered; traditionally they have been hunted for their flesh, reputedly tender and delicious, and for their very tough hides. Manatees move west toward more remote lagoons seeking quiet places to mate and are rarely seen. Affectionate animals, they kiss each other, sometimes swim with linked flippers, and always make solicitous parents. The animals, sometimes called sea cows, can be huge, growing to four meters long and weighing as much as a ton. They're at home in brackish rivers and lagoons, where they eat as much as 45 kilos of aquatic vegetation a day.

The **park headquarters** is at the southern end of Tortuguero village (entrance 60 cents). It has a small exhibition center. **Estación Jalova,** at the park's southern end (45 minutes by boat from Tortuguero village) is a center for nature study. Short day-trips to hike the rustic trails from Estación Jalova provide a satisfying adventure for those with only limited time.

Entrance is $15 walk-in, $7 advance purchase.

Turtles

The park protects a vital nesting ground for green sea turtles, which find their way onto the brown-sand beaches every year June-Nov. (the greatest numbers arrive in September). Mid-February through July, giant leatherback turtles also arrive to lay their eggs (with greatest frequency April-May), followed, in July, by female hawksbill turtles. Tortuguero is the most important green-turtle hatchery in the entire western Caribbean.

During the 1950s, the Tortuguero nesting colony came to the attention of biologist-writer Archie Carr, a lifelong student of sea turtles. Carr enlisted sympathy through his eloquent writing (particularly *The Windward Road;* Gainesville: University of Florida Press, 1955). His lobby—originally called the Brotherhood of the Green Turtle—worked with the Costa Rican government to establish Tortuguero as a sanctuary where the endangered turtles could nest unmolested. The sanctuary was established in 1963 and the area was named a national park in 1970. The Brotherhood, now the Caribbean Conservation Corps, maintains a research station and natural history visitors center (the complex replaces the old Casa Verde) at the north-

ern end of the beach. The CCC also publishes *Velador,* a quarterly update on turtle projects in the region.

Limits were established in 1994 to control visitor impact. Only 150 people are allowed at night on the beach sector called 4 Esquinas; 100 on the Jalova sector; and 15 each on the Caño Negro and El Gavilán trails. Local guides—trained by the National Parks Service and now organized into a local cooperative—offer guided walks at 8 each evening in turtle-nesting season ($5; you can buy tickets in advance at the information kiosk in the village center). At press time it appeared that no one was allowed on the beach at all after 10 p.m. If you are allowed to go alone (you will probably be denied permission), check with the park ranger for instructions. Strict rules and guidelines are enforced for turtle watching. Turtles are endangered: respect them! Three rules you must adhere to: Do not use cameras or flashlights. Keep quiet, as the slightest noise can send the turtle hurrying back to sea. Keep a discreet distance.

When to Go

Rain falls year-round. The three wettest months are January, June, and July. The three driest are February, April, and November. Monsoon-type storms can lash the region at any time; rain invariably falls more heavily in the late afternoon and at night. August through November are best for turtle watching. The interior of the park is hot, humid (*very* humid on sunny days), and windless. Bring good rain gear; a heavy-duty poncho is ideal. **Note:** It can be cool enough for a windbreaker or sweater while speeding upriver under cloudy weather. *Take insect repellent—the mosquitoes and chiggers can be fierce.*

Exploring Tortuguero

Hiking: You can walk the entire length of the beach. Trails into the forests—frequently waterlogged—also begin at the park stations at both ends of the park and offer an excellent chance of seeing copious animal and bird species. The northern trail leads to Cerro Tortuguero (elev. 119 meters), two km north of Tortuga Lodge; from here—the highest point for miles around—you have a superb perspective over the swamps and coastline. The rusting

lookout tower at the top was assembled during WW II.

Canoes: You can hire dugout canoes *(cayucas* or *botes)* from the **Snake Tourist Social Center** at the south end of Tortuguero village ($3 per person per hour with guide; $1.50 without a guide). Many local villagers, including Mister Dama, Ruben Aragón, and Juan José Artencio, will rent you their *cayucas* (they'll also rent themselves out as guides—hire one, as on your own you'll not see 10% of the wildlife you'll see in their company). Give the canoe a good inspection before shaking hands on the deal: paddle around until you feel comfortable and have ascertained that there are no leaks and that the canoe is stable. Alternately, consider a *panga,* a flat-bottomed boat with outboard motor, or a *lancha* (with inboard motor), which will cost more. It's also a good idea to check on local currents and directions, as the former can be quite strong and it's easy to lose your bearings amid the maze of waterways. And don't forget to pay your park entrance fee before entering Tortuguero National Park.

Guided Tours

I highly recommend a guided tour offered through one of the lodges, or through tour companies in San José. Guides have binocular eyes: in even the darkest shadows, they can spot caiman, birds, crocodiles, and other animals you will most likely miss.

The guides will lead you deep into the narrow *caños* where you can see wildlife galore: giant iguanas and basilisk lizards basking atop the branches, toucans and aracarias, the pendulous nests of oropendulas, swallow-tailed hawks and vultures swooping over the treetops, and caimans luxuriating on the fallen raffia palm branches at the side of the river (they're difficult to spot, as their black and brown bodies provide perfect camouflage). That hair-raising roar? A male howler monkey that had misjudged a leap and—*"thwuwwuump!"*—hit a tree with legs spread apart! Well, that was the explanation given by one irrepressible guide.

Exploring at night is a particularly exciting adventure. I went on a guided night tour from Tortuga Lodge. We chugged up the side streams, where the waterways narrowed down to a murky closeness, and shone halogen searchlights on the riverbanks seeking the reflections of crocodilian eyes in the inky-black night. My favorite reward was seeing bulldog bats skimming through the mist that rose from the water: one scooped up a fish right on cue. Amazing! Our guide cut the motor and poled us deeper into the jungle. The succession of creatures—some virtually at arm's reach—seemed almost to have been installed for our benefit: a diminutive pygmy kingfisher, an agouti snoozing on the riverbank, owls sitting as still as statues, transfixed by the beams. I felt as if we were in a museum instead of a wilderness.

green macaw at
Tortuguero

The following offer guided tours:

Costa Rica Expeditions (Apdo. 6941, San José 1000, tel. 257-0766, fax 257-1665; in the U.S., contact P.O. Box 025216, Dept. 235, Miami, FL 33102) operates a variety of tours with overnights at its Tortuga Lodge. It provides rain ponchos, plus lunches for day-trips to Barra del Colorado. Three-day/two-night packages with private flight from San José to Tortuguero cost $299 per person (based on four-person minimum); boat tours into the park are extra.

Cotur (Apdo. 26-1017, San José 2000, tel. 233-6579) has a three-day/two-night package from San José, including a bus ride to Moín, then a journey to Tortuguero aboard either the *Miss Caribe* or the *Miss América*. A half-day tour of the park is included. Accommodation is at the Jungle Lodge. Departure on Friday, return Sunday.

Agencia Mitur (Apdo. 91, San José 1150, tel. 255-2031, fax 255-1946) operates its three-day/two-night Tortuguero Jungle Adventures aboard the *Colorado Princess,* with accommodation at the Hotel Ilan Ilan on Tuesday, Friday, and Sunday. **Sol Tropical** (Apdo. 153-1017, San José 2000, tel. 232-9041, fax 232-9062) features one-, two-, and three-day packages from San José, as do virtually all other major tour companies.

The **Mawamba Lodge** operates a launch—the *Mawamba*—twice weekly from Puerto Limón to Tortuguero (in San José, tel. 233-9964, or in Puerto Limón, tel. 758-1564). **Tico Tours** (tel. 222-8521, fax 222-8429) has a one-day "Tortuguero Monkey Jungle Tour" from San José. **Parismina Tarpon Rancho** (tel. 257-3553), **Laura's Tropical Tours** (tel. 758-2410), and **Caribbean Magic** (tel./fax 758-1210) also offer Tortuguero tours from Puerto Limón. **Caribbean Comfort** operates tours from Moín (tel. 758-1210). Most other hotels in Puerto Limón can arrange tours to Tortuguero.

BARRA DEL COLORADO

Unexciting and ramshackle Barra sits astride the mouth of the Río Colorado. The village once prospered as a lumber center, but its fortunes declined with the demise of lumbering and the river trade. Today it is a sportfishing center. Until recently there was no other reason to visit, except perhaps to look for crocodiles, which lounge on the sandbars of the wide and murky Río Colorado, or to explore Barra del Colorado Wildlife Refuge.

Barra's fortunes are slowly returning as cargo traffic with Nicaragua increases since the peace settlement in that country (the village became a haven for refugees from Nicaragua during the 1980s). For now, locals predominantly rely on lobster fishing or serving as guides for the sportfishing lodges. More and more, however, are becoming engaged in tourism as the Río Colorado and Río San Juan are being opened up for sportfishing and nature trips (see the Northern Lowlands chapter). The village has no roads, just a broken concrete walkway down its center.

Sportfishing "Paradise"

The rivers hereabouts are famous for their game fishing. Barra has four of the busiest sportfishing camps in Costa Rica—**Isla de Pesca, Río Colorado Lodge, Casa Mar,** and **Silver King Lodge**—and a handful of lesser accommodations for fishingfolk. The lodges are simple but well-maintained and comfortable. They are perfect oases after a day in the sun fighting tarpon and snook. Tarpon are so abundant and feisty hereabouts that a two-meter whopper might well jump into your boat! Gar—one of the oldest fish on earth, with an ancestry dating back 90 million years—are also common; growing up to two meters long, these bony-scaled fish have long, narrow, crocodile-like snouts full of vicious teeth. A recently discovered blue water fishery is "offering some big surprises."

Despite the end to the contra conflicts, tensions with Nicaragua run high here. In May 1994, for example, a Nicaraguan navy gunboat arrested five U.S. sportfishermen and three Costa Rican guides at the mouth of the river for "violating Nicaraguan territorial waters." Those arrested claim they were inside Costa Rican waters. The incident occurred amid the dispute over the Río San Juan—the international border—which becomes the Río Colorado as it approaches the sea. Nicaraguans dispute Costa Rica's territorial rights to land north of the Río Colorado. Fortunately an agreement signed in 1994 between Presidents Figueres and Chamorro aimed at more con-

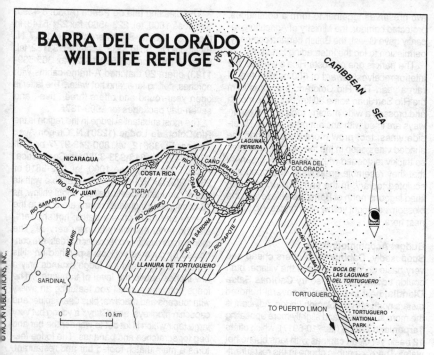

BARRA DEL COLORADO WILDLIFE REFUGE

CARIBBEAN SEA

NICARAGUA

RÍO SAN JUAN

RÍO SARAPIQUI

RÍO MARIS

SARDINAL

COSTA RICA

TIGRA

RÍO CHIRRIPO

RÍO LA SARDINA

RÍO ZAPOTE

RÍO COLORADO

CAÑO BRAVO

LAGUNA PENIERA

BARRA DEL COLORADO

CAÑO LA PALMA

BOCA DE LAS LAGUNAS DEL TORTUGUERO

TORTUGUERO

TO PUERTO LIMON

TORTUGUERO NATIONAL PARK

LLANURA DE TORTUGUERO

0   10 km

© MOON PUBLICATIONS, INC.

vivial relations. The Río San Juan is entirely Nicaraguan territory, but Costa Ricans have right of use. Still, Nicaraguan authorities began charging for use in 1994 at $5 per person, plus $7 per boat (you must also now carry your passport on the river).

In addition to the sportfishing lodges (see below), a 20-meter a/c houseboat—the **Rain Goddess** (Blue Wing International, Apdo. 850, Escazú, tel. 231-4299, fax 231-3816)—offers fishing on the San Juan, Colorado, and adjacent Nicaraguan rivers, and offers the advantage of mobility. Six double bed cabins each have a queen-size and single bed, sinks, and vanities. Three shared bathrooms have hot water and showers. It has an observation deck and dining room, plus TV and VCR. Two outboards are towed for fishing otherwise inaccessible areas. Rates: $1350 per person, five-day package including all meals plus air transportation from San José. Guided nature trips are also offered.

Barra del Colorado Wildlife Refuge

One of the biggest of Costa Rica's wildlife preserves, Barra del Colorado (91,200 hectares) protects a large wildlife population, including more than 240 species of birds. Great green macaws wing screeching over the canopy, mixed flocks of antbirds follow advancing columns of army ants, and jabiru storks with two-meter wingspans circle above, flying so high that they are no more than white motes in the sun. Cruising the small sloughs you might see caiman, manatees, peccaries, sloths, three species of monkeys, pacas, and, deep in the shadows, perhaps a jaguar or tapir.

Barra del Colorado is a model for other parks because of the many small communities with roots in the region: although it is virtually without roads, a maze of navigable waterways has spawned tiny farmsteads and communities along the rivers. As with Tortuguero, Tico conservationists are struggling to protect the wildlife refuge from illegal logging. Though plans exist to link the

two preserves together to form a continuous, protected corridor, the Ministry of Agriculture recently gave Geest, the British banana company, permission to log the interceding forest.

The park is one of Costa Rica's wettest: the interior receives upward of 600 centimeters of rain a year. The Río Colorado branches from the Río San Juan some 30 km before its mouth and crosses a wide marshy region. The waterways are lined with ancient raffia palms. Riverside vines, too, grow more densely than the shaded vines deep in the forest, their host trees so thickly festooned with cascades of greenery that they resemble great walls of clipped and sculpted topiary. In the early winter, the tree-lined lagoons north of Barra are ablaze with the blossoms of bright yellow allamandas. No turtles nest here.

Budget Accommodations
Supposedly, **Cabinas Leo** offers cheap and very basic accommodation in the village, but I couldn't confirm this. Also try **Cabinas Salsa Olandia,** next to the airstrip several hundred meters north of Río Colorado Lodge. Adjacent is the more substantial and slightly more appealing **Tarponland Lodge** (tel. 710-6917), which offers 12 basic yet clean cabinas with fans but no hot water. There's a public phone in the restaurant-cum-bar. Owner Guillermo Cunningham can arrange fishing trips and nature tours. Rates: $25 d.

Moderate Accommodations
Just north of Barra village is the somewhat spartan **New Tropical Tarpon** (tel. 225-2336; in Canada tel. 514-469-4861), with five basic cabins on swampy land crossed by narrow raised walkways. Each features a basic restaurant and bar.

Upscale Accommodations
Going up the social scale, options include the **Casa Mar Fishing Lodge** (Apdo. 825, San José, tel. 441-2820, fax 433-9287; or, in the U.S., P.O. Box 787, Islamorada, FL 33036, tel. 800-327-2880 or 305-664-4615), which offers 12 comfortable duplex cabins set in attractive landscaped grounds in fishing season, Sept.-Oct. and Jan.-May. As in most lodges, rates are for multiday packages.

The pleasing **Isla de Pesca** (Apdo. 8-4390, San José 1000, tel. 223-4560, fax 221-5148; in the U.S., Costa Sol International, 1717 N. Bayshore Dr., Suite 3333, Miami, FL 33132, tel. 800-245-8420 or 305-539-1632, fax 305-539-1123) offers 20 thatched A-frame cabins with porches, ceiling fans, and hot water. The latter is open year-round and offers three-, five-, and seven-day packages for $999-1375.

The most substantial lodge in the region is the **Río Colorado Lodge** (12301 N. Oregon Ave., Tampa, FL 33612, tel. 800-243-9777 or 813-931-4849, fax 813-933-3280); in Costa Rica, Apdo. 5094, San José 1000, tel. 232-8610 or 232-4063, fax 321-5987), unmistakable with its roof of corrugated plastic painted bright yellow. Its 18 comfortable individual rooms are open to the breeze and have private baths, hot showers, electric fans, and daily laundry service. The rooms, plus dining and recreation areas, are connected by covered walkways perched on stilts (when the river rises the lodge extends only a few inches above the level of the water). The lodge contains a small zoo featuring an aviary with toucans and macaws, plus deer, spider and capuchin monkeys, and "Baby," a young but very large tapir which is let out to wander the bar and beg for scratches and bananas. The lodge features a main thatch-roofed bar and restaurant, plus an open-air restaurant-cum-bar on the riverfront, complete with hammocks. The lodge is equipped with a complete tackle shop, plus a large fleet of 5.5-meter boats with two fighting chairs. The lodge offers five-, six-, and seven-night packages, including air transfers from San José ($1275-1945). Extra fishing days are $375. Rate for nonfishing guests is $75 per day.

Upriver 300 meters is the **Silver King Lodge** (tel. 288-0849, fax 288-1403; in the U.S., Aerocasillas, Dept. 1597, P.O. Box 025216, Miami, FL 33102, tel. 800-847-3474 or 813-942-7959, fax 813-943-8783), with 10 spacious duplexes, widely spaced and linked by covered catwalks. All cabins have queen-size beds with orthopedic mattresses, plus private baths with their own water heaters and large showers. Other features include a Jacuzzi, well-equipped tackle shop, plus a spacious bar and restaurant (with "gourmet chef," they say) in hardwoods with a wide-screen TV and VCR. Free beer, rum, and soft drinks are included. Fishing is from 10 six-

meter Carolina skiffs and offshore boat (and five-meter aluminium canoes for rainforest fishing). Package prices—from $1195 (single) for three days fishing to $2245 (double) for five days—include roundtrip air from the U.S., alcoholic drinks, meals, transfers, and laundry service. Ray Barry is the friendly manager, ably assisted by his pet peccary, Solito.

Services

You'll find a bar in the village center, plus a *soda* and bar (with **public telephone**) at the south end of the soccer field; there's another public telephone in the bar of the Tarponland Lodge. The village has two *pulperías*, a *librería*, and **Bazar a Missy**, which carries basics. The ramshackle **police station** is located at the wharf for Tarponland Lodge, near the airstrip, on the south shore of the river. A local guide and canoe cost $3 per person per hour.

Transportation

By Air: SANSA operates flights from San José on Tuesday, Thursday, Saturday, and Sunday at 5:30 a.m. ($41). Return flights depart Barra del Colorado at 6:15 a.m. **Travelair** offers flights from San José's Pavas Airport, daily at 6:00 a.m., continuing to Tortuguero and San José

at 6:45 a.m. ($66). You can also charter a light plane from San José.

By River: A rough road leads from Puerto Viejo de Sarapiquí to Pavas, at the juncture of the Toro and Sarapiquí rivers. From here, you can charter a boat down the Río San Juan to Barra del Colorado. The **Río Colorado Lodge** (Apdo. 5094, San José 1000, tel. 232-8610 or 232-4063; in the U.S., tel. 800-243-9777) recently reinstituted its boat trip between Barra del Colorado and Sarapiquí. It may also be possible to hire a boat from Los Chiles. You can also hire boats from Tortuguero (do not attempt to reach Barra without a guide, as there are several braided channels to negotiate and it is easy to get lost).

By Road: Many of the plantation villages southwest of Barra del Colorado have bus service. Reportedly, buses depart Guápiles to Cariari (21 km north), from where in dry season another bus journeys to a place called Puerto Lindo, on the Río Colorado. A boat apparently leaves Puerto Lindo for Barra at 4:50 a.m.

Tours: The **Río Colorado Lodge** (see above) offers a two-day, one-night package from San José, including bus to Moín, canal cruise to Barra del Colorado, and return flight to San José.

PUERTO LIMÓN TO CAHUITA

South from Puerto Limón, a succession of sandy shores leads the eye along the Talamanca coast toward Panamá. The beaches, popular with surfers for a decade, are now being discovered by tourists, and hotels are beginning to rise in large numbers beside the crystalline sands. Eight of Costa Rica's 34 "protected zones" lie in Talamanca, including the nation's only true coral reef.

The coast is sparsely settled, with tiny settlements (few villages) spaced far apart. The region, a mellow melting pot, has long been a cultural bastion for Bribrí and Cabecar Indians, who lived in the mountains, and English-speaking black immigrants from the Caribbean islands who settled along the coast and centered on a village originally called The Bluff. In 1915 a presidential decree changed the name to Cahuita, a combination of the Miskito Indian words *cawi* (a small tree with red wood that flourishes in coastal lowlands and is used to make dugouts) and *ta* (which means point of land): hence, "mahogany point." Paula Palmer's book *What Happen* depicts the traditional lifestyle of the Talamanca coast.

Life along the southern Caribbean is lived at an easy pace, services are minimal, and locals complain of being neglected by government (which perhaps explains why a significant percentage can be surly). Making a telephone call can take all afternoon. The weather is always humid. Though the region is slightly drier than the northern Caribbean, heavy rains can fall virtually any time of year. Then, the sea and sky are whipped into blending shades of gray, horses and cows stand about aimlessly, and water lies everywhere.

A decade ago, the *Monilia* fungus destroyed the cacao plantations which had sustained the region for generations. The April 1991 earthquake and a series of devastating floods that same year struck the region a severe blow, wiping out half a dozen bridges on the road south from Limón. A sturdy bridge over the Río Estrella was only reopened in July 1992; the original bridge and three provisional bridges were washed away by subsequent floods.

It has traditionally been hard to get to Talamanca, which remained isolated from national commerce before the opening of the coast road in the late 1970s. The paved road hugs the shore as far south as Puerto Viejo before continuing inland to Bribrí. From Puerto Viejo, a dirt road reaches into Gandoca-Manzanillo National Park; another dirt road extends south from Bribrí to Sixaola, on the Panamanian border. Keep your speed down south of the Río Estrella: there are some lethal potholes. About 30 km south of Puerto Limón, the road briefly leads away from the shore near Penshurst, from where a branch road leads into the valley of the Río Estrella, dominated by banana plantations of the Standard Fruit Company. You'll gain no idea of the vastness of these plantations driving south to Cahuita. To do so, take a sidetrip to Estrella (a back-to-basics option is to journey on the rusty ol' passenger train that runs daily from Limón to Estrella; see "Río Estrella," below). The banana plantations are an interesting study. Otherwise there is not much of tourist interest, although guided boat trips up the Estrella provide good wildlife viewing.

You'll see signs along the route for services such as **Jungle River** which rents fishing boats for trips up the Río Negro.

If you're coming for the beaches, I recommend Feb.-March and Sept.-Oct., the driest months.

Accommodations and Food

Only limited accommodation lies between Puerto Limón and Cahuita, but for food you can take your pick from a dozen or so *sodas*.

Cabinas Westfalia, on the left two km south of the airfield, is basic but adequate. **Selvamar Hotel & Club Campestre Cahuita** (tel. 758-2861; or Apdo. 214, La Uruca, San José 1150, tel. 233-1911), 22 km south of Puerto Limón, is a surprisingly attractive resort 200 meters from a lonesome beach that seems to stretch to eternity. The lobby sets the mood, providing a touch of Tahiti with its attractive bamboo furnishings in bright floral prints and soaring *palenque* roof.

Likewise, the restaurant. The pool is Olympic-size. Choose from pretty a/c cabinas or more basic rooms (52 in all) set amid shade trees and boasting color TV and room service (some with kitchenette). Rates: $40 s, $68 d, $80 t, $91 q, including tax and breakfast.

The **Anexo Hotel,** which offered camping and basic cabinas beside the estuary of the Río Negro in 1993, was closed for an upgrade when I passed by in spring 1995. **Cabinas Lemari** (tel. 758-2859), five km south of Selvamar, has six cabinas (no hot water; $8), plus a bar, a restaurant, and a public telephone; fishing trips can be arranged.

Transportation

The San José-Sixaola bus (Autotransportes MEPE, tel. 221-0524) leaves from Avenida 11, Calles Central/1 at 6 a.m. and 1:30 and 3:30 p.m. for Penshurst, Cahuita, and beyond (you may hop off the bus at any point that takes your fancy). Local buses depart Puerto Limón (Calles 3 and 4 and Avenida 4) for the Valle de Estrella and Pandora every two hours 5 a.m.-6 p.m.

HITOY-CERERE BIOLOGICAL RESERVE

Virtually undeveloped and distinctly off the beaten track, the 9,050-hectare Hitoy-Cerere National Park is the nation's least visited park. It is surrounded by three indigenous reservations—Talamanca, Telire, and Estrella—and backed by the steep and rugged Talamanca mountains, which make the reserve seem all but inaccessible. Dense evergreen forests are watered by innumerable rivers, including the Hitoy, an Indian name for a moss-bedded stream, and the Cerere, meaning "River of Clear Waters."

Take your pick of arduous trails or moderately easy walks from the ranger station along the deep valley of the Río Hitoy-Cirere to waterfalls with natural swimming holes. Large sections of the park's western and southern flanks have not been explored, and trails into the interior are overgrown, unmarked, and challenging (Indian guides are available for local hikes,) conditions that will appeal to the fit and adventurous. The park is a starting point for trans-Talamanca journeys to the Pacific via a trail that leads south to the Indian village of San José Cabecar and up the

margay

BOB RACE

valley of the Río Coén and across the saddle between Cerro Betsú (elev. 2,500 meters) and Cerro Arbolado (elev. 2,626 meters) to Ujarrás, in the Valle de El General.

Rainfall is prodigious: seven meters of rain a year is not unknown. When the sun shines, the park is spectacular. However, there is no defined dry season (March, September, and October are usually the driest months; July-Aug. and Nov.-Dec. are marked by torrential rains and storms). The result: one of the best specimens of wet tropical forest extant in the country. Large cats are also found throughout the reserve, as well as healthy populations of margays, tapirs, peccaries, agoutis, pacas, otters, and monkeys. The park is one of the last remaining strongholds of the harpy eagle. And Montezuma oropendolas, rare blue-headed parrots, toucans, and squirrel cuckoos are common.

Entrance: $15 walk-in, $5 advance purchase.

Accommodations

You can reserve basic lodging at the ranger station (tel. 233-5473); researchers get priority. Most likely, you'll not be able to get through to the ranger station microwave telephone, so check with the National Parks Service headquarters in San José (tel. 323-4070, or toll-free information tel. 192). Camping is permitted, but there are no facilities.

Javier Martín, a naturalist guide, offers packages that include a night at the Hotel Matama in Puerto Limón, plus three meals, transport to Hitoy-Cerere, and guided hikes ($135; tel. 758-1123, fax 758-4409).

Getting There

From Puerto Limón, turn right at Penshurst and follow the unpaved road via Pandora to the park

BANANAS: FRIEND OR FOE?

Stop banana expansion! That's the demand of Costa Rican environmentalists. Sadly, no one appears to be listening.

In 1967, banana plantations covered some 10,000 hectares, and about nine million bunches a year were being exported. In 1991, Costa Rica had 32,000 hectares planted in bananas, 18,800 workers were employed in the industry, approximately 57 million boxes were grown for export, and bananas earned $473 million in hard currency for Costa Rica. By 1995, more than 40,000 hectares were raising bananas and Costa Rica was well on its way to overtaking Ecuador as the world's largest banana exporter.

Tremendous, you may say. So what's wrong?

Let's start with soil productivity: Banana production is a monoculture that can cause tremendous ecological damage. Banana plants deplete ground nutrients quickly, so that heavy doses of fertilizer are required to maintain productivity over the years. Eventually, the land is rendered useless for other agricultural activities.

Pesticides are blamed for poisoning and sterilizing plantation workers, and for major fish kills in the Tortuguero canals. Fertilizers washed down by streams have been blamed for the profuse growth of water hyacinths and reed grasses that now clog the canals and wildfowl habitats, such as the estuary of the Río Estrella. And silt washing down from the plantations is acknowledged as the principal cause of the death of the coral reef within Cahuita National Park and, more recently, of Gandoca-Manzanillo.

Even marine turtles are threatened. Plastic bags are wrapped around the fruit stems and filled with insecticides and fungicides, which kill the fungus responsible for the black marks on skins. Once the stems are cut, the banana companies have traditionally dumped the plastic bags in streams—you can see them washed up at flood levels on tree branches throughout the lowlands—to be washed out to sea, where turtles mistake them for jellyfish, eat them, and suffocate.

Campaigns by local pressure groups and the threat of international boycotts are beginning to spark a new awareness among the banana companies. The plastic bags are now supposedly being saved for recycling (for every ton of bananas, 2.14 tons of waste is produced). A project called Banana

---

entrance. The road is reportedly passable even in rainy season, though a 4WD is needed even in dry season. Even then, you may not be able to make it all the way. It's a 90-minute drive from both Puerto Limón and Cahuita. Taxis from Cahuita are $30 each way (you will need to arrange your return pick-up in advance if you stay overnight in the park). Reportedly, the local banana company (tel. 587-0753) may be able to provide transport.

By Bus: A local bus departs every two hours 5 a.m.-6 p.m. from Puerto Limón (Calles 3/4, Avenida 4) to the Estrella Valley Standard Fruit Co. banana plantation, 10 km from the park entrance. Taxis from Finca 6 in the Estrella Valley cost about $5.

RÍO ESTRELLA

The Río Estrella is spawned in the foothills of the Matama mountains, where it collects the runoff of some 700 centimeters of rainfall and irrigates the banana plantations of the Estrella Valley as it crosses the plains in search of the Caribbean. Near the coast, the river gives rise to a dense network of channels and lagoons that provide shelter for 180 species of birds, including great flocks of snow-white cattle egrets, which roost at dusk on the riverbanks. The **Caribbean Biological Bird Station** (30 km south of Puerto Limón, near the bridge over the Río Estrella) protects this ecosystem. You can arrange guided river trips upriver ($40; check with the El Pizote Lodge in Puerto Viejo, or the Aviarios Rio Estrella—see below). **Rancho del Sol,** immediately north of Aviarios de Caribe (see below), offers birdwatching and fishing and has boats for rent.

Orchid-lovers may thrill to **Orquídeas Mundo** (Apdo. 575, Limón 7300, fax 758-2818), a very funky botanical nursery where French-Canadian botanist Pierre Dubois hybridizes rare orchid species. Pierre will happily give you a tour,

Amigo recommends management guidelines. Companies that follow the guidelines will be awarded an Eco-OK seal of approval to help them export bananas; companies continuing to clear forests will not. The Eco-OK program is a joint project between the Costa Rican environmental group Fundación Ambio and the international Rainforest Alliance. (The sticker shows a yellow sun rising behind a map of the world.) The government-backed National Banana Corporation (CORBANA) has mounted a campaign to prove that it is cleaning up its act. Bananas, it claims, are going green.

The Río Sixaola plantation in Bribrí became the first Costa Rican producer to receive an Eco-OK label in 1994. Owner Volker Ribniger uses a minimum of pesticides and herbicides; contaminated water is run through a special filtering system; organic wastes are recycled; and plastic bags are collected for recycling.

Green or not, massive tracts of virgin forest continue to be put to the blade to meet the expansion of banana plantations. In mid-1992, for example, Chiquita Brands International announced a massive banana expansion of 6,000 hectares in the economically depressed areas of Limón, Sarapiquí, and Sixaola. Banana producers assert that the industry provides badly needed jobs. Environmentalists claim that devastating environmental effects are not worth the trade-off for a product for which demand is so fickle. The multinational corporations, too, are hardly known for philanthropy. Workers' unions, for example, have historically been pushed out of the banana fields, and some banana companies have even been accused of operating plantations under virtual slave-labor conditions.

The Calderón administration sided with the *bananeros,* supporting expansion by improving the infrastructure in areas desirable for banana plantations. This, despite pleas from the local government of Limón—which derives its greatest source of income from bananas—to stop banana companies from clearcutting the forests of the Caribbean zone. The pleas have fallen on deaf ears. The Limón government and environmentalists, for example, recently denounced the clearcutting of forests separating Barra del Colorado and Tortuguero National Parks by the British banana company Geest. The fragile region was supposedly protected by a management plan. The Ministry of Natural Resources issued permits to Geest anyway.

or guide you on a nature hike into nearby forests ($5). Turn right at the sign for Penshurst after crossing the Río Estrella. The nursery, based around an old school bus-turned home, is on the right after 500 meters.

Dole and other fruit companies have gargantuan banana plantations in the Estrella Valley ("Valley of the Stars"), reached via **Penshurst,** a small village a few km south of the Río Estrella. Life hereabouts is an intriguing study. I recommend that to glimpse it you ride on the local **banana train,** a passenger service that operates daily at 4 a.m. and 2:30 p.m. from Puerto Limón ($1.20 each way; tel. 758-3314). The roundtrip journey takes about five hours. Don't expect comfort! Seats are of the old-school-bus variety, bolted to the floors. Your companions will be local plantation workers and perhaps the odd backpacker. The weary iron horse groans along past ramshackle villages and lonesome corrugated-tin shacks interspersed between row upon row of banana plants and orderly plantation villages with names such as Finca 6 and Finca 8, where it lurches to a stop before jerking along past Penshurst, winding west down the valley of the Río Estrella. The train returns for Limón at 6 a.m. and 4:30 p.m. If you want to take it one way only and continue to Cahuita or Puerto Viejo, get off at Bonifacio, 38 km south of Limón; from here, it's a 10-minute walk to the coastal highway, where you can hail a bus running between Limón (tel. 758-1572) or San José (tel. 221-0524) and Sixaola.

Accommodations

Aviarios del Caribe (Apdo. 4011, San José 1000, tel. 224-7822, fax 224-6895 or 798-0374), one km north of the Río Estrella, offers one of the best bargains on the Caribbean coast. The beautiful modern lodge (a replacement to one that collapsed in the 1991 earthquake; the new lodge used the latest anti-quake designs) is set amid a privately owned 75-hectare wildlife sanctuary. It protects a marshland ecosystem of freshwater lagoons threatened by the effects of fertilizers washing down from nearby banana plantations (the fertilizers

have caused the marsh grasses to bloom prodigiously). The lagoons are a haven for caimans, river otters, and river turtles, as well as more than 200 bird species, plus monkeys and sloths; jungle trails lead to a lookout blind. You don't even need to head off into the sloughs, however, to spot wildlife—the owners have a veritable menagerie on site, including Buttercup, an orphaned sloth, Pink Cheeks the boa constrictor, Coco the crocodile, a couple of tame toucans, and dozens of poison-arrow frogs spawned in the hatchery.

Five spacious, superbly furnished rooms have tiled floors, king-size beds, and ultramodern bathrooms. The lodge features a small gym,

laundry service, a TV and video room with library, and a screened upstairs restaurant with beautiful hardwood floors. Owners Luis and Judy Arroyo offers canoe rentals ($5 per hour; $10 with resident guide, Luis) and can arrange tours into the Talamanca mountains. Highly recommended. Rates: $50 d, low season, $60 high season, including breakfast. First-come, first-served.

Hospedaje Nohelyn (tel. 284-9089), just beyond the Penshurst turnoff, has four clean but dark rooms (two with a bunk and double bed; two with a double and single) with fans, and private bath with cold water. Rates: $15 s/d including breakfast.

CAHUITA AND VICINITY

This funky, seemingly down-at-the-heels village (pop. 3,000), 45 km south of Puerto Limón, is an in-vogue destination for the young backpacking crowd and others for whom an escapist vacation means back to basics. It gets very crowded on holidays but for much of the rest of the year is free from the hordes that descend on, say, Manuel Antonio National Park (typically, no more than 50 people a day enter Cahuita National Park). Cahuita is totally laid-back and definitely not for those who like their luxuries (although that is changing as Cahuita inexorably goes upmarket). The village itself is no more than two parallel unpaved streets crossed by four rutted streets overgrown with grass, with ramshackle houses spread apart . . . much as it was in the years following 1828, when it was founded by a Panamanian named William Smith. The area suffered major damage during the April 1991 earthquake, which raised the coast hereabouts, exposed most of the coral reef, toppled the trees that now litter the beach, and dealt a devastating blow to the local economy. The area has finally recovered. Alas, a gang of thugs who culminated their brief predation on tourists in 1994 by murdering one before being caught left Cahuita with an unfair reputation for being unsafe; the crimes actually occurred near Estrella. In March 1995, tourists were still staying away because of the bad publicity while Puerto Viejo, down the road, was booming. By some reports, hotel occupancy in

Cahuita nose-dived as much as 80%.

What you get is golden sand beaches backed by coconut palms and an immersion in Creole culture. One of the most endearing aspects of life on the southern Caribbean coast is the large number of Rastafarians, with their broad smiles, dreadlocks, and a lifestyle that revolves around reggae, rasta, and—discreetly!—*ganja* (marijuana). Bob Marley is God in Cahuita! Alas, the "rent-a-Rasta" syndrome well-known to Jamaica (European blonde femme fatales with local gigolos in tow) has inspired a reputation for "free love" that other women travelers must contend with. Women are advised *not* to walk around at night on their own.

North of Cahuita is a black-sand beach (Playa Negra) that runs for miles. Cahuita's more famous beach south of the village is fringed by tall palms and, behind, by the dense, wet tropical forest of Cahuita National Park, an ideal place to relax and observe nature close-up. Best time to visit is March-April, or Sept.-Oct., when rains subside.

Two dirt roads (marked with signs for various hotels) lead to Playa Negra just before the turnoff for Cahuita, which lies to the right once you reach the beach. Entering Cahuita directly from the main road, you come to a T-junction at the water's edge; the left fork leads back toward Playa Negra; Cahuita village is to the right, with the main street coming to a halt at the entrance to the national park.

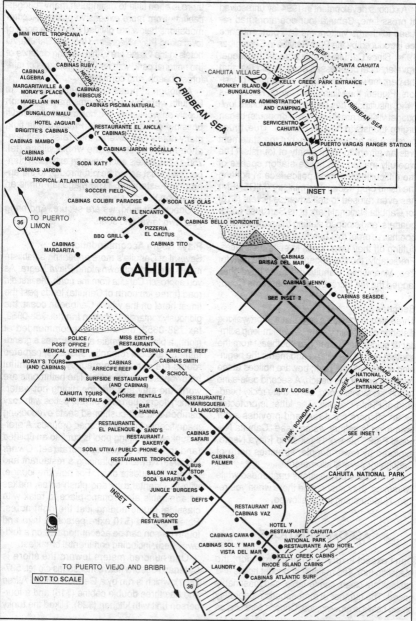

MINI HOTEL TROPICANA

CABINAS RUBY

CABINAS ALGEBRA

MARGARITAVILLE & MORAY'S PLACE

MAGELLAN INN

BUNGALOW MALU

HOTEL JAGUAR

BRIGITTE'S CABINAS

CABINAS MAMBO

CABINAS IGUANA

CABINAS JARDIN

TROPICAL ATLANTIDA LODGE

CABINAS COLIBRI PARADISE

CABINAS MARGARITA

CABINAS HIBISCUS

CABINAS PISCIMA NATURAL

RESTAURANTE EL ANCLA (Y CABINAS)

CABINAS JARDIN ROCALLA

SODA KATY

SOCCER FIELD

PLAYA NEGRA

CARIBBEAN SEA

SODA LAS OLAS

EL ENCANTO

PICCOLO'S

CABINAS BELLO HORIZONTE

PIZZERIA EL CACTUS

BBQ GRILL

CABINAS TITO

CABINAS BRISAS DEL MAR

CAHUITA

CABINAS JENNY

CABINAS SEASIDE

SEE INSET 2

TO PUERTO LIMON
36

POLICE / POST OFFICE / MEDICAL CENTER

MISS EDITH'S RESTAURANT

CABINAS ARRECIFE REEF

MORAY'S TOURS (AND CABINAS)

CABINAS ARRECIFE REEF

CABINAS SMITH

SCHOOL

ALBY LODGE

NATIONAL PARK ENTRANCE

WHITE SAND BEACH

KELLY CREEK

SURFSIDE RESTAURANT (AND CABINAS)

CAHUITA TOURS AND RENTALS

HORSE RENTALS

BAR HANNIA

RESTAURANTE / MARISQUERIA LA LANGOSTA

PARK BOUNDARY

SEE INSET 1

RESTAURANTE EL PALENQUE

SAND'S RESTAURANT / BAKERY

SODA UTIVA / PUBLIC PHONE

RESTAURANTE TROPICOS

CABINAS SAFARI

CABINAS PALMER

CAHUITA NATIONAL PARK

BUS STOP

SALON VAZ
SODA SARAFINA

JUNGLE BURGERS

DEFI'S

INSET 2

EL TIPICO RESTAURANTE

RESTAURANT AND CABINAS VAZ

CABINAS CAWA

CABINAS SOL Y MAR

VISTA DEL MAR

HOTEL Y RESTAURANTE CAHUITA

NATIONAL PARK RESTAURANTE AND HOTEL

KELLY CREEK CABINS

RHODE ISLAND CABINS

TO PUERTO VIEJO AND BRIBRI

LAUNDRY

CABINAS ATLANTIC SURF

NOT TO SCALE

36

INSET 1

CAHUITA VILLAGE

REEF

PUNTA CAHUITA

MONKEY ISLAND BUNGALOWS

KELLY CREEK PARK ENTRANCE

PARK ADMINSTRATION AND CAMPING

CARIBBEAN SEA

SERVICENTRO CAHUITA

CABINAS AMAPOLA

PUERTO VARGAS RANGER STATION

36

A curious development in 1994 lay unresolved at press time. Cahuita tour operators had refused to charge visitors the $15 park entrance fee introduced by the Park Service in September 1994. Since Cahuita mainly attracts the budget traveler, local businesses have a valid fear that the park fee will deter a large percentage of visitors. Piqued, the Minister of Natural Resources (who, insultingly, has implied that Cahuita's low-budget visitors are drug-crazed dropouts) began urging tourists to boycott Cahuita. True, drugs here are an easy purchase, but the statement was an affront to the majority of tourists. (The woefully inadequate police station speaks of the difficulties the local police face in fighting the rising drug trade.) The ministry (MIRENEM) has even refused to sell advance tickets ($10) for Cahuita National Park at its San José headquarters, and stopped staffing the park entrance booths . . . proof that bureaucrats are experts at cutting off their own noses to spite their faces. Predictably, tourists began to enjoy the park for free. Meanwhile, Cahuita residents have challenged the fee increase in the Supreme Court.

Beaches
Three slender beaches lie within a short walking distance of Cahuita village. A two-km-long scimitar of golden sand stretches southeast from the eastern end of the village and marks the beginning of the national park; beware riptides at the northern end of this beach. A second pale-sand beach lies farther along, beyond the rocky headland of Punta Cahuita. The latter is protected by an offshore coral reef and provides safer swimming in calmer waters (see "Cahuita National Park," below). Black-sand Playa Negra, explored by fewer people, stretches north of Cahuita for several kilometers.

Do not leave possessions unattended while swimming; they may not be there when you return. Nude bathing is not allowed.

ACCOMMODATIONS

Don't expect luxury (with one exception: the Magellan Inn). The majority of budget hotels and cabinas are clean, comfortable, and reasonably priced. The number of atmospheric moderately priced hotels is growing, too. Choose carefully, as there is often little to distinguish many "budget" cabinas from more expensive places. Accommodations below are divided into those north of town along Playa Negra and those in Cahuita. All hotels in the village are within walking distance of the national park, with its 1,067 hectares of rainforest, beach, and coral reef.

Although at press time, tourist numbers in Cahuita were low, hotel rooms may be in short supply on weekends and holidays; call ahead if possible or visit midweek. Prices are in flux; many hotels had lowered their rates. One telephone number serves the whole village (tel. 758-1515). Hotels each have an extension number; you must ask to be put through to the appropriate extension. (The Magellan Inn is an exception.)

Check that windows are secure. And bring your own towel and soap.

Playa Negra Accommodations
Several of Cahuita's more appealing establishments are north of town along Playa Negra. As you approach Cahuita from the north, the first dirt road (three km north of Cahuita) leads past the finest hotel on the whole Caribbean coast: the gloriously romantic **Magellan Inn** (tel. 758-0652, fax 798-0652; the latter is recommended at night), a place as intimate and warm as a grandfatherly hug. Six romantic, spacious, carpeted rooms are done up in mauves, with plentiful hardwoods in counterpoint. The bathrooms are worth the stay and provide piping hot water. French doors open onto private patios with cozy bamboo and soft-cushioned seats overlooking magnificently lush landscaped grounds. A pretty sunken swimming pool is cut into an uplifted (and therefore deceased) coral reef. Owner Elizabeth Newton is planning a restaurant and full bar (for guests only). For now the lounge, with its Oriental rugs and plush sofas, makes an admirable atmospheric place to relax with classical music adding just the right notes. Rates: $55 s/d ($10 extra person: a third and fourth person can be accommodated on a fold-away bed), including continental breakfast.

One hundred meters toward the shore is **Cabinas Algebra** (leave messages c/o tel. 587-2861), which is run by a German named Alfred and has three double cabins ($15) and a four-person unit with kitchen ($26). I liked the funky

feel of the restaurant with its veranda festooned with epiphytes; Alfred cooks tasty, wholesome dishes. Turn left on the shorefront road and you'll arrive at **Mini Hotel Tropicana,** an Italian-run hardwood two-story structure with four large rooms with private baths and hot water. Two more buildings are being considered. The grassy grounds are expansive. Rates: $20 s, $25 d, $30 t.

Opposite Algebra is a pretty green cottage housing the very basic **Cabinas Ruby.** Heading south toward Cahuita along Playa Negra you'll almost immediately come to **Moray's Place Bed & Breakfast,** a romantic stone-and-hardwood two-story house. The second-floor restaurant is none other than the acclaimed **Margaritaville,** whose meal of the day is posted. A bedroom next door has a king-size bed and private bathroom and wide windows. Four rooms are below, each with beautiful stone walls, fan, and private bath (except one room) with hot water. Rates: $25 s/d including breakfast. Moray's allows camping.

A stone's throw south is **Cabinas Hibiscus** (tel. 239-4485 in San José), one of the best places in Cahuita, with three pleasing cabinas ($30 double) and a chalet for six ($75). No restaurant, but it has hot water and a spiral staircase up to the second floor, where rockers and hammocks allow a balcony siesta. Next is **Cabinas Piscina Natural,** run by a friendly chap called Walter and so-named for the natural seawater coral cove with sandy bottom good for swimming. It's a modest place with five cabins (each has a double bed and bunk) with private baths and hot water, plus patios. Rates: $18 s/d.

Farther along are **Bungalow Malu,** a pretty thatched cabina enclosed in landscaped grounds and *still* only half-complete (as in the first edition), and the **Hotel Jaguar** (Apdo. 7046, San José 1000, tel. 758-1515, ext. 238, or tel. 226-3775, fax 226-4693), which is one of the best hotels around. It is set in seven hectares of modestly landscaped grounds, and has 44 beachfront rooms: spacious and light, with screens, queen-size bed (firm as a handshake), fans, and hot water. The restaurant is in the remains of an old farmhouse. Jaguar's creator, Don Harkness, died, alas, but the renowned breakfasts are still good (though not "phenomenal," as before). Trails behind the hotel lead into the nearby rainforest. You can rent boogie boards and snorkeling equipment in the well-stocked souvenir shop run as a separate business by Susan and Wayne. A swimming pool and tennis court may be added. Rates: from $30 s, $55 d, including full breakfast and tax.

A dirt road leads along the side of **Restaurant El Ancla** (which offers pizzas and spaghetti, as well as basic cabinas; it's a cool place to hang at night, with plenty of local color and lots of reggae riffs) to **Brigitte's Cabinas,** run by Swiss-born Brigitte. Two run-down rooms are somewhat dingy and have shared bath ($11 d). She cooks, offers horseback tours ($19, half day), and supposedly has a large collection of poison-arrow frogs. Opposite Brigitte's is **Cabinas Mambo,** a handsome two-story hardwood structure with four large rooms, each with mosquito nets, fan, and hot water, and spacious veranda ($20 s/d). Again, fishing, horseback rides, etc. are offered. Fifty meters brings you to **Cabinas Iguana.** Three all-hardwood budget rooms share toilets and shower outside but are handsome and have verandas with hammocks. At $10 d, a bargain. Larger cabins are very attractive and have mosquito nets and kitchenettes (the German owner provides fruits free) and wide balconies with hammocks ($25-40, up to four people). It offers a laundry service, plus large book exchange, and you can rent horses. Nearby is **Cabinas Jungle Paradise,** offering four simple but attractive cabinas ($10 per person).

Fifty meters south on the coast road into Cahuita is **Jardín Rocalla** (formerly Cabinas Black Sand; ext. 251), which has an open-air restaurant serving Italian dishes, and attractive stone-and-hardwood, two-story, Swiss-style cabins ($12 per person). Upstairs rooms have balconies. More appealing yet is the **Atlántida Lodge** (ext. 213), which has 15 pleasing bamboo-roofed duplex cabins with private terraces, fans, and hot water, plus a restaurant under thatch with hammocks, set in a well-tended four-acre garden with tame parrots, toucans, and Emilio, the pet white-faced monkey. A little arched bridge spans a pool filled with carp. There's a "boutique" and book exchange, secure parking, and above all, a friendly, "home-with-the-family" ambience. Highly recommended. Rates (high season): $50 s, $62 d, $75 t.

Passing the soccer field on your right, you'll come to the **Cabinas Colibri Paradise** (ext. 263), with pleasing cabinas with private baths and fans. Beyond, a dirt road leads back toward the Puerto Limón-Bribrí road: 200 meters on the right is **Cabinas Margarita** (ext. 205), with 10 double cabins, each with fans, hot water, and tiled floors ($25 per cabin). Owner John Henry Lewis is a friendly soul.

Continuing south of the soccer field along the dirt road fringing the coast is **El Encanto** (Apdo. 1234, Limón), a bed and breakfast run by Michael and Karen Russel, who offer three two-story cabinas in a pretty garden. It's modern and pleasing, with lots of hardwoods, queen-size orthopedic mattresses, ceiling fans, private baths, and hot water. It also has a small patio restaurant and secure parking. Rates: $40 s, $45 d, including breakfast. Next, you'll come to **Cabinas Bello Horizonte** (ext. 206 or 258), which has three simple cabinas with private bathrooms on the beach ($25 double), plus eight rooms with communal baths ($5). The very basic-looking **Cabinas Tito** is opposite. Cahuita village begins about 200 meters farther south, at the end of Playa Negra. **Grant's Cabinas** (ext. 206), with two basic cabinas (with private baths) and rooms (communal bath), is on the Playa Negra road north of Cahuita.

Cahuita Village Accommodations
Suddenly Cahuita village is sprouting hotels with charm. Leading the pack is **Kelly Creek Cabins** behind a white picket fence immediately overlooking the park entrance. Four very large rooms are in a single handsome all-hardwood Thai-style structure with heaps of light pouring in through tall jalousied (louvered) windows. Elegant bed linen adds a bright note. A second, similar, structure houses the restaurant (serving Spanish cuisine), and five identical cabins were being built behind. Tables on the lawn overlook the beach. Rates: $60 d, $65 t, $70 quad.

The other romantic gem is the very private and peaceful German-run **Alby Lodge**, where you'll find four beautiful thatched Thai-style cabins sitting on stilts and widely spread apart amid lawns and bougainvillea. All have heaps of character, with high-pitched roofs, screened and louvered windows, hardwood floors, mosquito nets pendant from the ceiling, nice bathrooms, and private pa-

tios with hammocks and marvelous tables hewn from logs. A *ranchita* restaurant should be complete by the time you read this. Rates: $31 s/d, $36 t, $41 quad with tax.

Another reasonable option is the **Hotel Cahuita** (ext. 201), one block west of the park entrance. The place is well managed by Ingo and Cora Kolonko, and offers 12 spacious motel-style cabinas with fans ($10 per person) but no hot water, plus two "houses," one for four people and one for six ($15 per person). The hotel has a small swimming pool, a bar (live music Friday and Saturday) and restaurant, plus hammocks. Rooms above the restaurant have balconies and communal bath.

A tad more sophisticated is the **Hotel National Park** (ext. 244), above the restaurant of that name directly in front of the park entrance. The 15 rooms are pleasant: clean and bright, with private baths and cold water (hot water is being installed). Rates: $15 s, $20 d.

Across the street from Hotel Cahuita is **Cabinas Vaz** (ext. 28), with a clean restaurant popular with locals. The accommodations could use what my father used to call a "damn good clean out." Rates: $12 s, $15 d. Next door, and of similar quality and price, is **Cabinas Cawa,** with six cabinas. Also here is **Cabinas Sol y Mar** (ext. 237), with eight basic rooms for four to six people (from $13 d), with pleasing private bathrooms but no hot water. Rooms upstairs catch the breeze.

Past Sol y Mar, the side road leads to the fairly basic **Rhode Island Cabins** (ext. 264), with eight small rooms ($10-15), and **Cabinas Atlantic Surf,** with six very handsome all-hardwood rooms in a two-story building. The reception for both is in two cottages on the right, 20 meters beyond Sol y Mar. The footpath beyond Atlantic Surf leads to Alby Lodge.

Near the shoreline are several reasonable options beginning with the newly constructed **Cabinas Arrecife Reef,** whose seven rooms have breezy verandas and are clean and roomy if gloomy. Bathrooms have hot water. Rates: $15 per person. (A little cabin opposite Arrecife has a very basic room for rent: the sign reads Backpackers Welcome!). Fifty meters west is **Cabinas Smith** with six pretty little rooms with fan and hot water and patios with seats. Rates: $15 s/d, including taxes.

I like the seafront setting of **Cabinas Jenny** (ext. 256), which has 15 basic rooms on two levels, all with comfy mattresses, mosquito nets, and fans plus private bathrooms with cold water ($16-26). Seven rooms face the beach. Upstairs rooms have balconies. Just being completed nearby in April 1995 was **Cabinas Seaside,** whose superb location only 20 meters from the waves with marvelous views along the shoreline makes a mockery of the construction laws. Hammocks are strung between the palms. At least a dozen rooms were planned, some being small cabinas, others in a two-story building. Rates: $12 s, $15 d.

Also on the shore is **Cabinas Brisas del Mar** (ext. 267), with clean and modest cabinas with private baths but no hot water. Rate: $22 d.

Surfside Cabinas (ext. 246) has 12 modern and clean yet basic rooms, each with refrigerator, louvered windows, fan, and private bath. You can choose between doubles, bunks, and twin beds. Rate: $12 d. The restaurant offers meals from $2.50 upward and is popular with the locals.

One block toward the beach from the bus stop is **Cabinas Palmer** (Apdo. 123, Puerto Limón, tel. ext. 243), which has 20 rooms (13 with hot water) that include small but clean rooms with fans, plus three larger four-person rooms with refrigerator and kitchenette. The friendly owner Rene accepts credit cards. There's parking, and a sunny garden out back. Rates: $12-15 s, $20-25 d, $30 for larger rooms. Opposite is **Cabinas Safari** (ext. 277), with seven clean and pleasant rooms, each with a tiny garden. Rates: $12 s, $18 d.

Moray's, the tour agency at the northern end of Cahuita's main street (ext. 216), also has basic cabinas for $10.

Somewhat out of the way, 1.5 km south of Cahuita, on the road to Puerto Viejo, is **Hotel Playa Blanca,** with six clean cabins in a field backed by the forest of Cahuita National Park. **Cabinas Amapola** ($15 per person) and a bungalow called **Quetzal Jardín** ($25, four people) are close to the Puerto Vargas park entrance, as is **Monkey Island Bungalows** with six cabins just off the main road ($20 d).

Camping
You'll find a campground inside the national park, one km along the trail from the Puerto Vargas park entrance. Closer to town, **Vishnu's Camping Inn** ($1.50 to camp) is one-half km north of Cahuita, about 50 meters on the right along the dirt road leading from Playa Negra back to the Limón coastal highway. You can also reportedly camp at **Cabinas Brigitte** (see above).

Note: You don't want to pitch your tent on the beach. The "no-see-ums" are vicious.

FOOD

There's excellent eating to be enjoyed in Cahuita.

Alas, the acclaimed Cafetería Vishnu, which once served the most delicious and healthy breakfasts in town, looked closed in March 1995. Check it out. If I'm wrong, it's a true breakfast treat! The **Hotel Jaguar,** however, serves filling breakfasts. Another recommended breakfast spot is **Soda Kukula,** where American owner Bill Toneo serves up tremendous North American standards: pancakes, fresh fruit, etc. (5 a.m.-5 p.m. daily). Cheap, too!

A good choice for lunch is **Restaurante El Ancla,** farther along Playa Negra. This colorful hangout for local Rastas offers a good selection of basic Italian and local dishes, enjoyed to the accompaniment of reggae music. There are several good bets in town, too, including the **Restaurant Cabinas Vaz, Restaurant Sol y Mar,** and **Vista del Mar** (all popular with locals), and—in front of the park entrance—the **Restaurant National Park** (a steadfast favorite of travelers), which has a cosmopolitan menu with sandwiches, fresh seafoods, and desserts, but which has lost all its charm since owner Richard Wray replaced his thatched, hardwood hangout with a soulless concrete restaurant. All are good bets for dinner, too. Another favorite with locals is the restaurant at **Cabinas Surfside** (meals from $2.50), where games of dominoes stir quite a noise. **Pizzeria el Cactus** (also recommended; ext. 276) has live music on weekends. Pizzas and spaghetti dishes from $4.

Cahuita is one place McDonald's hasn't yet reached, but Rene Palmer conjures sizzling **Jungle Burgers** at the restaurant of that name next to Defi's. Lunches and dinners at **Bananas Restaurant** at Cabinas Algebra on Playa Negra are also recommended; so too the sea bass (corvina) in garlic ($6) at the **Hotel Cahuita.**

Salon Vaz, Cahuita

JOHN ANDERSON

Don't leave Cahuita without having dinner at **Miss Edith's, Defi's,** and/or **Margaritaville.** The latter is on Playa Negra. Owner Sandra Johnson offers a set dinner special each evening—no breakfasts or lunches—with local cuisine washed down with piña coladas and killer margaritas ($5, including salad, main course, bread, dessert, and coffee). Jimmy Buffett riffs mingle with the rush of the waves. Sandra offers a taxi service from Cahuita.

On a par is **Miss Edith,** who, ably assisted by her two daughters, will create inexpensive, spicy, aromatic Caribbean specialties such as "rundown" (a spiced stew of fish, meat, and vegetables simmered in coconut milk) at lunchtime and dinner. She also serves breakfast 7-10 a.m. Meals are complemented by Miss Edith's own herbal teas. She offers a vegetarian menu. And weekend meals are highlighted by homemade ice cream. Expect to pay $5-10.

Though the old **Defi's** (ext. 204) made entirely of driftwood burned down, the new Defi's has lost none of its charm and still serves one of the best meals in Costa Rica! Fabulous seafoods and West Indian dishes include roasted fish in curry sauce ($5), filet mignon with mushroom and vegetable sauce ($4), octopus in garlic ($11), and the house special (jerk chicken in spicy coconut milk). Tremendous! Also with heaps of ambience, yet tiny and funky, is the very rustic **Restaurante Trópicos** (opposite Soda Vaz),

which also doubles as a bakery. Other options include **Restaurante El Palenque,** with a large menu in the $2-5 range; **San Key Solo Restaurante** and **Restaurante/Marisquería La Langosta;** and what I call the **Restaurante Sin Nombre** attached to Cahuita Tours and held aloft by treetrunks (it has a vegetarian breakfast for $3, and a "tropical" breakfast for $4).

The **Kelly Creek** restaurant promises to be a winner with its Spanish cuisine.

The **El Típico Restaurant,** 50 meters up the street, serves delicious *refrescos* and crab dishes from $8, but you can dine on a filling *casado* special for $3.

If catering for yourself, sometimes a fruit-and-vegetable stand sets up in front of the National Park Restaurant. There's a small bakery next to the small "park" opposite Salon Vaz on the main road where you can stock up on delicious pies, breads, and corn pudding, all for less than $1. You can also buy inexpensive foodstuffs and meals at **Soda Jardín Cervecero,** at the junction of the dirt road to the Puerto Vargas entrance; or at **Soda Katy.**

ENTERTAINMENT

There's not much night action in Cahuita. **Salon Vaz** is a laid-back bar with a funky plank-floored disco complete with flashing lights at the back.

DRUGS, SEX, AND THEFT

Before I begin, let me say: *don't get paranoid* . . .

Theft
A lot of tourists get ripped off in Cahuita and Puerto Viejo. An American and a European who have each lived in Puerto Viejo for several years told me of being repeatedly ripped off in crafty scams. Don't trust locals to handle your money. Particularly beware of credit. Don't exchange money before receiving the services or goods you're paying for: I've heard more than once of locals saying they needed your money to pay someone in advance to arrange a boat ride or horseback trip . . . then disappearing for a few days.

Watch, too, for pickpocketing. And there are reports of night-time muggings. Be cautious at night, particularly if you intend to walk on the beach or park trail. Stick to the well-lit main streets if possible. Be aware that the cheaper the cabinas, the more susceptible you are to burglary. Make sure you have bars on the window (your own door lock is a good idea) and that your room is otherwise secure.

Don't leave valuables in your room or on the beach.

Sex
If you're looking for love beneath the palms, you'll probably have better luck if you're female. Local Afro-Caribbean men are very forward with their advances toward women, and judging from the number of blond beauties on the arms of local males, their approaches are often warmly received. Reportedly, many men charge for love on the equator. Despite this, the local community is basically conservative: cover up in town, as bathing suits are frowned on.

Drugs
Ganja (marijuana) is also part of the local scene, and cocaine is readily available; trading has increased in leaps and bounds since the fall of Noriega in Panamá. However, Costa Rican authorities are getting increasingly serious in their attempts to counter drug trafficking. Many supposed dealers are undercover policemen. A new effort to counter narcotics trade was recently launched.

It's a popular hangout for dreadlocked Rastas (village elders sit out front), who also favor the **Ancla** on Playa Negra. Across the road from Salon Vaz, **Soda Sarafina** is a slightly more upscale version on the theme. **Bar Hannia** is a ramshackle saloon one block north of Vaz. Many people hop down to Puerto Viejo, where the discos pack 'em in at night.

SERVICES

Tours and Activities
Cahuita Outdoor Sports & Adventure (tel. 758-1515, ext. 232, fax 758-0652), **Moray's** (tel. 758-1515, ext. 216), **Jaguar Tours** (tel. 226-3775), and **Sea Tours & Cahuita Information Agency** all offer glass-bottomed boat tours to the reef ($10 for four hours, drinks included). You can also arrange boat trips up the Río Estrella, guided hikes, horseback rides, and trips to Tortuguero. Cahuita Tours also has **jeep tours** (owner Antonio also acts as a reservation agent; credit cards accepted). José McCloud, a local

guide trained by the Talamanca Association for Ecotourism and Conservation, can also take you snorkeling on the reef (ext. 256); while Walt Cunningham, also trained by ATEC, offers guided hikes in the park and local cacao plantations (tel. 758-1515, ext. 58 or 229; his house is the blue one next to the soccer field).

Cahuita Outdoor Sports and Moray's both charge $75 for six hours' guided scuba diving, with tanks included; both also rent scuba gear. Cahuita Tours, Moray's, Sea Tours, and the Hotel Cahuita all rent snorkeling masks and fins (approximately $5 a day). Cahuita Tours has **bicycles** for $1.25 per hour or $6 a day; Moray's charges $5 a day. You can rent **horses** from Brigitte's Cabinas for $6 a day, or $45 with guide. For the ultimate thrill, Cahuita Tours rents **dune buggies.**

Souvenirs
Cahuita Tours sells T-shirts, postcards, postage stamps, etc. A store next door is fully stocked with clothing, hammocks, embroidered vests, sandals, carvings, model ships made of wicker,

etc. It features a Guatemalan room and a Costa Rican room.

Another excellent boutique called **Coco Miko** sits opposite Cabinas Vaz. Letty Grant of Cabinas Bello Horizonte runs the **Tienda de Artesanía,** a women's cooperative crafts shop selling T-shirts and other souvenirs. A souvenir store sells hair beads, jewelry, and clothing next to Cabinas Cawa. Other little stalls are by the Kelly Creek park entrance.

Other

Many local women wash clothes; there are plenty of **laundry** signs. The **police station** (Guardia Rural) and **post office** (Mon.-Fri. 7 a.m.-11 a.m. and noon-4 p.m.) are at the north end of town. There are no **banks;** the nearest one is in Bribrí, about 20 km farther south. Cahuita Tours, however, offers dollar exchange, as will most hotels. You can pay almost everywhere with dollars. There is one **telephone** number for the whole village (tel. 758-1515). All calls are received by an operator who will transfer your call to the extension you want. There's a public phone at Soda Uvita, opposite the bus stop. Cabinas Iguana has a very well-stocked **book exchange.** You can buy **gas** (petrol) at several places (watch for the makeshift signs), including 50 meters east of Cabinas Margarita; at a hut that bills itself as "Servicentro Cahuita," three km south of Cahuita; at Bar Las Bromelias, one km before the turnoff for Puerto Viejo; and Geronimo's Place, 200 meters along the dirt road after the turnoff.

TRANSPORTATION

From San José

Direct buses to Cahuita and Sixaola depart from Avenida 11, Calles Central/1, daily at 6 a.m. (and 8:30 a.m., Saturday and Sunday), and 1:30 and 3:30 p.m. (four hours; Autotransportes MEPE, tel. 221-0524). They will drop you off in Cahuita village center or at the road leading to the Park Vargas park entrance. Fare is about $4. Return buses depart Cahuita at 7, 7:30, and 9:45 a.m., and 4 p.m. (3:50 weekends) from opposite Soda Vaz.

Saragundí Specialty Tours (tel. 255-0011, fax 255-2155) was due to introduce a daily tourist shuttle, departing San José 7 a.m. via Puerto Limón, continuing to Puerto Viejo.

From Puerto Limón

Buses depart from Radio Casino, one block north of the municipal market (Avenida 4, Calles 3/4) at 5 and 10 a.m., and 1 and 4 p.m. daily (one hour). Buses are usually crowded; get to the station early. Departures for Puerto Limón are at 6:30 a.m., 10 a.m., noon, 1:30 and 5 p.m. Buses for Puerto Viejo, Bribrí, and Sixaola depart at 6 and 11 a.m., and 2 and 3 p.m.

CAHUITA NATIONAL PARK

Cahuita's 14 kilometers of beaches are shaded by palm trees, lush forests, marshlands, and mangroves. Together they make up Cahuita National Park (1,067 hectares), created in 1970 to protect the 240 hectares of offshore coral reef that distinguish this park from its siblings (see special topic, "Coral-Reef Destruction). Animal life abounds in the diverse habitats behind the beach—an ideal place to catch a glimpse of tamanduas, pacas, raccoons, sloths, agoutis, armadillos, and, of course, the ubiquitous monkeys that come down to the shore.

A footbridge leads into the park from the Kelly Creek Ranger Station at the eastern end of Cahuita village. Kelly Creek is shallow and easily waded. A shady seven-km nature trail leads from the Kelly Creek Ranger Station to another at Puerto Vargas, three km beyond Cahuita Point at the southern end of the park. You must wade the Perozoso ("Sloth") River—its waters stained dark brown by tannins—just west of Punta Cahuita.

Both entrance stations are open 8 a.m.-4 p.m. ($15 walk-in, $7 advance purchase; entrance fees were not being collected at the Kelly Creek entrance at press time). You can stay at a camping area with picnic tables, water, toilets, and showers at the administrative center beside the beach, one km north of the Puerto Vargas Ranger Station ($1 per day). You can either walk the beach to Puerto Vargas, or drive to the site from the Puerto Vargas entrance off the main road to Puerto Viejo (the Sixaola-bound bus will drop you off near the entrance; it's a one-km hike from the road). A gate across the

road is locked after hours. The reef lies offshore north of Puerto Vargas.

The nature trail walk takes about two hours with time to stop for a swim in the warm Caribbean waters, watch the tree-dwelling sloths, iguanas, and troops of howler and capuchin monkeys, and focus your binoculars on a green ibis, rufous kingfisher, or low swooping Swainson and keel-billed toucans. Other birds include the Central American curassow and large groups of nesting macaws Dec.-February. Cahuita's freshwater rivers and estuaries are also good places to spot caimans and herons. Coatis, raccoons, and poisonous snakes—watch your

CORAL-REEF DESTRUCTION

The most complex and variable community of organisms in the marine world is the coral reef. So complicated are the relationships of the coral reef complex that "they would make the largest computer in the world blanch," says Dr. Frank Talbot, a marine ecologist with the California Academy of Sciences.

Corals are animals that secrete calcium carbonate ($CaCO_3$, better known as limestone). Each individual soft-bodied coral "polyp" resembles a small sea anemone and is surrounded by an intricately structured calyx of calcium carbonate, an external skeleton that is built upon and multiplied over thousands of generations to form fabulous and massive reef structures.

The secret to coral growth is the symbiotic relationship with single-celled algae—zooxanthellae—which grow inside the cells of coral polyps and photosynthetically produce oxygen and nutrients, which are released as a kind of rent directly into the coral tissues. Zooxanthellae must have sustained exposure to sunlight to photosynthesize. Hence, coral flourishes close to the surface in clear, well-circulated tropical sea water warmed to a temperature that varies between 21 and 27° C (70 and 80° F). The Caribbean's clear waters expose the submerged coral gardens to a long and fruitful growing season for the algae and other plants that form the base of the food chain in this fertile world.

The reef is a result of a balance between the production of calcium carbonate and a host of destructive forces. Though stinging cells protect it against some predators, coral is perennially gnawed away by certain snails and fish, surviving by its ability to repair itself and at the same time providing both habitat and food for other fauna.

To untrained eyes, Cahuita's coral reef may look pristine, an aquatic version of the Hanging Gardens of Babylon. On the sea floor are the massive brain corals and the delicate, branching sea fans and feathers; nearer the surface are elkhorn corals, frondlike gorgonians spreading their fingers up-ward toward the light, lacy outcrops of tubipora, like delicately woven Spanish mantillas, and soft flowering corals swaying to the rhythms of the ocean currents. Up to 500 species of fish gambol among the exquisite reefs. Here, amid sprawling thickets of bright blue staghorn, great rosettes of pale mauve brain coral, and dazzling yellow tubastras almost luminescent in the bright sunlight, a multicolored extravaganza of polka-dotted, piebald-dappled, zebra-striped fish protect their diminutive plots of liquid real estate among the reef's crowded underwater condominiums.

Sadly, man's incursions threaten the fragile ecological balance. Twenty years ago, Cahuita had a superb fringing reef. Today, much of it is dead—smothered by silt from mainland rivers. Coral growth is hampered by freshwater runoff and by turbidity from land-generated sediments—from banana plantations and deforestation—which clog their pores so that zooxanthellae can no longer breathe. Along almost the entire Talamanca coast and the interior, trees are being logged, exposing the topsoil to the gnawing effects of tropical rains. The rivers bring agricultural runoff, too: poisonous pesticides used in the banana plantations and fertilizers that are ideal for the proliferation of seabed grasses and algae that starve coral of vital oxygen. It is only a matter of time before the reef is completely gone.

Prospects for the reef at Gandoca-Manzanillo are equally grim. The region's isolation is already a thing of the past, and hotel developers are moving in fast. More than a dozen major projects are planned, most slated to be built facing the beach. Ronal Umana, a marine biologist with the conservation group ANAI, fears that sedimentation and pollution could devastate the reef and tarpon and lobster nurseries.

Coral is a very resilient creature: a coral reef will grow back again if left alone. Alas, the Costa Rican government must move more quickly and conscientiously than it has to date if it is to save what little coral remains.

step!—are commonly seen along the trail. And red land crabs and bright blue fiddler crabs— the latter with oversized claws—inhabit the shores. Don't forget your insect repellent and sunscreen.

The reef off Punta Cahuita protects the northern stretch of the beautiful scimitar beach to the south. Smooth water here provides good swimming; it's possible to wade out at knee level. At the southern end of the park, beyond the reef, huge waves lunge onto the beach—a nesting site for three species of turtles—where tidepools form at low tide. Check with rangers about currents and where you can walk or snorkel safely.

The waters offshore abound with angelfish, blue parrot fish, moray eels, lobsters, and even green turtles, which feed on the fields of swaying turtle grass. Snorkelers can try their luck near Cahuita Point or Punta Vargas (you must enter the water from the beach on the Punta Vargas side and swim out to the reef); you can also hire a local resident to take you out farther by boat. Besides what remains of the beautiful coral, there are two old shipwrecks about seven meters below the surface, both with visible ballast and cannons; one wreck has two cannons, and the second, a more exposed site, has 13. The average depth is six meters. The best time for diving and snorkeling is during the "dry" season, Feb.-April; water clarity during the rest of year is not very good beacause of silt brought by rivers emptying from the Talamanca mountains.

PUERTO VIEJO AND VICINITY

About 13 km south of Cahuita the road forks just after Home Creek (also spelt "Hone Creek"). The paved road turns inland toward Bribrí; the unpaved road leads to Puerto Viejo, Punta Uva, and Manzanillo. Puerto Viejo is three km down the bumpy unpaved road, which parallels Playa Negra—an endlessly curling black-sand beach—on your left.

The village encloses a small bay with a capsized barge (now sprouting a tree) in its center. The tiny headland of Punta Pirikiki at its southern end separates Puerto Viejo from the sweep of beaches—Playa Pirikiki, Playa Chiquita, etc.—and offshore coral formations that run all the way south to Manzanillo and Panamá. You can walk along the beach from Cahuita in a day.

Puerto Viejo is very low-key, very funky. Its laid-back way of life is still almost innocent, though changing fast as the younger surf, backpack, and college crowd is flocking in increasing numbers. Everyone walks around barefoot. Vultures hop around lethargically on the streets, taking to reluctant flight only when you approach within a meter or two.

The village was the most "happenin'" place in spring 1995. The discos are hoppin'! Many Europeans and North Americans seeking an alternative lifestyle have settled here and now run bistros and restaurants alongside the locals.

It should take you at least three or four days to get in the groove—to absorb the flavor and get friendly with the locals. Don't expect things to happen at the snap of your fingers.

Until only a year or two ago, most of the people lived a traditional, modest life of subsistence farming and fishing as generations had done before them. Before the growth of tourism, 95% of the area's income was derived from lobster fishing, which is highly seasonal. Telegraph poles and high wires today import the power of the 20th century (the electricity and water supply are still not reliable; bring a flashlight), and the sudden influx of tourists threatens to sweep away the last of the old ways. Every second person now seems to have cabinas to rent; the others are opening restaurants, each on a unique theme. A few Afro-Caribbean farmers, however, still grow cacao; the coconut palm, too, is the "tree of life." Sweet and juicy citrus fruits fill the gardens, lobsters are plentiful, and large, tasty shrimp live in the rivers that rush down from the mountains. Drugs—cocaine and marijuana—are abundant in these parts.

Puerto Viejo

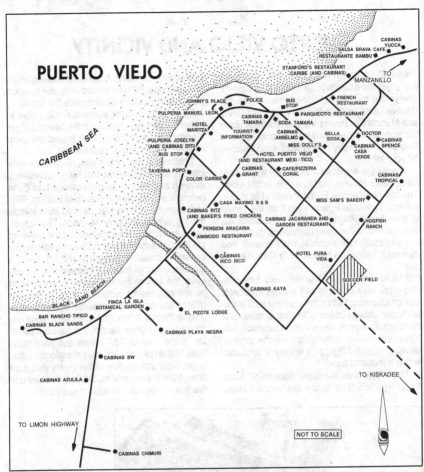

PUERTO VIEJO

CARIBBEAN SEA

CABINAS YUCCA
SALSA BRAVA CAFE
RESTAURANTE BAMBU
STANFORD'S RESTAURANT
CARIBE (AND CABINAS)
TO MANZANILLO

JOHNNY'S PLACE POLICE BUS STOP
PULPERIA MANUEL LEON
FRENCH RESTAURANT
CABINAS TAMARA SODA TAMARA
PARQUECITO RESTAURANT
HOTEL MARITZA
TOURIST INFORMATION
CABINAS ANSELMO
BELLA SODA
DOCTOR
CABINAS SPENCE
PULPERIA JOSELYN (AND CABINAS DITI)
MISS DOLLY'S
CABINAS CASA VERDE
BUS STOP
HOTEL PUERTO VIEJO (AND RESTAURANT MEXI-TICO)
TAVERNA POPO
COLOR CARIBE
CABINAS GRANT
CAFE/PIZZERIA CORAL
CABINAS TROPICAL
CASA MAXIMO B & B
MISS SAM'S BAKERY
CABINAS RITZ (AND BAKER'S FRIED CHICKEN)
CABINAS JACARANDA AND GARDEN RESTAURANT
HOGFISH RANCH
PENSION ARACARIA
AMIMODO RESTAURANT
CABINAS RICO RICO
HOTEL PURA VIDA
SOCCER FIELD
CABINAS KAYA
BLACK - SAND BEACH
FINCA LA ISLA BOTANICAL GARDEN
BAR RANCHO TIPICO
CABINAS BLACK SANDS
EL PIZOTE LODGE
CABINAS PLAYA NEGRA
CABINAS BW
CABINAS AZULILA
TO KISKADEE
TO LIMON HIGHWAY
CABINAS CHIMURI

NOT TO SCALE

Paula Palmer's *What Happen: A Folk History of Costa Rica's Talamanca Coast* (Ecodesarrollos, 1977) and *Wa'apin Man* (Editorial Costa Rica, 1986) provide an interesting insight into the traditional Creole culture of the area. Another useful reference is *Welcome to Coastal Talamanca,* published by ATEC, the **Talamanca Association of Ecotourism and Conservation** (you can buy the book in Puerto Viejo and in San José), which runs an excellent tourist information bureau opposite Soda Tamara. Visitors are welcome to attend the association's weekly meetings in the Hotel Maritza (Monday 6 p.m.), when development and conservation issues are discussed. One of the group's concerns is that the bulk of tourist dollars flowing into the more upscale resorts south of town bypassing the local community. To help counter this, they recently initiated a program to train locals as "approved" guides to lead trips into the jungle.

Puerto Viejo has no dry season, although March, April, and May tend to be less rainy.

Surfing

Puerto Viejo is legendary among the surfboard set. December through April the village and beaches are crowded with surfers, who tell tall tales about a killer six-meter storm-generated wave called La Salsa Brava, reputed to be for experts only. It washes ashore in front of Stanford's Restaurant. November and December are supposedly the best months, though it was cookin' when I called by in March. Beach Break is good for novices and intermediates.

Surfboards and surfing equipment can be rented (soon, I'm sure, a dedicated surf shop will open), and you might be able to buy a board from someone closing out his vacation (many surfers find it easier to sell their boards rather than carry them back home). Kirk, a Yank who owns the Hotel Puerto Viejo, is a surfing aficionado and can repair broken boards.

ACCOMMODATIONS

You'll find plenty of small and cozy cabins to choose from in Puerto Viejo, although most places do not have hot water. You'll want a room with a ceiling fan (otherwise, check that the hotel provides mosquito nets). A lot of cabinas seem to be changing hands or are being upgraded; the names and ownership may have changed by the time you arrive.

The only public phones in town are at the Hotel Maritza (tel./fax 758-3844), Pulpería Manuel León (tel. 758-0854), and ATEC office (tel./fax 798-4244). The Maritza and ATEC had the town's only faxes. It is wise to write a month or two in advance to secure reservations, or call the above numbers and leave a message for the owner of the hotel of your choice to call you back.

Many other cabinas and some excellent hotels lie south of Punta Cocles within walking distance of Puerto Viejo (see "Punta Cocles, Punta Uva, and Manzanillo," below).

Budget

Just beyond Home Creek, before the turnoff for Puerto Viejo, is **Cabinas El Monte**, advertising trips to Talamanca. At the end of the dirt road into town, some 200 meters before reaching the coast, is **Cabinas Azulil** (tel. 228-6748; in San José, tel. 255-4077), the best self-catering ac-commodation around and a superb deal for several people together. Two two-story family-size "cabins" provide lots of light, beamed ceilings, and attractive hardwoods; two bedrooms and two bathrooms upstairs, two bedrooms and a shower downstairs ($10 s, $50 for up to eight people).

In the village, Mr. Vincent Guthrie has seven rooms at **Cabinas Ritz**. Rooms have fans and hot water. Rates: $8 s, $15 for three to four people, $20 for a large room for six. The **Hotel Puerto Viejo**, above the Restaurant Mexi-Tico, has small and spartan rooms without even fans. Upstairs rooms are preferable. It is run by two friendly Americans, Dan and Kirk, and is popular with surfers. Most rooms have communal bathrooms. Rates: $5 per person d, $20 for a large room with private bath. **Cabinas Stanford** has nine clean cabinas with hardwood walls, fans, and pretty carved beds ($14 d). Also try **Cabinas Manuel León**, another popular hangout for surfers. Rooms ($10), which sleep four, are basic, and the water supply is reputedly inconsistent.

At **Cabinas Jacaranda** are four cabins set in a pretty landscaped garden; three with shared bathroom. Japanese paper lanterns, mats, and mosquito nets are nice touches. The fourth cabin is for four people. Best yet, it's a 10-second walk to the Garden Restaurant (see "Food," below). Highly recommended. Rates: $15 d.

A five-minute walk up the hill behind the soccer field (follow the sign) is **Kiskadee's**, a fairly basic but popular dormitory-style hotel run by an American, Alice Noel. One room has double beds. Bird lovers can admire the brightly colored tanagers and kiskadees that throng hereabouts. Don't forget your flashlight, and be prepared to get muddy hiking to and fro. Rates: $4, or $5 with use of the kitchen. Nearby, down the hill near the soccer field, is **Cashew Jungle Lodge**, with cabinas plus a dorm room in the family home of two friendly Americans, Amy and Mike.

Cabinas Diti has four cabinas off the street next door to the *pulpería* opposite the bus stop (contact Taverna Popo for information). **Cabinas Tamara** also has four basic cabinas with furnished porches, some with stoves, some without; one block up from Hotel Puerto Viejo. Both are in the $10 range. Set back from town, the very funky, tumbledown **Hogfish Ranch** is popular with the young surf crowd and is run on a communal basis with small kitchen plus bunk

beds and shared toilets and shower outside; inside it looks like an after-the-party scene from a John Belushi movie. Rates: $6.

More salubrious is **Cabinas Black Sands,** with three simple rooms, each with twin beds, in a bamboo-and-thatch hut with communal bathroom right on the black-sand beach, just before entering Puerto Viejo ($8 s, $12 d). You can rent all three units ($30). It's 200 meters along a dirt road (the last 100 meters can be very muddy); the turnoff is opposite Pulpería Violeta, which also advertises rooms for rent. Basic, too, at a lonesome location on the south edge of town, is **Cabinas y Restaurante Rico Rico.**

Just east of Restaurante Bambú is **Salsa Brava Café y Cabinas,** right on the beachfront and a favorite of surfers. Simple, dark, dingy rooms have private bath and fans and veranda ($15 s/d). The very Caribbean-style restaurant is a cool place to hang.

The following are aligned along the dirt that swings southeast to Punta Cocles: **Vista Verde** offers basic cabinas, as does **Vilas Monte Sol,** with four musty rooms from $15 d. New attractive, thatched cabinas were being built next door, as was the **Hotel Casablanca,** farther down the road. Nearby, too, set in landscaped gardens to left and right of the road, is **El Escape Caribeño,** with clean and very attractive brick-and-stucco cabins with screens and communal kitchen (bring your own utensils); some rooms have refrigerators. The very basic **Cabañas Banana** is 100 meters further.

Inexpensive

The Swiss-run **Cabinas Casa Verde** is of an excellent standard. It has 12 large rooms in three units, each with fans, mosquito nets, and lots of light, plus hot water. Four rooms share two spotlessly clean showers and bathrooms. Wide balconies have hammocks. Owner Renée, who mixes his time between lazing in a hammock and fussing over running his place, has maps and an info service. Features include a laundry, secure parking, and a book exchange, plus a tiny poison-frog garden, and you can arrange horserides. There's also a small cabin, romantic as all get-out, for a family or small group. Rates: $15 s, $20 d.

Cabinas Girasol has eight clean cabinas with fans, screened windows, heated water and tiled showers, and a small store and laundry. Rates: $15 s, $21 d, $25 t. The **Hotel Pura Vida,** around the corner from the Garden Restaurant, is nice: well-kept, with large, pleasing rooms for $13 s, $18 d. An airy outside lounge has hammocks and easy chairs.

The **Hotel Maritza** (tel. 758-3844) on the beachfront has 10 rooms with private bath with hot water; some with a/c, the others with fans ($15 d, $18.50 t). All have private bathrooms with hot water. On weekends, the bar and disco downstairs make the walls throb. The rooms were being renovated and upgraded. Also, 14 simple but comfortable cabinas have fans and private baths with hot water, plus motel-style parking ($18 d).

Cabinas Tropical opened in February 1995 with five pleasing rooms: clean, airy, with ceiling fans, huge showers, and wide French doors onto little verandas. Smaller single rooms are dingier. It's quiet and secure. A restaurant was being built. Rates: $10 s, $15 small room; $20 s/d, large; $25 d, cabin. A bargain.

Moderate

A pleasant option is the Belgian-run **Pensión Aracaria:** a pretty yellow-and-white clapboard house on the edge of town. It offers five small rooms with shared bath above the restaurant, with porch views out to sea. Rates: $25 s, $30 d. I can't speak for **Casa Máximo Bed and Breakfast,** as there was no one there when I called by this pleasant looking three-bedroom hostelry.

Another good deal is the **Cabinas Playa Negra** (tel. 556-1132 or 556-6396), which has four two-story villa-style units, one-half km west of Puerto Viejo ($33 for up to six people). Owner Alexis Coto Molina is very friendly. Downstairs in each unit is an airy living room, a fully equipped kitchen complete with refrigerator, plus a bathroom; upstairs are two bedrooms, plus a screened veranda with rockers—an ideal place for a siesta. Alas, no hot water.

Cabinas Grant (tel. 758-2845) has also been recommended. Rates: $20 s, $30 d, $45 t, including breakfast.

If you're a nature lover and don't mind being out of town, I highly recommend **Cabinas Chimurí** (a Bribrí word for "ripe bananas") for a more "authentic" traditional experience. It's a 15-minute walk from town, set back from the

dirt road leading into Puerto Viejo. A trail (200 meters) leads uphill through forest and banana plants to four small, charming A-framed thatched cabins with private balconies overlooking a forested valley. Each has two single beds with mosquito nets. Bring mosquito repellent; mosquitoes around here defend their territory fiercely. A small kitchen and airy, attractive open-air communal area provide for dining alfresco. Owner Mauricio Salazar offers guided day-trips into the KekoLdi Indian Reserve (seven hours, $25 per person, including box lunch and a contribution to the Indian Association). Guided walks, including night walks, in Chimurí Nature Reserve ($10, three hours), and horseback rides on the beach ($15) are also offered. Nearby are a waterfall and a pool, good for a refreshing dip.

About 100 meters along the road to Punta Cocles is **Cabinas Yucca,** with four cabins with private bath and a veranda facing the beach. A plus point is king-size beds, though the rooms are rather dark. Rates: $25 s/d, $30 t. Farther south comes **Cabinas Casas Risas,** a quartet of small, hardwood cabins on stilts with floor-to-ceiling glass windows to three sides (three more were being added). Each comes with ceiling fan, little refrigerator, and heated water. They're clean, attractive, and peaceful, and have verandas with hammock and table. Rates: $30 s/d/t, $40 quad.

Upscale

About 400 meters before entering Puerto Viejo from Cahuita is **El Pizote Lodge** (Apdo. 230, Coronado 2200, tel./fax 229-1428, direct tel. 758-1938). Owner Carr Pechtel has sculpted magnificently landscaped grounds complete with giant hardwoods and sweeping lawns—a fine setting for eight small but clean and atmospheric rooms with shared bathrooms with huge screen windows ($40 d). There are also six bungalows ($66) and a two-bedroom bungalow ($80-110). Units have overhead fans and bedside lamps you can actually read by. The lodge even has a volleyball court. Popular with an older crowd. The restaurant gets good reviews. Recommended.

Camping

You can pitch tent next to Cabinas Soda Brava, south of town. Miss Trish will charge about $2 nightly; so will Hotel Puerto Viejo, which allows tents in its backyard.

FOOD

Puerto Viejo is blessed with a surprisingly cosmopolitan range of cuisines and even-yes!-gourmet cuisine. Don't expect napkins and candelabras, however . . . with one exception.

First and last, dine at the **Garden Restaurant** at Cabinas Jacaranda, where the food makes a journey to the Caribbean well worthwhile. Vera Khan—a Trinidadian described by one resident expatriate as "a bit of a character"—makes superb curries, vegetarian, Thai, and Caribbean dishes ($3-8) to true international standard, with flower petals and sauces artistically flourished for flair. Wolfgang Puck would be proud! And the candlelit setting is romantic and tranquil. Expect to wait at peak hours, for diners flock from far and wide. The cocktails are powerful indeed! And there's self-service coffee. Open 5-9:30 p.m.

The **Cafe Pizzeria,** on the same block, serves good food but is pricey ($6 and upward for dinners). Also serving Italian dishes (of what standard I can't say) is the **Amimodo Italian Restaurant.** A good bet for seafood is **Cabinas Grant** (tel. 758-2845), and you can't go wrong for sandwiches and basic fare at **Salsa Brava Café.**

Soda Tamara (closed on Tuesday) is another good find: clean, pleasant, and surprisingly cosmopolitan—it even has a TV—with a shaded outside patio. You can have burgers and fries here, or *típico* Costa Rican dishes such as fried fish with *patacones* (plantain). Most meals cost $4 or less. Come early; it gets busy, and closes at 9 p.m. **Stanford's Restaurant Caribe,** on the beachfront facing "La Salsa Brava," has a highly regarded upstairs restaurant, where you can nibble on Caribbean seafood specialties while enjoying the views. A vegetarian meal here will cost $2. Also on the beach nearby are the ramshackle **Restaurante Bambú** and the **Parquecito,** popular with local Rastas and the budget crowd.

Soda Coral, on the northern corner of the soccer field, is highly rated for its health-food breakfasts and homemade pizzas.

For Oriental food, check out **Johnny's Place,** serving voluminous meals at a fair price. The **Restaurant Mexi-Tico** offers genuine Mexican food and food off the grill. **Pizzeria Coral** serves moderately tasty but good-size pizzas. Salivating for fried chicken? Try **Baker's Fried Chicken** next to the Taverna Popo. There's even a **French Restaurant** of that name on the beachfront, 50 meters before Stanford's. Around the corner from Mexi-Tico is **Bela Soda,** *the* place for breakfast on the palm-fringed veranda surrounded by lush bougainvillea with classical music as background. French owner Lucas alas is selling the place. For now he serves huge portions of granola with fruit, yogurt, and honey ($2.50), plus banana bread ($1), omelettes ($3), and other natural foods.

One of the pleasures of eating in Puerto Viejo is having one of the local ladies cook for you; you'll need to give at least a day's advance notice. Miss Biggy makes steak and chips (French fries) in true English fashion (she has a kitchen at the back of the Taverna Popo); Miss Dolly makes delicious ginger biscuits and bread, plus Caribbean dishes such as "rundown" stew; Miss Sam bakes tarts and bread; while Miss Daisy is renowned for her *pan bon,* ginger cakes, and meat-filled patties. Ask around.

A growing number of good eateries are opening their doors south of town and are well worth the short drive.

If you're cooking for yourself, a vegetable truck reportedly parks opposite the Soda Tamara every Wednesday afternoon.

ENTERTAINMENT

What Cahuita lacks in raging nightlife Puerto Viejo more than makes up for. It's well known among the surf crowd for its hot and hopping discos on weekends, and folks travel down from Cahuita and even as far afield as Limón to bop. The prize contenders are **Stanford's,** the large mirrored disco—reggae! reggae! reggae!—and the even more popular beachfront **Johnny's Place,** which plays reggae and rock hits and has the craziest barstaff in the world. Wear your tank top, 'cos you're gònna sweat! **Restaurante Bambú** is a popular Rasta hangout. **Taverna Popo** is the quietest of the breed and plays

Latin tunes and North American pop. **Lapa Lapa,** at Playa Cocles south of town, also has a lively disco plus music videos.

SERVICES

Puerto Viejo has no banks—the nearest is in Bribrí—but you can change traveler's checks and cash at **Pulpería Manuel León, Johnny's Place** next door, and **Stanford's.** The **police station** is next to Johnny's Place. There are only three public **telephones** in town: at the Hotel Maritza (758-3844), Pulpería Manuel León (758-0854), and outside the ATEC office (798-4244), opposite Soda Tamara. You can have incoming messages left here.

There's a **doctor**—Dr. Rosa León—and health clinic (hours: Mon.-Fri. 7 a.m.-4 p.m.) at the house with the red roof next to Casa Verde. For serious problems you should visit the Red Cross evacuation center in Bribrí.

Color Caribe stocks a fabulous selection of clothing, jewelry, and souvenirs. You'll also find hand-painted T-shirts and jewelry on sale at stalls along the beachfront. For general items, the *pulpería* next to the Taverna Popo is well-stocked.

Activities and Information
Soda Tamara maintains a bulletin board with tourist information, including private house rentals. The **ATEC** office (see above) provides tour information and sponsors environmental and cultural tours of the Talamanca coast using local guides in an effort to promote "ecologically sound tourism and small-scale, locally owned businesses." Options include "African-Caribbean Culture and Nature Walks," trips to the KekoLdi Reserve that include the Iguana Farm, rainforest hikes, snorkeling and fishing, bird and night walks, and overnight "Adventure Treks" into the Gandoca Reserve. Trips are limited to six people. Be prepared for rain! The ATEC office also has a gift store, plus maps and a fax service and public telephone. Open Sunday 8:30-11:30 a.m. and 1-8 p.m., Mon.-Fri. 7:30 a.m.-noon and 1-9 p.m., Saturday 8 a.m.-noon and 1-8 p.m.

Plenty of locals will take you fishing, diving, or hiking, or if you wish a guided tour to Gandoca-Manzanillo Wildlife Refuge or into one of the

nearby Indian reserves. Ask around. Also, check the notice boards in the Hotel Maritza and Pulpería Manuel León.

Buceo Aquatour, five km south of town at Punta Uva (no telephone), offers scuba diving, including four-day PADI certification courses ($350); also, kayaking to Gandoca, snorkeling, and river excursions. Two-tank morning dives cost $60; one-tank afternoon dives cost $40. Night dives are $60. "Virgin" dives ($35) are also offered for the novice diver. No phone.

Deep-sea fishing and **snorkeling** can be arranged with advance notice through Earl Brown, Daniel Brown at Soda Acuario, or "Papi" Hudson. The El Pizote Lodge also offers boat trips and snorkeling. Rumor has it that a powerful fishing boat is available for charter trips to off-shore reefs and to Bocas del Toro, in Panamá.

You can rent **bicycles** at Bela Soda, or with Jaco Brent at Cabinas Kaya, and at El Escape Caribeño ($6-12 per day). Don Antonio's stables, 600 meters south of town, rents **horses.** You'll see lots of other signs advertising horse rentals. Mauricio Salazar (Cabinas Chimurí) also offers scheduled horse riding trips and hikes into the KekoLdi Indian Reserve (seven hours, $25 per person, including box lunch and a contribution to the Indian Association). Physically grueling three-day trips can be arranged with several days' notice. He also offers guided walks, including night walks, in Chimurí Nature Reserve ($10, three hours).

A local botanical garden and farm—**Finca La Isla**—welcomes visitors and offers lunches (by arrangement). Peter Kring grows spices, exotic fruits, and ornamental plants for sale. He has acres of native and introduced fruit trees. You can sample the fruits and even learn about chocolate production. Toucans, sloths, poison-arrow frogs, and other animals are commonly seen. It's 200 meters before El Pizote Lodge and is signed (entrance is $3, or $8 with guided tour; open 10 a.m.- 4 p.m daily except Tuesday and Wednesday).

GETTING THERE

From San José
Direct buses (Autotransportes MEPE, tel. 221-0524) to Puerto Viejo depart San José at 1:30 p.m. (reportedly, 8:30 a.m. weekends); returning from Puerto Viejo at 7 a.m. (3:30 p.m. weekends). Additional buses via Cahuita to Bribrí and Sixaola depart San José from Avenida 11 and Calles Central/1 at 6 a.m., and 1:30 and 3:30 p.m. (four hours; tel. 221-0524). Return buses depart Puerto Viejo at 5 and 8 a.m., and 2:30 p.m.

The bus used to drop you off at El Cruce ("The Crossroads"), the beginning of the dirt road into Puerto Viejo, but may now go all the way into town. It's easy to hitch the five km into the village; otherwise call ahead to either Johnny León at Pulpería Manuel León (tel. 258-0854) or José Luis Fernández at the Hotel Maritza (tel. 258-3844) to arrange a taxi ride along the dirt road into Puerto Viejo; you'll need to call a day or more in advance and know for sure which bus you'll be arriving on.

From Puerto Limón
Puerto Viejo-bound buses depart from Avenida 4 and Calles 3/4 (one block north of the municipal market) at 5 and 10 a.m., and 1 and 4 p.m. (one hour). The bus reportedly continues past Punta Uva to Manzanillo. The Puerto Limón-Puerto Viejo buses are usually crowded; get to the station early. Buses depart Puerto Viejo for Cahuita and Puerto Limón from opposite Taverna Popo at 5, 8, and 10 a.m., and 3 p.m.

PUNTA COCLES,
PUNTA UVA, AND MANZANILLO

"Where the road ends and the jungle begins," says a sign for Hotel Playa Chiquita on the pot-holed dirt road that leads from Puerto Viejo along the coast, past Punta Cocles and Punta Uva, and into Manzanillo and the Gandoca-Manzanillo Wildlife Refuge. Well, almost! Hotels are rising, and while the road to Manzanillo is still an ordeal in places, the tour buses have begun to arrive. No wonder—the beaches are fabulous! Long, lonesome, and breathtakingly beautiful in a South Pacific kind of way. The road stopped at Puerto Viejo until June 1984. Then it arrived at Manzanillo, a fishing village of just a few houses within the refuge itself.

Development is sweeping in and changing the face of the region. Electricity was a major change, arriving at Punta Uva and Manzanillo for Christmas 1989. Cabinas and small hotels are sprouting up like mushrooms on a damp log. And in 1991, the cacophony of chainsaws began in earnest on the western side of Gandoca-Manzanillo, followed by the roar of flatbed trucks loaded with cativo and cedar logs. Independent loggers are reportedly buying trees from local farmers, then cutting them down and carrying them off to sell to lumber companies. Many trees—particularly the fine mahoganies—are being cut illegally on the borders of, and even within, the refuge itself. And banana plantations are pushing up against the refuge from the west (two banana companies, País and Chiriqui, have bought land rights on the park border).

There are no settlements to speak of between Puerto Viejo and Manzanillo, just a paternoster-string of shacks and cabinas along the dirt road. And Manzanillo hardly deserves the moniker; it, too, is just a few wooden shacks and houses. The very beautiful, kilometers-long, coral-colored Playa Cocles runs south from Puerto Viejo to the rocky shore of Punta Uva. Separating Punta Uva from Manzanillo is a magnificent five-km-long black-sand crescent beach with dramatic ridgeback mountains in the distance, marching down to the coast. The beach imme-diately facing the hamlet is littered with trash.

From Manzanillo you can follow a five-km coastal trail south to the fishing hamlet of Punta Mona ("Monkey Point"), from where you can walk the beach to Gandoca Lagoon, just south of Gandoca village, virtually within a stone's throw of the Panamanian border; alternatively, an inland trail runs between the base of the mountains and Manzanillo swamps to Gandoca. Gandoca has no facilities except one unmarked store. Beyond the lagoon, a trail winds through the jungle—thick, hot, and teeming with monkeys, parrots, sloths, and snakes—ending at the Río Sixaola and the Panamá border. Trails are often obscure and slippery with mud. A guide is recommended.

According to local legend, Christopher Columbus himself named Monkey Point for the population of howler monkeys that still inhabits the swampy area, and Manzanillo for a great old manzanillo tree that once towered over the coast. The tree died in the 1940s and finally toppled into the sea in 1957.

The primarily black population has lived for generations in what is now the wildlife refuge, using the land between Puerto Viejo and Manzanillo to farm cacao until 1979, when the *Monilia* fungus wiped out the crop.

Rainfall is particularly heavy July-Dec.; March-April and Sept.-Oct. are generally the driest months.

ACCOMMODATIONS

The following are from Punta Cocles south, arranged separately by category.

Tent Camp
The **Almonds & Corals Lodge Tent Camp** (c/o Geo Expediciones, Apdo. 681, San José 2300, tel. 272-2024, fax 272-2220) is three km north of Manzanillo, with a lonesome setting a few leisurely steps from the beach. Each of 24

tent-huts is raised on a stilt platform, is protected by a roof, and features two singles or one double bed, a locker closet, night lamps, table and chairs (with reading light), plus mosquito nets and deck with hammock—a touch of Kenya come to the Caribbean. Very atmospheric! Each cabin has its own shower and toilet in separate wash houses (an environmentally friendly "bio-digester" gobbles up your waste, which—voila—reappears as light from methane lamps lining the walkways). Trees tower over the tent-cabins. Raised walkways lead between the huts and also to the beach, pool, snack bar, and restaurant serving Costa Rican food. You can rent kayaks, bicycles ($10) and snorkeling ($8) gear, and take guided trips into Hitoy Cerere Biological Reserve and the Indian village of Volio. Rates: $35 s, $45 d.

Budget and Inexpensive
La Isla Inn is a two-story all-hardwood structure that opened March 1995 with four rooms (three up, one down) just 50 meters from Playa Cocles. The wide, upper-story veranda replete

with hammocks grants views over the ocean. Rooms are large, with lots of light pouring in through screened windows, plus fans and nets to keep mosquitoes at bay. Rates: $15 per person, $50 for a big room sleeping four.

Next door is the basic **Cabinas Surf Point** and, 200 meters beyond, a funky house called **Cabinas Garibaldi.**

Immediately south of Hotel Yaré are **Cabinas Katy,** with two four-person units with private baths ($10 per unit), and the attractive **Cabinas Picasso,** with cabins, plus rooms in a two-story wooden home on the beach (from $30 d). Within calling distance is the basic **Cabinas Tio Lou.**

Half a kilometer beyond Tio Lou are a bevy of budget properties: the **Cabinas Cocori, Aguas Claras,** which has pretty cottages, and **Cabinas Yemanya,** with rustic yet atmospheric rooms on the shoreline and chickens running loose. Beyond Hotel Punta Cocles is **Ranchita Blanca,** offering small yet pretty rustic cabins with wide verandas and hammocks (it also rents mountain bikes)

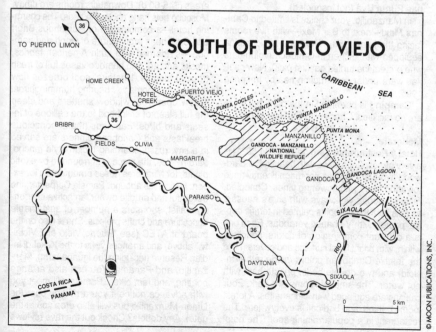

Irie, a stone's throw south of Miraflores, offers camping and cheap cabinas. Also here is **Villas Paradiso**, a rather grandly named budget establishment that opened in early 1995 with 12 cabinas, eight with private bath. It caters to surfers. Rates: $10 shared bath, $25 private, d.

Playa Chiquita Lodge (tel. 233-6313), 1.5 km south of Punta Cocles, is one of the nicest places on the coast in its category. Eleven clean, spacious rooms offer sunken bathrooms (no hot water), fans, and Sarchí's famous leather rocking chairs on a wide veranda. You can dine alfresco under thatch in the restaurant. Narrow walkways lead through landscaped gardens to the golden sand beach. Watch your toes! Bright blue sand crabs the size of a dessert plate defend the terrain with fearsome claws. The lodge arranges diving and snorkeling trips, boat trips to Punta Mona, plus bike and horse rentals. Rates: $15 s, $30 d.

One km beyond Playa Chiquita are **Cabinas Valerie's Happy Times** and **Cabinas Selvyn**, the latter with at least four funky cabins and a small open-air restaurant ($10 d). Also try **Cabinas Punta Uva** (not inspected).

In Manzanillo, your choice is limited to **Cabinas Maxi**—next to Bar Maxi—with five rooms facing the beach ($8). There's a basic cabina equipped with kitchen in Gandoca (volunteers who protect the turtles get first pick). New cabinas were under construction nearby in spring 1995.

Camping is permitted in the park, but there are no facilities. Check with Cabinas Maxi.

Moderate

Hotel y Restaurante Yaré (tel./fax 284-5921) is a very atmospheric place with beautiful all-hardwood two-story houses set magnificently amid towering trees with flowering vines. Canopied, raised wooden walkways with ship's hausers as rails lead to tall cabins painted in terrific tropical pastels with V-shaped verandas. Each unit is a different combination of colors, spacious within, with bright floral curtains and covers (I find the festive Caribbean colors *inside* rather insipid) and two double beds, private bath with hot water. The smaller rooms are dark. Four cabinas are equipped with kitchenettes. A forest looms behind, and bird call is everywhere. The restaurant is a popular dining spot. The hotel

offers a wide range of tours. Rates: $30 s, $36 d, standard; $42 s, $48 d, superior; from $48, family-size ($10 extra for kitchenette).

At Playa Chiquita, on Punta Uva, about four km south of Puerto Viejo, is **Hotel Kasha** (tel. 284-6908), an attractive place with six bungalows set back from the road amid the forest. The handsome hardwood units are spacious, with plenty of light, screened windows, ceiling fans, two double beds, and pleasant bathrooms with heated water and beautiful Italian ceramics. The hotel boasts a small *ranchita* restaurant and a basic gym and Jacuzzi. Rates: $42, including tax and breakfast.

Next door is **Jardín Miraflores Lodge** (Mail Stop SJO 2385, P.O. Box 025216, Miami, FL 33102-5216; or Apdo 6499, San José 1000, tel./fax 233-2822 or tel. 798-1844), a true nature lover's paradise. It has a basic six-bed dormitory with outside bathrooms ($10 per person), double rooms with shared bathroom ($40 s, $50 d) or private bathroom ($45 s, $55 d) and balcony with hammock, and suites with king-size beds, private bathrooms and living areas ($45-60 d). Downstairs rooms are dingy. Mosquito nets hang above the beds. The charming hotel—a combination of indigenous Bribrí and Caribbean architecture of wood and bamboo—is adorned with Latin American fabrics, masks and art, and bamboo vases full of fresh tropical blooms. Upstairs, cool breezes flow through the rooms . . . bearing hummingbirds! Throw open your window shutters and sleep the full sleep of childhood to the calliope of insects and birds. Fabulous health-conscious breakfasts and Caribbean dinners are served in a tiny, rustic, charming Indian-style rancho. *Jardín?* Yes, the place is surrounded by exotic plants, for Miraflores raises ornamentals for export. Heliconias abound. Pamela Carpenter, the delightful and erudite owner, an active environmentalist, sponsors a number of sustainable agriculture and crafts projects. She is also on the board of ATEC (see "Puerto Viejo and Vicinity," above) and arranges visits to the KekoLdi Indian Reserve (including the iguana farm), Manzanillo, and Panamá. You can also arrange boating, and rent bikes. Pamela will meet you with advance notice if you arrive by bus (the Limón-Manzanillo bus will also drop you at the gate). Any doubts? Check out the rave reviews

in the guest book. Rates include a hearty breakfast. Seventh day free.

Also at Punta Cocles is **Lapa Lapa Beach Hotel** (Apdo. 459, San José 1000, tel. 221-9592, fax 255-3941), with comfortable beachfront rooms with private bath and hot water. It's set in landscaped gardens and has a popular bar and disco. Not reviewed.

Another two km brings you to **Walaba Lodge** (tel. 234-2467 or 225-8023), a delightful three-story lodge with large carved sea-horse motifs on the facade. It sits in pleasing landscaped grounds. Owner Alejandro Rodriguez rents four airy rooms ($13.50 per person) with fans, plus beds in a dorm ($8).

Upscale

About four km south of Puerto Viejo, on the road to Punta Uva, is the relatively upscale **Villas del Caribe** (Apdo. 8080, San José 1000, tel. 233-2200, fax 221-2801), with eight attractive rooms—each with private second-floor balcony—lined along a beautiful veranda with potted plants, set in landscaped gardens 50 meters from the beach. Fully equipped kitchen, hot water, and fans are standard. Very pleasant. The modern two-story "resort," however, was a point of contention when first opened. The place became a cause celebre when the local Indian community accused owner Maurice Strong—coordinator of the June 1992 Earth Summit held in Rio de Janeiro—of building the hotel within KekoLdi Indian Reserve lands without permits. To be fair, so have several others. Most important, it seems Strong had acted in good faith. The good news is that the hotel is eco-conscious—even the soaps and toiletries are biodegradable! You'll find an ox-driven sugarcane mill and an oxcart for rides on site! Rates: $69 d, including tax. Possibly it's overpriced compared to other properties in this bracket. Let me know!

One of the more pleasing places on the Caribbean, **Hotel Punta Cocles** (Apdo. 11020, San José 1000, tel. 234-8055, fax 234-8033; in the U.S., tel. 800-325-6927), five km south of Puerto Viejo, is hidden in the lowland rainforest. Set 500 meters back from the beach, it sprawls over gently rising lawns and gardens covering 10 hectares, all but 2.4 still forested. The only sounds are the incessant buzz of insects, the call of birds, and the hushed sound of distant waves. Access to Punta Uva beach is via a path that leads past towering tropical trees. Nature trails lead into the private reserve.

Guided tour programs include the "Cocles Indian Reserve Jungle Tour" ($45), "Hitoy-Cerere Reserve Jungle Hike" ($60), "Cahuita National Park" ($60), "Punta Mona Walking Tour" ($45), plus biking and snorkeling at Punta Uva ($45). This oasis of tranquility features an attractive open-air restaurant with a beautiful hardwood roof and a sunken, open kitchen-cum-bar overlooking a swimming pool and sundeck for alfresco dining. The hotel's 60 modern cabins (some with kitchenettes) are spaced wide apart and connected by thatched walkways. They're also very spacious and clean, with air conditioning, hot water, ceiling fans, large closets, and supremely comfortable—but noisy—beds (plan on lovemaking and your neighbors will follow every move). Wide wooden porches are good for armchair birdwatching. Rates: $63 s, $69 d, $80 t.

About four km south, on the nape of Punta Uva, a rough track off the dirt road leads to **Resort Hotel Las Palmas** (Apdo. 6942, San José 1000, tel. 255-3939, fax 255-3737). The expansive resort—claimed with undue bravado to be the "only full-service beach and jungle resort on the Caribbean"—nestles up to a stunning white-sand beach cleaned of driftwood with hammocks in the palms. A reef lies just offshore. The resort offers 83 rooms, a small discotheque and shopping center, plus 60 lots for private cottages. The rooms I inspected were modest, though nicely appointed. An open-air restaurant overlooks the grounds and a large octagonal swimming pool with swim-up bar. The hotel rents snorkeling and diving equipment, and has 25 horses on site. The hotel has had an on-going battle with conservationists and the government and is accused of having been built without permits. The government even ordered removal of most of the structures and restoration of damaged ecosystems, though the Supreme Court later ruled for the hotelier. Neighboring hoteliers complain of other abuses. Rates: $60 s, $70 d, $85 t. Two-night packages with roundtrip transportation cost $150 per person; three nights, $185. Las Palmas offers full-day excursions from San José ($60).

FOOD

Hotel y Restaurante Yaré is a good option; so, too, **Restaurante Lapa Lapa,** a stone's throw away, strongly recommended (French chef Françoise conjures tremendous dishes) and doubling as a disco after 10 p.m. Nearby, **Restaurante Elena Brown,** I'm informed, offers Caribbean dishes that border on gourmet. Two km farther is **El Duende Felíz,** a highly recommended Italian restaurant.

French-run **La Paloma Café,** about four km from Puerto Viejo, serves pasta, steak, and lobster in an open-air dining room with chairs in bright tropical colors. It serves American breakfasts and features a chess night, video night, and backgammon night.

A few diminutive *sodas* squat beside the road between Punta Cocles and Manzanillo. The most substantial is **Soda Restaurant Naturales,** offering basic breakfasts as well as **bike rentals.**

Bar Maxi is the only place in Manzanillo that remotely resembles action. This gloomy bar is enlivened by the slap of dominoes and the blast of Jimmy Cliff and Bob Marley. Several local ladies will cook meals with advance notice. Ask for Miss Alfonsina, Miss Edith, Doña Cipriana, and Miss Marva.

SERVICES

In Manzanillo, you can rent **horses** from Jácamo; Willie Burton arranges boat rides and **snorkeling;** Miss Alfonsina offers guided botany tours; and local guides for hikes into Gandoca-Manzanillo can be arranged through Florentino Renald, who acts as park administrator. He'll also help arrange a boat ride to the beaches at the southern end of the park.

TRANSPORTATION

Buses from Puerto Limón to Puerto Viejo continue past Punta Uva to Manzanillo (see the "Puerto Viejo" section for information on bus service from Puerto Limón). Two buses a day make the journey. Departures from Manzanillo are at 9 a.m. and 4:30 p.m. Check for current schedules. Hitchhiking from Puerto Viejo is relatively easy; an informal pick-up and delivery service operates among drivers. Just wave and they'll stop. Alternatively, rent a bicycle. **Note:** A series of well-worn old wooden bridges have wide gaps between the planks, and even have planks missing. Walk your bike! If you're driving, drive slowly—there are no warning signs. Locals would appreciate a ride if you're driving.

GANDOCA-MANZANILLO WILDLIFE REFUGE

One of Costa Rica's best-kept secrets, Gandoca-Manzanillo protects a spectacularly beautiful, palm-fringed, nine-km-long, crescent-shaped beach where four species of turtles—most abundantly, leatherback turtles—come ashore to lay their eggs (Jan.-April is best); Playa Gandoca is black sand, but I've nonetheless seen it referred to as Costa Rica's most beautiful beach. The waters here are quite dangerous.

Turtle Patrol
Volunteers are needed for the **Marine Turtle Conservation Project,** which conducts research and protects the turtles from predators and poachers. The tour of duty is one week. You patrol the beach at night, measuring and tagging turtles, camouflaging their nests, and discouraging egg-bandits. Conditions are harsh: lots of rain and insects, and long hours walking the beach. Lodging is either in your own tent on in closely packed bunk beds in a small earth-floored rancho that acts as refuge headquarters. It has no electricity or running water. Mosquitoes will eye you greedily, awaiting a signal to pounce (bring a mosquito net). Local families prepare meals. Contact either **ATEC** (Puerto Viejo's environmental "chamber of commerce") or Jesús Valenciano (tel. 224-3570, fax 253-7524). Non-volunteers: $15. Another option is **ASACODE Lodge,** deep in the forest. The simple lodge accommodates groups ($7 per person; $5 per meal) and is run by a local farmers' association (Asociación Sanmigueleña de Conservación y Desarrollo, tel. 745-2165, c/o Teodoro, who speaks only Spanish) on its private reserve within a reserve.

Exploring the Park

The park—which is 65% tropical rainforest—also protects rare swamp habitats, including the only mangrove forest on Costa Rica's Caribbean shores, two holillo palm swamps (important habitats for tapirs), a 300-hectare cativo forest, and a coral reef 200 meters offshore. The reef system covers five square kilometers and is rarely dived by outsiders because of the difficulty of reaching the refuge. The hill forests, with their thick understories, harbor many tall mahoganies. The hamlets of Punta Uva, Manzanillo, Punta Mona, and Gandoca form part of the refuge. Because local communities live within the park, it is a mixed-management reserve; the locals' needs are being integrated into park-management policies.

The park is easily explored simply by walking the kilometers of white-sand beaches; trails also wind through the flat, lowland rainforest fringing the coast. It's possible to hike through the reserve to Gandoca Lagoon, about six km from the ranger station, where refuge manager Florentino Renald can describe in glowing detail the reserve's treasures. The large freshwater lagoon has two openings into the sea and runs up to 50 meters deep.

The Gandoca estuary comprises red mangrove trees: a complex world braided by small brackish streams and snakelike creeks, which sometimes interconnect, sometimes peter out in narrow cul-de-sacs, and sometimes open suddenly into broad lagoons that all look alike (see "Flora" and "Fauna" in the Introduction chapter). The mangroves shelter both a giant oysterbed and a nursery for lobster and the swift and powerful tarpon. Manatees also swim and breed here. With luck, too, you'll be able to spot crocodiles and caimans. The park is also seasonal or permanent home to at least 358 species of birds (including toucans, red-lored Amazon parakeets, and hawk-eagles) as well as margays, ocelots, pacas, and sloths.

You can hire a guide and boat in Sixaola to take you downriver to the mangrove swamps at the rivermouth (dangerous currents and reefs prevent access from the ocean). If you pilot yourself, stay away from the Panamanian side of the river, as the Panamanian border police are said to be very touchy.

Getting There

You must hike (two hours) from Manzanillo, from where you may also be able to hire a boat and guide. By road, take the Sixaola road via Bribrí; about four km beyond Daytonia, a dirt-and-mud road to the left leads to the tiny hamlet of Gandoca. A 4WD is essential.

BRIBRÍ AND VICINITY

The road beyond the Puerto Viejo turnoff near Home Creek winds uphill through foothills of the Talamancas before suddenly revealing a spectacular vista: bright green banana plantations spread out in a flat valley backed by tiers of far-off mountains with veils of courtesan clouds drifting among the valleys and shrouding the peaks. At the base of the valley sits Bribrí, 60 km south of Puerto Limón, and the administrative center for the nearby Indian reserves. The Indian influence is noticeable. The paved road south from Puerto Limón ends here.

The drive is worthwhile, and so, too, a visit to the nearby Indian reserves, but the town is not worthy of a visit, except for two rarities in this part of the world: a **Banco Nacional** and **post office** (there's also a Red Cross evacuation center for emergency health needs). The bank offers a discounted rate (eight percent less than in San José) but has a $100 limit; it can take half a day to get money changed. Buses run from here to the Indian villages of Amubre and Shiroles, from where trails lead into the reserves (see below).

Accommodations and Food

Just before town is the **Restaurant El Socia** and **Restaurant Mango** (tel. 258-3353); the latter has dancing and has been recommended by Peace Corps volunteers (thanks, guys, for stealing my maps!). In town are the **Restaurante King-Giang** and **Restaurante Bribrí**. The only place to stay is **Cabinas Picuno** (tel. 258-2981; $7), with private bathrooms. The **Bar Tiliri Bribrí** looks like the most "happening" place.

Getting There

Buses depart San José from Avenida 11 and Calles Central/1 daily at 6 a.m. and 1:30 and 3:30 p.m. and pass through Bribrí en route to Sixaola. Buses depart Bribrí for Limón at 6:30, 9, and 11:30 a.m. and 12:30 and 4 p.m.; for San José at 6, 9, and 11 a.m. and 4 p.m.; and for Sixaola and the Panamanian border at 7:30 a.m., noon, and 3 and 5:30 p.m.

INDIAN RESERVES

West of Bribrí are three reserves—KekoLdi, Talamanca-Bribrí, and Cabecar—incorporated into La Amistad International Peace Park, on the slopes of the Talamanca mountains. The parks were established to protect the traditional lifestyle of the indigenous people. Though the Indians speak Spanish and wear Western clothing, what the reserves offer is a rewarding insight into a lifestyle in harmony with nature, including customs and beliefs passed down through millennia.

The 3,547-hectare KekoLdi reserve, created in 1977, is home to some 200 Bribrís and Cabecars. They have no villages of any substance as the Indians prefer to live apart. The reserve extends to the borders of the Gandoca-Manzanillo refuge and the coast. Less than half of the reserve land is in Indian hands today. Apparently, aerial surveys used to demarcate the reserve failed to take into account preexisting cacao plantations on land later sold to private developers, to whom titles have reverted. Government proposals to build a trans-Talamanca Highway and a hydroelectricity dam are being fought by the Indians, who are well aware that their fate hangs in the balance. To sway the odds, to protect their land, they have formed the Indigenous Association of Talamanca and are preparing their reserves as tourist destinations.

Reforestation and other conservation projects are ongoing in all three reserves, and the KekoLdi people are participating in an experimental project to raise green iguanas and other endangered species. They supplement their income by selling baskets, etc., and organically grown cacao is an increasingly important source of revenue. And two Bribrí guides, including Gloria Mayorga, coauthor of *Taking Care of Sibo's Gift,* are on hand to educate tourists on indigenous history and ways.

Permits are necessary to enter the parks, although things are easing and this may have changed; contact ATEC (Talamanca Association for Ecotourism and Conservation) opposite Soda Tamara in Puerto Viejo. Mauricio Salazar, a Bribrí Indian who owns the Cabinas Chimurí in Puerto Viejo, can also arrange permits, as can Jaguar Tours in Cahuita. The journey can be arduous, and the accommodations are very, very basic. Gifts for the locals would be appreciated: cigarettes and *guaro* are both powerful currency.

If you go, enter with a sense of humility and respect. Do not attempt to treat the community members as a tourist oddity. Remember: You have as much to learn from the indigenous communities as to share.

"Capital" of the reserve is **Shiroles** (public tel. 754-2064), little more than a Guardia Rural station, a couple of *sodas,* and a few tumbledown houses, with banana plantations that provide employment down by the Río Sixaola. You can walk 15 minutes uphill to La Finca Educativa Indígena, an administrative center for the Bribrí people, who hash out their differences here and plan their futures. It has a 44-bed dorm and cafeteria.

In contrast, the Cabecar Indians remain cautious of any tourist influx. Any visit to Calveri or other remote Cabecar villages must be by invitation or prior permission.

Getting There

Buses depart Bribrí for Shiroles at 8 a.m., noon, and 5:30 p.m. It's a bumpy ride along an unpaved road.

ATEC (see "Puerto Viejo," above; tel./fax 798-4244) arranges visits ($13 half-day; $19 full-day) with reservations. Hiking and horseback trips into KekoLdi Indian Reservation are offered by Mauricio Salazar (Cabinas Chimurí, Puerto Viejo de Talamanca, Puerto Limón, tel. 258-3844), whose cabinas feature a trail directly into the reserve. The demanding trips (one-day trips cost $22; three-day trips cost $140, including overnight stays with the Indians) require notice. **American Wilderness Experience** (P.O. Box 1486, Boulder, CO 80306, tel. 303-444-2622 or 800-444-0099, fax 303-444-3999) offers a 10-day journey through the Talamancas using canoes (hiking and horseback riding are

also featured) and native guides ($1676 land only). You can also arrange canoe trips through ATEC in Puerto Viejo.

Aerovías Talamanqueñas Indígenas reportedly flies to Amubre, where local nuns run the Casa de Huéspedes.

SIXAOLA

You can cross into Panamá at Sixaola, on the banks of the Sixaola River marking the international border, 34 km south of Bribrí. You reach the dour, gutsy border town along a deeply rutted dirt road with banana plantations to left and right. Like Sixaola, the graceless hamlets along the way exist only to serve the banana industry. You'll see a Texaco **gas station** about 10 km from Bribrí, and *sodas* and restaurants at regular intervals. There are no banks.

Lots of people walk the road, including children who have to walk kilometers to school; help them out with a ride if you have room. The turnoff for the hamlet of Gandoca is at Noventa y Seis, three km before Sixaola.

Border Crossing

The border post (atop the railway embankment next to the metal bridge) is open daily 7-11 a.m. and 1-5 p.m. (see "Border Crossings" under "Getting There" in the On the Road chapter for details). There's little reason to cross into Panamá here, as links with the rest of the country are tenuous. However, the Sixaola crossing is growing in favor as the northern Caribbean coast of Panamá develops as a resort region.

Most international travelers cross into Panamá at Paso Canoas, on the Pacific coast. Remember to advance watches by one hour.

If you want to go to Guabito or Changamora, in Panamá, to shop, you can do so without getting exit stamps from Costa Rica (the bus from the Panamanian side of the border to Changamora costs $1). You will have to leave your bags at Panamanian customs after walking across the bridge. You can also hire a boat in Sixaola to take you on a trip up the Sixaola River with notice.

Accommodations and Food

The Chinese-run **Restaurant Central** (just before the ramp up to the border post) has a large menu and reportedly offers very basic accommodation. On the same block are the **Restaurant China**, **Restaurant Yeleski** (with discotheque), and **Restaurant Hang Wung**. Also in town is the **El Siquerreno**. The **Hotel el Imperio** is on the left as you come into town (one room only, $4; tel. 754-2289).

Transportation

From San José: Express buses depart from Avenida 11 and Calles Central/1, daily at 6 a.m. and 1:30 p.m. (four hours; $5).

From Puerto Limón: Sixaola-bound buses depart from Avenida 4 and Calles 3/4 (one block north of the municipal market) at 5 and 10 a.m., 1 and 4 p.m. (one and a half hours). Check for latest schedule. Also see "Bribrí," above.

From Sixaola: buses depart for Puerto Limón at 5 a.m., 8 a.m., 10 a.m., and 3 p.m.; for San José at 6 a.m. and 2:30 p.m. They're normally full by the time they reach Cahuita.

CATHY CARLSON

PACIFIC SOUTHWEST
INTRODUCTION

Relatively off the tourist's beaten path, the Pacific southwest has many fine jewels to display. A larger proportion of the region is protected as national park or forest reserve than in any other part of the country. Much remains inaccessible and unexplored—no bad thing, for huge regions such as Chirripó National Park, La Amistad International Peace Park, and Corcovado National Park harbor healthy and incredibly diverse populations of Central American flora and fauna. Of late, though, the region has been coming on strong as a place of attraction, and nature lodges, hotels, and tour services are being added at a healthy pace.

The Pacific southwest is also home to the nation's largest concentration of indigenous people—especially Guaymís and Borucas, around Buenos Aires. Like native people worldwide, they are caught in a vicious cycle of poverty. But, according to Gail Hewson Gómez, associate director of the Wilson Botanical Gardens, "These people are not at all preoccupied by the fact that they are poor. In fact [they] are extravagantly rich in spirit and cheerfulness." I have many pleasing memories of the glee and sense of good fortune that creased many a *campesino*'s face in response to my offers of a ride of even a few kilometers along a dusty road. You'll pass many Indian women walking barefoot along the roads, their small frames laden with babies or bulging bags. Do give a ride if you have space.

The waters of the Golfo Dulce are rich in marlin and other game fish (black marlin have been caught here in the 400-kg class), and the area is understandably popular with sportfishers. Surfers flock for fabulous waves. Cocos Island, 300 km offshore, is acclaimed as a world-class dive site. Corcovado National Park and adjacent wildlife reserves boast many of the nation's greatest wildlife treasures. And there are a couple of stunning drives.

The region is well served by air service from San José, and by road via the Pan-American

Hwy., which connects the central valley with the "Zona Sur," cutting through the heart of the Pacific southwest en route to Panamá.

LAND

This area is divided into three regions. To the east rises the great bulk of the Talamanca massif, sometimes called the Blue Mountains for the haze that often smothers them. Along the Pacific coast is a narrow plain backed by low mountains and broadening to the south, from which the Osa Peninsula hooks around to enclose the Golfo Dulce. The plains backing onto the gulf are highly fertile and have supported banana plantations for much of this century.

Between mountains and coast are the **Valle de El General** and **Valle de Coto Brus**. The former is basically a tectonic depression about 100 km long by 30 km wide. The Valle de El General is a center of agroindustry, with pineapples increasingly predominant, and groves of citrus, the latest crop, covering the flatlands and hillsides. Coffee has the upper hand on the slopes of Coto Brus.

CLIMATE

Climate alone can define the region. As you move south you begin to realize you're in the tropics. Be prepared for progressively more rain, stifling humidity, and a lingering wet season. This is particularly so of the Golfo Dulce and Osa, where trade winds from the southeast discharge their rains on the Fila Costeña mountains year-round. The area receives 375-762 centimeters of rain annually. Infamous thunderstorms move in Oct.-Dec., lashing the region and dumping torrents of rain. They're followed by clear blue skies and brilliant sunshine, which turn the sopping jungle into a steaming sauna. In fact, Caño Island gets struck by lightning more often than any other part of Central America; it was considered sacred by pre-Columbian peoples, who used it as a burial ground. The Valle de El General sits in a rain shadow and receives less rain than the coast and Talamancas.

HISTORY

Spaniards combed the region for the legendary gold of Veragua. They searched in vain, and forsaking the region for the more hospitable terrain and climate of Guanacaste and the central highlands, never heavily settled the Pacific southwest to any degree. They did, however, settle the inland valley of the Coto Brus as early as 1571 and shortly afterward opened a mule trail between Cartago and Panamá.

The Indians of the area had cultural traits distinct from people farther north. Their historical links were with South America. Despite a plethora of unusual and intriguing phenomena—notably perfectly spherical granite balls found throughout the Osa region—the archaeological background of the region is less complete than for the rest of the country. The spheres—*bolas*—and occasional small tombs are the only physical legacy of cultures past. They range from a few centimeters to three meters across and weigh as much as 16 tons. They litter the forest floors in no perceptible order. No one is certain when they were carved or for what purpose. Erich von Daniken in his *Chariots of the Gods?* calls the spheres "projectiles shot from star ships."

The region was already a center of gold production when the Europeans arrived. Indeed, it was and still is the largest gold source in the country. Goldsmiths pounded out decorative ornaments and used a lost-wax technique to make representations of important symbols: crocodiles, scorpions, jaguars, and eagles. Like contemporary prospectors, each Indian village had a stake on a section of a river or stream. The Tigre and Claro rivers still produce sizeable nuggets—the largest to date weighs over three kilos. In the early 1980s, gold fever destroyed thousands of hectares of the Osa forests, and Rincón, Puerto Jiménez, and Golfito were rife with prostitutes and drunks. The physical devastation was a deciding factor in the creation of Corcovado National Park.

Though coffee production arrived in Coto Brus only in 1949, today it is the nation's largest coffee-producing region. It wasn't until the mid-1950s that a paved road was cut across the mountain ridge known as Cerro de la Muerte

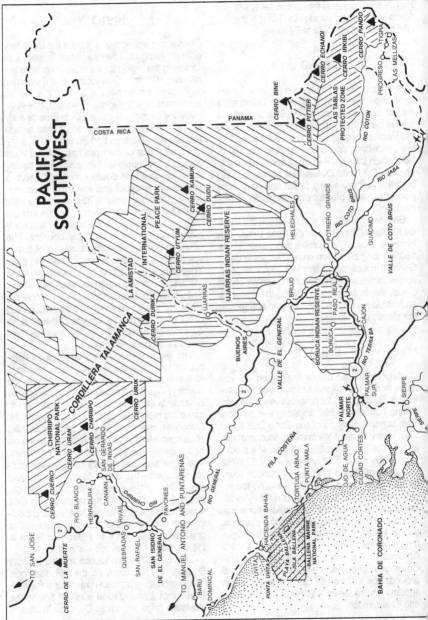

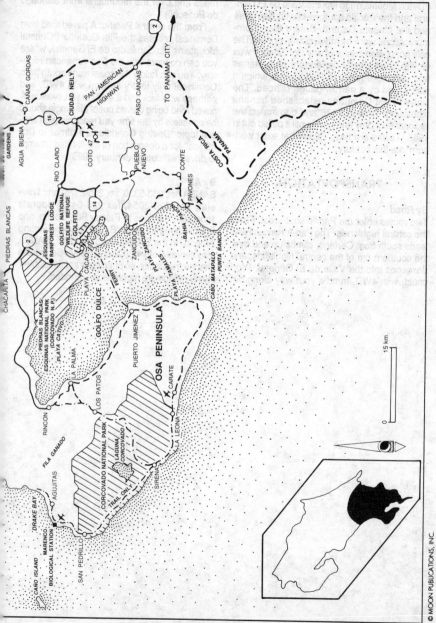

© MOON PUBLICATIONS, INC.

("Death Mountain") to link the Valle de El General and the Pacific southwest with San José and the Meseta Central. Before then, communications were by mule, plane, or sea. The only population center of any significance was Golfito, then wholly dependent on bananas and tied more firmly to Panamá, to which it was linked by a narrow-gauge railroad. The United Fruit Company established banana plantations here in 1938 and dominated the regional economy and polity until it pulled out in 1985. Towns are few. Those that exist were born late this century.

TRANSPORTATION

By Road
Two routes enter the Pacific southwest. **From the central highlands:** The Pan-American Hwy. leads south from Cartago, climbs up and over the southern rim of the central highlands, and descends into the Valle de El General. (You could, with 4WD, trundle your way along dirt roads and over the mountains from Santiago de Puriscal.)

From the central Pacific: A paved road from Dominical crosses the Fila Costeña ("Coastal Mountains") to San Isidro de El General, where you can connect with the Pan-American Highway. You can follow the coast route south from Dominical only in dry season with 4WD, and perhaps with *luck* and a 4WD in wet season. A paved road being carved out of the jungle should be complete by the time you read this (see special topic "Driving Conditions, Palmar to Dominical" for a description of my ill-fated attempt to drive this route in January 1993).

By Air
SANSA (tel. 233-5330, fax 255-2176) and **Travelair** (tel. 220-3054, fax 220-0413) operate scheduled services to Palmar Sur, Golfito, and Puerto Jiménez (see "By Air" under "Getting Around" in the On the Road chapter). SANSA also serves Coto 47 (Ciudad Neily). Schedules change frequently, so check current timetables. Reservations are highly recommended.

SAN ISIDRO AND VICINITY

CERRO DE LA MUERTE

From the 3,491-meter summit of Cerro de la Muerte, about 100 km south of San José (see "Cañon and South" at the end of the Central Highlands chapter), the Pan-Am Hwy. drops steeply to San Isidro, at 709 meters, in the Valle de El General. If possible, avoid this road at night. The route is often fog-bound and there are many large trucks—some without lights! Fortunately, there are few hairpin turns. But there are frequent landslides, fathoms-deep potholes, and too many accidents for your own safety. If you do drive at night, take extreme care. Your reward, once you drop below the cloud level, will be a fabulous vista, with the whole Valle de El General spread out before you, twinkling with orange lights far below.

No, the summit gets its name not from the dozens who have lost their lives through auto accidents, but from the many poor *campesinos* who, often shoeless and in nothing more than shirt and pants, froze to death in days of yore while carrying sacks of wild blackberries, dried corn, and rice to trade in San José.

The actual summit is marked by a forest of radio antennae at Km 89, where there's a restaurant suitably called **Las Torres** ("The Towers"). A dirt road leads up to the antenna, from where you'll have miraculous views, weather permitting, of the scintillating golden beaches of the Caribbean and Manuel Antonio, and a strong feel for the damp forest conditions and stunted flora. At 3,000 meters the vegetation is Andean *páramo* complete with wind-sculpted shrubs, peat bogs, and marshy grasses. Be prepared for high winds. Note, too, the vegetative changes as you descend from the heights past great stands of bamboo and oak forest, good for spotting quetzals and other birding, and past plantations of agaves (*cabuya*), from which sisal fibers are extracted for twine, "the golden fibers," says one writer, "overflowing from dump trucks taking them to market, diesel fumes coughing." If the sun is shining, you may see a statue of Christ balancing precariously on the cliff face above the highway two km north of San Rafael (Km 104). A small traditional *trapiche*—ox-driven sugar mill—is still in operation a little way down the road.

Accommodations and Food

Five km below the summit at **Villa Mills** is **Las Georginas** restaurant, popular with buses, which unload their passengers for meals. Reportedly, it has basic cabinas ($5). Locally grown apples and other produce are sold by the roadside.

Las Quebradas Biological Center

The 2,400-hectare Centro Biológico Las Quebradas research station and nature reserve (Apdo. 44, Quebradas 8000, Pérez Zeledín, tel. 717-0530) was established to protect the cloud-shrouded watershed of San Isidro. It is in the upper basin of a ravine on the southern flanks of the Cerro de la Muerte. It's open to ecotourists who, with luck, might see a quetzal. The Foundation for the Development of Las Quebradas Biological Centre (FUDEBIOL) is installing trails and camping and picnic sites.

SAN ISIDRO DE EL GENERAL

San Isidro, regional capital of the Valle de El General, is an important crossroads and a pleasant place to rest your head. The town is the gateway to Chirripó National Park via San Gerardo de Rivas and to Dominical and the central Pacific via the Fila San Antonio mountain range (the **Restaurant La Fiesta**, on the left just before **Tinamaste**, has cabinas; see "Dominical and Vicinity" in the Central Pacific chapter for more details). San Isidro is also a base for rafting trips on the Ríos Chirripó and General. Attesting to its lack of classical lineage (the town was founded in 1897, though most of it is post-WW II) is an ugly cathedral of concrete that looks like the German fortifications of Normandy. Nearby, next to Café el Teatro, there's a cul-

tural complex, including a museum, art gallery, and theater, plus artisans' workshops. In a cultural mood? Check out the **Southern Regional Museum,** Calle 2 and Avenida 1, which tells the story of the local indigenous peoples.

The town comes alive late January and early February for its **Fiestas Cívicas,** when agricultural fairs, bullfights, and general festivities occur. Best time of all, however, is 15 May, for the **Día del Boyero** ("Day of the Oxcart Driver"), featuring a colorful oxcart parade.

Budget Accommodations

There's no shortage of budget options. **Hotel/ Restaurante El Chirripó** (tel. 717-0529, fax 717-0410), on the south side of the square, has 41 rooms with hot water, plus a pleasing outdoor restaurant. Rates: $5-8 s, $8-15 d. The **Hotel Iguazú** (tel. 717-2571), behind the Banco Nacional, has 21 rooms with private and shared baths with hot water. It's clean and appealing. Rates: $10 s, $15 d. **Hotel Lala** (tel. 717-0291), opposite the Banco Nacional, is run-down. It has 26 rooms with fans and cold water. Rates: $3 per person; $7 d with bath. The **Hotel El Jardín** (tel. 717-0349) is of a similar price but higher standard.

Maria Morales, the friendly owner of the **Rincón de Papa** (see "Food," below), has converted a beautiful bamboo cabin into a cabina,

SAN ISIDRO DE EL GENERAL

with one room up and one down, plus hot water and natural ventilation. In town, also try **Cabinas El Prado** (tel. 717-0578), **Cabinas Río Mar** (tel. 717-2333), and **Pensión Eiffel** (tel. 771-0230), near the new bus station. All are in the $4-8 per person range.

Moderate Accommodations
Hotel Amaneli (tel. 717-0352), on the right immediately after you enter town from the north, is a condo-style hotel with 40 rooms with fans, private baths, and hot water. Rooms facing the highway are noisy through the night. Rates: $13 s, $18 d. **Hotel Astoria** (tel. 717-0914), facing the square, has 48 rooms with cold water. Rates: $9-10 s, $12 d.

The **Hotel del Sur** (Apdo. 4-8000, Pérez Zeledín, San Isidro, tel. 717-0233 or 234-8871, fax 717-0527), six km south of San Isidro, is the best hotel nearby. The 35 a/c rooms were dowdy when I called in, but also spacious and clean (a brochure published since I visited suggests the place may have been refurbished). It also has 12 deluxe rooms plus self-sufficient cabinas. A large restaurant and bar opens onto a swimming pool and landscaped grounds with volleyball court and tennis. You can rent horses and mountain bikes. A spa and casino were planned. My dinner was spoiled by a radio blaring, and at night the disco was loud enough to wake the dead. Rates: $25 s, $30 d, $35 t, $60 suite.

About 200 meters north of the Hotel del Sur is the **Hotel El Tecal** and **Apartotel El Tecal** (tel. 717-0664).

Food
Rincón de Papa (tel. 717-2042) beats all contenders. This elegant eatery has bamboo furniture beneath a large open-air *palenque* beside the Río Paja, one km south of San Isidro. Superb meals! Turn off the Pan-American Hwy. to the left. Follow the road about two km to a stop sign where the road turns right. The restaurant is hidden behind trees, on the right 100 meters before the stop sign.

In town, try the restaurant of the Hotel Chirripó, recommended for an early breakfast; the **Café el Teatro**, two blocks west and one block north of the church; or—for Chinese—**Restaurant Hong Kong**, facing the park. **Restaurante/Pizzería El Tenedor** (tel. 717-

SAN ISIDRO EMERGENCY TELEPHONE NUMBERS	
Hospital	717-0318
Red Cross	717-0990
Police (Guardia Rural)	117 or 717-0447
Transit Police	717-1313

0881) is recommended for pizzas and has a balcony overlooking the park, next to Hotel Iguazú. The **Hotel del Sur,** south of town, has a reasonable restaurant, though nothing to write home about. **Marisquería y Bar Marea Baja** (tel. 717-0681) is recommended for seafood. You can buy fresh fruit and vegetables at a new public market.

Rumor has it there's a **rollerskate disco** for post-prandial pleasure!

Services
Tourist information is provided by the San Isidro Chamber of Commerce (tel. 717-2525), on the plaza. You can get information on Chirripó National Park or La Amistad International Peace Park at the regional **parks service office** (tel. 771-1115), on the Pan-Am Hwy. opposite Calles 2/4. The **Banco Nacional** is two blocks northeast of the plaza; the **Banco Anglo Costarricense** faces the plaza. **Pharmacies** include Farmacia El Valle (tel. 717-0207) and Farmacia La Fuente (tel. 717-0602). **Doctors** include Dr. Gerardo Mora (tel. 717-1798), and Dr. Edgar Calderon Gonzalez, who has a clinical laboratory (tel. 717-2030). You'll pass more **gas stations** than you would care to count along the Pan-Am Highway.

Transportation
Express buses depart San José from Calle 16, Avenidas 1/3 ($3.50) hourly, 5:30 a.m.-5 p.m. (Musoc, tel. 222-2422 or 771-0414). Buses depart San Isidro for San José from a new bus station, between Calles Central/2 and Avenidas 4/6 (some buses may still depart from the Pan-Am Hwy. and Calle 2). Buses fill up fast—buy tickets in advance, especially on weekends and holidays.

Buses also depart Quepos via Dominical for San Isidro at 5:30 a.m. and 1:30 p.m. (tel. 717-

1384); returning from San Isidro at 7 a.m. and 1:30 p.m. You can also catch Tracopa buses to Buenos Aires, Ciudad Neily, David in Panamá, Golfito, Palmar, Puerto Jiménez, and San Vito.

Rafting Trips

The Ríos Chirripó and General are both popular for whitewater rafting. The rivers' enormous volume of water creates superb class III and IV rapids with gigantic waves. **Costaricaraft** (Apdo. 812, San Pedro, San José 2050, tel. 225-3939, fax 253-6934) offers three-day ($305) and four-day ($410) rafting trips on the Ríos General and Chirripó, August through December. **Costa Rica Expeditions** (Apdo. 6941, San José 1000, tel. 257-0766, fax 257-1665) and **Pioneer Raft** (Apdo. 29, Sabanilla, San José 2070, tel. 253-9132, fax 253-4687; in the U.S., P.O. Box 22063, Carmel, CA 93922, tel. 408-626-1815, fax 408-626-9013) offer three- to five-day trips on the Chirripó (from $305), June through December.

SAN GERARDO DE RIVAS AND VICINITY

San Gerardo is a small mountain village at 1,300 meters, 20 km northeast of San Isidro. The route to San Gerardo offers spectacular scenery and great birding. Quetzals nest hereabouts: local guides can show you where, as well as point the way uphill to a hot spring and waterfalls. The **ranger station** for Chirripó National Park is here. The park begins two miles east of San Gerardo (see below).

En route to San Gerardo you'll pass through **Rivas,** a pleasing little village with a series of *sodas* and *cantinas* and a Guardia Rural office opposite Soda Prisma; and **Canaan,** a small hamlet where an office (tel. 717-0433, ext. 101) next to Bar Estrella sells souvenirs and T-shirts and arranges guided trekking up Chirripó.

Three km north of San Gerardo is **Herradura,** a tiny village reached by rough dirt road. Here you'll find hot springs, but you'll need to hike along a steep path to reach them (look for the sign: Aguas Termales a 300 metros). You can hike from here to the hamlet of Río Blanco and beyond to Chirripó and Cerro Urán (3,333 meters).

Accommodations

Midway between San Isidro and San Gerardo is **Talari Auberge de Montagne** (Apdo. 517, San Isidro 8000, tel./fax 771-3102), a small mountain "resort" set in a river valley on an eight-hectare *(talari)* property partially reforested with secondary forest good for birding. Much of the balance is made up of orchards. The eight rooms have private baths and hot water; four have mini-bars and terraces proffering grand vistas. There's a restaurant and swimming pool. Rates: $20-25 s, $29-34 d. Nearby, in Canaan, halfway to San Gerardo, is the **Chirripó Lodge** (you can leave messages at the nearby *pulpería,* tel. 771-0433, ext. 101) offering basic rooms for $5 per person.

In San Gerardo, **Cabinas y Soda Marín** has two rooms with cold water for six people ($3). **Posada del Descanso** (tel. 717-0433, ext. 106; leave a message), 200 meters beyond the ranger station, has four slightly more appealing cabinas with doubles, plus three dorms with bunks, both with shared baths with cold water. Walls are extremely thin, and the rooms have just enough room for two beds, but the owners are super-friendly. The Elizondo family will welcome you warmly ($10-15, including meals). Farther up the road on the hillside near the church is **Cabinas y Soda Chirripó,** with three rooms with shared baths and hot water (approximately $3); and the **Cabinas Elimar,** with private baths, hot water ($15 d), and a restaurant. **Roca Dura** ("Hard Rock") is popular with trekkers. Alas, I missed it on my visit.

There are no rooms in Herradura. However, the **Pensión Quetzal Dorado** (tel. 717-0433, ext. 109) is an hourlong hike away in Río Blanco. It has beds for 45, plus two toilets, in its dorm ($3; or $10 including meals). Reportedly, you can rent horses here.

Food and Services

Soda Marín is a *pulpería* (general store; tel. 771-0433, ext. 106) where you can buy food for the hike up Chirripó if you forgot to stock up in San Isidro. You can call the store and leave a message for accommodations. The locals gather to play pool in the local *cantina,* and will gladly hire themselves out as *arrieros* or porters ($28 a day); you can also hire **horses** ($24 a day) here or at any of the cabinas. Prices are

fixed by the *arriero* association. You can buy a trail map at the visitor information center.

Transportation

Buses depart from San Isidro for San Gerardo de Rivas at 5 a.m. and 2 p.m., returning at 7 a.m. and 4 p.m. A 10:30 a.m. bus from San José (Calle 16, Avenidas 1/3; $1 each way) to San Isidro will get you there in time for the 2 p.m. bus. There's another San Gerardo nearby; specify San Gerardo de Rivas.

If driving, the turnoff for San Gerardo and Chirripó National Park is opposite the **Pollo Brasilia,** one km south of San Isidro. The road to Rivas is paved; it's a further nine km uphill

along an unpaved road from here to San Gerardo de Rivas. A 4WD taxi from San Isidro will cost $22.

CHIRRIPÓ NATIONAL PARK

Chirripó National Park protects 50,150 hectares of high-elevation terrain surrounding Chirripó (3,819 meters), Central America's highest peak. The park is contiguous with La Amistad International Peace Park to the south; together they form the Amistad-Talamanca Regional Conservation Unit. Much of the area remains *terra incognito*—a boon for flora and fauna, which

CLIMBING CHIRRIPÓ

You can do the 16-km hike to the summit in one day, but normally it takes two days, three days roundtrip. You should call the National Parks Service (tel. 233-4160) three days in advance and register and pay your fee at the ranger station upon arrival at San Gerardo. There are distance markers every two kilometers. Though you must hike with a guide (see "Guides" under "Chirripó National Park"), you might want to back up the pamphlet and map supplied by the ranger station with 1:50,000-scale topographical maps (sections 3444 II San Isidro and 3544 III Durika, available from Lehmann's or Librería Trejos in San José; if you plan on hiking to nearby peaks, you may also need sections 3544 IV Fila Norte and 3444I Cuerici). Note: Pack out all your trash; bury human waste.

Day One

Today is 14 km, mostly steeply uphill. Less fit hikers should begin not long after dawn, as it can take 12 hours or even longer in bad conditions (fitter hikers should be able to hike this section in six or seven hours using a shortcut called Thermometer, described here). You can hire local porters to carry your packs to base camp. Leaving San Gerardo, walk east over two bridges, staying to the right at each of two forks. At a sign marked Sendero al Cerro Chirripó, climb the fence and ascend across the pasture for approximately two km to where the official trail begins. You'll pass a sign reading "Trail

to Chirripó. Good luck!" There's a stream (the first water supply on the trail) one-half kilometer beyond the Llano Bonito marker, beyond which you begin a grueling uphill stretch called La Cuesta del Agua. Allow at least two hours for this. The climb crests at Monte Sin Fé ("Faithless Mountain"). You'll see a rudimentary wooden shelter at the halfway point, beyond which you pass into dwarf cloud forest adorned with old man's beard. Expect to see plentiful toucanets, trogons, monkeys, etc. lower down.

About six km below the summit is a cave large enough to sleep five or six people if rains dictate. From here a final climb—La Cuesta de los Arrepentidos ("Repentants' Hill")—takes you to the three huts (two km uphill), which are sheltered snugly beside the Río Talari beneath an intriguing rock formation called Los Crestones. The farthest hut, painted yellow, has a wooden floor and a stove. The huts have capacity for about 50 people. Note: Burning wood is now illegal. The huts (only two were in use at last report) have solar-powered lights, flush toilets, large bunk beds, and *very* cold showers. Be prepared for an uncomfortable night, as it freezes up here at night.

A new lodge capable of accommodating 80 people was in the offing to replace the huts.

Day Two

The early bird catches the worm! Today, up and onto the trail by dawn to make the summit before the

thrive here relatively unmolested by humans. One remote section of the park is called Savannah of the Lions, after its large population of pumas. Tapirs and jaguars are both common, though rarely seen. And the mountain forests protect several hundred bird species.

Cloud forest above 2,500 meters covers almost half the park, which features three distinct life zones topping off with subalpine rain *páramo,* marked by contorted dwarf trees and marshy grasses that dry out on the Pacific slopes January to May (presenting perfect conditions for raging fires fanned by high winds). Much of this area still bears the scars of a huge fire that raged across 2,000 hectares in April 1992, causing such devastation that the park was closed for four months. The region is still

trying to recover from this and even worse fires in 1976 and 1985.

The mountain was held sacred by pre-Columbian Indians. Tribal leaders and shamans performed rituals atop the lofty shrine; lesser mortals who ventured up Chirripó were killed. Magnetic fields are said to swing wildly at the top, particularly near Los Crestones, huge boulders thought to have been the most sacred of Indian sites.

Just as Hillary climbed Everest "because it was there," so Chirripó lures the intrepid who seek the satisfaction of reaching the summit (the first recorded climb was made by a priest, Father Agustín Blessing, in 1904). More than 2,000 visitors entered the park in 1994—the majority bound for the top. Many Ticos choose to

fog rolls in. It's about a 90-minute hike from the hut via the Valle de los Conejos ("Rabbits' Valley;" alas, the creatures were burned out in 1976 and haven't returned). On clear days the view is awesome! With luck, you'll be able to see both the Pacific and the Caribbean. Take time, too, if you can stand the cold, for a dip in Lago San Juan (if it's sunny, you'll quickly dry off and warm up on the rocks). You'll pass waterfalls en route to the top, giving you an understanding of why the Talamancan Indians called it Chirripó—"Place of Enchanted Waters."

You can head back to San Gerardo the same day, or contemplate a roundtrip hike to Cerro Ventisqueros, the second-highest mountain in Costa Rica: the trail begins below the Valle de los Conejos. You can spend your second night at another hut in the Valle de las Morenas, on the northern side of Chirripó (reportedly you need to obtain the key from the ranger in San Gerardo). With a local guide, you could also follow the Camino de los Indios, a trail that passes over Cerro Urán and far northern Talamancas. Do not try to follow this or any other trails without an experienced guide!

What to Bring
• Warm clothes—preferably layered clothing for varying temperature and humidity. A polypropylene jacket remains warm when wet.

• Raingear. A poncho is best.
• Good hiking boots. The path is wet and slippery.
• Warm sleeping bag—good to 0° C.
• Flashlight with spare batteries.
• Camping stove (kerosene, propane, or alcohol).
• A compass and map.
• Water (one liter minimum). You will lose body fluids. Avoid dehydration at all costs. There is no water supply for the first half of the hike.
• Food, including snacks. Dried bananas and peanuts are good energy boosters; bananas have potassium (good for guarding against cramps).
• Bag for litter/garbage. Take only photographs, leave only footprints.
• Wind/sun protection.

Tours
Jungle Trails (Apdo. 2413, San José 1000, tel. 255-3486, fax 255-2782) offers a guided five-day trek March, April, June, and July. Horses carry gear. Highlight is a summit picnic. Universal Tropical Nature Tours (Apdo. 4276, San José 1000, tel. 257-0181, fax 255-4274) has a four-day guided trek ($310). Camino Travel (tel. 234-2530, fax 225-6143) has a three-day trekking program departing San José each Tuesday ($315). L.A. Tours (Apdo. 492, San José 1007, tel. 224-5828, fax 221-4951) also offers a tour.

hike the mountain during the week preceding Easter, when the weather is usually dry. Avoid holidays, when the huts may be full. The hike is no Sunday picnic but requires no technical expertise. The trails are well-marked, and basic mountain huts are close to the summit (see special topic). You must stay overnight in San Gerardo de Rivas, from where you begin your hike early the next day.

Every February a **marathon** is held from San Gerardo to the peak of Chirripó and back to San Gerardo! The owner of the Posada del Descanso has won the trophy several times (the walls of his restaurant are covered with trophies and certificates from various marathon races). His best time? Up and down in four hours!

Information
Park headquarters is next to Cabinas Marín in San Gerardo de Rivas. Hours: 5 a.m.-5 p.m.

Park admission is $15 walk-in or $10 advance purchase, plus $1.50 each additional day and $3 for each night's use of mountain huts (you may be told there's a waiting list; experienced hikers recommend showing up anyway as there are usually lots of no-shows). Geiner Ureña Navarro, the park ranger, is very helpful. He has a basic map (25 cents) showing trails and landmarks to the summit. The **La Amistad Biosphere Reserve** office in San Isidro (tel. 717-1775) can supply general information on park conditions and current regulations for hikers.

Guides
Excessive wear and tear on the trails led the National Parks Service to begin phasing in new regulations in 1993. Only 30 visitors are allowed each day. You are no longer allowed to hike without a guide. The park service is pushing the less-known Herradura Trail, with the first

night camping atop Cerro Urán. Check for current regulations. You can hire guides in San Gerardo or Herradura (about $35 per day for guide and mule).

Weather

The weather is unpredictable and potentially dangerous—dress accordingly. Indeed, the hike to the summit from the park headquarters at San Gerardo ascends 2,500 meters. When the bitterly cold wind kicks in, watch out. Winds can approach 160 km/h: the humidity and wind-chill factor can drop temperatures to -5° C. Rain is always a possibility, even in "dry season," and a short downpour usually occurs midafternoon. Fog is almost a daily occurrence at higher elevations, often forming in midmorning. And temperatures can fall below freezing at night (some of the lakes near the summit are a legacy of the glacial ages). Time your hiking right, however, and you should be close to shelter when needed. Who knows, you may have good weather the whole way! February and March are the driest months.

BUENOS AIRES AND VICINITY

BUENOS AIRES

About 40 km south of San Isidro the air becomes redolent of sweet-smelling pineapples, the mainstay of Buenos Aires, a small agricultural town three km north of the Pan-American Hwy., 63 km south of San Isidro (there are *sodas* and a Texaco gas station at the junction). Reportedly, it's possible to take a tour of the Pindeco pineapple-processing plant; check with the regional chamber of commerce (tel. 717-2525) in the Hotel Chirripó in San Isidro. **Tropical Rainbow Tours** (Apdo. 774, San José 1000, tel. 233-8228, fax 255-4636) includes a tour of the plantation as part of a two-day tour to La Amistad ($175).

A dirt road leads 10 km northeast from Buenos Aires to **Ujarrás,** where you can hike into La Amistad International Peace Park (see below).

Accommodations and Food

Two km before Buenos Aires, at a fork leading from the Pan-American Hwy., is a sign for **Cabinas Mary** and **Cabinas El Buen Amigos,** both 200 meters up the dirt road to the right. The latter has two cabinas with baths ($5) and three without ($3); they're clean and all have fans but no hot water. There's a *pulpería* next door. Funkier Cabinas Mary has a small restaurant. In the center of town, the **Cabinas la Redonda Familiares** offers cheap accommodation. **Restaurant Ling Cheng** is an Italian restaurant—just kidding! The **Panadería Santa Marta** is opposite. **La Restaurante la Flor de Sabana** (tel. 730-0256) serves tasty *típico* dishes. (Also see "Finca Anael," below.)

Services

You'll find a **Banco Nacional** on the southeast corner of the plaza and a **Banco de Costa Rica** to the northwest. The **police** (Guardia Rural, tel. 117 or 730-0103) are one block east of the Banco Nacional. There are three **pharmacies** in town. The **Red Cross** is at 730-0078.

Transportation

Buses depart San Isidro for Buenos Aires every two hours. The Zona Sur bus to Ciudad Neily and Panamá departs San José from Avenida 18, Calle 4 (tel. 221-4214) and will drop you at Buenos Aires if you ask.

From Buenos Aires, the Pan-American Hwy. drops into the valley of the Río General and follows its course to its confluence with the Río Coto Brus. The rolling flatlands beyond **Brujo** are an ocean of endless sea-green pineapple plantations. Beyond **Paso Real,** both road and river turn southwest and descend through a deep ravine in the Fila Costeña mountains. The road is winding and prone to landslides.

FINCA ANAEL

If you're depressed by the extent of deforestation on the slopes of the Talamanca mountains, take heart. Despite being severely denuded, these mountains are home to a very special project:

FIESTA DE LOS DIABLITOS

Every year on 30 December a conch shell sounds at midnight across the dark hills of the Fila Sinancra. Men disguised as devils burst from the hills into town and go from house to house, where they perform skits and are rewarded with *tamales* and *chicha,* the traditional corn liquor. The Fiesta de los Diablitos has begun. Drums and flutes play while villagers dress in burlap sacks and traditional balsa-wood masks, energizing a pantheon of chiseled supernatural beings. Another dresses as a bull. Plied with *chicha,* the man becomes the animal and the animal the man, just as in the Roman Catholic tradition the sacrament becomes the body of the Lord. The *diablitos* chase, prod, and taunt the bull. Three days of celebrations and performances end with the symbolic killing of the bull, which is then reduced to ashes on a pyre. The festival reenacts the battles between Indian forebears and Spanish conquistadores with a dramatic new twist: the Indians win.

Finca Anael, a self-sufficient agricultural community that is working on behalf of harmony and conservation. Its 20 or so members operate this 50-hectare farm on land contiguous with the Durika Reserve, part of La Amistad International Peace Park. It's an oasis of greenery amid the bare mountains (project members hope to buy surrounding forest). The community was founded by a group of city folks who wanted to escape the rat-race for a stress-free, more peaceful existence.

In early 1995 the community opened its doors to ecotourism. A guide will be assigned to you. Besides the opportunity to milk the goats, feed the kids (goats, that is), make yogurt and cheese, try your hand at carpentry, and learn—and even participate in—organic farming, you can attend classes in martial arts, meditation, and art. The surrounding forests provide excellent opportunities for spotting quetzals, trogons, toucans, and monkeys. Animals such as pumas and jaguars, not seen for many years, have recently been spotted, suggesting that the community's efforts may be paying off. Guided hikes include one to a fabulous waterfall, another to Indian villages, and a third, five-day camping trip to

the summit of remote Cerro Dúrika.

You'll stay in one of three simple, candlelit cabins with fantastic views (one has two beds and a bathroom; the others each have four beds and share a bathroom). Rates: $30-35, including all vegetarian meals (don't fail to try the *chicha,* a heady home-brew of fermented corn and sugar), plus transfers. For information and reservations, call Annie McCormick (tel. 240-2320, fax 223-0341).

At press time, Finca Anael was a two-hour uphill journey from Buenos Aires to a trailhead that leads steeply through cloud forest to the hamlet. The dirt road will eventually reach the *finca* itself.

BORUCA INDIAN RESERVE

About 10 km beyond Paso Real, a dirt road on the right leads uphill to Boruca, a slow-paced hamlet set in a verdant valley. It's the center of a series of Indian villages and tiny *fincas* scattered throughout these mountains. A visit here offers a very different perspective on traditional life. Here, you can watch delicate female fingers weaving tablecloths, purses, and belts on traditional hand looms, while men carve balsa-wood masks. Gourds *(jícaras)* are made too, carved with intricate pastoral scenes. Apparently there's an **eco-museum,** which I've not seen.

North of the Boruca turnoff is the Indian village of **Rey Curré,** looking much like most small villages in the country but also with a strong hint of an indigenous heritage. There's a crafts cooperative next to the school where you can buy carved gourds and other Indian crafts.

Accommodations

There are no hotels in Boruca, but it is possible to stay with families by prior arrangement through **Tur-Casa** (tel. 225-1239). Alternately, ask at the *pulpería.*

Transportation

A school bus departs Buenos Aires for Boruca at 1:30 p.m. (two hours away). Alternatively, the Zona Sur bus from San José will drop you off at the Entrada de Boruca (a trailhead, two km south of Brujo), or at the road to Boruca south of Paso Real, from where you can hike uphill to the village.

SAN VITO AND VICINITY

About eight km northeast of the Boruca turnoff (one km south of Paso Real), a turnoff from the Pan-American Hwy. leads down to the Río Térraba, where a small ferry ($1.25) provides a link with the ridge-crest road to San Vito. It's one of the most scenic drives in the country, with magnificent views across the Valle de Coto Brus to the Talamancas. It's easy to miss the sign to San Vito; a larger sign—on the left when you're driving south—reads "Proyecto Paso Real." You'll find *sodas* at the dock. The wiry ferry men—often bare-chested—who operate the motor look as if they were born in the reeds of the river edge with the crocodiles, which wait for morsels thrown from the ferry. Someday soon a bridge will put the ferry men out of work.

Three km beyond the ferry, a turnoff on the left leads to **Potrero Grande** (five km) and **La Amistad International Peace Park.** The Estación Tres Colinas Ranger Station is 28 km from here. Another road at **Guácimo** leads to **Altimira** (21 km) and La Amistad Ranger Station (26.5 km; see "La Amistad International Peace Park," below).

Accommodations
Monte Amou Lodge (c/o Tucan Ecological Tours, tel. 234-0934, fax 224-3029), 12 km east of Potrero Grande, lies at the foot of Mt. Fallas, at an elevation of 1,000 meters and in a transition zone between humid tropical forest and tropical cloud forest on the edge of La Amistad. Stupendous views! Trails penetrate the park. The lodge and cabinas have thatched roofs, with locally handmade furniture. The lodge has four guest suites, each with three beds, desk, and private shower (hot water at night only, when the generator is turned on). There's a cozy lounge, and family-style dinners are served in a large dining room. Bring warm clothing. Tucan Ecological Tours offers guided nature tours to La Amistad using Monte Amou as a base. Four-day package rates per person: $484 s, $424 d, $404 t, including transport from San José, three meals daily, plus guided tours.

SAN VITO

San Vito is a pleasant little mountain town that nestles on the east-facing flank of the Fila Costeña, overlooking the Coto Brus Valley, at 990 meters above sea level. If you surmise an Italian air it's because the town was founded by Italian immigrants in the early 1950s. When entering by car from Buenos Aires, take the right hand (uphill) fork at the bus station. This leads to a tiny park, from where you can turn left into the town. A larger park has been named Parque Ecológico and rehashed to resemble a tropical rainforest complete with rushing river.

Budget Accommodations
Cabinas Las Mirlas (tel. 773-3054), next to the Ministry of Agriculture on the road to Cañas Gordas, has pretty landscaped grounds overlooking a valley, plus seven cabins with hot water but no fans. Rates: $4 per person; a bargain. **Albergue Firenze** (tel. 773-3206), on the left just north of the gas and bus stations at the fork at the entrance of town from Buenos Aires, has six rooms with private baths and hot water but no fans. It is small but pleasing. Rates: $4 per person. **Hotel Colona** (tel. 773-3461) has 25 very basic rooms with hot water but no fans. Rates: $3 per person. **Hotel Collina** (tel. 773-3173) has six pleasant rooms with private baths, hot water, and fans, plus a lively bar and open-air restaurant upstairs. Rates: $6 per person.

Hotel Tropical (tel. 754-2473) has 16 rooms with cold water and fans, and—be warned!—a disco downstairs ($2.50 per person). **Hotel Pittier** (tel. 773-3027), on the outskirts of town on the road to Cañas Gordas, has 12 rooms with hot water but no fans. It was terribly run-down when I called by. The office is hidden around the corner. Rates: $4 s, $7 d. Also try the **Hotel El Jardín** and **Cabinas Las Huacas** (tel. 773-3115); the latter has private baths with hot water, and a disco on weekends.

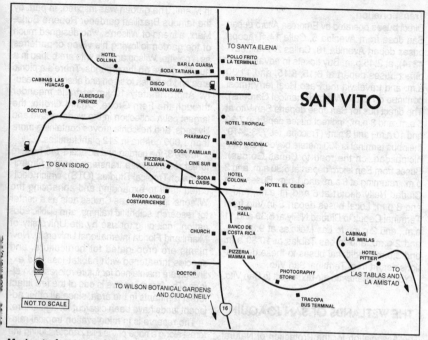

TO SANTA ELENA

HOTEL COLLINA

CABINAS LAS HUACAS

ALBERGUE FIRENZE

DOCTOR

BAR LA GUARIA
SODA TATIANA

DISCO BANANARAMA

POLLO FRITO LA TERMINAL

BUS TERMINAL

SAN VITO

HOTEL TROPICAL

PHARMACY

BANCO NACIONAL

SODA FAMILIAR

CINE SUR

PIZZERIA LILLIANA

SODA EL OASIS

HOTEL COLONA

HOTEL EL CEIBO

BANCO ANGLO COSTARRICENSE

TO SAN ISIDRO

TOWN HALL

BANCO DE COSTA RICA

CABINAS LAS MIRLAS

HOTEL PITTIER

CHURCH

PIZZERIA MAMMA MIA

DOCTOR

PHOTOGRAPHY STORE

TO LAS TABLAS AND LA AMISTAD

TRACOPA BUS TERMINAL

TO WILSON BOTANICAL GARDENS AND CIUDAD NEILY

16

NOT TO SCALE

Moderate Accommodations

A good bargain and the nicest place in town is **Hotel El Ceibo** (tel. 773-3025), behind the Municipalidad. It has 38 modern rooms with private baths and hot water, a large restaurant, a lounge with TV, plus a small bar. Each room has one double and a single bed. Rooms at the back face Parque Ecológico. Rates: $11 s, $18 d, including breakfast.

Food

Pastas and pizzas sum it up! San Vito's Italian heritage shines. **Pizzeria Mamma Mía** has a large menu of Italian dishes, from lasagne and ravioli to gnocchi, *orechiette a la Mamma Mía,* and *cotolette a la bolognesa,* all under $4. The **Hotel El Ceibo** restaurant serves cannelloni, lemon scalloppini, and fresh tuna spaghetti. **Pizzeria Lilliana** is another option, as is the upstairs restaurant of the **Hotel Collina,** which serves Italian and Chinese. Costa Rican fare is served at the **Pollo Frito la Terminal, Soda Tatiana,** and **Soda Familiar.**

Entertainment

Nightlife centers on the bar of the **Hotel Collina, Bar Hermanos Ureña,** and the **Disco Bananarama,** 50 meters east of Collina, next to the gas station. There's also a **cinema.**

Services

Doctor Cesari Consumi (tel. 773-3206) has an office next door to Albergue Firenze; hours are 10 a.m.-noon, and 2 to 6 p.m. You'll find a **pharmacy** (Farmacia Coto Brus, tel. 773-3076) on the main street, and a reasonably well-stocked **photography store. Banco Nacional** and **Banco de Costa Rica** have branches on the main street.

SAN VITO EMERGENCY TELEPHONE NUMBERS

Hospital	773-3103
Red Cross	773-3191

Transportation

Direct **buses** operated by Empresa Alfaro depart San José from Avenida 5, Calle 14. Tracopa buses depart Avenida 18, Calles 2/4 (tel. 221-4214), at 2:45 p.m. Buy tickets in advance. Indirect buses depart at 6:15, 8:15, and 11:30 a.m. and travel via the Paso Real ferry (most continue on to the Wilson Botanical Gardens). The direct bus for San José departs San Vito at 5 a.m. and 3 p.m.; indirect buses depart at 7:30 and 10 a.m., and 3 p.m. (Tracopa, tel. 773-3410; their bus terminal is 400 meters beyond the Municipalidad, on the road to Cañas Gordas). Buses from San Isidro depart at 5:30 a.m. and 2 p.m., returning at 6 a.m. and 1 p.m. Buses from Ciudad Neily depart at 6 and 11 a.m., and 1 and 3 p.m. Local buses depart San Vito from Terminal Cepul: to Ciudad Neily at 5:30 and 11 a.m., and 2 p.m.; to Las Mellizas at 9:30 a.m. and 2 p.m.; and to Las Tablas at 10:30 a.m. and 3 p.m. Additional buses to these destinations depart from Terminal San Vito.

You can charter an **air-taxi** direct to San Vito.

THE WETLANDS OF SAN JOAQUÍN

The Association for the Protection of Natural Resources of Coto Brus (APRENABRUS) was recently formed to preserve and stabilize a species-rich freshwater wetland—a habitat now rare in Costa Rica—three km east of San Vito. In addition to fish, reptiles, and insects that live only in aquatic environments, the area attracts more than 100 species of birds. The goal is to make the wetlands more accessible. Facilities will include parking areas, observation platforms, benches, and trails. If you're interested in contributing or visiting, contact the Wilson Botanical Gardens.

WILSON BOTANICAL GARDENS

The Wilson Botanical Gardens (also known as the Las Cruces Biological Station), six km south of San Vito, is much more than its name suggests and well worth the drive south in itself! Foremost are the 10 hectares of cultivated gardens established in 1963 by Robert and Catherine Wilson, former owners of Fantastic Gardens in Miami. The garden was inspired, in part, by the famous Brazilian gardener Roberto Burle-Marx, a friend of Wilson's, who designed much of the garden following his vision of parterres as a palette. Wilson and his wife are buried in a humble grave on the grounds. There's a picnic area and benches to sit on and absorb the beauty. Approximately 10 km of trails meander through the Fern Grove, Orchid Grotto, the largest palm collection in the world, agave and lily beds, and heliconia groves containing more than 1,000 genera in 212 plant families.

In 1973, the garden and adjacent 145-hectare forest reserve were transferred to the Organization of Tropical Studies (OTS), which dedicated itself to expanding and enhancing the Wilsons' life work. Las Cruces acts as a center for research, scientific training, and public education, including for use by the University of Miami and Florida International University. New plants are propagated for horticulture, and species threatened with habitat loss and extinction are maintained for future reforestation efforts. The forest reserve is one of the few intact forest remnants in the area, since all other adjacent lands have been clearcut for agriculture.

The reserve is in midelevation tropical rainforest along a ridge of the Fila Zapote. During the wet season, heavy fog and afternoon clouds spill over the ridge, nourishing a rich epiphytic flora of orchids, bromeliads, ferns, and aeroids. The forest is a vital habitat for pacas, anteaters, opossums, kinkajous, porcupines, armadillos, sloths, tayras, monkeys, deer, small cats, and more than 35 species of bats. Birdwatching at Las Cruces is especially rewarding: 315 species have been recorded.

Maintaining the reserve—proclaimed part of La Amistad Biosphere Reserve—is the cornerstone of a larger effort to save the watershed of the Río Java. OTS is trying to acquire a contiguous virgin rainforest of 91 hectares. Paul and Anne Ehrlich, famous population biologists, state that the overwhelming biological evidence is that it would be devastating to the Garden and Forest Reserve if the adjacent forest were cut. Not only would the carrying capacity of the Las Cruces forest diminish with regard to species, but the opening of edges would increase exposure to wind and sun, further affecting species that rely on moist, dark areas. In-

evitably, many larger species would die off. You may send donations to OTS (see "Accommodations," below), earmarked for the Las Cruces Land Purchase.

More critical, however, the research laboratories and guest housing were destroyed by a fire in November 1994. Alas, the research station was not insured for replacement value. OTS is desperately short of money. Contributions for the rebuilding can be sent to the OTS address below or to OTS/Save the Garden Fund, Duke University, P.O. Box 90630, Durham, NC 27708-0630.

When to Go
Dry season is mid-December through mid-April (afternoon showers are not unknown); the rainiest period is Sept.-November. Annual rainfall is about 400 cm.

Accommodations
Temporary facilities are replacing the dormitories, private cabins, and kitchens that were destroyed in late 1994. Las Cruces will accept drop-by overnighters on a space-available basis. It's advisable to reserve. Contact the OTS for current rates. By the time you read this, permanent structures may be in place. Special discount rates apply for researchers and students with accredited projects. Researchers can also rent cars ($40 daily). Reservations: Organization for Tropical Studies, Apdo. 676, San Pedro 2050, tel. 240-6696 or 240-9938, fax 240-6783.

Cabinas La Cascada, 800 meters north of the gardens, has basic cabins with cold water ($6).

Information and Services
You'll find a very spacious and atmospheric lounge opening onto a porch with grand views toward the Talamancas, plus a research library and laboratory for students. Entrance: $4.50 half day; $6 full day; $12 with lunch; students, special rate. Reservations not required for day visits. Hours: 8 a.m.-4 p.m., closed Monday. For more information contact Wilson Botanical Gardens, Apdo. 73, San Vito de Java, Coto Brus, tel./fax 773-3278.

Getting There
Local buses stop at the gardens and operate from San Vito at 7 and 11 a.m., and 1:30 and 4 p.m.; and from the garden gate to San Vito at 6:30 and 7:30 a.m., and 1:45 and 4 p.m. Buses depart Ciudad Neily for the gardens at 7 a.m. and 1 p.m. A **taxi** from San Vito costs about $3; from Golfito reckon on $40 or so.

LA AMISTAD INTERNATIONAL PEACE PARK

The 193,929-hectare "Friendship Park" is shared with neighboring Panamá. Together with the adjacent Chirripó National Park, the Hitoy-Cerere Biological Reserve, Las Tablas and Barbilla Protective Zones, Wilson Botanical Gardens, and a handful of Indian reservations, it forms the 600,000-hectare Amistad Biosphere Reserve, a UNESCO World Heritage Site also known as the Amistad-Talamanca Regional Conservation Unit—the largest biological reserve in the isthmus.

The park transcends the Cordillera Talamanca ranges, rising from 150 meters above sea level on the Caribbean side to 3,554 meters atop Cerro Kamuk. The Talamancas are made up of separate mountain chains with only a limited history of volcanic activity; none of the mountains is considered a volcano. La Amistad's eight life zones form habitats for flora and fauna representing at least 60% of the nation's various species, including no fewer than 450 bird species (not least the country's largest population of resplendent quetzals and 49 endemic species), as well as the country's largest density of tapirs, jaguars, harpy eagles, ocelots, and many other endangered species. The park protects such important watersheds as the Ríos Térraba, Estrella, and Sixaola, whose valleys harbor the largest stands of tropical rain- and moist forests in the isthmus. Cloud forests ex-

ocelot

tend to 2,800 meters, with alpine *páramo* vegetation in the upper reaches.

Trails and Access

Much of this massive park remains unexplored. It has no facilities, and those few trails that exist are unmarked and often barely discernible. Unless you're an experienced trekker, don't even think about hiking into the park without a guide. Weather is extremely fickle. And—with the exception of the Las Tablas Forest Reserve section—you'll be many kilometers from human contact in case of an emergency.

The park has four official access points (entrance is $15 walk-in, $5 advance purchase). **Park headquarters** is at Progreso, about 30 km northeast of San Vito, and reached via the road through Sabalito, Unión, Río Negro, La Lucha, and Làs Mellizas. Four-wheel drive required. From here, trails lead to the Las Tablas Ranger Station (camping, but no facilities); it's about 10 km to the station.

You can also enter via **La Escuadra Ranger Station,** 14 km northeast from Agua Caliente, reached by a dirt road from Santa Elena, in the Cotón valley, about 20 km north of San Vito.

The **Estación Tres Colinas Ranger Station** at Helechales is about 12 km northeast of Potrero Grande (the turnoff for Potrero is four km south of the Río Térraba ferry and is signed as 28 km to Helechales); 4WD required. There are no facilities at Helechales.

The **La Amistad Ranger Station** is 26.5 km northeast of Guácimo, 18 km south of the ferry on the road to San Vito; the rough dirt road leads via Altimira (neither the road nor Altimira are marked on road maps).

Another trail from Ujarrás, 10 km northeast of Buenos Aires, crosses the Talamancas via Cerro Abolado and the valley of the Río Taparí, ending in the Hitoy-Cerere Biological Reserve on the Caribbean side (you can catch a bus to Sixaola and thence to Puerto Limón from Shiroles). It is a very strenuous, 54-km, five- or six-day hike. *Do not attempt this hike without an indigenous guide.* Register in advance at the CONAI (Indigenous Affairs) office at Ujarrás. The San José CONAI office (tel. 221-5496) can provide updated information on restrictions and protocol.

Accommodations

There are no accommodations in the park. **La Amistad Lodge** (formerly Las Mellizas Lodge) (tel. 221-8634 or 233-8228) is on a 1,215-hectare farm within Las Tablas Protective Zone, a private wildlife reserve adjoining La Amistad near the Panamanian border. It is built of multi-hued *cristobal,* a beautiful hardwood that lends the A-framed lodge a warm glow. It has 10 rooms, a stone fireplace, a third-floor aerie for cozy relaxation, and family-style dining where hearty and healthy meals are turned out by husband-and-wife managers Carmen and Roy Arroyo. You'll need a sturdy 4WD to get there in the wet season. Horseback rides and guided hiking are offered along 40 km of trails graded according to difficulty and ranging from 700 meters to 1,500 meters above sea level. A 24-room lodge, similar in appearance, was under construction (the original lodge will revert to family use by the owner). Rates: $65 per person, including meals. **Universal Tropical Nature Tours** (Apdo. 4276, San José 1000, tel. 255-4274, fax 551-4270) and **Costa Rica Expeditions** (Apdo. 6941, San José 1000, tel. 257-0766, fax 257-1665) both offer four-day packages with three nights at La Amistad Lodge ($425, including all meals). **Tropical Rainbow Tours** (Apdo. 774, San José 1000, tel. 233-8228, fax 255-4636) offers a two-day tour to La Amistad International Park, with accommodation at La Amistad Lodge ($175). **Rico Tours** (Apdo. 883, San José 1002, tel. 233-9658, fax 233-9357; in the U.S., 13809 Research Blvd. #606, Austin, TX 78750, tel. 512-331-0918, fax 512-331-8765) offers a similar four-day package.

Five km south of Tigra is **Finca Las Tablas** (La Lucha, Sabalito, Coto Brus 8257), where the Sandí family offers **camping** and meals. The fruit farm and surrounding forest have a healthy population of quetzals. Horseback and hiking tours are offered.

Also see "Finca Anael" under "Buenos Aires and Vicinity," above.

Information

Contact the Amistad Bisophere Reserve Office (tel. 717-1775), in San Isidro, or the toll-free National Parks Service information line (tel. 192) in San José.

Transportation
Buses depart San Vito for Cotón at 3 p.m., Progreso and Las Mellizas at 9:30 a.m. and 2 p.m., for Las Tablas at 10:30 a.m. and 3 p.m., and for Santa Elena at 10 a.m. and 4 p.m. Buses depart Buenos Aires for Potrero Grande at 6:30 a.m. and noon. **Jeep-taxis** will run you there in dry season from Buenos Aires or San Vito (about $50 roundtrip).

CIUDAD NEILY AND VICINITY

CIUDAD NEILY

Ciudad Neily squats at the base of the File Costeña mountains, beside the Pan-American Hwy., 18 km northwest of Panamá and 15 km east of Río Claro and the turnoff for Golfito. If you're descending from San Vito and the Wilson Botanical Gardens, be warned that the rough gravel road plummets steeply to Ciudad Neily, 31 km south of, and 1,000 meters lower than, San Vito. It has many hairpin bends. Drive slowly! After the cool of San Vito, the sudden humidity seems oppressive. The town is surrounded by banana plantations and functions as the node for plantation operations. The airport is four km south of town, at Coto 47.

Accommodations
There's no shortage of budget hotels, with little to choose between them. Hot water is a luxury. The most pleasing is **Cabinas Heyleen,** a nicely kept home festooned with epiphytes. She didn't want to give prices or let me inside, but the place looked nice. Otherwise, in the $5-10 s/$8-12 d range, try the **Hotel Musuco** (tel. 783-3048), **Cabinas Fontana** (tel. 783-3078), or **Cabinas El Rancho** (tel. 783-3201), with rooms with private baths. The more basic options include the **Hotel Central, Hotel Las Vegas** (tel. 783-3205), **Pensión Familiar, Hotel Bulufer** (tel. 783-3216), and **Hotel El Viajero** (tel. 783-3034). I welcome readers' comments.

About six km south of Neily is **Cabinas y Restaurante Guaymi** (tel. 783-3127), with a thatched *palenque* on the left. You can reportedly camp at **Camino Real,** about six km north of Paso Canoas.

Food and Entertainment
The two best places are **Soda de López,** a nice, tiny open-air restaurant facing the park, and **Restaurante La Moderna** (tel. 783-3097), whose eclectic menu includes burgers and pizza. Options for Chinese include **Restaurante Huang Guen** (tel. 783-4055) and **Restaurante Mei San** (tel. 783-3214), facing the park.

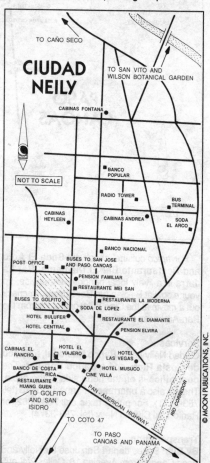

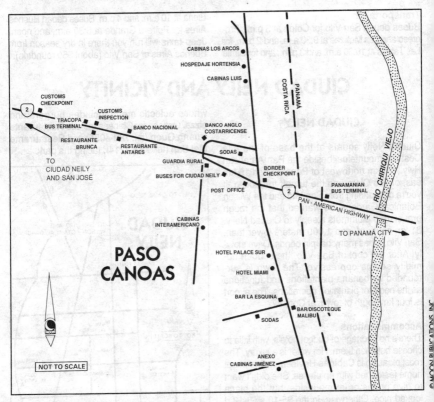

CABINAS LOS ARCOS

HOSPEDAJE HORTENSIA

CABINAS LUIS

CUSTOMS CHECKPOINT

CUSTOMS INSPECTION

TRACOPA BUS TERMINAL

BANCO NACIONAL

BANCO ANGLO COSTARRICENSE

RESTAURANTE BRUNCA

RESTAURANTE ANTARES

SODAS

TO CIUDAD NEILY AND SAN JOSÉ

GUARDIA RURAL

BUSES FOR CIUDAD NEILY

BORDER CHECKPOINT

POST OFFICE

PANAMANIAN BUS TERMINAL

CABINAS INTERAMERICANO

PAN - AMERICAN HIGHWAY

TO PANAMÁ CITY

PASO CANOAS

HOTEL PALACE SUR

HOTEL MIAMI

BAR LA ESQUINA

BAR/DISCOTEQUE MALIBU

SODAS

ANEXO CABINAS JIMÉNEZ

COSTA RICA

PANAMÁ

RÍO CHIRIQUÍ VIEJO

NOT TO SCALE

For *típico* cuisine, check out **Soda El Arco** and **Restaurante/Bar El Diamante. Bar La Jarra** is a lively local hangout. Otherwise, tip your elbow at Belgian-run **Bar Europa,** or check out a movie at the **Cine Villa,** one block from the Pan-American Highway.

Services

Ciudad Neily has a **Banco Nacional,** a **Banco de Costa Rica,** and a **Banco Popular.** The **post office** is on the north side of the plaza. There's also a **pharmacy,** Farmacia Ibarra (tel. 783-3171). For public **taxis** call 783-3862, or Radio Taxi Ciudad Neily (tel. 783-3374).

Transportation

By Bus: Buses depart San José for Neily and Paso Canoas from Avenida 18, Calles 2/4, at 5 and 7:30 a.m., and 1, 4:30, and 6 p.m. (eight hours). Buses depart for San José from the terminal, next to the market on the northeast side of town. Buses to Golfito ($0.75) depart hourly 6 a.m.-7 p.m.; to Paso Canoas (on the Panamá border) hourly 6 a.m.-6 p.m.; to Puerto Jiménez at 7 a.m. and 2 p.m.; and to San Vito at 6 and 11 a.m., and 1 and 3 p.m.

By Air: SANSA (tel. 233-3258, fax 255-2176) flies twice daily from San José to Coto 47 on Tuesday, Thursday, and Saturday at 8 a.m., and on Monday, Wednesday, and Friday at 8:45 a.m. ($24 one-way). Flights to San José depart Coto 47 via Palmar Sur and Puerto Jiménez at 9 and 9:45 a.m. **Travelair** (tel. 232-7883, fax 220-0413) may have introduced service by the time you read this. **Note:** Reduced schedules operate in off season.

PASO CANOAS

There's absolutely no reason to visit ugly Paso Canoas unless you intend crossing into Panamá—a straightforward affair (see "Border Crossings," under "Getting There" in the On the Road chapter). Endless stalls and shops selling personal goods are strung out along the road paralleling the border. The place is popular with Ticos, who pour in to buy the duty-free goods. **Note:** Even if you don't cross into Panamá, you must get a clearance from the customs officials adjacent to the Tracopa bus terminal before leaving town, otherwise you'll be turned back by officials. (There's another border post at **Cañas Gordas,** 16 km north of Neily; turn right at Agua Buena. Foreigners are not allowed into Panamá there.)

Accommodations
Accommodation is motley, and often full on weekends. All the hotels below are in the $5-10 price range; none have hot water. The following have private baths: **Cabinas Interamericano, Cabinas El Hogar** (tel. 732-2301), **Cabinas Los Arcos, Cabinas Evelyn** (tel. 732-2229), **Cabinas Velise** (tel. 732-2302), **Cabinas Luis, Anexo Cabinas Jiménez** (tel. 732-2258), **Hotel Azteca** (tel. 732-2217), and **Hotel Palace Sur.** Other budget options include **Hotel el Descan-**

so (tel. 732-2261), **Hotel Miami,** and **Hospedaje Hortensia.**

Services
The **immigration** office (tel. 732-2150) is next to the bus terminal. Get there early; the interminable line moves at a snail's pace. The **Costa Rican Tourism Institute** (ICT) has an office here (tel. 732-2035). **Agencia de Aduana Aimi** (tel. 732-2171) is a customs broker. The two banks, **Banco Anglo Costarricense** and **Banco Nacional,** close at 4 p.m. and weekends. There are plenty of **moneychangers** lingering (rates are reportedly good). You're advised to get rid of *colones* before crossing into Panamá.

Taxis wait at the triangle in front of the border crossing. A taxi from Ciudad Neily will cost about $10. There's a **pharmacy,** Farmacia Paso Canoas (tel. 732-2293). The **police** station (tel. 732-2106) is on the south side of the triangle.

Transportation
See "Ciudad Neily" (above) for bus departures from San José. Weekend buses to and from Paso Canoas fill up early; reservations are recommended. Buses depart Paso Canoas for San José at 4, 7:30, and 9:30 a.m., and 2:45 p.m. (eight hours; approximately $6.50; Tracopa, tel. 732-2119). Local buses depart for Neily every hour. Taxis to/from Neily cost $10.

GOLFO DULCE

The Golfo Dulce region fringes the huge bay of the same name encompassed by the Osa Peninsula to the west and the Fila Costeña mountains to the north and gently sloping to the east, where flatlands planted with bananas fade off to the border with Panamá. South of these flatlands is the virtually uninhabited Peninsula de Burica, the southernmost tip of Costa Rica. The region is centered on the town of Golfito. It, and the much smaller Puerto Jiménez, are the only towns of any consequence. The bay is rimmed by swamplands, lonesome beaches (several with nature and/or fishing lodges at which to rest your head), and remote tracts of rainforest accessible only by boat.

GOLFITO

Golfito is for travelers who love adventures in forlorn ports. Its setting is pleasing, but the town itself is a disappointment unless you like funky, semi-down-at-the-heels places. Character it has. Charm, no. Use it as a jumping-off point for the Osa Peninsula and Corcovado National Park, Wilson Botanical Gardens, and the surf spots of Zancudo and Pavones.

The town was born in 1938, when the United Fruit Company moved its headquarters here after shutting down operations on the Caribbean coast. By 1955, over 90% of the nation's banana exports were shipped from Golfito. Back then both sailors and prostitutes struck it rich, especially when World War II came along and Allied sailors came ashore to spawn. "Men in fatigues had parties with our women for $100 a night. After a while the women wouldn't go out with Costa Rican men," says Louis Vinicio Elizondo Arguello, the municipal administrator. The United Fruit Company closed its doors and pulled out of Golfito in 1985 after a series of crippling labor strikes. Today Golfito attracts its fair share of tropical vagabonds, yachties, and roughneck military-type expatriates who appear when the sun goes down. There are still plenty of prostitutes around to part them from their money.

The town is slung along a single road on the estuary of the Río Golfito, which opens onto the Golfo Dulce. Forested mountains form a backdrop a few hundred meters inland, a part of which forms Golfito National Wildlife Refuge, abutting to the north onto the recently formed Piedras Blancas National Park. There are two distinct parts of town. First entered, to the south, is the **Pueblo**

Golfito

CHRISTOPHER P. BAKER

Civil, the run-down working-class section full of cheap bars and hotels that still—at least the odd one—act as brothels. The only interesting site is the derelict locomotive behind a fence at the side of the road. To the north is the **Zona Americana,** a more tranquil, upscale quarter where the administrative staff of United Fruit used to live. Today, it houses mostly North American retirees. It reminds me of a scene from the British Raj, with brightly painted, two-story wooden houses raised on stilts to catch the breeze, and tall shade trees hung with epiphytes and lianas.

The town is growing popular as a sportfishing center. The bay is not recommended for swimming. Take a water-taxi to a nearby beach, such as Playa Cacao, a popular relaxation spot for locals about 10 km north of town (the road curls around; Cacao actually faces Golfito across the bay, is two km as the crow flies, and can be reached by water-taxi for $1).

Golfito National Wildlife Refuge
This 1,309-hectare Golfito National Wildlife Refuge, created to protect the city's watershed,

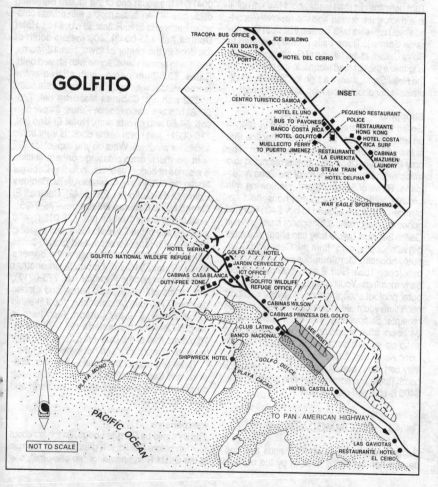

is formed of primary rainforest covering the steep chain of low mountains behind the harbor. Abundant year-round rains feed the insatiable jungle. Many endangered tree species such as butternut, plomo, and purpleheart thrive and attract 146 bird species, not least scarlet macaws. Trails lead through the reserve. With patience, you might spot an anteater, an agouti, a margay, a raccoon, or a jaguarundi. All four species of Costa Rican monkeys live in the refuge.

You'll find a sign at Barrio Invu across from the Plaza Deportes soccer field in the Pueblo Civil. Turn right; the dirt road leads about five km uphill to a microwave station and the reserve (reportedly, you can also take a steep trail from Restaurante Samoa). Three trails off the road lead to Playa Cacao, at the far end of Golfito (the easiest is to follow the dirt road alongside the airstrip from the Hotel Sierra; there's a sign for "Senderos Naturales" after about three km). Ask directions.

Shopping

Golfito was declared a duty-free port in 1990—an attempt to offset the economic decline that followed United Fruit's strategic retreat. The duty-free zone, Depósito Libre, is restricted to a massive shopping mall north of the Zona Americana. Rows of 52 shops are overflowing with luxury goods, electronics, and household appliances. Ticos are allowed to buy $400 worth of goods each six months. Shoppers must arrive in Golfito 24 hours before they can shop. You must get a "shopping card" from the Centro de Computo, opposite store number one in the complex (open Tues.-Sun. 8 a.m.-4:30 p.m.). Avoid early mornings. You'll need to present your computer printout shopping card plus your passport each time you make a purchase. Keep the sales receipts. Supposedly, you must leave Golfito 24 hours after shopping. If you think you can snap up superb bargains, forget it. This isn't Hong Kong. Yes, foreigners can buy as much as they can carry, but you can do just as well back home (there is a nominal tax) and anything over $400 is charged regular duty.

ACCOMMODATIONS

Golfito gets very busy on weekends and holidays, when Josefinos flock in by the busload

to splurge on electronics and the like. If you plan on overnighting here, it's best to plan a weekday visit.

Budget
Hotel del Cerro has $5 "backpacker" rooms with shared baths (see "Inexpensive," below). **Hotel Castillo** (tel. 775-0437), on the left at the south end of town, has nine fairly basic but clean rooms with cold water and fans. Rates: $9 per person.

Hotel Golfito (Apdo. 80, Golfito, tel. 775-0047), at the south end of the Muelle Bananero dock, has 14 very basic rooms with private cold-water baths and fans. Rates: $9 s/d, $14 t. **Hotel Delfina** (tel. 775-0043), 400 meters south of the dock in the center of town, has 12 rooms, some with ocean views, some with shared bath. Rates: $3.50 per person with shared baths (some without windows), $10 with private bath; or $22 with a/c. **Cabinas Mazuren** (tel. 775-0058) has two basic rooms. Rates: $4 per person, $4.50 with private bath. **Hotel El Uno** (tel. 775-0061), just north of the dock, is very basic and lacks windows. What do you expect for $2?

In the much more pleasing northern section is a series of budget cabinas, including **Cabinas Marlin** (tel. 775-0191), **Cabinas Adelia, Cabinas Princesa del Golfo** (tel. 255-0442), **Cabinas El Manglar,** and **Cabinas Wilson** (tel. 775-0795).

Cabinas Casa Blanca (tel. 775-0124), 400 meters south of the Depósito Libre, has pleasing cabinas with fans, screens, and private baths with cold water in a house below the owner's home. Rates: $10 s/d. Opposite, in another home, is **Hospedaje Familiar** (tel. 775-0217), with rooms with a/c, shared baths, and kitchen access. If you love ornamentals, you'll like this place. Rates: $10 per person. Also here is **Jardín Cervecero Alameda** (tel. 775-0126), 75 meters east of the Duty-Free Zone, with cabins with private baths and hot water plus fans.

Three *very* budget *pensiones*—**Familiar, Minerva,** and **Cabinas Villa Mar**—sit next to each other in a block midway between the north and south sections.

Inexpensive
The ill-named **La Purruja Lodge,** on the left about four km before Golfito, is a great bargain (*purruja* is the Costa Rican name for "no-see-ums"; see

"Insects" under "Health Problems" in the "Health Care" section of the On the Road chapter). It has two very pleasing modern cabinas, with two more planned. They're very breezy, have lots of windows, and are set amid landscaped lawns on a hill overlooking a forested valley. Swiss owner Walter Rosenberg offers hiking tours to Corcovado and is building a mini-golf course. Rates: $10 per person.

Hotel del Cerro (tel. 775-0006, fax 775-0551), opposite the old United Fruit dock (Muelle Bananaero), has 20 spotlessly clean rooms with private baths, hot water, fans, and large single beds. There's an open-air restaurant upstairs. The owner crams in more beds and bunks for the weekend shoppers. There's a TV in the upstairs lounge and funky art on display. On the premises is an old movie house, which the owner has restored—complete with old film posters and original theater seats—into a bar with a "gourmet" restaurant in the balcony. Movie previews supposedly are screened. The Chinese owner offers boat tours to a private island where you can see birdlife and caimans in the mangrove swamps. Rates: upstairs, $10-25 per person with private bath.

Hotel Costa Rica Surf (Apdo. 7, Golfito 8201, tel. 775-0034) has 29 dark rooms, plus sidewalk restaurant and bar. The hotel is the current favorite of the surfing and budget crowd and supposedly was once a high-class brothel. It's still easy to imagine, as you walk through the front door, that rooms may rent by the hour. The American Legion meets here the first Tuesday of each month. Rates: $9 s, $15 d with shared bath; $15 s, $20 d with private bath and a/c. Two unknowns to me are **Koktsur Cabins** (tel. 775-0327) and **Rancho Katuir**, on the road to the duty-free zone. Both are said to have rooms with private bathrooms and fans. The latter also serves "classic and international food."

Moderate

Centro Turístico Samoa del Sur (tel. 775-0233), on the waterfront, has cabinas next to its thatch-roofed restaurant, Le Coquillage. There's a disco here at night. The owners rent bicycles and boats. **Hotel y Restaurante El Ceibo** (tel. 775-0403), on the shoreline at the foot of the hill as you enter Golfito, has eight cabinas with cold water and fans. There's a pleasant open-air restaurant. The *playa* in front

of the hotel is okay for swimming. Rates: $18 s/d, $25 with a/c. The modern **Golfo Azul Hotel** (formerly the Hotel Costa Sur, tel. 775-0871, fax 775-0832), at the southern end of the airstrip, has 24 pleasing rooms (eight with a/c) with fans and private baths with cold water. Rates: $24 s/d, $27 t; from $46 quad, with a/c.

Upscale

Las Gaviotas (alias the Yacht Club, Apdo. 12, Golfito 8201, tel. 775-0062, fax 775-0544), on the waterfront at the entrance to town, is fairly elegant and has 21 pleasant cabinas with private porches and nice, spacious tiled bathrooms with large showers. The outdoor restaurant overlooks the gulf and serves excellent seafood plus expensive breakfasts. You'll also find a pool, a sunbathing balcony, and a souvenir shop, plus scarlet macaws in the garden. Yachts anchor at the mooring. Rates: $35 d, $45 with a/c and kitchenette.

The modern and very elegant **Hotel Sierra** (Apdo. 5304, San José 1000, tel. 233-9693, fax 233-9715; or Apdo. 37, Golfito, tel. 775-0666, fax 775-0087) is between the airport and the duty-free zone, next to the airstrip. It has 72 luxurious rooms, each with a/c, TV, private bath, and telephone, and room service. Two restaurants serve grilled and international cuisine. The hotel features a pool with wet bar, a children's pool, plus a restaurant, a bar, and a disco. Rates have dropped markedly since the first edition. A bargain! Check rates before booking, however. Rates: $39 s, $47 d, $54 t.

Fishing Lodge

Golfito Sailfish Rancho (tel. 235-7766; in the U.S., P.O. Box 290190, San Antonio, TX 78280, tel. 800-531-7232, fax 512-377-0454) is a sportfishing lodge run by a lively Texan lady named Ginny Cotner. It has 10 rooms, each with beamed ceilings and soaring roofs. The landscaped grounds contain sea-view terraces and paved trails leading back into the jungle. The lodge offers a guarantee for anglers spending more than three days at the lodge: if you don't get at least one sailfish, you come back and stay free. It's a 15-minute boat ride from Golfito aboard the lodge's 6.5-meter Makos. The lodge operates catch-and-release sportfishing trips. Rates: $1395 d for three days; $2395 d seven days, all-inclusive of alcohol, laundry, meals, etc.

Playa Cacao and
Punta Encantado Accommodations

The most unusual hotel for kilometers around is the aptly named **Shipwreck Hotel**—a beached 19-meter-long trawler—west of town at Playa Cacao. The three rooms are strewn with icons of a mariner's life. A one-legged sailor, Thomas Clairmont (alias Captain Tom), built this Popeye-like place when he washed ashore in 1954 after his boat capsized. Alas, Tom died in 1993 and the infamous bar where Tom told his tales is no longer operating. Tom's wife, Rocío, still rents rooms (she also plans to reopen the bar when her son, Tommy, is old enough to run it). But there's no electricity, telephone, hot water, or fans. You share the toilet in Captain Tom's house, nearby. John Wayne anchored here in 1966 and left his signature in the guestbook. There's no road link; you'll need a boat to get there. Rates: $5 to $10. You can **camp** in the front yard.

There are also basic cabinas at Playa Cacao, including **Rancho Not-so-Neato, El Fin del Camino,** and the far more charming and rustic-yet-upscale American-owned **Cabinas Palmas** (Apdo. 98, Golfito, tel. 775-0357, fax 775-0373), with six octagonal thatch-roofed, tile-floored cottages eccentrically designed and decorated with heaps of plants within. Three cabins have kitchenettes, but there's also a restaurant. Rates: $35 d. You can rent canoes.

A new American-run hotel, **Punta Encantado/Enchanted Point** (tel. 735-5062 or 789-9713, fax 735-5043; in the U.S., P.O. Box 481, Chautauqua, NY 14722) recently opened beside the beach at Punta Encantado, west of Playa Cacao. This comfortable yet casual log-and-bamboo lodge with matching rattan furniture is tucked into the jungled shoreline and has six rooms with private baths and ceiling fans. Somerset Maugham would have felt at home. Family-style meals and beach barbecues keep you fed. You'll find a *ranchita* bar down on the beach, which has a small coral reef offshore. It offers scuba, snorkeling, and sportfishing. The week after full moon, the phosphorescent bay is a spawning ground for *aguja* (needlefish). The only way to get here is by water-taxi. Not inspected. Rates: $95 s, $65 d per person, including all meals and transfer from Golfito (three-day package only).

FOOD AND ENTERTAINMENT

The coolest place to eat is the **El Balcón Pizzeria,** which has gourmet dishes conjured by Terry Moore, who once was galley hand on the Alaskan fishing fleets. El Balcón is above the Hotel Costa Rica Surf and is advertised by a windsurf sail hanging outside. An old jukebox plays equally outdated tunes. For ambience of a different note, try **Cinema Studios,** where you can dine in the balcony of an erstwhile movie theater adjacent to Hotel del Cerro; the bar stays open until the wee hours.

Alternatively, try the thatch-roofed, French-owned **Le Coquillage,** which offers a wide choice, from burgers ($2) and pizzas to quality paella and seafood. It's part of the pleasing Centro Turístico Samoa del Sur (tel. 775-0233), which also has a lively bar overlooking the water. Or try the restaurant at **Las Gaviotas** (relatively pricey and not great). Also for pizza, try **Pizza Restaurante Fermary** in the old railroad station. The American-run **Rio de Janeiro Restaurant** cooks burgers, barbecued ribs, and steaks. Also popular with locals is **Pequeño Restaurant** (tel. 775-0220). **Restaurante La Eurekita** is popular for its superb *refrescos* and bay vistas. **Restaurante Siete Mares, Jardín Cervecero Alameda,** and **Bar Mariscos del Sur Restaurante** serve good seafood. For Chinese, try **Restaurante Hong Kong,** which also has rooms, or the venerable **Restaurante Uno.**

You can even eat at sea aboard the *Fiesta,* a floating barge-cum-restaurant that sails from Sandbar Marina (tel. 775-0874).

A number of *sodas* are clustered together just north of the Banco Nacional, 100 meters north of the dock. Several open-air places overhang the frontage road, including **Restaurant Ballesta,** opposite the Gulfo Azul Hotel. The **Jungle Club,** south of Punta el Cabro, is popular with yachters and has reasonably priced meals; hire a boat at the municipal dock to get there.

Discos include the **Palanque, Club Latino,** and the **Centro Turístico Samoa.** The **El Balcón** is a popular watering hole, as is the **Marea Baja Discotheque** (tel. 775-0139). The latest addition is the **Gemini Disco** (tel. 775-0681) with its own seafood restaurant.

GOLFITO EMERGENCY TELEPHONE NUMBERS

All emergencies 911
Police . . . . 117 or 786-6320
Red Cross 786-6204
Hospital (Ciudad Cortés) 788-8148

SERVICES AND INFORMATION

Sportfishing

Golfito Sailfish Rancho specializes in sportfishing packages (see "Fishing Lodge," above). **Sandbar Marina** (tel./fax 775-0874) has a sportfishing fleet, rents jet boats, and offers snorkeling, scuba diving, and fishing trips on *Fiesta,* a 14-meter barge ($75 including lunch). It also offers trips to Caño and Cocos Island aboard the motorcruise *Phoenix,* which sleeps six. **Leomar Sportfishing and Diving** (Apdo. 14, Golfito, tel. 775-0230, fax 775-0373) offers sportfishing aboard a seven-meter Aquasport. The 16-meter *War Eagle* (tel. 775-0838; in the U.S., tel. 714-632-5285, fax 714-632-1027) is available for charter: you'll see it on the left when entering town.

The 35-meter *Coral Star* (tel. 800-862-1003, fax 222-1760) based in Golfito, runs fishing charters to the Hannibal region of Panamá. You fish from smaller gameboats and return to the mother ship to dine and sleep in comfortable, air-conditioned staterooms. Accommodates 25 guests. The fishing at Hannibal is said to be fantastic! Rates: from $2695 one-week, all-inclusive. The *Coral Sea* also operates diving trips to Cocos Island. For information in the U.S., contact Adventure Sportfishing, tel. 800-356-2533 or 619-739-9903, fax 619-739-9906.

Plenty of other options are listed around town.

Information

Golfito Centro (tel. 775-0449), next to the Hotel Costa Rica Surf, is run by an American expat called Ron. **Surfari Souvenirs** (tel./fax 775-0220), opposite the Hotel Costa Rica Surf, also serves as a tourist information center (open 9 a.m.-noon weekdays; Anita McIntyre, the owner, also represents Rainbow Adventures Lodge; see "Playa San Josecito and Playa Cativo," below). It also sells locally made souvenirs and even gold nuggets fished out of local rivers. The **Costa Rican Tourism Institute** (ICT) office (tel. 775-0496) is opposite Cabinas Casa Blanca, at the north end of town. Rodolfo Hernandez (tel. 775-0230) will act as local guide for virtually any need.

Other

You'll find a **laundry** service next to Cabinas Mazuren. Golfito has an **immigration office** (tel. 775-0487). A **police** (Guardia Rural) post is in front of the gas station, next to **Banco Costa Rica** (tel. 775-0323). Eager for a good paperback? Two restaurants—El Balcón, above Hotel Costa Rica Surf, and El Jardín—each have a **book exchange.**

Reports are that "Banana Joe," an amiable California who ran a water-taxi service and offered tours and marine sport rentals, has left town.

TRANSPORTATION

Getting There

By Bus: Direct buses depart San José (Tracopa, tel. 775-0365 or 221-4214) from Avenida 18, Calles 2/4 daily at 7 and 11 a.m., and 3 p.m. (eight hours, $5); an indirect bus leaves at 6:30 a.m. The Zona Sur bus to Ciudad Neily and Paso Canoas will drop you at Río Claro, where you can catch an hourly bus from Ciudad Neily to Golfito. Tracopa buses depart Golfito for San José at 5 a.m. and 1 p.m. Buses depart for Ciudad Neily hourly from Club Latino; buses to Zancudo depart the Muellecito at 1:30 p.m.; and for Puerto Jiménez from the Muelle at 11 a.m.

By Air: SANSA (tel. 775-0303 or 233-3258, fax 255-2176) offers flights to Golfito daily except Sunday at 6 a.m., and Wednesday, Thursday, and Friday at 1:45 p.m. ($47 one-way). Return flights depart Golfito at 7 a.m. and 2:45 p.m. **Travelair** (tel. 232-7883, fax 220-0413) flies from San José's Pavas Airport to Golfito daily at 11 a.m. ($76 one-way). Return flights via Puerto Jiménez depart Golfito at 12:05 a.m. Advance reservations are essential. **Note:** Reduced schedules operate mid-April through mid-December. **Aeronaves** (tel. 775-0278; in San José, tel. 232-1413), **Aero Costa Sol** (tel. 775-0607; in San José, tel. 441-1444) and other air charter companies have offices at the south end of the airstrip (Aeronaves flies to Puerto Jiménez daily; see "Puerto Jiménez" under "The Osa Peninsula," below).

By Car: The turnoff for Golfito from the Pan-American Hwy. is at Río Claro, where you'll come across a plethora of restaurants and *sodas,* plus a gas station. It's about 23 km from Golfito.

By Sea: Golfito is a popular port-of-call for yachters. **Immigration** and the **port captain** (tel. 775-0487; open Mon.-Fri. 7-11 a.m. and 12:30-4 p.m.) are beside the old Muelle Bananero dock. Most yachties berth at either the Sanbar Marina or Eagle's Roost Marina ($30 daily; longer rentals $10 per foot per month).

By Ferry: Two small ferries alternate daily service to Puerto Jiménez at 11:30 a.m. (9:30 a.m. on Sunday; 90-minute journey) and return to Golfito at 6 a.m. (tel. 775-0472). The ferries hold 30 people but no vehicles. With luck you might see bottlenosed dolphins playing in the bow waves. The ferries have a shortage of life jackets.

Getting Around

Buses run between the two ends of town. *Colectivo* taxis are abundant and will run you anywhere in town for 75 cents. They pick up and drop off passengers along the way. **Association ABOCOP** (tel. 775-0712), opposite the ICE, operates water-taxis from the Muelle Bananero. Other water-taxis operate a regular schedule to Playa Cacao (about $3), Playa Zancudo (about $8), and other beaches from the dock just south of Banco Costa Rica. Many locals also offer boat services to Zancudo and Playa Cacao; try **Rodolfo** (tel. 775-0348) or the **Burbujas de Amor** (tel. 775-0472).

PIEDRAS BLANCAS NATIONAL PARK/ "RAINFOREST OF THE AUSTRIANS"

In 1991, a tract of the Esquinas Forest north of Golfito and centered on the village of **La Gamba** was named Piedras Blancas National Park (also known as Esquinas National Park) and incorporated with Corcovado National Park. It remains a paper park only, as land within its bounds is still in private ownership, and logging permits issued before 1991 apparently remain valid. That year, Michael Schnitzler, a classical violist, founded the Regenwald der Osterreicher ("Rainforest of the Austrians") to raise funds to buy land in the Esquinas Forest. By 1993, more than 10,000 Austrians had donated money and

1200 hectares had been purchased and donated to the nation.

Local farmers in La Gamba decided to turn to ecotourism as an alternative source of income. In turn, in 1993 the Austrian government decided to underwrite the local population's efforts to save the forest, and "Rainforest of the Austrians" was appointed to oversee and direct the project. A cooperative was formed to provide income for 25 families whose members are employed at Esquinas Rainforest Lodge (see "Accommodations," below) and on fruit farms and a botanical garden. In time, the cooperative will become owner of the lodge. Plans are to create a "megapark" linking Esquinas to Corcovado National Park and Golfito National Wildlife Refuge. Trails are being opened up through the forest. A guide ($15) is strongly recommended.

The "Rainforest of the Austrians" also operates **La Gamba Biological Station** in conjunction with the University of Vienna through a grant of the Austrian government. The station, on land adjoining the Esquinas Rainforest Lodge, is open to any student or biologist wishing to study there.

Accommodations

At La Gamba Biological Station, a small, self-contained farmhouse accommodates eight people ($6 per person; Regenwald der Osterreicher, Sternwartestrasse 58, A-1180 Vienna, Austria, tel. 431-470-4297, fax 431-470-4295).

Esquinas Rainforest Lodge (tel. 775-0131, fax 775-0631; in San José, tel. 227-7924, fax 226-3957) opened in late 1994 next to a burbling stream amid landscaped grounds, a stone's throw from the entrance to Piedras Blancas National Park. It's built of natural stone and tiles to minimize use of tropical hardwoods. Five cabins sit atop a hill and are connected by a covered walkway to the main lodge. Each of 10 rooms has rattan furniture and bright tropical colors, plus private bath, fan, tiled floor, and shady veranda with easy chairs and hammocks. The main building features a tall, thatched, open-walled lounge offering views of the forest. Highlights include a bar, gift shop, library, and splendid thatched dining room (Andrea, the Brazilian chef, was trained by renowned gourmet chef Hubert Hepfel), plus naturally filtered swimming pool. Trails lead through the cacao and bananas groves and botanical gardens (which attract toucans, parrots, and other exotic birds), and beyond into the rainforest. No

more than 25 people at a time are allowed, to minimize impact on wildlife. Excursions include half-day coast, Río Coto mangroves, and Playa Cacao tours and a full-day rainforest hike. Three- to 10-day packages are offered in combination with nearby lodges. The lodge is six km from the Pan-American Hwy. turnoff at Km 37 in Villa Briceño. Alternately, you can hike in from Golfito. Rates: $65 d per person, including three meals and transfers from Golfito.

PLAYA SAN JOSECITO AND PLAYA CATIVO

Playa Cativo, about 20 km and a 45-minute boat ride north of Golfito, is a lonesome beach, popular for day-trips from town. The jungle sweeps right down to the shore. **Casa de Orquídeas** is a private botanical garden (Apdo. 69, Golfito, tel. 775-0353, leave a message) midway between Golfito and Cativo, at Playa San Josecito about 10 km northwest of Golfito. This labor of love culminates the 20-odd-year efforts of Ron and Trudy MacAllister, who lead fascinating and illuminating tours (school groups are encouraged). Masses of ornamental plants attract zillions of birds. There's a trail through the jungle. Hours: Sun.-Thurs. 8-11 a.m. ($5 entrance, with guided tour). Accommodations are limited to a lone cabin for four people, with kitchenette and solar electricity ($150 weekly); bring your own food. Zancudo Boat Tours has tours to the garden (see "Services" under "Playa Zancudo," below); otherwise take a water-taxi from Golfito or any of the local lodges.

Accommodations
Rainbow Adventures Lodge (Apdo. 63, Golfito, tel. 775-0220; in the U.S.—and recommended by the owner for faster replies—5875 N.W. Kaiser Rd., Portland, OR 97229, tel. 503-690-7750, fax 503-690-7735) is on a private nature reserve at Playa Cativo, 20 km northwest of Golfito (much of the property lies within Corcovado National Park). The sturdily handsome three-story lodge—run by a Virginian, John Lovell—is constructed of hardwoods and set in a lush, landscaped garden. It comes as a surprise for somewhere so remote. Antiques and beautiful rugs adorn the walls, and vases are full of fresh-cut flowers. Three double rooms with private baths open onto ocean-view ve-

randas. There's a penthouse suite on the third level, plus exquisite, hand-crafted cabinas (with two bedrooms and private bathrooms) in the grounds. Solar heating provides warm water. There's also an open-air dining terrace. I've received rave reviews on the meals (and the lodge)! The lodge offers frée use of snorkeling gear, boats for hire ($35 per hour with guide and fishing equipment), and guided tours to Corcovado ($4 per person), which begin virtually on the back doorstep. No road access; instead, it's a 45-minute boat journey. Be warned: There's no dock at the lodge and you may need to hike in over sandy tidal flats after jumping into thigh-deep water (you may wish to take into account any physical infirmity). You can request a video of the lodge and region. Rates: $100-150 s, $150-180 d, including all meals and transportation from Golfito (you're picked up from the boat dock near Las Gaviotas in Golfito). Children under four free. Yachts anchor free.

Rainbow Adventures Lodge's owner, Michael Medill, was building the **Buena Vista Beach & Jungle Lodge** on his private beach about 800 meters away (inquiries and reservations as above). The following is provided by Medill: "The open-air main house has the lounge and dining area. Nearby are two, two-story buildings each with four double rooms with private baths. All are constructed of hardwoods and have spectacular jungle and ocean views. The grounds are lush, with the jungle at your doorstep. Solar-heated water." The beach boasts sand, not shingle, as in front of the existing lodge. Facilities and rates same as Rainbow Adventures Lodge.

Less splendid but not without charm is **Cabinas Caña Blanca** (Apdo. 34, Golfito; David Corella, c/o fax 775-0373), with two handsome cabins on the next cove north of Cativo. Each cabin has a stove and refrigerator (don't forget to bring your own food). Rates: $70 d, or three-day packages for $449 d, including breakfasts, dinners, and transfers.

Nearby is **Dolphin Quest** (Apdo. 141, Golfito, tel. 775-1481, leave a message for Raymond; in the U.S., P.O. Box 107, Duncan Mills, CA 95430), a unique, rustic, back-to-basics getaway for folks whose idea of a good time is swimming with dolphins and hangin' with the alternative-lifestyle set. The wooden nature lodge, 13 km north of Golfito, is run "in harmony with nature" by Amy Khoo and Raymond Klchko,

who operate New Age scientific studies (telepathic communication, etc.) on dolphins, which swim thick as sardines hereabouts. They offer scuba, snorkeling, kayaking, and horseback rides. Plans included a hot spa and swimming pool. The lodge is accessible only by boat and you *must* call ahead to arrange transportation. Lodging includes five ranchos, three *casitas*, four rooms, and a dormitory for 15. Rates: $10-35. Reductions for work-share.

RÍO COTO SWAMPS

This swampy estuary south of Golfito harbors plentiful waterfowl. With luck, too, you may see crocodiles and caimans basking on the riverbanks, motionless as logs, as well as monkeys and river otters. It's also known as El Atrocha. You'll pass it by water-taxi en route to Zancudo. Mosquitoes will eye you hungrily as you pass by; at some secret signal, they'll descend en masse around dusk, but be prepared for forays at any time. You can hire guides and water-taxis in Golfito for cruise-tours of the swamps.

PLAYA ZANCUDO

Playa Zancudo is a small village that stretches along a spit backed by marshland at the estuary of the Río Coto Colorado. Zancudo has good fishing and a eight-km-long black-sand beach good for swimming, windsurfing and, when the waves are up, surfing. Many American residents have chosen to live here in homes back of the beach behind the palms. It's also popular with locals from Golfito on weekends, when it can get quite crowded. If action is your thing, stay in San José. This place is laid back! There's plenty of local color, though, at the *cantinas* and *sodas*.

Monika Hara, of Cabinas Sol y Mar, accepts donations for the local school—chip in!

Accommodations

El Coquito, 200 meters south of Estero Mar (see below), has basic rooms with private baths (cold water only). Things can get very noisy when the music is cranked up in the thatched bar. Rates: $8 per person. Similarly priced **Río Mar** (tel. 775-0350), near the northern point of Zancudo, has cabins with private baths and

fans. Another option is **Cabinas Zancudo** (tel. 773-3027), with simple yet adequate cabinas facing the beach for $20 d.

Cabinas Los Almendros/Zancudo Lodge (Apdo. 41, Golfito, tel. 775-0515 or 800-515-7697), 400 meters north of Estero Mar, has 10 screened cabinas with private baths (no hot water) and fans, plus balcony views. There's also a restaurant. Owner Roy Ventura arranges boat cruises and fishing trips and will ferry you by boat from Golfito. Rates: $15-25. **Cabinas Sol y Mar** (Apdo. 87, Golfito, tel. 775-0353, fax 775-0115), half an hour's walk south, has a pleasant casual ambience. Cabinas (some of them geodesic domes) and larger rooms are furnished in Oriental fashion, each with canvas sofas and fans, and private tiled bathrooms have hot water. There's volleyball, plus a small restaurant popular with locals. It's run by Bob and Monika Hara (he from San Francisco, she from Germany). Rates: about $25 d, for cabinas, $40 for "honeymoon" suites. The Haras also rent three self-catering cabins—**Cabinas Los Cocos**—owned by Susan and Andrew Robertson. The houses are venerable, refurbished banana company properties. Verandas have tables and chairs. Rates: $30 per night, $175 per week.

Casa Tranquilidad Bed & Breakfast (fax 775-0373) was to open with four rooms. It's run by Steve and Dee Lino (see below). Rates: $30 d. Also here, and not to be confused, is **Restaurante y Cabinas Tranquilo** offering four rustic rooms ($7 per person) with shared bath and hammocks on the veranda above the restaurant, which serves unusual but tasty German-cum-*típico* dishes ($5 upward). The eccentric German owner, Rainer Kremer, also owns **Cabinas La Vista**, two-story beachside stilt-cottages ($10 per person) about two km south of town.

Lastly, try **Hotel Pitier** (tel. 773-3027), which also has basic but clean cabins ($7); or the unique **Cabinas Río Mar**, which is an old caboose divided into six very basic guest "rooms" with bath and fan ($10 per person).

Services

Estero Mar (tel. 775-0056), opposite the dock in the center of town, is a lively bar and restaurant with the only public telephone in Zancudo. For **fishing trips**, contact Cabinas Los Almendros (see above) or **Steve and Dee Lino** (tel. 288-5083 or 775-0268, fax 775-0373), who have

a nine-meter sportfishing boat for charter ($350 a day for two people, including lunch and drinks). **Zancudo Boat Tours,** next to Cabinas Sol y Mar south of the village, rents surfboards, paddleboats, and snorkeling equipment. Owners Susan and Andrew Robertson also offer nature trips up the Río Coto (a good chance to spot caiman, monkeys, and otters), as well as to the Casa de Orquídeas botanical gardens and to prime snorkeling spots (from $15 d, per hour). You can rent **mountain bikes** from Wally Hastings ($10 a day, $50 a week).

Transportation

By Car: The paved road to Zancudo begins about eight km from the Pan-Am Hwy., midway along the road to Golfito; turn right at El Rodeo Salon. An aging two-car ferry will transport you across the Río Coto, 18 km beyond El Rodeo (the ferry operates on the high tide as late as 10 p.m.; $2). Turn right at Pueblo Nuevo for Conte, then right at Conte for Zancudo Beach. In Conte, continue straight along the newly paved road for Pavones and Punta Banco—the end of the road.

By Bus: A bus runs between Golfito and Zancudo in dry season.

By Boat: A water-taxi departs Golfito for Zancudo on Monday, Wednesday, and Friday at noon, and originating in Zancudo at 6 a.m. (about $5). **Zancudo Boat Tours** also offers service ($8). Another local boatman, **Fernando Sandé** (tel. 783-4090) reportedly goes to Zancudo Monday, Wednesday, Friday, and Saturday, midafternoon. You can also hire a private boat at the dock (about $15).

PAVONES

The bumpy potholed road parallels the beach south from Zancudo to Pavones, a legend in the surfing world for possessing the longest wave in the world . . . more than a kilometer on a good day! The waves are at their best, apparently, during rainy season, when dozens of surfers flock for the legendary very-fast-and-very-hollow tubular left. Best surfing months—April through October—are also the rainiest.

Pavones is no more than a string of houses and cabinas (multiplying in numbers year by year), a restaurant, and a *pulpería* next to the soccer field. There are no phones. Surfboards are available for rent. The place recently went through a period of drug trafficking and land disputes. The problem began in 1991 when a U.S. citizen bought a lengthy stretch of coastal property and began selling it in parcels to other gringos. When the developer ended up in jail for drug dealing, squatters—*paracaidistas*—rushed in to claim the land, contending that the developer's criminal status nullified his original title. A violent showdown between those who had bought parcels and the local squatters ended in the death of a North American in 1992, and one local resident recently told me that the tensions still simmer. Tourists passing through should have no problem.

Accommodations

Two cheap options include **Esquina del Mar,** a *soda* with basic rooms above the bar ($8 d); and **Pavón Tico,** another *cantina* with four basic rooms. If they're full try Doña María Jiménez, who has a couple of cabinas; or **Pensión Maurem** for about $4 per person.

Cabinas la Ponderosa (tel. 775-0131, fax 775-0631; in the U.S., tel. 407-783-7184) offers two-story cabins with private baths. There's a basic dining room and lounge with bar and TV. Rates: $35, including three meals.

Nearby is **Cabinas Mira Olas** (Apdo. 32, Golfito; radiotel. 775-0120; VHF channel 74): two cabinas with private baths and warm water (one with kitchenette) for $10-15 s, $15-20 d.

Bahía Pavones Surf Lodge, two km south of Pavones, squats atop a huge rock with a wooden deck overhanging the beach. Rooms in the main building are basic and small; separate cabinas are larger and have their own porches and private baths. Meals are provided. Make reservations at the Tsunami Surf Shop (tel. 222-2224, fax 222-2271) in San José. Rates: about $18 s, $28 d including breakfast.

Transportation

By Bus: A bus departs Golfito from the La Bomba Bar at the municipal dock at 5 a.m. There may also be a morning service. Buses for Golfito leave Pavones at 2 p.m.

By Boat: Water-taxis from Golfito cost about $65 one-way. Walter Jiménez in Pavones reportedly has a water-taxi service (about $35 to Zancudo).

By Taxi: A 4WD taxi will cost you about $50.

PUNTA BANCO

The dirt road leads south from Pavones through jungle-covered hillsides to the tiny beach community of Punta Banco, which has been roused from torpor by the recent arrival of tourists. Punta Banco has one of many beautiful beaches that line the coast from Golfito south to Panamá.

It boasts the requisite *pulpería* and *cantina*, plus a church, school and soccer field. Electricity was due to be installed in early 1995. The beach is good for swimming and snorkeling, though surfing is far better at Pavones. A waterfall and swimming hole next to Rancho El Borica provides cooling dips if you tire of the sea.

Accommodations and Food

A number of locals rent rooms. Patrizio Baltadano rents rooms ($7) at the entrance to the village. The Vargas family offers three basic cabinas with outside bathroom at **Rancho El Borica** ($9 per person). Meals are served in a thatched *cantina* popular with locals (breakfast costs a whopping $1, twice that for lunch or dinner). **Casa Punta Banco** (tel. 775-0006, fax 775-0087; in the U.S., Continental Associates, 202 W. Fifth Ave., Royal Oak, MI 48067, tel. 313-545-8900, fax 313-545-0536) is a six-bedroom house with fully equipped kitchen, hot water, washer/dryer, and its own generator and caretaker. Rates: $700 d, $50 each additional person, per week.

Nature Lodge

Farm. Nature lodge. Seaside retreat. Combination exotic-fruit station and biological reserve. **Tiskita Lodge** (Costa Rica Sun Tours, Apdo. 1195, Escazú 1250, tel. 255-3418, fax 255-4410) is all these and more. Situated atop Punta Banco, the last major point of land before Panamá, the lodge garners gentle sea breezes and proffers sweeping panoramas of the Pacific and Osa Peninsula. A farmhouse serves as main lodge and dining room. Nine rustic but comfortable cabins can accommodate up to 18 people in a combination of double, twin, and bunk beds (and even a resident iguana in one). Each cabin is screened and has a private bathroom and shower. Bedding and towels are provided. A water-powered Pelton wheel and solar panels provide electricity.

The lodge is surrounded by 40 hectares of virgin rainforest, with pools for swimming and extensive trails for nature lovers; one leads to the beach. Sixteen stops along the rainforest trail describe the vegetation and ecology of the region. A booklet helps birders identify scarlet-rumped and blue-gray tanagers, toucans, laughing hawks, blue parrots, macaws, and othres; a similar one describes Tiskita tidepools for beachcombers.

Owner Peter Aspinall's pride and joy is his tropical-fruit farm, which contains the most extensive collection of tropical fruits in Costa Rica.

All meals—"Costa Rican country-style"—are included and served family style (I've heard complaints on food quality). Packed lunches are provided for hikers. The lodge sells straw hats and other crafts made by local Guaymi Indians. (*Tiskita* is the Guaymi name for "fish eagle.") You can arrange trips to the adjacent Guaymi Indian reserve can be arranged. Rates per person: $93 s, $67 d, $58 t including all meals.

Services

You can hire a boat at Rancho El Borica for fishing trips or to reach Matapalo, on the Osa Peninsula ($70 for four people). Patrizio Baltanado rents horses for $20 a day.

Getting There

The Golfito-Pavones **bus** serves Punta Banco (see "Pavones," above). Buses depart for Golfito at 5 p.m. If driving, it's about a two and a half hour drive from Golfito; 4WD recommended. Wet season is tough going! Beyond Punta Banco, the rugged dirt road continues along the surf-swept shore for 30 km to Las Peñas. Even more arduous going.

A private **airstrip** allows direct access to Tiskita Lodge from San José by chartered plane (55 minutes).

THE OSA PENINSULA

This massive horsehead-shaped peninsula lies west of Golfito, across the Golfo Dulce. Its bulk and heretofore inaccessibility protect major tropical rainforests, preserved as Corcovado National Park. A single road provides access to Puerto Jiménez (the only town of significance) and the peninsula, dead-ending at Corcovado National Park. The turnoff from the Pan-American Hwy. is at Chacarita, about 26 km northwest of Río Claro (the turnoff for Golfito); the **Bar y Restaurant Chacarita** and a Texaco gas station are at the junction. The road to Puerto Jiménez is in excellent condition as far as Rincón, where you get your first sense of the cathedral-like immensity of the rainforests of the Osa Peninsula. The magnificent coastal vistas are spoiled only by the patches torn up by loggers, exposing soils as red as bright lipstick. The paved road ends at the coast at Rincón. It's dirt thereafter.

As everywhere in Costa Rica, the region, which as late as 1990 was almost entirely off the tourist map, is experiencing a bit of a tourism boom.

LA PALMA

La Palma is a little hamlet five km south of Rincón. Turn left for Puerto Jiménez; beyond La Palma the dirt road smoothes out and you can happily cruise along at the speed limit. To the right, the gravel and mud road leads 12 km up the valley of the Río Rincón to the Los Patos Ranger Station, easternmost entry point to Corcovado National Park.

Accommodations and Food
Cabinas El Tucáno (tel. 775-0522 or 775-0033) has six small cabins for $5 double, with private baths (cold water) and fans. There's a tiny restaurant. Next door is **Soda Centro Social.** Two km south of La Palma a dirt road leads to **Playa Blanca,** with a small *soda* and, reportedly, cabinas next to an unimpressive beach.

On the road to Los Patos is **Cabinas Corco-** **vado** (tel. 774-0433, message only), which has basic rooms, private baths and cold water, plus a platform where you may sling a hammock. There's also a restaurant. Rates: $8 per person. About 10 km further, beyond the Los Patos trailhead, is the rustic **Cerro de Oro Lodge** run by a gold-mining "communistic" cooperative of ex-gold miners: Coope Unioro (tel. 225-8966, fax 735-5073). Rooms have shared baths with cold water. Coope Unioro is experimenting with sustainable use of jungle products, and the cooks conjure tasty meals from local produce, including wild plants, nuts, and herbs. The lodge offers guided hikes and horseback trips to Corcovado. Rates: $24, including meals.

Services
A self-proclaimed **tourist information center** and guide service operates 50 meters beyond El Tucáno. **Buses** operate four times daily between La Palma and Puerto Jiménez. The earliest departs Puerto Jiménez at 5:30 a.m.

DOS BRAZOS DE RÍO TIGRE

About three km before Puerto Jiménez, a turnoff to the right follows the Río Tigre 14 km west to Dos Brazos, a small community of gold miners at the easternmost entrance to Corcovado National Park. When the gold petered out, the miners found themselves without a livelihood and turned to ecotourism rather than abandon their riverside homes. In 1990 they formed the **Asociación de Productores Villa Nueva** to organize tours and provide lodging. You can see them still panning for *oro* in the soupy rivers, and maybe even try your hand yourself. But be careful . . . gold fever is contagious! The association members will even take you 270 meters deep into their mining tunnels ($20).

The hamlet is one km from the border of Corcovado National Park. Guided trips to the park ($20) are offered daily at 7 a.m., returning around 3 p.m. Buses service Dos Brazos from Puerto Jiménez.

Accommodations and Food

The **El Tigre Lodge** (c/o Aeroviajes, Apdo. 12742, San José 1000, tel. 233-6108, fax 233-6293) is an "ecotourist shelter" with six rooms of varying sizes (the largest sleeps six people) with private baths plus a large open restaurant that serves Costa Rican dishes and looks out over the river. Hand-crafted highlights include the fretwork on the wooden balustrade and murals painted on the bedroom walls. The lodge is run by the Asociación de Productores. Horseback rides lead to the park, where guided hikes are offered. Rates: $12 s, $18 d. Aeroviajes offers weeklong tour packages from $775).

PUERTO JIMÉNEZ

This small town, 50 km south of the Pan-American Hwy., is the gateway to Corcovado National Park. I like this laid-back place. It's popular with the younger backpacking crowd and until recently untainted by tourists, though this is changing fast in the swell of the recent tide. It has a considerable population of down-to-earth gringos, who have introduced some very intriguing tours (sea kayaking in search of alligators, and the like) and lead the way in attempts to manage tourism development conscientiously. An Ecotourism Chamber oversees the attempt. During the gold-boom days in the 1980s it briefly flourished. Locals have colorful tales to tell of gambling and general debauchery. To the south lies a string of beautiful white-sand beaches, including good surfing at American, Backwater, Pan Dulce, and Carbonera beaches.

Accommodations

Hotel Las Manglares (Apdo. 255-8203, Puerto Jiménez, tel. 735-5002, fax 735-5121), near the airstrip, is the best place in town. It has 10 rooms surrounded by mangroves, where crabs scurry about. Reportedly there's an alligator on the grounds. The rooms have private baths with showers and hot water. The restaurant is popular with locals. The owner is very friendly and has a travel agency—**Corcovado Tours**—which represents Aeronaves. Rates: $25 s, $30 d.

Cabinas Marcelina (tel. 735-5007, fax 735-5045), 200 meters south of the soccer field, has

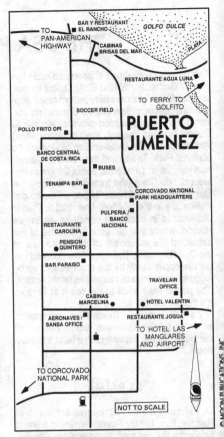

basic rooms with private baths and fans. It can arrange fishing trips, horseback rides, and even gold-panning expeditions. Rates: $8 s, $12 d. North of the soccer field is **Cabinas Brisas del Mar** (tel. 735-5028, fax 735-5012), between the town and dock. It has nine basic rooms with fans and private baths with cold water, plus views out over the gulf. Rates: $12 d. **Vivero y Jardín Joyosa,** near the Texaco station, has basic bunks and shared baths with cold water but no fans. **Pensión Quintero** (735-5087) is a bargain at $4 per person, though it, too, has shared baths but no fans. If all else fails, or you're flat broke, $3 will buy a box with a bed at the **Hotel Valentín. Iguana Iguana Cabins** (tel.

CHIP MILL FOR OSA

The Osa Peninsula is about to get Central America's largest chip mill courtesy of Ston Forestal, a Costa Rican subsidiary of the paper giant, Stone Container Corporation of Chicago. The mill, it is proposed, will export more than one million tons of chipped wood each year to the U.S. and Asia for paper pulp.

Instead of clearing primary forest, the company plans to grow and harvest a nonnative tree species called *gmelina*. The ecology of the Osa Peninsula, nonetheless, will be threatened.

The chip mill will operate 24 hours a day, causing excessive pollution and dramatically increasing truck traffic. Seeds dispersed from Stone's 30 million trees may well displace native species, changing the local ecosystem. The fruit of the *gmelina*, opponents argue, will attract birds and mammals from nearby habitats, creating abnormal migration patterns with unknown consequences to the ecosystem. And the marinelife of the Golfo Dulce may be seriously threatened.

The gulf is an anoxic (lacking oxygen) body because of its limited water circulation. The weak dispersion makes the gulf especially susceptible to a buildup of chemical pollution and sediment runoff from the chip-mill project. Coastal estuaries, mangroves, and coral reefs could well be destroyed, and the offshore waters that are breeding grounds for whales, dolphins, and many species of fish may be irretrievably altered.

A coalition of environmental, indigenous, and community organizations called the Puerto Jiménez Comite de Pro-Defensa de Recursos Natural is working to have the Golfo Dulce region named a national aquatic park. In 1994, the group's efforts forced Ston Forestal to agree to relocate the mill farther away from Golfito. Alas, the environmentalist movement suffered a severe blow in December 1994 when its three leading advocates died in a fire. To support their effort, write to Sr. Orlando Morales, Ministry of Natural Resources and Energy (MIRENEM), Apdo. 10104, San José 1000.

735-5158) opened in 1994; seven basic but comfortable rooms have private baths with cold water and fans ($6 s, $9 d, low season). Three more share a bath ($4 per person). A restaurant, swimming pool, and six cabinas were in the works . **El Castillo Cabins,** 100 meters east of the entrance to town, has rooms for one to four people, with private baths.

Carlos Dominick, a well-known local environmentalist, offers beds at **Dormitorio Cockadoodledoo** ($1; fax 735-5073) for one-hour's labor in his reforestation nursery, Vivero y Jardines Joyosa.

Five km south of Jiménez, at five-km-long Playa Platanares, are the **Playa Presi-Osa Cabinas,** due to open with great fanfare (read, liberal imbibing of *guaro* and beer) at press time. The cylindrical, six-meter-wide cabinas with conical thatched roof a la African *rondavels* sleep three people apiece and have ceiling fans and private bathrooms with gravity-fed showers. By the time you read this, a horse-drawn cart should be functioning as transport from Jiménez. Rates: $50 per cabina, including breakfast. Inquire at Souvenir Corcovado (tel. 735-5005).

Food and Entertainment

The place to hang out is **Bar y Restaurant El Rancho** (tel. 735-5120, fax 735-5073), run by an affable Canadian-Scot named Andrew (alias André) Gray. The open-air bar, with its bamboo roof, catches the breezes and is replete with orchids and plants. The place was infamous in the days of the gold-mining boom, when gold miners would buy bottles of whisky just to throw at the walls! Said Andrew: "I want you to write that you can be as wild and crazy as the gold miners!" The place rocks at night. It serves good music and *bocas.* Happy hour is 5-6 p.m. More sedate folks can relax in hammocks. The restaurant opens at 5 pm.

Giving El Rancho a run for its money is Keith Elliott's **Banana Bar** on Playa Platanares. You can't miss Keith—he's the crazy dude with a prosthetic leg who zips around town on a three-wheel motorbike. Listen for the rock 'n' blues music and you can't miss the Banana.

Agua Luna has good seafood dishes; try the *pescado al ajillo* (fish with garlic) for about $3. It's next to the dock opposite El Rancho, and has little thatched-roof *ranchitas.* **Pollo Frito Opi** is a

tiny open-air diner next to the soccer field. Other options include the popular **Restaurante Carolina, Restaurante Jogua,** and **Restaurante La China.**

Several bars are popular with locals: **Tenampa Bar, Bar Manglares, Bar Paraíso,** and **Restaurante Carolina** (tel./fax 735-5073), which doubles as a tourist-information service.

Tours
Escondido Trex (tel./fax 735-5073) offers half-day sea-kayaking trips ($30) through the mangrove "swamps" of the Río Platanares. You stand a superb chance of seeing caiman (alligators), white-faced monkeys, freshwater turtles, rays, and heaps of birdlife. It also offers mountain biking and nature treks. The office is in Restaurante Carolina, on the main street. Local guide **Taboga Loaciga** (tel. 735-5092, or marine radio channel 12) also offers fishing and boat trips, plus water-taxi service to virtually any point you wish.

Corcovado Tours, at the Las Manglares Hotel (Apdo. 255-8203, Puerto Jiménez, tel. 735-5002, fax 735-5121), offers sportfishing, gold mining, hiking, and natural history trips into Corcovado, as well as visits to the Guaymis Indian reserve.

Finca Franceschis (tel. 735-5007, fax 735-5045; or at the Souvenir Corcovado shop, tel./fax 735-5005) is a family-owned farm and private wildlife refuge opened up to horseback tours in January 1995. You'll roughly follow the course of the winding Río Platanares past mangroves and through primary rainforest to Playa Platanares, where you can canter along the deserted beach or relax at a shady rancho with hammocks. Tours include lunch and the services of an English-speaking guide, possibly Doña Lidiette, the distinguished-looking *patrona* of the family farm.

Services
The *pulpería* will change traveler's checks and money. A **Banco Central de Costa Rica** and a **Banco Nacional** (tel. 735-5020) will happily buy any gold you may find in the Osa. The **Corcovado National Park Office** (tel. 735-5036) is opposite Banco Nacional. Hours: Mon.-Fri. 7:30 a.m.-noon and 1-5 p.m. You must register here if you plan on visiting Corcovado. **Fundación**

Neotrópica (tel. 735-5116) has an office here. Oscar Blanco offers **taxi** service. Cecilia Solano at **Restaurante Carolina** (tel. 735-5138, fax 735-5073), and **Souvenir Corcovado** (tel./fax 735-5005) serve as local **information** services and booking agents for hotels, plane tickets, and local transportation. There's also **Travelair** agency (tel. 735-5062) on the main street.

Transportation
By Bus: Buses depart San José for Puerto Jiménez from Calle 12, Avenidas 7/9 (Transportes Blanco, tel. 771-2550) daily at 6 a.m. and noon (eight hours; $8); and from San Isidro de El General at 5:30 a.m. and noon (five hours). The Zona Sur bus from San José to Ciudad Neily intercepts a bus from Neily to Puerto Jiménez at Chacarita/Piedras Blancas (departs Neily at 7 a.m. and 3 p.m.). Buses to San Isidro and San José depart from the Restaurante Carolina at 5 and 11 a.m.; and to Ciudad Neily at 5:30 a.m. and 2 p.m. Buses depart Golfito for Puerto Jiménez from the municipal dock daily at 11 a.m. Buy your tickets in advance.

By Air: SANSA (tel. 223-4179, fax 255-2176) offers service from San José via Coto 47 on Tuesday, Thursday, and Saturday at 8 a.m., and on Monday, Wednesday, and Friday at 8:45 a.m. **Travelair** (tel. 220-3054, fax 220-0413) offers daily service via Golfito, departing San José at 11 a.m. (return flights depart Puerto Jiménez at 12:05 p.m.). **Aeronaves de Costa Rica** (tel. 575-0278 or 232-1413; in Golfito, tel. 775-0278) offers daily flights between Golfito and Puerto Jiménez at 6 a.m. and 2 p.m. ($12; note the 10 kg limit). You can charter flights from Golfito (about $40). **Note:** Reduced schedules operate mid-April through mid-December.

By Ferry: The famous *Arco Iris* ferry between Golfito and Puerto Jiménez was retired in 1991 after 30 years' service and has been replaced by two small ferries, which alternate daily service ($4) at 11:30 a.m., and 9:30 a.m. on Sunday; and return to Golfito at 6 a.m. (tel. 775-0472; $2.50; 90-minute journey). The ferries hold 30 people, but no vehicles. You might see bottlenosed dolphins playing in the waves. Private **water-taxis** (tel. 775-0712 or 775-0357) charge about $50 and are available in Golfito from Muelle Bananero.

Taxis: Taxis from Golfito charge about $80.

PUERTO JIMÉNEZ TO CARATE

The road south to Carate and Corcovado National Park takes about two hours under good conditions. Just as the Río Reventazón is no place for birchbark canoes, the road between Puerto Jiménez and Carate is no place for a Ford Escort or Honda Civic. It gets gradually narrower and bumpier and muddier. There are about a dozen streams to ford. I was told you need to cross the Río Tamales at low tide; however, both times I've driven through the river there was no sign that it was tidal. You pass through cattle *fincas* much of the way. The U.S. Corps of Engineers began building bridges and improving the road in 1993.

Surfing

Cabo Matapalo, at the southeast tip of the Osa Peninsula, is becoming popular with the longboard surf set. A string of beaches offers a variety of wave types, all left breaks. According to local surf expert Mark Kelly, deep water close to shore and a southerly swell can generate powerful six-foot waves, usually in late July through August.

Accommodations

Emerald Bay Inn (tel. 775-0131, or c/o Arco Iris, tel. 289-6227) is the splendid home-cum-hostelry of ex-musician Brett Harter of the rock group Route 66. Twenty km south of Puerto Jiménez, near Matapalo, it commands 37 hectares of rainforest overlooking the southernmost part of the Golfo Dulce. The inn has three bedrooms, each with private bathroom and furnished in bamboo. Swim in the pool fed by a local creek (at night you can follow the lanterns for a moonlit dip). You can hike, or rent horses, for nature trips along forest trails, and a splendid beach awaits a five-minute walk away. Harter was adding cabinas. Rates: $75-100 d, per person, including transport, meals, beers, and horse rental.

New Age

Tierra de Milagros (Lista de Correos, Puerto Jiménez, Peninsula de Osa, tel. 233-0233, fax 735-5073; or in the U.S., P.O. Box 35203, Siesta Key, FL 34242, tel. 813-349-2168) or "The Land of Miracles" is a "counterculture" earth-worship kinda place (yoga, moon rituals, and lots of drumming are the order of the day) about 20 km south of Puerto Jiménez. Very holistic . . . and a fantastic place for an alternative travel experience. Basically, you're sharing the vegetarian, peace-and-harmony lifestyle of founders Nicky and Edie. The very basic accommodations have hammocks slung beneath eight open-air, thatched *ranchitas* spread throughout the five-hectare property. Even the bathrooms have minimal privacy. No electricity, and running water means a boy with a bucket! Meals are mostly vegetarian, with plenty of fish; shared kitchen (you're expected to help). Trails lead to local waterfalls as well as to the beach, and there are horses for use. "Volunteers" participate in the reforestation work. Edie and Nicky encourage groups interested in art, yoga, Tai Chi, holistic medicine, and the like. A water-taxi reportedly runs here from Playa Sombrero, about 15 km south of Puerto Jiménez. There are no signs, so you'll need to ask locals on the road (look for a wooden gate with bull's horns). Rates: about $30 per night, including all meals.

Also near Matapalo is **Encanta La Vida** (tel. 735-5062, fax 735-5043), a beautiful lodge where you can look out over both the ocean and jungle. It requires a two-day minimum stay.

Upscale

Lapa Ríos (Apdo. 100, Puerto Jiménez, tel. 735-5130, fax 735-5179; in the U.S., P.O. Box 025216, SJO 706, Miami, FL 33102-5216) is the most sensational hotel south of Manuel Antonio! This exquisite "Mexican-style" hotel, set in a 400-hectare private reserve, enjoys a fabulous location atop a hill overlooking the ocean. It offers a small swimming pool, a sundeck, and a poolside bar that catches the breezes. Fourteen romantic bungalows are luxuriously appointed, each with two queen-size beds, a patio garden complete with outdoor shower, and a private terrace overlooking the forest. The coup de grace is a spectacular thatched *palenque* lodge with a soaring roof and a twisting spiral staircase to an all-around walkway *mirador* (lookout platform), with a restaurant below. What views! You'll dine to the accompaniment of a Renaissance motet playing over the very real cries of monkeys, *lapas* (macaws), and cicadas.

Walks in the rainforest are complemented by a tree-planting program in the 100 hectare Volunteer Rainforest. John and Karen Lewis, who own Lapa Ríos, are active environmentalists (no live trees were cut, for example, to make the lodge; the couple even built a school for local children). Kayaking and horseback riding are offered, as is massage, and trails lead into the jungle and to nearby waterfalls. The resort attracts the rich and famous. Transfers are offered. Rates: $127-179 s, $96-126 per person d, plus $45 "food package."

Bosque del Cabo (tel. 222-4547, fax 735-5073), at the tip of the Osa Peninsula, is another winner. Walkways lined by poinsettias lead through expansive landscaped grounds (140 hectares, 50% of which is forested) to four pretty, thatched, clifftop cabinas with superb ocean views over Playa Matapalo. Screened open-air showers have their own little gardens. Verandas with hammocks. Lanterns light the place at night. Very romantic! Owner Phil Spear planned to build a "cooling-off" pool and sundeck. Meals are eaten family-style under a *palenque,* which has a small raised bar. There are lots of shade trees, including one where a pair of scarlet macaws nest. Your reveille call is a symphony of songbirds and the barking of howler monkeys.

You can enjoy hikes and horseback rides ($20 all day, including lunch) to waterfalls, a Jacuzzi-like tidepool, and prime wildlife-viewing areas. The walk to the beach is 150 meters up and down. Phil provides 4WD taxi pick-up from Puerto Jiménez. Two more cabinas are planned. Rates: $75 s, $55 per person double, $50 t, $45 quad, including all meals.

CARATE

Carate, at the end of the road, is no more than an airstrip and a single *pulpería* festooned with shark jaws. Grab an ice-cold Coke or *refresco.* Linger long enough and an *orero* might appear bearing gold and tall tales. If you intend on staying at Corcovado Tent Camp (see below), Mayor Morales, who owns the *pulpería,* will radio the camp to send a guide with a horse; it's a 30-minute ride along a magnificent, kilometers-long black-sand beach. You have to leave your vehicle at the *pulpería* (it should be safe; the owner

sleeps here). Alternately, you can camp on the beach in front of Mayor's place, which has bathrooms, showers and water faucet.

The La Leona Ranger Station, at the entrance to Corcovado National Park, is about two km along the beach.

Accommodations
Corcovado Tent Camp is a "safari-style" tent camp flush against the border of the national park, 1.5 km west of Carate. It's operated by Costa Rica Expeditions (Apdo. 6941, San José 1000, tel. 257-0766, fax 257-1665). Eighteen roomy tents sit on a low rise fronted by palms immediately behind the beach. Guests sleep on sturdy bamboo cots raised well off the floor and share two shared bathhouses (cold water only). Electricity is supplied by a small generator and is limited to certain hours in the dining area and bathhouse. Large bullfrogs gather to catch insects beneath garden lamps. Bring flashlights. Family-style meals are eaten in a screened *palenque* restaurant. An atmospheric bar has a large veranda on tall stilts. Quite rustic, but it's a fabulous experience being lulled to sleep by the sound of surf and good-night wishes from the Pacific screech owl. *The perfect base for exploring Corcovado.* A 10-meter inflatable pontoon vessel, *Guacamaya,* designed to navigate through the crashing Pacific surf, is available for reaching Corcovado National Park. Recommended. Rates: three-day/two-night package $295-395 for two or four people, including roundtrip air from San José; extra nights, $31-34 s, $38-43 d, including breakfast and dinner.

Getting There
A **taxi** runs to Carate from Puerto Jiménez daily at 7 a.m., but Monday, Wednesday, Thursday, and Saturday in "green season" ($5). You can hire 4WD taxis (about $40).

CORCOVADO NATIONAL PARK

Corcovado—the Amazon of Costa Rica—is the final stronghold of primary forest on a Pacific coastline that has been all but destroyed from Mexico to South America. Its 41,788 hectares (excluding Piedras Blancas) encompass eight habitats, from mangrove swamp and jolillo palm

Corcovado

groves to montane forest. The park protects more than 400 species of birds (20 are endemic), 116 of amphibians and reptiles, and 139 of mammals—representing 10% of the mammals in the Americas . . . on only 0.000101777% of the landmass! Its healthy population of scarlet macaws (about 1,200 birds) is the largest concentration in Central America. Depending on the trails you choose, you can expect to see large flocks of macaws in flight or feeding on almond trees by the shoreline.

Corcovado is one of only two places in the country that harbor squirrel monkeys (the other is Manuel Antonio). It's one of the last stands for the harpy eagle. Four species of sea turtles—green, Pacific ridley, hawksbill, and leatherback—nest on the park's beaches. And the park supports a healthy population of big cats and crocodiles, which like to hang around the periphery of the Corcovado Lagoon. If you want to see either, tether yourself to a stake at night. Just kidding! Jaguar paw prints are commonly seen in the mud trails, and the cats are often sighted.

A shower of vegetation and dead wood usually calls attention to a tamandua, or banded anteater, feeding in the canopy. Corcovado is a good place to spot the red-eyed tree frog (listen for his single-note mating "cluck"), the glass frog with its transparent skin, and enamel-bright poison-arrow frogs. And you can watch fishing bats doing just that at night over such rivers as

the Río Claro. You can even try your own hand for snook inside the mouths of the coastal rivers on incoming tides, where snook in the 22-kilo class have been taken. They strike plugs all year and during the fall become very aggressive.

The Osa Peninsula bears the brunt of torrential rains from April to December. It receives up to 400 cm per year! The driest months, Jan.-April, are the best times to visit.

There are trails for lengthy hikes and some fabulous beaches. Beware of riptides. Swim only where rangers advise it may be safe. **Note:** Sharks reportedly cruise the inshore waters, and crocodiles inhabit the Río Claro and Río Sirena.

Peccaries

Corovado has a large population of peccaries. These wild pigs are very aggressive, and attacks by groups of a dozen or more peccaries are common. If attacked, climb a tree and stay there until they tire and disappear. Don't try to frighten them away—that's a sure way to get gored. One guide told me of being surrounded by them in a clearing for 20 minutes. The dominant male bluff-charged him a few times. He stood stock-still. Eventually they got bored.

Gold Mining

Pre-Columbian Indians sifted gold from the streams of the Osa millennia ago. But it wasn't until the 1980s that gold fever struck. After gold

panners—*oreros*—found some major nuggets, prospectors poured into the region. The Banco Central established an office in Puerto Jiménez just to buy gold. At the boom's heyday in the early '80s, at least 3,000 miners were entrenched in the park. Because of the devastation they wrought—dynamiting riverbeds, polluting rivers, and felling trees—the Park Service and Civil Guard ousted the miners in 1986. The *oreros* were promised indemnity for their lost income, but it went unpaid for over a year. In a dramatic protest, they camped out in the parks of San José until the government upped the money. Gold mining is slowly creeping back into Corcovado, and it is not unusual to bump into a lucky (or luckless) *orero* celebrating (or commiserating) his luck over a beer in a bar.

For now, the government has decided to let things be.

Information and Entry

The park **administration office** (tel. 735-5036, fax 735-5011) is in Puerto Jiménez, next to the Banco Nacional. Hours: Mon.-Fri. 7:30 a.m.-noon and 1-5 p.m. Most tour operators in San José can arrange tours. Costa Rica Expeditions is recommended.

The park has three entry points: **La Leona,** on the southeast corner near Carate; **Los Patos,** on the northern perimeter; and **San Pedrillo,** at the northwest corner, 18 km south of Drake Bay. You can hike or fly into **Sirena,** a large research station set back from the beach at the end of a long, grassy airstrip in the heart of the

park. The park headquarters is here. There's also a remote ranger station at **Los Planes,** on the northern border midway between San Pedrillo and Los Patos. All are linked by trail. Entrance: $15 walk-in, $7 advance purchase.

Hiking Trails

Several short trails (two to six hours) make for rewarding half- or full-day hikes from, say, Corcovado Tent Camp (guided hikes are offered; contact Costa Rica Expeditions, see above). Each trail has its own points of interest.

Corcovado's longer hiking trails grant excellent opportunities for an in-depth backpacking experience in the rainforest. You'll come across occasional shelters in addition to the ranger stations. Allow about three days to hike from one end of the park to the other. Expect to get hot and sweaty. Horseflies and mosquitoes can be a pain in the butt and webs of poisonous spiders span the trails. Trails are badly eroded, poorly maintained, and in places poorly marked. I strongly recommend buying the Instituto Geográfico 1:50,000 scale maps (see the section on "Maps" under "Other Practicalities" in the On the Road chapter).

From La Leona: It's 15 km to Sirena following the beach for most of the way. Beyond Salsipuedes Point, the trail cuts inland through the rainforest—good for spotting monkeys and coatimundis. Don't try this at high or waning tide: you must cross some rocky points that are cut off by high tide. Don't trust exclusively to the ranger's statements: buy a tide table before you arrive! Allow up to eight hours.

From Sirena: A trail leads northeast to Los Patos (see below for details) via Corcovado Lagoon. Another trail leads to the San Pedrillo Ranger Station (23 km), where there are showers, beds, and water, and seats placed strategically under shady palms for sunset viewing. There are three rivers to wade. Time your hike for low tide. Sharks—mostly hammerheads—like to come up the rivermouths in the hours immediately before and after high tide. The trick is to reach the Río Sirena and slightly shallower Ríos Llorona before the water is thigh-deep. Watch for the crocodile upstream! Don't let me put you off . . . dozens of hikers follow the trail each week.

Halfway, the trail winds steeply into the rainforest and is often slippery—good shoe tread

is essential. The last three kilometers are along the beach. The full-day hike takes you past La Llorona, a 30-meter high waterfall that cascades spectacularly onto the beach. From San Pedrillo, you can continue another 10 km to Drake Bay and Marenco Biological Station.

From Los Patos: From Los Patos the trail south climbs steeply for six km before flattening out for the final 14 km to the Sirena Research Station. The trail is well marked but narrow, overgrown in parts, and has several river crossings where it is easy to lose the trail on the other side. You must wade. Be especially careful in rainy season, when you may find yourself hip-deep. There are three small shelters en route. A side trail will take you to Corcovado Lagoon. Allow up to eight hours. Another trail reportedly leads from Los Patos to Los Planes.

Accommodations

Basic rooms are available at Sirena (about $1.50): reservations essential. Other ranger stations may be able to squeeze you into one of their basic rooms and provide meals (about $10 per day) with notice. Contact the National Park headquarters in San José or the Corcovado park headquarters in Puerto Jiménez (see above) as far ahead as possible. **Camping** is allowed at ranger stations (50 cents). Rangers can radio ahead to the various stations within the park and book you in for dinner and a tent spot. No-see-ums (pesky microscopic flies you'll not forget in a hurry) infest the beaches. Take a watertight tent, a mosquito net, and plenty of insect repellent.

Transportation

By Bus: A bus departs Puerto Jiménez for La Palma daily at 5:30 a.m. You must hike or hitch the 12-km dirt-and-mud road to the park entrance at Los Patos. You'll cross the Río Rincón 19 times! The last bus from La Palma to Puerto Jiménez is at 2 p.m. There is no bus to Carate. Take a taxi (see below). Budget travelers might try hitching; otherwise it's a full-day walk.

By Air: You can charter an air-taxi to fly you to Sirena or Carate. **SAETA** flies from San José (tel. 232-1474; $400 per planeload). **Aeronaves de Costa Rica** (tel. 575-0278) offers charter flights from Golfito ($110 per planeload). I've heard it has a reputation for stranding passen-

gers. Air charters may not operate in "wet" season, May to December.

By Taxi: A truck-taxi departs Puerto Jiménez for Carate early every Monday, Thursday, and Saturday morning ($5); ask for Cirilo Espinosa at the *pulpería* next to Restaurante Carolina. You can also rent a jeep-taxi (about $50 per carload). The park administration office can assist.

By Boat: Boats from Marenco Biological Reserve and Drake Bay will take you to either San Pedrillo or Sirena.

MARENCO BIOLOGICAL STATION

This 500-hectare nature reserve is five km north of Corcovado. The wilderness lodge (Apdo. 4025, San José 1000, tel. 221-1594, fax 255-1340) serves as a center for scientific research and welcomes ecotourists, too. The hilltop lodge is set in beautiful gardens and accommodates up to 40 people in rustic thatched bamboo-and-wood cabins, each with four bunks, a private bath, and a terrace offering panoramic ocean views. Meals are served family-style in a large, folksy dining hall overlooking a rocky shore.

Marenco's reserve forms a buffer zone for Corcovado National Park and is home to all four monkey species and other wildlife species common to Corcovado. The area's 400-plus bird species include the scarlet macaw, great curassow, toucans, and several species of brightly colored tanagers, not least the endemic black-cheeked ant-tanager. Watch for whales out at sea.

Resident biologists lead nature hikes along the rocky shore to the Río Claro, where a refreshing deep freshwater pool behind the beach is perfect for a swim (the ocean here is the warmest I've ever experienced), and to Corcovado National Park. A self-guided tour booklet is available, as are horses. September and October are the rainiest months. Reserve well in advance. Rates: for room about $85 s, $55 d per person; $65 for bungalow per person, including three meals; $575 for a three-night package, $690 four-night, including air transportation and all meals.

Many tour operators feature packages to Marenco. **Halintours** (P.O. Box 49705, Austin, TX 78765, tel. 800-695-2968, fax 512-472-1896;

in Costa Rica, tel. 472-1895), for example, offers a weeklong "Osa Adventure" featuring four nights at Marenco, plus visits to Corcovado and Caño Island, as well as charter flights to and from San José.

Getting There
Tour packages include air transportation. You can charter a small aircraft from San José; planes drop onto a private dirt airstrip. You can charter a boat at Uvita, Dominical, or Sierpe (see "Getting There" under "Drake Bay").

DRAKE BAY

Drake Bay (pronounced "DRA-cay" locally) has changed little since the day in March 1579 when Sir Francis Drake sailed past Caño Island into the tranquil bay that now bears his name. Sailboats still find the calm bay a popular place to anchor.

Now, though, a village—Agujitas—stretches along the two-km-wide crescent bay. It's good for forays into Marenco Biological Reserve (eight km) and Corcovado National Park (13 km south), or to Caño Island, which dominates the view out to sea. The village is famous as one of only two places in Central America that make reverse-appliqué stitched *molas* (the other place is the San Blas islands in Panamá) featuring simplistic designs and motifs of birds, animals, and fruit in bright colors.

The beach is mediocre, but there are good tidepools and the wilderness surrounding Drake Bay is replete with wildlife, including scarlet macaws, toucans, and tanagers. Humpbacks and other whale species pass by close to shore. You'll find good snorkeling at the southern end of the bay. A trail leads south through small coffee, cacao, and guava plots to the mouth of the Río Agujitas, good for swimming and jungle exploration by canoe.

Moderate Accommodations
Albergue Jinetes de Osa (tel. 273-3116 or 253-6909), at the edge of Agujitas, offers five rooms, each sleeping three people with shared baths with cold water. Private bathrooms were being built. A very rustic open-air cafe serves Costa Rican cuisine as well as great burgers

and hot dogs. You can rent horses here ($20 up to four hours) and arrange guides plus stays with local *campesinos*. Rates: $30-35 per person (low-high season). **Casa Mirador** (tel. 227-6914) has simple but pleasing rooms atop a hill at the southern end of the bay, with private baths and cold water. Meals included. Rates: about $15. North American Cecilia Steller runs the basic **Cabinas Cecilia** (Apdo. 84, Palmar Norte, tel. 717-2436 or 717-3336), otherwise known as Cabinas Sir Francis Drake. Twelve bunks in two rooms have shared bath with cold water. Cecilia rents horses ($25 full day), offers hiking trips, and can arrange a cruise to Caño Island. Rates: $25 per day, including three meals; $20 for dorm.

Upscale Accommodations
Águila de Osa Inn (P.O. Box 025216, Dept. 250, Miami, FL 33102; or Apdo. 10486, San José 1000, tel. 296-2190, fax 232-7722), is on the north bank of the Río Agujitas. Seven double rooms with private baths, fans, and ocean views are set in a landscaped garden containing ancient Indian rock spheres. And what rooms! Bamboo beds, hardwood floors, and tropical furnishings add just the right hint of romance. The focal point is the circular open-air restaurant with high-pitched *palenque* thatched roof and beautiful hardwood floors. There's a small boutique. A veranda offers good ocean views. A cheery Dominican named Edgar Coolson—"Cookie"—cooks great food, including sashimi with ginger and horseradish sauce. Louise Young oversees scuba-diving trips to Caño Island (I've heard negative reports on the dive operation), and there are Garrett 31s for sportfishing. It's run by amiable Americans Rob and Mary Messenger. A nice touch is free wine with dinners. (It was formerly known as El Caballito de Mar, and before that Phantom Island Lodge.) Rates: $80 s, $130 d, including three meals (no credit cards); transfers from Sierpe, $15 per person.

Across the river from Águila de Osa is **Drake Bay Wilderness Camp** (Apdo 98-8150, Palmar Norte, Osa, tel./fax 771-2436, beeper, 223-3333, radiotelephone 220-2121), owned and operated by American Herb Michaud. It, too, has pleasant two- and four-person cabinas with ceiling fans and solar-heated hot showers. Some cabins have ocean-view patios; double-occupancy cabins

have private baths and ceiling fans. Roomy tents with electricity and comfortable folding beds are provided for campers. American-Tico food is served on a screened veranda (a playful squirrel monkey has adopted the camp and likes to slip into the dining room). There's an open-air bar and clubhouse slung with hammocks. The camp specializes in diving expeditions to Caño Island in the company of a master diver ($90, one-day, including two tanks). Fins and masks are available for rent (Punta San Josecito, eight km south, offers good snorkeling), plus horseback riding ($30) and tours to Corcovado and Caño Island. One reader has written to complain about the professionalism of the nature tours. Rates: $68 per person cabinas; $48 per person tents. Transfers from San José ($160, including charter flight, Palmar-Sierpe taxi transfer, and Sierpe-Drake Bay boat transfer).

Another option, more serene, is **La Paloma Lodge** (Adpo. 97, San Antonio del Belén 4005, tel./fax 239-0954; in the U.S., P.O. Box 025216, Miami, FL 33102, tel. 305-785-2260, fax 305-785-2372; the lodge radio-telephone number is 239-2801). The lodge, built by Mike and Sue Kalmbach from Ohio, is perched atop a cliff overlooking Playa Cocalito and offers a superb view of nearby Caño Island. Three spacious thatched ranchos and five comfortable cabins perched on stilts have private baths and balconies overlooking the sea and jungle. The thatched clubhouse is a perfect spot for dining and relaxing. Meals are family-style. Hikes and horseback rides ($20) are accompanied by resident guide and naturalist Vanessa Amsbury. La Paloma has three boats fully outfitted for trips to Caño Island, sportfishing ($325 half day, $600 full day), and light-tackle fishing ($150 half day, $275 full day). Be warned: There's an uphill hike to close your arrival, though you can arrange a tractor/trailer ride. Rates: $70 s, $55 per person double. Four- and five-day packages with air transfers are available.

Cocalito Lodge (fax 786-6335; in Canada, tel. 519-782-4592), operated by siblings Marna and Mike Berry, is the southerly neighbor to La Paloma and sits between forest and beach amid gardens with orchids, lilies, and bright red roses. The node is the rustic Cocalito Lodge, a model ecological project on the edge of a 14-hectare

property (most of the meals prepared here, for example, are made of organically home-grown products). Simple but clean cabinas have private baths with cold water, and electricity supplied by a stream-driven generator and solar panels. Monkeys, toucans, and other critters call in to sneak fruit from the trees, while local inhabitants pop in to eat, sup, and chat in the popular restaurant/bar. Hikes, horseback rides, and scuba-diving packages are available. Rates: $39 s, $50 d (low season), $50 s, $65 d (high season), including meals.

Nearby Accommodations

At press time, **Esperanza Fishing Lodge** was due to open a few kilometers north of Drake Bay. Owner Dennis McDermid has two 10-meter Dawsons. And Marna and Mike Berry, owners of Cocalito Lodge, were building a rainforest lodge near Los Planes, on the border of Corcovado National Park, in the Ganada mountains east of Drake Bay. Alas, I have no further information on either. Readers' comments welcome.

Camping

Corcovado Adventures Tent Camp (tel. 238-2726, fax 260-4434; in Quepos, c/o Hotel Dorado Mojado, tel. 777-0368, fax 777-1248) lies within the forest on a 14-hectare property beside Playa Caletas, about one hour hike south of Drake Bay. Two-person tents are pitched on wooden platforms, protected by tarps, and are big enough to stand up in. Each has a closet, wooden beds made up with cotton sheets, plus two armchairs for quiet meditation. Washrooms have showers and toilets, and hearty meals are served in a rancho-style dining room. A trail leads into the jungle, though monkeys, macaws, toucans, etc., come into camp to feast on fruits of almond and water-apple trees. Owner Larry Hustler also offers guided hikes and horseback rides ($45) to Corcovado National Park. You can also rent sea kayaks ($10 per hour). A butterfly garden was in the works. Hustler arranges boat transfers via Sierpe from Palmar. The property is used as a day stop-over by the *Temptress* cruise ship, which is how I arrived. Rates: $399 d (low season; two nights), including all meals, transfers, and guided tour to Caño Island and Corcovado; $60 per person, high season, including meals.

Water Sports

Angling Adventures (in Drake Bay, tel./fax 717-2436; in San José, tel. 233-8090, fax 222-2238; in the U.S., tel. 708-931-1608, fax 708-931-1719) offers fishing charters. It's operated by husband-and-wife team Skip and Elizabeth Foulk.

Kapper Dau, once "king of the Santa Cruz, California, line-up," offers a charter **surfing** service aboard a custom-designed seven-meter cabin cruiser built for surfing and overnighting. He can take you to some excellent breaks, many rarely surfed. Half-day trips are to Caño Island ($125), or to Violin and Rincón breaks ($80); overnight trips including two days' surfing cost $600 double. Contact the Drake Bay Wilderness Camp (tel. 717-2436).

All the lodges can arrange scuba diving, snorkeling, sportfishing, horseback rides, and jungle hikes into Corcovado National Park or Caño Island. Scuba divers must bring their own buoyancy compensators and regulators.

Getting There

By Road: A "road" has recently been opened from Rancho Quemado westward over the Fila Ganado to Drake Bay (20 km; Rancho Quemado is reached via Rincón, on the eastern shore of the Osa Peninsula; there's bus service between the two). It's heavily rutted and mountainous: 4WD is essential. The track is frequently impossible to negotiate, but plans are to upgrade it despite local protests (many locals enjoy their relative inaccessibility).

By Boat: Boats travel downriver to Drake Bay from the village of Sierpe, 10 km south of Palmar Sur (see "Sierpe" under "Palmar and Vicinity," below). Board a boat from behind the Las Vegas Bar for the two-hour trip down the jungle-draped Río Sierpe (about $15): choose from everything from weatherbeaten dugout canoes to smoking river steamers. Watch for crocodiles and caimans (alligators) in the mangroves. At the river's mouth, smaller boats make a daring run past the surf (ensure you have an experienced local guide, as dugouts and other light craft have been known to capsize at the rivermouth; larger vessels are fine). On the 20-minute journey across Drake Bay to the mouth of the Río Agujitas you sometimes pass whales and dolphins. If you book with one of the lodges, it can arrange transportation from San José to Sierpe.

A sportfisherman, Steve Wofford, offers a water-taxi service—**Taximar** (tel. 777-1170 or 771-1903)—from Quepos ($55) via Dominical ($35), continuing to Playa Caletas and Caño Island. The 22-seater boat will reportedly do a speedy 30 knots.

By Bus: Buses for Palmar Sur depart San José from Calle 4, Avenida 18 (tel. 221-4214), daily at 5 and 7 a.m. From Palmar, take a taxi to the banana village of Sierpe for a boat ride to Drake Bay (see above).

By Air: See "Palmar and Vicinity," below for information on scheduled air service. You can charter a small plane direct to Drake Bay; there's a landing strip near La Paloma.

By Sea: The 68-passenger eco-cruise ship *Temptress* includes Drake Bay on a six-day nature cruise from Puntarenas to national parks and wildlife refuges on the Pacific coast. The full-day Drake Bay visit includes lunch at the Águila de Osa Inn plus a river trip up the Río Agujitas. The day ends with folkloric dancing by the local schoolchildren dressed in traditional costume on board. Contact **Cruceros del Sur** (Apdo. 1198, San José 1200, tel. 220-1927, fax 220-2103).

PALMAR AND VICINITY

PALMAR

Palmar, at the foot of the Fila Costeña, 125 km south of San Isidro and 81 km north of Golfito, is a service center for the banana plantations of the Valle de Diquis and an important stop on the Pan-American Highway. The Chinese presence is strong. The town is divided in two by the Río Térraba. Palmar Norte is the most important, with all the hotels. Palmar Sur, south of the bridge, has pre-Columbian Indian granite spheres—*bolas grandes*—in the plaza, plus a venerable and rusty steam locomotive that once hauled bananas.

A grid network of roads serving the banana plantations south of Palmar Sur leads to Sierpe, the "port" upriver from Drake Bay.

Accommodations

Restaurante Wah-Lok has basic but adequate rooms with private baths for $12. **Cabinas Ticos Alemán** (tel. 575-0157 or 786-6232), on the Pan-American Hwy., has 18 very basic motel-style rooms for $10 d. In town is the basic and dingy-looking **Hotel Xinia** (tel. 786-6129), with shared bath; and **Hotel y Cabinas Casa Amarilla** (tel. 786-6251), which has 19 pleasant and clean but basic rooms with shared bath ($5 per

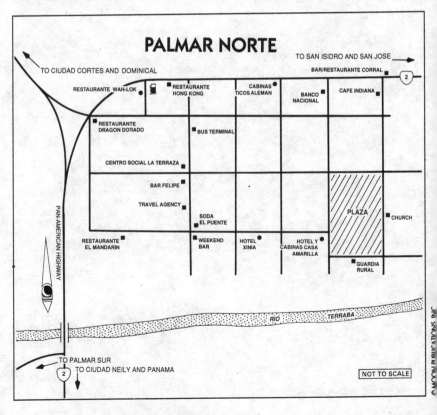

PALMAR NORTE

TO SAN ISIDRO AND SAN JOSE

TO CIUDAD CORTES AND DOMINICAL

BAR/RESTAURANTE CORRAL

2

RESTAURANTE WAH-LOK ●

RESTAURANTE HONG KONG

CABINAS TICOS ALEMAN ●

BANCO NACIONAL

CAFE INDIANA ■

■ RESTAURANTE DRAGON DORADO

■ BUS TERMINAL

CENTRO SOCIAL LA TERRAZA ■

BAR FELIPE ■

TRAVEL AGENCY ■

SODA EL PUENTE ■

PLAZA

■ CHURCH

PAN-AMERICAN HIGHWAY

RESTAURANTE EL MANDARIN ■

WEEKEND BAR ■

HOTEL XINIA ●

HOTEL Y CABINAS CASA AMARILLA ●

■ GUARDIA RURAL

RIO TERRABA

TO PALMAR SUR

2

TO CIUDAD NEILY AND PANAMA

NOT TO SCALE

© MOON PUBLICATIONS INC

person), plus 12 cabins with private baths (two have a/c; $18 d).

Food
Two Chinese restaurants, **Restaurante Dragon Dorado** and **Restaurante Wah-Lok,** are immediately north of the bridge over the Río Térraba. **Restaurante Hong Kong** (tel. 786-6230) is 100 meters east, next to the gas station, and **Restaurante El Mandarin** (tel. 786-6183) is in Palmar Norte. On the Pan-American Hwy., about 400 meters east of the bridge, is **Bar y Restaurante Corral** and, a little farther, **Cafe Indiana,** which also has souvenirs. The **Soda El Puente** is clean and pleasant (it's the only place in town serving breakfast). Alternately, try the **Restaurant Las Tinajes.**

Services
A Chevron gas station lies immediately north of the bridge and a **Banco Nacional** just is off the Pan-American Highway. Hidanuel Lopez Valerín (tel. 786-6065) represents **Travelair** and also operates **Chino Taxi** service and travel agency, in Palmar Sur. The **police station** (Guardia Rural) is on the south side of the park.

Transportation
SANSA (tel. 233-3258, fax 255-2176) flies from San José to Palmar Sur via Coto 47 (Ciudad Neily) and Puerto Jiménez on Monday, Wednesday, and Friday at 8:45 a.m., and on Tuesday, Thursday, and Saturday at 8 a.m.; and via Quepos on Monday, Wednesday, Friday, and Saturday at 9:30 a.m. **Travelair** (tel. 232-7883, fax 220-0413) flies from San José's Pavas Airport to Palmar Sur via Quepos, daily at 11 a.m. ($45 one-way); return flights depart Palmar Sur for San José at 12:15 a.m. **Note:** Reduced schedules operate mid-April through mid-December.

Buses depart San José for Palmar from Avenida 18, Calles 2/4 (Tracopa, tel. 221-4214) at 5, 6:30, 8:30, and 10 a.m., and 2:30 and 6 p.m. Buses leave from Supermercado Térraba for Sierpe five times daily (50 cents).

SIERPE

Sierpe, 15 km south of Palmar, is a tiny village on the banks of the Río Sierpe. It has no inherent interest except as the "port" from which boats

travel downriver to Drake Bay and, en route, for exploring the delta of the Ríos Sierpe and Térraba. These two rivers demarcate a vast network of mangrove swamps harboring crocodiles, alligators, and myriad wading and water birds. You can try hiring a boat to take you through the delta from Sierpe, Palmar, or Cortés (see below). Dugouts and *"especiales"* (motor boats) leave from the dock behind the Las Vegas bar. You'll be able to negotiate one at dockside; otherwise the Hotel Pargo can make arrangements if needed. Buses and taxis (about $12) operate from Palmar Norte.

Accommodations
The American-owned **Hotel Pargo** (tel. 786-6092, fax 232-9578), about 50 meters from the dock, has rooms with private baths with hot water, some with a/c. A veranda and *ranchita* restaurant overlook the river. Rates: $16-25 s, $24-35 d. The **Hotel Margarita**, next to Bazar Jennifer, has basic rooms with shared bath ($8). **Cabinas Estero Azul** (tel. 233-2578, fax 222-0297), two km north of town, has basic cabinas with fans and refrigerators. It offers sportsfishing and boat tours. Rates: $30 d.

Nature Lodge
Río Sierpe Lodge (Apdo. 149, Moravia 2150, tel. 223-9945, fax 233-2886), 25 km downriver from Sierpe on the Río Sierpe north of Drake Bay, specializes in fishing and diving excursions (the lodge provides dive tanks, weights, boat transport, and guides) using a 14-meter three-decked yacht and seven-meter airboat. Guides and equipment are provided. The 11 rooms are basic but large. Each has a private bathroom. There's a large dining and recreational area with a library. The lodge also has trails into the nearby rainforests, and offers hiking, horseback trips, and a range of excursions, including some to nearby islands, plus overnight camping trips. Rates: $65 per person, including meals and transfers from Palmar; packages from $345 (three days/two nights, including transfers from San José).

PALMAR TO BALLENA MARINE NATIONAL PARK

The turnoff for Dominical is to the left, immediately north of the Río Térraba bridge. This paved

DRIVING CONDITIONS, PALMAR TO DOMINICAL

"Best turn around now, mate. If you get through I'll buy you a pint . . . and I'll throw in my missus for free!"

Now, I'm not generally a gambling man. And I don't normally risk my life for a beer and another man's woman. When a worldly Australian says a road can't be driven, I'm prepared to believe him. He described the route—a 50-km stretch of Pacific coast midway down the western seaboard of Costa Rica—in several ways, the most polite of which was "a daggy!" (a dirty lump of wool at the back end of a sheep).

I took a more charitable view. I'd spent the last month perfecting my four-wheel-driving techniques over, around, and across terrain that would have challenged a goat. As long as I could resist being carried off into the mangroves by the mosquitoes, I reckoned, I could get through. Sure, it was still the wet season, when according to all the guidebooks only horses and tractors could negotiate the track along the jungled shoreline. My alternative was to follow the Australian and take a 240-km detour along the paved road via the banana town of Palmar Sur and the flatlands of the Valle de El General, then back to the coast. But that felt like cheating.

It wasn't long before my pulse began to quicken. Rain had been belting down for two days, and the mud was inches deep. I encountered two cars and a truck destined to spend the night in a ditch, including a Toyota Tercel full of anguished-looking young surfers outskating Torvill and Dean.

Now there were no more vehicles. No villages or farms. Not another soul for miles. The only sounds were the bellows of howler monkeys, the screechings of toucans and parrots, and the crashing of surf where the track briefly came down to the coast. A claustrophobic tangle of rainforest had closed over my head. And for all the world I could have been the only person in it.

The level road designed to shake the fillings from my teeth had deteriorated into a trail best described as steeper than a dentist's bill and with twice as many cavities.

Remembering advice I'd been given years before in the Sahara, I pulled out the foot pump stowed in the back and bumped the tire pressures up to what I guessed was around 45 pounds. Hardly ideal for sealed roads but a good precaution on the razor-

edged flint that now covered the trail. Grateful for permanent 4WD, and with low ratio still to fall back on, I walked the vehicle up and over the boulder-strewn mountain. It was a case where the argument in favor of a V6 was very persuasive. The car seemed not to notice. I blessed the engineers who had designed the Range Rover. Surely these were the conditions they had in mind when they conceived the car.

I inched along the map through more mud. More clifflike hills. More boulders. A small landslide. A fallen tree to manhandle out of the way. More bruising rain. More raging streams to ford. And mile after mile of really wild country that had been barely explored.

"Aaawright! I'm through!" I chimed, looking down into a canyon that seemed to descend into the Stone Ages, but which I knew would disgorge me onto the surfaced road, which began at the coast near Uvita.

Instead, the gorge descended into a morass of fathoms-deep, vacuumlike mud. My stomach tightened sickeningly as my vehicle sank until the doors wouldn't open. Yikes! There really was a Shit Creek, and this was it.

I climbed out of the window, sank—bloop!—up to my knees, and began dripping sweat like a faucet. Somewhere beyond the forest canopy the sun heliographed the heavens and sank from view. Blackness descended. And the rainforest was suddenly silent.

Then the night noises began.

I curled up in the back of the Range Rover and listened to my stomach rumble. Why hadn't I stocked up on food? When dawn came, rain was drumming down from a sky as dark as Costa Rican coffee. I groaned miserably.

Fortunately, even atheists have their angels of mercy. Mine was a giant earth-mover that miraculously appeared around noon and plucked me from my muddy grave. The giant "Cat" was one of several tearing up the rainforests for the long-awaited Costanera Sur Highway, a four-year project that will be a final link in coastal communications along the Pacific coast. I had followed the newly cut path through the mountains and become stuck at its furthermost point. Beyond lay impenetrable forest. My foolhardy attempt to drive through the pool had been futile.

CHRISTOPHER P. BAKER

*negotiating the
Fila Costanera*

I retraced my tracks and—tail between my legs—arced around the Fila Costanera mountain range to Dominical.

"Told ya ya'd nivver git through, ya great dill," the Aussie said, likening me to a sexual aid, as we swigged beer together at a bar called Jungle Jim's.

"You remind me of something Paul Theróux once wrote," I replied, "about how when things were at their most desperate and uncomfortable, he always found himself in the company of Australians, a reminder that he'd touched bottom."

That was in 1993. Since then, the government has made significant headway in carving the Costanera Sur highway through the coastal mountains . . . the missing link in communications along the Pacific coast. If it's not completed, maybe enough progress will have been made by the time you read this that you can travel directly from Palmar to Uvita and Dominical without having to spend the night eating your fingernails while the mosquitoes and God knows what other beasts press their noses up against your car window, eyeing you greedily.

road leads west to Ciudad Cortés, where there's a hospital (tel. 788-8148) and Red Cross (tel. 788-8171). Cortés is a perfect point from which to explore the mangrove swamps at the mouth of the Río Térraba. Turn left at the T-junction for Cortés; the road to the right (follow the sign for Casa Papagayo), where the road, now dirt-and rock, leads to Punta Mala (20 km), where the road hits the coast at the southern end of **Ballena National Marine Park** (see "Dominical and Vicinity" in the Central Pacific chapter). Three km farther, at the hamlet of Tortuga Abajo, the road deteriorates into a muddy track that leads to Uvita and Dominical. The track is passable with 4WD in dry season only. Believe me, it's truly horrendous! (See special topic "Driving Conditions, Palmar to Dominical.")

By the time you read this, the long-awaited Costanera Sur Hwy.—a new, paved road—may

have been completed; if not, and if you don't want to tackle the challenging drive along the shore, you'll have to travel via the Valle de El General and San Isidro to reach Dominical.

Accommodations

Casa Papagayo (alias the Hotel Posada Tortuga) is at Punta Mala. Another hotel—**Casa Pura Vida**—should be open just north of Punta Mala by the time you read this.

Las Ventanas de Osa (P.O. Box 1089, Lake Helen, FL 32744, tel. 904-228-3356, fax 904-228-0181), near Tortuga Abajo, is a clifftop nature lodge in a private wildlife refuge, big with birders. The modern lodge is a private club open to members only (life membership costs $500). It is open Dec.-March plus mid-July only (the lodge may open year-round after completion of the Costanera Sur Hwy.). Six rooms have twin

beds and private baths. The lodge has a swimming pool and an open-air dining room with meals prepared by a professional chef. Also nearby are beaches good for swimming, and trails lead through the surrounding forest. Ca-

puchin and howler monkeys are common. More than 380 bird species have been recorded, along with a boat-billed heron rookery. Rates: six-day package $900 including all meals, plus transfers from San José.

COCOS AND CAÑO ISLANDS

COCOS ISLAND

The only true oceanic island off Central America and the world's second-largest uninhabited island (52 square kilometers), Cocos Island—500 km southwest of Costa Rica—is a mountainous chunk of land that rises to 634 meters at Iglesias Peak. The island is the northernmost and oldest of a chain of volcanoes, mostly submarine, stretching south along the Cocos Ridge to the equator, where several come to the surface as the Galápagos Islands. These islands were formed by a "hot spot," which pushes up volcanic material from beneath the earth's crust. The hot spot remains stationary while the sea floor moves across it (see special topic "Plate Tectonics" in the Introduction chapter). Over time, a volcano is transported away from the hot spot and a new volcano arises in the same place.

Cliffs reach higher than 100 meters around almost the entire island and dramatic waterfalls cascade onto the beach, fed by 800 cm of rain a year. The island was discovered in 1526 by Juan Cabezas and first appeared on a map in 1542. Prisoners lived here in watery solitude in the late 1800s, and occasional settlers have tried to eke a living. Today it is inhabited only by national park guards who patrol the park equipped with small Zodiacs. The only safe anchorage for entry is at Chatham Bay, on the northeast corner, where scores of rocks are etched with the names and dates of ships dating back to the 17th century. Even Jacques Cousteau has left his indelible mark: a substantial and beautiful engraving made in 1987.

There are no native mammals. The surrounding waters, however, are home to four unique species of marine mollusks. One endemic plant is christened Franklin Roosevelt, after the U.S. president who made several vis-

its to the island. The island has one butterfly and two lizard species to call its own. And three species of birds are endemic: the Cocos Island finch, Cocos Island cuckoo, and Ridgeway or Cocos flycatcher (the Cocos Island finch is a subspecies of the famous Galápagos finches, which inspired Darwin's revolutionary theory of evolution). Three species of boobies—red-footed, masked, and brown—live here, too. Cocos is also a popular spot for frigate birds (arch-rivals of boobies) to roost and mate. The white tern, which may hover above your head, is the *espíritu santu*, or Holy Spirit bird. Feral pigs introduced in the 18th century by passing sailors today number about 5,000 and have caused substantial erosion. The island's isolation attracts poachers seeking black coral, seashells, and lobster, and fishermen who violate the no-fishing zone to net sharks for fins treasured in the Orient. Access to the island is restricted.

Treasure

Coco's forested hills supposedly harbor gold doubloons. More than 500 expeditions have sought in vain to find the Lima Booty, gold and silver ingots that mysteriously disappeared while en route to Spain under the care of Captain James Thompson. The pirate William Davies supposedly hid his treasure here in 1684, and Portuguese buccaneer Benito "Bloody Sword" Bonito his in 1889. The government has placed a "virtual moratorium" on treasure hunts, although the Ministry of Natural Resources sanctioned a hunt in January 1992 by North American computer company owner John Hodges—for a rights fee of $100,000! Most recently, Turismo 2000 de Limón was granted permission to look for treasure . . . for a mere $25,000. Christopher Weston's book, *Cocos Island—Old Pirate's Haven* (San José: Imprenta y Litografia Trejos, 1990), tells the tale.

Diving

The island is renowned as one of the world's best diving spots. It is famous for its massive schools of white-tipped and hammerhead sharks (sometimes hundreds together), and eerie manta rays, which haunt these waters at deeper depths. Pilot whales, whale sharks, and even sailfish are also abundant. Cocos is for experienced divers only. Drop-offs are deep. Currents are continually changing. And beginning divers will freak at the huge shark populations! Converging ocean currents stir up such a wealth of nutrients that the sharks have a surfeit of fish to feed on, and taking a chunk out of divers is probably the last thing on their minds. Snorkelers swimming closer to the surface can revel in moray eels, white-tipped sharks, and colorful reef fish.

Information

For information on visiting, contact the National Parks Service (tel. 257-0922). There is no accommodation, and camping is not allowed.

Transportation

The *Okeanos*, a 36-meter luxury power cruiser especially equipped for diving, operates one-week and longer trips out of Puntarenas. The journey usually takes 32 hours. It sleeps 20 divers. *Okeanos* also operates a three-week cruise combining Cocos with the Galápagos Islands. The vessel is heavily booked up to two years ahead. Contact: **Cruceros del Sur** (Apdo. 1198, San José 1200, tel. 220-1927, fax 220-2103; in the U.S., P.O. Box K, Morgan City, LA 70381, tel. 504-385-2416 or 800-348-2628).

Dive packages are also offered aboard the *Undersea Hunter*, a 27-meter dive ship with 50 tanks and compressors. It can accommodate 12 divers in seven cabins. Contact: **Escenarios Tropicales** (Apdo. 2047, San José 1000, tel./fax 224-2555). Ten-day packages cost about $2500.

See & Sea Travel (50 Francisco St., Suite 205, San Francisco, CA 94133, tel. 415-434-3400 or 800-DIV-XPRT) operates dive packages aboard both vessels from the United States.

The 35-meter *Coral Sea* (tel. 800-862-1003, fax 222-1760) operates diving packages from Golfito, June-August.

A twin-masted motor-sailing yacht, the *Pollux*,

offers a 10-day diving package ($2285), plus an eight-day nondiving excursion ($1429) to Cocos. The vessel sleeps six people and is available for charter. Contact **Pollux de Golfito** (Apdo. 7-1970, San José 1000, tel. 661-1224, fax 661-2061). **Ocean Voyages** (1709 Bridgeway, Sausalito, CA 94965, tel. 415-332-4681) offers chartered yacht cruises to Cocos.

CAÑO ISLAND
BIOLOGICAL RESERVE

Caño Island is 17 km off the western tip of the Osa Peninsula. It is of interest primarily for its inshore coral reefs and its importance as a pre-Columbian cemetery. Many tombs and artifacts—pestles, corn-grinding tables, and granite spheres *(bolas)*—gathering moss in the rainforest undergrowth. The 300-hectare island is ringed with secluded white-sand beaches that attract olive ridley turtles. Among its residents are boa constrictors (the only poisonous snakes here are sea snakes), giant frogs, a variety of hummingbirds, and three mammal species: a marsupial, the paca (which was introduced), and a bat. Surprisingly, only 13 terrestrial bird species are found here. Snorkelers can see brilliant tropical fish and moray eels among the coral beds. Offshore waters teem with common and bottle-nosed dolphins, and sperm, pilot, and humpback whales, which migrate from Alaska.

In 1973 Caño was leased to a Spanish developer with plans to build a megaresort. The island, however, was heroically saved by an outburst of popular displeasure led by University of Costa Rica students and the Association of Biologists. Although now administered as part of Corcovado National Park, uncontrolled sportfishing and poaching of coral goes virtually unchecked because of under-funding and -staffing.

A wide and well-maintained trail leads steeply uphill from the ranger station and provides an excellent entree into a rainforest environment. Pre-Columbian tombs are scattered along the trail.

Entrance: $15, or $10 advance purchase.

Accommodations

You can camp near the ranger station on the beach. No facilities.

A STRANGE PROCESSION

If you think you see the beach moving, it's not the heat waves nor last night's excess of *guaro* messing with your mind. Daily, whole columns of seashells—little whelks and conchs of green and blue and russet—come marching down from the roots of the mangroves on to the sand. Scavengers only an inch long, soldier crabs are born and grow up without protective shells. For self-preservation they move—"lock, stock and abdomen," says one writer—into empty seashells they find cast up on the beach. Although they grow, their seashell houses do not; thus whole battalions of crabs continually seek newer and larger quarters. When threatened, a soldier crab pulls back into its shell, totally blocking the entrance with one big claw.

Transportation and Tours

You can hire a boat from Drake Bay. Alternately, the park rangers might squeeze you into their boat from San Pedrillo or Sirena, in Corcovado National Park.

Cruceros del Sur (Apdo. 1198, San José 1200, tel. 220-1927, fax 220-2103) offers a four-day/three-night cruise to Caño aboard the 68-passenger *Temptress* ($595 low season, $745 high season). The company also includes a full-day visit to Caño Island on its one-week nature cruise. Guided nature hikes, sea kayaking, and scuba diving highlight the visit. Highly recommended. Many U.S. tour operators offer packages that include the *Temptress*.

Pollux de Golfito (Apdo. 7-1970, San José 1000, tel. 661-1224, fax 661-2061) operates a four-day trip to Caño Island aboard the twin-masted motor-sailing yacht *Pollux* ($561; charter rate, $1500 per night).

CENTRAL PACIFIC

INTRODUCTION

The central Pacific region—defined as Puntarenas south to Punta Uvita—offers something for everyone along the coastal littoral. The region boasts its share of long beaches renowned for killer surf (for surfers that means the kinds of waves they love to ride; for others it means dangerous swimming conditions). Jacó, a favorite of Canadian package charter groups, is famous in surf lore, though its appeal is otherwise limited. The best-known—and most beautiful—beaches are the white-sand beaches of Manuel Antonio National Park, just south of the sportfishing town of Quepos. The clear water here makes it a favorite among snorkelers, while bordering the beach is a lush tropical forest home to abundant wildlife. Carara Biological Reserve and a growing number of private nature reserves, too, offer a feast of wildlife wonders.

Puntarenas, the nation's preeminent coastal town, has long been favored by Josefinos seeking R and R, as are even the most remote

beaches along the Pacific coast, to which they flock with camp gear on weekends. (For tourists, Puntarenas is merely a curiosity en route to destinations farther afield).

The resort industry is better developed here than anywhere else in the country except Nicoya. There are haciendas-turned-hotels to enjoy. In Escaleras, Finca Brian y Milena and its neighbor, Bella Vista Lodge, exemplify the best in rustic mountain retreats. And though there are only a handful of top-class hotels in the region, any journey is worth the distance to stay at the finest hotel in the country: Villa Caletas.

The months of Dec.-April anywhere along the Central Pacific coast are particularly busy, when tour groups flock in from Canada, and Costa Ricans take their "summer" holidays (the long school break is January and February). Reservations are recommended during the dry season, especially for Christmas, New Year's, and Easter. Consider visiting in the "green sea-

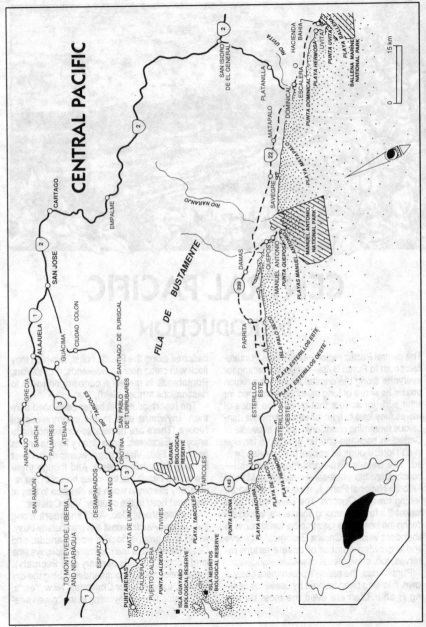

CENTRAL PACIFIC

son" (May-Nov.), when many hotels entice with discounts.

Climate

The region marks the boundary between the tropical dry zone farther north and the tropical wet to the south. It has distinct wet and dry seasons:

May-Nov. and Dec.-April, respectively. As you move south be prepared for progressively more rain and a lingering wet season. The region is humid year-round. You'll feel it away from the shore, where breezes keep you pleasantly cool. Temperatures average about 30° C in dry season, a little lower in wet season.

SAN JOSÉ TO PUNTARENAS

Three routes descend from the central highlands to the coastal plains of the central Pacific. The first, and most trafficked, is via the Pan-American Hwy. through San Ramón to Esparza, gateway to Puntarenas and Guanacaste. The second more southerly route, along Hwy. 3 (also heavily trafficked), leads via Atenas to Orotina, gateway to Carara Biological Reserve and the beach resorts of the central Pacific. Whichever route you select, road conditions are the same— a steep drop with plenty of hairpin bends, slow-moving trucks holding everyone up, and Costa Ricans driving like suicidal maniacs. Both are single-lane affairs in each direction. Drive cautiously: These two routes are among the most dangerous in the country!

If you're wise, you'll take a newly laid, more southerly route west from San José through the valley of the Río Turrubares via Santa Ana, Ciudad Colón and Santiago de Puriscal (the exit through town is unclear: the route is to the south side of the plaza, up the hill; ask if unsure). The well-paved road sidles magnificently along a mountain ridge to San Pablo de Turrubares before dropping in a zig-zag to Orotina, where it joins Hwy. 3. (I've driven this route only as far as San Pablo.) Nary a car in sight! See "Santiago de Puriscal and La Garita" under "West of Escazú" in the Central Highlands chapter.

ESPARZA

Esparza, on Hwy. 1 (the Pan-Am Hwy.), 20 km east of Puntarenas, is a good place to stop for a soda, fruits, and/or *gallo pinto*. Buses operate hourly between Esparza and Puntarenas.

Accommodations and Food

The **Motel Calypso**, near Angostura, about five km east of Esparza, is the only accommoda-

tion between the central highlands and Esparza. Not reviewed. In Esparza is the motel-style **Las Castañuelas** (tel. 635-5105), on the left at the turnoff into town. It looks modestly upscale on the outside but is basic inside. Some rooms have a/c. Bargain. Rates: $10 s, $12 d; $15 d with a/c. Budget options include the **Hotel Cordoba** (tel. 635-5014) and **Pensión Fanny** (tel. 635-5158).

Services

Here you'll find a **Red Cross** post (tel. 635-5172), a **Banco Nacional,** plus a **taxi** service, Taxis de Esparza (tel. 635-5810).

OROTINA

Orotina enjoys a strategic location as a transportation hub and is replete with roadside restaurants and *sodas*. The local seasonal specialty is *toronjas rellenas* (candied grapefruit stuffed with white milk fudge). You can buy traditional ceramic pots and vases from roadside stalls.

Accommodations

Palenque Machucha, beside the bridge, has cabinas and a pleasant riverside restaurant under thatch. Two superb upmarket lodges lie outside Orotina. **Hacienda Doña Marta Lodge** (Apdo. 23, Santa Bárbara de Heredia 3009, tel. 253-6514, fax 269-9555) is a fully restored and thoroughly charming Arizona-style hacienda on hundreds of acres of cattle pasture, in Cascajal de Orotina, about seven km east of Puerto Caldera. No landscaping here; the hacienda has been very much a working farm with prized Brahmas since the 1930s. The cattle sheds and corral are adjacent to the bedrooms. The six light and airy rooms—among the most romantic in the country—are as warm as a hug. High-

lights include bamboo ceilings and tiled floors, large showers, and lots of rustic, country-style adornments. Two rooms have trompe l'oeil walls showing *finca* scenes, with old hacienda wrought-iron gates and cartwheels as bed-steads. Some rooms have semi-canopied beds. There's a small pool. The ranch is overseen by a friendly manager, Carlos Sánchez. Horse-back riding is offered. It's a perfect base for vis-iting Carara or Monteverde and it's run by the same folks who operate Finca Rosa Blanca (see special topic of that name in the Central Highlands chapter). Great bargain. Rates: $50 s, $60 d or $160 d including all meals, farm tour, and horseback riding.

A stone's throw away is the equally distinc-tive and appealing **Dundee Ranch** (Apdo. 7812, San José 1000, tel. 267-7371, fax 239-1050), another working mango plantation and cattle *finca*. The 11 very appealing red-tiled rooms have fans, TVs, and two double beds, plus tiled bathrooms with showers, and sur-round a small garden. A beautiful kidney-shaped pool has a small cascade. A plank walkway leads out into a lake with a viewing platform and a breezy bar from where you can seek out the resident crocodile.

An elegant screened restaurant with lots of fans and open grill serves from a wide menu. The grounds have lots of old trees festooned with epiphytes. Ana Astorga, the delightful Eng-lish-speaking manager, is extremely accom-

modating. Horseback rides are offered, as well as tours through the farm in a canopied "cart" towed by a tractor. Highly recommended. Dundee Ranch is well signposted along the highway between Orotina and Puntarenas. Rates: $76 s/d, $10 each additional person.

Another upscale option is the **Rancho Oropendola** (Apdo. 159, Orotina, tel./fax 428-8600), set in four acres of tropical gardens just outside picturesque San Mateo, a couple of miles north of Orotina. Rustic yet pleasingly decorated cabins have private baths, and a choice of king, queen or two doubles. Rooms in the main house share a bath; they have a dou-ble bed. Choose, too, from either a junior or grand suite. Ranch highlights include a 12-meter swimming pool with sundeck plus a games room, video movies at night, and meals on a dining veranda. Trails wind through the gardens and forest. Rates: $30 rooms, $50 cabins, $60-70 suite, including breakfast.

IGUANA PARK

This innovative conservation project, on a 285-hectare farm (Apdo. 692, San José 1007, tel. 240-6712, fax 235-2007) on the banks of the Río Turrubares, southeast of Orotina, is the brain-child of a German-born biologist named Dagmar Werner. Dagmar, popularly called "Iguana Mama," created the **Pro Green Iguana Foun-**

*Iguana Park raises
your future meal.*

dation in 1985 to research and promote the raising of iguanas by small farmers. Once abundant throughout Costa Rica, the iguana is endangered throughout much of its former range because of deforestation. Dagmar's project—a "pasture in the trees"—is aimed at helping to reverse deforestation and protect the iguana population by raising the dragonlike reptilian livestock for the dining table. The leaf-eating lizard, which can reach a meter in length and weigh six kilos in three years, has long been considered a tasty treat among Central Americans, who refer to the reptile as *gallina del pollo,* or tree chicken (it tastes like a cross between chicken and fish; "a most remarkable and wholesome food," recorded one early conquistador). If Costa Rica plants more trees—or preserves what primary forest remains—iguanas will increase, and farmers will have a steady diet of iguana meat. Remarkably, the lizards yield more than 10 times the amount of meat per hectare as cattle! Iguana Mama's farm is home to thousands of iguanas kept in large pens. Already, more than 100,000 have been released to the wild. Entrance: $15.

An airy, rancho-style dining room serves iguana ribs, tail, and breast, and, eventually, iguana sausages and smoked ham. Also planned is a shop where you can buy iguana paraphernalia, including dandy iguana leather shoes.

Canopy Tour
An intriguing way to get eye-to-eye with the harmless dragons is on a "Canopy Tour," which departs from the center daily at 8:15 and 10:30 a.m. and 1:45 p.m. ($69, including transportation from San José). Special dawn and dusk departures are offered on request. After hiking the trails, you'll ascend to the treetops and traverse from platform to platform using pulleys on horizontal cables; an expert guide will be there with you (tel. 255-2463, fax 255-3573; or contact ECHO, tel. 255-2693, fax 255-0061).

PUNTARENAS

What to make of this sultry, slightly sleazy port, 120 km west of San José? Five km long but only five blocks wide at its widest, the town is built on a long narrow spit—Puntarenas means "Sandy Point"—running east to west and fronted to the north by a mangrove estuary; to the south are the Gulf of Nicoya and a plain beach cluttered with driftwood "waiting for an artist's inspired hand." In past years there were health warnings against bathing in the estuary; the gulf waters were once considered unsafe. Fortunately, both have recently been cleaned up. Indeed, the city as a whole is on the up-and-up.

The town is hot and modestly decayed, but it is finally pulling itself up because of the current tourist boom. The old wharfs on the estuary side could be straight out of Robin Williams's *Popeye* movie, with their decrepit fishing boats leaning against ramshackle piers popular with pelicans. Roseate spoonbills, storks, and other birds pick among the shallows. You can watch the locals, too, knee-deep in mud, hunting for *chuchecas* (clams) amid the mangroves. You might want to visit for curiosity's sake—it's a fascinating walking town, an intriguing sociological study—and to watch the sun set magnificently behind the Nicoya Peninsula.

In my first edition, I stated that: "Otherwise the town's only usefulness is as the departure point for day cruises to islands in the Gulf of Nicoya and for the ferries to Playa Naranjo and Paquera, on the Nicoya Peninsula." I'm not ready to eat my words. Still, in 1993 the city fathers initiated a valiant effort to boost Puntarenas' fortunes by giving it a major facelift. The kilometers-long beach has been transformed from a dump to a pleasant stretch of sand with the aid of a mechanized cleaner that makes regular forays (alas, the biggest battle is to reeducate the Ticos who flock on weekends; they're litter louts). The Rotary Club has planted trees and installed a fountain near the newly opened Casa de Cultura. An aquarium and artisans' market are planned. The old dock-pier that juts out into the gulf was in its final stages of being transformed into a tourist boardwalk, with restaurants, shops and cafes . . . New Jersey and Brighton all over again!

HISTORY

The area around contemporary Puntarenas was colonized by the Spaniards as early as 1522. The early port grew to prominence and was de-

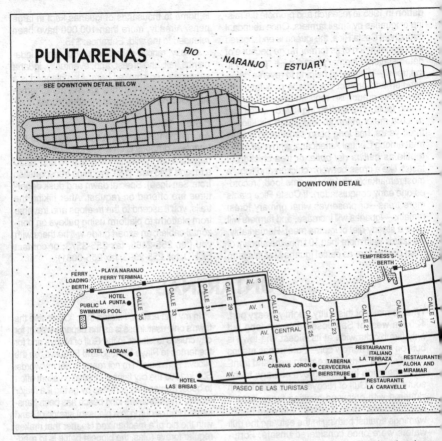

PUNTARENAS

RIO NARANJO ESTUARY

SEE DOWNTOWN DETAIL BELOW

DOWNTOWN DETAIL

TEMPTRESS'S BERTH

FERRY LOADING BERTH

PLAYA NARANJO FERRY TERMINAL

HOTEL LA PUNTA

PUBLIC SWIMMING POOL

CALLE 35 · CALLE 33 · CALLE 31 · CALLE 29 · AV. 3 · AV. 1 · CALLE 27 · CALLE 25 · CALLE 23 · CALLE 21 · CALLE 19 · CALLE 17

AV. CENTRAL

HOTEL YADRAN

AV. 2

HOTEL LAS BRISAS

AV. 4

CABINAS JORON

TABERNA CERVECERIA BIERSTRUBE

RESTAURANTE ITALIANO LA TERRAZA

RESTAURANTE ALOHA AND MIRAMAR

RESTAURANTE LA CARAVELLE

PASEO DE LAS TURISTAS

clared a free port in 1847, a year after completion of the oxcart road from the Meseta Central launched Puntarenas on its path to relative prosperity. Oxcarts from the central highlands made the lumbering descent to Puntarenas in convoys; coffee beans were shipped from here via Cape Horn to Europe. At its height Puntarenas had streetcars like those of San Francisco. It remained the country's main port for most of the 19th century until the Atlantic Railroad to Limón, on the Caribbean coast, was completed in 1890 (the railroad between San José and Puntarenas would not be completed for another 20 years). A new port was recently opened a few kilometers south at Puerto Caldera, and it is

there that freighters and the occasional cruise ship now berth.

Earlier this century, Puntarenas developed a large conch-pearl fleet. Pearlers would spend months at sea earning money to spend on women and booze (prostitution is still common on the streets of Puntarenas, as in any seaport worldwide). Some 80% of Porteños, as the inhabitants of Puntarenas are called, still make their livings from the sea, often going out for days at a time to haul in corvina, wahoo, dorado, shrimp, lobster, and tuna.

Secure as the country's principal port, Puntarenas even enjoyed favor as a *balneario*—a place for Josefinos to sun and bathe on week-

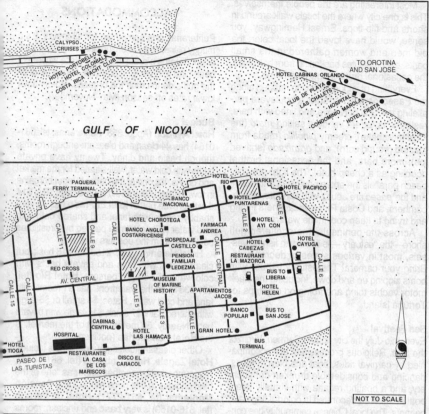

CALYPSO CRUISES
HOTEL PORTOBELLO
HOTEL COLONIAL
COSTA RICA YACHT CLUB
TO OROTINA AND SAN JOSE
HOTEL CABINAS ORLANDO
CLUB DE PLAYA
LAS CHALETS
HOSPITAL
CONDOMINIO MAROLA
HOTEL FIESTA

GULF OF NICOYA

PAQUERA FERRY TERMINAL
HOTEL RIO
MARKET
HOTEL PACIFICO
BANCO NACIONAL
HOTEL CHOROTEGA
HOTEL PUNTARENAS
FARMACIA ANDREA
BANCO ANGLO COSTARRICENSE
HOTEL AYI CON
HOSPEDAJE CASTILLO
HOTEL CAYUGA
HOTEL CABEZAS
PENSION FAMILIAR LEDEZMA
RESTAURANT LA MAZORCA
BUS TO LIBERIA
RED CROSS
AV. CENTRAL
MUSEUM OF MARINE HISTORY
APARTAMENTOS JACOB
HOTEL HELEN
BANCO POPULAR
BUS TO SAN JOSE
CABINAS CENTRAL
HOTEL LAS HAMACAS
GRAN HOTEL
BUS TERMINAL
HOTEL TIOGA
PASEO DE LAS TURISTAS
RESTAURANTE LA CASA DE LOS MARISCOS
DISCO EL CARACOL

CALLE 11, CALLE 9, CALLE 7, CALLE 5, CALLE 13, CALLE 15, CALLE CENTRAL, CALLE 2, CALLE 4, CALLE 6, CALLE 3, CALLE 1

NOT TO SCALE

© MOON PUBLICATIONS, INC.

ends. It was "New Jersey to San José's New York or Brighton to its London," says writer Michael Tunison. Alas, when international tourists began to arrive in numbers in the 1970s, and resorts sprang up elsewhere to lure them, Puntarenas was left behind in the tourism sweepstakes. By the time you read this, once-shabby Puntarenas may have proudly put itself back on the map.

SIGHTS AND EVENTS

Only a fistful of buildings are of interest, although many are the bright-painted old houses that re-

tain latticework below the eaves to welcome the breeze. The first is the **historic church** (Avenida Central, Calles 5/7) built in 1902 of flagstones; it's supposedly the only Catholic church in the country that faces east. Second, and next door, is the recently renovated old city jail, a mock-fortress-style building complete with tiny battlements and bars on its windows, which today houses the **Casa de la Cultura** (tel. 661-1394), with a library, art gallery, a museum, and a 204-seat auditorium for hosting plays and concerts (hours: Mon.-Sat. 9 a.m.-noon and 1-5 p.m.). A blossoming of craft stores adds color to the scene. The **Municipal Market** is also worth a look for its vitality and color.

Most interesting are the people themselves. This is one city where the locals walk around in shorts and flip-flops. Ernest Hemingway, you sense, would have loved the local color: the old men and women gathered in the small parks, the prostitutes beckoning from balconies, the occasional drunk staggering home.

Everything of import seems to happen along the **Paseo de las Turistas,** a boulevard paralleling the Gulf of Nicoya and lined with bars, restaurants, street vendors selling *mató* (the local milkshake), creamy *pinolillo* (made from toasted ground corn), and *granizado* (shaved ice), more bars, and the occasional brothel doubling as a cheap hotel. The light-gray city beach parallels the entire peninsula and both it and the *paseo* are abuzz with vendors, beachcombers, and Costa Rican vacationers flirting and trying to keep cool in the waters.

Across the peninsula, the sheltered gulf shore—the "estuary"—is lined with fishing vessels, most in various states of decrepitude. Bring your camera! The estuary is busy with boats zipping up and down, including the sleek motor yachts toing and froing on day-trips for Tortuga Island.

Sea Festival

Every mid-July the city honors Carmen, Virgin of the Sea. Religious processions are accompanied by carnival rides, boat and bicycle races, dancing and considerable drunken debauchery, and a boating regatta with virtually every boat in the area decorated in colorful flags and banners. The local Chinese community has contributed significantly to the celebration with its dragon boats, although one rarely sees the papier-mâché marine birds that were once a colorful feature.

The festival was started in 1913, when four fishermen narrowly escaped drowning during a storm in the Gulf of Nicoya. According to local superstition, one of the seamen offered the following prayer: "Sweetest little virgin, Carmen, excellent saint of the navigators, provide us salvation and I promise you that when I return to Puntarenas I will give a party in your honor using all my boats and fellow fishermen in return for your help."

ACCOMMODATIONS

Puntarenas has something for all tastes. It's a muggy place, so try to ensure that ventilation is efficient (I loathe a/c, but this is one place where I've been glad to have it). If possible, take a hotel on the gulf side to catch the breezes. Hotels have lower rates off-season (May-November).

Budget

Hotel Ayi Con (Apdo. 358, Puntarenas, tel. 661-0164) has 44 clean and pleasant-enough rooms, though basic and dingy. Twenty have private baths with cold water, well-situated for the market and docks. It's one of the better budget bargains in town. Rates: $6 s, $10 d shared bath; $9 s, $14 d with private bath. **Hotel El Prado** has 42 very shabby rooms with fans, and shared bath with cold water ($5); last time I passed by, prostitutes beckoned from the upstairs windows.

Hotel Helen (tel. 661-2159) has 16 basic but clean rooms with fans and private baths with cold water ($4.50 per person). **Hotel Río** (tel. 661-0331), on the waterfront, has 91 rooms with fans and cold water. Rates: $4 small or $6 large with shared bath; $7 small, $11 large with private bath. Nearby, 50 meters west of the market, is the **Hotel Puntarenas** (not inspected).

Other pleasant-looking budget hotels include **Hotel Zagala, Hotel Cabezas** (tel. 661-1045), recommended by another author as "one of the best choices in this price range," and **Pensión Montemar** (tel. 661-2771). **Hotel de Verano** (tel. 616-0159) is very basic and unclean; rooms can be rented by the hour ($12 double). The **Pensión Familiar Ledezma** (tel. 661-1468), next door, is a better bet in the same price range.

Very basic options include **Hotel Condor** with shared bath; **Hospedaje Castillo** (tel. 661-0771); **Pensión Juanita** (tel. 661-0096), on Avenida Central and Calles Central/1; and **Pensión Gutierrez,** opposite Cayuga. **Hotel Imperial** (Apdo. 65, Puntarenas, tel. 661-0579) doesn't live up to its name: the funky Caribbean architecture with high ceilings and wide halls belies its seedier side: sailors and hookers rent rooms by the hour. Avoid the **Hotel Pacífico,** a volatile refuge of drunks and cheap hookers.

Hotel Cabinas Orlando (tel. 663-0064), in the suburb of San Isidro, has roomy but rather run-down-looking cabins under shade trees. Another out-of-town option is the **Hotel Río Mar** (tel. 663-0158), 400 meters south of the Hotel Fiesta near Playa Doña Ana. Farther out is **Cabinas Cecil** (tel. 663-7148), near Puerto Caldera.

Inexpensive

Hotel y Restaurant Cayuga (Apdo. 306, Puntarenas, tel. 661-0344, fax 661-1280) is pleasant, clean, and well kept; an excellent bargain, rightfully popular with gringos. The 31 rooms have a/c and private baths with cold water. The restaurant is popular, the parking secure. Rates: $12 s, $18 d, $22 t, $35 suite with kitchenette.

Gran Hotel (tel. 661-0998), on Paseo de las Turistas and Calle Central, is very clean and well-run, with 36 rooms (13 with private bath) with hot water. Take an upstairs room with balcony and light (downstairs rooms are dingy). Rates: $8-13 s, $16-22 d, $21-28 t. Nearby, in the same price range and standard, is **Cabinas Central** (tel. 661-1484), at Calle 7 and Paseo de las Turistas. **Hotel Las Hamacas** (tel. 661-0398), on Paseo de las Turistas and Calles 5/7, has simple rooms (some with a/c) with private bath and cold water. It also has a pool and a disco that might keep you awake at night. Rates: $12 s, $20 d.

Cabinas El Jorón (tel. 661-0467), on Calle 25 and Avenidas 2/4, has rather gloomy rooms with a/c, hot water, and kitchenettes. It has a restaurant. Rate: $20 d. **Hotel Chorotega** (tel. 661-0998), on Calle 1 and Avenida 3, once popular with the backpacking crowd, has rooms with shared or private bath but has boosted its prices since a facelift. Rates: $16 d with shared bath, $25 d private bath.

Moderate

The American-owned and -run **Hotel La Punta** (Apdo. 228, Puntarenas, tel. 661-0440), at Avenida 1, Calles 35/37, is a good place to rest your head if you want to catch the early-morning ferry to Nicoya, and thereby is popular with tourists. The 10 pleasant if spartan rooms have fans and spacious private baths with hot water. The hotel has a small pool and a breezy restaurant, plus indoor parking. Upper rooms have balconies. Rates: $35 d, including tax ($7 each additional person).

The venerable **Hotel Tioga** (Apdo. 96, Puntarenas 5400, tel. 661-0271, fax 661-0127) has 45 rooms surrounding a pleasing but very compact courtyard with tiny swimming pool graced by its own tiny palm-shaded island. Air-conditioned rooms vary in size. Some have cold water. Rates include breakfast in the fourth-floor restaurant, with views over the gulf. Rates: $30-40 s, $40-55 d.

Hotel Las Brisas (Apdo. 83, Puntarenas 5400, tel. 661-4040) is a modern hotel near the end of Paseo de las Turistas. The 19 spacious rooms with a/c are clean. Some rooms face the Gulf of Nicoya but, though adequate, are spartan and soulless. Cold water. The hotel has an open-air bar and restaurant, plus a small pool. The owner is multilingual and friendly (though I found him rather ingratiating). Rates: $25-35 s, $30-45 d. Also on Paseo de las Turistas, at Calles 3/5, is **Hotel Oasis del Pacífico** (tel. 661-0209, fax 661-0745), a Tico favorite with 18 funky-looking cabins and an open-air restaurant and disco under thatch, plus pool. Rates: $25 s, $35 d.

Club de Playa San Isidro (Apdo. 4674, San José 1000, tel. 221-1225, fax 263-0031) and the slightly newer **Villas del Mar/Las Chalets** (Apdo. 1287, San José 1000, tel. 663-0150), are really the same complex, on opposite sides of the road five km east of downtown in the San Isidro suburb. The 50 two-bedroom cabinas (they sleep up to eight) with rather grubby kitchens and small bathrooms are set in shady and pleasingly landscaped grounds and are laid out military-barrack style. Newer units are of a higher standard. Scattered around the complex are five pools, a volleyball court, and soccer and basketball courts. Supposedly, the place is part of the Costa Rican Youth Hostel Association. Also here are a children's playground and pool. Rates: $45 for four, $62 for six, $82 for nine.

Casa Canadiense (Apdo. 125, Puntarenas, tel./fax 663-0287) offers self-contained units, plus a pool. It's a few hundred meters west of the Hotel Fiesta. Not reviewed.

The **Yacht Club** (Apdo. 2530, San José 1000, tel. 661-0784, fax 661-2518), next to Portobello a few km south of town, offers accommodation

for yachters and others in 28 rooms with a/c, private baths, and hot water. There's an open-air restaurant-cum-bar, plus a pool spanned by a bridge. Often full. You may find a vacancy on a space-available basis, especially on weekdays. Rates: $31 d standard, $41 with a/c.

Upscale

Hotel Fiesta (Apdo. 171, Puntarenas 5400, tel. 239-4266 or 239-4205, fax 239-0217 or 663-1516; in the U.S., tel. 800-662-2990; in Canada, tel. 800-264-1952) is an attractive large-scale resort complex at San Isidro, five km east of downtown. The 174 rooms are spacious and elegantly furnished, with a/c and satellite TV. Also offered are five master suites, 120 junior suites in a new (rather soulless) wing, plus the opulent presidential suite, and two excellent restaurants and a seafood bar. The massive El Mastil bar is shaped like an old square-rigged schooner. An immense and beautiful free-form swimming pool with island bar, plus two other sizeable pools (one with Jacuzzi jets), are surrounded by expansive grounds with volleyball and tennis courts. At the end of the day you can rouse yourself from the day's poolside torpor and try your hand with Lady Luck in the casino (gamblers get free drinks) before hitting the disco. Lately added is a private pier where guests can enjoy sea kayaking, windsurfing, scuba diving, or jet skiing. There's even an a/c gym. The resort caters to families (there are kiddies activities throughout the day) and is very popular with Ticos who know a good thing when they see it. Not for those seeking serene sanctuary, but a great choice for the gregarious. Rates (s/d): $99 standard, $109 deluxe, $109-119 suites, $155 junior suite (six people), $350 presidential suite (six people). A "Green Season Deluxe Special" (from $369 pp) includes three nights' acccommodation at Cariari or Corobicí hotels in San José, three nights at the Fiesta, plus transfers, breakfasts, and taxes.

Hotel Yadran (Apdo. 14, Puntarenas 5400, tel. 661-2662, fax 661-1944), at the tip of the peninsula, is as pretty as it is breezy. Its superb location provides views across the bay to Nicoya. The 42 double rooms have private baths, hot water, a/c, cable TV, and balconies or verandas. The hotel has two small pools, plus an upstairs restaurant with vistas across the gulf.

Some rooms face the estuary. The hotel features its own discotheque and sailboat. Pricey. Rates: $95 d, including tax; $110 upstairs.

Hotel Colonial (Apdo. 368, Puntarenas, tel. 661-1833, fax 661-2969), facing the estuary at Cocal, three km east of downtown, has a Spanish colonial feel. The 82 modestly decorated rooms have a/c, balconies, and hot water. There's live mariachi music on weekends in El Bambú restaurant, plus a delapidated tennis court, a pleasing pool, mini-golf, and a dock for yachts. Lots of shade trees. Rate: $60 d, including breakfast and tax.

Hotel Portobello (Apdo. 108, Puntarenas, tel. 661-1322, fax 661-0036), next door to the Colonial, has 35 nicely decorated high-ceilinged rooms with a/c and private baths with hot water. Private patios and balconies open onto lush grounds with a nice pool beneath shade trees. A pleasing restaurant serves grilled meats and seafoods. The Italian owners hauled in tons of sand to create an artificial beach. Rates: $58 d, $70 t.

Apartments and Condominiums

Condominio Marola (tel. 253-0007), in the residential area known as San Isidro, 800 meters west of Hotel Fiesta, is a new condominium complex with Western-style houses 50 meters from the beach. **Apartamentos Jacob** (tel. 661-0246) has very basic and small "tourist apartments"; monthly rates preferred.

FOOD

You're sure to find something that appeals along Paseo de las Turistas. One of the best restaurants in town is the highly regarded **La Caravelle** (Calles 19/21), a very pleasant wood-paneled restaurant with outside terrace, serving French cuisine. Closed Monday and Tuesday. Next door is the **Bierstrube Beer Tavern** (tel. 661-0330), where a huge beam-ceilinged room tries to replicate the beer halls of Munich. Also nearby are **Restaurant La Mazorca,** with a lively bamboo bar at the back; the open-air, touristy **Restaurant Aloha** (tel. 661-0773); and the charming **La Casa de los Mariscos,** serving good seafood and open to the beach. For Italian seafood, try the **Restaurant Miramar,** on the

waterfront at Calles 17/19. There's no shortage of Chinese restaurants, highlighted by **Chung San Restaurant** (tel. 661-0068), one block east of Parque Victoria. Cheap *sodas* abound near the Central Market and along the Paseo de las Turistas, between Calles Central and 3. **Bar Mar-Marina Restaurant** (tel. 661-3064), on the second floor, 50 meters east of the ferry terminal and handy for a meal if you're catching the ferry, serves Spanish paella and Costa Rican seafood specialties (open 6 a.m.-8 p.m.). **Restaurante Italiano La Terraza,** in a pretty wooden building painted yellow, has been recommended.

ENTERTAINMENT

In summer, concerts and plays are put on at the Casa de la Cultura. You'll find a couple of **discos,** including at Hotel Yadran, and at the Oasis del Pacífico on Paseo de las Turistas. There's also a Saturday night disco-party at Hotel Colonia. The **Cine Central** shows movies in English; and **Cinema del Pacífico,** at Avenida 1, Calles 4/6, shows movies in Spanish. Otherwise, the local bars provide plenty of color—guard against pickpockets! By day you can swim at **Balneario Municipal,** the public swimming pool set amid lawns on Paseo de las Turistas at the end of the peninsula. Hours: Tues.-Sun. 9 a.m.-4:30 p.m. ($1, 50 cents children).

SERVICES

La Cámara Puntarenense de Turismo (tel. 661-1985), which offers local tourist information, is in the Casa de la Cultura on Avenida Central and Calle 3. You can call AT&T US-ADirect here. The **Costa Rican Tourism Institute** (ICT, tel. 223-1733) has an office at Avenida 4, Calles 5/7.

Banks include Banco Nacional (Avenida Central, Calle Central, tel. 661-0233), Banco Anglo Costarricense (Avenida 3, Calles 1/3), and Banco de Costa Rica (Calle Central, Avenida 3, tel. 661-0444). The **post office** is 50 meters south and 50 meters west of the Casa de la Cultura. Coopepuntarenas (tel. 663-0053, 663-1635) offers **taxi** service. **Discovery Rent-a-Car** (tel. 661-0328) and **Elegante Rent-a-Car**

PUNTARENAS EMERGENCY TELEPHONE NUMBERS

All emergencies	911
Coast Guard	661-1859
Police	117 or 661-0640, 661-0740
Red Cross	661-0184
Hospital (Monseñor Sanabria)	663-0835
Immigration	661-1446
Coast Guard	661-1859

(tel. 661-1958; opposite Banco Nacional) have offices here. **Sportfishing Costa Rica** (tel. 255-0791 or 661-0697) offers fishing tours. Cyclists can find supplies at **Ciclo Gaby** (tel. 661-0348).

Medical
The **Monseñor Sanabria Hospital** (tel. 663-0033) is eight km east of Puntarenas, in the suburb of San Isidro. There's a branch hospital at Paseo de las Turistas and Calle 9. **Farmacia Andrea** (tel. 661-2866, fax 661-1438) is at Avenida 1, Calle 1 (hours: 7 a.m.-9 p.m.); **Farmacia Central** (tel. 661-0361) is at Calle Central and Avenida Central.

TOURS

Several cruise companies offer popular day-trips across the Gulf of Nicoya to Tortuga Island and lesser-visited islands. Cruises generally include buffet luncheon and several hours at palm-shaded Tortuga Island, plus roundtrip transfers from San José. **Calypso Cruises** (Apdo. 6941, San José 1000, tel. 233-3617, fax 233-0401; or Apdo. 138, Puntarenas, tel. 661-0585) originated day cruises aboard its motor yacht *Calypso;* today it operates Tortuga Island trips aboard the 21-meter *Manta Ray,* a space-age catamaran that goes like the wind ($84 day-tour)! The venerable *Calypso* now operates cruises further afield. The company's office—a former beach house used to tan shark skins—is at Calle 66, near the Hotel Colonial. See "Cruises/Yachting" under "Special-interest Travel and Recreation" in the On the Road

chapter for more details, including other cruise-tour companies (also see "Tortuga Island" under "The East Coast" in the Nicoya Peninsula chapter).

Pacific Ocean Winds (c/o Hotel Fiesta, tel. 663-0808, ext. 472) operates another high-tech catamaran, the *Lohe Lahi,* from the pier of the Hotel Fiesta. The 18-meter cat zips through two-hour cruises Wed.-Sat. at 11 a.m. and 1:30 and 4 p.m.

Fred's Folly offers sportfishing trips (tel. 288-2014; $275 per day for two people).

TRANSPORTATION

By Bus:
Buses depart San José from Calle 16, Avenidas 10/12 (Empresarios Unidos, tel. 222-0064 in San José, 661-2158 in Puntarenas), daily every 40 minutes 6 a.m.-7 p.m. (direct), and at 7:30 a.m. and 9 p.m. (indirect, $2). Buses depart Puntarenas for San José from Calle 2 and Paseo de las Turistas. The indirect bus departs Puntarenas at 8 p.m. Buses can get horribly crowded.

Exotur (tel. 227-5169, fax 227-2180) has been slating a daily express bus service—the Silver Bullet—from San José. It wasn't in service at press time.

Buses depart Puntarenas from Calle 2 and Paseo de las Turistas for many destinations, including Tilarán at 11:30 a.m. and 4:30 p.m.; Monteverde at 2:15 p.m.; Jacó and Quepos at 5 and 11 a.m. and 2 p.m.; and Liberia at 6 and 9:30 a.m. and 5 p.m. Check times ahead.

By Air
You can charter an air-taxi to Chacarita Airport, east of town. There are no scheduled services.

By Ferry
The ferry from/to Playa Naranjo (tel. 661-1069), midway down the east coast of the Nicoya Peninsula, holds 50 vehicles and 500 passengers. It departs the tip of the Puntarenas peninsula (Avenida 3 and Calles 33/35) daily at 3:15, 7, and 10:50 a.m., and 2:50 and 7 p.m. (90 minutes). Return ferries run at 5:10 and 8:50 a.m., and 12:50, 5, and 9 p.m. Fares: $2 adult passenger; $3 motorbikes; $9 car and driver. A bus marked "Barrio Carmen" or "Ferry" travels along Avenida Central to the ferry terminal ($2). Get there early—two hours ahead is not unwise on weekends and holidays. Ferry times change, so check schedules in advance. Buses marked "Ferry" operate along Avenida Central to the Playa Naranjo ferry terminal.

The **La Paquereña ferry** (tel. 661-3034 or 661-2830) to Paquera, at the southeastern tip of the Nicoya Peninsula, departs daily at 4:15 and 8:45 a.m., and 12:30 and 5:30 p.m. from the Muelle Banana at Avenida 3 and Calle 9 ($1.50 passengers; $12 car and passenger). Return ferries depart Paquera at 6 and 10:30 a.m., and 2:30 and 7:15 p.m. Note that this once passengers-only ferry now takes cars, and that it no longer departs from the wharf on Calle 2.

There's also direct service to Montezuma (see "Montezuma" under "The East Coast" in the Nicoya Peninsula chapter). Taximar (tel. 661-0331 or 661-1143) also operates a **water-taxi** service ($40 per hour).

PUNTARENAS TO JACÓ

The highway south from Orotina and Puntarenas is in good condition as far as Carara. Beyond Carara, the paved road is riddled with some of the worst potholes in the country. *Drive slowly.* The holes are big enough to bend a rim.

PLAYA DE DOÑA ANA

At the southern end of Bahía de Caldera, two km toward Puerta Caldera along the coastal highway, is the Paradero Playas de Doña Ana, built by the Costa Rican Tourism Institute. The two beaches—Boca Barranca and Doña Ana—are the site of the Costa Rican world invitational surfing championships. You'll find a camping area, lockers, plus restaurant and bar. Entrance: 75 cents (plus 75 cents for parking).

Buses depart Puntarenas for Playa de Doña Ana hourly from the Central Market.

MATA DE LIMÓN

Amazingly, Mata, near Puerto Caldera about 15 km southeast of Puntarenas, was one of the country's original beach resorts, built on an estuary—the Boca del Caldera—surrounded by mangroves across from the port of Caldera. It is a reasonable surf spot, with good tubular waves at the jetty. Not my first choice for a beach vacation, but the mangrove swamps harbor scarlet macaws and alligators. You can charter a boat in the village to go birding and in search of caimans; Ringo Lastro at the Costa El Sol is a good source. A unstable wooden bridge leads across the estuary to another part of the village, where there are additional cabinas.

At press time, Mata was positioned to boom. A company called Pacific Banut S.A. was about to break ground on a $175 million **La Roca Beach Club and Country Resort**, a 215-hectare beachfront development to include 1,000 condominium apartments, a luxury hotel, a theme Spanish-colonial village complex that includes a four hectare center of shops and restaurants, plus a championship 27-hole golf course and 24 tennis courts. The course was scheduled to open for play in 1997, with nearly a dozen lakes plus signature holes overlooking the ocean. The first phase will involve 24 tennis courts, volleyball, basketball and racquetball courts, two swimming pools, a soccer field, and an equestrian center. Owners will be able to lease their condo apartments to vacationers.

Accommodations and Food
Hotel Viña de Mar (tel. 663-4030) is a budget option, just south of the footbridge. **Cabinas María Cecilia** has basic cabinas plus a small pool. Other budget accommodations include **Cabinas Las Santas** (tel. 441-0510), which has three bedrooms, and **Villas Fanny, Hotel Casablanca** (tel. 222-2921), and **Villas America**.

Restaurant La Lede overlooks the estuary on the north side of Puerto Caldera. **Restaurant Puerto Nuevo** is across the railroad tracks on the right, immediately as you enter the village. You'll see several other restaurants along the road and waterfront. **Costa El Sol** (tel. 654-4008) is the best.

Getting There
Buses pass Mata regularly en route to and from Puerto Caldera.

TIVIVES

Tivives has a pleasant and peaceful four-km-wide beach lined by vacation homes and surrounded by 670 hectares of mangrove swamps at the mouth of the Río Jesús María. The white mangrove here grows to a height of 35 meters. Good birding! Howler and white-faced monkeys live here. And jaguarundis and ocelots have even been sighted on the beach. You can reach the northern side of the estuary via a rough, eight-km-long dirt road from Caldera harbor. You can reach Tivives from the paved road to Orotina (nine km; follow the sign for Proyecto Vacacional Bajamar).

Two km south of Tivives is **Playa Guacalillo,** site of Proyecto Vacacional Bajamar, centered on the hamlet of Bajamar. The unremarkable gray-sand beach is backed by a lagoon full of wading birds. Alligators—toothy and fast—cool off in the mangroves, which stretch south to the mouth of the Río Tárcoles and Carara Biological Reserve.

Accommodations and Food

There's only one restaurant/bar, and no cabinas or hotels at Tivives. It's possible to camp at the southern end of the beach (no facilities).

Hotel Marazul (tel./fax 221-8070) is a new resort complex about 800 meters from Playa Guacalillo. It has 10 hotel rooms, plus 10 spacious self-catering units with lots of light (cabinas each sleep up to six people). Centerpiece is an Olympic-size pool and a large sundeck fronting a restaurant under thatch set in landscaped grounds. You can rent bikes and horses, or get a game going on a soccer field and tennis and volleyball courts. Rates: $50 d for rooms, $75 for self-catering units.

CARARA BIOLOGICAL RESERVE

Rainforest exploration doesn't come any easier than at Carara Biological Reserve, 20 km south of Orotina. The 4,700-hectare reserve borders the Pan-American Hwy., so you can literally step from your car and enter the last significant stand of primary forest of its kind on the Pacific coast.

Carara is unique in that it lies at the apex of the Amazonian and Mesoamerican ecosystems—a climatological zone of transition from the dry of the Pacific north to the very humid southern coast—and is a meeting place for species from both.

Carara was once part of the huge Finca La Coyola, one of the biggest haciendas in Costa Rica. The Cervantes family protected the area for generations before the land passed to the National Parks Service. The land was expropriated in 1977 as part of an agrarian resettlement program for landless *campesinos;* in April 1979, 4,700 hectares were pared off to form the reserve. This island in a sea of agriculture remains the only forested area of significance to

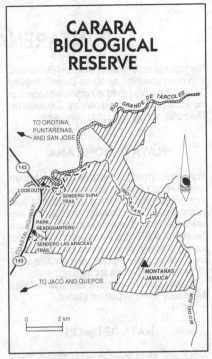

survive the deforestation that occurred early in colonial history in Costa Rica's Pacific northwest.

Carara protects evergreen forest of great complexity and density. The diversity of trees is one of the highest in the world; some of the most striking characteristics are the giant trees that stand out from the high canopy. The 10 rarest hardwoods in the country are here, as are some of the rarest and most spectacular animals of tropical America: American crocodile, great anteater, ocelot, spider monkey, and poison-arrow frog.

Carara is also one of the best birding localities in all Costa Rica. Fiery-billed aracari and toucan are common. Boat-billed herons, with their curious keel-shaped beaks, are common along the watercourses. And toward dusk, scarlet macaws—there are at least 40 breeding pairs—can be seen in flight as they migrate daily from the wet forest interior to the coastal mangrove

swamps. The bridge over the Río Tárcoles is a good place to spot them. The pulloff on the south side of the bridge (on the Pan-American Hwy.) is also the best place in the country for spotting crocodiles, which bask on the muddy banks. **Restaurante Eco Cocodrilo** is a pleasant *ranchita* where you can dine and sup while watching the crocs staring hungrily at the well-fed tourists staring down at the crocs from the bridge.

The name Carara is supposedly derived from the Huetar Indian name for "crocodile." Carara has numerous pre-Columbian archaeological sites: studies indicate 15 sites corresponding to different periods dating back at least 2,000 years.

The reserve was closed for a short period in 1993 because the National Parks Service did not have enough funds to employ staff. In an attempt to avoid despoilation, in 1994 the Park Service introduced a limit of 60 people at any one time on each of the two trails. Be prepared to wait to enter if the reserve is full when you arrive.

Note: If you come across a band of monkeys while hiking, stop! Be patient. It may take 30 minutes for them to pass by, one by one. After a while, other animals may appear in their wake—coatis, peccaries, agoutis—feasting on the fruit dropped by the monkeys. Silence is imperative.

Driest months are March and April. Bring insect repellent!

Information

The Quebrada Bonita Ranger Station (park headquarters) sits beside the Coastal Highway, three km south of the Río Tárcoles. You'll find picnic tables and restrooms here, plus Las Araceas Nature Trail, a one-km loop. Another short trail—4.5 km long—begins at the highway, two km north of Quebrada Bonita, and follows an old road paralleling the Río Tárcoles. The rest of Carara is off-limits. Entrance: $15 walk-in; $7 advance purchase. Camping is not allowed, although I've heard a rumor of camping facilities being installed.

Guides

You'll be amazed how much more wildlife you see in the company of an experienced guide. Of all the guides I've had as my teachers, Rudi Zamora—my guide at Carara—outshone them all. To walk in Carara with Rudi is to explore as if with David Attenborough. His engaging de-

scriptions are rich in imagery and imagination. He uses marvelous metaphors to explain the complex web of nature, and his theatrical passion will awaken the most docile. Book him if you can (Apdo. 347, Santa Ana 6150, San José, tel. 282-8538).

Tours

Most tour operators in San José arrange tours to Carara. **Geotur** (Apdo. 469 Y Griega, San José 1011, tel. 234-1867, fax 253-6338) specializes in tours to Carara.

Fantasy Tours (tel. 643-3231) arranges a "Jungle Crocodile Safari," a two-and-a-half-hour boat tour on the Río Tárcoles ($30, including drinks and snacks). No children under 12. The safari leaves from Cabinas y Restaurant la Guaria (tel. 661-0455), in Tárcoles. Departure times vary according to high tide. **J.D.'s Watersports** (tel. 669-0511, ext. 34), based at Punta Leona, also offers jungle river cruises.

Getting There

Take any bus between San José or Puntarenas and Jacó, Quepos, and Manuel Antonio (see relevant sections). They all pass by the reserve and will let you off. **Note:** Buses at weekends may be full. Saragundí Specialty Tours (tel. 255-0011, fax 255-2155) operates a daily **Pura Natura** tourist shuttle from San José, departing at 7 a.m. (departs Carara for San José at 5 p.m.), and continuing to Jacó and Manuel Antonio.

TÁRCOLES

Immediately west of Carara, hidden off the road, is the down-at-the-heels fishing village of Tárcoles, with a pebbly beach. Mangrove swamps, reached via a dirt road along the coast north of the village, extend 15 km northward to Punta Loros and the mouth of the Río Tárcoles, providing ample pleasure for birders. The turnoff for Tárcoles is two km south of the ranger station; turn left here (at the sign for Hotel Villa Lapas) for the Manantial de Agua Viva Waterfall.

Manantial de Agua Viva Waterfall

French Canadian Daniel Bedard has cut a three-kilometer trail that drops steeply to this spectacular 183-meter-high waterfall on his 70-

hectare property. There are *miradors* and benches for wildlife viewing. Side trails lead to natural pools good for swimming. Best time is rainy season, when the falls are giving it hell! They don't tumble in one great plume, like Angel Falls in Venezuela, but rather tumble down the rockface. Alas, the trail—a stiff 45-minute hike—is closed April through December. A water bottle and strong shoes are recommended. Entrance: $8 (tel. 236-4140, fax 236-1506). The entrance is on the dirt road that leads past Hotel Villa Lapas (see below). Bedard is building an eco-lodge near the top of the falls. You can get there via a bus from Orotina to Bijagual (departs 11:30 a.m.; returns from Bijagual at 5:30 p.m.), a small mountain village a few kilometers beyond the shack that marks the entrance to the waterfall trail. The bus will drop you at the "front gate."

Accommodations and Food

In Tárcoles, try the very simple **Cabinas El Dorado,** behind Bar El Dorado; **Cabinas y Restaurant la Guaria** (tel. 661-0455); and **Cabinas Villa del Mar** (tel. 661-2478), whose basic albeit adequate rooms for $25 d show that the law of supply and demand is in effect. One kilometer north, at Playa Tárcoles, is **Hotel El Parque,** with basic rooms for about $12.

Hotel Carara (formerly Las Palmas, tel. 661-0455) has 17 basic rooms, some with shared or private bath and fan or a/c. Rates: $20-35 d.

Nature Lodges

Hotel Villa Lapas (Apdo. 419, Ciudad Cariari, San José 4005, tel./fax 239-4104) is a nature lodge just outside Carara reserve (turn east opposite the turnoff for Tárcoles village). It has 48 clean and comfortable albeit stuffy cabinas with queen-size beds and private baths (10 have a/c), plus a restaurant/bar, swimming pool, and nature trails that lead into a 280-hectare private reserve of secondary forest bordering Carara. There's plenty of wildlife, including—in the restaurant—a free-flying macaw and toucan. Rates: $75 s/d, $83 t.

Not reviewed is **Tarcol Lodge** (tel./fax 239-7138), a birder's haven (heaven?) sitting behind the beach on the bank of the Río Tárcoles. It's affiliated with the Rancho Naturalista in Turrialba (see the Central Highlands chapter) and thereby geared to the nature-loving crowd. At

last count there were five rooms with shared bath in a two-story wooden lodge. Guests see scarlet macaws "migrating" each dawn and dusk. The lodge offers birding and nature tours. Rate: $85 per person. Multiday package rates include meals and guided nature hikes.

PLAYA MALO AND PUNTA LEONA

A series of small coves and beaches sheltered by shade trees lines the coast from Tárcoles south to the headland of Punta Leona. The most prominent is Playa Malo, a scenic cove with lots of little fishing boats popular with pelicans. The beach at Punta Leona, 10 km north of Jacó, is dominated by the planned resort of that name (see below).

Star Chaser

The sleek *Star Chaser*—the fastest commercial catamaran in the world—leaves from Playa Malo daily for an afternoon-'n'-sunset cruise that'll have you screaming for more ($49 at the boat; $79 including transfers from San José). The vessel is as sharp as a cut diamond and wide as a city block. You fly along with New Age music as a backdrop. When I sampled the wares on a moderately breezy day, we cut the waters at a crisp 13 knots. The vessel is so stable (perfect for landlubbers) you don't notice the warp-speed pace. It's a superb way to get a tan, feel the breeze in your hair, gain a different perspective of the coast, *and* have fun. Piña coladas, fruits, and snacks are served on board.

Star Chaser is operated by Calypso Cruises (Apdo. 6941, San José 1000, tel. 233-3617, fax 233-0401; or Apdo. 138, Puntarenas, tel. 661-0585). The owners are introducing a nighttime "star chaser's" cruise with a professional astronomer on board.

Accommodations and Food

Steve N' Lisa's Paradise Cove (tel. 228-9430), a breezy restaurant overlooking the beach, has great burgers, grilled chicken and tuna-melt sandwiches ($2), lobster ($12), fettucine ($4), and salads, and a whole lot more. Lisa—an American—oversees the kitchen herself. They rent four two-story oceanside cabinas—**Villa Lilly**—with kitchens, and **Paradise Cabinas**

VILLA CALETAS

Take a steep, 500-meter headland. Construct a Louisiana-style gingerbread Roman villa and self-contained matching *casitas* overlooking the sea. Surround each with sensuous, tropical greenery: bougainvillea, fuchsia for fragrance, palms, and Classical vases with cacti. Then add sublime decor, stunning museum pieces, and an aquarium a zoo would be proud of. The result is Hotel Villa Caletas (Apdo. 12358, San José 1000, tel. 257-3653, fax 222-2059), a glory in stone dreamed up and run by Denis Roy, an effusive Frenchman with an infectious *joie de vivre* and schoolboy charm. The hotel, two km south of Punta Leona, is the *best resort hotel in Costa Rica*. There's a chauffeur for airport transfers.

Centerpiece of this splendid, fabulously breezy oasis is the sensational, deep-blue "horizon" pool (filtered by ionization) and huge wooden deck suspended miraculously as if in midair. A whimsical waterfall adds its own fairytale note. It's the kind of set Hollywood might have come up with . . . or adopted. Which, I suspect, it just might.

Spacious public lounges in black, grays, and whites are graced with black wicker furniture, hand-painted terra-cotta tilework, tasteful turn-of-the-century paintings, Renaissance antiques, giant clam shells, and Oriental rugs, with hints of ancient Rome around every corner. You'll think you've entered the Louvre! *Vogue* magazine or *House Beautiful* could not have done better. No wonder: Denis was a professional interior designer for Arabian princes and the European elite. In Villa Caleta, he's displayed his exemplary aesthetic vision.

Eight huge, high-ceilinged, individually styled bedrooms vibrate with color. Each is done up in warm tropical peaches, papaya, and pinks, with antique-style beds, Japanese-style lampshades, floor to ceiling silk French curtains and bedspreads of Indian provenance, and verandas opening onto stunning ocean vistas. No TVs or a/c. Twenty separate bungalows (including two junior suites and a suite) follow the theme. Wall-to-wall mirrored bath-rooms have minimal shelving, and at press time the bungalows were without telephones or room service (some, being a hefty hike up and down pathways lined with natural stone walls, desperately need both), although I'm told these are in the works.

A splendidly skilled chef and no-expense-spared kitchen guarantee ambitious French cuisine a la Costarricense—*crevettes à l'anis* (shrimps in anise), *noix de marlin au citron* (marlin in lemon), *mousse de maranchaja* (passion fruit)—on a breezy open-air terrace that commands views across the Gulf of Nicoya. Cuisine occasionally reaches sublime heights. The menu changes daily ($20 lunch/dinner, average; breakfasts $9). Nonguests are welcome.

When I called by in April 1995 finishing touches were being made to a stunning Greek amphitheater complete with Corinthian columns set on the cliff-face as a setting for sunset jazz and classical concerts. Sublime! It is pure intoxication itself to gather at sunset with the breezes and tasteful music. One can almost imagine Apollo—the god of light par excellence—stepping onto the stage. A second restaurant, too, serving lighter food has been added.

A 4WD trail leads steeply down to lonesome Playa Caletas. It's a stiff hike without a vehicle, but a beach-shuttle service was to be introduced. Service, hit-and-miss on my first visit, remains so. I thought the bow-tied English-speaking waiters were prompt, courteous, and mustard-keen to please (as did other guests) on my last visit, but a fellow travel writer thought the service "appalling" (she also was unimpressed by the decor and amenities, which I admit are few, and the bugs, which I admit are many). A boutique sells only the finest quality ceramics and jewelry.

I overheard one guest say, "we're coming back, and we're bringing friends." Another exclaimed, "you can't help but be happy here; it's so wonderful!" To experience the contrast between the spectacular and the intimate is a special pleasure. Book now! Rates: $115 s/d, $136 bungalows.

(both are $15 per person) overlooking Playa Malo. They also have eight cabins in Jacó. They also run a souvenir ship, tourist information service, and sportfishing service. You'll pass a couple of other attractive *ranchita* restaurants further south.

A beachfront a/c home, **Casa del Mar** (tel. 288-2199), is for rent at Playa Agujas, just north of Punta Leona. It's signposted two km off the coast road.

Punta Leona (Apdo. 8592, San José 1000, tel. 231-3131 or 661-1414, fax 232-0791) is an ex-

pansive planned resort beside the ocean. The reception gate is just off the roadway three km south of Punta Malo. The road winds through a 300-hectare private nature reserve to the self-contained resort (what in England is called a "holiday camp"), until recently a private club. You can follow mountain trails into the forest, with occasional views over the fabulous bays fringed by white-sand beaches. An **RV and camping** area is right beside the scalloped, 800-meter-wide beach; 73 more expensive apartments, plus Selvamar, a large bungalow complex, are five minutes' walk away. The 108 a/c bungalows and rooms are modern and spacious, with TV and very large showers. Modest cabañas are also an option. A small bar fronts a large kidney-shaped swimming pool and sunning area. The resort also has a small discotheque and a children's video arcade. Particularly good for families. Popular with Ticos. **J.D.'s Watersports** (tel. 669-0511, ext. 34) is on site and offers sportfishing, sunset cruises, and diving aboard its 44-foot Striker, *Resourceful.* Rates: $107 condominiums, $78 cabañas, $49-98 chalets, $93-122 bungalows.

PLAYA HERRADURA

South of Punta Leona the road climbs steeply before dropping down to Playa Herradura. At the crest of the rise is the entrance to **Villa Caletas,** my choice as the best resort hotel in Costa Rica (see special topic).

About seven km north of Jacó, just beyond the Río Caña Blanca, is a turnoff for Playa Herradura. I find its gray-sand beach appealing. It is swarmed by litter-*un*conscious Ticos on weekends on holidays. For now—but surely not for long—marine turtles come ashore to lay their eggs July-December. The beach recently gained attention as a film set for the movie *1492,* starring Gerard Depardieu as Columbus and Sigour-

ney Weaver as Queen Isabella. (Even Columbus's departure from Spain was filmed at Playa Herradura, at sunset along the jetty in front of a false-front palace.) Filming lasted about 10 weeks and pumped an estimated $8 million into the local economy. More than 150 local indigenous people played the parts of native Indians (extras were paid $15 a day; women who appeared topless received $45); another 350 locals were hired for on-site work constructing a cathedral and a replica Indian village.

Accommodations

Bay y Cabinas Herradura (tel. 643-3144) is on the left, at the turnoff for the beach. **Cabinas Romance** (tel. 643-3689) has simple cabins midway between the Pan-Am Hwy. and the beach. **Cabinas Herradura** (tel. 643-3181) has basic but large beachfront *casitas* with kitchenettes, fans, and private baths with cold water. Rate: $30. It also operates sportfishing through **Herradura Bay Charters** ($425 per day, four people). **Cabañas del Río** (tel. 643-3029 or 643-3275) has pleasing little self-catering cabins with verandas and twin bedrooms upstairs, raised on stilts set back from the beach. You'll also see four cabinas with fans and private baths on the coast road, half a kilometer beyond the turnoff for Playa Herradura.

A huge upscale condominium and villas complex, **Los Sueños Resort,** was under construction.

Camping

Ticos pour onto the beach at holidays with their tents, which they erect anywhere there's space; much of the detritus is theirs. **Campamento Playa Herradura** (tel. 221-4491), 200 meters from the beach, has campsites and bathrooms ($2 per person). The lively **Bar La Puesta del Sol,** midway down the beach, has a large camping area with bathrooms.

JACÓ

Jacó is the closest beach resort to San José and therefore popular with Josefinos as well as backpackers, surfers, and the North American beach-party crowd. It's the country's most developed beach area, with accommodations to suit every taste and a full panoply of tour and transportation options and heaps of boutiques found at popular resorts worldwide. I've never understood its appeal. Jacó has been particularly popular with Canadian charter groups: on prior visits lots of Canadian flags flew in tribute to the power of the maple-leaf dollar. But few Canadians were in evidence in early 1995. It looks as if they've wisely moved on for better things. Nature abhors a vacuum . . . and so do empty hotels, now occupied by Ticos. The three-km-long beach is not particularly appealing, and swimming is discouraged: signs warn of dangerous rip currents. Everything lines the single main street, which parallels the beach. If peace and quiet are your thing, give Jacó a wide berth.

Businesses are fluid in Jacó, and many boutiques etc. mentioned here are likely to have closed their doors or moved to new locations by the time you read this.

Surfing
A series of beaches and rivermouths south of Jacó are famous in surfing lore, including Playa Hermosa (known as "Boom Boom Beach" to the locals), site of an annual international surfing contest. Esterillos Oeste and Esterillos Este are equally popular. A chap called Chuck does surfboard repair, including 24-hour fin repair; he also offers a surf report, board rentals, and lessons. His house is down the side road leading to Hotel Copacabana. He has funky cabinas. **Safari Surf Shop** sits at the southern end of the beach, opposite Hotel Marapaíso.

ACCOMMODATIONS

Prices in Jacó tend to be higher than elsewhere on the coast. Many hotels are overpriced. Look at standards as much as prices. Many units are self-catering. Consider the wet ("green") season, when discounts are offered. Reservations are virtually essential over Easter and weekends in dry season. Many hotels offer surfers' discounts.

Budget
Cabinas Antonio (tel. 643-3043), adjacent to Restaurante La Fragata, is a popular bargain for budget travelers, with 11 rooms with private baths, fans, and cold water from $10. **Cabinas Emily** (tel. 643-3328) is also a good budget option popular with surfers. Rates: $11 shared bath, $16 with private bath.

Cabinas Alice (tel. 643-3061) has 22 motel-style rooms. Older rooms are basic. Five newer rooms with kitchens and hot water are far more pleasant (by the week only). Large mango trees shade a popular tiny open-air restaurant. Rates: $15 for four people, cold water; $35 with kitchens and hot water.

Others include **Cabinas El Recreo** (tel. 643-3012), which has basic cabinas with private baths with cold water. Rate: $15. **Cabinas La Sirena** (tel. 643-3193, fax 235-4310) has nine rooms with fans and private baths with cold water. It looks pleasant enough. Rate: $30 for five people. **Cabinas Cindy** has basic rooms with private baths with cold water. A sign reads *Perro Bravo:* "Beware of the Dog." Rate: $10. **Cabinas Garcia** (tel. 643-3191) has 16 small roadfront cabinas with private baths with cold water. Soulless. Rate: $15. **Cabinas Heredia** (tel. 643-3131) has bunk beds; not inspected. Also to consider (but not reviewed) are **Cabinas Karilyn** (tel. 643-3215); and **Cabinas Los Balcones** (recognized by its logo—Captain Haddock from the Tintin cartoons). (This might otherwise be known as the **Hotel Balcón del Mar**—tel. 643-3251, fax 283-2283.)

Reports are that the Hotel Marapaíso (see "Moderate Hotels," below, tel. 221-6544) operates a hostel for $9 (members; $15 nonmembers). **Hospedaje Canguro** ("Kangaroo"), near Restaurante Peruano, is also a budget hostel.

Places of last resort include: **Cabinas Las Brisas** (very unclean; reportedly, the house has been ordered closed by the health inspectors); **Cabinas Las Tres Marías,** also very funky;

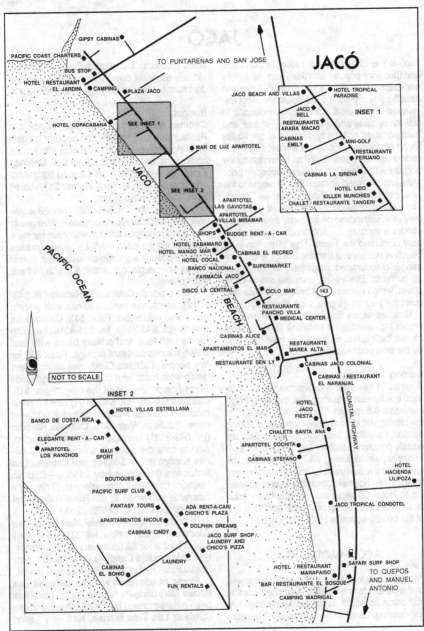

JACÓ

TO PUNTARENAS AND SAN JOSE

PACIFIC OCEAN

NOT TO SCALE

INSET 1

GIPSY CABINAS
PACIFIC COAST CHARTERS
BUS STOP
HOTEL / RESTAURANT
EL JARDIN
CAMPING
PLAZA JACO
HOTEL COPACABANA
SEE INSET 1
MAR DE LUZ APARTOTEL
SEE INSET 2

JACO BEACH AND VILLAS
HOTEL TROPICAL PARADISE
JACO BELL
RESTAURANTE ARARA MACAO
CABINAS EMILY
MINI-GOLF
RESTAURANTE PERUANO
CABINAS LA SIRENA
HOTEL LIDO
KILLER MUNCHIES
CHALET / RESTAURANTE TANGERI

APARTOTEL LAS GAVIOTAS
APARTOTEL VILLAS MIRAMAR
SHOPS
BUDGET RENT-A-CAR
HOTEL ZABAMARO
HOTEL MANGO MAR
CABINAS EL RECREO
HOTEL COCAL
BANCO NACIONAL
SUPERMARKET
FARMACIA JACO
DISCO LA CENTRAL
CICLO MAR

143

RESTAURANTE PANCHO VILLA
MEDICAL CENTER
CABINAS ALICE
RESTAURANTE MAREA ALTA
APARTAMENTOS EL MAR
RESTAURANTE SEN LY
CABINAS JACO COLONIAL
CABINAS / RESTAURANT EL NARANJAL
HOTEL JACO FIESTA
CHALETS SANTA ANA
APARTOTEL COCHITA
CABINAS STEFANO
HOTEL HACIENDA LILIPOZA
JACO TROPICAL CONDOTEL
SAFARI SURF SHOP
HOTEL / RESTAURANT MARAPAISO
BAR / RESTAURANTE EL BOSQUE
CAMPING MADRIGAL
TO QUEPOS AND MANUEL ANTONIO

COASTAL HIGHWAY

JACO BEACH

INSET 2

HOTEL VILLAS ESTRELLANA
BANCO DE COSTA RICA
ELEGANTE RENT-A-CAR
APARTOTEL LOS RANCHOS
MAUI SPORT
BOUTIQUES
PACIFIC SURF CLUB
FANTASY TOURS
APARTAMENTOS NICOLE
ADA RENT-A-CAR /
CHICHO'S PLAZA
CABINAS CINDY
DOLPHIN DREAMS
JACO SURF SHOP /
LAUNDRY AND
CHICO'S PIZZA
CABINAS EL BOHIO
LAUNDRY
FUN RENTALS

Gipsy Cabinas; and Cabinas y Restaurante Clarita (tel. 643-3013), with basic and dingy waterfront rooms with fans and private baths with cold water.

Inexpensive

Cabinas y Restaurante El Naranjal (tel. 643-3006) has six clean and pleasing cabinas with fans and private baths; three cabins have hot water. Rates: $28 t, $38 quad.

The Belgian-owned Hotel y Restaurante El Jardín (tel. 643-3050) has seven rather dark rooms with fans and private baths with hot water. Highlights include a large pool in a tight but pleasing courtyard with coconut palms, and a small restaurant with excellent food cooked by a French chef. Live jazz on weekends. Rates: $35 d ($25 in winter), including breakfast.

Los Ranchos (tel./fax 643-3070) is popular with surfers, who receive a 20% discount. It has 12 rooms with kitchenettes and queen-size beds from $35, larger cabins with kitchenettes from $50, and upstairs rooms for $25, all with private baths with hot water. There's a pool, plus laundry service. The Disco Papagayo next door cranks out decibels to wake the dead.

Cabinas Las Palmas (Apdo. 5, Jacó, tel. 643-3005) has 23 rooms with private baths with hot water, surrounded by a small garden. Older rooms are dark; newer rooms are slightly nicer. Most rooms have two doubles; some have kitchenettes and laundry sinks. Rates: cabins from $25; rooms with kitchenettes, $35.

Restaurant y Cabinas El Flamboyant has 18 cabinas with private baths and fans ($20), plus apartamentos with kitchens, fans, and cold water ($38 for four) in landscaped grounds. The beachfront restaurant is pleasing.

Restaurant y Chalet Tangerí (Apdo. 622, Alajuela, tel. 643-3001, fax 42-1160) has 10 three-bedroom cabinas, plus three apartments with kitchens in pleasing landscaped grounds (weekly rentals preferred). There's a bar and restaurant, plus a small swimming pool in the neatly manicured grounds. Good bargain. Rate: $35 for up to four people.

Also try Cabinas Gaby (tel. 643-3080, fax 441-5922); approximately $30 for rooms with private baths with hot water and fans, $40 for self-catering units. Chalets Santa Ana (tel. 643-3233) has 10 simple rooms with private baths with hot water. Rate: $35. Cabinas Pacific Sur (tel. 643-3340) has simple cabinas with private baths with cold water and fans. They're clean but pricey at $25. And Cabinas La Cometa (tel. 643-3615), opposite Villas Miramar, has 12 modern, clean, pleasing rooms. Rate: $30 d.

Cabinas El Bohio (tel. 643-3017) reportedly has eight funky beachfront cabinas with private baths with cold water ($16), plus seven apartments with kitchenettes ($35). The thatched restaurant and bar has a very loud sound system. The Hotel Lido is soulless, cramped, basic, and overpriced ($25). Rooms have private baths with cold water, plus kitchenette (alas, no refrigerators). There's a small pool.

Cabinas Jacó Colonial (tel. 643-3359) is a new, Spanish colonial-style structure with 10 rooms. Rate: $30 d. Not inspected. Two other unknowns are Casa de las Cuadraciclos (tel. 643-3035), which bills itself as a bed and breakfast in the center of town; and Cabinas Mar del Plata (tel. 643-3580).

Moderate

Hotel y Restaurante Marapaíso (Apdo. 6699, San José 1000, tel. 221-6544, fax 221-6601) is a pleasant if older and somewhat run-down colonial-style property with a swimming pool and Jacuzzi. Rooms are a bit dowdy. The place smelled strongly of grilled fish! Rooms are at the back, away from the beach; they have private baths with cold water. It's popular with Ticos. Rates: $45 s, $55 d.

Zabamaro Hotel (tel./fax 643-3174), owned by American Ed Morse, is very popular with surfers. Its 20 very clean and modern cabins (10 with fans; 10 with a/c) have hammocks on the patios; some have refrigerators. The hotel has a swimming pool and a small bar and restaurant under thatch. Rates: $30 s, $35 d, $40 t, $45 for four; or $45 s, $50 d with a/c.

Also to consider is Jacó La Costa (tel. 643-3465). Not reviewed.

Upscale

Hotel Jacó Fiesta (Apdo. 38, Jacó, tel. 643-3147, fax 643-3148; or in the U.S. 800-327-9408, fax 407-588-8369) is a somewhat sterile upscale resort whose 80 rooms with a/c and cable TV surround a pleasing pool and tennis court. It's 200 meters from the beach at the mouth of a small river. You can't miss it. It now wears a hideous facade; when you see the pink-

and-turquoise architectural carbuncle you'll understand. The landscaped grounds lack shade trees. It was popular with Canadian charter groups. Rates: $289 s, $219 d per person for a three-night package.

Jacó Beach Hotel & Casino (Apdo. 262, San José 1000, tel. 220-1441 or 800-CR-BOOK-H, fax 232-3159; in the U.S., c/o Costa Rica Fantasy Travel, tel. 800-832-9449, fax 305-871-6631) offers 160 a/c rooms. Superior rooms have TVs and refrigerators. A TV in the lobby pipes in 24-hour CNN. Amenities include El Muelle restaurant and bar, a discotheque, car rental, a swimming pool, a floodlit tennis court, plus a volleyball court, mopeds, bicycles, sailboats, sea kayaks, and surfboard rentals. Daily transportation to and from the Hotel Irazú in San José. Bargain, but double-check rates. Rates: $65-80 s, $65-90 d, $65-96 t.

Hotel Copacabana (tel./fax 643-3131), 100 meters west of Restaurant La Hacienda, metamorphosed from a disco and though now a hotel remains popular with the party crowd. It has 30 pool-side standard rooms, each with one double bed and single bed (it also claims "ocean-front" rooms, but this is stretching the truth; only the public facilities are ocean-front). Beautiful, spacious suites with kitchenette (some with a/c) sleep five. Hardwoods abound. And lively tropical murals dance on the walls. The hotel boasts a pool with swim-up bar, restaurant specializing in Italian cuisine, and a sports bar with TV that can remain lively into the wee hours. Weekends, live jazz and rock 'n' roll bands play. Sleep? Are you crazy! The hotel's own "Sunset Booze Cruise" weaves a liquidy course to sea at 3 p.m. Rates: $68 d ($78 with a/c), $108 suite, including breakfast. Overpriced!

Hotel Club del Mar (tel./fax 643-3194), nestled beneath the cliffs at the very southern end of Jacó, has 10 tasteful cabin-suites with kitchenettes, living rooms, and private sea-view balconies surrounded by pretty landscaped grounds and lots of palms. American owners Philip and Marilyn Edwardes also offer eight rooms with two queen beds. They have a souvenir shop, a small pool and sunning deck, and the breezy Las Sandalias restaurant. You can rent bicycles and boogie boards. Rates: $57 d, $77.50 with a/c, $108 suite; low season rates (May-Nov.) are 40% less.

If you were wondering what that red-tile-roofed little village was dominating the view toward Jacó as you drop down from Punta Leona, its **Las Villas Tropical Paradise Condominios** and **Condo-Villas Paradise Hotel and Resort** (tel. 296-2022, fax 296-2023, or tel. 643-3211 for the condominiums; in the U.S., tel. 305-861-2501 or 800-277-6123, fax 305-864-7487), which together form a reclusive but rather soulless enclave in the heart of town. Little *ranchitas* and pools and bars and a Jacuzzi are scattered about this huge complex of 153 one-, two- and three-bedroom a/c apartments with kitchens and satellite TV. Rates: from $75 d, $89 t, $103 t; six-night packages from $136.

Hotel Cocal (tel. 643-3067, fax 643-3082) is very elegant, intimate, and appealing. The Spanish hacienda-style hotel was popular with Canadian charter groups: book early to avoid disappointment. Arched porticos grace 26 spacious rooms surrounding a courtyard with two pools and a bar. Hot and cold water, private bath, and fan. An upstairs restaurant overlooking the beach serves international cuisine; there's a small downstairs restaurant too, along with a small casino. German-owned. No children. Recommended. Rates: $44 (a/c, $5 extra).

Hotel Tangerí (Apdo. 622, Alajuela 4050, tel. 643-3001) has rooms with a/c and private baths with hot water. It shares a swimming pool with the chalets of the same name. Rooms have refrigerators. Pricey. Rate: $85 d.

Hotel Pochote Grande (Apdo. 42, Jacó, Puntarenas, tel. 643-3236) has 24 attractive beachfront rooms in shaded grounds with a pool. Rooms have kitchenettes, plus private baths with hot and cold water. Rate: $55.

At **Hacienda Uzite Jacó** (tel. 643-3404, fax 643-3284), opposite the Texaco gas station, are magnificent thatched, three-bedroom, two-bath castlelike villas seemingly inspired by Finca Rosa Blanca (see special topic "Finca Rosa Blanca" in the Central Highlands chapter). Each has a little pool and outside veranda. Rate: $500 per week.

Deluxe

Hotel Hacienda Lilipoza (Apdo. 15, Jacó 4023, tel. 643-3062, fax 643-3158) offers 20 hacienda-style units amid beautiful and expansive landscaped grounds on a slope about 600 meters from the coast road and half a kilometer from the

beach. Each individually decorated room has two double beds, a/c, and a large TV. Some are done in wicker, some in modern Tudor style. Voluminous bathrooms have twin sinks, reclining bathtubs, and bidets. Some have Jacuzzis. Spacious closets. A Swiss chef conjures international dishes at the Banyan Bar Restaurant. Other highlights are a tennis court, and a small swimming pool with a bar and barbecue arena screened by tall trees, many festooned with epiphytes. Very tranquil and secluded.

The hotel rents mopeds and cars, and has a shuttle bus into Jacó. Rate: $167 including breakfast and dinner.

Apartments and Villas

Jacó Princess Villas (tel. 220-1441 or 800-CR-BOOK-H, fax 232-3159; in the U.S., c/o Costa Rica Fantasy Travel, tel. 800-832-9449, fax 305-871-6631) has 28 deluxe villas for five people. Each has a large bathroom, dining and living rooms, a terrace, and a kitchenette. There's a swimming pool. Rates: $78-99.

Apartotel Las Gaviotas (tel. 643-3092, fax 643-3054) has 12 units with patios, kitchenettes, a/c, fans, and private baths with hot water. Rate: $60. **Casas de Playa Mar Sol** (tel. 643-3008) has rooms with kitchens, fans, and private baths with cold water. Rate: $35. **Apartamentos El Mar** (tel. 643-3165) has 12 well-furnished units built in a C shape around a tiny pool and garden. Clean and spacious rooms have kitchens, plus private baths with hot water. Rate: $60.

Apartotel Villas Miramar (Apdo. 18, Jacó, tel. 643-3003) has 12 pleasing rooms with kitchens, fans, and hot water set in landscaped grounds 50 meters from the beach. Rates: $35 d, $42 t. The French-owned and rather dowdy **Hotel Villas Estrellana** (Apdo. 33, Playa Jacó, tel. 643-3102 or 643-3702) has 24 cabinas with kitchens with a/c, each with a refrigerator and a stove, plus one double and one single bed. Set in large landscaped grounds. The hotel has a pool and a small bar. Popular with an older crowd. Rate: $55 t. A recent addition is **Apartotel El Cisne** (tel. 643-3395), with ten fully equipped rooms 100 meters north and 150 meters east of the Banco Nacional.

Apartotel Catalina (tel. 643-3217, fax 643-3544) recently opened with "new rooms with kitchenettes plus private bath, patio or balcony." Also new is **Hotel Mango Mar** (tel./fax 643-

3670), in neoclassical Spanish colonial-style, with two apartments ($75) and 12 a/c rooms with kitchenette ($45 s, $50 d). Nice furnishings. It offers a pool with Jacuzzi and redbrick sun terrace, plus private parking. When all else fails, try the **Apartamentos Flamboyant,** next to Villas Miramar; the basic **Apartamentos Nicole** (tel. 643-3501), opposite Ada Rent-a-Car; the basic **Apartotel Los Ranchos** (tel. 643-3070); and the more salubrious **Mar de Luz Apartotel** (tel. 643-3259), **Apartotel Sol D'Oro,** and **Apartotel Cochita** (tel. 643-3589).

Camping
Camping Madrigal (tel. 643-3230), at the southern end of the beach, is a large, well-developed campground with picnic tables beneath shade trees about 100 meters from the beach ($2 per night). It has toilets and showers. Madrigal also has a few grubby cabinas with private baths and cold water ($10). Alternately, try **El Hicaco** (tel. 643-3004), offering oceanfront camping for $2 per person and RV space from $3.50 a night. It has bathrooms, plus an open-air restaurant and a disco next door. **Tropical Camping** offers showers, picnic tables, and shady lawns for camping ($3). Another campsite sits opposite Hotel El Jardín, at the northern end of the beach, and you'll find another site on the side road behind Restaurante Peruano.

FOOD

A favorite rustic eatery is **Killer Munchies** serving just that, as well as great pizza. Within earshot is **Capitan Cococ's,** good for seafood. Another good option is **Restaurant Peruano,** serving paella ($6), *arroz chaufa especial* ($5), *lomito saltido* ($5) and other Peruvian dishes in a shady patio setting. **Restaurante Arara Macao** has a European menu and a rustic thatched setting. **Bar/Restaurante La Hacienda** is a very popular *marisquería* serving seafoods. **Restaurante La Fregata** also has splendid seafood, while **Jungle Bar** is a rustic eatery serving grilled chicken and similar local fare from a *leña,* or wood-fired stove.

One of the best restaurants is **El Jardín,** in the hotel of the same name, serving highly regarded French cuisine on an ocean-view terrace. Reservations are recommended. **Restaurant Maris-**

quería **Los Manudos** is another favorite beachside restaurant with tremendous seafoods (Canadian charter groups often arrive en masse). Surf-n'-turf (steak and lobster) is a specialty of **La Hacienda** (tel. 643-3191), in the Rayito Celeste supermarket. Fancy some ribs? **Susie Q's BBQ** can oblige. In an Italian mood? Try **Ristorante Esperanza** (tel./fax 643-3332), dishing out pizzas and ice creams along with pastas and related fare. **Pizzeria Bribri** and **Chico's Pizza** both reportedly also have good pizzas, as does **Pizzeria Verona**. **El Bosque** (tel. 643-3009), on the highway south of Jacó, has been recommended for breakfast beneath shady mango trees. It's also popular for its seafood dishes and a local favorite, beef tongue in salsa. **Jaco Bell** offers Mexican food such as enchiladas, tostadas, and even steak and lobster under a thatched *palenque*. For Chinese, try **Restaurante Sen Ly**.

ENTERTAINMENT

Jacó has no shortage of bar action. Simply close your eyes and follow the noise. **Disco La Central** (tel. 643-3076), on the beach, is replete with flashing lights for John and Jane Travoltas. It's the travelers' choice; locals favor **Disco Papagayo**. Alternately, try the disco in the Hotel Jacó Fiesta (a little more dressy). If the woman of your dreams eludes you on the dance floor, you can try your hand with Lady Luck in the casinos of the Hotel Cocal (open 4 p.m.-3 a.m.) and Hotel Jacó Beach. **El Jardín** offers jazz. Surprisingly, there's no cinema. For more sedate pleasure, try **Mini-Golf de Jacó**, with 36 holes to keep you amused ($4 adults; $3 children)

SERVICES

Tours and Activities
Save the Rainforests Expeditions and School (tel. 643-3493) is a private nonprofit conservation and education group that offers whitewater rafting on the Nunawachi River, 43 km from Jacó, as well as other nearby rivers. Full-day $70. **Tropical Rainbow** (tel. 643-3151 or 233-8228, fax 255-4636) has placid "rafting safaris" on the Río Tulin, which boasts plenty of wildlife along its banks ($70).

Three operators whose future was uncertain include **Fantasy Tours** (tel. 643-3221 in Jacó,

tel. 220-0042 in San José), which offers tours to Carara and elsewhere, and also handles reservations for the *Star Chaser*, a large catamaran that offers afternoon and sunset cruises from Playa Malo. Likewise **Unicornio Ranch** (tel. 643-3211), which rents horses and offers horseback-riding excursions into the nearby forests; and **Viajes Jaguar** (tel. 643-3242), offering boat trips and scuba diving.

Pacific Coast Charters (tel. 643-3129), at the extreme north of Jacó, offers sportfishing charters. **Dolphin Dreams** (tel. 643-3510) offers snorkeling tours daily at 10 a.m., plus a half-day cruise aboard its 11-meter yacht. It also has a water-taxi service to various beaches, plus fishing ($45 per person).

Fun Rentals (Apdo. 28, Jacó, tel. 643-3242; in the U.S., tel. 800-780-2364) has a wide range of Yamaha scooters (from $15 first hour, $45 day, $150 week), mopeds (from $10 first hour, $30 day, $100 week), and mountain bikes for rent. It also offers sportfishing and scuba trips. The last rental of the day is at 5 p.m. for "sunset special" overnight rentals. You can rent four-wheel "bi"cycles with shade canopies at the **Casa de las Cuadraciclos;** and motorbikes and from **To'oy's** and bicycles (two wheels) from **Pinguis Ship,** both next to Restaurante Arara Macao. **Ciclo Mar** (tel. 643-3344) also offers bicycle rental, as does a shop next to Marisquería El Pelicano.

New Wave (tel. 643-3387), behind Restaurant Peruano, has a range of nature trips, including kayaking and hiking, plus a **water-taxi** to transport surfers to Playa Escondida. It also offers full **spa treatments** that include facials, massage, and even sunburn relief.

Souvenirs
Among the many boutiques is **Bali Batik,** selling quality clothing from Indonesia and elsewhere. A new shopping center—**Plaza Jacó**—has gone up opposite the Hotel Jacó Beach. And there's

even a trendy art gallery, **La Heliconia,** opposite La Piraña restaurant.

Other
Ada Rent-a-Car (tel. 233-7733), **Elegante Rent-a-Car** (tel. 643-33224), and **Budget Rent-a-Car** (tel. 643-3112 or 223-3284, fax 255-4966) all have offices. **Economy Rent-a-Car** (tel. 643-3147) has an office in the Hotel Jacó Fiesta.

Banco de Costa Rica and **Banco Nacional** (tel. 643-3072) are both in the town center. Expect long delays.

The **Red Cross** (tel. 643-3090) post is opposite Cabinas Alice. **Farmacia Jacó** (tel. 643-3205) can fulfill pharmaceutical needs. Hours are 8 a.m.-8 p.m. There's a **laundry** service in the same complex as Jacó Surf Shop, and another across the street. **Núcleo·Turístico Bribrí,** next to Pizzeria Bribrí, is a small ICT-built complex with showers, somewhat unclean bathrooms, and parking for day visitors. For taxis, call **Taxi Jacó** (tel. 643-3009) and **Taxi 30-30** (tel. 643-3030).

TRANSPORTATION

By Bus
Buses depart San José from Calle 16, Avenidas 1/3 (tel. 223-1109, 233-5567, or 643-3074) at 7:15 a.m. and 3:30 p.m. (two and a half hours). Alternatively, buses between San José and Quepos and Manuel Antonio stop at Restaurant El Bosque in Jacó. From Puntarenas, buses to Jacó and Quepos depart from near the train station at 5 a.m. and 2:30 p.m. Return buses depart Jacó for San José at 5 a.m. and 3 p.m., and for Puntarenas at 6 a.m. and 4 p.m., from the bus terminal at the north end of town. Buses are crowded on weekends—get there early!

Check with **Exotur** (tel. 227-5169, fax 227-2180) to see if it has reinstated its daily express bus service—the Silver Bullet.

A microbus operates from the Hotel Irazú in San José to its sister hotel, the Hotel Jacó Beach, departing San José daily at 9:30 a.m. (return, 2 p.m.; $12 one-way). Reservations are advised (tel. 232-4811), but note that hotel guests get priority.

Sarangundí Specialty Tours (tel. 255-0011, fax 255-2155) operates the **Pura Natura** tourist shuttle, departing San José at 7 a.m. ($14) and continuing to Manuel Antonio; the return bus departs Jacó for San José at 4 p.m. Another "Beach Shuttle" operated by **Dos Océanos** (tel. 282-8400, fax 282-2899) operates daily from San José ($15 one-way, $28 roundtrip).

Getting Around: Simple! Rent a scooter, mountain bike, or four-wheel "bi"cycles (see above). A shuttle bus operates between the Hotel Jacó Beach in the north and the Terraza del Pacífico, south of town at Playa Hermosa (southbound departures are at 9 and 10:30 a.m. and 2, 3:30, 5, and 7 p.m.; check times).

By Air
You can charter an air-taxi to the airstrip at the northern end of Jacó.

JACÓ TO QUEPOS

A string of fabulous beaches marches south from Jacó to Quepos. They're separated from one another only by the occasional mangrove swamp where rivers come down to the coast, and separated from the coast highway by ranchland and—farther south—by endless groves of African palms. Despite their beauty, these beaches are remarkably untrammeled by Man Friday footprints. If you fancy beach seclusion, this could be the place. You have several options for budget to moderate accommodations.

Drive slowly—the potholes are horrendous! South of Parrita, the road is so thick with dust in dry season that you need your headlamps on.

Violence flared in 1993 when local residents barricaded the road to protest the rotten road conditions. Consequently, a section of the road was paved. With luck, the rest will have been by the time you read this. Swimmers should beware of dangerous riptides.

PLAYA HERMOSA

The road south from Jacó crests a steep headland, beyond which Playa Hermosa comes into view, 10 km long and arrow straight with surf pummeling ashore along its whole length. The beach is the

setting for an international surfing championship each August. There's a pulloff atop the headland; the view through the trees is incredible, but don't get close to the unstable cliff edge! Access to the virtually undeveloped beach is at its northern end. The road cuts inland from here.

Accommodations and Food

At the extreme northern end of the beach is **Terraza del Pacífico** (Apdo. 168, Jacó, tel. 643-3222, fax 643-3424, or direct 643-3222, fax 643-3424; in the U.S., P.O. Box 31288, Raleigh, NC 27622, tel. 800-835-1223), a modern, upscale complex. This very appealing contemporary Spanish colonial-style property has a superb location, with cliffs immediately to the north and the vast expanse of beach disappearing into the distance to the south. The 43 rooms, including three suites, have a/c, satellite TVs, telephones, and sofa beds and double beds. A red-tiled causeway leads downhill through pretty landscaped grounds surrounding a beautiful, circular pool with a swim-up bar in the center. You'll also find a casino, and a restaurant and bar that open onto the beach. Sunbathing chairs are provided beneath tiny beach *ranchitas*. Super bargain! Rates: $65 s, $75 d, $85 t, $100 suite.

Nearby is **Hotel Villas Ballena** (tel. 225-7802), also very appealing for more modest budgets. Twelve spacious, fully furnished self-catering cabins, each complete with kitchen, one double and two single beds (some have two singles), are set in delightful landscaped grounds with a small pool in the shape of a whale. Only 50 meters from the beach. For nightlife, there's the **Bar Las Palmereños**, 100 meters north, on the coast road.

Cabinas Olas (tel./fax 643-3687), 200 meters south, is a modern two-story structure with kitchenettes in its pleasing beachfront rooms. There's a pool. Rate: $40 d. The more basic **Cabinas Vista Hermosa** are next to **Soda Surf.**

ESTERILLOS OESTE

Another favorite with surfers, Esterillos Oeste is barely two km from the highway, but it's a million miles away in seclusion. The seven-km-long beach has tidepools at its northern end, where a sculpture of a mermaid sits atop the rocks. Strong currents preclude swimming, al-

though you can swim safely in the lee of rocks at the northern end of the beach at low tide. When the tide recedes, you can delight in treasures the earth has kept hidden for millions of years: an ancient mosaic of mollusk fossils embedded in the rock strata. Most are so tiny you can see them only with a microscope, while others are visible to the naked eye. Leave them for others to enjoy! The **National Museum** organizes educational trips to Esterillos Oeste for fossil hounds ($3.50; tel. 257-1433).

Accommodations and Food

You have several budget options. **Cabinas y Restaurant Greco Mar,** next door to **Bar y Restaurant El Ranchito,** has four cabins with fans and cold water ($12), plus two family-size *casitas* ($55). A road to the right at Esterillos Oeste leads to **Fandango Club** (tel. 779-9184), with cabinas and a restaurant; I couldn't find it. The same road leads to **Se Alquilan Cabinas,** which has six rooms with fans, shared bath with cold water, and bunks and screens open to view (no curtains), prison-style ($15 for four people). You dine alfresco on a small shady terrace. Farther along is **Cabinas Famoso** (tel. 779-9184), with 18 very nice cabins with fans, private baths with cold water, and verandas ($24 d, $7.50 additional). Spacious grounds front the beach; there's a laundry house in the grounds, plus **Jardín de Pulpo Restaurant** on the front lawn, open to breezes. Two other budget options are **Cabinas Fernando Mora** and **Cabinas Caletas.**

The very atmospheric **Shake Bar Musical,** at the end of the road, is the place to hang out. It's set on a small rise—just high enough to catch the breezes—with thatched roof, mariner's ropes, an old surfboard hanging from the ceiling, and outdoor dining on a thatched-canopied terrace.

Continuing past the sign for Fandango when approaching Esterillos Oeste from the coast road, you come to **Cabinas, Restaurant y Disco Las Caleteras** (tel. 717-2143), at the beachfront, a disco complete with flashing lights, a jukebox, and a DJ's booth. It has a three-room *casita* with kitchen and cold water ($12 s/d; $15 t).

Follow the sandy beachfront road south. About 800 meters away is **Camping Oceano,** which also has **sportfishing,** the **Bar y Restaurant El Barrilito,** and, next door, **Cabinas Las Brisas** (tel. 717-1513), with an open-air restau-

rant. The latter, writes reader Heinrich Maier, have "double room without fan with extremely run-down disgusting shared bath for $12." It also has rooms with private baths but no fans ("recommended") for $15. Many homes line the beach. The road ends after about two km; the beach continues south and merges with Esterillos Este. You must return to the coast road to reach Esterillos Este.

ESTERILLOS ESTE

Virtually identical to its northerly sibling: kilometers long, straight as a ruler, gray sand cleansed by high surf, and virtually unspoiled by Man Friday footprints. Several dirt roads lead from the Pan-Am Highway to the beach. Taking the most northerly, you reach a Y-fork; to the left, the dirt road parallels the beach with a grass airstrip on the other side. The accommodations are down here. The southern end of the beach is known as **Playa Bejuco,** reached via another dirt road from the Pan-Am Hwy.

(See "Parrita," below, for information on the beach's southerly extension.)

Accommodations and Food
Auberge du Pélican (Apdo. 47, Parrita 6300, tel. 779-9108) is operated by French-Canadian hosts Mariette Daignault and Pierre Perron and is simple but pleasing. There are eight rooms in a two-story house, plus two rooms in a separate *casita.* Each has ceiling fan, hot water, and safety box. Upper-story rooms have heaps of light and are breezy. Some have shared baths, which are spacious and clean. There are hammocks beneath shady palms, plus a tiny pool and a shuffleboard court. Three meals daily ($15) are served in a large dining room. Rate: $30 d.

The **Fleur de Lys** (tel. 779-9117, fax 779-9108), 200 meters farther south, is similar in price and standard, though with cabinas rather than rooms. Not reviewed.

The University of Costa Rica has basic cabinas and a restaurant (open to the public) at Playa Bejuco. Here, too, is **Centro Turístico Bejuco** offering camping, simple cabins, plus bathrooms and a *ranchita* restaurant.

The beachfront, Spanish colonial-style **Hotel Delfín** (Apdo. 37, Parrita 6300, tel. 779-9246; in the U.S., tel. 407-367-9306, fax 407-367-9308) is very popular with Ticos. It has a pool shaded by palms, and a highly praised restaurant. At last count, there were 15 tile-floored rooms with fans and private baths. Mundane decor within, but how the beach makes amends! Rates: $60 and upward s/d.

Away from the beach is the very basic **Cabinas Los Angeles** for true budget travelers.

PARRITA

This small town, 45 km south of Jacó, is a center for the huge (1,700 hectares) African oil palm ranch established by United Brands Fruit Co. in 1985. According to local lore, the town got its name for a woman called Rita whose business was handling mail packages for the region. Hence the phrase *"Para Rita!"* ("It's for Rita!"). The road south of Parrita is paved in parts and lined with oil-processing plants and plantation villages of gaily painted, two-story stilt houses set around a soccer field.

About four km north of Parrita, a dirt road leads west, zigzagging through the palms until you emerge at **Playa Palma,** a long, ruler-straight, utterly lonesome extension of Playa Esterillos Este, from which it is separated by a rivermouth (Playa Palma is known as Playa Bandera at its southern end), and which is known only to Ticos and readers of this book. Another road immediately south of Parrita leads to **Playa Palo Seco,** another gray-sand beach (separated from Playa Bandera by a river) that seems to go forever and is backed by the mangrove swamps of the Palo Seco and Damas estuaries.

Hacienda El Tecal (tel. 223-3130) hosts a "forest recreational facility" known as **Bosque y Villas Margarita,** with cabinas and camping, a pool, hiking trails, horses, etc. It is 12 km inland, and you reach it via a dirt road about two km north of Parrita.

Accommodations
At Playa Palma is **Rancho Estel** (tel. 225-2500), a popular bar and restaurant, also with 10 rooms with private baths and hot water. Rate: $30 for four. One km south is **Cabinas y Restaurante Concha Mar,** more rustic but still popular. Farther down the beach is the funky **Ruta del Sol** (tel. 779-9075) and the slightly better **Cabinas Alexis.**

In Parrita itself are the **Hotel Los Alemendros, Hotel Nopal** (tel. 779-9216), and **Cabinas Calova** and **Cabinas Parrita** (tel. 779-9057, fax 779-9163), opposite each other on the main street. I can't think of a reason to stay in Parrita. Better bets are the nearby beach hotels.

At Playa Palo Seco, **Complejo Villas Las Flores** (tel. 779-9117, fax 779-9108) is a Canadian-owned apartotel complex with units spread out amid a large field, 150 meters from the beach. Not reviewed. There are also basic cabinas 100 meters east of where the road meets the beach. **Restaurant y Cabinas Mar y Sol,** immediately when you reach the beach, has cabinas and **camping** beneath palms on the beachfront lawn. Two km south along the beach is **Cabinas Brisas del Mar,** behind a blue picket fence. It wasn't open when I passed by. Another two km brings you to **Cabinas San Francisco.**

The best place, however, is **Beso del Viento** (Apdo. 86, Parrita 6300, fax 779-9108; in Canada, tel. 514-383-7559, fax 383-0971), a handsome Spanish colonial-style home operated as a bed-and-breakfast hotel by an amiable French Canadian couple, Jean and Brigette. They offer five rooms and two spacious loft apartments, the latter with kitchen. Rooms share very nice bathrooms with a deep tub/shower with hot water. A large lounge-cum-dining area boasts wide, wide windows and a pool table. Artwork abounds. It's simple yet elegant, but most important is that you feel like a guest in a friend's home. The pool and wide sundeck with hammocks are good for lazing. Monkeys come down from the forest behind the hotel (you may see them on guided boating trips into the nearby *estero*). An eight-meter sportfishing boat is available for charter and tours to Manuel Antonio and further afield. Windsurfing, water-skiing, snorkeling, and even banana boat rides are available. Rate: $45 d, including breakfast. Lunch and dinner are offered a la carte.

Apartotel La Isla (Apdo. 472, San José 1007, tel. 222-6561 or 779-9016, fax 233-5384), at the end of Playa Palo Seco, has 18 very spacious twin-bedroom cabins with kitchenettes spread out among lawns, 100 meters from the beach. A large open-air barbecue restaurant has a swimming pool adjacent. It's backed by a river and mangroves. You can rent canoes and horses. Rate: $40 d.

Services

Parrita has a **Banco Nacional, Banco de Costa Rica,** and a **gas station.**

DAMAS ESTUARY

The Palo Seco-Damas mangrove swamp south of Parrita covers many square kilometers south of Parrita and is home to crocodiles, monkeys, pumas, coatimundis, and wading and water birds by the thousands. Several tour operators in Quepos offer trips, including **Kanals Kayaking** (tel. 777-0082), which has paddle trips and motor-launch trips around Damas Island, with lunch at the floating restaurant, **La Tortuga.** (See "Quepos," below, for further options.) You can also visit Damas Island by renting a boat with guide ($20 per hour, up to eight passengers) at the waterfront dock immediately west of the Pueblo Real hotel (see below), one km west of the Pan-American Highway.

Accommodations

The **Pueblo Real** (tel./fax 777-0536; or Apdo. 1136, San José 2000, tel. 232-2211, fax 232-0587) resort community features an 18-hole golf course, two tennis courts, a free-form swimming pool, a country club and a marina, and fully furnished Spanish-style condos. The complex spreads across 120 hectares on the banks of the river with access to isolated beaches via a dwarf Malaysian coconut plantation. The rooms are very elegant, with modern furnishings. Rate: $136 per night. It might be overpriced.

Cabinas La Isla (tel. 777-0514), opposite, offers more modest rooms, as does **Cabinas El Tucán,** between the Pan-Am Hwy. and the river.

Flotante La Tortuga is a floating restaurant serving seafoods and "international dishes."

QUEPOS

This erstwhile fishing town (population 11,000) has been catapulted to fame among sportfishers and is a lively stopover for travelers heading to Manuel Antonio National Park, seven km south. There's nothing of interest to see in town, expect perhaps the dilapidated fishing village with rickety plank walkways connecting the warren of houses built on stilts and extending over an unappealing muddy beach called Blue Bay, and the old residential compounds of the Standard Fruit Company, whose clapboard homes, shady grounds, and great views are impressive. There's plenty of life in town, however, especially for younger folks enamored of the laid-back lifestyle. Goodness . . . there's even a casino!

Besides being a base for sportfishing and visits to Manuel Antonio, river rafting is becoming popular hereabouts. One of the most important runs is on the **Río Naranjo,** which flows down from the rainforest-clad mountains to wind through plantations and eventually fan out into an estuary in Manuel Antonio National Park. In high water it offers extremely challenging class V whitewater action. At other times the river falls and slows and becomes too low for running.

The 1994 season brought a drop-off in tourist arrivals who'd got used to the boom. Experts say the boom in hotel construction combined with negative publicity about Manuel Antonio National Park caused many tour operators to steer travelers elsewhere. But in April 1995, things were hopping. The roads had even been paved.

Note: The tourism boom has created numerous sewage problems for Quepos and neighboring Manuel Antonio. Recent tests show a high level of contamination: Quepos's El Cocal beach is considered high-risk for swimmers. The beach also has dangerous currents. Save your swimming for Manuel Antonio.

HISTORY

In February 1563, the conquistador Juan Vásquez de Coronado arrived in the region. One of the first missions in Costa Rica was established here in 1570; you can still see the ruins up the Río Naranjo. Vásquez found the area populated by Quepoa Indians, a subtribe of the Borucas. In addition to farming, the Quepoa fished and trapped sea turtles. The Spanish soon forced them onto less fertile lands, and it wasn't long before European diseases and musket balls had decimated the indigenous population. Many local inhabitants still bear the facial features of their aboriginal forebears.

Toward the end of the 19th century, agricultural colonies were established in the Parrita, Paquita, Quepos (Boca Vieja), and Savegre zones, followed by banana plantations in the 1930s. Bananas came to dominate the economy, and Quepos rose to prominence as a banana-exporting port. The plantations were blighted by disease in the 1950s and the bananas were replaced by African palms, which produce oil for the food, cosmetic, and machine-oil industries. The trees stretch in neatly ordered rows for miles north of Quepos. The oil is high in cholesterol and now the African-palm industry is in decline, a victim of these health-conscious times.

Banana boats have given way in recent years to sportfishing boats, and Quepos is gaining new stature thanks to the growing tourist trade.

ACCOMMODATIONS

Quepos is a popular place that sells out in dry season Dec.-April; reservations recommended. Wet-season discounts are offered, and travelers will find accommodations in Quepos generally better value than at Manuel Antonio (see "Manuel Antonio National Park," below, for hotels south of Quepos). **Note:** Quepos is developing so rapidly that hotels are constantly raising their prices; prices quoted may be low.

Budget
Hotel Ramus (tel. 777-0245) has clean rooms, private baths, and ceiling fans. Rates: from $8 per person; weekend rates are higher. **Hotel Pueblo,** in the heart of the bus station, has four simple but adequate rooms. Better yet is the

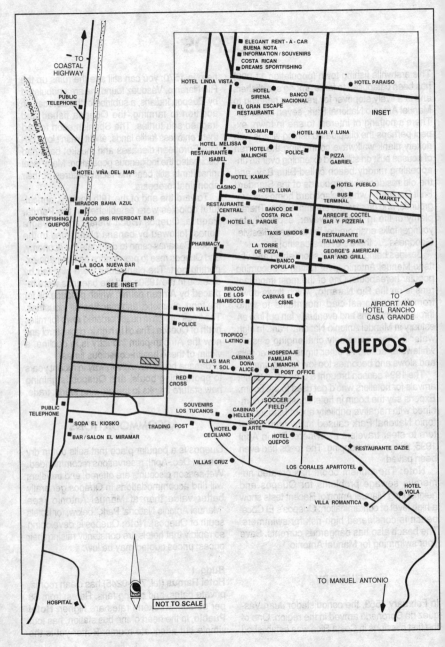

QUEPOS

new **Hotel Melissa** (tel. 777-0025), with 14 rooms with private baths and fans; simple, clean, adequate. Rate: $9 per person.

The basic though clean **Hotel Linda Vista** (tel. 777-0001) has rooms facing the street. Rates: from $9. The **Hotel Mar y Luna** (tel. 777-0394) has small, basic upper-floor rooms with communal baths; ground floor rooms have private baths but no windows. The owner is friendly and helpful. Rate: $12 s/d.

Travelers on a really tight budget might try the **Hotel Luna**, whose ascetic rooms offer little more than beds and showers; or, next door, **Hospedaje El Único**; the **Hotel America**; the **Hotel Majestic**; **Cabinas Hellen** (tel. 777-0504); or **Cabinas Doña Alice** (tel. 777-0419), above the *soda* north of the soccer field.

You'll also find several fairly basic cabinas north of the bridge: **Hotel Familiar** (tel. 777-0078), half a kilometer from town; **Cabinas Los Horcones** (tel. 777-0090), next to Quepos Sportfishing; **Cabinas Almuedaba** (tel. 777-0426); **Hospedaje Familiar La Mancha** (tel. 777-0216); and **Cabinas Mary** (tel. 777-0128).

The following are on the outskirts on the road to Manuel Antonio: **Cabinas Primo** (tel. 777-0134), pleasant but basic; **Cabinas Geylor** (tel. 777-0561), 25 meters beyond Primo, with basic rooms with private baths ($20 triple); **Cabinas Delicia** (tel. 777-0306); **Cabinas Tauro** (tel. 777-0014), basic but modern and clean; **Cabinas Ipakarahi** (tel. 777-0392); **Cabinas Cruz** (tel. 777-0271); and **Cabinas El Cedros** (tel. 777-0950).

Inexpensive

The oceanfront **Hotel El Parque** (tel. 777-0063) has 12 relatively spacious but vastly overpriced rooms at $28 s/d (a 400% increase since the first edition). **Hotel Malinche** (tel. 777-0093), inside an arched brick entrance, is relatively clean and has 24 rooms, 12 with a/c. Rates: $17 s/d without a/c; $18 s, $30 d with a/c. **Hotel Quepos** (Apdo. 79, Quepos, tel. 777-0274), above the SANSA office, has 23 rooms, 13 with private baths. Rooms are clean and airy, with fans and hardwood floors. Rates: $10-14 s, $15-20 d. The family-run **Hotel Ceciliano** (tel. 777-0192) has 20 light and airy rooms—12 with private baths—with immaculately clean tiled floors, a little garden with caged birds, and a nice patio restaurant. Laundry service. Rates: $15 s/d, $20 t.

Two new options near the bus station include **Hotel Villas Morsol** (tel. 777-0307) and, offering cabins and camping options, **Mirador del Río** (tel. 777-0290). Also consider the **Villas Mar y Sol Inn** (tel. 777-0307), whose a/c rooms have lots of light, refrigerators, private baths with hot water, and secure parking; and of a similar standard, at the northeast corner of town, **Cabinas El Cisne** (tel. 777-1570), also with secure parking. Also try **Club Caribe** (tel. 777-0134), with simple cabins for $25 d.

Moderate

The **Hotel Viña del Mar** (tel. 777-0070; or Apdo. 5527, San José, tel. 223-3334), north of the bridge over the Boca Vieja, has 20 spacious a/c rooms with ceiling fans and private baths. You'll find a small bar and restaurant on a veranda overlooking the estuary, plus a boutique selling beachwear and souvenirs. Rates: $20 s, $30 d; $30 s, $40 d with a/c, including breakfast. Nearby, aside the estuary, is **Hotel Itzamana** (tel./fax 777-0351), popular with Ticos. It has a pool, but there's nothing special about this hotel. Rates: $30 s, $45 d, $60 t, including breakfast.

On the road out of town to Manuel Antonio is the brand-new **Hotel Viola** (tel. 777-0124) with seven very clean rooms with fans and private baths with hot water. Rates: $35 s/d, $40 t, $45 quad.

Expensive

The **Hotel Kamuk** (Apdo. 18-6350, Quepos, tel. 777-0379, fax 777-0258) is the only real class-act in town. It has 28 spacious and elegant, nicely furnished a/c rooms (some with balconies; all with TVs and telephones), all beautifully decorated in light pastels. The **Miraolas Bar and Restaurant** on the third floor has vistas over El Cocal Beach and serves good international cuisine. There's a small boutique. The hotel can organize day tours. Owner Luis Alberto Bolanos also operates an English-style pub and an elegant casino next door. Rates: $60 s/d standard, $80-115 d "deluxe."

Hotel Rancho Casa Grande (Apdo. 618, Zapote, San José 2010, tel. 777-0330, fax 253-2363) is set in 73 hectares on the road to the Quepos airport, with 14 luxuriously furnished a/c rooms and 10 fully equipped cabins. Highlights include a swimming pool, a Jacuzzi, horse riding,

nature trails into the surrounding forest, and guided tours. Rates: $95 d, $110-125 bungalows.

The aptly named and reclusive **Hotel Villa Romántica** (tel./fax 777-0037) opened in 1994 on the edge of town on the road to Manuel Antonio. The two-tier Mediterranean-style building is set in pretty landscaped grounds. Sixteen simply yet nicely appointed rooms have spacious bathrooms, heaps of light, and lots of whites and purples, with murals of bamboo arching to form faux-headboards. Balconies and dining terrace (breakfasts only) overlook a swimming pool. Recommended. Rates: $45 s, $60 d.

Hotel Sirena (tel./fax 777-0528) is clean and pleasant, with 14 double rooms with a/c, private baths and hot water. A central sundeck offers a pool. The hotel specializes in horseback trips on Savegre Ranch and also offers rafting and fishing. Overpriced. Rates: $50 s, $68 d, including tax and breakfast.

Apartments
Opposite Delicia is **Los Corales Apartotel** (tel./fax 777-0006), with pleasing modern units. Half a block east of Costa Rican Dreams is the **Apartotel El Coral** (tel. 777-0528/fax 777-0044). **Villas Cruz** (tel. 777-0271), 100 meters up a dirt road south from the Trading Post, has a fully equipped villa and cabins for rent. **Restaurant Nahomi** rents two apartments in the center of Quepos, both with TVs, parking, and full kitchens: one (for four people) rents for $600 per month; the other (for three) rents for $450. **Troy's** bar and restaurant has a wooden *casita*-style house for rent on the hill south of Quepos (contact Mrs. Andersson, tel. 222-6756). Anita Myketuk of the Buena Nota gift shop has a house for rent near Hotel La Mariposa, with a stunning view toward Manuel Antonio.

The **Hotel Paraíso** (tel. 777-0082) has six very pleasant apartments with a/c, kitchens, refrigerators, and hot water. Lots of light. Rates: $35 d, $85 quad. Other apartments (for five people) are offered for rent in **Pueblo Real** (tel. 777-0171; $20 per person).

FOOD
Quepos is replete with cheap places to eat and drink. The spacious and airy **Restaurante Isabel,** on the beachfront "strip," has a comprehensive menu for $2-7. Next door is **Café Triángulo** (also known as Restaurante Ana). At least four restaurants offer Italian food, including **La Torre de Pizza, Pizza Gabriel,** and **Arrecife Coctel Bar** and, next door, **Restaurante Italiano Pirata** (tel. 777-1976). I loved the homemade pasta at **Trópico Latino,** which serves a full range of Italian dishes and offers a "daily special double dish" for $4.50. The **Mira Olas Bar and Restaurant** (tel. 777-0379), atop Hotel Kamuk, has a fairly expensive international menu; the hotel's open-air patio soda serves *refrescos* and ice creams. Craving a really good burger or barbecue? Try **George's American Bar and Grill,** an almost authentic recreation of Texas, with barbecue ribs, burgers, and eggs benedict on the breakfast menu. **El Gran Escape Restaurante and "Fish Head" Bar** (tel. 777-0395) serves good *típico* meals. Fancy fish-n'-chips? Then head 100 meters past the soccer field (on the road to Manuel Antonio) to the rustic and atmospheric **Restaurante Dazie,** where a Californian exile—Dazie Zeddies—fries her fare "Australian-style" in beer batter (a healthy portion, best enjoyed with malt vinegar, costs $4.50). Quepos runs the international gamut. There's a Mexican place, too: **Dos Locos** (tel. 777-1526). And a Spanish-style **Café Quijote** (tel. 777-1446) for chicken to go.

La Boca Nueva Bar offers a pleasing setting under a *ranchita* at the mouth of the river; it serves Costa Rican fare. Other inexpensive eateries include **Soda la Única,** next to the Hotel Luna; **Bar/Salon el Miramar,** at the southern end of the oceanfront road; **Restaurant Nahomi,** with a romantic airy setting on the road to Manuel Antonio; and **Soda El Kiosko,** on the harbor road south of Quepos.

Craving good coffee? Head to **Café Milagro** (tel. 777-1707), which roasts its coffee fresh, and sells iced coffee, espresso, and capuccino.

ENTERTAINMENT
North of the bridge, **Mirador Bahía Azul** and **Arco Iris Riverboat Bar/Disco** over the water (it's not really a riverboat) are popular nightspots with dancing. The **Gran Escape Bar,** in Restaurant Ana, and the **Pub Kamuk** are also favorite drinking spots, as is **El Banco Bar,** with satellite

TV and good music. You can try your hand with Lady Luck at the Hotel Kamuk's elegant casino. **La Portentina** and the **Mar Blue** are both small bars popular with the locals, who also pack the **El Banco Pool Hall.**

Quepos's famous **Carnivale** is back! It's not as debauched as Rio de Janeiro's famous bacchanal, nor as colorful as Trinidad's, but the three-week event (mid-Feburary to early March) offers plenty of fun and cultural entertainment.

SERVICES AND INFORMATION

Rafting and Sea-Kayaking

Iguana Tours (alias Ríos Tropicales, tel./fax 777-0574; in San José, tel. 233-6455, fax 255-4354) offers one-, two-, and three-day sea-kayaking trips to the adjacent mangrove lagoons of Damas Island and Manuel Antonio National Park, plus kayaking and river-rafting trips down the Río Naranjo (class III). The company also rents sea kayaks. Its office is in Hotel Si Como No, in Manuel Antonio. **Ríos Locos** (c/o Lynch Tourist Service, in the Quepos Center, tel. 777-1170, fax 777-1571) also offers trips on the Río Naranjo ($75, full-day including lunch) plus "Crocodile Kayaking" in the estuary of the Naranjo. (Lynch also represents **Save the Rainforest Expeditions and School,** which has whitewater trips locally.) **Amigos Del Río** (tel. 777-0082), kitty-corner from Banco Nacional, offers rafting on the Río Savegre ($55), a trip to Damas Island ($65), plus jungle hiking, mountain biking, etc. **Ocean Kayak Tours** (tel./fax 777-0403) also offers wildlife trips to Damas.

Horseback Riding, Cruises, and Tours

Jungle Adventures (tel. 777-1286) and **Estrella Tours** (tel. 777-1286) offer off-the-beaten-path mountain bike and horseback trips for the hardy. **Unicorn Adventures** (Apdo. 158, Quepos, tel. 777-0489) offers horseback-riding tours with a focus on natural history. **Punta Quepos Trail Rides** (tel. 777-0566) also offers half-day guided horseback rides, including lunch on the beach. **Eco-Fan** (Apdo. 618, Zapote 2010, tel. 777-0330, fax 777-1575) offers some intriguing tours, including one to the Palma Tica Oil Processing Plant, and horseback riding at Rancho Casa, plus nature tours at Manuel Antonio and private reserves.

Tarzan's Mother (tel. 777-1257, in San José tel. 257-2904) is a 19-meter twin-deck cruise-ship that offers daily cruises to Manuel Antonio. **Costa Rican Dreams** (see "Sportfishing," below) runs multiday charter trips to Drake Bay and Caño Island, plus half-day coastal sightseeing trips to Manuel Antonio. **Paraíso Acuático** (Apdo. 145, Quepos, tel. 777-0514), in the Hotel Paraíso, offers parasailing, water-skiing, deep-sea fishing, surfboard and boogie-board rentals, and boat rentals ($180 half day, $300 full day), as well as tours to the Damas Caves, which have stalactites and stalagmites.

Planes Turísticos Nahomi (Apdo. 110, Quepos 6350, tel. 777-0161, fax 777-0562) offers tours into the Nara Hills behind Manuel Antonio, with a visit to a fruit farm and lunch plus afternoon cruise through the mangroves of Isla Damas aboard the *Tortuga* cruise boat ($65). **Olman Nature Tours** (tel. 777-0497) also offers tours.

The 17-meter *Byblos I* offers full-day and sunset cruises, plus sportfishing and diving trips; contact the Hotel Byblos, on the road to Manuel Antonio (or Apdo. 112, Quepos, tel. 777-0411, fax 777-0009). **Corcovado Adventures** (tel. 777-0368, fax 777-1248; in San José, tel. 238-2726, fax 260-4434) offers tours to Corcovado and Caño Island, plus kayaking, horseback riding, and sportfishing.

Sportfishing

Protected from the heavy winds that restrict fishing on the northern Guanacaste coast for much of the year, the Quepos region offers outstanding sportfishing for marlin and sailfish through the peak season, December through August. The inshore reefs are also home to large populations of snapper, amberjack, wahoo, and tuna.

QUEPOS EMERGENCY TELEPHONE NUMBERS	
All emergencies	911
Police	117 or 777-0196
Red Cross	777-0116
Hospital	777-0020

Costa Rican Dreams (Apdo. 79, Belén, Heredia 4005, tel. 239-3387 or 777-0593, fax 239-3383 or 777-0592) operates four boats: two twin-diesel fly-bridge sportfishermen and two single diesel center-console boats. The company specializes in flyfishing. Half-day trips (nine-meter boats) cost $275 (offshore) and $200 (inshore); full-day trips from $395.

Quepos Sportfishing (tel. 777-0106) is on the left, 200 meters north of the bridge. **Sportsfishing Quepos** (tel./fax 777-0221) has an office in a small *ranchita* on stilts over the water in front of the bridge into town (from $325 full day).

Sportfishing Treasure Hunt Tours has a seven-meter boat with center console and Bimini cover ($180 half-day, $300 full-day, for three people); La Buena Nota gift shop has information and handles reservations. Other companies include **Tours Cambute Sportfishing** (tel./fax 777-0082); **Skipmar Sportfishing & Diving** (tel. 777-0275), next to Buena Nota; **Sportfishing Costa Rica** (tel. 237-8312, fax 238-4434); and **Blue Marlin Sportfishing** (tel. 777-0191), below the Hotel Quepos, next door to which is a "tourist information center" that also arranges sportfishing.

Safari 1 is an 11-meter custom-built walk-around boat that charters for $675 (five people; tel. 777-0106); the super-deluxe *Venecia II*, with shaded lounge area on the bridge, a/c salon, and even hot showers, charters for $900 per day (up to eight anglers; tel./fax 777-0275).

Car Rental

Budget (tel. 777-0186) has an office in the lobby of the Hotel Kumak. **Elegant Rent-a-Car** (tel. 777-0115) has an office next to Buena Nota. Only a limited number of cars are available; make reservations in San José. **Moto Affaire** (tel. 777-1489) rents motorbikes.

Banks

The **Banco Nacional de Costa Rica, Banco de Comercio,** and **Banco de Costa Rica** all have branches. There's a **Western Union** office opposite the Banco de Costa Rica.

Other

The **post office** is on the north side of the soccer field. Beyond the docks south of Quepos is

Paradero Turístico Nahomi. Built onto the rocks, the complex features a shaded open-air restaurant, two public swimming pools, and scuba-diving service. If you need **laundry** done, call 777-0048 for same-day delivery. Kelly Potter runs **Lavanderías de Costa Rica** (tel. 777-0128), which offers a next-day service. **Public telephones** face the ocean in front of the park. For taxis call **Taxi Quepos** (tel. 777-0277). **Farmacia Botica Quepos** (tel. 777-0038) is next to the Hotel El Parque. The **Hospital Dr. Max Teran V** (tel. 777-0020) is three km south of town on the Costanera Sur.

Information

Buena Nota (Apdo. 15, Puerto Quepos, tel. 777-0345), run by American owner Anita Myketuk, is a tourist-information bureau. It also has a book exchange. **Villas Selva Real Estate** (tel. 777-0495), on the road for Manuel Antonio, also acts as an information bureau, as does the lobby of the Hotel Kamuk.

Souvenirs

Buena Nota gift shop has a very good selection of beachwear, as well as maps, books, international magazines, and some handicrafts. **Souvenirs Los Tucanos,** next to Cabinas Hellen, has T-shirts, sandals, etc. The **Trading Post** sells Guatemalan clothing and artifacts, while **Galería Costa Rica** has fabulous print dresses and batiks. **Shock Arte** has a marvelous array of carvings, etc. You'll find several other very good small boutiques opposite the soccer field on the road leading to Manuel Antonio.

TRANSPORTATION

By Bus

Buses depart San José for Manuel Antonio via Quepos from Calle 16, Avenidas 1/3 (tel. 223-5567, 223-1109 or 777-0318), at 6 a.m., noon, and 6 p.m. (three and a half hours); return buses depart Quepos at 6 a.m., noon, and 5 p.m. Indirect buses (five hours) depart San José at 7 and 10 a.m., and 2, 4, and 6 p.m., returning at 5 and 8 a.m. and 2 and 4 p.m. Direct buses originate in Manuel Antonio and fill up fast. Buses depart Puntarenas for Quepos daily (tel. 777-0138) at 5 and 11 a.m. and 2 p.m., returning via Jacó

at 4:30 and 10:30 a.m. and 2 p.m. Check times ahead. Buses operate from Quepos to Dominical and San Isidro at 5:30 a.m. and 1:30 p.m.

Buy your ticket as far in advance as possible. The ticket office is open 7-11 a.m. and 1-5 p.m daily (Sunday 7 a.m.-2 p.m.).

Exotur (tel. 227-5169, fax 227-2180) may have reinstated a daily express bus service—the Silver Bullet—that used to run from San José via Jacó. Likewise, the **American VIP Coach Service** was slated to offers deluxe service aboard a Greyhound (see "Manuel Antonio National Park" for details). Another "Beach Shuttle" is operated by **Dos Océanos** (tel. 282-8400, fax 282-8899) daily ($25 one-way, $48 roundtrip).

Buses depart Quepos almost hourly for Manuel Antonio (5:30 am.-9:30 p.m.; $0.25), with schedules varying by season and weekday or weekend. **Quepos Taxi** (tel. 777-0277) charges about $4 to Manuel Antonio.

By Air
SANSA (tel. 323-5330, fax 255-2176; in Quepos, tel. 777-0161) operates flights to Quepos from San José daily except Sunday at 8:15 a.m.

and 3:45 p.m.; on Monday, Wednesday, Friday, and Saturday at 9:30 a.m. (with onward service to Palmar Sur); and on Sunday at 11 a.m. ($24 one-way). Return flights depart 35 minutes later. **Travelair** (tel. 232-7883, fax 220-0413) operates flights from San José's Pavas Airport daily at 7 a.m., noon, and 3:30 p.m., and at 11 a.m. with onward service to Palmar Sur ($35 one-way); return flights depart Quepos 40 minutes later. **Sportfishing Costa Rica** (tel. 237-8312, fax 238-4434) reportedly offers daily charter flights from San José during dry season. **Note:** Buy your ticket as far in advance as possible, and reconfirm your flight!

By Boat
Taximar (tel. 777-1647 or 777-0262; or c/o Lynch Travel Service, tel. 777-1170) is a sea shuttle service operating between Quepos, Dominical ($20 one-way), Drake Bay ($55 one-way) and Caño Island ($85 roundtrip, including lunch and drinks) four times a week aboard a canopied seven-meter boat that makes a nifty 30 knots. Departs Quepos Tuesday, Thursday, Saturday, and Sunday at 7 a.m.

MANUEL ANTONIO NATIONAL PARK

Tiny it may be, but this 682-hectare national park epitomizes everything tourists flock to Costa Rica to see: stunning beaches (undoubtedly among the best in the country), a magnificent setting with islands offshore (bird sanctuaries for marine species), lush rainforest laced with a network of welcoming trails, wildlife galore, and—could this be true?—all this within walking distance of your hotel.

First the good news: Manuel Antonio, seven km south of Quepos, lives up to its reputation. It has four lovely beaches, each with its own personality: Espadilla Sur, Manuel Antonio, Escondido, and Playita. Outside the park, and the least attractive, is Playa Espadilla, a perfect crescent that arcs north for two km.

The prettiest of park beaches is Playa Manuel Antonio, a small scimitar of coral-white sand with a small coral reef. It's separated from Playa Espadilla Sur by Punta Catedral, an erstwhile island now linked to the mainland by a *tombolo,* a natural land bridge formed over eons through

the accumulation of sand. The hike to the top of Punta Catedral (100 meters) along a steep and sometimes muddy trail takes about an hour from Playa Espadilla Sur (also known as the Second Beach). Espadilla Sur and Manuel Antonio offer tidal pools brimming with minnows and crayfish, plus reasonably good snorkeling, especially during dry season, when the water is generally clear. The sergeant major is the most common fish. (There are other beaches tucked into tiny coves at the base of the "mountain" and reached by dirt trails from the main road; one such leads from Hotel Villa Teca to **Playa La Macha,** for example.)

Between bouts of beaching, you can explore the park's network of wide trails, which lead into a raw swatch of humid tropical forest. Manuel Antonio's treetop carnival is marvelous. Howler monkeys bound from branch to branch, iguanas shimmy up trunks, toucans and scarlet macaws flap by. Capuchin monkeys welcome you at treetop height on Espadilla Sur Beach;

Manuel Antonio
National Park

JEAN MERCIER

they play to the crowd and will steal your sandwich packs given half a chance. The Perezoso Trail is named after the lovable sloths, which favor the secondary growth along the trail (*perezoso* means "lazy"). You might see marmosets, ocelots, river otters, pacas, and spectacled caimans.

And about 350 squirrel monkeys live in the park, another 500 on its outer boundaries. The titi or squirrel monkey is in great danger because of loss of environment. The park's small area is too small to sustain a healthy and viable population. If the monkeys do not have access to areas outside the park, the population will decline because they cannot breed. Yet hoteliers are building closer and closer to the park. Corridors that allow animals access to areas outside the park have been taken up by hotels, so that the park has in recent years become an island. As a result, the squirrel monkey population is declining.

Note: Do not feed the monkeys! Recent studies have found a worrying increase in heart disease and heart failure among the local monkey population. This is attributed to tourists feeding the monkeys with scraps of food such as cheese sandwiches, peanut butter, potato chips, etc. Unfortunately, the animals are much more prone to rises in cholesterol than humans. Do not leave food lying around.

Outside the park, midway from Quepos, is the **Jardín Gaia,** a wildlife breeding and reha-

bilitation center open to visitors 9 a.m.-noon and 1-5 p.m. (closed Wednesday). Entrance: $1.25 (children free).

Overuse
Despite its diminutive size, Manuel Antonio is one of the country's most popular parks (more than 150,000 visitors annually). Too many tourists threaten to spoil the very thing they come to see. Park director José Antonio Salazar believes the park can withstand no more than 300 visitors a day. In recent years, however, Manuel Antonio has averaged about 1,000 people each day, with significantly more on some peak-season days, when hundreds of people were walking the trails at any one time.

The Park Service considered closing the park for a while to let it recover from all those human feet. In early 1994 it began limiting the numbers of visitors to 600 per day (800 on Saturday and Sunday). More successful in reducing visitation has been the $15 entrance fee ($10 with advance purchase) introduced in September 1994 for parks nationwide; this scared the more pecunious traveler away. Plans were afoot at the executive level to make Manuel Antonio and the surrounding area a model sustainable region.

If you wish to do your bit to help preserve Manuel Antonio, consider visiting in the "green" or wet season. Litter and pollution are additional problems. Remember: Pack out what you pack in. **Note:** The park is closed on Monday ("to

clean up after the throngs of weekend partiers," reckons reader Sally Lourd).

A Brief History
In 1968 the land was bought by an American, who erected gates to keep the locals out. Costa Rican law, however, guarantees beach access for all. After locals tore the gates down, the municipal council ruled that the road must remain open. A Frenchman bought the property in 1972. When *he* tried to bar outsiders from the land and initiated plans to develop a resort, locals rallied in support of demands to create a national park. Eventually, the land was expropriated and Manuel Antonio National Park created in November 1972. Additional land was added in 1980.

The Beach Apple
The "beach apple" *(manzanillo)* or manchineel tree is very common along the beaches. It's highly toxic and possesses a sap that irritates the skin. Its tempting applelike fruits are also poisonous. Avoid touching any part of the tree and don't use its wood for fires: the smoke will irritate your lungs. Ask the ranger at the park entrance to show you an example.

A guide can show you other interesting tree species: among them, the *gaupinol negro,* an endemic species that is in danger of extinction; *cedro maria,* which produces a yellow resin used as a traditional medicine; and *vaco lechoso,* which exudes a thick white latex that also has medicinal properties.

Turtle Traps
If you look closely at the rocks at the far right on Playa Manuel Antonio, you can see ancient turtle traps dug out of the rocks by pre-Columbian Quepoa Indians. Female sea turtles would swim over the rocks to the beach on the high tide. The tidal variation at this point is as much as three meters; the turtles would be caught in the carved-out traps on the return journey as the tide level dropped. The Indians also used female-turtle decoys made of balsa to attract male turtles over the rocks. Olive ridley and green turtles still occasionally come ashore at Playa Manuel Antonio.

Information
The park **entrance** is at the southern end of Playa Espadilla, where you wade across the shallow Río Camaronera and pay your park entrance fee ($15 walk-in, $10 advance purchase; you can buy an entrance ticket for $7-10 locally, including from Iguana Tours and Hotel El Plinio). At high tide you may be thigh-deep. You'll find a small open-air natural-history **museum** and information center on Playa Manuel Antonio.

Some maps show a ranger station at Finca Quebrada Azul (reached from the crossroads for London, seven km south of Quepos) and a trail to Playa Playita, which faces Isla Mogote. This trail has been closed for some time. Check with the Park Service. **Camping** is not allowed in the park.

Cautions
Theft is a major problem on the beaches, not least by the monkeys. Don't leave your things unguarded while you swim. I've also heard several reports of stealth burglaries in the hotels. Take whatever precautions you can to protect your goods. There are **riptides** on Playa Espadilla. Watch your children, as there are no lifeguards.

ACCOMMODATIONS

An army of hotels marches up and over the hill separating Quepos and Manuel Antonio. A few hotels enjoy fabulous ocean views. Budget hotels are mostly found down near Manuel Antonio village. More expensive hotels have loftier, breezy perches. Many hotels are vastly overpriced and/or prove to be less appealing than their brochures and prices suggest. Many offer substantial off-season discounts (in fact, prices have dropped since 1993 because of overcapacity and a fall-off in visitors). Hilltop hotels may have steep steps; inquire. It can be a tough, hot walk back up the hill from the beach if you don't want to wait for the bus. Check to see if your hotel offers van service to/from the beach. Alas, many hotels have been built without regard to existing legislation (in 1993, for example, then-Tourism Minister Manuel Chacón demanded that 23 hotels be razed because they had been built within the inviolable 50 meters of the high tide mark). **Note:** Hotels in each price category are listed as they appear along the road from Quepos.

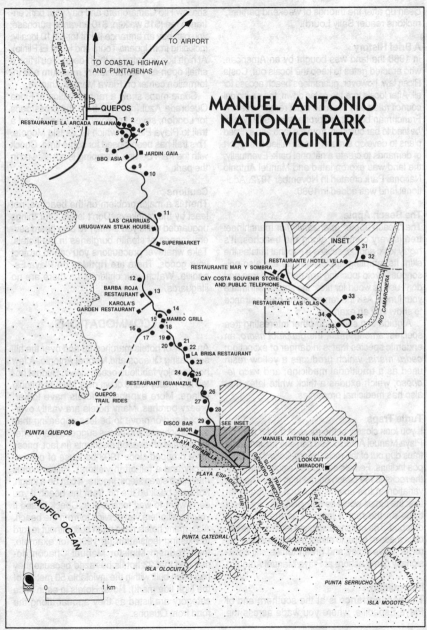

MANUEL ANTONIO
NATIONAL PARK
AND VICINITY

TO AIRPORT

TO COASTAL HIGHWAY
AND PUNTARENAS

BOCA VIEJA ESTUARY

QUEPOS

RESTAURANTE LA ARCADA ITALIANA

JARDIN GAIA

BBQ ASIA

LAS CHARRUAS
URUGUAYAN STEAK HOUSE

SUPERMARKET

BARBA ROJA
RESTAURANT

KAROLA'S
GARDEN RESTAURANT

MAMBO GRILL

QUEPOS TRAIL RIDES

LA BRISA RESTAURANT

RESTAURANT IGUANAZUL

DISCO BAR
AMOR

SEE INSET

PUNTA QUEPOS

PACIFIC OCEAN

PLAYA ESPADILLA

PLAYA ESPADILLA SUR

MANUEL ANTONIO NATIONAL PARK

LOOKOUT
(MIRADOR)

(SENDERO PEREZOSO) SLOTH TRAIL

PLAYA ESCONDIDO

PLAYA MANUEL ANTONIO

PUNTA CATEDRAL

ISLA OLOCUITA

PLAYA PLAYITA

PUNTA SERRUCHO

ISLA MOGOTE

INSET

RESTAURANTE / HOTEL VELA

CAY COSTA SOUVENIR STORE
AND PUBLIC TELEPHONE

RESTAURANTE MAR Y SOMBRA

RESTAURANTE LAS OLAS

RIO CAMARONERA

0   1 km

© MOON PUBLICATIONS, INC.

MANUEL ANTONIO NATIONAL PARK AND VICINITY

1. Hotel Plinio
2. Hotel Mirador del Pacífico
3. Hotel California
4. Mimo's Hotel
5. Cabinas Pedro Miguel
6. Bahía Hotel
7. Sula Bya Ba Villas
8. Villa Teca
9. Valle Verde Lodge
10. Hotel Tres Banderas
11. El Lirio
12. Villa Osa
13. Divisamar Hotel
14. Hotel Casa Blanca
15. Byblos
16. Makanda by the Sea
17. Hotel La Mariposa
18. Hotel Si Como No
19. Hotel and Villas Mogotes
20. Villa La Roca
21. Apartotel El Colibri
22. Hotel Casitas Eclipse
23. Costa Verde
24. Hotel Arboleda
25. Villas de la Selva
26. Hotel and Villas Karahé
27. Cabinas/Restaurante Piscis
28. Hotel del Mar
29. Cabinas Ramirez
30. Hotel and Beach Club El Parador
31. Cabinas Espadilla Anexo
32. Hotel Villa Bosque
33. Cabinas Espadilla
34. camping
35. Hotel Manuel Antonio
36. Cabinas Manuel Antonio

Inexpensive

Cabinas Pedro Miguel (tel. 777-0035), tucked away from the road amid the forest, one km south of Quepos, has eight small, basic cabinas with fans and private baths with hot water. Four are fully furnished, with kitchenettes sleeping four to eight ($30-50). They have cement floors and cinderblock walls. There's a small cooling-off pool in shady grounds. Owners José Astóa and his wife, Nuvia, are on-hand and happy to run errands, etc. Rates: $22 d ($4 extra bed).

Cabinas/Restaurante Piscis (tel. 777-0046) has six clean and spacious but basic cabinas with fans and private baths with cold water. There's a wide patio veranda plus a funky and atmospheric restaurant. Rate: $26 d.

Flor Blanca (tel. 777-1633, fax 777-0032) has pleasant rooms in a two-story unit; each has refrigerator plus private bathroom with hot water. Rates: $25 d, $30 with a/c.

Cabinas Ramirez (tel. 777-0003), at the bottom of the hill, has 18 rooms with fans and private baths with cold water. Hardy low-budget travelers may love the shady, cool rooms with tiny little patios behind cages. I see them as basic, dingy, cramped, and overpriced. The beach is two minutes' walk away. Rates: $26 d ($4 extra).

Moderate

The venerable **Hotel Plinio** (Apdo. 71, Quepos, tel. 777-0055, fax 777-0558), near Quepos, has long been a favorite of budget travelers. It has a very tropical ambience: *palenque* roof, hardwoods surrounded by banana groves, and an upstairs open restaurant and bar with hints of an East African treehouse. Some of the 14 rooms have two beds; three have a/c. Rooms are dark but clean. Hot water. A nature trail leads uphill through 10 hectares of primary forest to the highest point around, where a wooden *mirador* proffers a stunning 360-degree vista. I saw several poison-arrow frogs hopping around on the trail. Rates: $50 d, $60 with a/c, $75 two-story suite, $90 three-story suite, including buffet breakfast and tax.

Recently opened **Hotel Mirador del Pacífico** (Apdo. 164, Quepos, tel./fax 777-0119) has 20 very beautiful rooms, with fans and private baths with hot water, lots of light, and private patios and verandas. Rooms are in rough-hewn wood structures raised on stilts amid lush tropical grounds. A plank walkway leads to the swimming pool. A funicular will carry you up the steep hill. Little Polynesian-style tikis peek from behind tropical plants. Rates: from $40.

Bungalows Las Palmas (tel. 777-0051; or in the U.S., c/o Interlink #185, P.O. Box 526770, Miami, FL 33152) are shady, detached bunga-

TWO SEASIDE GEMS

Hotel and Beach Club El Parador

Arriving at a hostelry rarely sparks the excitement El Parador conjures at first sight: guests approach via a long winding drive along the forested peninsula of Punta Quepos where, cresting the saddle, sits this commanding white flashback to the romantic *pousadas* of Spain. The hotel occupies five acres overlooking Playa Beisanz, a five-minute walk to the north, with Playa Espedilla to the south.

Harry Bodaan, general manager, has applied his lavish taste and attention to period detail to oversee the creation of a Spanish *parador* so authentic that he's come close to his goal as "a hotelier seeking perfection." Guests enter through a hall full of glinting chandeliers, ceiling moldings, and typical Manchegan (from La Mancha, in Spain) decor—a knight in shining armor, antique farm implements, and weaponry—that place you immediately under the Quixotic spell and, indeed, it is easy to imagine the guileless hero of Cervantes's novel entering dementedly on his scrawny steed, Rozinante.

The hub is the main hall, breathtaking in its splendor, with hefty oak beams, Spanish tiles, magnificent antique wrought-iron chandeliers, balustraded staircase, tapestries, Persian rugs, and deep-cushioned sofas to help keep things cozy, and a priceless collection of European art, antiques and historic artifacts, including more than 60 17th-century paintings, intricate model ships, and even thick-timbered wooden doors and shuttered windows flown in from ancient Spanish castles. The hall doubles as a two-story restaurant that promises *recherché nouvelle* Costa Rican cuisine.

The main building measures 2,000 square meters, including two palatial suites; the Christopher Columbus suite may well be the most sumptuous hotel room in the country! The 25 standard rooms, 20 deluxe rooms, and 15 suites (complete with Jacuzzi) will seem cramped after the immensity of the public arenas. I toured the property before the rooms had been furnished, but got a sense they would be furnished in more contemporary vogue (the hotel was scheduled to open in June 1995), with every concession to modernity.

Facilities include a huge terrace bar, winetasting room and private club room, and a *mirador ranchita* bar-cum-restaurant offering a marvelous, almost 360-degree panorama of jungle-rimmed beaches, and dolphins and whales out to sea. El Parador is destined to be a favorite for conference business. It offers a full business center and a banquet room with full audiovisual set-up, a helicopter landing pad, plus mini-golf course, two swimming pools (one with cascading waterfall and swim-up bar; the other exclusively for the suites), a stage for cultural events, a hair salon, and a dedicated health spa. Golf carts will be on hand to whisk you around.

A tree will be planted for each reservation. You would expect this kind of grandeur to cost dearly, yet prices are reasonable. A green-season bargain! Rates: $88-140 standard d, $108-180 deluxe, $148-260 junior suite (low season-high season rates).

lows with complete kitchens with hot water. Rate: $59 d.

El Mono Azul ("the Blue Monkey") has cabinas for $40.

Living it up at the **Hotel California** (Apdo. 159, Quepos, tel. 777-1234, fax 777-1062) is easy. The French-run, three-story, jade-green hotel with the name you'll never forget has 22 rooms with queen-size beds, a/c and fans, cable TVs, piping hot water, kitchenettes, and marvelous views north along the coast from the balconies overlooking a kidney-shaped pool with wooden deck above the forest, with lush plants all around. The rooms are simply, if nicely, furnished, with lots of light, French doors opening onto private verandas, and—the coup de grace—trompe l'oeil walls representing individual national parks. Choose carefully . . . some of the paintings are overbearing. I like the Tortuguero Room. The hotel has a cold Jacuzzi. Yes, you *can* leave after check-out! It's 200 meters off the road, just beyond Bungalows Las Palmas. Rates vary according to view, top story being most expensive. Rates: $45-65.

Sula Bya Ba Villas (tel. 777-0597, fax 777-0279) has 14 rooms with intriguing yet somewhat ascetic decor that blends 1950s utility with a hint of modern Japanese! Light pours in through sliding doors at both front and back. There's a tiny open-air restaurant and bar. Rate: about $50.

Hotel Villas Si Como No

The strangely named hotel (Apdo. 5, Quepos, tel. 777-1250, fax 777-1093) is a jungle fantasy come alive. The handsome, thoroughly contemporary villas are "supported" by corner columns of concrete designed and painted to resemble palm trees, complete with leaves as support eaves for the roof. All the rails and fences are shaped and painted (by a Hollywood make-up artist) to resemble thick bamboo; so, too, the trims inside the rooms. Faux-bamboo, faux-palms abound to tremendous effect, like something from a Walt Disney movie (Greek-American owner Jim Damalas, formerly a Hollywood producer, admits to the cartoon influence).

Si Como No ("Yes, of course") looks as if it fell from its own picture postcard. The amoeba-shaped terrace pool is set like a jewel on the hillside, with a deck clinging to the cliff-face and greenery all around. The pool features a water slide, cascades, Jacuzzi, and swim-up bar. The adjoining bar-cum-restaurant is small but as intimate as a bouquet of roses; it's a cool place to hang, sampling an assortment of special cocktails and creative Costa Rican dishes.

The compact property, amid 2.63 hectares of rainforest overlooking the beach, has 32 spacious suites in split-level luxury villas, plus junior suites and apartments with splendidly equipped kitchens. All boast terra-cotta floors, warm tropical colors, rich tropical prints, and white tiles inset with hand-painted motifs of tropical creatures. Two-bath villas have living room, master bedroom, dining room, and kitchen; apartments also have kitchens, master bedroom, dining room; suites have kitchen or wet-bar. Tall French doors open to a balcony with wide awnings for shade. No need to step out, however, for you can indulge in the views from your king-size beds of rustic teak, with mosquito nets adding a romantic note. Halogen reading-lamps are inset in the ceiling high above. Bathrooms (festooned with fluffy towels) have octagonal Tiffany windows of underwater scenes, plus bench seats and glass-brick walls; it's like showering in an aquarium!

The whole complex could have been designed by Friends of the Earth, with waste- and water-recycling, biological marsh sewage systems, low voltage solar lighting, computer-programmed a/c, and double-paned windows and doors to deflect heat and keep cool air in. Nature plays its part. Si Como No sits in a valley between two ridges and benefits from the breezes that flow downhill.

In the complex you'll find a delicatessen plus beach-store, "convenience market," and pharmacy. Iguana Tours is also here, offering rafting, biking, etc. A shuttle to the beach was to be introduced. Damalas was planning a lobby, video theater, and conference center that promises to be something only Hollywood could have thought up . . . which I suppose it did! Nature trails lead through the 14-hectare rainforest across the road. Rates: $50-75 d, room, $72-95 d suites and apartment room, $124-165 d villas (low-high season).

La Colina (tel. 777-0231), near Quepos, has six simple rooms in a two-story *ranchita*-style house with black-and-white check floors. Rooms are dark but pleasant enough. Rate: $25 d.

El Salto Mountain Hotel (Apdo. 119, Quepos, tel. 777-0130, fax 441-2938) is a rustic inn with ocean view and four km of nature trails in a private reserve replete with waterfalls. Cabins have large bathrooms with hot water, plus terraces. A swimming pool sits amid flowering gardens, and there's an open-air restaurant. Not inspected. It's up a road leading east, south of Bahía Hotel.

Villa Osa (Apdo. 128, Quepos, tel. 777-0233, fax 777-0233) looks like a Scandinavian chalet; appropriately, it's owned by an amiable Norwegian called Bjorn. The two-story unit offers a beautiful ocean view across the bay to far mountains. It has lots of planters and creepers, plus a wide wraparound veranda with hammocks. Six rooms vary. Run to Scandinavian standards of cleanliness and efficiency. Laundry service. Rates: $50 s/d standard, $60 deluxe, $70 superior.

Tulemar Bungalows (Apdo. 225, Manuel Antonio 6350, tel. 777-0580, fax 777-1579) has ocean-view octagonal bungalows with a/c, in-room safes, TVs and VCRs, telephones, fans, hair-driers, kitchenettes, and beautiful interiors highlighted by wide windows, French curtains, and strange UFO-like bulbous skylights. You'll find a swimming pool plus shop and snack bar.

Villa El Oasis, just before Villas Nicolas, has a room ($35) and a condo ($55) for rent.

Villa La Roca (tel. 777-1349) is a whitewashed Mediterranean-style villa run by two

Germans. The five units—each different—hold two to four people, with terraces overlooking the ocean. Some have kitchenettes. Very pleasing. No telephones. Laundry service. Rates: $35-70 d.

Apartotel El Colibri (Apdo. 94, Quepos, tel. 777-0432) has 10 cozy duplex rooms with kitchenettes, fans, and private baths with hot water. Compact and basic, but light and clean. French doors open onto private terraces with hammocks. A beautiful colonial-tiled cooling-off pool sits amid lush, secluded grounds. Rates: $56 s, $68 d, $79 t, including tax. About 200 meters away is the **Comfort Lodge Hotel** (not reviewed).

Villa Niña Hotel (tel. 777-1628, fax 777-1497) is an attractive, three-story, salmon-pink, thatched structure: part-Mediterranean, part indigenous. All nine rooms (some with a/c) have a terrace with lounge-chairs for enjoying the views over Manuel Antonio. Each, too, has a private bathroom, terra-cotta tiles, coffee maker, plus double bed and a bunk. There's a pool and restaurant. Rates: $30-75 d, low season; $45-90 high season.

Hotel del Mar, at the bottom of the hill near the beach, has adequate though relatively small rooms with balconies, fans, and private baths with cold water. It's a great location for the beach, right on the road and without views. Rates: from $25 d. **Villas Mar y Sol** (Apdo. 256, Quepos 6350, tel. 777-0307, fax 777-0562), 125 meters east of the bus stop, has eight "South American style" a/c rooms with private baths.

Upscale

Mimo's Hotel (Apdo. 228, Manuel Antonio 6358, tel./fax 777-0054) is a new, very beautiful Spanish-style villa on a slope. Very spacious and attractive a/c rooms have private verandas with hammocks. Each room has a double-bed and futon, plus kitchenette. Rate: $65.

Bahía Hotel (Apdo. 186, Manuel Antonio 6350, tel. 777-0350, fax 777-0171) has 10 whitewashed rooms with a/c and private baths with hot water; two rooms each have a Jacuzzi next to the bed. Lovers' heaven! Shaded setting. The hotel has a small pool and snack bar, laundry and parking, plus a restaurant that blends elegance and rusticity. Rates: $65 d, $80 with Jacuzzi, including breakfast.

Villa Teca (Apdo. 180, Quepos 6350, tel. 777-1117, fax 777-1578 or 777-0279) is an exquisite, aesthetically appealing modern property with daffodil-yellow, red-tile-roofed villas scattered throughout the lushly vegetated hillside. There are 40 rooms in 20 a/c bungalows, each with two twin beds (with beautiful tropical floral spreads), telephone, terrace, plus private bath with hot water. Other highlights include an attractive pool and sundeck plus thatched restaurant serving Italian fare, and a free shuttle to and from the beach. Rates: $65-100, including breakfast.

By the time you read this, **Valle Verde Lodge** (tel./fax 777-0040) should have opened with 16 rooms and 12 one-bedroom apartments with living rooms and kitchens. The fairly large complex has covered walkways that lead to jungle cabinas. A large *ranchita* restaurant was planned. Rates: $80 d, one-bedroom cabinas; $500 per week, one-bedroom apartments.

Also recommended is **Hotel Las Tres Banderas** (tel. 777-1521, fax 777-1478), a handsome two-story Spanish colonial-style property abounding in hardwoods. Its 16 a/c rooms come in three types, including three suites. They're roomy and pleasant, with frilly spreads, lots of light, big balconies, and beautiful bathrooms with pretty tiles and deep tubs (suites only). Friendly Polish owner Andrzej Nowacki is proud of the water pressure in the showers! You'll also find a small *rosteria* (grill) and hardwood bar, plus a nice lap pool with cascade. Rates (high season): from $55 d, $95 suites.

El Lirio (Apdo. 123, Quepos, tel. 777-0403) has nine pretty rooms with a/c, fans, and private baths with hot water. It features a pool with sundeck plus a tiny *mirador* in lush, secluded grounds. Rate: $49 d, including breakfast and tax.

Divisamar Hotel (Apdo. 82, Quepos 6350, tel. 777-0371, fax 777-0525) is a three-story unit with 12 only moderately appealing a/c rooms, 12 junior suites and one master suite around a small kidney-shaped swimming pool. The hotel has a whirlpool, plus souvenir shop and an open-air bar and restaurant with a pleasant outside dining terrace (continental dishes). Overpriced! Rates: $85 s/d, $95 t.

Hotel Casa Blanca (Apdo. 194, Quepos, tel. 777-0253) has four very bright and pleasing though simply furnished double rooms plus two suites with terraces, fans, and private baths with hot water. Large and well-kept bathrooms. It's very tranquil. Bougainvilleas surround a small cooling pool. Rates: $60 d, $140 suites.

Villas El Parque (Apdo. 111, Quepos, tel. 777-0096, fax 777-0538) has 16 villas (no kitchens) plus one suite (with kitchen) in colonial style. Large balconies offer views out over the park. There's a restaurant plus a triple-level swimming pool. Rates: $71 villas, $82 suite.

Villas Nicolas (Apdo. 236, Quepos, tel. 777-0481, fax 777-0451) has 12 one- and two-bedroom villa suites, all with private ocean-view verandas overlooking lush grounds. Upper-story verandas have concrete benches with soft-cushioned sofas. Rooms are large and pleasantly furnished in hardwoods, with fans and private baths with hot water. Smaller bedrooms upstairs have no kitchens. There's a narrow swimming pool and a sundeck. Choose from six types of room, including suites. Rates: $59-156 d.

Next door is **Hotel Si Como No** (see special topic "Two Seaside Gems").

Hotel and Villas Mogotes (Apdo. 120, Quepos, tel./fax 777-0582) has two a/c villas with kitchenettes, plus rooms and suites, all with fans, hot water, telephones. Most rooms and all suites have ocean-view balconies. You'll find a pleasing little colonial-tiled bar and restaurant under thatch, plus a small pool on a concrete veranda with wide ocean views. The hotel has its own nature trail. The place, in early form, was once home to folk-rock singer Jim Croce. Rates: $60 s, $80 d, $95 t for rooms; $95 s, $110 d, $125 t for villas, including breakfast.

Hotel Casitas Eclipse (tel./fax 777-0408 or 777-1738) is one of the most exquisite and intimate properties in the area, and highly recommended. It offers 18 rooms in nine beautiful, whitewashed Mediterranean-style two-story a/c villas set in a hollow around a pool with redbrick sun terrace and bougainvillea cascading over white walls. The effect is stunning. You can rent the entire villa or one floor only. The spacious rooms have heaps of light and fully equipped kitchens and are brightly decorated with South American covers, etc. French owned. Mar-

velous! Rates: $91 standard, $109 suite, $193 house, including tax.

Rustic and intimate **Cabinas La Quinta** (Apdo. 76, Quepos, tel. 777-0434) was the third hotel to open in Manuel Antonio. It has seven spacious rooms with large private baths with colonial tiles. Triple and quad rooms have a/c and kitchenettes. It nestles in its own grove, with a tiny swimming pool and pleasant vistas. Rates: $45 s, $65 d, $72 t, $80 quad.

Costa Verde (tel. 777-0584, fax 777-0560; Apdo. 6944, San José, tel. 223-7946, fax 223-9446; in the U.S. tel. 800-231-RICA) is a three-story modern unit of 14 studio apartments, 12 two-story villas, and two two-bedroom apartments, with lots of space and heaps of light. Sliding doors backed by screen doors open onto verandas with leather rockers and views over the beach. Some rooms face away from the ocean. A restaurant has views over Manuel Antonio. Rates: about $70 for "efficiency" apartments, $120 villas (family-size), $95 with ocean view, including tax.

Hotel Arboleda (Apdo. 55, Manuel Antonio, tel. 777-0092, fax 777-0414) has 40 rooms with fans and private baths with hot water. Older units on stilts are dingy and overpriced. More modern units down near the beach are more pleasing, with a/c and wide patios. A breezy open-air restaurant is close enough to the sea that you can hear the waves. You can rent horses, catamarans, and surfboards. Rates: $65, $85 a/c.

Villas de la Selva (Apdo. 359, San José 2070, tel./fax 253-4890) has one master bedroom with a double and a single bed, and another room with two bunk beds and a single. A smaller apartment sleeps two people ($94 d). There's a fully equipped kitchen plus a terrace with ocean view. Rates: $125 s/d, $150 for three or four, $175 five or six, $200 seven or eight.

Hotel and Villas Karahé (Apdo. 100, Quepos 6350, tel. 777-0170, fax 777-0152) has 32 modern a/c rooms, including nine cabinas. They're large and light but lack ambience. Very nice bathrooms, good views, and beautiful grounds. The rustic restaurant's house specialties include shish kebabs. A private trail leads to the beach, where there's a pool and a snack bar. One reader has written to say that the rooms are dirty; I found them to be clean. The hotel offers sport-

fishing. Rates: $65 s, $70 d cabinas; $75 s, $80 d rooms; $95 s, $100 d junior suites.

Deluxe

Byblos (Apdo. 112, Quepos, tel. 777-0411, fax 777-0009) is a flamboyantly stylish quasi-Swiss lodge in lush landscaped grounds. A wonderful amoeba-shaped pool and sundeck are set in a hollow surrounded by jungle. Seven white-washed stone bungalows are spaced widely apart and have private balconies overlooking banana groves and primary forest. Nine spacious junior suites in the main unit enjoy large triangular bathrooms. Small windows do not take advantage of the lofty position. Rooms have private baths with hot water, refrigerators, TVs, and telephones. Bamboo furniture. A pleasant breezy restaurant overlooks the grounds. Rates: $120 d rooms and suites; $200 presidential suite.

Hotel La Mariposa (Apdo. 4, Quepos, tel. 777-0355, fax 777-0050; or in the U.S. tel. 800-223-6510) has been lauded by so many travel magazines over the years it has become an institution as the "best hotel" in the country. Surprise! In the first edition, I stated that the hotel rested on its laurels. Alas, it still does, though now under new ownership. First the good points: The delightfully romantic hotel, dramatically perched on cliffs above the sea, commands stunning views. Luxuriant grounds include bougainvillea bowers. And an airy restaurant centered on a little fountain overlooks a *palapa*-roofed bar and pool enhanced by subdued, romantic pink lighting at night. Steps inlaid with pretty hand-painted tiles lead down through lush hillside gardens to 10 split-level Mediterranean-style cottages, each with its own deck suspended over the steep hillside and a massive skylit bathroom with enough flora to stock a greenhouse.

The disappointments: The simple furnishings are dowdy and a bit moth-eaten for a hotel with such a reputation (and prices): the January 1993 issue of *Condé Nast Traveler* likened the decor to Hitchcock's Bates Motel! Nothing has changed under new management. And guests deserve far better in the dining room. Service, once notable, has more recently been reported as fair, and the food is still blasé. There's a table d'hôte menu and a single set dinner at 7 p.m. (too bad if you feel like a snooze). And there's no

room service: if you want a cocktail on your veranda, you climb the stairs. A sign in the lobby quotes Somerset Maugham: "There are two kinds of travel—first class and with children." No children under 15. No telephones. No TVs. A nature trail leads to the beach. Reservations essential. Vastly overpriced. Rates: $140 s, $200 d, $260 t, $320 quad, including breakfast and dinner ("add 25% for taxes and gratuity").

Makanda by the Sea (Apdo. 26, Quepos, tel./fax 777-0442) gives La Mariposa a run for its money. Three modern villas and three studios are each quite different, but all of stunning design. The minimalist decor has hints of Milan and Tokyo: suave and contemporary decor with simple Japanese statements. Number 3 is my favorite: the high-ceilinged, timbered bedroom opens directly onto a wraparound veranda. No doors or windows. Fans and mosquito nets keep bugs at bay. Kitchens, too, are of beautiful hardwoods. No restaurant or views (the hotel is surrounded by virgin forest and a Japanese garden). Facilities include a fathoms-deep pool and a Jacuzzi. Thumbs up! Rates: $90 to $155 s/d.

The dirt road leads past Makanda to the remarkable **Hotel and Beach Club El Parador** (see special topic "Two Seaside Gems").

El Dorado Mojado (tel. 777-0368, fax 223-6728) has eight attractive modern rooms—some with kitchens—with private baths, hot water, and a/c. The hotel specializes in fishing. A swimming pool was being added. A larger house has attractive modern units. Pricey. Rates: $125 d, $135 t.

Accommodations by the Beach

Most hotels and cabinas here charge for location, not standards. **Hotel Villa Bosque** (tel./fax 777-0401), set back from the beach close to the park boundary, has 13 pleasant, atmospheric rooms for three people, with private baths with hot water, plus veranda/patio with chairs. Restaurant. Nice, but pricey. Rates: $70 d; $80 a/c, including tax.

Cabinas, Bar y Restaurant Los Almendros (Apdo. 68, Quepos, tel./fax 777-0225) has 21 modern and clean though sparsely furnished a/c rooms (nine have fans), with private baths with hot water. A pleasing breezy restaurant is fronted by palms. The hotel offers horses for rent, fishing trips, and tours. Rates: $40 with fan; $45 a/c.

Cabinas Espadilla (Apdo. 30, Heredia, tel. 777-0416) has 16 cabinas, all with refrigerators (eight with kitchenettes), fans, and private baths. They're basically furnished but spacious; each sleeps up to four people. There are *pilas* (laundry sinks). An extra 16 large units with a/c are next to Villa Bosque. Rates: from $35 s, $45 d.

Cabinas Manuel Antonio (tel. 253-2103 or 777-0212) has 18 very basic beachfront units—all with private baths with cold water—barely hanging onto their foundation against the predations of the Pacific. Check that fans, etc., work before accepting your room. It has a *soda* and a public telephone. Though gloomy, both it and the Hotel Manuel Antonio, across the street, are popular with the youth crowd. Rate: $17 up to four people. **Hotel Manuel Antonio** (Apdo. 88, Quepos, tel. 777-0290) is a small hotel right beside the park entrance. Definitely for budget travelers, though the four rooms upstairs are clean and bright. A bar and restaurant are at the back. The downstairs is boarded up. Rates: $21 s/d, $25 t.

Restaurante/Hotel Vela (Apdo. 13, Quepos, tel. 777-0413), otherwise known as the Cabinas Vela-Bar, has nine cabinas with fans and private baths, plus a house and an apartment with kitchen. It has a quasi-Mediterranean-meets-Switzerland feel, plus a very popular thatched restaurant and bar with creative seafood dishes and daily specials. Rates: $16, or $60 d for a *casita*.

Cabinas Costa Linda (tel. 777-0304), near Hotel Villa Bosque, is a self-proclaimed youth hostel with very basic rooms for about $8 with shared bath, $20 with private bath. Deplorably dirty! About 200 meters away, **El Grano de Oro** (tel. 777-0578) has 10 rooms with shared bath. Clean and quiet. Rate: $10 d. The other option is the very basic **Cabinas Aymara.**

House Rentals

Two companies that specialize in house rentals are **Blue Marlin** (tel. 777-0295) and **Manuel Antonio House Rentals** (tel. 777-0560). Also check with **Buena Nota** souvenir store in Quepos (tel. 777-0345); Anita rents a house near the Hotel La Mariposa. **Residencia Alejandria** (tel. 777-0495) is a large house for rent opposite Byblos. A notice board outside the **Restaurante Mar y Sombra** (see below) also advertises houses for rent (tel. 777-0003 and 777-0406). Rates begin at about $250 per week. **Villas Residencia el Tucán** has villas for rent and sale.

Camping

No camping is allowed in the park. You can camp along the beach north of Restaurante Mar y Sombra. Campers may pitch tents on lawns under shade trees at the back of the Hotel Manuel Antonio ($2 per person; showers cost 25 cents); it will supply tents ($6). You'll also find a campsite 100 meters north of Mimo's.

FOOD

The best bets are the hillside restaurants. Pricey, but a good range of foods. **Byblos** has excellent French dishes. For Italian food at reasonable rates, try the **Plinio,** which also has a buffet breakfast for all-comers. Nearby, and another good place for breakfast, is **El Acuario,** a very atmospheric *ranchita* with rough-hewn furniture. For meats, check out the **Las Charruas Uruguayan Steak House** (tel. 777-0501, fax 777-0409), a very elegant restaurant with open-air terrace offering ocean views and candlelight dining. A lot of people have heard raves about the **La Mariposa,** but I found its food very disappointing; two readers have written to the same effect.

Restaurante La Arcada Italiana (tel. 777-1297) enjoys a beautiful hillside setting with views over Quepos and the coast; dinner only. If Italian is your thing, also check out **Italian Club Spaghettería** next to Jardín Gaia. Also here is **BBQ Asia,** highly recommended for its oriental seafoods and ambience.

Barba Roja Restaurant (tel. 777-0331), 100 meters beyond Villa Osa, offers delicious seafoods, daily specials, and ocean-view alfresco dining. Great for sunset dining. Good breakfasts include whole-wheat toast. There's an art gallery and a gift shop upstairs. Just down the road is **Karola's Bar and Garden Restaurant,** with a similar setting. Other options include the very atmospheric **Bar y Restaurant Iguanazul,** with terrace dining and ocean view; the elegant **La Brisa Restaurant,** with terrace and French cuisine at reasonable rates; and the exciting if expensive **Mambo Grill** (tel. 777-0096), for-

merly the Sukia Restaurant, serving Tex-Mex and Spanish seafood dishes and tapas in a dashing setting whose focal point is the triple-tier swimming pool with water cascades. Yes, you can buy a burger, but watch the stuffed jalapeños—they're hotter than Hades! "Monkey Hour" is 4-7 p.m.

A string of open-air budget restaurants by the beach serves fresh fish and local specialties. **Mar y Sombra** (tel. 777-0003) is the focal point of Espadilla Beach. Here you can sit at palm-shaded tables on the sand, talk to the tame macaw, and eat a whole fried fish for under five dollars (no prizes for quality, but adequate enough). The bar doubles as a disco at night. The neighboring **Vel Mar Bar**, sitting in its own little pocket of palms, rents surfboards and snorkeling equipment, presumably so you can work up an appetite. **Bar y Restaurant Disco Amor** also has beachfront dining. **Costa Linda** has been recommended for its health-food breakfasts.

SHOPPING AND SERVICES

Souvenirs
Cay Costa Souvenirs, on the beachfront, sells T-shirts, film, postcards, and toiletries. A handful of beach hawkers sell earrings and hash pipes carved in grotesque faces. **Tienda "Si Como No,"** also has souvenirs and clothing. The best stocked place, though, is **Buena Nota** selling swimwear, T-shirts, you name it, along with souvenirs. Several stalls sell jewelry down by the beach.

Tours
Most hotels can arrange sportfishing, horseback trips, and guided nature hikes. (Also see "Quepos," above) **Tikal Tours** (Apdo. 6398, San José 1000, tel. 223-2811, fax 223-1916) offers an in-depth three-day "Wildlife and Beaches" tour of Carara Biological Reserve and Manuel Antonio ($245). The **Iguana Tours** office is at Hotel Si Como No. The **Pacific Group**, at El Mono Azul, offers boat trips to Corcovado, Drake Bay, etc.

Horses
Marlboro Stables is on the left at the bottom of the hill, 200 meters before Manuel Antonio

beach. **Quepos Trail Rides** (tel. 777-0566) offers guided horseback rides along the beach; follow the trail that begins next to Barba Roja Restaurant. **Equus Stables** (tel. 777-0001) is midway between Quepos and the park.

Other
There's a **public telephone** (777-0303) outside Cay Costa Souvenirs. **Marley's Tropical Mini-Golf** is a rather pathetic little course where you hit balls through tires, etc. Good fun? Why not? You can rent boogie boards ($1.50 per hour; $8 per day) and snorkeling gear ($1.50 per hour; $6 a day) at **Café Mermaid.**

TRANSPORTATION

By Bus
See "Quepos" for bus schedules from San José. Local buses operate between Quepos and Manuel Antonio (depart Quepos 5:45, 7, 8, 9:30, 10:30, and 11:30 a.m., and 12:30, 2, 3, 4, 5, 7 and 10 p.m.; return 30 minutes later). Buses will pick you up along the road if you flag them down, but note that space sells out early. They'll also drop you at any hotel you request.

The future of **American VIP Coach Service** (Apdo. 896, Escazú 1250, tel. 222-8134, fax 221-4596; in Quepos, tel. 777-0017) was uncertain. The luxury, a/c Greyhound bus service to Quepos and Manuel Antonio (four hours) departs San José from the Gran Hotel at 7 a.m. The bus from Manuel Antonio departs at 3 p.m. The bus features reclining seats, TV and VCR, plus bar and restroom. Free drinks and appetizers are served on the return journey.

Saragundí Specialty Tours' Pura Natura tourist shuttle departs San José for Manuel Antonio at 7 a.m. ($19; arrives 1:30 p.m., tel. 255-0011, fax 255-2155).

By Air
See "Quepos," above. A bus will meet the SANSA plane for the short ride to Manuel Antonio.

By Sea
Cruceros del Sur (Apdo. 1198, San José 1200, tel. 220-1927, fax 220-2103) includes Manuel Antonio National Park on weeklong natural-history cruises aboard the 68-passenger eco-cruise

ship *Temptress* (see special topic, "Natural-History Cruise Tours" in the On the Road chapter). Other destinations include Palo Verde National Park, Drake Bay, Manuel Antonio, Marenco Biological Station, Corcovado National Park, and Caño Island. Highly recommended. The same company also offers one-day cruises to Manuel

Antonio from Puntarenas aboard the 11-meter *Georgiana* Tuesday and Saturday (plus Thursday in high season, Dec.-March). The six-meter catamaran *La Mamá de Tarzán* operates half-day trips from Quepos at 9 a.m. and 2 p.m., with drinks and food provided ($35, children $20; tel. 777-1257 or 777-0191).

MANUEL ANTONIO TO DOMINICAL

PLAYAS SAVEGRE AND MATAPALO

South of Quepos, a bumpy dirt and rock road leads to Dominical, 45 km southeast of Quepos. It's rough going. For several miles south of town the region is a sea of African palms broken only by oil-processing plants belching out sickly smoke. You'd hardly know that away from the ruler-straight road a network of dirt roads links various hamlets serving the plantations. Some of these unsigned roads lead to lonesome beaches. **Playa Matapalo,** for example, is a fabulous long gray-sand beach, two km east of the coast road, midway between Manuel Antonio and Dominical. The beach is a surfer's paradise; truly stunning, despite being gray-sand. The mouth of the Río Savegre separates Playa Matapalo from the equally beautiful and unspoiled **Playa Savegre** to the north. The river is a popular whitewater option. **Savegre Ranch** (tel. 777-0528), 10 km south of Manuel Antonio, is popular for horseback riding through the riverine lowlands, which shelter monkeys, crocodiles, and other rare fauna ($55 full-day tour; $40 half-day). Trails also lead down to little-visited Playa El Rey (contact tour operators in Quepos and Manuel Antonio).

South of Matapalo, habitation is very sparse and you'll find yourself driving the lonesome rutted road with nary a sight of humans all the way to Hacienda Barú, just north of which you'll find a **gas station.**

Accommodations and Food
Hotel Rancho Casa Grande has handsome *casitas* in lush grounds, 400 meters south of the hospital, three km south of Quepos. Not reviewed.

At Playa Matapalo, where you reach the beach, **Soda Cabinas Oasis** has a row of tiny,

basic cabins with private bath and cold water, set in a garden. Rates: $12-22. The dirt road extends along the beach, with basic cabinas spread well apart at regular intervals. Most are in the $20-30 d range and have private baths with cold water. Among them are **El Ranchito; El Coquito del Pacífico,** with pleasant cabinas amid rows of palms; **Terraza del Sol,** which has four cabinas and bills itself as a "hotel, restaurant, and beach club"; and the charming **Soda Kattia,** opposite Terraza del Sol, with cabinas and a popular yet funky little restaurant. **Cabinas Matapalo** also has budget rooms. Nearby is **Restaurant La Casa Nostra,** on the beachfront, with tables shaded by trees.

Hacienda Casa Grande is a large hotel project reportedly under construction at Playa Savegre.

Getting There
Saragundí Specialty Tours (tel. 255-0011, fax 255-2155) operates the **Pura Natura** tourist shuttle via Manuel Antonio (departs San José 7 a.m.; departs Manuel Antonio 1:30 p.m.).

HACIENDA BARÚ/NATURÍSTICA S.A.

Hacienda Barú (Apdo. 215, San Isidro de El General 8000, tel. 717-1903, fax 717-0441), one km north of Dominical, has its own private rainforest preserve, better known as Naturística S.A., plus three km of protected beach. The 330-hectare ranch protects several ecosystems, including mangrove swamp and at least 40 hectares of primary rainforest: a safe haven for anteaters, ocelots, kinkajous, tayras, capuchin monkeys, and jaguarundis. More than 220 bird species have been recorded: roseate spoonbills, magnificent frigate birds, boat-billed herons, kingfishers, curassows, falcons, cormorants, anhingas, and

owls, among others. Olive ridley and hawkbill turtles also come ashore to nest at the wide and isolated Playa Barú. Trails and guided birding and nature hikes lead through pasture, fruit orchards, cacao plantations, and forest.

Archaeologists are excavating a site on a crest of a hill overlooking the Río Barú north of Dominical. More than a dozen petroglyphs carved onto large rocks are the most obvious remains of what may be an ancient ceremonial and urban site. It's thought to have been wiped out by early Spanish conquest. Contact Jack and Diane Ewing at Hacienda Barú (see above) for permission to visit.

There's a three-bedroom house for rent 400

meters from the beach, with hot water, fans, and kitchen. There are also six two-bedroom cabins, each with two doubles and single bed, fans, hot water, refrigerator, and cooking facilities, plus a restaurant serving Italian and Costa Rican dishes. Camping is allowed. You can rent horses (from $15, two hours). A series of guided hikes include "A Night in the Jungle," ($15-60). And, to see the beasts at eye-to-eye level, explore the canopy (with guide) in either a bosun's chair with a winch or using rappeling equipment ($70). A canopy platform is planned. Rates: cabins, $50 d, $10 extra person.

The bus from Quepos to San Isidro will drop you here.

DOMINICAL AND VICINITY

A favorite of surfers and backpackers, Dominical, 45 km southeast of Quepos, is a tiny laid-back "resort" surrounded by magnificent coastal scenery, immediately south of the bridge over the Río Barú. There's little to it except a tiny church, school, the odd restaurant, and assorted cabins, but things are beginning to happen down here. The Costera Sur roadway being cut between Uvita and Palmar is helping bring new developments to the area and a boom in resorts and other facilities is under way south of town. Ror example, a water sports complex was under construction at Rancho de la Felicidad (see "Uvita," below).

The four-km beach is beautiful, and the warm waters attract whales and dolphins. Swimming reportedly can be dangerous because of rips, and the Río Barú supposedly empties polluted waters into the sea near the beach north of Dominical. Locals say the town's name is derived from the name of a local banana-like fruit. At dusk check out the riverbank, where egrets roost en masse.

Several isolated beaches offer good breaks and points for surfers farther south, as do Barú and Guapil beaches to the north. The reef-protected waters of Ballena Marine National Park, a 30-minute drive south, are perfect for swimming and snorkeling.

If you O.D. on the sun, sand and surf, a popular option is to hire a guide and horse for journeys through the forested mountains to **waterfalls** such as the Emerald Pool Falls or Santo Cristo (called "Naullaca" by old-timers).

The area has been notorious as a marijuana-growing area. "All the *campesinos* were growing it," says one source. It went unchecked for years. Now the police are cracking down (no pun intended).

ACCOMMODATIONS

Budget
Cabinas Coco (tel. 717-2555) has small, basic but clean beachfront cabinas with fans and shared baths with cold water. There's a disco on weekends. Rates: $7 s, $10 d.

Inexpensive
Cabinas Rio Lindo (tel. 771-2009, fax 771-1725), next to Restaurant Maui, on the right as you enter Dominical, has 10 rooms with fans and very large double bathtubs-cum-showers with hot water. It's brand new and very pleasing. Upstairs rooms catch the breeze. Rates: $23 d ($12 extra). **Posada Del Sol** (fax 771-3060) has four rooms with private bathrooms (hot water, perhaps, by the time you read this). They're pleasant, with plenty of light, fans, patios, plus laundry service. Rates: $15 s, $27 d.

Cabinas Willdale (tel. 717-1903, fax 717-0441) has four small cabinas and a spacious and atmospheric house with views over the river estuary. Rooms are clean, screened, and have fans plus private baths with hot water. Rates: $20 s, $25 d, $50 for the house.

Restaurante y Cabinas Boca Verde (tel. 717-1414) is on the beachfront beside a small estuary, one km south of Dominical. You can drive along the beach to reach it. Screened cabinas have fans and cold water. A reader reports "austere rooms with shared dingy bathroom and thin walls." The pleasing open-air restaurant is very popular with Ticos and has a great house specialty: grilled fish filled with potato and sour cream, plus salad and garlic bread ($5). Rates: $13 s/d, shared bath; $25 private bath.

Also see Cabinas San Clemente, below.

Moderate
La Residencia (tel. 717-2175) has eight small but clean rooms with fans, screens, and shared baths with hot water. Rate: $24 d. **Cabinas Narayit** (tel. 717-1878) has 18 a/c beachside cabins and rooms—some in a two-story unit—with fans and private baths with cold water. Nice! The restaurant is handsome. Rates: $30 d without a/c, $35 d with a/c and hot water.

DiuWak Hotel (tel./fax 223-8195) opened in January 1995 with eight simple but tasteful cabins plus four suites, amid a landscaped garden 50 meters from the beach. DiuWak has borrowed elements of design from Villas Río Mar (see below) to grace the spacious cabins; each

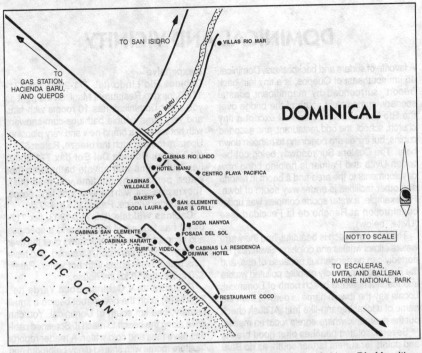

DOMINICAL

TO SAN ISIDRO

VILLAS RIO MAR

TO GAS STATION, HACIENDA BARU, AND QUEPOS

RIO BARU

CABINAS RIO LINDO
HOTEL MANU
CENTRO PLAYA PACIFICA
CABINAS WILLDALE
BAKERY
SODA LAURA
SAN CLEMENTE BAR & GRILL
SODA NANYOA
CABINAS SAN CLEMENTE
CABINAS NARAYIT
POSADA DEL SOL
SURF N' VIDEO
CABINAS LA RESIDENCIA
DIUWAK HOTEL

PACIFIC OCEAN

PLAYA DOMINICAL

RESTAURANTE COCO

NOT TO SCALE

TO ESCALERAS, UVITA, AND BALLENA MARINE NATIONAL PARK

© MOON PUBLICATIONS, INC.

has a double and single bed, ceiling fan, and charming porch plus private bath with hot water. Four a/c suites have kitchenettes and dining area plus living room, bathroom, and bedroom with bamboo furniture. A pool and large Jacuzzi are planned, and the restaurant was almost complete when I passed by. The hotel has a souvenir shop. Rates: $41 d, $60 suite.

Cabinas San Clemente (tel. 717-0866 or voicemail/fax 771-1972) offers 15 rooms in a handsome two-story unit with a bamboo roof, natural stone, and thatched veranda, also copied from Villas Río Mar. Large airy rooms have hardwood floors and shuttered windows and fans. Very attractive! Rate: $35 d. Additional, cheaper rooms are above the San Clemente Bay & Grill restaurant. Rate: about $20 with shared bath.

Upscale
Villas Río Mar Hotel & Resort (Apdo. 1350, San Pedro Montes de Oca 2050, tel. 771-2264 or 224-2053, fax 225-5712) opened in 1994 on

the site of the former Cabinas Río Mar. It's a Polynesian-style village magnificently secluded beside the Río Barú, 800 meters north of Dominical, surrounded by forest and lush landscaped grounds. It's the most elegant hotel for miles around, with heaps of bamboo furnishings, lanterns casting warm glows, and lacy mosquito-net curtains enhancing the tropical decor: *muy* romantic! Ten thatch-roofed bungalows house 40 junior suites with comfortable king-size beds, louvered windows, and French doors, plus three rarities: hair dryers, telephones, and steaming hot water. Each has a spacious and elegant veranda with heavy-bamboo-framed sofas and a hammock . . . wherein I relaxed one night with torrential rains pouring down. Tremendous! Thatch-canopied walkways lead between bungalows, which are spaced well-apart. A restaurant with soaring *palenque* roof and planters full of tropical blooms features local and international cuisine served at tables with elegant place settings. The hotel boasts a conference room,

plus tennis courts and an attractive pool with swim-up bar and Jacuzzi. It provides shuttle service to the beach. If you prefer tubing down the Río Barú, the hotel provides the inner tubes, or you may prefer to rent a mountain bike. Six adjacent condominium units were under construction. Rates: from $60 s, $75 d.

Houses
Pisces Pacific Boat Tours (tel. 717-1903 or 221-2053) has houses for rent. **Cabinas Nayarit** has two fully furnished houses ($45 for six people; $50 for seven). The gas station north of Dominical has a three-bedroom house with kitchenette for rent near the beachfront at Playa

FINCA BRIAN Y MILENA

This 10-hectare *finca,* located 300 meters above sea level, is my number-one choice for a totally reclusive, private, get-away-from-it-all, very rustic escape. The farm is run by Missouri transplant Brian and his Tica wife Milena. "One of the few genuine experiences available to tourists who would like to see true Costa Rican home life," reports one reader. "I know of no other tour that can offer such an intimate and delightful experience," says another. A third writes, "We loved it so much! Their guest cabin was so incredibly ULTIMATE!" I recommend at least two or three days here (write Apdo. 2, San Isidro de El General 8000; fax 771-1903 or 771-3060; allow at least four weeks for a reply).

Your home-away-from-home is a rustic yet remarkably cozy, well-fashioned, and utterly romantic cabin, with private bath and cold water. It sleeps three; a folding cot on the balcony could accommodate a fourth person. Farther up the mountain is a more basic hut—the "birdhouse." Brian and Milena planned to add a small bamboo shelter. At night, after Milena's superb Costa Rican-style all-natural meals cooked outside on a wood-fired stove (a private tip for her might be in order); you can soak by starlight in the streamside rock pool heated by a wood-fired oven.

Brian and Milena don't rent their cabin to those seeking only shelter. They think of themselves as *campesinos* and an educational enterprise rather than a tourist facility. Brian has developed an economically sustainable fruit farm, cultivating neglected fruit trees that prove productive in wetter areas of Costa Rica. At least 3,000 species of fruit trees may be available in tropical forests, according to *National Geographic,* and of these 200 are in actual use. Brian has about 90 in production, as well as nuts and spices such as ginger and vanilla. He will share his enlightened perspective, enthusiasm, and textbook knowledge on a fascinating tour of the orchard.

Brian and Milena are codirectors of a neighborhood conservation group that aims to protect a rainforest area of about 48 hectares. Brian sees his *finca* as a key to conservation. He is experimenting with imported cash-crop trees so that the whole area may someday benefit ecologically and economically by his example.

Most of his fruits are sold to local fishermen. As the commercial viability of exotic trees bears fruit, Brian hopes to form producers' cooperatives so that export becomes viable. Key fruits include mangosteen (a fruit described by a turn-of-the-century botanist as "so delicate that it melts in the mouth like a bit of ice cream") and durian (described as "as intoxicating as a fine liqueur"), the most important commercial fruit in Southeast Asia.

There's more! The birding is fantastic (rare chestnut-mandibled toucans and king vultures are common). Plus Brian will guide you on hikes to waterfalls with superb swimming holes. Overnight trips to Salto Diamante—a multiple waterfall of seven cataracts terminating in a final fall of 137 meters—include overnights and meals with *campesino* families. Bring heavy-duty pants and waterproof footwear (ideally, rubber boots) for hikes.

When I visited, it was a 45-minute journey by horseback along a steep trail (even 4WDs were prohibited). Now vehicles—4WD recommended—can make the journey. If you prefer the fun way to get there, simply radio the *finca* from Cabinas Willy, San Clemente, Hacienda Barú, or Bomba Ceibo in Dominical. (Note: It's often difficult to reach them in midday hours because of interference; early morning and evening are best.) Brian will bring horses and meet you at the turnoff for Escalera for an additional charge.

Rates: $36 per person (double occupancy); $8 for children under 12. A $2 per person discount applies for each additional day and for each additional person. Day visit is $26 including lunch and farm tour. Discounts are offered for anyone willing to work.

Guapil, north of the gas station ($35 d/$10 additional). Check out the bulletin board at San Clemente Bar & Grill for more houses.

FOOD AND ENTERTAINMENT

San Clemente Bar & Grill, formerly Jungle Jim's, is the center of action. Jim Bray no longer runs the place (pity—he picked the prettiest waitresses on the Pacific coast), but fellow Californian Mike McGinnis is doing an equally fine job. The large restaurant and open-air bar serves hearty breakfasts, plus Tex-Mex and Cajun and Italian dishes that earn rave reviews (dinner special costs $8). Where once burgers were the main fare, imagine grilled mahi mahi with honey, rosemary, and orange sauce served with fresh vegetables. Good burgers and seafood. Check out the pool table and large TV showing videos. By night everyone gets into the groove on the dance floor.

Opposite is **Soda Laura,** for *típico* food. Also try **Restaurant y Bar Maui, Soda Nanyoa, Restaurante Coco,** or **Restaurante Boca Verde,** reached via the beach south of Dominical. **Restaurant El Manó** (tel. 235-6895) has also been recommended for "California-style" food (I'm not sure where this is). The **Mare Nos Trum** deli, in the Playa Pacífica commercial center, has a salad bar, pizzas, sandwiches, ice cream, etc.; a full-service restaurant was to be added. A *panadería* (bakery) and deli stand opposite San Clemente.

Don't neglect **hotel restaurants,** especially those of Villas Río Mar, Hotelera Dominical, Cabinas Escondidas for vegetarian food, and Las Casita de Puertociti (the latter three are south of Dominical; see below).

SERVICES

The only **public telephone** is outside San Clemente, which also has a radio telephone. The **Selva Mar Reservation Service** (tel. 717-1903 or 771-2311, fax 717-0441) acts as a tourist-information and hotel-reservation service. Selva Mar also offers a series of **tours,** including ones to Ballena Marine National Park and to Oro Verde (see below), a local *finca*

where a traditional *trapiche* (ox-powered sugar mill) is still in use and from where the Duarte brothers lead horseback trips into the virgin jungle of their family's private reserve. **Pisces Pacific Boat Tours** (Apdo. 239, San Isidro de El General 8000, tel. 717-1903 or 221-2053) offers sportfishing trips plus overnight trips to Caño Island and Drake Bay. **Tropical Waters** is a tour information service; it's along the river near Villas Río Mar.

The **gas station,** about one km north of Dominical, sells maps, film, and fishing supplies. It also rents beach umbrellas and boogie boards. You can rent **bicycles** at Cabinas Narayit. Next door is the office for **Reel N' Release Sportfishing** (tel. 717-1903), which has a fully equipped seven-meter center-console boat. It also offers horseback rides and jungle tours. **Surf-n-Video** has bike and surfboard rental plus a board repair service.

Playa Pacífica is a **commercial center** 200 meters south of the bridge and the turnoff into the village. It has a supermarket, clothes boutique, real estate office, and small vegetarian deli/restaurant.

Transportation

Buses depart San Isidro for Dominical daily at 7 a.m. and 1:30 p.m. Buses depart Quepos for Dominical (continuing to San Isidro) daily at 5:30 a.m. and 1:30 p.m. (Transportes Blanco, tel. 771-1384). Supposedly a bus originating at Uvita departs Dominical at 7:30 a.m. for San Isidro. Buses to Quepos depart Dominical at 8:30 a.m. and 3 p.m.

Taximar (tel. 777-0262 or 777-1170 in Quepos) offers a water-taxi service between Quepos and Dominical ($20 one-way) aboard a 22-seat boat, Tuesday, Thursday, Saturday, and Sunday at 7 a.m. (the service continues to Drake Bay and Caño Island).

DOMINICALITO, ESCALERAS, AND PLAYA HERMOSA

The gravel road continues south from Dominical to **Dominicalito,** a little fishing village in the lee of Punta Dominical, five km south of Dominical at the southern end of the bay, where there is apparently safe mooring within the protection

of the Dominicalito reef. Vultures congregate on the beach. Opposite the turnoff for Dominicalito, signs point the way inland to **Escaleras** ("Staircases") along a rough road that leads steeply into the mountains (the turnoff is marked). All the lodges at Escaleras will provide horses.

Farther south are lonesome out-of-sight beaches culminating in **Playa Hermosa,** a magnificent kilometers-long gray-sand beach, totally undiscovered by tourists. There are no facilities. The beach ends at the headland of Punta Uvita, which marks the northern boundary of Ballena Marine National Park. A signed road leads through ranchland to the southern end of Playa Hermosa; there's another access road at the northern end of the beach.

The coast road, which deteriorates as you go south, has a propensity for landslides in wet season. About four km south of Uvita, it deteriorates into no more than a narrow track that can be impassable in wet season, although all this is about to change with the construction of the new paved coast road that begins two km south of Uvita.

Dominicalito Accommodations
Three kilometers south of Dominical is **Costa Paraíso Bed and Breakfast** (not reviewed), reached via a steep trail that leads to a staggeringly beautiful rocky shore.

Hotelera Dominical (Apdo. 196, San Isidro de El General 8000, tel. 717-0866 or 225-5328, fax 253-4750), alias Cabinas Punta Dominical, reached via a dirt road one km south of the turnoff for Escaleras, has four rustic but cozy tropical hardwood cabinas amid landscaped grounds surrounded by ocean atop Punta Dominicalito, where they catch the breezes. Each is shaded by trees and has screens, fans, and a private bath with hot water. Cabins sleep seven. A thatched open-air restaurant reportedly has excellent food and marvelous ocean views to left and right. The rocky shoreline is good for tidepools. The place is popular with Ticos. Rate: $45 d.

You'll find two basic cabinas—**Cabinas Sadu** and **Coco Tico Cabins**—behind the horseshoe-cove south of Punta Domincalito.

American-owned **Cabinas Escondidas** (Apdo. 364, San Isidro de El General, tel. 272-2904, fax 771-0735), two km farther south, has three cabi-

nas with private baths (no fans), plus splendid views over the Pacific from the hillside location. The landscaped gardens offer tranquility. Massage and Tai Chi classes are offered ($35 per hour). Guided nature walks and horseback rides are available into the surrounding 85-hectare rainforest. And you can rent snorkeling equipment. Patty Mitchell conjures "exquisite vegetarian cuisine" ($8 per meal; open for breakfast and lunch, but dinner by reservation), but be careful that Shanti, the lovable pet howler monkey, or the two affectionate *sainos* (wild pigs) don't make off with your meal. Book through Selva Mar (see "Services," below). There's also a guest suite in the main house. Rates: $40 d cabins, $25 suite, including breakfast.

Las Casitas de Puertocito (c/o tel. 771-1903), one km south, is a delightful little property run by a charming Italian and set amid a lush garden at the head of a valley on the peninsula. Six split-level cabins have a queen-size bed on an open loft, plus a single bed on the ground floor, with bamboo furniture and Guatemalan prints, a bathroom with hot water, and a wide patio complete with tiny kitchenette. A tiny *ranchita* restaurant serves genuine Italian dishes. You can arrange a full range of activities (hiking, horseback rides, snorkeling, fishing, etc.). Rates: $29-39 d, according to season. A four-day "Horseback Adventure" costs $295 per person.

Escaleras Accommodations
Finca Brian y Milena (see special topic) and the three properties below are all highly recommended.

Louisiana brothers Woody and Mike Dyer's **Bella Vista Lodge** (Apdo. 459, San Isidro 8000, tel. 771-1903 or CB Radio Channel 7; in North America, tel. 305-254-7592) is a working cattle ranch nestled in the Escalaras mountains. The converted farmhouse has four simple but comfortable and quaint rooms with shared bath and solar-heated water (dividing bedroom walls stop short of the ceiling; if you're lucky, you'll be spared snorers or amorous adventures—unless that's your thing!—next door). Some private cabinas were being added. The lodge has a restaurant and magnificent views from the airy veranda of the mahogany farmhouse, which commands a priceless position. The lodge offers horseback tours to nearby waterfalls and can

arrange transfers. One reader has raved about this rustic, environmentally conscious getaway (solar-heated water, septic-tank sewer system, etc.); another tells of the Dyers' "warmth and hospitality." Marvelously tranquil, I'm assured. Alas, I still haven't made it there . . . for which, apologies to both readers and Woody and Mike, who have been cited for their contributions to conservation. Book through Selva Mar (see "Services," above). Rates: $20 s, $35 d. Horseback rides cost $40.

Another marvelous option is **Escaleras Inn** (Suite 2277 SJO, P.O. Box 025216, Miami, FL 33102-5216, tel. 771-5247), a three-story classically contemporary structure commanding the hillside one km south of Bella Vista. It offers three deluxe, vaulted-ceiling bedrooms in the main lodge, plus two large cabins. Decor highlights include purple-heart floors and colorful fabrics, with a bar and library, swimming pool and terrace, plus sweeping coastal vistas for amusement. Tiled bathrooms feature pressurized hot water. "Gourmet" meals—the menus are mouthwatering—can be washed down with choice wines. The owners donate $1 per room per night to one of three environmental causes of your choice. Rates: $85 d, including breakfast; $125 for cabins.

Slightly more rustic but no less appealing is **Pacific Edge** (Apdo. 531, San Isidro de El General 2000), reached via its own steep dirt road (4WD recommended) half a km south of the turnoff for Bella Vista. It's simple and secluded, with three cabins stairstepping down a slope on a lower ridge of the mountains, from where you can enjoy grand vistas northward. Wooden walkways lead to the rustic yet comfortable cabins, which have all-around screened windows, as well as hammocks on their verandas. Each cabin has "half-kitchenette," but who needs it when you can hang out in the thatched *ranchita* bar-cum-*cocina*? It's run by an amiable ex-Valley Girl, Susie, and her affable Limey husband, George Atkinson (described, correctly, in *Condé Nast Traveler* as a "merry Londoner . . . 'Appy day!' he keeps croaking like a parrot," and, indeed, he does). Sound effects, in addition to George's twisted Cockney accent, include the cry of howler monkeys and a zillion squawks, whistles, and chirps of birds. Susie reportedly whips up mean cuisine spanning the globe (the

Asian influence is paramount) in her funky restaurant, complete with ice chest as refrigerator. These former mariners work with Bella Vista Lodge in arranging hikes and horseback trips, and also offer fishing, sailing, etc. Reservations through Selva Mar. Rates: $40 d ($5 extra).

Villa Cabeza de Mono is a mountain home for rent at Escaleras. It has a pool, a fully stocked kitchen, maid service, and ocean views. Book through Selva Mar (see "Services," above). Rates: $80-150.

UVITA

This tiny hamlet, 16 km south of Dominical, is the northern gateway to the mangroves and gray-sand beaches of Ballena Marine National Park. It has plenty of natural attractions, even crocodiles in the lagoons south of Uvita! And hiking or traveling by horseback, you may head into the mountains along trails that offer possible glimpses of spider and howler monkeys. This is best done at Oro Verde, with 300 hectares of primary forest ($35, including lunch) and attractions such as remote waterfalls and even a huge pre-Columbian *bola,* or stone sphere. Fortunately, citizens of Uvita have formed a 24-guard patrol and established a de facto ban on hunting and deforestation.

At press time, the Costanera Sur Hwy. from Dominical to Cortés, in the Pacific Southwest, was half complete. It may have been finished by the time you read this, providing direct road access for the first time and putting Uvita and Ballena Marine National Park on the map. (See "Palmar to Ballena Marine National Park" under "Palmar and Vicinity" in the chapter on the Pacific Southwest for driving conditions north from Palmar.)

Accommodations

A little way north and three km inland of Uvita, in the tiny hamlet of San Josecito de Uvita, is **Oro Verde** (tel./fax 771-3015), owned by real *campesinos*—the Duartes—and highly praised by reader Stéphane Tourangeau. The property, set amid jungled mountains at about 600 meters elevation in the valley of the Río Uvita overlooking Ballena Marine National Park, has been

in the Duarte family for three decades. You can watch and even participate in the farming (they raise cattle, grow coffee, beans, rice, etc., and even have a *trapiche,* or traditional sugar press). Two basic yet comfortable bungalows feature a kitchen and two bedrooms, each with two single beds. There's a cool-dip pool. Doña Eida will cook for you if you prefer ($10 per day). You can reach Oro Verde by 4WD (alternately, rent a horse at Rancho Merced; it's about 45 minutes by horse from the road; Oro Verde is signed). (Book through Selva Mar Reservation Service, tel. 717-1903 or 771-2311, fax 717-0441.) Rate: $12 per person.

Opposite the turnoff for Oro Verde is **Rancho La Merced** (tel./fax 771-1903), another private biological reserve—this one on a cattle ranch close to the shore—offering horseback riding, hiking, and a boating tour to Ballena Marine National Park. A cabin with kitchen (cold water only; $30 d) is for rent on a hillock overlooking the ranch and corral. Mangroves by the shore are good for birding.

In Uvita is the rustic yet simple **Cabinas Los Laureles** (tel. 771-1903), set amid a grove of laurel and sugarcane at the foot of the mountains. The four twin-story, thatched, pitched-roofed cabinas have rustic timbered beams and private baths, and come with parking space and porch. A horse-powered *trapiche* presses sugarcane juice. Congenial owner Victor Pérez offers horseback trips into the mountains, plus boat rides to Ballena Marine National Park. His wife serves tasty breakfasts at the family table in their home. Rates: $13 s, $23 d, with breakfast. **Coco Tico Lodge,** 100 meters farther up the dirt road, has rustic cabinas next to a charming little *soda.* It offers boat trips and horseback rides. **Cabinas Punta Uvita** (contact Selva Mar), nearby, has four wood-and-bamboo cabins surrounded by an orchard. Rates: $5 with shared bath; $9 s, $15 d, private bathroom.

Two other places offering beds are **Cabinas María Jesús** and **Cabinas Bejuco** (tel. 771-1182), about one and two km south of Uvita respectively.

Just south of Bejuco, at the entrance to Ballena National Park, is **Hotel El Chamán** (fax 771-7441), which has 11 small, basic cabins and a **campsite** ($3 or so) spread out beneath a palm grove behind the long beach. Each cabin has a double bed and bamboo furnishings (six have private indoor showers; a row of six outside showers serves the rest). True budget travelers can room in a large dorm for $3. The place is German-owned and popular with both Germans and Ticos. It has a small pool and restaurant. You'll function without electricity, drinking and dining by candlelight, though a string of battery-powered lights is strung from trees to light the paths at night. Rate: $30 for four people.

Nearby, at Bahía, **Cabinas Villa Hegalba** and a local resident, Victoria Marín, both have basic cabins with private bath and cold water for about $15.

At press time, Klaus Gudowius, owner of El Chamán, was developing a hotel and theme park complex in the foothills. **Rancho de la Felicidad** should be open, though not complete, by the time you read this. Centerpiece will be a cliffside 600-square-meter swimming pool from which a 300-meter-long water slide will spiral down through the forested and landscaped hill to another pool. Gudowius plans to install an alpine chairlift to whisk you up the mountainside. A botanical garden is also planned, along with a children's adventure playground. A 20-room hotel is also planned.

Camping

You can camp by the park ranger station, but this was of late being discouraged. You are encouraged, instead, to camp with locals at such places as Cabinas Punta Uvita, which has outside bathrooms and cooking facilities; Cabinas Los Laureles, also with cooking facilities; and Hotel El Chamán.

Food

Uvita has several *sodas,* including Cooperativa, Salon Familiar Bahía, and Salon Los Almeneros, a spacious bamboo restaurant. You can buy food at the *pulpería* (tel. 717-2311), where you can also arrange boat trips to Isla Ballena and the coral reefs with León Victor González. Most of the hotels mentioned above open their restaurants to nonguests.

Getting There

Buses depart Dominical for Uvita and Bahía at 8:30 a.m. and 4:30 p.m. (check schedules at San Clemente in Dominical). Buses depart San

Isidro from Calle 1, Avenidas 4/6, at 3 p.m. (return buses depart Bahía at 7 a.m.).

BALLENA MARINE NATIONAL PARK

This national park was created in February 1990 to protect the shoreline of Bahía de Coronado and includes the Uvita tombolo (a narrow sandbar connecting an island to the mainland), several splendid beaches, plus 4,500 hectares of water surrounding Isla Ballena. The beaches sweep south for 15 km or so, backed by palms and steep green, green mountains—the Fila Tinomastes.

The park, which stretches along 13 km of coast, harbors within its relatively small area important mangroves and the largest coral reef on the Pacific coast of Central America. A particular curiosity are the green marine iguanas that live on algae in the saltwater pools. They lit-ter the golden-sand beaches like prehistoric jetsam, their bodies angled at 90 degrees to catch the sun's rays most directly. Pretty smart: Once they reach 37° C they pop down to the sea for a bite to eat. Olive ridley and hawksbill turtles come ashore May-Nov. to lay their eggs (September and October are the best months to visit). Common and bottlenosed dolphins frolic offshore. And the bay is the southernmost mating site for the humpback whale, which migrates from Alaska, Baja California, and Hawaii. December through April they are often spotted performing ballet maneuvers with their young.

There's an irony in the tale of protection. Gill nets used by local shrimp fishermen were indiscriminate about the species they trapped, and the erosion and sedimentation resulting from an ill-fated attempt to build a coastal highway in the mid-1980s is claimed to have killed off 60% of the coral reef. Though the government created the park to protect the area, its earth movers are once more tearing up the rainforest for the Costanera Sur Highway. The project, begun in January 1992, is to be completed by the late '90s at a cost of some $100 million. In places it runs close to the shoreline of the bay; elsewhere it slices through the coastal mountains. Massive volumes of disturbed earth are again washing out to sea. Marine biologists believe that construction of the highway may kill the remaining coral reef.

Snorkeling is good close to shore during low tides. You can also reach the tombolo of Uvita at low tide; at its tip are corals, sponges, and sea anemones. A paternoster of caves is worth exploring. And Isla Ballena, and the rocks known as Las Tres Hermanas ("Three Sisters"), are havens for frigate birds and boobies as well as pelicans and even ibises. Whales tend to congregate here.

The ranger station and park headquarters is beside the

SIPAREMA

In response to ever-increasing threats to the fragile marine habitats of the Pacific coast, the System of Marine Parks and Reserves (SIPAREMA)—a part of the National Parks Service—was formed in 1991 within the Costa Rican Ministry of Natural Resources. The body represents a belated attempt to shield the precious coral reefs and offshore wildlife habitats from a final demise. According to a SIPAREMA publication, "fish, turtle, and sea-faring bird migrations are decreasing in size and frequency [and] calving whales, a common sight not long ago, are abandoning some tropical bays . . . and of greatest concern, sedimentation from coastal development and inland erosion is seriously damaging the coral reefs."

SIPAREMA must design and then execute sophisticated resource-management plans to set catch limits, control tourism, and balance all the competing demands on the marine resources against the needs of the marine fauna itself. It must build park monitoring facilities, hire park rangers, and buy boats and communications equipment.

Donations

SIPAREMA is underfunded and understaffed. Donations (specify Costa Rica Marine Parks Fund) may be made through: Fundación de Parques Nacionales (Apdo. 1108, San José 1002, Costa Rica), The Cousteau Society (930 West 21st St., Norfolk, VA 23517), or The Nature Conservancy (1815 North Lynn St., Arlington, VA 22209).

HUMPBACK WHALES

Throughout the last two centuries, humpbacks (and other whales) have been hunted with rapacious greed. Not long ago these leviathans were close to extinction. In recent decades, however, the economics of dead whales has given way to the economics of good will. August through March, you may dependably spot humpbacks playing up and down the Pacific coast of the Americas. Increasingly, they're showing up off the coast of Costa Rica.

Remarkably little is known about the ecology of whales. Until recently, for example, scientists believed that North Pacific humpbacks limited their breeding to the waters off Japan, Hawaii, and Mexico's Sea of Cortez. New findings, however, suggest that whales may get amorous, too, off the coast of Costa Rica. Individual whales are identified by the white markings on the underside of their flukes, and some of the whales sighted off California have been showing up in Costa Rican waters.

To learn more about humpback habits and activities, the Oceanic Society has an ongoing study to identify individual creatures and trace their migrations. The society needs volunteers on weeklong midwinter trips ($1734) offered through ElderHostel (P.O. Box 1751, Wakefield, MA 01880, tel. 617-426-7788). It's a marvelous opportunity for eyeball-to-eyeball encounters with the gentle giants of the deep.

dirt road to the right at the Uvita "crossroads" leads three km coastward to the Río Uvita, which pours onto the beach at Hacienda Bahía, "gateway" to the park. You must cross the river twice (no problem at low tide or in the dry season). See "Getting There" under Uvita, above, for bus service.

You can hire a **boat** and guide at any of the fishing hamlets between Palmar and the park, or in Dominical or Uvita, to take you to the reef or Isla Ballena (about $30 per hour, $45 two hours). In Uvita, ask for Captain Jenkin Mora Guzmann, or Victor Pérez, of Cabinas Los Laureles.

DOMINICAL TO SAN ISIDRO

The paved road from Dominical to San Isidro winds through the valley of the Río Barú before climbing magnificently up into the Fila Costanera mountains, where the climate cools and you may find yourself, within one hour of the hot, humid lowlands, high amid swirling clouds. Fruit orchards abound and the mountain road, which is heavily potholed, is lined with fruit stalls.

Just north of the village of Barú signs point the way east to the **Cataratas de Nauyaca**, magnificent waterfalls reached via a dirt road to, then trails from, the hamlet of Libano. Tour companies in Dominical offer trips to the falls, as do the various rustic lodges in Escaleras (see above).

beach at Hacienda Bahía, three km south of Uvita. There's another ranger station at Playa Piñuela, at the southern end of the park, which you reach from the town of Palmar (see "Palmar to Ballena Marine National Park" under "Palmar and Vicinity" in the Pacific Southwest chapter). Nominally the entrance fee is $15 walk-in, $5 advance purchase; recent news was no fee was being charged.

You can **camp** on the beach, though there are no facilities (a campsite is supposedly planned). The ranger stations have water.

Getting There
It's a straight shoot south along the rough dirt-and-rock road from Dominical via Uvita. The

CATHY CARLSON

GUANACASTE
AND THE NORTHWEST
INTRODUCTION

Travelers who emerge from the verdant central highlands or southern Pacific and enter the arid northwest might think they're in a new country. For the most part the region is a vast alluvial plain of rolling hills—the southern extent of the Mesoamerican plain—broadening to the north and dominated by giant cattle ranches interspersed with smaller pockets of cultivated cotton, rice, sorghum, and soy. To the east rises a backbone of mountains—the Cordillera de Guanacaste and Cordillera de Tilarán, separated by Lake Arenal—and, farther north, symmetrical volcanic cones spiced with bubbling mud pits and steaming vents. Rivers cascade down the flanks and slow to a meandering pace, halted—it seems—by the ravaging heat.

The name Guanacaste derives from *quahnacaztlan,* an Indian word meaning "place near the ear trees," for the tall and broad *guanacaste* (free ear or ear pod) tree—the national tree—whose seedpods spiral gracefully to earth. The tree spreads its gnarled branches long and low to the ground, and all that walks, crawls, or flies gathers in its cool shade in the heat of midday. Then, too, people take shady siestas or sit around drinking beer; local activity revolves around the cooler hours of early morning and late afternoon.

The **Pan-American Highway** (Highway 1) descends from the central highlands (see the Central Pacific chapter for route description) and cuts northwest through the heart of Guanacaste, following the foothill contours of the cordilleras, ruler-straight almost all the way to the Nicaraguan border. North of Liberia the route is superbly scenic. Almost every site of importance lies within a short reach of the highway. If traveling by bus, sit on the right for the views of the volcanoes.

CLIMATE

It's no coincidence that the majority of Costa Rica's resort hotels are nestled along the shores of the Pacific northwest, where sun is the name of the game. Guanacaste's climate is in total contrast to the rest of the country. For half the year (Nov.-April) the plains and rolling hills receive no rain, it is hotter than Hades, and the sun beats down hard as a nail. Cool winds bearing down from northern latitudes can lower temperatures pleasantly along the coast Dec.-February. The dry season usually lingers slightly longer than elsewhere in Costa Rica. The province averages less than 162 cm (65 inches) of rain a year. Certain rain shadows receive much less: the Tempisque Basin is the country's driest region and receives less than 45 cm (18 inches) in years of drought, mostly in a few torrential downpours during the six-month rainy season. In the wet season, everything turns green and the air is freshly scented.

HISTORY

The Guanacaste-Nicoya region was the center of a vibrant pre-Columbian culture—the Chorotegas. Descended from the Olmecs of Mexico, they had arrived in Costa Rica around the 8th century and soon established them-

Olmec-influenced axe-shaped jade pendant

A PALETTE IN BLOOM

In the midst of dry-season drought, Guanacaste explodes in Monet colors. Not wildflowers, but a Technicolor blossoming of trees as fervent flowers burst onto bare branches. In November, the saffron-bright flowering of the *guachipelín* sets in motion a chain reaction that will last for six months. Individual trees of a particular genus are somehow keyed to explode in unison, often in a climax as brief as a day. Two or three bouquets of a single species may occur in a season. The colors are never static. In January, it's the turn of pink *poui* (savannah oak) and yellow *poui* (black bark tree). By February, canary-bright *Corteza amarillo* and the yellow trumpet-shaped blossoms of *Tabebuia chrysanta* dot the landscape. In March, it's the turn of delicate pink *curao*. As *curao* wanes, *Tabebuia rosea* bursts forth in subtle pinks, whites, and lilacs. The *malinche*—royal poinciana or flame tree—closes out the six-month parade of blossoming trees with a dramatic display as red as bright lipstick.

selves as the most advanced in what would be Costa Rica. They alone, for example, developed art and writing schools. Their culture was centered on *milpas,* or cornfields. Many of the stone metates (small stool-like tables for grinding corn) on display in the National Museum in San José are from the region; elaborately carved with turtles, crocodiles, monkeys, and jaguars, they speak of the culture's strength. Some of the most beautiful pieces were delicately shaped into anthropomorphic axe-gods and two-headed crocodiles—totems derived from the Olmec culture.

The Chorotegas were particularly skilled at carving jade, and traded with the Mayan and Olmec empires to the north. They achieved their zenith in working jade between the last century B.C. and the 5th century A.D. Blue jade was considered the most precious of objects. Archaeologists, however, aren't sure where blue jade came from. Interestingly, there are no known jade deposits in Costa Rica, and the nearest known source of green jade, supposedly, was more than 800 km north, at Guatemasal, in Guatemala.

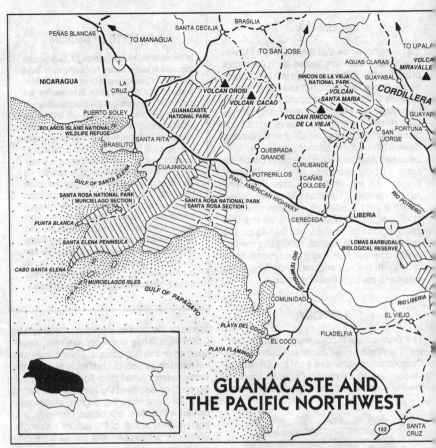

GUANACASTE AND
THE PACIFIC NORTHWEST

Archaeologists continue to unearth ancient gravesites. Although the culture went into rapid decline with the arrival of the Spanish, the Chorotega weren't decimated as were indigenous cultures elsewhere in the region and today one can still see deeply bronzed wide-set faces and pockets of Chorotega life.

Between 1570 and 1821 Costa Rica was part of the Captaincy General of Guatemala, a federation of Spanish provinces in Central America. In 1787, Guanacaste—then an independent province—was annexed to Nicaragua; in 1812 Spain awarded the region to Costa Rica. In 1821, when the Captaincy General was dissolved and autonomy granted to the Central

American nations, Guanacaste had to choose between Nicaragua and Costa Rica. Rancor between Liberians—cattle ranchers with strong Nicaraguan ties—and Nicoyans who favored union with Costa Rica lingered until a plebiscite in 1824. Guanacaste officially became part of Costa Rica by treaty in 1858.

CULTURE

No region of Costa Rica displays its cultural heritage as overtly as does Guanacaste. The culture owes much to the blending of Spanish and Chorotega. The *campesino* life here revolves

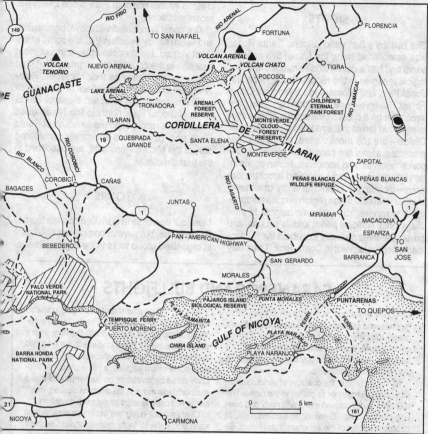

around the horse and cattle ranch, and dark-skinned *sabaneros* (cowboys) shaded by wide-brimmed hats and mounted on horses with lassoes at their sides are a common sight. Guanacaste has been called Costa Rica's "Wild West." Come fiesta time, nothing rouses so much cheer as the *corridas de toros* (bullfights) and *topes,* the region's colorful horse parades in which the Guanacastecans show off their meticulously groomed horses and the horses' fancy footwork. Guanacastecans love a fiesta: the biggest occurs each 25 July, when Guanacaste celebrates its independence from Nicaragua.

Costa Rica's national costume, music, and

even the national tree—the *guanacaste*—all emanate from this region, as does the *punto guanacasteco,* the country's official dance. Even the regional foods of Guanacaste have made their way into the national fare. Local specialties include *frito guanacasteco* (a local version of *gallo pinto*), *sopa de albondigas* (spicy meatball soup, with chopped eggs), and *pedre* (carob beans, pork, chicken, onions, sweet peppers, salt, and mint), plus foods based on corn, such as tortillas, *rosquillas,* corn rice, and the famous *yoltmatal.* And the regional heritage can still be traced in the creation of clay pottery and figurines.

SIGHTS

The country's first national park, Santa Rosa, was established here, the first of five national parks and half a dozen wildlife refuges and biological reserves in the region. Santa Rosa National Park and Monteverde Biological Cloud Forest Reserve—one a parched dry forest environment on a coastal plateau, the other a cool misty cloud forest that straddles the Continental Divide—are the most visited, although other protected areas are coming on strong. Many parks, reserves, and attractions, however, are little visited despite some splendid accommodations—definitely a plus! The array of ecosystems and wildlife in the region is quite astounding and ranges from volcanic heights to pristine shores. National parks, wildlife refuges, and private reserves preserve just about every imaginable ecosystem within Costa Rica. The newly

created Arenal National Park is one of several recent additions.

The coast is indented with bays, peninsulas, and warm sandy beaches that are some of the least visited, least accessible, and yet most beautiful in the country. No surprise, then, that sea turtles use many as their nurseries. Relatively few facilities, however, are on the beaches discussed in this chapter: those of Santa Rosa National Park north to the Nicaraguan border. The resort beaches lie south of Santa Rosa and, being more accurately considered part of the Nicoya Peninsula, are described in the that chapter.

TOURS

Most tour operators in San José operate tours to Guanacaste, but several companies specialize in organized group tours in the region. **Guana-**

SABANEROS AND BULLFIGHTS

Cowboys are a common sight on the big cattle ranches (and streets) of Guanacaste, Costa Rica's grassy Wild West. They have been since Spanish colonial days, when a *sabanero* (cowboy) culture evolved, much as a cowboy culture evolved on the North American plains.

At round-up time, the cowboys of various ranches would get together to gather in the cattle. The round-up usually closed with a wild party and cowboy competitions. Breaking in wild broncos, of course, was part of the *sabanero*'s daily work. By the turn of the 19th century, bull-riding had developed as a way for *sabaneros* to prove who was the toughest of the hard-drinking, fist-fighting breed. Fortified with *guaro*, they hopped onto wild bulls to pit their wits and courage against the bucking fury.

The tradition evolved into the Festejos Populares, or "Folk Festivals," in which bull-riding and bull-running are the main features for paying spectators. These festivals, held throughout Guanacaste, keep alive a deep-rooted tradition of Costa Rican culture: bull-riding, bronco riding, homestyle "Tico" bullfighting, and demonstrations of the Costa Rican saddle horse. Today's Festejos Populares—more commonly called Fiestas Cívicas—usually raise revenue to finance community projects.

At first, *sabaneros* rode bulls using uncured leather saddles *(albardas)*. The bulls were enraged before being released into the ring, where *vaqueteros* are on hand to distract the wild and dangerous bull if a rider is thrown or injured. The word comes from *vaqueta*, a piece of leather originally used by cowboys on haciendas to make stubborn bulls move in the direction desired, much as the red cape is used by Spanish matadors.

Over time bull-riding has become a professional sport and evolved to its modern style. Cowboys ride bareback and hang on to angry, jumping, twisting, 680-kilo bulls with only one hand or none at all (free style), while the *vaqueta* has given way to red cloth (called a *capote* or *muleta*) or even the occasional clown.

Rancho JAIZA (Apdo. 469, San José 1007, tel. 232-8480, fax 231-4723) offers a "Typical Rodeo and Costa Rican Fiesta Tour" at Quinta el Coyol (15 miles west of San José; see "West from Alajuela" in the Central Highlands chapter) with demonstrations of ropin' 'n' ridin' as well as saddle horse demonstrations during quieter interludes. There's plenty of marimba music, and the mood recreates that of a typical Fiesta Cívica. Also see "Liberia and Vicinity," this chapter.

*traditional carreta
(oxcart), Guanacaste*

caste Tours (Apdo. 55, Liberia 5000, tel. 666-0306, fax 666-0307) specializes in one-day tours of Guanacaste, including pick-up and return to hotels in Guanacaste. Tours include "Arenal Volcano and Coter Rain Forest" ($90); "Río Tempisque and Palo Verde" ($75); "Ostrich Ranch and Liberia City Tour" ($50); "Casona Santa Rosa and Hacienda Inocente" ($70); nighttime turtle-watching tours to Playa Grande (Nov.-Feb.; $40) and Playa Ostional (July-Nov.; $50); and "Tamarindo and Guaitil" ($75).

CATA Tours (tel./fax 669-1203) offers a "Guanacaste Nature Paradise" series featuring similar one-day tours, as well as birdwatching and kayaking trips in Bebedero and Palo Verde, and whitewater rafting trips. Its office is in the forecourt of La Pacífica (see "Cañas," under "Las Juntas, Palo Verde, and Cañas," below).

Frontera Tours (Apdo. 1177, Tibas 1100, tel. 670-0472, fax 670-0403) offers a range of tours in Guanacaste, including to most national parks and wildlife refuges, plus rafting, deep-sea fishing, horseback riding, sailing, etc. Its head office is at Playa del Coco (see "The Northern Beaches" in the Nicoya Peninsula chapter).

VICINITY OF PUNTARENAS

North from Esparza (see Central Pacific chapter) and Puntarenas, the horizon broadens as the Pan-American Hwy. (single lane each direction) glides north, virtually straight the whole way, through wide grassy plains with the foothills of the Tilarán and Guanacaste cordilleras to the east. Already the land is dominated by large cattle ranches and the large umbrella-like *guanacaste* trees that give the province its name.

PEÑAS BLANCAS WILDLIFE REFUGE

This 2,400-hectare refuge, 33 km northeast of Puntarenas, protects the watersheds of the Ríos Barranca and Ciruelas, on the forested southern slopes of the Cordillera de Tilarán. The mountain slopes rise steeply to 1,400 meters from rolling plains carved with deep canyons. Vegetation ranges from tropical dry forest in the southerly lower elevation to moist deciduous and premontane moist forest higher up. The region has been extensively deforested, however, and wildlife is scarce. That said, this is the only place in the country where I've seen a coatimundi in the wild: it bounded across the road like a cat. You may be lucky enough to see howler or white-faced monkeys, red brocket deer, kinkajous, and any of 70-plus species of birds. Gold was once mined hereabouts; you can still visit mines near **Miramar** (ask in the village), whose current mainstay is sugarcane. Geologists might be excited by the "white cliffs" of diatomaceous rocks which lend the park its name. The sedimentary rocks were laid down before the Central American isthmus rose from the sea and, like limestone, originated from the "skeletal" remains of subaqueous creatures—in this case microscopic algae.

Steep trails follow the Río Jabonal. Camping is permitted. There are no visitor facilities . . . and very few visitors!

Food and Accommodations
You can dine beneath shady trees at **Restaurant 4 Cruces,** on the Pan-Am Hwy. on the corner of the turnoff for Miramar, a pleasant agri-

cultural town with two reasonable eateries serving Costa Rican dishes (**Bar/Restaurant El Patio** and **Bar/Restaurant Las Huncas**). **Cabinas Katya Carolina** (tel. 639-9055) is in Miramar; not inspected.

Services
There's a **Banco Nacional** (tel. 639-9090) on the plaza in Miramar. If you need medical assistance, call the **Red Cross** (tel. 639-9060). For the **police** (Guardia Rural), call 639-9132 or 117 (emergencies).

Getting There
You reach the reserve by a dirt road from Macacona, three km east of Esparza. Another route is via a paved road to Miramar, eight km from the Pan-American Hwy. (the turnoff, at the Restaurant 4 Cruces, is four km north of the highway split for Puntarenas), and from there east 15 km along a rutted dirt road via Sabana Bonita and Cerrillo (turn left at the T-intersection) to Peñas Blancas. It's a very pretty drive up to Miramar.

ISLA PÁJAROS BIOLOGICAL RESERVE AND VICINITY

At San Gerardo, on the Pan-Am Hwy., 40 km north of Puntarenas, a paved road leads west to Punta Morales and the Isla Pájaros Biological Reserve, about 600 meters offshore. The 3.8-hectare reserve protects a colony of brown pelicans and other seabirds that live on this scrub-covered rocky islet rising 45 meters above the Gulf of Nicoya. Supposedly, it can be reached at low tide via a rocky platform, but access is restricted to biological researchers. You can hire a local fishing boat and guide in Morales or Manzanillo to take you there, but you are not allowed to step ashore.

A dirt road leads northwest from Punta Morales to Playa Camarita (12 km) and thence via Colorado to the Tempisque Ferry (37 km). There's fabulous birding inland of the mangroves that line the shore north of Manzanillo; the shore-

line is known as the Costa de Pájaros ("Bird Coast"). **Universal Tropical Nature Tours** (Apdo. 4276, San José 1000, tel. 257-0181, fax 255-4274) offers a three-day "Cowboy Country and Chira Island Adventure," which includes a boat trip through the Abangaritos River mangrove swamps—home to ibis, herons, pelicans, parrots, egrets, and caiman—plus a boat trip to **Isla Chira** and two nights' accommodation at La Ensenada Lodge (see below); $295, including roundtrip transfers from San José.

About seven km north of San Gerardo on the Pan-American Hwy., 100 meters before the bridge over the Río Lagarto, a road to the right leads 35 km uphill to **Monteverde,** nestled high in the Tilarán mountains. There's a small *soda*/restaurant at the junction. The gut-jolting, vertiginous dirt road (recently improved) is almost as famous as the place it leads to. Take it slowly and enjoy the spectacular mountain scenery. The drive takes one and a half to two hours. You'll stop at a tollbooth operated by the Monteverde Road Commission just before Santa Elena (the 50-*colones* fee goes to help maintain the road). This small agricultural community is gateway to the world-famous Monteverde Cloud Forest Preserve and the more recently established Santa Elena Forest Reserve. Santa Elena

and Monteverde are for most intents one and the same. (Service information for both has been amalgamated; see "Information" under "Monteverde Biological Cloud Forest Reserve," below.) Another road to Monteverde (35 km) leads via Sardinal; the turnoff from the Pan-Am Hwy. is about 10 km south of San Gerardo.

Accommodations
La Ensenada Lodge (tel. 228-6653, fax 228-5281), near Abangaritos on the shore of Punta Morales, 20 km west of the Pan-Am Hwy., is a family-run cattle *finca* and salt farm (papayas and watermelons are also grown) with rustic yet comfortable wooden cabinas with two double beds, private baths with cold water, and verandas with hammocks. The Italian-owned property is fronted by mangroves and *salinas* (salt pans) and has a tennis court. The lodge offers boat trips to Palo Verde, water-skiing, windsurfing, and horseback tours, including to Monteverde and Arenal. Rates: $60 per person, including all meals.

Los Vaqueros (Apdo. 627, San José 2100, tel. 233-3435, fax 221-5884) is a working ranch near Punta Morales where guests can help herd cattle. Accommodation is in a rustic lodge. I haven't had a chance to inspect either.

MONTEVERDE AND VICINITY

Monteverde means "Green Mountain," an appropriate name for one of the most idyllic pastoral settings in Costa Rica. Cows munch contentedly, and horse-drawn wagons loaded with milk cans still make the rounds. Most of the homes are hidden from view in the forest, accessible only by foot trail.

This sprawling agricultural community, on a secluded 1,400-meter-high plateau, was founded in 1951 by a group of about 40 American Quakers—most from Fairhope, Alabama—who as a matter of conscience had refused to register for the draft. Led by John Campbell and Wilford "Wolf" Guindon, they chose Costa Rica for a new home because it had done away with its army. With the help of their Costa Rican neighbors, the Quakers began developing the community that exists today. They built roads and cleared much of the virgin forest for dairy farm-

ing. They decided to make cheese because it was the only product that could be stored and moved to market (without spoiling) along a muddy oxcart trail. Cheese is still a mainstay of the local economy. The cheese factory now has more than 350 employees and produces more than 900 kilos pounds of cheese daily. The Quaker organization is still active in Monteverde (it meets every Wednesday morning at the Friends' Meeting House; visitors are welcome), but Productores de Monteverde has evolved into an operation in which the shareholders today are predominantly Costa Rican.

The town's founders were environmentally conscious and set aside a heavily timbered region near the headwaters of the Río Guacimal to be held undisturbed and in common to safeguard the water source for their small hydroelectric plant. The area attracted scientists, es-

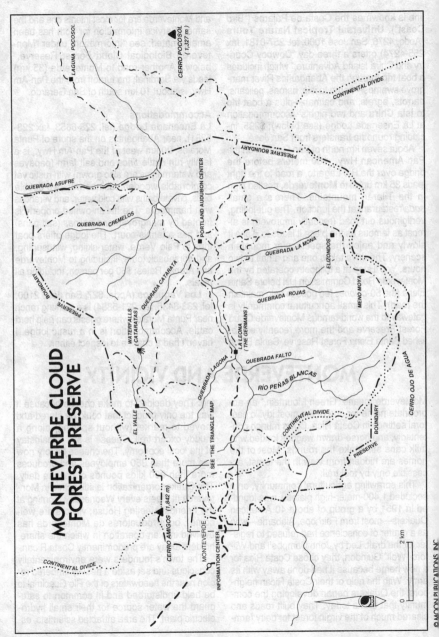

MONTEVERDE CLOUD
FOREST PRESERVE

LAGUNA POCOSOL

CERRO POCOSOL
(1,327 m)

CONTINENTAL DIVIDE

PRESERVE BOUNDARY

QUEBRADA ASUFRE

QUEBRADA CREMELOS

PORTLAND AUDUBON CENTER

QUEBRADA LA MONA

ELIZONDOS

QUEBRADA CATARATA

QUEBRADA ROJAS

MENO MOYA

BOUNDARY

WATERFALLS
(CATARATAS)

LA LEONA
(THE GERMANS)

PRESERVE BOUNDARY

CERRO OJO DE AGUA

QUEBRADA LAGONA

QUEBRADA FALTO

RÍO PEÑAS BLANCAS

EL VALLE

"SEE "THE TRIANGLE" MAP"

CONTINENTAL DIVIDE

PRESERVE BOUNDARY

CERRO AMIGOS
(1,842 m)

MONTEVERDE

INFORMATION CENTER

CONTINENTAL DIVIDE

MOON

0   2 km

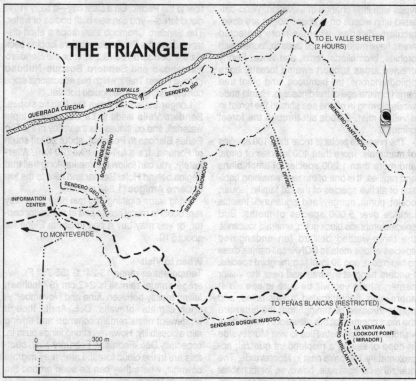

pecially after a small brilliantly colored frog—the golden toad—was discovered in 1964. In 1972, under threat of homesteading in the surrounding cloud forest, visiting scientists George and Harriet Powell joined forces with longtime resident Wilford Guindon and, overcoming local resistance, established a 328-hectare wildlife sanctuary. In 1975, the 554-hectare community watershed reserve was annexed with the aid of a $40,000 grant from the World Wildlife Fund. Together they formed the initial core of the Monteverde Biological Cloud Forest Preserve, a 10,500-hectare private reserve owned and administered by the Tropical Science Center of Costa Rica.

The fame of the preserve has spawned an ever-increasing influx of birders and nature-loving tourists. There are now more than 30 lodges, which catered to more than 30,000 vis-

itors in 1994. Community members are divided about the issue of tourism growth.

Note: Although the Monteverde Biological Cloud Forest Preserve steals the limelight, it isn't the only such preserve hereabouts. Consider the other options.

MONTEVERDE BIOLOGICAL CLOUD FOREST PRESERVE

The preserve (Reserva Biológica Bosque Nuboso Monteverde) is acclaimed as one of the most outstanding wildlife sanctuaries in the New World tropics. It extends down both Caribbean and Pacific slopes, encompassing eight distinct ecological zones. Temperature and humidity change dramatically over relatively short distances, producing a great diversity of forest

types with little change in elevation. Wind-battered elfin woods on exposed ridges are spectacularly dwarfed, whereas more protected areas have majestically tall trees festooned with orchids, bromeliads, ferns, and vines. Poorly drained areas support swamp forests, huge philodendrons, tall bamboos, and giant tree ferns from the age of the dinosaurs. Humid trade winds blowing in off the sea shroud the forest in a veil of mist. Clouds sift through the forest primeval.

The preserve protects more than 100 species of mammals, more than 400 species of birds, and more than 1,200 species of amphibians and reptiles. It is one of the few remaining habitats of all five species of the cat family: jaguar, ocelot, puma, margay, and jaguarundi. Insects include over 5,000 species of moths. Bird species embrace black guan, emerald toucanet, the three-wattled bellbird (an endangered species whose metallic BONK! call carries close to two miles), and 30 local hummingbird species. Feeders hang at the trailhead near the visitor center, where you will be sure to see violet sabre-wing, fiery-throated, rufous-tailed, and purple-throated hummingbirds; the latter are the most common at this elevation. Hundreds of visitors come to Costa Rica to visit Monteverde in hope of seeing a resplendent quetzal; approximately 100 pairs nest in Monteverde. The quetzal is far from safe, however, for its habitat extends past the boundaries of the reserve, into forests threatened with deforestation (see special topic "Monteverde Conservation League").

Trails

The preserve has kilometers of trails, sections of which are not for the weak-hearted. Parts ooze with mud; other sections have been magnificently covered with raised wooden walkways. Knowledgeable locals wear rubber boots. Because of the fragile environment, the preserve allows a maximum of 100 people on the trails at any one time. The paths are strewn with exotic blossoms, such as "hot lips." Shorter nature trails are concentrated in an area called "The Triangle."

The **Sendero Chomogo** trail leads steeply uphill to a wide clearing ringed with thousands of pink and white impatiens, where a *mirador* (lookout) straddles the Continental Divide. Rivers to the north flow to the Caribbean, those to the south flow to the Pacific. On a clear day—a rarity in the cloud forest—you can see both bodies of water. The Sendero Chomogo then drops a short distance down the Pacific slope before looping back via the **Sendero Río** (3.2 km); or the **Sendero Pantanoso** and **Sendero Bosque Nuboso** ("Cloud Forest Trail"), which has educational stops corresponding to a self-guide booklet.

Longer trails lead down the Pacific slopes. **Sendero Valle** leads to **La Cascada,** a triple waterfall, and continues via the valley of the Río Peñas Blancas to **Pocosol,** about 20 km south of Fortuna. It's a full-day hike (20 km). Alternately, you can follow a three-km-long trail that begins behind Hotel Belmar and hike to the top of **Cerro Amigos** (1,842 meters).

Bring warm clothing and rain gear. You may rent boots in many hotels and at the visitor center, or you may buy a pair in Santa Elena for about $10.

When to Visit

Temperatures range 13-24° C (55-75° F). Average annual rainfall is 242 cm (97 inches), falling mostly between June and November. A drier climate prevails Dec.-April, though windswept mists remain common and driving rain a possibility. However, strong winds push in, especially Dec.-February. February-May, quetzals are in the cloud forest. Later, they migrate downhill, where they can be seen around the hotels of Monteverde. The wet season is one of best times to visit: there are fewer people—a vital consideration, for the reserve limits entry to only 100 people every three hours!

Early morning and late afternoon are the best times to see birds, including hummingbirds, which can be seen feeding outside the information hut. Just after dawn is a good time to spot quetzals, which are particularly active in the early morning, especially in the mating season (April and May). Midmorning peak hours are to be avoided.

Guides

Hike with a guide! Although you can hike through the preserve on your own, you increase your chances of seeing quetzals and other wildlife if you hike with a guide. Guided tours are offered daily at 7:30 a.m. (minimum three people, $24 per person, including admission and

GOLDEN TOAD

One of Monteverde's several calls to fame is the inch-long golden toad, an endemic species that is supposedly both deaf and dumb. Monteverde is the only known home of this brilliant, neon-orange toad—supposedly the brightest toad in the world. Don't expect to see one. It may already be extinct. Although in 1986 it was seen in large quantities, by 1988 very few remained. To my knowledge, no confirmed sightings have been made since. No one is sure whether the demise of *sapo dorado (Bufo periglenes)* is related to the global diminution of frog populations during the last decade. (Also see "Amphibians and Reptiles," in the Introduction chapter.)

slide show). Tours at other times may be arranged through your hotel or directly with the guides recommended below (upward of $12 per person, half-day). You can arrange a guide at the information center or through your hotel. Most are fluent in English. Recommended guides include André (Verny) Werner (tel. 645-1001), Gary Diller (tel. 645-5045), Thomas Guindon (tel. 645-5118), and Richard and Mel Laval (tel. 645-5052).

Information

The park entrance is at the end of the road southeast from Santa Elena. **Hours:** 7:30 a.m.-4:30 p.m. daily. **Entrance:** $8 adults, $4 students and residents, children under 15 free. The preserve is traditionally closed 6 and 7 October. There's a visitor center and store at the entrance. It offers a free self-guide pamphlet and trail map; you can also buy more detailed maps plus wildlife guides. If you want to hike alone, buy your ticket the day before and set out before the crowds. You can rent rubber boots at the visitor center, which also offers slide shows daily.

Accommodations

The visitor center and field station includes simple laboratory facilities and dormitory-style lodging and kitchens for up to 30 people ($5, $15 with meals). Of course, scientists and students get priority. A small research post with basic ac-

commodations has been built on the Caribbean slope to provide access to Monteverde's tropical rainforest. Basic backpacking shelters are located throughout the preserve; no facilities. For reservations, contact the Monteverde Biological Cloud Forest Preserve, Apdo. 10165, San José 1000, tel. 645-5122. A deposit is required, 45 days in advance. A wide range of accommodations is available in Santa Elena and along the road to the reserve. The closest hotel is about 1.2 km below the reserve.

Getting There

There's no public transportation to the reserve, and parking near the entrance is limited. Most hotels can arrange transportation. You may need to walk up the muddy hill. A taxi from Santa Elena will cost about $5 one-way. A bus for local workers departs from the Hotel Imán at 6:30 a.m. and goes all the way to the reserve, stopping en route for anyone flagging it down (workers travel free; tourists quite rightly pay, about $1). The return bus departs the reserve around 3 p.m.

Donations

You may make contributions to the preserve c/o the Tropical Science Center (Apdo. 8-3870, San José 1000). U.S. citizens wishing to make tax-deductible donations should make checks payable to the National Audubon Society, earmarked for the Monteverde Biological Cloud Forest Preserve (National Audubon Society, 950 Third Ave., New York, NY 10022).

CHILDREN'S ETERNAL FOREST

A Monteverde Conservation League project that has caught the imagination of children and adults around the world is the Children's Eternal Forest (El Bosque Eterno de los Niños), the first international children's rainforest in the world. The dream of a rainforest saved by children began in 1987, at a small primary school in rural Sweden. A study of tropical forests prompted nine-year-old Roland Teinsuu to ask what he could do to keep the rainforest and the animals who live in it safe from destruction. Young Roland's question launched a group campaign to raise money to help the Monteverde Conservation

MONTEVERDE CONSERVATION LEAGUE

Monteverde provides an excellent example for the Costa Rican government to learn how to make money from tourists while protecting an area from the adverse impacts of tourism. Despite its success, however, the preserve needs a bigger area to protect many animal species. The fact that the majority of sites used by local quetzals are outside the reserve shows the importance of protecting adjacent lands threatened by loggers and farmers. Recent efforts have gone into expanding the protected area. The Monteverde Conservation League—a nonprofit community conservation organization founded in 1986—is gradually buying back deforested land and virgin rainforest on the slopes of Monteverde. Since 1988, the reforestation program has helped almost 200 farmers plant more than 300,000 trees as windbreaks for pasture and crops, as well as supplying firewood, fence posts, and lumber.

Land purchase is only the first step toward long-term forest preservation. The next is to provide an alternative means for local communities to earn money. The league—which has 40 employees, 90% of them Costa Rican—is developing programs to train local residents to become naturalist guides so that the surrounding community can profit from tourism. It is also using tourism as a focus for educating local children, including taking youngsters into the reserve for natural-history education. The environmental-education staff works in 10 primary schools in Monteverde and La Tigra to implement ecological programs. Training for teachers as well as community leaders and organized women's groups is also under way. The league is seeking an easy and effective method of teaching English and needs better materials than government schooling provides. Suggestions and assistance are welcomed.

child's imagination. Children have collected aluminum cans and glass, baked cookies for sale with rainforest ingredients (ginger, chocolate, vanilla), or asked for a parcel of rainforest as a Christmas or birthday gift (land-purchase cost is $100 per 0.4 hectare). One-fifth of every donation goes into an endowment fund for protection and maintenance of the forest.

The original six-hectare preserve, established near Monteverde in 1988, grew to 7,285 hectares within two years, thanks to donations from around the world. By June 1992 the Children's Forest had grown to 14,302 hectares, bordering three sides of the Monteverde Biological Cloud Forest Preserve. Remaining to be purchased was a 5,800-hectare slice of forest.

The Monteverde Conservation League plans to create an educational center where children from around the world can join Costa Rican children in environmental workshops and outdoor leadership training. The Children's Eternal Forest was not open to visitors at press time, but may be for educational tourism by the time you read this.

League buy and save threatened rainforest in Costa Rica. With the guiding hand of teacher Eha Kern and her husband Bernd, and the assistance of tropical biologist Sharon Kinsman, who introduced the Monteverde project to the school, Roland and his classmates raised enough money to buy six hectares of rainforest at a cost of $250 per hectare, including surveying, title search, and legal fees connected with purchase.

Out of this initial success a group of children dedicated to saving the tropical rainforest formed Barnens Regnskog ("Children's Rain Forest"). The vision took hold. As the spirit sweeps across other lands, groups are forming to send contributions from the far corners of the globe. Fundraising projects have been as varied as a

Donations should be sent to the following addresses:

In Costa Rica: Bosque Eterno de los Niños, c/o Monteverde Conservation League, Apdo. 10165, San José 1000.

In the U.S.: The Children's Rainforest, P.O. Box 936, Lewiston, ME 04240.

In the U.K.: Children's Tropical Forests U.K., The Old Rectory, Church Street, Market Deeping, Peterborough PE6 8DA.

In Sweden: Barnens Regnskog, Pl 4471, Hagadal, 137 94 Västerhaninge.

In Japan: Nippon Kodomo no Jungle, 386-22 Minenohara-Kogen, Suzaka, Nagano.

In Canada: World Wildlife Fund, 60 St. Clair Avenue E., Suite 201, Toronto, ON M4T 1N5.

The League's office is opposite the gas station in Monteverde (tel. 645-5003, fax 645-5104). For **information,** contact Ree Strange Scheck (Apdo. 10165, San José 1000, tel. 645-2953, fax 645-1104). Scheck, author of *Costa Rica: A Natural Destination*, edits the League's bimonthly newsletter *Tapir Tracks* (free with donations of $25 or more).

SANTA ELENA FOREST RESERVE

This 600-hectare cloud forest reserve is five km northeast of Santa Elena, north of and at a slightly higher elevation than the Monteverde Cloud Forest Preserve (4WD required). The reserve is owned by the Santa Elena community. It has virtually all the species claimed by its eastern neighbor—quetzals, deer, sloths, ocelots, howler and capuchin monkeys—plus spider monkeys, which are absent from the Monteverde Cloud Forest Reserve. It receives far fewer visitors: it may thus be easier to see a greater diversity of birds. It has four one-way trails (from 1.4 to 4.8 km) and a lookout point with views toward Volcán Arenal. At a higher elevation than Monteverde, it tends to be cloudier and wetter.

The reserve is the site of the Monteverde Cloud Forest Ecological Center (tel. 645-3550), a forest farm started in March 1992 to educate youngsters and local farmers on forest ecology and conservation. There's also a visitor/information center. Guides are available. Dormitory accommodation for students was under construction. Organizers hope to expand this to include a laboratory, library, and kitchen. The accommodation will eventually be available to tourists. The Santa Elena community was hoping to raise $225,000 to buy land adjacent to the reserve and to reforest this to create a buffer zone, prevent hotel development, and protect the vital nesting areas for endangered species. Donations are welcome. The foundation is appealing to high schools to "adopt" the project.

The foundation offers guided tours (including night tours). For information, contact Monteverde Cloud Forest Ecological Center Foundation, Santa Elena Reserve, Apdo. 75, Santa Elena 5655, Monteverde, tel./fax 645-5238.

Hours: 7 a.m.-4 p.m. daily. Entrance: $5 ($3 students). You can buy trail maps and rent rubber boots at the information center.

Canopy Tour

An intriguing way to explore the Santa Elena Reserve is by ascending into the forest canopy on a "Canopy Tour" (tel. 645-5243 or 255-2463, fax 255-3573; or, contact ECHO, tel. 255-2693, fax 255-0061). The two-hour tour departs daily from Canopy Tour Base Camp in Santa Elena. You'll ascend to the treetops, then traverse from platform to platform using pulleys on horizontal cables before finally rappeling back to earth, all in the company of an experienced guide. Tours ($40; $30 students; $25 children) are offered daily at 7 and 9:30 a.m. and 1 and 3:30 p.m.

OTHER ATTRACTIONS

Bajo del Tigre/Jaguar Canyon

This private 30-hectare preserve, contiguous with the Monteverde Reserve and administered by the Monteverde Conservation League, is at a lower elevation than the Cloud Forest Preserve and thus offers a different variety of plant and animal life. Quetzals are more easily seen here, for example, than higher up in the wetter, mistier cloud forest. The same is true for the three-wattled bellbird and long-tailed manikin. It is crisscrossed by a network of easy trails and has strategically located picnic spots. Access is off the main road, near the Pensión Quetzal. A booklet corresponds to a self-guided walk. Guided tours are offered Mon.-Wed. at 7 a.m. and 1 p.m., plus guided night tours Thurs.-Sun. (7 p.m.). Hours: 8 a.m.-4 p.m. daily. Entrance: $5, including map (tel. 645-5003, fax 645-5104).

Reserva Sendero Tranquilo

This 200-hectare reserve is operated by the Lowthers, one of the original Quaker families, whose home is beside the Quebrada Cuecha stream behind the cheese factory. Only 12 people at any time are allowed on the trail, led by either David Lowther or Julie Kraft, who give detailed explanations of the habitats and wildlife ($15). Make reservations through the Hotel Sapo Dorado (tel. 645-5010).

Monteverde Butterfly Garden ("El Jardín de las Mariposas")

Founded by North American biologist Jim Wolfe, the garden features a nature center, three gardens, a 450-square-meter netted flyway, and two greenhouses, one representing lowland forest habitat, the second set up as a midelevation forest understory, darker and more moist than the first. Together, they are filled with hundreds of tropical butterflies representing about 40 species. A guided tour begins in the visitor center. Refreshments and snacks are offered. Butterfly-shaped signs point the way from the Hotel Heliconia. Hours: 9:30 a.m.-4 p.m. daily. Entrance: $5.

Finca Ecológico

This private reserve, on the same road as the Butterfly Garden, opened to the public in 1993 as the Finca de Aves ("Bird Farm"), but changed its name after visitors expressed delight at the number of mammal species they saw. Because the reserve is at a lower elevation than the Cloud Forest Reserve, it receives less rain and is also less cloudy. The vegetation is also less dense and you have an excellent chance of seeing coatimundis, sloths, agoutis, porcupines, and white-faced monkeys, as well as butterfies and birds. Four signed trails lead through the 17-hectare property. One leads to a waterfall and the Bajo del Tigre canyon. An information booth has an English-speaking attendant; the guide—Jorge Rodríguez—speaks only Spanish. Night tours offered. Open 9 a.m.-5 p.m. Entrance: $5.

Hummingbird Gallery ("Galería Colibrí")

The Hummingbird Gallery (tel. 645-1259), 100 meters south of the visitor center, features the fabulous photography of Monteverde residents Michael and Patricia Fogden. Prints, slides, T-shirts, and handicrafts from throughout Central America are for sale. Feeders outside the gallery attract a wide variety of hummingbirds. Slide shows are shown at 9:30 a.m. and 4:30 p.m. daily.

Sarah Dowell Watercolor Gallery

A path just west of the cheese factory leads 400 meters uphill to Sarah's home, where she displays her distinctive artwork. Her watercolors decorate the walls of many local hotels. Admission is free.

The Sugar Mill ("El Trapiche")

This 100-year-old ox-driven sugar mill (tel. 645-6054) is near Cañitas, about two km northwest of Santa Elena. After witnessing how sugarcane is processed, you can tour the 24-hectare family farm and—Nov.-Feb.—even join in harvesting coffee. A pleasant patio restaurant lit by a skylight serves typical Costa Rican cooking and features marimba music and dancing on Thursday and Friday. A souvenir shop sells T-shirts, fresh cane sugar, and other traditional dishes. You'll see a botanical garden and EcoPark immediately next to El Trapiche. Alas, the latter is merely a rather sad display of animals caged to cull a tourist buck; a Machiavellian example of jumping on the "eco" bandwagon. Maybe it will have improved by the time you read this. Hours: daily 10 a.m.-7 p.m. Entrance: $2.

Cheese Factory

The cheese factory (La Lechería, tel. 645-2850) in Monteverde is famous throughout Costa Rica for its quality cheeses, which are on sale. Production began in 1953 when the original Quaker settlers bought 50 jersey cattle; that year they produced 76,000 liters of milk, which they turned into pasteurized Monteverde Gouda cheese. In 1993, the factory, which employs 110 workers (all shareholders), processed more than 10 million liters and produced 14 types of cheese—from parmesan, baby Swiss, emmantel, Danish-style "dambo," and edam, to Monte Rico, the best seller, popular in fondues. You may observe cheesemaking through a window in the sales room. Alternately, you can take a guided farm and factory tour, initiated in December 1994. Hours: Mon.-Sat. 7:30 a.m.-4:30 p.m.; Sunday 7:30 a.m.-12:30 p.m.

Serpentario Monteverde

This den of snakes (tel. 645-5238, fax 645-5216), next to Hotel Finca Valverde, opened in 1994 and lets you get up close and personal with a repertoire of coiled constrictors and venomous vipers and their kin, as well as their prey: frogs, lizards, and the like. The dreaded fer-de-lance is here. So, too, the equally deadly eyelash viper, plus a host of less lethal brethren. Fortunately there's a thick piece of glass between you and the serpents. Guided tours cost $3. Hours: daily 9 a.m.-5 p.m.

ACCOMMODATIONS

Monteverde is a *very* popular destination. Accommodations may be difficult to obtain in dry season, when tour companies block space. Book well ahead if possible, especially for Christmas and Easter. A deposit may be required. **Note:** Unless otherwise noted, mail all correspondence to the generic Monteverde postal box number: Apdo. 10165, San José 1000.

Budget
Not much to choose below $10 around Monteverde and Santa Elena. **Pensión A Different Place,** close to Monteverde Lodge, is about as far from the latter in style as you can get. Plain cubicle-type rooms cost $5 with breakfast. There's also a small single cabina 50 meters south of El Bosque restaurant, owned by Enrique Hurtado, which rents for $15 a day. It has a small kitchenette, plus a laundry sink outside. Call the restaurant for reservations. Next door to Pensión Manikin is **Pensión Piñas** (not to be mistaken for Cabañas los Pinos), with simple rooms with bunk beds and shared bath for $6.

Options in Santa Elena include the **Pensión Santa Elena** (tel. 645-5051, fax 236-4361), which has 10 clean though small and basic rooms of varying sizes (some dark). Some have private baths, others share, with separate baths for men and women. Very colorful decor and super-friendly hosts! There's a TV in the small reception lounge. The hotel provides free use of kitchen services, plus laundry service and a slide and video show. It also offers horseback riding. Rates: $8 per person; $15 with home-cooked breakfast and dinner. **El Tucán** (tel. 645-6058 or 645-5017, fax 661-1206) has 11 rooms, seven with shared bath, four with private baths. There's a large but dingy restaurant. Rates: $10 per person shared bath, $14 private bath.

Pensión Hummingbird, also in Santa Elena (tel. 645-1007), has four small but pleasing rooms (two doubles, two triples) with shared bathroom with hot water. A budget bargain! Rates: $5 per person. **Pensión el Iman** (tel. 645-1255), opposite El Tucán, has eight funky rooms with shared bath. Rates: $4. **Cabinas Marin,** 400 meters north of Santa Elena, is pleasant. Rooms with shared bath and hot water cost $6 per person. **Hospedaje Esperanza** (tel. 645-5068), above the *pulpería* opposite the police station, has 10 clean rooms with shared bath with hot water (from $5 per person). Three other options are **Cabinas Las Cañitas** (tel. 458-4133), on the left, two km northwest of Santa Elena on the road to Tilarán; **Cabins Don Taco** (tel. 645-6023), reportedly "pleasant with private, hot water baths"; and **Pensión Colibri** (tel. 645-5067) with very basic rooms with shared bath ($5). Horse rentals are offered. Also consider the basic **El Tauro,** opposite Pensión Santa Elena, with rooms with shared bath for $4.

Inexpensive
The **Monteverde Inn** (tel. 645-5156), tucked at the bottom of the road past the Butterfly Garden, is a simple rustic lodge with 10 very basic cabinas (four doubles, six singles), all except two with private baths with hot water, plus hardwood floors. A redeeming factor is the view out across the Gulf of Nicoya. Rates: $10 per person, including meals.

Pensión Manikin (tel. 645-5080) is a basic bed and breakfast with nine rooms with bunk beds and shared bath (two have private baths) with hot water. Rates: $10 or $20 d. Meals extra. **Cabinas Mariposa** (tel. 645-5013) has three very simple cabins, each with a double and a single bed and a private bath with hot water. Rates: $29 d, including breakfast.

Albergue Bellbird (tel. 645-2652) is an all-wooden structure with a balcony and very pleasing but basic rooms in hardwoods. Some are larger than others; some share very nice tiled bathrooms with roomy showers and hot water. There's lots of storage space, plus a basic restaurant and bar downstairs. Rates: $15 s, $25 d with shared bath; $30 d with private bath.

Hotel Finca Valverde (tel. 645-5157, fax 645-5216), amid a setting of forest and pasture immediately after you leave Santa Elena for Monteverde, has five cozy if spartan double-unit wooden cabins with single beds in lofts and spacious bathrooms with bathtubs marvelous for soaking after a crisp hike ($35 s, $45 d). There's a restaurant, and you can rent horses ($7 per hour).

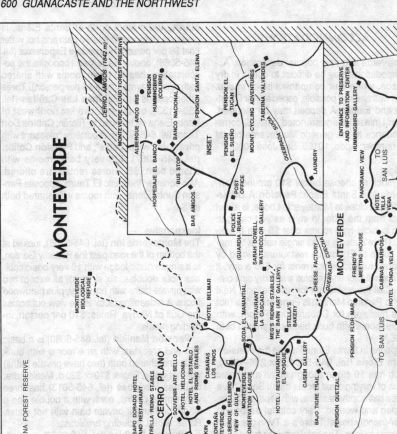

MONTEVERDE

CERRO AMIGOS (1842 m)

MONTEVERDE CLOUD FOREST PRESERVE

ALBERGUE ARCO IRIS
PENSION HUMMINGBIRD (COLIBRI)
PENSION SANTA ELENA

BANCO NACIONAL
PENSION EL TUCAN

HOSPEDAJE EL BANCO
BUS STOP
ALBERGUE EL BANCO

PENSION EL SUEÑO
MOUNT CYCLING ADVENTURES
TABERNA VALVERDES

BAR AMIGOS

POST OFFICE

POLICE (GUARDIA RURAL)

QUEBRADA SUCIA

SARAH DOWELL WATERCOLOR GALLERY

INSET

ENTRANCE TO PRESERVE AND INFORMATION CENTER
HUMMINGBIRD GALLERY

PANORAMIC VIEW

TO SAN LUIS

HOTEL VILLA VERDE

MONTEVERDE

FRIEND'S MEETING HOUSE

CABINAS MARIPOSA

CHEESE FACTORY

QUEBRADA CUECHA

HOTEL FONDA VELA

PENSION FLOR MAR

MONTEVERDE BIOLOGICAL REFUGE

HOTEL BELMAR

RESTAURANT LA CASCADA

SODA EL MANANTIAL

MEG'S RIDING STABLES / THE BARN (ART GALLERY)

STELLA'S BAKERY

HOTEL / RESTAURANTE EL BOSQUE

CASEM GALLERY

TO SAN LUIS

BAJO TIGRE TRAIL

PENSION QUETZAL

CERRO PLANO

SAPO DORADO HOTEL AND RESTAURANT

LA ESTRELLA RIDING STABLE

HOTEL HELICONIA

CABAÑAS LOS PINOS

SOUVENIR ARY BELLO

HOTEL EL ESTABLO AND RIDING STABLES

PENSION MANIKIN

HOTEL DE MONTAÑA MONTEVERDE

ALBERGUE BELLBIRD VIEW OF GULF

MONTEVERDE CONSERVATION LEAGUE

TO SANTA ELENA FOREST RESERVE

MONTEVERDE LODGE

BULLRING PLAZA DE TOROS

SANTA ELENA

HEALTH CLINIC

MONTEVERDE INN

BUTTERFLY GARDEN

QUEBRADA MAQUINA

SEE INSET

BULLRING (PLAZA DE TOROS)

TO TILARAN

TO LAGARTO AND PAN-AMERICAN HIGHWAY

QUEBRADA SUCIA

TOLL BOOTH

400 m

0

© MOON PUBLICATIONS, INC.

Pensión Flor Mar (tel. 645-5009, fax 645-5088) has three rustic but clean rooms with private baths (one with double bed, one with two bunks, a third with double and bunk), plus nine rooms with shared bath. Some rooms are dark. It's popular with scientists and student groups. It offers laundry service plus a small restaurant. It's owned by Marvin Rockwell—one of the original Quaker settlers—and his wife Flory (hence the hotel's name). Rates: $24 per person shared bath, $28 private bath, including three meals.

Hotel El Bosque (tel./fax 645-5129) has 21 cabins surrounded by open lawns, each with private bath and hot water. Fairly simple. No atmosphere. Rates: $20 s, $28 d, $34 t, $38 quad. **Pensión Quetzal** (tel. 645-0955) is a popular though rustic lodge—no smoking!—with 10 rooms (seven with private bath) with wood-paneled walls. It offers a small library and family-style dining. Hummingbirds gather in the flower-filled gardens. Rates: $25 per person; $35 with private bath and hot water.

The following are in Santa Elena. **Albergue Arco Iris Ecolodge** (Apdo. 003-5655, Santa Elena de Monteverde, tel. 645-5067, fax 645-5022) has 11 roomy rooms amid a spacious garden on a hillside, with an airy restaurant with a large menu at very reasonable rates. The restaurant, serving Costa Rican cuisine using fresh produce from the organic garden, has a TV. One room has four bunk beds. All have private baths and hot water. Horses are offered for rent, and **camping** ($3 per person) is available. Rates: $10-20 per person double. **Hospedaje El Banco,** behind Banco Nacional, has four small, simple rooms with communal bath and hot water. Home-cooked meals are served in a tiny restaurant. The small lounge has a TV. Rates: $15 per person.

Pensión El Sueño (tel. 645-5021) has eight double rooms with private but basic baths with hot water. One room sleeps six in bunks. There's a TV in the lounge, plus a small restaurant. Rates: $5 dorm, or $15 private room, per person, including breakfast. **Sunset Hotel** (tel. 645-3558), northwest of Santa Elena, has three rooms with private baths with hot water. It was adding more. It has a panoramic view and restaurant but was not inspected. Rates: $18 per person, including breakfast.

A dirt road about two km west of Santa Elena leads uphill to **San Gerardo Abajo** (three hours by horse from Santa Elena), where you can reportedly stay in basic cabinas offered by the Quesada family (tel. 645-2757). Not inspected. 4WD required. Also at San Gerardo Abajo, and accessible in rainy season only by horseback, is **El Mirador** (tel. 645-5087), a rustic lodge with a large dormitory with shared baths, plus private rooms with baths. Home-cooked meals are provided, as are horseback rides. The lodge offers views towards Arenal volcano.

Moderate
Hotel de Montaña Monteverde (Apdo. 70, Plaza G. Víquez, San José, tel. 645-5046 or 224-3050, fax 645-5320 or 222-6148) is more basic than the upscale properties. It's set in expansive grounds, which include a lake and 15-hectare private reserve. Spacious rooms—30 doubles and suites, each with private bath with hot water—have hardwood floors and verandas with rockers. Otherwise sparsely furnished. Rooms in the newer block are slightly more elegant. Suites get higher marks for their fireplaces and king-size beds. The hotel has a Jacuzzi and a sauna, plus a large restaurant, a bar, and a lounge with TV and veranda offering views over the gulf. Rates: $45 s, $65 d, $76 t, $120 honeymoon suite, with its own Jacuzzi.

Sapo Dorado (Apdo. 9. Monteverde 5655, tel. 645-5010, fax 645-5180) has 10 large rooms in five duplex cabins, each with private bath, two queen beds, fireplace, and private balconies. Small bathrooms. My friend Gregg Calkins reports: "No hot water in the sinks" and "simply built . . . and very noisy when the neighbors so much as coughed. There was no fooling around that night let me tell you." Honeymooners stay away: the hotel rules include "no moving of furniture or gymnastics after 9 p.m." Chalets are spread through landscaped, hilly grounds. The pleasant restaurant with open-air terrace and views out across the gulf is famous for its vegetarian and natural-food meals. Classical music accompanies dinner. Five km of self-guided trails lead through pastures and forest. There's professional massage, too. Rates: $60-70 d ($10 each additional person).

Cabañas Los Pinos (Apdo. 70, San José, tel. 645-5005, 645-5252) has five cabinas in an

alpine setting with lots of cedars. Each unit has a kitchenette and a private bath with hot water. Varying sizes sleep up to six people. Rates: $34 d, $42 t, $60 quad, $85 for a three-bedroom unit, including tax.

Hotel Villa Verde (Apdo. 16 C.P., Monteverde 5655, tel. 645-5025, fax 645-5115) has compact, rustic cabinas, plus new apartment rooms with hardwood floors, roomy kitchenettes, a small lounge with fireplace, and large bedrooms, each with four beds (one double, three singles). Suites have fireplaces and tubs. Voluminous tiled bathrooms have hot water. The pleasing restaurant offers a homey atmosphere. Two new blocks feature 18 rooms, plus an atrium restaurant and bar. Rates: $45 d, $65 suites.

Upscale

Monteverde Lodge (Apdo. 6941, San José 1000, tel. 257-0766, fax 257-1665; direct line, tel. 645-5057, fax 645-5126) is the most outstanding hotel in the area, and also the best bargain. A cavernous entrance foyer leads up to a spacious and elegant dining room with a soaring wooden-beamed roof (fresh-cut carnations on the tables, and excellent cuisine served by waiters in dress shirts and bow ties). To the left is a glass atrium over a large Jacuzzi (open 24 hours). Architecture is modern. Wraparound windows offer wonderful views over landscaped grounds and forested valley. Hardwood furniture and leather chairs from Sarchí contrast with the modern brick and wooden structure designed in an attractive theme of repeated "pyramids." Rooms are very spacious and elegant, with large V-shaped windows from which to watch the wind bowing down the trees while a virtually constant light drizzle falls beneath a blue sky framed by rainbows. Two large double beds. No TVs—thank goodness! Bathrooms are stocked with heaps of fluffy towels. Snacks are served in the bar at 5 p.m. Smoking is allowed in the bar and a designated smoking wing only. The lodge offers transportation to the Cloud Forest Preserve with advance notice ($4 one-way). The lodge is operated by Costa Rica Expeditions and is very popular with birding and nature groups. Rates: $89 d, including all meals. A three-day package with personal guide and transfers from San José costs $499 per person double, $349 quad.

Hotel Heliconia (tel. 645-5109, fax 645-5007) is an appealing Swiss-style chalet built almost entirely of lacquered cedar. Rooms, too, have abundant hardwoods and lots of light. Home-style comforts include deep-cushioned sofas in the lobby, curtains in hand-painted watercolors of local wildlife, and double and single beds with orthopedic mattresses in the 22 bedrooms, which have rocking chairs on the veranda. Otherwise basically furnished. Private bathrooms have hot water. The hotel boasts lots of epiphytes and hanging plants, plus a spacious and elegant restaurant, and a Jacuzzi. It is set in pretty landscaped grounds at the foot of the sloping 10-hectare Finca Heliconia, which boasts virgin forest at its upper elevations. Rate (per person): $45. Breakfast $5.

Hotel El Establo (Apdo. 549, San Pedro 2050, tel. 645-5033 or 645-5110, fax 645-5041) offers traditional Quaker hospitality, dude-ranch style! The new, two-story wood-and-stone structure is set on a private 48-hectare farm adjacent to the reserve. The 20 carpeted rooms have cinderblock walls. Rooms on the ground floor open onto a wood-floored gallery lounge with deep-cushioned sofas and an open fireplace. Each room has a double and a single bed, plus a pleasing bathroom with hot water. Heaps of light from the wraparound windows. The beautiful dining room has fresh-cut flowers and bright red tablecloths. El Establo has its own horse stable (see "Services," below). Rates: $48 s, $58 d, $65 t, $70 quad; breakfasts $5, lunch and dinner $8.

Hotel Belmar (tel. 645-5201, fax 645-5135) is a beautiful, ivy-clad, Swiss-style hotel with 34 clean, comfortable rooms, each with private bath and hot water. French doors in most rooms and lounges open onto balconies with grand views over the valley. A west-facing glass wall catches the sunset. The large and breezy restaurant reputedly serves good hearty meals and also has a veranda with a lookout over the gulf. The hotel will prepare box lunches for hikers. A larger unit has been added across the road in the same style. The road up to the hotel is very steep. Rates: $50 s, $60 d, $70 t, including tax; breakfast $5.

Hotel Fonda Vela (tel. 257-1413 or 645-5125, fax 257-1416 or 645-5119) has 28 rooms (junior suites), including five master suites. Hardwoods

abound. Some rooms have hardwood floors; others have flagstone floors. A highly recommended restaurant with an open-air balcony overlooks very forested grounds, through which a narrow trail leads to a Swiss-style chalet. All rooms are wheelchair accessible. Rates: $57 d, standard; $66 d, junior suites; $75 d for master suites.

The latest addition is the **Cloud Forest Lodge** (tel. 645-5058, fax 645-5168). The lodge, 1.5 km northeast of Santa Elena, has trails into the nearby forests. No smoking! Not reviewed. Rates: $70 s, $88 d. Breakfast $7, dinner $11.

Camping
Hotel Fonda Vela has a shady camping area. Several other hotels allow camping on their grounds. Try Hotel Villa Verde, Cabinas El Bosque, and Pensión Flor Mar.

FOOD

If you're a late diner, as I am, you'll be disappointed by the early closing hours most restaurants keep (most close at 9 p.m.). But the options are good. **Monteverde Lodge** (see above) offers excellent cuisine at reasonable rates ($6.50 breakfast, $11 lunch and dinner). The **Sapo Dorado** (tel. 645-2952) is also highly recommended. It specializes in vegetarian dishes, including whole-grain pizza, banana bread, and vegetarian pâté. Very romantic: Classical music is played every evening at sunset, followed by live music and dancing. Late diners note: Dinner is 7-9 p.m. **Restaurant El Bosque** (tel. 645-1258) is good for basic *típico* fare (average, $5); alternatively, for cheap grub, try **Soda El Manantial**, across from **Restaurant La Cascada**, 300 meters east of the gas station. La Cascada is a pleasant little restaurant in landscaped grounds with a small waterfall and balcony for dining alfresco (most dishes below $10). Music and dancing follow. **Bar y Restaurante Miramonte**, 400 meters north of the turnoff for the Santa Elena reserve, has views over the gulf. **El Daiquiri Restaurant**, in Santa Elena, has also been recommended.

The **cheese factory**, of course, sells 14 types of cheeses (hours: Mon.-Sat. 7:30 a.m.-4:30 p.m.). You can also buy homemade cookies and bread, and gouda and jack cheese at a dairy store next to the police station in Santa Elena. **Stella's Bakery** (tel. 645-5052; open 10:30 a.m.-4:30 p.m.), next to the CASEM gallery, sells homemade bread, cookies, granola, sticky buns, and doughnuts.

ENTERTAINMENT

Two **slide shows** are offered daily at the Hummingbird Gallery ($3). "Natural History of Cloud Forest Animals" is shown at 3:15 p.m. and "Colors of Tropical Animals" at 4:30 p.m. A **multimedia show**—"Sounds and Scenes of the Cloud Forest"—is also offered at 6:15 on Monday, Thursday, and Saturday at the Monteverde Lodge (tel. 645-5057).

The **Monteverde Music Festival,** each January and February, features live music to accompany the sunset offered by members of the National Symphony Orchestra and other leading artists at a villa above the Hotel Belmar (5 p.m. daily except Sunday and Wednesday; $7). A festival shuttle bus departs Santa Elena at 4:20 p.m. and runs between the hotels. Call or fax 645-5125 or 645-5114 for reservations. You can buy tickets in advance at the Monteverde Lodge. Dress warmly and bring a flashlight.

Monteverde is a Quaker community: hence, no bars! You can wet your whistle at the hotel bars, however, or at the **Taberna Valverdes** (tel. 661-2557) and **Bar Amigos** in Santa Elena. The **Sapo Dorado** also has dancing and live music at night.

SERVICES

Horseback Rides
Meg's Stables (tel. 645-5052) is highly recommended for its guided tours ($20 for two hours);

MONTEVERDE EMERGENCY TELEPHONE NUMBERS

All emergencies	911
Police	645-1002
Red Cross	645-1156

it also rents horses ($7 per hour). Notice is usually required. **Hotel El Establo** (tel. 645-5110) has 30 horses, which rent at $7 per hour with guide. **La Estrella** (tel. 645-2751) has 30 horses, with guided tours from one-hour to full-day ($7 per hour; tel. 645-5075 in Spanish, tel. 645-5067 in Dutch, English, German, or Italian). Also try **Rancho Verde** (tel. 645-1003) and **Pensión Santa Elena.**

Souvenirs

The **Artisans' Co-operative** of Santa Elena and Monteverde (CASEM, tel. 645-5190, fax 645-5006) features the handmade wares of 140 local artisans whose work focuses on the natural beauty of the area. Sales directly benefit the artists (closed Sunday May-Nov.). Next door is the coffee roaster of **Café Monteverde,** where you can taste locally produced coffee and watch beans being roasted and packaged ($2 per half-pound). Roaster Victorina Molina will be happy to tell you all about the local coffee cooperative. To order Café Monteverde in the U.S., call (800) 345-JAVA. **Souvenir Ary Bello** (tel. 645-2558) sells local handicrafts, plus film. You can also buy souvenirs—locally made hand-carved woodenware and embroidered placemats, wall hangings, and blouses—plus posters, postcards, and color transparencies at the Hummingbird Gallery and visitor center.

Other

The **post office** is in the dairy store on the southwest corner of Santa Elena, next door to the **police** (Guardia Rural). **Mount Cycle Adventures** (tel. 645-1007) rents mountain bikes and offers guided cycling tours. Lavandería Patricia (tel. 645-2653) offers **laundry** service. There's a small **health clinic** (tel. 645-1156) in Santa Elena. For **information,** contact the Monteverde Tourist Board (Apdo. 10165, San José 1000, tel. 645-1001).

GETTING THERE

By Bus

From San José: Autotransportes Tilarán (tel. 222-3854 in San José, 645-1152 in Santa Elena) operates an express bus from Calle 14,

Avenidas 9/11, twice daily at 6:30 a.m. and 2:30 p.m. (four hours; $4.50). The return bus departs Monteverde at the same times.

Buy your ticket in advance. Watch your luggage! Buses will drop you by your hotel. The cheese factory (about 2.5 km before the reserve) is the end of the route; buses to San José depart from here and pick up passengers along the road. Buy your return bus ticket from the Hotel El Bosque or Hotel Finca Valverde (other hotels may be able to supply tickets) as soon as you arrive in Monteverde, otherwise you might be out of luck!

From Puntarenas: The Santa Elena/Monteverde bus departs at 2:15 p.m. daily from the beachfront stop between Calles 2 and 4. You can pick it up at the Río Lagarto turnoff for Monteverde at around 3:30 p.m. Return buses depart Santa Elena from outside the Banco Nacional at 6 a.m. A bus to Tilarán departs San José from Calle 12, Avenidas 9/11 (tel. 222-3854) at 12:45 p.m. and usually arrives at Río Lagarto around 3:15 p.m., in time to connect with the bus from Puntarenas. Alternately, a bus departs Tilarán daily for Santa Elena at 1 p.m. (the return bus departs at 7 a.m.). Buy tickets in advance.

Exotur (tel. 227-5169, fax 227-2180) has been slating an express bus service—the Silver Bullet—daily from San José. It wasn't in service at press time; check to see if it has been reinstated. Evelio Fonseca Mata runs a private **minibus** service (tel. 645-0958) to/from San José for four people for around $200 roundtrip.

Note: Many rental-car companies used to refuse to allow their vehicles to be driven to Monteverde. The road was recently upgraded. It's still in rough shape, however, so check with your rental company. Drive slowly through Santa Elena and Monteverde. There are a lot of pedestrians, horses, and children playing along the road, which has many blind bends. Speed limit in the area is 20 km/h.

Monteverde to Tilarán

If traveling to Lake Arenal, you can avoid the long descent to the Pan-Am Hwy. and the 67-km journey via Cañas to Tilarán by following the rough dirt road west from Santa Elena via Cabeceras and Quebrada Grande (you cut out a lot of mileage, but unless you have a power-

ful 4WD vehicle you'll probably not save any time; allow two hours). The roads are in a terribly muddy state. Worse, there are lots of junctions, and the roads are unsigned. Ask directions at every opportunity! Follow your instincts and keep heading west and you're sure to emerge in Tilarán or onto the paved road from Cañas, just below Tilarán. A 4WD is recommended but not essential. It's beautiful scenery all the way!

LAKE ARENAL AND VICINITY

This picture-perfect lake—12,400 hectares (48 square miles)—might have been transplanted from the English Lake District, surrounded as it is by mountains kept perpetually emerald-green by winds from the Caribbean that sweep through the gap in the cordillera. The looming mass of Volcán Arenal (see Northern Lowlands chapter) to the east adds a tropical note. About two to three million years ago, tectonic movements created a depression that filled with a small lagoon. In 1973, the Costa Rican Institute of Electricity (ICE) built a dam at the eastern end of the valley, raising the level of the lagoon and creating a narrow 32-km-long reservoir. Recent satellite photos have identified several ancient Indian settlements at the bottom of the lake; archaeological studies suggest they may be as much as 2,000 years old.

The volcano is most easily reached from Fortuna in the northern lowlands. You can, however, follow the paved road from Tilarán that swings west around the lake (don't go careening along, as is temptation, as the next bend may deliver you into an almighty pothole). Beyond the small town of Nuevo Arenal, alas, this road deteriorates into an unpaved eight-km-long section that is surely one of the most abysmal roads in the country. The road is so bad that it effectively divides the western part of the lake from the volcano and Tabacón Hot Springs to the east as effectively as any international border. At press time, the road—a true torment—had still not been paved, despite promises that it will soon be completed. (You can also drive east along the southern rim of the lake via Tronadora, where there are basic cabinas; from here the rough dirt and rock road deteriorates rapidly and is best tackled in a 4WD. You'll pass only a few homesteads and two tiny hamlets. I once drove the "road" at night in a Range Rover during torrential rains but could get no farther than the Río Chiquito, where a bridge was being washed away!)

The lake and volcano are enveloped within recently created Arenal National Park, a polyglot assemblage encompassing the pristine cloud-forest terrain that extends westward to Monteverde. The road along the northeastern corner of the lake is backed by thick primary forest. Luuuush! And the views from here are fantastic.

The area is enjoying a tourism boom, and hotels are springing up like weeds, backed by tours of every description, many based out of Fortuna in the northern lowlands.

Note: Everything *west* of the hydroelectricity dam at the eastern end of the lake is included in this chapter. Tabacón and Volcán Arenal are included in the chapter on the northern lowlands, from which they are more readily accessible.

NUEVO ARENAL

The tiny town of Nuevo Arenal, on the north shore, was created only in 1973, when the lake flooded the original settlement. It is the only settlement between Tilarán and Fortuna, in the northern lowlands. In March 1994, local citizens destroyed the local telephone exchange in protest over what they considered an inadequate system. They were without phone service for some time. Officials even called in the National Guard to quell the uprising! That's in the past, but if you still need to request phone numbers, do so by calling information: 113.

Field of Dreams

Otherwise called the Arenal Botanical Garden (tel. 695-5266, ext. 273, fax 694-4273), five km east of Nuevo Arenal, this marvelous botanical garden blooming on the Continental Divide harbors rare tropical species, including a panoply of Costa Rican plants: anthuriums, bromeliads, heliconias, ferns, even roses, plus orchids galore, not least all six species of gorguras. There's

LAKE ARENAL

Map labels:
TO SAN RAFAEL
RIO COTE
143
4
ECO-ADVENTURE LODGE
LAKE COTER
RIO PIEDRA
ALTURAS DEL ARENAL LODGE
MIRADOR LOS LAGOS
ROCK RIVER LODGE
VISTA LAGO INN
RESTAURANTE CHICO Y MERI
TORONTO CABINS
HOTEL EL CAFETAL
HOTEL PUERTO LAJAS
CHALET NICHOLAS
NUEVO ARENAL
CABINAS RODRIGUEZ
LA CASONA DEL LAGO
VILLA DECARY
XILOE LODGE AND EQUUS BBQ
VILLAS ALPINO
TICO WIND WINDSURF CENTER
MYSTICA LAKE LODGE
TILAWA VIENTO SURF CENTER
LAKE ARENAL
ARENAL BOTANICAL GARDEN
HOTEL TILAWA
LA CEIBA
COMPLEJO TURISTICO LA ALONDRA
HOTEL BAHIA BLUE BAY
QUEBRADA AZUL
TRONADORA
MARINA CLUB HOTEL
TOAD HALL
LOS HEROES
TO FORTUNA
RIO ARENAL
142
ARENAL LODGE
TABACON HOT SPRINGS
TO CAÑAS
142
142
TILARAN
145
ARENAL VOLCANO
RIO CHIQUITO
CHIRIPA
RIO CHIQUITO
RIO AGUA CALIENTE
QUEBRADA GRANDE
ARENAL OBSERVATORY LODGE
ARENAL VISTA LODGE
RIO CAÑO NEGRO
RIO PIEDRAS NEGRAS
RIO NEGRO
0   5km
NUBES
145
TO MONTEVERDE
SANTA ELENA

© MOON PUBLICATIONS, INC.

even an Asian garden with waterfalls. Should you be awed and need to rest and absorb it all, benches plus a fruit and juice bar provide the means. Visitors are limited to 20 per hour. A booklet corresponds to the numbered displays. Trails also lead through the adjacent farm, also owned by Michael LeMay. Open daily 9 a.m.-5 p.m. (closed October). Entrance: $4.

ACTIVITIES

You'll find a local tour office opposite the bus stop in Nuevo Arenal. Also see hotel listings for additional information on activities, rentals, and tours.

Windsurfing

In the morning the lake can look like a mirror. The calm is short-lived. More normal are nearly constant 30- to 80-km/h winds, which whip up whitecaps. November-April, winds up to 100 km per hour turn the lake into one of the world's top windsurfing spots. Although promoted as "a rival to Oregon's Columbia Gorge," avid windsurfers tell me that Arenal doesn't live up to that billing: it's too choppy. I'm also told it's not a good place for beginners to learn. Water temperatures re-

main at 18-21° C (65-70° F) year-round. Swells can top one meter. Says local windsurfing aficionado Jean Paul Cazedessus: "None of this, '*Last* week it was ripping!' to be heard at Lake Arenal . . . It's every day, all day . . . Twenty-five mph is the *average* winter day's wind speed." Nov.-Jan. are best; June and October are the worst months. Adds local surf expert Norman List: "Out here I've seen people get 30 feet of air . . . Speed is boring. We're out trying to do loops, jumps, jibes, and acrobatics!"

The **Tilawa Viento Surf High Wind Center** (Apdo. 92, Tilarán, tel. 695-5050, fax 695-5766), on the lake's southwest corner, has a rental fleet of ready-rigged high-wind, transitional, and beginner boards (daily and weekly rates). The center is on a leeward-access peninsula with side-shore wind, grassy rigging area, and protected cove. It features a flatwater port jibe area, chop rollers in sets of three, and port ramps with up to 2.5-meter faces. Bilingual staff offer complete lesson programs for all levels. The center also rents Hobie-cats ($10 per person, per hour).

On the western shore is **Tico Wind** (fax 695-5387; in the U.S., tel. 800-678-2252 or 503-386-5524, fax 503-387-3300), a windsurf center open Dec.-April 9 a.m.-6 p.m. Rentals are $45 a day, $250 per week, including wet suits, harnesses, and choice of board and sail. Instruction is offered from beginner to advanced (private lessons: $20 first hour, $15 additional).

Most other local hotels rent windsurf equipment. The Rock River Lodge is recommended.

Fishing

The lake, 1,800 feet above sea level, is stocked with challenging game fish—*guapote, machaca,* and (for lighter tackle enthusiasts) *mojarra*—and is understandably popular with anglers, including locals who fish with simple handlines from rafts of balsa logs. *Guapote* (rainbow bass indigenous to Central America) is the most fierce fighter among the freshwater fish; a four-kilo catch would be a trophy. The *machaca* (Central America's answer to American shad) is a relative of the piranha, whose voracious temperament it apparently shares. They come up to three kg and are supposedly very difficult to hook. *Mojarra*—described by angler Chet Young as "Costa Rica's bluegill with teeth!"—are also tricky

to hook but are tasty. Most of the hotels in **Fortuna** offer fishing tours (see "Fortuna and Vicinity" in the Northern Lowlands chapter). A local resident, **Natanael Murrillo** (tel. 479-9087), also offers fishing trips.

Tours

Agencia Mitur (Apdo. 91, San José 1150, tel. 255-2031, fax 255-1946) has a two-day/one-night package that includes a cruise on the newly introduced *Arenal Prince* and overnight on the shores of Lake Arenal (approximately $100). The tour is led by a bilingual guide and leaves daily from the Plaza de la Cultura at 7:30 a.m. A stop at Zarcero is included. **Tico Tours** (tel. 222-8521, fax 222-8429) has a two-day tour to Lake Arenal with a visit to Caño Negro ($195). **CATA Tours** (tel. 221-5455, fax 221-0200) has a one-day Lake Arenal and volcano tour, offered Tuesday and Sunday ($70). **Aventuras Arenal** (tel. 479-9133) has a sunset cruise on the lake ($15; see "Fortuna and Vicinity" in the Northern Lowlands chapter). You can even enjoy a sunset cruise aboard the *El Sueño Imposible* (tel. 228-9200), which is docked at Los Héroes Hotel.

A novel way of touring the region is with **Impossible Dream,** combining a tour by double-decker bus and boating. It takes four hours ($27), including dinner and drinks. Information from Hotel Burio Inn or Hotel Aurora in Fortuna.

The Stable (tel. 253-3048), just outside Nuevo Arenal, has horses for rent ($30 half-day) on a 200-hectare farm with primary forest. A ring displays dancing horses and you can enjoy a terraced garden and small *soda* for a cool *refresco* after your ride.

Most other tour operators in San José offer, or can arrange, tours to Arenal. Several hotels and tour companies in **Fortuna** offer inexpensive tours.

ACCOMMODATIONS

Hotels are listed by category in clockwise order from Tilarán.

Inexpensive

Cabinas Chico y Meri (tel. 695-5427 or 695-5430), offered by the restaurant of that name,

has six basic cabinas with private baths and hot water. Rates: $18 d, $28 t. Unless an improvement has been made since I last saw them, they're funky and overpriced.

By the time you read this, **Toronto Cabins,** with ten spacious, rustic cabinas ($15 d, including breakfast) perched on a hill amid a coffee *finca* immediately north of Nuevo Arenal, will have been complemented by a full-fledged hotel next door.

In Nuevo Arenal, **Hotel/Restaurante Lajas** has six basic but clean rooms; private bathrooms have rock walls and hot water ($8 per person). Also in town is **La Cage des Tigres** (tel. 695-5266), opposite the bus stop. All three rooms have private baths. Rate: $15 d. In the same price range, on the south side of the church, is **Cabinas Rodriguez,** with private baths and hot water.

La Casona del Lago (tel. 695-5008 or 231-4266), also known as Albergue Tilarán, is affiliated with the youth hostel system and has four rooms, each with four bunks. It's about two km east of Nuevo Arenal. Rates: $15 for IYHF members, $25 for nonmembers, including breakfast.

You'll also find cheap cabinas for rent in the hamlet of Guadalajara, at the lake's western extreme.

Moderate
Hotel Bahía Blue Bay (Apdo. 2, Tilarán, tel. 695-5750, fax 695-5387), formerly Hotel Puerto San Luis, nestles in a sheltered cove on the south shore and has 19 rooms, all with private baths, roomy showers, and hot water, on sloping landscaped grounds. Basic and somewhat dated rooms are sparsely furnished and have TVs, plus verandas with lake views. A small restaurant overlooks the grounds and a larger one overlooks the lake. You can rent paddleboats, water-skis, and sailboards. To get there, take the road to the right at the Y-fork as you approach the lake from Tilarán. Rates: $35 s, $42 d, $50 t.

Mystica Lake Lodge (fax 695-5387) was opened by an Italian couple, Moglia and Francesco Carullo, in early 1994. They have six large rooms and equally spacious bathrooms. Each has desks, open closets, and odd, delightful touches. You can sit on your veranda and contemplate the universe. Moglia cooks wholesome breakfasts, served in the kitchen, while dinners—including pizzas—are served in a cozy, high-ceilinged restaurant complete with a big fireplace at the bottom of the garden. Rate: $35 double, including breakfast.

Xiloe Lodge (Apdo. 35, Tilarán, tel. 259-9806, fax 259-9882) is a family ranch offering very pleasant, rustic ranch-style cabinas set amid lawned grounds up a gradual rise overlooking the lake. Options include spacious three-bedroom cabinas with kitchenettes; an older bungalow under a massive shady tree, with kitchenette, terrace, and its own barbecue pit; or two basic two-bedroom cabinas sleeping four. Each unit has a private balcony and a private bath with hot water. There's a small circular swimming pool, plus a river that runs through the property. The **Equus BBQ**—a cozy "corral guanacastero"—offers delicious smoked chicken and grilled meats. Horseback rides are guided by *vaqueros.* You can hire surfboards. Rates: $40-50.

Rock River Lodge (tel. 222-4547, fax 221-3011) has six aesthetically pleasing and romantic cabins, plus 10 more modern Santa Fe-style cabins with private baths and hot water. A very beautiful open-air restaurant has a magnificent stone fireplace in a Western-style lounge, with hardwood tables and chairs overlooking the lake. A large bar features an open-stove barbecue pit (beers and rum run $1). The lodge rents mountain bikes and a catamaran. Owner Norman List runs the Tico Wind windsurf center. Rates: $35-50 d ($10 additional).

Villas Alpino (fax 695-5387) has five rustic yet marvelous self-contained Swiss-style cabins stairstepping up the hillside, each with abundant hardwood decor, tasteful Guatemalan fabrics, plentiful light, and verandas for enjoying the views. Each room has a double bed and bunk. Dutch owner, Ernesto de Leones, operates to high standards. Rate: $35.

Mirador Los Lagos (Apdo. 97, Tilarán 5710, tel. 695-5484 or 695-5169, fax 695-5387) has 15 cabinas with private rock-walled baths and verandas with chairs for enjoying one of the best views around. The open-air restaurant high above the lake is very popular with locals and serves freshly caught seafood. There's a *mirador* nearby on a separate hilltop. Biking ($10 per hour) and horseback rides ($8 per hour) are offered, as well as boat trips on the lake, plus

tours to Cote Lagoon, Monteverde, Venado Caves, and Arenal volcano. Rates: $35 s, $45 d with private bath; $25 s, $35 d with shared bath ($15 additional).

Albergue and Club Alturas del Arenal (Apdo. 166, San José 1007, tel. 222-6455, fax 222-8372) is an upscale and elegant bargain. It offers 12 small rooms with private baths, plus a beautiful upscale restaurant with terra-cotta tiles and log supports to the roof. The small lounge has a large TV. The lodge overlooks landscaped gardens and offers fishing, boat, and horse trips, plus windsurfing. The restaurant is popular with locals, especially on weekends when they "get down" with foot-stomping music and dancing. Rate: $25 per person, including breakfast.

Next along is Chalet Nicholas and then Puerto Lajas, two bed-and-breakfast inns that I highly recommend (see "Bed and Breakfast," below).

Hotel El Cafetal (tel. 695-5266, ext. 288), north of Nuevo Arenal, offers 27 rooms, five bedrooms in the main lodge, plus rustic cabinas on a three-hectare working coffee plantation overlooking Arenal and the lake. Rooms have telephones, TVs, and private baths; they vary from "regular" (two twins or a double) to elegant suites accommodating four adults. Highlights include a restaurant, lounge, billiard room, and sauna. The views are marvelous. Walking paths lead to secluded spots good for meditation. There's a pool with spacious sundeck and a tennis court. The hotel offers laundry service, tours, and horse rentals. The complex was built to be eco-sensitive (solar heating, wind generation, "micro-biodigester," etc.). It's Canadian owned and run. Rates: hotel $15, cabins $10.

In Nuevo Arenal is the rather faceless, American-run **Hotel Aurora Inn Bed & Breakfast** (tel. 694-4245, fax 694-4262), with seven rooms in the main building—complete with deck on which to relax—and six cabins facing the lake. The lobby has a satellite TV. Rooms are carpeted and comfortably furnished but homely, even dowdy. Rates: $30 s, $36 d, including breakfast.

East of town are several properties, beginning with **Villa Decary** (Nuevo Arenal 5717, Tilarán; fax 694-4086), a small, American-owned home-turned-inn converted from a fruit and coffee *finca* on three hilly hectares, two km west of the botanical gardens. The thoroughly contemporary structure glows with light pouring in through French doors and windows. Hardwood furniture gleams. Five large bedrooms each have bright Guatemalan covers, plus a private bath and balcony with a handy rail that serves as bench and table. There's also a bungalow with kitchenette. Gardens were being planted, trails were being cut for birding and nature hikes in the surrounding forest, and a spa and deck are planned. Peaceful. Rates: $49 d, including full breakfast; $275 bungalow. A bargain! Telephone service may have been added by the time you read this.

Next is **La Ceiba** (Apdo. 9, Tilarán, fax 695-5387), a small German-run bed and breakfast amid a 16-hectare farm that swathes the hillside about six km east of town. It's reached via a very steep, very narrow lane lined with tropical flowers. Four large rooms have heaps of light, plus private baths with hot water. Ursula's oil paintings abound. Go hiking or birding in the private forest reserve, help milk the goats, or simply relax on the veranda beneath the huge ceiba tree and watch the profusion of birds. The place is popular with birders, who head off along nearby trails. You can rent a sailboat. Rates: $30 s, $50 d, including breakfast.

Complejo Turístico La Alondra has a restaurant plus 10 pretty, modern cabinas with verandas. Not reviewed. Approximately $40 d.

Upscale

Hotel Tilawa (Apdo. 92, Tilarán 5710, tel. 695-5050, fax 695-5766; in the U.S., tel. 800-851-8929) can't and shouldn't be missed! This stunner—a piece of the Mediterranean carried into the hillsides of the Americas—was inspired by the Palace of Knossos on Crete. It opened in December 1992 with 28 rooms, including four junior suites, that command magnificent hillside views over the lake. Thick bulbous columns, walls painted with flowers and dolphins, and ochre pastels play on the Cretan theme. All very atmospheric! The rooms are spacious, simple, and beautiful, with hardwood ceilings, orthopedic mattresses, decor of subdued rough-painted pastels, and stunning bedspreads from Guatemala. Each has two queen-size beds and private bath with hot water. Junior suites have kitchenettes, couches, and TVs. Very airy bathrooms (those upstairs are lit by skylights).

A bar and restaurant upstairs have floor-to-ceiling windows offering superb vistas. The Delfin bar offers drinks and snacks beside a swimming pool that is a model of Minoan simplicity. The hotel has its own rental-car agency and a tennis court. It also operates the Tilawa Viento Surf High Wind Center (see above), offering the largest and finest selection of rental equipment on Lake Arenal. Tilawa also offers mountain biking ($10 per hour) and horseback rides ($10), plus fishing. Rates: $54 s, $71 d, $87 t; $112 d suites.

Giving Tilawa a run for its money, but in altogether different guise, is the **Marina Club Hotel** (tel./fax 239-0040, fax 479-9178), eight km east of Nuevo Arenal. Its stunning setting—grassy meadows sweeping down the hill and grazed by horses—is complemented by bougainvilleas clambering over bamboo rails and seven supremely novel luxury cabinas with views over the lake (18 more were planned). Within is a mezzanine bedroom with king-size bed, low-lit lamps, and timbered ceilings, with small lounge below. Radio and CD (no TVs) are standard. Kitchenettes are to be installed. Each cabina has its own color scheme of tropical pastels. French doors open onto a veranda with Sarchí rockers. Each, too, has its own sheltered carport. The former barn is now an open-air bar (shaped like a ship's prow) and restaurant, rustic as all-get-out and decorated with nautical motifs. The property has horses and even its own marina with two catamarans and windsurfers for hire. Rates: $75 d.

Next is the Swiss-owned **Hotel & Restaurant Los Héroes** (tel. 441-8585, fax 441-4193), a chalet-style hotel with hints of the Alps at every turn. Twelve nicely appointed rooms feature brass beds. Some have bathtubs and balconies. Upper story rooms are larger. International cuisine is served in the restaurant. Highlights include a pool and Jacuzzi, plus stables for horseback rides, and even a boat—"Impossible Dream"—for dinner and sunset cruises. The hotel gets rave reviews; owner Hans Ulrich maintains the place to Swiss standards. Yes, your bed is turned down each evening, and a little chocolate sits on your pillow! Rates: $55-75 d, including continental breakfast. Two fully furnished apartments are available; $112 for up to six people.

Arenal Lodge (Apdo. 1195, Escazú 1250, tel. 228-2588, fax 228-2798; in the U.S. tel. 800-235-3625) is a ranch-style lodge that combines rusticity, elegance, and a warm, inviting atmosphere. It looks out over the volcano but has no lake view. The 15 spacious and beautiful rooms include doubles, junior suites, and a full suite, all with private baths and hot showers, and all in wood, with wall-to-wall louvered windows. You'll also find an atrium courtyard, a library, a lounge bar with a large stone fireplace and a full-size pool table, plus a beautiful restaurant with an all-around window facing toward Arenal and a deck on which to rock and contemplate the view. The lodge specializes in fishing ($225 double per day, with guide), but an evening volcano tour ($100) and a "birding by boat" tour ($25) are also available. You reach the lodge via a very steep and daunting gravel road (about three km). Rates: $60-80 d.

The **Arenal Vista Lodge** (Apdo. 818, San José 1200, tel. 220-2121 or 231-2808, fax 232-3321), on the southeast corner of the lake near the village of El Cairo, perches on a landscaped terraced hill with forest behind. Twenty-five Swedish-inspired cabins are grouped on the slopes and feature niceties such as window boxes and small balconies. Each has a private bath with hot water. A dining room and terrace offer panoramic lake and volcano views. There are wide options for activities and touring. Food from the set meal has been rated "OK." You'll need 4WD, as you cross three rivers (no bridges) to get there. **Note:** Your easiest approach to this hotel is probably via Fortuna, in the northern lowlands. Rates: 79 d.

Bed and Breakfast

Vista Lago Inn, just west of Rock River Lodge, has pretty if rustic chalets with decks on the hillside. Not reviewed.

Two enormous yet friendly Great Danes—Max and Minka—welcome guests to the American-run **Chalet Nicholas** (Apdo. 72, Tilarán 5710, tel. 694-4041, fax 695-5387), a splendid three-bedroom bed and breakfast guest house reached up a bougainvillea-lined driveway two km west of Nuevo Arenal (at road marker Km 48). It exudes charm and all the comforts of home—including private bathrooms festooned with fluffy pillows and towels, rareties indeed in

Costa Rica. Two bedrooms are downstairs. However, clamber the spiral staircase and you emerge into another, larger loft bedroom with cozy sitting room boasting a deck. The inn proffers a video library and fabulous views plus horseback riding ($20, three hours) and birding. The meals get rave reviews. Americans owners John and Catherine Nicholas top it all with fine hospitality. A splendid bargain! Rates: $39 d, including breakfast, $10 extra person.

Puerto Lajas (fax 695-5387), 400 meters east of Chalet Nicholas, is a small inn with spacious, gracious rooms done in bright ceramic tiles and reached by a rock-lined walkway (it continues downhill to the lake shore, where a dock was being built). In time, the inn will offer boats, horses, and windsurfing rentals. Rate: $30 d, including breakfast. Not reviewed.

FOOD AND ENTERTAINMENT

The upscale and moderate hotels all have reasonable restaurants (see above).

Equus Bar, adjoining the Xiloe Lodge, is a corral-style open-air barbecue restaurant serving chicken, pork, and beef cooked in an open-hearth oven. Very atmospheric. Closed Monday. **Restaurante Chico y Meri,** at the northwest corner of the lake, offers inexpensive *típico* meals (lunches average $2) served on a breezy open-air terrace; **Pico's Discotheque** used to crank it up here seven nights a week. The place looked forlorn when I last passed by. The **Full Moon Disco** behind the Xiloe Lodge attracts folks from far and wide for Latin and disco dancing under the moonlight. By the time you read this, owner Fernando Calderón should have initiated informal **horseraces** on a "country-style track" near the lodge.

In Nuevo Arenal, try **Restaurant Los Arcos** (tel. 695-5266, ext. 196) for Costa Rican fare; and **Tramonti** (tel. 695-5266, ext. 282) for highly praised pizzas baked in a wood-burning oven. Two places favored by locals include the restaurant of the **Albergue Alturas del Arenal** and **Mirador Los Lagos** (see hotel listings, above, for these and additional hotel restaurants).

The harrowing road east of Nuevo Arenal is worth the ordeal simply to visit **Toad Hall,** whose attractions, besides the fact that it stocks the

Costa Rican Handbook, are many. Kim West runs this Aladdin's Cave . . . in equal part, deli/cafe/gallery/book shop/general store. After browsing the superb selection of arts, crafts, clothing, etc., settle on the outside balcony and admire the view over coffee and divine chocolate and macadamia cookies. A full-service restaurant serving organic salads and pastries should be in service by the time you read this.

On the southeast shore, the rough road that leads to Arenal Observatory Lodge (turn right at the Y-junction for Tronadora from Tilarán) winds to the hamlet of El Castillo, where turning right, or south, brings you to **Café de Crepe,** where you can enjoy *típico* meals or coffee and desserts while taking in the views of lake and volcano.

SERVICES

You'll find a branch of the **Banco Nacional** (tel. 695-5266, ext. 122) on the west side of the church, plus a **gas station** as you enter Nuevo Arenal from Tilarán. You'll find another gas station 400 meters south of the Y-junction to Tronadora, just north of Quebrada Azul.

GETTING THERE

Buses depart San José for Nuevo Arenal via Ciudad Quesada and Fortuna from Calle 16, Avenidas 1/3 (Garaje Barquero, tel. 232-5660) at 6:15, 8:40, and 11:30 a.m. (4½ hours). Additional buses depart Ciudad Quesada (San Carlos) for Tabacón and Nuevo Arenal daily at 6 a.m. and 3 p.m. and continue on to Tilarán. Buses depart Cañas for Tilarán and Nuevo Arenal at 7:30, 9, and 11 a.m., and 3 p.m. You can also get to Tilarán direct from San José with Autotransportes Tilarán (tel. 222-3854); they have buses departing from Calle 12, Avenidas 9/11 at 7:30 a.m., and 12:45, 3:45 and 6:30 p.m. (four hours). An express bus departs Nuevo Arenal for San José via Ciudad Quesada at 2:45 p.m.; additional buses depart for Ciudad Quesada at 8 a.m. and 2 p.m. A bus marked "Guatuso" also departs Arenal at 1:30 p.m. for San Rafael, Caño Negro, and Upala in the northern lowlands.

Schedules change. Check times.

I'm often asked about day excursions to Arenal. I don't recommend it; it's about three hours each way. Plan on staying overnight.

LAKE COTER

Lake Arenal's smaller neighbor, five km northwest of Nuevo Arenal, presents opportunities for hiking and horseback rides. Fishing is not great. You can reach Coter via a partially paved road (4WD recommended); follow the signs for Eco-Adventure Lodge.

Accommodations
Eco-Adventure Lodge (Apdo. 6398, San José 1000, tel. 223-2811, fax 223-1916) is an extremely elegant hardwood-and-brick structure in expansive landscaped grounds next to heart-shaped Lake Coter. A cozy lounge with deep-cushioned sofas is centered on a large open-hearth fireplace. The lodge has a games room, a lounge bar, and a pleasing restaurant. The 30 rooms with hardwood walls are fairly small and modest, each with double bed and bunk. All share his-and-hers communal baths. A better bet are the newer four-person duplex cabins atop the hill, with heaps of windows and patios offering great views. The lodge is operated by Tikal Tours and has hiking, horseback and mountain-bike rides, and water sports (oh, and *lots* of tourists). A nature trail leads through rainforest. Rates: about $80-100, including meals.

TILARÁN

The road east from Cañas (Avenida 1) climbs steadily to Tilarán (23 km), a well-kept town with a very pretty square and a park with cedars and pines in front of the church. It's the kind of place where after a full day of touring you might rest beneath a tall tree in the park until the tropical odors and the chime of a church bell or the distant braying of a mule lull you to sleep. At this elevation (550 meters) you begin to notice the breezes that work their way over the crest of the Cordillera de Tilarán from Lake Arenal, five km to the northeast. The countryside hereabouts is remarkably similar to the rolling hill country

of England—the Mendips or Downs. The last weekend in April (and again in mid-June) Tilarán plays host to a rodeo and a livestock show, and the town fills up.

Accommodations
Cabinas Lago Lindo has seven spotlessly kept rooms with shared bath, plus one with a private bath and hot water. It's superbly run by the same folks who own El Sueño (see below). Lots of light. A recommended bargain. Rates: $6 s, $11 d, $16 t with shared bath. The **Hotel Grecia** (tel. 695-5043), on the west of the plaza, has 20 adequate though simply furnished rooms, some with private baths but no fans. Rates: $6 per person, shared bath; $12 private bath. **Hotel Central** (tel. 695-5363) has 12 basic rooms with shared baths, plus eight cabins with private baths. Rates: rooms $5 per person, $12 cabins. Alternately, try **Cabinas Mary** (tel. 695-5479), on the south side of the park, with basic rooms with private baths with warm water. Rates: $7 s, $12 d; $5 per person with shared bath.

Albergue Tilarán (tel. 695-5008), opposite the Windsurf Hotel, is part of the Costa Rican Youth Hostel chain. Eight beds, shared bath. Reservations are handled by the Aventuras Tilarán tour company, which has an office and a small boutique below the Windsurf Hotel. Rates: $15 s, $25 d. (Aventuras also has a house with a kitchen and a garden 12 km west of town at Río Picas, with views of the mountains and lake; $300 per week.) Rates: $5 rooms, $7 cabins.

Cabinas El Sueño (tel. 695-5347), next door to Lago Lindo, is one of the best hotels for its price in the country. Twelve rooms, all with private baths with hot water, surround a sunlit second-floor courtyard with a fountain. There's a hammock in the courtyard. Downstairs is the hotel's **Restaurant El Parque,** with good seafood dishes. Herman and Sonia Vargas, the super-friendly owners, provide fruit and toiletry baskets that include shaving implements. Impeccable! *Highly recommended.* Rates: $15 s, $25 d, $30 t.

Cabinas Naralit (tel. 695-5393), on the south side of the church, has very pleasing cabinas with glass-enclosed porches, private baths, and hot water. It's small but ultraclean and well run. Some cabins have TVs. You'll find a restaurant

next door. The cabins are run by the Spot tourist information service (tel. 695-5711; see below). Rates: $22 s, $28 d, $35 t.

The **Windsurf Hotel** has very appealing rooms with lots of potted plants and pretty lace curtains. The office was closed when I passed by.

Food

Restaurant El Parque, below Cabinas El Sueño, is a good bet. **Mary's Restaurant** (tel. 695-5891) is also recommended and doubles as a tourist information center. Across the street, on the west side of the plaza, is **Bambú Bar/Restaurante Catalá. Soda Stefanie** is also reportedly popular; it's 50 meters west of Hotel Grecia. Chef Don Raoul at **Restaurant Catalá,** in the Spot, is recommended for delicious meals: tender roast chicken, creamy mashed potatoes, yucca, etc.

Services

Lake Arenal Tours (tel. 695-5292) offers sportfishing, boat rental, and water-skiing. **Aventuras Tilarán** (tel./fax 695-5008) and the **Spot** (tel. 695-5711) act as self-proclaimed tourist information centers, rent windsurfers and mountain bikes, and offer mountain biking, windsurfing, fishing trips, and horseback rides. In town are a **Banco Nacional** (tel. 695-5028) on the southwest corner of the park, plus a **Banco Anglo Costarricense** (tel. 695-5259) and a **Banco de Costa Rica** (tel. 695-5117). If you need a **pharmacy,** try Farmacia Tilarán (tel. 695-5064) or Farmacia Santa Teresita (tel. 695-5372).

Getting There

Buses depart San José for Tilarán from Calle 14, Avenidas 9/11 (Autotransportes Tilarán, tel. 222-3854) daily at 7:30 a.m. and 12:45, 3:45, and 6:30 p.m. (four hours via Cañas). The bus continues to Nuevo Arenal. Local buses depart Cañas for Tilarán at 7:30, 9, and 11 a.m., and 3 p.m. Buses depart Ciudad Quesada (San Carlos) for Tilarán via Fortuna, Tabacón, and Nuevo Arenal daily at 6 a.m. and 3 p.m. (tel. 460-0326; four hours). Return buses depart Tilarán for San José at 7 and 7:45 a.m., and 2 and 5 p.m.; and for Ciudad Quesada at 7 a.m. and 1 p.m. Buses also depart for Puntarenas at 6 a.m. and 1 p.m. The bus station is one block north of the plaza.

From Monteverde: You can drive to Tilarán from Monteverde (see "Monteverde and Vicinity," above). The road is paved west of Quebrada Grande. **Auto Transportes Soto Mena** operates a bus between Monterverde and Tilarán, departing Santa Elena at 7 a.m. daily (three hours; return 1 p.m.); check with Restaurante Iman (tel. 661-1255) for current schedule.

LAS JUNTAS, PALO VERDE, AND CAÑAS

LAS JUNTAS DE ABANGARES

A turnoff from the Pan-American Hwy. at Km 164, about 12 km north of the Río Lagarto, leads northeast to the pretty village of Las Juntas, splashed with colorful flowers and trim houses. Small it may be, but Las Juntas once figured big in the region's history. When gold was discovered in the nearby mountains in 1884 it sparked a gold rush. Hungry prospectors came from all over the world to sift the earth for nuggets. The locals' facial features play every note on the racial calliope . . . a reflection of the disparate peoples who flocked, rooted, and produced offspring in this remote quarter.

That pint-size locomotive—the *María Cristina*—that sits in the town plaza once hauled ore for the Abangares Gold Fields Company. It was named after Minor Keith's wife (see special topic "Coffee, Bananas, and Minor Keith" in the Introduction chapter). Inflated gold prices have lured many *oreros* back to the old mines and streams, but today the pickings are thin.

With 4WD, you can continue uphill along a rough road all the way to Monteverde, Tilarán, and Lake Arenal.

Abangares Mines Ecological Museum

The small open-air Eco Museum (tel. 662-0129) displays mining equipment and the ruins of a turn-of-the-century mining center at the hamlet of **La Sierra,** five km beyond Las Juntas (turn left about 100 meters beyond the park and then right, across the bridge, at the Cantina Caballo Blanca, and right again at the Y-junction; the road is appalling). Trails run through tropical

---

LAS JUNTAS DE ABANGARES EMERGENCY TELEPHONE NUMBERS

Red Cross 662-0382
Police (Guardia Rural) . . . . . 117 or 662-0161

---

dry forest. Hours: 6 a.m.-5 p.m. You can follow the unpaved and relatively untraveled road to the left at the Y-junction to Monteverde via **Boston,** where a cooperative of *oreros* may be happy to lead you down the dank candlelit tunnels to show you their operation. **Geoaventuras** (tel. 221-2053, fax 282-3333) offers tours.

Food and Accommodations

Cabinas Las Juntas (tel. 662-0069 or 662-0153) has basic rooms with cold water ($8). Several *sodas* serve basic Costa Rican fare. Try **La Familiar,** on the plaza, or **Restaurante Soda Nuri** (tel. 662-0116). **Restaurante Ji Lam Mun** (tel. 662-0005) has reasonable Chinese food.

Services

There's a branch of **Banco Nacional** (tel. 662-0172) in the center of town. You can hire **horses** and 4WD **taxis** in Las Juntas.

Getting There

Buses depart San José for Las Juntas from Calle 12, Avenida 9 (tel. 222-1867), daily at 11 a.m. and 5 p.m.; and from Cañas at 9:30 a.m. and 2:50 p.m. Return buses to San José depart Las Juntas at 6:30 a.m. and 12:30 p.m.

TEMPISQUE FERRY

The turnoff for the Tempisque ferry (tel. 685-5295) and the Nicoya Peninsula leads west from Km 168 on the Pan-American Hwy., four km beyond the turnoff for Juntas (20 km south of Cañas). The ferry takes perhaps 15 vehicles plus passengers and runs back and forth across the wide Río Tempisque (400 *colones*—$2.50—per car; 200 *colones*—$1.25—passengers). Hours: daily every 45 minutes 6 a.m.-7 p.m. The journey takes 20 minutes. Weekends and holidays are busy and delays can be two hours or even more. Get there early. You'll see a small **tourist information office,** plus a shady *soda* and a *mirador* restaurant on a high bluff overlooking the river,

CHRISTOPHER P. BAKER

Tempisque ferry

500 meters before the ferry wharf. If you're traveling by bus, you'll still need to buy a ferry ticket as a passenger to step aboard. You must buy your ticket before boarding.

"Ganado sin guia no pasa," reads one sign: "No cattle allowed without guide."

Beginning in mid-1995, the government was to begin construction of a bridge over the mouth of the Tempisque, to be completed by the end of 1996.

The small estuary and marshlands on the east side of the river teem with waterbirds, especially December through March, and it's amusing to watch the various fowl plunging and diving in the wake of the ferry.

PALO VERDE NATIONAL PARK

Palo Verde National Park protects 13,058 hectares of floodplains, marshes, limestone ridges, and seasonal pools in the heart of the driest region of Costa Rica—the Tempisque basin, at the mouth of the Río Tempisque in the Gulf of Nicoya. The tidal river rises and falls up to four meters and is navigable for about 36 km, as far as the confluence with the Río Bolsón. There are 15 different habitats (including several types of swamp and marshland) and a corresponding diversity of fauna. Plump and lengthy crocodiles wallow on the muddy riverbanks, waiting no doubt for coatis, porcupines, white-tailed deer,

and other mammals that come down to the water to drink.

Palo Verde is best known as a birders' paradise. More than 300 bird species have been recorded, not least toucans, great curassows, and the only permanent colony of scarlet macaws in the dry tropics. At least a quarter of a million wading birds and waterfowl—including up to 20,000 black-bellied tree ducks, 25,000 blue-winged teals, and 750 roseate spoonbills—flock here in fall and winter, when much of the arid alluvial plain swells into a lake. **Isla de Pájaros,** in the middle of the Río Tempisque, is particularly replete with waterbirds, not least white ibis, roseate spoonbills, anhingas, and wood storks, which prefer the isolation, and jabiru storks, the largest storks in the world. Isla de Pájaros is also home to the nation's largest colony of black-crowned night herons.

The park is laced by well-maintained trails that lead through deciduous tropical forest and marshland. One leads to a lookout over the Tempisque floodplain. Others lead to limestone caves and large waterholes such as Laguna Bocana, which are gathering places for a diversity of birds and animals. Limestone cliffs rise behind the old Hacienda Palo Verde, now the **park headquarters,** eight km south of the park entrance (entry is $15 walk-in, $7 advance purchase). Ask a ranger to point out the mango trees nearby. The fruits of the mango are favored by peccaries, monkeys, coatimundis,

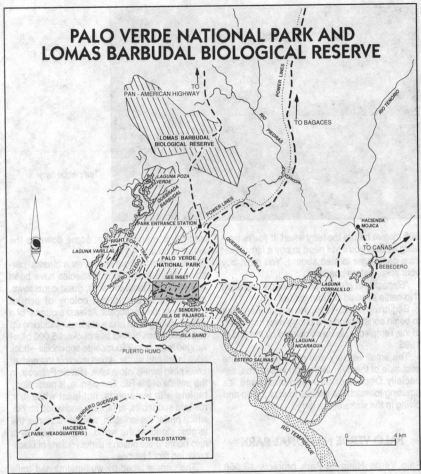

PALO VERDE NATIONAL PARK AND LOMAS BARBUDAL BIOLOGICAL RESERVE

© MOON PUBLICATIONS, INC.

deer, and other mammals. The banks of the Tempisque are also lined with many hundreds of archaeological sites for the curious. The Tempisque basin can get dizzyingly hot in dry season. When the rains come, mosquitoes burst into action—bring bug spray!

Much of the parkland was originally part of Finca Wilson, a huge cattle ranch, and was expropriated in 1975 for the park, which was created in 1977. The park, which derives its name from the *palo verde* or horsebean shrub, is con-

tiguous with the remote Dr. Rafael Lucas Rodríguez Caballero Wildlife Refuge and, beyond that, Lomas Barbudal Biological Reserve, to the north. The three, together with Barra Honda National Park and adjacent areas, form the Tempisque Megapark.

Dr. Rafael Lucas Rodríguez Caballero Wildlife Refuge

This 7,354-hectare wildlife refuge abuts Palo Verde to the north. The two parks are adminis-

tered jointly. Like Palo Verde, it consists of a variety of habitats—from swampland to evergreen forest and dry forest—and has a similar diversity of wildlife, including crocodiles and white-faced and howler monkeys. Hacienda Palo Verde, the park headquarters, is here.

When to Visit

Dry season is by far the best time to visit. Access is far easier then. Wildlife gathers by the waterholes. There are far fewer mosquitoes and bugs. And deciduous trees lose their leaves, making bird viewing easier. Bring binoculars.

Accommodations

The park administration building has a campsite ($2.50) beside the old Hacienda Palo Verde. Water and showers are available. You may be able to stay with rangers ($10) with advance notice: for information call the **Tempisque Conservation Area** office (tel. 671-1062) next to the gas station in Bagaces (hours: 8 a.m.-4 p.m.); Spanish-speakers might try the ranger station radio-telephone (tel. 233-4160). Camping is allowed throughout the park: no facilities. Biting insects abound. Visitors can sometimes stay at the **Palo Verde Biological Research Station** ($50), operated by the Organization of Tropical Studies (OTS, Apdo. 676, San Pedro Montes de Oca 2050, tel. 265-6696, 240-5033, or 240-9938, fax 240-6783; in the U.S., P.O. Box DM, Durham, NC 27706, tel. 919-684-5774). The station is at the northern end of Palo Verde. Approximately $40 with meals. **Rancho Humo,** across the Río Tempisque, is the closest commercial hotel (see "Puerto Humo" under "Nicoya and Vicinity" in the Nicoya Peninsula chapter).

Tours

CATA Tours (tel. 221-5455 or 690-1203, fax 221-0200) has a full-day Palo Verde boat trip that includes Isla de Pájaros, a three-hour "birdwatchers' special" on the Río Bebedero, plus kayaking on the Río Bebedero. The trips begin and end at La Pacífica (see "Cañas to Liberia," below). The Palo Verde adventure is also offered with transfers to/from San José ($89). **Guanacaste Tours** (Apdo. 55, Liberia 5000, tel. 666-0306, fax 666-0307) offers a full-day Palo Verde trip from San José, including a cruise

to Isla de Pájaros, on Tuesday and Friday. **Transportes Palo Verde** (tel. 669-1091, fax 669-0544), in the lobby of the Hotel El Corral in Cañas, has a birdwatcher's tour (three hours; $33) and a half-day Palo Verde tour ($50, including lunch). Most tour companies in San José and local hotels offer river tours in Palo Verde. One, **El León Viajero** (tel. 233-9398, fax 233-9432), has a guided "Tempisque River Adventure" that includes a river journey and hikes in Palo Verde. **Cruceros del Sur** (Apdo. 1198, San José 1200, tel. 220-1927, fax 220-2103) includes a day-trip to Palo Verde National Park as part of a six-day nature cruise aboard the 68-passenger eco-ship *Temptress*. Highly recommended. Many U.S. tour operators offer packages that include the *Temptress*. On the West Coast, contact **Delta Tours** (291 Geary St., Suite 406, San Francisco, CA 94102, tel. 415-421-7447); on the East Coast contact **Temptress Cruises** (1600 N.W. LeJeune Rd., Suite 301, Miami, FL 33126, tel. 305-871-2663 or 800-336-8423, fax 305-871-2657).

Getting There

The main entrance is 35 km south of Bagaces, along a dirt road that begins at the gas station (the office of the Tempisque Conservation Area is at the junction; there's a sign for the park). The route is confusing; follow the power lines past the turnoff for Lomas Barbudal. No buses. A jeep-taxi from Bagaces costs about $15 one-way.

You can also reach Palo Verde by driving to the depauperate village of **Bebedero,** reached by a paved road west from Cañas. A bus departs Cañas for Bebedero from Calle 1, Avenidas 9/11, at 11 a.m. Bebedero is dependent on the local sugar haciendas and was for many years a river port; reportedly, there's been talk for years of turning it into a tourist center, though nothing to date has been done. I couldn't find a road route across the wide Río Tenorio, although I'm told this is possible; in Bebedero, the road north crosses a rickety wooden bridge beyond which is the gate of Hacienda Mojica; to the south it leads to Hacienda Taboga. I suspect the access route is via Hacienda Mojica, to which a plantation worker told me there was no access (I bet he's wrong). However, you can hire local boatmen or join a tour with **Bebedero and Tempisque**

Wildlife Adventures, which has an office on the riverbank in Bebedero; it offers birding and wildlife trips by canopied boat. The ramshackle office is signposted just before the wooden bridge.

From Nicoya: In dry season, you can drive from Filadelfia or Santa Cruz to Hacienda El Viejo. The park is four km east from El Viejo, and the Río Tempisque two km farther. Easy to get lost! A local boatman will ferry you upriver to the park dock; the park headquarters is then an hour's walk east along a rough track that is very muddy and swampy in wet season. A bus reportedly operates from Nicoya to Puerto Humo, 27 km north of Nicoya. You can hire a

boat and guide to take you to Isla de Pájaros—one km downriver—or three km upriver to the Chamorro dock, the trailhead to park headquarters (it's a two-km walk). Note that boats are not allowed within 50 meters of Isla de Pájaros: don't pressure your guide to get closer. Another option is to take the Tempisque ferry to Puerto Moreno, where you can hire a boat to the Chamorro dock.

CAÑAS

Cañas is nothing to write home about, but it makes a pivotal point for exploring Palo Verde

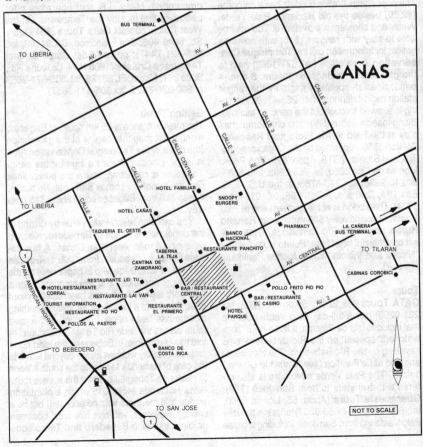

National Park or Lake Arenal. The city was named for the white-flowered wild cane that still grows in patches hereabouts and is otherwise known as Ciudad de la Amistad ("City of Friendship"). It is indisputably a cowboy town, as the many tanned *sabaneros* shaded by wide-brimmed hats attest. Japanese, Italians, and Israelis supposedly have added their bloodlines to that of Spaniards and Corobicí Indians.

Accommodations
Hotel Corral (tel. 669-0622) has 12 clean and spacious rooms with a/c and private baths with cold water; three rooms have TV. It's on a noisy junction. Rate: $20 per person. The popular **Hotel Cañas** (tel./fax 669-0039), on Calle 2 and Avenida 3, has 48 clean, simple, but pleasant cabinas, some with a/c, all with private baths with cold water. Large showers. An atmospheric restaurant features cowboy paraphernalia on the walls. Rates: $10 s, $16 d, $20 t, $24 quad, including tax. **Cabinas Corobicí** (tel. 669-0241) has 15 small and basic but very well-kept cabinas with fans and private baths with cold water. Take the two cabinas on the left: they're larger. Rates: $7 s, $9 d. Cheaper yet are the **Hotel Parque** and **Hotel Guillén** (tel. 669-0070) on the southeast of the park. Both are basic and charge about $4 per person. Budget hounds might also try the **Gran Hotel,** on Avenida 2 and Calle 5, but the surly owner refused me information about her run-down property.

Food
You have a variety of Chinese restaurants to choose from. I recommend **Restaurante El Primero, Restaurante Ho Ho,** and **Restaurante Lei Tu,** all with meals below $5. **Restaurante Panchito** and **Bar y Restaurante Central** both have reasonable local fare. If ya gotta have a burger, try **Snoopy's,** one block northeast of the plaza. **Pollo Frito Pio Pio** and **Pollos al Pastor** might satisfy fried-chicken fans—then again, they may not! I tried neither.

Services
There are two **banks** in town: Banco de Costa Rica (tel. 669-0066) is on the southeast corner of the plaza; Banco Nacional (tel. 669-0128) has a branch on the northeast corner. There's a pharmacy—**Farmacia Cañas** (tel. 669-0748)—on Avenida 1, two blocks east of the plaza. **Dr. Juan Acon** (tel. 669-0139) has an office in the center of town. **Taxis Unidos de Cañas** (tel. 669-0898) has taxis on call.

Getting There
Buses depart San José for Cañas from Calle 16, Avenidas 3/5 (Transportes La Cañera, tel. 222-3006 or 669-0145) daily at 8:30 and 10:30 a.m., and 1:30, 2:15, and 4:30 p.m.; Tralapa also operates buses from Calle 20, Avenida 3. Three hours; $3. An express bus departs Puntarenas for Liberia via Cañas at 5:30 p.m. (Empresa Arata, tel. 666-0138).

Buses for San José depart from the new terminal at Calle 1, Avenidas 9/11 at 4:30, 5:25, and 9:15 a.m., and 12:30 and 2 p.m. (5:30 p.m. on Sunday). Buses depart Cañas for destinations throughout Guanacaste from the new terminal, including to Arenal and Tilarán (6, 9, and 10:30 a.m., and 1:45, 3:30, and 5:30 p.m.); Bebedero (5, 9, and 11 a.m. and 1, 3, and 5 p.m.); Las Juntas (9:30 a.m. and 2:50 p.m.); Puntarenas (6, 6:40, 9:30, and 11 a.m., and 12:30, 1:30, and 4:15 p.m.); and Upala (5:45, 9, and 11 a.m., and 2 and 5 p.m.). Check against current schedules.

CAÑAS TO LIBERIA

The first impression as you drive north from Cañas is of Costa Rica at its least welcoming: a vast barren plain, burning hot in dry season, with lone palms rising like tattered umbrellas over the scrubby landscape. But the view is not a fair one. Away from the main highway, the villages of whitewashed houses are as welcoming as any in the country. For the traveler interested in history or architecture, there are some intriguing sites. And the area is charged with scenic beauty. Looking at this austere landscape, shimmering, phantasmagoric in its infinity, conjures images of the wanderings of the demented Don Quixote across stark La Mancha. Indeed, it is easy to come under the quixotic spell that inspired the knight-errant to cut his despairing swath, for here in the far northwest of Costa Rica are opportunities for what he called "adventures elbow-deep."

LAS PUMAS "MINI ZOO"

Three km north of Cañas is the home and "mini zoo" of Lily Bodmer de Hagnauer, a Swiss-born environmentalist (original owner of La Pacífica; see below) whose passion has been raising big cats: ocelots, a jaguar, cougars, margays, jaguarundis, and "tiger" cats. She has healthy specimens of all six cats housed in large chain-link enclosures. Most of the cats were either injured or orphaned and have been hand-reared by Lily, who will gladly share the trials of being a foster mum to felines. The cougars—which Lily raised from three weeks old (she bottle-fed them using a mixture of chamomile tea and baby formula)—act like giant housecats, purring loudly and rubbing up against Lily and licking her face, which they do while standing on hind legs! The jaguar once belonged to the San José zoo.

Don't get within paw-swipe range if you're perusing these magnificent creatures in their cages.

Although keeping indigenous cats is illegal, Hagnauer works with various forestry agencies to care for and reintroduce trapped or injured

animals. The few animals that are released are radio-tracked by Hagnauer's research assistants. She accepts donations to ease the burden since she receives no official funding (many cats, though, are delivered by the Ministry of Natural Resources after being confiscated from illegal hunters); each jaguar costs $1,200 a year to feed, a puma $500, an ocelot $275, etc. Hagnauer also raises hundreds of Australian budgerigars, parrots, and scarlet macaws for sale.

Lily welcomes visitors, but not on Monday. No entrance fee, but donations are welcome. A band of fearsome dogs will greet you. Don't be alarmed. Act as their friend, hold your hand palm up in greeting, and they'll calm down. The zoo is tucked secretly behind the roadside office of Safari Corobicí, beside the Pan-American Hwy. six km north of Cañas. Follow the dirt road 100 meters. The zoo is on the left.

LA PACÍFICA

La Pacífica (Apdo. 8, Cañas 5700, tel. 669-0050, fax 669-0555), 200 meters north of Las Pumas, is a farm, hotel-restaurant, and Ecological Center on 2,000 hectares, most of it devoted to dairy and beef cattle production, but more than one-third still covered with tropical dry forest. The Ecological Center was founded in 1986. Its objective is to "implement a model of sustained development on an ecological basis," combining agricultural production with forestry, research, education, and ecotourism. The project includes reforestation of prairies and construction of small swamps to attract native wildlife. Its 39 archaeological sites date back as much as 2,000 years; you can visit two of them. La Pacífica publishes a useful "Ecology Guide Book" about the project, including descriptions of the various species to be seen.

A trail along the Tenorio River takes you to **La Casona de la Pacífica,** at the northern boundary. The old house was once owned by ex-president Don Bernardo Soto and now func-

tions as a small eco-museum. The Las Garzas and Chocuaco nature-study trails along the Río Corobicí offer a chance to see howler monkeys and some of the property's 225 bird species. The call of the male howlers can scare you silly! I recommend exploring other trails by horseback, of which there are many options for tours. You'll need mosquito repellent! Note that the land is north of the Río Corobicí and the hotel is on the south side. Get a trail map at the office.

Boat trips on the Río Bebedero take guests to Palo Verde National Park. Other options include raft safaris on the Corobicí or bike trips to Lake Arenal. You can hire guides ($25, half day) and horses ($7 per hour).

The hotel's 32 clean and well-lit bungalows are distributed throughout the landscaped grounds. It has a large swimming pool, an elegant bar and restaurant serving international cuisine, plus a large library on ecological themes. Fat toads gather by the pool at night to catch flies attracted to the lights. Rates: $56 s, $76 d, $86 t.

CATA Tours (Apdo. 8, Cañas 5700, tel. 669-0050, fax 259-0555) has an office on the premises. Its Guanacaste Nature Paradise series includes one-day tours to Rincón de la Vieja, Miravalles, and Arenal volcanoes and Santa Rosa National Park, birdwatching in Bebedero and Palo Verde, plus kayaking and rafting trips.

Food
About 400 meters north of La Pacífica is **Restaurante Corobicí**, a very pleasing place to eat, with good seafood dishes and a porch over the river where you can watch rafters go by. **Campers** may be able to pitch a tent here for a small fee.

RÍO COROBICÍ

The 40-km-long Río Corobicí runs down from the Cordillera de Guanacaste to the Gulf of Nicoya and is rightfully popular among rafters. It's fed by Lake Arenal, providing a good rush of water year-round. The trip, however, is a relatively calm run described as a "nature float." I sampled a trip with **Ríos Tropicales**. It was fabulous: though it cuts through cattle country and

rice paddies, the river is lined with a narrow ribbon of mahogany, ceiba, and palm forest the entire way. Wildlife gathers by the watercourse—a veritable tropical *Fantasia*. Motmots, herons, crested caracaras, egrets, and toucans are common, as are howler monkeys, caiman, and iguanas basking on the riverbanks. The river averages a drop of 3.5 meters per km: class II. Still pools provide excellent swimming.

One km north of the Río Corobicí, a road leads northeast to **Upala** (see the "Fortuna and Vicinity" in the Northern Lowlands chapter) via the saddle of Tenorio and Miravalles volcanoes. **Los Tigres** (30 km) is a private reserve on the Caribbean side of the saddle protecting 800 hectares of premontane rainforest and its denizens: sloths, howler and white-faced monkeys, agoutis, ocelots, toucans, tanagers, and many other bird species. There's no accommodation, but you may be able to camp near a small waterfall with special permission. **Wildland Adventures** (3516 N.E. 155th St., Seattle, WA 98155, tel. 800-345-4453 or 206-365-0686, fax 206-363-6615) offers 13-day nature tours that include visits to Los Tigres, La Pacífica, Palo Verde, Arenal, and other parks and reserves ($1765).

Tour Companies
The following companies offer one-day trips ($65 per person) year-round on the Corobicí: **Costa Rica Expeditions** (Apdo. 6941, San José 1000, tel. 257-0766, fax 257-1655); **Ríos Tropicales** (Apdo. 472, San José 1200, tel. 233-6455, fax 255-4354); **Pioneer Raft** (Apdo. 29, San José 2070, tel. 253-9132, fax 253-4687); **Costaricaraft** (Apdo. 812, San Pedro 2050, tel. 225-3939, fax 253-6934). **Safaris Corobicí** (tel./fax 669-0544) has an office and souvenir shop beside the Pan-American Hwy., 400 meters south of the river. It offers a three-hour birdwatching float (12 km/two hours; $33), plus a full-day "family float," including lunch ($55). Trip participants can take a sapling along to plant on behalf of reforestation.

Getting There
The **Pura Natura** tourist shuttle operated by **Saragundí Specialty Tours** (tel. 255-0011, fax 255-2155) calls at Corobicí ($14); departs San José at 7 a.m. and continues to Liberia.

BAGACES

Bagaces is a somewhat run-down town, 22 km north of Cañas. Many of the houses are quite ancient, and several adobe-brick houses date back several centuries. Pretty, perhaps, but even the most diligent search will not turn up anything more interesting than a bust of ex-president General Tomás Guardia on a pedestal in the park honoring the city's most illustrious child.

A dirt road leads southwest from the gas station on the Pan-American Hwy. (at the entrance to Bagaces) to Dr. Rafael Lucas Rodríguez Caballero Wildlife Refuge and Palo Verde National Park (see above). At the junction is the National Parks Service headquarters (tel. 671-1062; Mon.-Fri. 8 a.m.-4 p.m.) for the Area de Conservación Tempisque, made up of Palo Verde, Lomas Barbudal, Barra Honda, and adjacent reserves. The road to Lomas Barbudal Biological Reserve is six km north of Bagaces, near the tiny hamlet of Pijije.

The **Friends of Lomas Barbudal** (tel. 671-1062 or 671-1029, fax 671-1203) has a visitor center in town. See special topic on "Dry Forest Restoration," this chapter.

Food and Accommodations

Budget travelers can choose between **Cabinas Miravalles** and **Cabinas Eduardo Vargas,** each with basic rooms with fans and private baths and cold water (about $8). Eight km north of Bagaces is **Albergue Las Sillas Lodge,** on the Pan-American Highway. Not inspected.

Services

There's a **Banco Nacional** (tel. 671-1049). For the local **police** (Guardia Rural), call 671-1173; for the **Red Cross,** call 671-1186.

LAS HORNILLAS
AND MIRAVALLES VOLCANO

A road leads northeast from the center of Bagaces to Las Hornillas ("Little Ovens"), an area of geothermal activity with lots of bubbling mudpots and fumaroles expelling foul gases and steam. The Costa Rican Institute of Elec-

tricity (ICE) harnesses geothermal energy for electric power, with two plants (one opened in 1994; the other was scheduled to open in 1996) that tap the super-heated vapor deep within the bowels of Miravalles volcano.

About 12 km from Bagaces, a road to the right leads to **Fortuna.** A sign for **Bar/Restaurant Pasatiempos** and a plaque honoring Oscar Arias Sánchez mark the T-junction. You'll see the ICE geothermal sites on the right. Beyond, continuing straight, you'll come to a dirt road with signs directing you to Las Hornillas; you'll eventually come to another geothermal site, from where you can hike to Las Hornillas. Alternately, passing the T-junction and continuing straight you'll arrive at **Guayabo** (30 km), where there are restaurants and cabinas. Las Hornillas is signposted to the right three km north of Guayabo. If you continue straight from Guayabo, the road north leads via Aguas Claras and deteriorates as it drops into the northern lowlands toward Upala.

Las Hornillas is on the southwest flank of Volcán Miravalles (2,026 meters), the highest in the Cordillera de Guanacaste. Some 10,850 hectares of important watershed surrounding the volcano forms the Miravalles Forest Reserve. The western slopes are covered with savannah scrubland; the northern and eastern slopes are lush, fed by moist clouds that sweep in from the Caribbean. The slopes are cut with deep canyons and licked by ancient lava tongues.

To visit the geothermal plant or any of the sites around it, you should make arrangements through **Miratur** (tel. 673-0260), which runs a "geotour" of the thermal plant. It also has ecological packages that feature mountain trail hikes plus a visit to the energy plant and the steaming fumaroles. **CATA Tours** (Apdo. 8, Cañas, tel. 669-1026, fax 669-1995) offers horseback riding tours of Miravalles and Las Hornillas.

Food and Accommodations

The **Finca La Reina** (tel. 666-0040), near Fortuna, rents rooms and horses. Reportedly, you can help milk the cows. **Parador Las Nubes** (reservations tel. 671-1011, ext. 280; information tel. 666-1313; fax 666-2136), a *finca* at Guayabal (or El Carmen de Upala), four km north of Guayabo, has rudimentary rooms. **Cabinas Ca-**

ballos, in Guayabo, rents basic rooms for about $4. Next door is **Restaurant La Amistad,** which offers inexpensive dishes, including excellent chicken and fries ($1.50). **Restaurant La Choca,** about one km north of Guayabo, is another good place to stop for a bite.

Services

There's a **Banco de Costa Rica** in Guayabo. **Bravo Tropical Tours,** next to Restaurant La Amistad, offers tours to Las Hornillas and nearby nature reserves.

LOMAS BARBUDAL BIOLOGICAL RESERVE

Lomas Barbudal ("Bearded Hills") is a 2,279-hectare reserve fed by protected river systems, some of which flow year-round, among them the Cabuya, which has sandy-bottomed pools good for swimming. The "beards" at Lomas Barbudal are patches of dry forest that once extended along the entire Pacific coast of Mesoamerica. Dry forest was even more vast than the rainforest, but also more vulnerable to encroaching civilization. For half the year, from November to March, no rain relieves the heat of the Tempisque basin, leaving plants and trees parched and withered. Fires started by local farmers eviscerate the tinder-dry forests, opening holes quickly filled by ecological opportunists such as African jaraguá, an exotic grass brought to Costa Rica in the late 19th century to grow pastures. Jaraguá rebounds quickly from fire and grazing pressures, reaching four-meter-high combustible stands. Today, dry forests cover only two percent of their former area in Central America. Its rolling, rocky terrain spared Lomas Barbudal from the changes wrought on the rest of Guanacaste Province by plows and cows. Here, the dry forest remains largely intact.

Several endangered tree species thrive here: mahogany, Panamá redwood, gonzalo alves, rosewood, sandbox (popular with scarlet macaws), and the cannonball tree *(balas de cañón).* A relative of the Brazil nut tree, the cannonball tree produces a pungent, nonedible fruit that grows to the size of a bowling ball and dangles from a long stem. Several evergreen tree species also line the banks of the waterways,

creating riparian corridors inhabited by species not usually found in dry forests.

Unlike Costa Rica's moist forests, the tropical dry forests undergo a dramatic seasonal transformation. In the midst of drought, the dry forest explodes in Monet colors, and vibrant yellow and pink flowers burst onto bare branches. Myriad bees—at least 250 species—moths, bats, and wasps pollinate the flowers. And moist fruits ripen throughout the dry season, feeding monkeys, squirrels, peccaries, and other mammalian frugivores. Lots of birds live here, including such endangered species as the great curassow, yellow-naped parrot, and king vulture. Lomas Barbudal is also one of the few remaining Pacific coast forests that attract the colorful scarlet macaw. The macaws are fond of the seeds from the sandbox tree's segmented fruit, whose inner tissue contains a caustic latex strong enough to corrode flesh!

The reserve adjoins Dr. Rafael Lucas Rodríguez Caballero Wildlife Refuge to the south and therefore serves as a vital migratory route. Unfortunately, the corridors of swamp forest linking Palo Verde and Dr. Rafael Lucas Rodríguez Caballero with Lomas Barbudal continue to shrink; local farmers have invested in permits to clear the swamp forest and plant crops, increasing the isolation of both reserves. In 1987, the **Friends of Lomas Barbudal** was organized to promote the reserve and raise funds for its protection (691 Colusa Ave., Berkeley, CA 94707, tel. 510-526-4115).

The park has many excellent trails. Time your visit for the dry season, when the trees burst into fiery red, blinding yellow, pink, blue, and purple blossom.

Look for an educational and amusing field guide, *A White-faced Monkey's Guide to Lomas Barbudal,* published in 1993 by the Friends of Lomas Barbudal. Its thoroughly simian perspective explains, for example, why monkeys *really* pee on tourists!

Services

The **park office** and information center (Casa de Patrimonio) is on the banks of the Río Cabuyo. Note that it's open on a 10 days on/four days off schedule. Picnic benches sit under shade trees. Camping is permitted ($2.50). No facilities. Entrance: $15 walk-in, $5 advance purchase.

Getting There

The unpaved access road is off the Pan-American Hwy., at the Km 221 marker near Pijijes, about ten km north of Bagaces. A dirt road leads six km through scrubby cattle pastures until you come to a lookout point with views over a valley whose hillsides are fully clad with dry forest. The road descends steeply from here to the park entrance and information center (you can't drive across the river and into the park, but you can parallel the river for a ways and even, it is said, circumnavigate the reserve; about two-thirds km from Casa de Patrimonio is the home of the Rosales family, who reportedly are very helpful). If conditions are particularly muddy you may wish to park at the lookout point and hike to the ranger station. A jeep-taxi from Bagaces will cost about $25 roundtrip.

U.C. Berkeley entomologist Gordon Frankie leads an annual "Preserving Biodiversity" tour to Lomas Barbudal. Participants assist with field research (University Research Expeditions Program, University of California, Berkeley, CA 94720, tel. 510-642-6568).

LIBERIA AND VICINITY

Liberia is the provincial capital and a social, economic, and transportation hub of Guanacaste. It is called the "White City" because of its houses made of blinding-white ignimbrite. There's a rich simplicity, a purity to the surrounding landscape, to the craggy, penurious hills and the cubist houses sheathed in white light like a sort of celestial glow. Many old adobe homes still stand to the south of the landscaped central plaza, with high-ceilinged interiors and kitchens opening onto classical courtyards. Old corner houses have doors—*puertas del sol*—that open onto two sides to catch both morning and afternoon sun. The leafy plaza itself has bright blue benches where you may rest and admire the modern white church and older town hall flying the Guanacastecan flag, the only provincial flag in the country.

The town fills on Saturday evenings, when everyone dons his or her finest clothing to socialize in the plaza.

As you enter Liberia from the south you'll see a sign for the **Area de Conservación Guanacaste** pointing you in the direction of various parts of the park. For example, to the right, 23 km is the "Sector Santa María" of Rincón de la Vieja National Park.

The **Tomás Guardia International Airport** (tel. 666-0695) was recently opened 12 km west of Liberia and was to be fully operational by 1996. For now it lies fallow, but officials hope that charter vacation operators from North America and Europe will soon start using the airport, bypassing San José. This may be optimistic, as there are many entrenched political and economic elites with vested interests in keeping air traffic flowing to San José.

The road past the airport leads to the resorts and towns of the Nicoya Peninsula, including the huge (and stalled) Papagayo development, which promises to turn Bahía Culebra into the Cancún of Costa Rica. The Papagayo Project (see the special topic "Gulf of Papagayo Project" in the Nicoya Peninsula chapter) provided a major impetus for completion of the Tomás Guardia airport, but the latter's inception, critics claim, had more to do with U.S. foreign policy against the Sandinistas in Nicaragua (the airfield was probably seen as a nifty base for supplying the contras, and the U.S. thereby pressured the Costa Rican government to have it built; see special topic "Costa Rica and the Nicaraguan Revolution" in the Introduction chapter).

SIGHTS AND ENTERTAINMENT

The only two attractions are the **Museo de Sabanero,** housed in the Casa de Cultura (see "Services," below), which honors the local cowboy tradition with saddles and other *sabanero* memorabilia; and, at the far end of Avenida Central, also known as Avenida 25 Julio, **La Agonía Church** ("Little Church of the Agony"), which, though its stuccoed adobe suggests the colonial era, was built in 1852. Behind the church is Parque Rodolfo Salazar, surrounded by old cottages. There's also a statue honoring the *sabaneros* in the divide along Avenida Central (Calle 10) near the Pan-American Hwy. Finally,

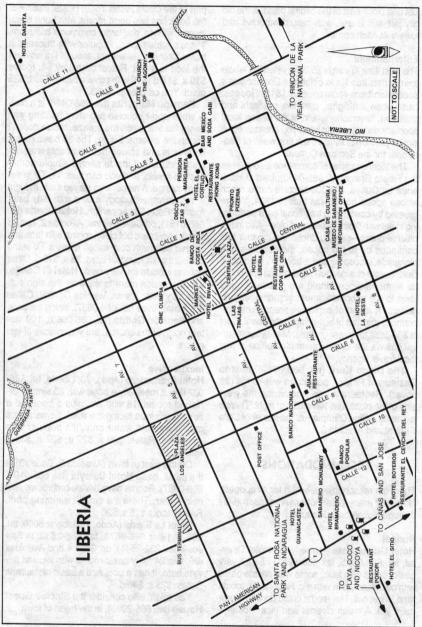

LIBERIA

© MOON PUBLICATIONS, INC.

NOT TO SCALE

TO RINCON DE LA
VIEJA NATIONAL PARK

RIO LIBERIA

QUEBRADA PANITE

HOTEL DASYTA

CALLE 11

CALLE 9

CALLE 7

CALLE 5

CALLE 3

CALLE 1

Little Church
of the Agony

CALLE

CENTRAL

CALLE 2

CALLE 4

CALLE 6

CALLE 8

CALLE 10

CALLE 12

Bar Mexico
and Soda Gabi

Pension
Margarita

Hotel El
Cortijo
Restaurante
Hong Kong

Pronto
Pizzeria

Disco
Star 2

Banco de
Costa Rica

CENTRAL PLAZA

Casa de Cultura /
Museo de Sabanero /
Tourist Information Office

Hotel
Liberia

Restaurante
Copa de Oro

Market

Hotel Rivas

Cine Olimpia

Las
Tinajas

Hotel
La Siesta

Juaja
Restaurante

Banco Nacional

Post Office

LOS ANGELES
PLAZA

Bus Terminal

Sabanero Monument

Banco
Popular

Hotel Boyeros

Restaurante El Ceviche del Rey

Hotel
Guanacaste

Hotel
Bramadero

Restaurant El Sitio

Restaurant
Pokopi

AV. 7

AV. 5

AV. 3

AV. 1

CENTRAL

AV. 2

AV. 4

AV. 6

PAN-AMERICAN
HIGHWAY

TO SANTA ROSA NATIONAL
PARK AND NICARAGUA

TO
PLAYA COCO
AND NICOYA

TO CAÑAS AND SAN JOSE

just one block east of the central plaza, is the old city jail, still in use, with barred windows and towers at each corner.

Entertainment

The best time to visit is 25 July, when the whole town bursts into life to celebrate Guanacaste's secession from Nicaragua in 1812. Rodeos, cattle show, bullfights, parades, mariachi and marimba, firecrackers, and stalls selling local specialty dishes should keep you entertained. A similar passion is stirred each first week of September for the Semana Cultural.

The local chamber of commerce also pushes the **Fiesta Brava** (tel. 666-0450), held at Hacienda La Cueva, a 3,000-hectare cattle ranch whose adobe house was built in 1824. You're greeted by cowboys in traditional garb performing tricks with their lassoes, and girls—also in traditional dress—serving drinks. As the tour bus continues up to the house, the cowboys ride alongside, whooping and a-hollerin'. Traditional Guanacaste cuisine, beer, and *chicha* (the popular fermented-corn drink) are guzzled on the lawn to the accompaniment of marimbas and guitars. A round of explosive firecrackers announces the start of bull-riding in the corral. Cost is $69 (less for larger groups). Make your reservations via the tourist information office or any local travel agency.

The **Disco Kurú** (tel. 666-0769), next to Restaurant Pókopí, pulses on weekends ($3 cover). Restaurant Las Tinajas, on the west side of the plaza, has live music at night. There's a cinema—**Cine Olimpia**—at the corner of Calle Central and Avenida 3.

ACCOMMODATIONS

There's a reasonable selection for all budgets. Note that many hotels offer wet-season (May through November) discounts.

Budget

Hotel Guanacaste (formerly the Hotel Oriental, tel. 666-0085, fax 666-2287) has 27 very basic rooms with fans, some with private baths with cold water, one with a/c. Reportedly, rooms tend to get hot. The rooms could do with a new paint job. A much cleaner and nicer hostel—

part of the Costa Rican Youth Hostel chain—at the back has two dorm rooms with bunk beds, lounge, kitchen, and large, communal bathroom. There's table tennis. Popular with truckers. It has a Chinese restaurant, though I'm advised the food is bland. Rates: dormitory $8; rooms $10 s, $16 d ($19 with private bath), $20 t, $25 quad. You can camp for $3.

Pensión Margarita (tel. 666-0468) is a pretty white-and-turquoise two-story building with verandas that catch the breeze. Inside doesn't match the external billing. The 38 basic rooms have fans and shared bath with cold water. A small restaurant inside serves simple home-cooked meals, and you can watch a TV in the dingy lounge. A reader who stayed there thought it "run-down, with dingy rooms with dirty bathrooms." Rate: $6 per person. **Hotel Liberia** (tel. 666-0161), on Calle Central, Avenida 2, has 28 small, very basic but clean rooms with fans and shared bath with cold water. It has a TV in the pleasant skylit lounge. Rates: $6 s, $10 d. Other options include the very basic **Hotel El Cortijo**, which is much more funky than the sign outside suggests. It's on Avenida Central, Calles 3/5. **Hotel Rivas** (tel. 666-0037), facing the park, and **Pensión Golfito** (tel. 666-0963), 100 meters north of the church, are your places of last resort.

Inexpensive

Hotel Bramadero (Apdo. 70, Liberia, tel. 666-0371) is a motel-style hotel with 25 simply furnished rooms, 18 with a/c, plus a pool and a large restaurant facing the road. Some rooms may have cold water only. It's popular with Josefinos. Rates: $20 s, $27 d; $27 s, $38 d with a/c.

On the east of town (Avenida 3, Calle 13) is the small, basic **Hotel Daisyta** (tel. 666-0197, 666-0927). Rooms have private bathrooms with cold water. There's a small swimming pool. Rates: about $15 s, $20 d.

Hotel La Siesta (Apdo. 15, Liberia 5000, tel. 666-2118 or 666-0678, fax 666-2532; in San José, tel. 232-2541), on Calle 4 and Avenidas 4/6, has 24 fairly basic rooms with a/c and private bath. It has a pool and a basic restaurant. Rates: $25 s, $40 d.

You might also consider the **Sinclair Guest House** (tel. 666-2088), in the heart of town.

About eight km north of town is the unappealing **Motel Delfín.**

Moderate
Hotel El Sitio (Apdo. 471, San José 1000, tel. 666-1211, fax 233-6883), about 100 meters on the road to Playa Coco, is a modern convention-type hotel with 52 spacious rooms with private baths, 18 with a/c. The uninspired design is countered with atmospheric Guanacastecan trimmings: red-tiled roofs, local landscape paintings, wagon-wheel chandelier, and the El Rancho bar by the pool. Rates: $45 s, $55 d, or $60 s, $75 d with a/c.

The Spanish-style **Hotel Boyeros** (Apdo. 85, Liberia 5000, tel. 666-0995, fax 666-2529) has 60 rooms with a/c and private baths with hot water surrounding a large pool and a *palenque* bar in landscaped grounds. All rooms have a private patio or balcony. Next door is a restaurant and bar that can get very noisy on weekends. It's popular with Ticos. Rates: $42 d, $48 t, $53 quad.

Two km south of town is **Hotel La Ronda** (tel. 666-2799). Not reviewed, but word is it is (or was) unkempt. Rooms are reportedly large and have private baths and fans. Rates: approximately $18 s, $25 d.

Upscale
Hotel Las Espuelas (Apdo. 1056, San José 1007, tel. 666-0144 or 233-9955, fax 225-3987) is a modern and modestly elegant family-operated hotel amid tropical gardens facing the Pan-American Hwy. two km south of Liberia. The 35 spacious rooms and three suites have a/c, telephones, color TVs and so-so decor. Private baths. A country-style, beam-ceilinged restaurant serves expensive seafoods and bread fresh from the oven. The hotel has a pleasant lounge with sofas and lots of potted plants, plus a large pool, hammocks under trees, and a poolside *palenque* bar. Nightly entertainment includes marimba players, folksingers, and folkloric dancing. A 12-passenger minivan with a driver is available for hire for exploring Guanacaste. The hotel also offers special tours to Rincón de la Vieja volcano, fishing at Cuajiniquil, tours to Los Juncos Biological Station, Tropical Trail horse rides from San Antonio Cattle Ranch, and a three-day tour including two nights at Las Es-

puelas, a trip to Santa Rosa National Park, plus a day of horseback riding at San Antonio ($289). Rates: $60 s, $80 d ($10 additional).

FOOD

Jauja Restaurante (Apdo. 17, Liberia 5000, tel. 666-0917), on Avenida Central, Calles 6/8, has tasty Mexican food and wonderful fresh-fruit salads. **Restaurant Pókopí** (tel. 666-1036), one block west of the fire station—opposite Hotel El Sitio—on the road to Santa Cruz, is a tiny restaurant serving suprisingly varied and inventive continental dishes selected from a cutting board used as a menu. Burgers and sandwiches cost $2 or $3, and steaks and seafood dishes less than $10.

Las Tinajas has outdoor tables where you can eat pizzas and deep-fried chicken while watching the activity across the road in the park. Two other options for pizza are the atmospheric **Pronto Pizzeria** and **Da Beppe Pizzeria & Ristorante Italiano** (tel. 666-0917). Better yet is **La Casona,** on Calle 1 and Avenida 4. Pizzas here are served in a delightful rustic ambience that includes a wood-fired oven and art gallery.

For cheap *típico* dishes, try **Soda Gabi.** You'll find a wide selection of Chinese restaurants in the town center. Try the popular **Gran China,** opposite the Hotel Boyeros; the **Restaurante Copa de Oro** on Avenida 2, Calle Central; **Restaurante Hong Kong** at Avenida Central, Calles 3/5; or **Restaurante Chun San** on Avenida 1, Calle 3. Lastly, **Restaurante El Ceviche Del Rey,** on the left of the Pan-Am Hwy. as you enter Liberia, serves Peruvian seafood.

For ice cream to counter the Guanacastecan heat, try **Monpik,** two blocks north of the park on Calle 2.

SERVICES AND TRANSPORT

Information
The helpful and efficient **Liberia Chamber of Commerce Tourist Information Center** (tel. 666-1606) is three blocks south of the plaza in the Casa de Cultura, a pretty colonial-era building that is a perfect example of a structure with doors on each corner (hours: Tues.-Sun. 9 a.m.-noon

LIBERIA EMERGENCY TELEPHONE NUMBERS

Police . . . . 117 or 666-0409

Transit Police 666-1116

Hospital 666-0318

Red Cross 666-0994

and 1-6 p.m., Sunday 9 a.m.-1 p.m.). It has a 24-hour phone with AT&T USADirect access.

Banks
Liberia has four banks: **Banco Anglo Costarricense** (tel. 666-0355), on Calle Central, Avenidas 1/3; **Banco Nacional** (tel. 666-0996), at Avenida Central, Calles 6/8; **Banco de Costa Rica** (tel. 666-0148), on Calle Central, Avenida 1; and **Banco Popular**, at Avenida Central, one block east of the Pan-American Highway.

Medical
Pharmacies include **Farmacia Liberia** (tel. 666-0747), on Avenida 1, Calles 3/5, and **Farmacia Lux** (tel. 666-0061). **Hospital Dr. Enrique Baltodano Briceño** (tel. 666-0011) is at Avenida 4, Calles Central/2.

Getting Around
Aventura Rent-a-Car (tel. 239-4821, fax 666-2885) has an office in the Hotel Bramadero. **Sol Rent-a-Car** (tel. 666-2222, fax 666-2898) also has an office in Liberia. A place called **Cantarranas**, four km west of Liberia, has a rent-a-jeep office and sells souvenirs, crafts, and swimwear. **Heat Rent-a-Moto** rents scooters and mountain bikes (they're in Centro Comercial El Quijongo). **Guanacaste Tours** (tel. 666-0306, fax 666-0307) also has its office in the Bramadero; see the chapter introduction for complete details of tours. There are four **gas stations**—one on each corner—at the junction of Avenida Central and the Pan-American Highway. **Taxis** gather at the northwest corner of the plaza. You can hire one for local touring (expect to pay perhaps $20 per cab to visit Santa Rosa National Park; double that to Rincón de la Vieja National Park). You may, instead, choose to rent a bicycle for $12 daily including

helmets and water bottle from **Guanaventura Mountainbike** (tel. 666-2825), 200 meters north of the INS building. You can also sign up here for guided bike tours (from $45).

Other
The **post office** is on Calle 8, Avenida 3 (open 7:30 a.m.-8 p.m.). You can make international telephone calls and send faxes from a **communications office** on Calle 8 and Avenidas Central/2. If craving communication with the outside world, you can buy international magazines at **Galería Fulvia,** in Centro Comercial Bambú, 100 meters north of the church.

GETTING THERE

By Bus
Buses depart San José for Liberia daily from Calle 14, Avenidas 1/3 (Pulmitán, tel. 222-1650 or 666-0458) at 7, 9, and 11:30 a.m. and 1, 3, 4, 6, and 8 p.m. (four hours; $3). Return buses depart Liberia for San José from the new Tralapa bus terminal at Avenida 7 and Calle 12 at 4:30, 6, and 7:30 a.m., and 12:30, 2, 4, 6, and 8 p.m.

Empresa Arata (tel. 666-0138) operates a bus from Puntarenas to Liberia daily at 5:30 p.m. (two and a half hours); it returns at 8:30 a.m. Buses from Nicoya and Santa Cruz depart for Liberia hourly, 5 a.m.-8 p.m.

Buses also depart from the new bus terminal hourly for Filadelfia, Santa Cruz (5:30 a.m.-7:30 p.m.), and Nicoya (5 a.m.-7 p.m.); and Playa Coco, Playa Panamá, and other destinations in the Nicoya Peninsula. Local buses also depart regularly for La Cruz and Peñas Blancas via the entrance to Santa Rosa National Park. The express bus from San José departs Liberia for Peñas Blancas at 5:30, 8:30, and 11 a.m., and 2 and 6 p.m.

Saragundí Specialty Tours (tel. 255-0011, fax 255-2155) operates the Pura Natura tourist shuttle from San José) (departs 7 a.m.; $18), continuing to Playa Flamingo and Tamarindo. A second shuttle departs Fortuna at 8 a.m. for Liberia via Lake Arenal ($18; departs Liberia for Fortuna at 3 p.m.).

By Air
Scheduled **air service** to the new international airport (tel. 666-0695), 12 km west of town, is

provided by Travelair (tel. 232-7883); flights depart San José's Pavas Airport on Monday, Thursday, Friday, and Saturday at 7:30 a.m. Return flights depart Liberia at 8:40 a.m. ($82 one-way, $136 roundtrip). **Note:** Schedules may change in "green season," mid-April to mid-December.

RINCÓN DE LA VIEJA NATIONAL PARK

Rincón de la Vieja (1,895 meters), an active volcano passing through a period of relative calm, is one of five volcanoes that make up the Guanacaste mountain range. It is composed of nine separate but contiguous volcanic craters, including Von Seebach and Santa María (1,916 meters), the tallest. The last serious eruption was in 1983. Rincón, however, spewed lava and acid gases on 8 May 1991, causing destructive *lahores* (ash-mud flows). The slopes still bear reminders of the destructive force of the acid cloud that burnt away much of the vegetation on the southeastern slope.

The volcanic attractions are protected in the 14,083-hectare Rincón de la Vieja National Park, which extends from 650 to 1,965 meters' elevation on both the Caribbean and Pacific flanks of the Cordillera de Guanacaste. The two sides differ markedly in rainfall and vegetation. The Pacific side has a distinct dry season (if you intend climbing to the craters, February through April is best). The Caribbean side is lush and wet year-round, with as much as 500 cm of rainfall falling annually on higher slopes. The park is known for its profusion of orchid species.

The diverse conditions foster a panoply of wildlife species. More than 300 species of birds include quetzals, toucanets, the elegant trogon, eagles, three-wattled bellbirds, and the curassow. Mammals that inhabit this remote mountain refuge include cougars, howler, spider, and white-faced monkeys, kinkajous, sloths, tapirs, tayras, and even jaguars. Monkeys may make themselves known along the trails. Don't be surprised if one of the resident spider monkeys throws something at you!

Hiking to the Summit
The hike is relatively straightforward. You can do the roundtrip from the Las Pailas Ranger Station

to the summit and back in a day; two days from the park headquarters. The main crater still steams. The dormant Santa María crater harbors a forest-rimmed lake popular with quetzals, linnets, and tapirs. Icy Lake Los Jilgueros lies between the two craters. The lower trail begins at the Santa María Ranger Station, leads past Las Hornillas and the Las Espuelas Ranger Station, and snakes up the steep, scrubby mountainside through elephant grass and dense groves of twisted, stunted copel clusia, a perfumed tree species common near mountain summits. En route, you cross a bleak expanse of shingly purple lava fossilized by the blitz of the sun. Trails are marked by cairns, though it is easy to get lost if the clouds set in; consider hiring a local guide. The upper slopes are of loose scree. Be particularly careful on your descent.

It can be cool up here, but—if it's clear—the powerful view and the hard, windy silence make for a profound experience. From on high, you have a splendid view of the wide Guanacaste plain shimmering in the heat like a dreamworld between hallucination and reality, and, beyond, the mountains of Nicoya glistening like hammered gold from the sunlight slanting in from the south. On a clear day, you can see Lake Nicaragua. Magical! You have only the sighing of the wind for company.

It will probably be cloudy, however, in which case you may need to camp near the top to ascend to the summit next morning before the clouds set in (there's a campsite about five km from Las Espuelas; it's about two hours to the summit of Von Seebach). The beach of Linnet Bird Lagoon—a whale-shaped lagoon filled with very cold water, southeast of the active volcano—is recommended for camping. Bring waterproof tent and clothing, plus mosquito and tick repellent. The grasses harbor ticks and other biting critters: consider long pants.

Fill up with water at the ranger station before your uphill hike.

Attractions
Lots of attractions lower down the slopes are reached by relatively easy trails from the park headquarters. The **Sendero Encantago** leads through cloud forest full of *guaria morada* orchids (the national flower) and links with a 12-km trail that continues to **Las Pailas** ("Cal-

drons"), 50 hectares of bubbling mud volcanoes, boiling thermal waters, vapor geysers, and the so-called Hornillas ("Ovens") geyser of sulfur dioxide and hydrogen sulfide. The hot bubbling mud has minerals and medicinal properties used in cosmetology. Be careful when walking around: It is possible to step through the crust and scald yourself! This trail continues to the summit.

Between the cloud forest and Las Pailas, a side trail (marked Aguas Thermales) leads to soothing, hot sulfur springs called **Los Azufrales** ("Sulfurs"). The thermal waters (42° C) form small pools where you may bathe and take advantage of their curative properties. Use the cold-water stream nearby for a two-minute cooling off after a good soak in the thermal springs. **Las Hornillas** are sulfurous fumaroles on the devastated southern slope of the volcano. Another trail leads to the **Hidden Waterfalls,** four continuous falls (three of which exceed 70 meters) in the Agria Ravine. You'll find a perfect bathing hole at the base of one of the falls. The various trails link the volcanic attractions.

Park Headquarters

The park headquarters is an old adobe hacienda—**Hacienda Santa María**—supposedly once owned by Lyndon Johnson. It contains an exhibition room and is linked by a six-km trail to Las Pailas ranger station. Entrance: $15 walk-in, $7 advance purchase! You can rent horses ($2.50 per hour) from the ranger station by calling Cigifredo Marín, the head ranger of the Guanacaste Regional Conservation Area at Santa Rosa National Park (tel. 695-5598). You can reach the Las Espuelas Ranger Station, on the western flank of the volcano via the road from Curubande.

Tours

Jungle Trails (Apdo. 2413, San José 1002, tel. 255-3486, fax 255-2782) offers a three-day tour from San José, including a horseback ride and a hike to the crater, plus a second horseback ride to the thermal springs at Azufrales.

Most tour companies in San José can arrange tours to Rincón. **Private guides** Rodrigo and Sergio Bonilla escort tours and can provide horses, camping equipment, etc., as needed (tel. 223-0628).

Accommodations

You may be able to stay in basic accommodations at the **ranger stations** ($2.50). The two bunk beds have mildewed mattresses, or you can sleep on the floor. No bedding or towels. Bring a sleeping bag and mosquito netting. Call the park headquarters in Santa Rosa (tel. 695-5598) or the National Park radio-communications office in San José (tel. 233-4160) to inquire and/or make reservations.

Camping: A shady campsite next to an old sugarcane-processing plant, 500 meters from Santa María ranger station, has a bathroom. You'll find another campsite on the banks of the Río Colorado, near the Las Espuelas Ranger Station. Camp here if hiking to the summit. Take water from the creek. Otherwise you may camp where you like though note that there are lots of ticks. It can get cold at night; come prepared. You'll be better off camping in dry season, January to April being best.

Haciendas outside the Park

Hacienda Lodge Guachipelín (Apdo. 636, Alajuela, tel. 441-6545 or 441-6994, fax 442-1910, or tel. 257-0433 at night) is a centenarian working cattle ranch that doubles as a rustic lodge (see "Getting There," below). It offers 25 nice if somewhat small bedrooms in the homey hardwood lodge, plus a "suite" with more elegant decor. A bunkhouse offers more basic accommodation and is part of the Costa Rican Youth Hostel system; you can make reservations through the Toruma Hostel (headquarters of the hostel system) at Avenida Central, Calles 29/31, in San José (Apdo. 1355, San José 1002, tel./fax 224-4085). Pleasing tiled communal bathrooms have cold water. The lodge has a very comfortable lounge with deep-cushioned sofas and a TV, plus breezy verandas with Sarchí rockers. *Típico* food is served in a dining room overlooking the corral, where you can watch cattle and horses being worked.

The lodge has more than 1,000 hectares of terrain from dry forest to open savannah, plus a 1,200-hectare pochote and melina tree-reforestation project. There are more than 70 horses for guided horseback rides (the lodge gives riding lessons), and even an eight-day horse-riding tour around Rincón de la Vieja. The lodge also has hikes to waterfalls, bubbling *pailas* (mud-

pots), sulfur springs, and natural pools for swimming, plus a "monkey trail" tour to see howler and capuchin monkeys. The owners had planned to introduce mountain bikes and open a *mirador* with a bar facing the ocean; an old coffee-drying trough was to be turned into a swimming pool; 4WD vehicles were to be introduced for exploring farther afield; and a bullfight plaza was planned. However, a reader wrote to say new owners had dropped these plans.

The lodge is 18 km from the Pan-American Hwy., eight km south of the Santa María Ranger Station, and has views out towards the volcano. Extremely hospitable staff. Highly recommended by some past guests; another thought it "overpriced." Rates: $15 s ($9 bunkhouse), $35 d, $45 suite. Horses are $15 half day, $22 full day. A minibus from the Hotel Guanacaste in Liberia costs $7 one-way.

Rincón de la Vieja Mountain Lodge (Apdo. 114, Liberia 5000, tel. 253-8431, 233-4578, or 666-2369, fax 223-5502 or 666-0473), five km beyond Hacienda Lodge Guachipelín, is another superb base for exploring the park. The rustic all-hardwood lodge was converted from the main family hacienda-home of Alvaro Wiessel (one of the volcano's craters is named Wiessel after Alvaro's German immigrant grandfather). The two-story structure has six pleasing though dark bedrooms and two bathrooms with cold water, plus three rustic cabins near the lodge for six to eight people each with shared bath. There are two small pools in the gardens and, beyond that, forest. The property, part of the Hacienda Guachipelín, also includes a roofed corral and a dairy farm, plus scientific library and a butterfly collection on display. Electricity is generated by a stream. Options for exploring include guided horse tours ($45) and nature tours to the volcanic attractions. The lodge is adjacent to the park boundary, 500 meters beyond the Río Colorado, which you can safely cross by 4WD. It's 1.5 km to the right from the fork for the park. Meals average $10 for breakfast; $12 dinner. Rate: about $50 per person, including meals. Adventure package: two days $137, three days $195, four days $252. Discounts for IYH members. A **tent-camp** with showers and dining room

should have been added a 30-minute hike away, near Las Hornillas, by the time you read this (about $20 per person).

Also see Buena Vista Lodge, in the "Accommodations" section of "North of Liberia," below.

Albergue Rincón del Turista, in the village of **San Jorge** near the park's southern border, has rustic cabinas with cold water and outhouse bathroom in a forested valley ($10 per person). You can rent horses and guides. Make reservations and arrange transportation through the Casa de Cultura tourist information office in Liberia (tel. 666-1606). You reach it via a side road (dirt all the way) that leads east from a point three km south of the park entrance on the road east from Liberia.

Not reviewed is **Rinconcito Lodge** (tel. 666-0636), "17 kilometers out of Liberia" along "a spur track," according to another guidebook. Apparently it has "rudimentary lodging" in a cement blockhouse, plus horses and guides. Rate: $10 per person.

Getting There

Two routes lead to Rincón de la Vieja National Park and the Santa María Ranger Station. Avenida 6 leads east from Liberia via Colonia La Libertad and San Jorge to the park headquarters. The 27-km dirt road is deeply rutted; 4WD is recommended. Alas, no buses. A second (much better) road leads to Rincón from the turnoff for Cereceda, about six km north of Liberia on the Pan-American Highway. The road winds past small oak groves and is in excellent condition. Two km beyond the village of Curubandé, you come to the gates of Hacienda Guachipelín: you pay a $2.50 fee for the right to use the private road. The dirt road leads past Hacienda Guachipelín (the toll fee is reimbursed if you stay here) and a turnoff for Rincón de la Vieja Lodge to the secondary ranger station (Santa María is about eight km from the lodge). A bus departs Liberia for Curubandé at 2 p.m. on Monday, Wednesday, and Friday.

Take your sunglasses, especially if you walk: the roads are blinding white. The rock is ignimbrite, the white volcanic rock used to build the houses of Liberia.

NORTH OF LIBERIA

Driving north from Liberia to La Cruz, you'll see that the area is surprisingly rich in forest. Settlements diminish to the north. The Pan-American Hwy. is moderately lightly traveled and traffic picks up speed north of Liberia. I don't recall ever seeing a police car between Cañas and the Nicaraguan border, but don't push your luck. The scenery is magnificent, with volcanoes—one, two, three—marching in a row to the east, convex-curved, like the volcanoes of childhood vision.

LAS IMÁGENES BIOLOGICAL STATION

Las Imágenes (reservations c/o Hotel Las Espuelas, Apdo. 88, Liberia, tel. 666-0144 or 225-3987) is a 1,000-hectare working cattle ranch and biological station with 100 hectares of virgin tropical dry and moist forest and riverine habitat. The station is a former hacienda recently opened to tourists. A rustic cabin can accommodate 20 people, with shared bath. There's a working water well. Horseback trips are offered to Rincón de la Vieja. Not inspected.

SUTTON OSTRICH RANCH

Sutton Ostrich Ranch (tel. 228-6646 or 331-5068), about 15 km north of Liberia, on the western fringe of Quebrada Grande (marked on some maps as Garcia Flamenco), claims to be the only commercial ostrich ranch outside of Africa. The hot, windy, dry climate of Guanacaste is perfect for breeding the comical, gawky, long-necked bird. A path behind the ranch house leads uphill to corrals, each with a trio of birds. Young chicks are prone to infection. Hence, visitors are asked to shower, change into sterile clothes, and step into an antiseptic dip before entering the hatchery, which contains electronically controlled incubators. Each hen lays 50 to 100 eggs a year. Each egg weighs 1.5 kilos (about the equivalent of 25 chicken eggs)

and takes an hour to boil! You can hope the adults will be in a good mood: their kick delivers a punch of 35 kg per square centimeter (adults weigh 90 to 160 kg apiece, making them the biggest birds in the world). Vivian Gonzalez and Joe Sutton opened the 160-hectare farm in May 1992 after importing 100 of the blueneck and black ostrich varieties. At press time, they had multiplied threefold, with 500 eggs incubating in the wings, so to speak. With luck, December to April you might see the magnificent mating dance of the luxuriantly plumed male. The birds are to be slaughtered for meat, hide, and feathers (the meat is high in protein but low in cholesterol and fat).

Turn right at the Guardia Rural station at Potrerillos and follow the signs (the village of Quebrada Grande is about six km). Scheduled tours (from $20) are offered on weekends at 10 a.m. and 1 and 3 p.m. Groups can make advance arrangements for midweek visits, although the guided tours are in Spanish (tel. 695-5355). Guanacaste Tours (Apdo. 55, Liberia 5000, tel. 666-0306, fax 666-0307) offers a guided tour to Liberia and the ostrich ranch every Monday ($50).

FINCA SAN ANTONIO

This 2,024-hectare working cattle ranch, near Quebrada Grande, offers horseback trail rides. It's east of the Pan-American Hwy. (the junction is nine km south of the turnoff for La Casona in Santa Rosa National Park and 23 km north of Liberia). There's no accommodation. Scheduled rides are offered every Wednesday and Saturday. You can arrange rides on other days through Hotel Las Espuelas (tel. 666-0144, fax 225-3987). A one-day tour with barbecue lunch includes a visit to Santa Rosa National Park ($65).

Valle Dorado (Apdo. 340, San José 1002, tel. 220-4250, fax 232-2027) offers a three-day trail-ride tour to Hacienda San Antonio, which includes an afternoon at Playa Hermosa, an evening of folkloric dancing, and a visit to the In-

dian craft village of Guaitil, plus transfers from/to San José ($289); accommodation is at Hotel Las Espuelas. **L.A. Tours** (Apdo. 492, San José 1007, tel. 221-4501, fax 224-5828) has a three-day tour from San José that combines a half day at San Antonio with a visit to Santa Rosa National Park, a half day at the beach, plus a boat ride on Lake Arenal.

ACCOMMODATIONS

Buena Vista Lodge (Apdo. 373, Liberia, tel. 695-5147, fax 666-0090), part of the Youth Hostel system, nestles at the foot of the volcano 13 km northeast of Cañas Dulces (reached via a turnoff from the Pan-Am Hwy., 12 km north of Liberia), on the 1,600-hectare Hacienda Buena Vista. Its 15 dorm-style rooms can accommodate 40 people, though there are a handful of private rooms with baths. The rooms face a courtyard bright with blossoms. Rough-hewn timbers and locally crafted rockers add to the atmosphere. The lodge offers a variety of guided hikes and horseback trips to Rincón de la Vieja, to local waterfalls, or into the secondary forest behind the lodge, though you need not venture from the property to admire the splendid views . . . you can do so while

soaking in the natural steam bath ringed by volcanic stone. Rate: $20 d. You can camp for $15. Students receive a 10% discount. Transfers from Cañas Dulces cost $15 roundtrip.

Santa Clara Lodge (Apdo. 17, Liberia, tel. 226-4921, fax 666-0475), near Quebrada Grande, is a working cattle ranch—you'd never know it!—with four rooms with shared bath, plus one room for three people with a private bath. It's very well kept. Though basically furnished, rooms have extremely pretty decor, louvered windows, and towels laid out in the shape of hearts. Home-style meals are served alfresco on a veranda with carnations and pretty tablecloths. A *palenque* bar overlooks a small duck pond. A mineral spring feeds a soaking pool, said to be therapeutic. When the electricity fails, candles provide a romantic touch. Horse riding is available, as well as tours to Santa Rosa National Park and Orosí volcano. Popular with Ticos, it is reached via a very scenic dirt road (10 km) from Potrerillos, 24 km north of Liberia. Rates: $34 s, $62 d, $87 t with shared bath; $39 s, $68 d, $91 t, with private bath.

Centro Social La Mata de Caña, in Quebrada Grande, has cabinas with shared bath and cold water ($6 per person), and is recommended for stews and other Guanacasteco dishes. The popular bar has a pool table.

SANTA ROSA NATIONAL PARK

Santa Rosa, founded in 1972 as the country's first national park, has special significance: all three times the country has been invaded, the usurpers have been routed here. The 49,515-hectare park, which incorporates much of the Santa Elena peninsula, is perhaps most famous for Hacienda Santa Rosa—better known as La Casona—the nation's most cherished historic monument. It was here in 1856 that the mercenary army of American adventurer William Walker was defeated by a ragamuffin army of Costa Rican volunteers. The old hacienda-turned-museum alone is well worth the visit. Santa Rosa National Park has other treasures, too.

The wide range of habitats—the park is a mosaic of 10 distinct habitats, including mangrove swamp, savannah, and oak forest—attracts a wide range of animals: more than 250

bird species; countless insect species (including 3,800 moth species); and relatively easily seen mammals such as white-tailed deer, coatimundis, howler, spider, and white-faced monkeys, and magnificent anteaters. Jaguars still roam Santa Rosa, as do margays, ocelots, pumas, and jaguarundis; they're all shy and seldom seen. Half of the 115 mammal species are bats, including two vampire species. Santa Rosa is a vitally important nesting site for ridleys and other turtle species. In the wet season the land is as green as emeralds, and wildlife disperses. In dry season, however, when the parched scrubby landscapes give an impression of the East African plains, wildlife congregates at watering holes—such as those on the Naked Indian Trail—and is easily seen. Be patient. Sit still for long enough and some inter-

esting creatures are sure to appear. Keep an eye out for snakes.

The park is divided into two sections: the Santa Rosa Sector and the Murciélago Sector. The park entrance for the former is 200 meters off the Pan-American Hwy., at Km 269, 37 km north of Liberia. Another road from the Rural Guard station 10 km farther north leads via Cuajiniquil to the Murciélago Sector.

Information

The park entrance station sells detailed maps (1:50,000 scale; 75 cents) showing trails and campgrounds. Hours: 7 a.m.-5 p.m. Both the natural-history museum in La Casona and the park administration office (tel. 695-5598) can provide additional information. Entrance: $15 walk-in, $10 advance purchase.

Getting There

Buses depart San José for Peñas Blancas from Calle 14, Avenidas 3/5 (Carsol, tel. 224-1968) daily at 5 and 7:45 a.m., and 1:30 and 4:15 p.m., passing the park entrance (35 km north of Liberia) en route to the Nicaraguan border. Six hours. Buy your ticket in advance. Buses depart Liberia for Santa Rosa and Peñas Blancas from Avenida 5, Calle 14 at 5:30, 8:30, and 11 a.m. and 2 and 6 p.m. You'll have to walk or hitchhike from the park entrance (seven km to La Casona and the park headquarters, another 13 km to Playa Naranjo). Hitchhiking is easy. The return bus schedule for La Cruz, Liberia, and San José is posted both at the park information center at the park entrance and in the natural-history room at La Casona.

To Murciélago: Buses depart La Cruz for Cuajiniquil at 5 a.m. and noon, and reportedly from Liberia for Cuajiniquil at 7 a.m and 3 p.m. It's about eight km from here to the Murciélago park entrance. Hitchhiking to Cuajiniquil isn't a problem; from here, you may have to walk the eight km to the park entrance (take lots of water). You can rent a boat from a local fisherman ($25-50 per boatload) to explore the coastline of Murciélago. Try in Cuajiniquil or at the wharf at the end of the road, three km west of the village.

Note: The journey can be quite rough in the rainy season because of high winds. **Cruceros del Sur** (Apdo. 1198, San José 1200, tel. 220-1927, fax 220-2103) has included a one-day

stop in the area as part of a four-day natural-history cruise, June-Oct. only, aboard the 68-passenger eco-cruise ship *Temptress* (also see special topic "Natural-History Cruise Tours" in the On the Road chapter). Their itineraries have been subject to changes recently, and in 1994 no "northern" itinerary was offered.

SANTA ROSA SECTOR

The Santa Rosa Sector is the more important and accessible of the two sectors. On the right, one km past the entrance gate, a rough dirt road leads to a rusting armored personnel carrier beside a memorial cross commemorating the Battle of 1955, when Somoza, the Nicaraguan strongman, made an ill-fated foray into Costa Rica.

La Casona

Six km farther on the paved road is La Casona, a magnificent colonial homestead with a beautiful setting atop a slight rise overlooking a stone corral where the battle with William Walker was fought. The farmstead was rebuilt in 1895 and was in use in 1972 when the land was expropriated for the national park. Inside the house are photos, illustrations, carbines, and other military paraphernalia commemorating the battle of 20 March 1856 (see "History" in the Introduction chapter). Battles were also fought here during the 1919 Sapoá Revolution and in 1955. One room is furnished in period style. Another is a small chapel. Large wooden mortars and pestles are on display, along with decrepit chaps and centenary riding gear. There's also good nature exhibit. Bats fly in and out. Forget *Dracula*—they're totally harmless. There's a large *guanacaste* tree outside, by the parking lot.

Trails

The **Naked Indian** loop trail (1.5 km) begins just before the house and leads through dry-forest woodlands with streams and waterfalls and gumbo-limbo trees whose peeling red bark earned the nickname "naked Indian trees." The **Los Patos** trail, which has several watering holes during dry season, is one of the best trails for spotting mammals. The **Laguna Escondida and Caujiniquil River Trail** (14 km roundtrip)

SANTA ROSA
NATIONAL PARK
(SANTA ROSA SECTOR)

also takes you to a pond that is a magnet for thirsty wildlife. Other good spots for wildlife are **Platanar Lake, Laguna Escondida,** and **La Penca,** reached by trails north from the park administrative area.

Trails are marked in detail on the map sold at the park entrance.

Playas Nancite and Naranjo

The paved road ends just beyond the administration area. From here, an appalling dirt road drops steeply to Playa Naranjo and Playa Nancite, 13 km from La Casona. It's a good road to break your springs. Ordinary vehicles

do make it down this road, but having bounced loose the hood bolts of my Range Rover, I consider taking anything other than a 4WD with good ground clearance totally foolhardy. Park officials reportedly have closed the road at times because they get tired of towing vehicles out!

Playa Nancite: The virtually deserted white-sand beach at Playa Nancite is renowned as the site for the annual *arribadas,* or mass nestings of olive ridley turtles which occur only here and at Ostional, farther south. More than 100,000 turtles will gather out to sea and come ashore over the space of only a few days, with the possibility of up to 10,000 reptiles on the

La Casona
Historic Museum

BOB RACE

beach at any one time in September and October. Although the exact trigger is unknown, *arribadas* seem to coincide with falling barometric pressure in autumn and are apparently associated with a waxing three-quarter moon. You can usually see solitary turtles at other times August through December. Stephen E. Cornelius's illustrated book, *The Sea Turtles of Santa Rosa National Park* (National Park Foundation, Costa Rica, 1986; 80 pages), provides a thorough insight into the life of the ridley turtle (also see "Turtles," in the section on "Fauna" in the Introduction chapter).

You might spot a vulture, a coatimundi, peccaries, or coyotes greedily gorging on the still-warm eggs. Visitors frequently see white-faced monkeys. A boa constrictor has made his home in the ceiling of the ranger's hut. Reportedly pumas live here also.

Getting There: Playa Nancite is about a one-hour hike over a headland from Estero Real, at the end of the dirt road. Access is restricted and permits are needed (see "Camping," below).

Playa Naranjo: This very popular and beautiful kilometers-long light-gray sand beach is legendary in surfing lore. Steep, thick, powerful tubular waves and "killer beautiful Witches Rock rising like a sentinel out of the water, make this a must stop in the world for top-rated surfers," says surf expert Mark Kelly. The beach is bounded by craggy, penurious headlands and frequently visited by monkeys, iguanas, and other wildlife. Alligators and reportedly even a croco-

dile lurk in the mangrove swamps at the southern end of the beach. The 85-meter *Nordic* runs day-trips from Playa Tamarindo. It's a two-hour hike from Naranjo to Playa Nancite at low tide. You have to cross a river south of Estero Real, where you take the main trail to Nancite. If you're walking to Playa Nancite or Naranjo, it's at least a two-hour hike before you reach drinking water—take water!

Surfing

In addition to Playa Naranjo, **Playa Portrero Grande** and other beaches on the central Santa Elena peninsula reportedly offer some of the best "machine-like" surf in the country, with double overhead waves rolling in one after the other. The makers of *Endless Summer II,* the sequel to the classic surfing movie, caught the Portrero Grande break perfectly. The beaches are inaccessible by road. You can hire a boat at Jobo or any of the fishing villages in the Golfo Santa Elena to take you to Portrero Grande or Islas Murciélago ("Bat Islands").

Accommodations

Costa Rica Adventures and Wildlife (tel. 223-5595; in the U.S., tel. 800-497-3422) has opened a lodge and restaurant in the heart of Santa Rosa. Eight rooms come with fans. Not inspected. Rates: $32 s, $39 d. Also new and not inspected is **Centro de los Investigaciones Daniel Janzen** (Apdo. 169, Liberia, tel. 695-5598), a science center that accommodates

guests ($10 per person, or $25 with meals). Reservations recommended.

Camping

The Santa Rosa sector has four campsites (75 cents per person). **Note:** Fires are a serious hazard in Santa Rosa. Take extra precautions (the Parks Service issues a pamphlet, *Preventing Forest Fires*).

La Casona campsite is 0.5 km before the hacienda, to the right on the road to Playa Nancite. Beneath shady *guanacaste* trees are barbecue pits, picnic tables, and bathrooms. It can get muddy here in the wet season. There's another campsite at the north end of **Playa Nancite.** No more than 20 people at a time are allowed to camp at Nancite. You need a permit (free) obtained from the Ecotourism Office at the park administration area. Raccoons abound, so you'll need to be creative to keep your food safe.

Estero Real has a shady campsite behind a mangrove swamp with lots of wading birds and fish with luminous eyes. There are camping tables, barbecue pits, and latrines. Bring a hammock to sling between the trees. There's no piped water here; you take it from the lagoon—boil it!

The shady Argelia campsite at **Playa Naranjo** has individual sites, each with a fire pit, a picnic table, and a bench. Showers, sinks, and outhouse toilets are near the ranger cabin. Get water from a windmill pump well. The raccoons will stop at virtually nothing to get at your food. Do *not* leave food in your tent.

Services

The park administration area north of La Casona has a small *cocina* (kitchen) serving park rangers. The staff is not supposed to sell to tourists, but you usually won't be turned away if you want to buy a soda. You might be able to buy meals here between 6 and 7 a.m., noontime, and 5 to 6 p.m. (breakfast $2.50; dinner $3.50). Best with advance notice. Lately I was informed that meals with the park rangers are no longer allowed. Things change: It's worth asking.

MURCIÉLAGO SECTOR

The entrance to the Murciélago Sector of Santa Rosa National Park is 15 km west of the Pan-American Hwy., 10 km north of the Santa Rosa Sector park entrance (there's a police checkpoint at the turnoff; have your passport ready for inspection). The road winds downhill to a coastal valley through spectacularly hilly countryside to **Cuajiniquil;** the paved road continues past Cuajiniquil and dead-ends at a wharf where fishing boats berth. The village itself is hidden off the paved road: look for an unsigned dirt road to the left. (See "Bahía Junquillal Recreation Area," below for accommodation; see above for bus service.)

The road to the Murciélago park entrance (eight km) and Punta Blanca is to the left from the Y-fork in Cuajiniquil. You'll have to ford two rivers en route. You'll pass the old CIA training camp for the Nicaraguan contras on your right. The place—Murciélago Hacienda—was owned by the Nicaraguan dictator Somoza's family before being expropriated in 1979, when the Murciélago Sector was incorporated into Santa Rosa National Park. It's off-limits (it's now a training camp for the Costa Rican Rural Guard). Armed guards may stop you for an ID check as you pass. A few hundred meters farther, the road runs along the secret airstrip that Oliver North built to supply the contras. It's worth the journey just to have your photo taken here! The park entrance is just beyond the airstrip.

It's another 15 km to **Playa Blanca,** a beautiful horseshoe-shaped white-sand beach—one of the most isolated in the country—about five km wide and enjoyed only by pelicans and frigate birds. Waterfalls are surrounded by ferns and palms in **Cuajiniquil Canyon,** which has its own moist microclimate. The **Poza El General** watering hole attracts waterfowl and other animals year-round and is reached along a rough trail.

Camping

You can camp (75 cents per person) at the ranger station (there's a bathroom and water plus picnic tables) or at Playa Blanca (no facilities).

GUANACASTE NATIONAL PARK

This recent addition to the park system was created in 1989 to protect more than 84,000 hectares of dry forest, rainforest, and savannah extending from mangrove swamps at the tip of the Santa Elena peninsula to cloud forests at 1,659 meters atop Volcán Cacao. The park is part of a mosaic of ecologically interdependent parks and reserves—the 110,000-hectare Guanacaste Conservation Area—that incorporates Santa Rosa National Park, Rincón de la Vieja National Park, Bolaños Island Wildlife Refuge, the Junquillal Bay Recreation Area, and the Horizontes Experimental Station, which abuts Santa Rosa and performs agricultural research. It is contiguous with Santa Rosa National Park and protects the migratory routes of myriad creatures: jaguars, tapirs, sloths, monkeys, three-wattled bellbirds, and other species, many

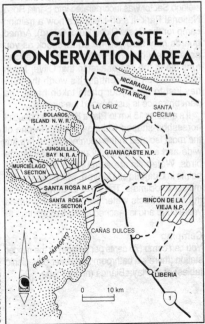

of which move seasonally between the lowlands and the steep slopes of Cacao (1,659 meters) and Orosí (1,487 meters) volcanoes, whose wind-battered and rain-drenched eastern slopes contrast sharply with the flora and fauna on the dry plains. Orosí long since ceased activity and interestingly shows no signs of a crater.

The park is administered from the Guanacaste Regional Conservation Unit Headquarters at Santa Rosa (tel. 695-5598). Hours: 8 a.m.-4 p.m.

Accommodations

Visitor facilities are gradually being developed. Reportedly you can camp at any of the stations ($2.50 per day). Four biological stations on the slopes of Cacao provide spartan dormitory accommodation ($20 per day, including meals; contact the park headquarters in Santa Rosa National Park, tel. 695-5598), although students and researchers get priority. You can also arrange transportation through the Park Service.

The rustic lodge at **Cacao Field Station,** at the edge of a cloud forest at 1,100 meters on the southwestern slope of Volcán Cacao, offers staggering views. To get there, hike or take a horse from the **Gángora Station,** at Quebrada Grande (also known as Garcia Flamenco) on the Río Gángora; it's about 10 km along a rough dirt trail. The turnoff from the Pan-American Hwy. is at Potrerillos, nine km south of the Santa Rosa National Park turnoff, from where it's about seven km to Quebrada Grande, which you can also reach by bus from Liberia (departs daily at 3 p.m.). You'll pass hot springs en route. Four-wheel-drive vehicles can make it in dry season, with permission.

A dirt road to the right at the Cuajiniquil crossroads on the Pan-American Hwy. leads to **Maritza Field Station** (15 km), on the lower southern flanks of Volcán Orosí. Don't worry about the barbed-wire gates: simply close them behind you. Four-wheel drive is essential in wet season. There are beds for 18 people, with shared bath. The station has a research laboratory. From here you can hike to **El Pedregal** on the Llano

© MOON PUBLICATIONS, INC.

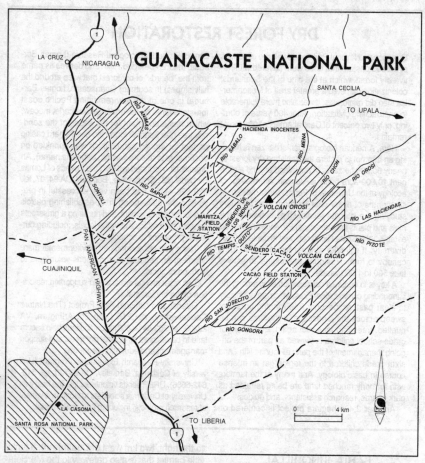

GUANACASTE NATIONAL PARK

de los Indios, where almost 100 Indian petroglyphs representing a pantheon of chiseled supernatural beings lie half-buried in the luxurious undergrowth that cloaks the mountain's hide. Another trail leads to Mengo Biological Station.

Mengo Biological Station, surrounded by cloud forest at 1,100 meters halfway up Volcán Cacao, can also be reached by a 4WD trail that begins approximately 10 km east of Quebrada Grande; the last two km have to be done on foot or horseback. Five rustic dormitories shelter up to 40 people. No towels or electricity. The

Pitilla Biological Station, with accommodations for 32 people, is on the Caribbean side of Cacao and can be reached by 4WD. No electricity. Even if you've stayed at one of the other stations, Pitilla is worth the visit for its lusher vegetation reflecting Caribbean influences. It is reached via a rough dirt road from **Santa Cecilia,** 28 km east of the Pan-American Hwy. (see "East of La Cruz," below); 4WD recommended. It's a nine-km drive via Esperanza. Don't blithely drive east from Santa Cecilia as that route goes to Upala. Ask locals for the correct route.

DRY FOREST RESTORATION

Guanacaste National Park includes large expanses of eroded pasture that once were covered with native dry forest, which at the time of the Spaniards' colonization carpeted a greater area of Mesoamerica than did rainforests. It was also more vulnerable to encroaching civilization. After 400 years of burning, only two percent of Central America's dry forest remains.

Here, American biologist Daniel Janzen is heading an attempt to restore the vanished dry forest to nearly 60,000 hectares of ranchland around a remnant 10,000-acre nucleus. Janzen, a professor of ecology at the University of Pennsylvania, has spent six months of every year for more than 30 years studying the intricate relationships betweeen animals and plants in Guanacaste Province and helped establish the Costa Rican National Institute for Biodiversity. It will take at least two decades for a canopy to form. Restoring the original forest will take 500 to 1,000 years!

A key is to nurture a conservation ethic among the surrounding communities. Fires, which are set initially to clear pasture, become free-running fires that sweep across the landscape. If the fires can be quelled, trees can take root again. Education for grade-school children is viewed as part of the ongoing management of the park; all fourth-, fifth-, and sixth-grade children in the region get an intense course in basic biology. And many of the farmers who formerly ranched land are being retrained as park guards, research assistants, and guides.

Another 2,400-hectare project is centered on Lomas Barbudal Biological Reserve (Lomas Barbudal means "Bearded Hills" and derives its name from the "beards" of dry forest that wrap around the hilly slopes) in southern Guanacaste. Lomas Barbudal is one of the few remaining Pacific coast forests favored by the endangered scarlet macaw, which has a penchant for the seeds of the sandbox tree (the Spanish found the seed's hard casing perfect for storing sand, which was sprinkled on documents to absorb wet ink; hence its name). An organization founded in 1987, the Friends of Lomas Barbudal (691 Colusa Ave., Berkeley, CA 94707, tel. 510-526-4115), has been very successful in preventing the devastating fires, establishing patrols and forest management, and nurturing a grassroots conservation ethic among the locals, including outreach programs to schools.

The group raises funds for environmental management and education and needs volunteers to work on projects.

Two other groups are active in supporting restoration of the dry forests:

Guanacaste National Park Project (The Nature Conservancy, 1815 N. Lynn St., Arlington, VA 22209, tel. 703-841-4860). Contributions help secure land to be restored as tropical dry forest and support management and education programs.

University Research Expeditions Program (University of California, Berkeley, CA 94720, tel. 510-642-6586). UREP sends volunteers into the field with University of California scientists to work on a variety of research projects, including Lomas Barbudal.

BAHÍA JUNQUILLAL RECREATION AREA

The 505-hectare Bahía Junquillal Recreation Area, in Bahía Junquillal north of Murciélago, is part of the Guanacaste Conservation Area ($1.50 entrance). The calm bay is backed by tropical dry forest. The bay is a refuge for seabirds as well as the olive ridley, hawksbill, green, and leatherback turtles, which come ashore to lay their eggs on the beautiful, two-km-wide half-moon beach of coral-colored sand. Paths lead along the shore to mangrove swamps. The recreation area is reached via a deeply rutted dirt road

to the right, two km west of **Cuajiniquil**, a funky little hamlet that is also gateway to the Murciélago sector of Santa Rosa National Park (see above). You can also reach the northern end of the bay via Puerto Soley, southwest from La Cruz (see below). There's a ranger station.

Food and Accommodations

There's a very popular camping area under shade trees ($2.50 per person), with basic latrines. Water is reportedly rationed to one hour daily. You'll see a bar—Coco Loco—and **Restaurant Cuajiniquil** as you enter Cuajiniquil. Both may have rooms. Inquire by calling the public telephone (679-9030). The local *pulpería* reportedly has two rooms with

shared bath and cold water—**Cabinas Santa Elena** (tel. 679-9112, leave a message). Two **campsites** are in the hamlet of Brasilito, at the northern end of the beach.

The dirt road to Playa Junquillal continues 4.5 km to **Finca Bavaria** (tel. 253-6942, fax 225-7763), a pretty and tiny but very rustic homestead that sits on stilts atop a breezy hill, surrounded by bougainvilleas and shade trees. It advertises rooms. It's quite funky: there's lots of litter on the ground and an outhouse at the back. No one was there when I called by. It offers guided hikes and horseback rides, as well as diving with a professional instructor.

LA CRUZ AND VICINITY

LA CRUZ

This compact gateway town to Nicaragua is dramatically situated atop a plateau, although there's no hint of this unless you turn left at the plaza and walk 100 meters to the Mirador Ehecatl Restaurante, on the crest of the escarpment, for the incredible views over the Bahía Salinas and Bolaños Island. From here the road drops to Puerto Soley. You'll pass an **ecological museum** in an old customs house at Agua Buena, four km south of La Cruz on the Pan-Am Hwy., just south of the turnoff for Hacienda Los Inocentes and Santa Cecilia. La Cruz is the last town of any significance before the Nicaraguan border (19 km). A good time to visit is May, when it hosts its annual and lively **Fiesta Cívica**.

Accommodations
Amalia Inn (tel./fax 679-9181) is a newly opened American-run hostelry operated by Lester and Amalia Bounds, boasting fabulous clifftop views over Bahía Salinas and north along the Nicaraguan coast. Its seven rooms have private bathrooms. A pool is handy for cooling off, though the inn's setting is breezy enough. You can prepare picnics in their kitchen. They offer horse and boat rentals. Rates: $25-35 s, $35-45 d, including American breakfast.

Hotel El Faro (tel. 679-9009) on the left, 100 meters west of the gas station, has 17 basic rooms in need of a spring cleaning. Shared bath with cold water. The large and dingy restaurant downstairs doubles as a disco. Rate: $5 per person. A much better bet is **Cabinas Santa Rita** (tel. 679-9062), 300 meters west of El Faro, opposite the Tribunales de Justicia. The 14 rooms with private baths (three with shared bath) with cold water and fans are very clean though basic. Much nicer and larger units at the back have lots of light and roomy showers. Private parking. Rates: $5 for small units; $12 d, $18 t, for larger units.

Not reviewed is the newly opened **Iguana Lodge** (tel. 679-9015, fax 679-9054), described as having "a variety of rooms ($50 double, including breakfast) with green areas, a recreation area for children, and incredible views of Bahía Salinas." It's next to Amalia Inn. Reports are that the old wooden house is "worn around the edges." Don't worry about the iguana on the living room table. He's stuffed, as are the others!

Hospedaje Pensión La Tica, opposite the new bus station, has very basic, tiny but clean rooms with communal bath. Rate: $3. The **Cabinas Maryfel** (tel. 679-9096), nearby, is said to be better.

Colinas del Norte (tel. 679-9132, fax 679-9064) is a cattle *finca* about three km north of La Cruz. Its rustic lodge has private baths. Not reviewed. It offers horseback rides.

Food
The elegant **Mirador y Restaurante Ehecatl** (Ehecatl is a Chorotega Indian name meaning "God of Wind") sits atop the scarp slope with superb vistas across Bahía Salinas—a fabulous place to enjoy superb seafoods and salads. **Bar y Restaurante Thelma** (tel. 679-9150) is clean and has reasonably priced food; the friendly owner is Thelma Jiménez Reyes. Also recommended for cheap *casados* and *gallo pinto* is **Restaurante Dariri**, two blocks south of the main square. It's 200 meters beyond the gas station, on the road to Peñas Blancas. Other options include **Restaurante Pan Americano, Soda La Esquina,** and **El Churassco,** three km north of town, along a dirt road to the east.

Services
A **Banco Nacional** (tel. 679-9110) is opposite the gas station immediately as you enter town. The **police** (Guardia Rural) telephone is 679-9197.

Getting There
Buses depart San José for La Cruz from Calle 16, Avenidas 3/5 (Carsol, tel. 224-1968) daily at 5 and 7:45 a.m., and 1:30 and 4:15 p.m. The bus continues to the Nicaraguan border at Peñas Blancas. Buy your ticket in advance. Slower buses also operate from Liberia. Buses for San José depart La Cruz at 7:15 and 10:30 a.m., and 3:30 and 6 p.m., though these originate at the Nicaraguan border and are often full by the time they pull into La Cruz. You can buy tickets from the *pulpería* (tel. 679-9108) next to the bus station.

BAHÍA SALINAS

Beyond Mirador Ehecatl, 100 meters west of the plaza in La Cruz, a rugged dirt road drops steeply to the horseshoe-shaped Bahía Salinas, complete with a fabulous beach and staggering views that cry out for resort development. The coastal plains are lined with salt pans that attract wading birds. **Isla Bolaños** lies offshore (see below). If you fancy peace and tranquility, go now! The resort boom that is turning Bahía

Culebra, a few miles south, into a mini-Acapulco threatens to spread north to Bahía Salinas. An ambitious resort plan has been unveiled that will encompass a windsurfing village, golf course, and big hotels. Construction was slated to begin in mid-1995.

Beyond the hamlet of **Puerto Soley,** the road splits. The right fork leads to **Jobo,** a funky little fishing village just inland from Bahía Jobo. Continue straight and you'll reach Manzanillo. Colorful fishing boats—perches for pelicans—and views across the Golfo de Santa Elena make up for the pebbly beach; the road to the left leads to Brasilito, on Bahía Junquillal (see above). Turn right in Jobo and then left at a Y-junction for the exquisite beach at Playa Rajada; turn right for Playa Jobo.

Accommodations and Food
Las Salinas (Apdo. 449, San José 1007, tel. 233-6912 or 228-2447) is a trailer park with cabinas in pretty grounds right next to the beach. The three cabinas hold five people each ($38). The super-friendly owner may have added 10 rooms by the time you read this. Private bathrooms outside. RVs and campers are charged $4 per person. Horseback rides are offered. Salt ponds behind the site are good for birding; the sheltered bay is superb for swimming. Very peaceful. The restaurant is basic but was slated for an upgrade. You can also eat at **La Fonda Restaurante,** a funky *soda* that serves the salt-pan workers. There are

Bahía Salinas

two **campsites** at the hamlet of Brasilito. If you want to stay in Jobo, ask: someone is sure to offer to put you up for the night.

El Diamante, just before reaching Puerto Soley, has been recommended for its seafood dishes.

Getting There
Buses depart La Cruz daily at 5:30 and 10:30 a.m., and 1 p.m. for Puerto Soley and Jobo. Return buses depart Jobo 90 minutes later. A taxi will cost about $3 one-way to Puerto Soley, $8 to Jobo.

BOLAÑOS ISLAND WILDLIFE REFUGE

Bolaños Island is a rugged, oval-shaped rocky crag, 25 hectares in area, in Salinas Bay, about one km off Punta Zacate. The island rises dramatically to a height of 81 meters and looks, as Herman Melville described the Galapagos, "much as the world at large might, after a penal conflagration." This pocket of northwest Guanacaste is one of the driest in the country, with less than 150 cm of annual rainfall. It is grown over with drought-resistant shrubs, which feed on the mists and occasional rain. The predominant species are the *paira,* which sheds its leaves during the dry season, and lemon wood, a woody vine that forms dense thickets that serve as nesting sites for island birds.

Bolaños Island was declared a national wildlife refuge to protect one of only four nesting sites in Costa Rica for the brown pelican, and the only known nesting site for the American oyster-catcher. As many as 200 frigate birds also nest here during the Jan.-March mating season. The birds nest on *alfaje* trees, predominantly on the southwestern cliffs. Strong winds are the primary reason the frigate birds nest here. Because they have small bodies and tiny feet with very wide wings and extremely long tails, they cannot run to take off but need a high ledge from which to launch themselves into flight. High winds blow almost nonstop Dec.-April, giving strong lift to their large wingspans.

Visitors are not allowed to set foot on the island, but you can hire a boat and guide in Puerto Soley or Jobo to take you within 50 meters.

EAST OF LA CRUZ

A turnoff at the police security checkpoint three km south of La Cruz leads east to Upala, in the northern lowlands. Volcán Orosí looms to the south. About 15 km along the road you begin to feel the influence of the Caribbean. Vegetation and microclimates can change dramatically within a few kilometers. East of Hacienda Los Inocentes and the Río Sábalo, dry deciduous forest gives way to evergreen forest cloaked in epiphytes, while flatlands give way to rolling hills covered with citrus plantations and grasslands that are green year-round. The palette-bright blossoming trees of Guanacaste fade away. In a span of some 10 kilometers you pass into the realm of the northern lowlands.

Hacienda Los Inocentes
This beautiful hacienda (Apdo. 1370, Heredia 3000, tel. 265-5484 or 679-9190, fax 237-8282 or 265-5217), 16 km east of the Pan-American Hwy., has one of the most stunning settings in Costa Rica, with the great ascendant bulk of Orosí looming ominously to the south, cloud-shrouded and thick with tropical moist forest. The vintage lodge—built in 1890 of gleaming teak by the grandfather of Violeta de Chamorro, president of Nicaragua—is made of magnificent hardwoods and has 11 modest but pleasant rooms surrounded by a wide veranda with wicker rockers and hammocks for relaxing and savoring the views and sunsets. Two suites have private bathrooms upstairs; the other rooms have private bathrooms downstairs. A newly built annex offers four extra rooms, and there are two new cabins down the hill. Rates: $56 per person including three meals ($28 room only). Economy cabins are also on the grounds. The restaurant serves pleasing meals, and there's a small bar.

The lodge, now a dedicated eco-lodge, specializes in horseback nature rides ($10 half-day with guide) to see howler, capuchin, and rare spider monkeys, sloths, anteaters, coatimundis, and white-tailed deer. Birds—especially toucans, oropendolas, and collared aracaris—are prolific. Garrulous parrots hang around the hacienda grounds, as does a small deer, which will feed from your hands. Alas, when I returned

Hacienda Los
Inocentes, near La
Cruz, with Orosí
volcano in
background

CHRISTOPHER P. BAKER

in 1995, the mooing was gone, for in 1994 Los Inocentes, once the center for 8,000 head of cattle, ceased operations as a working hacienda. The estate once belonged to the Inocentes family, which owned almost one-third of Guanacaste. Instead of getting up at dawn to help milk the cows, you can do so now for horseback rides to the very summit of Orosí. A taxi from La Cruz costs about $15 one-way.

Santa Cecilia

The village of Santa Cecilia straddles the regional boundary at the end of the paved road. A rough road continues east to Upala (51 km) and Caño Negro National Wildlfe Refuge (see the "Ciudad Quesada to Los Chiles" in the Northern Lowlands chapter). Another dirt road leads north from Santa Cecilia (you pass a bullfighting arena) to the hamlet of **La Virgen** (seven km). The drive is worth it for the stupendous vistas down over Lake Nicaragua, with classically conical volcanoes in the distance.

The communal **telephone** (tel. 679-9105) is in the *pulpería* next to Bar El Pescadito. The only place to stay in Santa Cecilia is the **Hotel /Bar/Restaurante Chuli,** with five clean, simple, and breezy rooms (no fans) with large beds and shared bath ($4 per person). The lively restaurant has walls painted with parrots, etc., in bright pastels.

A bus departs La Cruz for Santa Cecilia daily at 5 and 10:30 a.m., and 1:30, 7, and 7:30 p.m.

PEÑAS BLANCAS

Peñas Blancas, 19 km north of La Cruz, is the border post for Nicaragua. The Costa Rican border post is open 8 a.m.-noon, and 1-6 p.m. A minibus operates between the Costa Rican border post and Nicaraguan immigration, four km away. The bus stop is 800 meters north of the Costa Rican post. There's no village at Peñas Blancas.

Accommodations

The Italian owner of a nearby cattle ranch was due to open a deluxe lodge and resort—**Las Colinas del Norte** (tel. 679-9132)—about three km south of the border. Plans included a large pool, tennis courts, a disco (converted from a cattle pen), and even a casino, plus horseback riding through 270 hectares of tropical forest and plains. A spacious restaurant will feature a clay oven and serve pizzas, pastas and seafood. Cheeses are homemade on site using milk from the ranch's heifers. The bar has a resident pianist and singer, Al Moreno. A yacht will be on hand for cruises, and tours will be offered across the border. Let's hope the disco isn't a cattle market! Rate: $25 per person.

Border Crossing

A tourist visa into Nicaragua costs $2. U.S. citizens do not need visas. Entry visas for Canadi-

ans and others cost $25 and take a minimum of 24 hours to obtain in San José. Contact the Nicaraguan Consulate (tel. 233-3479 or 233-8747; hours 8 a.m.-noon, weekdays) at Avenida Central, Calle 27, in the Barrio La California suburb, in San José.

You can cross into Nicaragua for 72 hours and renew your 30- or 90-day Costa Rica visa if you want to stay in Costa Rica longer. A three-day transit visa costs $15. If your visa has already expired, you will need to get an exit visa in San José, otherwise you will be turned back at the border. You can obtain the visa—$40 for exiting by land, plus $2.50 per month fine—from the immigration office at Calle 21, Avenidas 6/8 in San José (hours: Mon.-Fri. 8:30 a.m.-3:30 p.m.).

When you arrive, you must get your passport stamped at the window outside the border post. Change money into Nicaraguan *córdobas* here ($1 = six *córdobas* = about 165 *colones*). You must then walk the 600 meters of No-Man's Land to the Nicaraguan side, where shuttle buses take you to the Nicaraguan immigration building. Here you'll receive two slips of paper (five *córdobas* and US$2, respectively), and then complete a Spanish-language information sheet before receiving your entry visa.

There's a basic restaurant near the Nicaraguan immigration office. **Buses** (66 cents) depart from here every hour for **Rivas,** a small town about 40 km north of the border.

Services
The Peñas Blancas **bus terminal** contains the **immigration office** (tel. 679-9025), a **Banco Anglo Costarricense** (tel. 679-9029), and the **Restaurante Peñas Blancas,** which is well-stocked with essentials such as batteries, cookies, and booze. There's a **Costa Rican Tourism Insitute** office (ICT, tel. 679-9025) here, too. Change your money before crossing into Nicaragua: You get a better exchange rate on the Costa Rican side.

Getting There
Buses depart San José for Peñas Blancas from Calle 14, Avenida 3/5 (Carsol:, tel. 224-1968) daily at 5 and 7:45 a.m., and 1:30 and 4:15 p.m. Six hours. Buy your ticket in advance. Buses depart Liberia for Peñas Blancas from Avenida 5, Calle 14 at 5:30, 8:30, and 11 a.m., and 2 and 6 p.m. Buses depart Peñas Blancas at 6, 7:15, 9:30 and 10:30 a.m., and 12:30, 2:30, 3:30, 5, and 6 p.m.

CATHY CARLSON

NICOYA PENINSULA
INTRODUCTION

The Nicoya Peninsula is a broad, hooked protuberance—130 km long from Playa Panamá to Cabo Blanco, and 60 km wide at its broadest—separated from the Guanacaste plains by the Río Tempisque and Gulf of Nicoya. The region has traditionally been one of the country's least developed. However, more than 70% of Costa Rica's coastal resort infrastructure is in the province and the services (including paved roads) that have long lagged behind are now arriving posthaste. A long dry season, warm waters, and the nation's finest beaches lure visitors seeking the joys of the tropics. Italians are particularly enamored of Nicoya's beaches and from Tamarindo south they, along with Swiss, recently opened some splendid hotels, restaurants, and bars. The peninsula has very few large towns (none on the coast), and long lonesome stretches of coast help preserve an atmosphere of serenity, though this is changing quickly.

The government, anxious to reap the tourist boom, has targeted Nicoya for the kind of resort developments that have swallowed up whole oceanfronts elsewhere in the isthmus of Central America. Costa Rica is positioning itself to compete as a beach resort destination on a par with Mexico's Cancún and Ixtapa. The center of this frenzy is Bahía de Culebra, where the Gulf of Papagayo Project is turning a 2,025-hectare swath into a massive resort complex complete with marina, golf course, and (eventually) as many as 20,000 hotel rooms!

Beaches here come in every hue and every shape, although only a select few compare with those of Cancún, Tahiti, or the Caribbean islands. And don't expect the same wide selection of romantic resorts as you'll find on the Mexican Riviera or in the Caribbean. That, too, is changing as a fistful of five-star resorts emerge. Budget travelers are well served throughout, though prices are higher than elsewhere in the country, often inordinately so. Reservations are highly recommended for weekends and holiday periods.

Away from the coast, the region is mostly hills and low mountains, cut by deep valleys and much denuded for pasture. The region is not blessed with the diversity of natural attractions found elsewhere in the country. But two nature experiences stand out as shining stars: a visit to the Guanacaste Marine Turtle National Park to see the leatherback turtles laying eggs, or the Ostional National Wildlife Refuge during a mass invasion of olive ridley turtles. These are, for me, singularly the most momentous guaranteed wildlife encounters in Costa Rica. And Curú and Cabo Blanco wildlife refuges offer their own nature highlights.

Gas stations are in short supply away from Route 21, bus service between beaches is ephemeral, and there is as yet no single road linking the northern beaches, so it is often necessary to backtrack inland to travel to the next beach north or south. This, too, is an area where a good wad of cash is advisable, as banks are few and far between. A growing number of hotels will gladly exchange traveler's checks or dollars. Campers should take all supplies with them.

Climate

It's no coincidence that the majority of Costa Rica's resort hotels are nestled along the shores of the Pacific northwest, where sun is the name of the game. Best time to visit is Dec.-April, when rain is virtually unheard of (average annual rainfall is less than 150 centimeters in some areas). The rainy season generally arrives in May and lasts until November. September and October are the wettest months. The so-called Papagayo winds—heavy northerlies *(nortes)*—blow strongly January (sometimes earlier) through March. Gusts of 100 km/h are not uncommon. Surfers rave about the rainy season (May-Oct.), when swells are consistent and waves—fast and tubular—can be 1.5 meters or more. When the Papagayo winds roar ashore, however, swells become inconsistent, with waves normally around one meter high.

History

The peninsula was colonized early by Spaniards, who began the cattle industry that predominates in the region to this day. At that time, the Nicoya Peninsula had long been the heartland of the culturally advanced Chorotega Indians, who celebrated the Fiesta del Maíz ("Festival of Corn") and worshiped the sun with the public sacrifice of young virgins and ritual cannibalism. Nicoya is today, as then, the capital of the region: the Spaniards found well-defined trade routes radiating northward from this small village all the way to Nicaragua.

The people who today inhabit the province are tied to old bloodlines. They live and work on the cusp between cultures. In Guaitil, for example, Chorotega women have kept stirred the spark of a nearly dead culture by making pottery in the same fashion their ancestors did one thousand years ago (the battle to maintain traditional influences has also kept kindled the matriarchal hierarchy: women run the businesses and sustain families and village structures). Fortunately, a renaissance of cultural pride is emerging, fostered by tourist interest.

During the colonial era, the area formed part of Guanacaste, a separate province. The province was delivered to Nicaragua in 1787, and to Costa Rica in 1812. After independence, Guanacaste's loyalties were split, with the Nicoyans favoring union with Costa Rica while the rest of Guana-

Oxcarts are among the road hazards in Nicoya.

CHRISTOPHER P. BAKER

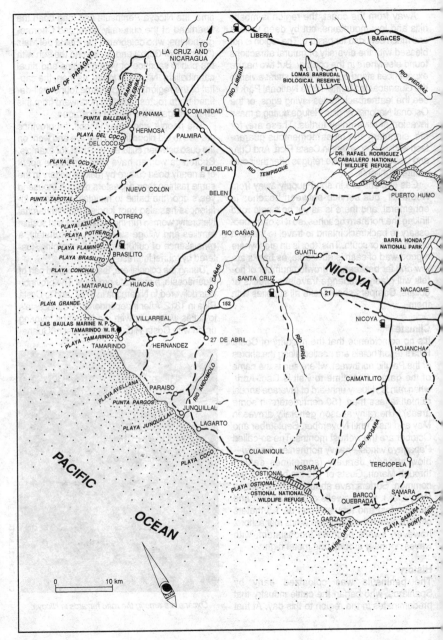

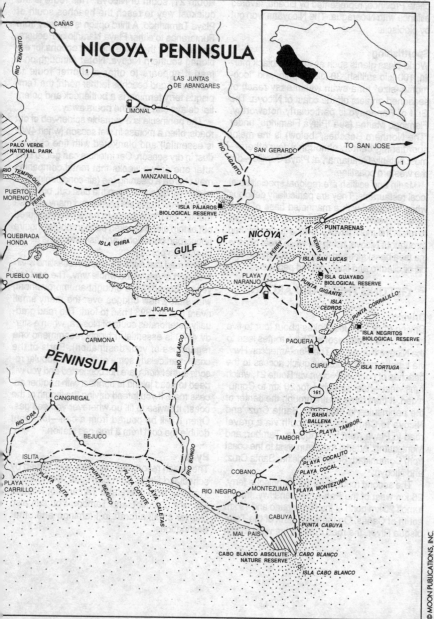

NICOYA PENINSULA

caste Province, represented by Liberia, favored alliance with Nicaragua. The Nicoyans won out by plebiscite.

Sportfishing

World-class giants such as 400-kilo black marlin, 100-kilo sailfish, 30-kilo dolphin, and "locomotive-size" tuna swim within easy reach of seasoned anglers off the coast of Nicoya. The Gulf of Papagayo is particularly noteworthy. Flamingo Marina (see "Playa Flamingo" under "The Northern Beaches," below) is the major sportfishing center, although a few others—most notably Guanamar, at Playa Carrillo—dot the western coastline.

Marlin and sailfish are regional specialties at local restaurants. They are particularly delicious when prepared with a marinated base of fresh herbs and olive oil, and seared over an open grill to retain the moist flavor. Ceviche is also favored throughout Nicoya, using the white meat of corvina (sea bass) steeped in lemon juice mixed with dill or cilantro and finely cut red peppers.

GETTING THERE AND AROUND

Driving

Driving from San José takes about four to five hours to the coast resorts. Three routes lead to the Nicoya Peninsula. The Pan-American Hwy. via Liberia gives relatively quick access to the beaches of northern Nicoya via Route 21, which runs west—ruler straight—for 20 km to Comunidad. It then turns south through the center of the peninsula via Filadelfia, Santa Cruz, and Nicoya to Carmona, then south via a gravel road to Playa Naranjo, Paquera, Tambor, and Montezuma. Arterial roads run west to the coast from Comunidad, Belén, Filadelfia, Santa Cruz, and Nicoya.

The second route is via the Tempisque ferry, 26 km west of the Pan-American Hwy. from a turnoff 20 km north of the Río Lagarto and 19 km south of Cañas. On the west bank of the Tempisque River, the road runs 15 km west to join Route 21, south of Nicoya. This route is the quickest way to reach the beaches south of Playa Tamarindo. A third option is the ferry from Puntarenas to either Playa Naranjo or Paquera, farther south; these are the best options for exploring southern Nicoya. **Note:** Although on a map it appears to offer a shorter route to Tamarindo and beaches farther north, the Tempisque ferry terminal is a bottleneck and potential delays can steal the hours away.

The peninsula is a veritable spiderweb of dirt roads, often a morass in wet season (when 4WD is essential) and blanketed with fine choking dust in dry season. Car interiors can get so dirty after one or two weeks that rental companies may charge a cleaning fee (air-conditioning and sealed windows will keep the dust out, but that's no fun). Few roads are paved, and many of those marked on maps seem to have been conjured out of thin air by drunken cartographers. Inquire about road conditions, and ask directions as frequently as possible.

The road that skirts the western coastline is virtually dirt or gravel the whole way. The past few years, though, have brought an improvement, with sturdy new bridges over the many small rivers that in 1993 I had to ford. The road gradually deteriorates south of Nosara, when a sturdy 4WD is essential (I highly recommend one regardless of your destination). Parts of the coast, particularly some of the more popular resorts farther north, are not connected and you will need to head inland to connect with another access road. If you intend driving the length of the coast, it's wise to fill up wherever you see gas. Often it will be poured from a can—for about double the cost from a true gas station.

By Air

The beach resorts are relatively well served by scheduled flights from San José. SANSA and Travelair both operate to Tamarindo, Nosara, Sámara (Carrillo), and Tambor. You can also charter small aircraft to Flamingo and other destinations.

NICOYA AND VICINITY

From Puerto Moreno, on the western bank of the Tempisque, a paved road leads west for 15 km to the main highway, which runs north to south through the peninsula. You'll find a **gas station** at the junction at **Pueblo Viejo,** plus a restaurant, **Las Girasolas,** two km before Pueblo Viejo. Nicoya, the regional capital, is 15 km north of the junction; Playa Naranjo is 54 km south (another car and passenger ferry operates to Puntarenas from there). The paved road runs south as far as Paquera (a third ferry serves Puntarenas from here), where a dirt road continues to Montezuma and Cabo Blanco. To the north it leads via Nicoya to Santa Cruz, Filadelfia, and Liberia and the Pan-American Highway. Smaller roads reach out like fingers to the coast.

NICOYA

Nicoya, about 78 km south of Liberia, is Costa Rica's oldest town and a pleasant place to stay overnight. It was the nation's first colonial city. The beautiful colonial **Church of San Blas,** built in the 16th century, contains a museum of pre-Columbian silver, bronze, and copper icons, and other objects (hours: 8 a.m.-noon and 2-6 p.m.; closed Wednesday and Sunday). Two calcified skeletons were recently found beneath the church during restoration.

Try to visit on 12 December, when villagers carry a dark-skinned image of La Virgen de Guadalupe through the streets accompanied by flutes, drums, and dancers. The festival combines the Catholic celebration of the Virgin of Guadalupe with the traditions of the Chorotega Indian legend of La Yeguita ("Little Mare"), which honors a legend about a mare that interceded to prevent twin brothers from fighting to the death for the love of an Indian princess.

The religious ceremony is a good excuse for bullfights, explosive fireworks *(bombas),* concerts, and general merriment. Many locals get sozzled on *chicha,* a heady brew made from fermented corn and sugar and drunk from hollow gourds. Ancient Indian music is played, and it is easy to imagine a time when Nicoya was the center of the Chorotega culture.

Accommodations

By far the nicest place to stay in town is **Hotel Curime** (tel. 685-5238), on the road to Playa Sámara. It has 20 a/c cabinas and five rooms with private baths with hot water in landscaped grounds. It has a swimming pool and children's pool surrounded by little *ranchitas,* plus a restaurant. Rates: $26 s, $50 d, $61 t.

The **Hotel Yenny** (tel. 685-5245 or 685-5050) reportedly offers good value. It has 24 rooms with a/c, private baths, and TV. Rates: $15 s, $20 d. Also try **Cabinas Loma Bonita** (tel. 655-5269), which has 11 rooms with private baths (about $20).

The pleasing **Hotel Las Tinajas** (tel. 685-5081 or 685-5777) has 24 spacious, light, and clean rooms with fans and private baths with cold water. Family rooms are very large. Rates: $10 s, $13 d (students with ID get $2 discount). **Hotel Elegancia** (tel. 685-5159) has six large, well-kept rooms with lots of light plus fans, and private baths with cold water. Rate: $2.50 per person.

Another basic but adequate option is the **Pensión Venecia** (tel. 685-5326), next to the Hotel Elegancia. It has 28 clean and airy rooms with fans, some with private baths. Secure parking. Rates: from $5 s, $8 d. More basic is the **Hotel Alí** (tel. 685-5148), with 10 dingy rooms with smelly bathrooms ($6 d). Perhaps the best budget bet in town is the **Hotel Chorotega** (tel. 685-5245), with 24 spic-and-span rooms with private baths ($10 d).

You might want to give **Pensión Familiar** a miss: it's supposedly a nest for love (or is it lust?) by the hour.

Food

The town's significant Chinese population makes itself felt. I recommend **Restaurante Cecilia,** on the plaza. It has friendly owners and reasonably priced dishes (e.g., rice and shrimp for $2). **Restaurante Jade** and the **Restaurante Teyet,** in front of Hotel Jenny, are also recom-

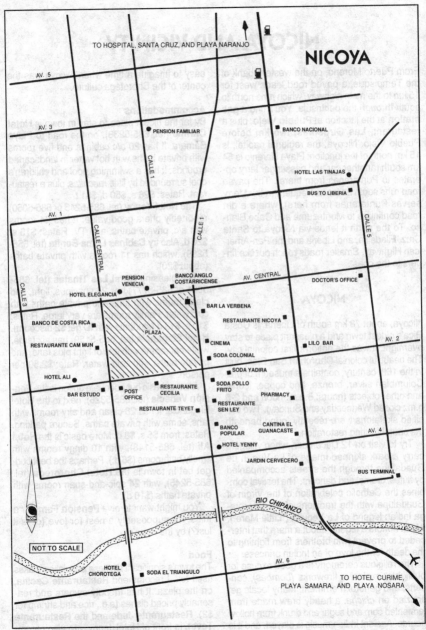

NICOYA

TO HOSPITAL, SANTA CRUZ, AND PLAYA NARANJO

AV. 5

AV. 3

CALLE 1

PENSION FAMILIAR

BANCO NACIONAL

HOTEL LAS TINAJAS

BUS TO LIBERIA

CALLE 5

AV. 1

CALLE CENTRAL

CALLE 1

CALLE 3

PENSION VENECIA

HOTEL ELEGANCIA

BANCO ANGLO COSTARRICENSE

AV. CENTRAL

DOCTOR'S OFFICE

BAR LA VERBENA

RESTAURANTE NICOYA

BANCO DE COSTA RICA

PLAZA

CINEMA

LILO BAR

AV. 2

RESTAURANTE CAM MUN

SODA COLONIAL

SODA YADIRA

HOTEL ALI

BAR ESTUDO

POST OFFICE

RESTAURANTE CECILIA

SODA POLLO FRITO

PHARMACY

RESTAURANTE TEYET

RESTAURANTE SEN LEY

CANTINA EL GUANACASTE

BANCO POPULAR

HOTEL YENNY

JARDIN CERVECERO

BUS TERMINAL

RIO CHIPANZO

NOT TO SCALE

HOTEL CHOROTEGA

SODA EL TRIANGULO

AV. 6

TO HOTEL CURIME, PLAYA SAMARA, AND PLAYA NOSARA

mended. There are *sodas* on three corners of the plaza: **Kiosko Alí,** opposite Restaurante Cecilia, looks the best. **Restaurante Nicoya** is also recommended; it has a pleasant ambience, as does the open-air **Café Daniela** (tel. 686-6148), which serves pizzas, fresh-baked breads and cookies, and has reasonable Costa Rican fare at ludicrously low prices ($2 at most to fill up). More interesting yet is the **Cantina El Guanacaste,** a working-class bar with fantastic decor: deer hides and antlers on the walls, which are painted with cowboy scenes.

Services

There's a **tourist information** office at Bar El Molino (tel. 685-5001) next to the hospital. The town is replete with banks. Take your pick: **Banco Popular** (tel. 685-5167), **Banco Nacional** (tel. 658-5366) on the road into town from San José, and **Banco Anglo Costarricense** (tel. 685-5267) and **Banco de Costa Rica** (tel. 685-5110), both on the main square. Dr. Hugo Lopez Rodas has a **medical clinic** (tel. 685-5805). You'll find a **pharmacy,** Farmacia Ramirez (tel. 685-5539; hours: 7:30 a.m.-7 p.m., Saturday 7:30 a.m.-6 p.m.), 75 meters north of the Central Market.

Transportation

Buses depart San José for Nicoya from Calle 14, Avenidas 3/5 (Empresa Alfaro, tel. 222-2750), at 6, 8, and 10 a.m, noon, and 1, 2:30, 3, and 5 p.m. (six hours; $5). Return buses depart Nicoya for San José at 4, 7:30, and 9 a.m., noon, and 2:30 and 4:55 p.m. Buses also depart for Santa Cruz hourly, 6 a.m.-9 p.m.; for Liberia hourly, 5 a.m.-7 p.m.; for Playa Naranjo at 5:15 a.m. and 1 p.m.; for Sámara and Carillo at 8 a.m. and 3 and 4 p.m.; and for Nosara at 1 p.m. Buses also serve other towns throughout the peninsula from

---

NICOYA EMERGENCY TELEPHONE NUMBERS

Police
   (Guardia Rural) .... 117 or 685-5559
Red Cross 685-5458
Doctor 686-6372
Hospital 685-5066

---

here. The bus terminal is at the southeast corner of town, on Calle 5.

BARRA HONDA NATIONAL PARK

Seeking a Jules Verne adventure? Then this 2,295-hectare park, 13 km west of the Río Tempisque, is for you. Distinct in the Costa Rican park system, Barra Honda is known for its limestone caverns dating back some 70 million years. Remarkably, the caverns have been known to modern man for only two decades; 42 have been discovered to date. Pre-Columbian peoples, however, knew of them, and skeletons, utensils, and ornaments dating back to 300 B.C. have been discovered inside the Nicoa Cave. Access to the cavern is via a 10-meter chute and a vertical 20-meter descent to the floor of Hall Number One.

The deepest cavern thus far explored is the Santa Ana Cave, which is thought to be at least 240 meters deep (descents have been made to 180 meters). One of its features is the handsome Hall of Pearls, full of stalactites and stalagmites. Another cavern with decorative formations is Terciopelo Cave, named for the snake of that name found dead at the bottom of the cave during the first exploration, and reached via an exciting 30-meter vertical descent to a sloping plane that leads to the bottom, 63 meters down.

Mushroom Hall is named for the shape of its calcareous formations. The Hall of the Caverns has large Medusa-like formations, including a figure resembling a lion's head. And columns in Hall Number Five, and "The Organ" in Terciopelo, produce musical tones when struck. Beyond the Hall, at a point called the Summit, you can sign your name in a book placed there by speleologists of the University of Costa Rica. Some of the caverns are frequented by bats, including the Pozo Hediondo ("Fetid Pit"), which is named for the quantity of excrement accumulated by its abundant bat population. Blind salamanders and endemic fish species have also evolved in the caves.

The caves are not easily accessible and are risky for those not duly equipped. You must be accompanied by a guide, who can be hired from **Proyecto Las Delicias** at the entrance (tel. 685-5580; see "Accommodations," below), or by calling 685-5455 or 685-5406 (Spanish only). You

can also arrange guides through the Park Service or the Speleology Group of the University of Costa Rica (tel. 225-5555 or 253-7818). Groups will need to call the National Parks office in San José (Calle 25, Avenidas 8/10, tel. 233-5284) or the regional headquarters in Bagaces (tel. 671-1062) several days in advance for authorization to enter the caves. Descents are allowed during dry season only, but, reportedly, not during Holy Week. (Also see "Tours," below.) Note: Two German tourists died of dehydration in 1993 after getting lost while hiking without a guide.

Above ground, the hilly dry forest terrain is a refuge for howler monkeys, deer, macaws,

agoutis, peccaries, kinkajous, anteaters, and many bird species, including scarlet macaws. The park tops out at Mount Barra Honda (442 meters), which has intriguing rock formations and provides an excellent view of the Gulf of Nicoya. While here, check out Las Cascadas, strange limestone formations formed by calcareous sedimentation along a riverbed. Hire a guide; the pathways leading throughout the park are convoluted.

Entrance: $15 walk-in, $5 advance purchase.

Accommodations
Proyectos Las Delicias is a community pro-

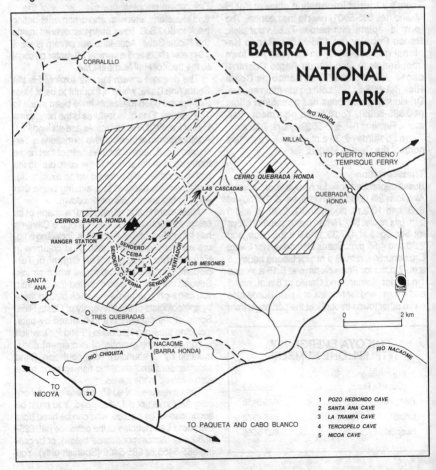

BARRA HONDA NATIONAL PARK

CORRALILLO

RIO HONDA

MILLAL

TO PUERTO MORENO / TEMPISQUE FERRY

CERRO QUEBRADA HONDA

LAS CASCADAS

QUEBRADA HONDA

CERROS BARRA HONDA

RANGER STATION

SENDERO CEIBA

SENDERO CAVERNA

SENDERO VENTADOR

LOS MESONES

SANTA ANA

TRES QUEBRADAS

0   2 km

NACAOME (BARRA HONDA)

RIO CHIQUITA

RIO NACAOME

TO NICOYA

21

TO PAQUETA AND CABO BLANCO

1 POZO HEDIONDO CAVE
2 SANTA ANA CAVE
3 LA TRAMPA CAVE
4 TERCIOPELO CAVE
5 NICOA CAVE

ject to provide employment for the local populace and engage it in conservation. In addition to providing guide services and tasty meals cooked in a *leña* (wood stove), the project offers three basic cabins with bath ($12 per person). **Hawkview Mountain** (tel. 237-8959) is a campsite also offering guided tours; it's beside the main road near the turnoff for Barra Honda.

Camping
You can camp at Proyectos Las Delicias ($2). There's a campsite close to the Terciopelo Cavern, about 400 meters from the ranger station. It has showers and toilets (dirty), plus picnic tables and water ($1 per day). The ranger station has basic trail maps.

Tours
Costa Rica Adventures and Wildlife (tel. 800-497-3422; in Costa Rica, tel. 255-2463, fax 255-3573) has a four-day caving trip, with accommodation at Rancho Humo ($437). Equipment and support is provided. **Intertur Agencia de Viajes** (Apdo. 2150, San José 1000, tel. 253-7503, fax 324-6308) has a three-day caving tour (on request). Also try **Ríos Tropicales** (tel. 323-6455) and **Turinsa Receptivo** (tel. 221-9185) for spelunking. **Olman Cubillo** (tel. 685-5580) is a private guide; he speaks no English.

Getting There
An all-weather gravel road leads to Nacaome (Barra Honda), four km north of the Nicoya-Tempisque highway (the turnoff is one km east of Pueblo Viejo, on the road between Nicoya and the Tempisque ferry; watch for the signs). Beyond Nacaome, the road climbs steeply in place^, all the while deteriorating (4WD recommended); signs point the way to the entrance, about six km further via Santa Ana. A bus departs Nicoya for Santa Ana and Nacaome daily at noon; you can walk from either to the park entrance. You can also enter the park from the east via a road from Quebrada Honda; not recommended.

PUERTO HUMO

A road leads northeast 27 km from Nicoya via Corralillo to Puerto Humo, on the Río Tempisque. Puerto Humo is the gateway to Palo Verde National Park. A bus leaves Nicoya daily at 2 p.m.

The newly constructed **Hotel Rancho Humo** (Apdo. 322, San José 1007, tel. 255-2463, fax 255-3573), above the riverside, has 24 a/c rooms, a swimming pool, and a *palenque*-roofed restaurant. Rates: $78 s/d, $19 extra person. At the bottom of the hill on which the hotel sits is **Zapanti Lodge,** with eight rustic rooms with fans and shared baths. Part of the Rancho Humo complex, it is built as a vivid re-creation of an Indian village and features meals prepared in traditional mud ovens at the restaurant. Rates: $21 s, $38 d, $43 t. The Rancho Humo Ecotourist Center offers boat tours up the Tempisque and Bebedero rivers.

CHIRA ISLAND

Despite its size—10 km east to west, six km north to south—Isla Chira is virtually uninhabited. It has no hotels. The island, Costa Rica's second largest, is separated from the Nicoya Peninsula by the one-km-wide Estero Puncha. It is surrounded by a maze of mangroves popular with pelicans and frigate birds. A few dozen fishermen and farmers eke out a meager living, including Gerardo Seas, who oversees the *salinas*, or salt pans, on the shores of **Hacienda Encantato.** His father came to the island in 1932 with little more than two oxen and a cart. He bought the salt pans and built a processing plant using his own ingenuity. Gerardo welcomes groups. I explored Chira while cruising aboard the *Temptress* (see below); Gerardo gave us a tour of the farm and *salinas* on a flatbed towed by a tractor! Very interesting. Especially noteworthy were the bats in the salt shed. The salt pans are popular with roseate spoonbills and other wading birds. Gerardo's wife, who raises chihuahuas, served ceviche and cold beers. Gerardo will rent horses.

Local legends about the island include that of La Mona, a woman who turns into a monkey after midnight to haunt drunks and men cheating on their wives.

Transportation
Local fishermen in Puntarenas, Puerto Moreno (on the west bank of the Río Tempisque), or

frigate birds
at Chira Island

CHRISTOPHER P. BAKER

Puerto Jesús (20 km southeast of Nicoya) may rent a boat to take you there. **Cruceros del Sur** (Apdo. 1198, San José 1200, tel. 220-1927, fax 220-2103) includes a day visit to Chira as part of a one-week natural-history cruise of the Pacific coast aboard the 68-passenger eco-cruise ship *Temptress*. Highly recommended.

Blue Sea Cruises (Apdo. 64, San José 1000, tel. 233-7274, fax 233-5555) includes Chira on a one-day cruise of the Gulf of Nicoya from Puntarenas. **Universal Tropical Nature Tours** (Apdo. 4276, San José 1000, tel. 255-4274, fax 257-0181) features a visit to Chira as part of its three-day "Cowboy Country Adventure" ($295).

SANTA CRUZ

This peaceful and colorful town, 20 km north of Nicoya, is gateway to Playas Tamarindo and Junquillal, 30 km to the west. The ruin of an old church (toppled by an earthquake in 1950) stands next to its modern replacement—a quasi-miniature version of the modern cathedrals of Liverpool and Brasilia. The gracious Plaza de Los Mangos is shaded by mango trees and bright bougainvillea, whose warm tropical hues match those of the magnificent stained-glass windows in the new church. Alas, a ruinous fire swept through the historic center in March 1993, claiming many fine buildings.

Santa Cruz—declared the National Folklore City—is renowned for its traditional music, food, and dance (such as the Punto Guanacasteco), which can be sampled during fiestas each 15 January and 25 July, when the town's cultural heritage blossoms. Afterward, life returns to normal . . . which seems to consist of sitting on rockers on verandas. For entertainment, take your pick of the local bars. If your Spanish is good, you might check out a movie at **Cine Adelita,** on the east side of the old church tower.

The road from Nicoya is lined with stalls selling pottery from Guaitil, 10 km east of Santa Cruz, which has revitalized its Indian pot-making heritage.

Accommodations

The casually elegant, motel-style **Hotel Diriá** (Apdo. 58, Santa Cruz, tel. 680-0080, fax 680-0442) is centered on a pool and grounds full of palms. Some cabina-style rooms have doubles, others have two single beds. The breezy El Bambú restaurant has bamboo walls and overlooks the pool. Pleasant decor. It also offers a video room and live marimba bands. Rates: $24 s, $35 d, $40 t. A slightly cheaper and second-best motel-style option is **Hotel La Estancia** (tel. 680-0476), which has 17 very pleasing modern units with fans, TVs, and private baths with hot water. Spacious family rooms come with four beds. Some rooms are dark. Secure parking. Laundry service. Rates: $16 s, $22 d ($4 additional).

There's not much to choose from in the way of budget options. The hardy can try **Pensión Pampera,** five blocks east of the old plaza: it's very basic and dingy. Rooms ($4 per person) have shared baths. **Hospedaje Avellanas** (tel. 680-0808) offers rooms in a family home; some shared, others with private baths with cold water. Rates: $5-8. Other basic hotels to consider are **Pensión Anatolia, Hotel Isabel** (tel. 680-0173), and the **Hotel Santa Cruz,** next to the Tralapa bus terminal.

Food

Soda Versalles (tel. 680-0144) and **Restaurante Campeón** (tel. 680-0033) are both next to the soccer field. The **Bar y Restaurante La Plaza** (tel. 680-0169), next to Soda Versalles, has a disco. **Restaurante Bárbara** (tel. 680-0646), one block west of the soccer field, also looks pleasant. **Bar y Restaurante Nuevo Mundo,** two blocks west of the soccer field, and **La Taberna,** on the plaza, are recommended for Chinese food.

Other appealing-looking restaurants include **Restaurante El Parque,** on the east side of the plaza, and the **Sea Horse Soda Bar y Restaurante,** half a block east of Banco Anglo Costarricense. The **Coope-Tortilla** factory-restaurant, near the central plaza, offers corn tortillas and other Guanacastecan dishes cooked over open wood fires (hours: 5 a.m.-7 p.m.). There's often a long line outside.

Services

A **tourist information** office (tel. 260-0748) is 100 meters north of the plaza. **Banco Nacional** (tel. 680-0544) has a branch on the left as you enter town, opposite the Hotel Diría; a branch of **Banco Anglo Costarricense** (tel. 680-0075) is on the northeast corner of the plaza. Photographers in need will find a reasonably well-stocked store—**Foto Bazar Persa** (tel. 680-0463)—on the south side of the plaza. There's a **gas station** one block west of the Hotel Diría.

For doctors, try the **Centro Médico Santa Cruz** (tel. 680-0681). Alternately, Dr. Allan Arayan has a clinic one block east of the soccer field; **Farmacia Chorotega** (tel. 680-0818) is next door. Dr. Pablo Briones has a clinic one block from the old plaza (hours: 11:30 a.m.-12:30 p.m. and 4-6 p.m.). Another pharmacy—**Farmacia Rojas** (tel. 680-0096)—is also in town. The **Red Cross** is on the north side of the plaza.

Transportation

Buses depart San José for Santa Cruz from Calle 20, Avenidas 1/3 (Tralapa, tel. 221-7202, or tel. 680-0392 in Santa Cruz) at 7:30 and 10:30 a.m., and 2, 4, and 6 p.m. Buses depart Liberia for Santa Cruz hourly, 5:30 a.m.-7:30 p.m., returning at the same time. Buses depart Nicoya for Santa Cruz hourly 6 a.m.-9 p.m., returning at the same time.

Buses depart Santa Cruz for San José at 4:30, 6:30, 8:30 and 11:30 a.m., and 1 p.m. Local buses depart Santa Cruz for Brasilito, Playa Flamingo, and Playa Potrero at 9 a.m. and 5 p.m., Playa Junquillal at 6 p.m., and Playa Tamarindo at 8:30 p.m.

GUAITIL

A trip to Guaitil, 12 km east of Santa Cruz, is a richly rewarding journey and well worth the effort for those seeking ethnic pottery. The turnoff is about two km southeast of Santa Cruz (the road is paved). Guaitil is a pretty and very tranquil little village surrounding a soccer field, with the usual chickens that get under your feet. Many of the village inhabitants—descendants of Chorotega Indians—have been making their unique pottery of red or black or ochre the same way for generations, turned out on wheels beneath shady trees and displayed on roadside racks and tables.

More than a dozen women work at the ancient craft of pottery making. Together they form the Guaitil Art Cooperative. You are welcome to watch villagers such as Marita Ruíz or Marielos Briseño and her mother Flora (every family co-

---

SANTA CRUZ EMERGENCY TELEPHONE NUMBERS

Police
(Guardia Rural) . . . . 117 or 680-0136

Red Cross 680-0330

operative seems to be attended by the family matriarch) molding ceramics by hand with clay dug from the hills above the hamlet. They use the same steps as did their ancestors, including polishing the pottery with small jadelike grinding stones taken from nearby archaeological sites and said by the local women to have been made by shamans.

The women happily give lessons to tourists and will take you to the back of the house to see the large open-hearth kilns where the pots are fired. Look closely and you'll note that everyone has a slightly different style. A children's cooperative offers surprisingly high-quality work hand-crafted by youngsters. I bought a wonderful three-legged vase in the shape of a *vaca* (cow) for $10. It's difficult to bargain the price down more than 10% or so. Note that plates and dishes have a tendency to crack.

The road (dirt) continues southeast to Nicoya through the valley of the Río Viejo.

Practicalities
The only place to eat in town is **Soda Tamarindo**, on the right as you enter Guaitil. **Guanacaste Tours** (Apdo. 55, Liberia 5000, tel. 666-0306, fax 666-0307) offers a one-day guided tour to Guaitil and Playa Tamarindo each Sunday, including hotel pick-up and return ($75). Guaitil is also included in a four-day "Chorotega Culture" tour ($339) offered by **Costa Rica Adventures and Wildlife** (tel. 800-497-3422; in Costa Rica, tel. 255-2463, fax 255-3573); and in a half-day "Guaitil Artisan Market" tour offered by **Flamingo Tours** (tel. 654-4238, fax 654-4039; in San José, tel. 222-6762).

Getting There: Buses depart Santa Cruz for Guaitil every two hours 7 a.m.-5 p.m.

FILADELFIA

There's little reason to recommend Filadelfia, other than as a stop for a bite to eat perhaps en route to the beaches. The pleasing town plaza has lots of seats under shade trees. The annual Civic Fiesta with bullfighting is held during the first week of January.

Accommodations and Food
Salon Hawaii, on the west side of the plaza, is a popular *campesino's* bar with pool tables. An alternative for Costa Rican fare is **Soda/Restaurante Miriam,** one block farther west. **Cabinas Tita** (tel. 688-8073), two blocks north of the town plaza, has seven clean and adequate cabinas with fans and private baths with cold water ($6.50 per person). The shower I saw was in need of a good scrubbing. The **Tanquera Bar** is next door. Alternately, try **Cabinas Amelia** (tel. 688-8087), one block west of Tita.

Services
There are two **gas stations** on the main road and a **Banco Nacional** (tel. 688-8146) two blocks west of the town square. The **bus station** is one block west of the town plaza; the **Red Cross** (tel. 688-8224) building is also here, next to Soda Miriam. There's a **pharmacy,** Farmacia Cristal (tel. 688-8336), and a **police** station (Guardia Rural, tel. 688-8229). For **taxis,** call Taxis Filadelfia (tel. 688-8256).

Getting There
Buses pass through Filadelfia en route between Nicoya, Santa Cruz, and Liberia (see relevant towns for details).

THE NORTHERN BEACHES

GETTING THERE FROM LIBERIA

The road from Liberia is ruler straight. You'll pass the new Tomás Guardia Airport 12 km west of Liberia. About 18 km west of Liberia, in the village of Guardia, you cross over the Tempisque, and two km farther pass through **Comunidad,** where there's a gas station. Immediately beyond the river, a road to the right leads to Marina Papagayo, the huge and controversial resort development (see special topic on "Gulf of Papagayo Project"). This road is a fast, sweeping, freshly paved, lonesome beauty of a drive that dead-ends after 15 km or so in an arterial network of dirt roads that lead down to a dozen beaches that await the developers' jackhammer.

South of Comunidad, the main road (Hwy. 21) continues via Filadelfia, Santa Cruz, and Nicoya (turn east here for the Tempisque ferry), and, continuing around the south of the peninsula, to Playa Naranjo, Curú Biological Reserve, Montezuma, and Cabo Blanco Absolute Nature Reserve. From Comunidad, a road leads west to the beach resorts of the Gulf of Papagayo: Playas del Coco (15 km), Ocotal, Hermosa, and Panamá.

Pack your sunscreen, a towel, and camera, for awaiting your pleasure are some of the prettiest beaches Costa Rica can offer. Note, however, my previous comments about water color (dull blue rather than brilliant turquoise) and clarity (murky rather than scintillating), with one added caveat: snakes! Yellow-and-black-striped *Pelamys platurus,* to be exact. Sea-snakes. Slithery and—gulp!—lethal. Fear not, though, for these beautiful creatures have far better things to do than mess with humans. Indeed, it would take some provocation to elicit a bite. The wise swimmer will leave 'em alone. Should you decide to test Pelamys's patience, be warned that there's no known antidote.

Accommodations and Food

The pleasing **Turista Bar** is at the junction for Playa del Coco in Comunidad. About 800 meters down the road to Cocos is the basic **Bar y Cabinas El Recreo** (not inspected). **Villas de Playa Nacazcol** (tel. 670-0416 or 257-2993), 10 km west of Comunidad, has comfortable and pleasing a/c villas/cabinas with large kitchenettes. It also has a tennis court, pool, and bar. Half a km farther is the **Bar y Restaurante Costa Alegre,** where a disco under a *palenque* pumps out very loud music day and night. The grounds have a pool, a children's playground, and **camping** is allowed ($3).

About 12 km west of Comunidad (three km before Cocos) is the moderately upscale **Cabinas Costa Alegre,** with a pool and a thatched *palenque* bar and restaurant. Rooms have private baths with cold water. Rate: $20 per person.

PLAYA DEL COCO

Playa del Coco, 35 km west of Liberia, is the most accessible beach in Guanacaste, and therefore one of the most visited. Locals claim that the sun "shines longer and more brightly here than anywhere else in Costa Rica." Maybe, but the place can be crowded and dusty, and the two-km-wide gray-sand beach gets disgustingly littered during busy weekends and holidays when Ticos flock. The college crowd likes to think of Coco as its playground. The plaza is crowded at night with youngsters "cruising." Avoid during Christmas and New Year's, when it is impossibly overrun. There's a shortage of nice places to stay in Coco and an abundance of overpriced hotels. Check around to make sure you get what you pay for. You'll either love it or hate it. A funky wooden footbridge links the western end of the beach; you can drive across the small creek that empties into the horseshoe-shaped bay where fishing boats lie anchored. **Note:** Don't buy coral from the hawkers in the town plaza as this only encourages destruction of the tiny offshore coral reef.

The coast road south from Coco dead-ends after two km at Ocotal.

PACIFIC OCEAN

PAPAGAYOS BAR

MARISQUERIA LA GUAJIRA

BAR COCOS

PLAZA
TAXIS
BUSES

DISCO / BAR
COCO MAR

CABINAS
COCO
MAR

CABINAS
EL COCO

BAR
BOHIO

LAUNDRY

TELEPHONES

HOTEL ANEXOS
LUNA TICA

POLICE

MONPIK

SODAS

BAR/RESTAURANTE EL ROBLE

SUPERMARKET

SOCCER FIELD

SOUVENIRS / BOATING

COCO PALMS

BAR / RESTAURANTE OASIS

SUPERMARKET

LAUNDRY

MARIO VARGAS EXPEDITIONS

CABINAS/BAR
EL POZO

CIAO

HOTEL VILLA
FLORES

BAR/RESTAURANTE SHADY

CAMPING

CALIFORNIA
CAFE

TO DOÑA ANA COCO LODGE

CONDOMINIUMS
DEL PACIFICA

BUCCANERO COSTA RICA/
RICH COAST DIVING

NEW HOTEL

ROSTICERIA DON HUMO

TO PLAYA EL OCOTAL

CABINAS LAS BRISAS

PLAYA DEL COCO

PRONTO PIZZERIA

MAMA'S MUFFINS

DIVING SAFARIS

FRONTERA TOURS

DOCTOR

DISCO/HOTEL ASTIRELLO

HOTEL FLOR DE ITABO

BOATYARD

NOT TO SCALE

TO RANCHO
ARMADILLO

TO LIBERIA

CASA ALBA
BED & BREAKFAST

© MOON PUBLICATIONS

Budget Accommodations

Cabinas El Coco (Apdo. 2, Playa del Coco 5059, tel. 670-0167), next to Cabinas Coco Mar, has 76 small and basic but clean rooms. The office is in the Restaurante Coco Mar. Light sleepers be warned: the disco next door is a giant boom box. Avoid rooms at the back. Rates: $12 single, $18 double. A better bet is **Cabinas Catarino** (tel. 670-0156), with six well-lit and clean rooms, each with two double beds, fans, and large private baths with cold water. Rate: $7 per person.

A dirt road to the right as you enter town leads to **Cabinas Chale** (tel. 670-0036), which has 17 simply furnished rooms with private baths with tiled floors and fans. There's a large pool. Rate: $10 per person. Alternately, try **Cabinas Keystone** (Apdo. 10, Playa del Coco, tel. 232-0210), which reportedly has seven very basic cabinas with kitchenettes; or **Doña Ana Coco Lodge,** one km down the dirt road to the right as you approach the plaza.

Coco Beach Hostel (tel. 225-1073, fax 234-1676), part of the Youth Hostel chain, has 18 beds, a recreation room, plus bicycle rentals and water sports. Not inspected.

At the bottom of the pile—a true hovel—is the **Mar Azul Hospedajes.**

Inexpensive Accommodations

Hotel Luna Tica (Apdo. 67, Playa del Coco 5059, tel. 670-0249, fax 670-0392) has 18 rooms with fans and private baths with cold water. The older cabinas on the beach are dark, stuffy, and funky. Newer rooms in the annex across the street are nicer. Meals are served in the beachfront **Restaurante Luna Tica,** across the road. Luna Tica has rent-a-car service and offers fishing and boating tours. Rates: $18 s, $24 d, $30 t, $38 quad, including breakfast and tax ($6 more for a/c).

Small, dingy, and overpriced describes **Cabinas Coco Mar** (tel. 670-0110), next to the restaurant and disco of the same name. The reception desk is in the restaurant. Some rooms are beachfront; others—noisier and no breezes—are at the back. All have private baths and fans. Rates: $12 s, $15 d. Despite its name, **Cabinas Las Brisas** (tel. 221-3292) does not catch the breezes. Its 13 very basic and simple rooms are sparsely furnished with double and single beds, side tables, and fans, plus spacious private baths with cold water. The owner is not a particularly friendly soul. Overpriced. Rate: $27.

Apparently just west of the soccer field is **Pirate's Cove Hotel** (tel. 670-0367, fax 670-0117); alas, I missed it. Likewise, **Rancho Armadillo** (tel. 223-3535 or 670-0108). Guidebook authors aren't infallable!

Moderate Accommodations

Hotel Villa Flores (tel./fax 670-0269) is a very handsome Spanish colonial-style hostelry run to All-American standards. Ceramics abound. It has nine rooms that are, unfortunately, more basic than the public arenas, though with lots of light. A restaurant overlooks lawns with hammocks slung beneath the palms. Rates: $40 d, $50 suite, including tax and breakfast.

Condominiums del Pacífica (tel. 670-0157 or 228-9430), 400 meters west of Coco on the road to Ocotal, has 10 cabins in shady grounds with a small pool a short distance from the beach. Each of the clean though simple cabins has kitchen, fans, and private baths with cold water. Rates: $32-90 first day (two to 12 people); rates drop for consecutive days. One of the better places to stay—but overpriced—is **Coco Palms** (tel. 670-0367, fax 670-0117), which has 20 spacious, adequately furnished rooms with

fans, and roomy private bathrooms with hot water. There's also a pleasing restaurant and bar. Rates: $45 s/d, $50 t, $55 quad.

About 800 meters east of the turnoff for Playa Hermosa as you approach Coco is **Costa Alegre** (tel. 670-0218). It's popular with Tico families and can be quite lively on weekends. Costa Alegre has 14 fully furnished apartments with kitchens, beds for five people, plus private baths with cold water. A swimming pool, a volleyball court, and a small soccer field, plus a large open-air restaurant with barbecue grill round out the attractions. Rates: $45 per unit.

A new option—not reviewed—is the **Villa del Sol** (Interlink 2107, P.O. Box 025635, Miami, FL 33102, tel./fax 670-0085), a contemporary, Canadian-run bed-and-breakfast. Five rooms have ceiling fans, tile floors, "cathedral" ceilings, private balconies, and "semi-private" bathrooms. A large pool and Jacuzzi are on site. Rate: $45 d, including breakfast.

Upscale Accommodations

The nicest place in town is **Hotel Flor de Itabo** (Apdo. 32, Playa del Coco, Guanacaste, tel. 670-0011, fax 670-0003), which is under German-Italian management and is big on sportfishing, as the paraphernalia on the walls attests. The eight very pretty and spacious rooms have lofty hardwood ceilings, a/c, satellite TVs, and beautiful Guatemalan bedspreads, plus large tiled bathrooms with hot water; five bungalow apartments come with kitchens but have fans only. There are also 10 economy rooms reached via a spiral staircase. The Da Beppe Italian restaurant is renowned locally for excellent cuisine. It opens onto a pool in landscaped grounds full of giddy bougainvillea, palms, and birdlife, including parrots and macaws, many of which were rescued from various traumas and arrived with ruffled feathers. There are caged peccaries, too. When you've eaten, the casino will keep you amused. The hotel specializes in fishing trips. Its 10-meter sportfishing boat rents for $560 per day (four passengers); an eight-meter boat rents for $450, including lunch and sodas. It also rents mountain bikes for $4 per hour, $20 per day. Rates: $50 s, $65 d; $35 economy; $85 apartments, including tax.

Rancho Armadillo (Apdo. 15, Playa del Coco 5019, tel. 670-0108, fax 670-0441; in San José,

tel./fax 223-3535) is a beautiful home with rooms for rent on a 10-hectare *finca* owned and run by an erstwhile Texan mariner, Jim Procter. Spacious well-lit rooms with fans (two also have a/c; one has a kitchen) boast magnificent hardwood furniture and heaps of atmosphere. The honeymoon suite is voluminous. Plans include a hilltop *mirador* and a second house for families or groups. The Wahoo Sportsbar and Grill is a lively adjunct, with country music first and foremost. You can sip a cocktail on the sundeck or settle on the veranda and take in the coastal views. No, the ranch isn't named for the armadillo of Jim's native Texas. Real-life critters abound on the ranch, though mostly at night. Ceramic, stone, and wood miniatures of the beast pop up all over the house. The place is a menagerie: it boasts a parrot, several rottweilers, and even a spider monkey. Want to arrive in style? Take the helicopter! Rates: $35-60 d, $10 extra person, including breakfast.

Houses

You'll find at least three large houses for rent by the week in the village at the southern end of Playa del Coco, halfway between Coco and Ocotal. **Cabaña Tamarindo** (tel. 231-3107), opposite Bar Pacífico, has a house for eight people ($148) plus two cabinas for six people ($55), all with kitchens, fans, refrigerators, and private baths with cold water. Turn right where you see a large boat and a telephone kiosk at a triangle in the middle of the road. A similar two-story house (tel. 556-0139) is on the road (marked, San José) that loops back to Coco. There's also a pleasant **cabaña** painted sea-green (tel. 670-0170), on the left farther along the road to Ocotal.

Camping

The only campsite is next to the **Albastedor Las Brisas** in shady but funky grounds ($3 per person). Facilities include bathrooms, laundry sink, and water.

Food

There's no shortage of reasonable places to eat. The most popular place in town is the breezy **Restaurante Coco Mar**, which overlooks the beach: a good place to check out the Ticos and Ticas showing off their bodies to best effect. An

old man plays mariachi. The **Bar Coco** has good seafood dishes, including an excellent mahimahi *al ajillo* (with garlic). Next door is **El Bohio,** under new American ownership, with dining by karaoke! **Bar El Roble** has a shady but funky outside dining terrace where you can eat to *salsa* music from speakers hung in branches. **San Francisco Treats** (tel. 670-0484) bills itself as "a California café"; as you'd expect, it serves brownies, fudge pie, banana nut bread, cheesecake, and the like. Fabulous. Highlights from the gifted hand of ex-attorney Michale Salinsky are rum and walnut cake, killer ice-cream shakes, and the brownie sundae. **Mama's Muffins** contends with pancakes and waffles.

Rosticeria Don Humo (tel. 670-0144), at the turnoff for Playa El Ocotal, is a modern structure with glass walls that trap the heat (at least they keep the dust at bay). You can also sit outside on a small terrace under shade trees to enjoy your American cocktail—a house specialty. You'll find a well-stocked boutique next door.

Heavy Italian aromas mingle with the breezes, too. **Pronto Pizzeria** (tel. 670-0305), next to Cabinas Las Brisas, serves reasonably priced pizza and other Italian dishes alfresco (hours: 11:30 a.m.-10 p.m., closed Tuesdays). It will deliver. It also has a souvenir shop and art gallery. **El Pozo** offers the usual Italian fare, but has good options for vegetarians. Also try **Ciao.** Another Italian restaurant—**Da Beppe**—is in the Hotel Flor de Itabo.

Entertainment

Disco Coco Mar, next to the town plaza on the beachfront, is the liveliest place in town. The **Papagayos Bar,** also on the plaza, is popular with skippers and boaters from Canada and California; most gringos hang out here, and next door at **Bar Cocos,** which has a moray eel in a tank and fishing nets hung over the bar. If you like '70s rock, this is the place. If you want to try your hand at Lady Luck, check out the little casino in Hotel Flor de Itabo.

Sportfishing, Diving, and Boat Tours

Most hotels can arrange fishing trips and boat tours. **Frontera Tours** (tel./fax 670-0403) offers nature tours, plus sailing trips aboard a 13-meter yacht, and fishing charters aboard a 13-meter motor yacht operated by Aqua Rica Yacht

Charters. **Diving Safaris** (tel. 670-0012) has an office opposite; it also rents sea kayaks. **Mario Vargas Expeditions** (tel. 670-0351) offers trips around the bay ($250 half day, $450 full day, per boatload), offshore fishing ($300 half day, $500 full day, per boatload), plus scuba-diving lessons, including PADI certification. **Tienda Maria** (tel. 670-0354) is a well-stocked store that also arranges a three-hour boat tour ($30 per person) and fishing trips ($35 per hour, $85 full day, including sodas and lunch). **Bar El Roble** (tel. 670-0256) also offers diving and sightseeing trips. **Hotel El Ocotal** (see below), **Rich Coast Diving** (tel. 670-0176, fax 670-0165), and **Buccanero Costa Rica** also offer diving packages and will rent equipment.

Other Services

Mi Tiendita, a little store on the road to Ocotal, sells Kodak film. **Boutique Chichicastenango,** next to San Francisco Treats, has a tremendous clothing supply. Dr. Elizabeth Benavides has a small **clinic** on the left beyond Hotel Flor de Itabo as you come into town. **Sol Rent-a-Car** (in Libera, tel. 666-2222, fax 666-2898) has an office in town. The **police station** (Guardia Rural, tel. 670-0258) is opposite the bus stop on the east side of the plaza, where you'll find **public telephones.** There's a coin-op **laundry** next to Restaurante El Bohio.

Getting There

Buses depart San José from Calles 14, Avenidas 1/3 (Pulmitán, tel. 222-1650) daily at 10 a.m. (five hours; $3). Buses depart Liberia (Arata, tel. 666-0138) for Coco at 5:30 a.m. and 12:30 and 4:30 p.m. (plus 2 p.m. on weekends). Buses depart Coco for San José at 9:15 a.m., and for Liberia at 7 a.m. (and 9:15 a.m. weekends) and 2 and 6 p.m. **Dira Expediciones** (tel. 223-3443, fax 223-3666) offers a/c shuttles from San José, departing daily at 8 a.m. (from $33 one-way; return to San José at 2 p.m.).

PLAYA EL OCOTAL

This relatively secluded gray-sand beach (almost black at its northern end), three km west of Playa del Coco within the cusp of steep cliffs, is much smaller than Coco—barely half a km

long—and less crowded. It gets the overflow from Coco on busy weekends. Its position at the entrance to the Gulf of Papagayo makes it ideal for sportfishing. Two major sportfishing lodges are located here. At Las Corridas, a dive spot only a km from Ocotal, divers are sure of coming face-to-face with one of the 90- to 180-kilo jewfish that make this rock reef their home. Tiny sea horses and hawk fish are among the many species who live among the soft corals. And divers have even seen black marlin cruising gracefully in the area. Rick Wallace, the owner of El Ocotal dive resort, is selling adjacent lots for development, so expect Ocotal to change considerably in the next few years. (Diria Expediciones offers scheduled shuttle service from San José; see "Playa Coco," above.)

Upscale Accommodations

The bay is dominated by **El Ocotal** (Apdo. 1, Playa del Coco, Guanacaste, tel. 670-0230, fax 670-0083), a gleaming whitewashed structure that stairsteps up the cliffs at the southern end of the beach. The elegant hotel gets mixed reviews from past guests. It has 40 rooms, all with a/c, fans, freezers, two queen-size beds each, satellite TV, direct-dial telephones, and ocean views. The original 12 rooms are in six duplex bungalows stepped into the hillside down to the water's edge; newer rooms with dramatic views open up to the horizon and have their own Jacuzzi, sunning area, and pool. The lobby and restaurant (I've heard several reports that the food is a letdown) sit atop a knoll surrounded by water on three sides, with views along the coast. You can even see Orosí and Rincón volcanoes cloud-covered in the distance, beyond the bays receding in scalloped relief. The property is surrounded by very beautiful landscaped grounds with lots of palms, cacti, and bougainvillea floodlit at night. There are three small pools, each with a small *ranchito* for shade, plus tennis courts and horseback riding.

El Ocotal is *big* with divers. **Diving Safaris de Coco** (Apdo. 121, Playa del Coco, tel./fax 670-0012), an independent company based at the resort, operates a fully equipped dive shop with daily two-tank dive trips and night dives. It offers special trips to Murciélago or Catalina islands, 34 and 23 km from El Ocotal, for more experienced divers using its 11-meter, air-conditioned, V-

hull yacht *Georgiana.* The rocky headland below the restaurant is good for tidepooling. Elegante Rent-a-Car and Guanacaste Tours are represented in the reception lobby. El Ocotal also has a fleet of five sportfishing boats. Rates: $70 s, $80 d, $105 bungalow, $120-150 suite (low season). Special package rates available.

Vista Ocotal Beach Hotel (Apdo. 230, San José 1007, tel. 255-3284, fax 255-3238; or, in Ocotal, tel. 670-0429, fax 670-0436; in the U.S., tel. 800-662-1656) is a new property behind the beach. The project—which is described as "a kind of Club Med"—was semi-complete and open at press time. Scheduled for completion in 1997, it will include villas, condo-type studios, and a separate hotel and casino complex, plus a health spa, clinic, and shops. Each fairly small unit includes a fully equipped kitchen, a king-size bed in the master bedroom, two singles in a mezzanine bedroom, and a sofa bed in the tiny lounge. Vista Ocotal plans to operate **Club Náutico Ocotal,** with the largest fleet of small boats in Costa Rica for rental and personal use. The club will offer water-skiing, windsurfing, and sailing lessons, plus sea kayaks, pedal boats, catamarans, and regular sailboats. Check if these features have been installed before booking. Rates: $85 for one to three people; $96, three to six people. A "Special Two-Day Offer" is $45 per person (minimum group of four in one villa or suite), including breakfast and half-day fishing.

My friend Shirley Miller told me of a new condo "beach house" on the beachfront next to Father Rooster restaurant. It sleeps six comfortably. It comes complete with satellite TV, Jacuzzi, and full-size community pool. Rates: $150 nightly, less on weekly basis. Contact Jerry Merrick, P.O. Box 206, Palmer Lake, CO 80133, tel. 719-481-2133. It may be part of Los Almendros . . . **Los Almendros** (tel./fax 670-0442, or tel. 221-3250, fax 255-1845) consists of 43 fully furnished, privately owned two-story villas and condominiums (all with ocean view) available as short-term rental units. Each villa features three bedrooms, two baths, kitchen, living and dining area, carport, two bathrooms, and all the luxuries of home. Furnishings are bamboo. A fabulous thatched bar (alas, no restaurant) is perched loftily over a pool with huge wooden sundeck and hammocks. Rate: $130 per night.

Bed and Breakfast

Hotel Villa Casa Blanca (Apdo. 176, Playa del Coco 5019, tel./fax 670-0448) sets the standard for Costa Rica's beachside bed and breakfasts. A stay here is like being a guest in a personal home. The family atmosphere is conducive to intermingling. Canadian-born owners James and Jane Seip have two children of their own, and families are welcome. The hotel—a pretty and petite Spanish-style villa on a slope about 800 meters from the beach—is surrounded by a lush landscaped garden full of yuccas and bougainvillea. The small swimming pool, rimmed with colonial tiles and crested by a bridge, has a swim-up bar and a sundeck with lounge chairs. Inside, the hotel epitomizes subdued elegance with its intimate and romantic allure. Eight rooms include three suites with private Jacuzzis. Rooms at the back don't catch the breezes but have a/c. Upstairs rooms are cooled by fans and natural ventilation through louvered windows. Best yet are the prices—a superb bargain! Rates: $45 s, $50 d, $7.50 additional.

Okay, so you've been wondering about that fantastic white Spanish-colonial house—surely a millionaire's? you guess—atop the hill. No, it's yours, if you wish. It consists of three rental units, including an open-plan, two-bedroom upper apartment decorated with the same supremely tasteful panache as Villa Casa Blanca, of which it's an adjunct. Heaps of bright light pours in through wall-to-wall arched windows. And bright Caribbean bed covers might have been painted by David Hockney, who you may imagine by the pool, barefoot, cocktail at his feet, hair tousled, with easel and paints. Two thumbs up!

Sportfishing Resort

Over the headland from El Ocotal is **Bahía Pez Vela** (Apdo. 7758, San José 1000, tel. 221-1586, fax 221-3594), a sportfishing resort that nestles in its own tiny, secluded cove. Six basic but adequate a/c cabinas on a small rise catch the breeze. Each has two double beds, lots of light, and a private bathroom with hot water, plus a veranda looking out over the ocean. The very elegant oceanfront restaurant and lounge has hardwood furniture and leather chairs from Sarchí and a small tree-shaded veranda where you can settle and listen to the noise of waves washing upon the rocks.

Sportfishing runs are made in fully equipped nine-meter Boston Whalers and 11-meter Blue Marlins. Package rates (per boat), include transfers, accommodation, meals, liquor, tackle, and fishing. When I first visited in 1992, I said it was vastly overpriced. In 1994, new owners quite rightly reduced rates 35%. Rate: $1575 (four nights, three days fishing).

Food

There're only two places to eat. First is the fabulously rustic **Father Rooster Restaurant,** which looks as if it fell from a movie set. It serves seafood dishes and Roosterburgers ($2.50) and Roosterfrankfurters ($2). It has a sand volleyball court. By night it gets into the groove as a disco. If you're feeling flush, try the cuisine at El Ocotal (see above).

PLAYA HERMOSA

Three km east of Playa del Coco, a turnoff to the north leads to Playa Hermosa, a pleasant two-km-wide, curving gray-sand beach, very similar to Coco but far less developed. There are good tidepools at the northern end of the beach, where you'll find most of the hotels and development. The southern end of the beach (reached by the first turnoff to the left from the main road) is like a piece of rural Mexico: Funky red-tile-roofed shacks . . . Old fishing boats drawn up like beached whales . . . Nets hung out to dry . . . Cockerels scurrying around . . . Pigs lazing beneath the shade trees . . . Fantastic! Laid-back to the max. Pity about the horse-shit on the beach!

Budget and Inexpensive Accommodations

Cabinas Vallejo (tel. 670-0050) has been recommended. Reportedly, it offers rooms with both private and shared baths.

Cabinas Los Corales (Apdo. 1158, San José 1002, tel. 670-0255 or 257-0259) has 12 cabinas with fans and a/c and private baths with cold water ($7.50 per person), plus apartments with kitchens ($41). It also has a large pool, a volleyball court, and a bar under thatch. The open grounds have no shade, though there's parking under shade trees. **Aqua Sport** (see "Services," below) also has basic cabinas for rent, as

does **Eco-Tours/Southern Exposure** (tel. 670-0458), 50 meters south.

At the southern end of the beach are the very basic **Cabinas Playa Hermosa** and **Cabinas Vallejos.** Great if you're seeking barefoot, carefree, $5-a-night living.

Moderate Accommodations

Popeye's & Daddy O's (tel. 670-0245) opened in May 1995: a daffodil-yellow and sky-blue bar/restaurant/"hotel" with 10 airy rooms (some with kitchenettes and two bedrooms) boasting lots of light in a two-story unit that promises to become a favorite of the surfing and college-kids-on-vacation crowd. The bar, too, promises to be a noisy winner. Also, a dorm-style unit sleeps 10, with kitchen and spacious, albeit rustic, living area. There's a small pool. Duarto, the Canadian-Italian manager, is a cool dude, as are the two Canadian owners. Rates: $25 d; $50 per night, entire dorm.

Villas Huetares (tel. 460-0963, fax 284-9410) is an apartment-style complex of 15 bungalows. They're spacious, with lounge (modestly furnished) and well-stocked kitchen and one bedroom. Geez! they get hot, though, despite the a/c. And whoever designed the tiny bathroom sink (crammed into the corner of a doorway) should go back to the drawing board. Still, the whole is pleasant enough, with a pool and sundeck, and small bar. It's popular with Tico families. Rates: $25 s, $40 d, $50 quad, $60 six.

Nearby, I'm told, is **Bed and Breakfast Oasis** (tel. 670-0224), with rooms for $45. Not inspected.

Tucked 150 meters behind the southern end of the beach is the Canadian-run **Villa del Sueño** (Interlink 2059, P.O. Box 02-5635, Miami, FL 33102, tel./fax 670-0027). It offers eight rooms with tiled floors, lofty hardwood ceilings, large picture windows, and private bathrooms in a two-story, whitewashed stone building surrounded by cactus, banana plants and papaya trees. You can dine alfresco and dip in a landscaped pool. Rates: $25-35 s, $22-45 d, $43-55 t.

Upscale Accommodations

American-born Manny operates **Villa Boni Mar** (tel. 670-0397, fax 228-7640), with six pleasing and modestly elegant units. One sleeps four and has a kitchen; two other units have dinner

sets. All feature ceiling fans, refrigerators, and private baths with cold water. It has a pool and a barbecue. Rates: $50 and $65 for small units, $75 for the larger unit.

For ambience, try **Hotel El Velero** (Apdo. 49, Playa del Coco 5019, tel. 670-0330, fax 670-0310), a small, intimate, and distinctly romantic Spanish colonial-style hostelry 50 meters from the beach. It boasts 14 modestly elegant rooms. The Canadian-owned and -operated hotel has both upstairs and downstairs restaurants open to the breezes (see "Food," below), plus a boutique and a small pool surrounded by shady palms. The hotel offers tours to Rincón de la Vieja and Playa Grande, as well as boat trips and scuba diving using its 12-meter sailboat, *L'Embellie*. Rate: $45 d.

Playa Hermosa Inn (Apdo. 112, Liberia, tel./fax 670-0163; in North America, tel. 800-GET-2-SJO), at the southern end of the beach, has eight modestly furnished but pleasant rooms and four cabinas (plus an a/c apartment) set in shady landscaped grounds shaded by palms on the beach. Some have two doubles; some have one double and one single. Rooms are simple but charming. All have fans, private baths with hot water, and wide, shady terraces with wicker seats. You'll find a breezy Italian restaurant with rough-hewn hardwood furniture and an aviary, plus white-faced monkeys, on the grounds. American owned and operated. Rates: $55 s/d, $65 t, $75 quad, including breakfast. Apartment: from $95 s, $100 d. It might be overpriced.

Deluxe Accommodations

Playa Hermosa is dominated by **Condovac La Costa** (Apdo. 55, San José, tel. 221-8949, fax 222-5637), which sits atop a hill at the northern end of the beach. The modern and attractive large-scale complex enjoys a marvelous breezy setting with superb ocean views. It offers a hotel complex with 54 deluxe rooms and a separate hillside complex of 101 a/c villas stairstepping down to the beach amid lawns and bougainvilleas. Golf carts ferry hotel guests up and down the steep hill. Each complex has its own pool and adjacent *palenque* bar. There's a selection of bars and restaurants, plus the **Chico & Pepe** discotheque. The magnificent open-air *palenque* bar and restaurant,

Bar Las Lapas, sits on stilts over the beach—an ideal spot from which to enjoy the sunset. The hotel offers a full complement of tours, sportfishing, and scuba diving (there's a full-service dive shop). Dozens of new villas were being built when I called by in April 1995. Rates: hotel rooms and cabinas from $100 d ($15 for an extra bed).

A new property, **El Cacique del Mar,** was under construction south of Hermosa.

Houses

The small but pleasant-looking cabaña (tel. 231-2305) with pool sits on the left, 50 meters beyond Villa Boni Mar.

Camping

Several places allow campers use of their grounds. You'll see two such properties opposite each other 50 meters from the beach, to the left at the junction with the sign for Hotel Velero.

Food

Rancho Nando (tel. 670-0050) is a delightfully funky bar and *soda* favored by locals. Its eclectic ornamentation includes a decrepit fishing boat turned into tables and chairs, a concrete bartop curved like a wave, an ocelot pelt, saddle, stuffed caiman, and other dusty miscellany. Good *casado* and seafood. It has video games. Next door is **Popeye's & Daddy O's** (tel. 670-0245), famed for its pizzas.

The best bet for breakfast (average $5; portions are large) is Hotel Velero, whose French-Canadian owners take their cuisine seriously. At night, treats in their modestly elegant setting reflect various European influences, including kebabs and barbecues. Happy hour (2-4 p.m.) includes blackberry daiquiris.

A very pleasing thatched restaurant faces the beach behind Aqua Sport (specialties include crepes, paella, lobster provençal, and shrimp a la diabla). Less expensive ($2 for seafood lunch) are two restaurants near Cabinas Hermosa; food is basic Costa Rican fare. You'll find an ice cream store behind Aqua Sport.

For fabulous funky ambience, stroll to the southern end of the beach, where **Rancho Hermosa** and **Soda y Café Pizza Home** serve simple meals in an unbeatably simple setting.

Services

Aqua Sport (tel. 670-0158 or 670-0050) offers kayaks and windsurfers ($3.50 per hour), parasailing, plus boat tours ($33 per hour; eight people); its **telephone** is also the public telephone for Hermosa. There's a well-stocked general store and a souvenir shop next door, halfway along on the beach, where you can mail letters and cash traveler's checks. Dr. Enrique Guillermo Aragon has a **medical clinic** (tel. 670-0119). Several locals, including Corinsa (tel. 670-0244), will rent **horses.**

Transportation

A bus departs San José for Playa Hermosa from Calle 12, Avenidas 5/7 daily at 3:20 p.m. (five hours). A bus departs Liberia for Playa Hermosa daily at 11:30 a.m. and 7 p.m. (Empresa Esquivel, tel. 666-1249). Both buses continue to Playa Panamá (see below). Buses depart Hermosa for San José at 5 a.m., and for Liberia at 5 a.m. and 4 p.m. Hitchhiking from Coco should be no problem since there are lots of cars. A taxi from Coco will run about $5 one-way; from Liberia about $15. Diria Expediciones also offers scheduled shuttle service from San José (see Playa Coco, above).

PLAYA PANAMÁ

The road from Coco to Hermosa crests a headland and drops down to Playa Panamá, a narrow, two-km-wide gray-sand beach encusped by the low, scrub-covered hills that encompass Bahía Culebra. Playa Panamá is very popular with Ticos who camp among the shady sarno, brazilwood, manchineel, and mesquite trees along the full length of the beach. Weekends and holidays get crowded, but midweek you should have the place virtually to yourself. Go now if you love to camp, before the bulldozers move in.

Before reaching Playa Panamá, a branch road leads west along a headland to **Playa Buena,** where nestles the deluxe and gleaming Smeralda Resort and the skeleton of Le Wafou Resort (see "Bahía Culebra," below).

Accommodations and Food

Costa Congrejo is a handsome hacienda-style restaurant—with cabinas in the offing—at the apex where the road meets the beach. The place is crafted of gleaming hardwoods and surrounded by bougainvillea, with a pleasing pool and sundeck to boot. Good *típico* dishes. The dirt road to the left at a Y-fork leads along the shore to **Sula Sula Beach Resort** (tel. 670-0492). It offers 34 pleasing Thai-style thatched cabins for up to five people ($57.50, including tax), and camping with showers and toilets ($3 per person). A new hotel, **Hotel La Playa,** should be complete by the time you read this. **Jardín del Mar** (tel. 231-7629) offers camping ($3 per person). It has a small store and a restaurant, plus showers and toilets, and it rents tents ($5).

BAHÍA CULEBRA

Playa Panamá is the most southerly of several beautiful beaches that ring the massive horseshoe-shaped Bahía Culebra ("Snake Bay"), sheltered from the Pacific Ocean by the Nacascolo Peninsula (actually, Panamá is separated from the bay by a headland, but let's not quibble over technicalities). The water is so deep here that U.S. submarines apparently anchored unseen during World War II. There are several small mangrove swamps good for birding, plus the remains of a pre-Columbian Indian settlement on the western shore of the bay at Nacascolo.

The huge bay is a natural amphitheater rimmed by a scarp cliff cut with lonesome coves sheltering deserted pocket-size gray- and white-sand beaches. Behind, the plateau extends for kilometers, flat as a pancake, with volcanoes—Rincón de la Vieja, Miravalles, and Orosí—in the distance, veiled with courtesan clouds. Magnificent!

The road dead-ends at the northern end of Playa Panamá, but miles and miles of dirt roads newly cut by bulldozers for the Papagayo Project (see special topic) lace the plateau that rims the bay farther north (see "Transportation" under "Playa Hermosa," above, for information on the main access road). The next few years will see a mini-Cancún rise from the dusty earth.

Until recently Bahía Culebra's tiny coves were popular with Ticos who found them perfect spots for isolated camping. Unfortunately, signs have recently gone up all over reading "STRICTLY NO ADMITTANCE." If you ignore these and

GULF OF PAPAGAYO PROJECT

Playa Panamá was recently renamed Playa Chorotega by the Costa Rican Tourism Institute (ICT), which in 1993 began to push roads into the two more northerly beaches—Playa Iguanita and Playa Cabuyal—and beyond, to Playa Prieta and an endless string of adjacent beaches. The government also leased 2,000 hectares surrounding the bay as part of the long-troubled Gulf of Papagayo Tourism Project of the ICT, begun in 1974 but left to languish until a few years ago, when development suddenly took off exponentially. The mini-Cancún that is emerging will push Costa Rica into the big resort-tourism league.

Mexico's Grupo Situr, a conglomerate of independent companies, is heading the project and will build as many as 15,000 hotel rooms on its 911-hectare, 88-km-long coastal concession (almost the entire Nacascolo Peninsula) in a 15-year development. Grupo Situr alone is planning to build more than a dozen major hotels, along with two golf courses, a 300-yacht marina at Playa Nacascolo, an equestrian center and tennis center, timeshare condominiums, private villas, forest-canopy tour, water sports, and other amenities. Grupo Situr is developing a master plan for the peninsula, which will be linked by a new road to the recently completed Llano Grande airport in Liberia.

The development—and flagrant environment abuses—has raised quite a stink (see "Tourism" in "Economy" section of the Introduction chapter). Developers and environmentalists squared off over the project, which featured prominently in the presidential election debate in 1994. An independent review panel created by the victorious Figueres administration expressed particular concern about illegal activities, unlawful exemptions, social problems, and environmental degradation, including sedimentation in the bay caused by poorly managed movement of topsoil. In March 1995 the former tourism minister and 12 other senior ICT officials were even indicted as charges of corruption began to fly!

The government has created a permanent Environmental Monitoring Plan to oversee the project and at press time intended to declare Bahía Culebra a "coastal marine zone for special management." And the Nacascolo Peninsula is an area of archaeological importance with many pre-Columbian sites. When it was discovered that the bulldozers were plowing heedlessly, the government issued an executive decree to declare the peninsula a place of historic importance (now development sites must be inspected before construction can continue). To improve its image, Grupo Situr has changed the name of the project to "Ecodesarollo Papagayo," or Papagayo Eco-Development!

Stalled for months by environmental arguments and postponed by politics, the bulldozers began to roll again in May 1995.

Existing commitments include: Altamira Condominiums (27 houses), Bay Balconies (24 condominiums and 40 townhouses), Bel-Air (60 rooms), Bramadero Papagayo (50 suites), Caribbean Hotel Village (300 rooms), Continental Plaza Hotel (300 rooms), Continental Villas, Ecological Country Villas (21 condominiums), Guanacaste Crown Plaza Hotel (250 rooms), Golf Villas (27 houses), Holiday Inn Sunspree (120 rooms), Pueblo Bonita (250 rooms), Royal Forte Orquídea (250 rooms), Sodak Group (1,000-room hotel), Tico Papagayo (120 suites), and Fiesta Papagayo, Jerry Howard, Omni International, Pointe International, and Royal Turtle Hotel, all with 250 rooms each. Also see "Bahía Culebra," in this chapter.

---

camp on any of the beaches, be aware that there are no facilities. Reportedly, a rustic **ecolodge** at Playa Cabuyal (tel. 666-1497) has four rooms with 20 beds, and provides horses and guides. This, too, may be history by the time you read this.

Accommodations

An Italian company called Corporation 358 signed a 20-year lease for a 10-hectare project at the southern end of Playa Panamá and thereby got the ball rolling with the **Smeralda Hotel** (Apdo. 12177, San José 1000, tel. 670-0044, fax 670-0379), a splendid and expansive upscale, all-inclusive resort that opened in 1995. The airy lobby sets the tone for the contemporary Spanish-colonial resort, with its terra-cotta tile floor and elegant wicker furniture. The 68 beautiful a/c bungalows stairstep grassy lawns, with sweeping views across the bay. Golf carts

will whisk you there along winding pathways. Hardwoods and terra-cotta tiles abound. Closet space is plentiful, and good lighting and huge mirrors adorn the bathrooms. Plate-glass walls and doors proffer priceless vistas. Suites have a mezzanine bedroom and king-size bed, plus deep sea-green marble in the bathroom complete with Jacuzzi. The large restaurant is open to breezes and view, as is the large amoeba-shaped pool, set like a jewel on the slopes. There's a tennis court and shops. Rates: $110 s/d, $240 suite.

Le Wafou (Apdo. 944, Pavas 1200, tel./fax 231-3463) was scheduled to open in mid-1994 on a hill overlooking Playa Buena (the entrance is adjacent to Smeralda Resort; curiously, this hill is uniquely graced by tall organ-pipe cactus). As of April 1995, construction at the half-complete resort was idled. Supposedly it will feature 50 junior suites, 50 bungalows, and two presidential suites, plus a casino and Le Cobra Bleu discotheque. All rooms will have a/c, satellite TV, direct-dial telephone, and mini-bar. A highlight will be architecture on a Chorotega Indian theme. Tennis courts and water sports, including scuba diving, are also planned. Projected rates: rooms from $85 s, $95 d; bungalows $140 s, $205 d.

Ground-breaking had just begun on the **Hotel Papagayo Resort** (Apdo. 1077, Monte de Oca, San José 2050, tel./fax 221-7204), near Le Wafou at the southern end of Playa Panamá, when I called by.

Malinche Real Marina Hotel & Beach Resort (Way to Go Costa Rica, tel. 800-706-1900 or 800-835-1223) opened in May 1995 as an all-inclusive, five-star property with 96 Spanish-colonial-style duplex bungalows nestled amid bougainvillea, shade trees, and palms on the scarp face overlooking Playa Arenilla, immediately north of Playa Panamá. All units have marble floors, pine ceilings, a/c, TVs, and direct-dial telephones. Amenities include a casino, three swimming pools, Jacuzzi, tennis courts, and a wide range of water sports including scuba diving. Malinche is Nicoya's answer to the health and fitness craze with its steam room, sauna, and gym. Now take those well-honed buns to the beach . . . a water-taxi is available to whisk you to any local beach of your calling. Buffet-dining alfresco in the casual La Fonda or "gourmet"

Italian cuisine in the a/c Da Vinci Restaurant are your options.

Due to open in November 1995 was the 300-room **Caribbean Village Costa Rica**, owned by Allegro Resorts, and part of the Grupo Situr development. The all-inclusive facility overlooks Playa Manzanillo, on the north side of Bahía Culebra, and features one-, two- and three-story, a/c villa-style complexes. The 300 rooms feature satellite TVs. In the village are two swimming pools, three tennis courts, a disco, children's playground and activities, plus a panoply of water sports. Rates include all meals, alcoholic beverages, activities (including water sports), gratuities, and taxes.

In early 1995 Grupo Situr began construction on a 300-room **Continental Plaza** with three-story, red-tile units spreading up the hillsides of Playa Nacascolo. It will have a beach club, two restaurants, tennis courts, and a conference center. When I called by in April, the development was on hold while judges and legislators in San José wrangled over the legal complications in which Papagayo has become embroiled. Likewise, **Club Las Velas**, an all-inclusive, 300-room village that according to literature opened in spring 1995 (alas, I couldn't find it) amid gardens, plazas and waterfalls on nine hectares adjacent to Playa Prieta. It features (or will feature) a casino, health club, and marina, plus a swimming pool designed to resemble a lake.

PLAYA BRASILITO

There is no direct road connection from Playa del Coco or Ocotal to the beaches farther south (see "Transportation" under "Playa Flamingo," below). Unless you have a sturdy 4WD and a sense of adventure, you must return to Comunidad and turn south via Filadelfia, from where a road leads west to **Huacas**, gateway to Brasilito, Flamingo, Conchal and Playa Grande. (En route to Huacas, an artisan's store on the left, just before El Llano, sells fabulous pottery.)

From Huacas, a wide paved road leads four km north to the hamlet of Brasilito. The place is on the verge of a tourism boom. The light-gray-sand beach fades off to the north of the village. It's pretty, though nowhere near so as Playa

Flamingo to the north, or Playa Conchal to the south. Playa Brasilito is divided from Playa Flamingo by a small headland, and from Playa Conchal by a rocky promontory, Punta Conchal (you can negotiate a track to Conchal along the beach by 4WD; be prepared for some deep sand in parts). The entrance to the Melía Conchal Resort is about one km north of Huacas en route to Brasilito.

Accommodations
Hotel Conchal (tel. 654-4257), south of the village, has pretty, ochre-colored Spanish colonial-style cabins with private baths set in a landscaped garden full of bougainvillea. It offers horse and bike rentals. Rate: $38 s/d. **Rancho el Coracol** is next door. Two other properties (not inspected) are **Cabinas Doña Olga** (tel. 654-4013) and **Cabinas Mi Posada** (tel. 680-0953).

A German couple, Josef Compes and Manuela Klasen, run **Hotel Brasilito** (tel./fax 654-4237), 50 meters from the beach. This well-run hotel has a very atmospheric, breezy, bougainvillea-festooned restaurant made of hardwoods, plus 10 pretty though simple rooms with fans and private baths with cold water, in a delightful home of daffodil-yellow adorned with boxed bougainvilleas and other *veraneras*, flowers that bloom in the dry season. Rate: $40 d.

Several hotels are spaced well apart along the dirt road between Brasilito and Playa Potrero. **Bar/Restaurante La Perla,** just outside Brasilito, has three clean, tiled cabinas with fans, small kitchens, refrigerators, and private baths with cold water, plus a larger cabin for up to seven. There's a small swimming pool. It's 300 meters from the beach. The owner offers horseback rides, boat tours, and taxi service. The restaurant doubles as a large dance hall and is a popular hangout for expatriate gringos. Miss your "downhome" breakfast? Try here. Rates: $22 s, $29 d, $36 t, $44 quad, including tax; $44 large cabin.

Cabinas Christina (Apdo. 121, Santa Cruz 5051, tel. 654-4006), 200 meters beyond La Perla, has clean, spacious rooms with kitchenettes, double and bunk beds ("hard," by one account), plus rockers on verandas. There's a small pool and a thatched *palenque*: A five-minute walk to the beach. Rates: $25 s, $35 d.

You can **camp** on the beach, 100 meters south of Hotel Brasilito.

Food
Best bet is the **Restaurant Hotel Brasilito.** You'll find a couple of basic eateries on the beachfront, both selling seafood and rice dishes. **Bar y Restaurante Camaron Dorado** (tel. 654-4028) is a favorite of locals; try the filling specials or Camaron Dorado Salad ($8, for which you get lobster, shrimp, calamari, cheese, and ham heaped in with the greens). South of the village is **Marisquería Bar Odisea,** an attractive thatched seafood restaurant. It has cabinas for rent, too.

A budget alternative is the **Rancho Bar La Playa,** on the soccer field (you'll find a water faucet here for those camping on the beach).

Horses
Hotel Brasilito offers horse excursions. **Jalisco U Tours** (tel. 654-4106) also has horses for rent.

Getting There
See "Playa Flamingo," below, for bus and air schedules.

PLAYA FLAMINGO (PLAYA BLANCA)

Two km beyond Brasilito, a dirt road to the left passes **Tio's Bar and Grill** (complete with tennis court amid a pasture) and climbs over a headland to Playa Flamingo (officially and more accurately called Playa Blanca; it was renamed by developers); if you were to continue straight, you'd arrive at Playa Potrero. The two-km-wide scimitar of white sand that forms part of Bahía Flamingo is one of the most magnificent beaches in Costa Rica. There are no flamingos, however. The area has long been favored by wealthy Ticos and gringos (North Americans now own most of the land hereabouts), and expensive villas sit atop the headlands and line the beach. A great many private homes are under construction along the headland to the north; it's well worth the walk to check out the architectural styles and fabulous views. Many of these fortunates have their own little coves as private as one's innermost thoughts.

Playa Flamingo has been called the "Acapulco of Costa Rica." Alas, while well-heeled Ticos vacation here, the moniker is about a decade too soon. There's little nightlife to speak of, although that is changing fast. More appro-

priate is its reputation as the nation's sportfishing capital (the annual **International Sportfishing Tournament** is held here each May and June). Flamingo is home to Costa Rica's largest sportfishing fleet, which anchors in what is supposedly the largest marina between Acapulco and Panamá. A bridge connects the marina with Playa Potrero.

A golf course is to be built between Brasilito and Flamingo. Not too soon, perhaps, for I'm reliably informed that the lack of action has spawned a considerable cocaine trade to keep the wealthy expat gringos amused.

Upscale Accommodations

Flamingo Tower Bed & Breakfast (tel. 654-4109, fax 654-4275), opened in early 1995, is a contemporary Spanish-colonial home-turned-hotel sitting fairytale-like atop the headland at the southern end of the beach. It's reached by a steep winding road. It has five rooms, each as individual as a thumb print, yet each with a/c, refrigerator, and private bath. One room has a kitchenette. The octagonal tower—there really is one—was built by Harvard University for an astronomer but now caters to honeymooners and would-be honeymooners. It's now a suite with windows to all sides, reached by a spiral metal staircase. South American tapestries, hardwood ceilings, and tiled floors all add charm. Enjoy American breakfasts on a breezy veranda overlooking the beach. Rates: $50 d, $60 suite, including breakfast. A bargain!

The **Flamingo Marina Resort** (Apdo. 321, San José 1002, tel. 257-1431 or fax 221-8093), behind the Presidential Suites about 300 meters from the beach, has pleasing rooms but lacks the beachside appeal and class of the Flamingo Beach Hotel. All rooms are spacious, with fans, a/c, refrigerators, TVs, and telephones. Sportsman's suites have Jacuzzis and bars. A circular swimming pool with poolside *ranchito* bar on a terrace overlooking the marina pool has a marvelous setting overlooking the Bahía Potrero. The pleasant restaurant, furnished in bright tropical colors, opens onto the pool and is more reasonably priced than the Flamingo Beach Hotel. The hotel has a tennis court. Rates: from $95 d to $160 suite.

The **Mariner Inn** (tel. 654-4081) is a new 12-room Spanish colonial-style hotel overlooking the marina. Dark hardwoods fill the a/c rooms that feature color TV, blue-and-white tile work, and terra-cotta tile floors. A suite has a minibar and kitchenette. A pool and sundeck sit next to a moody, elegant bar of dark hardwoods. The restaurant specializes in seafood. Rates: $50 s/d, $100 suite.

Deluxe Accommodations

Two km south of the turnoff for Flamingo, just north of Brasilito, is **Villas Pacífica** (Apdo. 10, Santa Cruz, tel. 680-0932, fax 680-0981; in the U.S., 6387-B Camp Bowie Blvd., Suite 333, Fort Worth, TX 76116, tel. 817-738-1646, fax 817-738-9240), the closest thing to an upscale Arizona resort in this quarter of the world. The complex enjoys a lofty and luxurious setting about one km inland from the beach at the end of a palm-lined drive. It overlooks the ocean amid tranquil tropical surroundings full of bougainvilleas.

The resort has five deluxe two-bedroom villas (two people per room minimum), each with a/c, twin bathrooms, full American kitchen, dining room, large living room, and veranda. Each sleeps six guests. The very elegant and atmospheric curved dining room with its walls of dark volcanic rock defies superlatives and is overseen by Karen Bean, a restaurateur from Pennsylvania. After dinner you can enjoy your favorite cocktail at the large rotunda Marlin Bar, which is done up in rosewood and Australian walnut burl. The open, breezy terrace offers stunning views along the coast. A tennis court and a large pool await the active.

The hotel specializes in anglers' packages (inquire for special rates) and offers a wide range of charter boats from eight-meter Grady Whites to 18-meter Bertrams from $550 to $950 half day; $750 to $1250 full day. Rates: $105 s/d, $125 t, $150 quad.

Villas Flamingo (tel./fax 654-4215) is a complex of 24 very spacious villas about 50 meters from the southern end of Flamingo beach. Each sleeps six people and has a large lounge-cum-bedroom and a good-size kitchen. There's a small pool. Daily rates: $100 d, $110 t, $130 quad, $140 for five, $150 for six. Weekly rates: $650 d/t, $700 quad, $750 for five/six. Monthly rates: $1600 d/t/quad, $1700 for five/six.

The **Aurola Playa Flamingo** resort (tel. 233-9233, fax 654-4060 appears to be a condo deve-

lopment fronting Villas Flamingo (I mistook it for an expansion) and was only half-complete at press time. Apartments are reportedly deluxe, and the resort has all the trimmings. Rates: from $120 rooms, $200 apartments.

The nicest place close to the beach is the **Flamingo Beach Hotel** (Apdo. 692, Alajuela 4050, tel. 680-0444, fax 680-0916; for reservations, tel. 239-1584, fax 239-0257), a large-scale and very elegant modern hotel complex. Centerpoint is a voluminous pool with a swim-up bar and expansive sunbathing areas. It has 134 spacious rooms, including eight surfside suites, five ocean-view suites, and 23 luxury two-bedroom apartments. The rooms have a/c, fans, telephones, satellite TVs, and private balconies. When hungry, you can choose from the shaded open-air Barefoot snack bar or Catalina restaurant (prices are Tokyo-expensive). The hotel has a very well-stocked souvenir shop, plus a rental-car agency and a sportfishing office. Rates: $96 s, $105 d ($10 additional for poolside rooms; $9 for each additional person); $160 surfside suites.

The same company runs the **Presidential Suites**, on a bluff facing south above the hotel. Luxurious one- and two-bedroom condominiums feature fully equipped kitchens, living and dining rooms, two bathrooms, color TVs, and telephones. All suites have private balconies overlooking the ocean. Rates: $160 s/d, $180 t/quad ($10 each additional). I find them overpriced, and a reader agrees, though he over-reacts by calling them worse than any motel in the United States.

Hotel Fantasías Flamingo (Apdo. 4518, San José, tel. 231-0701 or 222-9847, fax 257-5002) was under construction on the headland at the north end of the beach (opposite the Presidential Suites). Some 42 rooms and 18 two-room apartments are planned. Also under construction half a kilometer farther was **Club Talolinga,** with apartments with huge plate-glass windows in an eight-story tower.

House Rentals

Several of those beautiful hilltop and beach-front villas you admire can be rented. Most come with maids and gardeners, towels, fully equipped kitchens, and laundry service. One delightful

option is **Casa Mega,** which has its own tiled spa, three bathrooms, brick patios, two a/c bedrooms, and a tempting ocean view. Contact Megadventures (tel. 654-4091) or Fred Schultz of **Sea View Rentals** (Apdo. 77, Santa Cruz, tel. 654-4007, fax 654-4009; in San José, tel. 226-0901). Schultz handles virtually all the house rentals around, with prices ranging from $50 a day to $7500 a month.

Food and Entertainment

Marie's Restaurant (tel. 654-4136), 50 meters beyond Flamingo Beach Hotel, offers basic but tasty seafood, plus daily specials and a large selection of sandwiches under a *ranchito* with tree-trunk slabs for tables. The **Bar/Restaurante/Disco Amberes** (tel. 654-4001), up the hill opposite the Marina Trading Post, is the only place to party in town. It has a spacious lounge bar, plus a lively disco with tunes from a DJ booth.

The **Sunset Bar y Restaurante** of the Presidential Suites offers fabulous views over the bay. Expensive! Even better, and much cheaper, is the **Mar y Sol Restaurant** (tel. 257-4151; cocktails 4-6 p.m., dinner 6-9 p.m.; closed Sunday), set up high atop the flank of the headland between Flamingo and Potrero. This is the place to settle into wicker furniture to watch the sun go down. Mariners prefer to booze in the **Mariner Inn,** which features cable TV. **Villas Pacífica** offers free transportation to *its* restaurant.

Alas, Hal's American Bar & Grill fell foul of a legal dispute and was razed. In a similar vein, though, is **Tio's Sports Bar** (tel. 654-4236), a Tex-Mex restaurant with driving range, tennis court, and softball stadium. Adult games are played each Sunday at 10 a.m. Little Leaguers play on Saturday. All comers welcome. Don't play? Then watch the big game on satellite TV.

Sportfishing

Flamingo Bay Pacific Charter (tel. 654-4015, tel./fax 234-0906; in the U.S., 1112 East Las Olas Blvd., Fort Lauderdale, FL 33301, tel. 800-992-3068 or 305-765-1993), above the lobby of the Flamingo Beach Hotel, offers sportfishing charters aboard its custom Palm Beach 31 Sportfishermen ($550 half day, $696 full day for four people). It publishes the quarterly

Flamingo Bay's Saltwater Digest, listing what's happening on the local sportfishing scene. For free subscriptions, contact *Saltwater Digest* (address same as above, tel. 800-654-8006 or 800-467-0531).

Sportfishing Costa Rica (Apdo. 11, La Uruca, San José 1150, tel. 220-1115); **Blue Marlin Sport Fishing** (Apdo. 109, Santa Cruz, tel. 654-4043), opposite the Presidential Suites; **Club Villas Pacífica** (tel. 654-4137; see "Deluxe Accommodations"); and **Bahía Flamingo Beach Resort** (Apdo. 45, Santa Cruz 5051, tel. 654-4014, fax 654-4183), on Playa Potrero, also offer fishing packages. You can also charter sail- and motorboats at the marina and through the chamber of commerce.

Flamingo Marina

The marina (tel. 654-4203), supposedly the largest south of Acapulco, is tucked in the southern end of Playa Portrero bay, with a rock breakwater enclosing a dredged basin. It has dock space for 80 yachts up to 24 meters long, with plans for 250 slips by 1997. Additional docking for larger yachts was under way, as was a shopping center on adjacent land. The fuel dock (with diesel, gasoline, and 120-volt and 220-volt electricity and fresh water) is on the finger pier jutting from the southern breakwater. The marina also has a floating dry-dock for maintenance, and a 20-ton crane, plus marine mechanic on duty. Wax-n'-wash crews are available. Reportedly, the approach is very shallow. Dockage is $10 per foot for stays of less than three months. A "lease," with first and last month payable in advance at $7 per foot, is offered for longer stays. Moorings inside the breakwater cost $3.50 per foot. Call the **dock master** on channels 16, 86 or 87. Office hours: Mon.-Fri. 7:30-11:30 a.m. and 12:30-4:30 p.m., Saturday 7:30-11:30 a.m. Closed Sunday.

Boats arriving from international waters to the north reportedly must clear customs and immigration at Playa del Coco (Thomas Patrick reports that they'll come to you in Flamingo by arrangement). There's a bonding service ($100) if you wish to leave your yacht for extended periods. You'll need four copies of your passport plus the Certificate of Entry (Certificado de Entrada) obtained from immigration in Playa del Coco.

Services

You'll find a small **shopping center** behind the Mariner Inn, plus a well-stocked general store, the **Marina Trading Post** (tel. 654-4156), across the road. The **Surfside Way Liquor and Grocery Store** (tel. 654-4291), across from the marina on Playa Portrero, specializes in imported and gourmet foodstuffs. The marina office has a product list—you can fax your order to the store and it'll deliver! Or call, and someone will come pick you up.

Papagayo is a 14-meter sailboat offering sunset cruises ($40 with dinner on-board) nightly. Fabulous!

Flamingo Divers (tel. 654-4014) has a dive center on the grounds of the Bahía Flamingo Beach Hotel, at Playa Potrero. **Sol Rent-a-Car** (in Liberia, tel. 666-2222, fax 666-2898) has an office in Flamingo. There's a **gas station** on the road from Brasilito. **Tio's Information Hotline** (tel. 654-4236) can provide general information, as can Ann at the **chamber of commerce** (tel./fax 654-4229), behind the Mariner Inn. Ann can also arrange a wide variety of trips throughout Nicoya and Guanacaste. Restaurante Amberes offers a **moneychanging** service. If you need the **Red Cross,** call 680-0522, ext. 168.

Transportation

Buses depart San José from Calle 20, Avenida 3 (Tralapa, tel. 221-7202), daily at 8 and 11 a.m. (six hours; $3). The buses travel via Matapalo and Playa Brasilito and continue to Playa Potrero. Buses depart Santa Cruz for Playas Brasilito, Flamingo, and Potrero (Tralapa, tel. 680-0392) at 6:30 a.m. and 3 p.m. Buses depart Flamingo for San José at 9 a.m. and 2 p.m., and for Santa Cruz at 9 a.m. and 5 p.m.

The Flamingo Beach Hotel offers direct bus transfers from San José from the Herradura and Cariari hotels Monday, Wednesday, and Friday, at 8 a.m. (tel. 239-1584; $60 roundtrip). Return trips to San José depart at 2 to 2:30 p.m.

To get to Flamingo from Playas Coco, Hermosa, or Panamá, take a bus to Comunidad (at the junction of Route 21), where you can catch a southbound bus for Santa Cruz or Nicoya; get off at Belén, where you can catch a bus for Flamingo (buses from San José pass by around 10:30 and 2:30 p.m.).

You can charter a private **air-taxi** from San José (about $400 for five people). The **Turistas Amigo** (tel. 654-4238) tour office in the Flamingo Beach Hotel can arrange private air transfers. Playa Flamingo is five miles from Tamarindo airstrip. Bus shuttle service to and from the airstrip can be prearranged. SANSA no longer flies to Flamingo. An amphibious air service—**Alas Amphibious Air**—was recently initiated using a seaplane that lands right in the marina ($80 one-way to/from San José's Pavas Airport, tel. 232-9108 or 654-4203).

PLAYA POTRERO

This wide whitish-sand beach immediately north of Playa Flamingo is now up-and-coming, with several new hotels and cabinas concentrated at the crossroads at the northern end (the road to the right here leads to Playa Azúcar). The beach is also the site of a proposed 400-hectare tourist project—Project Zapotal—to be styled after a Spanish colonial town. Construction was due to begin in 1993 on a hill overlooking the beach, but there was still no sign of it in early 1995. The project was to include three hotels, golf courses, equestrian facilities, shops, and narrow streets overhung by tiny balconies, tiled roofs, patios, and fountains. The beach is popular with campers during holidays but is virtually deserted on weekdays.

For now, Playa Potrero is relatively unspoiled: savor it while you can. The calm sheltered waters are safe for swimming, and a small islet lies a short swim offshore. About 10 km offshore is **Isla Santa Catalina**, nesting site for bridled terns and other seabirds. A small saltwater forest at the estuary of the Río Salinas is home to monkeys, parrots, and other animals and birds.

The tiny hamlet of Potrero, one km north of the beach, is built around the perimeter of a soccer field. The village is a rustic charmer! From its southwest corner, follow the road 50 meters and you'll reach two rustic bars (the locals take a little time to warm to gringos), where you can sup a beer and take in the views south across the bay. From here, the dirt road leads north to **Playa Penca**, a beautiful almost-white-sand beach that begins immediately after the

village and is also backed by a protected mangrove estuary replete with birdlife, including roseate spoonbills and egrets.

Inexpensive Accommodations

Two basic rooms with fans and shared baths with hot water are available at **Rosalee's Beach Bar and Restaurant** (tel. 654-4269; about $30, including breakfast). **Cabinas Ocho Hijos** (named in honor of Jim 'n' Liz's eight little 'uns), 300 meters east of Bahía Potrero Beach & Fishing Resort, also has basic cabins. **Cabinas La Penca** (about $10) is just behind the beach of that name.

Moderate Accommodations

The following are in order of appearance, south to north. **Salty Pelican Bed & Breakfast** (tel./fax 654-4227) is a simple home, the first house on the left, where you reach the beach. The next house also doubles as a hotel: **Tara's Terrace Bed & Breakfast** (tel. 654-4184). Neither were reviewed. There's a small house for rent (tel. 654-4213) next door to Costa Rican Diving, which you'll pass 300 meters beyond Tara's.

The Italian-run **Cabinas Isolina** (no tel.), on the road to Playa Azúcar, has 10 attractive if simple and somewhat dark cabins (two with kitchenette) with a double and a single bed with beautiful spreads. Rates (low season): $25 d, $30 t; $40 d with kitchenette. **Cabinas Cristina** (tel./fax 654-4006), nearby, is of a similar standard and price, with the benefit of a small pool.

The **Rancho Costa Azul** (tel. 654-4153), on the north side of the soccer field in the village of Potrero, is a handsome, rustic, red-tile-roofed restaurant with four simple rooms with private bath and cold water. Rate: $24 d.

At Playa Penca is **Cielomar Hotel** (tel. 654-4194), behind a picket fence, with lawns and lots of palms, plus 11 a/c rooms, whitewashed, with bright pinks and blues in counterpoint. Each has private bath but cold water. Overpriced but nice. Rate: $50 d.

The best bargain around is **Casa Sunset Bed & Breakfast** (tel. 654-4265), on the hill behind Playa Penca. It's the home and brainchild of Martha and John, ably assisted by their half-dozen cats, two Great Danes, and two English Boxers (one of which nips at guys in long pants). No ordinary B&B, this. Casa Sunset is a true

home-away-from-home. Where else are you invited to pull a beer from the ice chest and flop on the couch in front of a giant screen TV? Maybe I got special treatment. Still, it seems there are always friends and neighbors popping in to shoot the breeze, pop a beer, etc. I didn't want to leave! The house sits midway up the hill with, below—the node of events—a marvelous *ranchita* bar (still in evolution when I stayed here) that promises to be *the* place of choice for locals to hang out at night. *Bocas* will be served. Note the fine workmanship of the heavy-duty tables, chairs, and bartop. The same craftsmanship is displayed in the seven simple yet splendid cabins sleeping four and cascading down the hill. One has a kitchen. Each has a double (or two singles) and bunk, plus ceiling and floor fans, and large bathrooms with hot water. Verandas have Sarchí rockers. There's a pool and sundeck. Horseback rides are offered and guests have free use of boogie boards. Rates: $40 d, $10 additional, including breakfast. Highly recommended!

Upscale

Bahía Potrero Beach & Fishing Resort (Apdo. 45, Santa Cruz 5051, tel. 654-4183, fax 654-4093) abuts the northern end of the beach (supposedly it has a title to the high-water mark granted by the King of Spain in 1812) in enclosed landscaped grounds. The 18 rooms have fans and private baths with hot water. Standard rooms have two double beds. Deluxe rooms have one queen bed and private patio. All rooms have a/c and refrigerators. The resort features a pleasant restaurant and bar serving pizzas and pastas, plus a modest library, a souvenir store, a small swimming pool and children's pool, plus hammocks under small *ranchitas.* The hotel offers special fishing packages ($350 half-day, $500 full-day charter; or $700 per person for seven nights' accommodation and four days' fishing). Horseback tours cost $40 per half day. **Flamingo Divers** has a dive center at the hotel. Overpriced? Rates: $75-95 d standard, $85-115 deluxe.

There are also six fully equipped two-bedroom condominiums at the northern end of the beach ($525 per week; tel. 670-0108). Another new upscale condominium development, **Endless Beach** (tel. 654-4164), was under way. And a spectacular, super-deluxe hotel is also planned for Playa Potrero. I saw the architect's drawings

of the grand conception: a beachfront Moorish style castle-cum-Alhambra—to be called Playa Turístico El Paso—complete with columns and arches and classical busts on pedestals. The owner claims it will be the most ostentatious resort in the country. We'll see! Meanwhile, a large all-inclusive resort called **Club Las Velas Resort** was semi-complete in April 1995 on a pocket-size beach north of Playa Penca.

Camping

You can camp along Playa Potrero (no facilities) and opposite Costa Rica Divers.

Food

There are two budget places to eat in Potrero hamlet: **Soda y Restaurante Playa Potrero** and **Las Brisas Restaurante.** Both are basic. The **Surfside Bakery** (tel. 654-4271), 50 meters from Bahía Potrero Beach & Fishing Resort, is recommended, particularly for its chocolate chip cookies! Within shouting distance is **The Bistro** (tel. 654-4014), serving Italian cuisine.

PLAYA AZÚCAR

The dirt road deteriorates north of Playa Penca and comes to an end just beyond Sugar Beach (Playa Azúcar), a narrow, 400-meter-wide spit of sun-drenched coral-colored sand that just might have you dreaming of retiring here. It is separated from an even more lonesome beach—Playa Danta—by steep cliffs. Catalina Islands, Chocoyas Islands, and Plata Island lie offshore. Reportedly, there's good snorkeling here. (Actually, you *can* continue north from here all the way to Playa Coco along a *very* rough dirt road known as the "Monkey Trail.")

Accommodations

Hotel Sugar Beach (Apdo. 90, Santa Cruz 5051, tel. 654-4242, fax 654-4239) offers something sadly diminished in Costa Rica—the privacy of a secluded setting. The hotel commands the entire beach, perched just high enough to catch the breezes, with bungalows set in a hollow sloping down to the beach. Shade trees run down to the shore but not in such numbers that they obscure the views south beyond Islas Chocoyas and the bays of Potrero and Brasilito to Cabo Velas.

When I called by in April 1995, 16 elegant new rooms in eight handsome Spanish colonial-style duplexes had been added to the 10 older (and recently renovated) units. The place is owned and run by super-friendly owners Jon Mechem and his wife Soni. The very spacious rooms have two queen-size beds, verandas, a/c, fans, pleasing wicker furniture, and tiled floors, plus beautiful hand-carved wooden doors with bird motifs. Also available are a three-bedroom beach house and an apartment suite. A large open-air restaurant with views is centered on an impressive radial-spoked hardwood-beamed ceiling. A helipad was recently added. Horseback rides are offered ($30). However, you don't need to go far to see monkeys, birds, and iguanas; they abound on the grounds! Recommended. Rates: $90-100 d ($10 extra persons); $2750 per week, beach house; $200 per night, suite. A free transfer to/from Tamarindo airport is included.

Transportation

There is no bus service. Those with sturdy 4WD might be able to negotiate the rough track—known to locals as the "Monkey Trail"—that leads south from the Comunidad-Coco road at a point two km west of Sardinal; the track emerges in Bahía Potrero, north of Playa Flamingo. The more advisable route is via a paved road that turns west from the Liberia-Nicoya highway, five km south of Filadelfia. At Huacas, 21 km west of Filadelfia, the road divides for Playas Brasilito, Flamingo, and Azúcar (north), Playa Grande and Playa Conchal (straight ahead), and Playa Tamarindo (south).

If you continue west from Huacas, instead of turning north for Playa Flamingo, the wide dirt road will take you to **Matapalo**, where it turns left at the soccer field for Playa Grande (four km); the road leading from the northwest corner of the soccer field leads to Playa Conchal (four km). If you wish to continue to Playa Tamarindo from Playa Grande, you'll need to return to Huacas and follow the road south via Villarreal.

PLAYA CONCHAL

This scintillating white-sand beach—one of Costa Rica's finest—lies in the cusp of a scalloped bay with proverbially turquoise tropical

waters, a rarity in Costa Rica. You can walk (or drive by 4WD) to Playa Conchal from Playa Brasilito by a path that fringes the shore. The beach is composed, uniquely, of zillions of tiny seashells that move with soft rustling sounds as you walk; the waters are of crystalline Caribbean quality perfect for snorkeling. Wading out to Conchal Point to the north, you'll find larger shells and crustaceans, too, scurrying around. It's illegal to remove shells. *Leave them for future generations to enjoy.*

Conchal has at last been "discovered." The time is now if you value relative peace and quiet, for the bulldozers are already at work. Conchal is included in the Gulf of Papagayo Project (see special topic).

The large gates on the left as you approach Conchal look like those of a private estate. In fact, they lead uphill to the tiny hamlet of Conchal, and the luxurious and stunning Conchal Condor Club, which resembles a manicured southern California residential community in a tropical setting. Beyond the gates you'll see a car half buried on end with a sign for **Disco Pacha.** The entire community is enclosed behind stone walls.

Beyond the wall, a dirt road to the left leads past tumbledown *bohios* (farmers' and fishermen's shacks) to **Playa Real,** a stunning little beauty of a beach, perhaps 400 meters wide, in a sculpted bay with a tiny tombolo leading to a rocky island. Venerable fishing boats make good resting spots for pelicans. It's the only place in Costa Rica where I can recall exclaiming, "Aah! this is where I want to build my home!"

Accommodations

Hans, of Pizzeria La Gondola, has three cabinas (more like houses)—**Hotelito La Paz** (tel. 654-4259)—up the hill. Each has a sitting room and a kitchen, plus fans and large verandas and large private baths with hot water. They're airy and light. One has a/c and a suite. There's also a swimming pool. Hans offers **fishing tours.** Rates: $35 suite, $55 large units for six.

Deluxe

"Stunning" fittingly describes the **Condor Club Hotel** (Apdo. 102, San José 2300, tel. 231-7328, fax 220-0670), a study in good taste that sits atop a hill about half a km from the beach. Every-

thing is blazing white, very modern, and *muy elegante*. The 41 comfortable and tastefully decorated rooms are set in landscaped grounds bright with bougainvillea. They come with a/c, fans, cable TV, telephones, and private bathrooms. There are also two- and three-bedroom houses with kitchens (one-week minimum). The ocean-view, open-terrace dining room is topped by a lofty lounge bar. A wonderfully landscaped pool with *ranchitas* overlooks the beach far below. There's basketball, volleyball, and horseback riding. A free shuttle runs down to the beach. Highly recommended and bargain priced. Rates: $65 standard, $80 superior.

The Spanish-owned, 300-room **Meliá Conchal Beach & Golf Resort** (Playa Conchal, Santa Cruz, tel. 654-4181, fax 654-4123; in the U.S./Canada, tel. 800-336-3542) was scheduled to open in fall 1995 on a 285-hectare property at the southern end of the beach. At press time it was the largest resort in the country (the PR department, of course, also claims it is the "most sophisticated"). The resort encompasses 310 suites contained in 37 bungalows on the flatlands behind the beach. Each has all modcons: satellite TV, hair drier, telephone, minibar, safety box, and a/c. It has three restaurants, two bars, a disco, tennis courts, plus a 18-hole golf course designed by the king of designers, Robert Trent Jones, Jr. Two swimming pools are designed to look like lakes to blend with the surroundings. You can rent sportfishing boats and cars. Hiking, horseback riding, bicycle tours, and a full panoply of water sports are other options. The resort caters to children. Note that the entrance is on the Huacas-Brasilito road.

Playa Real is the setting for the **Bahía de Los Piratas Resort** (tel. 222-7010, fax 223-4386), under construction when I called by in April 1995. This complex of Spanish colonial-style condos and villas enjoys a hilltop setting amid landscaped grounds. There'll be two pools, a casino, and more. It's sure to bring a big change to this previously sequestered quarter.

Food

You'll find two restaurants at the beach: the inexpensive **Restaurante Encanto,** serving basic Costa Rican cuisine, and a slightly more ritzy outdoor restaurant that belongs to the Condor Club and has a more cosmopolitan menu. If you fancy some *schweinefleisch und apfelstrudel,* check out the **Restaurante Biergarten,** on the left 50 meters uphill from the half-buried car. The **Pizzeria La Gondola** is, of course, good for Italian dishes. If you're feeling flush, splurge at the restaurant of the Condor Club Hotel—the view alone might be worth it.

Getting There

The Flamingo-bound buses from San José (10:30 a.m.; see above) and Santa Cruz (10 a.m. and 2 p.m.) stop in Matapalo, from where you can walk or catch a taxi.

PLAYA GRANDE

Costa Rican beaches don't come more beautiful than this seemingly endless curve of coral-white sand with water as blue as the summer sky. Alas, no palms or shade trees grow down by the beach itself. A beach trail to the north leads along the cape through dry forest—good for birdlife. You'll see a few tidepools for snorkeling and bathing, and a 400-hectare mangrove estuary at the southern end, where you might encounter crocodiles eyeing you covetously. And with hunting by locals a thing of the past, the wildlife population is increasing; monkeys and deer, even cats, are being seen with greater frequency. Superb surf pumps ashore at high tide. Playa Grande is renowned among surfers for its consistency and good mix of lefts and rights. Surfing expert Mark Kelly rates it as "maybe the best overall spot in the country."

The beach has been the site of a raging battle between developers and conservationists. Much of the land backing the beach has been sold to developers, who had until recently been prevented from constructing homes and hotels. At issue is the fate of the leatherback turtle, and the fact that humankind stands on the brink of terminating forever a miracle that has played itself out annually at Playa Grande for the past several million years. Fortunately, the beach was incorporated into the national park system in May 1990 after a 15-year battle. However, developers have also won their battle: the Villa Baula Beach Resort opened in mid-1994, and the ribbon had just been cut on the Casas Playa Grande condominium project when I stopped by

in spring 1995. Work was half-complete on the Rancho Las Colinas Golf and Country Club development project, which will include 220 residential sites plus a 7,000-meter golf course, and much of the remaining shorefront was bought by an Iranian and sold off in parcels that await development, much of it already under way. How this will affect the turtle population is anyone's guess! Louis Wilson believes the greatest threat is from the lights at Tamarindo, whose shoreline—entirely built up by hotels—faces perpendicular to Playa Grande. See Playa Grande now. In five years it will be an entirely different place.

Camping is not allowed on the beach. (See "Las Baulas Marine Turtle National Park," below, for accommodations.)

LAS BAULAS MARINE TURTLE NATIONAL PARK

The 445-hectare Las Baulas National Park, which incorporates the Tamarindo National Wildlife Refuge, protects not only the prime nesting site of the leatherback turtle on the Pacific coast, but also the mangrove estuary behind the southern part of Playa Grande, plus 22,000

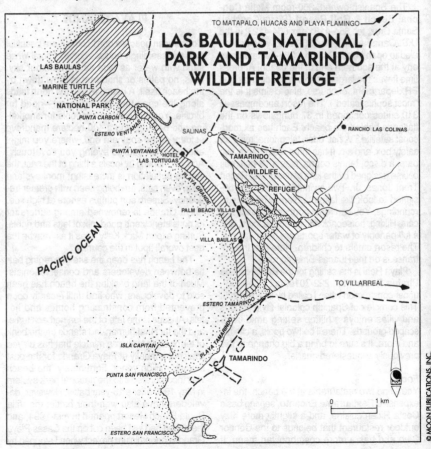

LAS BAULAS NATIONAL PARK AND TAMARINDO WILDLIFE REFUGE

TO MATAPALO, HUACAS AND PLAYA FLAMINGO

LAS BAULAS MARINE TURTLE NATIONAL PARK

PUNTA CARBON

ESTERO VENTANAS

SALINAS

RANCHO LAS COLINAS

PUNTA VENTANAS

HOTEL LAS TORTUGAS

TAMARINDO WILDLIFE REFUGE

PLAYA GRANDE

PALM BEACH VILLAS

PACIFIC OCEAN

VILLA BAULAS

TO VILLARREAL

ESTERO TAMARINDO

ISLA CAPITAN

PLAYA TAMARINDO

TAMARINDO

PUNTA SAN FRANCISCO

0   1 km

ESTERO SAN FRANCISCO

© MOON PUBLICATIONS, INC.

hectares out to sea. Turtles call at Playa Grande year-round. The nesting season for the giant leatherback is Oct.-April, when females come ashore every night at high tide. Often, more than 100 turtles might be seen in a single night. Olive ridley turtles can sometimes also be seen here, as may the smaller green turtles, May-August. Sept.-Nov. is best for avoiding hordes of tourists.

The park was formed because of the efforts of Louis Wilson and Marianel Pastor. In the 1970s, a cookie company was harvesting the turtles' eggs. The beach was subdivided among 30 or so egg-poachers, who sold Louis and Marianel "rights" to take tourists on to their sections of sand. Once the tourists left, the *hueveros* would steal the eggs. In the 1980s, Asians began harvesting eggs here. The government agreed to support the couple's efforts only if they could show that it was economically viable as a tourist destination. Things have come full circle. The locals have taken over all guiding (each guide is certified through an accredited course), and Las Baulas is now a model for similar experiments worldwide. The conservation group Earthwatch monitors the turtle population.

A visit here is a humbling, reverential experience. One turtle, having patiently withstood the intrusive gawking eyes through her labor, halted and turned to face me as I walked by her side down to the sea. Who knows what sentiment she may have tried to express. Watching her lumbering exertions as the mother-to-be hauled

herself back to sea was like saying a final, tearful farewell to a loved one. The experience was so sublime, so profound, that tears welled as I typed in my notes the next day.

Rangers from the local community roam the beach and lead groups to nesting turtles, guided by other rangers who spot for turtles and call in the location via walkie-talkies. Visitors are no longer allowed to walk the beach unescorted. Groups cannot exceed 15 people. And except for Christmas and holidays when the gates are opened and the beach is flooded with people, only 60 people are allowed at any time on the beach. Boy and Girl Scout groups often form patrols to protect against poaching. A large sign at the park entrance (by the Hotel Las Tortugas) gives instructions for turtle-watching. *Heed these instructions.* Resist the temptation to follow the example of the many thoughtless visitors who get too close to the turtles, try to touch them, ride their backs, or otherwise display a lack of common sense. Refrain from using flashlights or camera flash. And watch your step. Newborn turtles are difficult to see at night as they scurry down to the sea. Many are inadvertently crushed by tourist feet. No flashlights!

Information

You'll see a small **information booth** at the park entrance. Entrance: $15 walk-in, $7 advance purchase. During periods of high demand you must buy a ticket for a specified time. The guides

leatherback turtle, Playa Grande

WILDLAND ADVENTURES

police the beach and check for tickets at random (I'm told that people sneaking onto the beach without paying are dealt with harshly). Camping is not permitted. Hiking is allowed on the north side of the estuary and along the beach. Trails are not marked. The Hotel Las Tortugas (see below), by the park entrance, serves as the wildlife center for the marine park, but gradually all functions related to the refuge are being taken over by local community members.

Donations

The park is sadly underfunded. You can make donations earmarked for Las Baulas National Park through Fundación Chorotega (Apdo. 189, Santa Cruz de Guanacaste, tel. 255-2122 or 231-2608), Fundación de Parques Nacionales (Apdo. 1008, San José 1002, tel. 220-1744 or 232-0008), Fundación Neotrópica (Apdo. 236, San José 1002, tel. 253-2130); or via the Nature Conservancy International Program (1815 North Lynn St., Arlington, VA 22209, tel. 703-841-5300).

Budget Accommodations

Centro Vacacional Playa Grande (reservations, tel. 237-2552, fax 260-3991), on the left, about 400 meters before the beach, has 11 a/c cabinas (eight with kitchenette) with private baths, two bedrooms, kitchens, refrigerators, and fans. They sleep up to six people. You'll find reclining beach chairs under shade trees on the lawn, plus a popular outdoor restaurant with tasty and inexpensive seafood dishes. Free laundry service. Rates: $10 s, $20 d, $50 for six. You can camp here, too ($2). **Cabinas Las Baulas,** behind Centro Vacacional, also has six basic cabinas ($25 up to four people) plus camping.

Upscale Accommodations

Hotel Las Tortugas (Apdo. 164, Santa Cruz 5150, tel. 680-0765) is run by delightful owners, Louis Wilson and Marianel Pastor, who were instrumental in creating the refuge. Their hotel is a comfortable, ecotourist destination (indeed, much more comfortable than the brochure suggests). Since turtles are sensitive to light (newborn turtles are attracted to light; adults can be disoriented by it), there are no ocean views to the south, where the nesting beach is. Rooms have orthopedic mattresses plus private baths with hot water. The restaurant is mar-

velous: black stone floor, sextagonal tables of gleaming hardwood, an outdoor patio, plus a marvelous view over the beach through wall-to-wall windows. Hey! the food ain't bad either. Take your pick of burgers, sandwiches, tenderloin, shrimp, and chicken in wine or garlic sauce. And you *must* try the apple pie with ice cream! The hotel, described as "a mirthful combination of colonial and modern architecture," is bleached-white stucco throughout and has a turtle-shaped swimming pool with sundeck, plus a large hot-water Jacuzzi. An expansion was planned. The hotel rents surfboards and two-passenger canoes for trips into the estuary ($30 half day) and also has horseback riding. "We're an ol' Hemingway kind of place," says Louis, who tempts his willing Queensland Heelers (Australian cattle dogs) to perform a pantomime for guests. "I ruv roo!" barks June, after Benny sits up and begs her. Rate: $80 d.

Villa Baula Ecological Beach Resort (Apdo. 111-6151, Santa Ana 2000, tel. 228-2263, or 680-0869) is a resort with 20 rooms in five Thai-style, thatched hardwood bungalows raised on stilts within the dry forest behind the beach and in front of the Tamarindo Wildlife Refuge. Gosh! It almost feels like Africa, but it's far more humble than the artist's images in the brochure suggest. Twin rooms have two single beds; double rooms have a double bed. Bungalows sleep four. The Jaguarundi Restaurant and Malinche Bar face onto a swimming pool, plus there are trails for hiking and horseback riding, and mountain bikes, ocean kayaks, and surfboards for rent. The place seems to have been built without any attempt to shield the lights from the nesting turtles. In fact, there doesn't seem to be much that's "ecological" about it. Rates (high season): $80 twin/double, $95 t, $120 bungalow.

Half a kilometer north and likewise between beach and estuary is the **Casas Playa Grande/Palm Beach Village** complex, with fully furnished two-bedroom houses for purchase and rent. This little self-contained village of a/c Spanish colonial-style homes has a pool, and maid service is available. Rates: $85 d, or $500 weekly.

Linda Vista is a "private hilltop retreat with panoramic views," 400 meters to the right from Centro Vacacional. Another villa, this one on the beach, is for rent: **Villa Pura Vida.**

Deluxe Accommodations

Inland of Playa Grande is **Rancho Las Colinas Golf and Country Club** (SJO 893, P.O. Box 025216, Miami, FL 33102-5216; in Costa Rica, tel. 293-4644), which has turned an erstwhile cattle hacienda into a lush greensward. Many of the 220 condominium units under construction when I called by in April 1995 will be available as rented vacation units. Work began in 1994 on the 18-hole championship golf course, designed by internationally renowned golf course architect Ron Garl. The private club will have a limited membership . . . for $10,000 apiece for Full Membership! Palm Springs comes to Costa Rica, eh? The first nine holes were scheduled for completion in mid-1995, the balance by mid-1996. The course encircles Rancho Las Colinas and features artificial lakes. Members can enjoy the beach vistas and spectacular sunsets from the lounge, as well as sampling the swimming pool, tennis courts, and equestrian facilities. The self-contained resort includes a convenience store, small boutiques, and service-oriented businesses. A very snazzy but *private* beach club was also under construction north of Hotel Las Tortugas.

Tours

Virtually all the hotels in Playa Tamarindo and Flamingo can arrange turtle tours. **Rico Tours** (tel. 233-9658, fax 233-9357) offers a three-day all-inclusive "Las Baulas" package including lodging at Las Tortugas. **CATA Tours** (tel. 221-5455, fax 221-0200) offers a "Turtles under the Full Moon" tour, Nov.-April ($35). **Guanacaste Tours** (tel. 666-0306, fax 666-0307) offers a similar tour, Nov.-March ($40, including transfers from select hotels in Liberia and Playas Hermosa, Coco, Ocotal, Flamingo, Conchal, Tamarindo, Junquillal). **Papagayo Excursions** (tel. 680-0859, fax 223-3648), in Tamarindo, offers a nocturnal "Turtle Nesting Safari" throughout the nesting season ($25); so does **Flamingo Tours** (tel. 654-4238, fax 654-4039; in San José, tel. 222-6762), in Playa Flamingo. (see "Tamarindo," below, for tours to Tamarindo Wildlife Refuge.)

A "Jungle Boat Safari" aboard a 20-passenger, environmentally sound pontoon boat (i.e. low pollution, silent engine) takes you into the mangrove-rich Tamarindo Wildlife Refuge; $20 per person. It's operated by the local community. Ask at any hotel.

Getting There

The Flamingo-bound buses from San José (10:30 a.m.; see "Playa Flamingo," above) and Santa Cruz (10 a.m. and 2 p.m.) stop in Matapalo, where you can walk or catch a taxi.

TAMARINDO

Playa Tamarindo, eight km south of Huacas, is one of the most popular beach destinations for foreign travelers, especially North American surf dudes. Tamarindo is blessed with an array of accommodations for every budget. Still, it gets very full in high season, when a room in cheaper hotels is often hard to find. Reservations are recommended. The massive gray-sand beach is very deep when the tide goes out, and somewhat pebbly. It's backed by tamarind trees, which give the beach its name. No-see-ums, tiny sand flies that pack a jumbo-size bite, are a problem around dusk. More appealing is a smaller beach south of the main beach, with tidepools and relatively few people. The estuary that separates Tamarindo from Playa Grande to the north is a nirvana for birders; the estuary is protected as the **Tamarindo Wildlife Refuge,** now incorporated into the Guanacaste Marine Turtle National al Park (see above) and featuring crocodile and monkeys in the star-billed cast.

If swimming, beware of riptides. Tamarindo is popular with surfers. The beach has three surf breaks: a rocky right-point shore break named Henry's Point in front of the Restaurante Zully Mar, a left shore break named Pico Pequeño 100 meters north, and a superb rivermouth break. Local boats will also run surfers to difficult-to-reach surf spots nearby, including **Playa Langosta** (three km south of Tamarindo), **Playa Avellana** (10 km south; see below), and **Playa Negra** (12 km south). Langosta is famed for its rocky left and reefy shore breaks and is frequented by turtles. Langosta is undeveloped (you can camp beside the Río San Francisco) and now used for turtle-watching tours.

Real estate prices in Tamarindo have been inflated significantly, as the area has seen a decade of popularity among wealthy Europeans

and North Americans with cash in hand; a good percentage of the local hotels, restaurants, and businesses are operated by Canadians, Americans, Italians, and Swiss.

Budget Accommodations

A backpacker's beachfront favorite, **Hotel/Bar/Restaurante Dolly** (tel. 680-0174) has 12 small and basic cabinas. They're simple and totally bland, but clean. A restaurant on the ground floor is open on one side. One report says beware of paying a deposit. Rates: $16 d ($12 subsequent nights).

Inexpensive Accommodations

The best bargain in its price range is **Cabinas Zully Mar** (Apdo. 68, Santa Cruz, Guanacaste; San José, tel. 226-4732), a very well-run property with 27 clean rooms (eight with a/c) with private baths with cold water. It's understandably popular with backpackers. A curving outside staircase leads to upstairs rooms. Rates: $20 with fan and private bath, $24 for slightly larger rooms with refrigerator, $40 double with a/c.

Cabinas Pozo Azul (tel. 680-0147) has 27 spacious and clean rooms with fans and private baths with cold water; some have a/c and kitchenettes. Ask for a room with covered parking. No shade, but at least there's a pool. Rates: $24 s/d, $33 with a/c. **Cabinas Marielos** (tel. 441-4843), reached by a short palm-lined drive, has eight simple but pleasing cabinas with fans, verandas, and private baths with cold water. They're set in a natural garden with lots of shady palms. Rate: $22.50 per person. The owners also rent out a sparsely furnished two-story house for 10, with kitchen and large living area (available Feb.-Nov. only; $750 per week).

Moderate Accommodations

Finca Monte Fresco (tel. 680-0776), near Villarreal, offers fully furnished apartments with kitchens and a fabulous view over Playa Grande.

The **Hotel/Bar/Restaurante El Milagro** (Apdo. 145, Santa Cruz 5150, tel. 441-5102, fax 441-8494) has charm. The 30 modern rooms—set in soothing, breezy, landscaped grounds with swimming pool—have a/c, fans, and private baths with hot water. A very nice restaurant serves European cuisine under the

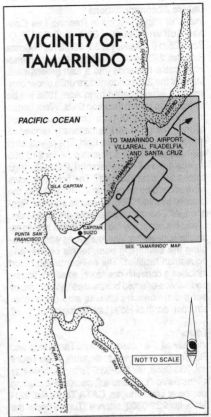

watchful guidance of European management. El Milagro means "the Miracle." Where they'll find the room heaven knows, but more rooms are slated. Rate: $50 d, including breakfast.

Hotel Tropicana (tel./fax 654-4261) is a gleaming white, 44-room, two-unit Spanish colonial-style complex; one unit features a spiral staircase that conjures images of the double-helix staircase of Chateaux Chambord. Within, rooms are pleasant and roomy with heaps of light. The hotel has a swimming pool and restaurant. Rates: $45 d, $50 t.

Despite its grandiose name, the **Tamarindo Resort Club** (Apdo. 73, Santa Cruz 5150, tel. 680-0883, fax 255-3785) is not as salubrious as one might think. It offers 40 basic cabinas

spread across barely landscaped grounds. Cabins have fans and private baths with hot water. Three have a/c. The club has a small pool, plus a bar and restaurant that doubles as a disco. The place offers water-skiing, scuba diving, snorkeling trips, and coastal cruises, plus rents surfboards ($4 half day, $7 full day) and boogie boards ($3.50 half day, $6 full day). Rate: $93 up to five people.

Upscale Accommodations

On the approach road to town, directly opposite the airstrip, is **Hotel La Reserva** (Apdo. 167, Santa Cruz, Guanacaste, tel./fax 654-4182), a very impressive Italian-owned proper-

ty about to open. The bungalows, comparatively modest within, have ochre-washed walls and intriguing Thai-style roofs (actually, Tyrolean I'm told). Each has a/c, ceiling fan, telephone, mini-bar, safety box, plus terra-cotta tile floors and rough plaster white walls. They look down over a fabulous pool measuring more than 1,000 square meters and fringed by a wide sundeck. Nearby is Harry's Bar & Cocktail Lounge and an elegant *ranchita* restaurant. Work up a sweat on night-lit tennis courts or the sand volleyball court. Rates: $60 d, $95 suite.

Down by the shores, **Hotel Tamarindo Diría** (tel./fax 654-4031; or Apdo. 4211, San José 1000, tel. 289-8616, fax 289-8727) is a com-

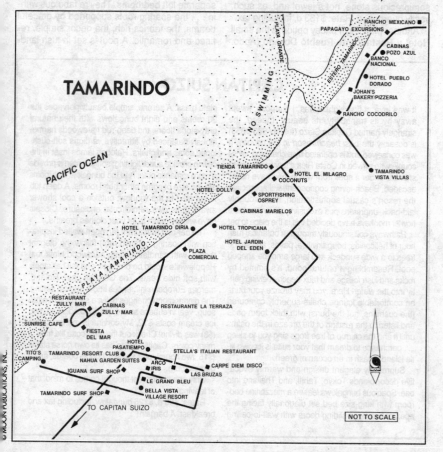

TAMARINDO

PACIFIC OCEAN

PLAYA GRANDE

NO SWIMMING

ESTERO TAMARINDO

RANCHO MEXICANO

PAPAGAYO EXCURSIONS

CABINAS POZO AZUL

BANCO NACIONAL

HOTEL PUEBLO DORADO

JOHAN'S BAKERY/PIZZERIA

RANCHO COCODRILO

TIENDA TAMARINDO

HOTEL EL MILAGRO

COCONUTS

TAMARINDO VISTA VILLAS

HOTEL DOLLY

SPORTFISHING OSPREY

CABINAS MARIELOS

HOTEL TAMARINDO DIRIA

HOTEL TROPICANA

HOTEL JARDIN DEL EDEN

PLAYA TAMARINDO

PLAZA COMERCIAL

RESTAURANT ZULLY MAR

CABINAS ZULLY MAR

RESTAURANTE LA TERRAZA

SUNRISE CAFE

FIESTA DEL MAR

TITO'S CAMPING

TAMARINDO RESORT CLUB

HOTEL PASATIEMPO

NAHUA GARDEN SUITES

IGUANA SURF SHOP

ARCO IRIS

STELLA'S ITALIAN RESTAURANT

CARPE DIEM DISCO

LAS BRUZAS

LE GRAND BLEU

BELLA VISTA VILLAGE RESORT

TAMARINDO SURF SHOP

TO CAPITAN SUIZO

NOT TO SCALE

© MOON PUBLICATIONS, INC.

pact hotel with 70 rooms, recently refurbished with terra-cotta tile floors, heaps of storage, pleasing if '60s-style furniture, a/c, private bathrooms, hot water, cable TV, and telephones. Some have a Jacuzzi. A very large and airy restaurant with a beautiful hardwood ceiling opens onto an expansive bar, an outside cocktail terrace, and a large swimming pool in shady grounds. There are tennis courts plus a small casino (open 6-11 p.m.). The Boutique Papagayo offers sportfishing and tours. The hotel is popular with the senior crowd. There are rocky tidepools in front of the hotel. It reminds me of Honolulu resorts a decade ago. Prices are deluxe, though the property is not. It's more a semiprecious stone, not a jewel and, as such, vastly overpriced. Rate: $133 d, including tax.

Another pleasing if pricey option is the small **Hotel y Restaurante Pueblo Dorado** (Apdo. 1711, San José 1002, tel./fax 222-5741), a Spanish-style "villa" with 22 rooms with a/c and private baths with hot water. The place is simply furnished in very elegant modern decor of grays, blacks, and whites. A small bar and restaurant overlooks a pool and a tiny landscaped courtyard garden. Maya-style motifs abound. The hotel rents kayaks ($10 per hour) and has a minibus service to San José ($150 one-way for 12 people). Rates: $50 s, $60 d, $70 t.

Looking like a South African *kraal* is the **Bella Vista Village Resort** (Apdo. 143, Santa Cruz 5150, tel./fax 654-4036), featuring six hilltop, thatched, four-person bungalows with fully furnished kitchens, living rooms, dining areas and separate loft bedrooms. They're fabulous within . . . the soaring roofs supported by graceful beams, the fabrics rich, the decor simple, refined and romantic. A pool is set in lush land-

CAPITÁN SUIZO

It was love at first sight. I was, I suppose, swept away by its tranquility, its beauty. Indeed, the strangely named Capitán Suizo (tel./fax 680-0853) is possibly the *best beach resort in the country*. It was conceived and is operated by a charming Swiss couple who arrived in Costa Rica a few years ago to stumble under a spell from which they have never escaped. Beach-loving cognoscenti will appreciate the resort's casual sophistication, its thoroughly laid-back, unpretensious exclusivity. Even the local howler monkeys have decided this is the place to be!

Pathways coil sinuously through a botanical rush hour of heliconias, bougainvillea, palms, and shade trees to a wide sundeck and large amoeba-shaped pool. Resembling a natural pond, it's rimmed by rocks and lush foliage and faux-beach shelving gently into the water. Here, you may bronze your buns on comfortable lounge chairs superbly contoured (the cushions, not the buns) with thick foam pads and listen to the rustling of the breeze in the palms until it and the chirrup of tree frogs sing you to sleep . . . perchance to dream that your suite is its own little island awash in an ocean of green.

Supremely elegant design and warmly evocative decor blends Tokyo, Tahiti, and Thailand into one. Spacious bungalows feature a mezzanine bedroom with king-size bed set diagonally facing the apex of two huge sliding doors with wall-to-ceiling plate glass. A serene, simple beauty pervades the 20 rooms and eight bungalows with their natural gray-stone floors and deep-red hardwoods harmoniously balanced by attractive verdigris soft-cushioned sofas and chairs. Halogen lamps inset in the ceiling provide super lighting; soft-lit lanterns provide a more romantic note. And the bungalow bathrooms are the size of some other hotel rooms. A deep tub is set next to the window; outside a cool shower awaits in its own semicircular enclosure. Closets have wicker-mesh to let your clothes breathe.

The bar and restaurant (an open-walled inspiration with soaring pyramid roof) follow the elegant theme, with candlelit dining, hardwood hints that Hepplewhite would be proud of, and tall bar stools with soft hide seats. The German chef, Roland, merges European influences into a tropical setting. The dinner menu changes daily: a set meal of oxtail soup, veal in cheese sauce, rosti, mixed salad, and ice cream costs $12. My corvina in mango sauce ($8) was divine! Check out the terra-cotta tile floor of many colors. Capitán Suizo has its own horse stable ($15, two hours), plus kayaks, boogie boards, and a games room.

Only one bittersweet thought comes to mind: that of leaving!

Rates: $90 d, $125 bungalow, including tax and breakfast. A bargain!

scaped grounds. Very attractive. The "kraal" commands marvelous views over the treetops to the ocean. Rates: $50-80 s, $55-90 d (low-high season).

Another newcomer is **Hotel Pasatiempo** (tel. 680-0776), with 10 attractive, spacious, well-lit thatched cabins around a pool in pretty grounds full of bougainvillea, bananas and palms. Note the beautiful hand-carved doors. It has a book exchange, and you can rent snorkeling gear. The Yucca Bar is a good place to sup. Rates: $59 d, $10 extra.

Across the road is **Nahua Garden Suites** (tel. 654-4223), with very attractive suites boasting terra-cotta floors, kitchenettes with gleaming white tiles with colonial-tile hints, plus futon, a queen-size bed on a mezzanine, and hardwood accents. Lush gardens have a lap pool. In all there are five suites (11 more are planned).

Farther up the road **Las Bruzas** restaurant has three very atmospheric, native-style cabinas with loft bedrooms. Nearby, **Carpe Diem** is a cabin complex that should be complete by the time you read this.

Not reviewed, but recommended to me, is **Tamarindo Vista Villas** (tel./fax 654-4298), with ocean-view one-bedroom Executive Suites and three-bedroom Imperial Suites, with spacious verandas and balconies centered on a twin-turreted lounge area. I'm informed these are are elegant enough for Hollywood to have dreamed up. There's a pool and spacious solarium deck.

Deluxe Accommodations

There're two places in Tamarindo where you get what you pay for, and more. The first is Capitán Suizo (see special topic). The second is the **Hotel Jardín del Edén** (Apdo. 1094, San Pedro 2050, tel./fax 220-2096; in Tamarindo, tel./fax 654-4111), on a bluff overlooking Tamarindo. The "Garden of Eden" comprises a group of five supremely handsome, salmon-pink Spanish-style villas with 18 independent rooms, and two fully equipped apartments owned and managed by a congenial Italian couple, Marcello and Aurora Marongiu, and their equally amiable partner Etienne. This place earns laurels for its evocative design, its amorous tenor. All rooms have spacious terrace porches offering fabulous views out to sea.

A stunning, amoeba-shaped pool with swim-up bar and magnificent blue-tiled Jacuzzi, and a large sundeck with shady *ranchitas* are surrounded by gardens fit for Adam and Eve. The lush foliage is floodlit at night, creating a colorful quasi-*son et lumière*. A cool, shady restaurant has heavy-duty hardwood tables inlaid with beautiful Spanish tiles, plus a changing menu that pays special attention to its Mediterranean-inspired seafood dishes. Pop in at breakfast for a fresh croissant from the *patisserie*. A lamp-lit pathway leads down to the beach. Very atmospheric—so paradisical it's almost Biblical. When I called in in 1995 it was even better than I remembered. Six smaller rooms and two suites may be added. Highly recommended! Rates: $80 s (small), $100 d (large), $135 d (apartments), including buffet breakfast. Children under 10, $10.

House Rental

There are several houses for rent locally, especially south of town. Look for notices, or ask at **Tienda Tamarindo, Palm Shop,** or the office opposite Papagayo Excursions. One property (in the U.S., tel. 800-874-7522 or 619-529-1365; in Costa Rica, tel. 654-4223) features three private rooms with "Bali-style bath/shower" and kiddies' loft, plus a guest cottage with kitchen and kiddies' loft. Another three-bedroom/2.5-bath house is available for $95 nightly with maid and cook (2300 Via Fernandez, Palos Verdes, CA 90274, tel. 310-378-3580). Also try Mike Stoker (tel. 310-378-3580).

Camping

The **Tamarindo Resort Club** allows camping by the beach ($3 per person). **Tito's,** a funky campsite under shade trees, lies further south.

Food

If Tamarindo has anything going for it, it must be its restaurants, which include some of the most creative of any beach resort in the country. Two Indonesian-inspired eateries stand out. **Fiesta del Mar** is a very atmospheric and romantic restaurant with a lofty Indonesian-style ceiling of rough-hewn timber and thatch. Pretty floral tableclothes and carnations on the tables hint at the quality of the food: steak and seafood dishes—and cocktails—are the house specialty. On a

par is **Coconuts,** which feels like something out of a Somerset Maugham novel. The restaurant is set on stilts, with an open-air lounge terrace and *palenque* bar. Candle-lit dining is very romantic, with vases full of orchids and soothing music. The unusually inventive menu has moved toward French cuisine of late, but retains a hint of Indonesia in its *dorado teriyaki,* red chicken curry, and *pato à la Thaki).*

Stella's Italian Restaurant, 400 meters beyond the Tamarindo Resort Club, offers very elegant dining under a pretty *palenque.* It has tempting vegetarian and seafood dishes (fettucine, fish in basic martini sauce, and linguine with shrimp with wine sauce). The **Restaurante El Jardín del Edén,** in the hotel of that name, offers surefire winners: a fabulous menu daily, with dishes such as jumbo shrimp in whiskey, lobster in lemon sauce, peppered tenderloin, etc. enjoyed in a setting that may well inspire you to check into the hotel! When the owner of Jardín tells you, however, that the best place in town is **La Terraza,** you believe him! The latter is a pizza restaurant with breezy upstairs dining in a circular restaurant with bamboo furnishings; chef Stefano knows his stuff. So, too, does Roland, the German chef at **Capitán Suizo,** where you should also eat before leaving town. Another option for Italian food is the rustic **Las Bruzas.**

Sunrise Cafe & Nogui Bar and **Zully Mar,** on the beachfront, are also recommended. For European cuisine, try **El Milagro** (see "Moderate Accommodations," above) or **Le Grande Bleu.** **El Girasol** serves health foods (7 a.m.-3 p.m.; closed Tuesday) in a beautiful setting; **Arco Iris** serves vegetarian food. Craving a burger and fries? The **Junglebus** serves "Killer Burgers and Munchies" down by the traffic circle.

Johan's Bakery, opposite the Pueblo Dorado, is a shady, open-air eatery overlooking the estuary. Johan, the Belgian owner, conjures real European croissants, chocolate eclairs, pizza, waffles, and bread.

Rancho Cocodrilo is a cool place to hang out for beers and *bocas.*

Activities and Tours

Papagayo Excursions (Apdo. 35, Santa Cruz de Guanacaste, tel. 680-0859, fax 225-3648) has an office on the right as you enter town. It runs sportfishing trips (half day from $250, full day from $350), windsurfing, water-skiing, scuba diving (from $60 for two guided dives), and nature tours, including a "Jungle Boat Safari" up the Tamarindo Estuary and nocturnal "Turtle Nesting Tours" ($25) that visit Playa Langosta. **Tienda Tamarindo** (tel. 680-0776) is a store selling virtually everying a tourist wants (souvenirs, clothes, magazines, etc.); next door is an adjunct offering turtle tours by boat ($12) or kayak ($25), horseback rides ($20, two hours), helicopter tours ($25, 10 minutes), and a sunset cruise ($35). They also rent kayaks and mountain bikes. **Iguana Surf Shop** rents surfboards ($10 half-day) and kayaks and has surf tours and kayak trips into the estuary ($25), plus catamaran trips. **Río del Pacífico** (tel. 680-0883, fax 255-3785) offers parasailing and surfing trips to Witch's Rock (Playa Naranjo), water-skiing, and bucking-bronco banana-tube trips (you ride the waves on a long yellow tube that is pulled behind a fast-paced speedboat). The shop is located on the beach in front of the Tamarindo Resort Club. **Tamarindo Sportfishing** (Apdo. 188, Santa Cruz, tel./fax 680-0280) has a large variety of modern boats, from a seven-meter Boston Whaler ($250 half day, $350 full day) to a 12-meter Topaz ($500 half day, $800 full day). **Flamingo Tours** (tel. 654-4238, fax 654-4039), in Playa Flamingo, offers boat trips into the Tamarindo Wildlife Refuge.

Fancy the snap of the wind in the sails? *Surfari* (tel. 680-0883 or 228-6380), run by the brothers Brown, is an 11-meter sloop that operates day and multiday tours ($75-95 per day) and charters along the Pacific coast, including surf tours to Witch's Rock and Pavones. You can help trim the sails or even take the helm if you wish. A full-day snorkeling trip to Playa Conchal costs $50; a two-hour sunset cruise is $25. Other vessels offering sunset and day cruises include *Samonique,* a 16-meter ketch (sunset cruise Tuesday and Thursday, $33), which is advertised locally.

Services

The **Tamarindo Information Center** is at the end of the road, in the heart of Tamarindo. The **Palm Shop,** 50 meters beyond Hotel/Restaurante Dolly, has a **tourist information service,** plus a small souvenir shop and tours; it rents

surf boards and also represents SANSA airline (tel. 654-4223). **Galería Doña Luna,** on the traffic circle, has a marvelous eclectic array of arts and crafts. **Tienda Tamarindo** has more conventional souvenirs, plus magazines, swimwear, etc. Next door is an **Artesanía** selling Guaitil pottery, Guatemalan clothing, straw hats, and the like. Johan's bakery, of all places, has a **rent-a-car** service. You can rent mopeds from **Tienda Tamarindo** ($12 half-day; $20 full-day), and motorbikes from **Moto-Sprint,** at the entrance of Tamarindo Resort Club ($40 per day; $200 per week). It also has mountain bikes. You'll find **public telephones** outside the Hotel Tamarindo Diriá and the Fiesta del Mar. **Sol Rent-a-Car** (in Liberia, tel. 666-2222, fax 666-2898) has an office in town. There's no **gas station** in town but you can buy gas at inflated prices at a funky shack on the right as you enter town.

Transportation

Buses depart San José daily from Calle 14, Avenidas 3/5 (Empresa Alfaro, tel. 222-2750), at 3:30 p.m.; and Calle 20, Avenida 3 (Tralapa, tel. 221-7202), at 4 p.m. Return buses depart Tamarindo at 5:45 a.m. (Alfaro) and 6:45 a.m (Tralapa). Buy tickets in advance, especially for weekends and holidays. Buses depart Santa Cruz daily at 10:30 a.m. and 3:30 p.m. and return from Tamarindo at 6 a.m. and noon.

SANSA (tel. 233-0397 or 233-3258, fax 255-2176) operates flights to Tamarindo from San José on Monday, Wednesday, and Friday at 6 a.m., continuing to Nosara and Sámara; and daily (except Sunday) at 11:15 a.m. and Sunday at 8 a.m. via Tambor, continuing to Sámara and Tambor. **Travelair** (tel. 232-7883 or 220-3054, fax 220-0413) flies direct to Tamarindo ($82 one-way) from Pavas Airport, daily at 7:30 a.m. and 2 p.m.; return flights depart Tamarindo at 8:40 a.m. and 3:40 p.m. **Note:** Reduced schedules operate mid-April through mid-December.

SANSA also offers package tours to Tamarindo, including airport transfers, accommodations, and local tours. Papagayo Excursions offers private air charters ($380).

TAMARINDO TO PLAYA NOSARA

PLAYA AVELLANA

You must backtrack to Villarreal from Tamarindo to continue southward along the coast. The dirt road from Hernandez, three km east of Villarreal, leads to Playa Avellana (11 km from Villarreal), a very beautiful and as-yet-undiscovered coral-colored beach with lots of tidepools. Avellana is renowned for its barrel surf. A break named Guanacasteco is described as a "bitchin' beach break." You can also reach Avellana and Playa Junquillal (10 km farther south) directly by paved road (via the village of 27 de Abril) from Santa Cruz, off the main road between Nicoya and Liberia.

Accommodations and Food
Camping is allowed on the beach just north of **Freddy's Restaurante & Surf Camp,** a very funky eatery with hammocks and tumbledown tables and chairs. Freddy offers cheap **cabinas** ($8-12). I've received two separate reports of thievery here, and sanitation leaves much to be desired. **Bar y Restaurante Gregorio's,** a pleasant bar and restaurant under thatch, has three basic cabinas 100 meters from the beach ($23 per night for four people).

A three-story all-hardwood place called **Mono Congo Lodge** sits between Playa Avellana and Playa Negra and has been described as "a mixture of Swiss Family Robinson tree house and Australian outback bed and breakfast." I drove straight by without realizing it was a hotel. Not reviewed.

PLAYA GARTILLO

Virtually undiscovered Playa Gartillo, beyond Punta Pargos, just south of Playa Avellana, is another white-sand beach with tidepools. The dirt road cuts inland from Playa Gartillo to the tiny hamlet of **Paraíso,** from where another dirt road leads back to the coast and dead-ends in Playa Junquillal. A self-appointed **tourist information center** can be found on the soccer field where you turn left of Junquillal. You'll also find a gas station here.

Accommodations
The **Lagartillo Beach Hotel** (Apdo. 1584, San José 1000, tel. 257-1420, fax 221-5717), atop a hill about 200 meters from the beach, is surprisingly pleasant for being so far off the beaten track. Ten pleasant all-wood cabinas come with fans, private baths, and hammocks on private verandas. A spacious and atmospheric bar and restaurant overlooks a small swimming pool. The hotel has bicycles and horses for rent. Rate: about $50 double.

JUNQUILLAL

Playa Junquillal, four km southwest of Paraíso, is a very beautiful four-km-long light-gray-sand beach without shade trees. There is virtually no development and only very limited services. You can **camp** along the beach; bring your own water and supplies. The beach gets whiter to the north and has extensive rock platforms for tidepooling. Beware the high surf and strong riptides; swimming is not recommended. The beachfront road dead-ends to the south at the very wide and deep Río Andumolo. The mangrove estuary offers plentiful birdlife and reportedly a crocodile or two. There are no budget accommodations. Junquillal is 29 km west of Santa Cruz via 27 de Abril and Paraíso.

Moderate Accommodations
El Castillo Divertido, 300 meters from the beach, is a little white castle-like structure in a breezy hilltop setting. It has a restaurant and souvenir shop. Rate: $37. Nearby is the Swiss-run **Guacamaya Lodge** (tel. 223-2300), with six clean, octagonal cabinas with private bath, hot water, and hammocks on the porch. The small pool and bar-cum-restaurant have ocean views. Rate: $45 d, including tax.

Within shouting distance is the **Hibiscus Hotel** (tel./fax 680-0737), run by Danielle and

Gilberto Farha—he Costa Rican, she an affable French hostess. It has five rooms with private baths with hot water set amid landscaped grounds full of palms and plantains. The genteel and spotless rooms have hammocks on the terraces. Good-quality French cuisine is served in a pretty little dining area. Rates: $35 s, $40 d.

Upscale Accommodations
The **Iguanazul Beach Resort** (Apdo. 130, Santa Cruz 5150, tel./fax 680-0783, tel. 232-1423, or tel. 680-0335) enjoys a breezy clifftop setting overlooking the beach, about two km south of Paraíso and two km north of Junquillal. The cabinas are set around a pleasant amoeba-shaped pool surrounded by lawns. They're pleasing enough but a bit short on light. The resort has a volleyball court and a small souvenir store. An elegant restaurant and bar open onto the pool. The hotel offers a shuttle from San José on Saturday, Tuesday, and Thursday. ($30 one-way; for reservations, tel. 227-2180). Rates: $48 s, $60 d, $70 t, $80 quad or $85 with a/c.

In the center of the beach is the German-run **Villa Serena** (Apdo. 17, Santa Cruz 5150, tel./fax 680-0737), which has nine modern bungalows (one family-size) and a new two-story unit with 12 rooms, each with its own private terrace. The spacious, light, and airy rooms—all with fans and private baths with hot water—are spread out among palms and surrounded by emerald-green grass and flowery gardens. The villa has a cozy lounge overlooking the beach, a library with a VCR and video library, and—for the active—a dive shop, a swimming pool, and a hibiscus-encircled tennis court. Dinners are served on an elevated veranda overlooking the ocean. No great distinction over lesser priced competitors. Overpriced! Rates: $120 d, $140 t, including all meals and tax.

The **Antumalal Hotel** (Apdo. 49, Santa Cruz 5150, tel./fax 680-0506), 200 meters from the shore near the southern end of the beach, is rather jaded. Expansive landscaped grounds help make amends. The 23 spacious but basically furnished cabins have oodles of light and bright color schemes with birds painted on the walls. The bungalows are spaced well apart, with hammocks on private patios, good for watching the resident parrots and monkeys play-acting. Amenities include a large pool with water

slide, a beautiful tennis court, a small open-air gym, and even an open-air disco. Enjoy dinner in an elegant and pleasing restaurant under a thatched *palenque* roof. The hotel offers horseback riding, fishing, and diving. The owners plan to add 10 upscale villas. Rates: $60 s, $75 d ($10 each additional person).

Camping
Camping Los Malinches can be found by following the road to the right, south of Iguanazul.

Transportation
A bus departs San José for Junquillal from Avenida 3, Calle 20 (Tralapa, tel. 221-7202; in Junquillal, tel. 680-0392) daily at 2 p.m. (five hours; $5). A bus departs Santa Cruz at 6:30 p.m. Return buses depart for Santa Cruz and San José at 5 a.m.

PLAYAS LAGARTO, MANZANILLO, PITAYA, AND AZUL

To continue south along the coast you must return to Paraíso. The turn off for the coast road, three km east of Paraíso, is easy to miss. A small hand-written sign reads "Lagarto." It's directly opposite a thatched *ranchita* called **Pochotes Pamperos** on the north side of the road.

The dirt road leads south via the hamlets of Lagarto, Marbella, and San Juanillo (28 km south of Paraíso) and is in excellent shape—flat and without potholes—and quite possible for an ordinary car in dry season. It had been newly widened and leveled by a bulldozer when I drove it in April 1995, and if your driving skills are up to it and you don't mind raising a pall of dust, you can put your foot down and run the road in top gear; not recommended for relaxed touring, but for a travel writer on a tight schedule and for those who thrill to fast driving, a helluva lot of fun on the dirt and gravel (the best way to tackle the appalling corrugations is *not* to go slow, which can shake loose your teeth, but to attain a minimum speed—probably around 65 km/h—where you ride *atop* the ridges; the speed can vary with wheelbase of the vehicle). New bridges have been built over most of the little rivers where a few years ago you had to stop

and check their conditions before driving over them.

Goodness knows how many fabulous beaches lie hidden along this route, which for most of the way is out of sight of the shore. There are no hotels for miles! Just forest, cattle pasture, lonesome rustic dwellings, and an occasional ramshackle fishing village.

Eventually you'll pass a sign for **Matapalo Bar,** a rustic yet welcome *soda* with chickens underfoot. Refresh yourself here with a beer and *casado* and views of the wide crescent beach, **Playa Pitaya.** The surf and tidepooling are good, and turtles come ashore in winter. There are simple cabinas here ($12), too, just past the village of **Marbella.**

About five km farther south, a turn off leads to the fishing hamlet of **San Juanillo,** where within the secret cove at the bottom of a very steep, rutted dirt road you'll find **Giants of the Deep Sportfishing** (tel. 680-0797) down by the tiny white-sand beach. Surprise! This horseshoe cove has several yachts and motor-launches at anchor.

OSTIONAL
NATIONAL WILDLIFE REFUGE

The 248-hectare Ostional National Wildlife Refuge begins at Punta India, about two km south of San Juanillo, and extends along 15 km of shoreline to Punta Guiones, eight km south of the village of Nosara. It incorporates the beaches of Playa Ostional, Playa Nosara, and Playa Guiones. The refuge was created to protect one of two vitally important nesting sites in Costa Rica for the *lora,* or olive ridley turtle (the other is Playa Nancite, in Santa Rosa National Park). Ostional was named by the World Conference for the Conservation of Sea Turtles as one of the world's most important sea turtle hatcheries. A significant proportion of the world's Pacific ridley turtle population nests at Ostional, where they head for a narrow sandy strip between Punta División and Ostional estuary, invading the beach en masse for up to one week at a time July-Dec. (peak season is August and September), and singly or in small groups at other times during the year.

Time your arrival correctly and out beyond the breakers you may see a vast flotilla of turtles massed shoulder-to-shoulder, waiting their turn to swarm ashore, dig a hole in sand, and drop in the seeds for tomorrow's turtles. The legions pour out of the surf in endless waves until they are so densely packed that, in the words of the great turtle expert Archie Carr: "One could have walked a mile without touching the earth . . . [you] could have done this, literally, with no metaphoric license at all. You could have run a whole mile down the beach on the backs of turtles and never have set foot on the sand."

It's a stupendous sight, this *arribada,* this "arrival." Of the world's eight marine turtle species, only the females of the olive ridley and its Atlantic cousin, Kemp's ridley, stage *arribadas:* synchronized mass nestings are known to occur at only nine beaches worldwide (in Mexico, Nicaragua, Honduras, Surinam, Orissa in India, and Costa Rica). Playa Ostional is the most important of these.

So tightly packed is the horde that the turtles feverishly clamber over one another in their efforts to find an unoccupied nesting site. As they dig, sweeping their flippers back and forth, the petulant females scatter sand over one another and the air is filled with the slapping of flippers on shells. By the time the *arribada* is over, more than 150,000 turtles may have stormed this prodigal place and 15 million eggs may lie buried in the sand.

Leatherback turtles also come ashore to nest in smaller numbers Oct.-January.

You can walk virtually the entire length of the beach's 15-km shoreline, which is littered with broken eggshells. Although turtles can handle the very strong currents, humans have a harder time: swimming is not advised. Much of the coastline south of the tiny village of Ostional has been developed and there's not a great deal of wildlife. Howler monkeys, coatimundis, and kinkajous, however, frequent the forest inland from the beach. The small mangrove swamp at the mouth of the Río Nosara is a nesting site for many of the 190 bird species hereabouts. The road parallels the dark-gray-sand beach, although for most of the way you don't have a view of the ocean. There is no shade on the beach.

Wealthy foreigners are buying land surrounding the refuge, with plans to build hotels to profit off the natural spectacle of the turtles. En-

RESPITE FOR THE RIDLEY

As the female ridley covers her nest with toeless flat feet and pounds back to the sea without ever looking back, does she know that she was herself hatched at Ostional 20 or more years ago? In those 20 years, the little boys who watched her mother come up to shore and then stole her eggs have grown up. A generation has passed, but the grown men who have not gone to the city to make it big will still take her eggs and sell them to *cantinas* to be drunk raw so that men might have strength in their loins. At dawn the whole village will descend on the beach. The men of Ostional will feel for the nests with their heels in a sort of two-step fashion. And the women and girls, all nicely dressed and with combs in their hair, will dig deep and remove the eggs and place them in rice sacks ready for shipment to bars to boost egos.

Though guards were first placed at Ostional in 1979 to protect the endangered ridley, still the egg harvest continues. But all is not what it seems. Elsewhere in Costa Rica, harvesting turtle eggs is illegal and usually occurs in the dead of night. At Ostional it occurs legally and by daylight.

The seeming rape of the ridley—called *lora* locally—is the pith of a bold conservation program that aims to help the turtles by allowing the local community to commercially harvest eggs in a rational manner. "The main goal . . . is to achieve social growth of the community through controlled removal of eggs without compromising the reproduction and conservation of the species," says Claudette Mo, professor of biology at the National University of Costa Rica.

Dramatic declines of ridley populations are evident throughout Central America. Nowhere is the ridley left in peace. During the late 1970s massive commercial exploitation of ridleys developed in Ecuador, where a significant proportion of Costa Rica's nesting population spends the nonnesting season feeding on macroplankton. Up to 150,000 adult ridleys were being killed to make "shoes for Italian pimps," in the words of Archie Carr. Ecuador banned the practice in 1981, but "resource pirates" from Asia still fish for turtles off Ecuador in violation of the latter's territorial rights. Mexico continued the slaughter until 1990. And tens of thousands of ridleys are still caught by shrimp trawlers along the coasts of Central America.

Legislative efforts throughout Central America have attempted to regulate the taking of eggs, but none have been very effective. Costa Rica outlawed the taking of turtle eggs in 1966. But egg poaching is a time-honored tradition. The coming of the first *arribada* to Ostional in 1961 was a bonanza to the people of Ostional. Their village became the major source of turtle eggs in Costa Rica.

Coatis, coyotes, raccoons, and other egg-hungry marauders take a heavy toll on the tasty eggs, too. Ridley turtles have thus hit on a formula for outwitting their predators, or at least of surviving despite them: they deposit millions of eggs at a time (in any one season, 30 million eggs might be laid at Ostional). Since the *arribada* follows a strategy that assumes that only a fraction of eggs will successfully incubate, the turtle invasions vary in size and timing year by year: *arribadas* are unpredictable, which is why ridleys do it—to confuse predators.

Ironically, the most direfully efficient scourge are the turtles themselves! Since Ostional beach is literally covered with thousands of turtles, the eggs laid during the first days of an *arribada* are often dug up by turtles arriving later (up to 70% of turtles nesting on the fourth and fifth nights of large *arribadas* destroy an existing nest). Often before they can hatch, a second *arribada* occurs. Again the beach is covered with crawling reptiles. As the newcomers dig, many inadvertently excavate and destroy the eggs laid by their predecessors and the beach becomes strewn with rotting embryos. Even without human interference, only one percent to eight percent of eggs in a given *arribada* will hatch.

In 1972, when the Nancite and Ostional hatcheries were discovered, their destruction was far along. The turtle population seemed to be below the minimum required to maintain the population, and uncontrolled poaching of eggs would ultimately exterminate the nesting colony, scientists concluded after a decade of study. They also reasoned that a *controlled* harvest would actually rejuvenate the turtle population. Such a harvest during the first two nights of an *arribada* would *improve* hatch rates at Ostional by reducing the number of broken eggs and crowded conditions that together create a spawning ground for bacteria and fungi that prevent the development of embryos. More eggs would incubate to full term.

In 1987, the Costa Rican Congress finally approved a management plan that would legalize egg harvesting at Ostional. The statute that universally prohibited egg harvesting (Wildlife Conservation Law, No. 4551) was reformed to permit the residents of Ostional to take and sell turtle eggs—but

(continues on next page)

RESPITE FOR THE RIDLEY

(continued)

only after the Ostional community had formed an economic development association.

The unique legal right to harvest eggs is vested in members of the Associacion Desarrollo Integral de Ostional (ADIO). The University of Costa Rica, which has maintained a biological research station at Ostional since 1980, is legally responsible for preparing an annual plan and review and for providing the scientific criteria to guide the Ostional community toward a sustainable cash-based use of their awe-inspiring natural resource. "Our role is to prepare studies and regulate the project, but the community administers the project. It is their project. They control the sale and marketing . . . and they police the beach," says Annie Chavez, a professor at the University of Costa Rica and director of the Sea Turtle Project.

The biologists judge when harvesting may begin after approval by the Ministry of Agriculture and Livestock. A quota is established for each *arribada*. Sometimes, no eggs are harvested; in the dry season (Dec.-May), as many as 35% of eggs may be taken; when the beach is hotter than Hades, the embryos become dehydrated, and the hatching rate falls below one percent. "The idea is to save eggs that would be broken anyway, or that otherwise have a low expectation of hatching," notes Chavez.

The egg collectors are organized into 10 work groups, each directed by a platoon leader and each with its own tract of beach. The men mark the nests with a tag. The women follow, extract the eggs, and place them in sacks to be hauled to the shore and washed in the sea. The eggs are then carted to the village packing center and placed—200 at a time—into small plastic bags pre-stamped with the seal of ADIO. By law, eggs may be taken only during the first 36 hours of an *arribada*. After that, the villagers protect the nests from poachers and the hatchlings from ravenous beasts.

The project has seeded a conservationist ethic among community members. When scientists arrived in 1972 to initiate the first studies, a field assistant was beaten, and the locals punctured the scientists' tires and interfered with tagging the turtles. Today, the villagers help biologists count and monitor the turtles. Even the mayor of Nicoya was taken to court by AIDO after villagers caught him with two bags of poached turtle eggs! The Guardia Rural (police) used to confiscate the poachers' eggs and sell them themselves. Now the police, too, are en-

thusiastic beneficiaries of the program—income from the sale of legally harvested eggs paid for construction of a Guardia Rural office at Ostional.

Today the whole community benefits from the profits (annual sales top $95,000). The eggs are dealt to four distributors who disburse the eggs to 81 "resellers," who then sell on a smaller scale at a contract-fixed price of four *colones* (two cents—many of the buyers are bakeries, which favor turtle eggs over those of hens; turtle eggs give dough greater "lift"). The commercial establishments—*cantinas*, brothels, and street vendors—sell the eggs as *bocas*—"tidbits" served with beer or *guaro*, the local firewater—for eight *colones* (six cents) or less.

The law stipulates that net revenues from the sale of eggs be divided between the community (80%) and the Ministry of Agriculture. AIDO distributes 70% of its share among association members as payment for their labors, and 30% to the Sea Turtle Project and communal projects. AIDO also pays the biologists' salaries. Profits have funded construction of a health center, a house for schoolteachers, the ADIO office, an egg packing center, and a Sea Turtle Research Lab. The school has been remodeled. And running water is no longer a boy with a bucket.

The project also has the potential to stop the poaching of eggs on other beaches, claim scientists. It's a matter of economics. Poachers sell green and leatherback eggs for 25 *colones* (15 cents). A report in 1992 found that cheaper eggs from Ostional had captured 94% of the market (local dealers get documentation to indicate that this is a legal transaction).

Studies at Ostional show that the turtle population has stabilized. Recent *arribadas* have included as many as 200,000 turtles. And hatch rates are up to eight percent.

Key to defining a future from the chaos of the *arribadas* is an integrated Management and Development Plan. Initiated in 1992, the plan aims to stimulate other economic activities so that the community doesn't come to depend exclusively on egg exploitation. AIDO, for example, is promoting microenterprises that take advantage of the women's craft skills. And a honeybee enterprise is under way. The integrated plan will also regulate development, including construction of buildings within the refuge, land ownership, fishing, and tourism.

vironmentalists fear that hotels will bring too many people to this sacred refuge, and the lights and human activity will discourage the turtles from nesting. The local community is hostile to tourism development, certainly on the model of Nosara, its southerly neighbor, where foreign land purchases have forced land values out of the reach of local residents. This unwanted development threatens to remove the community's control over its resources. The developers are pushing hard to get permits, but so far Ostional residents have had the courts on their side. The priority is the purchase of the land adjacent to Ostional to establish buffer zones and ensure the protection of the nesting grounds. Only then can the indigenous community be assured that it has taken command of a sustainable egg-harvesting program that meets the challenge of protecting the turtles while addressing the community's needs.

You should check in with the local **turtle cooperative** in the village center before exploring the beach.

Food and Accommodations

Cabinas Ostional, 50 meters south of the soccer field, has four clean, pleasing rooms sleeping three people, with fans and private baths. Rate: $6 per person. About 100 meters south is the **Pulpería y Hospedaje Las Guacamayas,** with eight rooms (some with shared bathroom). Rooms are small but clean and have two single beds ($9 d). **Soda Brisas del Pacífico,** next door, is the eatery of significance. Next door a local named Melvin reportedly rents rooms for $3.50. A home on the southwest corner of the soccer field has a **camping** area. Call the National Wildlife Directorate (tel. 233-8112) to see if camping is permitted on the beach, and where.

An American couple, Darin and Kim McBratney, are developing a "Caribbean-style retreat" a few miles south of Ostional and will rent surfboards, motorcycles, and horses (P.O. Box 2628, Saratoga, CA 95070, tel. 408-450-9764).

At the north end of Ostional is **Hotel Rancho Brovella** (tel. 680-0459), with 48 rooms and two presidential suites, plus restaurant, bar, pool, tennis courts, horse riding and "ecological trails." It was under construction in April 1995.

Information

The **ADIO** (see special topic "Respite for the Ridley") office is beside the road, on the corner of the soccer field. It doesn't have much information, but Geraldo Ordez, the community leader, can assist (his house is first on the right as you enter Ostional from the north), and there's a **Tourism Orientation Place,** run by ADIO, 200 meters south of the soccer field, at the junction of the path to **Laboratorio de Investigación Tortuga Marinos.** The rustic hut houses research volunteers and scientists. See special topic "Volunteer Programs to Save the Turtles" under "Amphibians and Reptiles" in the Introduction chapter, for organizations with volunteer programs.

Services

You'll find a **public telephone** (680-0467) by the *pulpería* at the northern end of the soccer field. You can reserve accommodations by calling this number and leaving a message.

Tours

CATA Tours (tel. 221-5455, fax 221-0200) offers a "Turtles under the Full Moon" tour June-Nov. ($45), including hotel transfers. **Guanacaste Tours** (tel. 666-0306, fax 666-0307) offers a similar tour ($50), including transfers from select hotels in Liberia and Playas Hermosa, Coco, Ocotal, Flamingo, Conchal, Tamarindo, and Junquillal. So does **Flamingo Tours** (tel. 654-4238, fax 654-4039; in San José, tel. 222-6762).

Transportation

A bus departs Santa Cruz for Ostional daily at noon (three hours); it may not run in wet season.

The newly cut road south from Ostional has three sturdy bridges over the rivers and merges with the main road south from Nosara about two km south of the village. The old dirt road still fords the Río Nosara just before entering Nosara. It's not as daunting as it looks and was only about half a meter deep when I last crossed it. You can also reach Ostional via a dirt road from Nicoya (35 km east) that leads through Curime, Dulce Nombre, Guastomatal, and Nosara.

NOSARA

The village of Nosara, five km inland from the coast, offers little of appeal, although it has a couple of lively bars and eateries. The two beaches make amends! A series of convoluted dirt roads winds south to and along the stupendously beautiful beach of **Playa Guiones,** a ruler-straight expanse of white sand washed by surf (Playa Pelada is north of the Río Nosara: see "Ostional National Wildlife Refuge," above). The beaches have rocky tidepools, a small coral reef, and the seawater is heated by the sun. Great for soaking! There's virtually no shade, however, on Playa Guiones. For that, check out Playa Pelada.

Much of the land backing Playa Guiones has been divided into lots and sold for development during the past two decades. The roads are an intestinal labyrinth. Like any maze, it's easy to enter but getting out is sheer puzzlement, with dirt roads coiling and uncoiling like a snake. Many of the residents are North American retirees. Much to the credit of the developer, Nosara's land-use policies are a model for others to follow. The Nosara Civic Association, the property owners' organization, maintains trails, shelters, and camping facilities and fosters preservation of natural vegetation cover (compare the area to Sámara, farther south, where forests have been cleared). The maritime zone fronting the beach is protected by the Forest Service. Hence, wildlife abounds in the sprawling primary forest.

Budget Accommodations

Chorotega Cabinas (tel. 680-0836) is a handsome complex just south of the village. Rooms have private baths with cold water. It's clean and well-run. Rate: $8 per person. **Cabinas Agnnel,** nearby, also has six basic but well-kept cabinas with fans and private baths with cold water ($6). **Casa Río Nosara** has rooms in a rustic *palenque* lodge. Not inspected.

Domus is a stunning stone-and-thatch "hostel" that was nearing completion down by Playa Guiones. Nearby is **Cabinas Giardino Tropicale.**

Heinrich Maier, of Weil am Rhein in Germany, recommends **Cabinas Angel** for its clean cabinas with private bath and fan ($8 s/d), although it is five km from the beach.

Moderate Accommodations

If setting is foremost in mind, there is but one choice you can make: **Lagarto** (tel./fax 680-0763). Though the road that climbs steeply is enough to make you weep (or at least turn around), the hotel's hilltop setting offers one of the most miraculous vistas in all Costa Rica—north along Ostional—with the estuary below and mountains far off in the distance. Coatimundis and howler monkeys abound nearby. Settle in a high seat or Sarchí rocker and relax. The dining table, made from a single piece of hardwood, must be six meters long. Four rooms are in a two-story house (the upper story reached by a spiral staircase) and two in a smaller unit. The latter, with one entire wall a screened, glassless window, have a mezzanine bedroom overlooking a voluminous open shower and bathroom. Some have a king-size bed. The stone wall and wooden gates of Teutonic proportion hint at the German ownership. Rates: $25-40 s, $35-50 d, including tax and breakfast.

The **Rancho Suizo Lodge** (Apdo. 14, Bocas de Nosara 5233, no phone; reservations via Eco-Tours, tel. 233-1888) is very popular with backpackers and naturalists. It has 10 thatched cabinas with small but pleasant rooms and private baths with hot water. Hammocks swing under *ranchitas* in the *muy* tropical grounds, which contain a tiny aviary. Trails lead directly to the beach. It is run by René Spinnier and Ruth Léscher, who have created an agreeable ambience. The pleasing thatched bar-cum-restaurant with bamboo furniture is open for breakfast and dinner only. A Jacuzzi was recently added. A notice in the cabinas reads "No opposite sex visitors"; or, as two female German guests put it: "Sex is *verboten!*" Although I thought this was a joke, a reader wrote in March 1995 to report that when he was checking in, two Swiss couples were being ejected for not heeding this regulation. Strange! Rate: $45 d, including tax.

The newly constructed **Hotel Villa Taype** (tel. 680-0763), within spitting distance of Playa Guiones and otherwise known as Hotel Estrella del Pacífico, offers 16 a/c cabinas and slightly larger private *ranchita*-style bungalows with fans and private baths with hot water. They're set off by delightful grounds including an inviting pool, a

tennis court, plus a large bar and restaurant. Rates: $40 d, $60 bungalows, including tax.

Another atmospheric place, but a ten-minute walk to the beach, is **Estancia Nosara** (Apdo. 37, Nosara 5257, tel./fax 680-0378), which has beautiful rooms surrounded by tropical gardens. All rooms—each for four people—have minibars, plus private baths with hot water. Some have small kitchenettes. The hotel has a small swimming pool, satellite TV in the *palenque* lounge, and pleasing bamboo furnishings in the romantic bar-cum-restaurant, open on all sides. The hotel offers tennis ($5 per hour), horseback rides ($8 per hour), and bicycles ($7 per hour), plus a tree farm tour ($25), a turtle tour ($25), and tours to Barra Honda and Palo Verde. A bargain. Rates: $40 s, $46 d, $54 t, $62 quad.

Almost Paradise (Apdo. 15, Nosara; fax 685-5004) is another German-owned property that enjoys a hilltop setting above Condominiums de las Flores. Its haphazardly and utterly charming construction is enhanced by creeping vines and flowers bedecking the place. Six rooms are of different size, though all have private baths with hot water, plus access to a wide balcony with hammocks and splendid vistas. Original paintings from Haiti and the Dominican Republic adorn the walls. The restaurant is pretty and catches the breezes. Rates: $35-45 d, including breakfast.

Upscale Accommodations
Nosara Retreat (Centro Comercial El Pueblo, #120, San José, tel. 233-8057, fax 255-3351; in the U.S., tel. 800-999-6404) is the most enriching place around; the perfect place to relax and recharge. The focus at this hilltop villa is health and spiritual reneweal. Co-founders Don and Amba Stapleton and four full-time professional staff offer yoga, meditation, nutrition counseling, fasting and detoxification, Danskinetics, Yogassage (Amba's own technique, combining vigorous massage with Hatha yoga), and such other pleasures as hiking, boogie boarding, and mountain biking. My first visit to Costa Rica was as a participant in a holistic health retreat led by Amba. Since 1988 she has taught at the renowned Kripalu Center for Yoga and Health in Massachussetts, of which Don is CEO. Imagine! Sunrise yoga on the beach! Five rooms are tastefully furnished, with

deep tubs for soaking and doors opening to wide balconies overlooking the beach. A pool perches on the hillside. After sunset—accompanied by classical tunes or panpipes—stargazers can make the most of a telescope. The retreat offers three-day and weeklong courses. Three-day/two-night "Rejuvenation Retreats" cost $250-275, including yoga, body treatment, guided walks, and all meals.

Hotel Playas de Nosara (Apdo. 4, Nosara 5257, tel. 680-0495) squats atop a headland—Punta Pelada—with the sweeping arc of Playa Guiones stretching away in endless relief below to the south. Steps lead down to a tiny cove good for beachcombing to the north. What a transformation! When I first came here in 1986, the hotel was a fairly simple structure with a modest restaurant built over a wooden deck. In 1993, it had metamorphosed into a charming whitewashed Spanish-colonial-style villa whose restaurant is graced by arches and columns. The young plants on the grounds had flourished into lush foliage which threatens to take over the hotel. In early 1995 inspirational additions, including a fabulous pool, seemed inspired by Gaudi . . . its walls awash in surflike waves and a *mirador* resembling a fairytale castle. The 20 newly renovated rooms—all with fans and private baths with hot water—enjoy a fabulous setting facing south over Playa Guiones and have private verandas. Hammocks hang under tiny thatched miradors. The cabins atop the cliff are recommended; the new rooms in the main building don't have cross-ventilation. Despite the hotel's youth, the tropical climate has gone to work, and the place already looks a century old. It's complete with restaurant and swimming pool. Horseback rides cost $8 per hour. The hotel may go all-inclusive soon. Rates: $50-65 d, including tax.

At the southern end of the beach is **Playa Guiones Lodge** (tel. 231-3637, fax 231-6346; in the U.S., tel. 800-998-8864), a sturdy stone affair with thatched cabinas atop the hill. Not reviewed. Reports are that as yet there is no road link and that you must drive along the sand to reach it; since Playa Guiones is a protected turtle-nesting site, concerns have been raised about turtle nests being destroyed by the traffic. I welcome your comments. Rate: about $80 d.

Apartments and Houses

Chatelle by the Sea (Apdo. 755, San José 1007, tel. 487-7781, fax 487-7095), down the hill from Hotel Playa de Nosara and behind Playa Pelada, offers spacious, two-bedroom/two-bath condominium suites with lounges, large kitchens and private balconies. The fully equipped suites are tastefully appointed with modern furnishings. Bed configurations differ; every permutation is there. Daily maid service is extra. A bargain; recommended! Rates: $100 low season, $120 high season.

Condominiums de las Flores (tel. 680-0696) also has modern furnished condos for rent from $60 per night. The rooms are pleasing and front onto landscaped gardens with profuse bougainvillea. The **Gilded Iguana** (tel. 680-0749) has "budget" apartments for rent (about $70). Also, many expatriate residents rent their houses (expect to pay about $200 per week).

Monkey Trail is the peculiar name of a fully equipped house for rent (tel. 227-0088) just a few minutes' walk from Playa Guiones. It sleeps four and has water sports equipment and "the jungle as its backyard." Rate: $375 per week.

Casa Tucán (fax 680-0856) is an attractive house across from Hotel Villa Taype, with wide lawns and a *ranchita* for shady lazing.

Food

In Nosara village, take your pick from **Restaurante Nosara, Bambú Bar, Soda Mon Río, Bar Sin No More,** and **Rancho Nosarito,** all around the soccer field. Bambú is the most atmospheric. Between the beach and the village is **Rancho Suizo Lodge,** which serves "Ruth's good cooking" at breakfasts and dinners (no lunches). **La Lechuza** is also popular with expatriate residents; it serves lunches Monday through Sunday. The **Gilded Iguana** is another favorite with locals who gather for bridge games on Saturday; it serves lunches Wednesday through Sunday. **Olga's,** a rustic place fronting the northern beach, is recommended for seafood

($5 average). The rustic **Pacholi Bar** is next to Hotel Villa Taype and offers German specialties ($6 and up) in a marvelously rustic "jungle" bar. Nearby is **Giardino Tropicale** pizzeria, and, two km south, also serving Italian dishes, **Ristorante La Dolce Vita. Piga's Bar** is a rustic eatery down by Playa Pelada; **Café Almost Paradise,** below Hotel Playa de Nosara, has good seafood and pastas.

Services

A funky little mechanic's hut (it bills itself euphemistically as "Servicentro Nosara") next to the Travelair office sells **gasoline.** Nearby is **Monkey Business** selling beachwear, jewelry, and fresh-baked breads, cookies, and pizzas. Next door, at Quinta Sirena, is **Pacific Aqua Adventures,** which offers diving. There are two **supermarkets,** plus a store—**Chorotega**—selling pottery from Guaitil. The **tennis courts** behind Chatelle by the Sea are for public use.

Transportation

A bus departs San José for Nosara from Calle 14, Avenidas 3/5 (Empresa Alfaro, tel. 222-2750) daily at 6:15 a.m., returning at 4 p.m. A bus departs Nicoya for Nosara at 1 p.m. (Transportes Rojas, tel. 685-5352), returning at 6 a.m. (reportedly one hour earlier in wet season).

SANSA (tel. 233-0397 or 233-3258) operates scheduled flights via Tamarindo departing San José on Monday, Wednesday, and Friday, at 6 a.m. ($47 one-way) and departing Tamarindo 6:55 a.m. Return flights depart Nosara at 7:25 a.m. via Sámara. **Travelair** (tel. 322-7883 or 220-3054, fax 220-0413) flights depart San José's Pavas Airport for Nosara daily at 8:45 a.m. via Sámara ($82 one-way). The Travelair representative (tel. 680-0836) is south of the soccer field in Nosara village.

The **Turi Nosara Center** (tel. 232-5626) in San José can arrange private air charters. The airstrip is to the south end of town. SANSA also offers packaged tours, including accommodation at the Hotel Playa Nosara.

NOSARA TO SÁMARA

BAHÍA GARZA

The dirt road from Nosara leads south to Playa Sámara (26 km) via the horseshoe-shaped Bahía Garza, rimmed by a marvelous though slightly pebbly white-sand beach. Beyond Garza the road cuts inland from the coast, which remains out of view the rest of the way. You can reach Bahía Garza from Nicoya via a partially paved road that goes through Belén and Terciopela; the dirt road is heavily corrugated south of Belén, and the bulldozers (which had made this section quite tortuous) were there in force in spring 1995, preparing a new road. A **gas station** lies two km south of Terciopela, where the road forks to the left for Sámara (six km) and to the right for Barco Quebrado, on the coast road, six km east of Bahía Garza.

Accommodations
Villagio Guardia Morada (Apdo. 860, San José 1007, tel./fax 680-0784, or tel. 233-2476, fax 222-4073), one of Costa Rica's most impressive beach resorts, has the bay to itself. Hints of Polynesia are all around, particularly in the stunning restaurant with a massive two-tier *palenque* roof, and a spiral wooden staircase up to the mezzanine casino. The imaginatively conceived resort combines elegance and rusticity. Accommodation is in 30 nicely appointed thatched cabinas surrounded by superbly landscaped grounds containing a 230-square-meter pool with waterfall cascade that reflects the candlelight at night. Two bungalows accommodate up to eight guests each. The beachside **La Tortuga** bar doubles as a dance hall. The hotel has two sportfishing boats ($65 per day) and offers water-skiing, jet-skiing, scuba diving, and horseback rides ($15 two hours). No access to nonguests. Rates: $85 s, $125 d, including tax.

Just south of Garza village is the down-to-earth **Casa Pacífico** with four nice rooms with king-size beds and a rustic beachside bar with tremendous ambience. Rates: $45 d, including gourmet breakfast.

Hotel Latino should have opened by the time you read this.

PLAYA SÁMARA

Playa Sámara, about 15 km south of Garza, is a very popular budget destination for Europeans and North Americans. It is gradually going upscale. Some accommodations are overpriced, but your choice of good-value hostelries is on the rise. Categories below reflect price, not standard. The lure is its relative accessibility and extremely attractive horseshoe-shaped bay with a light-gray beach, very wide and deep although not particularly pretty. Chora Island lies offshore. A few palms shade the beach, while manchineel and groundcover plants fringe the shore. Vultures and pelicans provide entertainment. Many Costa Ricans—including ex-president Oscar Arias Sánchez—have homes here. There are two parts to the village, which is divided by a large cattle *finca*. They are connected by road, but you can drive along the beach between them. The southern village is where the action is; the north—called Cangrejal—is funky, with only basic accommodations.

Budget Accommodations
A favorite among Ticos is the **Hotel/Restaurant Playa Sámara** (tel. 680-0750, fax 233-5503), a larger, older, and somewhat run-down unit with 54 rooms with fans, telephones, and private baths. Its *soda*-style restaurant is very popular with locals. Be warned: there's a disco downstairs. Rate: $8 per person.

The owner of **Cabinas Magalay**, behind Cabinas Comodor Arena, refused to give me information or let me inspect his rooms ($6 per person). I'm not surprised: the place looks shitty! The place seemed to have improved not at all when I passed by again in 1995. You can camp for $2. South of town is the **Cabinas El Mango** (not reviewed).

In Cangrejal is the **Hospedaje Tinajitas**, which has 13 very dark and cramped rooms (five with private baths) with bunk beds but no

fans ($4 per person shared bath, $5 private bath). On a similar funky scale is **Hospedaje Yuri** (tel. 680-0022), which has nine basic but pleasant-enough rooms; some have private baths, some share ($4 per person). Next door is the **Hospedaje Katia**, with seven rooms; only two have private baths ($5).

Moderate Accommodations
Albergue Casa del Mar (tel. 232-2241, fax 257-2272) is one of several good bargains in town. This relaxing and well-run bed and breakfast has seven rooms (four share a bath), with fans, hot water, and heaps of light. Attractive decor, good-size beds, and a balcony overlooking the ocean complete the picture. Extra rooms are being added. Recommended. Rate: $40 d, including breakfast and tax.

Another hot bargain is the German-run **Cabinas Belvedere:** three very pretty and intriguing Swiss-chalet-style cabinas with attractive bamboo furnishings, king-size beds with mosquito nets, whitewashed walls, fans, and private baths with hot water. More cabinas are to be added. Rate: $30 d, including tax and breakfast.

The **Hotel Marbella** (Apdo. 490, Heredia 3000, tel./fax 233-9980) is compact but charming. Its 14 rooms and six apartments all have fans and private baths with hot water. Rooms are basic but clean and adequate, with whitewashed walls and harmonious sea-green decor. They open onto a courtyard with a profusion of bamboo and thatch, and a tiny cooling-off pool in a neat little garden. There's a small restaurant. Marbella offers river-rafting on the Corobicí ($79). It also has three charming chalets (a mix of Switzerland and Thailand) across the road. Rates: $43 s, $47 d, $50 t. Bungalows cost $250 per week.

Another option is **Cabinas Comodor Arena,** next to the bus stop. Eight rooms in a modern two-story unit are simply furnished but clean, with fans and private baths with cold water. Upstairs rooms have verandas but catch the nocturnal noises from the disco next door; downstairs, you can almost hear the occupants above breathing. There's a tiny breakfast restaurant. Overpriced. Rate: $30 s/d, including tax.

Upscale Accommodations
Setting a standard is **Isla Chora Inn,** an architectural stunner with 10 beautiful rooms and four a/c apartments. The Italian owners have brought their native aesthetics to bear. The simple, elegant two-story units circle a pool and landscaped grounds. Within, the rooms have marvelous bamboo beds in Japanese style, with beautiful bed covers, plus showers of natural pebbles. All have wide verandas. A restaurant with soaring *palenque* roof serves natural health food, ice cream, and sodas; another serves Italian dishes. The open-air disco is *the* happenin' scene in Sámara. Rates: $50-60 d.

The striking gleaming white contemporary interpretation of a Spanish parador that commands the hill overlooking Sámara is **Mirador de Sámara** (fax 685-5004). Imagine the panoramic views, especially from the tower *(mirador)* containing open-walled restaurant and bar. Six large apartments each sleep five. They're clean within, almost clinical, with simple hardwood furnishings and floors. German-owned. Rates: $60 d ($10 extra).

Hotel Sámara Beach is a two-story complex with 20 rooms with private baths with hot water. Some have king-size beds and a/c. Rooms are spacious and bright, with private patios. The hotel has a small swimming pool, plus a bar-cum-restaurant under thatch. It plans to add three more rooms and a Jacuzzi. It offers tours and rents bicycles ($3 per hour; $18 per day). Overpriced. Rates: $75 d, $85 with a/c, including tax. More genuinely upscale is **Hotel y Villas Las Brisas del Pacífico** (Apdo. 129, Ciudad Colón 6100, tel./fax 680-0876; direct line, tel./fax 233-9840), about two km south of Sámara on the road to Playa Carrillo. The German-run hotel has 30 rooms (rather dark), with 10 more planned; 10 have a/c. All have private baths with hot water. An open-air restaurant which opens onto the ocean, a small swimming pool plus Jacuzzi, and a shady lounging area under palms, all add to the setting. Separate bungalows sit atop a hill, with ocean views and their own pool. Rates: $52 s, $95 with a/c; $72 bungalow.

At the southern end of Playa Sámara, three km south of the village, is **Villas Playa Sámara** (tel. 233-0223, fax 221-7222). The upscale "tourist village" has 72 one-, two- and three-bedroom villas with huge interiors, wicker furnishings, large, well-equipped kitchens, and voluminous bedrooms and bathrooms with hot

water and oodles of light. All have a/c. They're spaced well apart amid expansive grounds. The complex features a large pool with swim-up bar, Jacuzzi, and kiddies' pool, plus a souvenir shop, and a casino above the restaurant. It offers windsurfing ($8 per hour), water-skiing ($40 per hour), plus volleyball, badminton, and scooters for hire. Rates: $95 s, $125 d, $185 two bedrooms, $240 three bedrooms.

You'll find plenty of charm and character to **Hotel Giada** (fax 685-5004), in classic "tropical style." Its 13 rooms are very attractive, with faux-terra-cotta tile floors, ochre/cream decor, bamboo beds (some are king-size), and wide balconies. Rates: $38 s, $52 d, $62 t.

House Rental
There's a modest house for rent just before the Hotel Marbella.

Camping
Camping Playa Sámara has a beachside campground midway along the beach. **Camping Cocos** also has a clean campground on the beach with bathrooms, water, and sites under shady palms ($2.50 per person). Alternatively, you can camp on the grounds of **Bar Acuarios,** 100 meters south from the soccer field ($2).

Food
There's no shortage of options here. The appealing thatched **Bar y Restaurante Colocho's** serves excellent, reasonably priced seafood dishes. The **Restaurant Trattoria Al Manglar,** behind Isla Chora, is recommended for Italian food. Another quasi-Italian eatery—the **Soda Italian**—serves natural foods, including wonderful *refrescos.* **Bar El Lagarto,** on the beach just north of Camping Playa Sámara, is popular with younger gringos. Gosh! There's even a Chinese restaurant: **Restaurante Flor de Giruelo.**

The locals tend to hang out at the restaurant of Hotel Playa Sámara and at **Soda Mure,** a small thatched *ranchita* on the corner of the road to Carrillo. Other options include **Bar y Restaurante El Coracol,** behind the Hotel Playa Sámara, and the rustic but atmospheric **Bar Acuarios,** which has lively music and quality seafood dishes ($2-4).

There's a bakery next to Hotel Giada.

Entertainment
The thatch-roofed **Disco La Gondola,** opposite Hotel Sámara Beach, has a dance stage with a trompe l'oeil of the Ponte Vecchio in Venice; no wonder it's full of Italians! The **Disco Playa Sámara** is in the hotel of that name. But the disco at **Isla Chora** seems to have stolen the scene.

Services
The Hotel Sámara Beach has a **travel agency** that represents Travelair. **Excursiones Beppe,** in Soda Sindhy, offers boat tours and rents bicycles; a booth on the road behind **Bar Acuarios** also arranges horse riding and boating tours. The **post office** and **rural guard** are on the right, immediately before the beach. There's a **public telephone** at Pulpería Mileth, opposite the post office; and another at Hotel Lory, in the north section of town.

About 50 meters left from the post office is a place renting **sun chairs** ($2.50 half day, $4 full day). You can also rent sun chairs from next to Camping Coco, on the beachfront. You'll find a **supermarket** just beyond Albergue Casa del Mar.

Transportation
Buses depart San José for Sámara from Calles 14, Avenidas 3/5 (Empresa Alfaro, tel. 222-2750 or 223-8227), daily at noon, returning at 4 a.m. (six hours; $5). Buy tickets well in advance during holidays and weekends. Buses depart Nicoya (three blocks east of the park) for Sámara daily at 8 a.m. and 3 and 4 p.m. (Empresa Rojas, tel. 685-5352), continuing south to Playa Carrillo, and returning at 5:30 and 6:30 a.m. Schedules may change in wet season. The **bus stop** is behind Cabinas Arenas.

SANSA (tel. 233-0397 or 233-3258) operates scheduled flights from San José via Tamarindo and Nosara on Monday, Wednesday, and Friday at 6 a.m.; via Tambor and Tamarindo daily (except Sunday) at 11:15 a.m. and on Sunday at 8 a.m., returning to San José via Tambor (depart Sámara at 1:05 p.m. and 9:50 a.m. respectively). **Travelair** (tel. 232-7883 or 220-3054, fax 220-0413) flights depart San José's Pavas Airport for Sámara daily at 8:45 a.m. ($75 one-way, $122 roundtrip); returning via Nosara at 9:35 a.m. **Air Taxi Sámara** (tel. 232-1355, fax 220-4582) offers private charter ser-

vice for up to seven passengers in an a/c Cessna 421. The airstrip is at Playa Carrillo. **Note:** Reduced schedules operate mid-April to mid-December.

SANSA (tel. 222-6561) also offers package vacations including accommodation at Hotel Las Brisas del Pacífico.

PLAYA CARRILLO

The dirt road continues in reasonably good condition over **Punta Indio,** at the southern end of Playa Sámara, and drops down to coral-colored Playa Carrillo, one of the finest beaches in Costa Rica, fringed with palms trees, wooded hills, and cliffs. A dirt road midway down the beach leads uphill to **Bosque Puerto Carrillo,** a teak farm and "wildlife plantation."

The beach is undeveloped. An offshore reef protects the bay. The **camping** is superb under palms along the entire length of the beach. The tiny and funky fishing hamlet of Carrillo nestles around the Sangrado estuary at the southern end of the bay; the road rises over a small promontory before dropping to the sleepy village. Hotels are sprouting along this shore, the northernmost end of Nicoya's final frontier.

Budget Accommodations
Cabinas Mirador has eight basic, dark, and grungy triple rooms with private baths with cold water ($16) atop the headland above the village of Puerto Carrillo. They allow **camping** on the grounds. A funky green-and-yellow Caribbean-style house at the southern end of the beach also rents rooms. You'll also find basic cabinas for rent down the hill from the Guanamar Resort.

Upscale Accommodations
At the north end of the beach is **Inn at Puerto Carrillo** (c/o TAM Travel, Apdo. 1864, San José 1000, tel. 222-2642, fax 221-6465; in the U.S., tel. 800-848-5874), atop the cliffs of Punta Indio, with views to both Bahía Sámara and Bahía Carrillo. There are 21 cabinas with fans, satellite TV, and private baths with cold water. Owner Wayne Winter also runs Carrillo Sport Fishing and offers seven-day packages with three full days of fishing. Rate: $90 d.

Hotel Sunset (in Bagaces, tel. 680-1270) is about one km up a dirt road that leads into the hills from the beach. It enjoys a wonderful breezy hilltop setting with spectacular views over the bay. Each tile-floored cabin has two double beds with carved headboards, plus fans and pleasant bathrooms. Two cabinas have a/c. A tiny though pretty swimming pool is surrounded by an elevated wooden deck and *ranchita* bar. Rates: $75 d, or $85 with a/c, including breakfast. The American owner also has a fully furnished four-bedroom ocean-view house for eight people, including VCR ($100 per night). He also offers sportfishing.

Also see El Sueño Tropical, under "Playa Camaronal to Playa Bejuco" in the "Sámara South to Cabo Blanco" section.

Deluxe Accommodations
Guanamar Beach and Sportfishing Resort (Apdo. 7-1880, San José 1000, tel. 220-0722, fax 220-2095; in the U.S., Costa Sol International, 1717 N. Bayshore Dr., Suite 3333, Miami, FL 33132, tel. 800-245-8420 or 305-539-1630, fax 305-539-1123), on the hillside at the southern end of the bay, is one of Costa Rica's premier beach resorts. About 40 cabinas—some thatched—cascade down the hillside. Each has a private patio and satellite TV, plus room service. They're well spaced apart and connected by manicured walkways that lead through landscaped grounds full of bougainvillea. A splendid wooden balcony overlooking the bay opens onto a small swimming pool. The resort has a romantic rough wood-and-thatch restaurant, and even a small casino. Pity about the radio blaring! Quiet would be more appropriate for the perfect setting. Sportfishing is the Japanese-owned resort's main raison d'etre . . . a superb chance to test your skills against marlin, sailfish, tuna, dorado, snapper, and roosterfish. Boats regularly report "Super Grand Slams"—all three species of marlin and one or more sailfish taken on the same day. In early 1991, an angler out of Guanamar caught the first Pacific blue marlin ever taken on a fly (the 92-kg marlin is also the largest fish ever caught on a fly). **Note:** I've heard several complaints about upkeep of boats. It has a private airstrip for guests, plus sea kayaks, water-skiing, boogie boards, horseback riding, mountain bikes, and jet skis. Rates: $110-120 s/d, $165 suite, $10 each additional person.

Food

A clifftop restaurant at the top of the headland serves seafood dishes for about $3, breakfast for $1. Otherwise, you can blow your dollars at the Guanamar's upscale restaurant. The setting is worth it.

Services

You can rent **boats** in the village. There's a **public telephone** up the hill, just below the entrance to Guanamar Resort. Here, too, lives Rick Ruhlow, a "displaced California surf bum" who'll be happy to hire himself and his fully equipped nine-meter Palm Beach boat (about $650 per day) for fishing or to ferry surfers to the most classy waves; contact **Pacific Blue Water**

Adventures c/o Jerry Ruhlow, tel./fax 282-6743). Likewise, his pal Tad Cantrell of **CocoRico Verde**, 25 meters north of the church, offers kayak and surf trips locally and acts as a guide nationwide (Apdo. 107, Puriscal 6000; in the U.S., tel. 407-833-0909).

Getting There

A bus departs Nicoya for Playa Carrillo via Sámara Mon.-Fri. at 3 p.m., 8 a.m. on weekends (Transportes Rojas, tel. 685-5352). The schedule may change in wet season. There is no bus service from San José. **SANSA** and **Travelair** both operate scheduled service to Playa Carrillo (see "Playa Sámara," above). You can also charter private air-taxis.

SÁMARA SOUTH TO CABO BLANCO

South of Carrillo, the dirt road continues a few miles in reasonable condition, then deteriorates to a mere trail in places. In the words of the old spiritual, there are many rivers to cross. The route (about 70 km to Cóbano) can thwart even the hardiest 4WD in wet season, or after prolonged rains in dry season. However, the drive can be worthwhile if you're seeking a secluded hideaway. Be prepared to rough it. Don't attempt this section of the coast by ordinary car.

PLAYA CAMARONAL TO PLAYA BEJUCO

Playa Camaronal, beyond Punta El Roble about five km south of Playa Carrillo, is a remote gray-sand beach about three km long and a popular nesting site for leatherback and Pacific ridley turtles. Avoid camping along the beach in nesting season. You can **camp** by the mouth of the Río Ora, at the northern end of the beach. The river is tidal at this point and best attempted at low tide. In fact, you have to drive on the beach for a part of the way south—a pain at high tide!

South of Camaronal are two tiny but exceptionally beautiful beaches—**Playa Islita** and **Playa Corozalito**. Islita is hidden in a small cove, while Corozalito, with a large mangrove swamp,

is popular with hawksbill and leatherback turtles (reportedly, female turtles infrequently come ashore at Islita, mostly in October). This rarely traveled section of road is replete with wildlife, which, given the lack of human intrusion, is relatively easily seen. A mule track reportedly climbs inland from Hacienda Barranquilla to the top of **Cerro Potal** (618 meters), from where you can enjoy sweeping perspectives of the coast. At Barranquilla, the moody **Bar Barranquilla** (made of eclectic marine flotsam) sits on a coastal headland and is a favorite for local residents and the occasional gringo in-the-know.

Accommodations

Despite its "end-of-the-dirt-road" location, this area has two flawless gems.

About three km south of Carrillo, inland of Playa Camaronal, is **El Sueño Tropical** (fax 686-6501), which I call the "Three Brothers Inn," as it is run by three charming brothers from Verona, Italy. Their hospitality is boundless, blending European savoire faire with marvelously erudite conversations. The tropical motif is everywhere throughout this marvelous, lushly landscaped setting. There are 12 clean, simple rooms with terra-cotta tiles and king-size bamboo beds. The restaurant (surprisingly elegant with its bright pink table settings, candlelight, and colorful tropical mural) has a commanding presence, with its

soaring *palenque* roof commanding a hillock, and the bungalows spread out of sight in a hollow. Vanni, the Italian chef, is "outrageous" (his cooking, I mean). The bar and restaurant has become a popular hangout for local expats; it seems half of Verona has moved here! There's an amoeba-shaped pool and a kiddies' pool. Howler monkeys abound in the surrounding forest. It's one of the few places from which I've had difficulty tearing myself away, due mainly to the graciousness of the hosts. Highly recommended. Rate: $55 d, including breakfast.

Hotel Hacienda Punta Islita (Apdo. 6054, San José 1000, tel. 231-6122 or 296-3817, fax 231-0715) is a luxurious new hotel with 20 colonial Santa Fe-style bungalows and four junior suites (with Jacuzzis) scattered on the hill slopes above Playa Islita. Each is fully and luxuriously equipped with king-size beds, spacious bathrooms (complete with hair driers), ceiling fans and a/c, mini-bar, TV, and private terrace overlooking the beach. Terra-cotta tile and colorful ceramic tiles meld with thatch and rustic timbers, and additional intimate touches are lent by props from the movie *1492*—log canoes, old barrels, and huge wrought-iron candelabra. Cool off in the fabulous horizon pool, or relax at the wet bar and Jacuzzi, or restaurant-cum-bar that opens onto the pool. A private forest reserve has trails for horseback rides and nature hikes, and a panoply of water sports are available. Sea turtles nest nearby. Rates: $65-110, low-high season. A bargain! By the time you read this, sportfishing should be available. You can arrive in style using the ranch's private airstrip (30 minutes from San José; $108 roundtrip) . . . no bad thing, as the road south from Carrillo may stump you.

BEJUCO TO PLAYA COYOTE

The dirt road cuts inland to the village of Corazalito and continues south about two km from the coast. At the hamlet of Quebrada Seca, a dirt road leads to **Playa Bejuco**, a four-km-long white-sand beach with a mangrove swamp at the southern end. Another kilometers-long beach, **Playa Coyote**, which lies immediately

south of Punta Bejuco and the hamlet of San Miguel, is bordered by large mangrove swamps and backed by steep cliffs. The beach is fantastically wide at low tide. Excellent surfing here (as well as good snook fishing and birding in the mangroves at the rivermouth at the northern end of the beach).

Ticos appear out of nowhere during national holidays, but you'll have the beaches to yourself at other times of year.

Accommodations

The village of San Miguel has very basic thatched cabinas with outhouse toilet and bar-cum-restaurant ($4 per person). The 30-room **Hotel Jacienda Javilla** was being built on a hill south of Bejuco. You'll be able to explore 700 hectares of dry forest on the ranch where the hotel is being built.

Coyote is a **camping** beach, although cheap rooms are offered at **Bar/Cabinas Veranera**. You can also rent basic rooms at the **Soda Familiar** in the village of San Francisco de Coyote, a few km inland.

PLAYA COYOTE TO MAL PAÍS

South of Bejuco, the road turns into little more than a horse trail in parts, and I'm assured by several North Americans living hereabouts that in wet season the journey south is virtually impossible. Beyond the headland of Punta Coyote is another great surfing beach, **Playa Caletas**, which extends southward into **Playas Bongo** and *Manzanillo*, in reality one virtually uninhabited beach running ruler-straight for 11or so kilometers, broken only by the mouth of the Río Bongo.

You can either follow the power lines along an inland route via Río Negro direct to **Cóbano,** the gateway to Montezuma and Cabo Blanco Absolute Nature Reserve (see below), or follow a rough track along the coast south of the Río Bongo to **Playa Santa Teresa** and, beyond, the tiny fishing hamlet of **Mal País**, just north of Cabo Blanco Nature Reserve. Mal País is a long, pretty swath of gray-sand reportedly good for surfing. Riptides are common.

You have just reached the end of the line.

Accommodations and Food

At Caletas is **Rancho Loma Clara** (tel. 671-1236), which has basic rooms ($5) and serves meals. In Mal País, **Cabinas Mal País** has basic rooms ($25 d), and **Cabinas y Restaurante Mar Azul** (tel. 661-1122, ext. 203) offers eight basic cabinas with shared baths and reasonable *típico* meals. Golly! There's even an Italian-run **pizzeria** (Italians are everywhere along the southern Nicoya coast) serving espresso coffee. On weekends it doubles as a disco and locals press in to stare at the TV.

Of course, you can always buy fresh seafood from local fishermen and even hire a *panga* to catch your own dinner. You can hire horses here for rides to Cabo Blanco. At press time, entry to the park was *not* allowed via Mal País.

Getting There

You can reach Bejuco, Coyote, Caletas and Manzanillo via rough dirt roads from Carmona (30 km south of Nicoya) and Jicaral (18 km northwest of Playa Naranjo). You must cross several streams, and these roads may prove impassable in wet season.

Reportedly, a **bus** departs San José daily at 3 p.m. from Calle 12, Avenidas 7/9, and travels via the Puntarenas-Playa Naranjo ferry and Jicaral to Coyote, Bejuco and Islita (arriving around 11 p.m.). Return buses are said to depart Bejuco at 4 a.m., passing via San Francisco de Coyote at 5 a.m. Local buses reportedly also meet the Puntarenas-Playa Naranjo ferry and operate to Coyote and Bejuco.

THE EAST COAST

The road south from Nicoya and Quebrada Honda (16 km west of the Tempisque ferry) swings around the southern perimeter of the Nicoya Peninsula via Carmona, Jicaral, and Playa Naranjo. When I last drove it, the road was paved only as far as Carmona. The dirt road south from here was horrendously potholed as far as Jicaral. It is gradually being upgraded as part of an agreement with the Spanish-owned Barceló hotel group, which promised to provide much-needed infrastructure in the area in return for permission to build its megaresort at Tambor. My guess is that it will be paved all the way to Tambor by the time you read this.

There are very few hotels between Quebrada Honda and Playa Naranjo, 65 km farther south, though why you would stay here I don't know. **Hotel Guamale** (tel. 650-0073) and **Pensión San Martín** (tel. 650-0169), in Jicaral, are options.

PLAYA NARANJO

Despite its name, there's no *playa* (beach) worthy of the journey. The place is of note only as the terminal for the **ferry** to/from Puntarenas (see below) and, therefore, as gateway to southern Nicoya. The opening of a new car ferry service between Puntarenas and Paquera in 1993 led to a drop in traffic through Naranjo. In response, hoteliers have made efforts to stamp Naranjo on the tourist map. They're quick to point out that several unspoilt and pretty beaches lie a few minutes away, and that Naranjo is a good base for exploring islands such as San Lucas and Gitana, an old prison base and an Indian burial site, respectively.

You'll find a **gas station** and **supermarket** (plus rental car service) at the junction for the ferry. An old ferry lies half submerged in the bay. Isla San Lucas lies offshore, three km to the east (see below).

Accommodations

There are three quality places to lay your head. **Hotel El Paso** (Apdo. 232, San José 2120, tel. 661-2610), 600 meters northwest of the ferry, has 14 rooms—three with a/c—with fans, queen beds, and private baths with hot water. Rooms are basic but clean and pleasing enough. Cabinas have kitchenettes. The hotel offers **car rental** and has a swimming pool and a restaurant. A *mirador* overlooks the gulf. Rates: $20-24 s, $24-36 d, $27-34 t, $54 cabinas for five.

Better yet is the **Hotel Oasis del Pacífico** (Apdo. 200, Puntarenas 5400, tel./fax 661-1555; or P.L. Wilhelm 1552, P.O. Box 025216, Miami,

FL 33102-5216), a very relaxing and quiet gringo-run hotel with 36 comfortable chalet-type rooms with fans, double beds, and lots of hot water—a rarity in Nicoya. The large screened restaurant is pleasingly breezy—the *corvina al ajillo* (sea bass with garlic) is absolutely superb—and is decorated with timeworn toy sailboats and artwork from Bali. Cuisine is overseen by Aggie Wilhelm, who serves her native Singaporean dishes. There's a small library, plus a large swimming pool in the expansive landscaped grounds, where horses (available for rides) roam free. For a small day rate, nonguests can use the facilities ($3 to use the pool) while waiting for the ferry . . . a chance to relax in a hammock or stroll the not-very-appealing beach and take in the views across the gulf. Yachts are welcome to anchor at the 80-meter boat dock. Oasis del Pacífico specializes in sportfishing ($275 full day). Rate: $50.

The new kid on the block is **El Ancla** (tel./fax 661-4148), which opened in December 1994 just 200 meters from the ferry terminal abutting the gas station and supermarket. The 10 a/c rooms are fronted by a wide porch with hammocks. Within, you'll find bright decor. The grounds include a pool and thatched bar.

The **Centro Turístico Maquinay** (tel./fax 661-1763), 400 meters north of Spanish-hacienda-style Hotel El Paso, also has 10 more basic cabinas and a swimming pool. It hosts the lively **Disco La Maquinera** on weekends, when locals pour in from all around.

Food

You'll find several *sodas* next to the ferry terminal. The Hotel El Paso serves good quality food at reasonable cost. The best bet is the Hotel Oasis del Pacífico, which has wonderful seafood and good burgers.

Transportation

The car-and-passenger ferry departs Puntarenas for Playa Naranjo at 3:15, 7, and 10:50 a.m., and 2:50 and 7 p.m. The return ferry departs for Puntarenas at 5:10 and 8:50 a.m., and 12:50, 5, and 9 p.m. Schedules may change: call to check (tel. 661-1069). Cost: $8.50 car, $1.10 adult, 65 cents child, $3.50 motorbike. Buy your ticket from a booth to the left of the gates. Park in line first. Get there at least an hour before departure time on weekends (more at holiday time), as lines get very long. Buses meet the ferry for Jicaral, Coyote, Bejuco, Carmona, and Nicoya. Hotel representatives will pick you up with notice.

ISLA SAN LUCAS

This 615-hectare island, two km off the eastern tip of Nicoya Peninsula, has been called the Island of Unspeakable Horrors, the Island of Silence, and Devil's Island. From afar, it seems a pleasant palm-fringed place . . . a place, perhaps, where you might wish to be washed ashore and languish a few months or even years in splendid sun-washed isolation. Yet no matter how pleasant it looks from afar a term on Isla San Lucas once amounted to no less than an excursion to Hell.

Until a few years ago it was the most dreaded prison in the Costa Rican penal system, a legacy dating back 400 years. In the 16th century, the Spanish conquistador Gonzalo Fernandez Oviedo used San Lucas as a concentration camp for local Chara Indians, who were slaughtered on the site of their sacred burial grounds. In the 19th century, Japanese pearl divers reportedly briefly used the island before being ejected by the Costa Rican government, which turned it into a detention center for political prisoners in 1862. In 1991, the government closed the prison.

The island is now a sad, silent place, and should you deposit yourself on the grim bastion, the ghosts of murderers, miscreants, and maltreated innocents will be your guides. A cobbled pathway leads to the main prison building (the prisoner who built it was promised his freedom once he completed his task; reportedly it took him 20 years). The chapel has become a bat grotto, and only graffiti remains to tell of the horror and hopelessness. You can still see the underground solitary-confinement cell (a ghastly hole sure to evoke poignant images) and other structures, which the jungle has since mostly reclaimed. There are still guards here, however, though today their role is to protect the island's resident wildlife from would-be poachers. They'll happily escort you to the diminutive cells where two dozen or more men at a time rotted their lives away.

The Island of the Lonely Men, a biographical account written in 1971 by ex-prisoner José León Sánchez, tells tales of the betrayals, the madness, and the perpetual frustrations of attempts to escape this spine-chilling place.

Transportation

You can rent **motorboats** through the Costa Rica Yacht Club in Puntarenas (tel. 661-0784) or Oasis del Pacífico in Playa Naranjo (tel./fax 661-1555). You can also hire Rafael at the Hotel Río (tel. 661-1143), or Alan Maquinay, who offers a regular tour of the island from Hotel Maquinay (tel. 661-1763) in Playa Naranjo. **Pollux de Golfito** (Apdo. 7-1970, San José 1000, tel./fax 220-2074, or tel. 231-4055, fax 231-3030) offers a day tour to San Lucas and Playa Escondida from Puntarenas aboard the 16-meter twin-masted sailing yacht *Pollux;* $70, including roundtrip transfers from San José. **Blue Seas** (Apdo. 64, San José 1000, tel. 323-7274, fax 233-5555) recently introduced a cruise around the islands of the Gulf of Nicoya from Puntarenas, including Isla San Lucas, Isla Caballo, and Isla Chira.

There are no restrictions on visiting.

PLAYA NARANJO TO PAQUERA

The coast road turns south from Playa Naranjo and leads to Paquera (18 km). This section is one of the worst in Costa Rica: very hilly, with tortuous switchbacks, deep potholes, and needle-sharp rocks that give a truly jolting ride and threaten to tear your tires to shreds (it may have been upgraded by the time you read this). That's the price for marvelous views out over the Gulf of Nicoya, including toward Isla Guayabo, which comes into view to the northwest, about six km south of Playa Naranjo where the road meets the coast at Gigante. Beyond Paquera, the road to Montezuma improves considerably. The climate of this region grows increasingly humid; the vegetation is more like that of the southern Pacific than that of drier northern Nicoya and Guanacaste.

Accommodations

The North American-run **Hotel Bahía el Gigante** (Apdo. 1886, San José, tel./fax 661-2442) has four condos and 12 spacious, nicely decorated rooms with fans and large bathrooms with hot water. Hammocks are strung across private verandas and beneath little *ranchitas* in the landscaped grounds, which include a pool. Costa Rican cuisine, seafood, and burgers are served in an elegant restaurant under a *palenque* roof. Trails lead through a small patch of primal forest. The property is gradually being turned into a catch-and-release sportfishing lodge, with four 8.5-meter Grady-Whites. A new dock is being built, with fresh water and electricity for visiting yachts and motor launches. The shore is 200 meters away. The hotel offers horse rentals, plus guided horseback tours to waterfalls ($5 per hour), kayak rentals ($30 half day), and kayak trips to Isla Gigante. Rates: $36 s, $41 d, $46 t for rooms; $45-70 for condos.

ISLA GITANA

This tiny island was once a burial site for local Indians (they called it "Isla de los Muertos," or "Island of the Dead"), and crosses mark more recent graves (the Indians having adopted Christianity). The undergrowth is wild and cacti abound, so appropriate footwear is recommended. Gitana, off the coast near Punta Gigante (yet not marked on any maps I've ever seen) serves up a soupçon of tropical pleasures: a couple of atmospheric if rustic cabins, a totally funky palm-thatch beachside restaurant-cum-bar, plus a scintillating white-sand beach shelving gently into peacock-blue waters.

The place is run almost as a private island resort by residents Carl and Loida Reugg, who rent out two large cement-block cabinas with kitchens. This is *not* Fantasy Island, however; don't expect luxury! There's a large pool for cooling dips and anchorage for yachters, who seem to favor the place. The Reuggs also offer water sport options (kayaks, $25 per day; Hobie Cats, $12 per hour; sailboards $40 per day; rowboats, $4 per hour), and even a speedboat for trips to Islas Tortugas and Curú Reserve ($100) or any of 15 other tempting isles within view. Rates: $10 d cabinas; $50 per person, including all meals for large unit (tel./fax 661-2994; in the U.S., tel. 415-281-5906).

Unwind in a bar that looks like it washed up from the sea. Eclectic paraphernalia glued and tacked together seems to hold the ramshackle place together. Irregular mariners call in for beers. Regulars include a tame monkey (Minkey) and his bosom-buddy Gordo, the coatimundi (the two enjoy a good rough-and-tumble, reports writer Ashley Cavers), a parrot (Rico), and an alcoholic raccoon (Rocky).

Calypso Cruises (see "Tortuga Island," below) has recently added Gitana to its itinerary. Hotels along the Nicoya coast offer trips to Gitana and you can also reach it by sea kayak from Bahía Gigante, a 30-minute paddle journey.

ISLA GUAYABO AND ISLA NEGRITOS BIOLOGICAL RESERVES

These two biological reserves, which lie offshore of Costa de Pájaros ("Bird Coast"), protect nesting sites of the brown booby, frigate bird, pelican, and other seabirds. In winter, tiny (6.8 hectare) Guayabo is also a nesting site for the peregrine falcon. Negritos, which is less than half a kilometer from shore, was once settled by Indians, who left artifacts as evidence of their stay. The island (74 hectares) is actually two islands separated by a narrow channel and covered in a scrubby forest of spiny cedar, viscoyol palm, and frangipani. Dolphins are commonly seen offshore. The islands are off-limits to visitors.

Several cruise operators pass by Isla Guayabo and Isla Negritos on day cruises out of Puntarenas (average $70, including transfer from San José). These include **Bay Island Cruises** (Apdo. 49, San José 1017, tel. 296-5551, fax 296-5095); **Calypso Cruises** (Apdo. 6941, San José 1000, tel. 255-3022, or 661-0585 in Puntarenas, fax 323-0401); **Costa Sol Tropical Cruises** (Apdo. 7-1880, San José 1000, tel. 220-0722, fax 220-2095); and **Sea Ventures** (tel. 239-4719, fax 239-4666).

JESUITA ISLAND

Isla Jesuita (four km northeast of Paquera) and Isla Cedros lie between Guayabo and Negritos but are not protected. The small hotel—**Hotel Isla Jesuita** (tel. 661-0263)—has a lodge and cabinas with hammocks. It serves seafood dishes and offers water sports.

PAQUERA

This quiet village, 24 km from Playa Naranjo, is centered on the junction for the **Paquera ferry,** which shuttles to and fro from Puntarenas. The road to the left at the T-junction leads past a **gas station** (fill up here, as this is the *only* gas station in the whole southern region) and dead-ends at the ferry terminal. You can continue along a rough dirt track to the end of Punta Corralillo. The road to the right leads to Curú National Wildlife Refuge, Playa Tambor, Montezuma, and Cabo Blanco. **Note:** A direct shuttle ferry between Puntarenas and Montezuma was introduced in early 1995, negating the need to take the Paquera ferry for those without cars.

Accommodations and Food
The **Restaurante y Cabinas Ginana** (tel. 661-1444, ext. 119) is a pleasing and modestly elegant place to eat. It also has 19 rooms with fans, and private baths with cold water. Rate: $12 d. **Pensión Bengala,** next to the pool hall in the center of town, has basic rooms with shared baths and fans ($5). **Cabinas Rosita** (tel. 661-1444, ext. 102 or 206) also has basic rooms ($20 d). The road south from the ferry dock ends at **Fred's Folly** (tel. 288-2014). Not reviewed. Apparently cabins here cost about $40 d.

Rancho Lila is a very pleasant and popular place to eat. The **Bar El Bienvenido** is also good. **Salon Bar El Indico** is more down to earth.

Services
Paquera has a **Banco de Costa Rica** (tel. 661-1444, ext. 190) and a **Banco Nacional** (tel. 661-1444, ext. 101). The **public telephone** is next door to Restaurante Ginana.

Transportation
The easiest approach using public transport is via the Paquera ferry, which now carries cars and departs Puntarenas daily at 6 and 11 a.m., and 3 p.m. ($2 passengers, $6 cars or $27 first class with seating in an air-conditioned cabin; tel.

661-2830). Ferries depart Paquera for Puntarenas at 8:15 a.m. and 12:30 and 5:20 p.m. Check departures ahead of time. A bus marked Directo meets the ferry and travels to Paquera, Tambor, Cóbano, and Montezuma ($3; two hours). A **taxi** from Paquera will cost about $30. If you wish to head straight for Montezuma, note that there is now direct ferry service from Puntarenas (see "Montezuma," below).

Word is that a hydrofoil service from Puntarenas is to be introduced by the Tambor Beach Resort; it may be in service by the time you read this.

CURÚ NATIONAL WILDLIFE REFUGE

This private reserve forms part of a 1,214-hectare hacienda, two-thirds of which is preserved as primary forest. It is tucked in the fold of Golfo Curú, four km south of Paquera. The 84-hectare reserve includes 4.5 km of coastline with a series of tiny coves and three beautiful white-sand beaches: Curú, Colorada, and Quesera. Olive ridley and hawksbill turtles nest on the crystalline beaches. Mangrove swamps extend inland along the Río Curú, backed by forested hills. Diving is good close to shore, where lobsters and giant conches are abundant. Whales are often sighted offshore (January is reportedly the best month). Birds include motmots, white-fronted amazons, laughing hawks, lineated woodpeckers, and at least 150 other species. Mammals include agoutis, ocelots, margays, pumas, howler and capuchin monkeys, white-tailed deer, sloths, and anteaters. All rather remarkable for so small a place! Isla Tortuga lies three km offshore.

Call the owner, Doña Julieta Schutz (tel. 661-2392), for permission to enter, ideally with several days' notice. She has a microwave telephone, and getting through is often difficult. There's no sign for Curú. The gate is normally locked unless you're expected. Doña Julieta will give you instructions to find it. Guided tours are offered (your tip is their pay).

Accommodations
Basic research huts on the beachfront are sometimes available for overnight stays, meals included ($30 per night). Researchers and students get priority. Showers and toilets are primitive. No camping allowed.

Getting There
The bus from Paquera to Cóbano passes the unmarked gate. Ask the driver to let you off. Several tour companies in Montezuma and nearby hotels offer day tours. **Cruceros del Sur** (Apdo. 1198, San José 1200, tel. 220-1927, fax 220-2103) offers a one-day voyage to Curú from Puntarenas aboard the 11-meter *Georgiana* ($79), plus a four-day/three-night eco-cruise package aboard the 68-passenger *Temptress* ($595 low season, $745 high season).

TORTUGA ISLAND

This stunningly beautiful, 320-hectare island is a popular day-trip from Puntarenas. It's a 14-km (90-minute) journey aboard any of half-a-dozen cruise boats. Tortuga is as close to an idyllic tropical isle as you'll find hereabouts. The main attraction is a magnificent white-sand beach lined with tall coconut palms. Each of the cruise companies that put day-trippers ashore gets its own section of the beach. It can get a bit cramped on weekends, when three or four boats might disgorge their passengers at the same time. Still, it makes for a tremendous trip on a sunny day. You can snorkel, swim, play volleyball, hike, or simply snooze in the sun. The boats pass by Islas San Lucas, Guayabo, and Negritos en route.

Cruises
Calypso Cruises (Apdo. 6941, San José 1000, tel. 255-3022, or 661-0585 in Puntarenas, fax 233-0401) began the trend in 1979 aboard the venerable *Calypso*, which faithfully operated daily until 1994, when it was replaced by a vessel so stunning it will make your jaw drop in awe—the space-age *Manta Raya* catamaran ($84). It's more luxurious than any first class aircraft lounge, with soft leather seating, full bar, fresh-water showers, and even an underwater viewing window! Transfers from San José are provided, with snacks served en route, washed down by *coco locos* made of rum, coconut milk, and coconut liqueur served in a coconut. Your buffet lunch on the beach will be one of the best you'll have in Costa Rica, with fare such as

JOHN ANDERSON

Tortuga Island

mahimahi in shrimp sauce, salads, and tortillas. Another highlight of the trip is Abuelo, Calypso's octogenarian marimba player (the company paid for his eye surgery in 1987; now Abuelo says he's always smiling because he "can see the pretty young passengers in their bikinis").

Though Calypso sets the standard, the following companies also offer similar day cruises to Tortuga: **Bay Island Cruises** (Apdo. 145, San José 1007, tel. 239-4951, fax 329-4404); **Costa Sol Tropical Cruises** (Apdo. 7-1880, San José 1000, tel. 220-0722, fax 220-2095); **Fantasia** (tel. 255-0791); **Sea Ventures** (tel. 239-4719, fax 239-4666); and **S/Y *Pollux,*** a charming Dutch-built sailing yacht (tel. 231-4055, fax 231-3030).

TAMBOR

Tambor is a small and funky fishing village in Bahía Ballena ("Whale Bay"), 18 km southwest of Paquera. In town, there's a narrow and un-appealing gray-sand beach and a tiny church. Whales are sometimes sighted—hence the name. To the south the beaches get better and better; you can walk south to Tango Mar (eight km) and beyond along one of the country's more beautiful sections of coast. Monkeys and other critters hang out by the shore. Tambor was put on the map a few years ago by the publicity surrounding construction of the Hotel Playa Tambor. The controversy has since died down, and Spain's Barceló group is talking of adding more hotels near the site. Other hotels are rising. Choose from a brace of superb deluxe options.

Budget Accommodations

The **Hotel Dos Lagartos** (Apdo. 5602, San José 1000, tel. 661-1122, ext. 236), on the waterfront in Tambor village, has 19 rooms with shared baths, plus four cabinas with private baths. Rooms are clean but small, dark, and basically furnished. No towels. Rates: $10 s, $15 d, $18 t for rooms; $25 s/d for cabinas. A new hotel and cabinas were completed next door in 1993. **Cabinas El Bosque** has fairly basic accommodations, just before the turnoff into the village. Also try **Zorba's Place,** about three km east of Tambor, which has cabinas ($25 d, including breakfast) and a restaurant predictably selling Greek-inspired dishes.

Deluxe Accommodations

The Bahía Ballena is the setting for three of Costa Rica's most impressive deluxe hotels, including the controversial **Hotel Playa Tambor** (tel. 661-1915, fax 661-2069; or Apdo. 458, San José 1150, tel. 220-2034, fax 231-1990; in the U.S. at 150 S.E. Second Ave., Suite 806, Miami, FL 33131, tel. 800-858-0606 or 305-539-1167, fax 305-539-1160), the first megaresort in the nation: a contentious test case that helped obliquely to shape the future of oceanfront development in Costa Rica. The first phase opened in November 1992 after developers had raised the ire of environmentalists by violating protective laws.

Sprawling across a 2,400-hectare site, the planned resort is a "Club Med" of sorts in Costa Rica. Once settled, you need never put your hand in your pocket. It offers 402 rooms, each with terrace or balcony, a/c, refrigerator, cable TV, self-dial phone, and deep bathtub (the resort

may eventually contain 1,000 rooms). The rooms are housed in two three-story blocks. The grounds are ugly—they were once cattle pasture, which they still resemble. And the private gray-sand beach is unimpressive. The amenities make amends. An impressive 350-seat theater has a fully animated stage. Highlights include a two-million-liter pool, plus three poolside restaurants, five bars, a disco, a small open-air gymnasium, a children's playground, a solarium, a large shopping complex, and extensive sports facilities. Nature trails lead into an adjacent reserve featuring a botanical park and—sadly—a "zoo" with monkeys, squirrels, and tortoises. The resort has its own airstrip and a helicopter landing strip. Package rates (double occupancy): $539, three nights ($969 single); $1149 seven nights ($2069 single); extra night, $259 single, $149 double.

Much more appealing is the **Tango Mar** (Apdo. 2877, San José 1000, tel. 223-1864 or 661-2798, fax 255-2697), five km west of Tambor. This thoroughly romantic retreat—Costa Rica's finest beachside resort—embodies the essence of a relaxing vacation. Tango Mar whisks you 8,000 km to Hawaii, Tahiti, or Fiji! Imagine a beautiful beachfront setting: a long, lonesome strip of coral sand lined with tall palms and a sea as warm as bedtime milk. Add hectares of beautifully tended grounds splashed with color: bright bougainvilleas and potted hibiscus in blazing yellow and red. Include five Polynesian-style thatched cabañas raised on stilts, tucked neatly amid lush foliage, and a dozen hotel rooms raised over the shore, with large balconies overlooking the sea. Two-, three-, and four-bedroom villas are also available.

Although the hotel boasts a large pool, a 10-hole golf course, and water sports, the order of the day is a healthy dose of inactivity poolside or on the stunning beaches, with tidepools close by for warm-water soaks. There is talk of redesigning the course to 18 holes. It's the Pebble Beach of Costa Rica, with two holes bordering the cliffs. Greens fees are free to guests; others pay $25 per day for unlimited play. The resort also rents 4WDs—a good idea just for negotiating the rutted track that leads through the grounds! If you take the Paquera-Cóbano bus, you'll have to walk about one km along the abysmal, muddy track. Shame on the owners for

not upgrading this. Rates: $120 d for cottages and standard rooms, $131 with whirlpool bath; villas from $179.

Last but not least is the truly stunning **Tambor Tropical** (Public Affairs Counsel, 867 Liberty St. NE, Salem, OR 97301, tel. 503-363-7084; in Costa Rica, tel. 288-0491), designed, says its PR rep, "to create a union between modern facilities and the rejuvenating powers of traditional Costa Rican retreats." The result is a perfect place to laze in the shade of a swaying palm. Ten architecturally striking, hand-crafted beachfront cabinas nestle amid emerald forest and look transplanted from Bali. The two-story, hexagonal cabinas (one up, one down) are graced by intricately carved wood motifs, voluminous bathrooms, splendid balconies, and fully equipped kitchens for whipping up candlelight dinners or morning snacks. Of course, remarkably simple yet "fine cuisine" is also proffered by an international chef. Everything was handmade of native hardwoods at an on-site workshop. Windows are teak, walls are laurel and red oak, with floors and doors of exquisite purple-heart. Too lazy to get out of bed for the sunrise? No problem! The queen-size beds are raised so that you may revel in skies of carnal plum-purple and orange. A landscaped pool and Jacuzzi set in lush landscaped gardens add their own romantic notes. Fishing, snorkeling, horseback riding, and estuary boat trips are a few of the attractions. The bar is a popular hangout for locals. Oodles of atmosphere. Book now!

Camping
The **Salon/Bar Los Gitanos** allows camping.

House Rental
SIMA (tel. 661-3233, afternoons) has several houses for rent at Playa Pochote, about four km northeast of Tambor. The modern, fully equipped, two-bedroom homes rent for $65 daily, including laundry service plus use of bicycles, horses, and snorkeling gear.

Food
Restaurant Cristina, opposite the school, proffers good food for those on a budget. There's also a small restaurant in the Hotel Dos Lagartos. If seeking a treat, check out the restaurant of the

Bahía Ballena Yacht Club, where Louisiana's Chef Bob presents exceptional Mexican, Creole, and Cajun cuisine ($8 and upward).

Services

Salsa Boutique, on the left as you enter Tambor, sells Guatemalan clothing and souvenirs. The Salon/Bar Los Gitanos has a **public telephone.** The **Bahía Ballena Yacht Club,** on the marina at the southern end of the bay is equipped with a floating dock with 30 moorings, plus water, gas, and diesel. It also offers scuba diving, windsurfing, sunset cruises, and a **sea-taxi** service, plus Hobie Cat rentals. **Tropic World Diving Station** (tel. 661-1915, fax 661-2069) offers diving programs, including PADI certification, out of the Playa Tambor Beach Resort.

Transportation

For bus connections, see "Paquera," above. **Travelair** offers flights from Pavas Airport, San José, daily at 8:30 a.m. and 3 p.m. ($62 one-way, $98 roundtrip); return flights depart Tambor at 9:10 a.m. and 3:40 p.m. **SANSA** offers service from San José daily (except Sunday) at 11:15 a.m., and Sunday at 8 a.m., continuing to Tamarindo, Nosara, and Sámara ($36 one-way).

Two companies offer yacht cruises from Playa Herradura, north of Jacó (see the Central Pacific chapter). **Sea Ventures** (Apdo. 6941, San José; tel 255-3022, fax 233-0401) includes Playa Tambor on a three-day sailing adventure from Playa Herradura to Cabo Blanco (see below; $445). **Veleros del Sur** (tel. 661-1320) operates passenger service aboard the 516-meter *Pegasus,* a sailing yacht that departs Playa Herradura at 1 p.m. Monday and Friday (four hours; $30 one-way, $50 roundtrip).

CÓBANO

Cóbano, a small village 25 km southwest of Paquera, is the gateway to Montezuma and Cabo Blanco Absolute Nature Reserve. Turn left at the tiny road circle. If you continue straight, the horrendously rough road will take you to **Mal País** (see section "Sámara South to Cabo Blanco," this chapter).

Accommodations and Food

The **Bar y Restaurant Costena** (tel. 661-1122, ext. 219), opposite the Banco Nacional above the Costena Bar, has nine modest but well-kept rooms, four with private baths, five with shared. Rates: $5.50 per person with shared bath, $6 with private bath. Ask in the *pulpería* next door. Another option, reportedly, is **Cabinas Villa Grace.**

La Vida Natural has two basic cabinas (one sleeping six) on a farm two km east of Cóbano. You can dine here on vegetarian meals or cook for yourself. Rate: $5 per person.

Services

You'll find a **public telephone** at Soda Helena and a **Banco Nacional** at the junction for Montezuma, in the center of town.

Transportation

Buses to Montezuma depart Cóbano from outside the Costena Bar at 9 a.m. and 6 p.m., and for Paquera at 5:30 a.m. and 2 p.m.

MONTEZUMA

Montezuma is a charming, funky beachside retreat commonly described as being popular with "hippies," "drop-outs," and budget-minded travelers. Yes, it's favored by the backpacking, counter-culture crowd (I can't vouch for this, but it has a reputation for "free love"), and it's blessed with a range of good budget accommodations. It could be the most casual place in Costa Rica. But it also attracts its share of more elderly, monied, cultured folks to whom a vacation means lazing in T-shirts and boxers with beer in hand. Montezuma is also better organized and far cleaner than the majority of Costa Rica's beach villages, especially those popular with Ticos, the world's champion litter-louts (there are trash cans at regular intervals, for example). And local residents have of late taken less kindly to campers, many of whom have left garbage, felled trees, and a bitter taste in their wake.

A fantastic series of beaches east of Montezuma—Cocal, Cocalito, Quizales—is backed by forest-festooned cliffs from which streams tumble down to the coral-white sands. There are lots of rocks for tidepooling. And you can

often see monkeys frolicking in the forests behind the beach. Strong currents are a problem; Playa Grande, about two km northeast of Montezuma, is reportedly the safest. Cool off in the waterfall and swimming hole two km southeast of town, on the road to Cabo Blanco (the trail leads upstream from the Restaurante La Cascada). Note that you cannot drive to any of the beaches east of Montezuma. Bummer eh? being forced to walk barefoot with your feet in the warm water and the breeze in your hair.

The dirt road from Cóbano is in reasonably good condition, though occasionally muddy, even in the dry season (many of the soils around here are impervious). You drop down a very steep switchback hill into Montezuma. Drive with caution, especially when the road is wet, when it becomes treacherously slippy. You may need a 4WD in wet season just for this section. If all else fails, rent a horse. Dozens of signs advertise horse rentals and guided tours.

The town has only one phone (tel. 661-1122). Most hotels have their own extension: you'll need to ask the operator who answers to connect you. Montezuma gets very full in dry season. Reservations are recommended.

Budget Accommodations

The beachfront **Hotel Moctezuma** (ext. 258) has 22 very spacious and clean rooms, with fans; seven with shared baths, 15 with private baths, with cold water. The annex across the road is less appealing. The main unit has a restaurant and bar directly over the beach. A small boutique and store donates a share of its income to the Montezuma Ecological Fund. A bargain . . . if you can handle the noise from Chico's Bar. Rates: $8 s, $14 d with shared bath; $14 s, $20 d with private bath, including tax.

Cabinas Karen (tel. 661-2472, messages), next to El Sano Banano, has two cozy but very basic rooms. It offers cooking facilities and a *pila* (laundry sink). The owner, Karen Wessberg (wife of the late Olof Wessberg; see "Cabo Blanco Absolute Nature Reserve," below), also has three basic beachfront cabinas north of town on a separate 70-hectare reserve. Trails lead from shore to mountaintop. It's a wonderful escape, with monkeys sometimes outside your cabin. No electricity. Outside bathroom and open-air kitchen are shared. Rate: $6. The German-run **Cabinas El Pargo Feliz** has very pleasing, modern, and clean cabinas with hammocks on the verandas ($23 d). Its rustic but pleasant thatched restaurant opens at 6 p.m. You can also try **Cabinas Vilma,** which has two basic cabinas with tiny kitchens: not as appealing as other properties.

Hotel Lucy (ext. 273), the green-and-white building opposite Los Mangos west of Montezuma, has 10 basic rooms with fans, and shared bath with hot water. The veranda begs quiet contemplation while looking out to sea. In

beach at Montezuma

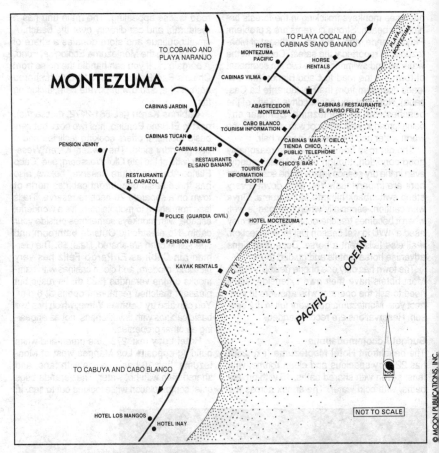

MONTEZUMA

TO COBANO AND
PLAYA NARANJO

TO PLAYA COCAL AND
CABINAS SANO BANANO

HOTEL
MONTEZUMA
PACIFIC

HORSE
RENTALS

CABINAS VILMA

CABINAS JARDIN

ABASTECEDOR
MONTEZUMA

CABINAS / RESTAURANTE
EL PARGO FELIZ

CABO BLANCO
TOURISM INFORMATION

PENSION JENNY

CABINAS TUCAN

CABINAS KAREN

CABINAS MAR Y CIELO,
TIENDA CHICO,
PUBLIC TELEPHONE

RESTAURANTE
EL SANO BANANO

CHICO'S BAR

RESTAURANTE
EL CARAZOL

TOURIST
INFORMATION
BOOTH

POLICE (GUARDIA CIVIL)

HOTEL MOCTEZUMA

PENSION ARENAS

KAYAK RENTALS

BEACH

PACIFIC OCEAN

PLAYA MONTEZUMA

TO CABUYA AND CABO BLANCO

HOTEL LOS MANGOS

HOTEL INAY

NOT TO SCALE

© MOON PUBLICATIONS, INC.

1993, Lucy's was targeted for razing by local officials eager to be seen enforcing environmental codes (like dozens of hotels along the coast, it is built within the inviolable 50 meters from the high-tide mark). The community got its dander up and squared off against the bulldozers. If it ain't there when you call, you'll know why! Rates: $8-14 per person.

Cabinas Las Rocas, four km west of Montezuma, has four rooms in a home, with meals provided by Natalie, the owner ($9 per person). She also has a two-bedroom house for rent ($15 per day). **Pensión Jenny** is hidden along a dirt road; rooms are small but clean ($6 s, $12 d).

Pensión Arenas and **Restaurante El Carazol,** also on the road leading toward Cabo Blanco, have basic rooms. You might also try **Cabinas Capitán,** though I've heard its rooms aren't too good (its *casados,* fixed-price lunches, however, are recommended).

Inexpensive Accommodations
Cabinas Linda Vista (ext. 274), atop the hill above Montezuma, has two modern brick cabinas, each for six people (four more will be added by 1994), with fans, kitchens, hammocks on the verandas, and cold water. It has views over the ocean. The owner lives in the house in front of

the gate to the cabinas. It's a steep climb down and up from the beach. Rate: $12 per person.

Another rustic but pleasing option is **Cabinas Tucán** (ext. 284), which has six fairly small and dingy cabins with fans, screens, and shared baths with cold water. It's raised on stilts: the shaded restaurant downstairs is a popular eatery. Rates: $10 s, $15 d. **Hotel L'Aurora** (ext. 200) is a pleasingly aged, whitewashed house surrounded by lush gardens. The five basic rooms have fans and private baths with cold water. Upstairs is an airy lounge with bamboo and leather sofas, a small library, and hammocks. Rooms downstairs are dark. Shared kitchen. There's a children's playground outside. Rate: $27 d.

Tienda Chico (tel. 661-2472) has six cabinas—**Cabinas Mar y Cielo**—behind the store, right on the beach. Each has fans and private bath. Chico offers tours to Cabo Blanco. Overpriced. Rates: $27 s, $30 d, $32 t. Another overpriced basic option is **Montezuma Pacific** (ext. 200), with 10 rooms with a/c, private baths, and hot water. The outside looks like a Bavarian home. Inside, rooms lack atmosphere but are clean with tiny balconies. Rates: $26-35 s/d ($6 each additional person).

Moderate Accommodations

One of the nicest places is **Cabinas Jardín** (ext. 284), which offers six hillside cabinas with fans and private baths with cold water. Each elegant cabina is individually styled in hardwoods and shaded by trees, with a magnificent ambience. Rate: $35 d. If you want to step out of bed and onto the beach, check out the 10 cabinas belonging to the **Restaurante El Sano Banano** (ext. 272); they back the beach, about one km east of the village. All have fans and private baths. Very private—you sense you have the beach to yourself. Rates: $40 rooms, $50 domes.

The most atmospheric place for miles is **Hotel Los Mangos** (ext. 259, fax 661-2320), on the road to Cabo Blanco, with 10 rooms and 10 thatched cabinas made of attractive hardwoods. The small but delightful octagonal bungalows under shade trees have all-around windows, wide porches, both single and double beds, and oodles of hot water. They're set on a marvelously landscaped slope complete with a three-tier waterfall. You'll find a clean pool, circular bar, thatched dining pavilion, and Jacuzzi on the grounds, and horses for forays into the forest. Greek owner Constantinas Jzavaras runs a great operation. Rates: $30 double in older rooms with shared baths, $60 triple in larger rooms with private baths.

Americans Richard and Doris Stocker will welcome you like family at the **Hotel Amor de Mar** (ext. 262), which enjoys a fabulous location on a sheltered headland, with views along the coast in both directions. The hotel is set in very pleasant landscaped lawns, one km west of Montezuma, with hammocks beneath shady palms. They have are 14 rooms (some with hot water) and one *casita*. Communal bathrooms are very clean. Rooms are entirely of hardwoods, open onto a large veranda, and have lots of light. An abundance of potted plants and beautiful tropical flowers enhance the relaxing atmosphere. Richard and Doris have three boys—families are welcome. Richard also asked me to mention the delicious homemade bread! Rates: $30 with shared bath, $45 *casita*.

Camping

Pensión Arenas, west of Montezuma, offers beachside camping, as well as basic rooms. You can also camp at **El Pargo Feliz** ($2). Camping is great under shade trees along the beaches northeast and southwest of the village. No facilities, and the community is trying to discourage camping on the beach. Too many campers are slobs! If you camp, leave only footprints. And don't leave things unattended—the local monkeys are, well . . . monkeys!

Food

Many of the hotels have restaurants: among the best options are the Hotel Moctezuma and Cabinas Tucán. **El Sano Banano** is a very popular natural-food restaurant serving garlic breads, lasagne, yogurts, and ice cream. It also sells filtered water and will prepare lunches to go. It offers a special of the day. **Chico's** reportedly had burned down since I last visited, but should have re-opened by the time you read this. Opposite is open-air **El Pargo Feliz** (the "Happy Red Snapper") belonging to the Abastecedor Montezuma; it has reasonably priced lobster ($12) and fish dishes (about $4). The **Marisquería La Cascada** is a good bet and has the

advantage of a nice streamside setting (a waterfall is half a kilometer upstream along a trail). You can also get tasty pastas and filling *casados* at **Soda Las Gemelas.** The restaurant of the Hotel Amor de Mar is a good bet for breakfasts and lunches—the homemade bread is delicious. Lots of funky shacks on the beach sell lemonade and *pipas*—freshly-opened coconuts. If you want to dine *on* the beach, pull up a chair at the **Restaurant El Parque.**

Entertainment

Sano Banano shows movies on laser disc nightly around 7:30 to 8 p.m. (free with dinner, or $2.50 minimum order). The in place to sup was **Chico's,** which could get quite lively (see above). **Kaliolin** is a new bar in the hills above town; I've not been, but it's been recommended.

Services

The Cabinas Jardín office doubles as a **tourist information** office, rents motorcycles ($70 per day) and bicycles ($12 per day), and also represents **Monte Aventuras,** whose tours include kayaking to Cabuya and Río Lajas ($41), speedboat tours to Jacó and Playa Sámara ($26-35 per person), and guided tours to Cabo Blanco ($15). The **Centro Regional de Información Turístico** (tel. 661-1122, ext. 257 or 258), opposite El Sano Banano, rents kayaks, horses, and bicycles, and offers a guided horseback trip to the waterfalls and a Tortuga Island tour, including snorkeling and lunch ($30 per person, full day), plus transport to Cabo Blanco ($5 roundtrip; guides are $20 per person, including car).

A hut on the left just before the beach rents horses and sells homemade whole wheat bread. Roger Nuñoz also rents horses and offers guided horseback trips to the waterfalls ($20, four hours); ask for him at the Hotel Amor de Mar. The **Casa del Mundo,** next to Cabinas Jardín, is a boutique selling hammocks, Guatemalan items, and T-shirts. **Tienda Chico** also sells Guatemalan clothes, sandals, etc., and has a public telephone (tel. 661-2472). Jenny, at the Hotel Montezuma Pacific, gives **massages.** You'll find a **public shower** behind Tienda Chico.

Transportation

A bus for Cóbano and Montezuma ($4) meets the Paquera ferry (see above; take the early ferry if possible, to avoid arriving in Montezuma after dark). Buses to Montezuma depart Cóbano from outside the Costena Bar at 9 a.m. and 6 p.m. In wet season, you may need to take a jeep-taxi beyond Cóbano (about $5). The return bus departs Montezuma (dry season) or Cóbano (wet season) at 5:30 a.m. and 2 p.m.

If the ferry-and-bus journey sounds like an ordeal, $15 will buy you a roundtrip direct passage between Puntarenas and Montezuma aboard *Simba,* a 16-meter version of the PT boats used by the U.S. Navy in World War II. The vessel departs Montezuma 7 a.m. daily, Dec.-April; return departure from Bar Bananas in Puntarenas at 1 p.m. You can buy tickets in Puntarenas from the Polar Bar (Avenida Central, Calle 4, tel. 661-0344). *Simba* also offers service to Tambor from Montezuma at 3:30 p.m. Reportedly, a local cooperative also offers **boat-taxis** to Puntarenas and points along the central Pacific, as well as north to Playas Sámara and Nosara. Check with the information booth opposite the Hotel Moctezuma. Plenty of people hitch along the road between Montezuma and Cabuya.

CABUYA

Cabuya is a tiny hamlet two km east of Cabo Blanco reserve. After years of isolation, sleepy Cabuya is waking up, stirred by the traffic to the nature reserve and the spillover from Montezuma. Isla Cabuya, about eight km west of Montezuma, is a cemetery for the village of Cabuya. You can walk out to the island at low tide to see perhaps two dozen graves marked with crude crosses. You'll find a shop plus a **public telephone** and fax in **Pulpería El Higueron,** which has a large open-air *soda.*

You can rent horses from Lolo, who'll act as guide; while locals such as Manolo or Pipo will be happy to take you fishing or even on a boat tour to Isla Tortuga. Alex Villalobos and his English wife, Fiona, (owners of the El Ancla hotel; see below) also rent horses ($20), mountain bikes ($10), and boats.

Accommodations and Food

Cabinas/Soda Cabo Blanco is on the beachfront, one km east of Cabuya. Rooms are dingy

and small; from $10. Next door is the **Hotel Cabo Blanco** (tel. 442-0785; in the U.S., tel. 800-721-4141), which opened 1 January 1995 as a more upmarket property with 10 a/c rooms with cable TV and orthopedic beds. You can rent kayaks. Rate: $40. Also for those with dollars to spare is **Hotel Celaje** (tel. 284-7562), whose seven simple yet beautiful beachfront thatched four-person cabinas have private baths and patios with hammocks. It has a nice pool with Jacuzzi as well as a tempting *ranchita* restaurant (yes, you can dip if you eat, even if you're not staying here). It offers kayak rentals and horseback and sportfishing rides. Rate: $60.

Restaurante y Cabinas El Ancla de Oro (tel. 642-0023 or 661-3234, fax 642-0025) has **camping,** plus three delightful thatched hardwood A-framed cabins on tall stilts with a restaurant beneath the largest, which sleeps five. Mosquito nets are provided. Rate: $10 per person. The Villaloboses also rent rooms in their house ($6) and have a self-contained thatched cabina with kitchen, available by the week or month.

Yugo Cabinas has three self-contained cabins facing the ocean. Rate: $23. You can also rent rooms with Doña Lila, whose thatched house is the last on the left before the park entrance ($10 including meals). Not reviewed but apparently quite adequate is the new **Hotel Sunshine,** on the Cabo Blanco side of Cabuya.

El Palenque Cabo Blanco restaurant, just before the park entrance one km west of Cabuya, allows **camping.**

CABO BLANCO ABSOLUTE NATURE RESERVE

This jewel of nature at the very tip of the Nicoya Peninsula is where Costa Rica's quest to bank its natural resources for the future began. The 1,172-hectare reserve—the oldest protected area in the country—was created in October 1963 thanks to the tireless efforts of Nils Olof Wessberg, a Swedish immigrant commonly referred to as the father of Costa Rica's national park system. (See David Rains Wallace's excellent book, *The Quetzal and the Macaw: The Story of Costa Rica's National Parks,* for a profile on Wessberg's influence.) Olof and his wife, Karen, settled in the area in 1955 when this cor-

ner of the Nicoya Peninsula was still covered with a mix of evergreen and deciduous forest, an island in a sea of rapidly falling trees, rising settlements, and cattle ranches. They bought a rocky mountainous plot of land and spent 10 years developing fruit orchards.

In 1960, when the first patch of cleared land appeared at Cabo Blanco, Olof launched an appeal—published in the April 1961 journal of the World League Against Vivisection and For the Protection of Animals—to save the land. "Only in one spot is there today some of the wildlife that was formerly everywhere in the northwest," Olof wrote. "Here live the puma and the *manigordo* (ocelot), deer, peccary, tepiscuintle, pizote, kinkajou, chulumuco (tayra), kongo (howler monkey), caraiblanca (capuchin monkey), and miriki (spider monkey). The jaguar and tapir are already extinct . . . When we settled here six years ago the mountain was always green. Today it has great brown patches, and in March and April it is shrouded in smoke, much of it on fire . . . Two years more, and the mountain will be dead. Who is going to save it? It can be had at the ridiculously low price of $10 an acre . . . But it has to be done immediately."

Although several international organizations responded with money, buying the land and protecting the area extracted blood, sweat, and tears. Conservation had not yet entered national consciousness. The first warden killed the last 10 spider monkeys for their fat; the third warden felled trees to grow crops. When one of Olof's supporters—Allston Jenkins, of the Philadelphia Conservation League—suggested the need for a national parks service to the Costa Rican government, they responded enthusiastically. "So then," writes David Rains Wallace, "they found two students in San José to be the national parks service, one of them twenty-seven years old and one twenty-four. That was Mario Boza and Alvaro Ugalde." Ugalde has been parks service director for most of the past two decades; Boza is famous for his beautifully written and illustrated book, *The National Parks of Costa Rica.*

Olof Wessberg was murdered in the Osa Peninsula in the summer of 1975 while researching the area in his attempts to have the region declared a national park. A plaque near the Cabo Blanco ranger station has been erected in his honor.

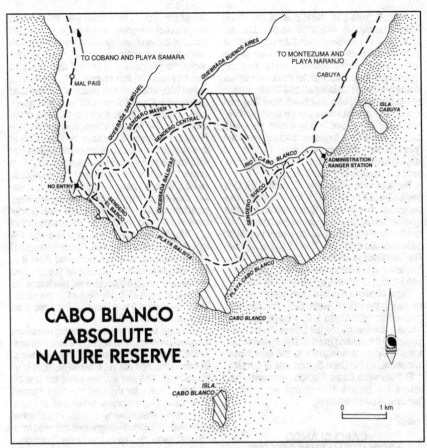

CABO BLANCO
ABSOLUTE
NATURE RESERVE

TO COBANO AND PLAYA SAMARA

MAL PAIS

QUEBRADA BUENOS AIRES

TO MONTEZUMA AND
PLAYA NARANJO

CABUYA

ISLA
CABUYA

QUEBRADA SAN MIGUEL

SENDERO MAVEN

SENDERO CENTRAL

QUEBRADA BALSITAS

RIO CABO BLANCO

ADMINISTRATION
RANGER STATION

NO ENTRY

SENDERO EL BARCO

SENDERO SUECO

PLAYA BALSITA

PLAYA CABO BLANCO

CABO BLANCO

ISLA
CABO BLANCO

0   1 km

© MOON PUBLICATIONS, INC.

The reserve is named after the vertical-walled island at its tip, which owes its name to the accumulation of *guano* deposited by seabirds, including Costa Rica's largest community of brown boobies (some 500 breeding pairs). Many of the wildlife species that Wessberg gave his life to protect—not least howler, spider, and capuchin monkeys, as well as tiger cats, agoutis, white-tailed deer, and plentiful snakes—can still be seen. The reserve was originally off-limits to visitors. Today, about one-third is accessible along hiking trails, some steep in parts. **Sendero Sueco** leads uphill and then down onto the totally unspoiled white-sand beaches of Playa Balsita and Playa Cabo Blanco, which are separated by a headland (you can walk around it at low tide). A **coastal trail**—Sendero El Barco—leads west from Playa Balsitas to the western boundary of the park. All have tidepools. Check tide tables with the park rangers before setting off, otherwise you could get stuck! Torrential downpours are common April-December. You cannot take horses in.

A substantial increase in visitation in recent years has spawned efforts to manage the influx and minimize the impact. Certain restrictions may be in effect by the time you read this.

Services

The ranger station sells a trail map and T-shirts. Hours: 8 a.m.-4 p.m. Closed Monday and Tuesday. Entrance: $15 walk-in, $7 advance purchase. Camping is not allowed, not even at the ranger station.

Transportation

The road is in very good condition most of the way from Montezuma; it deteriorates markedly just before Cabo Blanco and gets very muddy in wet season. Be prepared to cross a wide river about one km before Cabuya. Be very careful! Follow the tracks of previous cars to the left; if you try to go directly across, you'll end up in extremely deep water. Many people walk from Montezuma (11 km): it's a hot and tiring walk. Hitchhiking is easy. A jeep-taxi from Montezuma will cost about $25 roundtrip. Collective taxis depart Montezuma for Cabo at 7 and 9 a.m., returning at 3 and 4 p.m. ($5 per person).

Sea Ventures (Apdo. 6941, San José; tel 255-3022, fax 233-0401) offers a three-day sailing adventure from Playa Herradura (see the "Puntarenas to Jacó" in the Central Pacific chapter) to Playa Tambor and Cabo Blanco, including nature hikes, accommodation aboard a yacht, and transfers to/from San José ($445).

APPENDIXES

RECOMMENDED ITINERARIES

SELF-DRIVE—12 DAYS

Day 1: Arrive San José. Overnight San José or, better yet, outside the capital, where you can admire the Central Valley. Leave the capital city for later. Have rental car delivered. Recommended hotels: Grano de Oro (in town), a bed and breakfast in Escazú, Orquídeas Inn, or Finca Rosa Blanca.

Day 2: Tour Café Britt for an introduction to Costa Rica's most important traditional product. Drive to the summit of Poás volcano. Visit Zoo Ave for an introduction to the wildlife of Costa Rica, and the Butterfly Farm.

Day 3: Drive via Sarchí (the nation's handicraft center) and Zarcero (famed for its topiary) to Ciudad Quesada (San Carlos). Drop to the northern lowlands, via Fortuna, to Tabacón. Take a dip in the hot springs; view Arenal volcano. Recommended hotels: Tabacón Resort, Arenal Observatory Lodge (4WD highly recommended), or Chachagua Rain Forest Lodge.

Day 4: Via Lake Arenal, Tilarán, and Cañas to Pan-American Highway. Visit Las Pumas "Mini-Zoo." Drive north to Santa Rosa National Park; visit La Casona. Recommended hotels:

Hotel Las Espuelas (Liberia) or Hacienda Los Inocentes.

Day 5: Via Liberia, Filadelfia, and Huacas to Playa Conchal, Flamingo, or Tamarindo. Afternoon, relax on the beach. Nighttime visit to Playa Grande to see leatherback turtles. Recommended hotels: Jardín del Eden or Capitán Suizo (deluxe), or Las Tortugas (moderate).

Day 6: Day at rest on the beach. Perhaps take a guided boat tour of Tamarindo Wildlife Refuge.

Day 7: Visit Guaitil to buy Chorotega Indian pottery. Then, via Nicoya and the Tempisque ferry to the Pan-American Highway. Continue to either Monteverde Cloud Forest Reserve or, for a less touristed alternative, via Esparza and San Ramón to Los Angeles Cloud Forest Reserve (a long option with much late-afternoon mountain driving; good if returning to San José from here). Recommended hotels: Monteverde Lodge, Hotel Heliconia, Sapo Dorado (moderate), Villablanca Hotel (Los Angeles).

Day 8: Guided hiking in the cloud forest. Midafternoon, drive south to Orotina or Playa Herradura. Recommended hotels: Hacienda Doña Marta (Orotina), Dundee Ranch, Villa Caletas (Playa Herradura).

colonial church at Orosí

BOB RACE

FIVE FUN-FILLED DAY-TRIPS FOR THE LESS ACTIVE

Green Train: Full-day rail journey follows the route of the famous Jungle Train.

Cruise to Tortuga Island: A fabulous fun-filled day-trip across the Gulf of Nicoya, with beach barbecue, swimming, and snorkeling.

Cruise on the Star Chaser: An exciting, fast-paced, no-motion scenic half-day cruise down the central Pacific coast.

Ballooning: You're the passenger. A bird's-eye view of Costa Rica. Fabulous!

Sarapiquí Jungle Boat Tour: A great way to see wildlife without working up a sweat.

Travel agents and tour operators can arrange these and other trips.

Day 9: Morning hiking in Carara Biological Reserve. Return to San José via Orotina. Recommended hotels: See "Day 1."

Day 10: Via Rancho Redondo and Tierra Blanca to the summit of Irazú volcano. Then via Pacayas and Turrialba to Guayabo National Monument. Recommended hotels: Casa Turire (deluxe) or Guayabo Lodge (rustic).

Day 11: Via Juan Viñas to the colonial church ruins at Ujarrás, then circle Cachí Lake via Cachí and Río Macho to the colonial church at Orosí. Return to San José via Cartago, with a visit to the basilica. Recommended hotel: Grano de Oro.

Day 12: Explore San José (see "Sightseeing Highlights" in the On the Road chapter).

FOR WILDLIFE LOVERS—14 DAYS

Day 1: See above itinerary.

Days 2-3: Fly to Tortuguero National Park. Explore the coastal rainforest by boat. Nighttime, watch turtles nesting (in season). Return to San José via Los Canales.

Either:

Days 4-5: Drive via Cartago and San Isidro to Dominical. Perhaps detour to San Gerardo de Dota en route, to view quetzals. At Dominical, transfer to Finca Brian y Milena or Bella Vista Lodge. Guided hikes.

Day 6: Drive north to Manuel Antonio National Park. Afternoon in the park. Recommended hotel: Si Como No.

Day 7: Drive north to Carara Biological Reserve. Explore park, with rest of day for local birding. Recommended hotel: Tárcoles Lodge.

Days 8-9: Drive to Monteverde Cloud Forest Reserve or Los Angeles Cloud Forest Reserve. Guided hiking in search of the quetzal. Return to San José.

Or:

Days 4-5: As days 8-9 above.

Day 6: Via the Pan-American Hwy. to Cañas. Visit Las Pumas "Mini-Zoo." Check in La Pacifica (three nights). Organized nighttime tour to Playa Grande or Playa Ostional to see turtles nesting.

Day 7: Organized birding tour to Palo Verde National Park.

Day 8: Rafting on the Río Corobicí.

Day 9: Return to San José, possibly via Carara Biological Reserve.

Days 10-12: Fly to either Marenco Biological Reserve or Corcovado Tent Camp. Rainforest hiking, either guided or alone. Alternately, transfer to either Rara Avis or Selva Verde for guided montane rainforest hikes. Return to San José.

Days 13-14: Explore San José. Possible day trip(s) to Poás volcano; Guayabo Monument, CATIE, and Lankester Gardens; or the Butterfly Farm.

LIVING IN COSTA RICA

Peter Dickinson, author of *Travel and Retirement Edens Abroad* (American Association of Retired Persons, $16.95), considers the quality of life in Costa Rica among the highest in the hemisphere: "It's probably one of the easiest places in the world for Americans to settle," he says. More than 30,000 U.S. citizens share Dickinson's sentiments and have settled here for genteel retirement, a carefree lifestyle, or simply to escape the shoals of wrecked marriages.

For years, the Costa Rican government has wooed North American retirees through tax and customs incentives. To become a *pensionado,* or government-approved retiree, you must have a steady source of foreign income exceeding $600 a month and live in Costa Rica at least four months out of the year. Until April 1992, foreign income was exempt from Costa Rican income tax, there was no tax on interest from bank deposits, funds could be transferred in and out of the country without restriction, and you could import an automobile valued at up to $16,000 and up to $7000 in personal effects duty-free.

In 1992, things changed. Pressured by the International Monetary Fund, the Costa Rican legislature eliminated many of the *pensionado* tax breaks as part of a deficit-reduction austerity package. The *pensionado* program remains in place. Foreign retirees, however, now have to pay the same duties on imported cars and household goods as Costa Ricans.

Pensionados cannot hold salaried jobs in Costa Rica, but they are encouraged to start businesses. In all, *pensionados* contribute some $150 million annually to the local economy. Whatever you choose to do in Costa Rica, the first $70,000 of your local earnings will be exempt from U.S. income tax. After five years, you are eligible for Costa Rican citizenship. Benefits include access to the low-cost medical care by paying $50 a year into the Costa Rican social-security system.

If you wish to buy a vacation home, consider the Pacific coast, where land goes for $1000 to $20,000 an acre, depending on location. That will get you a verdant slope within walking distance of a pristine white beach. The price of a three-bedroom beach house ranges from $40,000 to $150,000. In Escazú, one of San José's most desirable outskirt neighborhoods, a four-bedroom Spanish-style stucco house with swimming pool, sauna, two-car garage, and a stunning view of the Escazú Mountains goes for as little as $100,000. Dealing with the bureaucracy can be maddening. But a good lawyer can do your paperwork for about $2000.

For more information, contact the Departamento de Jubilados/Instituto Costarricense de Turismo (Apdo. 777, San José 1000), located on the ground floor of the ICT Building (Calle 5, Avenida 4). The **Association of Foreign Residents** (Apdo. 700, San José 1011, tel. 233-8068, fax 222-7862) can help prepare the way with information to consider in making your decision. Its office is on the first floor of the ICT/Social Security Building (CCSS), on Calle 5 and Avenida 4. It recommends several extended visits as a tourist as a prelude to settling in Costa Rica. A provisional membership ($50) entitles you to the same information and services as full members. The association charges $500 to process your *pensionado* application. **Note:** The association suffered a few knocks in 1993-94 when some of its executives absconded and the spittle started flying over lost money, embezzlement charges, etc. Brief mayhem and chaos resulted, but it seems to have gained its footing (and respectability) under a new regime.

The **Costa Rican-American Chamber of Commerce** (Apdo. 4946, San José 1000, tel. 233-2133, fax 223-2349) publishes *The Guide to Investing & Doing Business in Costa Rica* ($30, including shipping). *Choose Costa Rica: A Guide to Wintering or Retirement,* by John Howells (Gateway Books, 1992), is a good resource, as is *The Official Guide to Living, Visiting, and Investing in Costa Rica,* published by Lawrence International (SJO 643, P.O. Box 025216, Miami, FL 33102-5216). Another is *Paradise Properties: Costa Rican Real Estate and Investment* (Apdo. 779, Escazú 1250, tel./fax 223-0331; in the U.S., SJO-1769, P.O. Box 025216, Miami, FL 33102-5216), a monthly magazine that lists

properties for sale and provides feature articles and news of interest to retirees and investors.

The publishers of the *Costa Rican Outlook* (P.O. Box 5573, Chula Vista, CA 91912, tel./fax 619-421-6002, or tel. 800-365-2342) bimonthly newsletter offer a weeklong "Costa Rican Fact-Finding Trip" each November for would-be retirees. An annual subscription special ($22) includes a free copy of the excellent 150-page book *The Golden Door to Retirement and Living in Costa Rica,* by Chris Howard.

Howard's book is also available from Costa Rica Books (P.O. Box 1512, Thousand Oaks, CA 91358, tel. 805-496-1625, fax 805-373-0686; $17.95 including shipping), which sells a wide range of books and videos on real estate, legal and medical issues, and retirement living in Costa Rica and Central America.

LANGUAGE

TIQUISMOS: COSTA RICAN SPANISH

Castilian Spanish, with its lisping *c*'s and *z*'s, is the Spanish of Spain, not Latin America. Costa Ricans do not lisp their *c*'s and *z*'s. They also speak more slowly than other Latin Americans, which makes understanding and learning easier. They have also evolved their own manner of speech, softening the Spanish language in the process, by the widespread use of the diminutive form. Thus *un momento*—"one moment"—becomes, in Costa Rica, *momentito*. *Tiquismos*, phrases peculiar to Costa Ricans, lace their conversations.

Most noticeable, perhaps, are the little affectations and teasing endearments given and taken by Ticos without offense: *flaco* (skinny), *gordo* (fatty), *chino* (Chinese), *negro* (dark-skinned) are common names of address. *Mi amor* (my love) is a common term of endearment, used by both men and women, much as Cockneys and Yorkshire folks call strangers "luv." Young men are usually called *maje* (literally "dummy," but more correctly "buddy" or "pal") among their peers.

Costa Ricans still use *vos*, an archaic form of second-person-singular address, and the personal *tú* instead of the more respectful *usted* common elsewhere in Latin America. Children, curiously, are normally addressed as *usted*.

Formal courtesies are also widely used when greeting someone. For example, you may be asked *"¿Como amaneció?"* ("How did you awake?"). The reply: *"Muy bién, por dicha; y usted?"* ("Very well, fortunately; and you?"); or *"Muy bién, gracias a Dios"* ("Very well, thank God"). God crops up in speech all the time. *Si Dios quiere* ("God willing") is a favorite expression. And *Hasta luego* ("See you later") is sometimes acknowledged with *Que Dios le acompañe* ("May God accompany you").

Confusingly, *adios!* (used as a long-term goodbye) is also used as a greeting in casual passing—the equivalent of *"Hi!"* You call *"Adios!"* across the street, or when passing someone in the road in rural areas.

A common courtesy when paying a call on someone, especially in the countryside, is to call *"Upe!"* from outside the house to let him or her know you're there. As you enter, you should say *"Con permiso"* ("With your permission"). Expect to be engaged by polite questions on the health of individual family members. It's a politeness to show the same concern toward your host.

Like all countries, Costa Rica has its slang words. You won't be in the country long without hearing *pura vida!* (great, terrific; literally "pure life"). *Tuanis* means cool. *Buena nota* also means cool or okay. *Mala nota* or *furris* means "uncool"). If Ticos really like something, they'll exclaim *"Qué bruto"* or *"Qué bárbaro"*; if they disapprove, you'll hear *"Qué horror," "Qué fatal,"* or *"Qué maje."*

Speaking the Language

Although learning the basics of Spanish will aid your travels considerably, you should still get along fine without it. Most Costa Ricans are well educated, and English is widely spoken, particularly in San José. Even in the most remote backwater village, there'll be someone around who speaks English. Most larger hotels have bilingual desk staffs, and English is widely spoken by the staff of car rental agencies, travel agencies, and tour companies. Of course, English—spoken with a lilting accent—is the lingua franca on the Caribbean coast.

Don't use that as an excuse, however, not to learn some Spanish. Costa Ricans warm quickly to those who make an effort to speak their language. Don't be bashful. Use what Spanish you know and you'll be surprised how quickly you'll pick up the language. If you put your foot in your mouth *(metida de pata)*, don't worry. Absolve yourself with a self-deprecatory *"¿Diay?"* meaning "What do you expect?"

At the least, you should learn some key words and phrases, such as *por favor* (please), *gracias* (thank you), and *buenas días* (good morning; good day). Consider a language course at your local community college before your vacation. Many local libraries also provide language tapes.

In San José, many fine language schools offer short-term programs for travelers, as well as longer courses for more serious students (see "Language Study," below). You'll also find a small phrasebook and dictionary helpful. The paperback *Spanish-English, English-Spanish Dictionary* published by the University of Chicago is a good choice: a handy size, comprehensive, and replete with Latin American phraseology. Also try the pocket-size *Berlitz Spanish for Travelers*.

Pronunciation

Compared with English, the Spanish written language offers a remarkably faithful representation of the sounds of the spoken language. Vowels are generally sharper and more vigorously pronounced than English vowels (where English tends to diphthongs, as in *coin*, each vowel is pronounced as a pure sound in Spanish, as in the English word *oasis).*

In words ending in a consonant (except n or s), the last syllable is stressed, as in *señor.* When words end in a vowel, n, or s, the next-to-last syllable is stressed, as in *mañana.* Any variation from the above is indicated by an acute accent, as in *difícil.*

The Spanish alphabet has 29 characters—three more than English. Actually, four more, since w isn't part of the Spanish alphabet (see "Spanish Alphabet" chart).

Grammar

Nouns in Spanish are either masculine or feminine. Most nouns that end in *o* are masculine; those ending in *a* are feminine. Articles must agree with the noun in gender and number. Thus, the definite article *la* (the) and the plural *las,* and the indefinite article *una* (a/an) and the plural *unas* (some), are used with feminine nouns. Masculine nouns are accompanied by the definite articles *el* (singular) and *los* (plural), and the indefinite articles *un* and *unos.* Adjectives also agree with the noun in gender and number. Thus, *la casa amarilla* (the yellow house) and *las casas amarillas* (the yellow houses). As a rule, nouns precede adjectives.

Questions are often formed by changing the inflection of your voice: it's the rising inflection of the last syllable of the sentence that transforms a statement into a question. Hence, *Habla es-*

pañol (He speaks Spanish) becomes *¿Habla español?* (Does he speak Spanish?). Nouns ending in vowels add an *s* to form the plural; words ending with a consonant add *es.* Negatives are formed by placing *no* before the verb: *Es caliente* ("It's hot") becomes *no es caliente* ("it's not hot").

THE SPANISH ALPHABET

Symbol	Name	Pronunciation
a	*a*	Like *a* in "cat."
b	*be*	At the beginning of a word, like *b* in "boy." Elsewhere, a "buzzed" sound (lips pursed for the English *b;* sound as for English *v*). Virtually same sound for *v.*
c	*ce*	Before *e* or *i,* like *th* in "think." Elsewhere, like *c* in "cat." In Costa Rica, the lisp is less pronounced.
ch	*che*	Like the English "child"; *muchacho* (boy).
d	*de*	At the beginning of a word, after nasal consonants and after *l,* like *d* in "darn." Elsewhere like *th* in "though," but lightly.
e	*e*	Like the first *e* in "elephant."
f	*efe*	Like *f* in "friend."
g	*ge*	Before *e* or *i,* like *ch* in Scottish "loch." Elsewhere like *g* in "gate," sometimes softly.
h	*hache*	Always silent (i.e., never pronounced)
i	*i*	Like *e* in "seen."
j	*jota*	Like *ch,* as in "loch." Thus, *hojas* (leaves) is pronounced "o-has."

Symbol	Name	Pronunciation
k	*ka*	Like *k* in kilo (found only in a few words of foreign origin).
l	*ele*	Like *l* in "lion."
ll	*elle*	Between y in "yacht" and lli in "million." Thus, *calle* (street) is pronounced "ca-yae."
m	*eme*	Like *m* in "marry."
n	*ene*	Like *n* in "noun."
ñ	*eñe*	Like *ni* in "onion," but with the *n* and *y* more closely associated, as in *señor*.
o	*o*	Like *o* in "for," but shorter and sharper.
p	*pe*	Like *p* in "potato."
q	*cu*	Like *c* in "cat."
r	*ere*	At the beginning of a word, two trills, as in "borrow"; elsewhere, one trill, as in "robin."
rr	*erre*	Three trills, as in "grrr!"
s	*ese*	Like *s* in "silver."
t	*te*	Like *t* in "table."
u	*u*	Like *u* in "under."
v	*ve* or *uve*	(See b.)
x	*equis*	Like *gs*, as in "exist."
y	*ye*	Like *y* in "young," but stronger.
z	*zeta* or *zeda*	Like *th* in "thing."

NUMBERS

1 — *uno, una*
2 — *dos*
3 — *tres*
4 — *cuatro*
5 — *cinco*
6 — *seis*
7 — *siete*
8 — *ocho*
9 — *nueve*
10 — *diez*
11 — *once*
12 — *doce*
13 — *trece*
14 — *catorce*
15 — *quince*
16 — *dieciseis*
17 — *diecisiete*
18 — *dieciocho*
19 — *diecinueve*
20 — *veinte*
21 — *veintiuno*
22 — *veintidos*
30 — *treinta*
40 — *cuarenta*
50 — *cincuenta*
60 — *sesenta*
70 — *setenta*
80 — *ochenta*
90 — *noventa*
100 — *cien, ciento*
101 — *ciento uno*
125 — *cien veinticinco*
200 — *docientos*
300 — *trescientos*
400 — *cuatrocientos*
500 — *quinientos*
600 — *seiscientos*
700 — *setecientos*
800 — *ochocientos*
900 — *novecientos*
1,000 — *mil*
100,000 — *cien mil*
1,000,000 — *un millón*

GREETINGS, COURTESIES, AND FAREWELLS

Good morning — *Buenos días*
Good afternoon/evening — *Buenas tardes*
Good night — *Buenas noches*
Pleased to meet you — *Mucho gusto de conocerle*
Hello — *Hola*
Hi! — *¡Adios!*
How are you? — *¿Cómo estás?* (familiar) or *¿Cómo está?* (formal)
Fine. And you? — *Perfectamente. ¿Y usted?*

Very well — *Muy bien*
It's a pleasure — *Con mucho gusto*
You're welcome — *De nada*
The pleasure is mine — *El gusto es mío*
You're very kind — *Usted es muy amable*
See you later — *Hasta luego*
Goodbye — *Adios*
Until we meet again — *Hasta la vista*

LANGUAGE STUDY

We all know that the best way to learn a foreign language is to take a lover who speaks no other. But you're married, let's say. Or engaged. In any event, why leave learning a language to the fickle whims of Cupid? What better, then, than combining classroom and culture in one; with verb conjugation by morning and dancing merengue by night? Learning Spanish in Costa Rica is guaranteed to turn academic pursuit into a vacation.

Costa Rica abounds in language schools. There's an appropriate school and course for every student, regardless of age, background, or language learning aptitude. The nation's two dozen or so accredited language schools operate on a similar basis, with only details to distinguish between them. All offer a span of courses for the novitiate and up, with programs normally consisting of beginner, intermediate, and advanced. Some schools also offer highly specialized courses lasting up to three months for those with "superior" Spanish. A few even have intensive Spanish for business. Most programs include homestays with Costa Rican families—a tremendous (and fun) way to boost your language skills and learn the local idioms. Many courses also feature workshops and lectures on Costa Rican culture, some with an emphasis on Latin American dancing. And some provide for a more rounded travel experience with tours and excursions.

Courses run an average of two to four weeks. The norm is three to five hours of instruction daily, more in intensive courses. Classes are generally small, rarely more than six people. Most schools also offer private tuition ($10-20 per hour). Any necessary visa extensions are generally handled by the school. Most schools offer courses beginning each Monday year-round.

Language schools advertise in the *Tico Times* and in the *Specialty Travel Index* (305 San Anselmo Ave., San Anselmo, CA 94960, tel. 415-459-4900, fax 415-459-4974). Several local language schools recently joined forces to form the **Union of Spanish Language Centers** (known by its Spanish acronym UCEEPE) to promote language study tourism in Costa Rica. For more information, contact UCEEPE, Apdo. 1001, San Pedro 2050, tel. 225-2495, fax 225-4665. The following language schools offer residence courses:

Academia Costarricense de Lenguaje (Apdo. 336, San José 2070, tel. 221-1624, fax 233-8670) has intensive language and culture programs designed for students and travelers ($850 for one month with homestay or hostel accommodation).

Academia Smith Corona (Apdo. 4592, San José 1000, tel. 222-4637) specializes in "survival courses" for tourists (private $9 per hour; two weeks $90).

Academia Tica (Apdo. 1294, Guadalupe, San José 2100, tel. 234-0622, fax 233-9393) offers language and culture courses (minimum 20 hours, three hours per day) that can be extended indefinitely ($120 for 20 hours group; $180 private). Many German-speaking students.

American Institute for Language and Culture (Apdo. 200, San José 1001, tel. 225-4313, fax 224-4244) has group or one-on-one language and cultural courses ($9-13 per hour individual instruction; $500-650 a month for group tuition; homestays $90-95 additional per week).

Central American Institute for International Affairs (c/o Educaturs, Apdo. 10302, San José, tel. 255-0859, fax 221-5238; in the U.S., P.O. Box 5095, Anaheim, CA 92814, tel. 714-527-2918, fax 714-826-8752). Offers Spanish and cultural courses, including dance. Two to four weeks ($560-840).

Centro Cultural Costarricense Norteamericano (Apdo. 1489, San José 1000, tel. 225-9433, fax 224-1480). Founded in 1945, this nonprofit institution offers a standard five-week Spanish course (three hours' tuition daily, $280). Shorter, more intense courses are available.

Centro Linguistica Conversa (Apdo. 17, Centro Colón 1007, tel. 221-7649, fax 233-2418) offers a conversational study program at its

campus in Santa Ana, west of San José. An intensive monthlong course, including homestay and meals, costs $1455.

Centro Linguistico Latinoamericano (Apdo. 151, Alajuela, tel. 441-0261) has four-week intensive courses ($900, including homestay and all meals; $1300 including excursions).

Centro Panamericano de Idiomas (Apdo. 151 San Joaquin de Flores, Heredia 3007, tel. 265-6866, fax 265-6213; in the U.S., tel. 409-693-8950 or 800-347-8087; e-mail cpi@huracan.cr). Offers two-, three- and four- week classes from $300. Private classes are $6 per hour. Also offers a one-day "survival course" for tourists. Highly recommended by past readers. Beautiful, quiet location next to coffee plantations in San Joaquín de Flores, near Heredia.

DALFA Spanish School (Apdo. 323, San Francisco de Dos Ríos, San José 1011, tel. 226-8584) offers a one-month "tourist" package including four weekend excursions and cultural activities ($1100 with homestay). Minimum of 15 weeks for Spanish courses ($790).

Forester Instituto Internacional (Apdo. 6945, San José 1000, tel. 225-3155, fax 225-9236) offers various classes, from a two-week language program ($590 with homestay) to a four-week language-and-culture program ($1120).

ICADS (Institute for Central American Development Studies, Apdo. 3, Sabanilla 2070, tel. 225-0508, fax 234-1337) has a one-month Spanish program with emphasis on politics, social conditions, and environmental issues ($892, including homestay).

ILISA (Latin American Institute for Language, Apdo. 1001, San Pedro 2050, tel. 225-2495, fax 225-4665; or c/o Megadventures, P.O. Box 2392, Toluca Lake, CA 91610, tel. 818-843-7554, fax 818-843-1226) offers a range of programs from two to 12 weeks (from $335, plus homestay at $105 per week).

Instituto Universal de Idiomas (Apdo. 219, San Francisco de Guadalupe 2120, tel. 257-0441) offers three-day ($95), two-week ($155), and four-week courses ($250, or $630 with homestay).

INTENSA (Apdo. 8110, San José 1000, tel. 225-6009; in the U.S., tel. 414-278-0631). One of the larger schools. Offers intensive Spanish programs of two, three, and four weeks ($260-545).

Instituto Britanico (Apdo. 8184, San José 1000, tel. 234-9054, fax 253-1894). Lists a three-week language-and-culture course with field trips to museums, archaeological sites, conservation projects, and other sites of ecological and cultural importance ($1000 with homestay).

Instituto de Español Para Extranjeros (Apdo. 1380, San José 1000, tel. 225-5878, fax 225-2907) offers four-week courses at the Universidad Autónoma de Centro América. Beginner and intermediate units involve 20 hours a week ($360); advance units involve 14 hours a week of language plus six hours of history, literature, and ecology ($385). "Spanish For Business" is also offered.

Instituto de la Lengua Española (Apdo. 100, San José 2350, tel. 227-7355, fax 227-0211) offers 15-week courses for missionaries ($635); others on request.

La Escuela Moravia (c/o Costa Rica Tours And Travel, P.O. Box 2645, Las Cruces, NM 88004, tel. 800-383-7859, fax 505-521-4324) opened in summer 1994 and offers two-, three-, and four-week courses ($360-620, homestay $80 extra).

Lisa Tec (Apdo. 228, San Antonio de Belén 4005, tel. 239-2225, fax 239-2225) is "dedicated to practical methods of teaching Spanish." Two-week courses cost $542, including homestay and two meals a day.

Pura Vida (Apdo. 890, Heredia 3000, tel. 237-0387, fax 237-0387; in the U.S., P.O. Box 730, Garden Grove, CÁ 92642, tel. 714-534-0125, fax 714-534-1201) has a wide range of courses. Language classes are $210 per week (including five days of school and seven days accommodation); an "Immersion Course" ($330) combines language lessons with excursions and cultural activities. Pura Vida also offers children's classes ($170) and a three-day "Survival Course" ($160) that provides basic preparation for travelers.

Rancho de Español (Apdo. 1880, La Guácima 4050, tel./fax 438-0071) is on a farm outside San José and offers three four-week programs. Four students maximum per class. The property has a swimming pool, basketball court, soccer field, and ping-pong.

Universidad Internacional de las Americas (Apdo. 1447, San José 1002, tel. 222-3640, fax 222-3216) offers beginner, intermediate, and advanced Spanish courses. Courses begin the first Monday of each month except May.

BOOKLIST

GENERAL

Chalfont, Frank. *Medical Systems of Costa Rica.* San José, Costa Rica: 1993. A heavily anecdotal review of Costa Rica's medical services.

Costa Rica at a Glance. San José: Market Date, 1990. Handy mini-compendium of statistical data.

Hall, Carolyn. *Costa Rica: A Geographical Interpretation in Historical Perspective.* Boulder, CO: Westview Press, 1985.

Jones, Julie. *Between Continents, Between Seas: Pre-Columbian Art of Costa Rica.* Detroit: Detroit Institute of the Arts, 1981.

Mayfield, Michael W., and Rafael E. Gallo. *The Rivers of Costa Rica: A Canoeing, Kayaking, and Rafting Guide.* Birmingham, AL: Menasha Ridge Press, 1988.

Moser, Don, ed. *Central American Jungles.* Amsterdam: Time-Life Books, 1975.

Ras, Barbara, ed. *Costa Rica: A Traveler's Literary Companion.* San Francisco, CA: Whereabouts Press, 1994. Twenty-six stories by Costa Rican writers that reflect the ethos of the country.

Trejos, Alonso, ed. *Illustrated Geography of Costa Rica.* San José: Trejos Editores, 1991. Coffee-table format. Lots of colorful photography belies matter-of-fact text covering everything from government structure and social aspects to industrial production.

NATURE AND WILDLIFE

Alvarado, Guillermo. *Costa Rica: Land of Volcanoes.* Cartago; Editorial Tecnológia de Costa Rica, 1993. A detailed guide to the volcanoes, with science for the layman and a practical bent for the traveler.

Boza, Mario, and A. Bonilla. *The National Parks of Costa Rica.* Madrid: INCAFO, 1981. Available as both a coffee-table hardback and a less bulky softback. Lots of superb photos. Highly readable, too.

Carr, Archie F. *The Windward Road.* Gainesville: University of Florida Press, 1955. A sympathetic book about the sea turtles of Central America.

Caulfield, Catherine. *In the Rainforest.* Chicago: University of Chicago Press, 1986.

Cornelius, Stephen E. *The Sea Turtles of Santa Rosa National Park.* San José: Fundación de Parques Nacional, 1986.

DeVries, Philip J. *The Butterflies of Costa Rica and their Natural History.* Princeton University Press, 1987. A well-illustrated and thorough lepidopterist's guide.

Dressler, Robert L. *Field Guide to the Orchids of Costa Rica and Panama.* Ithaca, NY: Comstock Publishing, 1993.

Emmons, Louise H. *Neotropical Rainforest Mammals—A Field Guide.* Chicago: University of Chicago Press, 1990. A thorough yet compact book detailing mammal species throughout the neotropics.

Forsyth, Adrian, and Ken Miyata. *Journey Through a Tropical Jungle.* Toronto: Greey de Pencier Books, 1988. An educational children's book that provides a lighthearted introduction to rainforest ecology.

Forsyth, Adrian, and Ken Miyata. *Tropical Nature.* New York: Scribner's & Sons, 1984. A

readable, lighthearted insight into tropical ecosystems.

Herrera, Wilberth. *Costa Rica Nature Atlas-Guidebook.* San José: Editorial Incafo, 1992. A very useful and readable guide to parks, reserves, and other sites of interest. Text is backed by stunning photos and detailed maps showing roads and gas stations.

Janzen, Daniel, ed. *Costa Rican Natural History.* Chicago: University of Chicago Press, 1983. The bible for a scientific insight into individual species of flora and fauna. Weighty, large format. 174 contributors.

Kricher, John C. *A Neotropical Companion: An Introduction to the Animals, Plants, and Ecosystems of the New World Tropics.* Princeton, NJ: Princeton University Press, 1989.

Lellinger, David B. *Fern and Fern-Allies of Costa Rica, Panamá, and the Choco.* Washington, D.C.: Smithsonian Institution. A scientific tome for botanists and fernophiles.

Mitchell, Andrew W. *The Enchanted Canopy.* New York: Macmillan, 1986.

Mitchell, Sam. *Pura Vida: The Waterfalls and Hot Springs of Costa Rica.* Beaverton, OR: Catarata Press, 1993. Not reviewed.

Perry, Donald. *Life Above the Jungle Floor.* New York: Simon & Schuster, 1986. A fascinating account of life in the forest canopy, relating Perry's scientific studies at Rara Avis.

Schmitz, Anthony. *Costa Rica Mammal Flip Chart.* San José: Educación Ambiental, 1994. Marvelous, handy, bound "flip chart" identifying more than 40 mammals, with pictures, vital statistics, and habitat maps for each.

Skutch, Alexander. *A Naturalist in Costa Rica.* Gainesville: University of Florida Press, 1971.

Stiles, F. Gary, and Alexander Skutch. *A Guide to the Birds of Costa Rica.* Ithaca, NY: Cornell University Press, 1989. A superbly illustrated compendium for serious birders.

Wallace, David R. *The Quetzal and the Macaw: The Story of Costa Rica's National Parks.* San Francisco: Sierra Club Books, 1992. An entertaining history of the formation of Costa Rica's national-park system.

Young, Allan. *Field Guide to the Natural History of Costa Rica.* San José: Trejos Hermanos, 1983.

POLITICS AND SOCIAL STRUCTURE

Ameringer, Charles D. *Democracy in Costa Rica.* New York: Praeger, 1982.

Ameringer, Charles D. *Don Pepe: A Political Biography of José Figueres of Costa Rica.* Mexico City: University of Mexico Press, 1978.

Barry, Tom. *Costa Rica: A Country Guide.* Albuquerque, NM: The Inter-Hemisphere Resource Center, 1989.

Bell, John P. *Crisis in Costa Rica: The 1948 Revolution.* Austin: University of Texas Press, 1971.

Biesanz, Richard, et al. *The Costa Ricans.* Englewood Cliffs, NJ: Prentice-Hall, 1987 (updated).

Edelman, Marc, and Joanne Kenen, eds. *The Costa Rican Reader.* New York: Grove Weidenfeld, 1988. An excellent compendium of extracts on politics, history, economics, the contras, etc.

Palmer, Pauline. *What Happen: A Folk History of Costa Rica's Talamanca Coast.* San José: Ecodesarrollos, 1977.

TRAVEL GUIDES

Baker, Bill. *Essential Road Guide for Costa Rica.* San José: 1992. A handy reference for self-drive exploring, especially strong on San José. The regional route charts are difficult to follow unless you have a navigator along.

Bell, Vern. *Vern Bell's Walking Tour of Downtown San José*. San José: Bell's Home Hospitality, 1994. A concise, entertaining pocket-size aid to exploring the capital city.

Beresky, Andrew, ed. *Fodor's Central America*. 2nd ed. New York: Fodor's, 1994. Good for travelers not seeking a detailed guide.

Berkeley Guide: Central America on the Loose. New York: Fodor's, 1993. Excellent, concise compendium for those on a shoestring. Very hip, very thorough, very well-organized. Money to blow? Forget it.

Blake, Beatrice, and Anne Becher. *The New Key to Costa Rica*. 12th ed. Berkeley: Ulysses Press, 1993. Solid, well-structured travel guide packed with information.

Box, Ben, ed. *Mexico and Central American Handbook*. New York: Prentice Hall, 1994. A bulky yet concise bible for those traveling throughout the isthmus. Written for British travelers. Amazing volume of information, if not always easy to find.

Bradt, Hilary, et al. *Backpacking in Mexico and Central America*. 3rd ed. Boston: Bradt Publications, 1992.

Castner, James L. *Rainforests—A Guide to Research and Tourist Facilities at Selected Tropical Forest Sites in Central and South America*. Gainesville: Fekine Press, 1990. Information on 39 sites throughout Central America for travelers intent on visiting rainforest preserves.

Drive the Pan-American Highway. Miami: Interlink, 1991. A do-it-yourself guidebook offering practical advice and tips on paperwork, routes, etc. for those driving to Costa Rica.

Franke, Josephs. *Costa Rica's National Parks and Preserves: A Visitor's Guide*. Seattle: The Mountaineers, 1993. Excellent guide specifically for those heading into protected zones. Detailed maps and trail routes of most parks and reserves, plus bare-bones information on preparing for your trip. No hotel or restaurant reviews.

Glassman, Paul. *Costa Rica*. 5th ed. Champlain, NY: Passport Press, 1994. A very good general guide, much improved over previous editions. Well organized, sound information. No photos.

Haber, Harvey. *Insight Guide to Costa Rica*. Hong Kong: APA Publications, 1992. Stunningly colorful photography and maps. A pleasurable read with in-depth coverage of the history, geography, and social aspects of Costa Rica. Armchair reading to accompany a more practical "how-to" guide.

Hatchwell, Emily, and Simon Calder. *Travellers Central America Survival Kit*. England: Vacation Work, 1991. A budget traveler's guide written in a literary vein. Solid.

Instituto Costarricense de Turismo. *Costa Rica: Tourist Orientation Guide*. San José, Costa Rica, 1993. Concise "guidebook" with hotel, tour operator listings, etc., arranged like *Yellow Pages*.

Instituto Costarricense de Turismo. *Real Guide of Costa Rica*. San José, 1992. A few useful maps and listings. Otherwise, forget it!

Itiel, Joseph. *Pura Vida! A Travel Guide to Gay & Lesbian Costa Rica*. San Francisco: Orchid House, 1993. An uninhibited anecdotal account of an experienced gay traveler's time in Costa Rica, including practicalities on accommodation, nightlife, etc.

Keller, Nancy, Tom Brosnahan, and Rob Rachowiecki. *Central America on a Shoestring*. Berkeley: Lonely Planet, 1992. Good resource for budget travelers exploring the isthmus. Lots of practical advice and maps.

Lougheed, Vivien. *Central America by Chickenbus: A Travel Guide*. Quesnel, B.C.: Repository Press, 1988. For those roughing it overland.

Meza Ocampo, Tobia, and Rodolfo Mesa Peralta. *Discover Costa Rica: A Historical Cultural*

Guide. San José: Universal, 1992. Home-grown perspectives on history, politics, etc. Pocket-size. Unfortunately, also pocket-size on practical advice.

Norton, Natascha, and Mark Whatmore. *Central America.* London: Cadogan Guides, 1993. Handy for those planning to explore the isthmus. Lacks regional details and the jolly literary style of other Cadogan guides.

Panet, J.P. *Latin America on Bicycle.* Champlain, NY: Passport Press, 1987. Anecdotal account of cycling through Latin America, including a chapter on Costa Rica.

Pariser, Harry S. *The Adventure Guide to Costa Rica.* 2nd ed. Edison, NJ: Hunter Publishing, 1994. A thorough, well-presented guidebook with solid coverage on history, the economy, politics, etc. plus comprehensive practical details. Color photos.

Price, Carolyn, ed. *Fodor's Costa Rica, Belize, Guatemala.* New York: Fodor's Travel Publications, 1993. Well-organized and concise guidebook. A boon to the traveler wanting easy reference, though treatment is lightweight. Minimal hotel and restaurant reviews and off-the-beaten-track information.

Pritchard, Audrey, and Raymond Pritchard. *Drive the Pan-Am Highway to Mexico and Central America.* Heredia, Costa Rica: 1992. Handy preparatory text with hints on packing, customs, etc.

Rachowiecki, Rob. *Costa Rica—A Travel Survival Kit.* 2nd ed. Berkeley: Lonely Planet, 1994. Well-written, comprehensive, and well-structured coverage of what to see, where to stay, and how to get there. Substantially larger than first edition. Detailed maps.

Red Guide to Costa Rica: National Map Guide. San José: Guias de Costa Rica, 1991. City maps and regional maps in one book; recommended for self-drive exploration.

Reisefuhrer, Peter Meyer. *Costa Rica: Reisehandbuch fur das Naturparadies Zurischen.*

Frankfurt: 1993. A thorough, handy, compact guide for German travelers.

Samson, Karl. *Frommer's Costa Rica, Guatemala & Belize on $35 a Day.* New York: Frommer Books, 1993. Concise and well-structured guide to the major destinations. Selective; not strong on off-the-beaten-track travel. Good for the grand tour of Central America.

Searby, Ellen. *The Costa Rica Traveler.* 3rd ed. Occidental, CA: Windham Bay Press, 1991. Venerable but less-detailed guide. Black-and-white photos.

Sheck, Ree S. *Costa Rica: A Natural Destination.* 3rd ed. Santa Fe, NM: John Muir Publications, 1994. Good guide to the national parks and reserves, substantially more detailed than prior editions.

Sienko, Walter. *Latin America by Bike: A Complete Touring Guide.* Seattle, WA: The Mountaineers, 1993. Splendidly organized practical guidebook to cycling in the Americas, including a chapter on Costa Rica.

Tattersall Ryan, Judy. *Simple Pleasures: A Guide to the Bed and Breakfasts and Special Hotels of Costa Rica.* San José, 1993. No photos or illustrations, but good descriptions of select hostelries. Order by writing to Apdo. 2055, San José 1002, or faxing 222-4336.

Tico Times. *Exploring Costa Rica: The Tico Times Guide.* San José: Tico Times, 1993. Excellent little compendium replete with information. A no-nonsense directory with feature articles, too.

Tucker, Alan, ed. *Costa Rica: The Berlitz Traveler's Guide.* New York: Berlitz Publishing, 1994. Handy, pocket-size guidebook in lively, upbeat style.

Verlag, Heller. *Costa Rica: Kreul Und Quer Durch.* Munich: 1993. Good pocket-size guidebook in German.

Wood, Margo. *Charlie's Charts of Costa Rica.* Surrey, B.C.,: Charlie's Charts. One-of-a-kind guide for sailboaters, with bays and moorings described and charted.

LIVING IN COSTA RICA

Howard, Chris. *The Golden Door to Retirement and Living in Costa Rica,* 6th ed. San José: C.R. Books, 1994. Another splendid comprehensive guide to making the break. Leaves no stone unturned. Also highly useful information for travelers passing through.

Howells, John. *Choose Costa Rica: A Guide to Wintering or Retirement.* Gateway Books, 1992. Well-written book that answers most questions asked by those thinking of settling in Costa Rica.

The Official Guide to Living, Visiting, Investing in Costa Rica. San José: Lawrence International Publishing.

United States Mission Association. *Living in Costa Rica.* San José, 1989. Comprehensive listings of services not covered by other books. Aimed at those already settled in Costa Rica.

VIDEOS

Adventures in Costa Rica. (Away From It All Press, P.O. Box 5573, Chula Vista, CA 91912-5573, tel. 800-365-2342.) Features 15 thrilling adventures, from hikes and horseback rides to bungee jumping and sportfishing. (55 minutes; $25.50 including shipping.)

Costa Rica: Making the Most of Your Trip. (Marshall Productions, P.O. Box 534, Carlsbad, NM 88221; 90 minutes; $35 including shipping.)

Costa Rica: The Key. (Videorama, Apdo. 6709, San José 1000, tel. 221-8110, fax 221-0540; 31 minutes.)

Costa Rica: The Land and Its People; Costa Rica: Sun, Water and Fun; Costa Rica: The National Parks. (Producciones La Mestiza, Apdo. 3011, San José 1000, tel. 253-8071, fax 253-5911; 25 minutes.)

Costa Rica Today. (Cota International, P.O. Box 5042, New York, NY 10185.) Includes information for potential residents. Widely available at hotels. (60 minutes; $30.)

Costa Rica Video. (Megaview Productions, 255 N. El Cieto, Suite 155, Palm Springs, CA 92262; 34 minutes; $25 including shipping.)

This is Costa Rica. (Swiss Travel Service, Apdo. 7-1970, San José 1000; 35 minutes; $25.)

The Video for Costa Rica. (The Young and New Tone of Costa Rica, Apdo. 6709, San José 1000; 60 minutes; $30.)

ENGLISH LANGUAGE NEWSLETTERS AND NEWSPAPERS

Adventures in Costa Rica. Monthly newsletter with "no punches pulled" and "no axes to grind." Strongly oriented to would-be residents. (Starflame Publications, P.O. Box 508, Jackson, CA 95642; $36.95 annual subscription.)

Costa Rica Adventure and Business. Full-color quarterly magazine on tourism and investment. (Publications & Communications, Inc., 12416 Haymeadow Dr., Austin, TX 78750; $19.95).

Costa Rica Report. Covers topics of interest to travelers and residents. (Apdo. 6283, San José; $42 annual subscription.)

Costa Rican Outlook. An upbeat newsletter with insightful background stories and handy tidbits for travelers. Highly recommended. Subscribers receive an Identification Card for discounts for restaurants, tours, car rental, etc., in Costa Rica. (Away From It All Press, P.O. Box 5573, Chula Vista, CA 91912, tel./fax 619-421-6002 or 800-365-2342; $19 annual subscription with money-back guarantee.)

Costa Rica Today. Excellent full-color newspaper geared to the foreign traveler. Widely available in hotels, etc. (P.O. Box 0025216, Miami, FL 35102; $59.95 annual subscription.)

The Tico Times. Superb weekly newspaper covering all aspects of Costa Rican life. Includes comprehensive listings of events. (P.O. Box 145450, Coral Gables, FL 33114; $40 annual subscription.)

OTHER

Americans Abroad is a newly updated U.S. government booklet that discusses many aspects of international travel, from visa and passport requirements to health and safety concerns. Ask for booklet 599W. (Consumer Information Center, P.O. Box 100, Pueblo, CO 81002.)

INDEX

Page numbers in **boldface** indicate the primary reference. *Italicized* page numbers indicate information in captions, charts, illustrations, maps, or special topics.

ABOUT THE AUTHOR

Christopher P. Baker was born and raised in Yorkshire, England. After receiving a B.A. (Honours) in Geography at University College London (including two Sahara research expeditions and an exchange program at Krakow University, Poland), he earned Master's degrees in Latin American Studies from Liverpool University, and in Education from the Institute of Education, London University. He began his writing career in 1978 as Contributing Editor on Latin America for *Land & Liberty*, a London-based political journal. In 1980, he received a Scripps-Howard Foundation Scholarship in Journalism to attend the University of California, Berkeley. Since 1983 he has made his living as a professional travel and natural-sciences writer. He

has been published in more than 150 publications worldwide, including *Newsweek*, BBC's *World Magazine*, *National Wildlife*, *Islands*, *Elle*, the *Christian Science Monitor*, *The Los Angeles Times*, the *Chicago Tribune*, the *San Francisco Examiner*, the California Academy of Sciences' *Pacific Discovery*, and *Writer's Digest*. For seven years, Christopher was also president of British Pride Tours, which he founded. He has escorted group tours to New Zealand, Hong Kong, Korea, England, and Cuba. He appears frequently on radio and television talk shows, and as a guest-lecturer aboard cruise ships throughout the Caribbean and further afield. Christopher is a member of the Society of American Travel Writers and has been honored with several awards for outstanding writing, including—twice—the prestigious Lowell Thomas Travel Journalism Award and the 1995 Benjamin Franklin Award for "Best Travel Guide" for the *Costa Rica Handbook*. In 1993 he was named "Best Travel News Investigative Reporter." His other books include the *Trav'Bug Guide to California*, *Passport Illustrated Guide to Jamaica*, *Frommer's America on Wheels: California & Nevada*, *Jamaica: Travel Survival Kit*, the *Cuba Handbook* (in progress), and *Mi Moto Fidel*, a literary account of his travels through Cuba by motorcycle (in progress). He has also contributed chapters to *I Should Have Stayed Home*, and *Writer's Digest Beginner's Guide to Getting Published*. He lives in Oakland, California.

MOON TRAVEL HANDBOOKS
THE IDEAL TRAVELING COMPANIONS

Moon Travel Handbooks provide focused, comprehensive coverage of distinct destinations all over the world. Our goal is to give travelers all the background and practical information they'll need for an extraordinary travel experience.

Every Handbook begins with an in-depth essay about the land, the people, their history, art, politics, and social concerns—an entire bookcase of cultural insight and introductory information in one portable volume. We also provide accurate, up-to-date coverage of all the practicalities: language, currency, transportation, accommodations, food, and entertainment. And Moon's maps are legendary, covering not only cities and highways, but parks and trails that are often difficult to find in other sources.

Below are highlights of Moon's Central America and Caribbean Travel Handbook series. Our complete list of Handbooks covering North America and Hawaii, Mexico, Central America and the Caribbean, and Asia and the Pacific, is on the order form on the accompanying pages. To purchase Moon Travel Handbooks, please check your local bookstore or order by phone: (800) 345-5473 Monday-Friday 8 a.m.-5 p.m. PST.

MOON OVER CENTRAL AMERICA
CENTRAL AMERICA AND CARIBBEAN TRAVEL HANDBOOK SERIES

> "Solidly packed with practical information and full of significant cultural asides that will enlighten you on the whys and wherefores of things you might easily see but not easily grasp."
> —*Boston Globe*

BELIZE HANDBOOK
by Chicki Mallan, 363 pages, **$15.95**
"Indispensable for those wanting to explore the Mayan ruins and other attractions of the interior."
—*Islands Magazine*

CARIBBEAN HANDBOOK
by Karl Luntta, 384 pages, **$16.95**
Famous for white beaches and crystal water, the islands of the Caribbean include such popular tourist destinations as the Virgin Islands, Barbados, and Guadeloupe. Author Karl Luntta covers these well-known spots, along with many not-so-famous island getaways in *Caribbean Handbook*. Travelers may choose among 38 Caribbean islands, including the volcanic craters of Montserrat, Saba's scuba diving, and the tropical rainforest of Sint Eustatius.

MOON TRAVEL HANDBOOKS

NORTH AMERICA AND HAWAII

Alaska-Yukon Handbook (0161) $14.95
Alberta and the Northwest Territories Handbook (0676) . . . $17.95
Arizona Traveler's Handbook (0536) $16.95
Atlantic Canada Handbook (0072) $17.95
Big Island of Hawaii Handbook (0064) $13.95
British Columbia Handbook (0145) $15.95
*Colorado Handbook (0447) $18.95
*Georgia Handbook (0390) $17.95
Hawaii Handbook (0005) $19.95
Honolulu-Waikiki Handbook (0587) $14.95
Idaho Handbook (0617) $14.95
Kauai Handbook (0013) $13.95
Maui Handbook (0579) $14.95
*Montana Handbook (0498) $17.95
Nevada Handbook (0641) $16.95
New Mexico Handbook (0153) $14.95
Northern California Handbook (3840) $19.95
Oregon Handbook (0102) $16.95
*Road Trip USA (0366) $22.50
Texas Handbook (0633) $17.95
Utah Handbook (0684) $16.95
*Washington Handbook (0455) $18.95
Wyoming Handbook (3980) $14.95

ASIA AND THE PACIFIC

Bali Handbook (3379) $12.95
Bangkok Handbook (0595) $13.95
Fiji Islands Handbook (0382) $13.95
Hong Kong Handbook (0560) $15.95
Indonesia Handbook (0625) $25.00
Japan Handbook (3700) $22.50
Micronesia Handbook (3808) $11.95
*Nepal Handbook (0412) $18.95
*New Zealand Handbook (0331) $19.95
*Outback Australia Handbook (0471) $18.95
*Pakistan Handbook (0692) $19.95
Philippines Handbook (0048) $17.95

Southeast Asia Handbook (0021) $21.95
South Korea Handbook (3204). $14.95
*South Pacific Handbook (0404). $22.95
Tahiti-Polynesia Handbook (0374) $13.95
*Thailand Handbook (0420) $19.95
Tibet Handbook (3905) $30.00
*Vietnam, Cambodia & Laos Handbook (0293) $18.95

MEXICO

Baja Handbook (0528). $15.95
Cabo Handbook (0285) $14.95
Cancún Handbook (0501). $13.95
Central Mexico Handbook (0234) $15.95
Mexico Handbook (0315) $21.95
Northern Mexico Handbook (0226) $16.95
Pacific Mexico Handbook (0323) $16.95
Puerto Vallarta Handbook (0250) $14.95
Yucatán Peninsula Handbook (0242). $15.95

CENTRAL AMERICA AND THE CARIBBEAN

Belize Handbook (0307). $15.95
Caribbean Handbook (0277) $16.95
Costa Rica Handbook (0358). $19.95
Jamaica Handbook (0129) $14.95

INTERNATIONAL

Egypt Handbook (3891). $18.95
Moon Handbook (0668) $10.00
Moscow-St. Petersburg Handbook (3913) $13.95
Staying Healthy in Asia, Africa, and Latin America (0269) . . $11.95

* New title or edition, please call for availability

PERIPLUS TRAVEL MAPS

All maps $7.95 each

Bali	Indonesia	Penang
Bandung/W. Java	Jakarta	Phuket/S. Thailand
Bangkok/C. Thailand	Java	Sabah
Batam/Bintan	Kuala Lumpur	Sarawak
Cambodia	Ko Samui/	Singapore
Chiangmai/N. Thailand	Lombok	Vietnam
Hong Kong	S. Thailand	Yogyakarta/C. Java

WHERE TO BUY MOON TRAVEL HANDBOOKS

BOOKSTORES AND LIBRARIES: Moon Travel Handbooks are sold worldwide. Please contact our sales manager for a list of wholesalers and distributors in your area.

TRAVELERS: We would like to have Moon Travel Handbooks available throughout the world. Please ask your bookstore to write or call us for ordering information. If your bookstore will not order our guides for you, please contact us for a free title listing.

> Moon Publications, Inc.
> P.O. Box 3040
> Chico, CA 95927-3040 U.S.A.
> tel.: (800) 345-5473
> fax: (916) 345-6751
> e-mail: travel@moon.com

IMPORTANT ORDERING INFORMATION

PRICES: All prices are subject to change. We always ship the most current edition. We will let you know if there is a price increase on the book you order.

SHIPPING AND HANDLING OPTIONS: Domestic UPS or USPS first class (allow 10 working days for delivery): $3.50 for the first item, 50 cents for each additional item.

EXCEPTIONS: *Tibet Handbook* and *Indonesia Handbook* shipping $4.50; $1.00 for each additional *Tibet Handbook* or *Indonesia Handbook*.

Moonbelt shipping is $1.50 for one, 50 cents for each additional belt.

Add $2.00 for same-day handling.

UPS 2nd Day Air or Printed Airmail requires a special quote.

International Surface Bookrate 8-12 weeks delivery: $3.00 for the first item, $1.00 for each additional item. Note: Moon Publications cannot guarantee international surface bookrate shipping. Moon recommends sending international orders via air mail, which requires a special quote.

FOREIGN ORDERS: Orders that originate outside the U.S.A. must be paid for with either an international money order or a check in U.S. currency drawn on a major U.S. bank based in the U.S.A.

TELEPHONE ORDERS: We accept Visa or MasterCard payments. Minimum order is US$15.00. Call in your order: (800) 345-5473, 8 a.m.-5 p.m. Pacific standard time.

ORDER FORM

Prices are subject to change without notice. Be sure to call (800) 345-5473 for current prices and editions or for the name of the bookstore nearest you that carries Moon Travel Handbooks • 8 a.m.–5 p.m. PST. (See important ordering information on preceding page.)

Name: _____ Date: _____

Street: _____

City: _____ Daytime Phone: _____

State or Country: _____ Zip Code: _____

QUANTITY	TITLE	PRICE

Taxable Total_____

Sales Tax (7.25%) for California Residents_____

Shipping & Handling_____

TOTAL_____

Ship: ☐ UPS (no P.O. Boxes) ☐ 1st class ☐ International surface mail

Ship to: ☐ address above ☐ other _____

_____

Make checks payable to: **MOON PUBLICATIONS, INC.**, P.O. Box 3040, Chico, CA 95927-3040 U.S.A. We accept Visa and MasterCard. **To Order:** Call in your Visa or MasterCard number, or send a written order with your Visa or MasterCard number and expiration date clearly written.

Card Number: ☐ **Visa** ☐ **MasterCard**

☐ ☐ ☐ ☐ ☐ ☐ ☐ ☐ ☐ ☐ ☐ ☐ ☐ ☐ ☐ ☐

Exact Name on Card: _____

Expiration date:_____

Signature:_____

F 95

COSTA RICA
HANDBOOK